ESTATE AND GIFT TAX DIGEST

FOURTH EDITION

JOHN CATHERALL
Member, New Jersey Bar

DANIEL E. FELD
Member, New York Bar

Warren,
Gorham &
Lamont

How to Use This Book

Estate and Gift Tax Digest, Fourth Edition, provides references to important federal estate, gift, and generation-skipping tax cases and rulings. The reported decisions of federal courts and the rulings of the Internal Revenue Service have been carefully reviewed, selected, and edited to present concise and easily understandable abstracts of complex cases.

Digest Contents and Citations. Each digest summarizes the facts, gives the holding, and states the name of the case or ruling and the volume and page number of the law reporters where the decision or ruling is printed. Citations to reporters published by Commerce Clearing House and Research Institute of America are provided for convenience.

Digest Organization and Finding Aids. The digests are arranged topically into twenty-six chapters. The following research tools are helpful in directing the reader to specific topics: a Table of Contents; a Table of Internal Revenue Code Sections; a Table of Treasury Regulations; a Table of Revenue Rulings and Revenue Procedures; a Table of Private Letter Rulings; a Table of Cases; and an Index.

Letter Rulings. Digests of private letter rulings and technical advice memoranda have been included for the reader's convenience.

Section 6110(k)(3) states that unless the Secretary of the Treasury rules otherwise, a written determination made available for public inspection under this section may not be used or cited as precedent. However, in the *Agents' Manual*, the IRS notes that letter rulings may be used as a guide with other research material in formulating a district office position on an issue.

Acknowledgments

The authors wish to thank Anne-Marie Nespoli, the book editor, and Jennifer Harris, the copy editor, for their work in editing the manuscript, as well as Prudence Conner, who provided clerical assistance.

Summary of Contents

Table of Contents

3   Annuities and Employee Benefits

4   Retained Estates and Powers

5   Joint Interests

6   Powers of Appointment

7   Life Insurance

PART II   TAXABLE ESTATE

8   Deductions From Gross Estate

9   Administration Expenses

10   Charitable Deduction

13   Income Tax

Part IV   GIFT TRANSFERS

14   Determining Taxable Gift Transfers

15   Valuation of Property

PART V   GIFT TAXATION

16   Applying the Gift Tax

17   Annual Exclusion

18   Compliance and Procedure

22   Trust Income

23   Trust Deductions

24   Compliance and Procedure in Reporting Income

25   Taxable Income

26   Expenses and Deductions

PART I

THE GROSS ESTATE

CHAPTER **1**

Includable Interests, Generally

¶ 1.01 BENEFICIAL INTERESTS

Gifts made under power of attorney were excludable from estate. Decedent executed a power of attorney on May 28, 1971, naming his only child as his attorney-in-fact. This power of attorney contained a general statement of authority that granted his son the power to

> execute and perform all and every act, matter and thing, in law or in the judgment of my said attorney needful or desirable to be done in relation to all or any part of my property, estate, affairs, and business of any kind or description, as fully and amply, and with the same effect, as I, myself, might or could do if acting personally.

This general grant of authority was followed by a provision empowering his attorney to perform certain specific acts. When this power of attorney could not be located, decedent executed a second durable power of attorney on January 12, 1987, granting his son the same powers. Decedent had a history of making partly tax-driven gifts to his family. Decedent suffered from congestive heart disease, and by March 20, 1987, he could no longer effectively communicate with others. Acting pursuant to the power of attorney, decedent's son made gifts from decedent's checking account of $9,500 to himself, his wife, his four children, and three grandchildren. He made these gifts to the natural objects of decedent's bounty to reduce the gross estate and minimize estate taxes. Decedent's son wrote the checks on March 27, 1987. The decedent died on April 15, 1987. On decedent's estate tax return, the $85,000 in gifts made under the power of attorney were not included in his gross estate. The IRS asserted that these transfers were includable in the estate, relying on the Fourth Circuit decision in Casey, 948 F2d 895 (4th Cir. 1991). Because no Virginia court had addressed the question raised in *Casey*, the Fourth Circuit opinion in that case was based on its prediction as to how the Virginia Supreme Court would resolve the question. In *Casey*, the circuit court determined that the power of attorney contained no express gift power and that the gifts were revocable and includable in the estate. The year after *Casey* was decided, Virginia enacted Code Section 11-9.5, which specifically provides for an implied gift power in a power of attorney that grants broad general powers, making such gifts irrevocable. The IRS in the instant case contended that since *Casey* was decided closer in time to the date of the gifts than to the effective date of the Virginia statute, *Casey* controlled. The Tax Court refused to rely on *Casey*, finding that the statute was intended to have retroactive effect and therefore controlled. Accordingly, the Fourth Circuit in the instant case was required to decide whether the Virginia statute had retroactive effect and whether it conflicted with *Casey*.

Held: Affirmed for the estate. The circuit court began its analysis by reviewing its holding in *Casey* and concluded that the statute and *Casey* could be reconciled. It noted that in *Casey*, the court recognized that the Virginia Supreme Court might not be disposed to adopt a flat rule that an unrestricted power to make gifts could not be found in a durable power of attorney that does not expressly grant that power. The court thus found that an appropriate method to resolve the question was to review the complete text of the particular instrument and the circumstances of its execution to determine whether the court could infer a power, though unexpressed, to make the gifts at issue. According to the circuit court, *Casey* stands for the proposition that to infer an implied gift power, the court must look to the intent of the person granting the power of attorney. While the instrument and circumstances involved in *Casey* did not indicate the principal's intent to confer a gift power on the attorney-in-fact, the court ruled that the evidence in the instant case did support such an intent. The power of attorney in *Casey* used language limiting the powers granted to business transactions. In addition, the principal's pattern of making gifts in *Casey* did not support an intent to confer a gift power on the attorney-in-fact. The Fourth Circuit stated that these circumstances were clearly distinguishable from those in the instant case. The court then reviewed the subsequent Virginia statute and found that the statute had retroactive effect. In addition, the court ruled that the statute validates both gift powers and actual gifts. In enacting the gift statute, the General Assembly incorporated the presumed intent of principals to permit their attorneys-in-fact to make gifts pursuant to the broad general powers expressed. According to the court, the statute not only applies powers of attorney executed but also validates gifts made before the effective date.

[Estate of Ridenour, 36 F3d 332, 74 AFTR2d 94-7492, 94-2 USTC ¶ 60,180 (4th Cir. 1994).]

Beneficiary's interest in plan was included in her estate. Decedent's father was a participant in a profit-sharing plan created by the McCarthy Well Company. Decedent's father designated his children or their issue per stirpes (i.e., by representation) as beneficiaries of his interest in the trust in the event of his death. His estate was designated as the contingent beneficiary. Decedent's father died on December 20, 1981. Under the terms of the profit-sharing trust agreement, the trustee was given absolute discretion to distribute a deceased participant's interest to the designated beneficiaries, either outright or in equal installments over the beneficiaries' life expectancy or ten years, whichever was less. Decedent, upon her father's death, was entitled to one third of his interest in the profit-sharing trust. The trustee elected to distribute the proceeds to decedent in ten equal annual installments. Decedent died approximately one year after her father, leaving three daughters and a husband. At her death, she received the first of the ten annual installments, but the unpaid balance remained at $143,129. Her husband disclaimed any interest in his intestate share, since decedent did not have a will. The trustee then paid the annual installments to decedent's three daughters until May 1988, when the trustee acceded to their request to distribute the remaining balance to them in lump-sum payments. Decedent's estate tax return did not include the unpaid balance of her interest in the profit-sharing trust. The IRS determined on audit that her one-third interest in the trust proceeds should be included in her gross estate. The district court upheld the deficiency.

Held: For the IRS. The Eighth Circuit stressed that it must look to the language of decedent's father's beneficiary designation form to ascertain his daughter's interest in the retirement plan proceeds. This form named the father's children or their issue per stirpes as beneficiaries and his estate as a contingent beneficiary. The taxpayer argued that the form was ambiguous and submitted evidence of the father's intention that if the benefits were not distributed to decedent during her lifetime, they were to be distributed to her issue, rather than to her estate. The court concluded that the form was unambiguous and that once decedent survived her father, she received a one-third interest in fee simple absolute. The form did not contain language expressing an intent to create a life estate in decedent or to limit her use of the proceeds. In addition, the court stated that the father's use of the term "per stirpes" demonstrated his intention that his children's issue were substitute takers if his children did not survive him. The court indicated that where the primary taker survives the donor, the gift vests in the primary taker and he takes to the exclusion of the substitutes. The words of substitution become inoperative by the vesting of the gift, devise, or bequest in the primary taker. (See First & Am. Nat'l Bank of Duluth v. Higgins, 293 NW 585 (Minn. 1940).) Because decedent survived her father, her interest vested in her to the exclusion of her issue. The court stated that the trustee's chosen manner of payment did not alter its conclusion. Where the right to receive the gift is immediate and only the time of payment is postponed, the court reasoned that the gift vests immediately. The court also determined that the so-called divide-and-pay-over rule was not applicable in this case. The father's words of gift, as stated in his beneficiary designation form, did not contain a direction to delay distribution or to divide and pay over at some future time or upon the happening of a specified event. The form contained no language indicating a condition that decedent must survive until all payments were made. Therefore, the judgment was affirmed.

[Stack, 23 F3d 1400, 73 AFTR2d 94-1967, 94-1 USTC ¶ 60,167 (8th Cir. 1994).]

Language in will overrides state's simultaneous death statute, thereby causing husband's assets to be included in wife's estate. Decedent and her husband were killed in a car accident. The husband died instantly, but decedent survived for thirty-eight hours. The husband's will named decedent as sole beneficiary. However, the will contained a survival clause stating that in the event that his wife died before him, at the same time, or under circumstances that made it doubtful who died first, the estate was to be awarded to alternate beneficiaries named in the will. The state version of the Uniform Probate Code provides that a beneficiary who does not survive decedent by more than 120 hours is considered to have predeceased him unless the will contains language dealing explicitly with simultaneous death. The Tax Court held that the clause in the will overrode the statute and that because decedent survived her husband by thirty-eight hours, his assets passed to her estate.

Held: Affirmed for the IRS. Even though the state's simultaneous death statute would have kept the husband's property out of decedent's estate, the detailed survivorship clause in the husband's will overrode the statute because the clause constituted language dealing explicitly with simultaneous death.

[Estate of Acord, 946 F2d 1473, 91-2 USTC ¶ 60,090, 68 AFTR2d 91-6071 (9th Cir. 1991).]

Tax Court resolves discrepancy between antenuptial agreement and spouse's subsequent testamentary scheme. Decedent, a resident of New York, died in 1975. In 1932, her husband and two other individuals had formed a trust that held approximately 53 percent of the stock in a family newspaper publishing corporation. Six years prior to her marriage, decedent had signed an antenuptial agreement with her husband. The husband agreed that during his lifetime, he would either give outright 16.75 percent of his interest to decedent in the trust or make a testamentary transfer of a portion thereof to decedent for life if his son did not predecease him. The husband died in 1946, leaving a will that granted decedent both a life and remainder interest in his stock held by the trust. In so doing, he followed neither course outlined in the antenuptial agreement, preferring instead to leave his wife a considerably larger legacy. Decedent's executor did not include the 16.75 percent share of the trust in gross income, on the ground that decedent received a life estate in such share by the terms of the antenuptial agreement, and that it was extinguished on the date of her death. The IRS contended that decedent's entire trust interest was bequeathed to her under the terms of the husband's will and that such interest was includable under Section 2031 or, in the alternative, under Section 2036.

Held: For the estate. The Second Circuit affirmed, per curiam, the Tax Court decision that decedent's interest in the trusted stock was obtained entirely from the husband's will. In the Tax Court's view, the antenuptial agreement simply created enforceable limitations on the husband's obligations to decedent, but did not curtail his testamentary privilege under New York law to increase decedent's legacy by subsequent testamentary disposition. In addition, the court found no evidence to establish that a life interest was conveyed to decedent in accordance with the antenuptial agreement, or that the husband's obligation was anything other than conditional. The court further determined that decedent did not renounce her interest at any time.

[Estate of Patterson, 736 F2d 32, 84-2 USTC ¶ 13,578, 54 AFTR2d 84-6464 (2d Cir. 1984).]

Trust corpus reverts to decedent and is included in estate. Decedent had established an inter vivos trust for his grandchildren, with farmland as the corpus. Decedent's son was the trustee. The trust was to terminate when the grandchildren reached age 21. No later disposition of the property was made. The trust terminated one year before decedent's death, but the grandchildren continued to report the rental income from the property. The IRS included the trust property and rental income in decedent's estate.

    Held: For the IRS in part. The property was included in decedent's estate because under state law, it reverted to the owner when no later disposition was made. The rental income was not included in the estate, because no evidence was introduced that decedent expected to be repaid.

[Estate of Watson, 94 TC 262 (1990).]

Gross estate includes property in which decedent had an interest. A husband and wife died intestate in a common accident. The wife survived the husband by three hours. The couple co-owned U.S. Savings Bonds, and the husband owned a certificate of deposit in his name followed by the designation "payable on death" to his wife. The husband's gross estate included the full value of the property. The probate court approved a final accounting granting decedent's wife's estate one third of the property under the Oklahoma intestate laws. This amount was reported on her federal estate tax return. The IRS determined that the full value of the property was includable in the wife's gross estate, arguing, with respect to the bonds, that federal statutes and regulations preempt any inconsistent state law, and that federal law states that "if one of the co-owners named on a bond has died, the surviving coowner will be recognized as its sole and absolute owner." With respect to the certificate of deposit, the IRS asserted that an Oklahoma statute would apply and would supersede the probate court's determination.

    Held: For the IRS. The full amount of the property was includable in the wife's gross estate. Federal law determined her interest in the savings bonds, and payable on death designations were valid under an Oklahoma statute in effect at the time of her death.

[Fletcher, 94 TC 49 (1990).]

Tax Court refuses to extend the relation-back doctrine to noncharitable gifts. Decedent died on February 22, 1982. Prior to his death, he had given his son a general power of attorney with respect to all of his assets. Decedent intended to make a gift of $10,000 to each of his children in 1982. He gave his son oral instructions to take the necessary steps to fulfill his intent. His son wrote checks to himself and to his siblings against decedent's checking account. Several checks were cashed prior to decedent's death, and others were cashed afterwards. Before decedent's death, his son instructed decedent's brokerage firm to sell some of decedent's securities and issue checks to each of decedent's children and to their spouses. The brokerage firm issued some checks before decedent's death and others after his death. Again several checks were cashed prior to decedent's death, and others were cashed afterwards. On the estate tax return, the various transfers were not included in decedent's gross estate, under the theory that they were completed gifts within the amount of the annual exclusion. The IRS contended that the transfers were includable in the gross estate.

Held: For the IRS, in part. With regard to the checks written against decedent's checking account, the court held that only the checks cashed prior to decedent's death were properly excludable from decedent's estate. With regard to the checks issued by the brokerage firm, the court stated that these amounts were excludable if, under local law, these checks constituted completed gifts. In order to effect a valid gift, local law required donative intent and actual or constructive receipt by the donee, so that the donor has relinquished all dominion and control. The brokerage firm acted as decedent's agent, and, as such, its authority terminated upon decedent's death. Thus, it had no authority to sell stock after decedent's death. The court therefore held that the funds represented by checks issued by the brokerage firm after decedent's death were improperly excluded from decedent's gross estate. However, the checks representing funds that were removed from decedent's account at the time the checks were issued were analogous to cashier's checks or certified checks and were properly excluded from decedent's estate.

[Estate of Gagliardi, 89 TC 1207 (1987).]

Tax Court rejects argument that implied resulting trust excludes farm from gross estate. Decedent's father conveyed a life estate in a farm to decedent, with the remainder to decedent's children. To allow decedent to borrow against the farm, his children transferred their remainder interests to him by quitclaim deeds. Upon decedent's death, his children argued that the farm should have been excluded from decedent's gross estate because he merely held their remainder interests as the trustee of an implied resulting trust.

Held: For the IRS. The court stated that decedent's children were the natural objects of his bounty and that they expected him to leave the farm to them was insufficient to imply a trust. Under state law, in order for a trust to exist, the entire transaction must imply that the holder of legal title had an obligation to hold the property for the benefit of others. The court concluded that the evidence in the instant case did not reflect an obligation. Consequently, the farm was includable in the gross estate.

[Estate of Spruill, 88 TC 1197 (1987).]

Tax Court rules that checks drawn in favor of charities and not cleared until after date of death are not includable in gross estate. On December 21, 1973, decedent had prepared and mailed thirty-six checks (totalling $94,960) made to the order of various charitable donees. As of that date, there had been sufficient funds on account to cover the checks. Ten days later, on December 31, 1973, decedent died. Each check cleared the drawee bank during 1974. On decedent's 1973 individual income tax return, charitable deductions were claimed under Section 170 and were allowed by the IRS. The estate, in turn, included in the gross estate only the net amount of cash on deposit in the account on the date of death, reduced by the $94,960 of charitable donations. The IRS insisted that the $94,960 was includable in the gross estate under Section 2033 because it was in the account on the date of death.

Held: For the estate. The Tax Court examined relevant decisional authority and Treasury regulations, but concluded that the situation presented by these facts "simply was not contemplated" by any precedent. Accordingly, the court, looking to "policy considerations" and the possibility that a Section 2055 deduction would create a wash, held that the disputed amount constituted binding obligations that need not be included in the gross estate.

[Estate of Belcher, 83 TC 227 (1984).]

Value of decedent's right to share contingent attorney fees is includable in estate. At the time of his death, decedent, an attorney, had a right to share in contingent legal fees that might be realized by another attorney in certain pending cases. The IRS argued that the value of that right was includable in decedent's gross estate.

Held: For the IRS. The contingent nature of the right did not prevent its inclusion, but merely affected its valuation. However, the court reduced the IRS's valuation.

[Estate of Curry, 74 TC 540 (1980), acq. 1981-1 CB 1.]

Estate does not include property on which decedent paid mortgage. After decedent had received custody of his children, his children moved in with decedent's sister. Decedent made the down payment on his sister's house, paid the mortgage, and was named the owner on the sales contract and the loan settlement statement. The title to the property was held in his sister's name. The IRS sought to include the house in decedent's gross estate, on the theory that he had retained the right to enjoyment of the property or to designate the persons who could possess or enjoy the property.

Held: For the estate. Decedent's sister was the true purchaser and owner of the property. The down payment and mortgage payments were consideration for allowing his children to live in the house.

[Estate of Stavrakis, RIA TC Memo. ¶ 92,229, 63 TCM (CCH) 2796 (1992).]

House is includable in decedent's gross estate, even though it was deeded to her by her son to avoid attachment by son's ex-wife and was returned to decedent's son under will. Decedent died on March 23, 1982. At that time, she still held the deed to a house, which she left to her son by will. She had gained ownership of the house through a series of transactions inspired by her son's fear that his ex-wife would attach the house (their marital residence) if ownership remained in his name. Decedent had allowed her son to live in the house after the transfer. Decedent had never resided in the house or rented it to anyone. Pursuant to decedent's will, the house was bequeathed to her son or, in the event that he did not survive her, to her daughter. The value of the house was not included in decedent's gross estate. The IRS claimed that under Section 2033, the value of the house should be included in decedent's gross estate.

Held: For the IRS. Decedent owned the house in fee simple absolute at the time of her death. The facts do not support the contention by the estate that the house was held in constructive trust by decedent for her son. Additionally, the estate did not prove that there existed an understanding between decedent and her son to establish an express trust. Further, because the son did not purchase the property at the time he had transferred it to decedent, no resulting trust arose.

[Estate of Saunders, TC Memo. (P-H) ¶ 89,537, 58 TCM (CCH) 282 (1989).]

Lawyer's contingent fee is included in gross estate. Decedent, a lawyer, had entered into an arrangement to share in the contingent fee of a medical malpractice suit. Upon decedent's death, the executrix elected the alternate valuation date. Before the alternate valuation date, the case was settled, and decedent's share of the fee was $80,000. The IRS included the full amount in the gross estate.

Held: For the IRS. The speculative nature of the fee has no bearing on includability, only on valuation. If an asset is disposed of during the six-month alternate valuation period, it is valued on the date of disposition. The fact that $80,000 was received is sufficient indication of its value for estate tax purposes.

[Aldrich, TC Memo. (P-H) ¶ 83,543, 46 TCM (CCH) 1295 (1983).]

Payments that are not secured by transferred property and not determined by income from property are not income from property. *A* conveys to *B* the right to remove timber from a tract of land for five years in return for cash plus four unsecured promissory notes due at annual intervals. One month later *A* conveys the property to *C* subject to *B*'s interest. *A* dies before one note reaches maturity. The IRS ruled that *A* has no interest or estate in the land, and its value is not includable in *A*'s gross estate.

[Rev. Rul. 77-193, 1977-1 CB 273.]

Property passing to government is not included in estate. Decedent died in a Veterans Administration hospital. Decedent did not dispose of his property by will. Consequently, decedent's property does not pass to his heirs under state law, but passes to the United States. As a result, such property is not included in the estate of decedent.

[Rev. Rul. 76-542, 1976-2 CB 282.]

Checks given while decedent is living, but not cashed until after her death, must be included in estate. On January 16, 1984, one of decedent's children, upon her instructions, had drawn ten checks for $10,000 each against decedent's trust account. The checks were gifts given to the individual's children within two days. They had been post-dated to January 27, 1984, because there had not been sufficient funds in the account until that time. Each check had been accompanied by a promissory note in consideration of the donee's promise to defer cashing the check until January 27, 1984. Decedent died February 9, 1984, on which date the trust account balance was $61,250. The checks were not presented for payment until approximately eight months after decedent's death.

    The IRS stated that the value of the ten checks drawn on decedent's trust account before her death, but not cashed until after her death, was includable in decedent's gross estate. The IRS reasoned that under Regulations § 20.2031-5, bank checks that are outstanding at death may be excluded from a decedent's gross estate if they are given in discharge of bona fide obligations that decedent incurred for an adequate and full consideration in money or money's worth. The IRS noted that a gift of a check is not complete until it has been paid, certified, or accepted by the drawee, or until it is negotiated for value to a third person.

[Priv. Ltr. Rul. 8706011.]

¶ 1.02 TRANSFERS FOR CONSIDERATION

Attempted remainder sale did not keep property out of estate. Plaintiff is decedents' daughter and is the executrix of her father's estate. Prior to their deaths, decedents conveyed remainder interests in three properties to their daughter. Plaintiff's mother conveyed a remainder interest in property located in Forest Township, Illinois ("Forest property"), for $124,995, which was paid for with $6,250 in cash and a promissory note of $118,745. The fair market value (FMV) of this property on the date of transfer was $543,338. Plaintiff's mother also conveyed to her daughter a remainder interest in property located in Indian Grove Township, Illinois ("Indian Grove property"), for $62,574, consisting of $3,129 in cash and a promissory note of $59,445. The FMV of that property on the date of transfer was $272,000. Plaintiff's father conveyed to plaintiff a remainder interest in property located in Eppards Point Township, Illinois ("Eppards Point property"), for $7,463, which was paid for with $373 in cash and a promissory note for $7,090. The FMV of this property on the date of transfer was $130,200. Apparently, plaintiff's parents each retained a life estate in the property transferred. When plaintiff's mother died on March 11, 1988, the FMV of the Forest property was $711,199, and the FMV of the Indian Grove property was $355,750. When plaintiff's father died on June 9, 1989, the FMV of the Eppards Point property was $207,203. The estate tax return for each decedent did not include these properties but did include the balances due on the promissory notes. The IRS assessed plaintiff's mother's estate $294,569 and her father's estate $90,169 in deficiencies, contending that the estates should have included the FMV of the properties on the date of death, less the consideration paid for the interest transferred, pursuant to Section 2036(a). Plaintiff paid the assessments and then claimed a refund. The government moved for partial summary judgment.

Held: For the IRS. The court stated that summary judgment is appropriate if the court is satisfied that "there is no genuine issue of material fact and that the moving party is entitled to judgment as a matter of law." To withstand summary judgment, a plaintiff must be able to establish that there exists a genuine issue of material fact about which a jury could find in her favor. Section 2036(a) generally provides that the gross estate includes the value of all property of which a decedent has made a transfer (except in case of a bona fide sale for adequate and full consideration), under which he has retained for life the possession or enjoyment of, or the income from, the property. Quoting the Fifth Circuit, the court said that "the purpose of this provision is to prevent circumvention of federal estate tax by use of intervivos schemes which do not significantly alter lifetime beneficial enjoyment of property supposedly transferred by a decedent." (Estate of Wyly, 610 F2d 1282 (5th Cir. 1980).) According to the court, the issue in the instant case was the adequacy of the consideration received by plaintiff's parents. Unlike common law, under Section 2036(a), the adequacy of the consideration received is measured against the value of the entire property, not just against the value of the interest transferred. This is to ensure that the property removed from the estate is replaced with an asset of equal value. Any other interpretation would allow a taxpayer to greatly reduce estate tax by removing a large portion of property from his estate through the sale of only a remainder interest, which generally has a small value in comparison to the total value of the property. If the transferor does not receive adequate and full consideration equal to the FMV of the property, the FMV at the time of death, reduced by the consideration actually received, must be included in the gross estate. In the instant case, the court determined that the transfers were not for full and adequate consideration. Plaintiff's mother conveyed the Forest property for $124,995 when it was worth $543,338 and conveyed the Indian Grove property for $62,574 when it was worth $272,000. Plaintiff's father conveyed the Eppards Point property for $7,463 when it was worth $130,200. In order for these properties to be removed from the transferors' estates, plaintiff's parents must have received at least the FMV of the properties at the time of transfer. Because adequate and full consideration was not received, the court found it was not necessary to address whether the transfers were bona fide within the meaning of Section 2036(a). The court then ruled that each of these properties must be included in the transferor's estate and valued at the FMV on the date of death, less (1) the cash received on the initial transfer and (2) subsequent cash payments on the promissory notes. Therefore, the Forest property was includable in plaintiff's mother's estate at $695,929 and the Indian Grove property at $348,105. The Eppards Point property was includable in plaintiff's father's estate at $205,433. The court then granted the government's motion for partial summary judgment.

[Pittman, 878 F. Supp. 833, 75 AFTR2d 95-520, 95-1 USTC ¶ 60,186 (EDNC 1994).]

Residence is included in estate, despite transfer to son, where full and adequate consideration is lacking. Decedent, an eighty-one-year-old widow with a history of cancer, had owned property in New York that consisted of two acres of land and a house with an attached two-car garage. On March 14, 1984, decedent had conveyed the residence to her son and to his wife. The transaction took the form of a sale for $270,000; decedent had received a $250,000 mortgage and had simultaneously forgiven $20,000 of principal. Although the property had been appraised at $280,000 by a real estate broker, the lower price was used because, according to the estate, the appraisal included the amount of commission a broker would have earned on a sale. In each of the following two years, decedent forgave an additional $20,000 of principal. On March 16, 1984, two days after the purported sale of the property, decedent had inserted a provision in her will that canceled the mortgage indebtedness. The mortgage note called for the monthly payment of interest, computed at the rate of 9 percent per year. This amount had apparently been paid each month by the son to decedent. Simultaneously with the sale of the property, decedent had signed a five-year lease as a tenant of the house. The monthly rent of $1,800 had approximately equaled the monthly interest payment owed by the son to decedent. There was no evidence that this amount constituted a fair rent. This rent also was paid until decedent's death, which occurred on July 30, 1986. Decedent had been the sole occupant of the residence from the time of the transfer until the date of her death. The son and his wife never attempted to rent the property to anyone other than to decedent or to sell the property before renting to decedent. Less than two months after decedent's death, the son and his wife entered into a contract to sell the property for $550,000 to unrelated persons. The property was not reported as an asset of the estate on decedent's estate tax return. The return did report, however, the mortgage note from the son and his wife in the amount of $210,000, an amount that reflected decedent's forgiveness of $20,000 per year over three years. The IRS did not recognize the transfer of the property for estate tax purposes and included the FMV of the residence, or $550,000, in the taxable estate. The note for $210,000 was eliminated from the taxable estate.

Held: For the IRS. Section 2036(a) provides that if a decedent makes a transfer of property (except in the case of a bona fide sale for an adequate and full consideration in money or money's worth) under which decedent retains until death the possession or enjoyment of the property, the value of the entire property is included in decedent's gross estate. Although the transaction in the instant case appeared to be a bona fide sale on the surface, the court looked to the substance of what occurred rather than to the form used. The court held that decedent had made a transfer to her son and daughter-in-law with the understanding, at least implied, that decedent would continue to reside in her home until her death and that the lease represented nothing more than an attempt to add color to the characterization of the transaction as a bona fide sale. An express or implied understanding between the parties at the time of transfer that decedent will retain the actual possession or enjoyment of the subject property is sufficient to trigger inclusion in the estate under Section 2036, even if decedent has no enforceable right to do so. The burden is on taxpayer to disprove the existence of any implied agreement or understanding, and that burden is particularly onerous when intrafamily arrangements are involved. The court cited numerous factors leading to its conclusion that decedent had transferred the house to her son without an adequate and full consideration. The court found that none of the parties had ever intended that decedent would receive the sale price of $270,000. The mortgage note had no value at all, because there was no intention that it would ever be paid.

[Estate of Maxwell, 98 TC 594 (1992), aff'd, 3 F3d 591, 93-2 USTC ¶ 60,145, 72 AFTR2d 93-6733 (2d Cir. 1993).]

"Transmutation agreement" changing items of both spouses' community property and will allocation agreement results in exchange of property for consideration. A husband and wife had executed a "transmutation agreement" changing community property into separate property and a will "allocation agreement." Under the allocation agreement, the wife's interest in her husband's individual retirement account (IRA) had become his separate property, and the husband's interest in their other assets had become his wife's separate property. They also had executed identical wills, each of which provided that assets of decedent's estate with a value equal to the allowable unified credit would pass to a family trust that would pay its income to the surviving spouse. The allocation agreement was effective only if the husband predeceased the wife. According to that agreement, if the husband, predeceased the wife, the wife would transfer all her interest in her separate assets to her husband's estate. In exchange, the wife would receive a lifetime annuity from the IRA. When decedent gives property to his spouse, the value of the gift is deductible under Section 2523(a). Here, pursuant to the agreement, when the wife had transferred her interest in her husband's IRA for separate ownership of other assets, the interest exceeded the value of the property she received in exchange. As a result, the wife will make a gift to her husband that qualifies for the marital deduction. Since the execution of the allocation agreement will not result in a present transfer of property, there is no transfer subject to gift tax. The transfer to the husband's estate will be subject to the gift tax at that time. Since the transfer will be to an estate, however, no marital deduction will be available. Therefore, though the signing of the allocation agreement produces no taxable gift, its future implementation will do so. With regard to whether the assets transferred to the husband's estate will be included in the wife's estate, taxpayer argued that because she will exchange the assets for a life estate, the assets should no longer be included in her estate. Under Section 2036(a), assets transferred as to which a life estate has been retained are not included in decedent's gross estate if the transfer was for adequate and full consideration. Thus, to avoid the inclusion under Section 2036, the value of the annuity that the wife receives from the IRA must be equal to or greater than the value of the other non-IRA assets. Since this can be determined only when the contingency of the husband predeceasing the wife occurs, the IRS declined to give an opinion as to the effect of Section 2036 on the estate plan.

[Priv. Ltr. Rul. 8929046.]

¶ 1.03 RECIPROCAL TRUSTS

Reciprocal trust rule not triggered by payout timing. A couple had two granddaughters. The husband established an irrevocable trust that named one granddaughter as beneficiary and his wife as trustee. The trustee had discretion to reinvest and time the distribution of trust corpus and income until the beneficiary reached age 21. The wife executed substantially identical trust documents that named the other granddaughter as beneficiary and her husband as trustee. When the husband died, the IRS sought to include the trust he had set up in his estate. Applying the reciprocal trust doctrine, the IRS argued that, in effect, the couple had each formed a trust and retained a power to reinvest and time distributions from the trust. Thus, the trust the husband had established should be included in his estate under Sections 2036(a)(2) and 2038(a)(1).

Held: For taxpayer. The court refused to apply the reciprocal trust doctrine. Citing Estate of Grace, 395 US 316, 23 AFTR2d 69-1954, 69-1 USTC ¶ 12,609 (1969), the court held that the reciprocal trust doctrine applies only if the trusts are interrelated and "the arrangement, to the extent of mutual value, leaves the settlors in approximately the same economic position as they would have been in had they created trusts naming themselves as life beneficiaries." The powers to reinvest and time distributions did not leave the couple in such an economic position.

One judge, however, sided with the IRS. This judge reasoned that the "same economic position" standard was not the central requirement to applying the reciprocal trust doctrine. Rather, the facts that the trusts were simultaneously executed and amended under the same terms, funded in equal amounts, and contained identical operative terms was enough to make them sufficiently interrelated for the doctrine to apply.

[Estate of Green, 68 F3d 151, 76 AFTR2d 95-7094, 95-2 USTC ¶ 60,216 (6th Cir. 1995).]

Reciprocal trust doctrine applies without retained interest. Decedent and his wife each had created four trusts for the benefit of their grandchildren. The trusts were identical, except that decedent had been the trustee for his wife's trusts and the wife had been the trustee for decedent's. Each trust gave the trustee the power to accumulate trust income or to distribute trust income or corpus in the trustee's sole discretion for the benefit of the trust beneficiaries. It was undisputed that if the powers had been retained by the grantors, the property would have been includable in their respective estates. The sole issue was whether the trusts should be uncrossed to treat each grantor as the "transferor" of property over which he/she retained the prohibited control. The taxpayer argued that decedent had not retained any economic interest in the trust assets and that the cross-trust rule therefore should not apply.

Held: For the IRS. In its reviewed decision, the Tax Court extended the reciprocal trust doctrine to encompass arrangements where the grantors retain no economic interest in the trusts. Thus, the cross-trust rule may be applied where Section 2036 or Section 2038 will cause property to be included in an estate. The Tax Court held that the reciprocal trust doctrine as articulated in Estate of Grace, 395 US 316 (1969), merely requires that the trusts be interrelated, and that neither a retained economic interest nor the intent to avoid taxes is a necessary prerequisite to application of the cross-trust doctrine.

[Estate of Bischoff, 69 TC 32 (1977).]

¶ 1.04 DISCLAIMERS AND RENUNCIATIONS

[1] Generally

Time for filing disclaimer begins on date of death. Decedent died on September 23, 1983, and his will was admitted to probate on January 26, 1984. His will bequeathed the residue of his estate to his wife, and if she did not survive him, to his children. Decedent's wife died on May 13, 1984, and her will was admitted to probate shortly thereafter. On July 19, 1984, the executor of decedent's wife's estate executed a petition to disclaim her interest in the assets of her husband's estate. This disclaimer was filed on August 1, 1984, with the probate court; the court granted that petition. Section 2518 provides in part that a qualified disclaimer must be in writing and must be received by the transferor of the interest, his legal representative, or the holder of legal title to which the interest relates not later than nine months after the day on which the transfer creating the interest in such person is made. The estate argued that the transfer of the husband's interest to decedent's wife for purposes of Section 2518 was made on the date that his will was admitted to probate. The IRS argued that if the transfer was made on the date of his death. If the transfer was made on the date of his death, the disclaimer under the facts in this case would be untimely. The estate argued that local (Illinois) law determined when the transfer of the assets was made. It asserted that these assets were transferred to decedent's wife after the will was admitted to probate, citing Illinois law: "Every will when admitted to probate as provided by this Act is effective to transfer the real and personal estate of the testator bequeathed in that will."

Held: For the IRS. The Seventh Circuit noted that the Illinois statute allows testamentary gifts to be transferred at death; it does not state that a testator's assets are transferred only after a will is admitted to probate or that a transfer of property for Section 2518 purposes cannot occur at death. The court then reviewed the legislative purpose of Section 2518, which was to create "definitive rules concerning disclaimers for estate and gift tax purposes to achieve uniform treatment" by providing a "uniform standard ... for determining the time within which a disclaimer must be made." Consequently, for the court to look to a variety of state laws to determine when a transfer is made would defeat the congressional goal of uniformity. In addition, as noted above, the court held that Illinois law does not directly address this issue. According to the court, the House Conference Committee report further indicated that a transfer is considered to be made on the date of decedent's death with respect to testamentary transfers. This is consistent with Regulations § 25.2518-2(c)(3), which similarly provides that a taxable transfer occurs on the date of decedent's death. Thus, the court concluded that the transfer of assets occurred on the date of the husband's death. As a result, the disclaimer was not filed within the required nine-month period.

[Estate of Fleming, 974 F2d 894, 70 AFTR2d 92-6226, 92-2 USTC ¶ 60,113 (7th Cir. 1992).]

Instruction to draft disclaimer not sufficient. The wills of decedent and her spouse each left virtually the entire estate to the other. The spouse died on May 31, 1986, and, absent a disclaimer, his property would pass to the wife, thus wasting his unified credit. On January 14, 1987, decedent instructed her attorneys to draft a legally enforceable instrument renouncing her bequest so that it would pass to the spouse's heirs. Decedent died on January 26, 1987, before the document was prepared. But within nine months of the spouse's death, a state court decided that her instructions to the attorneys created a legally enforceable obligation and that she had renounced a portion of her bequest. Decedent and her spouse had lived in a nursing home, and their finances had been managed by the spouse's brother. After the spouse's death, decedent remained in the home and the brother paid her expenses from an account in his name and that of decedent. Under state (Louisiana) law, this account was community property prior to the spouse's death and, afterwards, decedent and the spouse's estate each owned an undivided one-half interest in it. It did not occur to the brother to segregate or specifically to allocate the income and expenses between decedent's and the estate's interests in the account so as to pay her expenses only from her share. Decedent, by satisfying the requirements for a qualified disclaimer under Section 2518, would have been treated as never having received the bequest from her spouse and it would have passed directly to his heirs. A qualified disclaimer must meet all the following requirements:

1. It must be an irrevocable and unqualified refusal by a person to accept an interest in the property.
2. It must be in writing and signed.
3. The disclaimer must be made within nine months after the transfer creating the disclaimant's interest (or nine months after a minor attains age 21).

4. The disclaimant must not have accepted the interest or any of its benefits.

5. As a result of the refusal to accept the property, the interest must pass without any action on the part of the disclaimant to a person other than the disclaimant (or to the spouse of decedent (or donor)).

The IRS denied the disclaimer.

Held: For the IRS. The district court decided that decedent did not satisfy the second requirement since her refusal to accept the interest was never reduced to writing. Also, decedent's personal representatives had no authority under state law to renounce the interest. Therefore, once she died, the fifth requirement could not be satisfied because it implicitly requires compliance with state law (since the interest has to pass without action on the disclaimant's behalf). Moreover, the spouse's brother inadvertently caused her to accept the benefit of property she wished to disclaim (a violation of the fourth requirement), by paying decedent's expenses from the joint account. A portion of these payments necessarily came from her deceased spouse's undivided interest so decedent received a proscribed benefit, albeit one she would have preferred to do without. Decedent's estate, in an effort to obtain a tax benefit equivalent to a disclaimer, argued that the spouse's heirs had an enforceable claim against her that was deductible under Section 2053(c). This, however, overlooked the requirement of Regulations § 20.2053-4 that a claim founded on a promise must have been contracted for bona fide consideration in money or money's worth, which was obviously not the case.

[Estate of Delaune, 79 AFTR2d 97-1509, 97-1 USTC ¶ 60,266 (MD La. 1997).]

Estate tax filing deadline did not govern timeliness of disclaimer. Decedent died on February 13, 1988, survived by three children and her husband. Because decedent left no will, under the laws of Louisiana her half of the couple's community property passed to her three children. On November 10, 1988, surviving husband filed an Application for Extension of Time to File the Estate Tax Return, which was subsequently approved. The return was filed on May 13, 1989. On May 12, 1989 (one day before filing the estate tax return), decedent's three children executed disclaimers of their interest in the estate except for $600,000 in cash. The balance of the estate then passed to decedent's husband and was claimed as a marital deduction on the estate tax return thereby resulting in no estate tax due. After examining the estate tax return, the IRS determined that two of the three disclaimers were not timely filed, and therefore the portions of the estate covered by these disclaimers would not be exempted under the marital deduction. The IRS contended that Section 2518, which requires that qualified disclaimers be filed within nine months of the date of the transfer creating the interest, or when the person disclaiming reaches twenty-one years of age, whichever comes later, controlled in this case. Because the transfers were created by decedent's death, the disclaimers should have been filed within nine months after the date of her death unless the disclaimant was under age 21 on that date. Only decedent's youngest child was under age 21 on both the date the disclaimers should have been filed and on May 12, 1989. Consequently, the IRS took the position that only one of the disclaimers was timely filed. The IRS did not challenge the validity of the disclaimers but treated the property as though it had not passed to the surviving spouse for estate tax purposes. Accordingly, the IRS found a tax deficiency, plus interest. The surviving spouse paid the deficiency and sued to recover the payment of taxes. Taxpayer-surviving husband argued that the nine-month time limit in Section 2518 does not apply to disclaimers that affect the marital deduction. He contended that the timeliness of such disclaimers is governed by the deadline for filing the estate tax return that claims the marital deduction. It was his position that if the estate tax return is timely filed, as it was here, any disclaimers affecting the marital deduction that are executed before the return is filed are also timely. The IRS argued that the strict language of Section 2518 controlled.

Held: For the IRS. The court first reviewed the language of Section 2518, which sets forth the requirements for a qualified disclaimer. Of particular relevance here is Section 2518(b)(2), which generally states that a disclaimer (which must be in writing) must be received by the transferor of the interest, his legal representative, or the holder of legal title to the property to which the interest relates not later than nine months after the later of (1) the date on which the transfer creating the interest in the disclaimant is made or (2) the date on which the disclaimant attains age 21. The court noted that the language of Section 2518 is quite clear, and the only exception to the nine-month deadline is a requirement that the disclaimant be at least twenty-one years old when the disclaimer is executed. Absent another statutory provision to the contrary, the court reasoned that Section 2518 must govern the dispute. According to the court, the IRS was correct in relying on cases that refuse to look beyond the clear language of the statute. Only when a statute is unclear on its face will a court turn to the intent of those enacting the provision. The district court held that the Code requires that disclaimers be filed within nine months of the date of the transfer that created the interest being disclaimed unless the disclaimant is less than twenty-one years old. Thus, the disclaimers of the two older children were not timely filed, and the Code treats the estate as though the disclaimers had not been made. The court concluded that the clear language of Section 2518 supports no other interpretation and that the IRS correctly calculated the taxes due from decedent's estate.

[Fitzgerald, 94-1 USTC ¶ 60,152, 73 AFTR2d 94-2323 (WD La. 1993), aff'd, 35 F3d 562, 74 AFTR2d 94-6409 (5th Cir. 1994).]

For disclaimer purposes, transfer occurs at death, not when will is probated. Decedent's estate disclaimed her interest in her predeceased husband's estate. The disclaimer was made more than nine months after decedent's husband died. The IRS denied the disclaimer, asserting that it was untimely. The estate argued that under applicable state law, the transfer of an interest by will occurs on the date on which the will is admitted to probate. Further, the date of death rule would lead to a paradoxical result in the case of a will contest. Specifically, until the contest is resolved and a will is admitted to probate, no beneficiary has the determinable interest necessary for the transfer of property. In the absence of such a transfer, the nine-month period for measuring the time for making a disclaimer does not begin to run.

Held: For the IRS. A timely disclaimer must be made within nine months after the transfer creating the interest in question. The husband's date of death, rather than the date on which his will is admitted to probate, is the transfer date. No will contest was involved in this case, nor were there any circumstances that might suggest that the husband's death would be an unreasonable starting point for the nine-month disclaimer period.

[Fleming, TC Memo. (P-H) ¶ 89,675, 58 TCM (CCH) 1034 (1989), aff'd, 974 F3d 894, 92-2 USTC ¶ 60,113, 70 AFTR2d 92-6226 (7th Cir. 1992).]

Disclaimer executed by attorney under oral instructions of estate's personal representative is qualified disclaimer where state law allows such instructions to be given orally. The attorney of the estate's executrix had advised the executrix of the last day on which a disclaimer could be made. On that day, the executrix was on vacation and was unable to return due to inclement weather. She telephoned the attorney and authorized him to execute and file the disclaimer on her behalf, which he did. The next day the executrix filed the federal estate tax return reflecting the disclaimer. The IRS contended that the attorney did not have the authority to execute the disclaimer.

Held: For the estate. In order to determine whether the attorney was authorized to execute the disclaimer, it was necessary to look at state agency law. An agent may be appointed in writing or orally, except when a statute requires written authorization. State courts had indicated that an agency may be created orally. Here the executrix expressly authorized the attorney by telephone to execute the disclaimer on behalf of the estate. This action was confirmed the next day, when the executrix filed an estate tax return reflecting the disclaimer.

[Allen, TC Memo. (P-H) ¶ 89,111, 56 TCM (CCH) 1494 (1989).]

Disclaimer that is invalid under state law fails as qualified disclaimer for federal purposes. Under the Code, a person can make a valid disclaimer of property for federal tax purposes, even if the disclaimer does not qualify under state law. However, the disclaimer must satisfy certain requirements. In this instance, a trustee attempted to disclaim a beneficiary's interest in a trust. Applicable state law did not allow the trustee to take this action without either the beneficiary's consent or authorization under the trust. Because the beneficiary did not give his consent and the trustee was not authorized to take such action under the trust agreement, the disclaimer was not valid under state law. For this reason, the IRS ruled that the disclaimer was also not a qualified disclaimer for federal tax purposes.

[Rev. Rul. 90-110, 1990-2 CB 209.]

IRS rules on surviving spouse's disclaimer of elective share. The IRS has ruled that the disclaimer by a surviving spouse of a portion of the interest acquired as a result of the spouse's exercise of the statutory right of election is a qualified disclaimer if the interest is disclaimed within nine months of decedent's death.

[Rev. Rul. 90-45, 1990-1 CB 175.]

Disclaimer requires more than intent to be effective. In this ruling, decedent did not disclaim an interest in a predeceased spouse's estate, because he never documented a refusal to accept the property. In December 1992, decedent's spouse died with a probate estate of $475,000. Decedent had an additional $1.125 million of assets. Under the spouse's will, their child received a $75,000 bequest, with the residue reverting to decedent. Any interest disclaimed by decedent passed to a bypass trust for the benefit of decedent and the child during decedent's life, and then to the child. In January 1993, decedent completed a twelve-page ledger of his assets, which consisted of a residence, securities, and bank accounts. The ledger identified each asset; noted whether its source was the residue of the spouse's estate, a joint tenancy, or ownership by decedent; and recorded the total value. It also listed the maturity date and interest payment dates for securities and bank accounts. Decedent's attorney then prepared and filed with the probate court an inventory of the spouse's estate. The decedent renounced nothing in either document. A disclaimer of decedent's interest in the spouse's estate was logical under the circumstances. Her estate would have generated no federal estate tax. Therefore, the marital deduction (for property in her probate estate) was wasted, while the bypass trust was not includable in decedent's estate. On the other hand, absent a disclaimer, the residue of her estate would augment his estate and be subject to estate tax. The attorney had anticipated this possibility and explained in a 1988 letter that, after the death of the spouse or decedent, the survivor would have nine months to decide the amount of property to direct to the bypass trust. Decedent and the attorney, however, never pursued the matter after the spouse died; decedent never signed a document funding the trust or giving up any interest in the spouse's estate.

Under Section 2518, if the recipient of a gift or a bequest makes a qualified disclaimer (the "disclaimant"), the interest is treated as never having passed to the disclaimant. Instead, the property passes directly to the person entitled to receive it as a result of the disclaimer; the disclaimant is not charged with a gift under Regulations § 25.2518-1(b). To qualify, a disclaimer has to satisfy all of the following requirements:

1. It must be an irrevocable and unqualified refusal by a person to accept an interest in the property.
2. It must be in writing and signed.
3. It must be made within nine months after the transfer creating the disclaimant's interest (or nine months after a minor attains age 21).
4. The disclaimant must not have accepted the interest or any of its benefits.
5. As a result of the refusal, the interest must pass without any action on the part of the disclaimant to the spouse of the donor or decedent, or a person other than the person making the disclaimer.

Here, there is no evidence that decedent intended to make a qualified disclaimer. The only possibly relevant documents were the ledger, the inventory, and the attorney's letter. Nothing in the ledger or the inventory, however, even suggested a renunciation. Although the letter contemplated a disclaimer, it was only suggesting possible future action and did not bind decedent. Therefore, the first two requirements were not satisfied. The fifth requirement was also not met. The IRS stated that, for property to pass without action by a disclaimant, state law requirements for a disclaimer must be satisfied. Here, the applicable state law required an instrument clearly renouncing identified property, while decedent remained free to bequeath the property to anyone he wished. (Regulations § 25.2518-1(c)(ii) reserves the effect of state law on interests created after 1981, but apparently the IRS thought the result was clear without a regulation.) The IRS cautioned that the requirements for a qualified disclaimer must be strictly followed and satisfied within the four corners of one instrument. Thus, even if it were somehow possible to extract an intent to disclaim decedent's interest from a combination of the three documents, the result would be the same.

[Tech. Adv. Mem. 9640005.]

Agreement not to probate will has effect of disclaimer. Under decedent's will, her share of community property was placed in a trust for her surviving spouse, with the remainder to pass to her two sons. Within nine months of decedent's death, the surviving spouse and the sons entered into an agreement not to probate the will and to allow the estate to pass by intestacy. On the same day, the sons, as individuals and as guardians for their own children, disclaimed all interest in the estate, except for $400,000. The instruments were then filed with the state (Texas) probate court. The reason for the agreement and the disclaimers apparently was to qualify for the marital deduction. In Technical Advice Memorandum 9228004, the IRS concluded that the agreement not to probate the will and the disclaimers by the sons were qualified disclaimers under Section 2518. The disposition of the estate that resulted from the agreement and the sons' disclaimers could have been achieved by using only disclaimers. Moreover, the agreement was valid under state law.

[Tech. Adv. Mem. 9228004.]

IRS indicates that disclaimers are qualified and do not result in generation-skipping transfer tax. A settlor created an inter vivos revocable trust (trust) in August 1986. The trust provided that the trustee would distribute all or part of the income and principal to, or for the benefit of, the settlor's two adult grandchildren for their education after her death. The trust language provided that the trust terminates when the settlor dies and the surviving grandchildren are at least thirty years old. Following trust termination, the remaining trust assets will pass in equal shares to the two grandchildren or to their respective issue, per stirpes. If none is surviving when the trust terminates, the remaining trust assets will pass outright to the settlor's daughter. The settlor's predeceased husband had created a testamentary marital trust and residuary trust. The settlor was granted limited power of appointment under the residuary trust. She exercised her limited power of appointment over the assets in the residuary trust under her will, providing that a portion of the assets of the residuary trust be added to the trust. The terms of the settlor's trust did not postpone the vesting of any estate or interest in the residuary trust property for an ascertainable period. Both grandchildren were alive when the settlor's husband died, and the trust did not provide for the postponement of the vesting of the grandchildren's interest in the trust. No income or principal of settlor's trust has been distributed to or for the benefit of either grandchild. The grandchildren proposed to disclaim all of their respective rights, title, and interests in and to the settlor's trust, with certain exceptions. The IRS stated that the grandchildren's disclaimers would constitute "qualified disclaimers" under Section 2518(a), noting that they satisfy the requirements of Section 2518(b) and Regulations § 25.2518-3. The IRS further concluded that the proposed disclaimer would not result in a GSTT, assuming that the disclaimed property would pass to a nonskip person under local law. In order for there to be a GSTT, the disclaimed interest would have to pass to a skip person. The IRS also stated that the transfer of property to the settlor's trust under the limited power of appointment would not constitute a GSTT, citing Example 5 of Regulations § 26.2601-1(b)(1)(v)(D).

[Priv. Ltr. Rul. 9014005.]

Disclaimer of beneficial interest in trust is qualified disclaimer. Decedent died, survived by her husband, three adult children, and ten grandchildren. Decedent had bequeathed her personal effects to a family trust and the balance to a revocable trust. Under the revocable trust, the trustee is to establish a marital trust for the husband and a separate trust for each descendent, per stirpes. The aggregate value of property allocated to these trusts is to equal the amount of the wife's unused generation-skipping transfer tax exemption. The trust directs the trustee to divide the balance of the trust property into a number of shares equal to the number of descendants and to add these shares to the descendant's individual trusts. If a descendant disclaims an interest in the trust, the disclaimed property will pass to a separate trust, that is, a grandchild's trust, for the benefit of a living child of the disclaimant. Further, the trust provides that the three children are to serve as advisers to the revocable trust. The three children propose to disclaim a fractional share of their interest in the revocable trust and their rights to serve as advisors. The children will not have received or accepted any beneficial interest in any of the property, which would pass under the terms of the trust, and the children will deliver the disclaimers within nine months of the wife's death. The IRS stated that the proposed disclaimers will be treated as qualified disclaimers under Section 2518 if the disclaimers are timely delivered and if the children relinquish any rights that they may have to be advisers. Further, the IRS stated that the transfer of the property from the wife's probate and nonprobate estate to separate trusts for the grandchildren will be eligible for the $2,000,000 grandchild exclusion for the purposes of Section 1433(b)(3) of the Tax Reform Act of 1986, as amended by Technical and Miscellaneous Revenue Act of 1988, § 1014(h)(3).

[Priv. Ltr. Rul. 9007034.]

Disclaimers of all property and interests are qualified disclaimers. Decedent died testate, survived only by adult siblings. Under decedent's will, his sister would receive all of his property, and then she would distribute it according to decedent's previously expressed desire. The sister wanted to execute a written disclaimer of 85.7 percent of the beneficial interest in the property bequeathed to her under the will. She also proposed to disclaim any power of appointment and property that might pass to her under applicable state law. The disclaimed property would pass to a surviving brother. The brother would then disclaim 83.33 percent of the property bequeathed to him under the will. He also would disclaim a power of appointment and any property that would pass to him under state law. All of this property would then be distributed pro rata among the siblings. The brother and sister would not direct how the disclaimed property would pass. The IRS stated that the proposed disclaimers would qualify as qualified disclaimers, provided that the following circumstances were met. First, the disclaimers would have to be filed within nine months of decedent's death. Second, the brother and sister could not accept any interest or benefits from the disclaimed property. Third, each interest of property under the will would have to constitute a separate interest.

[Priv. Ltr. Rul. 8908022.]

[2] Acceptance of Benefits

Implied promise of gifts does not void heirs' disclaimers. Decedent died in 1989, leaving a multimillion dollar estate for her ninety-two-year-old husband/ executor to administer. Decedent made more than thirty specific cash bequests to longtime friends, employees, and extended family members. She also made $500,000 bequests in trust to two grandnieces and a grandnephew, and left the residuary estate to her husband. To help reduce the significant transfer tax burden on the individual bequests, the husband asked twenty-nine of the heirs to disclaim the bequests. The disclaimers would cause the property to pass directly to the husband and be covered—as property passing directly from decedent to her surviving spouse—by the estate's marital deduction. The husband personally asked one grandniece and some employees to renounce the bequests, and his nephew asked the others. The heirs were told that the bequests would be significantly reduced by taxes, and that the husband was upset by this. They were also reminded of the husband's past generosity, informed they would be giving up a legal right, and told that the disclaimers had to be voluntary and without consideration. All twenty-nine agreed and signed disclaimers that were indisputedly valid under state law. The total disclaimed amount was $892,781, which passed to the husband and was claimed as part of the marital deduction on the estate's return. Then, shortly after the disclaimers were made, the husband gave each disclaimant a gift approximating the individual disclaimed bequest (which he reported on his gift tax returns). The Tax Court invalidated twenty-eight of the disclaimers, ruling that they were not "unqualified" refusals under Section 2518. That section defines "qualified disclaimer" as an irrevocable and unqualified refusal to accept an interest in property in which the disclaimant has not accepted any interest or benefit. The Tax Court reasoned that the heirs agreed to the disclaimers in exchange for the implied promise that they would be in a better tax position by doing so, and with the expectation of receiving the gifts. The Tax Court found this implied promise to be impermissible consideration for the disclaimers and concluded that, because these disclaimers rested on an implied promise or expectation, they were not "unqualified" refusals under Section 2518.

Held: Reversed for the estate. The circuit court flatly rejected the Tax Court's implied promise/expectation interpretation of Section 2518's "unqualified" as impermissibly vague and "inconsistent with a holistic reading" of the statute, regulations, and the IRS's letter rulings. The circuit court first pointed out that this interpretation was purely subjective and would defeat the law's purpose of facilitating post-death tax planning. The circuit court noted that disclaimers are rarely made without some sort of expectation or inducement. The circuit court then turned to Regulations § 25.2518-2(d)(1), which provides that a disclaimer is not valid under Section 2518 if the disclaimant accepts, impliedly or expressly, the disclaimed interest or its benefits or receives consideration in exchange for the disclaimer. The circuit court agreed with the estate that, under the regulation, a disclaimant must have received actual consideration in return for disclaiming his or her interest to have accepted the interest or its benefits, and that the mere expectation of a future benefit does not rise to the level of consideration. Thus, the heirs' alleged expectation of receiving the gifts was not consideration received in exchange for their disclaimers. This finding was supported by the IRS's own prior rulings, which found that a disclaimant's expectation that he or she would be better off by renouncing a bequest in favor of a decedent's spouse did not invalidate his or her disclaimer (see Private Letter Rulings 9427030 and 9509003). The circuit court concluded that, rather than a mere expectation or an implied promise, the distinction rested with disclaimers that are based on mutually-bargained-for consideration. In those instances, the disclaimers are made in return for consideration within the meaning of the regulation, and are therefore no longer unqualified refusals under Section 2518. Applying this bargained-for-consideration test to this case, the circuit court rejected the Tax Court's analysis of the disclaimers on a group basis. The correct approach was to evaluate each individual disclaimer and determine if it was made for actual, bargained-for consideration. With respect to each of the disclaimers, the nephew's recitation of the bequests' tax consequences and the legalities of disclaiming did not rise to the level of consideration. Moreover, his reference to the husband's past generosity was not sufficient to invalidate the disclaimers unless a specific heir actually interpreted this reference as a promise. The circuit court concluded that most of the disclaimers were made without consideration. In fact, some of the disclaimers were made for personal reasons inconsistent with any inducement by the husband. Further, with respect to a few disclaimants who might have—due to their individual relationships with the husband—interpreted the nephew's representations as a promise, or agreed to renounce out of fear of aggrieving the husband, there was still no actual evidence that they did so. Thus, the heirs' disclaimers were unqualified refusals as well. The circuit court did, however, remand with respect to six individual heirs whose testimonies, that they disclaimed on the belief the husband "would take care of us" or because he "would see to it that we get the full amount of our inheritance," put the status of their disclaimers in question.

[Estate of Monroe, 124 F3d 699, 80 AFTR2d 97-6826, (5th Cir. 1997).]

Assets of wife's estate are accepted by husband or his estate; renunciation of wife's estate by husband's estate is barred by Colorado statute. A husband and wife had been married since 1930 and had two children. The wife died on July 5, 1976, and, pursuant to her will, all of her property passed to her husband, who was subsequently appointed personal representative of the estate. The husband died unexpectedly on December 17, 1976, and his son was appointed personal representative of both estates. On March 15, 1977, a federal estate tax return was filed on behalf of the wife's estate, reflecting that her entire estate had passed to the husband. On account of the federal estate tax marital deduction and estate tax exemption, no federal estate tax was shown as due on the wife's return. On June 16, 1977, a tax return was filed for the husband's estate showing a net tax payable of $36,693. On December 19, 1977, the son, as personal representative, petitioned a Colorado probate court for an order of disclaimer renouncing on behalf of the husband's estate all rights and interests that it possessed in the estate of the wife. The petition was untimely because it was made well beyond the state statute of limitations. The disclaimer would have had no influence in determining who ultimately would take the property and was made solely to reduce the federal estate tax imposed on the combined estates. On January 11, 1978, the probate court approved the disclaimer, citing extraordinary circumstances. The court then ordered the reopening of the wife's estate to allow the receipt of property previously distributed in error to the husband's estate. After filing amended estate tax returns that reflected the new disposition of assets, the husband's estate filed a formal claim for refund with the IRS. The district court upheld the action of the probate court, and entered judgment for the estate. On the first appeal to the Tenth Circuit, that court partially remanded the action to the district court so that it would receive additional evidence on the validity of the disclaimer. The district court, on remand, again approved the Colorado probate court's action.

Held: Reversed for the IRS. The district court had erred in upholding the action of the Colorado probate court. The assets of the wife's estate were accepted by either her husband or by his estate through the actions of the personal representative. By virtue of this acceptance, renunciation of the estate was barred by a Colorado statute. Hence, there was no justification in law for the probate court's grant of the order of disclaimer and the reopening of the wife's estate to receive the previously distributed assets. There was no authority under Colorado law for reopening a closed estate merely to reduce the amount of federal estate tax. Accordingly, the district court's judgment against the IRS for the refund of federal estate taxes had to be reversed.

[Estate of Selby, 726 F2d 643, 53 AFTR2d 84-1590, 84-1 USTC ¶ 13,556 (10th Cir. 1984).]

Account set up with death benefits that entitled beneficiary to their use cannot be disclaimed. Shortly after an individual had died, his daughter found in his effects a letter that provided information about decedent's group life insurance policy, the beneficiary of which was decedent's sister. After the sister prepared the claim of loss that entitled her to the death benefits and sent it along with a death certificate to the insurance company, an account containing the insurance benefits was set up by the insurance company in the sister's name. The sister proposed to disclaim one-half of the amount in the account, so that the amount would pass to the estate and the daughter would receive those funds.

The IRS stated that the sister could draw on the account containing the entire amount of the insurance proceeds and that her acts were affirmative acts consistent with ownership, so that her disclaimer would not be qualified under Section 2518. The IRS also indicated that the transfer by the sister to decedent's estate was a transfer subject to the gift tax under Section 2501, but that it qualified for the annual exclusion under Section 2503(b) and the unified credit under Section 2505.

[Priv. Ltr. Rul. 8702024.]

[3] Interests Subject to Disclaimer

Disclaimer of tax benefits adds to marital deduction. Decedent's will directed the executor to pay out of the probate estate the estate tax on life insurance proceeds passing to decedent's son. Decedent's son, however, who was the policy's beneficiary, disclaimed the benefit and, in addition, gave the estate a check for the estimated tax due. The estate then claimed that this amount was restored to the bequest to decedent's spouse and qualified for the marital deduction. The IRS contended that the direction to the executor was not an interest in property that could be disclaimed. It therefore argued that the amount did not qualify for the marital deduction.

Held: For the estate. If an insurance policy is included in a decedent's estate because decedent retained an incident of ownership in it, Section 2206 permits the estate to require that the beneficiary of the policy reimburse the estate for the allocable federal estate tax in the absence of a will direction to the contrary. Section 2518 provides that if a person makes a qualified disclaimer of an interest in property, it is as if that interest were never transferred to the disclaimant. The Seventh Circuit noted that under state (Wisconsin) case law, a direction that state inheritance taxes, which would otherwise be paid by the legatees, be paid out of the residue of the estate constitutes a transfer of an interest in the estate. Thus, such a direction is a bequest of an interest in property. The IRS conceded that if the will had bequeathed an amount to the son to reimburse him for paying the estate tax, there would have been no question that Section 2518 would apply to disclaimer of this bequest. The court concluded that no distinction existed between a direction and a bequest, because state law provided that the son's disclaimer was one of a property interest. The court noted that a common form of a bequest is the forgiveness of a debt owed the testator. If the intended recipient disclaims it and insists on repaying the debt, such a disclaimer should be effective under Section 2518. Thus, the court rejected the IRS's position that a direction in the will is not a bequest. Here, because it transferred an interest in property, it was.

[Estate of Boyd, 819 F2d 170, 59 AFTR2d 87-1272, 87-1 USTC ¶ 13,720 (7th Cir. 1987).]

Tax Court upholds charitable estate tax deduction, despite existence of voidable forced heir's rights in donated property. Decedent died in 1980 and was survived by children and grandchildren. Under the terms of her will, a charitable foundation was to receive approximately $12.5 million, for which the estate claimed a charitable estate tax deduction under Section 2055. The IRS disallowed the claimed charitable deduction on the ground that it was voidable by the exercise of a forced heir's interest under state law. A "forced heir's," or "legitime," "interest" is that portion of a parent's estate of which he cannot disinherit his children without legal cause. All of decedent's children and grandchildren had previously waived their rights to claim their forced heir's interests in the charitable bequest. Section 2055 allows a federal estate tax deduction for charitable devises and bequests to qualified donee organizations. Under Regulations § 20.2055-2(b)(1), however, where a charitable devise or bequest is contingent upon the happening of a precedent event or condition, or upon the happening of a subsequent event or condition, a charitable deduction is not allowed unless the possibility of the occurrence of the event or condition is so remote as to be negligible. The IRS argued that the possibility that decedent's forced heirs would exercise their legitime interests was not so remote as to be negligible. The IRS also argued that in order for the charitable devise to be deductible, the forced heirs would have had to file disclaimers of their legitime interests as provided under Section 2518. The estate argued that the cases that have considered the effect on charitable deductions of state statutes that protect forced heirs have allowed charitable estate tax deductions where the charitable bequest was explicit in the will, where under state law the bequest to charity was merely voidable, and where the charitable donee actually received the full amount of the bequest with respect to which the charitable deduction was claimed.

Held: For the estate. The Tax Court noted that under local law, a testamentary disposition that impinges on a legitime interest is not void, but merely voidable. The court found that the relevant case law and Example 6 of Regulations § 20.2055-2(e)(1)(i) supported the estate's position. Under Example 6, a testator devises real property to charity. The charitable devise can be defeated by the exercise of the surviving spouse's statutory dower rights. The example concludes that the surviving spouse's unexercised dower rights are to be ignored, and that the charitable deduction is to be allowed. The court stated that the cases and regulations look beyond the voidable character of the gifts or disclaimers, and treat the gifts or disclaimers as effective and final, at least in those situations where the gifts or disclaimers in question are never voided. In other words, the mere voidability of a gift or disclaimer in these situations is not regarded as creating a contingency that fails the "so remote as to be negligible" test of the regulations under Section 2055. With respect to the IRS's argument that each of the forced heirs should have filed disclaimers that qualified under Section 2518, the court stated that Section 2518(b)(4) makes it clear that the provisions apply only where the interest in the property being disclaimed will be transferred to decedent's spouse or to a person other than the person making the disclaimer as a result of the disclaimer. The court stated that under the will, the devise and bequest in question passed to the foundation immediately upon the death of decedent. The transfer of ownership to the foundation occurred as a testamentary gift from decedent, not as a result of disclaimers executed by the forced heirs. Therefore, Section 2518 disclaimers were not required. Accordingly, the court upheld estate's deduction.

[Longue Vue Found., 90 TC 150 (1988), acq. 1989-1 CB 1.]

Disclaimer of interest in tenancy by entirety is not valid. Several years before decedent's death, she and her husband had acquired real estate as tenants by the entirety. When decedent died, her husband attempted to disclaim the interest in the property that would have otherwise passed to him as a result of her death. The IRS stated that the disclaimer was not a qualified disclaimer under Section 2518, which generally requires that a disclaimer must be executed within nine months of the transfer creating the interest. Under state law, decedent could not have severed her portion of the tenancy by the entirety without the consent of her husband. Therefore, the IRS concluded that the interests were created when the couple acquired the property, not when the wife died. Accordingly, the disclaimer was not timely, because it was not made within nine months of the transfer creating the interests. The fact that state law permitted the disclaimer of an interest in entireties property was not significant for purposes of Section 2518.

[Tech. Adv. Mem. 9208003.]

Disclaimer by trustee of heir who died shortly after original beneficiary of trust is qualified disclaimer. An individual had established a trust, with her father and a trust company serving as trustees. Under the trust, the settlor would receive the net income until death, with the corpus passing to her children when they became thirty years old. If the settlor had no children at death, the corpus was to pass to her father. If her father predeceased the settlor, the trust would go to her brothers and sisters, or to their surviving issue, per stirpes. When the settlor established the trust, she was eighteen and her father was fifty. Based on the gift tax regulations then applicable, the value of the right of a male age 50 to receive $1.00 at the death of a female age 18, provided that the male survived her, was $0.04138. Therefore, at the time that the trust was established, the present value of the father's interest was less than 5 percent of its value. The settlor died, survived only by her brothers and sisters. One of settlor's sisters died shortly thereafter, survived by three children. The sister's executor proposed to disclaim on her behalf the interest she received in the trust. The IRS stated that the proposed disclaimer would be a qualified disclaimer under Section 2518, provided that it was received within nine months of the original beneficiary's death.

[Priv. Ltr. Rul. 8911028.]

Children's renunciation of trust principal during parent's lifetime, but not after her death, is qualified disclaimer. Under the terms of a trust created in decedent's will, the trustee was directed to pay the net trust income to the surviving spouse, for her life, as well as distributions of principal for her reasonable support. The trustee was also directed to pay trust principal during the spouse's lifetime for the support and education of decedent's children. Upon the spouse's death, the trust principal was to be distributed in equal shares to the children. Within nine months of decedent's death, each of the children, having attained the age of majority, renounced the right to receive distributions of principal for support and education during the spouse's lifetime. Each child, however, retained the right to receive trust principal upon the death of the spouse.

The IRS stated that the children's renunciation of the right to receive trust principal distributions during their mother's lifetime was a qualified disclaimer under Section 2518. The IRS reasoned that under the relevant local disclaimer statute, the children's right to the remainder interest in the trust and their right to principal distributions during their mother's lifetime did not merge. "Rather, under local law, each child acquired two separate interests in the trust principal that could be independently renounced," stated the IRS.

[Priv. Ltr. Rul. 8546007.]

[4] Joint Interests

Joint tenancy disclaimer made by executor is qualified disclaimer for estate tax purposes because it is valid under applicable state law. Decedent's husband died, leaving his entire estate to her, and decedent died eight days later. The couple held a money market account, stocks, bonds, and certificates of deposit as joint tenants with right of survivorship. About five and one-half months later, decedent's executor filed a written statement of renunciation disclaiming, among other things, decedent's survivorship interests in the jointly held property. The estate filed tax returns, relying on the validity of the disclaimer. Thus, one half of the property held as joint tenants was included in decedent's estate and one-half in her husband's estate. The state revenue department accepted the disclaimer, but the IRS did not. The IRS claimed that the full value of the property held in joint tenancy should be included in decedent's estate, and the Tax Court upheld this determination.

Held: Reversed for the estate. Under Section 2518, disclaimers are valid if they comply with state law, are in writing, and are made within nine months of the transfer creating the interest disclaimed. For interests created after 1981, disclaimers need not be valid under state law if they comply with the requirements of Section 2518(c)(3). The lower court held that the joint tenancies in the stocks and bonds were created before 1982 and that the disclaimer was not valid under state law. It further held that the other joint tenancies were created after 1981, but did not comply with Section 2518(c)(3). The Tax Court found that North Carolina did not specifically authorize disclaimers of survivorship interests in jointly held property, and thus the disclaimers on joint tenancies created before 1982 were not valid. The appellate court disagreed with the Tax Court's interpretation and held that the disclaimer was valid under North Carolina law by virtue of its acceptance by the Department of Revenue. The lower court found that as to the interests created after 1981, the disclaimer was not timely filed. The appellate court stated that the timeliness of the disclaimer depended on when the interests were created. The IRS contended that they were created when the couple acquired the jointly held property, whereas the estate claimed that decedent's survivorship interest was created upon her husband's death. The estate's contention was premised on applicable state law that allows unilateral elimination or impairment of a survivorship interest by partition or attachment for debts. Regulations § 25.2518-2(c)(4)(i) provides that for tax purposes, a surviving joint tenant cannot make a disclaimer after nine months from the time the joint tenancy was created. The regulation recognizes, however, that the survivorship interest in a joint bank account is created on the death of the cotenant. The court concluded that there was no true distinction between a joint tenancy with a right of survivorship that is subject to partition by either cotenant and a joint bank account with right of survivorship that can be depleted through withdrawals by either cotenant. In either case, it is impossible to determine whether a cotenant has any right of survivorship until the other tenant dies. The court relied on Kennedy, 804 F2d 1332, 862 USTC ¶ 13,699 (7th Cir. 1986), which held that the unilateral power of partition means that only one-half of the undivided interest has been irrevocably transferred to the joint tenants at the time the tenancy is created. Since the survivorship interest may be eliminated at the will of one joint tenant, the interest is created only when a cotenant dies without having partitioned the tenancy. Thus, the court in the instant case held that since the disclaimer was of decedent's survivorship interest, not of her original one-half interest in the property, the dis-claimer was timely.

[Estate of Dancy, 872 F2d 84, 89-1 USTC ¶ 13,800, 63 AFTR2d 89-1560 (4th Cir. 1989).]

Time for disclaimer is measured from date of joint tenant's death. Tax-payer and her husband had owned land under joint tenancies created before 1977. Within nine months of the husband's death in 1981, taxpayer disclaimed her survivorship interests in the joint tenancies. As a result, the property passed to three of decedent's children. Taxpayer contended that the transfer of her survivorship interest in the jointly held real property had occurred on the date of death of the first joint tenant, her husband. Thus, taxpayer argued that her disclaimer made within nine months of her husband's death was qualified under Section 2518, even though the joint tenancy had been created years before. Under Regulations § 25.2518-2(c)(3), applicable to disclaimers after 1976, a person to whom any interest in property passes because of the lapse of a general power of appointment may disclaim such interest within a nine-month period after the lapse. Regulations § 25.2511-1(c)(2) applies to transfers creating an interest in the disclaimant before 1977. It requires that the dis-claimer be made within a reasonable time after the transfer. The Tax Court had adopted the IRS's position that "transfer" for purposes of the disclaimer provisions refers to the transfer creating the joint tenancy. Since the joint ten-ancies were created prior to 1977, the disclaimer in 1981 was not made within a reasonable time. In reaching this conclusion, the Tax Court relied primarily on Jewett, 455 US 305 (1982). There the Supreme Court had ruled that the disclaimer of a not-yet-vested interest in a trust was not timely where it oc-curred thirty-three years after the trust's creation.

Held: Reversed for taxpayer in part. The Eighth Circuit agreed with the taxpayer that the relevant transfer in the instant case had occurred at the time of the husband's death. In so holding, the court followed Kennedy, 804 F2d 1332 (7th Cir. 1986). There the Seventh Circuit in distinguishing *Jewett* held that a deceased joint tenant's power of partition is equivalent to a general power of appointment over the survivorship interest. By partitioning the prop-erty, the joint tenant can defeat the survivorship interest and direct his or her interest to creditors and other devisees. Thus, the relevant transfer for purposes of the disclaimer provisions occurs at the death of the first joint tenant, not at the creation of the joint tenancy. Applying this reasoning, the Eighth Circuit held that because decedent in the instant case died in 1981, Section 2518 ap-plied. Taxpayer's disclaimer, made within nine months of decedent's death (when his power of partition lapsed), was timely.

[McDonald, 853 F2d 1494, 88-2 USTC ¶ 13,778, 62 AFTR2d 88-5995 (8th Cir. 1988).]

Disclaimer of interest in tenancy by entirety is not valid. Several years before decedent's death, she and her husband had acquired real estate as tenants by the entirety. When she died, her husband attempted to disclaim the interest in the property that would have otherwise passed to him as a result of her death. The IRS stated that the disclaimer was not a qualified disclaimer under Section 2518, which generally requires that a disclaimer must be executed within nine months of the transfer creating the interest. Under state law, decedent could not have severed her portion of the tenancy by the entirety without the consent of her husband. Therefore, the IRS concluded that the interests were created when the couple acquired the property, not when the wife died. Accordingly, the disclaimer was not timely, because it was not made within nine months of the transfer creating the interests. The fact that state law permitted the disclaimer of an interest in entireties property was not significant for purposes of Section 2518.

[Tech. Adv. Mem. 9208003.]

Joint interest in U.S. Savings Bonds may be disclaimed. When decedent died, he possessed U.S. Series E and H Savings Bonds registered in joint and survivorship form, with taxpayer as the other joint tenant. In addition, decedent had owned bonds registered in his name and payable to taxpayer upon decedent's death. Within nine months of decedent's death, taxpayer filed with the estate's executor a written disclaimer of her interest in the bonds. When a person makes a qualified disclaimer, it is as if the disclaimed interest had never been transferred to that person. Under Section 2518(b), "qualified disclaimer" is an irrevocable and unqualified refusal by a person to accept an interest in property if:

1. The refusal is in writing.
2. The writing is received by the transferor of the interest, his legal representative, or the holder of the legal title to the property to which the interest relates within nine months after the later of the day on which the transfer creating the interest was made or the disclaimant reaches age 21.
3. The disclaimant has not accepted the interest or any of its benefits.
4. The interest passes to decedent's spouse or to a person other than the disclaimant, without any direction from the disclaimant.

Under Regulations § 25.2518-2(d)(1), a qualified disclaimer cannot be made for an interest in property if the disclaimant has accepted the interest or any of its benefits, expressly or impliedly, prior to making the disclaimer. Merely taking delivery of an instrument of title, however, does not constitute acceptance of the interest or any of its benefits. A disclaimant does not accept property simply because, under applicable local law, title to the property vests immediately in the disclaimant when decedent dies.

Citing Revenue Ruling 68-269, 1968-1 CB 399, the IRS concluded that the disclaimer was effective. There an individual purchased savings bonds with his separate funds and had them registered in his name as owner, payable on death to an individual as beneficiary (e.g., John Jones, payable on death to Mary Jones). The revenue ruling concludes that there is no completed gift to the beneficiary, because the owner may redeem the bonds at will and does not have to account to the beneficiary for the funds. The revenue ruling also considers the situation in which the owner bought savings bonds with his separate funds and had them registered in his name and that of another individual in the alternative as co-owners (e.g., John Jones or Mary Jones). It concludes that there is no completed gift unless the second co-owner surrenders the bonds for cash, without any obligation to account for a part of the proceeds to the first co-owner. Here the disclaimer of decedent's bonds was timely and in writing. The disclaimant did not accept the interest disclaimed or any of its benefits and did not cash any of the bonds after decedent's death. Because decedent could have cashed in the bonds while he was alive, and without the disclaimant's consent, there was no completed gift of the bonds before decedent's death. The nine-month period for making a qualified disclaimer began to run for all of the bonds when decedent died, because that is the first date on which a transfer tax would have been imposed. Because the disclaimer was qualified, taxpayer was treated as never having received the bonds. In addition, she was not deemed to have made a gift to the beneficiary to whom the interest passed because of the disclaimer.

[Priv. Ltr. Rul. 9017026.]

Survivor may disclaim interest in brokerage account after making cash gifts from brokerage account. A married couple had owned a general brokerage account jointly with a right of survivorship. The husband died in 1987, designating the surviving spouse as the principal beneficiary of his estate. The survivor had not made any withdrawals from the account before the spouse's death and subsequently was confined to a nursing hospital with a debilitating sickness. The survivor's conservator applied for, and received, permission to make gifts of cash on the survivor's behalf from the account. The conservator proposed to file a disclaimer on the survivor's behalf for one half of the account passing because of the spouse's death plus the income on that half, less the gifts and the income attributable to them.

The IRS stated that the conservator could make a valid disclaimer on behalf of the invalid survivor because the disclaimed interest satisfied the requirements of Regulations § 25.2518-2(d)(1). The IRS noted that no part of the interest had inured to the survivor's benefit, that the disclaimer would be timely because it would be filed within nine months of the spouse's death, and that as a result of the disclaimer, the interest would pass, without direction by the disclaimant, to a trust for the surviving spouse and other descendants of decedent.

[Priv. Ltr. Rul. 8827072.]

Settlement between son and stepmother was qualified disclaimer, allowing for marital deduction. Following decedent's death in 1987, a will that left all his property to his son was probated. Before the estate tax return was due, however, the son and his stepmother moved to have the will set aside. They claimed that the probated document was only a copy of an original will, which had been destroyed, and that decedent had intended to make a new will leaving only $600,000 (the maximum amount sheltered by the unified credit) to his son and the remainder to his wife. The probate court granted a motion to settle the will contest by having the parties receive these amounts. The estate tax return likewise reflected these figures and, after applying the marital deduction and unified credit, indicated that no estate tax was due. The IRS, however, denied the entire marital deduction on the ground that the probated will left all the property to the son and the will contest agreement was invalid. The Tax Court agreed, sustaining deficiencies in estate tax of $1.63 million and gift tax (on the transfer of property from the son to his stepmother) of $1.3 million, plus a $324,438 addition to tax for failure to file the gift tax return. The case turned on whether the disclaimer was qualified.

Held: Reversed for taxpayer. Section 2518(b)(4) requires that the property pass to the surviving spouse "without any direction on the part of the person making the disclaimer." The Tax Court had found that the interest would not have passed to decedent's spouse without the son's direction. Under New Mexico law, disclaimed property passes as if the disclaimant predeceased decedent. For the year at issue, this meant that the property would have passed to the son's two illegitimate children, if they were his "heirs," instead of to his stepmother.

At that time, state law provided that an illegitimate child is an heir if the father "recognized the child in writing by an instrument signed by him, which shows upon its face that it was so signed *with the intent of recognizing the child as an heir.*" The Tax Court found that the son had done so, citing income tax returns on which he had listed the children as dependents and indicated "son" next to each of their names. The Tenth Circuit, however, faulted the Tax Court for equating "son" for federal income tax purposes with "heir" under the state's probate code, and held that income tax returns did not establish the requisite intention to recognize the illegitimate children as heirs. The appellate court also rejected the IRS's reliance on cases from other states whose statutes were not as specific in requiring that the parent recognize the child *as an heir,* rather than merely recognizing paternity. Thus, decedent's son did not have any heirs, and the disclaimed property would have passed by operation of law to the surviving spouse. Accordingly, the direction in the settlement agreement to that effect was not fatal and the disclaimer was qualified under Section 2518(b)(4). As such, the property passed from decedent to his surviving spouse, the marital deduction eliminated any estate tax liability, there was no gift from decedent's son to his stepmother, and there could be no addition to tax for failure to file a gift tax return.

[Estate of DePaoli, 62 F3d 1259, 76 AFTR2d 95-5881, 95-2 USTC ¶ 60,205 (10th Cir. 1995).]

[5] Judicial Reformation

Estate complies with time limitations for reformation of will. Decedent had executed a will in 1968 and died in 1982. The estate tax return was filed in March 1983. The will provided for a testamentary trust the net income of which was to be paid to decedent's sister, and the corpus was to be distributed on her death to charities and to one noncharitable beneficiary. The sister disclaimed her interest in the trust. Before October 16, 1984, the estate filed a petition with the local probate court to reform the will.

The IRS stated that the reformation of decedent's will was timely filed for purposes of Section 2055(e)(3)(C)(iii)(I). The IRS expressed no opinion on whether the reformation was a "qualified reformation" for purposes of Section 2055(e)(3)(B).

[Priv. Ltr. Rul. 8605003.]

[6] Marital Deduction

Disclaimer of direction restores marital deduction. A beneficiary of a life insurance policy on decedent disclaimed the right to have decedent's estate pay the estate tax on the policy's proceeds. The beneficiary was decedent's son, and the proceeds were an asset of the estate pursuant to Section 2042. The will directed the executor to pay out of the probate estate the tax allocable to the proceeds. The son disclaimed the benefit and gave the estate a check for the estimated tax due. Section 2518 provides that if a person makes a qualified disclaimer of an interest in property, for purposes of calculating estate tax, it shall be as if that person had never received the interest disclaimed. The IRS contended that the direction to the executor was not "an interest in property." The estate argued that the disclaimer operated to restore this amount to the assets qualifying for the marital deduction.

Held: For the estate. The Seventh Circuit noted that under state case law, a direction for state inheritance taxes (which would otherwise be paid by the legatees) to be paid out of the residue of the estate constituted a transfer of an interest in the estate. Thus, by state law, such a direction is a bequest of an interest in property. The situation was thus distinguishable from that in Jeschke, 814 F2d 568 (10th Cir. 1987), where there was no suggestion that state law treated the obligation of a surviving spouse to pay certain expenses as conferring property interest on other beneficiaries. The IRS conceded that if the will had bequeathed an amount to reimburse the son for paying the estate tax, there would have been no question that Section 2518 applied. The court concluded that no distinction existed, because state law provided that this was a disclaimer of a property interest. The court noted that a common form of a bequest is the forgiveness of a debt owed to the testator. If the intended recipient insists on repaying the debt, such a disclaimer should be effective under Section 2518. Thus, a direction may be a bequest.

[Estate of Boyd, 819 F2d 170, 59 AFTR2d 87-1272, 87-1 USTC ¶ 13,720 (7th Cir. 1987).]

Trustees' disclaimer cannot create marital deduction. Decedent's will poured the residue of the estate into an existing inter vivos trust. At the time of decedent's death, this trust was divided into two separate trusts—the Family Trust and the Memorial Trust. Under the terms of the Memorial Trust, the trustees were to pay the net income of the trust to the surviving spouse during her lifetime. The trustees were also authorized, however, to pay medical, funeral, and burial expenses for three relatives of decedent from either income or principal. In addition, the trustees were authorized to pay educational benefits for certain individuals from trust income or principal. The trustees had the right to terminate the trust if they determined that it was so small that it was difficult to manage and did not accomplish the purposes for which it was established under decedent's will. After decedent's death, in an effort to obtain a marital deduction for a portion of the Memorial Trust, the trustees disclaimed some of their powers under the trust agreement. Members of decedent's family also disclaimed specified trust benefits (e.g., certain medical benefits). A state probate court confirmed the disclaimers. A qualifying income interest for life, as required by Section 2056(b)(7), exists if (1) a surviving spouse is entitled to all of the income from the property, payable at least annually and (2) no person has a power to appoint any of the property to anyone other than the surviving spouse. The IRS disallowed the marital deduction on the ground that the surviving spouse did not have a qualifying income interest for life, because:

1. The trustees could pay the medical and educational benefits from the income of the trust.
2. The amount of the medical benefits and the number of educational beneficiaries were unlimited, and thus the trustees conceivably could appoint the entire trust to someone other than the spouse.

3. The trustees had the power to terminate the trust.
4. The trustees had the power to allocate income to principal and thereby defeat the spouse's income interest.

Although the estate conceded that the trust failed to meet the requirements of QTIP, the estate contended that the disclaimers cured the defects in the trust agreement to permit a marital deduction.

Held: For the IRS. The Tax Court agreed with the IRS that the trustees did not have the authority to change the unambiguous terms of the trust agreement. The court rejected the trustees' attempts, through renunciation of certain powers, to substitute their view of decedent's intent and to rewrite the trust agreement to allow a marital deduction that neither the will nor the trust agreement provided for. According to the court, the trustees sought to disclaim powers and duties that would amount to a renunciation of their trusteeships. Such a renunciation could not be effective, particularly if it was for the sole purpose of changing the tax results. The state probate court order confirming the disclaimers was not binding on the Tax Court. Thus, although disclaimers are frequently used to remedy a defective QTIP trust, the court refused to permit this where the result would be to rewrite the trust.

[Estate of Bennett, 100 TC (1993).]

Estate may deduct spousal allowance provided under state law. Two months after decedent's death, the surviving spouse petitioned the state court and received her statutory allowance. The surviving spouse also disclaimed her life estate in the homestead, which immediately passed to decedent's three children. The estate deducted the spousal allowance and the surviving spouse's one-third interest in the homestead. The IRS disallowed two-thirds of the statutory allowance and the entire homestead deduction. The estate argued that the spousal allowance was not a terminable interest under Section 2056 and that it qualified for the marital deduction. Furthermore, the waiver of the homestead resulted in a one-third fee interest under state law and was deductible.

Held: For taxpayer in part. The spousal allowance was deductible because state law was not discretionary and did not contain any contingencies. Thus, the allowance was a nonterminable interest. The waiver of the homestead passed the property directly to the children, however, and no marital deduction was allowed for that interest.

[Estate of Radel, 88 TC 1143 (1987), acq. 1987-2 CB 1.]

Wife's interest in residence fails to qualify as QTIP, despite disclaimer. Decedent left an interest in his personal residence to his wife, directing in his will that she could use and occupy the residence for her life unless she moved out or remarried. The remainder interest in the residence was left to decedent's sons. In an attempt to qualify the wife's interest for QTIP treatment, the sons and grandchildren executed disclaimers of any interest in the residence that they had that might arise during the wife's lifetime. The IRS stated that though beneficiaries may disclaim one interest in property while retaining another interest in the same property, they may not disclaim a part of a single interest. To qualify for a partial disclaimer, the interest disclaimed must be separately created by the transferor or must be a separate portion of an interest. The IRS concluded that there could not be a partial disclaimer of the remainder interest of the beneficiaries that might come into existence on the wife's moving or remarrying. Without such a disclaimer, the wife could not have a qualifying interest for life in the residence as required for QTIP treatment. Thus, her interest in the residence could not be a QTIP interest.

[Priv. Ltr. Rul. 9140004.]

Children's renunciations of interests in trust constitute qualified disclaimers; spouse's property interest qualifies for QTIP election. Decedent left a will that bequeathed the residue of his estate to a trust for the benefit of his spouse and their two children. The spouse was guaranteed a specific sum, and the children would receive the balance in equal amounts. Upon the death of the spouse, the assets in the trust would be distributed equally to the children or to their respective lineal descendants, per stirpes; neither of the children had accepted any benefits. The children proposed to execute a joint disclaimer in writing within nine months of their parent's death, by which disclaimer they would disclaim their right to receive any invasion of the principal during the life of the spouse. Upon the execution of the disclaimer, the trust would be split into two trusts. One trust would be for the benefit of the spouse and would pay out all of the current income, or, if less than $1,000, it would pay the spouse $1,000 per month. The other trust would provide for the payment of net income at least quarterly to the children, and the trustee could invade the corpus for the children's support and maintenance. Upon the spouse's death, the assets of both trusts would be distributed to the children in equal shares and per stirpes. Upon execution of the disclaimer and creation of the two additional trusts pursuant to a local court order, the executor of the estate would make an election under Section 2056(b)(7) to treat the trust so that it would be for the benefit of the spouse as qualified terminable interest property (QTIP).

The IRS stated that the proposed disclaimer was valid because the children would have delivered to the trustee a written notice of their renunciation of their right to invade up to one-half of the original trust during the life of the spouse, and because they have affirmed that they have not accepted any benefits from the trust. Therefore, the IRS indicated that the renunciations by the children would constitute qualified disclaimers under Section 2518. With respect to the trusts created by the renunciation, the IRS concluded that the surviving spouse's interests in trusts would be qualified terminable interest property within the meaning of Section 2056(b)(7). The IRS relied upon the facts that the spouse was entitled to receive, on a monthly basis, at least all of the net income from the trust for her lifetime, and that no income or corpus was payable to anyone else during her lifetime.

[Priv. Ltr. Rul. 8815038.]

Children's disclaimers are sufficient to allow interest to pass to surviving spouse who is entitled to marital deduction. An individual died in Oklahoma owning interests in bank accounts and savings certificates that had been held in joint tenancy with his surviving spouse and his children. Within nine months of decedent's death, the children filed valid disclaimers under Oklahoma law to their interests in the accounts and certificates.

The IRS stated that the disclaimed interests must be treated as passing directly from decedent to the surviving spouse, who was entitled to a marital deduction under Section 2056. The value of the accounts and certificates was includable in the gross estate of decedent under Section 2040, the IRS added. In its analysis, the IRS examined the disclaimers and determined that they complied with the four requirements for a valid disclaimer under Section 2518(b).

[Priv. Ltr. Rul. 8625001.]

IRS classifies qualified disclaimers and issues private ruling on marital deduction allowable to one estate. An individual had entered into a revocable trust agreement with his wife in 1962. The individual had executed his will at about the same time. The will and the trust agreement had been altered in 1965 but had not been amended after that date. The will passed the residue of the individual's estate to the trust. The trust agreement stated that the trust estate was to be distributed "in such a manner as will secure the maximum marital deduction and/or community property exclusion under the federal estate tax laws in force at the death of" the individual. Another trust provision stated that the trust should be divided into two parts, each to be administered as a separate trust. The individual died in 1984.

The IRS stated that the estate was not subject to the transitional rule of Section 403(a) of the Economic Recovery Tax Act of 1981, because the testator's intent was "to give his spouse the benefit of any post execution increases in the allowable deduction and to have any statute in effect at his death applied to the trust to accomplish this result." Accordingly, the estate qualified for an unlimited marital deduction. The state where the individual's will was probated had enacted a statute to allow wills drafted before September 13, 1981, to avoid the transitional rule.

[Priv. Ltr. Rul. 8610032.]

[7] Partial Disclaimers

Administrative expense allocation allowed after partial disclaimer. Decedent's surviving spouse made a timely waiver of a portion of her interest in a marital trust by using a formula disclaimer. The disclaimer stated that she accepted her interest in the portion of the trust required to reduce the taxable estate to the "pecuniary amount of $500,000." The will was silent as to how administration expenses should be charged. The estate allocated the expenses, which were claimed as an income tax deduction, to the successor beneficiary. The IRS argued that the expenses were allocable to the marital bequest.

Held: For taxpayer. The disclaimer provides for a formula amount subject to a maximum of $500,000 and is not a pecuniary bequest of that amount. In calculating the disclaimer amount, the estate correctly accounted for administrative expenses. Thus, the expenses did not reduce the marital bequest.

[Estate of McInnes, 64 TCM 840, RIA TC Memo. ¶ 92,558 (1992).]

Disclaimer of fractional portion of individual retirement account allows widow to maximize unified credit available to her husband's estate. When *A* died, he held an individual retirement account (IRA) of which his wife, *B*, was the beneficiary. Under Section 408(d)(3)(C)(ii), *B* could roll over the account when she inherited it. However, she decided to disclaim part of the account. The portion disclaimed was to go into a trust established by her husband for the benefit of *B* and their children. Because the trust was included in *A*'s taxable estate, exempted only to the extent of the unified credit, *B* wanted to disclaim only that portion of the IRA that would not have brought the trust above the credit limit. Although she was herself a beneficiary of the family trust, disclaimers of interests by spouses were not precluded, even if the spouse received another interest in the property disclaimed. Therefore, *B* was able to use a fractional disclaimer to assure that the maximum amount was included free of estate tax in the family trust.

[Priv. Ltr. Rul. 8922036.]

Disclaimants' retention of remainder interests in trust corpus does not disqualify disclaimers. An individual died testate on March 13, 1988, survived by his wife and five children. The residue of his estate was placed in trust, with the bank designated as trustee. The trust was to terminate on the death of the spouse, with the remaining principal to be divided among the children. It was represented that no child had accepted any interest or benefit from the estate property, but that each child was to accept an immediate distribution of 11 percent, to which each was entitled at decedent's death. Each of the children proposed to disclaim all rights to receive any portion of trust income or principal during his mother's lifetime. Afterward the personal representative of the estate was to make an election under Section 2056(b)(7) to treat the remaining assets as qualified terminable interest property. The bank that was named trustee merged with another financial institution subsequent to the execution of the will. The beneficiaries sought a declination from the institution renouncing its nomination as trustee, on the basis that real property owned by the estate and passing into the trust was in a state in which the institution was not qualified to do business. A court ordered that the wife and children be appointed cosuccessor trustees.

The IRS stated that the disclaimers by the children would be qualified disclaimers under Section 2518, provided that the requirements of Sections 2518(b)(1) and 2518(b)(2) were satisfied, and provided that the disclaimants did not accept any interest or benefit from the estate before the execution of the disclaimers. The IRS noted that the disclaimants' retention of remainder interests in the trust corpus would not disqualify the disclaimers under Regulations § 25.2518-3(d). The IRS also concluded that the trust constituted a QTIP under Section 2056(b)(7). The IRS noted that the disclaimant's retention of interests would not disqualify the trust under Section 2056(b)(7).

[Priv. Ltr. Rul. 8906036.]

Renunciation of interests in specified trust assets is not qualified disclaimer. Upon the death of the grantor of a revocable inter vivos trust, the grantor's spouse was to become the trustee. The trust was to continue for the lifetime of the surviving spouse, distributing to the surviving spouse any portion of the corpus that he requested. The remainder would pass to the children of the grantor and the surviving spouse. Within nine months of the grantor's death, the surviving spouse renounced his interests in specified assets of the trust corpus. Consequently, these assets passed to the children.

The IRS concluded in technical advice that a renunciation of a portion of an individual's lifetime income interest in, and general power of appointment over, trust property is not a "qualified disclaimer" under Section 2518 if the renunciation relates to specific trust assets.

[Tech. Adv. Mem. 8332014.]

¶ 1.05 TAX REFUNDS

Tax refund on joint income tax return is includable in decedent's gross estate. Decedent died in 1981, and his surviving spouse elected to file a joint income tax return for that year. On the estate tax return of decedent, no estate tax liability was shown. On its final audit of the estate tax return, the IRS determined that a portion of the tax refunded on the joint income tax return was includable in decedent's estate, and denied the estate's claim that it was entitled to an income tax deduction for taxes paid in 1981. The estate paid the deficiency and brought this suit for refund.

Held: For the IRS. Regulations § 20.2053-6(f) provides that unpaid income taxes are deductible from the gross estate if they are on income property properly includable in the income tax return of decedent for a period before death. The amount of the deduction, in cases where a joint return is filed by the surviving spouse, bears the same ratio to the joint tax liability as the amount of decedent's separate tax deduction bears to both spouses' separate tax liability if separate returns are filed. The regulation further states that in any event, the deduction cannot exceed the lesser of decedent's liability reduced by amounts already paid by decedent or by any amount payable by the estate toward joint tax liability pursuant to an enforceable agreement between decedent and his spouse. If a refund is due, the portion to which the estate is entitled is includable in the gross estate. Such amount is presumed to be the amount by which decedent's contributions toward payment of the joint tax liability exceeds the liability as determined by the above-mentioned ratio formula. The court held that because withholding credits available to decedent left no remaining balance of unpaid tax liability of decedent for assertion as a claim against the estate, no deduction for 1981 income taxes was available to lessen the gross estate. The court did not accept the estate's method of calculation, which included a negative tax liability for the surviving spouse resulting from a net loss incurred from a tax shelter partnership. The court explained that if a separate return was filed by the spouse, the net loss could provide only a zero income tax liability and would not have provided a negative tax liability. Thus, the IRS's method of calculation, which included a zero income tax liability for the spouse, was proper. Since a portion of the income tax refund obtained by the surviving spouse was attributable to withholding credits of decedent, such amounts were properly includable in the gross estate.

[Cherney, 89-1 USTC ¶ 13,799, 63 AFTR2d 89-1556 (D. Neb. 1989).]

¶ 1.06 COMMUNITY PROPERTY

No portion of post-marriage appreciation in value of decedent's stock is community property and thus is not excludable from gross estate. Decedent had inherited 35 percent of the stock in GHS, Inc., from her first husband. Decedent died in 1979, survived by her second husband, whom she had married in 1975. The principal asset in her estate was the block of GHS, Inc., stock that she had inherited. Decedent's spouse filed a petition in the California courts to establish that 50 percent of the appreciation in value of this stock during the marriage was his under the community property laws. This action was dropped during extensive settlement negotiations. The estate tax return was filed on September 11, 1980. In March 1982, decedent's spouse renewed his $4 million claim against the estate, and, in May 1982, a settlement in the amount of $375,000 was reached. The IRS audited the estate and, in the course of the audit, allowed the settlement payment to be deducted in full as a marital deduction. The estate paid the additional tax required as a result of the audit and, in 1984, filed a refund claim on the ground that the $4 million community property claim by decedent's spouse was excludable in its entirety from decedent's gross estate or, in the alternative, was deductible as a claim against the estate. The estate, at trial, conceded that the $4 million was not deductible, but then argued that the $375,000 settlement amount was deductible. The district court allowed the estate a deduction for the settlement.

Held: Reversed for the IRS. Under California law, any appreciation in the value of separate property is also considered separate property, unless it can be shown that all or a portion of the appreciation is attributable to the post-marriage efforts or skill of the spouse who owns the property. The estate had not shown that decedent had expended more than a minimal amount of time and effort on the enhancement of the stock's value. Furthermore, the settlement payment was not deductible as a claim against the estate, because it involved the relinquishment of the spouse's claim to a community property interest in the GHS, Inc., stock.

[Trust Servs. of Am., 885 F2d 561, 89-2 USTC ¶ 13,815, 64 AFTR2d 89-5920 (9th Cir. 1989).]

Ninth Circuit orders second remand in complex community property estate settlement. Decedent, who died in 1968, had been the founder and a principal owner of a savings and loan association. During decedent's lifetime, he had created a revocable trust that, by the terms of his will, became irrevocable on the date of his death. The trust provided, among other things, for a marital trust and for the payment of certain estate expenses. In addition, the trust was to include property having a value equal to the value of his wife's share of community property, not to exceed $5 million. She also received various smaller bequests plus $750,000 from the estate in settlement of her challenge to the testamentary dispositions. The IRS, in its original audit, allowed a marital deduction for the $750,000 payment, but later changed its position and disallowed the deduction. In the first trial of the case, the district court found that the wife had an enforceable right to receive more than $5.75 million in community property and that decedent apparently intended that she should receive all of her community property interest in addition to the marital trust. The Ninth Circuit, in a decision reported at 674 F2d 761, 48 AFTR2d 81-6317, 81-2 USTC ¶ 13,438 (9th Cir. 1981), held that such finding constituted a clear error, because the $750,000 paid in settlement of community property claims would be excludable from the gross estate only if the wife had an enforceable right under state law. Accordingly, the case was remanded to the district court in order to resolve the confusion on these issues. On remand, the district court held that the estate was not entitled to a community property exclusion, because of the $750,000 payment to the wife in settlement of her claims against the estate. In reaching this conclusion, the court determined that the wife had no enforceable right to receive the $750,000, because California law does not allow a surviving spouse to claim community property passing outside the will in addition to testamentary gifts intended to dispose of the surviving spouse's share of community property. On appeal, the estate claimed that there was, in fact, an enforceable right in favor of the wife to the extent of $5.75 million.

Held: Reversed for the estate. The Ninth Circuit concluded that an issue of material fact existed with respect to the value of the wife's community property interest, and that the lower court erred in its application of governing law. If the payment of $5.75 million was made to settle the wife's community property claims, and if the claim was worth that much, judgment would have to be entered for the estate, notwithstanding the fact that the settlement agreement did not expressly support the estate's argument.

[Ahmanson Found., 733 F2d 623, 53 AFTR2d 84-1648, 84-1 USTC ¶ 13,572 (9th Cir. 1984).]

Income derived from trusts during marriage is separate property of wife, not community property. Decedent, a resident of Texas, died during 1976 and was survived by his wife. The couple had been married in 1927 and had moved to Texas in the following year. At the time of decedent's death, his wife was the owner of certain shares of stock and bank accounts that she had acquired through the years with funds paid to her from seven separate irrevocable trusts. Six of the trusts were created by the wife's parents for her benefit, and the seventh had been established by decedent himself, naming his wife as sole income beneficiary. The IRS determined that the stocks and bank accounts constituted community property under Texas law, and, accordingly, the IRS sought to include half of their value in decedent's gross estate. The estate contended that the property in question was solely that of the wife under state law.

Held: For the estate. The court ruled that the issue whether the income from the seven trusts constituted the wife's separate property was to be determined with reference to state law, which determines questions of community property for federal tax purposes. Under Texas law, the income derived from the trusts during the marriage was not community property, because it was received by her solely as a gift. Accordingly, decedent had no recognizable property interest in the wife's trust income, and therefore no part of it was includable in his gross estate.

[Wilmington Trust Co., 4 Cl. Ct. 6, 53 AFTR2d 84-1556, 83-2 USTC ¶ 13,547 (1983), aff'd, 753 F2d 1055, 55 AFTR2d 85-1572, 85-2 USTC ¶ 13,625 (Fed. Cir. 1985).]

IRS construes will to divide community and separate property. Decedent died in Texas, leaving a holographic will declaring that all of his property was community property and that his wife owned half of it. The will provided that if a court declared that some of his property was separate property, his executor should "distribute my property . . . in a manner such that an equal share of the dollar value shall vest in (my wife) . . . and a like share shall vest in The . . . Bank . . . as trustee." The will also provided that when the wife agreed to the division of assets, she should hold them in fee simple.

The IRS stated that decedent's estate correctly construed the will to leave half of decedent's community property and half his separate property to his wife. The IRS commented that "[t]he alternative construction suggested that decedent intended to leave his surviving spouse none of his interest in the community estate, since she 'already owns' one-half of such property, is without merit."

[Priv. Ltr. Rul. 8513002.]

CHAPTER **2**

Valuation of Property

¶ 2.01 VALUATION FACTORS AND METHODS

[1] Generally

IRS can revalue gifts for estate tax purposes, rules Eighth Circuit. Decedent made two gifts of mineral rights in January 1981. He filed a gift tax return for that year, listing the taxable value of the interests at $14,769. The tax computed on the gifts was offset by his unified credit. Decedent died in 1985; his federal estate tax return included the $14,769 of adjusted taxable gifts. In August 1986, for reasons unrelated to this case, the estate filed an amended estate tax return, requesting a partial refund. Upon reviewing the return, the IRS decided that the value of the mineral gifts should be increased to $135,750, generating additional estate tax of $35,123. The estate paid the tax and then filed for a refund. The estate filed suit when its request for a refund was denied. The estate apparently did not dispute the accuracy of the IRS's valuation of the gifts. The estate's claim was based on the fact that the statute of limitations for assessing gift tax had passed and, therefore, the IRS was barred from revaluing the gifts for estate tax purposes. The district court agreed with the estate. Under the unified gift and estate tax system, the adjusted taxable gifts made during a person's lifetime are added to his estate at death to determine the tentative estate tax. This amount is reduced by a hypothetical tax computed on the adjusted taxable gifts. The estate in the instant case argued that the IRS could not revalue the gifts for estate tax purposes because the three-year statute of limitations had run, and the value of the gift was "fixed" pursuant to Section 2504(c). Section 2504(c) prohibits the IRS from challenging the valuation of gifts for gift tax purposes if the gift tax statute of limitations has expired and a gift tax has been assessed or paid. The IRS agreed that it could not revalue the gifts to assess additional gift tax. It did not agree, however, that the limitations in Section 2504(c) applied to revaluation for estate tax purposes. The IRS position was that Section 2504(c) applied only to gift tax calculations.

Held: For the IRS. Citing Levin (Estate of Prince), 986 F2d 91 (4th Cir. 1993), the Eighth Circuit stated that the unification of the estate and gift tax systems does not permit a taxpayer to reduce the value of his estate by undervaluing lifetime gifts. In *Levin,* decedent did not report on her gift tax return $20,000 in gifts of Atlanta, Georgia Project Notes that she made in 1984, because the notes were to be tax exempt under the Housing Act of 1937. In 1988, the Supreme Court ruled that the notes were not tax-exempt. When decedent died, the IRS included the project notes in the calculation of estate tax, even though the statute of limitations for imposing gift tax had expired. The Fourth Circuit agreed with the IRS, finding nothing in Section 6501(a) (the statute of limitations) that would prohibit taking the gifts into account in computing the estate tax. In the instant case, the estate contended that it was fundamentally unfair to allow the IRS to revalue gifts for estate tax purposes. According to the estate, taxpayer would be forced to keep records indefinitely. In addition, when the dispute over the valuation occurred, the person most knowledgeable about the gift and its value—the donor—would be dead. This argument was successful in Boatmen's First Nat'l Bank of Kansas City, 705 F. Supp. 1407 (WD Mo. 1988), but not in Estate of Smith, 94 TC 872 (1990).

In *Boatmen's,* the district court ruled that the IRS could not revalue a gift for estate tax purposes after the statute of limitations had passed. To allow otherwise would subject taxpayers to a statute of limitations that had no definite cutoff. This statute of limitations would make effective tax planning impossible because the IRS treatment of gifts in their estates could not be estimated. A contrary decision was reached by the Tax Court in *Smith,* which held that Section 2504(c) did not prevent the revaluation of gifts for estate tax purposes (particularly because this was a one-time event rather than an event that recurred with every future gift tax return). The effect of this holding was mitigated somewhat by the Tax Court's ruling under Section 2001(b)(2), that the estate would be allowed a credit for the gift tax that would have been paid if the revalued amount of the gift had been listed on the gift tax return. The reason for this ruling was to prevent the IRS from collecting the additional gift tax indirectly. The Eighth Circuit in the instant case followed *Smith* and *Levin.* The circuit court determined that laws establishing statutes of limitations must be strictly construed in favor of the government. Section 2504(c) states that the law applies to "taxes under this chapter." This statement can only refer to ¶ 12, which governs gift taxes (estate taxes are governed by ¶ 11). In addition, the court noted that Section 2001(b)(1), which relates to the calculation of estate taxes, refers to Section 2503 for the definition of "adjusted taxable gifts" and makes no reference to Section 2504(c). The Eighth Circuit found nothing in the statutes or case history that would allow it to incorporate gift tax provisions into the estate tax statutes. The IRS can, therefore, re-examine and revalue adjusted taxable gifts includable on the estate tax return.

[Evanson, 30 F3d 960, 74 AFTR2d 94-7459, 94-2 USTC ¶ 60,174 (8th Cir. 1994).]

Prior transfer credit is allowed for life interest. Before his death, decedent's husband had established both a marital and a nonmarital deduction trust for decedent. The trust instrument provided that the trustee's powers were to be liberally construed in allowing distributions of interest or principal. Because of this liberal construction, decedent could continue to maintain herself in the manner to which she had been accustomed. Her estate claimed that the value of her life estate in the nonmarital deduction trust, although not includable in her estate, was entitled to the credit on prior transfers. The IRS argued that the value of decedent's interest could not be determined because the trustee had the power to invest trust funds in nonproductive assets, to invade principal for the children's benefit, to accumulate income, and to distribute income to the children rather than to decedent. The IRS contended that if an interest is subject to contingencies that make it incapable of valuation in accordance with recognized valuation principles, there can be no credit.

Held: For the estate. Relevant state law indicated that although the trustee was granted broad investment powers under the instrument, the trustee was nevertheless required to exercise such powers in a fiduciary capacity. The instrument required that the trustee exercise his powers primarily for decedent's benefit, and only secondarily for the children's benefit. Consequently, investing in nonproductive assets for the children's benefit (as ultimate takers) would be a violation of the trustee's fiduciary responsibility under state law. Although the trustee was authorized to pay income or principal to beneficiaries other than the decedent, the instrument required that, first and foremost, she be maintained in her accustomed manner. This allowed a reasonable estimate of her needs. The court indicated that the situation was similar to that in Estate of Lloyd, 650 F2d 1197 (Ct. Cl. 1981), where the Court of Claims held that a life estate was reasonably capable of valuation, though the trustee was empowered to invade principal for the benefit of persons other than the surviving widow.

[Estate of Weinstein, 820 F2d 201, 59 AFTR2d 87-1279, 87-1 USTC ¶ 13,722 (6th Cir. 1987).]

IRS can revalue gifts for estate tax purposes. Decedent died in 1986. In 1977, 1978, 1981, 1982, 1985, and 1986, decedent had made various gifts of land and minerals to members of her family. Gift tax returns had been timely filed for the gifts made in 1977, 1978, 1981, and 1982. None of the returns had been examined or audited, although the IRS had corrected a mathematical error on the 1981 return. In 1977, the amount of the gift had been less than the annual exclusion, so no gift tax had been due. In 1978, 1981, and 1982, the gift tax owed had been offset by the unified credit. When decedent's estate filed the estate tax return, it valued the prior taxable gifts at $196,000. The IRS adjusted the value of the gifts to $1,068,600, an increase of $872,600. The estate paid the additional tax generated and filed for a refund, which led to the case being filed in federal district court. The estate argued that the statute of limitations applicable to the gift tax computation barred the IRS from revaluing the taxable gifts for estate tax purposes. The IRS claimed that the statute of limitations applied only to gift tax calculations.

Held: For the IRS. Estate tax is computed under Section 2001(b) by adding the value of adjusted taxable gifts made by decedent to the value of decedent's taxable estate, and subtracting the gift tax that would have been payable under Chapter 12 (the gift tax provisions in the Code). According to Section 2001(b), the term "adjusted taxable gifts" refers to the total amount of taxable gifts within the meaning of Section 2503. Section 2504(c) provides a limitations period of three years during which a gift can be revalued for gift tax purposes. The court examined the language of all the statutes and determined that Section 2504(c) did not apply to the estate tax calculation. In analyzing Section 2504, it noted that the statute stated that it applied "for the purpose of computing the tax under this chapter [Chapter 12]," which means that it does not necessarily apply to another chapter. The court then discussed the estate tax statutes, pointing out that in Section 2001(c), Congress could have defined "adjusted taxable gifts" by referring to Chapter 12, which would have included all of the gift tax statutes. Instead, Congress referred solely to Section 2503, which makes no reference to Section 2504 or to the gift tax statute of limitations. The court also noted that the credit given in the estate tax computation is for gift taxes that *would have been* payable under Chapter 12. If there were a prohibition on revaluing gifts for estate tax purposes, Congress could simply have given a credit for taxes that *had been* paid. The phrase "taxes that would have been payable" suggests that gifts can be revalued for estate tax purposes, but that the estate receives credit for taxes it would have paid, so that the IRS cannot indirectly recoup the lost gift tax by increasing estate tax. The court said that it was aware of the decision in Boatmen's First Nat'l Bank, 705 F. Supp. 1407, 89-1 USTC ¶ 13,795, 63 AFTR2d 89-1510 (WD Mo. 1988), but felt that it must follow the ruling in Smith, 94 TC 872 (1990).

[Stalcup, 792 F. Supp. 714, 91-2 USTC ¶ 60,086, 68 AFTR2d 91-6057 (WD Okla. 1991).]

Date-of-death value of claim for compensatory and punitive damages determined. At the time of decedent's death, she was a plaintiff in a pending lawsuit seeking compensatory and punitive damages from her broker for securities churning. The IRS placed a value of $2 million on the suit, while the estate argued that its value was $62,255. The case eventually settled for over $2.2 million.

　　Held: For taxpayer (in part). The date-of-death value of the claim was based on the facts reasonably foreseeable on the valuation date. The amount of the subsequent judgment was not determinative.

[Estate of Davis, 65 TCM 2365, RIA TC Memo. ¶ 93,155 (1993).]

IRS explains how to request Statement of Value to substantiate value of art. The IRS has issued a revenue procedure informing taxpayers how to request from the IRS a Statement of Value that can be used to substantiate the value of art for income, estate, or gift tax purposes. A taxpayer who complies with the procedure may rely on the Statement of Value in completing the tax return that reports the transfer of art. The procedure generally applies to an item of art that has been appraised at $50,000 or more and has been transferred (1) as a charitable contribution, (2) by death, or (3) by lifetime gift.

　　A taxpayer must submit to the IRS a request for a Statement of Value for an item of art before filing the estate or gift tax return that first reports the transfer of the item. The procedure sets forth the information (including an appraisal) that must be included in the request. A copy of the Statement of Value, regardless of whether taxpayer agrees with it, must be attached to, and filed with, taxpayer's return. The procedure applies to requests for Statements of Value submitted after January 15, 1996.

[Rev. Proc. 96-15, 1996-1 CB 627.]

Failure to enforce notes cannot avoid gain. When decedent died, he owned notes that his estate had not enforced and that the executors insisted were not marketable or immediately collectible. The notes were from the sale of property by decedent, the gain from which sale had been reported on the installment plan. The debtors were decedent's sons, who were also the executors of the estate. Although the notes remained in force after decedent's death, no interest payments were made, and the executors did not request payment. Under Section 691(a)(2), an estate realizes gain on the transfer of a right to receive income to the extent of the FMV of the right or, if greater, the consideration received. The gain is reduced by the basis the obligation had in the hands of decedent. A transfer includes a cancellation, a transfer to the obligor, or an unenforceability of the note instrument. The obligation is deemed to have been transferred upon the conclusion of the estate's administration if there was no prior disposition. Where the obligor is related to decedent, the value of the obligation is not less than its face amount. In the ruling, the executors had neither discharged the obligors (themselves) nor renounced their rights. The notes therefore had not been canceled. Further, under state law, the failure of the executors to enforce the note also did not result in a cancellation. Therefore, the ruling concluded that the previously unrecognized gain had to be recognized at the earliest of the following events:

1. The notes are distributed, either directly or indirectly, to the obligors.
2. The notes are canceled by operation of state law.
3. The notes become unenforceable.
4. The administration of the estate terminates.
5. Any other event occurs that may be considered a cancellation under Section 691 or Section 453B.

If principal payments were made while the estate held the note, gain was to be reported in the same manner as if decedent were still alive. The ruling specifically did not indicate what event would constitute an indirect distribution of the notes. Thus, the ruling gave the executors some leeway in determining the year in which the gain from the notes was to be recognized by controlling the year of distribution or termination of the estate.

[Priv. Ltr. Rul. 8806048.]

[2] Remainder Interests

The Tax Court calculates discounted value of two remainder interests where trustee had power to invade principal during life estate. The Seventh Circuit directed the Tax Court on remand to determine the value of two remainder interests that were required to be included in the gross estate as the result of taxpayer's appeal of a 1979 decision. The interests in question involved the life estate of decedent's spouse in the net income of a trust subject to the power of the corporate trustee to invade income or principal for the life beneficiary's support and maintenance. The IRS had erroneously convinced the Tax Court that the remainders were to be valued pursuant to the tables set forth in Regulations § 20.2031-7. The Seventh Circuit found error in the fact that the table failed to account for the corporate trustee's power to invade the principal.

Held: The proper method of valuation consistent with the Seventh Circuit's remand was to calculate the actual present value of the interests and to apply to such value a discount factor reflecting the likelihood that the trustee would exercise its invasion powers. The court evaluated the life beneficiary's income and other assets to arrive at a figure describing her standard of living. After analyzing this data, the court concluded that the invasion power rendered each remainder worth $16,360.

[Estate of Gokey, TC Memo. (P-H) ¶ 84,665, 49 TCM (CCH) 367 (1984).]

[3] Valuation Tables

Gender-based mortality tables used in calculating present value of reversionary interest in trust of decedent are unconstitutional. In 1923, an individual (decedent) had established a trust and retained the right to the trust's income for her life. At the same time, decedent had named her son as beneficiary, to receive the income from the trust after her death. Decedent had also retained a reversionary interest in the trust income, in the event that her son predeceased her. In 1976, decedent died at age 88 and was survived by her son, who was age 57. Section 2037 provides that the value of a decedent's reversionary interest in a trust is includable in decedent's gross estate if the value of that reversionary interest, immediately before decedent's death, exceeds 5 percent of the value of the corpus. The applicable regulations provide both the actuarial tables and formulas to be used to calculate the value of the reversionary interest. Under the regulations, the value of the reversionary interest is a function of the life expectancies of both decedent and the trust beneficiary. The tables employed give one set of life expectancies for men and another for women. The plaintiff (executor of decedent's estate), seeking a refund of federal estate taxes, challenged the IRS's use of gender-based mortality tables in calculating the present value of the reversionary interest in decedent's trust. The plaintiff argued that such tables (1) exceed the IRS's statutory authority to promulgate regulations concerning actuarial tables and (2) constitute impermissible gender discrimination in violation of the due process clause of the Fifth Amendment. The district court held that the promulgation of the regulations was not beyond the delegation of authority in Section 2037. However, the challenged regulations constituted impermissible gender-based discrimination in violation of the Fifth Amendment. Taxpayer appealed the decision.

Held: Reversed for the IRS. The Second Circuit held that although the challenged IRS practice classified taxpayers on the basis of gender, such a classification was substantially related to the important governmental objective of promoting equity in estate taxes through accurate valuation of reversionary interests. The court found that there was no evidence that the challenged practice distributed burdens or benefits in a way that disadvantaged women or men as a group. The gender classification did not demean the ability or social status of women or men, nor was it based on the assumption that women or men would choose stereotypical or traditional social roles. The court found that the gender-based mortality tables realistically reflected men's and women's different average life expectancies and that the government's use of these averages for determining values in estate taxation did not create an unacceptable risk of discriminating against those who were not within the statistical norm. The court felt that after taking all of those circumstances into consideration, it could find nothing unconstitutional about the challenged practice. Thus, the IRS was free to use the gender-based tables for decedents who had died prior to December 1, 1983.

[Manufacturers Hanover Trust Co., 775 F2d 459, 56 AFTR2d 85-6560, 85-2 USTC ¶ 13,640 (2d Cir. 1985), cert. denied, 475 US 1095 (1986).]

Use of expectancy tables is followed, despite actual death. Testatrix-decedent created a testamentary charitable remainder trust. The life estate was to be paid to decedent's eighty-four-year-old sister, with the remainder going to a hospital. The sister died within six months of decedent, and prior to the filing of the state tax return. The estate computed the value of the life estate by using the tables in Regulations § 20.2031-10, considering the sister's actual survival rather than her life expectancy. This increased the value of the charitable estate. The IRS argued that the tables should be applied.

Held: Reversed for the IRS. The value of a testamentary charitable remainder must be determined pursuant to the prescribed actuarial tables where the life tenant is not known to be terminally ill at the date of the testator's or testatrix's death. Valuing a charitable remainder for purposes of Section 2055 must be distinguished from valuing a reversion under Section 2037. In Section 2037(b), Congress provided a rule of administrative convenience that requires the application of actuarial tables, notwithstanding the physical condition of decedent. Obviously, the value of a reversion would be distorted if the estimated survival of a deceased person were used to compute the value. Therefore, most courts rely strictly on the IRS's actuarial tables. The basic rule in valuing life and remainder interests for estate tax purposes, however, is that the determination must be made from facts available at the time of decedent's death. Revenue Ruling 66-307, 1966-2 CB 429.

The fact that the life tenant may survive decedent by only a short time is not significant. On the other hand, where the life tenant is known to be afflicted with a fatal illness and can be expected to survive for only a brief period, then the life tenant's physical condition may be taken into account in determining the value of his interest. In the instant case, there was no expectation of imminent death, therefore the IRS valuation by actuarial tables was proper.

[Merchants Nat'l Bank, 583 F2d 19, 42 AFTR2d 78-6491, 78-2 USTC ¶ 13,257 (1st Cir. 1978).]

Health is not factor in valuing Section 2037 reversion. Decedent's estate was required to include a reversionary interest in gross estate pursuant to Section 2037. It valued the interest by using a rate lower than that provided in the

IRS actuarial tables, arguing that decedent's health had been a factor requiring a lower valuation.

Held: For the IRS. The health of a decedent should not be taken into account in determining the value of a reversionary interest for purposes of Section 2037. The correct method of valuing the reversionary interest is to use the mortality tables provided in Regulations § 20.2031-10. Any method that considers decedent's actual health or physical condition is improper. If one were to value decedent's residuary interest by taking into account her ill health, the value would be less than 5 percent; however, disregarding her health, the value was more than 34 percent. The court reasoned that the use of the prescribed mortality tables promoted ease of administration and evenhanded application of the tax law. Because the 5 percent rule was adopted as a matter of administrative convenience, the use of the tables seemed most suitable. Taxpayer argued that it was not the intent of Congress to restrict valuation solely to the method of the mortality tables. The court, however, looking at the language of Section 2037(b), found that the IRS was specifically authorized to issue regulations concerning such valuations. Although the Code merely enumerated the mortality tables as a possible means of valuing such interests, the IRS was acting within its authority in prescribing them as the sole means of valuation. The court specifically cited Estate of Roy, 54 TC 1317 (1970), which reached the same conclusion on similar facts.

[Estate of Allen, 214 Ct. Cl. 630, 40 AFTR2d 77-6220, 77-2 USTC ¶ 13,199 (1977).]

Valuation tables are required in all but rare instances, according to IRS. Taxpayer set up a trust with a life estate for a named beneficiary and an irrevocable reversionary interest. Taxpayer transferred to the trust 1,000 shares of common stock that had been averaging dividends of 3 percent over the past ten years. The question arose whether IRS valuation tables, which are based on a 6 percent rate, were appropriate.

To value any transferred interest for gift tax purposes, one must look to the tables at Regulations § 25.2512-9 (for tax years ending after 1970). Although the tables, which are computed by using an assumed yield of 6 percent, may produce a valuation in excess of the true value of the life interest, taxpayer must use the tables. The tables are recognized not as being a precise measure, but rather as a reasonable average that is convenient for administrative purposes. The IRS would allow departure from the strict application of the tables where their use "would violate reason and fact." Thus, if the income interest is definitely determinable, the tables need not be used. This would arise if the assets generated a fixed yield.

In the instant case, where the dividends were merely an average of dividends paid, there was no assurance that future payments would remain fixed at 3 percent. The IRS therefore distinguished between the yield on stock and the yield on municipal and government bonds. The IRS's position is supported by Hanley, 63 F. Supp. 73 (Ct. Cl. 1945), in which a 3 percent yield was upheld because "it was reasonable to expect that the future rate of return from the trust assets would be substantially less than, the [table] rate."

[Rev. Rul. 77-195, 1977-1 CB 295.]

Gravely ill individual cannot use IRS valuation tables. Before death, decedent had been gravely ill, and it had been almost certain that he would die within one year. Decedent had sold a remainder interest in certain assets to one of his children and to a trust in exchange for a lifetime annuity to be paid by the child and the trust. The estate sought to value the remainder and the annuity in accordance with the IRS valuation tables. The IRS ruled that in computing the value of the remainder and the annuity, the valuation tables of Regulations § 25.2512-5 were not applicable, because decedent's death had been imminent within a year and had been predictable. Instead, the value must be determined based on decedent's actual life expectancy.

[Tech. Adv. Mem. 9133001.]

IRS does not allow departure from valuation tables using 6 percent rate when prime rate is 14 percent. A divorce agreement had required an ex-husband to make payments to his former spouse. These payments consisted of a weekly amount followed by a lump sum on an undisclosed date. The payments were to be made regardless of the death of either party. The ex-husband died, and his representative valued the annuity and the right to receive the lump-sum payment by using a 12 percent interest rate. The estate asserted that this was justified because the then-current interest rate was "one of the highest in history . . . the prime rate was 14 percent per annum." The estate further argued that a valuation of the assets under the actuarial table in Regulations § 20.2031-10(f), which required a 6 percent interest rate to be used, would not result in the assets being valued at their FMV. The estate tax examiner proposed to adjust the taxable estate based on the 6 percent interest rate.

The IRS stated that the 6 percent tables under Regulations § 20.2031-10 may not be disregarded in the valuation of the annuity interest and the right to receive a future sum certain. The IRS reasoned that the instant case did not present facts under which there was "a substantial reason for departing" from the regulations, citing Revenue Ruling 77-195, 1977-2 CB 295. The revenue ruling cited examples when "there is a substantial reason for departure" from the use of the tables. There was no market for the right to receive the payments and the lump sum, so the commercial annuities table in Regulations § 20.2031-8 could not be used.

[Priv. Ltr. Rul. 8706013.]

¶ 2.02 VALUATION OF STOCKS, SECURITIES, AND REAL ESTATE

[1] Corporate Stock and Securities

[a] Generally

Securities restrictions reduce stock valuations. Decedent was the chief executive officer and chairman of the board of a corporation that had two classes of stock, one of which was not publicly traded but was convertible into publicly traded shares. Decedent owned more than two million shares of the non-publicly traded stock. Because of his position with the company and ownership interest, decedent was subject to federal securities law restrictions on the sale of these shares. His estate was not subject to these restrictions. With the restrictions, the value of a share was $12.34; without the restrictions, each share was worth $15.56. Decedent's estate used the $12.34 value on the estate tax return, but the IRS contended that the higher value must be used. The Tax Court agreed with the IRS's position, reasoning that the restrictions ended when decedent died, so the shares should be valued without the restrictions.

Held: Reversed for taxpayer. The Ninth Circuit reversed in a split decision. The majority framed the issue as whether the stock should be valued in the hands of decedent or the estate. In situations where death alone is the precipitating event that changes a property's valuation, the court said that the after-death value (i.e., in the hands of the estate) should be used. In the instant case, however, the stock's value changed because the estate was not subject to the restrictions—rather than simply because of decedent's death. The court pointed out that, under the IRS's view, whether the restrictions applied to the estate depended on the identity of the executor. Thus, if the IRS's position were upheld, the stock's value would vary depending on who was named as executor—and shares of stock owned by a decedent who was not subject to securities law restrictions could wind up being valued subject to those restrictions if the "right" executor were chosen.

[Estate of McClatchy, 81 AFTR2d 98-5001, 98-1 USTC ¶ 50,443 (9th Cir. 1998).]

Option price is disregarded for estate tax value. Decedent had granted three sets of purchase options for publicly traded stock to her children and grandchildren. In the first set, decedent had not specified that she intended to be legally bound by the options. In the following two sets, she did indicate her intention. Her intention in granting all three sets of options had been to transfer all appreciation in the optioned stock in excess of the option price as a gift. No consideration had been received for the options, and the option prices had been set in such a way that the value of the option had been within decedent's annual exclusion for gift tax purposes. As of decedent's death, none of the options had been exercised. The executors valued the stock at its option price rather than at the higher market price on the date of death. The IRS contended that the stock should have been valued at the market price. The second and third sets of options had been legally binding on decedent under state law, and the estate therefore contended that the stock to which they were applied was includable in decedent's gross estate at the option price.

Held: For the IRS. Although Regulations § 20.2031-1 generally requires that property, including securities, be valued at its FMV, an exception is provided in Regulations § 20.2031-2(h). That exception permits the value to be determined by an option to purchase if the following three conditions are met:

1. The option is legally binding on decedent.
2. The option is made pursuant to a bona fide business arrangement.
3. The option is not a device to pass the shares to beneficiaries for less than full consideration.

Further, an option that leaves decedent free to dispose of the securities during decedent's lifetime at any price is given little weight. The Third Circuit stated that when an option is given to a natural object of the bounty of the optionor, there must be substantial proof to show that the option rested on adequate and full consideration. The Third Circuit reasoned that this requirement was applicable, even where the option was exercisable before decedent's death. The Third Circuit concluded that decedent in the instant case had no valid business purpose for granting the stock options and that the granting of the options was a device to pass the shares for less than adequate and full consideration. Therefore, the market price of the stock was the value of the stock to be included in the gross estate.

[Dorn, 828 F2d 177, 60 AFTR2d 87-6135, 87-2 USTC ¶ 13,732 (3d Cir. 1987).]

Estate must pay tax on stock used to fund trust. Decedent purchased shares of appreciated stock from his father for which decedent had executed a promissory note for the amount of the father's basis in the shares. The father then transferred the shares to a trust under the terms of which decedent was to receive income for his life. The promissory note was paid with dividends from the stock. Decedent reported the income from the stock and took deductions for the interest on the note. When decedent died, none of the stock of the trust was included in the estate. The IRS contended that decedent's purchase of the stock and the transfer of the stock to the trust by his father was, in substance, a Section 2036(a) transfer by decedent with a retained life estate. Thus, the IRS argued that the FMV of the sale portion of the stock on the date of decedent's death was includable in his estate. The district court held that because decedent's father had established and controlled the creation and funding of the trust, decedent had purchased only a life estate in the trust corpus and had not made a transfer. Inasmuch as there had been no transfer for Section 2036(a) purposes, the district court held that the property was excludable from the estate. In the Sixth Circuit, the estate argued that decedent's father had been the grantor of the trust because the father had retained a right to dividends from the stock; the trust had paid off the note; decedent had been only a surety for the trust's repayment of the note; and the note had been between family members and thus was not true debt. The estate contended that because decedent had not paid the consideration, he could not have made a transfer.

Held: For the IRS. In rejecting all of the estate's arguments, the Sixth Circuit noted that the trust instrument itself stated that the stock was transferred to the trust in exchange for payment by decedent. Although the payment was in the form of a note that was repaid by the corporation withholding dividends from decedent and making payment directly to his father, decedent treated the withheld dividends as income and took interest deductions for the repayments. The court reasoned that only if decedent had really purchased the stock would interest deductions have been taken. The court then examined whether decedent had transferred the shares or had merely purchased an equitable life estate in the transferred stock. The court observed that the purpose of Section 2036 is to include in the estate transfers that leave the transferor a significant interest in or control over the property transferred during his life. Estate of Grace, 395 US 316, 69-1 USTC ¶ 12,609 (1969). The Sixth Circuit then rejected the testimony of decedent's family regarding the nature of the transfer and concentrated on the objective evidence of the transaction. Because the trust instrument indicated that decedent had purchased the stock that funded the trust in exchange for a promissory note, and because the note stated that it was in payment for the shares, then, clearly, decedent had intended to purchase the stock and fund the trust, and had not purchased a mere life interest. Thus, decedent had been in substance the grantor of the trust and had retained a life income interest, so that under Section 2036(a), the date-of-death value of the purchased portion of the stock was required to be included in his estate.

[Mahoney, 831 F2d 641, 60 AFTR2d 87-6152, 87-2 USTC ¶ 13,737 (6th Cir. 1987), cert. denied, 486 US 1054 (1988).]

Tax Court approves revaluation of gifts for estate tax purposes. Decedent made gifts of stock that were valued at $284,871 on the gift tax return. He died two years later, and the gifts were included on the estate tax return at the same value. Two years after the statute of limitations for gift tax purposes expired, the IRS asserted an estate tax deficiency based in part on revaluing the gifts of stock at $668,495. The IRS increased adjusted taxable gifts (added to the taxable estate in computing the estate tax), but did not increase the gift tax payable on those gifts (also an element in the estate tax calculation). Under Section 2504(c), gifts made in prior taxable periods cannot be revalued for gift tax purposes after a gift tax has been assessed or paid and the statute of limitations for assessment of gift tax has run. The estate argued that Section 2504(c) should be read into the estate tax provisions to prevent the IRS from revaluing prior taxable gifts for estate tax purposes when the gift tax statute of limitations is closed. Otherwise, the statute of limitations for gift taxes and the legislative intent in unifying estate and gift taxes would be thwarted. The IRS argued that Section 2504(c) prohibits revaluation of prior taxable gifts solely for tax purposes.

Held: For the IRS. Although the Tax Reform Act of 1976 unified gift and estate tax rates, it did not extend Section 2504(c) to valuation of prior gifts for estate tax purposes. Taxpayer's argument—that because the Section 2503 definition of "taxable gift" is incorporated into Section 2001(b) (dealing with computation of estate tax), Section 2504(c) should also be incorporated—was rejected for lack of support in the language of the statute. The court also declined to incorporate Section 2504(c) into Section 2001(b) by using the doctrine of in pari materia, which allows the same gift and estate tax phrases concerning the same subject matter to be interpreted in the same way. Consequently, in computing adjusted taxable gifts for estate tax purposes, the IRS may revalue prior gifts even if the statute of limitations for gift tax purposes has expired.

[Estate of Smith, 94 TC 872 (1990), acq., 1990-2 CB 1.]

Uncertainty over rights and privileges is relevant in valuing estate's stock in closely held corporation. Decedent had owned all of the outstanding shares of Class A voting and Class B nonvoting common stock in a closely held corporation. Other family members had owned all of the outstanding shares of the company's preferred stock. The corporate charter gave exclusive board of directors voting rights to the holders of the voting common stock. All three classes of stock participated pro rata in dividends declared out of earnings; the preferred stock had a liquidation preference; only common stock could vote on plans for merger; and the preferred stock was authorized by statute to vote on corporate liquidation. The estate and the IRS both submitted substantial and well-reasoned testimony and reports of numerous expert witnesses about the common shareholder's rights under state law to extract wealth from the corporation through redemption, dividends, merger, and liquidation. The testimony was in disagreement on almost all issues. The estate asserted that the uncertainties surrounding the respective rights of the corporate shareholders should be a relevant consideration in valuing the stock for estate tax purposes. The estate also owned 100 shares of another closely held corporation that represented 44.44 percent of the total voting stock. The IRS argued that the estate effectively controlled the corporation and that the stock's value should reflect a control premium. The estate argued that a percentage discount was in order, given its lack of control of the corporation.

Held: For taxpayer. Where state law cannot determine the relative rights and duties of different classes of stock with any certainty as evidenced by the conflicting arguments and profound differences of opinion of several experts, the willing buyer and seller would take into account the likelihood of protracted and unpredictable litigation in negotiating a purchase price. In addition, the estate's interest of 44.44 percent in the other closely held corporation, although substantial, was insufficient to create effective control, and therefore a control premium was insupportable. Similarly, a discount of 35 percent for lack of control and lack of marketability was reasonable.

[Estate of Newhouse, 94 TC 193 (1990), nonacq., 1991-2 CB 1.]

Shares transferred by decedent within three years of death are included in his estate as adjusted taxable gifts, but are not eligible for special-use valuation. Within three years of decedent's death, he had transferred stock in a corporation that owned a farm to his sons. Decedent's executor included the stock decedent owned on Schedule B of the estate tax return and listed the stock given to decedent's sons on Schedule G (entitled "Transfers During Decedent's Life"). The executor valued the combined holdings of decedent and his sons by using the Section 2032A special-use valuation method. The IRS determined that the stocks given to decedent's sons were adjusted taxable gifts that were includable in decedent's gross estate but did not qualify for special-use valuation. The IRS did allow that such stock was considered to be in decedent's gross estate for purposes of determining whether real property held by decedent at his death qualified for the Section 2032A special-use valuation, though it did not itself qualify for such valuation.

Held: For the IRS. Based upon the legislative history of Section 2035(d)(3), the stock given by decedent to his sons was "included in his gross estate for purposes of determining the estate's qualification for special ... valuation ... purposes." The stock did not qualify for special-use valuation, though the value of such gift was included (under Section 2035) in the gross estate for estate tax purposes.

[Estate of Slater, 93 TC 513 (1989).]

Marketability discount denied where stipulated value did not refer to stock's freely traded value. Decedent owned 100 percent of a close corporation. After appraisals, the value of decedent's stock was stipulated. All the appraisers considered the factors in Revenue Ruling 59-60, 1959-1 CB 237, but none referred to the price of stock of a comparable corporation that was listed on a public exchange. The issue was whether the marketability discount should be applied to the stipulated value of the stock.

Held: For the IRS. The court held that it was inappropriate to discount the value of the stock for lack of marketability where the stipulated value was not determined by reference to the stock's freely traded value. According to the court, the discount is confined to property that is valued by reference to prices paid for assertedly comparable property.

[Estate of Cloutier, 71 TCM 2001, RIA TC Memo. ¶ 96,049 (1996).]

Price in private offering used to value publicly held stock. Decedent owned a controlling interest in a publicly held communications company. The estate valued the stock based on the value that could be obtained in a secondary public offering. Although the value in a third-party private offering would be greater, the estate's valuation expert rejected this method because the risk of litigation by minority shareholders precluded such a sale.

Held: For the IRS (in part). The estate did not establish that there was a real threat of litigation in a private sale. The IRS valuation was based on a private offering but failed to account for the sizable minority interest and possible legal complications due to government regulation of the industry.

[Estate of Gray, 66 TCM 254, RIA TC Memo. ¶ 93,334 (1993).]

Tax Court finds no conflict of interest for appraiser. Decedent owned stock in the Chicago Bears football team, and his son had owned a different class of stock in the team. Decedent transferred his stock to a holding company prior to his death in 1983. The son predeceased the father in 1979. The team purchased stock from the son's estate and used three independent appraisers to value the stock. The IRS sought to use one of these appraisers to value decedent's stock in the holding company. The estate argued that a conflict of interest existed and that the appraiser should be disqualified.

Held: For the IRS. The appraiser was not disqualified, because there was no confidential relationship between the party seeking disqualification (the father's estate) and the appraiser.

[Estate of Halas, TC Memo. (P-H) ¶ 89,536, 58 TCM (CCH) 280 (1989).]

Estate valuation of small business corporation stock is upheld where IRS valuation does not consider cyclical nature of corporation's business. Decedent was the sole owner of a small corporation involved in the construction business. In compliance with decedent's will, the corporation was liquidated after his death, and the proceeds were distributed as part of the residue of his estate. In valuing the corporation for federal estate tax purposes, the estate's expert used the capitalization of earnings approach over a period of five years in its determination that the corporation had a value of between $198,255 and $255,557. The IRS, on the other hand, used a similar method, but looked only at the preceding three-year period of the corporation in concluding that the value of the corporation was $445,200. The estate argued that the IRS had used a time period that represented only the peak earnings of the corporation and that therefore the IRS calculations were inaccurate, because the calculations did not take into account the fact that the nature of the corporation's business was cyclical.

Held: For the estate. The court concluded that the approach used by the estate's expert witness most closely reflected the FMV of the corporation. There were identifiable common grounds between the testimony of the two opposing experts, but the court believed that the more accurate approach to take was to consider the corporation's earnings over the longer five-year period on which the estate's valuation was based rather than the IRS's three-year period. The period used by the IRS was a peak earnings period for the corporation, and thus its calculations did not consider the fact that the average earnings that the corporation could have expected would have been substantially lower than the amount predicted by the IRS. The only changes that the court found necessary to the valuation calculated by the estate involved small adjustments to the operating income of the corporation, which adjustments the estate did not take into account. One of the court's adjustments involved decreasing the imputed fair rental value that the corporation would have paid if it had paid the market rate for the property on which it was located, rather than the much lower rent that the corporation was paying to decedent's children, who owned the property.

[Estate of Giselman, TC Memo. (P-H) ¶ 88,391, 55 TCM (CCH) 1654 (1988).]

Guidance on valuing compensatory stock options for transfer tax purposes. Revenue Procedure 98-34 offers taxpayers welcome guidance on valuing certain compensatory stock options to purchase publicly traded stock. It establishes an option pricing method that considers factors similar to those established by the FASB in SFAS No. 123 (Accounting for Stock-Based Compensation). If the procedure's requirements are followed, the IRS will treat the value of covered options as properly determined for gift, estate, and generation-skipping transfer tax purposes. The procedure is applicable only to the valuation of nonpublicly traded compensatory stock options (i.e., options granted in connection with the performance of services, including options subject to Section 421) on stock that is publicly traded on an established securities market on the valuation date. Taxpayers may make such a valuation using a generally recognized option pricing model (such as the Black-Scholes model or an accepted version of the binomial model) that takes into account certain specified factors on the valuation date, provided the factors are reasonable, the model is properly applied, the option grantor is subject to SFAS No. 123 for the fiscal year encompassing the valuation date, the underlying stock is common stock, and no discount can be applied to the valuation produced by the pricing model. The following are specified factors that must be taken into account:

1. The option's exercise price and expected life.
2. The underlying stock's current trading price, expected volatility, and expected dividends.
3. The risk-free interest rate over the remaining option term.

The procedure generally requires taxpayers to use *either* the maximum remaining term of the option on the valuation date or the procedure's specific "Computed Expected Life" calculation (in Section 4.03) to determine the option's expected life. If, however, any one of the following conditions is present on the valuation date, the maximum remaining term must be used:

1. The option transferor is not the person to whom the company granted the option.
2. Excepting transfers at death, the transferor is not an employee or director of the company on the valuation date.
3. Excepting instances involving the transferor's death or disability, the option does not terminate within six months of the transferor's termination of employment (or service as a director).
4. The option by its terms is transferable to, or for the benefit of, persons who are not the natural objects of the transferor's bounty or charitable organization.
5. Excepting instances involving the transferor's death, the option's exercise price is not fixed on the valuation date.
6. Excepting instances involving the transferor's death, the option's terms and conditions are such that, if they applied to all options granted in the fiscal year encompassing the valuation date, the weighted-average expected life for the year would have been more than 120 percent of the weighted-average expected life actually reported for the year.
7. The company is not required by SFAS No. 123 to disclose an expected life of the options granted in the fiscal year encompassing the valuation date.

Revenue Procedure 98-34 also stipulates that the expected volatility and expected dividends factors must be determined using the expected volatility and expected dividends as disclosed in accord with SFAS No. 123 in the publicly traded company's financial statements for the applicable fiscal year. Further, the risk-free interest rate must be determined using the valuation date yield to maturity of zero-coupon U.S. Treasury Bonds with a remaining term nearest to the option's expected life. Finally, taxpayers must indicate their reliance on this procedure by writing "FILED PURSUANT TO REV. PROC. 98-34" on the applicable return.

[Rev. Proc. 98-34, 1998-18 IRB 15.]

[b] Buy-sell agreements

Shareholder purchase agreement is found not conclusive for estate tax valuation purposes. The shareholders of a family-owned moving and storage business entered into a restrictive agreement under which, at the death of a shareholder, the company and other shareholders had the option to purchase the shares at a price determined by a formula based on average earnings over a five-year period. Eight years later, the company sold its operating assets. Thereafter it engaged principally in the rental of real estate and began to show substantial net losses. Four years later decedent died, and taxpayer's estate reported the shares for estate tax purposes at zero per share, which was the value of the shares under the agreement. The district court granted taxpayer's motion for summary judgment.

Held: Reversed for the IRS. Although the agreement provided for a reasonable price at the time of adoption, and the maintenance of family ownership and control of the business was a bona fide business purpose, under the circumstances there was a genuine issue of fact as to whether the agreement was testamentary in nature and a device for the avoidance of estate taxes. Consequently, the agreement was not conclusive for estate tax valuation purposes.

[St. Louis County Bank, 674 F2d 1207, 49 AFTR2d 82-1509, 82-1 USTC ¶ 13,459 (8th Cir. 1982).]

Buy-sell agreement does not set estate tax value of stock. Decedent had established an inter vivos trust funded with stock of his corporation. The trustee subsequently entered into a buy-sell agreement for the trust's stock with decedent's sons and an employee. Decedent then withdrew the stock from the trust, sold some shares, and bequeathed the remainder to his sons. After decedent's death, the estate valued the stock for estate tax purposes at the price set forth in the buy-sell agreement. The Tax Court held that decedent had revoked the trust agreement by withdrawing stock, thereby terminating the buy-sell agreement. Therefore, the stock should have been valued at its FMV at the date of decedent's death.

Held: Affirmed for the IRS. The revocation of the trust did revoke the buy-sell agreement before the date of decedent's death. The IRS correctly valued the stock at its FMV on the date of decedent's death.

[Estate of Anderson, 619 F2d 587, 45 AFTR2d 80-1719, 80-1 USTC ¶ 13,351 (6th Cir. 1980).]

Price in buy-sell agreement upheld. Decedent was one of two shareholders of a closely held manufacturing company. The shareholders entered into a buy-sell agreement that provided that the corporation would purchase insurance on their lives. Upon the death of a shareholder, the corporation would purchase his shares. The corporation's accountant assured the shareholders that the agreement was valid but gave no advice as to its tax consequences. The agreement fixed the price of the stock at $1,000 per share, subject to review at annual shareholder meetings. When one of the shareholders died, the IRS argued that the price of the stock set by the buy-sell agreement was not controlling for purposes of estate tax valuation. The IRS further contended that the buy-sell agreement was not valid and that the stock should have been valued at its FMV on the date of death.

Held: For taxpayer. The buy-sell agreement was entered into for bona fide business purposes and was not a testamentary device to pass the stock to the natural objects of decedent's bounty for less than full consideration. The price of the stock was reasonable, based on the facts when the agreement was executed and absent unusual intervening circumstances.

[Rudolph, 71 AFTR2d 93-2169, 93-1 USTC ¶ 60,130 (SD Ind. 1993).]

Estate-planning buy-sell restrictions are held valid. Decedent had been the founder of a greeting card company. At the time of his death, he held a minority interest in the corporation, with holdings in two of its three classes of stock. Only the Class B common stock was voting, and this was held in a trust indenture that was estimated to remain in effect until year 2050. All stock was subject to transfer restrictions, and blocks of decedent's stock were subject to buy-sell and option agreements requiring that decedent's estate sell the stock to certain transferees at book value. The IRS, on audit, contended that the agreements purporting to fix the price of the stock should be disregarded in valuing it for estate tax purposes, because they were estate-planning devices that merely "incidentally coincided" with decedent's testamentary objectives. Although the stock was sold under the restrictions, it was conceded that the actual sales should not be considered in valuing the stock. Because of the transfer restrictions, the IRS pointed out that sales could have been made at a price higher than book value to certain permitted transferees. Under the hypothetical "willing buyer-willing seller" standard, however, decedent's stock cannot be valued by assuming that sales will be made to any particular person. Despite the existence of permitted transferees for over fifty years, there had never been a purchase or transfer of the corporation's stock for more than book value. The IRS also noted that by various changes in the transfer restrictions, decedent had been successful in changing the categories of permitted transferees.

Held: For the estate. The court stated that the value of closely held stock is based upon such factors as (1) the value of listed stock of corporations engaged in the same or a similar line of business and (2) the corporation's net worth, prospective earning power, dividend-paying capacity, goodwill, the economic outlook of the particular industry, the company's position in the industry, its management, and the degree of control represented by the block of stock to be valued. The court concluded that decedent could not unilaterally amend or terminate the transfer restrictions. Also, all changes in the restrictions had been within the general categories of decedent's family, corporate employees, and charities. There had never been a proposal to sell any stock to an outsider. In comparing the results of the various experts, the court noted that the IRS's expert was "particularly hampered" by the IRS's instruction that the transfer restrictions be ignored in valuing the agreements. The court criticized this expert for considering only one alternative "market comparable," the publicly traded stock of a competitor. The second expert was also criticized for deriving a market premium in a questionable manner from price-to-earnings ratios. The court found the experts of the estate more credible and adopted the value determined by the one that it found most persuasive. This expert did several things that the court singled out as significant in achieving an accurate valuation:

1. Since there was only one comparable greeting card company, additional comparable companies from other industries were selected.
2. From the estimates based on comparable companies, a percentage discount was deducted because of the closely held nature of the stock.
3. Another percentage discount was deducted because of decedent's minority interest.
4. Trends in sales, net income, and profit margins were calculated, and the effect of the changing nature of the industry was determined.

(The court warned, however, that caution is necessary in weighting expert valuations, particularly when they attempt to infuse a "talismanic precision" into an issue that is inherently imprecise.)

[Hall, 92 TC 312 (1989).]

Formula in restrictive sales agreement did not control estate tax valuation of stock. Decedent owned closely held stock in an international cosmetics company. Under a shareholders' agreement designed to maintain family ownership and control of the company, a formula price was established for the sale of stock. The IRS argued that the restrictive agreement did not apply for estate tax valuation.

Held: For the IRS. The formula price bore no relationship to the price an unrelated person would pay for the stock. In addition, although the shareholders' agreement, on its face, served the legitimate business purpose of preserving family ownership and control of the closely held business (a motivating factor for entering into the arrangement), the agreement was intended as a testamentary device, since younger generations had received a bargain purchase price.

[Estate of Lauder, 64 TCM 1643, RIA TC Memo. ¶ 92,736 (1992).]

Tax Court holds that terms of buy-sell agreement control valuation of shares in closely held corporation. Decedent owned 100 shares of stock in a closely held corporation at the time of her death. Pursuant to the terms of a buy-sell agreement entered into by all of the shareholders of the corporation, decedent's estate offered her shares to the corporation at book value. The corporation exercised its option and bought the shares. The estate reported the amount received as the value of the stock on its estate tax return. The IRS contended that this valuation was incorrect and that the stock should have been valued at the fair market price at the date of decedent's death. The IRS argued that the buy-sell agreement should have been disregarded for estate tax purposes, because it did not represent a bona fide business arrangement.

Held: For taxpayer. Under Section 2031(a), the value of a gross estate is generally the FMV of the property at the date of death or an alternate valuation date. An exception may, however, exist for shares that are subject to a buy-sell agreement. The effect of the agreement may be to reduce the FMV or to fix the value for estate tax purposes. Regulations § 20.2031-2(h) provides that the contract price is not controlling if the agreement does not represent a bona fide business agreement or if it is a device to pass decedent's shares to his family members for less than full consideration.

Courts have usually found that a desire to maintain ownership and control of a business constitutes a legitimate business purpose and thus supports the good faith of the agreement. In examining the facts of the instant case, the court found that the agreement was in fact entered into for the purpose of maintaining ownership and control of the corporation. The parties to the buy-sell agreement had strictly adhered to its terms for thirty years. Absent the agreement, restrictive ownership could not have been achieved. Thus, the agreement served a bona fide business purpose. The court went on to determine whether the buy-sell agreement fixed, or merely had an effect on, the value of the shares.

The court stated that the following factors should be considered:

1. Whether the price was determinable under the terms of the agreement.
2. Whether the owner of the interest was obligated to sell at the contract price and the company or other interest holders were obligated to purchase at that price.
3. Whether the obligation to sell at the contract price was binding both upon the owner of the interest during his lifetime and upon his estate at his death.
4. Whether the agreement was a bona fide business arrangement, not a testamentary device.

The court found that the agreement in question met all of these factors and that it thus fixed the value of the shares for estate tax purposes.

[Estate of Seltzer, TC Memo. (P-H) ¶ 85,519, 50 TCM (CCH) 1250 (1985).]

Buy-sell agreement determines price of stock for purposes of estate. Decedent had been the founder and major stockholder of a company that employed four individuals who were also stockholders. Decedent and the four stockholders had entered into a buy-sell agreement covering company stock. The agreement provided that upon the death of a shareholder, the company would buy a deceased shareholder's stock to the extent permitted by law. Any stock not purchased by the company was to be purchased by the remaining stockholders pro rata. The purchase price was set by a formula. The agreement also allowed a decedent's estate to sell decedent's stock to any other shareholder at any price, subject to a volume limitation.

The IRS stated that the formula set the value of the stock for estate tax purposes, but only for the stock that decedent owned at death. The IRS further indicated that the value of the stock set by the formula that exceeded the purchase price was not a gift but was made in the ordinary course of business to retain valued employees, to continue the business, and to facilitate the transfer of stock between shareholders.

[Priv. Ltr. Rul. 8634004.]

[c] Blockage rule

Shares to be considered for blockage discount include only those held by estate at alternate valuation date rather than at date of death. An individual died on September 4, 1976. The federal estate tax return was timely filed on June 1, 1977. The executors elected to value the gross estate as of the alternate valuation date, March 4, 1977, rather than as of the date of death. At the time she died, decedent owned 56,454 shares of stock in a certain company. The executors decided to liquidate 42,416 shares to pay various expenses and taxes owed by the estate. In February 1977, these shares were sold in three blocks. Thus, on March 4, 1977, the alternate valuation date, the estate held only 14,038 shares of the stock. The Tax Court determined that the relevant block of shares to be considered for a blockage discount was the block held by the estate at the alternate valuation date, rather than at the date of decedent's death, and that a blockage discount on those shares was not warranted. On appeal, the estate contended that the entire block of the stock should be valued on the basis of a blockage discount.

Held: Affirmed for the IRS. The Tax Court was correct in determining that only those shares remaining in the estate on the alternate valuation date could be considered for a blockage discount. Section 2032, which provides for an alternate valuation date, states unambiguously that property disposed of prior to the alternate valuation date must be valued at market price. The Tax Court also was correct in finding that taxpayer failed to show that the market price of the shares on March 4, 1977, did not accurately reflect the FMV of the block of stock held by the estate on that date. It was taxpayer's burden to establish that the block of stock at issue was so large in relation to the market that the market price was misleading. The remaining 14,038 shares represented only 0.36 percent of the outstanding stock on that date. The Tax Court's conclusion that the remaining shares could have been disposed of in an orderly manner at no less than the market price was not clearly erroneous.

[Estate of Van Horne, 720 F2d 1114, 53 AFTR2d 84-1549, 83-2 USTC ¶ 13,548 (9th Cir. 1983), cert. denied, 466 US 980 (1984).]

All shares in estate affect blockage factor. Decedent had originally owned 60 percent (600 shares) of a closely held corporation. Two years before his death, decedent transferred 300 shares to his son. The IRS determined that the transfer was made in contemplation of death, so it was includable in decedent's gross estate under the pre-1981 version of Section 2035. Thus, in valuing both blocks of stock, the two blocks must be combined. The son's shares are accordingly treated as though the transfer had never taken place. The value per share of stock is significantly increased because decedent is found to own a controlling interest in the business.

Although the IRS ruling in the instant case does not indicate whether this logic would apply to related situations, it seems that stock included in the gross estate for any reason should be considered in measuring blockage. Thus, transferred stock that is returned to the gross estate under Section 2036, Section 2037, or Section 2038 should be equally susceptible to this treatment.

[Rev. Rul. 79-7, 1979-1 CB 294.]

[d] Control premium

No minimum valuation limit can be imposed on jury. The IRS contended that the judge should have instructed the jury that in valuing decedent's controlling holding in a corporation, the minimum value that may be found is the amount decedent could have realized if he had chosen to liquidate the corporation.

Held: For taxpayer. The assumption of this argument is that a controlling shareholder can automatically realize the asset value of the corporation by liquidating it, unconstrained by fiduciary duties to the minority. Under state law, however, the power to liquidate may not be exercised without scrupulous loyalty to minority shareholders. Therefore, a liquidation value cannot be imposed as the legal minimum of the FMV of the stock.

[Estate of Curry, 706 F2d 1424, 51 AFTR2d 83-1232, 83-1 USTC ¶ 13,518 (7th Cir. 1983).]

Control premium is added to block of stock passing to surviving spouse for purposes of marital deduction. Decedent died in July 1982. At the time of his death, decedent owned 100 percent of the stock of a corporation. The stock was valued in his federal estate tax return at $2,834,033. Under decedent's will, his surviving wife received 51 percent of the stock, for which the estate claimed a $1,996,038 marital deduction under Section 2056. The estate arrived at the stock valuation for marital deduction purposes by adding a control premium of 38.1 percent to the stock's value as reported in the gross estate. The IRS determined a deficiency in the estate tax. The IRS contended that the estate was not entitled to increase the value of the controlling interest in the corporation for purposes of the marital deduction above a strict 51 percent share of the value of all stock as reported in the gross estate.

Held: For the estate. The Tax Court held that changes can be wrought in the value of an asset in a decedent's gross estate by provisions in his will that change some of the asset's characteristics. Decedent in this case, by severing his controlling interest and transferring it to his surviving spouse, created a new and different asset that carried the control premium for valuation purposes. The court stated that assets can be valued differently for purposes of Sections 2031 and 2046.

[Estate of Chenoweth, 88 TC 1577 (1987).]

Survivor's stock combined to form majority block. Stock in a qualified terminable interest property (QTIP) trust included in the estate of a surviving spouse had to be aggregated with stock owned outright by the spouse for valuation purposes, according to the ruling cited below. This created a controlling block of stock from two minority interests. Decedent had an income interest in a trust set up under the will of decedent's spouse. Their two children had the remainder interest. Decedent and one child were the trustees. A marital deduction was allowed for the trust in the spouse's estate because of a QTIP election under Section 2056(b)(7)(A). Consequently, the trust was included in decedent's estate. The trust held 30 percent of the stock of a closely held corporation. Decedent owned another 40 percent outright. The IRS said that the stock in the trust had to be regarded as actually owned by decedent. The IRS found support for its position in Revenue Ruling 79-7, 1979-1 CB 294, in which a decedent transferred 30 percent of a corporation's stock to a child within two years of death while retaining another 30 percent. The gift was included in decedent's estate under an earlier version of Section 2035 as a transfer in contemplation of death. For valuation purposes, the ruling combined the stock held by the child with the stock retained by decedent to form a majority interest.

Here, the QTIP trust provisions strengthened the argument for aggregation. Section 2044(a) includes in a surviving spouse's estate the value of any property for which a QTIP election was made, and such property is treated as passing from the decedent to the remainder beneficiaries under Section 2044(c). Therefore, reasoned the IRS, it is considered to have been actually owned by the surviving spouse. Accordingly, the stock held by the trust was indistinguishable from the stock in decedent's name, which, treated together, constituted a 70 percent controlling block for valuation purposes.

[Tech. Adv. Mem. 9550002.]

Blocks of stock are aggregated when determining estate tax values. In two rulings, the IRS addressed the issue of whether the valuation of stock for estate tax purposes should reflect a control premium or minority discount when the stock is currently held, or will be distributed, in multiple blocks. The IRS concluded that the blocks of stock should be aggregated to determine the value of the stock for estate tax purposes, but should not be aggregated when determining the value of the stock passing to the surviving spouse that is eligible for the marital deduction. As a result, the value of the stock for purposes of the marital deduction was less than the stock's value for purposes of inclusion in the gross estate.

In Technical Advice Memorandum 9403002, decedent, many years before his death, had transferred a block of stock of a closely held company to a trust. When he died, this block of stock was includable in his estate under Section 2038 because he had retained the power to alter the beneficial enjoyment of the trust. At his death, decedent also owned a separate block of the closely held company's stock outright. This block was includable in his estate under Section 2033. The question raised was whether the two blocks of stock should be aggregated for purpose of valuing the stock. In Revenue Ruling 79-7, 1979-1 CB 294, the IRS considered a similar situation. There, the IRS chose to aggregate stock included in decedent's estate under Section 2035 with stock included under Section 2033. Under prior law, the stock transferred by decedent within three years of death was includable in the estate under Section 2035. The IRS determined that for estate tax purposes, the stock included under Section 2035 should be treated as if decedent held the property at his death. Therefore, it was aggregated with the stock he actually did hold at death when determining the value of all the shares.

The IRS reached a similar conclusion in the instant ruling. Since decedent could control the enjoyment of the trust, and hence indirectly the enjoyment of the stock in the trust, the IRS ruled that decedent retained "a sufficient nexus" to the block of stock held by the trust and included in the estate under Section 2038 for it to be treated as if it passed outright from decedent. Accordingly, that block was aggregated with the stock held outright by decedent for purposes of determining the value of the stock.

Technical Advice Memorandum 9403005 examined this aggregation issue from a different angle. In this ruling, the decedent owned a block of 400 preferred shares and a block of 37,728 common shares, both in the same company. The IRS and the estate agreed that the value per share of each class of stock would be higher if the two blocks were combined into one, rather than being valued as separate blocks. Under decedent's will, the blocks were bequeathed to different beneficiaries; the common stock was left to a credit shelter trust for the benefit of decedent's spouse and children, and the bulk of the preferred shares passed to the surviving spouse outright. Two questions were raised. The first was whether the two blocks should be aggregated when determining the value of the stock includable in the estate so that the stock would be valued as a single controlling interest. The second question was whether, for purposes of determining the marital deduction, the value of the stock passing to the surviving spouse should be treated as a separate minority interest block of stock. As discussed above, other factors, such as whether the stock represents a controlling interest, are to be considered when valuing stock for estate tax purposes if a value is not readily available. The marital deduction, however, is limited to the net value of the deductible interest that passes to the surviving spouse.

The valuation of the marital deduction was an issue in Estate of Chenoweth, 88 TC 1577 (1987). There, decedent owned all the stock of a closely held corporation. Under his will, 51 percent of this stock passed to his spouse in a manner that qualified for the marital deduction. Because the spouse received the controlling interest, her shares were actually worth more than 51 percent of the value of the corporation included in the gross estate. The Tax Court held that when decedent transfers less than his entire interest in an asset, and the transfer is unrestricted, the interest transferred should be valued as a separate property interest rather than as an undivided portion of decedent's entire interest. Thus, the IRS approved a marital deduction that was greater than 51 percent of the value of the stock as included in the gross estate. In Ahmanson Foundation, 674 F2d 761 (9th Cir. 1981), a decedent who owned a controlling interest in a corporation bequeathed nonvoting stock to a charity and the stock with controlling interest to his son. The court held that for purposes of valuing the gross estate, the value of the stock was to be determined at the moment of death; but for purposes of the charitable deduction, the value of the stock passing to the charity was limited to the value actually received by the charity. Applying these principles to Technical Advice Memorandum 9403005, the IRS concluded that for purposes of valuing the property included in the gross estate, one does not consider the fact that the property may be divided and distributed to several beneficiaries. If the interest held by decedent comprised a controlling interest, the value of the stock should reflect that control by the inclusion of a control premium. For purposes of computing the marital deduction, if the stock passing to the surviving spouse represents only a minority interest, the value of that interest should include a minority discount to reflect the actual value of the assets the spouse receives.

[Tech. Adv. Mems. 9403002 and 9403005.]

[e] Minority discounts

[For additional cases discussing minority discounts, see ¶ 2.02[1][d] (Control premium).]

Special-use and minority discounts taken in tandem. Decedent owned a 26 percent interest in a family limited partnership that operated a cattle ranch in New Mexico. The partnership's real property was appraised at $10.5 million. In valuing decedent's interest, the estate first took 26 percent of $10.5 million ($2.73 million) and then applied a 30 percent discount factor because the minority partnership interest lacked marketability and control, bringing the valuation down to $1.91 million. The IRS did not dispute this calculation of the interest's FMV. It agreed that this would be the estate tax value if Section 2032A did not apply. Next, the estate considered the interest's special-use value. The estate and the IRS stipulated that the special-use value of the ranch was about $2.05 million, 26 percent of which is $533,548. Section 2032A permits estates to reduce the value of qualified use property to the special-use value—with a maximum valuation reduction of $750,000. In general, qualified use property is real property used in a farming or other business, provided at least 50 percent of the estate is made up of real or personal property used in such business and the real property accounts for at least 25 percent of the estate. In this case, the $750,000 cap controlled because the FMV exceeded the special-use value by more than $750,000. (The court indicated that the special-use tax break applies to property owned through a family partnership as well as property owned directly.) At this stage, the dispute arose. Taxpayer subtracted $750,000 from the $1.91 million FMV of the 26 percent interest; the IRS, however, said that the $750,000 must be subtracted from the $2.73 million FMV calculated without a minority discount. (No minority discount could be taken from the net figure either.)

Held: For taxpayer. While the Tax Court agreed with the IRS relying on Estate of Mattox, 93 TC 228 (1989), the Tenth Circuit pointed out that *Mattox* denied use of a minority discount on top of the special-use valuation discount in a somewhat different context. In *Mattox*, the estate elected to use the special-use value (since the valuation reduction was less than $750,000) rather than the FMV; it then wanted to reduce the special-use value by a 30 percent minority discount. Had there been no $750,000 limit on the special-use valuation reduction, this would be equivalent to taxpayer in the instant case taking a 30 percent discount on the $533,548 special-use valuation figure. In contrast, taxpayer was seeking to reduce the interest's FMV by the $750,000 maximum special-use valuation discount. The Tax Court's holding suggested that FMV has a different meaning when Section 2032A is involved. This concept was rejected by the Tenth Circuit, which held that the property's FMV must be accurately determined as if Section 2032A did not apply (i.e., using a minority discount, when appropriate) and then the $750,000 reduction taken. The court noted that the IRS has not issued regulations under Section 2032A, so there was no reason to presume a different definition of FMV for special-use valuation purposes.

[Estate of Hoover, 69 F3d 1044, 76 AFTR2d 95-7305, 95-2 USTC ¶ 60,217 (10th Cir. 1995).]

Post-transfer conditions do not affect value. All of the stock of a corporation was held by four members of a family: two brothers and two sisters. Each of them created trusts into which all of the voting stock of the corporation would be transferred. The grantors of the trusts (the four siblings) and their descendants were to be the beneficiaries for as long as the Rule Against Perpetuities would permit. It was estimated that under the Rule Against Perpetuities, the trusts would last for ninety-seven years. One sister died shortly after the agreement was made, and her stock was transferred into the trust. The stock of the other three siblings, who were still living, was transferred into the trusts shortly thereafter. In determining the value of the stock for estate tax purposes, the grantors contended that there should be a 90 percent discount, because anyone buying one sibling's stock interest would know that the balance of the stock would be out of his control for ninety-seven years, thus making it impossible for him to gain control of the company. Further, because the trusts were established to ensure family control, the dividends would likely have been kept to a minimum so that earnings could be placed back into the company to provide better employment and investment opportunities for the family members. The IRS took the position that for gross estate purposes, the stock should have been valued without regard to the trusts at the higher pretransfer figure. Because it was a family corporation, however, the IRS did concede that a 20 percent discount for lack of marketability was appropriate.

Held: For the IRS. The court demonstrated an unwillingness to take into account terms or restrictions in the instrument of transfer itself in determining value. At the moment of decedent's death, the shares were unencumbered; accordingly, the court held that the fact that the stock was transferred into a family trust that was to last for nearly 100 years could not be taken into account in determining the value of the stock.

[Citizens Bank & Trust Co., 839 F2d 1249, 61 AFTR2d 88-1335, 88-1 USTC ¶ 13,755 (7th Cir. 1988).]

Minority interest in family farm corporation is not entitled to minority discount after farm real estate is specially valued under Section 2032A. When decedent died in 1983, he owned a minority (35.5 percent) interest in an incorporated family farm. The value of the farm was substantially reduced by the application of the special-use provisions of Section 2032A. In addition, the estate claimed a 30 percent discount otherwise applicable in determining the FMV of decedent's minority interest in the incorporated farm. The IRS disallowed the 30 percent FMV discount, because the value of the minority interests had already been substantially reduced below their FMV as a result of the special-use valuation. The estate, however, contended that once the real estate had been revalued under Section 2032A, it was properly included at the reduced amount in computing the total assets of the corporation, and thereafter the stock in the corporation was properly valued like the stock in all other corporations, subject to a minority interest discount.

Held: For the IRS. The Tax Court concluded that the estate was entitled to include in the gross estate the value of decedent's interest in the incorporated farm at the reduced value under the Section 2032A recomputation, but without any further reduction for minority interest. The court stated that subsection (g) of Section 2032A (which makes Section 2032A applicable to the real estate of a corporation) was intended to extend to estates of stockholders in family corporations the rights otherwise available under Section 2032A; it was never intended to give them greater rights.

[Estate of Maddox, 93 TC 228 (1989).]

Discount is applied in valuing family corporation's stock. Following an IRS estate audit, a discrepancy developed between the IRS and an estate over the valuation of decedent's shares in four closely held corporations owned in basically equal proportions by decedent and his four siblings. The corporations had been managed entirely by decedent and his two brothers. The IRS argued that no minority discount should be applied in valuing the shares, relying in part on Revenue Ruling 81-253, 1981-2 CB 187, which states that no minority discount is allowed where a controlling interest in a corporation is owned by family members. The IRS reasoned that in such a case, there is unity of ownership, and the shares owned by a family member should be viewed as a part of the controlling interest owned by the family as a unit.

Held: A minority discount should be applied in valuing the stock of a closely held corporation where the shares are all owned by family members. The court reasoned that the analysis must be based on a hypothetical sale from a hypothetical seller, not on a sale from a particular party. In ruling for taxpayers, the Tax Court cited Estate of Bright, 658 F2d 999 (5th Cir. 1981), as the leading case on this question. The issue there was the application of the minority discount to the valuation of the decedent's one-half community interest in 55 percent of a corporation's stock. The other one-half interest was owned by decedent's husband, who was also the executor of the estate and the trustee of the testamentary trust that was the recipient of decedent's shares. The Fifth Circuit, in holding for taxpayers, could find no authority for attributing control among family members as the IRS maintained. Instead, it found authority for applying a minority discount where decedent had owned less than 50 percent of the shares, regardless of whether overall control lay within decedent's family. The court looked to Regulations § 20.2031(b) and interpreted the "willing seller" to be a hypothetical willing seller, not the actual seller. The willing seller therefore should not be considered the estate, and the actual identities of the parties who receive the stock should be disregarded.

[Estate of Andrews, 79 TC 938 (1982).]

Tax Court recognizes valuation discount for community property interests. Decedent and her husband had owned 4,000 shares (80 percent) of the common stock and 50,000 shares (100 percent) of the preferred stock of a corporation. The 7 percent noncumulative preferred stock was entitled to $200 per share on dissolution or redemption, but had no voting rights other than on dissolution, merger, or amendment of the articles. Decedent died in 1971, leaving a will in which the preferred stock was left to a charity and her husband was to receive the common stock. The estate valued the preferred stock at its $200-per-share dissolution value ($10 million) and the common stock at its $10-per-share par value ($40,000). The IRS argued for a preferred value of $1,973,296 and a common value of $2,870,440.

Held: The court, by valuing the surviving spouse's one-half community interest in both the preferred and common stock as a block, allowed what appears to be a 10 percent to 15 percent minority interest discount and concluded that the value of such shares as a block was $2,192,773. The court further concluded that the value of the preferred stock left to charity was 90 percent and that the value of the common stock was 10 percent of that value. Surprisingly, the value finally assigned to decedent's preferred stock was within $200 of the amount at which the IRS had previously valued the preferred stock. Decedent's 40 percent of the common stock and 50 percent of the preferred stock was determined, in the aggregate, to be worth 40 percent of the corporation's stipulated total value. Both the estate and the IRS had originally treated the value of decedent's one-half community interest in the common stock as one half of the entire value of the 4,000 shares of common stock. The court concluded, however, that each party had an undivided one-half interest, which was equivalent to each having a separate interest in a block of 2,000 shares of common stock and 25,000 shares of preferred stock. Although in the aggregate the marital community held a majority interest in the stock of the corporation, for estate tax valuation purposes, each held a separate minority interest.

[Estate of Lee, 69 TC 860 (1978), nonacq., 1980-1 CB 2.]

Deathbed transfer did not create minority discount. Decedent in this ruling was unable to manufacture a minority discount to reduce the size of her estate. She had contributed assets to a partnership in exchange for a controlling interest shortly before her death and then sold enough of that interest to her heirs to be left with a minority interest. Decedent's executor sought to claim a minority discount for the partnership interest that remained in her estate after the sale. Decedent held rental real estate and marketable securities in a revocable trust. Her two children were co-trustees of the trust. They also were beneficiaries of the trust following her death. Decedent also owned an income interest for life and a testamentary general power of appointment over a marital trust established by her deceased husband. If that power of appointment were not exercised, the trust property would pass to decedent's children. Assets in both trusts were includable in decedent's estate under Sections 2038 (for the revocable trust) and 2041 (for the marital trust). Two days before decedent's death, the family formed a limited partnership. The children contributed cash in exchange for one percent general partnership interests. The marital trust contributed property for an 82 percent interest, and the revocable trust contributed property for a 16 percent interest. That same day, the marital trust sold two 30 percent limited partnership interests to decedent's son and daughter for a small amount of cash plus thirty-year promissory notes. Thus, on the date of decedent's death, the marital trust had a 22 percent limited partnership interest and the revocable trust had a 16 percent interest. On decedent's estate tax return, minority discounts were claimed for the partnership interests held by the trusts. Also, the promissory notes were assigned a discounted value. The IRS, however, said that these discounts were improper on two grounds. The IRS said that the formation of the partnership and the transfer of partnership interests were parts of a single testamentary transaction. As such, it disregarded the partnership for estate tax valuation purposes. In so ruling, the IRS relied on Estate of Murphy, TC Memo. (P-H) ¶ 90,472, 60 TCM 645 (1990). That case involved a taxpayer who appointed a 1.76 percent interest in a closely held corporation eighteen days before her death, leaving her (and her estate) with a 49.65 percent interest. The Tax Court concluded that the sole purpose for the lifetime transfer was to reduce the estate tax on the entire block of stock by claiming a minority discount. The court pointed out that the transfer changed nothing regarding the management of the company; control remained in the family. Neither did it "appreciably affect" taxpayer's beneficial interest, aside from potential estate tax consequences. Furthermore, the court concluded that a minority interest should not be applied when the transfer that fragmented control was made solely to reduce transfer taxes.

In the situation at issue in the instant ruling, there was an intra-family transfer like the one in *Murphy*, entered into when decedent's death was imminent and when it was known that she would not exercise her general power of appointment. Furthermore, the parties anticipated that the notes would not be paid because they would be cancelled when distributed to the children. Thus, assets subject to the power would have gone to the children under the terms of the trust, and the "sale" had no real substance. Furthermore, the ruling referred to Section 2703(a)(2) as an alternative reason for denying a minority discount. That provision ignores restrictions on the right to sell or use property for transfer tax purposes unless the restriction meets each of the following requirements:

1. It is a bona fide business arrangement.

2. It is not a device to transfer property to decedent's family members for less than its full FMV.
3. Its terms are comparable to those that would be entered into in an arm's-length transaction.

The estate contended that the property in question was the partnership interest. Because there were no restrictions in the partnership agreement on the transfer or use of these interests, the estate contended that Section 2703(a)(2) did not apply. The IRS, however, ruled that the underlying partnership property was the property subject to Section 2703(a)(2); the children received the underlying property, subject to a partnership agreement, at decedent's death, and the partnership wrapper was created only for a tax-motivated purpose. The ruling went on to state that the transaction was a device to transfer property to decedent's family members, rather than a bona fide business arrangement. The children, as co-trustees, were dealing with themselves in structuring the arrangement. In an arm's-length deal, decedent would not have entered into a transaction that reduced her net worth as the estate claims the sale of the partnership interests did—especially given her ill health, which eliminated the opportunity to recoup the immediate loss.

[Tech. Adv. Mem. 9719006.]

"Swing vote" attributes of block of stock taken into account in valuation. The donor, who owned 100 percent of the stock of a corporation, gave 30 percent of the shares to each of his three children. For gift tax purposes, the donor valued the gifts of stock at a 25 percent discount for minority interest and lack of marketability.

The IRS ruled that in determining the value of the 30 percent blocks of stock transferred, the "swing vote" attributes of each block must be taken into account. The swing vote characteristic means that the owner of any one of the transferred blocks could join with the owner of any of the other transferred blocks and control the corporation. The swing vote attribute enhances the value of each block transferred, and this increase in value may wipe out any minority discount that would otherwise be available.

[Tech. Adv. Mem. 9436005.]

[f] Factors and methods

Closely held stock is valued by comparing earnings history, book value, and dividend history with those of similar companies. During his lifetime, decedent had given several lots of stock in his closely held corporation to his son and daughter. He had retained a CPA firm to appraise the value of the stock and file the requisite gift tax returns. On the timely filed returns, the stock had been valued at $40 per share. The stock of the corporation had been privately held at all times and had never been traded on an exchange. The CPA firm had computed the value of the stock by employing an analysis of three factors: the earnings factor, the dividend factor, and the book value factor. A publicly traded company had been selected as the most comparable in terms of products, markets, and types of business, and a comparison had been made between the closely held corporation and the publicly traded corporation for each valuation factor. A weighted average of the three factors had then been derived by assigning a 40 percent weight each to the earnings and dividend factors and a 20 percent weight to the book value factor. When the IRS audited the estate's returns, it determined that the stock should have been valued at $110 per share, and assessed a deficiency. The IRS based its valuation on the appraisal of a valuation consultant firm. This firm had arrived at the appraised value of the stock by comparing the closely held corporation to three comparable publicly held companies. It concluded that the closely held company was superior to the three comparables in earnings per share, after tax return on sales, and returns to equity and return on investment, but inferior in growth of sales. Taxpayer paid the deficiency and then filed a claim for refund.

Held: For taxpayer (in part). The court determined the value of the stock to be $87.64. The court stated that pursuant to Regulation § 25.2512-1, the value of property is the price at which it would change hands between a willing buyer and willing seller, neither being under any compulsion to buy or sell and both having reasonable knowledge of relevant facts. In the case of valuing stock for which there is no public market, the company's net worth, prospective earning power and dividend-paying capacity, and other relevant factors must be taken into consideration. The court also considered Revenue Ruling 59-60, 1959-1 CB 237, which specifically addresses the valuation of closely held corporate stock. The revenue ruling sets forth the following factors to be considered:

1. The nature of the business and the history of the enterprise from its inception.
2. The economic outlook in general and the condition and outlook of the specific industry.
3. The book value of the stock and the financial condition of the business.
4. The earning capacity of the company.
5. The dividend-paying capacity.
6. Whether the enterprise has goodwill or other intangible value.
7. Sales of stock and size of the block of stock to be valued.
8. The market price of stocks of corporations in the same or a similar line of business having their stocks actively traded in a free and open market.

In arriving at the final valuation, the court took the weighted average of the company's earnings for the five-year period immediately preceding the year of sale and multiplied it by the price-earnings ratio based on the comparable publicly traded corporations. It then took the book value of the company's stock and multiplied it by the market-to-book-value ratio based on the comparables and computed a dividend factor. It assigned a 60 percent weight to the earnings factor, a 30 percent weight to the book value factor, and a 10 percent weight to the dividend factor. After applying the percentage weights to each factor, the court added each result to arrive at the estimated company value. From this figure it deducted the preferred stock and divided the result by the number of common shares outstanding. Finally, it applied a 30 percent marketability discount to this quotient to arrive at its estimated value per share.

[Reilly, 88-2 USTC ¶ 13,782, 61 AFTR2d 88-1332 (SD Ind. 1988).]

Tax Court rebukes IRS, finding no expectation at time of death that decedent's stock would triple in value within six months. On November 17, 1979, decedent, a resident of Ohio, died in the crash of a small airplane. Included in his estate were 381,150 shares of stock in a corporation that had been formed by decedent to produce and market scientific instruments. These holdings represented approximately 23 percent of all outstanding stock and were subject to trading restrictions imposed by federal securities law. At the time of death, shares of the stock were actively traded in the over-the-counter market, selling for $12.25 per share on the day before the fatal plane crash. Within six months, the estate arranged to sell the stock in a single block to an outside company for $24 per share as part of a comprehensive reorganization (merger) plan. For estate tax purposes, the estate valued the stock at $7.35 per share. The IRS, in issuing its notice of deficiency, valued each share at $24.

Held: For the estate. The Tax Court, in a thorough analysis of the stock, the market, and the facts and circumstances surrounding the reorganization, concluded that the valuation methods used by the estate properly reflected FMV as of the date of death. The IRS position throughout was that the merger was foreseeable at the time of death and that such a factor was an appropriate element to consider in valuing decedent's 23 percent block. The Tax Court, however, rejected this approach, finding it unreasonable to require the estate to assume that such a merger would take place.

[Estate of Gilford, 88 TC 38 (1987).]

Value of decedent's 100 percent stock interests in two investment companies is held to be their net asset value reduced by liquidation costs. At the time of her death, decedent owned all of the stock of two investment companies. One of the companies had been active prior to 1955. All of the stock and securities held by the two companies were marketable and had readily ascertainable values on April 9, 1979, the date of decedent's death. The companies had no known liabilities. The estate filed its estate tax return, claiming a 30 percent discount of the value of the stock to reflect the lack of marketability. The IRS determined a higher value. The IRS used the combined values of the stock and securities held by each company, less the costs of liquidating the companies and selling such stock and securities.

Held: For the IRS. Although discounts on stock are frequently used to recognize minority holdings or the lack of marketability, no such impediments existed in the instant case, because the assets of both companies were liquid, neither company had any known liabilities (even with due consideration of the fact that one of the companies had an operating history that ceased more than twenty years prior to decedent's death), and decedent's 100 percent ownership of both companies gave her or any buyer the unqualified right to liquidate both companies and sell the assets.

[Estate of Jephson, 87 TC 297 (1986).]

IRS's valuation of stock in closely held bank holding company is reduced. Decedent had owned a minority interest in a closely held bank holding company. The bank was in a rural agricultural area that was experiencing financial difficulties during a period of high interest rates and low commodity prices. The IRS valued the stock at a higher FMV than did the estate.

Held: For the IRS (in part). The IRS valuation was reduced because the IRS failed to consider the economic problems of financial institutions in the farming area. In addition, the IRS's comparison of the company to banks in two metropolitan areas was inappropriate, and the stock was entitled to a minority discount.

[Estate of Titus, TC Memo. (P-H) ¶ 89,466, 57 TCM (CCH) 1449 (1989).]

IRS issues guidelines for valuation of restricted securities. The IRS apparently agrees with a Securities and Exchange Commission (SEC) conclusion that restricted securities generally are issued at a discount from the market value of freely tradable securities and should be valued accordingly. In its ruling, the IRS has issued guidelines for valuing such securities. These guidelines stress SEC valuation suggestions in addition to the IRS's own guidelines for valuing securities, contained in Revenue Ruling 59-60, 1959-1 CB 237, as modified by Revenue Ruling 65-193, 1965-2 CB 370. In weighing the factors and circumstances surrounding valuation of restricted stock, earnings, net assets, and net sales are to be given primary consideration. Other factors include resale provisions concerning the length of time that the buyer must wait to liquidate the shares and whether he must bear the expense of registration, the relative negotiation strengths of the buyer and seller, and the market experience of freely tradable securities of the same class as the restricted securities.

The ruling notes that though there are a variety of methods available to value restricted securities, the SEC rejects automatic or mechanical solutions (presumably formula approaches). The IRS specifically notes that the general valuation factors of Revenue Ruling 59-60 are to be considered. These factors include:

1. The nature of the business and its history from the beginning.
2. The economic outlook in general and for the specific industry in particular.
3. The book value of the stock and the financial condition of the business.
4. The earning capacity of the company.
5. The dividend-paying capacity.
6. The presence of goodwill or other intangible assets.
7. Sales of stock and the size of the block of stock to be valued.
8. The market price of stocks of similar corporations that are actively traded in an open market.

In connection with the above factors, Revenue Ruling 77-287 suggests the use of the following documents and facts:

1. A copy of any declaration of trust, trust agreement, or any other agreement relating to the shares or restricted stock.
2. A copy of any buy or sell offers or indications of interest in buying or selling restricted stock.
3. The latest prospectus of the company.
4. Annual reports of the company for three to five years preceeding the valuation date.
5. The trading prices and the volume of the related class of traded securities one month preceding the valuation date.
6. The relationship of the parties to the restricted agreement.
7. Whether the interest being valued is a majority or minority ownership.

[Rev. Rul. 77-287, 1977-2 CB 319.]

[2] Partnership Interests

Decedent's partnership interest in closely held family partnership is valued on basis of its going-concern value, not its liquidated value. When decedent died in 1978, she owned a 15 percent interest in an Oregon general partnership that had been engaged in the wood products industry for over thirty years. The remaining partnership interests had always been held by the same three families. The partnership agreement provided that the death of one of the partners would not result in the dissolution or termination of the partnership. Decedent's will, in conformity with the partnership agreement, provided that her interest was to be placed in trust, with the trustee having no authority to sell the interest except in a transaction sanctioned by a majority of the partners. On the estate return, decedent's 15 percent partnership interest was valued at $2,550,000, its going-concern value. On audit, the IRS determined that the FMV of the interest was $20,006,000, its liquidation value. The Tax Court concluded that the partnership's liquidation value was not the correct standard of valuation, because it found no intent on the part of the partners to alter the family ownership structure of the partnership or to liquidate the company.

Held: Affirmed for the estate. The Eleventh Circuit stated that the Tax Court erred to the extent that it relied upon the subjective intent of the surviving partners in determining that decedent's interest should be valued as part of a going concern. This error did not require a reversal, however, because the Tax Court's decision to value decedent's interest as part of a going concern was amply supported by the law governing Oregon partnerships and the contractual restrictions placed upon decedent's partnership interest by the partnership agreement. The circuit court found that the partnership agreement clearly provided that the death of a partner would not cause dissolution and that the business would continue in the event of a partner's death. Thus, though in the absence of such an agreement the partnership would have dissolved upon decedent's death, here the interest that passed to her estate was, by terms of the partnership agreement, an interest in an undissolved partnership.

[Estate of Watts, 823 F2d 483, 60 AFTR2d 87-6117, 87-2 USTC ¶ 13,726 (11th Cir. 1987).]

Estate tax value of partnership interest owned by decedent is established under buy-sell agreement. At his death in 1979, decedent was a 50 percent owner in a two-person business partnership. The partnership agreement contained a buy-sell agreement between decedent and the surviving partner that was to become effective upon the death of either. The agreement set forth a specific price that the living partner would be required to pay to purchase the deceased partner's share. There was to be a periodic appraisal of the current value of the partnership. The last purchase price set by the parties was $1,006,750. The partnership agreement also provided for the continuation of the partnership's name and business by the surviving partner. Decedent's partnership interest was sold to the surviving partner by the estate for the agreed-upon sum of $1,006,750. Estate taxes were paid on this valuation. The IRS audited the estate's return, filed a deficiency notice and claimed that the taxable estate should be valued at $2,190,100. The estate objected to the assessment, paid the tax assessed by the IRS, and filed suit for a refund. The estate claimed that the valuation established through the buy-sell agreement determined the proper value of the partnership for federal estate tax purposes. The valuation set forth in the agreement, according to the estate, was essentially the worth of the business as a continuing entity. The IRS, on the other hand, argued that the proper valuation for estate tax purposes was the liquidated value of the property of the partnership, even though the buy-sell agreement may, indeed, have controlled the rights of the estate and the surviving partner.

Held: For the estate. Based upon the following factors, the court concluded that the proper estate tax value of the partnership interest was the amount established under the buy-sell agreement:

1. There was a bona fide business purpose for entering into the buy-sell agreement.
2. There was no tax avoidance motive behind the buy-sell agreement.
3. There were lifetime and death restrictions on the transferability of each partner's interest.

Accordingly, the refund was granted.

[Estate of Novak, 87-2 USTC ¶ 13,728 (D. Neb. 1987).]

Value of interest in land trust partnership is determined. Decedent had an interest in a family-owned land trust partnership that held farmland. The IRS and the estate disagreed on the highest and best use of the land. Consequently, they arrived at drastically different estate tax valuations: $365,000 for agricultural use (estate) versus $1.4 million for residential and commercial use (IRS). All of the expert witnesses used the market data approach to value the property.

Held: For the estate. The highest and best use of the land was farming. Because of the economic recession in the area at that time, there was no demand for residential or commercial property. Accordingly, little weight was given to the government's expert's estimates, because the comparable sales on which he based his appraisal (1) involved use for a higher purpose than as farmland and (2) took place before the serious decline in the local economy. In addition, the value of the land was discounted to reflect the partnership's undivided one-half interest in a portion of the land.

[Estate of Feuchter, RIA TC Memo. ¶ 92,097, 63 TCM (CCH) 2104 (1992).]

Family partnership ignored for valuation purposes. The IRS held, in this ruling, that a decedent's estate could not get a valuation discount for assets transferred to a family partnership only weeks before her death. Instead, the transferred interests had to be valued without regard to the family's partnership agreement. Alternatively, the IRS said that the valuation discount being claimed could be a taxable gift. In December 1993, decedent executed a will and created a revocable trust. In June 1995, she and her family created a family partnership. She became a limited partner (with a 99 percent partnership interest), and two of her children became general partners (each with a 0.5 percent partnership interest). In September 1995, decedent transferred $1.7 million in securities, held by the revocable trust, to the partnership. She also transferred $145,000 from a money market fund. Then in October, the month in which she died, she transferred two pieces of real estate (including the home where she lived) and $90,000 in cash to the partnership. Her two children, the general partners, transferred $10,000 each that October. Decedent had transferred almost all of her assets to the partnership in the six-week period before her death. On its federal tax return, however, her estate valued her partnership interest at only about 60 percent of what she had transferred. The estate claimed the diminution of the mother's interest was not a gift to her children, but was merely the result of the partnership's form of organization. The IRS disagreed on several grounds.

Section 2033 states that the value of a decedent's gross estate includes the value of all property to the extent of decedent's interest in it at the time of his or her death. According to *Murphy*, 60 TCM 645, ¶ 90,472 RIA TC Memo. (1990), if the sole purpose of transferring an interest was to avoid tax liabilities, the transfer is ignored for tax purposes. In the present case, the mother transferred her assets only to avoid the estate tax. There was no legitimate business reason for the transfers. Therefore, the IRS viewed the transfer of the mother's assets as one single testamentary transaction occurring at her death, and any valuation discount from the partnership's holding the assets should be ignored.

The valuation discount at issue was attributable to restrictions inherent in the property's being owned by a partnership. Section 2703, however, provides that any restrictions on the right to sell or use property should be ignored for transfer tax purposes unless three conditions are met: (1) The transfer in question was a genuine business arrangement; (2) the transfer was not a device to transfer property to members of decedent's family for less than full and adequate consideration in money or money's worth; and (3) the transfer's terms are comparable to similar arrangements entered into by persons in an arm's-length transaction. Decedent's transfers clearly were not designed to maximize the value of the assets involved. The value of decedent's interest shrank from $2.24 million to $1.3 million following the contributions to the partnership. This was not a "business" transaction by any account and would not have occurred in an arm's-length setting. Rather, it was done to reduce artificially the value of the transferred interest for estate tax purposes. Further, Section 2704 states that if a decedent transferred his or her interest in an entity to a family member, and the family was in control of the entity before the transfer, any "applicable restriction" in determining the value of the transferred interest is to be disregarded. An applicable restriction (1) limits the ability of the partnership to liquidate, and (2) is one the transferor or the transferor's family can remove after the transfer of an interest. The IRS found that the partnership agreement's limitations on the assets of the partnership were such an "applicable restriction." Therefore, the restrictions could be ignored, and the mother's assets could be valued for tax purposes at their full value, $2.24 million. Alternatively, the IRS contended that the 40 percent decrease in the value of decedent's assets could be subject to gift tax. The lack of a specific donee does not preclude this result. Rather, Regulation § 25.2511-2(a) states that the gift tax is not imposed on the receipt of property by a donee, but is based on the transfer by the donor.

[Tech. Adv. Mem. 9842003.]

Interests again combined to form majority block. Partnership interests in a QTIP trust included in the estate of a surviving spouse were valued by aggregating them with partnership interests owned outright by the spouse, in this ruling.

Decedent and the surviving spouse held community property (i.e., undivided one-half) interests in real property and in securities. Decedent's estate and the surviving spouse contributed the property to a real estate limited partnership and a securities limited partnership, with the estate receiving limited partnership interests and all of the general partnership interests, and the surviving spouse receiving the balance of the limited partnership interests. The partnerships could be dissolved by a majority vote of the general and the limited partners. The estate transferred most of its partnership interests to a QTIP trust, but retained the general partnership interest in the securities partnership. The surviving spouse's interests were held in a revocable trust at her death in 1992. The revocable trust was included in the surviving spouse's estate under Section 2038, and the QTIP trust was included in her estate under Section 2044(a). The estate valued the partnership interests as separate blocks with neither having the power to liquidate the partnerships.

The IRS had combined stock owned outright by a surviving spouse with stock owned by a QTIP trust to form a majority block for valuation purposes, in Technical Advice Memorandum 9550002. Therefore, the IRS required aggregation when it came to the partnerships. The IRS, however, now found additional support for its conclusion in legislative history indicating that Congress viewed a surviving spouse as the actual owner of property in a QTIP trust. Thus, when property in a QTIP trust is included in a surviving spouse's estate under Section 2044, it is to be treated for transfer tax purposes as if the entire property had been transferred to the donee-spouse. Therefore, the partnership interests held by both the revocable trust and the QTIP trust were treated as individually owned by the surviving spouse for valuation purposes.

[Tech. Adv. Mem. 9608001.]

[3] Real Estate

[a] Generally

Survivor's property not aggregated with QTIP trust's. Taxpayer died on January 11, 1989, owning a 62.5 percent undivided interest in a ranch, a 50 percent undivided interest in other real property, and a 50 percent undivided interest in a fifty-six-foot pleasure boat. The remaining interests in each property were owned by a QTIP trust set up under the will of taxpayer's predeceased spouse and were included in his estate. The IRS and taxpayer's estate agreed that the values of 100 percent of the properties on the date of taxpayer's death were $1.8 million for the ranch, $175,000 for the other real property, and $30,000 for the boat. The estate, however, claimed a fractional interest discount. This reflected the lack of control of the owner of less than a 100 percent interest, the consequent diminished marketability, and the costs and fees associated with partition. The IRS asserted that the properties owned by the QTIP trust had to be treated as if they were actually owned by the surviving spouse and that therefore, for valuation purposes, he owned 100 percent of each property, and no discount was allowed.

Held: For the estate. The Fifth Circuit decided that the estate was entitled to a fractional interest discount. Although the properties in the QTIP trust were included in taxpayer's estate under Section 2044, and Section 2044(c) provides that property so included is treated as having passed from decedent, this ·did not require that the separate properties be treated as one interest. Neither taxpayer nor his estate could control who the properties in the QTIP trust passed to after his death. (Furthermore, the actual recipient was not relevant, since the estate tax value of property is determined at the moment of death and not by the interest held by the decedent before death or the interest held by his beneficiary after his death.) In the court's view, since the predeceased spouse had controlled the disposition of the properties in the QTIP trust after decedent's death, each was a separate interest for valuation purposes. When decedent died, his estate did not have the degree of control over the properties in the QTIP trust that would permit it to act as a hypothetical seller negotiating with willing buyers, and therefore, negate the existence of fractional interests.

[Estate of Bonner, 84 F3d 196, 77 AFTR2d 96-2369, 96-2 USTC ¶ 60,237 (5th Cir. 1996).]

Offer to purchase lease determines its value. Decedent died on November 12, 1988, owning a 67 percent (undivided) interest in a parking garage lease with a remaining term of almost sixteen years. Decedent's son owned the other 33 percent interest in the lease, and they operated the parking garage together. An appraiser valued the entire lease at $425,000 as of October 31, 1988. In

January 1989, a company offered to purchase the lease for $2.23 million, payable over fifteen years without interest, and it later raised its offer to $2.63 million. The estate tax return was filed while this offer was outstanding, and the estate used the present value of the offer ($1.46 million) as the value of the entire lease and then adjusted for decedent's interest. The $2.63 million offer was not accepted by the estate. Nevertheless, initially, the estate did not seek to reduce the reported value. In 1991, the estate sold the 67 percent interest in the lease to the son. The purchase price equated to a 1988 FMV that was virtually the same as that in the original appraisal. Several months later, the estate filed a refund claim relying on the sale and the appraisal. The trial court was not persuaded that the value had been overstated.

Held: Affirmed for the IRS. The Federal Circuit affirmed because the estate had not established that its version of the facts was the only plausible one. The estate argued that it had used the company's offer only because of concern about valuation penalties. The IRS said the estate had used the offer to value the lease because it thought the offer might reflect the FMV. The explanation of why a value was reported, however, was for the trial court to decide. Although there was strong evidence in favor of the estate, its version of the facts was not the only permissible one. Therefore, the appeals court refused to overturn the trial court's decision.

[Wrona, 79 F3d 1166, 77 AFTR2d 96-1434, 96-1 USTC ¶ 60,227 (Fed. Cir. 1996).]

Seventh Circuit finds substantial evidence to support Tax Court valuation of farmlands. Decedent died in 1973 seized of a 92-acre family farm in Illinois. The property was located 30 miles west of Chicago in an area that was then being rapidly developed. A shopping center was located two miles away from decedent's homestead, and a major property developer was actively buying land in the area. On its estate tax return, taxpayer valued the property at $2,000 per acre. The IRS, however, asserted that FMV was over $5,000 per acre. The evidence showed that property in the general area was being purchased for the average price of $6,000 per acre and that decedent's farm was located within the so-called development corridor. The Tax Court considered this evidence and entered judgment placing a $5,000-per-acre value on the property. The estate thereupon took an appeal to the Seventh Circuit, contending that the highest-and-best-use valuation presented by the government's experts was based on speculative investment activity rather than on proved market value.

Held: Affirmed for the IRS. The court ruled that there was substantial evidence in the record to support the Tax Court's valuation. The fact that the estate actually sold the property seven years after the date of death for the same price established by the Tax Court was not considered to be determinative of error.

[Estate of Frieders, 687 F2d 224, 50 AFTR2d 82-6201, 82-2 USTC ¶ 13,489 (7th Cir. 1982), cert. denied, 460 US 1011 (1983).]

"Common sense" is used to value timberland. At the time of his death, decedent owned over 3,300 acres of timberland that was subject to a long-term lease. The lessee had exclusive use and control of the property and was required to make annual lease payments based on the price of timber harvested from the land. The lessee also had a right of first refusal on the land, should it be sold. The estate's valuation expert assumed that the lessee would be a willing purchaser and applied a discount rate to the future value of the lease payments and the value of the reversionary interest. The IRS disputed the estate's valuation of the future lease payments.

Held: For taxpayer (in part). Both expert valuations were rejected. Rather, the FMV was to be determined based on what a willing buyer would pay to afford the seller a 10 percent rate of return on the future lease payments.

[Oettmeier, 708 F. Supp. 1307, 89-2 USTC ¶ 13,809, 64 AFTR2d 89-5895 (MD Ga. 1989).]

Ninth Circuit refuses to disturb jury verdict on valuation of real property for estate tax purposes. A jury in an estate tax refund case was asked to find the FMV of a parcel of real estate in Kenosha County, Wisconsin, as of March 13, 1978, the date of the property owner's death. The jury heard evidence valuing the property at a low figure of $500,000 and a high one of $1.4 million. The jury returned its verdict finding the value of the land in question to be $1.1 million. The estate then moved for judgment notwithstanding the verdict or, alternatively, for a new trial.

Held: For the IRS; motions denied. Although it can be argued that a system that permits an unschooled group of laymen to assess the value of real estate "is akin to throwing darts at a dartboard while blindfolded," it is the system that, for better or for worse, has been established for the resolution of such disputes. Because there was evidence in the record sufficient to support a verdict of $1.4 million, it reasonably followed that a finding of $1.1 million was supportable, although the trial judge indicated that he would have set the value at $800,000 if the case had been tried to the bench.

[First Nat'l Bank of Kenosha, 84-1 USTC ¶ 13,569 (ED Wis. 1984), aff'd, 763 F2d 891, 56 AFTR2d 85-6492, 85-2 USTC ¶ 13,620 (9th Cir. 1985).]

Basis not fixed by death date FMV. Taxpayer filed joint returns with her husband for 1987 and 1988 but his tax liability was determined and discharged in a bankruptcy proceeding. Taxpayer claimed a NOL deduction for both years, mostly attributable to a business loss from her husband's married-but-separate 1984 return. The IRS disallowed the 1984 loss as a carryover, asserting it was offset by unreported gain on the husband's sale of land inherited from his mother. The husband, in preparing and filing the mother's estate tax return as the personal representative, had included only one half of the land, at a FMV of $525,000. Several months after the mother died, the husband and his three brothers contracted to sell the land for $2.48 million, of which the husband received his one-quarter share in 1984. The IRS asserted an estate tax deficiency against the husband and his brothers, which was settled in 1989 by a stipulation that included the entire tract in the mother's estate at a $1.4 million FMV. Following State Farming Co., 40 TC 774 (1963), the IRS could recompute the husband's 1984 income, even though the limitations period had expired, because it affected the NOL for an open year. The IRS argued that the husband had a gain on the sale because his share of the proceeds ($620,000) exceeded his basis ($350,000), which was one fourth of the stipulated FMV. Under Section 1014, the basis of inherited property is its FMV on the date of decedent's death or on the alternative valuation date. The value determined for estate tax purposes, however, does not conclusively determine the value for income tax purposes. Nevertheless, when taxpayers have attempted to profit from an error or omission and claim a higher basis after the estate tax limitations period expired, courts have applied the doctrine of duty of consistency to hold them to the estate tax value. The doctrine applies under the following conditions: (1) Taxpayer reported an item (or made a representation) for tax purposes in one year; (2) the IRS acquiesced in, or relied on, the reported item (or taxpayer's representation); and (3) taxpayer desires to change position in a later year after the limitations period bars adjustment of the initial year. Taxpayer argued that the first requirement was not met, because her husband's income tax liability was not involved and she was not a party to the stipulation.

Held: For the IRS. The Tax Court rejected taxpayer's argument because of the closely aligned interests of the spouses. The duty of consistency doctrine has been applied when an individual was both a fiduciary and a beneficiary of the estate, in Belzer, 495 F2d 211, 33 AFTR2d-1173, 74-1 USTC ¶ 9373 (8th Cir. 1974), and in McMillan, 14 AFTR2d 5704, 64-2 USTC ¶ 9720 (DC W. Va. 1964). Although beneficiaries were not bound when they were minors at the time the estate tax return was filed, in Ford, 276 F2d 17, 5 AFTR2d 1157, 60-1 USTC ¶ 9375 (Ct. Cl. 1960), the same court applied the doctrine to a testamentary trust created by an estate, in Hess, 537 F2d 457, 38 AFTR2d 76-5429, 76-2 USTC ¶ 9539 (Ct. Cl. 1976), because the two entities were so closely related. The Tax Court concluded that a duty of consistency bound taxpayer since, by filing joint returns for 1987 and 1988, she had elected to be treated as part of a single tax-paying unit. Moreover, any loss was attributable to the husband and, since he would have been held to a duty of consistency, she should not be in a better position. Therefore, the court refused to reconsider the FMV of the tract.

[Cluck, 105 TC 324 (1995).]

Change in market conditions negates recent appraisal. Decedent's estate included one of ninety-five units in a general partnership that owned two secondary office buildings in midtown Manhattan (New York City), situated outside the most prestigious areas. The partnership's rental income increased from 1982 through 1988, and cash distributions increased from $10,000 a unit to $40,000 a unit. As of May 9, 1988, while the real estate market was still fairly strong, the properties were appraised at $110 million in connection with a mortgage refinancing that permitted a special distribution of $140,000 a unit. By December 31, 1989, the date of decedent's death, the real estate picture had changed dramatically. New York was in the grip of a recession, and this adversely affected the demand for office space. Moreover, a university that occupied 40 percent of the space in the partnership's buildings gave notice a few months before decedent's death that it would likely not renew most of its leases when they ended in 1992 through 1994. Another general partner controlled 54 percent of the partnership units, and this enabled him to manage the partnership and even require additional capital contributions. Also, since units could not be sold or transferred without the consent of a majority of the partners, this partner had the power to determine whether and to whom the partners could transfer their units. The IRS's experts valued decedent's unit at $594,000, based on a FMV of $120 million for the buildings. They arrived at this value by projecting a net lease income and dividing it by a 7.9 percent capitalization rate (i.e., the return that an investor would require). The net lease income was arrived at by assuming initial gross rents that exceeded the partnership's 1989 rent and projecting future increases of 5 percent a year and a vacancy rate of only 1 percent. The estate claimed a lower valuation.

Held: For the estate. The Tax Court decided that the IRS's experts' assumptions were too optimistic, since they ignored the depressed state of the real estate market, the assumption of lenders that recovery would be slow, and the likelihood that the partnership would be forced to replace most of its major tenant's space in this unfavorable environment. Instead, the court accepted the $100 million FMV determined by the estate's expert. This assumed a lower initial gross rental income, a 5 percent contingency vacancy rate, and a higher (8.5 percent) capitalization rate. Although the 1988 appraisal had fixed a higher FMV, its underlying assumptions were no longer accurate on the valuation date. The IRS, having determined the liquidation value of a unit (by subtracting partnership liabilities from the value of the buildings), had allowed a 28 percent discount. This consisted of a 15 percent minority discount and a 15 percent discount (applied to the discounted value) for lack of marketability. The 15 percent minority discount assumed that decedent, as a general partner, could meaningfully participate in the management of the partnership. This ignored the practical control that the majority partner exerted over the partnership's management and operations. Only by voting as a bloc could decedent and the other minority partners exert any influence, and then only on matters requiring a two-thirds vote, such as the sale of the partnership's properties.

The power of any general partner to dissolve the partnership had not been considered by the experts, but the court did not regard it as significant. Therefore, the Tax Court allowed the 19 percent minority discount that market studies showed was generally applicable when a purchaser of a real estate partnership interest would have little control. The court also allowed a 26 percent discount for lack of marketability at the low end of the 25.8 percent to 45 percent range that market studies showed as typical, since the partnership was well managed and made regular substantial distributions. Nevertheless, because there was no public market and the transfer of the unit was subject to the approval of the majority partner, the discount was far larger than the IRS conceded. In addition, the discounts were allowed independently of each other, so they totaled 45 percent, resulting in a FMV of $338,000 for the unit.

[Barudin, 72 TCM 488, RIA TC Memo. ¶ 96,395 (1996).]

Residential zoning did not control the valuation of decedent's realty. Decedent owned an undivided one-half interest in two parcels of real estate held in trust, both of which were zoned for residential use. Four appraisals were done, with two appraisers concluding that one parcel's highest and best use was commercial and the other two that it was residential, with the difference being approximately $2.8 million. Taxpayer and the IRS agreed that the highest and best use for the second parcel was commercial.

    Held: For the IRS (in part). The mere fact that the current zoning restrictions do not permit a particular use does not necessarily preclude a consideration of unpermitted use when conducting a highest-and-best use analysis. At decedent's death, re-zoning of the first parcel from residential to commercial use was quite likely. Adjustments to the IRS's values were made, however, on account of topography, highway and sewer access, and quality of landfill.

[Estate of Lloyd, 71 TCM 1903, RIA TC Memo. ¶ 96,030 (1996).]

IRS's valuation is accepted as highest and best use. Decedent had owned two parcels of land used for agricultural purposes. The estate's appraisal valued the land based on that use. The IRS's valuation, on the other hand, was based on residential use of the land.

    Held: For the IRS. The highest and best use of the property was for residential development. The property was located directly in the path of the expanding residential development. In addition, comparable sales in the area indicated that that was the likely use for the property.

[Estate of Pattison, TC Memo. (P-H) ¶ 90,428, 60 TCM (CCH) 471 (1990).]

Tax Court determines FMV of decedent's stock and real property. Decedent's estate and the IRS disagreed over the fair market value of decedent's

Florida property and his beneficial interest in a revocable trust owning stock. Both sides introduced expert valuations to support their determinations.

Held: For the IRS. The IRS's expert was more experienced and credible than the estate's expert. Because of liquidating expenses and the limited market for the stock, a 35 percent discount was applied to the IRS's valuation of decedent's interest in the trust.

[Estate of Dougherty, TC Memo. (P-H) ¶ 90,274, 59 TCM (CCH) 772 (1990).]

IRS expert is rejected as biased and inexperienced. Decedent's residence was valued on the estate tax return at an April 10, 1982, alternate valuation date FMV of $76,000. The estate relied on an appraisal by a local real estate appraiser, who had held a real estate broker's license since 1980 and had a thorough knowledge of the local market. When the property was subsequently sold in 1986 for $52,000, decedent's estate contended that the initial appraisal was in error and that the correct FMV of decedent's residence on April 10, 1982, was $52,000. In addition, the estate valued decedent's farmland at $113,000. The IRS disputed the value of the farmland and introduced expert testimony to establish that it was worth $278,000.

Held: For the IRS (in part). Both decedent's residence and the farm economy surrounding it deteriorated substantially between 1982 and 1986. Given the admission on decedent's estate tax return that decedent's residence was worth $76,000, and the fact that no significant evidence was introduced that demonstrated that the value of decedent's residence was less than $76,000 on April 10, 1982, the valuation would remain unchanged. The farmland was valued at $176,000. The IRS witness was acting more as an advocate than as an expert and displayed a general lack of knowledge and inexperience in valuing local farmland. Accordingly, his testimony was rejected and disregarded for purposes of deciding the value of decedent's farmland.

[Hatchett, TC Memo. (P-H) ¶ 89,637, 58 TCM (CCH) 801 (1989).]

Discount for farmland is approved because it was held in common. Decedent died in 1983 owning a one-half interest in Illinois farmland as a tenant in common with eight cotenants who resided throughout the United States. The value of the entire parcel of farmland was $572,000. On the estate tax return, the estate claimed a value of $250,000 for the one-half interest in the parcel, an approximate 12.5 percent discount. The IRS determined a deficiency in the estate tax based on its valuation of decedent's share of the parcel at its full FMV of $286,000. The estate argued that a discount should have been applied because of the difficulties associated with dispersed ownership, the undesirability of buying a partition suit, and the associated costs and difficulty of partitioning the property. The IRS countered that under local law, partition was a relatively simple procedure, that partition of the property would be simple because of a road running along its eastern boundary, and that, in any event, if partition was impossible, the whole parcel could have been sold at FMV and the proceeds could have been distributed.

Held: For the estate. The court stated that real estate valuation and the question of fractional interest discounts are questions of fact to be resolved on the basis of the entire record. The court stated that ownership and management of tenancies in common present unique problems. For example, all co-owners must agree to participate in the government farm program, without which the property would most probably be operated at a loss. The court further noted other operational problems, such as crop rotation, fertilization, and weed control, that are compounded by dispersed owners. In addition, the court observed that there are few arm's-length sales of fractional interests in property. As a result of these factors, it was common practice for appraisers in Illinois to discount fractional interests in real property by 20 or 25 percent. The court concluded that the facts in this case provided sufficient evidence to support the discounted amount claimed on the estate tax return.

[Estate of Youle, TC Memo. (P-H) ¶ 89,138, 56 TCM (CCH) 1594 (1989).]

Valuation date for property received upon lapse of special power of appointment is date of grantor's death. Taxpayer's grandmother had died in 1944. Under her will, certain real estate was devised to taxpayer's uncle for life with a testamentary special power of appointment. Upon the uncle's failure to exercise the power by his last will, taxpayer received title to the property. The uncle died in 1960. In 1979, taxpayer sold the property; thereafter, on audit, a dispute arose with the IRS concerning the proper date to be used for valuation of the property for the purposes of determining its basis for calculation of gain on the sale. Taxpayer contended that his interest in the property was conditional at the time of his maternal grandmother's death (1944) and that he was not entitled to its use, enjoyment, or possession until the time of his uncle's death and failure to exercise that power (1960). Therefore, taxpayer argued, the valuation of the property should be its higher FMV in 1960. The IRS contended that the property should be valued according to the real estate market in 1944, when his grandmother, the grantor of the special power of appointment, died, because taxpayer received his interest from her estate upon the lapse of the power.

Held: For the IRS. The court stated that under Section 1014(a)(1), the basis of property acquired from a decedent is its FMV at the date of decedent's death. That a recipient's enjoyment and possession of the property is delayed because of intervening interests, the passage of time, or some other condition or impediment is irrelevant. The court noted that the language of Section 1014(a)(1) left no room for doubt with respect to the valuation date, because the phrase "at the time of acquisition" had been replaced by "at the time of decedent's death." Accordingly, the valuation of taxpayer's property was set at its lower 1944 value, and the IRS's deficiency was upheld.

[Juden, TC Memo. (P-H) ¶ 87,302, 53 TCM (CCH) 1154 (1987), aff'd, 865 F2d 960, 63 AFTR2d 89-595, 89-1 USTC ¶ 9142 (8th Cir. 1989).]

Binding option to purchase sets gross estate value of property, regardless of higher FMV. Decedent, a resident of Kentucky at the time of her death in 1979, had devised her entire estate to her sisters in equal shares. Among the property in her estate was a 237-acre farm that she had acquired under joint survivorship rights upon the death of her husband in 1973. A 38-acre tract of the farm had been developed as a thoroughbred horse training center containing, inter alia, a horse barn, a racetrack, a paddock, and a six-room farmhouse. Beginning in 1970, decedent and her husband had leased the 38-acre tract to taxpayer, who operated the horse facility. In 1975, decedent and taxpayer had renegotiated and expanded the lease to provide for an additional term of years, as well as an option in taxpayer to purchase the entire farm for $100,000. After the filing of the estate tax return, the IRS assessed deficiencies on issues relating to the includability of transfers made within three years of death under former Section 2035. In the course of deciding the Section 2035 issue, the Tax Court was called upon to resolve a dispute between the estate and the IRS on the proper valuation of the farm, which had a stipulated FMV of $270,000, but which remained subject to taxpayer's $100,000 option. For its part, the IRS contended that the full FMV of the farm, $270,000, was includable in gross estate without regard to the $100,000 option price. The estate, however, complained that the option held by taxpayer reduced the value of the farm to the option price of $100,000.

Held: The estate tax value of the farm was the price that the estate received following decedent's death upon taxpayer's exercise of the option, even though the $100,000 amount was substantially less than the stipulated FMV of $270,000. The court based its decision on the well-established rule that an option agreement fixes the value of an estate asset only where the agreement in question is binding under state law on both decedent and, following the date of death, the estate. In the present case, the agreement had full binding effect, and therefore the court was constrained to conclude that the estate's valuation was proper.

[Cobb, TC Memo. (P-H) ¶ 85,208, 49 TCM (CCH) 1364 (1985).]

Discount for undivided interest in real estate was the cost of partition. The IRS has ruled that in valuing undivided interest in real property, the discount to reflect the dual ownership interest should be limited to the estimated cost of a partition of the property. From the perspective of the owner of an undivided interest, a lack of unity of ownership is a possible disadvantage if the owner wishes to sell his interest. If the co-owners refuse to join in a sale of the whole property, the seller of the undivided interest may be forced to accept a lower price or seek a partition. On the other hand, if all the co-owners join in the sale, the rationale for a discount disappears because 100 percent of the property could be conveyed.

The definition of FMV contemplates that a hypothetical buyer and seller will act in their own best economic interests. According to the IRS, the courts recognize that partitioning is an alternative that results in greater economic benefit to the owner of an undivided interest.

[Tech. Adv. Mem. 9336002.]

Two undivided interests in realty are valued as single interest. When decedent died, a 37.5 percent interest in real property that had been held in a qualified terminable interest property (QTIP) trust established by his predeceased spouse's will was included in his gross estate under Section 2044. (This interest had been part of the predeceased spouse's half of community property.) In addition, Section 2033 included in decedent's estate the 62.5 percent interest in the same real property that he owned individually. The IRS stated that two different undivided interests in the same real property that are included in a decedent's estate under two different Code sections are to be valued as a single consolidated interest, not as two interests. The IRS reasoned that because decedent was treated as owning outright the undivided interest in the real property in the QTIP trust, and because he actually owned outright the remaining interest in the realty, the undivided interests would be aggregated for valuation purposes. Because decedent was considered to own a 100 percent interest in the property, no valuation discount for a minority interest would be available.

[Tech. Adv. Mem. 9140002.]

[b] Mortgages and encumbrances

Value of Texas surviving spouse's homestead interest must be included in decedent's gross estate. Decedent, a resident of Texas, died in 1965 and was survived by her husband. On the date of her death, she owned, as noncommunity property, a parcel of improved real estate as well as a tract of farmland that she and her husband had used as their principal residence. By the terms of her will, decedent had devised the homestead property outright to her niece and nephew without making any provision for her husband's continued use thereof. In view of this, the husband asserted his rights under the Texas homestead statute and claimed entitlement to the continued use and occupancy of the property during his lifetime. When decedent's federal estate tax return was filed in 1975, the date-of-death value of the homestead property was reported in accordance with an appraisal that treated the property as encumbered by the surviving spouse's homestead interest. In the appraiser's view, the value of the homestead property at the time of decedent's death was substantially lower than it would have been if unencumbered. The IRS redetermined the date-of-death value without any deduction for the homestead interest and determined a deficiency of $51,687. The Tax Court entered judgment for the estate.

Held: Reversed for the IRS. Under Sections 2033 and 2034, the gross estate includes the date-of-death value of the interests in property owned by decedent, as well as the interests of the surviving spouse represented by dower or curtesy or an interest created in lieu of dower or curtesy. The interest of the surviving spouse created by the Texas homestead laws was "by virtue of a statute creating an estate in lieu of dower or curtesy" within the meaning of Section 2034. Thus, the surviving spouse's homestead interest had to be included in decedent's gross estate in accordance with Section 2034. For at least thirty-four years, the governing rule for estate tax purposes has been that Texas homestead property is includable in a decedent's gross estate without reduction for the value of any rights of the surviving spouse. In light of the historical development of dower and homestead under Texas law and in light of thirty-four years of congressional acquiescence, the Tax Court erred in departing from the long-established rule and in removing substantial amounts of property from the scope of the federal estate tax.

[Estate of Johnson, 718 F2d 1303, 52 AFTR2d 83-6462, 83-2 USTC ¶ 13,544 (5th Cir. 1983).]

Original purchase price of property does not include amounts allocable to independent lease. Decedent had purchased land for about $22 per square foot and at about the same time signed a lease to rent other property from the seller on a month-to-month basis. After decedent's death, the estate valued the purchased property at $12 per square foot. The IRS determined that the value of the land was $25 per square foot. The estate argued that the original purchase price was inflated because it included an amount paid to the seller for the lease.

Held: For the IRS (in part). An attorney's bill covering services for both the purchase and the lease was insufficient proof that any part of the purchase price was attributable to the month-to-month lease. The court did not believe the property's value had declined to $12 per square foot and valued it at $17 per square foot.

[Estate of Murphy, TC Memo. (P-H) ¶ 81,489, 42 TCM (CCH) 1010 (1981).]

Homestead rights do not reduce value of house for gross estate purposes. When decedent died, she owned real estate that was a "homestead" under state law for her two minor children. Upon her death, the property and other interests passed into a trust for the benefit of all decedent's children. Under the trust, each child, upon attaining age 21, was to receive a pro rata share of the accrued income and principal of the trust. The minor children's homestead rights to continue to occupy the residence could be asserted by their guardian against the rights of the children who were age 21 or over to dispose of their share of the residence and the rights of the trustee to transfer or otherwise dispose of the homestead property. On the estate tax return, the executor reduced the value of decedent's estate to reflect the potential transfer restrictions of the homestead. The Texas constitution provided that on the death of the husband or wife, or both, the homestead shall descend and vest in the minor children as long as they occupy the property. The IRS stated that the homestead property should be included at its full fair market value in decedent's gross estate, notwithstanding the homestead rights of her minor children.

[Priv. Ltr. Rul. 8651001.]

¶ 2.03 ALTERNATE VALUATION DATE

[1] Elections

Protective alternate valuation election can be made. Decedent had owned a farm as well as nonfarm property prior to his death in 1985. The co-executors of the estate timely filed the estate tax return and elected special-use valuation for the farm. A schedule in the return reflected the FMVs and special-use values as of the date of death. In response to the question on the return regarding election of alternate valuation, the executors attached a document titled "Protective Alternate Valuation Election." The alternate valuation method was to be used only if the special-use valuation election was disallowed. A related attachment listed the property values as of the alternate valuation date. The IRS argued that the estate's protective election was invalid for three reasons:

1. The use of date-of-death values on the estate return was an election against alternate valuation and was contrary to the requirement that an election under Section 2032(a) be irrevocable.
2. There is no statutory authority permitting a protective alternate valuation election.
3. The protective election would allow the estate to indefinitely postpone a decision regarding the applicable valuation date.

Held: For the estate. The court stated that the use of date-of-death values on the return was not an election. Such valuation is required under Section 2031 and applies unless an affirmative election is made to use alternate valuation. In addition, the irrevocability of a Section 2032 election was not violated. The election is irrevocable only after it is made. Under the estate's protective election, denial of special-use valuation would trigger the alternate valuation election, which then would be irrevocable. The court noted that the special-use valuation election also is irrevocable, and Section 2032A(d) provides for the filing of a protective election. Thus, a protective election is not incompatible with irrevocability.

The court agreed that there was nothing in the statute authorizing use of a protective election. But there was also nothing prohibiting its use. Regulations under related Section 2032A expressly permit a protective election. This, according to the court, implied that a protective election may be made under Section 2032. Finally, the court also rejected the IRS's third argument. The protective election was conditioned on disallowance of special-use valuation. This determination was totally beyond the estate's control. Thus, it did not seem possible that the protective election could allow the estate to indefinitely postpone a decision as to the applicable valuation date.

[Estate of Mapes, 99 TC 511 (1992).]

Alternative valuation date election deadline is strictly applied. Decedent's executor filed for, and was granted, an extension to file the estate tax return. A second request for an extension was filed, which, on its face, again sought extension to the same date as the first request. The return was filed after the extension due date, and the IRS denied the alternate valuation date election. Decedent's estate argued that the IRS, by comparing the first and second requests, should have known that the later request was in error.

Held: For the IRS. The estate tax return was not filed within the granted extension time. Consequently, the estate was not entitled to elect the alternative valuation date under Section 2032. The timely filed requirement is strictly construed in connection with the election of the alternative valuation date, and cannot be excused where the failure was due to a mistake, or, very often, even where there is reasonable cause for the late filing. Section 2032(d)(2), which grants an election within one year after the time prescribed by law (including extensions), took effect only after decedent's death and therefore was inapplicable.

[Dixon, TC Memo. (P-H) ¶ 90,017, 58 TCM (CCH) 1165 (1990).]

IRS rules on situation where executor of estate elects both alternate valuation and special-use valuation. The IRS has ruled that if the executor of an estate elects to use both alternate valuation under Section 2032 and special-use valuation under Section 2032A in valuing a decedent's farmland, the alternate valuation date under Section 2032 must be used in valuing decedent's farmland under Section 2032A. Also, in applying the limit described in Section 2032A(a)(2) for the estate tax saving due to special-use valuation, the limit is applicable to the difference between the FMV and the special-use valuation of the property, determined as of the alternate valuation date.

[Rev. Rul. 88-89, 1988-2 CB 333.]

Alternative valuation is denied to estate that fails to separate or segregate trust assets within six months of decedent's death. An individual's husband died in 1985. The husband had bequeathed one-half of his adjusted gross estate to one trust, with the residue going to a second trust. Under the terms of the first trust, the surviving spouse was entitled to all of the income for life. The trust was to terminate upon the death of the spouse, and the trustee was to distribute the corpus to the second trust. The trustee of the first trust was authorized to withhold from the distribution to the second trust any amount necessary to cover any liabilities owed by the spouse. The spouse died. The spouse had made several bequests in her will. Her daughter received the residue of her estate, and the executor was responsible for paying all necessary taxes on the property in the estate. The assets of the first trust were included in decedent's estate. Her coexecutors attempted to elect alternative valuation under Section 2032(a). The executors valued the trust assets based on their value on the date of death. Other assets were valued as of a date six months from the date of death. The trustee of the first trust made no distribution to the second trust during the two years following decedent's death.

The IRS stated that the coexecutors of decedent's estate may not elect alternative valuation under Section 2032. Noting that the value of the estate did not decrease as required under Section 2032(c), the IRS said that to use the alternative valuation election, the assets of the first trust must have been "segregated, separated, or delivered" to the successor trust before the lapse of six months, citing Revenue Ruling 66-272, 1966-2 CB 432. In this case, the trustee still had made no distribution to the second trust two years following decedent's death, the IRS reasoned.

[Tech. Adv. Mem. 9001001.]

[2] Distributions, Sales, and Exchanges

Oil and gas royalty payments are not includable in gross estate when received during alternate valuation period. At the time of her death in 1974, decedent owned royalty and working interests in a number of oil and gas properties, principally in the state of Texas. Her executor elected to value the gross estate on the alternate valuation date (six months after death), pursuant to Section 2032. During that six-month period, the sale of oil and gas generated net proceeds of $156,011 to the estate, on which amount the executor duly paid income tax. The IRS contended, however, that the proceeds should also have been included in the gross estate, and accordingly, it assessed a deficiency in the estate tax. The estate argued that federal estate taxes can be imposed only on property actually owned by decedent on the date of death and that income that subsequently arises from the corpus of the estate is taxable only as income. The IRS argued that the net production proceeds constituted a "fractionalization and piecemeal sale" of the oil and gas in place at the time of decedent's death. The district court held for the estate, basing its holding largely on Burnet, 284 US 103 (1932), in which the Supreme Court considered and rejected Texas law that treated an oil and gas lease as a present sale of the oil and gas. The Supreme Court held that bonus and royalty payments constituted income to the lessor rather than a conversion of principal, so that the amount received would not be eligible for taxation at the more favorable capital gains rates. The district court held that the decision in *Burnet* implied that state law is not determinative of whether a certain property interest is to be included in the gross estate.

Held: Reversed for the IRS. The court found that the Supreme Court decision in Maass v. Higgins, 312 US 443 (1941), compelled a different result. As construed by the Fifth Circuit, *Maass* directs that a review be made of each case on its own merits, "with an eye toward determining the common understanding whether the proceeds in question truly represent income produced by the estate or, rather, are the translation of the corpus of the estate into another form." According to the Fifth Circuit, the former would not be included in the estate tax inventory, whereas the latter would. All investment income, from whatever source, represents, to some extent, a portion of the investment principal. As a matter of common understanding, however, rents, dividends, and the like represent an income stream separate from the principal. The value of the principal is determined by viewing it as an entirety factoring in the income stream. This common understanding, ruled the court, results in large measure from the apparent perception that the principal generating the dividends and rentals is not diminished by the use that produces the income. For this reason, the court reviewed the extensive record before it and then ruled that the quantity of the reserves are to be determined as of the date of decedent's death; only the value to be assigned to that quantity of reserves may be changed by market variances when severed before the alternate valuation date.

[Estate of Johnston, 779 F2d 1123, 57 AFTR2d 86-1502, 86-1 USTC ¶ 13,655 (5th Cir.), cert. denied sub nom. Payne, 477 US 904 (1986).]

Passage of title is not distribution fixing alternate valuation date. Under the law of State *X*, title to real property passes immediately to a decedent's heirs or devisees. The executor may take possession of the realty, but only if authorized by the probate court. The executor's potential right of possession lasts until the final decree distributing the estate. The passing of title immediately after death is not a distribution fixing the alternate valuation date, which will be six months after decedent's death if the final decree is after that date.

[Rev. Rul. 78-378, 1978-2 CB 229.]

[3] Stock Interests

Estate distributes stock for valuation purposes when state law recognizes transfer as complete. Decedent, a resident of Missouri, died on October 10, 1978. On October 26, 1978, the trustee of decedent's revocable living trust delivered 40,000 shares of closely held stock to a broker, and, on October 30, requested that the broker transfer the stock to the remaindermen of the trust. On November 13, the trustee executed a stock assignment, and, on the next day, the broker sent a letter to the corporation's transfer agent requesting the transfer and registration of decedent's stock. The transfer agent indicated that it could not effect the transfer without an inheritance tax waiver from the state of Missouri. On December 19, 1978, the broker provided the transfer agent with the waiver, and, on December 20, the shares were transferred and registered in the names of the remaindermen. The estate elected to use the alternate valuation method set forth in Section 2032 and valued the stock on October 30, 1978. The IRS challenged the estate's use of this date, asserting December 20, 1978, as the appropriate date for valuing the stock.

Held: For the IRS. Section 2032 of the Code and Regulation § 20.2032-1 permit an estate to value a distribution of property within six months of decedent's death on the date of such distribution. Distribution occurs for this purpose when the property "becomes unqualifiedly subject to the demand" of the distributee. Under Missouri law, the agency agreement between the broker and the trustee did not effect a complete transfer to the remaindermen, because such an agency arrangement remains revocable. Further, under Missouri law, there can be no effective transfer of a decedent's property without an inheritance tax waiver. Accordingly, complete distribution to the remaindermen could not occur until an inheritance tax waiver was received and the transfer agent recorded the distribution in the corporate stock books.

[Estate of Sawade, 795 F2d 45, 58 AFTR2d 86-6330, 86-2 USTC ¶ 13,672 (8th Cir. 1986).]

Mutual fund capital gain dividend paid during alternate valuation period is not includable in decedent's estate. The IRS has ruled that a 5 percent capital gain dividend, which is not extraordinary in any sense, that is declared and paid by a regulated investment company during the alternate valuation period, is not includable in computing the value of decedent's gross estate under Section 2032.

[Rev. Rul. 76-234, 1976-1 CB 271.]

IRS reserves opinion on inclusion of postdeath capital gains dividend in decedent's gross estate. At the time of her death, a woman directly owned public utility stock and also held a general power of appointment over a trust that owned shares of the same utility. As a result, her gross estate included the value of all of the utility stock. Two days after she died, the utility declared a capital gain dividend for the third year since 1980. On the record date for the dividend distribution, the estate sold the shares that decedent had formerly owned. One week later the trust sold its shares. The estate's personal representative elected the alternate valuation date for the stock and asked the IRS if the dividend was includable in the gross estate under Section 2032. The IRS reserved resolution of the issue for the district director upon an audit of the estate tax return. The IRS discussed the issue and hinted that the dividend is income to the estate, but is not includable in the calculations of gross estate value under the alternate valuation method.

[Priv. Ltr. Rul. 8328052.]

¶ 2.04 SPECIAL-USE VALUATION

[1] Elections and Agreements

Duty of consistency binds taxpayers to improper election. Decedent died in 1983, leaving farmland to taxpayers. The estate timely filed a special-use valuation election under Section 2032A along with the estate tax return, which reduced the farmland's taxable value by $585,078. In short, this election permits estates to value farmland based on its current use rather than its most valuable use. One requirement of the election is that the heirs continue to put the property to a qualifying use for ten years; otherwise, the IRS has three years from the date it is notified that the property has been disposed of or put to a nonqualifying use to assess a virtual recapture of the tax not paid because of the election. The heirs are personally liable for this tax. In this case, the election was made even though the property was never put to a qualifying use. In 1990, the IRS sent a questionnaire to taxpayers as part of a program to evaluate whether taxpayers were properly using the election. Based on taxpayers' answers, the IRS mailed a second letter requesting additional information. Taxpayers' response indicated that the property was being cash-rented to non-family members, which is a nonqualifying use. In 1992, the IRS sent notices of deficiency to taxpayers for additional estate tax under Section 2032A. Taxpayers contended that the notices were not timely, because they were sent more than three years after the estate tax return was filed. The IRS argued that the relevant limitations period was governed by Section 2032A(f)—i.e., three years after the IRS was notified that the property was no longer being put to a qualifying use. Taxpayers' response was that the property was never put to a qualifying use, so Section 2032A did not apply.

Held: For the IRS. The court agreed with the IRS that Section 2032A did apply because of a duty of consistency. Under this doctrine, when a taxpayer makes a representation to the IRS on which the IRS relied, that taxpayer cannot change its position after the limitations period has run. Here, taxpayers affirmatively applied for the special-use valuation election in the estate tax return and made representations as to the property's use. The IRS accepted the return and permitted the estate to pay less tax on account of the election. The court said that in the Tenth Circuit, the duty of consistency can be applied even without a showing that a taxpayer made an intentional falsehood or wrongful misleading silence; it is sufficient if that taxpayer made a representation to obtain favorable tax treatment. Taxpayers also asserted that the duty of consistency did not apply in this case, because the estate's executor, not taxpayers, made the representations underlying the special-use valuation election. The court held, however, that the duty of consistency encompasses both taxpayers and parties "with sufficiently identical economic interests." Here, taxpayers provided information to the accountant who prepared the estate tax return, they both signed a consent form for making the election, and they had an economic interest in reducing the estate's taxable value. Thus, there was sufficient privity of interest to apply the duty of consistency. Finally, taxpayers asked to deduct from the gross estate the attorney fees incurred in contesting the additional tax. The court rejected this request because only attorney fees incurred in figuring the estate tax under Section 2001 can be deducted against the gross estate. The attorney fees that taxpayers incurred were with respect to tax under Section 2032A and were not essential to the proper settlement of the estate.

[LeFever, 100 F3d 778, 78 AFTR2d 96-7335, 96-2 USTC ¶ 60,250 (10th Cir. 1996).]

Special valuation election requires recapture agreement. Decedent died on December 15, 1985, owning farmland that passed to his two sons. A timely filed estate tax return included a Schedule N that listed each son as the recipient of $227,000 of specially valued property. An attached document supplied most, but not all, of the fourteen items of information required by Regulation § 20.2032A-8(a)(3) to elect special use valuation. The return did not include a recapture agreement, however. On audit, the estate was notified that its election was defective, primarily because of the failure to attach a recapture agreement. Within ninety days following the notice, the estate submitted a recapture agreement that complied with the regulations. The IRS rejected this attempt to perfect the election. Section 2032A provides an election to value qualified real property as a farm (or at its use in another trade or business) instead of at its actual FMV. Thus, a farm within commuting distance of an expanding city need not be valued based on what a developer would pay. The maximum reduction in value for an estate is $750,000. To qualify for the election, the real property must make up at least 25 percent of the value of the adjusted estate (i.e., without special use valuation and reduced by mortgages) and, along with other property used in a family business, must equal 50 percent of the adjusted estate. The real property generally must have been used in a business in which a decedent or another family member materially participated for at least five years during the eight-year period immediately before that decedent died, and it must pass to certain family members ("qualified heirs"). If a qualified heir disposes of the real property within ten years of decedent's death, or ceases to use it for a qualified use, the tax benefits from the lower valuation are recaptured. To ensure that the recapture tax will be paid, Section 2032A requires a recapture agreement. Section 2032A(d)(3) provides an opportunity for an estate to perfect a defective election that "substantially complies" with the regulations. The missing items must be furnished within a reasonable period (not to exceed ninety days) following notice from the IRS of the omission.

Held: For the IRS. The Eleventh Circuit decided that the estate's failure to provide a recapture agreement with the return precluded substantial compliance. The court pointed out that Section 2032A(a)(1) treats the filing of a recapture agreement as an integral part of the election, and Regulation § 20.2032A-8(a)(3) indicates that an election is not valid unless a recapture agreement is submitted contemporaneously with the return. The recapture agreement must be binding under local law and signed by all parties who have any interest in the specially valued property (whether present, future, vested, or contingent). The qualified heirs must expressly consent to be personally liable for the recapture tax, according to Regulation § 20.2032A-8(c). The legislative history suggests that substantial compliance leaves little room for omissions in a recapture agreement. The mistakes that are condoned are minor: failure to include the signature of a person with an insignificant interest in the property, a parent's signing for a minor with a remainder interest when state law requires a guardian, and similar omissions. Therefore, decedent's estate, by not filing any recapture agreement with its return, did not substantially comply with the regulations, so its defective election could not be cured under Section 2032A(d)(3).

[Estate of Lucas, 97 F3d 1401, 78 AFTR2d 96-6911, 96-2 USTC ¶ 60,247 (11th Cir. 1996), cert. denied, 117 S. Ct. 1468 (1997).]

Special-use and minority discounts taken in tandem. Decedent owned a 26 percent interest in a family limited partnership that operated a cattle ranch in New Mexico. The partnership's real property was appraised at $10.5 million. In valuing decedent's interest, the estate first took 26 percent of $10.5 million ($2.73 million) and then applied a 30 percent discount factor because the minority partnership interest lacked marketability and control bringing the valuation down to $1.91 million. The IRS did not dispute this calculation of the interest's FMV. It agreed that this would be the estate tax value if Section 2032A did not apply. Next, the estate considered the interest's special-use value. The estate and IRS stipulated that the special-use value of the ranch was about $2.05 million, 26 percent of which is $533,548. Section 2032A permits estates to reduce the value of qualified use property to the special-use value— with a maximum valuation reduction of $750,000. In general, qualified use property is real property used in a farming or other business, provided at least 50 percent of the estate is made up of real or personal property used in such business and the real property accounts for at least 25 percent of the estate. In this case, the $750,000 cap controlled because the FMV exceeded the special-use value by more than $750,000. (The court indicated that the special-use tax break applies to property owned through a family partnership as well as property owned directly.) At this stage, the dispute arose. Taxpayer subtracted $750,000 from the $1.91 million FMV of the 26 percent interest; the IRS, however, said that the $750,000 must be subtracted from the $2.73 million FMV calculated without a minority discount. (No minority discount could be taken from the net figure either.)

Held: For taxpayer. The Tax Court had agreed with the IRS. It relied on Estate of Mattox, 93 TC 228 (1989). As the Tenth Circuit pointed out, however, that case denied use of a minority discount on top of the special-use valuation discount in a somewhat different context. There, the estate elected to use the special-use value (since the valuation reduction was less than $750,000) rather than the FMV; it then wanted to reduce the special-use value by a 30 percent minority discount. Had there been no $750,000 limit on the special-use valuation reduction, this would be equivalent to taxpayer in the instant case taking a 30 percent discount on the $533,548 special-use valuation figure. In contrast, taxpayer was seeking to reduce the interest's FMV by the $750,000 maximum special-use valuation discount. The Tax Court's holding suggested that FMV has a different meaning when Section 2032A is involved. This concept was rejected by the Tenth Circuit. Rather, the Tenth Circuit held that the property's FMV must be accurately determined as if Section 2032A did not apply (i.e., using a minority discount, when appropriate) and then the $750,000 reduction taken. The court noted that the IRS has not issued regulations under Section 2032A, so there was no reason to presume a different definition of FMV for special-use valuation purposes.

[Estate of Hoover, 69 F3d 1044, 76 AFTR2d 95-7305, 95-2 USTC ¶ 60,217 (10th Cir. 1995).]

Special-use valuation denied by Fifth Circuit due to taxpayer's lack of substantial compliance. Decedent was a rancher who died in 1987. In his will, he left interests in several tracts of ranch property to five grandsons in various forms of joint ownership. The will placed several ten-year restrictions on their ability to mortgage, partition, sell, or lease their interest in the property. The estate tax return was prepared by decedent's long-time, experienced attorney who was also a co-executor of the estate. The attorney checked the box on Form 706 to indicate that special-use valuation was being elected. He included Schedule N and its required attachments with the return. A Notice of Election (the Notice) was also attached to the return, but not a Recapture Agreement. The Notice contained only nine of fourteen items required to be included or attached. The Notice contained a statement that "[i]t is considered that all requirements exist for special valuation of the qualified real property." Only three of the five grandsons signed the Notice because one grandson was in the military and another was "not presently available." The tax return included a statement that the preparer would obtain the additional signatures on a counterpart and send that to the Service Center; this was not done, however, until the audit had commenced. All the missing information was submitted to the IRS within ninety days after the estate received notice of the defective election. Nevertheless, the IRS denied special-use valuation because of the initial lack of substantial compliance. This caused the ranch property to be valued at its highest and best use, which increased the value of the estate by over $400,000 and created a tax deficiency. The Tax Court found that the estate had substantially complied with the requirements for electing special-use valuation and should be allowed to perfect its election. The IRS appealed.

Held: Reversed for the IRS. Section 2032A(d)(3) gives executors a reasonable time, not to exceed ninety days, to cure a defective special-use valuation election. Under this provision, a timely election must have been made and must have substantially complied with the regulations except that (1) the Notice did not contain all the requested information or (2) the Recapture Agreement was missing required signatures or information. Section 2032A(d)(3) implies that a Notice, a Recapture Agreement, and a considerable amount of the required information must be provided when the election is initially made. This interpretation of the statute is supported by the legislative history. The conference report makes clear that "[b]oth a notice of election and [a recapture] agreement that themselves evidence substantial compliance with the requirements of the regulations must be included with the estate tax return, as filed, if the estate is to be permitted to perfect its election." The report also states:

> To be eligible for perfection, the [recapture] agreement as originally filed must at a minimum be valid under state law and must include the signatures of all parties having a present interest or a remainder interest other than an interest having a relatively small value. The right to perfect agreements is intended to be limited to cases where, for example, a parent of a minor remainderman, rather than a guardian ad litem as required under State law, signs the agreement. Similarly, failure to designate an agent in the agreement as filed may be corrected under this provision.

The court focused on the fact that the legislative history emphasized that when the election is made, some sort of document must be filed that is binding under state law and signed by all the interested parties and that binds those persons to pay any additional tax owed if special-use status is forfeited. No such document was filed in the instant case. The court concluded by denying special-use valuation for the ranch property on the ground that the estate did not substantially comply with the requirements for making the election. The court said that the ninety-day grace period within which a flawed election can be brought into full compliance is primarily for corrections and for obtaining additional signatures needed on the Recapture Agreement. This grace period is not to be used to complete a partial filing.

[Estate of Hudgins, 57 F3d 1393, 76 AFTR2d 95-5401, 95-2 USTC ¶ 60,202 (5th Cir. 1995).]

Failure to attach appraisal is not fatal to special-use valuation election. Decedent's estate filed a timely estate tax return on which a special-use valuation election was made for ranch property. The IRS disallowed the election because the property appraisal was not attached. The Tax Court upheld the IRS's position.

Held: Reversed for the estate. Failure to attach the appraisal was not an incurable defect. The estate had substantially complied with the election requirements.

[Estate of Doherty, 982 F2d 450, 93-1 USTC ¶ 60,125, 71 AFTR2d 93-2155 (10th Cir. 1992).]

Estate is allowed to correct omission of signatures on recapture agreement. Decedent's estate elected special-use valuation under Section 2032A for a family ranch. The recapture agreement was not signed by the beneficiaries who had an interest in the property, but it was signed by the trustee of the three trusts holding the interests in the property. The estate argued for substantial compliance, and the Tax Court agreed.

Held: Affirmed for the estate. The regulations under Section 2032A were unclear as to the signature requirement. In addition, the estate had acted reasonably and with due diligence by amending the election and recapture agreement within ninety days after notice.

[Estate of McAlpine, 968 F2d 459, 92-2 USTC ¶ 60,109, 70 AFTR2d 92-6216 (5th Cir. 1992).]

No substantial compliance where recapture agreement is filed after return. The estate's attorney failed to attach the signed recapture agreement to the estate tax return and filed it ten days later. The estate claimed substantial compliance, but the district court held that the special-use valuation election was untimely.

Held: Affirmed for the IRS. The recapture agreement was essential to a valid election. Failure to include it could not be corrected after the filing deadline. The substantial compliance doctrine can be used to correct only minor errors.

[Bartlett, 937 F2d 316, 68 AFTR2d 91-6015, 91-2 USTC ¶ 60,078 (7th Cir. 1991).]

Special-use election is valid with late recapture agreement. Decedent died in 1981, and the estate filed an election under Section 2032A to value farmland included in the estate at the value of its farming use, $120,000. The market value of the land was approximately $375,000. Section 2032A(d)(2) requires that a valid election include an agreement, signed by everyone having a vested or contingent interest in the estate, consenting to the collection of any additional estate tax if the property is put to a use other than the qualified use. The agreement must also designate an agent for the signators in dealing with the IRS. Under Regulation § 20.2032A-8(a)(3), the agreement must accompany the return. Because of the difficulty in obtaining all of the necessary signatures, the agreement was not filed until four months after the return had been filed. The agreement complied fully with the regulatory requirements, other than timeliness. When the estate's lawyer filed the special-use valuation election, he attached a letter explaining that the recapture agreement was not attached, because it was not fully executed as "the heirs reside throughout the United States." The IRS denied the election, arguing that it was untimely.

Held: For the estate. Under Section 2032A(d)(3)(B), an estate that substantially complies with the regulations on making the election, but either (1) omits required information from the notice of election, (2) fails to obtain the signatures required for the agreement, or (3) files an agreement that lacks all required information, can cure the defects within ninety days of notice from the IRS. This does not mean that an estate could file a blank notice of election and obtain the benefit of this statute. "Substantial compliance is always required; the question is whether it always excuses." The estate's lawyer could have obtained an extension of time for filing the estate tax return. Also, if he had obtained the signatures of the principal beneficiaries of the estate on the agreement and filed this with the return, he would have been protected under Section 2032A(d)(3). He would not have been protected by filing an agreement signed by only one contingent remainderman, because this would not have been substantial compliance. There is no precise test for what "substantial compliance" is. Substantial compliance should be restricted to cases where taxpayer had a good excuse, though not a legal justification, for failing to comply. Because the estate could have filed a request for an extension, it lacked the kind of excuse that could have supported a substantial compliance argument. Section 1421 of the Tax Reform Act of 1986, however, provides that late filing of recapture agreements for decedents dying before 1986 is permitted and makes specific mention of those estates that had made the election on the March 1982 edition of Form 706, which had failed to state that the recapture agreement should be filed with the return. There was no March 1982 edition of the form, but the June 1982 version failed to state the requirement, and it was presumably to this version that Congress intended to refer. In this case, the court read the section broadly to excuse later filings on all decedents dying before 1986. Therefore, the estate was excused from the late filing.

[Prussner, 896 F2d 218, 90-1 USTC ¶ 60,007, 65 AFTR2d 90-1222 (7th Cir. 1990).]

Estate's failure to attach recapture agreement and notice of election to estate tax return is not substantial compliance with Section 2032A. When decedent died, she owned farmland for which her estate attempted to elect special-use valuation under Section 2032A. Neither the recapture agreement nor the notice of election was attached to, or included with, the estate tax return sent by the attorney for the estate. A cover letter stated that an election was being made for special valuation under Section 2032A, however, and included appraisals at FMVs and special-use values. The IRS discovered that the notice of election and recapture agreement were not attached to the return and requested these documents, which were then submitted. The IRS nevertheless issued a statutory notice of deficiency. The estate paid the alleged deficiency and filed suit for a refund of the entire amount paid. The district court, relying on amendments to Section 2032A contained in the Tax Reform Act of 1986, determined that substantial compliance was sufficient to qualify for a special-use valuation and that there had been substantial compliance in this case. On appeal, the IRS argued that the case was controlled by McDonald, 88-2 USTC ¶ 13,778, 853 F2d 1494 (8th Cir. 1988), where the court held that an estate was not entitled to special-use valuation, because the omission from the recapture agreement of the signatures of all persons with an interest in the property was not the type of slight technicality envisioned by the substantial compliance amendment to Section 2032A. In an effort to distinguish McDonald on the facts, the estate argued that the version of the U.S. estate tax return used by the McDonald estate included on its face extensive instructions concerning the need to attach a notice of election and a recapture agreement and the required contents of those two documents. The version of the return used in the instant case, however, did not include that information on its face. The form used by the estate merely stated: "Attach a statement that includes the information described in instruction 13."

Held: Reversed for the IRS. The Eighth Circuit stated that the estate was represented by an attorney whose training should have led him to an examination of instruction 13, and that the cases could not be distinguished on the basis urged by the estate. According to the Eighth Circuit, the facts were different, but the statements of law in McDonald applied to this case. The court said that even if it assumed that a distinction could be made because the instructions were not on the estate tax form itself, such distinction would not aid the estate here. It did not fail to furnish some of the information set forth in the separate instructions. The estate failed to "attach a statement" that the form does call for on its face. The estate need not have looked to the separate instructions to learn that it was required to attach a statement. The court reasoned that at least in *McDonald*, the required notice and agreement were attached to the tax return, even if they were not signed by the proper parties. Here there were no required statements either signed or attached to the return. Although it may have been possible to glean the information required by instruction 13 from the return itself, nothing was filed with the return containing the substance of the recapture agreement or the principal beneficiary's consent to be personally liable for the recapture tax. Accordingly, the refund was denied.

[Foss, 865 F2d 178, 89-1 USTC ¶ 13,793, 63 AFTR2d 89-1524 (8th Cir. 1989).]

Retroactive effect of ERTA reforms is held not applicable to untimely special-use election. At the time of his death in 1977, decedent was the owner of certain farm property that was included in his gross estate. Although the farm qualified for special-use valuation, the estate did not make an election, because the surviving spouse anticipated that she would not "materially participate" in farm management for the statutory fifteen-year period. Failure materially to participate during this period would make any estate tax benefit that the estate had obtained from special-use valuation subject to recapture. In 1981, Congress amended the special-use valuation rules under Section 2032A by relaxing the material participation rules and shortening the recapture period. Based on the retroactive transition rules contained in Section 421(k)(5) of the Economic Recovery Tax Act of 1981 (ERTA), the estate filed an amended return contending that the new rules entitled the estate to elect special-use valuation nunc pro tunc. The IRS opposed the refund, citing ERTA § 421(k)(5)(B), which restricts retroactive effect to those estates that make timely elections under Section 2032A of the Code. The estate argued in district court that ERTA § 421(k)(5)(D), by waiving the statute of limitations on refunds, preserved its right to make the later election.

Held: Affirmed for the IRS. ERTA § 421(k)(5)(B) is unambiguous in limiting the retroactive application of the 1981 amendments to those estates that had made a timely election of special-use valuation. ERTA § 421(k)(5)(D) is a clear waiver of the statute of limitations on refund claims, not of the timely special-use valuation election requirement separately treated in ERTA § 421(k)(5)(B). As a result, the waiver of the three-year limitation on refund actions cannot revive the right to make a timely election, and therefore the estate in the instant case was ineligible for Section 2032A treatment.

[Rath, 733 F2d 594, 53 AFTR2d 84-1656, 84-1 USTC ¶ 13,573 (8th Cir. 1984).]

Special-use valuation is denied where estate fails to attach recapture agreement. The instructions to Schedule N required that a notice of election as described in Regulation § 20.2032A-8(a)(3), and an "agreement to special valuation by persons with an interest in property" (the "recapture agreement") as described in Sections 2032A(a)(1)(B) and 2032(d)(2) and in Regulation § 20.2043A-8(c), to be attached to the estate tax return, Form 706. Neither the notice nor the agreement was attached to the return. The executor received a letter dated February 3, 1987, from an IRS attorney who had been assigned to audit the estate tax return, stating that the return did not qualify for special-use valuation. At the initial meeting with this attorney on July 9, 1987, the executor was told that the estate did not qualify, because a recapture agreement was not attached to the return. The attorney did not request, and was not given, any other information relating to the special-use valuation. By transmittal letter dated September 25, 1987, the executor sent to the IRS an "Agreement to Special Use Valuation Under Section 2032A," which was a purported recapture agreement dated August 25, 1987. At an appeals conference on February 16, 1989, the executor gave a copy of the agreement and the transmittal letter to an IRS appeals officer who requested the documents. In the course of his examination, the IRS attorney reviewed the Inventory and Appraisement located in the estate's probate file at the courthouse. According to this document, the nine parcels of real property described on Schedule A of Form 706 had a total appraised value of $536,817, which the parties stipulated was the FMV at decedent's death. The IRS appeals agent requested, and was given, a copy of this document. In a deficiency notice issued on June 20, 1988, the IRS stated that the estate had failed to make a timely and effective election for special-use valuation. Prior to this date, except for noting the omission of the recapture agreement, the IRS did not inform the estate that its support for the special-use valuation was insufficient, nor did the IRS request additional information. Apart from the Inventory and Appraisement, the executor did not submit to the IRS a written appraisal on the value of the real property. Both parties agreed that the estate did not make a protective election to specially value qualified real property within the meaning of Regulation § 20.2032A-8(b).

Held: For the IRS. Failure by the executor of an estate to substantially comply with the requirements for electing to specially value property as found in Section 2032A will cause the election to fail. To make the election, an estate must submit a notice of election and a recapture agreement. An estate is given time to modify its filings if it substantially meets the requirements, but does not properly complete the notice of election or the recapture agreement. Substantial compliance is not found, however, if the estate does not submit a notice of election or a recapture agreement. Furthermore, even without the omission of the recapture agreement, the estate had failed to adequately supply the information requested on Schedule N of Form 706. Although the estate may have been confused as to what certain headings meant, information was omitted also from clearly stated headings such as "Fair Market Value." Although it appears that appraisals of the FMVs of the property were not done until after the estate tax return was filed, the substantial compliance standard in Section 2032A does not allow for untimely obtained appraisals.

[Estate of Merwin, 95 TC 168 (1990).]

Minority interest in family farm corporation is not entitled to minority discount after farm real estate is specially valued under Section 2032A. Decedent died in 1983 owning a minority (35.5 percent) interest in an incorporated family farm. The value of the farm was substantially reduced by the application of the special-use provisions of Section 2032A. In addition, the estate claimed a 30 percent discount, otherwise applicable in determining the FMV of decedent's minority interest in the incorporated farm. The IRS disallowed the 30 percent FMV discount, because the value of the minority interests had already been substantially reduced below their FMV as a result of the special-use valuation of the real property. The estate contended, however, that once the real estate had been revalued under Section 2032A, it was properly included at the reduced amount in computing the total assets of the corporation, and thereafter the stock in the corporation was properly valued like the stock in all other corporations, subject to a minority interest discount.

  Held: For the IRS. The Tax Court concluded that the estate was entitled to include in the gross estate the value of decedent's interest in the incorporated farm at the reduced value under the Section 2032A recomputation, but without any further reduction for minority interest. The court stated that subsection (g) of Section 2032A (which makes Section 2032A applicable to the real estate of a corporation) was intended to give stockholders in family corporations the rights otherwise available under Section 2032A, not greater rights.

[Estate of Maddox, 93 TC 228 (1989).]

Timely mailed return electing special-use valuation is presumed received by IRS. When decedent died in 1981, he owned farmland for which his estate claimed special-use valuation under Section 2032A. The IRS disallowed special-use valuation on audit, however, arguing that it had not received a federal estate tax return making the Section 2032A election and that, under Section 7502(c), the estate could have proved delivery, and thus the election, only if the return had been sent by registered or certified mail. The estate countered that even though the return had been sent by registered or certified mail, delivery was established by a postal official who testified that she had accepted and postmarked the envelope prior to the due date of the return. The IRS, however, argued that under Section 7502, a timely mailed return is timely filed only if the return is actually, not presumptively, delivered to it. In general, a return is considered filed on the date on which it is delivered to the IRS. Section 7502(a)(1), however, provides that a return delivered to the IRS after its due date is timely filed if the following two mailing requirements of Section

7502(a)(2) are met: (1) The postmark date is on or before the filing or pay-ment due date, and (2) postage is prepaid, and the document or payment is contained in an envelope or wrapper that is properly addressed.

Held: For the estate. According to the court, neither Section 7502 nor its legislative history indicates that Congress intended to exclude the common-law presumption of delivery created by proof of a properly mailed document. The court indicated that Section 7502(c) appears to be a safe harbor by which tax-payers can be "assured of having prima facie evidence of delivery by present-ing the postmarked receipt." The court held that the timely mailed return was delivered, because the IRS was unable to present positive evidence to counter the testimony of the postal official. The court found it only coincidental that the corresponding state tax returns had not been received by the state tax au-thority. Accordingly, the estate was entitled to specially value the farmland.

[Estate of Wood, 92 TC 793 (1989), aff'd, 909 F2d 1155, 90-2 USTC ¶ 60,031, 66 AFTR2d 90-5987 (8th Cir. 1990).]

Failure to supply information and documentation to substantiate special-use valuation is fatal to Section 2032A election. When decedent died in 1982, she owned farmland in Oklahoma for which her estate attempted to elect special-use valuation pursuant to Section 2032A. In the notice of election, the estate failed to properly document and substantiate the special value based on the use of the property under Section 2032A(e)(7)(A) of the Code and Regula-tion § 20.2032A-4. The IRS contended that the estate's failure to properly doc-ument and substantiate the method used in determining the special value based on use was fatal to its claim for special-use valuation under the "substantial compliance" language of Section 2032A(d)(3)(B).

Held: For the IRS. The court held that the estate had not "substantially complied" with the regulations under Section 2032A in attempting to value the property of decedent under Section 2032A(e)(7)(A). According to the court, the estate had failed to identify comparable property, annual gross cash rentals, and state and local taxes for the requisite five years prior to decedent's date of death. Thus, it was impossible to compute average annual gross cash rentals under Section 2032A(e)(7)(A), even though the evidence established that com-parable tracts of land from which gross cash rental values could have been as-certained existed in the geographical area of the respective tracts. Because the estate had not "substantially complied" with the regulations, the court con-cluded that Section 2032A did not apply to the valuation of the respective tracts, and the estate had to value the land at the full FMV on the date of de-cedent's death.

[Estate of Strickland, 92 TC 16 (1989).]

Relief provisions do not affect untimely special-use election. A taxpayer at-tempted to elect special-use valuation under Section 2032A after the estate tax return was due. The IRS contended that the special-use valuation must be made not later than the time prescribed for filing Form 706.

Held: For the IRS. Relief is provided for returns that substantially comply with the requirements of the special-use valuation election. The legislative history does not indicate any intention to remedy untimely returns.

[Estate of Johnson, 89 TC 127 (1987).]

Tax Court holds substantial compliance with regulation insufficient to obtain benefits of special-use valuation. On decedent's original estate tax return, a mark was placed indicating election of special-use valuation under Section 2032A. In addition, fair market valuations and special-use valuations of decedent's interest in certain property were attached to the return. No recapture agreement was attached to the original return, however. An amended return, with the recapture agreement attached, was later filed. The IRS, on audit, claimed that the estate's failure to attach a recapture agreement to its original estate tax return defeated the estate's attempted election of special-use valuation.

Held: For the IRS. The Tax Court found that Regulation § 20.2032A-8(a)(3), which requires that the recapture agreement be attached to a timely filed estate tax return, is a legislative regulation expressly authorized by the statute. According to the court, even if that regulation were an interpretative regulation, it would still be valid because it is neither unreasonable nor inconsistent with the statute. The court concluded that substantial compliance with the regulation was insufficient to obtain the benefits of special-use valuation.

[Estate of Gunland, 88 TC 1453 (1987).]

Failure of tenants in common, who are not beneficiaries, to sign special-use agreement is held not fatal to Section 2032A(d) election. At the time of his death, decedent and his brother were tenants-in-common of farm property located in Virginia. Decedent had owned an undivided two-thirds interest in the property. He had also been the owner of a one-half interest as a tenant in common with his sister in yet another farm located in the same county. Neither sibling was a beneficiary under decedent's will. The property was left by testamentary devise to his daughter outright and to his grandchildren in trust. The estate filed a timely election under Section 2032A of special-use valuation of the two farm interests. The IRS agreed that the election was in all respects proper, except for the failure of the surviving tenants-in-common to execute the consent agreement required to be signed by all parties with an interest in the property under Section 2032A(d)(2). At trial, the issue was whether the estate was entitled to special-use valuation without including the signatures of the surviving tenants-in-common.

Held: For the estate. Section 2032A(d)(2) states that the agreement referred to in the preceding subsection in the Code must be "signed by each person in being who has an interest (whether or not in possession) in any property designated in such agreement." Because the statute refers only to property "designated in the agreement," it was evidently meant to include only such property as is subject to estate tax. This would therefore extend only to property owned by decedent, namely, to his separate undivided interest in the entire parcel of property. Accordingly, the court invalidated Regulation § 20.2032A-8(c)(2) and found that tenants-in-common were not required to be signatories under the statute.

[Estate of Pullin, 84 TC 789 (1985), acq. 1988-2 CB 1.]

Tax Court holds IRS discretionary denials of estate filing tax extension requests are fully reviewable. Decedent died testate on November 14, 1979. Her executrix retained competent counsel to prepare the estate tax return and promptly turned all necessary information over to him. The attorney died a few days later in an airplane crash, and his firm reassigned the estate to another lawyer. The deceased attorney had not followed the firm's scheduling procedures in respect of statutory deadlines, and the succeeding attorney, who was engaged in litigation in another city on August 14, 1980, the day on which the return was due, sent the IRS a request for extension on August 25, 1980. The return was signed by the executrix and mailed to the IRS on August 30, 1980. Thereafter the IRS routinely denied the estate's request for an extension, and the estate's attorney filed a written protest. The IRS District Director, noting that the estate had sought to elect special-use valuation under Section 2032A in respect of certain farmlands, sought technical advice from the national office as to the legal effect of the late filing. No ruling was ever issued on the question of late filing, and, after the filing of an adverse report from the examining agent, the IRS assessed a deficiency. The estate brought the matter to the Tax Court.

Held: IRS motion for summary judgment denied. Under Section 2032A(d)(1) prior to 1981, a special-use valuation election could be effective only if made not later than the due date of the return, including extensions thereof. Previous Tax Court decisions had consistently held that the timely filed return requirement was mandatory, leaving no room for reasonable cause exceptions. At the same time, however, Section 6081(a) provides that the IRS may grant a reasonable extension of time for filing any tax return. In Regulation § 1.6081-1(b)(1), there is a clear indication that in respect of estate tax returns, an extension may be granted, even though the request is filed after the ordinary due date. The IRS, citing supporting authority, argued that statutorily conferred discretionary powers are unreviewable. The Tax Court closely examined relevant case law and legislative history, and found as a general rule that agency action is exempt from judicial review only where the governing statutes expressly preclude such review or where the action is committed to agency discretion by law. Section 6081(a) does not, by its terms, preclude judicial review, and no recognized exceptions to the general rule apply. On this basis, the court held that IRS discretionary denials under Section 6081(a) are subject to full review by the Tax Court, and that summary judgment for such review was not proper, because there remained a genuine issue of material fact as to the reasons for the denial.

[Estate of Gardner, 82 TC 989 (1984).]

IRS rules on situation where executor of estate elects both alternate valuation and special-use valuation. The IRS ruled that if the executor of an estate elects to use both alternate valuation under Section 2032 and special-use valuation under Section 2032A in valuing a decedent's farmland, the alternate valuation date under Section 2032 must be used in valuing decedent's farmland under Section 2032A. Also, in applying the limit described in Section 2032A(a)(2) for the estate tax saving due to special-use valuation, the limit is applicable to the difference between the FMV and the special-use valuation of the property, determined as one of the alternate valuation date.

[Rev. Rul. 88-89, 1988-2 CB 333.]

Estate can elect both Sections 2032 and 2032A. The IRS has ruled that an estate may elect both the alternate valuation date under Section 2032 and special-use valuation under Section 2032A.

[Rev. Rul. 83-31, 1983-1 CB 225.]

Special-use election is held not to be gift, even though it increases residuary estate. Decedent had provided in a will, written before the marital deduction was made unlimited, that his wife was to receive an amount of property necessary to obtain the maximum marital deduction reduced by the largest amount needed to fund a trust for the couple's children that would result in no estate tax being imposed. The wife elected to specially value a farm property pursuant to Section 2032A that she received under the will. Section 2032A allows taxpayer to value farm property at its use as a farm rather than at its highest and best use. This reduced valuation in effect decreased the amount passing to the wife and increased the amount passing to the children. This was not, however, a gift from the wife to the children, because under Regulation § 20.2056(b)-4(a), any change in the amount of a marital bequest that results from use of an alternative valuation date is treated as passing from decedent. The IRS concluded that what applied to an alternative valuation election should also apply to a special-use election in that both involve a reduction in the value of the assets for purposes of determining the value of the estate. Consequently, making the special-use election was held not to be a gift to the residuary legatees, even though the election increased the residuary estate.

[Tech. Adv. Mem. 8943004.]

[2] Qualified Real Property

[a] Generally

Special-use regulation requiring election for at least 25 percent of value of gross estate is held invalid. Decedent died in 1985 owning real estate that included a tract of farmland. His estate elected special-use valuation under Section 2032A for the farmland, which had an adjusted value of 23.83 percent of the adjusted value of the gross estate. Although other real estate in decedent's estate (which, together with the farmland, had an adjusted value in excess of 25 percent of the adjusted value of the gross estate) qualified for special-use valuation, the estate sought to elect special-use valuation with respect to only the farmland. The IRS assessed a deficiency, claiming that the special-use valuation election could not be made with respect to real estate that had an adjusted value of less than 25 percent of the adjusted value of the gross estate as defined by Section 2032A(b)(3)(A). The IRS relied on Regulation § 20.2032A-8(a)(2), which states that an election under Section 2032A need not include all of an estate's real property that is eligible for special-use valuation, but property sufficient to satisfy the threshold requirements of Section 2032A(b)(1)(B) must be specially valued under the election. The estate argued that Section 2032A(b)(1)(B) requires that only 25 percent of the value of a decedent's gross estate must consist of a farm or property used in a trade or business. Thus, it argued that its election of only 23.83 percent was proper because the Code does not require a 25 percent election. According to the estate, the Treasury regulation at issue was invalid as an attempt to create an additional requirement to qualify for special-use valuation when no such additional requirement is found in the underlying statute or its legislative history. On the other hand, the IRS argued that the disputed regulation was promulgated pursuant to the IRS's express statutory authority under Section 2032A(d)(1) that it was a "legislative regulation" and that the rule of deference to the regulations required the court to find the regulation to be valid.

Held: For the estate. The court stated that the IRS's regulation impermissibly added a substantive requirement to the option of making an election. The court said that Section 2032A(d)(1) authorized the IRS only to promulgate procedural regulations dealing with the correct procedures for a taxpayer making an election (such as the proper forms to use and the information he must supply). Thus, the estate was entitled to elect special-use valuation for the farmland, even though it was less than 25 percent of the adjusted value of the gross estate.

[Estate of Miller, 680 F. Supp. 1269, 61 AFTR2d 88-1370, 88-1 USTC ¶ 13,757 (CD Ill. 1988).]

Section 2032A is inapplicable to unconnected personalty. Decedent died seized of a family farm of nearly 650 acres. The FMV of the farm real property at death was nearly $330,000, and the special-use value was approximately $60,000. Personal property associated with the farm had a date-of-death value of almost $15,000. Decedent had also owned as a sole proprietor a wholesale hardware business. This business was located in rented premises and included no real property owned by decedent. The personal property of the hardware business had a date-of-death value of approximately $94,000. The combined value of the farm and the hardware business was 53 percent of the adjusted value of the gross estate. The farm alone, however, including real and personal property, amounted to only 42 percent of the adjusted value of the gross estate. Taxpayers argued that the values of the hardware business and the farm could be aggregated to determine whether the 50 percent test of Section 2032A(b)(1)(A) had been met. The IRS contended that only the farm assets could be considered in determining whether the 50 percent test had been met and that the value of personal property used in an unrelated business could not be considered. The IRS's interpretation restricted the personal property that falls within Section 2032A to personal property connected to the real property eligible for special-use valuation.

Held: For the IRS. In a case of first impression, the court agreed with the IRS and concluded that under Section 2032A, there is no special-use valuation for personal property, regardless of whether it is connected to qualified real property. In the statute, the term "personal property" is used only where it is connected to real property in the phrase "real or personal property." The court further interpreted the language of Section 2032A(b)(1)(A) to mean a unitary use, not one use for the real property and a disconnected, separate use for the personal property. There is no implication that the real property could be a farm and the personal property could be connected with a wholly separate trade or business not involving real property included in decedent's estate. The legislative history indicates that real property physically connected to qualifying farmland is not necessarily qualified-use property. The court concluded that if real property connected to, but unrelated in use to, the qualified real property does not qualify, then personal property unconnected with the real property does not qualify.

[Estate of Geiger, 80 TC 484 (1983).]

IRS rules on application of special-use valuation where corporation owns farmland and portion of decedent's shares are redeemed under Section 303. Prior to his death, decedent had transferred farmland to a newly formed corporation in exchange for voting stock. At the time of decedent's death, his entire estate went to a qualified heir who also owned stock in the corporation. The executor elected special-use valuation for the indirectly held farmland. Prior to filing the estate tax return, the executor effected a redemption of a portion of decedent's stock pursuant to Section 303 (redemptions to pay death taxes). The remaining shares were distributed to decedent's heir. Generally, farmland that is owned indirectly by a decedent qualifies for special-use valuation.

The IRS ruled that decedent's estate:

1. Could not specially value the farmland represented by any increase, which resulted from the redemption, in the other shareholders' equity interests attributable to the shares that they owned prior to decedent's death.
2. Could not value the shares that were redeemed, by taking into consideration a proportionate amount of the specially valued farmland.
3. Could value the remaining shares received by decedent's heir, by taking into consideration the increased proportionate interest in the specially valued farmland that such shares represented because of the redemption.

[Rev. Rul. 85-73, 1985-1 CB 325.]

Community property is treated as individually held for purposes of special-use valuation. The full limitation on the reduction of the estate tax value allowable under the Section 2032A special-use valuation was available to an estate that elected to specially value decedent's interest in a farm, even though decedent had contributed nothing toward its purchase. The IRS reasoned that Congress intended the special-use valuation provisions to apply equally to community and individually owned property, and, in order to achieve this result, a community property interest must be treated as if it was owned by decedent as an individual.

[Rev. Rul. 83-96, 1987-2 CB 156.]

[b] Material participation

Managerial acts of conservator satisfy material participation requirement of Code. Decedent had been physically and mentally incapacitated and unable to handle her own affairs throughout the entire period at issue. Before decedent's death, the court-appointed conservator had leased decedent's farmland to a third party on a share-crop basis. At the time of her death, the estate elected to value the farmland under the special-use valuation provisions of Section 2032A. The district court upheld the IRS's refusal to permit special-use valuation of the farmland, holding that the conservator's activities did not constitute "material participation" in the operation of the farm as contemplated by Section 2032A(b)(1)(C)(ii). The district court found that the conservator's participation was no greater than that of a landlord in the typical share-crop lease arrangement and was not enough to constitute material participation under the statute. The estate argued on appeal that the district court had erred in concluding that the level of the conservator's activity was insufficient to constitute material participation. The estate further contended that the conservator's acts should have been attributed to decedent for the purpose of satisfying the material participation requirement. The IRS contended that attribution of the conservator's acts to decedent was impermissible, because the plain meaning of Section 2032A(b)(1)(C)(ii) limits eligible participation to acts by "decedent or a member of decedent's family."

Held: For the estate. The Eighth Circuit concluded that the conservator's activities constituted material participation in the lease of the farmland. The conservator's activities satisfied the minimum requirement of regular consultation and substantial participation in final management decisions. In addition to the minimum requirement, Regulation § 20.2032A-3(e)(2) lists four other factors to be considered in determining the presence of material participation. The district court weighed these four other factors against the activities of a landlord in a typical share-crop arrangement. The court of appeals stated that the regulation requires no such comparison, and that equating the material participation test of Section 2032A(b)(C)(1)(ii) with the managerial participation of a landlord in a typical share-crop arrangement imposed a burden of proof on the estate that was greater than that necessary to effectuate the purpose of the statute. The court then addressed the issue of whether the conservator's activities were attributable to decedent. The court held that attribution was permissible, stating that application of the "plain meaning" rule to Section 2032A(b)(1)(C)(ii) would impose a higher tax liability on decedent's estate merely because she had been placed in a conservatorship prior to death. The court reasoned that the consequences of such an interpretation would be absurd, because creation of the conservatorships would be discouraged, whereas by definition they should be encouraged as being in the best interest of a ward's estate. The court stated that its interpretation reasonably effected the basic intent behind the special-use provision. Accordingly, the court held that the estate was entitled to elect to value the farmland under Section 2032A.

[Estate of Mangels, 828 F2d 1324, 60 AFTR2d 87-6145, 87-2 USTC ¶ 13,734 (8th Cir. 1987).]

Rental of farmlands, where based in substantial part on production, does not necessarily disqualify resort to special-use valuation. Decedent died in 1977 owning certain farm property that she had rented to a tenant farmer. The governing lease provided that the tenant's cash rent would be based on gross income received at year's end, following the harvest. The estate included the farm in decedent's gross estate and elected to value it under Section 2032A, the special-use valuation statute. The IRS determined, however, that the election was void under Section 2032A, because the estate was unable to show that decedent had materially participated in an active farming trade or business. The district court held that decedent's activities amounted only to the passive rental of otherwise qualifying property, and that therefore the estate's election was voidable by the IRS. The court determined that as a matter of law, a tenant farming agreement based on the production of salable crops does not constitute an active trade or business on the part of a decedent.

    Held: Reversed for the estate. The Seventh Circuit placed great emphasis on the fact that the crop-sharing agreement was entirely dependent upon production, because even a slight change in crop yields or prices would have changed the rents payable to decedent. The evidence showed a variation in rental income of 32 percent over one three-year period. Citing Section 2032A(b)(1) and legislative history, the court noted that the qualified-use requirement is satisfied if the income from rental of farm property is substantially dependent upon production. Because the terms of the lease and the actual practice of the parties established production as a major determinant of rent, the court entered judgment for the estate.

[Schuneman, 783 F2d 694, 57 AFTR2d 86-1530, 86-1 USTC ¶ 13,660 (7th Cir. 1986).]

Estate does not qualify for special-use valuation under Section 2032A. An individual died on December 1, 1977. The executors of decedent's estate subsequently filed a federal estate tax return on which they reported that the estate included cash, life insurance, notes receivable, miscellaneous personal items, and thirteen groupings of real property, including 1,478 acres of land on which special-use valuation was claimed pursuant to Section 2032A. After an audit, the IRS issued a deficiency notice in which it was determined, among other things, that the special-use valuation provisions of Section 2032A were not applicable to any part of the 1,478 acres of land. The executors of the estate filed a timely petition for Tax Court review of the IRS's determination. The Tax Court held that the estate qualified for the special-use valuation on the 1,478 acres of land under Section 2032A, which permits certain qualifying farms and other real property used in a trade or business to be valued for estate tax purposes according to their actual use at the time of decedent's death. The value is arrived at by capitalizing the income derived from the actual use of the property rather than by adopting its FMV based upon its highest and best use. The disagreement of the parties in the instant case was limited to whether property representing 50 percent or more of the adjusted value of the gross estate was being used at decedent's death for a qualified purpose by decedent or a member of his family, and whether 25 percent or more of the adjusted value of the gross estate was represented by property that was used during five of the eight years preceding decedent's death for a qualified purpose in which there was material participation by decedent or a member of his family.

From 1952 until decedent's death in 1977, decedent and his son had had the acreage under their exclusive control and had made every management decision with respect to the property. The activities that had been performed by them and the manner in which the properties had been managed were consistent with the principles of good land management as recommended to and practiced by the owners of other property of a similar nature, size, and location. From 1952 through 1972, decedent had managed an active farm business that consisted primarily of planting, cultivating, growing, and caring for 1,108 acres of timber. The active farm business had also included the management of another 370 acres that were not suitable for timber but that constituted part of the total acreage on which the timber was located. The management of the 370 acres had been performed in such a manner that was an aid to, an integral part of, and inseparable from the management of the 1,108 acres of timber. From 1972 until decedent's death in 1977, the active farm business had been conducted by decedent's son as one of the trustees of a revocable trust that had been created by decedent and of which he was the sole beneficiary during his life.

Held: Reversed for the IRS. The Eleventh Circuit upheld the Tax Court's determination that decedent and his son had materially participated in the farm business during the entire twenty-five-year period. It did not, however, agree with the Tax Court's finding that the estate met the 50 percent threshold required by Section 2032A(b)(1)(A). The IRS conceded that part of decedent's land qualified for special-use valuation. This portion, however, constituted only 26 percent of the overall adjusted gross estate. Thus, the estate would be entitled to a special-use valuation only if sufficient additional property were deemed to be qualifying real property or related personalty to meet the 50 percent threshold. The Eleventh Circuit found that 68 acres of decedent's land were not used at all, and that an additional 270 acres were leased to unrelated parties for rent that was not based on the productivity of the land. There was no evidence that either decedent or his son had been involved in the managerial decisions concerning this land. On the contrary, the relationship had been merely that of a landlord passively collecting rent from an unrelated party. The Eleventh Circuit stated further that the Tax Court had erred in its determination that decedent's nontimberland was an inseparable unit of the timberland, because there was no showing that the timber-farming operation could not be performed without decedent or his son holding title to the nontimberland. Consequently, the 50 percent test was not met, and none of the estate's assets were entitled to special-use valuation.

[Estate of Sherrod, 774 F2d 1057, 56 AFTR2d 85-6594, 85-2 USTC ¶ 13,644 (11th Cir. 1985), cert. denied, 479 US 814 (1986).]

Lack of qualified use and material participation precludes special-use valuation. At the time of decedent's death in 1981, she owned a farm that was leased to nonfamily members. Her estate elected to use the special-use valuation provisions of Section 2032A to value the farm. On audit, the IRS determined that the estate was not entitled to value the farm under Section 2032A, on the grounds that the farm was not put to a qualified use by decedent or by a member of her family and that there was no material participation by same in the farm's operation.

Held: For the IRS. With respect to the issue of qualified use, Regulation § 20.2032A-3(b) provides that all specially valued property must be used in a trade or business, which includes an active business as distinguished from passive investment activities. The court concluded from the following facts that the farm was a passive investment: From 1976 until decedent's death, the farm had been leased to nonfamily members for rental amounts not substantially dependent upon crop production; the contract between decedent and her lessees had called for a flat rental of $10,080 per year, and the rental had been due and payable without regard to any production from the farm. Although the lease agreement had also called for a cash rental of $30 and delivery of twelve bushels of corn and three bushels of soybeans for each acre rented, there had been nothing in the lease that required corn and soybeans to be grown on the farm. The court also concluded that neither decedent nor her son had materially participated in the management decisions of the farm as required under Regulation § 20.2032A-39(e)(2). This regulation provides that no single factor is determinative of the presence of material participation, but that physical work and participation in management decisions are the principal factors to be considered. The court found that decedent neither had done physical work on the farm nor had participated in management decisions. Because her son had been compensated by the leases for his part-time work on the farm and because his income from the farm had been based on time worked, not on the level of crop production, his efforts had also failed to constitute material participation by a family member.

[Estate of Heffley, 89 TC 265 (1987), aff'd, 884 F2d 279, 64 AFTR2d 89-5909, 89-2 USTC ¶ 13,812 (7th Cir. 1989).]

Special-use value can apply to crop-shared land. Decedent died in 1978 owning a farm that she did not actually operate herself. Rather, the land was farmed under a crop-share arrangement. Her estate valued the farm under the special-use valuation provisions of Section 2032A. The IRS determined a deficiency in the estate tax on the ground that decedent had not materially participated in the operation of her farm within the meaning of Section 2032A(b)(1)(C)(ii).

Held: For the estate. Section 2032A permits land used as a farm or in a closely held business to be valued based on its use for that purpose rather than on its highest and best use. One of the conditions for using this section is that there must have been material participation by decedent or a family member in the farming operation for periods totaling five out of eight years ending on the date of decedent's death. Factors that indicate material participation as shown in Regulation § 20.302A-3(e)(2) include:

1. Physical labor.
2. Participation in management decisions.
3. Assumption of financial responsibility for a substantial portion of farm operating expense.
4. Regular inspection of farm production activities.
5. Furnishing of a substantial portion of machinery, equipment, and livestock used in farm operation.
6. Maintaining principal place of residence on the farm premises.

The court distinguished the instant case from Coon, 81 TC 602 (1983), wherein decedent had owned land that was farmed under a crop-share arrangement and discussed with the tenants the crops to be planted, directed them where to purchase his share of seed and fertilizer, and consulted with them regarding improvements or major repairs to the property, but permitted the operating decisions to be made without him. The court in that case held that decedent's activities had not amounted to material participation, and special-use valuation was denied. In the instant case, decedent, who was ninety-two years old when she died, had made decisions about when to harvest and market her share of the crops. She had also inspected the production activities on a regular basis. These activities, unlike those of taxpayer in *Coon*, constituted material participation in the farm, and therefore the estate was eligible for the special-use valuation.

[Estate of Ward, 89 TC 54 (1987).]

[c] Percentage test

Special-use valuation tests include predeath gifts. Decedent had given farmland to his children two years before he died. On the date of his death, he owned another farm, which by itself did not meet both tests for special-use property. Although decedent had given the farm to his children before his death, its value was includable in his gross estate for the determination whether the estate satisfied the special-use valuation requirements. Section 2032A allows land used for farming or in a closely held business to be valued on the basis of its actual use rather than its highest and best use. Section 2032A(b)(1) requires that to make the special-use valuation election, 50 percent or more of the value of the gross estate must be property that was being used for a qualified purpose by decedent or his family at the time of his death and that passed to a qualified heir. The section also requires that 25 percent or more of the value of the gross estate must be real property that passed to a qualified heir. Although Section 2035(d) generally excludes from the estate property that was given away within three years of death, Section 2035(d)(3)(B) makes an exception for special-use valuations. The purpose of the provision is to prevent taxpayers from making deathbed transfers of enough property not qualified for the special-use election so that more than 50 percent of the estate will be special-use property, thus allowing the estate to make the election as to this property. The provision also has the reverse effect, however, in that qualified property given away within three years of death will be included in the estate for purposes of the 50 percent test. The size of the gross estate is not affected by this, because Section 2035(d)(3) excludes such gifts from the gross estate in calculating estate tax liability. Although the excluded property counts for purposes of the 50 percent test, Regulation § 20.2032A-8(a)(2) makes it clear that only property actually included in the estate counts for the 25 percent test of Section 2032A(b)(1)(B). Because the qualified property not given away was more than 25 percent of the value of the gross estate in the instant case, special-use valuation was available.

[Rev. Rul. 87-22, 1987-1 CB 146.]

Estate may aggregate decedent's interest in closely held bank with interest in farm property to meet special-use valuation test. An individual and his family members had owned the stock of a closely held bank for more than ten years. The bank had owned various farm property and personal property. The individual's spouse had died in April 1987, leaving her stock in the bank to the couple's two children. In November 1987, the individual died, leaving all of his property to his spouse and the couple's children. The individual's property included farm property. The estate sought a ruling that the individual's interest in the bank may be aggregated with his interest in the farm assets to satisfy the 50 percent requirement of Section 2032A(b)(1)(A).

The IRS stated that the individual's interest in the closely held bank may be aggregated with the farm property for purposes of the 50 percent test. The IRS concluded that the individual's stock in the bank qualified under Section 6166(b)(1)(C) as an "interest in a closely held business," which may be aggregated with farm property under Section 2032A.

[Priv. Ltr. Rul. 8843023.]

Qualified farming property and qualified small business property may be aggregated for special-use valuation purposes. Decedent's estate included farm property and property used in a closely held retail furniture business. Valued separately, neither interest would qualify for special-use valuation under Section 2032A; but if they were valued together, the two interests would qualify.

The IRS stated that the estate could aggregate qualified farming property with qualified property in a closely held business to qualify for special-use valuation. The IRS also indicated that although the retail business was erroneously valued under Section 2032A(e)(7), the qualified use value of the real property in that business was its FMV, so that no adjustments to the value of the property were required.

[Priv. Ltr. Rul. 8433006.]

Special-use value is calculated by prorating excess Section 2032A(a)(2) limitation. Decedent's estate elected special-use valuation for five farms in the estate. The difference between the farms' FMV and their value under Section 2032A exceeded the limit on the allowable decrease in value under Section 2032A(a)(2). In technical advice, the IRS stated that the special-use value for each farm should be computed by prorating the excess to each farm on the basis of the portion of the total reduction under Section 2032A that is attributable to each farm.

[Priv. Ltr. Rul. 8404003.]

[d] Heirship requirement

Special-use election is still valid where there is remote chance of distribution to nonqualified heirs. Decedent's will devised her interest in farmland to her husband for life with a testamentary power to pass his interest to a nonqualified heir. The will also provided that if decedent's husband did not exercise the power of appointment and there were no surviving children or descendants of any deceased children of the wife, then nonqualified heirs might obtain an interest. Special-use valuation on the farmland was claimed on the estate tax return. The IRS disallowed the special-use valuation, arguing that the will, as written, created the possibility that the farmland might pass out of decedent's family members' hands within fifteen years of death.

Held: For taxpayer. Section 2032A(c)(1) is designated to provide substantial relief from the burden of estate taxes on family farms. It imposes a recapture tax however, if, within ten years (fifteen years under these facts) and before the death of the qualified heir, such heir disposes of his interest other than to a qualified heir, or ceases the qualified use. The possibility of divestment by power of appointment under decedent's will is so remote that it is not a reasonable basis for denying special-use valuation. A wait-and-see approach is in order, given that any future nonqualified use or disposition would trigger a recapture tax under Section 2032A(c)(1).

[Smoot, 892 F2d 597, 90-1 USTC ¶ 60,002, 65 AFTR2d 90-1177 (7th Cir. 1989).]

Special-use valuation of estate is allowed, despite interest of nonqualified heir. Decedent left four farms in trust, with instructions that the farming operation be continued. Although the income of the trust was to be distributed primarily to decedent's two daughters, the lesser of 2 percent or $2,000 a year was to go to an unrelated individual. This individual disclaimed the interest in return for a cash payment. The daughters had the power to leave their trust interests to their children or to a charity; they disclaimed this latter power. The Tax Court agreed with the IRS that the property was not eligible for special-use valuation pursuant to Section 2032A, because of the interest passing to the unrelated individual, a nonqualified heir. Under Section 2032A, property used in farming or in a trade or business may be valued for estate tax purposes at its current operating value, rather than at its highest and best use, if certain conditions, including the property being passed to a qualified heir, are met.

Held: Reversed for the estate. The Fourth Circuit disagreed with the IRS's strict interpretation of the last requirement, which would bar special use for qualified heirs when interests are also held by nonqualified heirs, noting that it was not supported by the legislative history. In Whalen, 826 F2d 668, 87-2 USTC ¶ 13,729, 60 AFTR2d 87-6127 (7th Cir. 1987), the Seventh Circuit allowed special-use valuation for the 75 percent of an interest that went to qualified heirs, even though the 25 percent passing to nonqualified heirs was ineligible. The IRS seemed to agree in Revenue Ruling 85-73, 1985-1 CB 325. There a family farm was held by a corporation. Decedent had owned an 80 percent share and a qualified heir and a nonqualified heir each owned 10 percent shares. After decedent's death, the corporation redeemed some of his shares, raising the interests of the other two shareholders to 11.1 percent each. The qualified heir received the balance of decedent's shares. All of the qualified heir's interest, except for that resulting from the redemption, was eligible for special-use valuation, even though 11.1 percent of the interest in the farm went to a nonqualified heir. The IRS distinguished this result from that in the instant case because the nonqualified heir in the instant case did not have an interest before decedent's death, whereas in the ruling, he did. The Fourth Circuit found this distinction to be specious. The Fourth Circuit then focused on the question whether special-use valuation was precluded because of the power of appointment given to decedent's daughters, allowing them to name charities as beneficiaries. Regulation § 20.2032A-8(a)(2) provides that all successive interests in real property must pass to qualified heirs in order for the property to be eligible for special-use valuation. The Tax Court had previously invalidated this regulation in Estate of Clinard, 86 TC 1180 (1986), a position adopted by the Fourth Circuit. The court noted that if, within ten years of decedent's death, the qualified heir disposes of the property or ceases to use it for its qualified use, a recapture tax will be imposed. The court felt that it was irrational to assume that Congress would put a limitation on the application of the recapture tax, yet insist that the property be held by qualified heirs indefinitely.

[Estate of Thompson, 864 F2d 1128, 89-1 USTC ¶ 13,792, 63 AFTR2d 89-1515 (4th Cir. 1989).]

Denial of qualified heir status to stepchild does not violate due process clause. Decedent died in 1977. In her will she had devised nearly 100 acres of Illinois farmland to her three sons and a stepdaughter. Her estate claimed special-use valuation under Section 2032A for all of the farmland. The IRS denied special-use valuation for the quarter-interest devised to her stepchild, finding that a stepchild was not a qualified heir as required by Section 2032A. Section 2032A allows certain property used in family farming and closely held businesses to be valued, for purposes of the federal estate tax, on the basis of its actual use at the time of decedent's death rather than its "highest and best use." On appeal, the estate conceded that the stepchild was not a qualified heir, but contended that Section 2032A did not require that property pass to a qualified heir until the section was amended by the Revenue Act of 1978. In the estate's view, the application of a 1978 law to the estate of a woman who died in 1977 violated the Fifth Amendment's due process clause.

Held: For the IRS. The court stated that the House and Senate reports made clear that Congress viewed the 1978 amendment to Section 2032A as merely correcting a technical defect rather than enacting a substantive change in the law. Therefore, the court concluded that Section 2032A, as originally enacted in 1976, required that property be passed to a qualified heir in order to qualify for special-use valuation. As such, the court noted, the 1978 clarifying amendment to that section did not change the law and was not retroactive in any substantive sense. Given this holding, the court determined that it need not address the constitutional question raised by the estate and held that due process was not offended by legislation that removed ambiguities from the law without changing its effect.

[Estate of Whalen, 826 F2d 668, 60 AFTR2d 87-6127, 87-2 USTC ¶ 13,729 (7th Cir. 1987).]

Property qualified for special-use valuations, even though remainder interest in decedent's grandchildren was subject to special power of appointment. Decedent died in 1980, owning land that qualified for special-use valuation under Section 2032A. Under decedent's will, this farmland passed to two trusts, one for her son and the other for her daughter. The trust for her son granted him a life-income interest that, upon his death, was to pass to his spouse, should he be survived by one. Then the trust income was to pass to his son. Upon the death of his son (decedent's grandson), the remainder was to pass as directed in his will (but not to his estate, his creditors, or his estate's creditors). If he failed to exercise this power, the remainder would vest in his then-living descendants. In the event that there were no such descendants, it would vest one-half to decedent's daughter's trust and one-half to the descendants of a named non-family member. The trust for decedent's daughter had substantially similar provisions concerning her interest and that of her descendants. Both trusts included a provision passing the remainder to a charitable organization in the event that no remainderman existed and the other trust, either the son's or the daughter's, had already terminated. Decedent's estate used a special-use valuation for this farmland. The IRS argued that such valuation was unavailable for two reasons. One was the special power in the grandchildren that enabled them to make a testamentary disposition of the farmland to a nonqualified person under Section 2032A. The other was the gift, in the event of complete failure of decedent's descendants, to the charity, a nonqualified person under Section 2032A.

Held: For taxpayer. When Congress enacted Section 2032A, it did not intend to deny special relief in instances where there existed only a remote possibility that qualifying property would pass to a nonqualified person after successive interests held by qualifying persons. Furthermore, the special sixteen-year recapture provision would protect the government in the event that a grandchild of decedent were to gain his income interest, die, and appoint the property to a nonqualified person within the sixteen-year period. Accordingly, the special power of appointment and the gift over to nonqualified persons upon the failure to exercise such power (or failure of the grandchild's descendants) did not prevent the estate's use of Section 2032A special-use valuation for the trusts' farmland. To the extent that Regulation § 20.2032A-8(a)(2) would require a different result, it was held to be invalid.

[Estate of Clinard, 86 TC 1180 (1986).]

Section 2032A special-use valuation is permitted, despite remote possibility that qualified property would pass through successive interests to nonqualified heirs. Decedent died on April 14, 1978, leaving a will that established two trusts with his son and daughter as trustees. One trust received farmland that was property qualifying for Section 2032A special-use valuation. The current beneficiaries of this trust were his children, who were given current income and corpus interests, with the remainder to be paid to the children's descendants. If no descendant of decedent were living at termination of the trust, the principal would go to certain named charities. The estate and the IRS agreed that the charities were not qualified heirs for purposes of Section 2032A and that there existed only an infinitesimal chance that the charities would inherit the remainder. The second trust was established for the benefit of decedent's wife, paying her net income for life and granting her a general testamentary power of appointment. If, however, she exercised this power in favor of her two children, the trustees of the first trust were directed to compensate decedent's daughter from his first marriage out of the first trust's corpus. The estate used the Section 2032A special-use valuation for farmland transferred to the first trust, and it claimed a marital deduction for property transferred to the second trust. The IRS asserted an estate tax deficiency on the grounds that the remote possibility that the farmland would be inherited by nonqualified heirs rendered special-use valuation unavailable under Section 2032A, and that the marital trust's provision for paying net income and the broad powers granted the trustees caused the marital deduction to be unavailable for this trust's property.

Held: For taxpayer. Although Congress did not include specific provisions in Section 2032A covering a gift of special-use property to a nonqualified heir after the default of successive qualifying interests, its intent was that Section 2032A of the Code nevertheless apply where inheritance by a "nonqualified" heir was remote. To the extent that Regulation § 20.2032A-8(a)(2) expresses a contrary policy, it is invalid. Second, the trust established for decedent's wife qualified for the marital deduction. The direction that the entire net income be paid to decedent's wife was substantially the same as the statutory requirement of "all of the income." Further, the broad grant of powers to the trustees (e.g., to borrow or to mortgage) that could undermine the marital bequest must be read in light of decedent's intent, as expressed in his will, namely, that his wife not be deprived in any manner of the beneficial enjoyment of the property placed in trust for her. Finally, the direction that the trustees of the first (or children's) trust compensate his ex-wife's daughter out of the first trust's principal, if his current wife exercised her general testamentary power in favor of the two children she had with decedent, was not a restriction or limitation on such general power. Accordingly, the property passing to the trust for decedent's wife qualified for the marital deduction under Section 2056(b)(5).

[Estate of Davis, 86 TC 1156 (1986).]

Special-use valuation is effective, despite possibility that property may pass to nonqualified individual. When decedent died on December 23, 1983, he owned real property that included a ranch held as a tenancy in common with his sister. Under decedent's will, the land was put into a trust for his two nieces until they reached age 30 when the trust was to terminate and the property was to be distributed to the nieces. Under the trust, income and principal could be expended for the nieces' health, education, maintenance, and support in the trustee's discretion. The estate elected to specially value the ranch land held by decedent and his sister as tenants in common. The estate filed a notice of election to specially value the property under Section 2032A. On the election, the nieces signed as "qualified heirs," and the sister and her husband signed as "other interested parties." The sister's duties as executrix of the estate and trustee of the testamentary trust were not indicated on the agreement or by her signature. The sister, as executrix of the estate, indicated that she wished to value the real property held in trust under Section 2032A. The district director was concerned that the property could pass from decedent to someone other than a qualified heir, violating the requirements of Section

2032A(b)(1) if both nieces were to die before they reached the age of 30. The district director also was concerned that the nieces' discretionary income, if one or both should die within ten years after the date of decedent's death, would pass through the niece's estate, so that the interest could pass to a non-qualified heir during the period that the additional estate tax under Section 2032A(c)(1) may be imposed.

The IRS stated that the real property specially valued under Section 2032A passed from decedent to qualified heirs under Section 2032A(e)(1), because no successive interest problems existed in this case. The IRS reasoned that the intention of decedent, which would be followed in the jurisdiction, clearly indicated that the trust should benefit only the two nieces, and, should one die, only the other would be entitled to benefit from the income earned by the trust. The IRS also indicated that the originally filed Section 2032A agreement was incomplete, but that it could be perfected under Section 2032A(d)(3). The IRS noted that neither the agreement nor the signature reflected the sister's capacity as executrix of decedent's estate or as trustee of the testamentary trust. The IRS reasoned, however, that because the sister had signed the agreement as an "other interested party," she would not be able to successfully deny her consent to the election, so that there was substantial compliance with the requirements of Regulation § 20.2032A-8(c).

[Priv. Ltr. Rul. 8713001.]

[e] Use requirement

Special-use valuation is denied where material participation and qualified use are lacking. Decedent's estate claimed special-use valuation for a farm, 100 of the 443 acres of which were leased for five years for use during the grazing season. During the nongrazing season, when the lessee did not use the land, the heirs were required to maintain the property. The Tax Court allowed special-use valuation for the 100 acres.

Held: Reversed for the IRS. The land was not used for farming by the heirs. The maintenance of land in the off-season did not satisfy the material participation requirement. The qualified use requirement was not met, because the property had not been used in a farming activity that had exposed decedent to the financial risks of farming.

[Brockman, 903 F2d 518, 90-1 USTC ¶ 60,026, 65 AFTR2d 90-1249 (7th Cir. 1990).]

Seventh Circuit, affirming the Tax Court, finds cessation of qualified use and imposes recapture, despite estate's showing of material participation by qualified heirs. Prior to his death in 1978, decedent was the sole owner of a 209-acre farm located in Posey County, Indiana. The property consisted of

166 acres of farmland, 23 acres of unmanaged woodlands, and 17 acres of woods and creeks, as well as the farmhouse. Decedent and his wife, who had predeceased him in 1977, personally had farmed the land for many years until their advanced years had forced them to retire in 1970. At that time, they had entered into an oral sharecrop arrangement with their son-in-law whereby he would farm some 95 acres in exchange for one-third of the net proceeds. In 1974, the oral lease had been modified to include the entire farm. By his will, decedent's seven surviving children received the farm as tenants-in-common, with the son-in-law continuing to operate under an extension of the 1977 lease. On its federal estate tax return, decedent's estate elected to value the farm pursuant to the special-use provisions set forth in Section 2032A. The return was accepted, and a closing letter was issued on June 16, 1980. Subsequent to the filing of the estate tax return, one of the sons, who was also their personal representative of the estate, determined that the lease arrangement was unsatisfactory, and, accordingly, he terminated the oral lease effective August 15, 1979. At the same time, he advertised for bids to lease the farm on a simple cash-rental basis. An unrelated farming concern was awarded a lease based on its rental bid of $21,060. The local probate court approved the lease, which extended only to the entire tillable portion of the property. During the cash lease term, the son and one of his brothers participated in the maintenance and operation of the farm by performing a number of duties, including the repair of field tile, the filling of a sinkhole, and the clearing of certain fence rows. In addition, the son regularly conferred with the lessee concerning fertilizer, planting, seed selection, and so forth. In the meantime, the disposed daughter commenced an action in partition, which was granted by the probate court in 1982. The IRS became aware of these developments, and it assessed a deficiency on the ground that the seven heirs of decedent had ceased to use the property for a qualified use by virtue of the cash lease agreement. The IRS proceeded under Section 2032A(c)(1), which provides for the imposition of additional estate taxes in any case where the qualified heir ceases to use the property for a qualified use.

Held: Affirmed for the IRS. Section 2032A(c)(7) provides that qualified property ceases to be used for a qualified use if, for an aggregate period of three years, there is no material participation by a qualified heir in the operation of the farm itself. In the legislative history, Congress expressly indicated that the mere passive rental of property is not to be regarded as material participation; therefore, the recapture tax will be imposed. The IRS argued, however, that the farm ceased to be used by the qualified heirs pursuant to Section 2032A(c)(1)(B), and at trial no objection was raised by the IRS in respect of the material participation issue under Section 2032A(c)(7)(B). In this way, the IRS was able to assert recapture solely by reason of the one-year cash lease, rather than by proof that there was no material participation by the heirs under Section 2032A(c)(7)(B). Citing its decision in Estate of Abell, 83 TC 696 (1984), the court found that the one-year cash lease to an unrelated party was sufficient ground to establish the failure to continue a qualified use, and therefore it held that recapture was properly asserted by the IRS.

[Martin, 783 F2d 81, 57 AFTR2d 86-1527, 86-1 USTC ¶ 13,659 (7th Cir. 1986).]

Lease of farm property blocks special-use valuation election. Decedent had owned a ranch in Kansas that consisted of 7,670 acres of grazing land and 580 acres of cropland. It had a FMV of $1.8 million on the date of decedent's death in 1979. The facts showed that decedent had lived on the ranch until the time of her death, but that shortly after her husband died in 1940, she had leased the ranch to a company that operated it continuously throughout her life. The per-acre rent had been set at considerably less than the fair rental value so that decedent could retain and exercise control over the manner in which the ranch was used. Decedent was regularly consulted on all decisions relating to ranch management, operation, and maintenance, and she personally supervised an employee who made necessary repairs. Following her death, the estate elected to value decedent's interest in the ranch under Section 2032A. The IRS, however, disallowed the claimed special-use valuation on the ground that decedent herself had not used the property in a farming business. The estate argued in the Tax Court that despite the fact that she leased the land to others, she participated actively in all ranch operations.

Held: For the IRS. Decedent had had no equity or financial interest in the business being conducted on her property, and because an unrelated party had the exclusive right to use and profit from the land, decedent could not be said to have satisfied the qualified use requirement under Section 2032A.

[Estate of Abell, 83 TC 696 (1984).]

Decedent's attempt to develop land did not bar special-use valuation. Decedent owned land that was used in a horse boarding and riding business operated by his son and granddaughter. Approximately two years before decedent's death, he and his son entered into a contract with a land development corporation to begin the planning and engineering necessary to convert the land into residential building lots. At the time of death, however, neither the preliminary plan of subdivision was approved nor the sewer authorization granted. After death, the land development contract was terminated, and no lots had been sold. The son and granddaughter continued to operate the horse boarding and riding business.

The IRS ruled that special-use valuation could be used to value the land. Even though decedent intended to develop the land, at no time during his life was any physical action taken that prevented the land from being used in the horse business. Thus, the business was not interrupted or restricted by the development plan, and the requirement of Section 2032A that land be used in a trade or business was met.

[Tech. Adv. Mem. 9433003.]

Lease is a production lease; hunting is not farming. A ranch owner had leased her ranch to a tenant for 30 percent of gross income from livestock operations and 50 percent of gross income from hunting activities. The rent was to be paid in semiannual installments, with the first installment of $7,000 being due on September 1 and the second installment being due the following March 1. The owner had paid property taxes on the ranch. The ranching operation had included the rearing, maintaining, and marketing of livestock. The hunting operation had consisted of determining the number of hunting permits to be sold, the provision of hunting guides and housing for hunters, wildlife disease control, and maintenance of food and water for the wildlife. When the ranch owner died, her estate elected to value the property under Section 2032A.

The IRS determined that the lease was a production lease, so the property qualified for special-use valuation. The IRS concluded that the $7,000 first installment of rent should not be viewed as a minimum payment, because of the express statements in the lease that rent would be based on a percentage of income. The IRS also determined that the hunting operation did not qualify as use of the property as a farm for farming purposes. The IRS noted that the activities of the ranching and hunting operations were different. The IRS concluded, however, that use of the property for hunting constituted use of the property in a trade or business other than farming under Section 2032A(e). Accordingly, the property should be valued under Section 2032A(e)(8), not under Section 2032A(e)(7).

[Priv. Ltr. Rul. 8516012.]

[f] Holding period

Duration of ownership of tracts of land is apportioned to replacement property for Section 2032A valuation. Decedent had owned two tracts of land (one for ten years and one for three years) that were condemned. Decedent had acquired replacement property with the condemnation proceeds and died one year later. Because the replacement property takes the holding period of the condemned property, the portion of the replacement property attributable to the original tract owned for ten years qualifies for Section 2032A valuation. The portion attributable to the original tract held for three years does not qualify. The condemnation proceeds are apportioned proportionately to the replacement tract.

[Rev. Rul. 81-285, 1981-2 CB 173.]

IRS takes position that holding periods may not be tacked. Decedent had owned 41 percent of a close corporation that engaged in farming. One of the corporation's parcels had been purchased three years prior to decedent's death with cash and land that decedent and his wife had owned. Part of the land that was eligible for special-use valuation was subject to a mortgage.

The IRS indicated in technical advice that the holding periods of consecutively owned pieces of otherwise qualified property cannot be tacked to meet the time requirements of Section 2032A. The IRS also determined that decedent's estate should apportion the value of the qualified property owned by the corporation according to decedent's stock interest. The apportioned value should then be used for the percentage tests in Section 2032A(b)(1). Further, the mortgage must be multiplied by the ratio of the property's use value to its FMV in order to arrive at the amount that is deductible.

[Priv. Ltr. Rul. 8108179.]

Holding period for replacement property may be tacked on to holding period for condemned farmland. Decedent had owned farm property that was condemned prior to decedent's death. With the compensation that he received for the condemned property, decedent had purchased four new tracts of farmland in an exchange that was tax-free under Section 1033.

The IRS stated that the holding period of the condemned farmland could be added to the holding period for the replacement property to meet the holding period requirements of Section 2032A(b)(1)(C). The IRS noted that the holding period for each of the four replacement tracts, when added to the holding period for the condemned property, met the Section 2032A requirements.

[Priv. Ltr. Rul. 8104030.]

[3] Recapture

[a] Calculations

IRS allows six months' grace period on interest on additional tax due on early disposition of specially valued property. Where property is disposed of by an estate within the recapture period, interest will not be assessed on the additional estate tax due until the period beginning six months after the disposition of the property and continuing until the tax is paid.

[Rev. Rul. 81-308, 1981-2 CB 176.]

IRS computes recapture tax on sale of farmland valued as special use property. When it filed Form 706 in 1980, an estate elected special-use valuation under Section 2032A with respect to four tracts of farm property. As a result of the election, the value of farm property includable in the estate was reduced by $500,000, the maximum reduction allowable in 1980. In the absence of the $500,000 limitation, an additional reduction of $36,329 would have been possible. The estate did not make a partial election to reflect that a reduction of $36,329 in the farm's value would not be allowed. On December 29, 1986, the estate sold 10 acres of farm property located on the second tract for $83,333. The date-of-death FMV of the 10 acres was $37,351, and the date-of-death FMV of the 144 acres in the second tract was $248,935. The estate would have increased its estate tax liability by $94,217 if it had not filed a Section 2032A election. The special-use value of the ten acres that were sold was $5,799.

The IRS determined that under Section 2032A(c)(1), an additional estate tax of $4,677 would be imposed on the estate as a result of the sale of the 10 acres. The IRS demonstrated two alternative methods under which calculation of the Section 2032A(c)(1) recapture tax could be made.

[Priv. Ltr. Rul. 8721052.]

IRS provides sample computation for recapture tax. An individual who inherited farmland from his father elected special-use valuation under Section 2032A. The heir planned to sell some of the qualifying property. The purchaser was not a member of the family. The IRS demonstrated by example how the recapture tax with respect to the sale would be computed.

[Priv. Ltr. Rul. 8438042.]

For recapture tax, value of specially valued land may be altered after estate tax limitations period runs. Decedent's estate elected special valuation of decedent's undivided interest in farmland. The estate reported the appraised fair market value of the farmland when it filed the election. The IRS did not examine the estate's federal estate tax return and election but stated in a closing letter that the estate had no estate tax liability. After the estate tax limitations period for the estate had ended, one tract of the farmland was sold to an unrelated party at a price higher than the appraised FMV. The recapture tax return was filed. The IRS's agent proposed to raise the FMV of the tract as of decedent's date of death for purposes of determining the recapture tax.

The IRS stated in technical advice that in determining the recapture tax under Section 2032A, the FMV of specially valued property may be altered after the federal estate tax limitations period has run. The alteration, however, must be limited so that the difference between the FMV of all decedent's Section 2032A property, including adjustments, and the special valuation value of that property does not exceed $500,000.

[Priv. Ltr. Rul. 8403001.]

[b] Cessation of use

Lease to family corporation did not defeat special-use valuation. Two sisters and their brother were the children of decedent and his wife. In 1947, the parents formed a family farming corporation, and because state law prohibited the transfer of farmland to the corporation, decedent's wife leased her farmland to the corporation for fixed cash payments. This leasing arrangement continued until her death in 1978. At the time of her death, decedent's wife owned 7 percent of the corporation's stock; her husband owned 10.5 percent; and her son owned the balance. Under the terms of the wife's will, her farmland and stock were placed in trust for the benefit of her husband and children. The husband, however, waived his right to receive trust income during his lifetime. Decedent's wife's estate elected special-use valuation for her farmland under Section 2032A. According to the government, there was no dispute at the time of decedent's wife's death that her farmland met the requirements for special-use valuation. Accordingly, her estate was permitted to reduce estate taxes by valuing the farmland based on the land's agricultural use rather than its highest and best use under the FMV method of valuation. Following the estate's transfer of the farmland and corporate stock, the trustee of decedent's wife's trust continued to lease the farmland to the family's corporation for fixed cash payments. After decedent died in 1982, his stock in the corporation was also placed in a trust, and the three children were the only beneficiaries of both trusts. The IRS conceded for purposes of Section 2032A that the children were to be treated as beneficial owners of the trust assets. Consequently, the two sisters each owned a one-third interest in their mother's farmland and approximately 6 percent of the corporation's stock, while their brother owned a one-third interest in the farmland and the rest of the stock. In 1988, the IRS asserted recapture taxes against the sisters even though this position was diametrically opposed to the posture taken by the IRS in the mother's estate. The IRS contended that the trustee's leases of the sisters' beneficial interests in the farmland to the corporation for fixed cash payments did not satisfy the sisters' obligation under Section 2032A(c)(1)(B) to use the farmland for a qualified use during the recapture period.

Held: For the estate. The Eighth Circuit placed a great deal of significance on the fact that the IRS conceded that decedent's wife's leasing arrangement with the family farming corporation qualified her estate to elect special-use valuation for her farmland. Decedent's wife had always leased her farmland for fixed cash payments to the family's farming corporation in which she owned stock. According to the court, the IRS necessarily concluded that decedent's wife was using her land under the leasing arrangement for farming purposes. The court cited Regulation § 20.2032A-3(b)(1), which states that farmland leased by a decedent to a farming corporation owned and operated by decedent and fewer than fifteen family members is eligible for special-use valuation. The Eighth Circuit concluded that although this regulation was written in terms of a decedent's predeath leasing activity, the regulation settles the broader question of whether farmland is being used for qualified use under Section 2032A(b)(2)(A). The regulation offers no distinction between decedent's wife's predeath leasing activity and the trustee's leasing activities after her death. Although the receipt of a fixed cash rent by a decedent's children may signal a passive investment, the children may nevertheless use farmland for a qualified use when their rent income is substantially dependent on production. The court held that cases such as Schuneman, 783 F2d 694 (7th Cir. 1986), and Heffley, 884 F2d 279 (7th Cir. 1989), make it clear that when a decedent's heirs enter into a fixed cash arrangement with another farmer who assumes the financial risk of farming, the rent income is not linked to the contingencies of production, because the heirs are mere landlords collecting a fixed rent. On the other hand, these cases also teach that when a decedent's children enter into a leasing arrangement in which their rent income is substantially dependent on production, the children have accepted the financial risks of family farming and retain the benefits of Section 2032A. Based on this reasoning, the court determined that the leases of the farmland to the family's farming corporation continued the use that qualified decedent's wife's estate for preferential treatment when the estate tax return was filed. As owners of the farmland and the family farming corporation, the sisters and their brother necessarily retained the financial risks of farming when their land was farmed by the corporation. The sisters' rent, like their mother's rent income before them, depended on the farmland's productivity and the variable risks of weather, disease, and fluctuating prices. The court held that the sisters assumed substantially the same risks under the leases as they would have incurred by farming the land themselves. The court dismissed the government's contentions that the sisters' minority shareholdings in the corporation were so minimal that it could hardly be said that they had leased the land to themselves.

[Minter, 19 F3d 426, 73 AFTR2d 94-1721, 94-1 USTC ¶ 60,160 (8th Cir. 1994).]

Cash rental arrangement was a disqualifying use. When decedent died in 1980, her estate elected under Section 2032A to value property based on its qualified use as a farm. Taxpayer, decedent's daughter, inherited an interest in the property and immediately leased it to her brother, who was also an heir, under a cash rental arrangement. In 1987, the IRS sent a questionnaire to the estate that was designed to monitor qualifying uses of specially valued property. The estate returned the questionnaire on January 11, 1988, and disclosed the cash rental. Based on "additional information," the IRS prepared substitute Forms 706-A (U.S. Additional Estate Tax Return) to impose recapture tax against the heirs on the ground that there had been a cessation of qualified use. The returns (unsigned by taxpayer or other qualified heirs) were completed by the end of November 1989. It was not until June 6, 1991, however, that the IRS issued deficiency notices to the heirs. Section 2032A permits an estate to value property that decedent or a family member used in farming or in a trade or business based on its agricultural or business use and not its highest and best use. This benefit is limited to a $750,000 reduction in the estate's value and applies only if:

1. Basically, at least 50 percent of the gross estate consists of qualified real or personal property, and the real property is at least 25 percent of the gross estate.
2. Decedent or a family member materially participated in a "qualified use" of the real property (i.e., farming or a trade or business) on the date of death and for five out of the eight preceding years.
3. The real property is left to a "qualified heir," which includes decedent's spouse and ancestors, and lineal descendants (and their spouses) of decedent and decedent's spouse and parents.

If specially valued property is disposed of or no longer used for a qualified use within ten years (fifteen years for decedents dying before 1982) after decedent's death, Section 2032A(c) imposes a recapture tax. Under Section 2032A(f), the period for assessing recapture tax on specially valued property expires three years from the date that the IRS is notified of the disposition or disqualifying use as prescribed by regulations (which have not been issued). Taxpayer contended that the statute of limitations had expired because the IRS failed to issue deficiency notices within three years of being notified of the cessation of qualified use, as required under Section 2032A(f). In the absence of regulations, taxpayer claimed that the questionnaire constituted the required notice. The IRS argued that the limitations period had not expired because (1) the questionnaire was not notice under 2032A(f); (2) the IRS did not determine the recapture tax based solely on the questionnaire; (3) the notices were timely because they were issued within three years of the Service's notification to taxpayer that there was a cessation of qualified use; and (4) notification under Section 2032A(f) can be accomplished only by filing Form 706-A and paying the recapture tax.

Held: For taxpayer in part. The Tax Court cited Sections 1033(a) (nonrecognition of gain on involuntary conversion) and 1034 (deferral of gain on sale of a residence), which include notice requirements similar to Section 2032(f). The regulations under those sections require only that notification contain all details of the transaction and be filed with the district office where the return was filed. The questionnaire submitted by taxpayer satisfied these requirements. The court found it irrelevant that the IRS acquired additional information before issuing the deficiency notices, since almost all examinations to some degree corroborate information that the IRS has. The IRS's contention that the limitations period ran from the date that the IRS notified taxpayer of its position was also rejected. Section 2032A(f) requires notification *from* taxpayer. Further, the absence of a return filing requirement to start the limitations period under Sections 1033 and 1034 rebutted the IRS's contention that only Form 706-A constituted required notice. Since the estate responded to the questionnaire on January 11, 1988, the limitations period expired on January 11, 1991, and the notices issued on June 6, 1991, were invalid. Taxpayer also argued that renting the land to a qualified heir was not a disqualifying use. The Tax Court rejected this argument based on Williamson, 92-2 USTC ¶ 60,115 (9th Cir. 1992), aff'g 93 TC 242 (1989), in which the Ninth Circuit concluded that Section 2032A(c)(1)(B) requires qualified heirs to put the property to the qualified use. The court noted that Section 2032A(b)(5)(A) permits only *spouses*, not other heirs, to rent to family members for cash without causing a cessation of qualified use.

[Stovall, 101 TC 140 (1993).]

Devisee of specially valued family farm is subject to recapture tax upon cash-leasing farm to his nephew, decedent's grandson. Decedent died in 1983 owning a farm that her estate properly elected to specially value under Section 2032A. Taxpayer, decedent's son and qualified heir, inherited the farm property. Thereafter he cash-leased it to his nephew, decedent's grandson, who continued to operate the property as a farm. The IRS assessed the recapture tax of Section 2032A(c)(1) against taxpayer, contending that there was a cessation of qualified use by taxpayer upon the cash lease to his nephew. That section imposes a recapture tax upon the early cessation of the qualified use. Taxpayer argued that a property continues to be used for a qualified use as long as it is used for farming by the qualified heir or by a member of his family. The IRS countered that the qualified heir himself must be the one who operates the farm in order for it to be used in a qualified manner.

   Held: For the IRS. The Tax Court concluded that a qualified heir ceases to use specially valued property for a qualified use if he leases it to anyone else for a cash rental, even if the lessee is a family member who uses it for farming. The court stated that Section 2032A(c)(6)(A) requires that the qualified heir himself farm the property. The court said that cash-leasing the property to someone else constitutes use of the property by the qualified heir in a passive rental activity, not use of the property as a farm for farming purposes. Accordingly, the recapture tax was properly assessed against taxpayer.

[Williamson, 93 TC 242 (1989), aff'd, 974 F2d 1525, 70 AFTR2d 92-6244, 92-2 USTC ¶ 60,115 (9th Cir. 1992).]

Cash lease of special-use property to qualified heir causes recapture. Decedent's six children each inherited a portion of a cattle ranch. The estate elected special-use valuation for the land, and each of the heirs executed the recapture agreement. Five of the heirs later entered into a cash lease with the sixth. The IRS imposed the recapture tax.

Held: For the IRS. Lease of the property to a qualified heir was not qualified use of the property.

[Fisher, 65 TCM 2284, RIA TC Memo. ¶ 93,139 (1993).]

Recapture tax imposed on lease of special-use land to qualified heir's son. Taxpayer was a qualified heir who received ranch property subject to a special-use valuation election and subsequently leased the land to her son. The IRS imposed recapture tax, contending that the special use had ceased.

Held: For the IRS. Upon leasing the ranch property to her son for cash, taxpayer was no longer a material participant with regard to the property. The cash lease was a passive rental activity and constituted a cessation of a qualified use.

[Shaw, TC Memo. (P-H) ¶ 91,372, 62 TCM (CCH) 396 (1991).]

IRS rules on recapture tax consequences of development of subsurface oil and gas interests in farm property that is subject to special-use valuation election under Section 2032A. In a revenue ruling involving three fact situations, the IRS ruled that the grant of the leasehold interest for oil and gas in place, the extraction of the oil, or the disposition of the oil and gas royalty rights does not constitute a disposition of specially valued real property for purposes of the recapture provision contained in Section 2032A(c)(1)(A), because oil and gas interests are not includable as part of farmland that can be specially valued under Section 2032A. To the extent that specially valued farmland is subsequently used for well drilling and extraction, however, this constitutes a cessation of use of specially valued farmland for purposes of the recapture provision in Section 2032A(c)(1)(B).

[Rev. Rul. 88-78, 1988-2 CB 330.]

Lease of inherited farm property does not trigger estate tax recapture. A son inherited a family farm following his mother's death. In 1984, the son executed a crop-sharing agreement with an unrelated farmer under which he leased the property to the farmer in return for a specified percentage of the crops grown. The lease obligated the son to participate in the farming activity personally by being consulted on all aspects of production and use of farm property. In a prior ruling, Private Letter Ruling 8444016, the IRS had concluded that neither the execution of nor the performance under the lease would trigger the imposition of a recapture tax under Section 2032A(c)(1). After the lease in the instant case expired, the parties sought to extend it through the remainder of the recapture period. The IRS stated that neither the execution nor performance under the extended terms of the lease agreement would trigger the imposition of additional estate tax under Section 2032A(c)(1). The IRS emphasized the property's continued use as a farm and the son's active participation in the farm's management.

[Priv. Ltr. Rul. 8939031.]

Additional estate tax is triggered by leases of farmland that are not substantially based upon production. Decedent's children, who were the estate's personal representatives, filed a timely estate tax return on which they elected to value under Section 2032A the farmland in which decedent had had an interest. Decedent's surviving spouse consented to the election. Upon the death of decedent, the surviving spouse became the outright owner of the specially valued property as the result of her survivorship interest in the property that was owned in joint tenancy. She also received an undivided one-half interest in farm property in satisfaction of a marital bequest under decedent's will. She was the life income beneficiary of the residuary trust created by decedent's will. Farmland held by decedent in fee simple was used to fund the residuary trust. Decedent's children were the trustees and remaindermen of the residuary trust. Decedent's children formed a closely held farm corporation in 1980. The specially valued farmland was the subject of a lease between the corporation and decedent's estate and surviving spouse during the 1980 and 1981 crop years. After decedent's estate was closed, the lessors of the farmland were decedent's surviving spouse and the trustees of the residuary trust for the crop years 1982 through 1984. The lease provided for the farm corporation to pay $50 per tillable acre fixed case rent, plus 5 percent of the gross profit from the farm.

The IRS stated that the leases of the farmland for the crop years 1980 through 1984 triggered an additional estate tax under Section 2032A(c)(1)(B). The IRS also stated that decedent's surviving spouse was the indirect owner of the specially valued property that passed to her under decedent's will and of the property that passed to her through the residuary trust. The IRS thus concluded that decedent's surviving spouse must satisfy the qualified-use requirement of Section 2032A with respect to the property that she owned outright and that she owned indirectly through the estate and the residuary trust. Based on Regulation § 20.2032A-3(b)(1), the IRS determined that decedent's surviving spouse was not engaged in the active trade or business of farming, because the leases for the crop years 1980 through 1984 were not substantially based upon production. The IRS stated that the terms of the leases, not the depressed farm economy, caused insignificant profit bonuses to be paid in two of the years at issue. The IRS also concluded that the full value of the qualified real property in the residuary trust was subject to the Section 2032A(c)(1)(B) recapture tax, because the surviving spouse had complete use of the trust property during her life. The IRS further stated that the recapture tax applied to the parcels of specially valued property that the surviving spouse owned outright, because she failed to use the property for a qualified use. The IRS indicated that in recomputing the estate tax liability under Section 2032A(c)(2)(C), the marital deduction was allowable for the value of the qualifying property that actually passed to the surviving spouse within the limitations of Sections 2056(b) and 2056(c). The IRS further stated that the additional estate tax under Section 2032A may not be deferred under Section 6166, and also that Section 6166 applies to the tax imposed by Section 2001, and that the estate tax under Section 2032A(c) is not the same as the Section 2001 estate tax.

[Priv. Ltr. Rul. 8652005.]

[c] Dispositions

Sale of farmland development rights triggers special use valuation recapture. Decedent owned and operated a dairy farm when he died in late 1984. At that time, the property had a FMV of $988,000 based on its highest and best use for development. Its value as a farm was $349,770. Decedent's son was the executor and sole heir of his father's estate. In 1985, he timely filed an estate tax return electing special-use valuation. This resulted in tax savings of $218,328. As required under the Code, decedent's son agreed to be personally liable for any additional estate tax due (the "recapture tax") if he disposed of any interest in the property within ten years of his father's death. On December 21, 1993, decedent's son and the State of New Jersey executed a "Deed of Easement." This gave New Jersey a development easement in the farmland. In return, decedent's son received over $1.4 million. The purchase was made under New Jersey's "Agriculture Retention and Development Act," which was enacted, among other reasons, to strengthen New Jersey's agricultural industry and to preserve farmland in the State. The Deed of Easement specified that the "Grantor" of the easement was decedent's son, both in his individual capacity and as executor of the estate, along with his daughter. It stated that "The Grantor, Grantor's heirs . . . successors and assigns grants and conveys to the Grantee a development easement" on the farmland: The deed expressly prohibited any development of the land for nonagricultural use and provided that the restrictions would be binding on any person to whom title is transferred. The IRS determined that the sale of development rights was a disposition of an interest in the property that triggered the recapture tax. Decedent's son disagreed but he paid the recapture tax and filed a claim for refund. After the IRS disallowed it, he sued in district court and won. The district court observed that, under the applicable New Jersey statute, a development easement is considered an "equitable servitude" and not a true easement. The district court determined that New Jersey treats equitable servitudes as creating contract rights, not property rights. Based on this, it ruled that decedent's son did not part with a real property interest in granting the development easement to the state and that the sale of the development easement was not a disposition of any interest in the farmland under the recapture provision. The IRS argued that the district court erred in holding that decedent's son did not owe the recapture tax because, under New Jersey law, a development easement purportedly gives rise to contract rights as opposed to property rights. The IRS said that once the district court determined that the development easement created rights that were recognized under state law, it should have turned to federal law to determine whether the transfer of those rights was a disposition of an interest triggering recapture tax.

Held: Reversed for the IRS. The Third Circuit agreed with IRS that the district court erred in predicating its decision on the manner in which development easements are classified under New Jersey law. The Third Circuit said that New Jersey law was relevant only to the extent that it defined the development easement that decedent's son deeded to the state. The state law consequences of that definition, however, as well as the state's doctrinal classification of the development easement as an easement, restrictive covenant, equitable servitude, or anything else, have no bearing on the application of the recapture tax provision. Having determined that the development easement is recognized under state law, the district court should have turned to federal law to decide whether the transfer of the development easement constituted a disposition of an interest in farmland for recapture purposes. Relying on well-established principles of property law and estate taxation, the Third Circuit concluded that the conveyance of the development easement was a disposition of an interest in the farm. The court observed that the real property that passed to decedent's son on the death of his father can be viewed in two portions: (1) the "bundle of rights" relating to the agricultural use of the land and (2) the additional value represented by the "bundle of rights" relating to development uses of the land. The Court stressed that if the special use provision did not exist, decedent's son would have been required to pay estate taxes on the entire bundle of rights associated with the farm. He avoided paying estate taxes on the bundle of rights associated with the development uses of the land by electing to value the farm under the special use provision. He did so on the understanding that he would not realize the value of those rights within the ten-year recapture period. In executing the Deed of Easement, however, decedent's son conveyed to New Jersey "all of the nonagricultural development rights and development credits appurtenant to the lands and premises." In exchange for these valuable development rights, he received over $1.4 million. Through this transaction, decedent's son disposed of valuable property rights that the Code would have otherwise taxed when those rights were passed from his father, but did not because of the special use valuation election. Because the disposition occurred within ten years of his father's death, the recapture tax was due.

[Estate of Gibbs, 161 F3d 242, 82 AFTR2d 98-7241 (3d Cir. 1998).]

IRS rules that recapture rules apply when qualified heir disposed of specially valued property to member of decedent's family who was not member of qualified heir's family. Decedent had devised farmland specially valued under Section 2032A to a child of decedent's older sibling. Subsequently, that child sold the farmland to his cousin, that is, to a child of another of decedent's siblings. Under Section 2032A, an executor may elect to value qualified real property used for farming or in a trade or business based on the property's value for its actual use, rather than on its highest and best use. Such an election is made on the federal estate tax return and is irrevocable. The estate tax savings that result from this election must be recaptured if the property is transferred to a nonfamily member. Sales of special-use property to nonfamily members may cause recapture of the estate tax. Under Section 2032A(e)(2), an individual's family includes:

1. An ancestor of the individual.
2. The individual's spouse.
3. A lineal descendant of the individual, of the individual's spouse, or of the individual's parent.
4. The spouse of any of these lineal descendants.

Here the final transferee was a member of decedent's family because he was a lineal descendant of decedent's parent. The family member requirement, however, relates to the qualified heir's family, not to decedent's family. Thus, property can be disposed of only during the recapture period without imposition of the recapture tax if the transfer is to a member of the qualified heir's family. Even though the two transferees were cousins, the second transferee was not a member of the first transferee's family under the definition described above. Therefore, the sale of the farmland by the first transferee to the second transferee was subject to the recapture tax imposed by Section 2032A(c)(1).

[Rev. Rul. 89-22, 1989-1 CB 276.]

IRS rules on sale of farmland by qualified heirs to avoid foreclosure. Decedent left a farm consisting of two tracts of land to qualified heirs. The estate elected both special-use valuation pursuant to Section 2032A and tax deferral under Section 6166. Both tracts were heavily mortgaged. Five years after decedent's death one of the farms was sold to avoid foreclosure. The proceeds were used to retire both mortgages. Under Section 6166(a)(1), if the value of an interest in a closely held business exceeds 35 percent of an estate, the executor may elect to pay the estate tax in ten annual installments starting not more than five years from the date on which the estate tax would otherwise be due. If 50 percent of the business is sold (at once or in installments), Section 6166(g)(1)(A) provides that the balance of the unpaid tax becomes due. In this ruling, however, the IRS concluded that where a sale of encumbered assets is necessary to preserve an ongoing business from creditors, accelerating the tax as a result of such a disposition would be inconsistent with the purposes of Section 6166. Thus, such a sale would not accelerate the tax unless the sales proceeds exceeded the mortgage and accrued interest. In that event, the excess would be an accelerating disposition. The situation was different for purposes of Section 2032A(c), however. According to the IRS, that section has no such flexibility. Thus, because the sale took place within ten years, an additional estate tax would have been imposed based on the increase in value of the property, had it not received special-use valuation. The value of the property, however, could not be more than the price for which it was sold.

[Rev. Rul. 89-4, 1989-1 CB 298.]

IRS rules on recapture tax consequences of development of subsurface oil and gas interests in farm property that is subject to special-use valuation election under Section 2032A. In a revenue ruling involving three fact situations, the IRS ruled that the grant of the leasehold interest for oil and gas in place, the extraction of the oil, or the disposition of the oil and gas royalty rights does not constitute a disposition of specially valued real property for purposes of the recapture provision contained in Section 2032A(c)(1)(A), because oil and gas interests are not includable as part of farmland that can be specially valued under Section 2032A. To the extent that specially valued farmland is subsequently used for well drilling and extraction, however, this constitutes a cessation of use of specially valued farmland for purposes of the recapture provision in Section 2032A(c)(1)(B).

[Rev. Rul. 88-78, 1988-2 CB 330.]

Donation of conservation easement on speciality valued land triggers estate tax recapture. A farm owner died before 1982, leaving the farm to his spouse in fee simple. Decedent's estate elected special-use valuation under Section 2032A. The spouse proposed to donate a conservation easement in perpetuity to a county agricultural preservation board. The IRS stated that the donation of a conservation easement to the preservation board constituted a disposition of an interest in property for purposes of Section 2032A(c)(1)(A). Therefore, the donation would result in the imposition of additional estate tax under Section 2032A(c)(1)(A). The IRS concluded that because the disposition was in the form of a gift, the amount realized was the FMV of the easement at the time of the disposition.

[Priv. Ltr. Rul. 8940011.]

Specially valued property is not subject to recapture tax liability when spouse dies. An individual had created a revocable trust on March 8, 1973. His sons and wife had served as cotrustees until one son died. The second son had continued to serve as trustee after his brother's death. The individual and the spouse had transferred real property to the trust by a warranty deed dated March 10, 1973. The individual died on April 2, 1982, leaving a will incorporating the trust as the device for distributing all of his real property. The trust provided that after decedent's death, the cotrustees were to set aside a separate trust fund equal to the allowable maximum marital deduction. The cotrustees were to pay the entire net income from this trust to the spouse during her lifetime at least quarterly. Additional funds could be distributed as needed. The spouse could distribute the entire accumulated principal in the trust to whomever she pleased through her will. The cotrustees elected to use special-use valuation for all property contributed to the trust by decedent passing under the trust to the spouse. The spouse died on December 1, 1986. A prospective buyer of the property was found, and the heirs requested a ruling on whether the sale of the specially valued property would invoke additional estate tax under Section 2032(A).

The IRS took the position that the sale of the property of the trust subject to special-use valuation would not result in the imposition of the recapture tax. The IRS noted that under Section 2041, when a spouse dies, the recapture tax liability is terminated because the property is included in the spouse's estate. The IRS cited HR Rep. No. 1380, 94th Cong., 2d Sess. 27 (1976), reasoning that the ten-year recapture period in Section 2032A(e)(1) does not apply if the recapture tax consequences at the death of the spouse are identical to the death of the owner of a fee interest, which was the case in the instant situation.

[Priv. Ltr. Rul. 8906033.]

[d] Family transfers and partition

IRS states that sale of farmland by three qualified heirs to one of qualified heirs and that heir's spouse, followed by construction of house thereon, did not constitute disposition or cessation of qualified use. The IRS has ruled that the sale of five acres of farmland from three qualified heirs to one of the qualified heirs and that heir's spouse, followed by construction of their house thereon, did not constitute a disposition or cessation of qualified use under Section 2032A(c) with respect to the five-acre parcel.

[Rev. Rul. 85-66, 1985-1 CB 324.]

Specially valued property can be partitioned without triggering additional tax under Section 2032A(c)(1). A quarter-interest in farm property that was included in an estate under special-use valuation could be partitioned into a fee simple interest without triggering the additional tax under Section 2032A(c)(1). The quarter-interest, originally held in trust for the benefit of a qualified heir, but transferred to her outright on the termination of the trust, would continue to be farmed by the husband of the qualified heir. Therefore, the IRS concluded that partitioning the quarter-interest into a fee interest was an exchange for a qualified interest under Section 2032A(i), with the result being that no additional tax would be imposed. The partition would necessitate a modification of the agreement required by Section 2032A(a)(1)(B), under which the persons having an interest in the specially valued property consent to the imposition of the additional tax under the conditions specified in Section 2032A(c)(1). However, the IRS declined to determine exactly how the agreement should be amended, noting that this responsibility lay with the district director, who would also have to determine whether the lien arising under Section 6234B as a result of the special-use valuation should be released.

[Priv. Ltr. Rul. 8933019.]

Recapture tax is not imposed on marital trust's lease of specially valued farm property to decedent's spouse. Decedent had owned a special-use valuation farm realty that, under his will, was administered by a marital trust. The trust would distribute its entire net income to decedent's wife for her life. At her death, some of the property would go to decedent's daughter, with the remainder being shared by the daughter and decedent's stepdaughter. A trust company was the trustee of the marital trust and the co-executor of the estate. The trustee proposed to execute a ten-year crop and livestock share lease under which the wife would perform all management duties and supply cash to operate the farm. The marital trust would supply the land. The lease would allocate profits and losses 90 percent to the wife and 10 percent to the trust.

The IRS concluded that the estate's distribution of the farm realty to the trust, with the trust's subsequent lease of the realty to the wife, would not result in the imposition of the recapture tax under Section 2032A(c)(1)(B). The IRS noted that the wife, as a qualified heir, had a present interest in the trust and an equity interest in the crop and livestock operation, because her return under the lease was a function of what the realty produced.

[Priv. Ltr. Rul. 8724017.]

Section 2032A(c) recapture provisions are inapplicable to exchange of one-half interests in farmland for separate parcels. An individual died, and his will provided for an undivided one-half interest in a parcel of land passing to a trust. The other undivided interest in the land was owned by decedent's grandson and his wife. The beneficiaries of the trust were decedent's children and grandchildren. The grandson, who owned the one-half interest, farmed the parcel under an oral agreement. Decedent's estate timely filed a federal estate tax return election to specially value decedent's agricultural real estate under Section 2032A. The IRS filed a federal estate tax lien on decedent's undivided parcel of land sixteen months after the estate tax return was filed. The grandson and his wife subsequently executed a mortgage on their one-half interest in the undivided parcel of land as security for the loan. The title opinion disclosed that the IRS claimed a lien on the one-half interest held by the trust. In 1986, the bank refused to grant an additional loan to the grandson and his wife based upon the security of their one-half interest in the land. The issue then arose whether the bank held a first mortgage on the one-half interest of the mortgagors. The parties proposed to resolve the issue by having the trust enter into a voluntary partition agreement with the grandson and his wife under which the trust would become the sole owner of the south half of the parcel and the couple would become the sole owners of the north half of the parcel. The partition would be completed through an exchange of deeds. The result would be a separation of interests, leaving each party the outright owner of a separate parcel of land. The partition would not impair the IRS's lien, in that the IRS could cause the lien to attach to the entire south half of the parcel. The separate interests would not have a lesser value than the undivided one-half interests.

The IRS concluded that no additional estate tax would be imposed, because the recapture provisions of Section 2032A(c) did not apply to the exchange. The IRS noted that the exchange would result in an interest in qualified real property being exchanged for an interest in qualified exchange property. Furthermore, "replaced property" would be exchanged for an interest in "qualified replacement property."
[Priv. Ltr. Rul. 8722046.]

Proposed partition of inherited farmland does not constitute disposition.
Two siblings inherited, as tenants in common, farmland consisting of three parcels. Since decedent's death, the property had been continuously and exclusively farmed by one of the siblings and his son. Decedent's estate elected special-use valuation for the farm property. The siblings proposed to partition the parcels as follows: Each sibling would acquire fee simple title to one parcel, and each sibling would also acquire fee simple in one-half of the acreage of the remaining parcel. Residences located on each of the parcels would be similarly transferred, and farming operations would continue on the land as before, but also pursuant to a crop rental agreement between the siblings.

The IRS stated that the proposed partition would not be a disposition under Sections 2032A(c) and 2032A(e)(2). The IRS also indicated that the continued farming operations by one of the siblings and his son would be a qualified use of the property. In addition, the IRS concluded that the siblings would be liable for any additional tax under Section 2032A(c) for parcels acquired in fee simple, but not for parcels disposed of in the partition. The IRS further concluded that the proposed partition would not cause acceleration of estate tax otherwise subject to the installment election under Section 6166(g). Finally, the IRS relied on Revenue Ruling 79-44, 1979-1 CB 265, to conclude that the proposed transfers of farmland incident to the partition would generate neither gain nor loss under Section 1031.
[Priv. Ltr. Rul. 8713029.]

CHAPTER 3

Annuities and Employee Benefits

¶ 3.01 ANNUITIES

[1] Generally

Ninth Circuit holds that Tax Court erred in recharacterizing annuity transactions as transfers in trust with retention of income. Taxpayers appealed from a Tax Court decision holding that transfers of common stock were not sales in exchange for annuities, but instead were transfers in trust subject to retained annual payments. Taxpayers decided to transfer common stock to foreign situs trusts in exchange for an undertaking to pay to the transferors a private annuity. Taxpayers sought thereby to obtain certain tax benefits. For purposes of calculating their income taxes, taxpayers treated the transfers of common stock to the two trusts as sales in exchange for annuities in which no gain or loss was recognized as of the date of the transfer. They maintained that the transaction should be taxed in accordance with Section 72. The Tax Court rejected taxpayers' contention that the transfers were sales in exchange for annuities and held that the transactions constituted transfers in trust with retained rights to annual payments. The Tax Court held that taxpayers were the true settlors of the two trusts. Consequently, the Tax Court concluded that the entire income of the trusts was taxable to them under the grantor trust provisions of Sections 671 and 677(a).

    Held: Reversed and remanded for taxpayers. The Ninth Circuit ruled that the case should be governed by LaFargue, 689 F2d 845 (9th Cir. 1982); the Tax Court had erred in recharacterizing the annuity transactions as transfers in trust with retention of income.

[Stern, 747 F2d 555, 54 AFTR2d 84-6412, 84-2 USTC ¶ 9949 (9th Cir. 1984).]

First Circuit strikes down attempt to use trust as "buyer" of property for later sale in exchange for "annuity." Taxpayer was an archbishop and the head of the Syrian Church of Antioch in North America. He owned the Dead Sea Scrolls. In 1951, he transferred the scrolls to a trust, naming himself and another individual as co-trustees with the power to sell, rent, exchange, or hold the scrolls at their discretion. He also reserved the power to deal in any way he saw fit with trust income, and provided that the trust was subject to his power to amend, revoke, or modify without restriction. In the following year, 1952, he amended the trust by relinquishing his rights to principal and income in exchange for an annuity in the amount of $10,000 per year and, on his death, $2,500 per year to his mother. In addition, the trust was to pay all excess annual income to his church. By express provision, the 1952 amendment also provided that taxpayer could no longer amend or revoke the trust, except to reduce the amount of his or his mother's annual payments. Nearly two years later the scrolls were sold for $250,000, and the proceeds were invested in securities. During taxable years 1951 through 1953, the trust made no distributions to taxpayer whatsoever. In 1954, the only distribution consisted of two $15,000 payments ostensibly for his expenses in effecting the sale. In both 1955 and 1956, the trust made $10,000 in distributions to him out of income or principal. Upon examining taxpayer's 1954 personal and fiduciary returns, the IRS determined that capital gains of $123,652 should have been reported and taxed. The case was first heard in the Tax Court, which found that taxpayer was personally taxable on the gain under the grantor trust rules set forth in Section 677(a). Section 677(a) provides that the grantor of trust property will be taxable where the trust's income is or may be either currently distributed to him or accumulated for his personal benefit. On appeal, taxpayer vigorously disputed the Tax Court's decision. He contended that the formation of the trust and the later provision for the payment of annuity should be characterized as a sale of the scrolls to the trust in return for the annuity.

Held: Affirmed for the IRS. Taxpayer's transfer of the scrolls to the trust was in no respect a sale. It was clear that taxpayer sought only to set up a trust to provide himself and his mother with income. Consequently, for tax purposes, the sale of the scrolls must be taxed to the taxpayer under the grantor trust rules in Section 677(a). The court observed that the creation of the trust and the subsequent amendment were two separate events that cannot be said to have been part of a single integrated plan. Furthermore, the amendment alone was ineffective to change the settlor-trust relationship into one of creditor and annuitant.

[Samuel, 306 F2d 682, 9 AFTR2d 1840, 62-2 USTC ¶ 9557 (1st Cir. 1962).]

Tax Court applies Ninth Circuit's view in upholding foreign trust and annuity plan. For two years prior to her death on February 21, 1977, decedent had been repeatedly hospitalized for treatment of serious heart problems. On September 19, 1975, five days prior to a coronary bypass operation, decedent had executed numerous documents, including her last will and testament and two agreements relating to the creation of a foreign trust and annuity plan. The trust was irrevocable, and decedent had named her four sons and their lineal descendants as beneficiaries. At the same time, decedent had entered into an annuity agreement with a foreign bank, which also served as her trustee. Under the terms of the annuity, the bank had agreed to pay her $2,378 per week for the rest of her life. In exchange, decedent had agreed to transfer assets to the trust totalling $1.15 million. Following the establishment of the trust and annuity, there had been "administrative problems" in carrying out the terms of the annuity agreement, and the bank on occasion had failed to make timely payments and missed some payments altogether. These missing and late payments had given decedent rights as a creditor against the bank. In addition, there had been delays in transferring decedent's assets to the bank, and as a result decedent had received some interest on investments that legally belonged to the trust. Following her death in 1977, the estate did not report the transfer of assets to the trust as a taxable transfer. The IRS assessed a deficiency, contending that for tax purposes, decedent had not purchased an annuity, but instead had retained a life estate in the transferred properties. On this basis, the IRS maintained that the value of the transferred properties was subject to U.S. estate tax under the provisions of Section 2036.

Held: For the estate. In the Tax Court's view, the critical question was whether the disputed transaction should have been treated as an annuity or as a retained life estate in the property. The court noted that the instant case was appealable to the Ninth Circuit, which had reversed the Tax Court in two dramatically similar cases, Stern, 77 TC 614 (1981), rev'd, 747 F2d 555, 54 AFTR2d 84-6412, 84-2 USTC ¶ 9949 (9th Cir. 1984); and LaFargue, 73 TC 40 (1979), rev'd in part, 689 F2d 845, 50 AFTR2d 82-5944, 82-2 USTC ¶ 9622 (9th Cir. 1982), aff'd, 800 F2d 936 (9th Cir. 1986). The Ninth Circuit adopted the position that despite any irregularities in the conduct of trust or annuity administration, the key test of an annuity's validity is whether the annuity payments were simply a conduit for trust income. In both *Stern* and *La Fargue*, the Ninth Circuit found that the annuities and trusts were valid because there was no tie-in between the amount of the annuity and the trust's income. In the instant case, the Tax Court concluded that the fixed and certain payments required under decedent's annuity plan were of the same type approved by the Ninth Circuit. Therefore, under Golsen, 54 TC 742, aff'd, 445 F2d 985 (10th Cir.), cert, denied, 404 US 940 (1971), the Tax Court was constrained to enter judgment for the estate without reference to the court's decision in Lazarus, 58 TC 854 (1972), which expresses a substantially different approach.

[Estate of Fabric, 83 TC 932 (1984).]

Tax Court, following reversal, enters judgment in case involving proper tax characterization of transfer to trust. In February 1971, taxpayer established a $100 trust. The trust agreement provided for independent trustees, and taxpayer's daughter was the named beneficiary. Taxpayer was neither a trustee nor a beneficiary under the terms of the trust. A few days after establishing the trust, taxpayer executed an annuity agreement with the trustees. Pursuant to that agreement, she transferred property worth $335,000 to the trustees in exchange for annual lifetime payments of $16,502. The property included non-income-producing land, proceeds from a business liquidation, and assorted stocks and municipal bonds. Both the initial creation of the trust and the subsequent transfer of the property were integral parts of a prearranged plan designed to minimize taxpayer's tax liability. The Tax Court characterized the $16,502 annual payments as distributions of trust income, taxable to the grantor under Sections 671 and 677(a). Taxpayer contended on appeal, however, that the Tax Court improperly characterized the transfer of her property to the trust, and the Ninth Circuit reversed, finding that the facts did not justify the Tax Court's recharacterization of the property. According to the Ninth Circuit, the formal agreement comported with the actual structure of the transaction and accurately reflected its substance. The formal agreement concerning the transfer of taxpayer's property to the trustees established her status as a creditor of the trust. Under the agreement, she was required to transfer the property, and in exchange, the trustees were required to pay her $16,502 annually. The $16,502 payments had been made each year, and the payments had not fluctuated with the trust income. The fundamental annuity obligation had not been ignored or modified. Absent some indication that the annuity payment agreed upon was a mere disguise for transferring the income of the trust to the grantor, rather than a payment for the property transferred, there was no justification for disregarding the formal structure of the transaction as a sale in exchange for an annuity. The Tax Court's conclusion that taxpayer had sold the property for less than she might have if the beneficiary of the trust had been a stranger did not alter the fundamental structure of the transaction as a sale in exchange for an annuity. The facts showed that the fundamental transfer and annuity obligations of the contract were being met and that taxpayer relinquished control over the property transferred. The case was remanded for a determination of the income tax consequences attending the annual annuity payments and the sale of the property to the trust.

Held: On remand, the Tax Court adopted the findings of the IRS and treated the transaction as a part-sale, part-gift undertaking, deciding that the present value of the annuity was $176,990. Accordingly, the court treated this amount as taxpayer's investment in the property. The court then applied an exclusion ratio of 52.8 percent, and $7,778 of the $16,502 annual payment was required to be included in gross income.

[LaFargue, TC Memo. (P-H) ¶ 85,090, 49 TCM (CCH) 839 (1985), aff'd, 800 F2d 936, 58 AFTR2d 86-5859, 86-2 USTC ¶ 9715 (9th Cir. 1986).]

Trusts that made annuity payments with funds borrowed from the grantors did not qualify as GRATs. *A* and his spouse, *B*, each established and funded multiple trusts with stock. These trusts purported to be grantor retained annuity trusts (GRATs). The grantors also created separate "administrative trusts" to coordinate the GRAT payments. Each quarter, *A* and *B* loaned cash to the administrative trusts. *A*, as trustee, would receive the cash and execute promissory notes to *A* and *B*. *A* would then use the cash to pay himself and *B* the required annuity payments. After the cash returned back to *A* and *B*, the net effect was that the trusts transferred notes to *A* and *B* in lieu of making the required annuity payments.

The IRS ruled that, in substance, *A* and *B* retained the right to receive an annuity payable in the form of notes from each trust. This retained interest was not a qualified annuity interest within Section 2702. Therefore, the trusts did not qualify as GRATs under Section 2702 because the annuity payments were to be made with funds borrowed from the grantors.

[Tech. Adv. Mem. 9604005.]

Grantor's reversion prevents gain on sales with trust. By retaining a reversion worth more than 5 percent of the initial value of a GRAT, a grantor ensured that she would not recognize gain on distributions of appreciated property from the trust in satisfaction of her annuity, or on a sale with the trust. Taxpayer transferred stock to separate trusts for her three children. (Her husband established identical trusts with the same results.) Each trust provided taxpayer with an annuity equal to 13.34 percent of the initial fair market value (FMV) of the trust, payable quarterly for eleven years or until her death, if earlier. The annuity was payable from income and then from principal. At the end of eleven years, each trust continued for the benefit of the child. If taxpayer died before the expiration of the eleven-year term, however, the trust property reverted to her estate. Taxpayer had a power, in a nonfiduciary capacity, to reacquire trust assets by substituting property of equivalent value.

The trusts incorporated the provisions for a qualified annuity under Regulations § 25.2702-3(b): (1) A fixed percentage of the initial value of the trust as determined for gift tax purposes was payable to the annuity holder at least annually (or the annuity could have been a stated dollar amount, and in either case the annuity could have increased within limits); (2) the annuity was payable for a specified number of years or the life of the annuity holder, or whichever was shorter; (3) additions to the trust were prohibited; (4) communication of the annuity was prohibited; (5) the annuity was prorated during short years; and (6) no distributions could be made to anyone other than the annuity holder during the annuity term.

Because each annuity was a qualified annuity interest under Section 2702, its value was subtracted from the FMV of the stock transferred to the trust in determining the gift; otherwise, the entire transfer in trust would have been a gift. Taxpayer was age 54 (on her nearest birthday) at the time of the transfer and, using the applicable federal rate (7.6 percent for September 1995), each annuity had a value equal to 94.86 percent of the initial corpus of the trust. In addition, each reversion to taxpayer's estate (if she did not survive the eleven-year term) had a value equal to 5.003 percent of the initial FMV. The reversions did not reduce the value of the gifts, but they did provide several advantages. Since each reversion exceeded 5 percent of the initial trust corpus, under Section 673 and Regulations § 1.671-3(b)(3), the trusts were entirely owned by the grantor (taxpayer) as to both capital gains and ordinary income. In this circumstance, the grantor is the actual owner of the trust's assets for income tax purposes and cannot recognize gain on a transaction with the trust, according to Revenue Ruling 85-13, 1985-1 CB 184.

Therefore, the IRS ruled that taxpayer would not recognize gain on the payment of an annuity with property or on a sale between herself and a trust. Thus, although the annuity was set at a high rate, taxpayer was assured that if there was insufficient income to provide for the annuity and it was paid by distributing appreciated stock in satisfaction of the shortfall, there would not be a taxable sale. Furthermore, taxpayer could repurchase the shares at FMV from the trusts, so there would be a step-up in basis in her estate for the shares, without recognizing gain. In addition, if taxpayer died before her interest terminated, there would be an inclusion in her estate. If there was no reversion to taxpayer's estate, the trusts would continue for the benefit of the children and estate tax would then be payable. The reversion enables taxpayer to take advantage of the marital deduction by providing the husband (if he survives) with a qualifying interest.

[Priv. Ltr. Rul. 9551018.]

[2] Valuation

Use of actuarial tables to value survivor annuity is upheld. For purposes of inclusion in decedent's gross estate, taxpayer sought to value a private joint and survivor annuity based on its FMV, which would be minimal, because the survivor was seventy-one years old. The IRS argued that a private joint and survivor annuity must be determined by reference to the actuarial tables in the regulations.

    Held: For the IRS. The value of a private joint and survivor annuity is determined by the actuarial tables in the regulations unless their use would be arbitrary.

[Estate of Bell, 46 AFTR2d 80-6148, 80-2 USTC ¶ 13,356 (ED Wash. 1980).]

Annuity value is not changed by annuitant's reduced life expectancy due to cancer. Decedent's spouse, who had an operation for breast cancer prior to her husband's death, received an annuity under an agreement between decedent and his employer. The IRS included that annuity in the estate. The estate asserted that the value of the annuity should be reduced because the spouse had only a five-year life expectancy.

    Held: For the IRS. The mortality tables for women who have had breast cancer cannot be used to determine the life expectancy of the widow for purposes of annuity valuation.

[Estate of Jones, TC Memo. (P-H) ¶ 77,087, 36 TCM (CCH) 380 (1977).]

IRS rules that annuity has no value. Taxpayer created a trust for the benefit of his relatives. The trustee has the power to appoint trust income and principal in amounts and at times as he sees fit. Taxpayer gave the trust an amount sufficient to purchase an annuity on his life at $800 per month, in return for the trustee's promise to pay taxpayer $800 per month out of the trust corpus.

The IRS ruled that the entire amount given to the trust is a taxable gift. Because the trust principal can be appointed at any time, the annuity has no value.

[Rev. Rul. 76-491, 1976-2 CB 301.]

IRS explains when valuation tables cannot be used. The IRS issued final regulations on exceptions to the use of the IRS actuarial tables for valuing annuities and other interests. The regulations modify a ruling defining a terminally ill individual, whose life expectancy cannot be determined under the tables. Section 7520(a) provides for the valuation of annuities, term interests, and remainder and reversionary interests under tables published by the IRS for income, gift, and estate tax purposes. The final regulations provide that the tables cannot be used for valuing an annuity, income, remainder, or reversionary interest relating to an individual who is "terminally ill" at the time of the transaction. An individual is terminally ill if known to be afflicted with an incurable illness or other deteriorating physical condition and there is at least a 50 percent chance of death within one year. This was the test under the proposed regulations. However, the final regulations add that an individual who survives for eighteen months is presumed not to have been terminally ill unless the contrary is shown by clear and convincing evidence. The 50 percent chance of death within a year test tightens the IRS's earlier standard, in Revenue Ruling 80-80, 1980-1 CB 194, under which an individual who had more than a negligible chance of surviving for one year was not terminally ill. Thus, a person with an incurable disease that was likely to prove fatal within a year could sell property for an annuity, valued under tables that assumed a normal life expectancy, provided there was a more than negligible prospect of survival for a year. The 1980 ruling is superseded for decedents who have died or transactions that have taken place after December 31, 1995, according to Revenue Ruling 96-3, 1996-1 CB 348. The regulations became effective December 31, 1995.

As a corollary to the terminal illness exception, the tables cannot be used if decedent and an individual who is a measuring life die as a result of a common accident. Thus, if a decedent's will provides for the payment of income to a surviving spouse for life and the spouses die in a common accident, a presumption in the will that the spouse survived a common accident, or even proof of the spouse's survival, will not permit the annuity tables to be used in valuing the spouse's interest. The regulations amplify the IRS position that an annuity that will be exhausted before an annuitant reaches age 110 (the maximum table life) must be valued as the right to receive an annuity for the shorter of the life of the annuitant or the date the corpus will be exhausted, following Revenue Ruling 77-454, 1977-2 CB 351. Thus, an annuity of 10 percent a year payable to charity for the life of a sixty-year-old donor from a $1 million trust (when the Section 7520 rate for the month of the transfer is 6.8 percent) has a value of only $867,000, under Regulations § 25.7520-3(b)(2)(v), Example 5. This figure results because the corpus will be exhausted after making seventeen full payments and one partial payment, and the payments must be discounted to present value. This approach makes it virtually impossible ever to "zero out" a GRAT. On the other hand, if an annuity, expressed as a percentage of the initial corpus, does not exceed the Section 7520 rate, but is payable from a trust consisting of nonproductive property that the trustee is authorized to retain, it is considered to be payable, and the tables can be used, under Regulations § 1.7520-3(b)(4), Example 1. The regulations provide that the tables cannot be used unless the degree of beneficial enjoyment is consistent with the character of the interest being valued. Section 2702 minimizes this issue because a retained interest is not deducted from the value of a gift unless it is an annuity interest. Nevertheless, it still may be necessary to value an income interest to determine the gift tax exclusion or the Section 2013 credit for a tax on a prior transfer. Therefore, additional guidance is provided on when the requisite beneficial enjoyment is present.

[TD 8630, 1996-1 CB 339.]

¶ 3.02 EMPLOYEE PLANS AND BENEFITS

[1] Excludable Benefits

Section 2039, prior to 1978 amendments, is held to exclude pension payments from insurance proceeds. At the time of decedent's death in 1978, he was a salaried employee of a stevedoring company with thirty-seven years of service. He had been a participant in a pension plan qualified under Section 401(a) that was funded by six life insurance policies on his life. Because he died prior to retirement, decedent's benefits were paid over to an inter vivos trust in the amount of $196,606, representing the full face amount of the life insurance policies. The trust had been created by decedent to provide support payments for his estranged wife. At no time did the trustee or the executor elect to have the insurance proceeds treated as a lump-sum distribution under Section 402(e)(4)(B). The IRS contended that the insurance proceeds were includable in the gross estate under Section 2042. The estate, however, argued that the proceeds fell within Section 2039(c), which excludes qualified plan annuities unless they are paid through a Section 402(e)(4) lump-sum distribution. The district court ruled for the estate.

Held: Affirmed for the estate. Both courts stated that the issue presented was whether the insurance policy proceeds constituted a Section 402(e)(4) "lump-sum distribution." Although Section 402(e)(4)(A), in defining the term, clearly embraces the policy payments in question, Section 402(e)(4)(B) further provides that the taxpayer must make an affirmative election in order for Section 402 to apply. For this reason, the estate, noting that there had been no such election, argued that the proceeds did not fall within the definition and that they were therefore excludable under Section 2039(c). The IRS maintained that only Section 402(e)(4)(A) was relevant for purposes of Section 2039(c) and that its position was supported by Regulations § 20.2039-3(b). The appeals court concluded that the reference to Section 402(e)(4) in Section 2039(c) must be read on its face to encompass all of Section 402(e)(4), including Sections 402(e)(4)(A) and 402(e)(4)(B). The court adopted the reasoning of Giardino, 47 AFTR2d 81-1580, 80-2 USTC ¶ 13,383 (D. Md. 1980), aff'd per curiam, 661 F2d 921 (4th Cir. 1981), and found no requirement that the disputed payments be included in the gross estate. The court also noted that subsequent amendments to Section 2039 were inapplicable to decedent's estate.

[Giardino, 776 F2d 406, 56 AFTR2d 85-6603, 85-2 USTC ¶ 13,647 (2d Cir. 1985).]

Election to exclude a lump-sum distribution of qualified plan annuities from gross estate is held not to be affected by nonfraudulent erroneous tax treatment of distribution by taxpayer. In 1981, the executors of decedent's estate elected to exclude from the gross estate the value of a lump-sum annuities distribution consisting of Keogh benefits and pension trust funds. The recipients of such distribution filed affirmations of their intent to treat the distribution, in accordance with Section 2039(f)(2), as ordinary income without benefit of ten-year income averaging or capital gains treatment. One of the recipients, however, filed a return claiming both capital gains treatment and ten-year averaging. The IRS requested that he refile his return in accordance with the election filed by the estate. The recipient asked the accountant who prepared the first return to prepare an amended return consistent with the IRS's instructions. The accountant prepared such a return without using ten-year averaging, but still using capital gains treatment of the distribution. The IRS then took the position that the estate's election was void and included the value of the lump-sum distributions in gross estate. Evidence indicated that the erroneous treatment of the distribution on the recipient's returns was not due to his fraud, deceit, or negligence.

Held: For the taxpayer. In the absence of fraud, deceit, or taxpayer negligence, the good faith attempts by an estate and its recipients to elect Section 2039(f)(2) tax treatment constitute a binding election, notwithstanding the subsequent erroneous treatment by a recipient's personal accountant of a portion of the annuities distribution.

[Martin, 638 F. Supp. 1220, 58 AFTR2d 86-6337, 86-2 USTC ¶ 13,679 (CD Cal. 1986).]

Municipal education board is held to be exempt organization for purposes of excluding annuity under Section 2039. Decedent had been a teacher employed by the New York City Board of Education prior to her death in 1976. As a participant in the Board's tax deferred annuity program, decedent had authorized the Board to withhold amounts from income for the purchase of her annuity contract, which was qualified for preferential income tax treatment under Section 403(b) because it had been purchased by the Board. After decedent died, an annuity benefit of $28,411 was paid to a named beneficiary. The estate initially reported the annuity payment in decedent's gross estate but later amended its estate tax return, contending that the benefit was excludable under Section 2039(c)(3). The IRS rejected the refund claim, and the matter was submitted to the Tax Court.

Held: For the estate. Section 2039(c)(3) provides an exclusion from a gross estate for the value of an annuity receivable by any beneficiary under a retirement annuity contract purchased for an employee by an employer exempt under Section 501(a). The IRS took the position that the Board was not an exempt educational organization, because it had never "established" its exemption by filing for a determination letter or ruling to that effect, and that the Board was not an "educational organization" as defined in Section 170. The Tax Court rejected both arguments. Without question, it held, a municipal board of education falls within the scope of Section 501(a) as evidenced by clearly stated legislative history and congressional intent. In addition, there was no basis for the IRS to impose harsh sanctions on annuity recipients where a public employer does not file for a ruling or administrative determination of its exempt status.

[Estate of Green, 82 TC 843 (1984).]

Beneficiaries cannot change their respective income tax treatment of decedent's lump-sum distribution from qualified plan. One of the assets of decedent's estate was a lump-sum death benefit under a qualified plan that he bequeathed to his son and daughter. On their respective 1980 income tax returns, the son treated his share of this amount as ordinary income, but the daughter reported her share as capital gain under Section 402(a)(2). The son subsequently amended his return to reflect capital gain treatment of his share under Section 402(a)(2). Subsequently, the IRS denied the estate's election of Section 2039(c) benefits to exclude from gross estate that portion of qualified plan payments receivable by a beneficiary. The IRS did so on the ground that decedent's son and daughter had both failed to elect Section 2039(f) treatment of their shares of the lump-sum payment as ordinary income under Section 402(a).

Held: The estate was permitted to elect Section 2039(c) benefits as to the son's share of such payment, but not as to the daughter's. Prior to the May 11, 1984 amendment of Regulations § 20.2039-4, the IRS took the position that a Section 2039(f) election must have been made on the beneficiary's income tax return reflecting treatment of his share of the distribution as ordinary income. Once the Section 2039(f) election was made, it could not be revoked. Accordingly, decedent's son could not revoke the initial ordinary income treatment of his share of the payment, and thus the estate was permitted to claim the benefits of Section 2039(c) as to the son's share. The daughter's willingness to change her initial treatment of her share arose after the statute of limitations had passed, and ordinary income treatment of her share of the distribution was never reflected in an income tax return for 1980. Accordingly, it was presumed that she never intended to make such an election, and no election was thereafter allowable.

[Estate of Bennett, TC Memo. (P-H) ¶ 86,425, 52 TCM (CCH) 425 (1986).]

Black-lung benefits payable to surviving spouse are not includable in decedent's estate. Pursuant to the Federal Coal Mine Health and Safety Act of 1969, decedent's spouse received monthly benefit payments after decedent died of black-lung disease. Decedent had no voice in the designation of beneficiaries. The benefits were payable from government appropriations or by the employer as in traditional workmen's compensation, and not from any fund in which decedent had a vested interest. As a result of these benefit characteristics the payments were not property in which decedent had an interest at the time of death within the meaning of Section 2033 and were not includable in decedent's estate.

[Rev. Rul. 76-102, 1976-1 CB 272.]

Decedent's individual retirement accounts payable to nonspousal beneficiaries are excludable from decedent's gross estate. An individual had taken no distributions from either of two individual retirement accounts (IRAs) that were located in two banks and that totaled less than $100,000 at the date of his death in 1984. The individual's will provided that distributions under the IRA plans should go equally to two nonspousal beneficiaries if the decedent were to die prior to receiving all of the distributions under the IRA plans. Each of the written plans governing the IRAs stipulated that the beneficiaries were required to withdraw the entire balance within a five-year period. The beneficiaries notified the banks where the IRAs were located to elect to have the account distributed to them over a thirty- to sixty-month period. They each asked that they be sent a monthly amount beginning after the date of decedent's death. The beneficiaries submitted affidavits indicating that these elections were irrevocable.

The IRS stated that the estate could exclude under Section 2039(e) the value of the IRAs, having found that the irrevocable elections to exclude the funds were properly made and that the election allowed for a "qualifying annuity" under Regulations § 20.2039-5(b). The IRS noted that the exclusions from the gross estate were allowed to the extent that distributions were not reduced by formula for contributions made by decedent to the IRAs for deductions disallowed under Section 219. The IRS also noted that the beneficiaries had submitted an affidavit of irrevocability of election to receive the periodic payments.

[Priv. Ltr. Rul. 8706007.]

[2] Includable Benefits

Survivor benefits payable to deceased employee's widow are held to be taxable under Section 2039(a) as part of deceased employee's estate. Decedent died in 1979 and was survived by his wife and daughter. He had been employed continuously since 1953 by International Business Machines Corporation (IBM). IBM maintained a variety of employee benefit plans, including a group life insurance and survivor's income benefit plan, a retirement plan, a sickness and accident income plan, and a total and permanent disability income plan. As a result of decedent's death, his surviving spouse received payments of $411 per month under the retirement plan, plus a life insurance benefit of $50,000 and $702 per month in survivor's benefits. The estate included the then-present value of the survivors' income benefit in the gross estate, resulting in estate taxes of $3,593. Subsequently, the estate filed for a refund, claiming that the present value of the survivors' income benefit should not have been included in the gross estate and that $3,593 was overpaid. The issue in the district court was whether the survivors' benefits payable by a company to its deceased employee's widow are taxable under Section 2039(a), dealing with the inclusion of annuities in the gross estate, where the deceased employee during his lifetime had contingent future rights to disability benefits while employed.

Held: For the IRS. It was appropriate to group the survivor benefits plan with the disability plan for purposes of applying Section 2039. Payments under the employer's disability plan could be characterized as post-employment benefits constituting an annuity or other payment under Section 2039. At the time of his death, decedent had the right to receive disability payments within the meaning of Section 2039. The inclusion of the present value of the survivors' income benefit in gross estate was proper in light of the legislative history of Section 2039 and relevant case law.

[Looney, 569 F. Supp. 1569, 52 AFTR2d 83-6451, 83-2 USTC ¶ 13,538 (MD Ga. 1983).]

Spouse's annuity is included in shareholder's estate. Decedent had been a director of a corporation in which he owned 83 percent of the voting stock. Approximately one month prior to decedent's death, the board of directors had adopted a plan providing for the payment of an annuity to the surviving spouses of corporate officers who met certain eligibility requirements and died while still employed by the company. The plan could have been amended or terminated by the board. At the time of adoption, decedent had been the only eligible officer. Upon decedent's death, the corporation began paying the annuity to his widow. The IRS contended that the benefit was includable in the estate of decedent as a revocable transfer under Section 2038. Section 2038 provides that a revocable transfer is includable in the decedent's estate where the decedent:

1. Held a property interest in the annuity.
2. Transferred the property interest.
3. Retained a power to amend or terminate the transfer.

Held: For the IRS. With respect to the first element of Section 2038, the court concluded that decedent, in remaining in the employment of the company, had effectively accepted the company's offer to make the annuity payments. This meant that the annuity was procured as a result of decedent rendering services to the company and was deferred compensation. The estate contended that the plan was revocable and was not a property interest, but merely an "expectancy" of a future benefit. The court noted, however, that (1) the plan's terms seemed to indicate that no amendment could be made having an adverse impact on the benefit without the written consent of the eligible officer and his spouse and (2) the fact that decedent owned 80 percent of the corporation's stock made it highly unlikely that the plan would be terminated without his approval. The third element for inclusion in an estate pursuant to Section 2038 is that decedent must have retained the power to "alter, amend, revoke, or terminate" the transfer. The court noted that though decedent did not have such a right in his individual capacity, as the majority shareholder he was able to do so in conjunction with other members of the board of directors. The court believed that the ability of the other board members to go against decedent's wishes was largely illusory. In rejecting the IRS's attempt to impose a gift tax, the court concluded, however, that because of this retained power, there had been no completed gift during decedent's lifetime.

[Estate of Levin, 90 TC 723 (1988), aff'd without published opinion, 891 F2d 281 (3d Cir. 1989).]

Survivor death benefit is includable in decedent's estate because of recipient's special capital gains treatment on his income tax return. Decedent had been an employee of the City of New York and a participant in a qualified pension plan. Decedent was entitled to a combination of retirement income and death benefits for his survivors. Moreover, he had been allowed to choose among specified options that would increase the death benefit to the detriment of his retirement income or vice versa. Upon his retirement in 1974, decedent had selected an option that set aside a total of $50,000 in lump-sum benefits for his son ($25,000) and his three grandsons ($8,333 each). Until the time of his death, decedent had been permitted to change the beneficiary of such benefits. Decedent died in 1981, and the lump-sum death benefits were paid to his son and grandsons. The estate did not include the lump-sum death benefits in decedent's gross estate. Upon receipt of his share of the death benefit, the son reported it as capital gain pursuant to Section 402(a)(2); however, he did not use ten-year averaging. The IRS included this $25,000 in decedent's gross estate.

Held: For the IRS. The general rule under Section 2039 is that death benefits such as these are includable in the decedent-employee's gross estate. Under Section 2039(c), however, certain benefits are excludable from the gross estate. Under the facts, the lump sum received by the son at least initially qualified for exclusion and would be excludable if Section 2039(f)(2) were inapplicable. Section 2039(f)(2) denies an exclusion where the recipient treats the lump-sum death benefit on his income tax return using the special capital gains treatment available under Section 402(a)(2) or the ten-year averaging permitted by Section 402(e). Here decedent's son used the Section 402(a)(2) special capital gains treatment. Accordingly, Section 2039(f)(2) required the benefit to be included in decedent's gross estate. The estate's position, that the caption suggests that Congress requires such treatment only if ten-year averaging is used, was invalid. The court held that the caption of Section 2039(f)(2) did not limit its scope. In addition, even though decedent elected his retirement option before the Section 2039(c) exemption was added in 1978, application of Sections 2039(c) and 2039(f)(2) in this case was not unconstitutional, because decedent retained the right, until his death in 1981, to revise his retirement plan option or the recipient of any death benefits thereunder.

[Estate of Rosenberg, 86 TC 980 (1986), aff'd, 812 F2d 1401, 59 AFTR2d 87-1220 (4th Cir. 1987).]

Death benefit payable to executors is included in estate. Decedent's estate received a death benefit from a state retirement system that decedent had made payable to the executors. Also, his will set up a marital deduction trust for his wife, allowing her to withdraw up to $50,000 of principal during her life. The estate argued the $50,000 of the death benefit should be excluded from the estate.

Held: For the IRS. Since the death benefit was paid to the executors, it did not qualify for the Section 2039(c) exclusion, but was included under Section 2039(a). The estate gave no valid reason why the $50,000 should be excluded.

•[Estate of Cohn, TC Memo. (P-H) ¶ 78,462, 37 TCM (CCH) 1847-88 (1978).]

Estate must include present value of survivor benefits for widow. An individual retired in June 1985 at age 61, at which time he elected to provide a survivor's annuity for his wife. When he retired, his contributions to the pension plan totaled $60,208. He died in 1987, after which the plan paid the wife a lump sum of $1,000 and monthly payments of $994 for the rest of her life. Had her husband died during his first year of retirement, the wife would have received $951 per month until her death.

The IRS stated that the estate was required to include the entire value of the survivor benefits from the plan, according to the calculation provided by Regulations § 20.2031-7; this calculation would result in a total includable benefit of $88,182. The IRS noted that the provisions of Section 1852 of the Tax Reform Act of 1986 did not apply the former exclusion rule of Section 2039(c) of the Code, because this employee did not quit work before January 1, 1985.

[Priv. Ltr. Rul. 8827042.]

Proceeds of IRA are includable in decedent's estate. A wife inherited the balance of a Keogh plan account from her husband and rolled it over into an IRA. At her death, the account passed to her sister.

The IRS stated that the full value of the IRA account is includable in the estate of the wife, because the rollover amount was the sole contribution to the IRA.

[Priv. Ltr. Rul. 8420060.]

¶ 3.03 MILITARY AND VETERANS' BENEFITS

Escheated veterans' funds are includable in gross estate. The IRS ruled that the value of Veterans Administration benefits that escheat to the United States for lack of heirs is includable in the deceased veteran's gross estate under Section 2033 as property beneficially owned at the time of death. Since the obligation to return the funds to the United States is imposed solely by law 38 USC § 3202(e)), the value of the funds is a liability that is deductible from decedent's estate within the meaning of Regulations § 20.2053-4.

[Rev. Rul. 78-14, 1978-1 CB 281.]

Veteran's benefits not included in estate. Veteran's benefits paid upon death from a service-connected disability are not included in decedent's estate.

[Rev. Rul. 76-501, 1976-2 CB 267.]

Value of serviceman's survivor benefits is not includable in his estate. An individual who was a member of the U. S. armed forces died in 1987 and was survived by his spouse. The individual had provided for a survivor annuity under the Armed Forces Survivor Benefit Plan. The individual began receiving retirement pay prior to December 31, 1982, and had irrevocably elected the form of benefit his beneficiary would receive under the plan prior to January 1, 1983. The individual made no deposits to the plan in addition to deductions from his retirement pay.

The IRS stated that the value of the survivor benefits should not be included in the individual's gross estate. The IRS noted that no deposits had been made to the plan and that the individual had met the requirements of Section 525(b) of the Tax Reform Act of 1984.

[Priv. Ltr. Rul. 8826028.]

Military survivor benefits are not includable in gross estate. Decedent, a retired member of the U.S. armed forces, died in 1987, leaving a survivor annuity for his spouse under the Armed Forces Survivor Benefit Plan. Decedent had started receiving retirement pay from the military prior to 1983 and had irrevocably elected the form of the benefit that his spouse would receive under the plan prior to 1983. Decedent made no deposits to the plan in lieu of deductions from retirement pay.

The IRS stated that the value of the survivor's benefits was not includable in decedent's gross estate for federal estate tax purposes. The IRS relied upon Section 525(b) of the Tax Reform Act of 1984 and stated that the facts of this situation fell squarely within the scope of the statute.

[Priv. Ltr. Rul. 8742027.]

Military survivor annuity is not includable in retiree's gross estate. An individual retired from the military on June 1, 1968, and went into pay status on that date. The individual made an election to receive retirement benefits in the form of an annuity and a survivor annuity that would be paid to his spouse after his death. The individual did not make any deposits into the military retirement plan under 10 USC § 1438 or 1452(d). The individual died. His wife asked for a ruling on the includability of the value of the military survivor annuity in his gross estate.

The IRS stated that no portion of the military survivor annuity was includable in the husband's gross estate. The IRS reasoned that the estate was entitled to the benefit of the unlimited Section 2039(c) exclusion in the transition rule of Section 525(a) of the Tax Reform Act of 1984. The estate was entitled to this benefit because the husband had received at least one payment before January 1, 1983, had been in pay status, and had not made any contributions to the plan.

[Priv. Ltr. Rul. 8741055.]

IRS states that survivor benefit annuity is excludable from decedent's gross estate. Individual retired from the military in 1980 and died on June 8, 1985. He had elected a survivor benefit plan that provided an annuity to his surviving spouse. The entire cost of the annuity was borne by decedent. The annuity became irrevocable on the date of decedent's retirement.

The IRS stated that the entire value of the annuity was excludable from decedent's gross estate. The IRS stated that under Section 525(b)(3) of the Tax Reform Act of 1984, the $100,000 limitation of Section 2039(c) was inapplicable, because decedent had been in pay status on December 31, 1982, and had elected the survivor annuity benefit plan before January 1, 1983.

[Priv. Ltr. Rul 8705011.]

CHAPTER 4

Retained Estates and Powers

¶ 4.01 RETAINED ESTATE INTERESTS

[1] Generally

Tax Court fails to find recognizable property interests as required by Section 2033. Decedent, who had been a resident of Limestone County, Alabama, died at age 82 on June 14, 1969. His executor filed a federal estate tax return stating that decedent had owned no real estate at the time of his death and further representing that in 1959, decedent and his wife had deeded all farmlands owned by them to their children. Following an investigation, the IRS determined that decedent had owned eighteen acres of farmland that he had gratuitously conveyed to his children and one grandchild while retaining actual possession, use, or income rights during his life. The IRS valued the eighteen acres at $417,526 on the date of death and asserted that such amount was includable in the gross estate under Section 2036(a)(1). Alternatively, the IRS determined that any parcels not effectively conveyed prior to the date of death were taxable under Section 2033. A second alternative position, that the conveyances were taxable gifts under Section 2501, was also asserted. The estate argued in the Tax Court that decedent had effectively conveyed the property to the respective grantees during his lifetime and that no amount was includable in the gross estate. The Tax Court sustained the IRS as to eleven parcels and determined that they were includable in the gross estate under Section 2033. It also found that six of the remaining parcels were gifts subject to gift tax, but that the last parcel had actually been sold by decedent during his lifetime.

Held: For the estate on the Section 2033 issue, but affirmed for the IRS under Section 2036. The Eleventh Circuit examined each of the eighteen separate findings with respect to the gift tax issues, but found that the court had erroneously concluded that the eleven parcels were subject to inclusion under Section 2033. The appeals court began with the proposition that the eleven parcels would have been includable under Section 2033 only if, under state law, decedent had been the owner of an equitable interest in them. Under Alabama law, decedent would have had an equitable interest if he had legal title and the equitable interest was not separated from the legal title, or if the property was impressed with the trust in his favor. Under the record before the Tax Court, there was simply no contention that the grantees were to hold the land in trust for decedent, and therefore decedent could have retained an interest in the properties under Section 2033 only if he had never conveyed legal title in the first place. The record showed, however, that the deeds were properly executed and recorded five years before decedent's death, and therefore the only bar to a finding of effective conveyance would be evidence that the deeds were never delivered to the grantees. The court noted that under state law proof of recordation creates a rebuttable presumption of delivery. However, the IRS was not required to overcome such a presumption, because it did not affirmatively determine that the property had been ineffectively conveyed. The court concluded that because the only evidence at trial was the recorded deed, the Tax Court had no basis for concluding that the property was includable under Section 2033. The court went on to find, however, that the estate had failed to show that decedent had not retained an implied use or income right within Section 2036, and therefore the value of the property was includable under this statutory provision.

[Estate of Whitt, 751 F2d 1548, 55 AFTR2d 85-1562, 85-1 USTC ¶ 13,607 (11th Cir. 1985), cert. denied, 474 US 1005 (1985).]

Section 2036 is held applicable to vacation home acquired by deed granting only life estate to decedent. Decedent died in 1974 at age 73, leaving two sons. In 1938 and 1939, the family had purchased vacation property in Massachusetts and had received deeds granting a life interest to decedent and his wife (who died in 1973), with a remainder passing to the two sons. The deeds contained a recital to the effect that the seller was in receipt of "one dollar and other valuable consideration" paid by decedent, his wife, and the two sons. On audit, the IRS determined that the entire value of the property was includable in the gross estate under Section 2036, which provides that property transferred by a decedent during his lifetime is to be included in the gross estate where decedent retained a lifetime interest. The estate contended that Section 2036 was inapplicable, because the deed showed that decedent had received a life estate only in the original conveyance, and that he therefore had never made a transfer as required by Section 2036. The Tax Court entered judgment for the IRS. Based on a factually complex record, the Tax Court found that the substance of the original conveyance was a purchase of the entire property by decedent, followed by the indirect transfer of a life estate to his wife and the remainders going to the two sons. The means of accomplishing this transfer was simply through the language of conveyance used in the deed. The court noted that the sons, as co-executors of their mother's estate, had signed earlier affidavits stating that the father had purchased the property outright for $1,200. These statements were made by the sons in connection with IRS inquiries on the includability of the property in the mother's gross estate. On the basis of various documents and affidavits, the IRS determined in the prior case that the father furnished the entire consideration and that consequently, nothing was includable in the mother's estate under Section 2036.

Held: On appeal, judgment for the IRS affirmed. The Sixth Circuit, in a thorough review of the Tax Court's decision, determined that decedent's direction to the grantor to convey the property in this particular manner had, in substance, been a transfer for estate tax purposes under Section 2036(a). The court noted that the inclusion or circumvention of an intermediate step does not make a difference in the tax effect of such transactions.

[Estate of Shafer, 749 F2d 1216, 55 AFTR2d 85-1531, 84-2 USTC ¶ 13,599 (6th Cir. 1984).]

Fifth Circuit finds no retained interest for gift to spouse in community property state. Taxpayer made a gift to his spouse in a community property jurisdiction. By operation of law, such property became the separate property of the donee-spouse, although the income from the property became community property. On audit, the IRS contended that the donor had a retained interest in the property under Section 2036(a) for estate tax purposes.

Held: For the estate. Regardless of the characterization of the income as separate or community property, the donor did not retain the possession, enjoyment, or the right to the income, and therefore Section 2036 does not require inclusion in the gross estate. The court noted that property given to a spouse becomes that spouse's separate property subject to the donee's sole management, control, and power of disposition. Thus, the donor-spouse's community property interest in that property is different from a general community property interest.

[Estate of Wyly, 610 F2d 1282, 45 AFTR2d 80-1737, 80-1 USTC ¶ 13,332 (5th Cir. 1980).]

Decedent's interest in family trust is held to be retained interest under Section 2036 because of informal agreement with nonadverse trustee and right of creditors to reach trust income and corpus. In 1967 and 1968, decedent had transferred to two trusts all of his assets, except for two patents. Included among these assets were the family residence and all of the stock in several corporations that had employed decedent and had licensed his patents. The trusts receiving these assets had issued certificates of beneficial interest to decedent, his wife, and his family. Distributions by the trustees, who were his sons or persons whom decedent had employed, were discretionary and were not required to be proportionate. After the transfers, decedent's principal source of income had been patent royalties ranging between $100,000 to $200,000 per year. These royalties would have ceased in 1982 when decedent was age 64. The transfers left no significant property in decedent's estate for his wife or children. Decedent died in 1975, and his wife began to receive substantial distributions from the trusts. No estate tax return was filed. The IRS asserted a deficiency, arguing that the property transferred to the trusts was includable in decedent's gross estate because decedent had retained an interest described in Section 2036.

Held: For the IRS. Decedent had retained an interest in the trust, which made the trust assets includable in the gross estate under Section 2036. Specifically, although no express interest had been retained by decedent, under the facts, an implied agreement existed with the trustees that required distributions to decedent if, as, and when he requested them. This implied agreement was evidenced by several facts. First, decedent had been a beneficiary of the trusts and had received several distributions from them. Second, decedent had transferred most of his property to the trusts under circumstances posing a substantial risk that he would become destitute after the cessation of his royalty income. Third, the beneficial interests in the trusts had been held by the natural objects of his bounty (indicating decedent's testamentary intent), and distributions to such beneficiaries increased substantially after decedent's death. Finally, decedent's close relationship with his oldest son, the principal trustee, indicated that the son would have honored an informal arrangement with decedent. Accordingly, decedent had retained life possession or enjoyment of the property that he transferred to the trusts by means of an informal arrangement. Therefore, the value of trust property was includable in the gross estate under Section 2036.

[Paxton, 86 TC 785 (1986).]

Sale of stock and option transaction upheld. Decedent, who died in 1991, owned shares in a professional football team. In 1983, he sold 117 of his 118 shares of stock in the team to S, an unrelated third party who already owned 213 shares of the team's stock. In exchange, S gave decedent a note and sold an option to decedent's sons to buy up to 329 shares of the team's stock (i.e., the 117 shares S bought from decedent plus 212 of S's shares). The option could be exercised from 1993 to 1996. In 1993, decedent's sons exercised the option for 329 shares of stock. Decedent's estate tax return reported that decedent owned one share of the team's stock when he died. The IRS contended that the estate included 312 shares of the team's stock. The IRS argued that, in substance, the 1983 transaction between S and decedent was a sale by S of his 212 shares of stock (or a remainder interest therein) to decedent in return for a ten-year income interest in decedent's 117 shares of stock, and an indirect transfer by decedent of 329 shares of the team's stock to his sons through S as a conduit.

Held: For taxpayer. Section 2036 did not apply because decedent (1) received full and adequate consideration for the 117 shares of stock and (2) did not make an inter vivos transfer of S's 212 shares of stock. The court also found that the option was not a sham. The option price was negotiated at arm's length.

[Estate of Brown, 73 TCM 2655, RIA TC Memo. ¶ 97,195 (1997).]

Property in which decedent had retained life estate was includable in gross estate without deduction for mortgage contracted for by remainderman. In 1976, D gratuitously conveyed a remainder interest in real estate to A, retaining a life estate. In 1976, a bank lent A $100x$ and as security received a mortgage on the property signed by both A and D. Under local law, D was a guarantor and, as such, had a right of reimbursement against A in the event that D was required to pay the loan directly or if D's life estate were sold in foreclosure. A was solvent at the time of the loan transaction, and D had a reasonable expectation of reimbursement from A in the event that D was required to pay the loan for A. D died in 1981. Because D had retained a life estate in the transferred property, the value of the property was subject to inclusion in D's gross estate under Section 2036 (transfers with retained life estate). The executor of D's estate sought to deduct the mortgage balance alternatively under Section 2053(a)(3), as a claim against the estate, or under Section 2053(a)(4), which provides a deduction for unpaid mortgages on property included in the gross estate. Advice was requested from the IRS as to what amount is includable in D's gross estate under Section 2036, and as to what amount is deductible in D's estate under Section 2053, if D is guarantor of a loan to A secured by a mortgage on property D previously transferred to A subject to a retained life estate.

The IRS ruled that since D is guarantor of a loan to A with a right of reimbursement and the loan is secured by a mortgage on property D had previously transferred to A subject to a retained life estate, the entire value of the property, unreduced by the mortgage, is includable in D's gross estate under Section 2036. If D's estate is not called upon to pay the indebtedness, no amount of the indebtedness is deductible under Section 2053. In the instant case, decedent had made a transfer described in Section 2036 of the full value of the unencumbered remainder interest. The property was encumbered after the transfer, and D had received no proceeds from the loan. Furthermore, the encumbrance of the property had no immediate effect on D's continued retention of the lifetime enjoyment of the property. Other than as a guarantor, neither D nor his estate was liable for the loan. Therefore, the entire value of the property was includable in D's gross estate under Section 2036, and no deduction was allowed for the mortgage under Section 2053(a)(4).

[Rev. Rul. 84-42, 1984-1 CB 194.]

Transferred reversion is excluded from gross estate. Decedent transferred property in trust with income to R for life. The remainder was to go to decedent if he should survive R, or, if not, to S. Thereafter decedent assigned his share of the remainder to S in a transfer that would qualify for Section 2035 treatment. The value of the relinquished reversion would be includable in the gross estate, however, only if the reversion would have been includable in decedent's gross estate if he had retained the interest until death. When decedent assigned the reversion, the value of the reversion exceeded 5 percent of the value of the trust property. Since the other requirements of Section 2037 were met, the reversion would have been included in his gross estate if he had died at that time. At the time he died, however, the value of the interest was less that 5 percent.

The IRS ruled that the determination of includability under Section 2037 (and, therefore, Section 2035) must be determined as of the date of decedent-transferor's death. Thus, the interest was not includable in decedent's gross estate.

[Rev. Rul. 79-62, 1979-1 CB 295.]

Death benefit derived from employment contract is includable in gross estate. The IRS ruled that decedent effected a Section 2037 transfer when he entered into an employment contract that provided for payment of the death benefit to decedent's spouse, *B*, in consideration of his performance of services. If *B* predeceased him, the death benefit was to be paid to decedent's estate. That *B* retained a reversionary interest in the death benefit, which exceeded 5 percent of the value of the payment immediately before his death, was noted by the IRS in including the value of the benefit in the gross estate under Section 2037.

[Rev. Rul. 78-15, 1978-1 CB 289.]

Trust set up for ex-spouse was includable in settlor's estate but was also deductible. Technical Advice Memorandum 9826002 concluded that a divorce-related trust was includable in the settlor's estate under Section 2036(a) but that the estate was allowed a deduction under Section 2053(a) for the value of the former spouse's interest in the trust.

The facts of the instant case involved a couple who divorced. They agreed on a division of their assets that gave the wife real estate, household furnishings, stock, a lump-sum payment, costs, and alimony. As part of the divorce, the husband also established a trust to secure his obligations under the divorce decree. The trust corpus consisted of stock and an insurance policy on the husband's life. The agreement, which was adopted by the divorce court in its entirety, provided that if the trust realized income from certain stock dividends, the alimony payments would increase by a formula amount. As long as the husband promptly paid the wife the monthly payments required by the agreement, he would receive the income from the trust. If the husband defaulted in his monthly payments, the trustee was to distribute to the wife the alimony payment due as long as the default continued. The husband remained primarily liable on all payments, whether in default or not. If the husband predeceased the wife, the life insurance proceeds were to be used to pay the monthly support obligation, the income from the trust was to be paid to the wife for her life, and the trustees were to pay her principal for her care, comfort, support, and welfare, regardless of her marital status. The wife also had a testamentary general power of appointment. If the wife predeceased the husband, the property would have been held in trust for the husband. Upon his death the trust would have been administered for the benefit of the couple's son. The husband predeceased the wife and issues arose as to whether the trust was includable in his estate and, if so, whether a claimed deduction was allowable for any portion of the trust.

Under Section 2036(a), property transferred by an individual during life is includable in his gross estate if he retained the lifetime right to the income from the transferred property. An exception, however, applies for a transfer made pursuant to a bona fide sale for an adequate and full consideration in money or money's worth. Under this exception, even though an individual may have retained a lifetime right to the income of the transferred property, no part of it is includable in his gross estate if he made the transfer in a bona fide sale and received an adequate and full consideration in money or money's worth. Similarly, if an individual received only a partial consideration in money or money's worth for the property, the value of the property that is includable in his gross estate is reduced by the amount of the partial consideration received (Section 2043(a)). Technical Advice Memorandum 9826002 noted that in the instant case, the husband transferred stock and life insurance to the trust and retained the lifetime right to income. The husband made the transfer pursuant to the divorce decree and the trust agreement. Under Section 2036(a), the value of the trust, on the date of the husband's death, is fully includable in his gross estate unless the transfer was made for an adequate and full consideration in money or money's worth. Technical Advice Memorandum 9826003 stated that the wife relinquished her marital rights in consideration for her interest in the trust and that this does not constitute a consideration in money or money's worth for purposes of Section 2036(a) and Section 2043(b)(1). Consequently, the husband is regarded as having received no consideration in money or money's worth for his transfer of property to the trust, and the full value of the trust property is includable in his gross estate.

The consideration for the husband's creation of the trust was based upon the wife's relinquishment of her marital rights in the husband's property. Ordinarily, this would not constitute a consideration in money or money's worth that would allow a deduction for a claim against the estate under Section 2053(a). There is, however, a statutory exception under Section 2043(b)(2) providing for deemed consideration under Section 2053(a) in the case of transfers of property under a spousal property settlement agreement meeting the requirements of Section 2516. Under this exception, a transfer of property or an interest in property to a former spouse in consideration of her relinquishment of marital rights under a property settlement agreement, followed by divorce within two years, is deemed made for an adequate and full consideration in money or money's worth for purposes of allowing a deduction for the obligation as a claim against the estate. Husband and wife divorced within two years after the written agreement concerning their marital rights was executed. Therefore, the husband was regarded as having received a full and adequate consideration for his transfers to the trust because the property settlement agreement met the requirements of Section 2516. Because the wife was the only permissible recipient of trust income and corpus and had a general testamentary power of appointment, the full value of the trust was considered transferred to the wife. Therefore, the full value of the trust property on the date of the husband's death was deductible by his estate.

[Tech. Adv. Mem. 9826002.]

Indirect transfer of stock did not prevent inclusion of shares in estate. Decedent sold shares in his closely held corporation to an unrelated shareholder who then gave decedent's children an option to purchase such shares plus other shares the shareholder already owned. Exercise of the option would give the children a controlling interest in the corporation. Under the terms of the transaction, the shareholder retained a ten-year right to income from the shares. At the end of ten years, decedent's children would obtain the shares at minimal cost. Execution of a new voting trust gave decedent the right to vote all the shares during the ten-year period. The IRS characterized the transfer of the remainders in the shares to the children as an intrafamily transfer from decedent to his children. Decedent provided nearly all the consideration for the transfer. Because decedent retained the right to vote the shares, Section 2036(b) applied. Accordingly, the value of the shares, less the present value of the shareholder's income interest at the date of death, was includable in decedent's estate.

[Tech. Adv. Mem. 9518002.]

Transferred stock was not included in transferor's estate despite his indirect retention of voting right. Decedent and his spouse created three trusts for their grandchildren and transferred stock of their closely held corporation to the trusts. Between the date of the gift and the date of death, the value of the stock declined. The estate took the position that the transferred stock was includable in the estate under Section 2036(b) because there was an oral understanding between decedent and the trustee that the trustee would vote the stock in accordance with his wishes. Consequently, on the estate tax return, the estate reported the stock not as an adjustable gift but as an asset of the estate valued at its lower date of death value. The IRS found that the form of the transfer to the trusts indicated that decedent had relinquished all his rights in the stock, including voting rights. The IRS concluded that the estate could not invoke the substance over form principal to disavow the form in which the transaction had been structured. Hence, the stock was an adjusted taxable gift and must be reported as its value on the date of the creation of the trusts.

[Tech. Adv. Mem. 9515003.]

[2] Income Rights

Sale of remainder eliminated property from estate. Decedent owned 470 shares of preferred stock in a family-owned corporation with a FMV of $2.35 million. On September 1, 1987, she sold the remainder interest in the shares (i.e., the ownership of the shares after she died) to the corporation for a private annuity with FMV equal to the FMV of the remainder interest. Decedent was age 80 at the time of the sale, and she died on May 25, 1990, having received only $590,000 in annuity payments. The Tax Court approved the inclusion of the FMV of the stock, minus the original FMV of the annuity in decedent's estate. Under Section 2036(a), property is includable in the estate if a decedent transferred an interest but retained the possession or enjoyment of, or right to income from, the property for life. Section 2036(a) does not apply, however, to a bona fide sale for an adequate and full consideration in money or money's worth. The Tax Court reasoned that, under the bona fide sale exception, the FMV of what was received had to equal the value that would have been included in the estate absent the sale. Thus, the removal of stock with FMV of $2.35 million from decedent's estate by the sale of the remainder interest for an annuity with a $1.3 million FMV was too favorable to be permitted. The estate appealed.

Held: Reversed for the estate. The Third Circuit reversed because, when decedent sold the remainder interest for its FMV, Section 2036(a) no longer applied. The court reasoned that an FMV sale of a remainder interest leaves the seller with the same wealth as before and, all things being equal, with the same estate. The court explained that if a young person sells a remainder interest for its FMV, the consideration will represent a small portion of the value of the property. Nevertheless, at the end of the seller's life this will have grown (assuming a normal life span and the same rate of return) to equal the value of the property. If the sale is made by a person of advanced years, the remainder interest will bring a higher price and, when combined with income from the retained life interest, should produce the same estate as if there were no sale. By contrast, if both the consideration received for the remainder interest and the entire property are included in the estate, there is double counting, which eliminates the sale of a remainder interest as a viable transaction. Yet, there is no indication that Congress wished to prohibit these sales. According to the Third Circuit, three cases the lower court relied on used the wrong analysis, beginning with Estate of Gregory, 39 TC 1012 (1963). There, the husband's one-half share of community property was transferred to a trust under his will. The will gave the wife a choice of receiving only her one-half share of the community property or transferring it to the trust, under which she would receive all the income for life. The wife elected the trust option, in effect retaining a life estate in her share of the community property, while transferring the remainder interest in her share in exchange for a life interest in her husband's share. The wife's contribution to the trust (the remainder interest) had a value of $66,000, but the Tax Court compared the higher value of what would have been includable in her estate with the income interest in her husband's share of the community property, which had a value of only $12,000. This was incorrect, but the Tax Court reached the same result since the $12,000 was not sufficient consideration even for the $66,000 FMV remainder interest. According to the Claims Court, in Gradow, 59 AFTR2d 87-1221 (Cl. Ct. 1987), aff'd, 897 F2d 516, 65 AFTR2d 1229 (Fed. Cir. 1990), the exception in Section 2036(a) for a bona fide sale refers to the property that would have been included absent a transfer. This, however, ignores the reference to "interest" in property (immediately before the bona fide sale exception), so the value of what is received has to equal only the value of the remainder interest. The Tax Court also relied on Past, 347 F2d 7, 15 AFTR2d 1422 (9th Cir. 1965), which had a fact pattern similar to that in *Gregory* and *Gradow*, but in the context of a divorce. The Ninth Circuit applied a similar analysis and, according to the Third Circuit, wrongly included the property. The Third Circuit acknowledged that some sales are beyond the pale, as in Allen, 293 F2d 916, 8 AFTR2d 1055 (10th Cir. 1961), cert. denied, 117 S Ct 1822 (1997). There, a remainder interest was disposed of by gift and the life estate was sold. Since the sale was clearly for tax avoidance, the Tenth Circuit was justified in including the entire property.

[Estate of D'Ambrosio, 101 F3d 309, 78 AFTR2d 96-7347, 96-2 USTC ¶ 60,252 (3d Cir. 1996), cert. denied, 117 S. Ct. 1822 (1997).]

Sale of remainder interest may not succeed in excluding property from estate. Decedent and her husband lived in California, a community property state. Her husband died in 1977. His will made provisions for disposing of both his and his wife's interests in their community property. He gave his wife the option either to reject his will and to take her share of the community property outright or to transfer her portion of the community property to a trust containing their community property in exchange for receiving all of the income from the trust. If decedent chose the latter option, she would also be entitled to take their residence outright and would receive her husband's jewelry and personal and household effects. Under either option, she retained her statutory rights to a probate homestead allowance and a widow's allowance. Decedent took the residence under the will. Fifteen months later decedent died. Her son, who was her executor and the remainder beneficiary of the trust, filed an estate tax return that referred to the trust, but did not include any of the trust corpus in her gross estate. The IRS asserted that under Section 2036(a), the estate should have included the value of the property that decedent had contributed to the trust. This amount could be offset, however, by the value of the life estate in the half of the trust corpus contributed by her husband, pursuant to Section 2043. The executor claimed that the transfer to the trust of decedent's half of the community property fell under the exception in Section 2036(a)for transfers made in a bona fide sale for adequate and full consideration. The Claims Court granted the IRS's motion for partial summary judgment and dismissed the estate's claim for a tax refund.

Held: For the IRS. The Federal Circuit began its analysis by examining Section 2036(a), which states that the value of the gross estate includes the value of all property transferred in which decedent retained a life interest. Pursuant to the election under her husband's will, decedent transferred her share of their community property to a trust while retaining a life interest in the property transferred. Therefore, under Section 2036(a), decedent's share of community property should be included in her estate. There is an exception under Section 2036(a) if the transfer was a bona fide sale for an adequate and full consideration in money or money's worth. If this exception applied, the property decedent transferred would not be included in her gross estate. The issue was whether there was a bona fide sale for adequate and full consideration. In addressing this issue, the Claims Court attempted to identify and value the "halves of the sale." In such a sale, there is consideration flowing to and from decedent. In the instant case, the parties agreed that decedent received, at a minimum, a life income interest in her husband's share of the community property. There was disagreement as to the consideration flowing from decedent—whether it was simply the value of the remainder interest in her share of the community property or whether it was the value of her entire share of such property. The Claims Court found that the consideration flowing from decedent was the property that would otherwise be included in her gross estate by virtue of her retention of a life estate in such property. This was her half of the community property, not just the remainder interest in such property. Because the value of her share of the community property exceeded the value of her life interest in her husband's share of such property, she did not receive full consideration for the amount she transferred to the trust. The Claims Court found support for its interpretation of the exception in Section 2036(a) in decisions of other courts and by examining the plain meaning and the legislative history of Section 2036(a). Although not bound by these cases, the Federal Circuit was persuaded by them. The executor claimed that requiring the consideration flowing from decedent to equal the combined value of the income interest and the remainder interest violates "commercial common sense, normal rules of statutory interpretation, the legislative history of Section 2036(a), and the long-term understanding of what constitutes 'adequate consideration.' The appeals court was not persuaded by the executor's arguments, which it considered to be primarily "general, conclusory statements by counsel not well grounded in fact or law." Affirming the holding of the Claims Court, the court stated that "[t]he Claims Court's well reasoned opinion indicates a complete consideration of the arguments raised here on appeal and we are unpersuaded of any legal error in the court's interpretation or application of Section 2036(a)."

[Gradow, 897 F2d 516, 90-1 USTC ¶ 60,010, 65 AFTR2d 90-1229 (Fed. Cir. 1990).]

Estate must pay tax on stock used to fund trust. Decedent's father sold him shares of appreciated stock for which decedent had executed a promissory note for the amount of the father's basis in the shares. The father then transferred the shares to a trust, under the terms of which decedent was to receive income for his life. The promissory note was paid with dividends from the stock. Decedent reported the income from the stock and took deductions for the interest on the note. When decedent died, none of the stock of the trust was included in the estate. The IRS contended that decedent's purchase of the stock and the transfer of the stock to the trust by his father was, in substance, a Section 2036(a) transfer by a decedent with a retained life estate. Thus, the IRS argued that the FMV of the sale portion of the stock on the date of decedent's death was includable in his estate. Under Section 2036(a), the value of property that a decedent transfers to a trust is includable in his estate if decedent retains a life income interest in the property transferred. According to National City Bank of Cleveland, 371 F2d 13, 67-1 USTC ¶ 12,440 (6th Cir. 1966), property is includable in the estate if: (1) decedent made a transfer of the property during his life; (2) decedent retained the right to income from the property; and (3) the retention was for decedent's life. The district court held that because decedent's father had established and controlled the creation and funding of the trust, decedent had purchased a life estate only in the trust corpus and had not made a transfer. Because there had been no transfer for Section 2036(a) purposes, the district court held that the property was excludable from the estate.

Held: For the IRS. In the Sixth Circuit, the estate argued that decedent's father had been grantor of the trust. The estate based this argument on the facts that the father had retained a right to dividends from the stock; the trust had paid off the note; decedent had been only a surety for the trust's repayment of the note; and the note had been between family members and thus was not true debt. The estate contended that because decedent had not paid the consideration, he could not have made a transfer. In rejecting all of the estate's arguments, the Sixth Circuit noted that the trust instrument itself stated that the stock was transferred to the trust in exchange for payment by decedent. Although the payment was in the form of a note that was repaid by the corporation withholding dividends from decedent and making payment directly to his father, decedent had treated the withheld dividends as income and had taken interest deductions for the repayments. The court reasoned that only if decedent had really purchased the stock would interest deductions have been taken. The court then examined whether decedent transferred the shares, or merely purchased an equitable life estate in the transferred stock. The court observed that the purpose of Section 2036 is to include in the estate transfers that leave the transferor a significant interest in or control over the property transferred during his life as espoused in Estate of Grace, 395 US 316 (1969). The Sixth Circuit then rejected decedent's family's testimony regarding the nature of the transfer and concentrated on the objective evidence of the transaction. Because the trust instrument indicated that decedent had purchased the stock that funded the trust in exchange for a promissory note, and the note stated that it was in payment for the shares, decedent clearly intended to purchase the stock and to fund the trust. Decedent had not purchased a mere life interest. Thus, decedent in substance, was the grantor of the trust and retained a life income interest. Therefore, under Section 2036(a), the date-of-death value of the purchased portion of the stock was required to be included in his estate.

[Mahoney, 831 F2d 641, 60 AFTR2d 87-6152, 87-2 USTC ¶ 13,737 (6th Cir., 1987) US 1054 (1988).]

Retained life estate triggers inclusion of divorce settlement trust. Decedent and his former wife were divorced in 1959. As part of the divorce proceedings, the parties entered into a property agreement and a trust settlement. In accordance with the settlement, the parties transferred their respective interests in certain real and personal property to a trust. Decedent was to receive $40 a month for life, and his wife was to be paid $300 a month for life. On the death of the survivor, the trust corpus was to be distributed to their children. In 1975, decedent, who had survived his ex-wife by five years, died at age 83. The estate did not report decedent's half-interest in the trust as property includable in gross estate. The IRS, however, determined that the trust was a transfer with a retained life estate subject to inclusion under Section 2036.

Held: For the IRS. The court concluded in its brief opinion that decedent retained a life estate in the trust property and that his transfer thereof had not been a bona fide sale for adequate consideration in money or money's worth. The fact that the transfer was made as part of the divorce settlement was found not to be determinative on the issue of adequate consideration.

[Estate of Ray, 54 AFTR2d 84-6497, 84-2 USTC ¶ 13,584 (ED Wash. 1984), aff'd, 762 F2d 1361, 56 AFTR2d 85-6496, 85-2 USTC ¶ 13,621 (9th Cir. 1985).]

Tax Court rules on overfunding of testamentary trust. A husband died and left his half of his community property in trust with income for life to his wife. During the period of administration, the property earned income and death taxes were paid from it. After adding the income and paying the taxes, the property was divided and half was placed in the trust. The wife later died, and the IRS included in her gross estate under Section 2036 half the amount of income and half the amount of death taxes paid.

Held: For the IRS. Under California law, all income earned during the period of administration was earned by the wife—half directly as owner and half as income beneficiary of the trust. When she added half the income to the trust (by adding all the income to the community property prior to division), she made a Section 2036(a)transfer includable in her gross estate. The death taxes should have been paid soley from the husband's share of the community property and charged against the trust assets. Thus, by charging the whole community property with these taxes, the wife made another Section 2036(a)transfer to the trust to the extent of half of the taxes paid.

[Estate of Hoffman, 78 TC 1069 (1982).]

Donor's estate includes bonds given without interest coupons. Decedent purchased a number of bearer bonds that provided for the payment of accrued interest on the presentation of attached coupons. In 1971, she transferred these bonds to a trust for the benefit of her grandchildren (and in which she retained no interest), but clipped and retained coupons representing the right to receive interest for the period 1971 through 1979. A gift tax return was filed for these transfers. Decedent reported as gifts the value of the bonds less the value of the interest coupons retained. The estate included the present value of the interest coupons retained, which were payable after the date of death, October 14, 1974. The IRS claimed, however, that the value of the bonds should also be included in her gross estate under Section 2036(a), because she had retained an income interest in them for a period that did not end before her death. Her estate argued that the bonds and interest coupons were separate property and that the bonds had independent intrinsic worth apart from the detached coupons.

Held: For the IRS. The right to receive interest was an integral part of the "bundle of rights" that taxpayer had purchased. Taxpayer originally acquired rights to both interest and return of principal; she retained only the former. What was transferred to the trust thus did not include one of the most important elements of that bundle of rights. Her situation is comparable to that in Fitzsimmons, 222 F. Supp. 140 (ED Wash. 1963), where decedent transferred a bond subject to the condition that the donee return the interest. Decedent was held to have retained an income interest in the obligation. A somewhat similar type of transfer with stock certificates was attempted in Estate of Fry, 9 TC 503 (1947). There decedent gave stock to his daughter subject to her giving him the first $15,000 of dividends. The court there had held that the value of the shares be included in decedent's gross estate under the 1939 Code provision comparable to Section 2036, because decedent had retained for a period that did not in fact end before his death the right to receive all of the income from the property.

[Estate of Cooper, 74 TC 1373 (1980).]

Assets of family partnerships were included in deceased parent's estate. A year before her death, decedent and her three adult children formed three family limited partnerships (FLPs), to which decedent transferred some of her assets. Decedent and each child were the general partners of each partnership. In addition, decedent functioned as the limited partner and the managing partner of all the FLPs. The partnership agreements required that all partnership income would be deposited into partnership bank accounts. Although the partnerships' initial capital was deposited into partnership accounts, all partnership income was deposited into decedent's personal checking account, where it was commingled with income from other sources. Decedent used this checking account to pay personal as well as partnership expenses. The IRS argued that the assets transferred to the FLPs were includable in decedent's estate.

Held: For the IRS. The value of the assets was includable in the estate under Section 2036(a)(1). The facts showed that an implied agreement existed among the partners that decedent would retain the economic benefit of the partnership assets.

[Estate of Schauerhamer, 73 TCM 2855, RIA TC Memo. ¶ 97,242 (1997).]

Promise to bequeath stock to children was not "adequate and full" consideration. Decedent and his father, owned the majority interest in the family's retail clothing business. In order to keep control of the business in the family, they entered into an arrangement in 1951 whereby the father agreed that, on his death, his stock would be left to decedent as lifetime trustee for the benefit of decedent and decedent's children. In exchange, decedent promised to bequeath all of his stock in trust for the benefit of his children. Decedent would retain voting rights in the first trust unless he violated the agreement. In addition, the agreement provided that except for a sale of all of the stock, at no time should the ownership of the stock by persons other than decedent and his father and children exceed 49 percent. In the event of a sale of any stock, the proceeds would be placed in a trust with a lifetime income interest to decedent and the remainder to decedent's children. The father died in 1953 and his stock was placed in trust in accordance with the 1951 agreement. Subsequently, all the stock was sold, and in 1971 decedent placed the proceeds in trusts, retaining an income interest for life with the principal to be distributed to his children on his death. He filed a gift tax return reporting the creation of the trusts and stating they were established in accordance with the preexisting agreement with his late father. Decedent died in 1988, and his estate excluded the 1971 transfers as bona fide sales for adequate and full consideration under Section 2036(a). The estate argued that when decedent obligated himself to transfer his shares in accordance with the 1951 agreement, he received consideration that exceeded the value of the remainder interest in his shares.

Held: For the IRS. The 1951 agreement included an element of bargained-for consideration. In determining the adequacy of the consideration received, however, it must be compared with the total value of the stock decedent agreed to transfer to his children and not merely the value of the remainder interest. Thus, the consideration was not "adequate and full" as required by the statute.

[Estate of Magnin, 71 TCM 1856, RIA TC Memo. ¶ 96,025 (1996).]

[3] Possession and Enjoyment Rights

Actuarial value deemed adequate and full consideration. In 1984, decedent deeded to his two sons the remainder interest in his ranch, in which he reserved a life estate for himself and on which he continued to live until he died in 1991. The sons paid for the remainder with a 7 percent interest bearing note for $337,790, secured by a deed of trust (which, along with the deed, was recorded). Using the appropriate factor in Regulation § 25.2512-5(A), the purchase price was determined by the actuarial value of the fee simple interest's appraised FMV. Decedent also started to give his sons stock in his solely owned corporation, of which the sons were employees, in 1983 and 1984, and continued to do so until and after the note was paid. The sons made the required periodic payments on the note throughout the term of the note, used $35,000 of their $50,000/$55,000 respective 1986 bonuses to pay down principal, and paid off the balance in 1988. The balance was paid on the same day decedent sold the sons additional stock and one day after they each received a $250,000 year-end bonus for 1987. Further, decedent gave them each $10,000 in 1986 by forgiving the amount due under the note, and he assigned the note to the corporation in partial payment of a debt he owed it. Finally, decedent's stock transfers ultimately diminished his interest in the corporation as of his death to a 50 percent ownership of the voting stock, with the other 50 percent, and all the nonvoting stock, owned by his sons. The IRS viewed the ranch, stock, and other intrafamily transfers as part of a single testamentary transaction intended to avoid estate taxes, even though decedent's death was not imminent in 1984, or even until 1991, and concluded that the ranch could not be excluded from the gross estate under Section 2036(a). Section 2036(a) provides that a gross estate includes the value of transferred property in which a decedent has retained a life estate, "*except* in the case of a bona fide sale for an adequate and full consideration" (the exception clause). The estate argued that the sons' payment of the full actuarial value of the transferred remainder interest met the exception clause's adequate and full consideration requirement. The IRS agreed that the sons paid full actuarial value, but countered that Section 2036(a)'s adequate and full consideration refers to the pre-transfer value of a full fee interest, not a transferred future interest's value. Thus, the exception clause did not apply, and the ranch was includable in the gross estate, to the extent of its date-of-death value less the amount the sons paid for the remainder.

Held: For the estate. The Fifth Circuit agreed with the estate, finding that adequate and full consideration under Section 2036(a) did refer to the value of the remainder interest transferred. The court distinguished a contrary line of cases holding that Section 2036(a)'s adequate and full consideration refers to underlying property. Those cases were decided in the widow's election context, where a surviving spouse transfers a remainder interest in his or her community property share for a life estate in deceased spouse's share. Those cases did not require inclusion of the value of the full fee interest in underlying property in all situations, but only where such a transfer depleted the gross estate, without a commensurate offset. The sale of a remainder interest for its actuarial value, however, does not deplete a seller's estate. The court then noted that the IRS's construction of adequate and full consideration under Section 2036(a) impermissibly differed from the meaning given that term in the gift tax statute, and the court found that Section 2036(a)'s "bona fide" language did not require heightened scrutiny of, or provide for differential treatment for, intra-family transfers that are perceived to have been entered in contemplation of death. By the statute's terms, so long as a family member allegedly paid full value for a remainder interest, as was the case here, the only ground for challenging such a transaction was whether decedent had actually parted with that interest and the sons had actually parted with the requisite consideration. The court went on to determine that the sale, which was indisputably for full actuarial value, was bona fide. The court found that the note's terms did not evidence any donative intent, and the fact that the sons did not have the cash to pay the full purchase price at the time of the transfer was not determinative. Furthermore, the sons' bonuses were not tied to the note's repayment, the lack of purchase price negotiations was not compelling, and there was no "testamentary synergy" arising from decedent's use of the gift-tax exclusion and other statutorily sanctioned tax-saving devices. Thus, decedent's sale of the remainder interest in his ranch for its full actuarial value was a bona fide sale for adequate and full consideration within the meaning of Section 2036(a). As such, and despite decedent's retained life estate, the ranch was not includable in decedent's gross estate.

[Wheeler, 116 F3d 749, 97-2 USTC ¶ 60,278, 80 AFTR2d 97-5075 97-2 USTC ¶ 60,278 (5th Cir. 1997).]

Decedent's estate included house that was purportedly sold to son. In 1984, when she was eighty-two years old and suffering from cancer, decedent "sold" her home of the past twenty-seven years to her son, who was her only heir, and his wife for $270,000. Decedent immediately forgave $20,000 of the debt, which qualified for the annual gift tax exclusion. Decedent's son and his wife executed a mortgage note for the $250,000 balance. Decedent leased the property back from decedent's son and his wife for a five-year term. The monthly rental of $1,800 was similar to the monthly payments made on the mortgage (which covered only interest expense). Decedent's son and his wife also paid other house expenses, such as taxes and insurance. Upon decedent's death, the outstanding balance of the note was forgiven. Decedent reported the sale of her home on her 1984 income tax return, but did not pay any tax on the gain due to the Section 121 one-time exclusion on the sale or exchange of a principal residence. Decedent occupied the house until her death in July 1986. Subseqently, decedent's son and his wife sold the house for $550,000. Decedent's estate did not include the value of the house on the estate tax return, reporting only the $210,000 outstanding balance on the mortgage note (decedent had forgiven an additional $20,000 in 1985 and 1986). The IRS assessed a deficiency against the estate for the difference between the FMV of the house at death ($550,000) and the value of the note ($210,000). The IRS contended that the 1984 transaction was a transfer with a retained life estate; therefore, the property must be included in the estate under Section 2036(a). The estate took the case to the Tax Court, which upheld the IRS's position.

Held: Affirmed for the IRS. On appeal, the Second Circuit stated that there were two questions to address in this case. Did decedent retain possession or enjoyment of the property following the transfer? If so, was the transfer a bona fide sale for an adequate and full consideration in money or money's worth? Section 2036(a) generally provides that the gross estate includes the value of all property of which decedent has made a transfer (except in case of a bona fide sale for an adequate and full consideration in money or money's worth), where a decedent has retained for life the possession or enjoyment of, or the right to the income from, the property. The court indicated that there are numerous Tax Court cases where the value of a home was included in a decedent's estate under Section 2036(a) when decedent transferred a home to a relative and continued to live there. In the instant case, the Tax Court found that, based on decedent's age and medical condition, and the terms and actual outcome of the sale and leaseback, the transfer to decedent's son and his wife was made with the understanding that decedent would continue to live in the house until her death. The lease was mere "window dressing" and of no substance or consequence. The court of appeals could overrule the Tax Court's decision only if it was clearly erroneous. The appellate court agreed that the Tax Court's analysis was not clearly erroneous. The Second Circuit stated that the fact that decedent lived in the house until her death, that decedent's son and his wife never attempted to sell the house until decedent's death, and that decedent's son and his wife demanded no rent from the estate after decedent's death and prior to the sale of the house supported the Tax Court's decision. The estate argued that decedent was simply a tenant; thus, "as a matter of law," the property was not includable in her estate. According to the court, decedent's status under the lease was not the deciding factor. The Tax Court's decision was based not upon the lease, but upon an implied agreement the court found between the parties to let decedent live in the house until her death. The appellate court then addressed the second issue—whether the transaction was a bona fide sale for adequate and full consideration. If so, the property would not be includable in decedent's estate even if decedent had retained possession and enjoyment of it. The estate argued that the mortgage note and the $20,000 initially forgiven by decedent constituted adequate and full consideration. The Tax Court held that neither the note nor the forgiven amount constituted consideration because neither party intended that the principal amount owed under the note would actually be paid. Though the note met all the requirements for a fully secured, legally enforceable obligation, the circuit court concluded that the note had no value because of the implied agreement between the parties.

[Estate of Maxwell, 3 F3d 591, 72 AFTR2d 93-6733, 93-2 USTC ¶ 60,145 (2d Cir. 1993).]

Attempted sale of remainder did not keep property out of estate. Plaintiff was the daughter of decedents and was the executrix of her father's estate. Prior to their deaths, decedents conveyed remainder interests in three properties to their daughter. Plaintiff's mother conveyed a remainder interest in property located in Forest Township, Illinois (Forest property), for $124,995, which was paid for with $6,250 in cash and a promissory note of $118,745. The FMV of this property on the date of transfer was $543,338. Plaintiff's mother also conveyed to her daughter a remainder interest in property located in Indian Grove Township, Illinois (Indian Grove property), for $62,574, consisting of $3,129 in cash and a promissory note of $59,445. The FMV of that property on the date of transfer was $272,000. Plaintiff's father conveyed to plaintiff a remainder interest in property located in Eppards Point Township, Illinois (Eppards Point property), for $7,463, which was paid for with $373 in cash and a promissory note for $7,090. The FMV of this property on the date of transfer was $130,200. Apparently, plaintiff's parents each retained a life estate in the property transferred. When plaintiff's mother died on March 11, 1988, the FMV of the Forest property was $711,199, and the Indian Grove property was worth $355,750. When plaintiff's father died on June 9, 1989, the FMV of the Eppards Point property was $207,203. The estate tax return for each decedent did not include these properties but did include the balances due on the promissory notes. The IRS assessed plaintiff's mother's estate $294,569, and her father's estate $90,169, in deficiencies, contending that the estates should have included the FMV of the properties on the date of death, less the consideration paid for the interest transferred, pursuant to Section 2036(a). The plaintiff paid the assessments and then claimed a refund. The government moved for partial summary judgment.

Held: For the IRS. The court stated that summary judgment is appropriate if the court is satisfied that "there is no genuine issue of material fact and that the moving party is entitled to judgment as a matter of law." To withstand summary judgment, the plaintiff must be able to establish that there exists a genuine issue of material fact about which a jury could find in her favor. Section 2036(a) generally provides that the gross estate includes the value of all property of which decedent has made a transfer (except in case of a bona fide sale for adequate and full consideration), under which he has retained for life the possession or enjoyment of, or the income from, the property. Quoting the Fifth Circuit, the court said that "the purpose of this provision is to prevent circumvention of federal estate tax by use of inter vivos schemes which do not significantly alter lifetime beneficial enjoyment of property supposedly transferred by a decedent." Estate of Wyly, 610 F2d 1282 (5th Cir. 1980). According to the court, the issue in the instant case was the adequacy of the consideration received by plaintiff's parents. Under Section 2036(a), unlike under common law, the adequacy of the consideration received is measured against the value of the entire property, not just against the value of the interest transferred. The reason for this is to ensure that the property removed from the estate is replaced with an asset of equal value. Any other interpretation would allow a taxpayer to greatly reduce estate tax by removing a large portion of property from his estate through the sale of only a remainder interest, which generally has a small value in comparison to the total value of the property. If the transferor does not receive adequate and full consideration equal to the FMV of the property, the FMV at the time of death, reduced by the consideration actually received, must be included in the gross estate. In the instant case, the court determined that the transfers were not for full and adequate consideration. Plaintiff's mother conveyed the Forest property for $124,995 when it was worth $543,338, and the Indian Grove property for $62,574 when it was worth $272,000. Plaintiff's father conveyed the Eppards Point property, worth $130,200, for consideration of only $7,463. In order for these properties to be removed from the transferors' estates, plaintiff's parents must have received at least the FMV of the properties at the time of transfer. Because adequate and full consideration was not received, the court found it was not necessary to address whether the transfers were bona fide within the meaning of Section 2036(a). The court then ruled that each of these properties must be included in the transferor's estate and valued at the FMV on the date of death less (1) the cash received on the initial transfer and (2) subsequent cash payments on the promissory notes. Therefore, the Forest property was includable in the plaintiff's mother's estate at $695,929, and the Indian Grove property at $348,105. The Eppards Point property was includable in the plaintiff's father's estate at a value of $205,433. The court then granted the government's motion for partial summary judgment.

[Pittman, 878 F. Supp. 833, 75 AFTR2d 95-520, 95-1 USTC ¶ 60,186 (EDNC 1994).]

Retained right to receive dividends from gifted stock triggers inclusion in gross estate. Following the filing of decedent's estate tax return, in 1983, the executor sought a refund on the ground that he erred in reporting a taxable estate of $812,525. In particular, he alleged that property having a value of $262,250 was improperly included in the gross estate. The disputed property consisted of the stock issued by a corporation of which decedent was president. Although the corporate records reflected an original stock subscription involving decedent and two other individuals, the only share actually issued was held by decedent. In the year preceding his death, he transferred the one share to his son. The corporation itself was in the business of purchasing and improving real properties. It appeared from the record that the unimproved realty, though recorded in the name of the corporation, was purchased by decedent with his own funds. The estate admitted that a majority of the expenses for improvements was borne by decedent and that the remainder was borne by corporate mortgages. Decedent reported the income generated by the improved properties and owed by the corporation on his personal income tax returns. In addition, on his tax return, he took advantage of the depreciation allowance and expense of the properties owned by the corporation. Upon raising the issue of the inter vivos transfer of stock in the refund action, decedent had contended that no part of the value thereof was includable in the gross estate. The IRS argued that ownership of the stock was not effectively transferred until decedent's death and that the entire value was thereby retained as a life estate and was therefore includable in the gross estate under Section 2036(a)(1).

Held: For the IRS. Section 2036(a)(1) contains two criteria for evaluating the presence of a retained life estate, retention of "the possession or enjoyment" or "the right to the income" from the property conveyed. According to the court, the "right to the income" factor was not applicable in the instant case and the term "right," under Section 2036(a)(1), connotes "an ascertainable and legally enforceable power." In this instance, decedent had no legal right to receive the income of the corporation, because he did not own any stock in the corporation and there was no evidence that he received the income as remuneration for his services either as president or as a director. Whether the value of the stock was required to be included in the estate had to be determined by application of the "possession or enjoyment of . . . the property" language. The court found that decedent purportedly transferred his stock interest to his son when the stock was conveyed to him. Yet it was undisputed that decedent enjoyed the property, because he received the income earned by the corporation. Decedent, having retained an interest in the property that did not terminate until his death, acted to ensure that the transfer of the stock was in fact a testamentary disposition, not an inter vivos disposition.

[Lee, 57 AFTR 2d 86-1548, 86-1 USTC ¶ 13,649 (WD Ky, 1986), aff'd, 815 F2d 78, 59 AFTR2d 87-1251 (6th Cir. 1987).]

Transfer of property with retained interest exists, even though transferor never held title. Decedent bought land, which the seller transferred to decedent's children subject to a life interest to decedent. The IRS included the land in decedent's gross estate under Section 2036 as property transferred with a retained interest. The estate contended that Section 2036 was inapplicable, because decedent could not retain an interest where he had no interest other than a life interest in the property in the first place.

Held: For the IRS. Regardless of the form, decedent made a transfer that was essentially testamentary, a disposition to which Section 2036 was intended to apply.

[Estate of Shafer, 80 TC 1145 (1983), aff'd, 749 F2d 1216, 55 AFTR2d 85-1531, 84-2 USTC ¶ 13,599 (6th Cir. 1984).]

Delay in vacating gifted residence results in gross estate inclusion. In August 1969, decedent made a gift of his personal residence to his two daughters. He took his regular winter vacation in Florida and considered buying a home there, but returned in the spring to the residence. Shortly thereafter he suffered a paralyzing stroke, from which he died three years later. He spent his final years in the residence. The IRS took the position that the facts showed an implied agreement at the time of transfer to allow decedent to remain in the home until he relocated. Thus, argued the IRS, decedent retained a life interest in possession of the property, compelling inclusion of the property in the gross estate under Section 2036.

Held: For the IRS. The court stated that the burden is on taxpayer to disprove the existence of an implied agreement and that this burden is particularly onerous on family members. The court noted that decedent made no real effort to find a new home after the transfer and that he continued to pay the real estate taxes on the property. No rent was paid to the daughters for the use of the property. Although there was evidence that one of the daughters made concrete plans to move into the home, the court held that this was contingent upon decedent's successful relocation. This illustrates that the court's decision was not based upon a family agreement that possession would be retained by decedent "for life," but rather that possession could be retained temporarily (until a new home was found). Because decedent had, in fact, retained possession for life when illness and death intervened, the property was includable under Section 2036.

[Estate of Rapelje, 73 TC 82 (1979).]

Decedent's estate includes house that she transferred to her daughter, but continued to live in until her death. Decedent, an elderly woman, transferred the house in which she lived to her daughter. The daughter, who lived elsewhere, sought to sell the house and contracted to buy a new home in which she, her family, and decedent would live together. Decedent died while still living in the house before its sale was completed and before title passed on the new home. The purchase of the new house was canceled. The IRS included decedent's house in decedent's estate under Section 2036.

Held: For the IRS. There was an implied agreement that the mother would continue to live in the house until the daughter sold it. Thus, decedent retained an interest that did not in fact terminate before her death.

[Estate of Honigman, 66 TC 1080 (1976).]

Part of value of transferred house that decedent occupied for one month is included in estate. Decedent transferred a vacation home to his adult children but retained the right either to use or to rent the house for one summer month each year. The rental value of the house for that month was 13.3 percent of the total annual rental income. Under Section 2036, 13.3 percent of the value of the house was includable in decedent's gross estate.

[Rev. Rul. 79-109, 1979-1 CB 297.]

Reservation of timber rights leads to inclusion in gross estate. The IRS ruled that where taxpayer-decedent reserved for ten years all timber rights to land that he gave to another party, the entire value of the underlying real estate, as well as the value of the timber rights, was includable in his gross estate under Section 2036. The fact that under state law the interest in the timber was separate from that in the land was held not to be controlling.

[Rev. Rul. 78-26, 1978-1 CB 286.]

Tenancy in common does not result in asset inclusion under Section 2036 or Section 2038. On March 3, 1980, a husband purchased 114.33 acres of land for $445,430. The deed as recorded gave the husband 77 percent of the land and the wife 23 percent of the land as tenants in common. The husband filed a gift tax return reporting a gift of $102,449 to the wife, but no tax was paid because of the gift tax marital deduction. On May 10, 1983, husband and wife executed a deed conveying thirteen tracts of land, some of which was owned separately by the husband, and some of which was owned in joint tenancy with the wife and was conveyed to themselves as tenants in common. On the same date, the wife conveyed her 23 percent interest in the previously acquired 114.33 acres to her husband. As a result of these two deeds, the husband owned 100 percent of the 114.33 acres and one half of the thirteen tracts as a tenant in common. Again, because of the unlimited marital deduction, no gift tax was paid on these transactions. On May 10, 1983, subsequent to the aforementioned conveyances, the wife executed her will. Under this will, she devised her interest in the thirteen tracts of land to her children or to their descendants in the event that the children predeceased her. She did provide in each instance that her husband was to have the use, possession, and income from these tracts during his lifetime if he survived her. The wife died on August 2, 1984, and the will was admitted to probate. A one-half interest in the thirteen tracts of land was included in her gross estate. The husband subsequently died on December 9, 1987, and the other one-half interest in the thirteen tracts was included as part of his gross estate. The question presented to the IRS was whether the other half-interest in the thirteen tracts (which was previously owned by the wife) should be included in the husband's gross estate under Sections 2036 or 2038, because the husband received, pursuant to the wife's will, a lifetime interest in that property. The critical question to be answered was whether, for purposes of Section 2036, the husband was the transferor of any of the property received as a life tenant under his wife's will that he had previously deeded to her as a tenant in common.

The IRS concluded that the property in which the husband received the lifetime enjoyment under his wife's will was previously owned by the wife as a tenant in common. Following the initial transactions, she owned a tenancy in common in property that she devised to her husband for life, and this tenancy in common interest was one that she could have unilaterally severed or conveyed for full and adequate consideration without his consent. In other words, she must be viewed for purposes of state law and for purposes of Section 2036 as the outright owner of that tenancy in common interest. The IRS reasoned that it could not be maintained that decedent was the legal or equitable owner of any portion of the wife's one-half interest between the date of acquisition and her death approximately one year later. The fact that she acquired a portion of her interest from decedent in one or more gift transactions was held to be irrelevant. Accordingly, the husband was not the transferor of any of the property under Sections 2036 or 2038. The half-interest in the thirteen tracts of land owned by the wife and devised to the husband for life was not includable in his gross estate under either of those IRC sections.

[Priv. Ltr. Rul. 9128005.]

¶ 4.02 RETAINED POWERS

[1] Alteration of Interests

Power to change trustees does not trigger estate inclusion. The settlor created a trust in which her son, decedent, was life beneficiary with the remainder passing to the son's children. The settlor reserved the power to change the trustee, and this power was passed to decedent upon the settlor's death. The trust agreement was ambiguous regarding whether the trustee could be replaced only with a corporate trustee. The IRS argued that decedent was given the right to name an individual as trustee, including himself, and thus possessed a general power of appointment over the trust corpus, causing it to be includable in his estate under Section 2041. The IRS, however, failed to argue that even the power to change corporate trustees was sufficient to render the corpus includable.

Held: For the estate. A life beneficiary's power to change corporate trustees does not constitute a general power of appointment under Section 2041, and thus does not cause the trust corpus to be includable in his estate. This view appears to differ from the IRS position in Revenue Ruling 79-353, 1979-2 CB 325, in which a decedent-settlor's reserved power to change corporate trustees caused the corpus to be included in her estate under Sections 2036 and 2038. The Tenth Circuit, in the instant case, found that the trust instrument gave decedent only the power to change corporate trustees (i.e., not to name himself trustee). More importantly, it concluded that such a power does not cause inclusion under Section 2041.

[First Nat'l Bank of Denver, 648 F2d 1286, 47 AFTR2d 81-1644, 81-1 USTC ¶ 13,408 (10th Cir. 1981).]

Trust assets are not includable in settlor's gross estate where he had power to appoint co-trustees, but could not appoint himself. Decedent was the grantor of a certain inter vivos trust for the benefit of named beneficiaries. By the terms of the trust instrument, the trustees were given broad powers and decedent retained the right to appoint trustees as the need arose. The IRS sought to include the trust corpus in the gross estate, arguing that decedent could have named himself trustee, thereby retaining the power to alter the respective interests of beneficiaries.

Held: For the estate. The court ruled that there is no requirement that the power of self-appointment be expressly withheld as long as, under controlling state law, such power would not be permitted under the terms of the trust indenture. The court pointed out, however, that "careful draftsmen will continue" to state that the grantor has no such power.

[Durst, 559 F2d 910, 40 AFTR2d 77-6232, 77-2 USTC ¶ 13,203 (3d Cir. 1977).]

Assets excluded despite power to replace trustee. Decedent created separate trusts for her daughter and two granddaughters. Each trust instrument provided for an independent corporate trustee that was replaceable at will by decedent. Any successor trustee, however, had to be an independent corporate trust company, and decedent could not appoint herself as trustee. The trustee's discretionary power to distribute assets to the beneficiaries was unlimited by any ascertainable standard. Decedent named the trust department of a local bank as initial trustee and, at her death, she had not exercised her power to replace the trustee. Under Section 2036(a)(2), transferred property is includable in an estate to the extent that decedent retained the right, singly or jointly, to designate who will possess or enjoy the property or the income therefrom. Section 2038(a)(1) requires the inclusion of transferred property if the enjoyment of the property is subject at decedent's death to any change through the exercise of a singly or jointly held power to alter, amend, revoke, or terminate. Taxpayer and the IRS agreed that the trustee's powers, if held by decedent, would result in inclusion of the trust assets in her estate. The issue was whether decedent's power to replace the trustee required attribution of the trustee's powers to decedent. Regulations §§ 20.2036-1(b)(3) and 20.2038-1(a)(3) provide in identical language that decedent has the powers of a trustee if decedent retained the power to remove or to discharge the trustee at any time and appoint himself as the successor trustee. The estate argued that these regulations set up a negative inference that attribution of a trustee's power to decedent was called for only when decedent had the power of self-appointment. The IRS's position was based on Revenue Ruling 79-353, in which it relied on O'Malley, 383 US 627, 17 AFTR2d 1393, 66-1 USTC ¶ 12,388 (S. Ct. 1966), to find that a distribution power not limited by an ascertainable standard resulted in inclusion of the property subject to the power in the estate, even though the power was retained solely in a trustee capacity. According to the ruling, courts generally have held that reserving the power to self-appoint as trustee, whether or not exercised, is equivalent to reservation of the trustee's powers. The ruling concluded that reservation of the power to remove a trustee at will and appoint another trustee was equivalent to reserving the trustee's powers.

Held: For the estate. The Tax Court rejected the implication in the IRS's argument that a grantor with the power to remove and to replace a corporate trustee exercises de facto control over the trustee. The court noted that general trust law precludes trustees from affecting the beneficial enjoyment of any interest in a trust merely to accommodate the grantor's wishes. A trustee's duty is to administer the trust in the sole interest of the beneficiary and to act impartially among multiple beneficiaries, and this duty has priority over the benefit of third parties, including the grantor of the trust. The court also cited Byrum, 408 US 125, 30 AFTR2d 72-5811, 72-2 USTC ¶ 12,859 (S. Ct. 1972), in which the Supreme Court indicated that a "right" to designate possession or enjoyment of property included under Section 2036(a)(2) must be an "ascertainable and legally enforceable power." Measured against this standard, decedent clearly had no right to designate the enjoyment of trust property under either Section 2036(a)(2) or Section 2038(a)(1). Absent such a right, the trust assets were properly excluded from her estate.

[Wall Estate, 101 TC 300 (1993).]

Tax Court holds that pre-1931 irrevocable trust over which grantor released certain powers in 1945 is not includable in grantor's gross estate. In 1927, decedent created an irrevocable trust under which she retained the right to income and the power to amend, alter, or change the distribution of income and the designation of beneficiaries. In 1945, she released the preceding powers. Nevertheless, at her death in 1983, she still retained the power to distribute income to herself, to approve the trustee's determination whether property received by the trust was principal or income, to appoint a successor institutional trustee, and to approve trust investments. Because the trust principal was not included in decedent's estate, the IRS determined a deficiency against it. The IRS argued that the trust principal was includable under Sections 2036(a) and 2038. Section 2036(a) provides for inclusion in decedent's gross estate of the value of property that decedent transferred while retaining the income for life. Section 2036(c) states, however, that Section 2036(a) does not apply to a transfer to a trust made before March 4, 1931. Under Section 2038, an estate includes the value of any interest transferred by decedent over which he retained the power to alter, amend, or revoke on the date of his death.

Held: For the estate. With respect to Section 2036(a), the court noted that in the 1927 trust agreement, decedent expressly relinquished her power to revoke the trust. In so doing, she irrevocably transferred legal title to the trust and made a Section 2036(c) transfer. Therefore, because the transfer in trust occurred before March 4, 1931, the court concluded that the trust principal was not includable in decedent's estate. The court noted that the fact that she reserved the power to designate beneficiaries did not require inclusion of the trust corpus in her gross estate. With respect to Section 2038, the court rejected the IRS's argument that the powers that decedent retained, when viewed cumulatively, were tantamount to the power to alter, amend, or revoke, even though no single power, standing alone, would have come within the purview of Section 2038. According to the court, at her death, decedent's powers did not enable her to direct trust principal to the income beneficiaries or otherwise effect changes with respect to the trust corpus. She had no power to alter the trust corpus. Accordingly, the deficiency against the estate was not sustained by the court.

[Estate of Graves, 92 TC 1294 (1989).]

Right to withhold payments is not power causing trust's inclusion in gross estate. Decedent was a trustee of a Massachusetts realty trust. He gave all of his common shares and most of his preferred shares in the trust to his children and descendants. The trust instrument provided for noncumulative dividends on the preferred stock, and for dividends on the common stock only if the preferred dividends were paid. The IRS argued that the trust assets were includable in decedent's gross estate under Section 2036(a)(2), because by paying or withholding dividends on the preferred stock, decedent, as trustee, could shift the enjoyment of income and principal between the classes.

Held: For the estate. The trust was a corporation for tax purposes. Under Byrum, 408 US 125 (1972), a de facto right to affect dividend policy is not includable in a gross estate if execution of the policy is subject to fiduciary restraint. Under state law, decedent did not have the power to withhold dividends arbitrarily and capriciously.

[Estate of Cohen, 79 TC 1015 (1982).]

Main trust is not includable because of supplemental trusts. Decedent created a family trust to pay annuities to certain individuals. If, at the beginning of any year, the income were insufficient to pay the annuities, the trustee could invade principal or the grantor or his son could elect to make up the deficiency. The trust gave the grantor the power to create annuity payments to other beneficiaries or to increase the annuity payments to the existing beneficiaries by creating a supplemental trust. In that event, the trustee had the power to combine the trusts. The IRS contended that the power made the corpus includable in the grantor's estate.

    Held: For the estate. Despite the grantor's ability to create supplemental trusts that would affect the beneficial interests of the original family trust, the corpus of the latter trust was not includable in his estate under Sections 2036 and 2038. Decedent did not have the power to increase payments under the trust just because the trusts could be combined. The provision would not have been necessary if decedent could have increased the family trust payments.

[Estate of Edmonds, 72 TC 970 (1979), acq. 1980-2 CB 1.]

Trust assets traced to one co-grantor are excluded from value of trust. Decedent's husband was the original and principal grantor of a trust for their daughters. When he established the trust, he named decedent a co-trustee. Later she gave the trust $1,500 and a $5,000 Treasury note. At the time of her gift, the $6,500 equaled 0.98 percent of the total trust assets. One of the trustees' powers was to invade principal to provide a daughter with funds "for a home, business, or for any other purpose believed by the Trustees to be for her benefit." The IRS contended that this power to control the time and amount of distributions to the beneficiaries was not limited by an ascertainable standard, so that part of the value of the trust corpus must revert to decedent's estate under Section 2038. At the time of decedent's death, the trust assets were worth more than $4 million. The IRS said that the inclusion should be in excess of $40,000. It reached this figure by applying to the value of the corpus on the valuation date the percentage of her personal contribution to the total trust assets at the time of her transfer.

    Held: Where trust assets can be traced to the gift of one grantor, the value of those assets should be excluded from the computation fixing the date-of-death value of another grantor's contribution. This decision is a logical extension of the rule announced in Estate of Kinney, 39 TC 728 (1963), in which it was held that where assets contributed by one grantor are still held by a trust, the value of these assets fixes the amount of the estate tax inclusion. The court did not agree with the IRS calculation of the includable amount, however. The court determined that the base figure in this computation should not include the value of trust assets that her husband had originally contributed and of assets that the trust had received in distributions because of its ownership of the original assets. By tracing stock dividends and spin-offs from the original corpus, the court found that over $3 million could be attributed to the husband's transfer. When it excluded this amount, it applied the 0.98 percent to the balance and the includable amount dropped to less than $14,000.

[Estate of Bell, 66 TC 729 (1976).]

Decedent's retention of power to substitute property of equal value does not result in retained power to "alter, amend, or revoke." In 1931, decedent created an irrevocable trust to which were transfered insurance policies on decedent's life, as well as certain other income-producing property. Decedent was one of three trustees. Premiums of the trust were to be paid from trust income, with the remaining income to be paid to decedent for life and then, after his death, to the daughter until she reached age 50, at which time the trust was to terminate. The trustees had the power to sell property if needed to pay the premiums and to borrow on the policies for premium payment purposes, and the trustees further had the power to select which policies should be maintained. Decedent retained the power to substitute property of equal value for that transferred to the trust. The IRS took the position that this power was a power to "alter, amend, or revoke," requiring inclusion in decedent's gross estate pursuant to Section 2038, or, alternatively, that the proceeds should be includable under Section 2042.

 Held: For the estate. The power to substitute was not a prohibited power under Section 2038, because property of equal value had to be substituted, and therefore, the corpus could not be depleted. This power is similar to a retained power to direct investments under a fiduciary standard of good faith. The interest of beneficiaries would be protected by New York law, and therefore, decedent did not have the power to deprive a remainderman of benefits by investing in highly productive property. Moreover, decedent did not possess incidents of ownership by reason of his policy dividends as an income beneficiary, because dividends are merely a reduction in premium paid.

[Estate of Jordahl, 65 TC 92 (1975), acq. 1977-1 CB 1.]

IRS rules on effect of power to replace trustee. Revenue Ruling 79-353, 1979-2 CB 325, concluded that the value of property transferred to a trust is includable in decedent-grantor's gross estate if the grantor retained the power to replace the corporate trustee. That conclusion does not apply to a transfer or an addition to a trust made before October 29, 1979, if the trust was irrevocable on October 28, 1979.

[Rev. Rul. 81-51, 1981-1 CB 458.]

Byrum ruling results in revocation of earlier revenue ruling. The IRS revoked Revenue Ruling 67-54, 1967-1 CB 269, in light of Byrum, 408 US 125 (1972), which overruled the proposition on which the revenue ruling was based, that is, that the voting control of a corporation, coupled with restrictions on the disposition of nonvoting stock, is equivalent to the right to designate the person who shall enjoy the income. Section 2036(b), affecting the retention of voting rights, does not apply where the transferor could not vote the transferred stock and thus does not change the effect _Byrum_ has on the earlier ruling.

[Rev. Rul. 81-15, 1981-1 CB 457.]

[2] Revocation of Interests

Trust gifts within three years of death not taxed in decedent's estate. In 1986, decedent amended a revocable trust she had created in 1981 to include provisions that gave her the power to create irrevocable fractional shares in the trust for her descendants and their spouses. The amendment also gave her the power to modify or to revoke the trust at will. Beneficiaries of these fractional interests were to receive any income attributable to their interests. In 1986 and 1987, decedent gave each of her children fractional interests in the trust worth about $10,000 per interest. She died in 1987, and her estate tax return did not include the interests given as lifetime gifts. The IRS sought to include the gifts as part of the gross estate under Sections 2035 and 2038.

Held: For decedent. The property would be includable under these provisions if decedent held a power on the date of her death to amend or to revoke the transfers or had relinquished such power within three years of death. The Eighth Circuit cited Jalkut, 96 TC 675 (1991), acq., in discussing the difference between (1) a taxpayer exercising a power to withdraw assets and then making gifts of those assets (which would not come under Section 2038) and (2) a taxpayer, directly or through a trustee, distributing assets as gifts by relinquishing the power to amend or revoke a trust with respect to the assets (which would be included in taxpayer's estate if death occurred within three years after the gifts were made). The court found that the terms of the trust permitted decedent to invade the corpus and make withdrawals without terminating the entire trust. She exercised that power to make transfers of fractional interests that were distinct from the remaining trust corpus, rather than relinquishing a power to modify a previously transferred interest. Thus, the interests given as lifetime gifts were not part of her estate.

[Kisling, 32 F3d 1222, 74 AFTR2d 94-7463, 94-2 USTC ¶ 60,176 (8th Cir. 1994), acq., 1995-2 CB 1.]

Gifts from revocable trust were not included in gross estate. Decedent executed a revocable trust agreement on December 17, 1984. Under its terms, she had the right to amend or revoke the trust. She also had the right to direct the trustee to (1) distribute income to her or to her order in monthly or other convenient installments and (2) distribute principal to her or one or more other persons as she might request in writing. Pursuant to such written requests, certain marketable securities were distributed to thirteen of her descendants in 1985 and 1987. Decedent died in 1987. The transfers made from the trust to descendants in 1985 and 1987, less the annual exclusion amounts, were reported on her 1985 and 1987 gift tax returns and as adjusted taxable gifts on the estate tax return. The balance of the assets in the revocable trust were listed on Schedule G of the estate tax return at date of death values. After auditing the estate tax return, the IRS determined that the 1985 and 1987 gifts should have been included in the gross estate. The IRS increased the value of the estate by the date of death value of the gifts and issued a notice of deficiency to the estate. The estate paid the additional tax and interest and then filed a refund claim. The estate sued when the claim was denied. The district court granted the IRS's motion for summary judgment and denied the estate's motion.

 Held: Reversed for the estate. Generally, gifts made by a decedent within three years of death are not includable in the gross estate, according to Section 2035(d)(1). There is an exception in Section 2056(d)(2), which provides that the general rule does not apply to a transfer of an interest in property that is included in the gross estate under Sections 2036, 2037, 2038, or 2042, or would have been included under one of these sections if the interest had been retained by decedent.

 The pertinent reference in this section is to Section 2038, which concerns revocable transfers. Section 2038(a)(1) generally states that the gross estate includes the value of all property of which a decedent has made a transfer but has retained the power to alter, amend, revoke, or terminate or has relinquished such a power within three years of death. Both parties agreed that the first part of Section 2038(a)(1), regarding retention of a power to revoke, applied only to the assets remaining in the revocable trust when decedent died. The question raised was whether the second part of the section, referring to a power that was relinquished within three years of death, applied to the gifts that were made in 1985 and 1987. The IRS contended that decedent relinquished her power to alter, amend, revoke, or terminate the trust with respect to the amounts given as gifts. The estate argued that the transfers were not a relinquishment, but rather an exercise, of decedent's withdrawal power as provided in the trust agreement. The Eighth Circuit compared the facts in the instant case to those in two other cases—Barton, 66 TCM 1547, RIA TC

Memo. ¶ 93,583 (1993), and Jalkut, 96 TC 675 (1991). The court recited a statement from *Barton*, in which the Tax Court said that "the determination of whether transfers occurring within three years of death are to be included in a decedent's gross estate pursuant to Section 2038 turns on the particular terms of the trust agreement and the specific powers granted therefrom." In *Barton*, decedent created a revocable trust that required the trustee to "pay any part of the principal of the trust estate as the Grantor may direct in writing." The IRS had claimed that transfers made by the trustee to various individuals at the grantor's request were relinquishments of Barton's power to revoke the trust agreement with respect to those assets. The Tax Court disagreed, ruling that the transfers were an exercise of decedent's power as grantor/trustee to invade the trust corpus at will, a power that she specifically retained for herself.

The facts are similar in *Jalkut*, where decedent established a revocable trust in which the trustees were directed to pay during decedent's life "such sums from the principal as he may request." Within three years of his death, Jalkut requested that amounts be transferred from the trust to six individuals. The court there ruled that the transfers could only have been made pursuant to Jalkut's power to withdraw principal from the trust because he was the sole permissible distributee. No one else was entitled to transfers from the trust. The transfers were, in effect, withdrawals by decedent, followed by direct transfers by him to the six individuals.

The IRS in the instant case attempted to distinguish *Jalkut* on the grounds that the trustee in the instant case was instructed to transfer assets to "one or more other persons," and that this trust language created a large class of permissible donees. The court did not agree that such language moved the case out of the realm of *Barton* and *Jalkut*, since no distributions could be made to anyone without decedent's consent and instruction. Alternatively, the IRS argued that the transfers should be included in decedent's estate because through Section 2035(d)(2), they would have been included in her estate under Section 2038 if she had retained the amounts transferred. The court found that the IRS was going too far with this argument. If accepted, such an argument would mean that every transfer from a revocable trust made within three years of death would be included in decedent's estate. This result contradicted the holdings in *Barton* and *Jalkut*.

[McNeely, 16 F3d 303, 73 AFTR2d 94-1168, 94-1 USTC ¶ 60,155 (8th Cir. 1994).]

Gifts made under durable power of attorney are held to be includable in estate. In December 1973, decedent, a resident of Virginia, executed a durable power of attorney appointing her son as her attorney-in-fact. The power of attorney was a typically broad power granting the attorney the power "to lease, sell, grant, convey, assign, transfer, mortgage and set over to any person, firm or corporation for any such consideration as he may deem advantageous any and all of my property." In addition, the following general power was granted to the attorney-in-fact:

> To do, execute and perform all and every other act or acts, thing or things as fully and to all intents and purposes as I myself might or could do if acting personally, it being my intention by this instrument to give my attorney hereby appointed, full and complete power to handle any of my business or to deal with any and all of my property of every kind and description, real, personal, or mixed, wheresoever located and howsoever held, in his full and absolute discretion.

The power contained no specific provision authorizing the attorney to make gifts or to convey without consideration. Approximately one year after the power of attorney was granted, decedent and her husband embarked upon an estate plan that consisted of making gifts to their sons within the scope of the annual gift tax exclusion. Typically, the husband would make yearly transfers to the three children and to trusts established for the benefit of their seven grandchildren. Decedent would join in these conveyances made by her husband and consented to treating the gifts as being made one-half by her. Between 1977 and 1980, decedent became incompetent to manage her affairs because of Alzheimer's disease, and she remained incompetent until her death in 1989. Consequently, when her husband made additional conveyances to take advantage of his gift tax exclusions in 1980 and 1981, the attorney-in-fact joined in the execution of these transfers to convey decedent's dower interest in real property. After decedent's husband's death, the attorney-in-fact continued to make gifts within the ambit of the annual gift tax exclusion pursuant to the power of attorney granted to him. After decedent's death in 1989, the estate tax return filed on her behalf did not include the gifts made by her son as attorney-in-fact. The IRS took the position that in the absence of an express grant of authority, a general power of attorney did not authorize gifts by an attorney-in-fact. The IRS determined that the gifts made by the attorney-in-fact were voidable transfers includable in her estate under Section 2038(a)(1). The Tax Court ultimately rejected the IRS's position and held that the gifts were not includable in decedent's gross estate.

Held: Reversed for the IRS. The Fourth Circuit acknowledged that there was no specific Virginia authority on this point, so it was compelled to determine how Virginia's highest court would decide this issue. The Fourth Circuit decided that the Virginia Supreme Court would conclude that the gifts were not authorized by the power of attorney. It reasoned that the Virginia Supreme Court might well adopt as a matter of policy a flat rule that an unrestricted power to make gifts will not be found in any comprehensive durable power of attorney that does not expressly grant this power. The Fourth Circuit next concluded that even if the Virginia Supreme Court would not adopt such a flat rule, it might decide, looking at the specific instrument and the circumstances of the situation, that the gifts were not authorized here. The guiding principle in determining whether an attorney-in-fact has certain powers is to examine the principal's intent as manifested in the instrument itself and to look to the surrounding circumstances only to clarify ambiguity in the instrument. The court noted that there was a glaring omission in the instrument, namely, the specific power to make gifts or transfers without adequate consideration. The other types of transfers (such as sale, lease, and mortgage) were specifically referred to in the power, hence, absence of the power to make a gift strongly suggested a specific intent to omit it, as opposed to an oversight. In addition, the court concluded that the expansive language authorizing the attorney-in-fact, in effect, to do everything that the grantor or the power might do was intended only to confer incidental interstitial powers necessary to accomplish objects as to which authority had already been expressly granted. Consequently, the Fourth Circuit determined that the omission of a specific gift power in the power of attorney was likely to be dispositive to a Virginia court. The Fourth Circuit concluded that compelling policy considerations require great care by courts that are asked to infer powers not expressly authorized by powers of attorney. This is especially so when the power is a "dangerous" one, such as a gift power, and when the power is a durable one that survives a principal's ability to monitor its exercise. Accordingly, the court ruled that the gifts were not authorized by the power of attorney in question and, hence, were voidable transfers included in decedent's estate for federal estate tax purposes.

[Estate of Casey, 948 F2d 895, 91-2 USTC ¶ 60,091, AFTR2d 91-6060 (4th Cir. 1991).]

Claims Court applies Section 2036 in requiring inclusion of value of decedent's community property that had been transferred to her husband's testamentary trust. Decedent, who died in 1980, was predeceased in 1977 by her husband. They had both been lifelong residents of California, a community property state. By the terms of her husband's will, decedent had an election whether to take under the will, in which case she could transfer her part of the community property into a trust along with her husband's estate and receive income for life, or, alternatively, to reject the will and receive only her part of the community property. After filing the estate tax return, she executed a written election to take under the will. Subsequent to decedent's death in 1980, her estate filed its estate tax return, which made reference to the trust established by the husband's will, but did not include any of the value thereof in decedent's gross estate. On audit, the IRS raised the issue of whether the gross estate should include, under Section 2036, the value of decedent's contribution to the trust assets. The IRS took the position that decedent's election had the effect of an exchange of her community property interest for a life estate, and that the value of the life estate was considerably less than the value of one-half of the community property. The estate, for its part, contended that the case was governed by Section 2036(a), which sets forth an exception to the inclusion of a life estate where it was transferred by decedent for adequate and full consideration. According to the estate, which stipulated that the value of the community property exceeded that of the life estate, the consideration flowing from decedent was merely the remainder interest that was left at her death, not the FMV of one half of the community property.

Held: For the IRS. The court rejected the estate's contention that decedent, by electing to take under the will, merely relinquished the interest that was left to the remainderman following her own life estate. The court considered previously decided cases on point and concluded that the corpus of decedent's community property, not just the remainder, had been transferred. Accordingly, the court found that the transfer was not for adequate and full consideration, and that Section 2036 required the inclusion of her life estate valued as of the time of her death, as adjusted.

[Gradow, 11 Cl. Ct. 808, 59 AFTR2d 87-1221, 87-1 USTC ¶ 13,711 (1987), aff'd, 897 F2d 516, 65 AFTR2d 90-1229, 90-1 USTC ¶ 60,010 (Fed. Cir. 1990).]

Tax Court rules on transfers from revocable trusts and annual exclusion. In September 1971, decedent, Lee D. Jalkut, created the Lee D. Jalkut Revocable Trust (the Revocable Trust). Jalkut funded the trust by transferring to it his entire estate, including his personal residence, bank and brokerage accounts, and publicly traded stocks. Jalkut appointed himself as trustee and retained the power to amend or revoke. In 1973, Jalkut amended the trust to authorize the trustees to pay the grantor any amounts of income or principal that the grantor requested. If the grantor became unable to manage his affairs, the trustees could use income and principal to care for the grantor or his descendants. The trustees were also authorized to continue to make any payments or gifts that the grantor had been making prior to becoming disabled. In 1984, Jalkut was diagnosed as having inoperable cancer. Later that year he amended the trust again to include instructions for the distribution of the trust property after his death. After making specific bequests, the balance of the property was to be held in trust for the benefit of Jalkut's children. This amendment to the Revocable Trust also named the replacement trustees.

In November 1984, Jalkut established an irrevocable trust for the benefit of his grandchildren (the Family Trust). The trust was funded by transferring to it $40,356 of mutual fund shares that had been held in the Revocable Trust. Jalkut set up a second irrevocable trust in December 1984 for the benefit of Anna S. and Jane Jalkut (the Jalkut Trust). This trust was funded by transferring $20,000 from the Revocable Trust. On January 25, 1985, the replacement trustees were notified by Jalkut's physician that Jalkut was no longer capable of managing the Revocable Trust. Rosehelen Klein-Fields and Nathan M. Grossman assumed the position of co-trustees. That same day they made the following transfers from the Revocable Trust:

1. $40,000 to the Family Trust
2. $20,000 to the Jalkut Trust
3. $10,000 to Michael Jalkut
4. $10,000 to Theresa Jalkut

Lee Jalkut died on February 6, 1985. Nathan Grossman was appointed as executor of Jalkut's estate. In November of that year, Grossman filed the federal estate tax return, on which the total gross estate was valued at $1,152,139. No transfers of assets were included in the gross estate under Sections 2035 or 2038. The IRS determined that there was a $55,184 deficiency in the estate tax due. It claimed that the $140,356 in transfers from the Revocable Trust in 1984 and 1985 should have been included in the estate under Sections 2035 and 2038. Grossman, as executor of the estate, contended that the value of the Revocable Trust was includable in decedent's gross estate only under Section 2033 (which excludes annual exclusion gifts). Sections 2035 and 2038 did not apply, he contended, because decedent did not divest himself of beneficial ownership of the assets when he transferred them to the Revocable Trust. The transfers made in 1984 and 1985 all qualified for the gift tax annual exclusion and were excludable from the gross estate under Section 2035(d)(1).

Alternatively, Grossman argued that the Service should look past the technical form of the transfers to their substance and treat all the transfers as if Jalkut had withdrawn the assets from the Revocable Trust and then made the transfers. Lastly, Grossman contended that it would be unjust to include transfers made within three years of death in the estate if deathbed transfers that qualify for the annual exclusion are not includable for decedents who die after 1981.

Held: For the IRS. The Tax Court began its response by stating that Section 2038, not 2033, determined whether property transferred to a trust was includable in an estate, and that generally, the value of a revocable trust at decedent's death was includable. The court next considered whether the transfers *from* the Revocable Trust were includable in the gross estate under Sections 2035(d)(2) or 2038(a)(1). Grossman claimed that annual exclusion gifts were not includable in the estate, because of Section 2035(d)(1). The court disagreed because of the provisions in Section 2035(d)(2). Grossman then claimed that Section 2038(a)(1) did not apply to annual exclusion gifts. He cited a number of letter rulings to support his claim. The court noted that such rulings have no precedential force, but said that "the number of rulings reveals that the issue is one of significant importance to estate planners." The court disagreed with Grossman's claim that annual exclusion gifts were beyond the reach of Section 2038. It decided that the determination whether the transfers would be included under Section 2038 depended on the particular terms of the trust agreement. While Jalkut was acting as trustee, he was the sole permissible beneficiary of the trust income and principal. The only way that trust assets could have been transferred to a third party was for Jalkut to withdraw the income or principal for his own use and then give it to the transferee; thus, the transferor was Jalkut, not the Revocable Trust. Therefore, the transfers in 1984 were not a relinquishment under Section 2038 of Jalkut's power to influence the enjoyment of trust property transferred, and they were excludable gifts under Section 2035(d)(1).

A different situation arose after Jalkut became disabled and could no longer act as trustee. At that point, the replacement trustees had authority to transfer trust principal and income to persons and entities other than Jalkut. Transfers made by the replacement trustees could not be treated as withdrawals by Jalkut for his own use. They were, however, relinquishments by Jalkut, through the trustees, of his power to alter, amend, revoke, or terminate the trust with respect to the assets transferred as described in Section 2038(a). Consequently, these transfers were includable in Jalkut's estate under Section 2035(d)(2).

[Estate of Jalkut, 96 TC 675 (1991).]

Gifts made under power of attorney were includable in estate. Decedent executed a durable power of attorney, naming his son as the attorney in fact. The power of attorney did not expressly authorize the son to make gifts on behalf of decedent. During the three years before decedent's death, his son made a number of annual exclusion gifts. The IRS argued that these amounts should be included in decedent's estate.

Held: For the IRS. Because the power of attorney did not explicitly authorize the attorney in fact to make gifts on behalf of the principal (as required by state (Nebraska) law), decedent-principal retained his power to revoke the gifts. Thus, the gifts were includable in his estate under Section 2038(a)(1).

[Townsend, 889 F. Supp. 369, 75 AFTR2d 95-1946, 95-1 USTC ¶ 60,192 (D. Neb. 1995).]

Estates included transfers from living trusts. In this ruling, decedent set up a trust in 1983 under which the trustee was to distribute income or principal to decedent or otherwise as she directed. If her doctor certified in writing that she was incapable of handling her financial affairs, the trustee could pay trust income or principal to her for her benefit or that of her dependents. In 1988 and 1989, decedent asked the trustee to make eleven gifts of $10,000 each and five gifts of $5,000 each from the trust to specified individuals. She died in 1989, and her estate included the date of death value of the trust, but not the value of the transfers, in the gross estate. Section 2035(a) provides that a gross estate includes the value of all property interests transferred by decedent within three years before death. Although under Section 2035(d)(1) this rule generally does not apply to decedents dying after 1981, Section 2035(d)(2) provides that it does apply to a transfer of an interest in property that is included in decedent's estate under Sections 2036 (transfers with retained life estate), 2037 (transfers taking effect at death), 2038 (revocable transfers), or 2042 (life insurance proceeds), or that would have been so included if decedent had retained the interest.

In addition, Section 2038(a) provides that the gross estate includes the value of property to the extent of any interest that decedent transferred without receiving adequate and full consideration in money or money's worth if, at death, the enjoyment of the interest is subject to any change through exercise of a power by decedent (alone or with any other person) to alter, amend, revoke, or terminate, or when such power is relinquished duing the three years ending on the date of death. According to Revenue Ruling 75-553, 1975-2 CB 477, if decedent creates a revocable trust with the remainder payable to decedent's estate, the corpus that is payable to the estate is decedent's property under Section 2033 (property in which decedent had an interest). In Estate of Jalkut, 96 TC 675 (1991), acq., decedent created a revocable trust that provided for the payment of all net income and principal as he requested during his life. If he became unable to manage his affairs, the trustee could pay income and principal to decedent or his descendants. During the three years before decedent's death, he became incompetent and transfers were made to persons other than decedent while he was competent and incompetent. At his death, the trust was distributed to third parties.

The Tax Court held that decedent was the sole permissible beneficiary while he was competent. Thus, the transfers to persons other than decedent during this period were withdrawals preceding gifts by decedent. Since transfers to or for the benefit of his descendants when he was incompetent were authorized by the trust, the court found no reason to recharacterize the transfers as withdrawals by decedent followed by transfers to third parties. Rather, they were relinquishments under Section 2038(a) of decedent's power to alter, amend, revoke, or terminate the trust with respect to the transferred property. Because the transfers would have been includable in the gross estate under Section 2038 if retained by decedent, they were held to be includable under Section 2035(d)(2).

In the ruling, the IRS held that the corpus remaining at decedent's death was includable in her gross estate under Section 2038, citing Revenue Ruling 75-553 and *Jalkut.* Since decedent's doctor never certified that she was incompetent, the trustee could distribute income or principal directly to any donees designated by decedent orally or in writing. Thus, the transfers were a relinquishment under Section 2038(a) of her power to amend or revoke the trust. In addition, since the transfers would have been includable in the estate under Section 2038 if retained by decedent, they were also includable under Section 2035(d)(2).

[Tech. Adv. Mem. 9318004.]

Predeath trust transfers are included in estate. Decedent set up a revocable trust, retaining the right to revoke, alter, or amend it. Two years before her death she directed the trustee to transfer $25,000 from the trust to each of three donees. When she died in 1988, though the trust assets were included in her gross estate, the $25,000 gifts from the trust were not. Under Section 2038(a), decedent's gross estate includes lifetime transfers, by trust or otherwise, if the enjoyment of the transferred property was subject at her death to any change through the exercise by her of a power to alter, amend, revoke, or terminate the trust. Section 2035(d)(2) includes in the gross estate any transfers made within three years of death if the transfer would have been includable under Section 2038 had the interest transferred been retained by decedent. Because the interest in the trust assets would have been included had the transfers not been made, these sections combined to include the gifts in the estate. The estate attempted to escape this logic by arguing that decedent's revocable trust was a vehicle to avoid probate and that decedent actually retained control over the assets. The estate also suggested that even if the trust arrangement could not be ignored, the trust was merely operating as the agent of decedent pursuant to her power to withdraw trust corpus for her own benefit.

The IRS disagreed, concluding that the estate was bound by the form chosen. Consequently, because decedent's directions to the trustee to transfer assets to certain parties was little different from decedent making direct gifts, the tax consequences were substantially different. Had the gifts been made directly, they would have been excludable from decedent's estate. The result of the direction to the trustee was that the transferred assets were includable in decedent's estate.

[Tech. Adv. Mem. 9049002.]

Distributions from grantor trust within three years of death are includable in gross estate. An individual established a revocable trust in 1976 and amended it several times. The net income of the trust was payable to the grantor for life. The trust principal was payable as directed by the grantor. When the grantor became physically or mentally disabled, the trustees were to continue to have the power to pay income and principal to or for the grantor. The trustees also were to have the power to distribute income or corpus to the children, the children's spouses, and grandchildren of the grantor. On the grantor's death, the property was to pass to his wife or to trusts created for the benefit of other members of the family. In the three years before the grantor's death, under the grantor's instructions, the trustees on several occasions distributed property directly from the trust to several individuals. When the grantor died in 1986, the trust assets were reported on Schedule G of the estate tax return as includable in the gross estate. The distributions to the various individuals, however, were not reported as includable in the gross estate for federal tax purposes.

The IRS concluded that the distributions of property within three years of the individual's death were includable in the gross estate under Sections

2035(a) and 2038. The IRS rejected taxpayer's argument that the distributions from the trust were comparable to distributions by the grantor personally, because he retained so much power and control over the trust. The IRS reasoned that the form of the gifts was significant in this context, because the form dictates the application of Section 2038, which triggers Section 2035(d)(2). The IRS refused to consider the transfer to have been made by an agent of the grantor or to treat the property as included in the gross estate under Section 2041.

[Tech. Adv. Mem 9015001.]

[3] Change of Beneficiaries

Revocable transfers are includable in gross estate. Decedent retained powers to add new beneficiaries and to change the respective beneficial interests in a trust he created. The Tax Court required inclusion of trust assets in his estate.

　　Held: Affirmed for the IRS. Parol evidence could not be used to establish that decedent did not intend to retain these powers. Thus, the trust assets were includable in the estate. The entire amount of payments made to the administrator of the estate was deductible, however, though decedent had stipulated that only $5,000 was to be paid to the executor.

[Estate of Craft, 608 F2d 240, 45 AFTR2d 80-1716, 80-1 USTC ¶ 13,327 (5th Cir. 1979).]

Grantor's position as director of charitable beneficiary is held to be sufficient retained power for purposes of Section 2036 inclusion. During 1961, decedent, who was the founder of a cosmetics empire, created a charitable trust primarily to reduce his income tax liability. The trust consisted of 35,000 shares of common stock in the cosmetics company in the form of voting trust certificates. Under the terms of the trust, the sole income beneficiary during decedent's lifetime was a charitable foundation previously organized by decedent. Although he never held a position as trustee, decedent served as an officer and director of the foundation with the power to designate the recipients of foundation grants. In 1972, however, the IRS released Revenue Ruling 75-552, 1972 CB 525, which held that Section 2036 compels the inclusion in gross estate of the value of trust corpus where a decedent-grantor was an officer of the trust's charitable beneficiary. On the advice of counsel, decedent resigned his position with the foundation, effective in April 1973. In August 1975, he died. The IRS asserted that the trust corpus—valued at $3.67 million—was includable in decedent's gross estate under Sections 2035 and 2036.

Held: For the IRS. The court upheld the position of the IRS that decedent's powers as director of the foundation, the charitable beneficiary, amounted to a retained power to control enjoyment of trust property within the meaning of Section 2036. The fact that decedent had no rights relating to the trust's distribution of funds was not determinative, because decedent possessed a fairly equivalent power in his other capacity. The court refused to grant the IRS's motion for summary judgment, however, finding that there was a triable issue of material fact regarding whether the 1975 resignation was "in contemplation of death" for purposes of Section 2035 as then in effect.

[Rifkind, 5 Cl. Ct. 362, 54 AFTR2d 84-6453, 84-2 USTC ¶ 13,577 (1984).]

Trust assets are includable in gross estate under Section 2036(a)(2). Prior to his death in 1977, decedent established an inter vivos trust for the benefit of his daughter. Until 1950, decedent served as trustee; but thereafter unrelated third parties were named as trustees, and decedent took no part in the trust administration. The trust instrument provided that all income would be "devoted for the sole benefit" of decedent's daughter "in such manner, and to such extent as I, or my successor, may desire." Any income not distributed during a given calendar year was to become part of the corpus of the trust. Upon reaching age 21, the daughter was to receive distributions from the trust in $5,000 installments every five years. Each payment was to include all accumulations added to the principal since the last disbursement in the event that the entire income had not been distributed. When the daughter reached age 66, the trust was to terminate, with the balance of the assets to be paid over to her. After examining the estate tax return, the IRS determined that the trust should have been included in decedent's gross estate under Section 2036(a)(2). In the IRS's view, he retained the right to designate which party was to possess and enjoy the trust income and corpus. The estate disputed the deficiency and brought the matter to the Tax Court.

Held: For the IRS. The trust assets were includable in the gross estate under Section 2036(a)(2). To avoid Section 2036(a)(2), it is not enough that the settlor-trustee has no retained right to determine to whom trust income or corpus will go in the event that the named beneficiary dies prematurely. The right of the settlor-trustee to deny to the named beneficiary the present enjoyment of the trust income is a right of designation within the scope of the statute. The court rejected the estate's contention that even if decedent retained a Section 2036(a)(2) "right" upon the original creation of the trust, he no longer held such "right" after he named a successor trustee in 1950. There was no indication in either the declaration of trust or any of the documents by which decedent appointed successor trustees that decedent at any time was precluded from again serving as a trustee. The right of designation was retained by decedent when the trust was created and was not thereafter released by him.

[Estate of Alexander, 81 TC 757 (1983).]

Trust property is not includable in estate, despite after-born children beneficiary provision. Decedent transferred property irrevocably in trust, with income going to his children for a specified period. After the specified period, there would be a distribution of principal to the children. The instrument automatically included subsequently born or adopted children as beneficiaries. The property was not includable in decedent's gross estate under Sections 2036 or 2038. The addition of more beneficiaries was only a collateral consequence of fathering or adopting more children.

[Rev. Rul. 80-255, 1980-2 CB 272.]

Employee's power to change beneficiary of death benefit results in inclusion of benefit in his gross estate. Taxpayer's employment contract provided that in consideration of his services, he would receive a stated salary and a death benefit payable to a beneficiary designated by him if taxpayer was employed by the corporation at the time of his death. Taxpayer had the power to change beneficiaries. The IRS ruled that this would result in the inclusion of the death benefit in decedent's gross estate under Section 2038(a)(1).

[Rev. Rul. 76-304, 1976-2 CB 269.]

CHAPTER **5**

Joint Interests

¶ 5.01 JOINT INTERESTS, GENERALLY

Jointly held property is partially included in estate. Decedent gave certain real property to her daughters, who held it for some years before selling it and buying stock with the proceeds. The daughters held the stock jointly with decedent. Upon decedent's death, her daughters sought to exclude the stock from her estate.

Held: For the IRS (in part). Jointly held property is includable in decedent's estate unless decedent did not supply the consideration. Here the appreciation in the real property is deemed to have been supplied by the daughters, and a ratio is applied to the FMV of the stock for inclusion.

[Estate of Goldsborough, 70 TC 1077 (1979), aff'd, 673 F2d 1310, 49 AFTR2d 82-1469 (4th Cir. 1982).]

Jointly held property conveyed through adequate consideration is excludable from gross estate. Decedent conveyed property under a "Joint Tenancy Grant Deed," which provided that she would receive all the income from the property, and her son performed all of the management activities associated with the property after transfer. If decedent predeceased her son, he would be sole owner, and vice versa. The son performed all of the management functions, and during decedent's life, she received and reported all of the income and claimed all of the deductions associated with the property on her income tax returns. Two limited partnership interests were also transferred, but the son provided only nominal services in exchange for his interest. The estate tax return included 50 percent of the value of the property and limited partnerships in decedent's gross estate. The IRS determined that 100 percent of the property should have been included.

Held: For taxpayer (in part). Decedent's gross estate includes the full date of death value of jointly held property, except for that part of the property conveyed for full and adequate consideration to the surviving joint owner. Decedent's son's management services performed with regard to the property were real and substantial, and included locating tenants, negotiating leases, collecting rents, and any other necessary management functions associated with the property. These services were sufficient to constitute full and adequate consideration for the receipt of his joint tenancy interest. Consequently, only 50 percent of the value of the property was includable in decedent's estate. With regard to the limited partnership interests, however, the services performed by decedent's son were minimal and part-time and insufficient to constitute full and adequate consideration for the joint tenancy interests he received.

[Anderson, TC Memo. (P-H) ¶ 89,643, 58 TCM (CCH) 840 (1989).]

State law determines jointly held interests. Decedent established a joint bank account that was in the sole possession of his son. The intention of the joint account was to allow the son to gain some investment experience under the direction of his father. The IRS argued that a completed transfer had not been made and that the entire account was includable in decedent's gross estate. The estate argued that a completed gift had been made and that no property should be included in the gross estate.

Held: For the IRS. A true tenancy was created under New York law. Because the father had contributed all the funds toward the joint tenancy, the entire amount was includable in his estate. In addition, the son's withdrawals exceeded his half-interest in the funds. Under New York law, he would owe this amount to decedent. Therefore, to this extent, there was a bona fide account receivable that was the property of the estate and that should also be included in the gross estate.

[Estate of Buchholtz, TC Memo. (P-H) ¶ 77,396, 36 TCM (CCH) 1610 (1977).]

Gross estate is included stock dividend on jointly owned stock. *X*, decedent, owned stock in corporation *A*, which he placed into a joint tenancy with *Y*. In 1972, *A* declared a stock dividend. In 1974, *A* declared a cash dividend but permitted shareholders to elect to receive stock instead. *X* elected the stock. The 1972 stock dividend was includable in *X*'s gross estate, because it did not increase the interest originally placed into joint ownership. The elective stock dividend resembled a cash dividend, however, requiring inclusion of one half of the shares in *X*'s gross estate.

[Rev. Rul. 80-142, 1980-1 CB 197.]

¶ 5.02 SPOUSAL JOINT TENANCIES

Court rules on disclaimer of survivorship interest in jointly held property. Decedent's husband died, leaving his entire estate to her. Decedent died eight days later. The couple held a money market account, stocks, bonds, and certificates of deposit as joint tenants with right of survivorship. About five and one-half months later, decedent's executor filed a written statement of renunciation disclaiming, among other things, decedent's survivorship interests in the jointly held property. The estate filed tax returns relying on the validity of the disclaimer. Thus, one half of the property held by the couple as joint tenants was included in decedent's estate and one half in her husband's estate. The state revenue department accepted the disclaimer, but the IRS did not. The IRS claimed that the full value of the property held in joint tenancy should be included in decedent's estate, and the Tax Court upheld this determination.

Held: Reversed for the estate. Under Section 2518, disclaimers are valid if they comply with state law, are in writing, and are made within nine months of the transfer creating the interest disclaimed. For interests created after 1981, disclaimers need not be valid under state law if they comply with the requirements of Section 2518(c)(3). The lower court held that the joint tenancies in the stocks and bonds were created before 1982 and that the disclaimer was not valid under state law. It further held that the other joint tenancies were created after 1981, but did not comply with Section 2518(c)(3). The Tax Court found that North Carolina law did not specifically authorize disclaimers of survivorship interests in jointly held property, and thus the disclaimers on joint tenancies created before 1982 were not valid. The appellate court disagreed with the Tax Court's interpretation and held that the disclaimer was valid under North Carolina law by virtue of its acceptance by the Department of Revenue. The lower court found that as to the interests created after 1981, the disclaimer was not timely filed. The appellate court stated that the timeliness of the disclaimer depended on when the interests were created. The IRS contended that they were created when the couple acquired the jointly held property, whereas the estate claimed that decedent's survivorship interest was created upon her husband's death. The estate's contention was premised on applicable state law that allows unilateral elimination or impairment of a survivorship interest by partition or attachment for debts. Regulation § 25.2518-2(c)(4)(i) provides that for tax purposes, a surviving joint tenant cannot make a disclaimer after nine months from the time the joint tenancy was created. The regulation recognizes, however, that the survivorship interest in a joint bank account is created on the death of the cotenant. The court concluded that there was no true distinction between a joint tenancy with a right of survivorship that can be depleted through withdrawals by either cotenant. In either case, it is impossible to determine whether a cotenant has any right of survivorship until the other tenant dies. The court relied on Kennedy, 804 F2d 1332, 86-2 USTC ¶ 13,699 (7th Cir. 1986), which held that the unilateral power of partition means that only one half of the undivided interest has been transferred to the joint tenants irrevocably at the time the tenancy is created. Because the survivorship interest may be eliminated at the will of one joint tenant, the interest is created only when a cotenant dies without having partitioned the tenancy. Thus, the court in the instant case held that because the disclaimer was of decedent's survivorship interest, not of her original one-half interest in the property, the disclaimer was timely.

[Estate of Dancy, 872 F2d 84, 89-1 USTC ¶ 13,800, 63 AFTR2d 89-1560 (4th Cir. 1989).]

Where property held in joint tenancy is subject of joint and mutual will giving surviving spouse life interest in decedent's joint interest, surviving spouse is held to have made gift of remainder interest in such property upon decedent's death. Taxpayer and his wife made a joint and mutual will in which each promised that the survivor would dispose of his or her interests in jointly held property according to the terms of the will. The will stipulated that in regard to real property held in joint tenancy, the portion of such property belonging to the first deceased would go to the children and grandchildren in fee simple subject to a life estate of the surviving spouse. Taxpayer's wife died first, and, under applicable state law, the will thus became irrevocable. The wife's interest in the jointly held real estate passed to the children and grandchildren subject to a life estate of taxpayer and was taxable to the wife's estate. The IRS claimed that by virtue of the will becoming irrevocable upon the wife's death, taxpayer made a completed gift of the remainder interest in his portino of the property. Taxpayer argued that there was no completed gift, because under the will, he had retained the right to consume the entire value of the property.

Held: For the IRS. The court held that the appropriate tax treatment under such wills depends on the language in the will. The court stated that a gift occurs only when the donor has parted with dominion and control, leaving him with no power to change its disposition. A gift does not, however, require donative intent; rather it requires only that beneficial ownership be conveyed for less than full consideration. Upon his wife's death, taxpayer became legally obligated to convey both his and his wife's interests in the property to the children and grandchildren according to the plan of the will. The court said that the effect of this was as if taxpayer had given all of his real property to his heirs, retaining a life interest. According to the court, such a scenario would have resulted in gift tax. Taxpayer argued that this scenario did not accurately portray the situation, because he retained the power to consume the entire value of the land. State law treats joint wills of this kind as reserving the right to consume corpus of the bequest only under certain circumstances, such as when the survivor incurs steep medical bills. Taxpayer contended that because he had this right to consume the corpus, there was no certainty that the remaindermen would take anything until taxpayer's death. The court rejected this argument, pointing out that under Illinois law, the surviving spouse does not have unlimited power to dispose of the property, unless the will clearly states otherwise. Rather, he has a duty to preserve the estate as well as to distribute what remains according to the will's directions. Because of this peculiarity in Illinois law, the court held that a completed gift was made when taxpayer's wife died.

[Grimes, 851 F2d 1005, 88-2 USTC ¶ 13,774, 63 AFTR2d 89-1526 (7th Cir. 1988).]

Ninth Circuit reverses Tax Court, holding that joint tenancy was severed by trust agreement. In 1977, decedent and his wife created a revocable trust. The terms of the trust provided that upon the death of one of the spouses, the trust assets would be divided into two separate trusts, the "Decedent's Trust" and the "Survivor's Trust." The survivor's separate property, the survivor's interest in the community property, and the amount necessary to obtain the maximum marital deduction were to be allocated to the Survivor's Trust, with the remainder going to the Decedent's Trust. The surviving spouse would retain the right to all principal and income and would have a general power of appointment as to the Survivor's Trust. The survivor's rights as to the Decedent's Trust, however, were substantially limited. A few months later, decedent died, and only his separate assets in the trust were listed on his estate tax return. The IRS determined that the couple held all of the property in the trust jointly and that the entire value of the trust, less the contribution of the surviving spouse, was to be included in decedent's gross estate. The estate petitioned for a redetermination, and the Tax Court upheld the IRS's decision. The court based its holding on the grounds that the couple had transferred their jointly held securities to a revocable trust, retaining unrestricted control over the principal and income, and that the survivor retained control over the assets in the Survivor's Trust. Thus, according to the court, the transfer to the trust was ineffective to sever the joint tenancy for estate tax purposes. The estate appealed the decision.

Held: Reversed for the estate. The Ninth Circuit focused its inquiry on the congressional intent behind Section 2040, which provides that joint interests held with a right to survivorship are includable in decedent's gross estate. The court found no express definition of the term "joint tenancy with right of survivorship"; thus, it looked to the common-law meaning of the term. Among the rules defining the term are those that determine the severance or destruction of a joint tenancy. The court found that a joint tenancy could be severed by express agreement or by implication if the parties contract in a manner inconsistent with the continued existence of the joint tenancy. One such inconsistency would be the modification of the right of survivorship. The court found that the creation of the revocable trust served to sever the joint tenancy in the trust assets because the terms of the trust agreement listed the assets contributed as separate property. Furthermore, the couple clearly agreed to alter the right of survivorship. The trust agreement placed substantial use restrictions on the survivor as to the assets in the Decedent's Trust. Those provisions substantially diminished the right of ownership that the survivor would have acquired at decedent's death had the joint tenancy not been severed. Thus, only decedent's interest under the trust agreement should have been included in the gross estate.

[Black, 765 F2d 862, 56 AFTR2d 85-6526, 85-2 USTC ¶ 13,628 (9th Cir. 1985).]

Termination of tenancy by entirety precludes inclusion in surviving spouse's estate. Decedent and his wife, owners of property as tenants by the entirety, executed a joint will under which the one-half interest of the spouse who died first would pass to their children. Decedent's wife died first and, less than three years later, decedent also died. The IRS argued that the wife's interest in the property passed to decedent under the terms of the tenancy by the entirety and that decedent had made a gift of the interest to the children, which gift was includable in his gross estate under Section 2035.

Held: For the estate. Under state law, execution of the joint will severed the tenancy by the entirety and converted it to a tenancy in common. Upon the wife's death, her interest passed directly to the children, and decedent made no gift.

[Estate of Stewart, 79 TC 1046 (1982), acq., 1984-1 CB 2.]

State law determines jointly held interests. The estate's executors discovered several nonregistered bearer bonds in an envelope on which decedent had written his wife's name. These bonds had been purchased partly through his spouse's brokerage account and partly through the joint account of decedent and his wife. All purchases were paid for by decedent with his own funds. An action was brought in Indiana probate court to determine the proper disposition of the assets. A settlement was arrived at and affirmed by the court. The bonds, which were purchased through the spouse's own account, were (according to the court order) the property of the wife and were not includable in decedent's probate estate, whereas the bonds purchased through the joint account were jointly held and passed to the spouse through survivorship. The IRS argued that no joint tenancy was created and that the estate was not entitled to a marital deduction, because the wife had received a terminable interest. The estate argued the Tax Court was bound by the state court decision.

Held: For the IRS. The Tax Court relied on Estate of Bosch, 387 US 456 (1967), in ruling that it was not bound by the state court decision. The court then made an independent study of Indiana law and determined that no joint tenancy had been created, because there was no adequate delivery or manifestation of intent to create jointly held property. The bonds were found to have passed to the wife as part of the residuary estate and were ineligible for the marital deduction, because she had received nondeductible terminable interests.

[Estate of Kincade, 69 TC 247 (1977).]

Post-1981 termination of tenancy by entirety created before 1982 does not result in interspousal gift to noncontributing spouse. In 1970, *D*, the donor, purchased real property and placed title in the names of *D* and *A*, *D*'s spouse, as tenants by the entirety. *D* did not elect, under former Section 2515(a), to treat the creation of the tenancy as a gift to *A*. Under former Section 2515(a), the creation of a tenancy by the entirety in real property, either by one spouse alone or by both spouses, was not deemed a transfer of property for purposes of the gift tax provisions, regardless of the proportion of the consideration furnished by each spouse, unless the donor elected to have such creation of a tenancy by the entirety treated as a transfer as provided in former Section 2515(c). In 1982, *D* and *A* executed a deed transferring the property to *B* as a gift, thereby terminating the tenancy by the entirety. Under applicable local law, *A* and *D* were each regarded as having owned one-half of the property from creation of the tenancy, with each tenant being entitled to receive a one-half share of the property upon a termination by partition. Thus, the termination by transfer to *B* was regarded under local law as a transfer of one-half of the property by each tenant to *B*. Advice was requested from the IRS with regard to whether the repeal of Section 2515 is effective with respect to the post-1981 termination of a tenancy by the entirety that was created before 1982, if the donor spouse did not elect to treat the creation as a gift. The IRS ruled that the repeal of Section 2515 by the Economic Recovery Tax Act of 1981 is effective with respect to post-1981 terminations of tenancies created before 1982 for which no Section 2515(a) election was made. Therefore, no interspousal gift resulted upon the post-1981 termination of the tenancy, whether the noncontributing spouse received one-half of the property or transferred it to a third person. However, the spouses' gratuitous transfer of their interests in the property to a third person resulted in a gift made by each spouse of one half of the property.

[Rev. Rul. 83-178, 1983-2 CB 158.]

CHAPTER 6

Powers of Appointment

¶ 6.01 GENERAL POWERS

[1] Definitions

Decedent had power of appointment over nonmarital trust even though marital trust had to be exhausted first. Decedent received annual income from a marital trust and a family trust. She also was entitled to as much principal of the marital trust as she wanted; the only requirement was that she notify the trustee in writing. In addition, she could withdraw 5 percent of the family trust annually if the marital trust was exhausted. The IRS contended that decedent had a general power of appointment over 5 percent of the family trust at her death and, therefore, that 5 percent of the value of the family trust was includable in her estate. The estate argued that the withdrawal power over the family trust was subject to a contingency that had not occurred (i.e., exhaustion of the marital trust), but the Tax Court agreed with the IRS.

　　Held: Affirmed for the IRS. Decedent exercised economic dominion over all the funds that could be withdrawn at any given moment. Until her death, decedent could have withdrawn all the funds in the marital trust and 5 percent of the family trust by notifying the trustee of her wish to do so.

[Estate of Kurz, 68 F3d 1027, 76 AFTR2d 95-7309, 95-2 USTC ¶ 60,215 (7th Cir. 1995).]

Pre-1942 powers of appointment. Decedent failed to exercise a general power of appointment over a trust that was created in 1931 and that he held until his death. The IRS included the trust in his gross estate under Section 2041(a)(1), applicable to powers of appointment created before October 21, 1942.

　　Held: For taxpayer. The question of whether the power of appointment is deemed exercised should be answered according to the state law to which the conflict-of-law rules of decedent's domicile look.

[White, 680 F2d 1156, 50 AFTR2d 82-6129, 82-2 USTC ¶ 13,472 (7th Cir. 1982).]

Decedent had no general power of appointment where her power of disposition was not, under state law, power to consume or appropriate property involved. The will of an individual who died in 1952 directed that his wife take the house, furniture, fixtures, utensils, and family automobile in fee simple, along with an undivided one-half interest in all of the residue of his estate. Debts, taxes, and administrative expenses were directed to be paid from the remaining half of the residue, and the remainder of that half was to be disposed of by the following provisions of the will: "If my said wife survive me I give,

devise and bequeath her a life estate in and to all of the rest, residue and remainder of my estate, real, personal and mixed, wheresoever situated or located, with full rights, powers and authorities to sell, convey, exchange, lease
for oil and gas and otherwise, assign, transfer, deliver and otherwise dispose of
any part or all of said estate during her lifetime, all without authority of or order from any court. Subject to said life estate I give, devise and bequeath all
of the remainder of my estate, or if my wife not survive me then all of the
rest, residue and remainder of my estate after payment of all items in [another
paragraph of the will] unto my children." This case was a suit by the executor
of the testator's wife's estate to force the refund of $90,306 in estate taxes that
were paid in 1979, because of the allegedly erroneous inclusion in the wife's
gross estate of certain life estate interests as general powers of appointment
under Section 2041. According to the wife's federal estate tax return, the property in which she received the interest specified in the will consisted of fourteen quarter-sections of land. The interest held by the wife was described as "a
life estate with power of sale," and her gross estate was augmented by
$294,698 by the inclusion of this property. The issue in the case was whether
the life estate interests were properly categorized as pure life estates or as general powers of appointment.

Held: District court judgment for the estate was affirmed per curiam. The
lower court held that it was necessary for a proper resolution of the case to
look to the law of Kansas to ascertain the substance and effect of the life estate and power of disposition, even though the taxability of the interest as so
determined was controlled by federal law. The issue had to be resolved by interpreting the language of the will to determine if the life estate and power of
disposition granted to the wife gave her the power, under Kansas law, to appoint the subject matter of the life estate to herself, her estate, her creditors, or
the creditors of her estate. Because the will provided no express authority for
the wife to appropriate and consume the life estate corpus, and because the
court could discern no basis under the language of the will or Kansas law for
implying such authority, the wife did not possess the power to appoint any of
the life estate property to herself or her creditors. She therefore had no general
power of appointment under Section 2041 and Regulation § 20.2041-1(b)(1),
and the inclusion of the $294,698 in her gross estate was an error.

[Gaskill, 561 F. Supp. 73, 52 AFTR2d 83-6433, 84-1 USTC ¶ 13,552 (D.
Kan. 1983), aff'd per curiam, 787 F2d 1446, 86-1 USTC ¶ 13,666 (10th Cir.
1986).]

**Different powers of appointment are necessary for marital deduction,
gross estate inclusion.** Decedent's husband created a trust with income to decedent upon his death and remainder to her estate. When the husband died, the
IRS disallowed a marital deduction because decedent did not possess a power
of appointment under Section 2056(b)(5). Upon decedent's death, the remain-

der was included in her gross estate because she had a power of appointment under Section 2041(a)(2). The estate argued that the IRS is equitably estopped from taking those inconsistent positions.

Held: For the IRS. Determination of the existence of a power of appointment for purposes of one Code section does not control the question of whether a power of appointment exists for purposes of another Code section. Thus, inconsistent positions were not taken by the IRS.

[Smith, 557 F. Supp. 723, 51 AFTR2d 83-1328, 83-1 USTC ¶ 13,511 (D. Conn. 1982).]

Donee's actual knowledge of general power of appointment is not necessary for inclusion of trust corpus. When decedent was ten years old, he was made income beneficiary of a trust with a power in himself or his guardian to terminate the trust at any time and to receive the corpus and accumulations. Upon decedent's death at age 28, the IRS sought to include the trust corpus in his estate.

Held: For the IRS. This was a general power of appointment under state law; although decedent had no actual knowledge thereof, he could easily have been informed of the power. Once he reached age 18, decedent was legally capable of exercising the power.

[Estate of Freeman, 67 TC 202 (1976).]

Distributions from marital trust were not subject to spouse's power of appointment. Decedent was the beneficiary of a marital trust that gave her all the income for life and gave the trustees the right to use principal for her well being. Decedent, who was one of the trustees, also had a testamentary general power of appointment over the remaining trust principal. The trustees transferred shares of stock from the marital trust to decedent, which she then (1) transferred to an irrevocable trust for her children and (2) gave as gifts to her descendants. The IRS argued that the stock was improperly transferred by the trustees to third parties before decedent's death and should be included in her estate under Section 2041.

Held: For taxpayer. The trustees acted with reasonable judgment, and the distributions were effective in removing the stock from the principal of the marital trust. Hence, the stock was not subject to decedent's power of appointment and was not includable in her estate.

[Estate of Hartzell, 68 TCM 1243, RIA TC Memo. ¶ 94,576 (1994).]

Power to use property during lifetime was limited power of appointment. Under the terms of decedent's predeceased husband's will, she was given a life estate "to do as she pleases" with his property, "and after her death the balance" was to be divided among designated beneficiaries. A district court upheld the IRS's denial of the marital deduction for this bequest, because decedent did not have unlimited power to dispose of the property. On the wife's death, the IRS contended that the district court's decision had been incorrect, and treated the interest as a general power of appointment, includable in her estate.

Held: For taxpayer. The estate's reliance on the district court decision was proper. Under Kentucky state law, the power to use the property for life without more was a limited power.

[Estate of Duvall, 66 TCM 164, RIA TC Memo. ¶ 93,319 (1993).]

Cotrustee's power not sufficiently adverse to negate general power of appointment. Decedent was the lifetime beneficiary and a trustee of a trust under which he was to receive the income with the remainder payable equally to his children, or to any one child as he directed. Additionally, at any time during his lifetime, decedent, with the consent of one of his children, also a trustee, could direct the trustees to distribute all or part of the trust property to anyone, including himself. The cotrustee's right of consent was not sufficiently adverse, and the entire value of the trust was included in decedent's gross estate under Section 2041.

[Rev. Rul. 79-63, 1979-1 CB 302.]

Cotrustee possessed general power of appointment over one-third of trust assets. A family trust was established to accumulate income until its termination. The three trustees could, however, by majority vote, distribute property to anyone, including themselves. Provision was made for the appointment of successor trustees. One of the cotrustees died.

The IRS stated that each trustee held a general power of appointment over one-third of the trust assets. The surviving trustees did not hold a substantial interest in the property that was adverse to the deceased trustee's power in favor of decedent. The surviving trustees were in no better position to exercise the power after decedent's death than they were prior to decedent's death.

[Rev. Rul. 77-158, 1977-1 CB 285.]

Power to mortgage asset caused its inclusion in estate. Although decedent's power to dispose of property was preempted by a joint will, the IRS ruled that he retained sufficient power over the property to include it in his gross estate. A joint will executed by decedent and his first wife provided that on the death of the survivor, half of their ranch was to go to charitable beneficiaries and half to a nephew. The survivor had the power to operate the entire ranch, however, and to mortgage or give away mineral interests in the part of the ranch going to the nephew. Decedent was the surviving spouse of that marriage. Decedent conveyed mineral interests to his second wife and gave her $100,000 from a mortgage on the ranch. The first wife's one-half community interest in the ranch was not included in decedent's estate on the ground decedent did not have a power to consume or to dispose of the property in favor of himself at his death. Rather, the estate viewed his power over the property as an administrative power exercisable only in preserving the ranch. Section 2041(a)(2) provides that property over which decedent had a general power of appointment is part of the gross estate, and Regulation § 20.2041-1(b)(1) says that this includes all powers that have the effect of powers of appointment. The IRS concluded that decedent possessed such powers:

1. He could execute a mortgage on the property that bound remainder interest holders. This was a general power of appointment in favor of creditors of his estate.
2. He had the unlimited power to make gifts of mineral interests.

The IRS pointed out that the estate's argument that the power was only administrative was undercut by decedent's having borrowed against the property and given the funds to his spouse. Thus, despite the joint will, decedent was able to reacquire equity in the property by mortgaging it.

[Tech. Adv. Mem. 9431004.]

IRS denies general power of appointment to Tennessee spouse because of marital trust's limitations. An individual died testate in 1986. A will and a trust governed the disposition of decedent's property. The trust created a marital trust that authorized the coexecutors to make an election under Section 2056(b)(7) or a similar Tennessee election. Decedent devised and bequeathed the residue of his estate to the cotrustees of the trust. Under the terms of the marital trust, the surviving spouse was entitled to receive the income from the trust for life, payable at least annually. The trust provided that if a Section 2056(b)(7) election was made, then all other powers granted by the trust must be exercised in a manner consistent with the election or with a similar Tennessee statute. The original trust provided that if any portion of the marital trust did not qualify for a marital deduction under Tennessee law because the surviving spouse did not have a general power of appointment over the assets, then the spouse would have a general power of appointment. The surviving spouse and bank were coexecutors of the estate and cotrustees of the original trust. Under the terms of the will and the original trust, the surviving spouse could replace the corporate executor and corporate trustee for any reason.

The IRS stated that the power of appointment granted to the surviving spouse does not qualify as a general power of appointment under Section 2056(b)(5). The IRS noted that a power of appointment that becomes exercisable only if the estate's executors do not make a special election on the state death-tax return does not meet the requirements of a general power of appointment. The IRS distinguished Revenue Ruling 75-350, 1975-2 CB 366, where a testamentary general power was exercisable at any time after decedent's death. The IRS also said that the spouse failed to survive the statutory time for making an election under Tennessee law, citing Tennessee Code Announcement § 67-8-315(6).

[Tech. Adv. Mem. 8952002.]

Widow's authority as income beneficiary and trustee does not constitute general power of appointment. Before an individual died, he established a testamentary trust designating his wife as trustee and beneficiary. The will directed the trustee to make quarterly income distributions to the beneficiary. The trustee was empowered to distribute to the beneficiary as much of the corpus as the beneficiary desired, provided that the distribution did not exceed, in any calendar year, the greater of $5,000 or 5 percent of the value of the corpus at the end of the calendar year. This right to invade the corpus was noncumulative and lapsed at the end of each calendar year for which no request was made. Upon the beneficiary's death, the trust's remainder was to be distributed to the deceased husband's children.

The IRS stated that none of the powers held by the widow in her capacity as trustee or beneficiary constituted a general power of appointment for Section 2041 purposes, with the exception of her power to take an annual share of the trust corpus. That portion, the IRS said, will be includable in the widow's estate in the year in which she dies.

[Priv. Ltr. Rul. 8949088.]

Whether surviving spouse has general power of appointment over trust property depends upon power to control trust at time of death. A husband and wife created an inter vivos trust in 1986. The couple transferred to the trust property in which each spouse had a one-half interest. The trust was to become irrevocable upon the death of the first spouse. At this time, the trust was to be divided into two separate trusts, a family trust and the survivor trust. At least one half of the assets of the corpus of the family trust was to consist of the joint assets contributed by the decreased spouse. Any additional assets could be contributed only with the consent of the surviving spouse. The surviving spouse was to receive all of the income from both trusts, and the trustee would be able, in its discretion, to distribute part of the corpus for health and maintenance. The survivor's trust was to terminate upon the death of the remaining spouse, and its assets would be distributed to the family trust. At this time, the family trust would be held and distributed primarily for the surviving children or their issue. Taxpayers designated themselves as the original trustees, and upon death, resignation, or incapacity, a corporate fiduciary was designated. The trust instrument provided for the removal and appointment of a successor trustee for either one of the trusts. The living person of a group consisting of the children or their guardians and the surviving spouse could, by majority vote, remove a trustee and designate a corporate trustee.

The IRS stated that if, at the time of death of the surviving spouse, the spouse were not to possess a majority of the votes, the spouse would not be regarded as possessing a general power of appointment over the portion of the corpus of the family trust that was contributed by the predeceased spouse, because of the removal power and the corporate trustee's power to make discretionary distributions to the minor children. If, however, at the time of the surviving spouse's death, the removal power were exercisable jointly with children (over which the spouse was a guardian) having a majority of votes, the surviving spouse would be regarded as having a general power of appointment by reason of the spouse's removal power being exercisable only with the joinder of persons having a substantial adverse interest and the corporate trustee's power to make discretionary distributions to minor children. The IRS concluded that if, during the spouse's lifetime, the spouse possessed a majority of the votes while a corporate trustee served as the trustee, and thereafter the spouse no longer possessed such majority (by reason of reduction in the number of votes held by the spouse), the reduction would be regarded as a lapse or release of a general power of appointment. The IRS further concluded that to the extent that such lapse or release was coupled with the retention, for the spouse's lifetime, of an income interest in the family trust or the property that was contributed by the predeceased spouse, this would be includable in the surviving spouse's gross estate under Section 2041(a).

[Priv. Ltr. Rul. 8916032.]

Power to pay late spouse's estate taxes out of residuary trust does not make trust includable in survivor's estate. A couple (*A* and *B*) executed an inter vivos trust. The trust instrument specified that the trustee was to pay the trust's net income to *A* and *B* until the death of one of them. Thereafter the trusts were to be split into a marital trust and a residuary trust, and the income from both was to be paid to the survivor. The trusts were to terminate at the death of the survivor. *B* died twenty years before *A*. *A* exercised a power of appointment over the marital trust and distributed assets from the trust to named individuals. Under the trust agreement, *A* was allowed to use the assets of the residuary trust to pay estate taxes.

The IRS stated that the residuary trust was not includable in *A*'s gross estate under Section 2041. The IRS reasoned that the facts were distinguishable from the situation where a decedent has provided by will that a trust may pay estate taxes. In the instant case, the power to pay estate taxes was contingent on the residuary trust being includable in *A*'s estate. In *A*'s case, the contingency did not occur prior to *A*'s death, and the IRS indicated that the power to pay estate taxes was not a power in existence on the date of *A*'s death. The IRS noted that "the power authorized by the trust agreement to pay estate taxes out of trust *B* is only exercisable if trust *B* assets are included in *A*'s gross estate. Absent inclusion of trust *B* in the gross estate through the action of another Code section . . . Section 2041 by itself will not trigger inclusion." [Priv. Ltr. Rul. 8551001.]

[2] Ascertainable Standards

Trust language did not result in general power of appointment. Decedent was appointed as a cotrustee of a revocable trust created by his mother, who died in 1965. At that time, the trust became irrevocable. Decedent and a bank served as cotrustees. Under the dispositive provisions of the instrument, decedent received all the income from the trust after his mother's death. Upon his death, the remaining trust assets were to be divided into two equal parts and passed to his two children or held for their benefit. Decedent developed Alzheimer's disease and entered a nursing home in 1984, but he did not resign as trustee. Prior to his death, a New Mexico court adjudicated him incompetent, but he was not formally removed as trustee. Although the estate argued that he was not a trustee at the time of his death because of the adjudication of incompetency, for purposes of this opinion the Tenth Circuit assumed that decedent continued as a trustee until death. The trust also provided that trustees were authorized to distribute to any of the beneficiaries (including decedent) "whatever amount or amounts of the principal of this Trust as may, in the discretion of the Trustees, be required for the continued comfort, support, maintenance, or education of said beneficiary." The IRS focused on the language that stated that the trust principal could be expended for the continued comfort of decedent and held that this did not establish an ascertainable standard as required by Section 2041(b)(1)(A). Consequently, decedent was held to have a general power of appointment over the trust corpus, and it was includable in his estate.

Held: Reversed for the estate. The Tenth Circuit looked to Florida state law to determine the rights created by the trust instrument. In reviewing such state law, the appellate court reasoned that the Florida Supreme Court would hold that a trust document permitting invasion of principal for comfort without further qualifying language created a general power of appointment. Here, however, the Tenth Circuit found that the modifying language in the trust would lead the Florida courts to hold that the term "comfort" in this context does not permit an unlimited power of invasion. The circuit court concentrated on the fact that the invasion of principal was permitted to the extent "*required* for the *continued* comfort" of decedent. This language was also part of a clause referencing the support, maintenance, and education of the beneficiary. The court focused on the words "required" and "continued," both of which implied providing more than the minimum amount necessary for survival but only to the extent reasonably necessary to maintain the beneficiary in his accustomed standard of living. Accordingly, it was held that the words in this context stated a standard essentially no different from the phrases "health, support and maintenance" as found in Regulation § 20.2041-1(c)(2). The court indicated that if decedent, during his life, had sought to use the assets of the trust to significantly increase his standard of living beyond that which he had previously enjoyed, his cotrustee would have been obligated to refuse to consent, and the remainder beneficiaries of the trust could have successfully petitioned the court to disallow such expenditures as inconsistent with the intent of the trust instrument. Therefore, the Tenth Circuit reversed the Tax Court's ruling that this was a general power of appointment includable in decedent's estate.

[Estate of Vissering, 990 F2d 578, 71 AFTR2d 93-2190, 93-1 USTC ¶ 60,133 (10th Cir. 1993).]

Seventh Circuit, applying state law, finds general power of appointment triggering Section 2041 inclusion. Decedent died in 1953 and was survived by his wife, his daughter, and four grandchildren. By his will, decedent created a trust with a power of appointment in favor of his wife, subject to a clause authorizing her to "use her own discretion as to how much of my property she will use for her own maintenance" and, further, to "use so much of my property as she desires for her own use and for whatever purpose she desires." In 1979, the wife died testate, and the appellant bank was appointed as the personal representative of her estate. In preparing the estate tax return, the bank excluded the value of the trust assets from the gross estate on the ground that the assets were subject to a nontaxable special power of appointment. Under Section 2041, only property subject to a general power of appointment is includable in the gross estate. Section 2041(b)(1)(A), however, provides that a power to consume, invade, or appropriate property for the benefit of decedent that is limited by an ascertainable standard relating to the health, education, support, or maintenance of the decedent may be excluded from the gross estate. The IRS determined that notwithstanding Section 2041(b)(1)(A), the trust created a general power of appointment and that it was fully taxable.

Held: For the IRS. Applying state law on the question of decedent's testamentary intent, the court found that the will in its entirety expressed decedent's clear and specific intent to create a general power of appointment in his wife's favor. By granting his wife the power to "use so much of my property as she desires for her own use and for whatever purpose she desires to use the same," decedent emphasized his intent to give his wife an unlimited power to invade trust corpus. The power was not limited to providing for her own health, support, or maintenance, but extended to "whatever purpose she desires." The court concluded that on the basis of this provision, the will created a general power of appointment, thereby causing the value of the trust to be includable in the wife's gross estate.

[Independence Bank Waukesha, 761 F2d 442, 55 AFTR2d 85-1593, 85-1 USTC ¶ 13,613 (7th Cir. 1985).]

Beneficiary's "right to encroach" is held to constitute ascertainable standard under state law, thereby qualifying for exclusion under Section 2041. Decedent, a lawyer, died on March 10, 1947, leaving a holographic will that had been executed the preceding December. The will provided for the creation of a residuary trust, which his wife administered as the sole trustee and life beneficiary. In addition to her life income interest, the wife had an unlimited right to "encroach" and was expressly relieved of all obligations to make an accounting to anyone, including the remainder beneficiaries. In 1975, at a time when the wife was incompetent to administer the estate, the local chancery removed her as trustee and appointed a bank to serve as trustee. The wife died on December 17, 1975, and the value of the residuary trust—more than $1 million—was not included in her estate for tax purposes. The IRS contended that the trust was includable, but the estate argued successfully in federal district court that the value of the trust was properly excluded. The lower court decided the case on cross-motions for summary judgment, ruling that the trust was not invalid by reason of a merger of the legal and equitable estates in the person of the wife and that the trust created a general power of appointment under Section 2041, with no limiting ascertainable standard. The court concluded, however, that the general power of appointment ceased to exist after the wife was removed as trustee, and therefore it entered judgment for the estate.

Held: Affirmed for the estate. The Sixth Circuit rejected the reasoning of the district court and found that the wife did not have a general power of appointment over the trust corpus, because her right of encroachment upon the corpus was limited by an ascertainable standard. Under state law, a bare right to encroach upon trust corpus confers upon a life tenant the right to dispose of or consume the property only if and when it is necessary for the life tenant's reasonable support and maintenance. Thus, decedent's will vested a life estate in the wife, coupled with a power of invasion limited by an ascertainable standard. As such, concluded the Sixth Circuit, the provisions of Section 2041 preclude the finding that there was a general power of appointment, and consequently the trust was property excluded from the gross estate.

[Finlay, 752 F2d 246, 55 AFTR2d 85-1546, 85-1 USTC ¶ 13,604 (6th Cir. 1985).]

Emergency is held permissible standard of invasion. Decedent was trustee of a trust in which she was also the income beneficiary. She had the power to invade the corpus of the trust for her own benefit "in cases of emergency or illness." Although the Tax Court determined that the word "emergency" was an ascertainable standard, it further determined that the word related to the timing of the invasion, not to any particular source of need. Accordingly, it brought into consideration standards different than those under which "health, education, support or maintenance" (the ascertainable standards listed in Regulation § 20.2041-1(c)(2)) were considered. The court therefore concluded that the power of invasion for emergency was not sufficiently limited and ruled that the corpus was includable in decedent's estate.

Held: Reversed for the estate. The Tenth Circuit concluded that the term "emergency" did not create a broad power that could be used for any purpose as long as an emergency existed, as the IRS had contended. The court analogized the term to the standard of "needs." In Funk, 185 F2d 127 (3d Cir. 1950), the court analyzed "needs" and concluded that though it could not be precisely defined, its use confined the trustees to subjectively determinable limits. In the instant case, the court held that the term "emergency" required a showing of actual financial or physical necessity. Accordingly, the court concluded that the term was restricted and would tolerate obtaining money from the trust only if the situation was extraordinary. Therefore, the corpus was not includable in decedent's gross estate.

[Estate of Sowell, 708 F2d 1564, 52 AFTR2d 83-6408, 83-1 USTC ¶ 13,526 (10th Cir. 1983).]

Power to invade corpus was limited by ascertainable standard. Under her late husband's will, decedent was given the use of his estate for life with the power to invade the corpus for her "maintenance, comfort and happiness." The IRS determined that the interest did not qualify for the marital deduction. Upon decedent's subsequent death, the IRS sought to include the corpus in her gross estate. The estate argued that the IRS's position would tax the same interest twice.

Held: For the estate. The court rejected the argument that Sections 2041 and 2056 should be construed in pari materia to prevent double taxation. Under local law, however, decedent's power to invade was limited by an ascertainable standard.

[Brantingham, 631 F2d 542, 46 AFTR2d 80-6223, 80-2 USTC ¶ 13,373 (7th Cir. 1980).]

Power to invade corpus of trust in event of emergency held to be ascertainable standard. Decedent was the life income beneficiary and cotrustee of a testamentary trust. The invasion clause of the trust provided that if the net income from the trust was "inadequate for the comfortable support and maintenance of any beneficiary therein, or should any emergency arise," then the trustees could invade corpus in their sole discretion as was deemed necessary for such purposes. The IRS contended that by the invasion clause, decedent possessed a general power of appointment over the trust corpus, resulting in the inclusion of the corpus in his gross estate under Section 2041. The estate paid the deficiency and sued for a refund.

Held: For the estate. The court held that decedent's power of appointment, and thus the corpus, was not includable in his gross estate. Section 2041(b)(1)(A) provides that a power "which is limited by an ascertainable standard relating to the health, education, support or maintenance of decedent shall not be deemed a general power of appointment." In this case, the issue was whether the trustee's power to consume corpus, "should an emergency arise," was related to health, education, support, or maintenance. The court held that the resolution of the issue was determinable under Pennsylvania law, but that it was not bound to follow decisions of Pennsylvania lower courts, and it was required to give only "proper regard" to such cases. Thus, the court did not follow, in re Dobbin's Estate, 148 Pa. Super. 177, 24 A2d 641 (1942), which held that an "emergency" encompassed "any pressing situation, personal to the donee, which the payment of money will relieve." Instead, the court followed a Pennsylvania Supreme Court decision that defined an "emergency" to mean "a sudden or unexpected event which creates a temporarily dangerous condition, usually necessitating immediate or quick action." Under this definition, the court could not visualize any situation where an emergency would not be reasonably measurable in terms of health or support. Thus, permitting an invasion of corpus in the event of an emergency met the "ascertainable standard" test of Section 2041(b)(1)(A).

[Hunter, 597 F. Supp. 1293, 85-1 USTC ¶ 13,601, 55 AFTR2d 85-1558 (WD Pa. 1984).]

Sole trustee-beneficiary's power to apply trust income and principal for his "support" and "general happiness" is general power of appointment, which is not excepted under Section 2041(b)(1)(A). Decedent was the sole trustee and sole beneficiary of a testamentary trust established in his deceased wife's will. Under the terms of the will, decedent had the power to invade, for his benefit, trust income and corpus to the extent necessary for his "proper support . . . and general happiness in the manner to which he was accustomed at the time of" his wife's death. The corpus of the trust was not included in decedent's gross estate. The IRS claimed the corpus was includable, under Section 2041(a)(2), as property over which decedent held a general power of appointment. The estate claimed this power was excepted from Section 2041(a)(2) by Section 2041(b)(1)(A), because it was limited to an "ascertainable standard" that related solely to decedent's "health, education, support or maintenance."

Held: For the IRS. Whether a power meets the criteria set forth in Section 2041(b)(1)(A) is determined by reference to state law. Although state law would hold the power held by decedent to be "limited to an ascertainable standard," the court doubted that such a standard would be found to relate to "health, education, support or maintenance." For example, decedent's "general happiness" might include an item such as travel that would not relate to his "health, education, support or maintenance."

[Estate of Little, 87 TC 599 (1986).]

Right under Uniform Gifts to Minors Act to petition court for payment to minor child is not general power of appointment. Under Section 4(c) of the Uniform Gifts to Minors Act, a parent of the minor child may petition a court for an order directing the custodian to pay to such minor custodial property for the support, maintenance, or education of such minor. The IRS ruled that this right in the parent did not constitute a general power of appointment under Section 2041(a)(2). Accordingly, the value of such custodial property is not includable in the estate of a decedent who dies prior to the minor's attaining age 21.

[Rev. Rul. 77-460, 1977-2 CB 323.]

Right to invade for "proper comfort and welfare" is ruled not to constitute Section 2041 ascertainable standard. Decedent's spouse directed that a testamentary trust be established and that decedent be given the power to invade corpus for her "proper comfort and welfare." The IRS ruled that in the absence of local New Jersey state law to the contrary, this standard of invasion would not be an ascertainable standard relating to health, education, support, or maintenance. Because there was no local law to the contrary, the IRS concluded that decedent possessed a general power of appointment over the trust assets.

[Rev. Rul. 77-194, 1977-1 CB 283.]

Power to invade for "comfort" is ruled not general power of appointment. Decedent was the life income beneficiary and trustee of a trust. The trustee had the power to invade principal for decedent's "maintenance, support, and comfort, in order to defray expenses ... of sickness, accidents and disability, and whether used for medical, dental, hospitals, nursing and institutional costs." The issue was whether the power of invasion constituted a general power of appointment, which would cause the trust to be included in decedent's estate. A power to invade that is limited by an ascertainable standard relating to decedent's health, education, support, or maintenance is not a general power of appointment. A power to invade for the decedent's "comfort" is usually not considered to be limited by the requisite ascertainable standard. Here, however, the power to invade for comfort was limited to amounts needed to defray health and related costs. Therefore, the IRS concluded that the power was limited by an ascertainable standard and was not a general power of appointment.

[Priv. Ltr. Rul. 9203047.]

[3] Release

Agreement did not result in release of power of appointment. Decedent died in 1986, a resident of Georgia. Her husband had predeceased her, dying in 1975. Under his will, three trusts were to be created—a trust for his great grandchildren funded with $125,000, and a marital trust and a residuary trust, each funded with half of the residue of the estate. Decedent was to receive all the income from the marital trust and had a testamentary power of appointment over the corpus. If not exercised, the corpus would pass to the residuary trust. The income from the residuary trust was to be paid to the husband's children and grandchildren for ten years; then, the trust was to terminate, with the principal being distributed to the income beneficiaries. The trust for the great grandchildren was to be administered in the same manner. None of these trusts was ever funded. Controversy arose over the administration of the husband's estate. During this time, new executors of the estate were appointed, and certain properties were transferred outright to decedent and other beneficiaries. In 1983, the beneficiaries of the husband's estate reached an agreement to terminate the various trusts established under his will and to distribute the estate's remaining assets directly to the appropriate beneficiaries or to a partnership in which they held partnership interests. In 1982, decedent transferred a 50 percent interest in nine tracts of property to nine named individuals who were some of the beneficiaries of the residuary estate (some interests were to be jointly held). The remaining 50 percent interest was transferred to those same beneficiaries in 1983. These gifts were properly reported on gift tax returns. On each return, decedent claimed twenty-five $10,000 annual exclusions under Section 2503(b). In 1984, decedent established two trusts for her children and their stepchildren and grandchildren. She transferred certain real property to the trusts, titling the deeds in the names of each of her two sons individually and as trustee.

Four issues came before the court:

1. Whether decedent released her power of appointment over the corpus of the marital trust when she entered into the agreement to terminate the trusts.
2. Whether she claimed too many annual exclusions on her gift tax returns.
3. Whether adjustment of the gift tax returns is precluded by expiration of the statute of limitations.

4. Whether the expiration of the statute of limitations for the gift tax returns prevents the IRS from limiting the number of annual exclusions allowed in those years for purposes of calculating "adjusted taxable gifts" for the estate tax return.

Held: For decedent (in part). Entering into the agreement did not cause decedent to release or exercise her power of appointment. The court said that her agreement to take outright ownership of one half of the assets in lieu of her rights under the marital trust was tantamount to converting her testamentary power of appointment into a lifetime one and exercising it in favor of herself. To release or exercise her power of appointment would entail transferring the property to someone other than herself, and this was not done. Though the beneficiaries of the residuary trust did receive outright ownership of certain property in lieu of its being placed in trust, decedent had no power of appointment over the corpus of the residuary trust, so that property was not transferred from her to the beneficiaries. The Tax Court did agree with the IRS that decedent claimed too many annual exclusions on her gift tax returns. The court rejected the estate's argument that under Georgia law implied trusts were created for decedent's great grandchildren.

Though the court determined that the estate was entitled to only nine annual exclusions, the estate asserted that the IRS could not assess a deficiency for the gift tax owed on account of this change in the number of annual exclusions because the period of limitations had expired. The IRS claimed that the six-year, rather than the three-year, statute of limitations applied. Section 6501(e)(2) allows a period of six years if the tax return omits an item or items valued in excess of 25 percent of the amount of total gifts stated on the return, unless taxpayer informed the district director of such item or items in some other manner. Decedent reported all gifts made and the number of exclusions she was taking. Though the calculation of the taxable amount of gifts was incorrect, the IRS could not claim that disclosure of pertinent information was inadequate. Although the court would not allow the gift tax returns to be adjusted, it did find that for estate tax purposes, the amount of adjusted taxable gifts could be altered to reflect the reduced number of allowable annual exclusions, since the limitations period for computing the taxable estate was still open.

[Estate of Robinson, 101 TC 499 (1993).]

¶ 6.02 EFFECT OF INCOMPETENCY

Incompetent's general power of appointment causes inclusion in estate. Decedent was left a life interest with an inter vivos general power of appointment in all of her husband's property. She was subsequently adjudicated incompetent and remained so until her death without having exercised the power of appointment. The IRS sought to include the value of the life estate in her gross estate. The district court found for taxpayer.

Held: Reversed for the IRS. Taxpayer failed to show that, under state law, the power of appointment could not have been exercised on decedent's behalf.

[Williams, 634 F2d 894, 47 AFTR2d 81-1596, 81-1 USTC ¶ 13,388 (5th Cir. 1981).]

Legal incapacity to exercise general power does not prevent inclusion of subject property. Under a trust instrument, decedent would receive the corpus on reaching age 21. She had general power to determine to whom it would pass if she died sooner. In default, it would pass to her estate. She died at age 16 without exercising the power. Under local law, she lacked capacity to exercise it because of her minority.

Held: For the IRS. Decedent's incapacity to exercise the power did not prevent inclusion of the subject property in her gross estate under Section 2041(a)(2).

[Estate of Rosenblatt, 633 F2d 176, 46 AFTR2d 80-6219, 80-2 USTC ¶ 13,374 (10th Cir. 1980).]

Incompetency held not to prevent inclusion of trust corpus in gross estate. Decedent's husband died in 1967, leaving property in trust that decedent could appoint at her death. The IRS asserted that under Section 2041(a)(2), such powers of appointment are includable in the gross estate. At all relevant times, however, decedent had lacked the requisite testamentary capacity to execute a will. In fact, she had been judicially declared incompetent six months after her husband's death. The taxpayer-estate argued that the property subject to the power of appointment should not be included in the estate, because the power could not have been exercised by decedent. The Tax Court ruled that decedent's incapacity had no effect on includability of the trust corpus in the estate, because the term "exercisable" for Section 2041(a)(2) purposes does not refer to the "capacity" to exercise, but rather to the "existence of the power" in decedent.

Held: Affirmed for the IRS. After an exhaustive review of case law, statutory language, and legislative history, the Second Circuit ruled that property subject to a general power of appointment is includable in decedent's gross estate, even though the donee was unable to make a valid will after the power was granted because of incompetency.

[Estate of Alperstein, 613 F2d 1213, 45 AFTR2d 80-1708, 80-1 USTC ¶ 13,327 (2d Cir. 1979).]

Power of appointment causes inclusion, though decedent is incompetent.
Decedent held a power of appointment over a trust but was not mentally competent to exercise it. Her will stated that she did not intend to exercise it. However, the district court held the trust was includable in her estate.

Held: Affirmed for the IRS. Under Section 2041, the scope of the power of appointment granted to decedent, not her capacity to exercise it, determines its includability.

[Pennsylvania Bank & Trust Co., 597 F2d 382, 43 AFTR2d 79-1332, 79-1 USTC ¶ 13,299 (3d Cir. 1979), cert. denied, 444 US 980 (1979).]

Mental incapacity of holder of general power of appointment does not preclude gross estate's inclusion of property subject to power of appointment. An individual began showing symptoms of a degenerative mental condition in 1974 and, by 1977, required professional help to aid her in her daily functions. In 1981, the individual was adjudged mentally incapacitated, at which time a guardian was appointed to handle her affairs. Under her deceased spouse's will, the individual received the right to use as much or all of certain property as might be necessary for her sickness, hospitalization, doctor's care, medication, support, maintenance, welfare, and general comfort in keeping with the manner and mode of living to which the individual had been accustomed. In the same paragraph, the individual acquired the power and authority to lease all or part of any real property for oil, gas, or other minerals for a term of years or on any conditions, without seeking the consent of any other party, including the surviving children. The individual did not exercise the power of appointment prior to her death. The IRS stated that the power in the will given to decedent was a general power of appointment under Section 2041. The IRS reasoned that decedent's legal or practical mental incapacity to exercise the power would not preclude it from being a general power of appointment, because the power could have been exercised by decedent's guardian. Accordingly, the IRS concluded that the right to use the property under the will was a general power of appointment over the property, causing the property subject to such power to be included in decedent's gross estate under Section 2041.

[Tech. Adv. Mem. 8901006.]

Instrument is controlling on whether power is includable. Decedent possessed an interest in his predeceased spouse's testamentary trust. Under the terms of the trust, the income was to be paid to decedent for life. Decedent also had the power to appoint to himself the entire trust principal at any time. Conservators were appointed for decedent, so his exercise of the power of appointment would have been voidable by his conservators.

In technical advice, the IRS has stated that the value of the trust was includable in decedent's estate regardless of decedent's inability to exercise the power of appointment. The IRS explained that under Revenue Ruling 75-350, 1975-2 CB 367, one must look solely to the terms of the instrument that creates the power of appointment to determine whether the property subject to the power is includable. Because the trust instrument did not state that the power of appointment was extinguished upon incompetency, the trust corpus was includable in decedent's estate.

[Priv. Ltr. Rul. 8233003.]

¶ 6.03 LAPSE AND FAILURE TO EXERCISE

Portion of trust subject to five percent power included in estate. Decedent's predeceased spouse set up a trust for the benefit of decedent, their children, and grandchildren in his will. During her life, income and principal could be used for the care, support, and maintenance of any of the beneficiaries. In addition, each calendar year decedent could withdraw cash or property with a value equal to the greater of $5,000 or 5 percent of the present value of the principal of the trust ("5/5 power"). The right was not cumulative, so it lapsed at the end of each year if it was not exercised during the year. Decedent never exercised her right of withdrawal. At her death, on July 12, 1992, the principal of the trust had a value of $1.35 million. The IRS included 5 percent ($67,500) of the trust in her estate. Property subject to a decedent's general power of appointment is includable in his or her estate under Section 2041(a)(2). Likewise, the transfer or release of the power of appointment may result in the inclusion of the property if Sections 2035 to 2038 (the retained-string provisions) would have applied to a similar transfer of the property. (A separate rule applies to lapses of powers created before October 22, 1942.) Decedent's withdrawal right was a general power of appointment under Section 2041(b) because she could exercise it in favor of herself. The estate argued that Section 2041(a)(2) could not apply, because the lapse of a 5/5 power is not a release of the power of appointment, according to Section 2041(b)(2). Therefore, the potential withdrawal in the final year was protected when the 5/5 power lapsed. This, however, ignored the fact that decedent's right of withdrawal for 1992 was in effect at her death.

Held: For the IRS. The court explained that ordinarily the exercise or release of a general power of appointment during the holder's life is a transfer subject to the gift tax under Section 2514(a) (there may be an inclusion in the holder's estate if a string is retained). There is an exception, however, for a 5/5 power. A lapse that does not exceed the 5 percent and $5,000 limits is not a release subject to the gift or estate tax, according to Sections 2515(e) and 2041(b)(2). Thus, the pre-1992 lapses that occurred when decedent did not exercise her 5/5 power were not transfers for the gift or estate tax. The $67,500, however, was another matter. The 5/5 power to make a 1992 withdrawal had not lapsed at the time of decedent's death, so Section 2041(b)(2) had no application. Instead, the 5/5 power was includable in her estate because it was exercisable at death, just as in an example in Regulation § 20.2041-3(d)(3).

[Estate of Dietz, 72 TCM 1042, RIA TC Memo. ¶ 96,470 (1996).]

Tax Court rules on estate and gift tax issues arising from settlement of bitter family business dispute. On the death of her father in 1964, decedent inherited all 5,000 shares of the stock outstanding in a commercial realty and management company. The will bequeathed the stock to decedent in trust "for life and at her death, share and share alike to her children." Over a period of years, decedent distributed all but 14 percent of the stock equally to her four daughters. Two of the daughters, representing one faction of the bitterly divided family, instituted a lawsuit in 1971 alleging that the other family members improperly formed a voting trust in order to gain control of the business and to arrange for loan guarantees in violation of earlier agreements. Decedent threatened to disinherit the two daughters, but eventually a comprehensive settlement was reached in 1972. The agreement required decedent to transfer her remaining shares to the four daughters and to divide the realty company into three separate corporations with different ownership interests. In addition, all of the parties entered into a trust agreement under which certain other property was conveyed to a trustee for the benefit of decedent for life. After her death, the trust was to be divided into four separate lifetime trusts for each of the daughters. The state probate court approved the settlement in 1974, and each separate provision was carried out thereafter. For reasons unclear in the record, however, certificates for 285 shares of stock in one of the newly formed corporations were issued to decedent, although the intended transferee held the stock and collected dividends. Four years following the settlment, decedent died. After an audit of the estate tax return, the IRS assessed tax deficiencies involving three separate aspects of the settlement: (1) the 14 percent stockholder interest, which the IRS argued was a taxable gift; (2) the 285 shares, which the IRS sought to include in the gross estate under Section 2036(a)(1); and (3) the corpus of the newly formed trust, a portion of which the IRS contended was subject to Section 2041.

Held: For the estate. On the gift tax issue, the Tax Court rejected the IRS's contention that it was transferred for less than adequate and full consideration and disallowed the deficiency. Decedent's broad release contained in the settlement freed her from future claims of breach of fiduciary duty as a life tenant of the stock and in her capacity as president and director of the original realty corporation. Regarding decedent's record ownership of the 285 shares of stock, the Tax Court determined that the estate was not required to include the value thereof in the gross estate. Under Section 2036(a)(1), a decedent with a retained life estate in transferred property must be shown to have retained some measure of enjoyment of the property pursuant to an express or implied understanding or agreement reached contemporaneously with the transfer. The fact that there was no evidence of any such arrangement, and that the surrounding circumstances of the settlement negated the actual retention of enjoyment rights, led the court to conclude that Section 2036(a)(1) was not applicable. Finally, the court ruled that though decedent held a general power of appointment over a substantial portion of trust income and corpus, such power was subject to an annual lapse provision effective for each year prior to the year in which decedent died. Accordingly, the amount includable in the gross estate was subject to the lapse limitation of Section 2041(b)(2).

[Estate of Noland, TC Memo. (P-H) ¶ 84,209, 47 TCM (CCH) 1640 (1984).]

Annual withdrawal from life insurance is taxable. Decedent, owner-beneficiary of a life insurance policy on his deceased spouse, selected a settlement option with income for his life and a noncumulative right to withdraw 5 percent of the face value. He never withdrew any of the proceeds. The property subject to the lapsed annual right was not includable in his gross estate under Section 2041. However, the value of the right in the year of death was includable. No amount was includable under Section 2036.

[Rev. Rul. 79-373, 1979-2 CB 331.]

CHAPTER **7**

Life Insurance

¶ 7.01 INCLUDABLE INTERESTS, GENERALLY

Policy assignment is no bar to inclusion of insurance proceeds in estate.
Prior to his death, decedent assigned an employer-provided life insurance policy to his spouse. The spouse later relinquished all rights under the policy as a
condition to decedent obtaining a larger policy. Decedent died four months after assigning the policy. The executor excluded the proceeds from decedent's
gross estate and argued that the surviving spouse was the owner of the new
policy under either a contractual theory or a constructive or resulting-trust theory. The IRS thereafter assessed a deficiency against the estate. The district
court held for the IRS in the estate's refund suit.

    Held: For the IRS. The Seventh Circuit held that the insurance proceeds
were includable in the gross estate. The new policy was neither a benefit nor
an advantage arising from the old policy. In addition, no trust arose, because
decedent and his spouse executed an election that assigned their rights in the
old policy without granting them ownership rights in the new policy.

[American Nat'l Bank & Trust Co., 832 F2d 1032, 60 AFTR2d 87-6164, 87-2
USTC ¶ 13,738 (7th Cir. 1987).]

**Court bars tracing of joint account funds in determining includability of
life insurance proceeds in gross estate.** Decedent was a key employee of a
business in which his wife held a substantial minority interest. Decedent's wife
handled both the financial affairs of the business and their personal finances.
In 1978, decedent's wife acquired a policy on decedent's life, naming herself
owner and beneficiary. Although decedent cooperated in the acquisition of this
policy, he acquired no rights therein. Premiums were paid by decedent's wife
out of their joint checking account. Evidence indicated that decedent's wife
wrote most of the checks on this account. Funds in the account were traceable
73 percent to decedent and 27 percent to the wife. Decedent died in 1979, and
his estate did not include the policy proceeds in the gross estate. The IRS assessed an estate tax deficiency, claiming that 73 percent of the proceeds were
includable in the gross estate.

    Held: For the estate. Although the payment of insurance premiums is im-
portant in determining includability, it is the act of making payment and maintaining control over the insurance transaction, rather than the source of the
funds used to pay premiums, that is determinative. Further, where persons
maintain a joint bank account, the withdrawing joint tenant is not necessarily
an agent of the nonwithdrawing joint tenant. Accordingly, the mere payment
of premiums with funds from a joint account does not of itself constitute payment by the nonwithdrawing joint tenant. Under the facts of this case, there
was no evidence that decedent's wife was acting as decedent's agent with respect to the insurance policy on decedent's life.

[Estate of Clay, 86 TC 1266 (1986).]

Insurance policy acquired through illegal rebate scheme, and consequent tort settlement for misrepresentation by insurance company, is not includable in decedent's gross estate. Decedent was approached by a life insurance agent. The agent told her that he could write a $1 million life insurance policy without charging for the first year's premium by borrowing against the impending cash value of the policy and by applying part of the agent's commission to the cost of the premium. This method of inducing potential clients to purchase policies is called premium rebating and was illegal in California, decedent's domicile state. Decedent and her husband both purchased policies with this agent and paid nothing for the first year's premium. During the first year of the insurance policy, decedent died, and her husband filed a claim for benefits under the policy. The life insurance company claimed that the contract was void because it was procured under an illegal premium-rebating scheme, and the state court ruled in the life insurance company's favor. Decedent's husband then brought suit for damages on the ground that the insurance company had engaged in fraudulent misrepresentation. The suit went to jury, which awarded decedent's husband $350,000 for mental distress and $10 million in punitive damages. The insurance company filed an appeal, and the parties finally settled out of court, with the insurance company paying decedent's husband $1.45 million for emotional distress. The IRS determined that the full face value of the life insurance policy should be included in decedent's gross estate under Section 2042. The IRS subsequently claimed that one half of the tort claim settlement should be included in decedent's gross estate as community property. Decedent's estate argued that because the insurance policy was void, it should not be included in the gross estate, and that decedent had no interest in the tort recovery.

Held: For the estate. Under Section 2042, insurance received by an executor of an estate from policies on the life of decedent is includable in the gross estate. Also includable in the gross estate are any amounts paid to any other beneficiaries if decedent possessed any incidents of ownership over the policy at the time of death. An incident of ownership includes any power to change the beneficiary on the policy, surrender or cancel the policy, assign the policy, revoke an assignment, or pledge the policy for loans against the surrender value. There was no dispute that decedent retained incidents of ownership over the life insurance policy, but the estate argued that the policy was void and therefore was not includable in the gross estate. The Tax Court decided that absent a ruling by the state's highest court on the issue, it was to apply state law after giving due regard to the rulings of other courts in that state. The California Supreme Court has not ruled on the validity of an insurance policy obtained under an illegal premium rebate scheme. The Tax Court stated that the California legislature has taken a strong stance against the practice of rebating to protect the public and preserve the financial integrity of the insurance industry. The court thus concluded that the purpose of the antirebate statute is best served in this case by denial of enforcement of decedent's insurance policy, because decedent knowingly accepted an unlawful rebate. The policy was therefore void, and no insurance proceeds were receivable under the policy or includable in decedent's gross estate. As to the IRS's contention that one half of the tort settlement was includable in decedent's estate as community property, the court made its own inquiry into the viability of the tort claim. It concluded that decedent and her husband did not have a legitimate claim against the life insurance company, because neither justifiably relied on the agent's representations. Thus, there was no claim to add to decedent's estate.

[Estate of Henderson, TC Memo. (P-H) ¶ 89,079, 56 TCM (CCH) 1332 (1989).]

No-fault survivors' loss benefits are not includable in gross estate. Decedent carried no-fault automobile insurance as required by his state. Survivors' loss benefits were paid pursuant to his no-fault policy. The benefits were reduced by Social Security and workmen's compensation as provided by state law.

The IRS ruled that survivors' loss benefits are not includable in decedent's estate under Section 2033 or Section 2042 because the benefits did not accrue until after decedent's death.

[Rev. Rul. 82-5, 1982-1 CB 131.]

Life insurance is not included in estate. Decedent's employer entered into an agreement with an insurance company providing that relatives of employees could purchase group life insurance on the employee's life if the employee declined to do so. Under state law, the relative who purchases the insurance is the sole owner of the policy purchased.

The IRS ruled that the insurance so purchased is not includable in decedent's estate.

[Rev. Rul. 76-421, 1976-2 CB 280.]

Assignment of life insurance policy to viatical settlement company produces taxable gain. Taxpayer, who was terminally ill, owned a whole life insurance policy. He irrevocably assigned the policy to a viatical settlement company in exchange for a payment from the company equal to roughly 63 percent of the face amount of the policy.

The IRS ruled that the transaction constituted a sale. Consequently, the payment received by taxpayer from the viatical settlement company minus his adjusted basis in the insurance contract was includable in his income. According to the IRS, no portion of the amount received was excludable from income under Section 101(a)(1) because the payment was not an amount received under a life insurance contract by reason of the death of the insured. This result should be contrasted with the treatment of accelerated death benefits, which are permitted to be received tax-free pursuant to proposed regulations under Section 7702.

[Priv. Ltr. Rul. 9443020.]

¶ 7.02 TRANSFERS MADE WITHIN THREE YEARS OF DEATH

Oral agreement was effective to transfer incidents of ownership in life insurance policies. Decedent was the chief executive of a food company that owned insurance policies on his life. The company later merged with Pillsbury. An officer of Pillsbury orally agreed that Pillsbury would sell the policies to decedent at the time of the merger. One week after the merger, on July 8, 1979, decedent gave the policies to a life insurance trust. He died on September 18, 1982. The district court held that the insurance proceeds were excluded from the estate because decedent had transferred all incidents of ownership in the policies more than three years from the date of death.

Held: Affirmed for the estate. Even though the oral agreement was unenforceable under the statute of frauds, it was valid to transfer all incidents of ownership from Pillsbury to decedent. The insurance trust agreement operated to transfer all incidents of ownership from decedent to the trust.

[Estate of O'Daniel, 6 F3d 321, 72 AFTR2d 93-6762, 93-2 USTC ¶ 60,150 (5th Cir. 1993).]

Insurance proceeds are excluded from decedent's estate where trust decedent created and owned policy and paid premiums. Decedent was a tax attorney who drafted an irrevocable trust agreement for himself as part of his personal estate planning. The agreement designated decedent as the settlor of the trust. His wife and three minor children were designated as primary beneficiaries. Decedent reserved to himself the right to remove any trustee at will and to appoint a bank as successor trustee. The beneficiaries had a limited power to withdraw trust property within thirty days of the contribution of such property. The trustee had the authority, but was not required, to invest in insurance policies on the life of decedent or a beneficiary and to hold such policies as trust principal. Decedent chose a bank to act as trustee. It was the bank president's understanding that decedent wanted the trust to be an insurance trust; however, establishment of the trust at the bank was not conditioned on the bank's commitment to acquire life insurance. Once the trust was executed, decedent irrevocably assigned $5,900 to the bank. On that same date, his wife executed, on behalf of herself and her children, a waiver of their right to withdraw any portion of that contribution. The next day, the bank applied for a $375,000 insurance policy on decedent's life. The bank, as trustee, was listed as the policy owner and the beneficiary. Decedent signed the application as the insured. The policy was approved on January 8, 1980. The bank, as owner of the policy, was given all rights under it, including the right to assign the policy, change the beneficiaries, change the owner, and exercise all the policy options. The bank paid the insurance company a monthly premium of $436. At the end of the next year, decedent made a second contribution to the trust corpus of $5,500. At the end of the third year, he made a contribution of $2,000. No portion of any of these contributions was withdrawn by the beneficiaries. The total amount paid by decedent covered all of the premium payments made by the bank. Several months after the trust was established, decedent was invited to join the bank's board of directors. He became a member and chairman of the bank's trust committee. The duties of this committee included reviewing and discussing new trust accounts and investments in those accounts. Decedent's trust was first reviewed on April 30, 1980, and was reviewed thereafter every three to four months as was the normal procedure. Decedent died on June 19, 1982, in an automobile accident, less than three years after he had executed the trust agreement. The insurance company paid $378,700 in death benefits to the bank as the owner of the policy on decedent's life. The insurance proceeds were not included in decedent's gross estate on the estate tax return. The IRS determined that the payment of the proceeds to the trustee constituted a transfer within the meaning of Section 2035(a) because the trust was created less than three years before decedent died; therefore, the proceeds should have been included in decedent's estate. The IRS assessed a deficiency against the estate, which the estate paid but challenged in Tax Court. The Tax Court ruled in favor of the estate, following its 1987 decision in Estate of Leder, 893 F2d 237, 90-1 USTC ¶ 60,001, 65 AFTR2d 90-1173 (10th Cir. 1989). The IRS appealed.

Held: Affirmed for the estate. The Sixth Circuit affirmed the Tax Court's finding that under Section 2035(d)(1), the proceeds of an insurance policy on decedent's life were not includable in his estate. The exception to Section 2035(d)(1), found in Section 2035(d)(2), did not apply, because decedent did not possess any incidents of ownership in the policy. The court refused to incorporate the constructive transfer doctrine into Section 2035(d)(2), because to do so would contravene Congress's intent in enacting Sections 2035(d) and 2042.

[Estate of Headrick, 918 F2d 1263, 90-2 USTC ¶ 60,049, 66 AFTR2d 90-6038 (6th Cir. 1990).]

Initiation of transaction and payment of premiums result in inclusion of insurance proceeds. Decedent and his wife lived in a community property state. He applied for an insurance policy on his life, naming his wife as owner and beneficiary. He also later executed a document disclaiming any interest in the policy or the proceeds. In addition, he authorized premiums to be paid by his spouse out of community funds, with his share of the funds constituting a gift to her. Decedent died within three years of the time the policy was issued, and the IRS included one half of the proceeds in his estate. The estate contended that the proceeds were excludable from the estate for one of two reasons: (1) Section 2035 requires a transfer of property, which did not occur here, and (2) in any event, the premiums came under the exception for small gifts under Section 2035(b)(2).

Held: For the IRS. Under Section 2035, transfers of property taking place within three years of decedent's death are includable in the estate. An exception is made in Section 2035(b)(2) for gifts not requiring a gift tax return. This exception, however, does not apply to transfers of life insurance policies. In Estate of Schnack, 848 F2d 933 (9th Cir. 1988), a case with similar facts, the court held that a transfer of a life insurance policy occurs when decedent transfers funds to a third party to pay a life insurance company. Based on that case, the life insurance proceeds in the instant case were included in the estate. Furthermore, Section 2035(b)(2), which excludes transfers for which no gift tax return was required, does not preclude the inclusion of insurance proceeds. The estate contended that the exception for life insurance policies did not apply to the transfer of funds for the payment of premiums. The court held that the language "with respect to" life insurance policies was broad enough to cover premiums. Consequently, even though decedent had never owned an insurance policy and had no incidents of ownership in one at his death, the proceeds still were includable in his estate. The court reached this conclusion because decedent initiated the transaction and paid the premiums.

[Knisley, 901 F2d 793, 90-2 USTC ¶ 60,037, 65 AFTR2d 90-1235 (9th Cir. 1990).]

Constructive transfer doctrine inapplicable to insurance proceeds under Section 2035(d)(2). Decedent died in May 1983 with a $1 million life insurance policy. The policy was purchased in 1981 by decedent's wife. The premiums were paid with preauthorized withdrawals from decedent's wholly-owned corporation. The wife never provided consideration to decedent or the company in exchange for these payments. Upon decedent's death, the policy proceeds were distributed and completely excluded from decedent's gross estate. The IRS determined a deficiency, asserting that the insurance proceeds were properly includable in decedent's gross estate under Section 2035(a) for gifts made within three years of death.

Held: For the estate. Decedent's payment of the premiums was irrelevant under the post-Economic Recovery Tax Act of 1981 (ERTA) provisions. ERTA added Section 2035(d)(1), which nullifies the three-year inclusionary rule of Section 2035(a), except for those transfers described in Section

2035(d)(2), which specifically references Section 2042. Decedent never possessed any incidents of ownership under Section 2042, having no ownership, economic, or contractual rights in the policy. In addition, the pre-ERTA constructive transfer doctrine is inapplicable to Section 2035(d)(2). Consequently, the insurance proceeds were excludable from decedent's gross estate.

[Estate of Leder, 893 F2d 237, 65 AFTR2d 90-1173, 90-1 USTC ¶ 60,001 (10th Cir. 1989).]

Portion of proceeds of two life insurance policies on decedent's life are included in her estate where decedent had sufficient control over purchase and retention of policies. Decedent was married, but for the most part, lived separately from her husband. She managed the businesses she co-owned with her husband and wrote most of the checks from a joint checking account that was funded with both spouses' earnings. On her initial application for insurance, decedent named her own estate as the beneficiary of her policy. Later, on the advice of insurance agents, she amended her initial application, naming her husband as the owner and beneficiary. The initial premium on the policy was paid with a check drawn by decedent from the joint bank account. Decedent also signed a release renouncing an interest in the money that was to be used to pay the future policy premiums. Later, an additional policy was obtained on decedent's life, which also listed decedent's husband as owner and beneficiary. This policy was approved and issued by the insurer and mailed to the husband on the same date that decedent died. On the federal estate tax return, the estate did not include any portion of the life insurance policies' proceeds in the gross estate. In a notice of deficiency, the IRS determined that one half of the proceeds of each policy on decedent's life should have been included in decedent's gross estate, because her interest in the policies was transferred within three years prior to her date of death. The estate argued that because decedent never owned the insurance policies, she could not have transferred an interest in them.

Held: For the IRS. The insurance policies' proceeds should have been included in the estate in accordance with Section 2035, because decedent transferred the insurance policies to her husband a short time prior to her death. Section 2035 provides that the value of the gross estate shall include the value of all property that decedent has an interest in and of which decedent had, at any time, made a transfer during the three-year period ending on the date of decedent's death. The court stated that because decedent exercised sufficient control over the purchase and retention of the policies and used her property to purchase the policies, she had ownership interests in the policies that were transferred to her husband. Such control was evidenced by the fact that decedent attended meetings with the insurance agents and took responsibility for making premium payments. In addition, the payments were drawn from a joint checking account, and no steps were taken to segregate her husband's funds into a separate account from which to pay the insurance policy premiums. The court's reasoning was based in part on its belief that Section 2035 was enacted to reach substitutes for testamentary dispositions and thus to prevent the evading of estate tax by structuring transactions as accomplished by decedent and her husband.

[Schnack, 848 F2d 933, 88-1 USTC ¶ 13,768, 61 AFTR2d 88-1386 (9th Cir. 1988).]

Retroactivity of 1978 amendment to Section 2035 is held constitutional, even though it caused inclusion of insurance policies in gross estate. In March and April 1978, decedent bestowed a gift to his wife of five life insurance policies with a total value of less than $3,000. Decedent died on May 13, 1978, and the policies had a date-of-death value of $484,611. In November 1978, Congress amended Section 2035(b)(2) to require inclusion in a gross estate of life insurance policies transferred within three years prior to death. This amendment was made effective retroactively to transfers made after December 31, 1976. The IRS challenged the estate's exclusion of the "death value" of the policies from decedent's estate. The estate argued that application of the 1978 amendment to decedent's transfer of the policies was a denial of due process, and thus Section 2035 was unconstitutional. The estate also contended that Section 2035 was unconstitutional, because it "unreasonably" created an irrebuttable presumption of a gift in contemplation of death.

Held: Affirmed for the IRS. A mere change in an existing tax law that increases the amount of a gift includable in a decedent's gross estate is not so harsh or oppressive as to be unconstitutional. Further, an amendment to a tax statute will not result in a violation of due process requirements if the change is reasonably foreseeable and if it causes a mere change in the amount of tax instead of a wholly new tax. Finally, Section 2035, as amended in 1976, rendered the donor's motive immaterial for application of Section 2035. Therefore, the affected statute does not make an irrebuttable presumption of a gift in contemplation of death, but it includes in the gross estate all gifts made within three years of the donor's death.

[Estate of Elkins, 797 F2d 481, 86-2 USTC ¶ 13,680, 58 AFTR2d 86-6357 (7th Cir. 1986).]

Retroactive application of Revenue Act of 1978 to 1977 transfer is held constitutional. On January 4, 1977, decedent purchased an insurance policy on his own life and transferred the policy to his wife, effective March 22, 1977. At the time of the transfer, the policy was worth less than $3,000, which at the time was the maximum gift tax exclusion under Section 2035(b)(2). In addition, such a transfer would have been effective under estate tax law to remove the policy and its proceeds from the donor's estate. Decedent died on June 13, 1977, and on November 6, 1978, the Revenue Act of 1978 became law.

Among other things, the 1978 Act took life insurance policies out of Section 2035(b)(2) altogether and further provided that it would be effective with respect to transfers made after January 1, 1977, by decedents dying after December 31, 1976. Thus, if the 1978 amendments were applicable, the proceeds of decedent's life insurance policy in the instant case were includable in the gross estate. The IRS applied the 1978 Act to the gift in question and included the proceeds of the policy in decedent's estate for tax purposes. The issue therefore was the constitutionality of the retroactive application of the 1978 Act to the 1977 transfer. The district court found such retroactivity constitutional, and the personal representative of decedent's estate appealed.

Held: Affirmed for the IRS. There is nothing unconstitutional or unusual about retroactive tax laws. Most of these laws have been upheld against due process challenges on the theory that retroactivity is necessary, as a practical matter, to prevent the revenue loss that would result if taxpayers, aware of a likely impending change in the law, were permitted to order their affairs freely to avoid the effect of the change. The retroactive application of a tax statute may be so unreasonable in a given case, however, as to amount to a deprivation of property without due process of law. In determining whether a tax meets this threshold, the Supreme Court has established a two-part test: (1) whether the change in the tax law was reasonably foreseeable and (2) whether it was only a change in the applicable tax rate or the imposition of a new tax. Under the facts presented, there was no showing of gross unfairness in violation of the Constitution, because decedent was not motivated by the estate tax laws when he bought, and later transferred, the policy. In addition, this was not a case concerning the imposition of a completely new tax. Accordingly, the retroactive application of the 1978 Act to the 1977 transfer was constitutional.

[Fein, 730 F2d 1211, 53 AFTR2d 94-1637, 84-1 USTC ¶ 13,567 (8th Cir. 1984), cert. denied, 469 US 858 (1984).]

IRS rules on assignment of life insurance policy by corporation within three years of death of corporation's controlling shareholder. The IRS ruled that life insurance proceeds are includable in a deceased stockholder's gross estate under Section 2035. For the proceeds to be includable, within three years of decedent's death and for less than adequate and full consideration, the corporation must assign an insurance policy on the stockholder's life. The stockholder must then dispose of control of the corporation. In addition, life insurance proceeds must be payable to a third party for other than a business purpose within the meaning of Regulation § 20.2042-1(c)(6). The IRS also ruled that life insurance proceeds are includable in a deceased stockholder's gross estate under Section 2035 if, within three years of death, and for less than adequate and full consideration, the stockholder disposes of the controlling interest in a corporation that owns a life insurance policy on the stockholder's life and if the life insurance policy proceeds are payable to a third party for other than a business purpose within the meaning of Regulation § 20.2042-1(c)(6).

[Rev. Rul. 90-21, 1990-1 CB 172.]

Transferred second-to-die policy was not in estate. In 1985, taxpayer and his spouse each created an irrevocable life insurance trust (*A* and *B* Trusts), naming the other spouse as trustee. Policies on the life of each grantor were transferred to his or her respective trust. In 1989, each person, as trustee of the spouse's trust, purchased a second-to-die policy insuring their joint lives. The trustees had various powers over the assets in the trusts, including the power to change beneficiaries, to pledge or assign the policies or their proceeds, and to distribute income and principal. This gave the trustees incidents of owner-ship over the second-to-die policies. In 1993, taxpayer and his spouse created a new trust, called the "Estate Reduction Trust," which had an unrelated third party as trustee. Neither taxpayer nor his spouse had any power over, or inter-est in, the income or principal of this trust. They did, however, have the right to reacquire all or part of the trust's assets by substituting property of equivalent value into the trust. In addition, the trust was to be amended to pro-vide that if it was determined to be a grantor trust under Sections 671 et seq., taxpayer and his spouse would be entitled to a yearly distribution from the trust of an amount equal to the increase in their personal income tax due to the inclusion of the trust income on their tax return. The Estate Reduction Trust purchased the two second-to-die policies from the *A* and *B* Trusts for the poli-cies' interpolated terminal reserve value plus the value of any unexpired pre-miums. Taxpayers requested that the IRS rule that (1) the second-to-die policies purchased by the Estate Reduction Trust would not be included in the estates of taxpayers (as trustees of the *A* and *B* Trusts) under Section 2035 if taxpayers died within three years of the transfer to the Estate Reduction Trust and (2) the corpus of the Estate Reduction Trust would not be included in the gross estate of either taxpayer or his spouse under Section 2036, Section 2038, or Section 2042.

According to this ruling, taxpayer/spouses who each serve as trustee of the irrevocable life insurance trust of the other could transfer second-to-die policies held in the trusts to a third trust whose trustee is an independent third party without causing the policies to be included in their estates if they die within three years of the transfer, provided the transfer is a purchase and not a gift of the second-to-die policies. The corpus of the third trust is not includable in their estates either, if they do not hold any incidents of ownership in the in-surance policies in the trust. The taxpayers' right to receive reimbursement for tax payments made by them on behalf of the third trust is not a retained right to income under Section 2036(a). Moreover, the right to reacquire trust assets by substituting assets of equivalent value does not constitute incidents of ownership. The IRS was also asked to rule that (1) taxpayer and his spouse would be considered the owners of the Estate Reduction Trust for income tax purposes under Section 675 and (2) the purchase of the second-to-die policies by the trustee of the Estate Reduction Trust was a purchase of insurance that is excepted from the transfer for value rule of Section 101(a)(2) and that, therefore, the proceeds would be excludable from income under Section 101(a). The IRS could not rule on these two issues, because the first issue was under extensive study, and until resolved, any ruling on the second issue would have involved a hypothetical situation, and the IRS cannot rule on hypothetical situations.

[Priv. Ltr. Rul. 9413045.]

¶ 7.03 EFFECT OF COMMUNITY PROPERTY LAWS

Estate does not include the full value of decedent's insurance proceeds. Decedent's and his predeceased wife's insurance policies and premiums were paid for with community funds (until the wife died). Decedent's wife and children were named as beneficiaries. When the wife died in 1978, her interest in the policies passed to her children, who did not exercise their right to receive half the cash surrender value. Decedent continued to pay the premiums until his death in 1988. Under Section 2042(2), a decedent's gross estate includes the proceeds of life insurance on his life that are receivable by beneficiaries other than the estate, to the extent decedent held any "incidents of ownership" in the policy at his death. Regulation §§ 20.2042-1(c)(2) and 20.2042-1(c)(5) provide that incidents of ownership generally refers to the insured's or estate's right to a policy's economic benefits, and that state law must be considered when determining incidents of ownership. It was undisputed that the policy and proceed rights were community property under Texas law where the policies were purchased with community funds during decedent's marriage, and that the wife held an undivided one-half interest therein when she died. Also, Texas law clearly provided that half those rights passed to decedent and the other half passed to the children, on his wife's death. The estate claimed that because half the incidents of ownership passed to the children, decedent held only a 50 percent interest in the policies when he died. The IRS maintained however, that the wife's interest in the policies was "settled" when half the cash surrender value was allocated to her estate and reported on her estate's return. The IRS concluded that the wife's interest was therefore extinguished before, and that decedent consequently held 100 percent of the incidents of ownership on his death.

Held: For the IRS. The Fifth Circuit looked to state law to determine the extent of decedent's incidents of ownership in the three policies. Although Texas law does provide that a pre-deceasing, uninsured spouse's remaining community interest in life insurance on her spouse's life may be extinguished on the settlement of her interest, that scenario did not occur in this case because the wife's interest was never settled. Specifically, the Fifth Circuit found that the position that reporting the wife's ownership interest on her federal estate tax return settled her policy interest for state community property law purposes lacked authority and was even contrary to state law. This position contradicted Revenue Ruling 75-100, 1975-1 CB 303, and Regulation § 20.2042-1(c)(5), which determined that in a factually similar situation, a decedent held only half the incidents of ownership. Furthermore, the IRS's position was contrary to established case law, such as Estate of Cavenaugh, 51 F3d 597, 75 AFTR2d 95-2049, 95-1 USTC ¶ 60,195 (5th Cir. 1995), which clearly did not interpret Texas law to mean that an uninsured, pre-deceasing wife's half interest in her husband's insurance could be settled by merely including the value of her interest on her estate tax return. Furthermore, Texas law provided that settlement occurs when half the cash surrender value is allocated or *paid* to the pre-deceasing spouse's estate. The children, however, testified that they never sought such allocation, so settlement could not have been effected. Consequently, the Fifth Circuit determined that the wife's interest was not extinguished; therefore, decedent only held half, not the entire, interest for estate tax purposes. Additionally, the estate was awarded litigation costs because the IRS was not substantially justified under Section 7430 in including the insurance proceeds in decedent's gross estate, or in its position on a separate issue regarding real property valuation.

[Estate of Cervin, 111 F3d 1252, 79 AFTR2d 97-2487, 97-1 USTC ¶ 60,274 (5th Cir. 1997).]

Assets included in estate because of prior QTIP election. Decedent and his wife were married residents of Texas, a community property state. In 1980, they purchased a renewable term insurance policy on decedent's life. In 1983, decedent's wife died testate; her will left decedent certain property interests that he, as executor of her estate, elected to deduct from her estate by making a qualified terminable interest property (QTIP) election. In 1986, decedent died, leaving his estate as the sole beneficiary of approximately $650,000 in life insurance proceeds. His personal representative excluded from the gross estate one half of the term life insurance death benefit paid to the estate and those property interests that passed from decedent's wife to decedent on her death in 1983. Decedent made a QTIP election in his wife's estate in 1983 and deducted the property at issue from her estate by claiming the marital deduction. Now, however, his estate advanced the argument that his election was defective. The estate took the position that the income interest decedent received could not constitute a "qualifying income interest for life," as required by Section 2056(b)(7)(B). Upon decedent's wife's death, decedent received two types of interests in property. She bequeathed him specifically defined interests in their home and other real property. Her will also created a residuary trust whose income was to be paid to decedent during his lifetime. Her will assigned him a life estate in the family home, but permitted him to sell it provided that the proceeds from such sale were invested in another home for him, with any balance to be added to her estate's residuary trust. Decedent's estate argued that since no provision of her will nor Texas law precluded the accumulation of trust income (as opposed to its current distribution), the possibility existed that some of this income might be distributed to someone other than decedent. His estate contended that the QTIP election was defective. Decedent's wife's will provided that all the income from the trust was to be paid to decedent for as long as he lived "monthly or at the end of such other periods as may be necessary or desirable in the discretion of the Trustee." The IRS issued a notice of deficiency, and the Tax Court held that both the life insurance proceeds and the other aforementioned interests were properly includable in decedent's estate.

Held: Affirmed for the IRS (in part). The Fifth Circuit held that although the provisions of the will plainly granted the trustee some latitude in determining when income distributions should be made, reading this clause to allow the trustee to exercise absolute discretion in choosing when to pay decedent income was unwarranted. Decedent's wife's will specifically stated that payments of income should be made periodically, and the inclusion of the word "monthly" evidenced an intent to distribute the income at more frequent intervals than "reasonableness" requires. There was no authorization in the will for the trustee to accumulate income during decedent's life, and decedent was also given "five and five" power. The court reasoned that since decedent was entitled to require distributions of principal annually under the "five and five" power, it was unlikely that decedent's wife did not intend him to take distributions of income as often. Consequently, the court ruled that decedent received a qualifying income interest for life.

With respect to the life insurance proceeds, the court concluded that half the insurance proceeds were excludable from decedent's estate because they represented decedent's wife's community property. Regulation § 20.2042-1(b)(2) excludes life insurance proceeds payable to the estate to the extent they belong to decedent's spouse under state community property law. Here, it was clear that under Texas law, if life insurance is purchased during a marriage and paid for with community funds, the policy rights or incidents of ownership and the right to receive the proceeds in the future constitute community property. The IRS argued that the marital community was dissolved at decedent's wife's death, and any community property interest in the policy terminated upon expiration of the last one-year term of the policy paid with community funds. Alternatively, the IRS asserted that her community interest was capped at half the cash surrender value or the interpolated terminal reserve value of the policy at her death, which would have been zero. The court examined community property law and concluded that community interest was not terminated by a zero cash surrender value at the time of decedent's wife's death. In other words, a number of valuable property rights continued for decedent's wife's estate, including the right to renew the policy annually at stated premiums with no evidence of insurability. In addition, the premium rates were fixed under the terms of the policy, and the dividends increased as the policy was renewed for extended terms. Therefore, by continuing coverage after decedent's wife's death, decedent apparently reaped some benefit from the prior four years of insurance. Based on this factor, the court held that half the proceeds should be attributable to decedent's wife's estate and, hence, excludable from decedent's estate.

[Estate of Cavenaugh, 51 F3d 597, 75 AFTR2d 95-2049, 95-1 USTC ¶ 60,195 (5th Cir. 1995).]

Life insurance proceeds are excluded from estates of spouses dying simultaneously. Decedents, husband and wife, died in a plane crash. Each owned an insurance policy, purchased with community funds, on the life of the other. The proceeds were excluded by the respective estates. The IRS included one half of the proceeds of each policy in each estate, contending that the proceeds were community property.

Held: For the estate. Each policy was the separate property of the noninsured spouse (the owner). Under Louisiana state law, where both the insured and the beneficiary die simultaneously, the insured is deemed to survive. Thus, the proceeds could never be included in either estate under Section 2042. The IRS did not raise the issue of includability under Section 2038 as separate property of the noninsured spouse. The IRS's theory that one half of the proceeds of the insured spouse's policy should be includable in the estate of the noninsured spouse was rejected.

[Estate of Marks, 94 TC 720 (1990).]

Half of the proceeds of an insurance policy owned by wife, but purchased with community funds, are includable in husband's gross estate. Decedent and his wife applied for an insurance policy on his life, with his wife designated as owner. Premiums were paid from a bank account containing community funds under Washington law. The IRS asserted that 50 percent of the policy was includable in the husband's gross estate.

Held: For the IRS. Taxpayer did not show by clear and convincing proof that the husband intended to make the policy the separate property of the wife by gift of his community interest. The court also rejected taxpayer's contention that Washington law made the policy her separate property, because she was the policy's beneficiary.

[Estate of Meyer, 66 TC 41 (1976), aff'd by court order, 566 F2d 1182 (9th Cir. 1977).]

Effects of paying life insurance premiums with community funds. Decedent, a Louisiana resident, purchased an insurance policy on his life. He designated his spouse as the owner of the policy. Therefore, she held all the incidents of ownership over the policy. The premiums for the policy were paid by the insured and his spouse out of community funds. When the insured died, the life insurance proceeds were paid to their child, who was designated as the beneficiary by the spouse. The issues of this ruling were (1) whether any of the proceeds were includable in the insured decedent's estate under Section 2042 and (2) whether, if the surviving spouse/owner designates a third party to receive the policy proceeds, the death of the insured and the payment of the proceeds cause the spouse to make a gift of the proceeds to the beneficiary under Section 2511.

Section 2042(2) includes in a decedent's estate the proceeds of an insurance policy on his life payable to a named beneficiary if decedent possessed any incidents of ownership in the policy at his death. Under Regulation § 20.2042-1(c)(2), the term "incidents of ownership" includes not only legal ownership but also the power to change the beneficiary; to surrender, cancel, or assign the policy; to revoke an assignment; to pledge the policy for a loan; or to obtain from the insurer a loan against the surrender value of the policy. The determination of whether a decedent held such incidents of ownership depends on state law. Generally, if an insurance policy is acquired by a spouse living in a community property state and the policy premiums are paid from community property funds, the proceeds of the policy are community property. The rule is different in Louisiana, however, where the presumption that property held by either spouse during a marriage is community property does not apply to a life insurance policy transferred from one spouse to another. In Catalano, 429 F2d 1058 (5th Cir. 1969), the Fifth Circuit ruled that an insurance policy unconditionally owned by the insured's wife was, as a matter of law, part of the wife's separate estate. In holding that insurance policies are contractual in nature, and not governed by the Civil Code, the court of appeals followed a long-standing position taken by the Louisiana Supreme Court. Later cases determined that the use of community funds to pay the premiums on such a policy would not alter the separate property status of the policy or cause incidents of ownership to be attributed to the insured. Applying these holdings to the facts of the ruling, the IRS concluded that the insurance policy was the sole property of the surviving spouse and that no incidents of ownership were attributable to the insured decedent. Consequently, under Louisiana law, no portion of the proceeds was includable in decedent's gross estate under Section 2042. The IRS noted, however, that if the insurance contract had specifically stated that the policy was to be held as community property, half the proceeds would have been included in decedent's estate.

The second issue in this ruling concerns the taxation of gifts. Section 2511 makes clear that taxable gifts include transfers in trust or otherwise, direct as well as indirect transfers, and property that is real, personal, tangible, or intangible. Under Regulation § 25.2511-1(a), the assignment of the benefits of a life insurance policy may be a taxable transfer. Regulation § 25.2511-1(h)(9) explains that if community funds are used to purchase insurance on the life of a spouse, and a third person is named as the beneficiary, then the payment of the proceeds constitutes a completed gift by the surviving spouse as to one half of the proceeds. The other half is considered to have passed to the beneficiary from decedent. This rule is inapplicable in Louisiana. In that state, the use of community funds to pay the premiums does not designate the policy as a community asset if the policy is owned by one spouse. Since all the proceeds are considered to be the separate property of the surviving spouse, upon the death of the insured the payment of the proceeds is treated as a completed gift by the surviving spouse to the beneficiary. The value of the gift is the total proceeds—not just half. Thus, the IRS found that because the surviving spouse in this ruling held all the incidents of ownership, including the right to designate and change the beneficiary, she made a gift to the beneficiary of all the proceeds upon her husband's death. This ruling revokes Revenue Ruling 48, 1953-1 CB 392, and Revenue Ruling 232, 1953-2 CB 268, which applied the general rule regarding the estate and gift tax treatment of life insurance proceeds in community property states to Louisiana and Texas. These earlier rulings can still be relied upon, however, for estate tax purposes by the estate of a Louisiana decedent who acquired a policy on his life prior to November 14, 1994, and died before May 15, 1995. For gift tax purposes, the prior rulings can be relied upon by the spouse of a Louisiana decedent who died before May 15, 1995, if the spouse acquired a policy on decedent's life before November 14, 1994.

[Rev. Rul. 94-69, 1994-2 CB 241.]

Gross estate includes one half of insurance proceeds where policy premiums are paid with community funds. Decedent was the "applicant, insured, and listed owner of the policy." The premiums were paid with community funds, and decedent's wife and children were the beneficiaries. The IRS stated that decedent's gross estate would include one half of the proceeds. The IRS reviewed the circumstances that must exist if one spouse is considered to have bequeathed a gift of his one-half of the policy to the other spouse. Whether there has been an effective transfer of all ownership in the policy to the other spouse depends, to a very great degree, on local law.

[Priv. Ltr. Rul. 8928003.]

¶ 7.04 INCIDENTS OF OWNERSHIP

Payment of insurance premiums by insured does not cause inclusion of proceeds in estate. Decedent applied for two life insurance policies within the one year before he died. Decedent's sons signed both applications as owners and beneficiaries, but decedent paid all the premiums for the two policies. The proceeds of the policies were paid to the sons at decedent's death. The Tax Court held that the insurance proceeds were not includable in decedent's gross estate, because he never possessed any incidents of ownership in the policies. The Tax Court declined to apply the "beamed transfer" theory of Bel, 452 F2d 683, 72-1 USTC ¶ 12,818, 29 AFTR2d 71-1482 (5th Cir. 1971), cert. denied.

Held: Affirmed for the estate. The Fifth Circuit agreed with the Tax Court and with the Tenth Circuit in Leder, 893 F2d 237, 90-1 USTC ¶ 60,001, 65 AFTR2d 90-1173 (10th Cir. 1989), and the Sixth Circuit in Estate of Headrick, 918 F2d 1263, 90-2 USTC ¶ 60,049, 66 AFTR2d 90-6038 (6th Cir. 1990). With the amendment of Section 2035 by the Economic Recovery Tax Act of 1981 (ERTA), Congress intended to do away with the premium payment test for inclusion of insurance proceeds. Since ERTA, the test for inclusion is the incidents of ownership test. The Fifth Circuit did not overrule *Bel*, but stated that subsequent action by Congress can have the effect of overruling a prior decision.

[Estate of Perry, 927 F2d 209, 91-1 USTC ¶ 60,064, 67 AFTR2d 91-1200 (5th Cir. 1991).]

Insurance proceeds are excluded from decedent's estate. Decedent was a tax attorney who drafted an irrevocable trust agreement for himself as part of his personal estate planning. The agreement designated decedent as the settlor of the trust and his wife and three minor children as primary beneficiaries. Decedent reserved to himself the right to remove any trustee at will and appoint a bank as successor trustee. The beneficiaries had a limited power to withdraw trust property within thirty days of the contribution of such property. The trustee had the authority to, but was not required to, invest in insurance policies on the life of decedent or a beneficiary, and to hold such policies as trust principal. Decedent chose a bank to act as trustee. It was the bank president's understanding that decedent wanted the trust to be an insurance trust; however, establishment of the trust at the bank was not conditioned on the bank's commitment to acquire life insurance. Once the trust was executed, decedent irrevocably assigned $5,900 to the bank. On that same date, his wife executed, on behalf of herself and her children, a waiver of their right to withdraw any portion of that contribution. The next day, the bank applied for a $375,000 insurance policy on decedent's life. The bank, as trustee, was listed as the policy owner and the beneficiary. Decedent signed the application as the insured. The policy was approved on January 8, 1980. The bank, as owner of the policy, was given all rights under it, including the right to assign the policy, change the beneficiaries, change the owner, and exercise all the policy options. The bank paid the insurance company a monthly premium of $436. At the end of the next year, decedent made a second contribution to the trust corpus of $5,500. At the end of the third year, he made a contribution of $2,000. No portion of any of these contributions was withdrawn by the beneficiaries. The total amount paid in by decedent covered all of the premium payments made by the bank. Several months after the trust was established, decedent was invited to join the bank's board of directors. He became a member and chairman of the bank's trust committee. The duties of this committee included reviewing and discussing new trust accounts and investments in those accounts. Decedent's trust was first reviewed on April 30, 1980, and was reviewed thereafter every three to four months as was the normal procedure. Decedent died on June 19, 1982, in an automobile accident, less than three years after he executed the trust agreement. The insurance company paid $378,700 in death benefits to the bank as the owner of the policy on decedent's life. The insurance proceeds were not included in decedent's gross estate on the estate tax return. The IRS determined that the payment of the proceeds to the trustee constituted a transfer within the meaning of Section 2035(a) because the trust was created less than three years before decedent died; therefore, the proceeds should have been included in decedent's estate. The IRS assessed a deficiency against the estate, which the estate paid but challenged in Tax Court. The Tax Court ruled in favor of the estate, following its 1987 decision in Estate of Leder, 893 F2d 237, 90-1 USTC ¶ 60,001, 65 AFTR2d 90-1173 (10th Cir. 1989). The IRS appealed.

Held: Affirmed for the estate. The Sixth Circuit affirmed the Tax Court's finding that under Section 2035(d)(1), the proceeds of an insurance policy on decedent's life were not includable in his estate. The exception to Section 2035(d)(1), found in Section 2035(d)(2), did not apply, because decedent did not possess any incidents of ownership in the policy. The court refused to incorporate the constructive transfer doctrine into Section 2035(d)(2), because to do so would contravene Congress's intent in enacting Sections 2035(d) and 2042.

[Estate of Headrick, 918 F2d 1263, 90-2 USTC ¶ 60,049, 66 AFTR2d 90-6038 (6th Cir. 1990).]

Initiation of transaction and payment of premiums result in inclusion of insurance proceeds, even though decedent had no incidence of ownership. Decedent and his wife lived in a community property state. He applied for an insurance policy on his life, naming his wife as owner and beneficiary. He also later executed a document disclaiming any interest in the policy or the proceeds. In addition, he authorized premiums to be paid by his spouse out of community funds, with his share of the funds being a gift to her. Decedent died within three years of the time the policy was issued, and the IRS included one-half of the proceeds in his estate. The estate contended that they were excludable for one of two reasons: (1) Section 2035 requires a transfer of property, which did not occur here and (2) in any event, the premiums came under the exception for small gifts under Section 2035(b)(2).

Held: For the IRS. Under Section 2035, transfers of property taking place within three years of decedent's death are includable in the estate. An exception is made in Section 2035(b)(2) for gifts for which a gift tax return is not required. This exception, however, does not apply to transfers of life insurance policies. In Estate of Schnack, 848 F2d 933 (9th Cir. 1988), a case with similar facts, the court held that a transfer of a life insurance policy occurs when decedent transfers funds to a third party to pay to a life insurance company. Based on that case, the life insurance proceeds in the instant case were included in the estate. Furthermore, Section 2035(b)(2), which excludes transfers for which no gift tax return was required, does not preclude the inclusion of insurance proceeds. The estate contended that the exception for life insurance policies did not apply to the transfer of funds for the payment of premiums. The court held that the language "with respect to" life insurance policies was broad enough to cover premiums. Consequently, even though decedent never owned an insurance policy and had no incidents of ownership in it at his death, the proceeds still were includable in his estate, because he initiated the transaction and paid the premiums.

[Knisley, 901 F2d 793, 90-2 USTC ¶ 60,037, 65 AFTR2d 90-1235 (9th Cir. 1990).]

Tax Court is reversed in holding that restriction in assignment instrument is retained incident of ownership over life insurance policies. In 1928, decedent, who died on October 16, 1978, purchased eight life insurance policies on his own life. Each policy contained a power granted to decedent by which he could freely revoke or assign the policy to another party. During 1929, decedent had made an assignment of all eight policies to his wife by means of a preprinted form furnished by the insurer. The form contained a clause providing that the assignment was effective in conferring and vesting all rights in the assignee, except that "without the written consent of the insured no one shall be designated as beneficiary or contingent beneficiary who has not an insurable interest in his life, nor shall the said policies be assigned to anyone who has not such insurable interest." As part of the same transaction, the wife assigned the policies to a trust created by her for the benefit of their children. The wife predeceased decedent on October 31, 1965, and the trustee, a local bank never changed the beneficiaries or exercised any other powers granted by the terms of the policies. Following decedent's death, the IRS sought to invoke Section 2042 and include the value of the policies in decedent's gross estate.

Section 2042 determines the includability of life insurance proceeds in decedent's gross estate and provides that the life insurance proceeds on a decedent, not receivable by or for the benefit of the estate, are includable in decedent's gross estate if decedent possessed any of the incidents of ownership in the policy at his death, exercisable either alone or in conjunction with any other person. With regard to the term "incidents of ownership," Regulation § 20.2042-1(c)(2) provides generally that the term has reference to the right of the insured or his estate to the economic benefits of the policy. Thus, it includes the power to change the beneficiary, to surrender or cancel the policy, to assign the policy, to pledge the policy for a loan, or to obtain from the insurer a loan against the surrender value of the policy. On the strength of these rules, the IRS contended that the wife's designation of an irrevocable beneficiary had no effect on decedent's power to prevent the owner of the policies from assigning the policies to anyone not having an insurable interest in his life. The IRS argued that although the wife did not reserve the right to change the beneficiary, the new beneficiary, the trustee bank, could assign its interest to a third party. From this the IRS concluded that decedent could have vetoed such an assignment if the assignee did not have an insurable interest in decedent's life.

The Tax Court held for the IRS, primarily because the assignment clause provided that the wife would receive her interest from decedent subject to a retained veto power, and therefore any interest that she assigned remained subject to his power. Hence, the clause remained in effect until decedent's death, providing him with an incident of ownership. In addition, the Tax Court gave great weight to its conclusion that the wife's designation of an irrevocable beneficiary did not strip decedent of his veto power, because the clause required his consent over the designation of a beneficiary or contingent beneficiary, as well as any assignment of the policies, to anyone who did not have an insurable interest in his life.

Held: Reversed for the estate. The Third Circuit, noting its previous decision in Estate of Connelly, 551 F2d 552 (3d Cir. 1977), stated the general rule that a decedent's power over a life insurance trust that gives no right to the economic benefits of the underlying policy does not constitute an incident of ownership. The court concluded that decedent's retained power to veto assignment of the policies on his life to a person lacking an insurable interest did not constitute an incident of ownership. In the more than fifty years since decedent drafted the power, he could not have enjoyed any economic benefit from exercising it. State law mandated the veto power retained at the time decedent created it. Whatever vitality, if any, the veto power may have had at one time, the wife's death and the terms of the trust agreement excluded decedent from any possible economic benefit. Congress's purpose in requiring the inclusion of policies in a gross estate when decedent retains incidents of ownership is to prevent taxpayers from enjoying property without paying tax on it. Decedent, by his retained power, neither enjoyed the benefits of nor exerted the sort of control that ordinarily accompanies ownership of life insurance policies.

[Estate of Rockwell, 779 F2d 931, 86-1 USTC ¶ 13,651, 57 AFTR2d 86-1491 (3d Cir. 1985).]

Insurance policy included in estate, absent proper planning. Decedent originally owned two $500,000 insurance policies on his life. Decedent converted them into one policy worth $1 million. Then decedent changed the policy beneficiary to his irrevocable trust, and the proceeds were paid to the trust following decedent's death in 1993. The insurance company's records listed decedent as the sole owner of the converted $1 million policy; the company never received a request to change the policy's owner. The estate contended that decedent's wife owned one of the original $500,000 policies, but she never questioned decedent's ownership of the $1 million policy or decedent's authority to name his trust as sole beneficiary. The IRS contended that the policy should be included in decedent's estate because decedent had incidents of ownership over it. Section 2042 states that the value of a gross estate for tax purposes must include the proceeds from a life insurance policy if the owner of the policy alone had incidents of ownership over it or in conjunction with another. Incidents of ownership includes the power to change the beneficiary of the policy, to pledge the policy for a loan, or to revoke an assignment of the policy, according to Regulation § 20.2042-1(c). The estate argued that the trust owned the policy, and decedent had no incidents of ownership over it.

    Held: For the IRS. The court stated that if decedent was not the owner of the policy, he could not have changed the beneficiary. By changing the beneficiary designation to the trust, he established that he possessed incidents of ownership. The estate also claimed that decedent's wife owned one of the $500,000 policies. This, however, had no bearing on the court's decision because the $1 million policy was the one at issue, and decedent was found to have incidents of ownership in that policy. Further, the court pointed out that even if decedent had transferred ownership of the policy to the trust as claimed in 1992, the result would be the same. Under Section 2035(a), an insurance policy given as a gift within three years of a decedent's death is included in decedent's estate. The estate also maintained that even if the policy proceeds were included in the estate, they should qualify for the estate tax marital deduction. This argument also was unpersuasive because decedent's spouse never retained the power to appoint the trust's principal, before or after her husband's death. Therefore, the policy did not qualify for the Section 2056 marital deduction.

[Salyer, 82 AFTR2d 98-5967, 98-2 USTC ¶ 60,326 (ED Ky. 1998).]

Tax Court rules on includability of insurance proceeds in trustee's estate. Decedent was trustee of a trust that owned several insurance policies on his life. The trust agreement conferred on him absolute powers to manage the policies, including the powers to pledge them for loans. Decedent-trustee subsequently pledged the policies as collateral for a loan to his 50-percent-owned corporation. Under Section 2042(2), the criterion for inclusion of insurance proceeds in gross estate turns on whether the insured possessed incidents of ownership in the policy. The IRS, in a reversal of its earlier position, agreed with the conclusion in Estate of Skifter, 468 F2d 699 (2d Cir. 1972), that powers held in a fiduciary capacity do not constitute incidents of ownership under Section 2042(2) where they have devolved on decedent after he has divested himself of any interest in the policies and where decedent cannot use the powers for his own personal benefit. The IRS contended, however, that inclusion of the proceeds in the estate was required because the trust agreement vested decedent with powers to use the policies for his own benefit. The estate claimed that decedent had possessed no incidents of ownership in either a personal or fiduciary capacity that would render the policies includable in his estate.

Held: For the estate. Exercise of the powers was limited by decedent's fiduciary duty. Thus, the powers were exercisable not for his own benefit, but only for the benefit of trust beneficiaries.

[Estate of Bloch, 78 TC 850 (1982).]

Group-term insurance is not includable, despite conversion right. Decedent was covered by a group-term insurance policy purchased by his employer. The provisions of the policy could be amended only by agreement between the insurance company and decedent's employer. Decedent had no control over the amount of benefits, the duration of payments, designation of beneficiaries, or the manner in which payments were to be made. The policy did grant decedent the right to convert his group insurance to individual insurance upon termination of employment. The IRS argued that the power to convert was an incident of ownership that required its inclusion in decedent's estate.

Held: For the estate. The court noted that not all rights in a policy constituted incidents of ownership and refused to distinguish the right to convert by voluntary termination from the power to cancel by voluntary termination, a right determined not to be an incident of ownership by the IRS itself in Revenue Ruling 72-307, 1972-1 CB 307. The court held that if "quitting a job is too high a price to pay for the right to cancel an insurance policy, it is likewise too high a price to pay for the right to convert to another policy." Thus, the court ruled that the insurance proceeds were not includable in the insured's estate when the insured has no control over a policy, other than the right to convert it upon termination of employment.

[Estate of Smead, 78 TC 43 (1982), acq., 1984-2 CB 2.]

Power to acquire policy from employer is not incident of ownership. Decedent's employer was the owner and beneficiary of two insurance policies on his life and in fact received the proceeds upon his death. The employment agreement gave decedent the right to purchase the policies for their cash surrender value if the employer elected not to pay the premiums on the policies, or to terminate or to surrender the policies. The IRS argued that the right to purchase the policy was an incident of ownership warranting inclusion of the proceeds in decedent's estate.

Held: For the estate. Decedent's rights were too contingent and beyond his control to be "incidents of ownership" for purposes of Section 2042. The court considered and rejected the IRS's reasoning in Revenue Ruling 79-46, 1979-1 CB 303, that the power to prevent cancellation of employer-owned insurance by an employee was an incident of ownership.

[Estate of Smith, 73 TC 307 (1979), acq. 1981-1 CB 2.]

Life insurance proceeds are excluded from gross estate. Decedent's daughter applied for life insurance on decedent ten months before his death. The daughter was the beneficiary, and the premiums were paid by preauthorized withdrawals from decedent's bank account. The IRS included the insurance proceeds in decedent's estate.

Held: For the estate. Decedent never owned or transferred the incidents of ownership in the policy. Under the applicable state law, the daughter was the policy owner.

[Estate of Ard, TC Memo. (P-H) ¶ 90,294, 59 TCM (CCH) 869 (1990).]

Life insurance proceeds are not part of gross estate, despite its purchase for estate-planning purposes. In 1982, decedent died and was survived by five children. A son was listed as owner and beneficiary of a $1 million insurance policy on the life of his mother. When purchasing the policy, the son stated that his purpose in being the owner and beneficiary of the policy was to prevent it from inclusion in decedent's estate. The estate subsequently brought suit against the son in order to claim the proceeds of the life insurance policy. Thereafter, the son and his siblings entered into a settlement agreement whereby the insurance proceeds were divided among them, and the suit was dismissed. The estate did not report as part of the gross estate the proceeds from the $1 million insurance policy. The IRS, on audit, contended that under Section 2042, the proceeds of the insurance policy were includable in the gross estate because decedent was the true owner of the policy under local law, and the son was merely decedent's agent, nominally designated as owner for the sole purpose of excluding the proceeds from the gross estate. The estate, on the other hand, argued that it was entitled to exclude from the gross estate the proceeds of the policy because no portion of the proceeds was payable to the estate or to the executor of the estate. In addition, the estate contended that decedent had not possessed any incidents of ownership in the policy, nor was she able to confer any economic benefits of the policy at the time of her death. Section 2042 provides that the gross estate includes (1) the proceeds of insurance on a decedent's life receivable by or for the benefit of the estate and (2) the proceeds of insurance on decedent's life receivable by other beneficiaries if decedent possessed at death any of the incidents of ownership in that insurance policy, exercisable either alone or in conjunction with any other person.

Held: For the estate. The court stated that in determining whether decedent possessed any incidents of ownership with respect to the insurance policy, the relevant question was whether decedent had the capacity to affect the disposition of the proceeds if she so desired. In making that determination, the court said that it would consider primarily the "policy facts," the rights given in the insurance contract, rather than the insured's subjective intentions. The court stated that it is the existence of a power, not the probability of its exercise, that controls. The court concluded that under local law, decedent had not possessed any incidents of ownership that would require the inclusion of the proceeds on her life in the gross estate pursuant to Section 2042(2). The court further found that there was no evidence of any legally binding commitment that obligated the son to provide any of the proceeds to the estate. Thus, the proceeds could not have been receivable by or for the benefit of the estate. Contrary to the IRS's contentions, the record simply did not establish that decedent was the true owner of the policy or that he was acting as an agent or other fiduciary or representative of decedent in regard to that policy. The court also rejected the IRS's contention that the proceeds were constructively received by the estate through the settlement agreement. There was no evidence that the son and the other beneficiaries of the estate were influenced by tax considerations in arriving at their settlement. Finally, the court found that the life insurance proceeds were also not includable in the gross estate under Section 2035(a), because decedent never had any property interest in the policy. Therefore, the court held that under both Sections 2042 and 2035, the proceeds were not includable in the gross estate.

[Estate of Chapman, TC Memo. (P-H) ¶ 89,105, 56 TCM (CCH) 1451 (1989).]

Decedent serving as trustee did not have incidents of ownership in policy. In 1960, decedent purchased an insurance policy on his own life and transferred all incidents of ownership to his spouse. The spouse designated their adult child as the policy beneficiary. The spouse died in 1978 and, by will, established a residuary trust for the benefit of the child. Decedent was designated as trustee. The insurance policy was included in the spouse's residuary estate and was transferred to the testamentary trust. The drafting of the spouse's will to provide for the residuary trust and the appointment of decedent as trustee were unrelated to his transfer of the policy to the spouse. As trustee, decedent had broad discretionary powers in the management of the trust property and the power to distribute or accumulate income. Under the terms of the policy, the owner could elect to have the proceeds made payable according to various plans, use the loan value to pay the premiums, borrow on the policy, assign or pledge the policy, and elect to receive annual dividends. The terms of the will did not preclude decedent from exercising these rights, although he could not do so for his own benefit. He paid the premiums on the policy out of other trust property. Decedent was still serving as trustee when he died in 1984. The IRS was asked to rule whether decedent had incidents of ownership in the policy sufficient to require inclusion of the proceeds in his gross estate pursuant to Section 2042.

After reviewing applicable law, the IRS noted that decedent completely relinquished all interest in the insurance policy on his life. The powers over the policy devolved on decedent as a fiduciary, through an independent transaction, and were not exercisable for his own benefit. Also, decedent did not transfer property to the trust. Thus, in the IRS's view, he did not possess incidents of ownership over the policy for purposes of Section 2042(2).

[Rev. Rul. 84-179, 1984-2 CB 195.]

Proceeds of partnership group-term life insurance policy are not includable in partner-decedent's estate where partner assigned all right, title, and interest in policy more than three years before death. *XYZ* was a partnership of thirty-five lawyers. *XYZ* employed forty associate lawyers and 100 administrative and clerical employees. In 1970, *XYZ* entered into an agreement with an insurance company providing for a master group-term life policy insuring the lives of the partners and the partnership employees. The insurance policy was group-term life insurance within the meaning of Section 79. In 1977, *D*, a partner of *XYZ*, created an irrevocable trust for the benefit of *D*'s children and assigned to the trust all right, title, and interest (including the conversion privilege) in the group-term life insurance policy insuring *D*'s life pursuant to the master policy. Pursuant to the master policy, however, *XYZ* retained the power to surrender or cancel the group-term life insurance policy with the insurance company.

D subsequently died in 1981. Under Section 2042(2), the gross estate includes the proceeds of life insurance on the decedent's life payable to beneficiaries other than decedent's estate under policies in which decedent possessed at death any incidents of ownership that can be exercised either alone or in conjunction with any other person. The power to surrender or cancel a life insurance policy is one such incident of ownership under Regulation § 20.2042-1(c)(2). Advice was requested from the IRS whether the value of proceeds received under the group-term life insurance policy of the partnership was includable in the partner-decedent's gross estate under Section 2042(2).

The IRS stated that the value of the proceeds was not includable in the partner-decedent's gross estate under Section 2042(2), because the partner did not die in possession of any incidents of ownership in the policy. The issue presented was whether the policy proceeds were includable in *D*'s gross estate under Section 2042(2) where the partnership's power to surrender or cancel the group-term life insurance master policy was attributed to *D* by virtue of *D*'s position as a partner. Regulation § 20.2042-1(c)(6) states that in the case of group-term life insurance, as defined in the regulations under Section 79, the power to surrender or cancel a policy held by a corporation shall not be attributed to any decedent through decedent's stock ownership. Similarly, a partnership's power to surrender or cancel its group-term life insurance policy shall not be attributable to any of the partners.

[Rev. Rul. 83-148, 1983-2 CB 157.]

Proceeds of life insurance policy owned by partnership, but payable other than to or for benefit of partnership, are includable in deceased insured partner's gross estate. *C, D,* and *E* were general partners in the *XYZ* partnership, each owning a one-third interest in the partnership profits and capital. On May 15, 1974, *XYZ* applied for and obtained a whole life insurance policy on the life of *D,* with *A, D*'s child, designated as beneficiary. The premium payments were made by the partnership in partial satisfaction of *D*'s distributive share of partnership income. On September 21, 1981, *D* died, and the face amount of the policy was paid to *A.* On the date of death, *D* did not possess, in an individual capacity, any incidents of ownership in the policy. All incidents of ownership were held by the partnership. Under Section 2042(2), the gross estate includes the proceeds of life insurance on the decedent's life receivable by beneficiaries other than the decedent's estate under policies in which decedent possessed at death any incidents of ownership that can be exercised either alone or in conjunction with any other person. Advice was requested from the IRS whether, for purposes of Section 2042(2), the insured partner would be deemed to have possessed incidents of ownership in the policy, so that the value of the proceeds was includable in the insured partner's gross estate.

The IRS ruled that for purposes of Section 2042(2), when a partnership owns a life insurance policy on a partner's life and the proceeds are payable other than to or for the benefit of the partnership, the insured partner possesses incidents of ownership in the policy in conjunction with the other partners, so that the value of the proceeds will be includable in the insured partner's gross estate. Regulation § 20.2042-1(c)(2) provides that the term "incidents of ownership" has reference to the right of the insured or the insured's estate to the economic benefits of the policy. For purposes of Section 2042(2), a partnership is generally regarded as an aggregate of its individual partners, and therefore any incidents of ownership in a life insurance policy held by the partnership are effectively held by the partners as individuals. In the present situation, the incidents of ownership in the policy were held by *D* in conjunction with the other partners. Thus, the value of the proceeds was includable in *D*'s gross estate under Section 2042(2).

[Rev. Rul. 83-147, 1983-2 CB 158.]

IRS reverses position on inclusion of split-dollar life insurance in estate. In Revenue Ruling 82-145, the IRS announced a change in its position with respect to split-dollar life insurance. The changed position results in unfavorable tax consequences for controlling and majority shareholders of close corporations. According to the revenue ruling, when a decedent's controlled corporation has the right at decedent's death to borrow against the cash surrender value of a policy on decedent's life, the proceeds of the policy, which are payable to a beneficiary other than the corporation, are included in decedent's gross estate. Revenue Ruling 76-274, 1976-2 CB 278, has been modified on the ground that it is inconsistent with this result. The distinction between Revenue Ruling 76-274 and Revenue Ruling 79-129, also affected by the IRS's change in position, seems to turn on which party—decedent or the controlled corporation—possessed the right to borrow against the policy. In Revenue Ruling 79-129, 79-1 CB 306, decedent assigned a policy on his life to a trust for the benefit of his spouse and children. Although the trustee was designated the owner of the policy, decedent had the right to borrow against the cash value to the extent of the premiums he paid. The estate received the portion of the proceeds equal to the cash value, and the trust received the balance.

The IRS ruled that the entire proceeds, not merely the cash value portion, were includable in decedent's estate. The right to borrow constituted an incident of ownership that required inclusion of the portion of the policy received by the trust under Section 2042(2). In Situation (3) of Revenue Ruling 76-274, decedent's controlled corporation possessed the right to borrow against the cash value of the policy to the extent of its premium payments and to assign the policy to a "sub-owner." The IRS allowed the portion of the proceeds payable to a third-party personal beneficiary (who was also the "sub-owner") to be excluded from decedent's estate. The IRS determined that the corporation held no incidents of ownership in this portion. Situation (3) of Revenue Ruling 76-274 has been reversed. Even though the controlled corporation, not the decedent, possesses the right to borrow against the policy, the proceeds payable to a personal beneficiary, not merely those payable to the estate, are included in the estate.

[Rev. Rul. 82-145, 1982-2 CB 213.]

Right to prevent cancellation of policy is ruled incident of ownership. Decedent's employer was the owner of an insurance policy on his life, with his wife designated the beneficiary. The employment agreement provided that the employee had the right to purchase the policy for its cash surrender value in the event that the employer elected to surrender and terminate the policy.

The IRS ruled that the right to prevent cancellation of the policy was an incident of ownership within the meaning of Section 2042. Thus, the insurance proceeds less the policy's cash surrender value were includable in decedent's gross estate. The IRS emphasized that includability was determined by the existence of the power rather than by the practical ability to exercise it.

[Rev. Rul. 79-46, 1979-1 CB 303.]

Split-dollar agreement gives rise to no transfer tax. Proceeds of second-to-die life insurance payable under a split-dollar agreement between a trust, which owned the policy, and married taxpayers, were not includable in the estate of the last spouse to die. Further, no taxable gift resulted from taxpayers' payment of a portion of the policy premiums, according to this ruling. Taxpayers, a husband and wife, established an irrevocable trust for the benefit of their three children. They initially funded the trust with a cash gift, which the trustee used to purchase and pay the first premium on a second-to-die life insurance policy covering taxpayers' lives. Taxpayers entered a collateral assignment split-dollar agreement with the trust with respect to the policy. Under the agreement, the trust—which was the designated policy owner and beneficiary—paid the portion of the premiums equal to the insurer's current premium rate for renewable term insurance, and taxpayers paid the balance. The agreement required that the estate of the second spouse to die (or surviving taxpayers, if the agreement terminated earlier) receive the policy's cash surrender value, less the initial year's cash surrender value, as reimbursement for taxpayers' premium payments. With respect to an early (i.e., before taxpayers died) termination of the agreement, the trust had the option of paying surviving taxpayer the cash surrender value within sixty days of termination and obtaining a release from the collateral assignment. If the trust opted not to do so, taxpayers were entitled to surrender the policy and receive that cash surrender value. All other policy rights were retained and exercisable only by the trustee.

Taxpayers requested a ruling to confirm that the insurance proceeds payable under the split-dollar agreement to the trust were not includable in the estate of the second spouse to die, and that the premium payments taxpayers made were not a taxable gift to the trust. The IRS agreed that the proceeds were not includable in taxpayer's estate under Section 2042(2). That section provides that the proceeds of life insurance policies on a decedent's life that are receivable by beneficiaries (other than the executor) are includable in decedent's gross estate to the extent decedent retained any "incidents of ownership" in the policies. Regulation § 20.2042-1(c)(2) clarifies that "incidents of ownership" does not just mean technical ownership. Rather, the term also refers to decedent's or the estate's rights to a policy's economic benefits in general, including the rights to surrender, cancel, assign, or pledge the policy, or the right to change the beneficiary. Here, the IRS found that, based on the agreement's terms, taxpayers retained no incidents of ownership in the policies. Because the trust had the option, in the event of the agreement's pre-death termination, of paying taxpayers the cash surrender value and obtaining a release from the collateral assignment, taxpayers could not force the policy's cancellation. Thus, taxpayers did not retain the right to cancel the policy, and as the trustee retained all other rights with respect to that policy, taxpayers did not possess any incidents of ownership under Section 2042 that would require the proceeds' inclusion in the estate of the second spouse to die. The IRS also found that no gift tax arose from taxpayers' premium payments under the split-dollar agreement. Because the estate of the second spouse to die (or taxpayers themselves) was entitled to reimbursement for the portion of the premiums taxpayers paid under the agreement, no taxable transfer occurred. The IRS distinguished this from its prior rulings finding a taxable gift in connection with premium payments under split-dollar life insurance arrangements that were made in the context of employer/employee relationships.

[Priv. Ltr. Rul. 9745019.]

Split-dollar policy approved for family trust. The favorable treatment of split-dollar insurance extended beyond the usual business context to cover a policy that was split between an insured's spouse and a family trust in Private Letter Ruling 9636033. A similar arrangement between a partnership and a partner qualified in Private Letter Ruling 9639053.

Spouse-trust. In September 1995, taxpayer created an irrevocable trust with his brother as the trustee and funded it with cash. Taxpayer reserved no powers over the trust or its assets, and he and his spouse were precluded from ever serving as a trustee. Under the trust, the trustee may make discretionary distributions of income and principal to taxpayer's issue during taxpayer's life and, at his death, to the issue and the spouse. The trust will terminate when the spouse dies or, if later, when taxpayer's children reach age 25. The trust purchased a life insurance policy on taxpayer's life and entered into a collateral assignment (or "reverse") split-dollar agreement with the spouse. The trustee agreed to pay the portion of each premium equal to the lesser of the P.S. 58 rate (shown in a table in Revenue Ruling 55-747, 1955-2 CB 228) or the insurance company's published rate for one-year term life insurance, and the spouse agreed to pay the balance of the premium. When taxpayer dies, the spouse will receive the total premiums she has paid, or the cash value of the policy if it is greater. If either the trustee or the spouse terminates the arrangement while taxpayer is alive, the spouse will receive the then cash value of the policy. The spouse's rights are secured under a collateral assignment of the policy, and she has the sole right to borrow against the policy. The IRS has provided extensive guidance on the consequences of a split-dollar insurance arrangement between an employer and an employee. An employee who pays no portion of the premium includes in income each year the one-year term cost of declining life insurance protection, according to Revenue Ruling 64-328, 1964-2 CB 11. This is the lesser of the P.S. 58 amount or the insurance company's published rate for generally available one-year term insurance (which usually is lower), under Revenue Ruling 66-110, 1966-1 CB 12. If the arrangement is between the employer and the employee's spouse (instead of the employee), the employee includes the value of the insurance protection (in excess of any payments by the spouse) in income and is treated as having transferred this to the spouse, according to Revenue Ruling 78-420, 1978-2 CB 67. The transfer falls under Section 2511, so it would be subject to gift tax if no exclusion or deduction applied. Here, applying the 1978 ruling, the IRS concluded that the spouse was not making transfers to the trust that could fall under Section 2511, because she would be reimbursed for her premium payments, and the trust was contributing the cost of annual term insurance. Thus, the spouse had the benefit of the long-standing IRS policy of not testing split-dollar arrangements as interest-free (or below-market) loans. (The fact that the spouse was a possible beneficiary of the trust had no effect, since she had no say in who would receive distributions from the trust.) The IRS stated that it had not considered the possible application of Section 7872. Under Section 7872, interest income is imputed to a lender on certain below-market loans, and the lender is deemed to transfer to the borrower the funds to pay the interest as a gift or compensation (or otherwise, in keeping with the transaction). Applying Section 7872 would remove a major advantage of the split-dollar arrangement. The IRS, however, apparently is not singling out the family split-dollar arrangement for special scrutiny under Section 7872. The IRS also decided that the proceeds of the insurance policy will not be included in taxpayer's gross estate. Under Section 2042(2), the proceeds of a life insurance policy payable to a beneficiary are included in a decedent's estate if, at death, that decedent possessed any incidents of ownership (alone or with any person). (A policy payable to the estate's personal representative is includable under Section 2042(1) without regard to incidents of ownership.) Incidents of ownership include the power to change the beneficiary, assign the policy, revoke an assignment of the policy, surrender or cancel the policy, or pledge it for a loan, according to Regulation § 20.2042-1(c)(2). Here, taxpayer possessed no incidents of ownership, because he retained no powers in the policy or the trust, and the powers held by the brother and the spouse were not imputed to him.

Partner-partnership arrangement. In the second ruling, a partnership entered into a split-dollar insurance arrangement with a general partner that was a revocable trust. The trust purchased a policy on the life of its grantor and agreed to pay the portion of the premiums equal to the annual cost of life insurance protection for the grantor under the insurance company's published rate for standard risks, and the partnership agreed to pay the balance of the premiums. The agreement followed the pattern in the spouse-trust ruling, with the policy assigned to the partnership as security and the partnership entitled to receive the greater of the cash surrender value or its cash outlay for premiums upon the death of the grantor. The IRS considered a split-dollar insurance arrangement between a corporation and a shareholder in Revenue Ruling 79-50,

1979-1 CB 138. The corporation provided the funds to pay the portion of the premium equal to the increase in the cash surrender value of the policy each year, and the shareholder provided the balance. The IRS applied the earlier split-dollar insurance rulings to determine whether the shareholder received a benefit and explained that any benefit to the shareholder was a distribution described in Section 301(a) (i.e., a dividend, if there were current or accumulated earnings and profits). Here, following the approach of the 1979 ruling, the IRS said that any benefit to the partner would be a partnership distribution. Since the trust paid the portion of the premium equal to the benefit as determined under Revenue Ruling 66-110, however, there was no distribution. The IRS added the same Section 7872 reservation as in the spouse-trust ruling and the additional caveat that the partnership had to have an insurable interest in the life of the grantor.

[Priv. Ltr. Ruls. 9636033, 9639053.]

Insurance excluded from estates of entity owners. The instant rulings illustrate two situations in which insurance policies owned by a partnership or a corporation are not included in the estate of a partner or a shareholder. In Private Letter Ruling 9623024, decedent was a partner in a partnership engaged in renting machinery and equipment. The partnership was the owner and beneficiary of insurance policies on the lives of all of its partners. Under the partnership agreement, following the death of a partner, any proceeds not required to pay partnership obligations or needed for reserves could be distributed to the remaining partners to the extent necessary to purchase the deceased partner's interest in the partnership and in two related partnerships. The policies did not have to be used to satisfy any obligation of decedent or his estate and did not secure any loan to decedent. The value of decedent's interest in the partnership included his proportionate share of the proceeds of the policies on his life. Under Section 2042(2), a life insurance policy is included in a decedent's estate (even though not payable to or for the benefit of the estate) if decedent possessed any of the "incidents of ownership" either alone or with another person. Incidents of ownership include the power to change the beneficiary, to surrender or cancel the policy, to assign the policy, to pledge the policy for a loan, or obtain a loan from the insurer against the cash surrender value of the policy, according to Regulation § 20.2042-1(c)(2). If a corporation owns a life insurance policy, the incidents of ownership (except for the power to cancel a group-term policy) are attributed to a controlling stockholder, i.e., the owner of more than 50 percent of its voting stock, under Regulation § 20.2042-1(c)(6). This rule, however, applies only when someone other than the corporation, for example the insured's child, is the beneficiary of the policy and the corporation does not benefit from the insurance. If the death benefit increases the net worth of the corporation because it is paid to the corporation or to a creditor of the corporation, the incidents of ownership are not attributed to the controlling shareholder, because this would be double counting the same insurance proceeds. If a partnership owns a life insurance policy, the IRS attributes the incidents of ownership to each partner regardless of the partner's interest in the partnership. Thus, when a decedent had a one-third interest in a partnership that owned a policy on his life, the proceeds were includable in his estate in Revenue Ruling 83-147, 1983-2 CB 158. The distinction drawn as to shareholders, between proceeds of a policy that augment the value of the corporation and those that do not, also applied in the 1983 ruling, but since decedent's child was the beneficiary, the insurance did not affect the value of decedent's interest, and there was no double counting in including the policy by way of the incidents of ownership attributed through the partnership. In Private Letter Ruling 9623024, the IRS applied the reasoning of the 1983 ruling to reach a different result. The policy was not includable in decedent's estate under Section 2042, because the policy proceeds were taken into account in valuing his interest in the partnership.

In Private Letter Ruling 9622036, a father and his son each owned 43 percent of a corporation's stock, and an unrelated shareholder owned 14 percent. A shareholders' agreement obligated the estate of a deceased shareholder to sell, and the surviving shareholders to buy, decedent's shares at a specified price. The agreement also required the purchase of two insurance policies. One policy insured the father and the son and was payable to the survivor and to the unrelated shareholder in proportion to their stock ownership. The other policy insured the unrelated shareholder and was payable equally to the father and the son. The proceeds of the applicable policy had to be applied to purchase a deceased shareholder's stock, and if the purchase price exceeded the proceeds, the corporation had to purchase the balance of the shares. If the purchase price of the stock was less than the proceeds, the excess could be kept by the beneficiaries, i.e., the surviving shareholders. The shareholders created an irrevocable trust and transferred the policies, including all the incidents of ownership, to the trust. The trustee was an unrelated third party. The trust was the beneficiary of the policies and the proceeds were distributable to the surviving shareholders in proportion to their stock ownership. The IRS concluded that the policies were not includable in the estate of a deceased shareholder, since the independent trustee, and not the shareholders, had all the incidents of ownership. (If the shareholders possessed the incidents of ownership, the insurance might still have been excludable from a deceased shareholder's estate if the shareholders' agreement fixed the value of the decedent's interest, but in light of Section 2703, the value may not be easily determinable.)

[Priv. Ltr. Ruls. 9623024, 9622036.]

Policy owned through split-dollar arrangement was not included in insured's estate. An irrevocable life insurance trust owned a second-to-die policy on taxpayer and his spouse. The trustee was a third party; neither taxpayer nor his spouse could act as trustee. Taxpayer, as trustee of his revocable trust, owned 50 percent of the stock of a closely held S corporation. The spouse, as trustee of her revocable trust, owned the other 50 percent. Thus, neither spouse was a controlling shareholder. At taxpayer's death, all the stock that was held by the revocable trust will be allocated to a QTIP trust that is also a QSST. Accordingly, the surviving spouse will own 100 percent of the corporation. The terms of the spouse's revocable trust are similar, except that if she dies first, taxpayer will be the beneficiary of the QTIP trust.

The S corporation and the trustee of the life insurance trust entered into a split-dollar agreement, which provided for a collateral assignment of the policy to the corporation to assure the corporation's security interest. The IRS ruled that although, after the first spouse's death, the surviving spouse will hold control of the corporation, the corporation will have no incidents of ownership in the second-to-die policy, and hence, no incidents of ownership will be attributable to the surviving spouse. According to the IRS, the proceeds of the policy will not be included in the estate of the second to die of taxpayer or his spouse.

[Priv. Ltr. Rul. 9511046.]

¶ 7.05 AMOUNTS PAYABLE TO EXECUTOR

Insurance proceeds are includable in murder victim's gross estate by operation of state forfeiture statute. On December 4, 1970, decedent was murdered by her husband, who was later convicted of voluntary manslaughter in a Kentucky state court. The husband had purchased four life insurance policies on decedent's life, with himself as the named beneficiary. In addition, the couple owned a home as tenants by the entirety. The IRS claimed that the proceeds of the life insurance policies, as well as the home, were includable in decedent's gross estate. The IRS noted that state law provides that the beneficiary of life insurance proceeds who murders the insured is not entitled to receive the proceeds, which are payable instead to the deceased's heirs-at-law. The law also prevents a convicted murderer from asserting an interest in property that he would receive from the victim by operation of a joint tenancy. The IRS contended that the state forfeiture statute caused the home and the insurance proceeds to pass to the estate, and that both were includable under Sections 2033 and 2042. The estate argued that the insurance proceeds were not "receivable by the executor as insurance under policies on the life of decedent," as required by Section 2042, and that the home was not includable as joint tenancy property.

Held: For the IRS. In providing that insurance proceeds must be "receivable by the executor," Section 2042 requires inclusion of only such insurance as comes into the hands of the executor for distribution as part of the assets of the state. The Kentucky statute does not provide for the payment of insurance proceeds directly to the heirs, but rather that such proceeds "descend" to the heirs unless disposed of by the will in a different manner. Consequently, insurance proceeds are payable to the executor under Section 2042 where, as in the instant case, such proceeds will pass to the estate for distribution. The court also found, without analysis, that the home was includable in the gross estate pursuant to Section 2033.

[First Ky. Trust Co., 737 F2d 557, 54 AFTR2d 84-6466, 84-2 USTC ¶ 13,581 (6th Cir. 1984).]

Proceeds of insurance policies held by husband on his wife's life are found to pass through wife's estate when husband feloniously kills her. Decedent-husband purchased two insurance policies on his wife's life, designating himself as beneficiary, and paid all of the premiums. He later killed his wife, then shot himself and died one month later. The local probate court awarded the proceeds to the children, who would have eventually taken under the wife's will. The IRS sought to have the proceeds included in decedent's gross estate. The Tax Court agreed, finding that the insurer's obligation to pay on the policy was not terminated by the felony, and the proceeds were taxable in the husband's estate.

Held: Reversed for the estate. The court, concluding that the insurer was still obligated to pay on the policies, interpreted local law as giving the wife an equitable right to dictate the manner of distribution of the insurance proceeds, and therefore viewed the proceeds as passing through the wife's estate.

[Estate of Draper, 536 F2d 944, 38 AFTR2d 76-6240, 76-2 USTC ¶ 13,142 (1st Cir. 1976).]

No-fault proceeds are includable in gross estate. In Revenue Ruling 83-44, the IRS ruled that the value of death benefits received under a policy issued pursuant to a state's no-fault insurance statute by the executors of a driver and a passenger killed in an accident are includable in their respective gross estates under Section 2042(1). The basic economic loss benefit paid to cover medical expenses is includable in the gross estate under Section 2033.

[Rev. Rul. 83-44, 1983-1 CB 228.]

¶ 7.06 ALLOCATION OF TAX LIABILITY

Eleventh Circuit reverses district court's erroneous application of Section 2206. Decedent died in 1983. His former wife survived him, and she was the beneficiary of several insurance policies on decedent's life. The estate included the life insurance proceeds in gross estate and paid taxes thereon. Subsequently, the estate brought suit in federal district court against the ex-wife to recover a pro rata share of the estate taxes paid by reason of the inclusion of proceeds in the gross estate. The ex-wife argued successfully that because decedent's will made no direction for estate taxes to be paid with respect to specific property, the entire tax was to be borne by the residuary estate alone. The lower court therefore concluded that the provisions of Section 2206, governing the allocation of liability as to estate tax on life insurance proceeds, were not controlling.

Held: Reversed for the ex-wife. The Eleventh Circuit found that the district court had erred in not applying the plain rule set forth in Section 2206. The fact that a decedent's will contains no provision specifying whether the beneficiary is to bear a tax burden in respect to life insurance leads conclusively to the application of the rule in Section 2206. State law does not control in such a case, because federal law governs where the life insurance proceeds do not pass under the will.

[McAleer v. Jernigan, 804 F2d 1231, 59 AFTR2d 87-1196, 86-2 USTC ¶ 13,705 (11th Cir. 1986).]

PART **II**

TAXABLE ESTATE

CHAPTER **8**

Deductions From Gross Estate

¶ 8.01　CLAIMS

[1] Creditors

No estate tax deduction for unpaid notes. Decedent made fourteen cash gifts to her sons and their wives, all but two of which were within the gift tax exclusion. A small gift tax was paid on the other two. The recipients then transferred the gifts back to decedent in exchange for unsecured, noninterest-bearing notes that were payable in 1995 or on her death. She died in 1986 without repaying any of the notes. The estate deducted the full balance due on the notes as a claim against the estate. Section 2053(c)(1) permits an exclusion from the gross estate for such claims only to the extent that the claims were contracted bona fide and for adequate and full consideration in money or money's worth. The IRS denied the deduction on the ground that the notes did not meet this test. The Tax Court agreed, concluding that the transactions were merely circular transfers of money from decedent to her children and back to her. Thus, rather than representing debts, the notes were unenforceable, gratuitous promises to make a gift, and were not based on money or money's worth.

　　Held: Affirmed for the IRS. In addition to noting extensive precedent that consistently has rejected taxpayers' attempts to use contemporaneous gifts and notes to avoid taxes, the court disagreed with the estate's argument that the Tax Court ruling violated Section 2504(c). That provision prohibits the IRS from challenging the value of gifts after gift tax has been assessed and paid and the gift tax statute of limitations has run. The estate argued that the IRS effectively revalued the gifts at zero. According to the Second Circuit, however, this case did not involve revaluation, and neither the gift tax paid nor the valuation of the property was at issue. Rather, the question was whether the notes were deductible claims against the estate for *estate* tax purposes. The contemporaneous gifts were merely highly relevant evidence that the notes did not reflect bona fide debts.

[Estate of Flandreau, 994 F2d 91, 72 AFTR2d 93-6711, 93-1 USTC ¶ 60,137 (2d Cir. 1993).]

Bank's claim was deductible under Section 2053(a)(3) as claim against estate. On May 28, 1974, decedent borrowed $50,000 from a bank, executing a promissory note in the principal amount of $50,000 with annual interest, due May 28, 1975. Decedent died in June 1974. On March 7, 1975, the executor filed a federal estate tax return in which the $50,000 note was listed as a deductible claim against the estate under Section 2053(a)(3). At the time of decedent's death, the estate did not have sufficient cash to pay either the $50,000 note or its federal estate tax. Consequently, the estate and the bank agreed that the interest accruing on the note would be added to the principal. In addition, the bank would loan the estate an additional $10,000. When the note matured, the estate would execute a renewal note in the amount of $50,000 plus accrued interest. On May 30, 1975, the estate executed a note payable to the bank in the amount of $54,332 plus interest, due on May 30, 1976. The proceeds of the note were applied by the bank in full payment of the principal and accrued interest on the note that decedent had executed prior to her death. In each of the next three years, the executor executed a renewal note on behalf of the estate. On June 1, 1979, the executor and the bank jointly petitioned the probate court for authority to satisfy an obligation of the estate. The probate court found that decedent's note dated May 28, 1974, and payable to the bank was a valid obligation of decedent at the date of her death, that the indebtedness was renewed by the executor on behalf of the estate, with interest, on May 30, 1975, and that the indebtedness should be paid by the executor as an obligation of the estate. On November 28, 1977, the IRS issued a notice of deficiency denying the deductibility of the original $50,000 note and assessing an estate tax deficiency. The estate sought review in the Tax Court, which approved the IRS's determination on the ground that in view of the bank's failure to file a claim with the probate court within six months from the date on which notice of death was first given to creditors, the claim was not deductible under Section 2053(a)(3). On appeal, the parties contended that the case turned on the question of whether, in deciding the deductibility of claims for a sum certain that is legally enforceable as of the date of decedent's death, the IRS may take into account post-death events.

Held: Reversed for the estate. It was not necessary to decide the issue of post-death events. Assuming the propriety of considering post-death events, the Tax Court reached an erroneous conclusion under state law as it related to the post-death facts in the case. Section 2053(a)(3) allows that deductions for claims against the estate are allowable by the laws of the jurisdiction under which the estate is being administered. Regulation § 20.2053-4 provides that only claims enforceable against the decedent's estate may be deducted. Thus, the Tax Court, absent compelling reasons to the contrary, should have considered all the post-mortem transactions and their approval by the state court. Even taking into consideration the events subsequent to decedent's death, her indebtedness to the bank was her personal obligation and was both "allowable" and "enforceable" against her estate under Indiana law within the meaning of Section 2053(a)(3) and Regulation § 20.2053-4. The indebtedness was thus deductible as a claim against the estate under Section 2053(a)(3).

[Estate of Thompson, 730 F2d 1071, 53 AFTR2d 84-1640, 84-1 USTC ¶ 13,568 (7th Cir. 1983).]

Full claim is deductible by estate. Decedent's estate partially consisted of a one-half community property interest in real estate that was encumbered by a lien of a trade association in an amount greater than $400,000. The estate negotiated for a compromise settlement, although at both the time of decedent's death and the time the return was filed, the association's bylaws prohibited the settling of claims for lesser amounts. The estate nonetheless deducted the full amount of the lien attributable to decedent's interest. Twenty-two months after the return was filed, the association's bylaws were amended, giving the association the power to negotiate compromise settlements, and the claim was subsequently settled for less than $135,000. The IRS limited the deduction to the amount actually paid under the settlement agreement. The estate paid the alleged deficiency and sued for a refund. The district court ruled in the IRS's favor.

Held: Reversed for the estate. The court ruled that for purposes of Section 2053(a), where a legal, enforceable claim for an undisputed amount lies against the decedent at the time of death, post-death events are not to be considered in computing the deduction. In holding for the estate, the court was influenced by the Supreme Court's decision in Ithaca Trust, 279 US 151 (1929), which held that post-death events had no effect on an estate tax deduction that had an ascertainable amount on the date of the decedent's death. Although *Ithaca Trust* dealt with charitable contributions and not claims against the estate, the Ninth Circuit saw this as a technical distinction that did not render it distinguishable. The court noted that there is an irreconcilable split between courts on this issue. In Estate of Hagmann, 60 TC 465 (1973), aff'd, 492 F2d 796 (5th Cir. 1974), the Tax Court held that to allow a deduction for a claim against an estate that subsequently became unenforceable would be to allow form to govern over substance. Other courts have reached similar holdings, for example, Gowetz, 320 F2d 874 (1st Cir. 1963), and Estate of Shively, 276 F2d 372 (2d Cir. 1960). The Ninth Circuit did not attempt to distinguish these cases, but refused to follow them, finding the opposite line of reasoning—that post-death events have no effect on the deduction—more persuasive.

The court in the instant case found authority for its decision in a line of cases that included Strauss, 77 F2d 401 (7th Cir. 1935), and Winer, 153 F. Supp. 941 (SDNY 1957). The court also refused to follow Revenue Ruling 60-274, 1960-2 CB 272, which ruled that a deduction was not allowed where a claim was never paid. A key element in this case was the fact that the claimant association had no authority to reach a compromise settlement for any outstanding claims at the time of the decedent's death. If it had, the claim would have run afoul of Regulation § 20.2053-1(b)(3), which states that no deduction may be taken on the basis of a vague or uncertain estimate. If that were the case, the settlement amount would figure in calculating the deduction.

[Propstra, 680 F2d 1248, 50 AFTR2d 82-6153, 82-2 USTC ¶ 13,475 (9th Cir. 1982).]

Tort claims paid by estate out of community property are fully deductible under Section 2053. Prior to his death, decedent, a resident of Texas, negligently shot two individuals who later sued decedent's estate for damages in state court. The plaintiffs were initially granted judgment, but the case was later reversed and a new trial was ordered on appeal. Thereafter the estate entered into a settlement pursuant to which judgment was entered against the estate for $354,500. The judgment specifically provided that if there was no separate property of decedent sufficient to satisfy the judgments, then community property could be used to make payment. The probate court eventually issued an order directing the estate to pay the judgment from community property. Following an audit, the IRS determined that because the tort judgments were payable out of community property, only one half of the amount so paid was properly deductible under Section 2053 for estate tax purposes.

Held: For the estate. Under Texas state law, it is well established that the community property of a husband and wife is subject to the payment of debts contracted by either of them during marriage. Even though one spouse is not personally liable for the torts of the other spouse, all of the community property is exposed to satisfaction of judgment. In addition, it is provided by state statute that a court may determine the order in which community property is to be used to satisfy judgments. The Tax Court concluded that, based on these principles of state law, the tort claims were in fact paid first out of decedent's share of community property, and that therefore the entire amount paid was deductible under Section 2053.

[Estate of Fulmer, 83 TC 302 (1984).]

Claims paid late may be deductible from estate. An estate made payments under a settlement agreement with decedent's creditor, where the creditor's claim was not timely filed. Applicable California state law provides a court-made exception to the filing deadline: An executor may not assert nonpresentation of a claim as a defense where the executor lulled the creditor into the belief that no formal claim was necessary. This question of misrepresentation was one to be decided by a state court. However, a state court was never given the opportunity to decide, because the parties settled before trial. Despite this, the IRS asserted a deficiency based on the disallowance of the estate's deduction of the claim. The IRS argued that the claim was not enforceable by the estate, and therefore it could not be deducted.

Held: For the estate. The court determined that its inquiry was limited to the question of whether (assuming that all of the creditor's allegations were true and absent any allegations that this is not so) the creditor would have been successful in state court. Here the court found a genuine contest by unrelated parties over the enforceability of a debt that was concededly valid at the time decedent died but was later not enforceable. This contest erupted into litigation and was followed by a settlement agreement approved by all beneficiaries with adverse interests and by the state probate court. The claim was in fact paid and was allowed for state inheritance tax purposes. The IRS contended that the settlement did not serve the estate. But it did serve the executor personally as well as the family business. Both the probate court and the Tax Court disagreed. The probate court determined the allowability of the creditor's claim by consent. Under Regulation § 20.2053-1(b)(2), it is presumed that such consent is a bona fide recognition of the validity of the claim on the merits, because consent was given by "all parties having an interest adverse to the claimant."

[Estate of Greenberg, 76 TC 680 (1981).]

No Section 2053 deduction is allowed for liabilities that were not existing and enforceable against decedent at time of his death. Decedent died on September 26, 1978. On the estate tax return, certain purported debts were listed as deductions. Two of the debts listed related to disputed claims that were settled by the estate for amounts that were less than the amounts deducted on the estate tax return. The other three debts were loans made by banks to various enterprises in which decedent was involved. Decedent was clearly a guarantor of one of these debts. Decedent's status as a maker or guarantor of the other two debts was in doubt. However, there was no evidence that the amounts loaned by the banks were overdue and that claims had been made against decedent before his death. The IRS disallowed the estate's deduction of these debts.

Held: For the IRS. A deduction is allowed from the gross estate only for claims for a sum certain legally enforceable at death. No deduction is allowed for potential, unmatured, contingent, or contested claims. The two settled claims were clearly in dispute at the time of decedent's death and were thus not deductible. The three bank loans were not matured liabilities of decedent. At the time of his death, there had been no default triggering his liability as a guarantor. His status as a guarantor was confirmed expressly in the case of one of the loans and impliedly for the two others. He did not personally receive loan proceeds. Events occurring after decedent's death that would have resulted in primary liability were not relevant to this determination.

[Estate of Cafaro, TC Memo. (P-H), ¶ 89,348, 57 TCM (CCH) 1002 (1989).]

Gratuitous transfer of legally binding promissory note is completed gift. On August 1, 1977, *D* gratuitously transferred to *A* a promissory note in which *D* promised to pay *A* a sum of money on December 31, 1982. The note was legally enforceable under state law. On May 30, 1982, *D* died. The note had not been satisfied at *D*'s death. The IRS was asked for advice regarding the gift and estate tax consequences of a donor-decedent gratuitously transferring a legally binding promissory note that has not been satisfied at decedent's death.

The IRS ruled that the gratuitous transfer of a legally binding promissory note is a completed gift under Section 2511. If the note has not been satisfied at the promisor's death, no deduction is allowable under Section 2053(a)(3) for the promisee's claim with respect to the note. The completed gift is not treated as an adjusted taxable gift in computing the tentative estate tax under Section 2001(b)(1). In the case of a legally enforceable promise for less than an adequate and full consideration in money or money's worth, the promisor makes a completed gift under Section 2511 on the date on which the promise is binding and determinable in value rather than when the promised payment is actually made. In such a case, the amount of the gift is the FMV of the contractual promise on the date on which it is binding. In this case, *D* made a completed gift under Section 2511 on August 1, 1977, the date on which *D*'s promise was legally binding and determinable in value. No deduction was allowable under Section 2053 for *A*'s claim as promisee on *D*'s note, because the note was not contracted for an adequate and full consideration in money or money's worth. Because the note had not been paid, the assets that were to be used to satisfy *D*'s promissory note were a part of *D*'s gross estate. Therefore, *D*'s 1977 gift to *A* was deemed to be includable in *D*'s gross estate for purposes of Section 2001. Thus, *D*'s 1977 gift was not an adjusted taxable gift as defined in Section 2001(b). Consequently, the value of *D*'s 1977 gift was not added under Section 2001(b)(1)(B) to *D*'s adjusted taxable gifts in computing the tentative estate tax under Section 2001(b)(1). The holding of this ruling applied only to the extent that the promissory note remained unsatisfied at *D*'s death.

[Rev. Rul. 84-25, 1984-1 CB 191.]

Post-death payment of guarantee was eligible for estate tax deduction. Decedent, the sole shareholder of an incorporated architectural firm, guaranteed the corporation's obligations under its office lease. At his death, the corporation was solvent and not in default on the lease. After decedent's death, however, the corporation eventually defaulted on the lease and ceased business. Approximately fourteen months after decedent's death, the estate paid the landlord pursuant to the guarantee.

The IRS ruled that the estate may take an estate tax deduction under Section 2053(a)(3), relating to claims against the estate, for the post-death payment under the guarantee agreement, even though at decedent's death, the primary obligor had not yet defaulted. According to the memorandum cited below, the estate's payment of its liability under the guarantee was made pursuant to a personal obligation of decedent existing at his death.

[Tech. Adv. Mem. 9321004.]

[2] Children

Amounts paid by estate to children of prior marriage were deductible as claims supported by consideration. Decedent and his wife were married in 1938 and had two children. The couple experienced marital difficulties and separated in 1950. After arm's-length negotiations in which each spouse was represented by legal counsel, decedent and his wife entered into a settlement agreement in 1951 that addressed all their property and support rights as well as child custody. As a part of this agreement, decedent's wife expressly released decedent from all claims and demands, both in law and at equity, and agreed to make no claim or demand other than as provided in the agreement. Notwithstanding the young ages of herself and the children, decedent's wife waived all rights to seek later modifications of this support award due to changed circumstances. Decedent's wife testified that the amount of these support payments was less than her living expenses had been during the marriage and, in fact, she had to obtain financial assistance from her father to maintain her household. In return for decedent's wife's agreement to accept this lower level of support payments, decedent agreed to provide a college education for the children and to leave two thirds of his estate in a trust for the benefit of his two sons and any children from any subsequent marriage. Decedent's wife testified that instead of seeking additional support payments in the face of decedent's protestations, she specifically bargained for his promise to provide for the children in his will. In 1984, decedent transferred virtually all his property to his second wife, and died approximately one month later. Contrary to the terms of the 1951 settlement agreement, decedent's will expressly excluded his sons from his prior marriage from sharing in the estate. In 1985, these children filed suit in a Florida court, alleging that their father had breached that portion of the 1951 settlement agreement in which he promised to leave two thirds of his estate to his children. In 1989, the estate reached a settlement with these two children, which called for the payment of $2 million to each son. The estate deducted the $4 million payments to the two sons as a claim against the estate. The IRS disagreed with this treatment and issued a notice of deficiency. The estate then filed a Tax Court petition. The court concluded that the facts before it were insufficient to make a finding that full and adequate consideration supported decedent's promise to make bequests to his sons from his first marriage. (The claim against the estate was based on this promise.) The Tax Court held for the IRS and disallowed the deduction for the $4 million payments. The estate appealed to the Eleventh Circuit.

Held: Reversed for the estate. The Eleventh Circuit reversed the Tax Court, holding that amounts paid by decedent's estate to two sons from a prior marriage were deductible from the estate as claims supported by full and adequate consideration. In so holding, the court relied on the fact that the children's mother, in a divorce settlement agreement, had bargained for decedent's promise to leave such a bequest to the children instead of seeking levels of spousal and child support at the time of the divorce.

[Estate of Kosow, 45 F3d 1524, 75 AFTR2d 95-1272, 95-1 USTC ¶ 60,190 (11th Cir. 1995).]

Settlement payment was not deductible claim against the estate. Decedent's stepsons contended that their deceased stepmother had promised, as part of a reciprocal will agreement with their father, that she would leave her estate in equal shares to them and to their stepsister. Decedent died intestate, leaving the sons without an inheritance. Their claim against the estate was settled, and the estate sought to deduct the settlement payment as a claim against the estate under Section 2053. The Tax Court held that the amount was not so deductible.

Held: Affirmed for the IRS. The mutual promises made by decedent and her spouse regarding the reciprocal will agreement did not create the sort of bona fide contractual obligation for which Section 2053 allows a deduction.

[Estate of Huntington, 16 F3d 462, 73 AFTR2d 94-2334, 94-1 USTC ¶ 60,157 (1st Cir. 1994).]

Post-death events are disregarded in determining deductibility of claims under Section 2053. At the time of his death in 1976, decedent, a resident of Ohio, was the sole owner of a farm. In 1959, decedent and his stepson entered into a contract by which the stepson agreed to provide all of the materials and labor necessary to repair and remodel a certain building located on decedent's property. In exchange, decedent executed a promissory note to the stepson. The note was expressly made payable on the date of decedent's death. Following decedent's death, the stepson was issued letters testamentary and served as the executor of the estate. By the terms of state law, however, an executor who himself has personal claims against the estate must present them to the probate court within three months from the date of his appointment in order to secure satisfaction. The stepson failed to comply with this procedure, but the state probate court nevertheless approved his untimely claim in full. The IRS denited the estate's Section 2053 deduction of the stepson's claim on the ground that he had failed to make a timely presentation thereof under state law.

Held: For the estate. The district court held that events that take place subsequent to the date of death have no bearing on the estate's entitlement to a deduction for claims actually paid. At the time of decedent's death, the note was valid and enforceable, and because the claim was eventually approved by the state court and satisfied by the estate, it was fully deductible under Section 2053(a)(3).

[Wilder, 581 F. Supp. 86, 53 AFTR2d 84-1563, 83-2 USTC ¶ 13,546 (ND Ohio 1983).]

Settlement payment for suit based on alleged promise not to revoke mutual will is not deductible claim. A husband (*H*) and wife (*W*) executed reciprocal wills, each providing that upon the death of the survivor, the estate would be distributed equally among their four children. After *H* died, *W* amended her will, cutting off the gifts to her children. After *W* died, the children sued to set aside the will, contending that *H* and *W* agreed not to revoke their mutual wills. The suit was settled and the children received $100,000. The executor of *W*'s estate deducted that amount as a claim against the estate; the IRS disallowed the deduction.

　　Held: For the IRS. The children were not creditors of *W*'s estate, because they did not give monetary consideration in money or money's worth for *W*'s promise to provide for them in her will.

[Luce, 444 F. Supp. 347, 41 AFTR2d 78-1494, 78-1 USTC ¶ 13,230 (WD Mo. 1977).]

"Gifts" to children followed by loan back do not give rise to estate deduction. Decedent made cash gifts to her children, who in turn loaned the money back to her. Noninterest-bearing unsecured notes were evidence of the loans. Repayment would not be made until decedent reached age 95 or her death, whichever occurred first. The IRS denied estate tax deductions for the notes.

　　Held: For the IRS. The decedent never intended to make any gifts, and the notes were nothing more than unenforceable gratuitous promises to make gifts to the children. Thus, they were not bona fide debt and could not serve as the foundation for estate tax deductions.

[Estate of Flandreau, RIA TC Memo. ¶ 92,173, 63 TCM (CCH) 2512 (1992), aff'd, 994 F2d 91, 93-1 USTC ¶ 60,137, 72 AFTR2d 93-6711 (2d Cir. 1993).]

Promise by decedent to son is held unenforceable for want of consideration, thus dooming deduction under Sections 2053(a)(3) and 2053(c)(1)(A). Decedent died in Massachusetts on June 21, 1981, at age 91. Prior to 1957, decedent and his wife owned all of the stock in a real estate business. During the following eighteen years, his son became involved in the business and acquired a 45 percent stock ownership interest. In 1974, decedent and his wife transferred all of the rest of their stock to the son in return for the son's written agreement to employ decedent as a consultant for the balance of his life and to make guaranteed payments of $27,000 per year for such services to decedent or his wife for life. At the same time, decedent and his wife executed new wills and a trust providing that upon their deaths, all of their remaining property would be transferred to their daughter. The daughter, however, voiced displeasure concerning the gifts of stock to her brother, and, in response, decedent wrote to the son and offered him full indemnity in the event of a lawsuit. The daughter filed suit a week later and decedent thereupon drafted a new will ordering his executors to pay the son's legal expenses. Decedent paid for such legals costs during his life, and the estate did likewise following his death. The estate asserted a deduction for the $110,000 that had been paid for legal fees, arguing that the item represented a claim against the estate under Sections 2053(a)(3) and 2053(c)(1)(A). The IRS opposed the deduction and the estate filed a petition in Tax Court.

Held: For the IRS. Under Section 2053(c)(1)(A), claims against an estate are limited to those that are contracted for under a bona fide agreement and for an "adequate and full" consideration. The estate argued that the son's agreement to provide lifetime support for decedent was full and adequate compensation. The Tax Court, based on the son's testimony and governing state law, voiced doubt about whether decedent's promise had actually been made at the same time as the son's pledge to provide support. Although the court might have found a want of consideration to bind the estate to decedent's promise, it based its holding instead on the estate's failure to show that the lifetime support promise had a value equivalent to legal fees of $110,000. In the absence of evidence, thus showing "adequate and full" consideration, the court held that the estate had failed to carry its burden of proof.

[Estate of Tofias, TC Memo. (P-H) ¶ 87,117, 53 TCM (CCH) 285 (1987).]

Claim against estate was disguised gift. Decedent's child sued decedent on a meritless ground; the suit was not contested and the state court awarded judgment to the child. When decedent died, the child presented a claim against decedent's estate based on the judgment. The estate paid the claim and deducted it from the gross estate under Section 2053(a)(3). The suit was instituted at the suggestion of a financial planner. The IRS ruled that the suit was merely a cloak for a gift and therefore was not deductible as a claim against the estate.

[Rev. Rul. 83-54, 1983-1 CB 229.]

[3] Ex-Spouse

Payments under marital settlement entered after divorce were deductible. Decedent and his ex-wife entered into a marital settlement two years after their divorce. Under North Carolina state law, the wife had a vested community property interest in one half of the marital property. The estate deducted the value of property going to the ex-wife, but the Tax Court held that the settlement agreement lacked consideration and disallowed the deductions for the payments.

Held: Reversed and remanded (in part). The wife parted with her community property interest in return for the agreement, and therefore adequate consideration existed. The estate, however, could not deduct a life insurance policy that was transferred to the ex-wife during settlement negotiations but not mentioned in the later agreement.

[Estate of Waters, Jr., 48 F3d 838, 75 AFTR2d 95-1356, 95-1 USTC ¶ 60,191 (4th Cir. 1995).]

Estate is entitled to deduction for full date-of-death actuarial value of lifetime spousal support obligation even where spouse of decedent died prior to filing of estate tax return. An individual died on September 4, 1976. The federal estate tax return was timely filed on June 1, 1977. The executors elected to value the gross estate as of the alternate valuation date, March 4, 1977, rather than as of the date of death. At the time of her death, decedent was obligated, pursuant to an interlocutory judgment of dissolution of marriage, to pay $5,000 per month for spousal support to her surviving ex-husband for the remainder of his life. The judgment provided that the award could not be modified, notwithstanding either his remarriage or her death. The judgment further provided that in the event of decedent's death, all payments thereafter falling due would be payable by the estate.

The ex-husband filed a creditor's claim against the estate on October 29, 1976. The executors filed a petition for court approval of this claim on November 29, 1976, and the claim was approved on December 27, 1976. The ex-husband died on April 20, 1977, having received only $35,000 from the estate in support payments. At the time of decedent's death, the ex-husband was aware that he had a liver ailment but had no reason to suspect that he was terminally ill with cancer. His fatal condition was not diagnosed until March 1977. The estate claimed a deduction of $596,386 for the value of the ex-husband's claim. This amount was calculated by reference to the actuarial tables included in Regulation § 20.2031-10. The government contended that actuarial valuation was not proper in this case, because the claim was actually extinguished after payment of only $35,000. The Tax Court determined that under Section 2053(a)(3), which allows deductions for claims against the estate, the estate was entitled to a deduction for the full date-of-death actuarial value of the lifetime spousal support obligation, even though the spouse of decedent died prior to the filing of the estate tax return.

Held: Affirmed for the estate. When claims against an estate are for sums certain, and are legally enforceable as of the date of death, post-death events are not relevant in computing the permissible deduction. Legally enforceable claims valued by reference to an actuarial table meet the test of certainty for estate tax purposes. Because decedent's spousal support obligation met that test, the Tax Court was correct in determining that the date of decedent's death was the proper time for valuation of the claim.

[Estate of Van Horne, 720 F2d 1114, 53 AFTR2d 84-1549, 83-2 USTC ¶ 13,548 (9th Cir. 1983), cert. denied, 466 US 980 (1984).]

Second Circuit disagrees with Tax Court on application of Section 2516. Section 2053(c)(1)(A) allows a deduction of a marital claim against an estate where it is based on an agreement and was contracted for an adequate and full consideration. Section 2516provides that transfers pursuant to a marital agreement are deemed to be made for such consideration if a divorce occurs within two years after the agreement. The Tax Court, in Estate of Satz, 78 TC 1172 (1982), held that Section 2516does not apply for Section 2053(c)purposes, because the former is a gift tax provision. The estate contended that it does.

Held: Reversed for the estate. The Tax Court decision is inconsistent with the Supreme Court's ruling in Harris, 340 US 106 (1950); the estate tax and gift tax are to be construed in pari materia.

[Natchez, 705 F2d 671, 51 AFTR2d 83-1346, 83-1 USTC ¶ 13,519 (2d Cir. 1983).]

Deduction is allowed for trust established to provide support for ex-spouse. Decedent who was married in 1938, entered into a separation agreement with his wife in 1950, which provided for decedent to make a $50,000 lump-sum payment to her "in partial discharge of marital rights." He was also bound to pay her $1,000 per month as support for such time as the wife remained living and did not remarry. The agreement further provided that decedent would make a lump-sum payment of $75,000 if the wife remarried, to be paid in release of all outstanding marital rights. Shortly after the agreement was signed, decedent obtained a divorce and paid the initial $50,000. He then set up a trust to provide for the monthly support and to serve as security for the contingent payment of $75,000. The wife never remarried, and the trust continued to make monthly payments up to the date of decedent's death in 1969. The estate sought to deduct the "statistical" value of the ex-wife's right to receive the $1,000 per month as a claim against the estate. The matter went on for trial in the Tax Court, which held that the ex-wife's claim was not deductible, because it was unsupported by consideration in money or money's worth within the meaning of Section 2043(a). Thus, the court upheld the IRS's argument and denied the claimed deduction in full.

Held: Reversed and remanded for the estate. The Third Circuit found that the establishment and transfer of assets to the trust as security for decedent's personal obligation to make monthly payments was not contracted for adequate and full consideration. It also concluded, however, that the subsequent $1,000 payments actually made to the ex-wife were themselves fully supported by consideration. State law provided that in the absence of an agreement, the ex-wife would have been able to assert a claim for a substantially larger amount in satisfaction of her claims. Thus, because the agreement was undertaken to avoid this possibility, decedent received more than mere inchoate marital rights; therefore, the ex-wife's claim against the estate is properly deductible.

[Estate of Iversen, 552 F2d 977, 39 AFTR2d 77-1643, 77-1 USTC ¶ 13,184 (3d Cir. 1977).]

Estate deduction for ex-spouse's property settlement is determined. Decedent had agreed to establish a trust for the lifetime benefit of his divorced wife. The trust proceeds, including one half the amount due to decedent under a profit-sharing plan, were in lieu of a division of the marital property. The trust was not established, and upon decedent's death, the estate paid the ex-wife the agreed amount and deducted it from the gross estate. The IRS asserted that the payment was not supported by consideration and therefore was nondeductible.

    Held: For the estate. The court held that the ex-wife's claim was supported by adequate consideration and was deductible. The deductible amount was limited to the legally enforceable obligation, however, and any amount above that was a voluntary distribution and was nondeductible.

[Estate of Scholl, 88 TC 1265 (1987).]

Section 2516 cannot be read into Section 2053(c)(a)(A). Decedent's former wife obtained a judgment to the effect that decedent breached a separation agreement (which was incorporated in the divorce decree) by failing to name her as the beneficiary of insurance policies on his life and that the proceeds of the policies be paid to her. The estate deducted the payment under Section 2053(a)(3).

    Held: For the IRS. The reduction to judgment of a claim originally founded on an agreement does not transform the claim into anything other than one founded on an agreement. Because the claim was founded on an agreement, not a decree, it was subject to the Section 2053(c)(1)(A)"adequate and full consideration" limitation on deduction of claims. The executor failed to show that the insurance provision was bargained for. The executor could not rely on the Section 2516gift tax provision by reading it as in pari materia with Section 2053(c)(1)(A).

[Estate of Satz, 78 TC 1172 (1982).]

Ex-wife's support rights are fully deductible under Section 2053. In 1960, decedent and his wife executed a separation agreement that provided $6,100 annually to the wife and a life estate in approximately 50 percent of decedent's estate after his death. The wife's annual support rights at that time amounted to $9,000, so that the excess multiplied by the appropriate annuity factor for joint lives resulted in a value for her postponed support rights at the time of the separation agreement of approximately $34,500. After the husband's death, the estate claimed a deduction for the value of the life estate that passed to the former wife, valued at nearly $162,000. The IRS sought to limit the deduction to $34,500, on the ground that the deduction should be limited to the consideration given up by the wife, because it was less than full and adequate consideration as required by Section 2053(c)(1)(A). The IRS reached this conclusion by comparing the value of the postponed support rights relinquished by the wife in 1960 with the value of her claims against the estate as of the date of decedent's death eleven years later. It contended that the life estate had no ascertainable value at the time the separation agreement was executed.

Held: For the estate. The Tax Court rejected what it referred to as a "fanciful and ridiculous" argument. The court reasoned that a wife who is bargaining away her right to support in the course of a divorce is engaged in serious negotiation and can be expected to know the value of what she is getting in return. Citing both the language of Section 2053(c)(1)(A) and Revenue Ruling 71-67, 1971-1 CB 271, the court held that the date on which the contract was made (here, the separation agreement) was the proper date to compare the value of the rights relinquished with the value of the claim against the estate. The revenue ruling provides that in determining whether the claim is in excess of the wife's reasonable support rights, the IRS is to consider elements such as the husband's annual income, the relative ages of the parties, and the probabilities of the wife's remarriage. In the court's opinion, these elements would be meaningless if the value of the claim against the estate were not valued until the husband's death. Based on the value of the wife's claim on the estate as of the date of the separation agreement, the court found that there had been full consideration and allowed the full deduction.

[Estate of Fenton, 70 TC 263 (1978).]

Life insurance paid to ex-wife under marriage settlement may be deductible estate claim. The IRS has taken the unusual step of reversing itself and broadening the estate tax deduction to include life insurance proceeds paid directly to decedent's former spouse. The deduction was permitted, under Section 2053(a)(4), for the amount paid under a policy that had been taken out as part of a divorce decree obligating the husband to maintain the policy until the wife's death or remarriage. The amount paid was included in decedent's gross estate. Under an earlier ruling, Revenue Ruling 71-482, 1971-2 CB 334, the possibility that the proceeds ultimately might return to decedent was viewed by the IRS as an incident of ownership that made the proceeds taxable under Section 2042(2). The IRS also ruled, however, that no deduction was permitted under Section 2053(a)(3) for those proceeds, albeit they were part of the taxable estate, because decedent's obligation was completely satisfied upon his death, and thus there was no remaining obligation surviving him that could form the basis of a claim against the estate by the ex-wife.

The IRS had a change of heart and issued Revenue Ruling 76-113 to supersede Revenue Ruling 71-482. The IRS says that the payment of the insurance proceeds to the ex-wife constitutes a satisfaction of the debt owed under the marriage settlement as embodied in the divorce decree. Because the reversionary interest causes inclusion of the proceeds in the estate, the obligation to pay the proceeds in indebtedness covered by Section 2053(a)(4), and the amount of the proceeds may be deducted under the authority of that provision.

[Rev. Rul. 76-113, 1976-1 CB 276.]

[4] Surviving Spouse

Widow's life interest in apartment was not deductible claim. In a prenuptial agreement, decedent agreed to give his fiancee a life interest in his apartment upon his death if they were then still married. In return, the fiancee gave up her rights to any of her future husband's property upon his death or their divorce. The husband later died. The issue was whether the widow's life interest in his apartment was a claim supported by adequate and full consideration and therefore deductible from his estate under Section 2053(c)(1)(A). The Tax Court held the claim was not deductible.

　　Held: Affirmed for the IRS. The Second Circuit agreed with the Tax Court that the widow's claim against the estate was not deductible for estate tax purposes. The right that she traded away in exchange for a life interest in her husband's apartment was not adequate and full consideration in money or money's worth under Section 2053(c)(1)(A). She waived only a potential right to an equitable distribution in her husband's property, which never actually ripened into an enforceable right.

Estate of Herrmann, 85 F3d 1032, 77 AFTR2d 96-2500, 96-1 USTC ¶ 60,232 (2d Cir. 1996).

The Tax Court finds that prenuptial relinquishment of community interest in spouse's earnings constitutes adequate and full consideration under Section 2053(a)(3). During 1972, decedent, a resident of California, created a revocable inter vivos trust with a reserved life estate. The trust agreement provided that upon decedent's death, the trust was to be divided into two portions, one for the benefit of decedent's son and the other for his grandchildren. As part of the plan, decedent transferred his personal residence to the trust and executed a will in which he bequeathed all of his tangible personal property to the son, with the residuary estate subject to a pour-over in favor of the trust. Two years later, when he was seventy-five years of age, decedent entered into a prenuptial contract with a woman whom he subsequently married. The agreement obligated decedent to amend the 1972 trust and will in order to provide his intended bride with a life estate in the residence, effective only if the parties were legally married at the time of decedent's death. In exchange, decedent's intended wife waived a number of rights she would have acquired by reason of marriage, including her community interest in decedent's earnings during marriage. Decedent died in 1977 without having amended either the trust or the will. In a subsequent agreement with the estate, the surviving spouse consented to a full relinquishment of her life estate rights in exchange for a payment of $10,000. Following settlement, the estate filed its federal estate tax return and claimed a marital deduction of $31,423 for the actuarial value of the life estate. It later abandoned this position and contended in the Tax Court that the value of decedent's interest in the residence should have been reduced by the value of the life estate in the amount of $31,423. The IRS, after disallowing the marital deduction, offered to permit a $10,000 deduction as a Section 2053 claim against the estate. It later changed its position and argued that no Section 2053 deduction had been proper.

Held: For the estate. The estate was entitled to a Section 2053 deduction equal to the settlement payment of $10,000. In the view of the Tax Court, the issue presented was whether decedent's promise of a life estate was supported by consideration and therefore enforceable under state law, not whether the value of the life estate was a proper offset against the fair market value (FMV) of the residence for Section 2031 gross estate purposes. Section 2053(e) states that in determining whether a claim founded on an agreement was contracted "for an adequate and full consideration in money or money's worth," the rule set forth in Section 2043(b) must be applied. Section 2043(b) provides that consideration in money or money's worth does not include an actual or promised relinquishment of dower, curtesy, or other marital rights. Applying these statutory rules, the court found that although the wife's waiver of her marital rights in the prenuptial contract was not adequate consideration, the fact that she also relinquished her community property interest in decedent's earnings during marriage was itself adequate and full consideration within the meaning of Section 2043(b). According to the court, in a case of an executory prenuptial contract, the requirement that the marital right relinquished must be presently enforceable should be interpreted as requiring that the right must be enforceable during the life of the spouse who benefits by the release or waiver, not at the time of the execution of the agreement.

[Estate of Carli, 84 TC 649 (1985).]

[5] Other Matters

Excessive professional fees are deductible as theft loss. After being appointed administratrix, decedent's sister hired an attorney and investment banker experienced with municipal bonds to locate approximately $2 million in bearer bonds that had been stolen from decedent shortly before his death. The sister signed a contingent fee agreement with the attorney, entitling him to one-third the value of any securities recovered before a lawsuit was filed, or 40 percent of the value for any securities recovered after a suit was filed. The sister's husband and daughter witnessed the agreement. The attorney then hired a stockbroker to help him locate the bonds and promised to pay him 15 percent of any recovered securities' face value. The attorney and broker traced the bonds to decedent's former housekeeper, who was charged but not convicted for theft and arson (for setting a fire at decedent's residence around the time he discovered the bonds were missing and which destroyed his bond ownership documentation). The estate subsequently filed a civil suit, but ultimately settled with the housekeeper and recovered bonds with a $1.6 million face value and $1.1 million FMV. The attorney placed the bonds in an investment account and then transferred some of them to his and the broker's individual accounts as payment for their services, with the sister's authorization. Based on a subsequently discovered will and pending will contest, however, the probate court deferred approving the fee payments. Ultimately, the fees were adjudged excessive, and the attorney and broker were ordered to pay back the estate—but they never did. The estate claimed the unrecovered excess payments were deductible as a theft loss.

Held: For the estate. Section 2054 allows an estate tax deduction for noncompensated losses from theft (as defined by state law). The issue here was whether the Pennsylvania state law's definition of theft required the estate to prove that the attorney or broker had a "thieving state of mind" when they charged the excessive fees. The circuit court decided that this state of mind was not an additional element of liability that had to be proved, and that the estate had in fact adequately proved theft. Notably, the moneys the attorney and broker withdrew from the estate were "property of another," and the attorney and broker knew their right to this property was subject to ultimate approval by the probate court. In addition, the attorney and broker improperly disposed of the funds for their own purposes, and did not comply with the court order to repay the estate. Finally, the estate's alleged failure to vigorously pursue collection did not prove that this was merely a fee dispute rather than a theft; Pennsylvania law measured theft on the basis of the thief's—not the victim's—actions, so the estate's subsequent retrieval efforts were irrelevant.

[Meriano, 142 F3d 651, 81 AFTR2d 98-1667, 98-1 USTC ¶ 60,310 (3d Cir. 1998).]

Post-death events considered in determining claim. Decedent died testate on November 16, 1990. Pursuant to a 1970 lease agreement, she retained royalty interests in oil and gas production obtained from a tract of land in Wood

County, Texas. In 1974, this land was approved for unitization (hereinafter, the "Unit") and, pursuant to a unit agreement effective January 2, 1975, Exxon became the sole unit operator and paid royalties to decedent. These royalties were based on the crude oil sold from the Unit. During the early operation of the Unit, the federal government regulated the price of domestic crude oil through the application of a two-tier pricing system under which "old" crude was required to be sold at a lower price than "new" crude. In June 1978, the Department of Energy (DOE) filed suit against Exxon for overcharges on the crude from the Unit which had resulted from violation of the DOE's price regulations. Exxon ultimately paid a judgment in the suit, plus interest, of just under $2.1 billion. On January 26, 1988, Exxon filed suit against the royalty interest holders of the Unit, including decedent, for reimbursement of the amounts that Exxon had paid to the Treasury as a result of the DOE litigation. Decedent vigorously contested Exxon's claim for reimbursement of her share of royalties received as a result of the overcharges; she denied that any amounts were owed to Exxon and argued that Exxon had not, in fact, suffered any loss in paying the judgment. Following decedent's death in November 1990, the District Court for the Eastern District of Texas issued an order on February 15, 1991, determining that the royalty interest owners were liable to Exxon for restitution of the overcharges received by them. The court appointed a special master to determine each royalty interest owner's share of the restitution; the resulting calculation showed that Exxon's claim against decedent was $2,482,719. On July 12, 1991, the executor of decedent's estate filed a federal estate tax return deducting the entire $2,482,719 sought by Exxon as a claim against the estate under Section 2053(a)(3), while continuing to object to the special master's calculations of restitution. Finally, on February 10, 1992, the estate and Exxon entered into a settlement agreement with respect to the litigation in which the estate agreed to resolve Exxon's disputed claim by paying $681,840. The Tax Court was faced with two issues. The first was whether decedent's estate was entitled to a deduction pursuant to Section 2053(a)(3) in the amount reported on the estate tax return ($2,482,719) or in the amount ultimately paid to Exxon in settlement of the claim ($681,840). Second, the court had to decide whether the income tax benefit derived by the estate as a result of the application of Section 1341(a) is an asset includable in decedent's gross estate. Taxpayer-estate argued that it should be entitled to a deduction under Section 2053(a)(3) for the entire amount reported on the estate tax return, based on the theory that post-death events may not be considered in determining the valuation of a decedent's estate. Although the court agreed that post-death events may not be considered where the valuation of a claim is valid and fully enforceable at the time of decedent's death, the court held that post-death events warrant consideration where decedent's creditor has only a potential, unmatured, contingent, or contested claim that requires further action before it becomes a fixed obligation of the estate.

Held: For the IRS. In the instant case, the Tax Court ruled that when claims under a contract are contested, as were Exxon's in this matter, the claims are not enforceable within the meaning of Regulation § 20.2053-4 until it is eventually determined whether and to what extent the claims have ripened into enforceable claims deductible under Section 2053(a)(3). The court relied on, and quoted approvingly, the Ninth Circuit's acknowledgement in Propstra, 680 F2d 1248, 50 AFTR2d 82-6153, 82-2 USTC ¶ 13,475 (9th Cir. 1982) that "[t]he law is clear that post-death events are relevant when computing the deduction to be taken for disputed or contingent claims." Accordingly, the Tax Court in the instant case concluded that the estate's Section 2053(a)(3) deduction was limited to the amount ultimately paid in settlement of Exxon's claim.

The fact that the estate ultimately paid restitution to Exxon on royalties previously included in decedent's income entitled the estate to relief under Section 1341(a) for repayment of amounts previously taken into income under a claim of right. This was the second issue decided by the Tax Court: whether the income tax benefit derived from the application of Section 1341(a) was an asset includable in the gross estate. The Tax Court in the instant case found that the facts giving rise to the estate's Section 2053(a)(3) deduction and its right to Section 1341(a) relief were "inextricably linked." The court concluded that under such circumstances, it would be inappropriate to consider one in the determination of decedent's taxable estate while excluding the other. As a result, the court ruled that the taxable estate must be increased by the amount of Section 1341(a) relief that is attributable to the amount the estate paid to Exxon in settlement of its claim.

[Estate of Smith, 108 TC 412 (1997)].

¶ 8.02 MORTGAGES

Balances due on mortgages are not deductible under Section 2053(a)(3) or Section 2053(a)(4). During 1974, decedents, husband and wife, were the owners of certain real property in Florida that they held as tenants-by-the-entirety. In November of that year, they made gifts of their respective survivorship interests to their two children but retained their complete life interests. On October 2, 1975, decedent-husband executed a mortgage on one of the properties pursuant to which the donees—but not decedent-husband—signed a promissory note in favor of the mortgagee-bank.

In the following year, a similar transaction was undertaken with respect to another parcel that had also been conveyed by gift. In this instance, decedent-husband signed the note. In neither case did decedents receive consideration for entering into the mortgages, and they did so merely to facilitate the donees' acquisition of mortgage money. Following their deaths, the estate of the husband took deductions under Section 2053equal to the outstanding mortgage indebtedness. The estate argued that even though the mortgagee had not asserted any claims, the indebtedness was fully deductible either under Section 2053(a)(3)as a claim against the estate or under Section 2053(a)(4)as estate indebtedness.

Held: For the IRS. The balance due on the mortgages was not deductible under either section. In order to fall within Section 2053, a debt not only must be the decedent's personal liability but also must be enforceable against the estate. Under state law, the failure of the husband to sign the first promissory note resulted in no personal liability to the mortgagee, and therefore the asserted claim was not deductible. As for the second mortgage, the court held that because no claim had been presented to the estate, there was no basis for a deduction where the liability had not yet matured and was nothing more than a potential future claim. In addition, the court held that the estate had not shown that the mortgages were contracted for bona fide consideration as required in Section 2053(c). Accordingly, because the estate was not able to show any primary liability, the deductions were properly disallowed by the IRS.

[Estate of Theis, 81 TC 741 (1983), aff'd, 770 F2d 981, 56 AFTR2d 85-6559, 85-2 USTC ¶ 13,639 (11th Cir. 1985).]

Deduction denied for full amount of mortgage where decedent owned only one-half interest in real estate. Decedent conveyed to his children a one-half interest in a ranch that he owned. Decedent had previously incurred an indebtedness secured by a deed of trust on the ranch. The estate included only decedent's one-half interest in the ranch in his gross estate but claimed a deduction for the entire balance of the note at the time of decedent's death.

Held: For the IRS. A deduction for the full amount of the mortgage is not allowed, since the full value of the mortgaged property was not included in decedent's gross estate. Moreover, the indebtedness is not deductible as a claim against the estate, because the creditor did not make any claim or demand against the estate for payment of the note. Additionally, the estate cannot elect to report decedent's net equity interest in the ranch under Section 2033, because the indebtedness and the interest in the ranch must be separately reported.

[Estate of Fawcett, 64 TC 889 (1975), acq. 1978-2 CB 2.]

Mortgage on Section 2032A property is fully deductible. Section 2053(a)(4) provides that a mortgage is deductible from the gross estate if the full value of the mortgaged property is included in the gross estate. The IRS ruled that a property with respect to which a Section 2032A special valuation election is in effect is fully includable in the gross estate, because the election does not effect the quantum of interest included, but only the valuation method. Therefore, the entire amount of the recourse mortgage on such property is deductible from the gross estate.

[Rev. Rul. 83-81, 1983-1 CB 230.]

Estate of decedent with life estate in children's mortgaged property may not claim debt deduction. A man and wife gave two jointly owned properties to their son and daughter, respectively, retaining a life estate in each parcel. Later, the man and wife, their daughter, and the daughter's husband signed a mortgage on the daughter's parcel, but the man and wife did not sign the accompanying promissory note. The daughter used the loan proceeds to build a house on her parcel. Still later, after the man's wife died, the man signed a mortgage with his son and the son's wife on the son's parcel. The son did not use the loan proceeds to improve his parcel. The man did not receive any of the proceeds of either loan. The man has since died, and the improved portion of the daughter's parcel was excluded from his gross estate on the ground that the man "had not retained a section 2036 right to a life estate" in the improved portion of the parcel.

The IRS stated in technical advice that the man's estate may not claim a deduction under Section 2053(a)(4) for the unpaid mortgages on the two parcels. The IRS noted that "the equities of this situation" would require liquidation of the daughter's house before the mortgagee could seek to satisfy the note from other sources, so "the lien is not a lien on property that is included in the decedent's gross estate." The IRS also said that to qualify as a deductible debt, some of the mortgage proceeds would have had to inure to the benefit of the man.

[Tech. Adv. Mem. 8206004.]

¶ 8.03 TAXES

Estate had right of recovery against QTIP. Decedent's gross estate included property in a qualified terminable interest property (QTIP) trust from his predeceased wife. Decedent's estate tax return included the QTIP trust but recovered from the QTIP its pro rata share of the estate tax. The IRS argued that, under decedent's will, the QTIP trust was exonerated from liability for its equitable apportionment of the estate tax; the IRS allocated the estate tax attributable to the QTIP trust to the residue of the probate estate. This reduced the decedent's charitable contribution and increased his taxable estate. The Tax Court agreed with the IRS, finding that under Ohio state law decedent's will expressed an intent that the state apportionment statute not apply. The estate appealed.

Held: Reversed for taxpayer. The Sixth Circuit, construing state law in an opinion designated as not for publication, ruled that decedent's will failed to sufficiently evidence his intent to exonerate the QTIP trust from its equitable apportionment of estate tax.

[Estate of Vahlteich, 69 F3d 537, 76 AFTR2d 95–7469, 95-2 USTC ¶ 60,218 (6th Cir. 1995)].

Eighth Circuit disallows deduction of income tax that resulted from donee's payment of gift tax where income tax was later forgiven by Congress. Decedent and his wife transferred stock to trusts established for their grandchildren on the condition that the trustees pay the gift tax due on the transfer. When the executors filed the estate tax return, they followed the then-established practice of subtracting the gift tax paid by the donee from the value of the gift. After the Supreme Court decided, in Diedrich, 457 US 191, 82-1 USTC ¶ 9419, 50 AFTR2d 82-5054 (1982), that a net gift resulted in taxable income to the donor, the estate filed an amended return recognizing the gift tax paid by the donees as income, deducting the income tax resulting from the donee's payment of the gift tax as a claim against the estate under Section 2053(a)(3). The additional tax liability was later forgiven by the Deficit Reduction Act of 1984 (DRA '84), however, and the estate received a refund of the tax. The Tax Court, interpreting the prior decision of the Eighth Circuit in Jacobs, 34 F2d 233, 1 USTC ¶ 420, 7 AFTR2d 9308 (8th Cir. 1929), determined that because the statutory elimination of the claim was not foreseeable at the testator's death, the claim was allowable.

Held: Reversed for the IRS. The Eighth Circuit declined to follow the Tax Court's interpretation of *Jacobs*, stating that the determinative factor in that case was not foreseeability, but rather whether a claim was actually paid or to be paid. Therefore, when claims against the estate disappear as a result of post-death events, the deduction disappears with them. A federal statute that forgives a tax obligation changes the law that imposed the liability on the estate in the first place. It does so with a retroactive effect. Thus, DRA '84 retrospectively declared that the claim never existed. The estate could not claim that the fact that the liability existed at one time justified a deduction under Section 2053(a)(3). There is nothing in the legislative history to suggest that Congress wanted taxpayers to receive the double benefit of an income tax refund that would also be exempt from estate tax. Regardless of the liability that existed at decedent's death, once the claim was unenforceable, the related deduction was lost. Section 2035(c) provides that in computing the amount of the gross estate, certain taxes paid by decedent or his estate are included. The estate claimed that the donees' payment of the gift tax should not have been included in the gross estate, because the tax was not paid by decedent or his estate. The court rejected this argument and, on this issue, affirmed the Tax Court. Just as the donees' tax payment was included in the donor's taxable income, the donee's tax payment was includable in the donor's gross estate under Section 2035(c),

[Sachs, 856 F2d 1158, 88-2 USTC ¶ 13,781, 62 AFTR2d 88-6000 (8th Cir. 1988).]

Decedent's prior tax years are netted for estate liability. Decedent had income tax overpayments for some prior tax years and liabilities for others. His final short-year return showed a net operating loss that could be carried back to prior years. Although there were overpayments in three of those years, the overpayments were more than offset by tax liabilities for the remaining four years. The testator's net tax liability at his death was approximately $745,000. The estate treated gross overpayments as an asset of the estate and gross outstanding liabilities as a debt of the estate. The IRS netted all overpayments and tax liabilities to produce a single debt. The estate's treatment resulted in a larger amount passing to the spouse and hence an increased marital deduction. The Tax Court determined that the estate was required to offset gross income tax overpayments against gross income tax liabilities within any single year, but was not obliged to offset net income tax liabilities against net income tax overpayments for different years.

Held: For the IRS. The Third Circuit stated that the estate could have no reasonable expectation that a refund would be awarded. Citing Bittker, Federal Taxation of Income, Estates and Gifts ¶ 124.7 (Warren, Gorham & Lamont, Inc., 1981), the court noted that mere expectancies do not rise to the level of property interests, which are generally includable as assets in an estate. Furthermore, the *Internal Revenue Manual* indicates that offsets are to be applied as a matter of course. Where the IRS has refrained from exercising its discretion to offset an overpayment against a tax liability, it was always to prevent recoveries of refunds and therefore solely to benefit the Treasury.

[Estate of Bender, 827 F2d 884, 60 AFTR2d 87-6123, 87-2 USTC ¶ 13,730 (3d Cir. 1987).]

Estate's relinquishment of right to contribution for joint tax liability does not affect deductibility of taxes paid. By the terms of her will, decedent, who predeceased her husband in 1975, left her entire estate to her foster son. Just prior to her death, the IRS sent a notice of deficiency to decedent and her husband based on assessments in respect of their joint income tax returns for 1968 through 1971. The deficiencies were attributable solely to the income of the husband, not to the income of decedent. The deficiency was settled with the IRS, although the agreed amount was not immediately paid. Eventually, the husband and the estate settled the question of their respective liabilities in connection with other matters of dispute that arose out of decedent's death.

The husband agreed to pay $261,250 of the tax liability and to release his claims against the estate, whereas the estate agreed to pay the remaining $179,865 and to release its right of contribution under state law. The estate paid the agreed amount and claimed it as an estate tax deduction under Section 2053(a). The IRS disallowed the deduction, contending that the amount of the joint tax liability paid by the estate was not attributable to decedent and that the estate's release of its right of contribution was irrelevant. The estate argued that it had no effective right of contribution, because its release of such right was necessary to preserve estate assets.

Held: For the IRS. Under Regulation § 20.2053-6(f), the IRS permits a deduction of payments of joint income tax liability only in an "amount for which the decedent's estate would be liable under local law ... after enforcement of any effective right of reimbursement or contribution." The court concluded that by the terms of the regulation, the amount covered by a right of contribution, whether exercised or not, must be excluded from any deduction claimed by the estate. Whether rights of contribution are enforced and whether they are retained by the estate have nothing to do with calculating the allowable deduction. Consequently, an estate's failure to enforce its rights of contribution has no bearing on the question whether such rights are "effective."

[Johnson, 742 F2d 137, 54 AFTR2d 84-6498, 84-2 USTC ¶ 13,585 (4th Cir. 1984).]

Deduction is denied for taxes paid on split gifts. Decedent's estate sought to take a deduction for gift taxes paid on prior gift transfers. The inter vivos gifts had been reported as a split gift by the executor after the date of death. The estate's principal contention relied on Regulation § 20.2053-6(d), which specifically allows estate tax deductions for gift taxes resulting from split gifts that are "enforced against the decedent's estate." These deductions, they argue, would be virtually eliminated if the preexisting claim requirement of Regulation § 20.2053-4 were applied to such taxes. The IRS responded by indicating that the limited application of Regulation § 20.2053-6(d) would not be considered, because, considering Regulation § 20.2053-4, plainly bars such a deduction and controls.

Held: For the IRS. The court reasoned that because decedent had no liability as of her date of death, there was no claim that would justify a deduction under Section 2053(a)(3). The court also rejected the estate's argument that the consent requirements of Section 2513 create an incongruous situation. Section 2513(b) indicates that the consent may not be made until after the fifteenth day of the second month following the close of the calendar quarter. If decedent dies in a calendar quarter during which his spouse made a gift, he could not make a consent himself. Thus, the gift taxes could never be deductible by his estate. The executor, on the other hand, could consent under Regulation § 25.2513-2(c). The gift tax could not be deductible, however, so the consent would amount to a depletion of the decedent's estate for the benefit of the surviving spouse. In many instances, this would constitute a breach of the executor's fiduciary duty. The court indicated that the proper remedy is to allow the spouse to record his consent at the time the gift is made. This is not currently permitted and would require a statutory modification by Congress.

[Proesel, 585 F2d 295, 42 AFTR2d 78-6517, 78-2 USTC ¶ 13,262 (7th Cir. 1978), cert. denied, 441 US 961 (1979).]

Property taxes paid by buyer are not deductible by estate. The purchaser of real property from an estate agreed to pay the property taxes attributable to the portion of the tax year following the date of purchase. The estate then tried to deduct the full year's taxes on its return. In technical advice, the IRS stated that the taxes paid by the buyer are not deductible by the estate. The IRS reasoned that although the full amount of taxes had been assessed against decedent at the beginning of the tax year, payment by the purchaser released the estate from liability for that portion of the tax claim.

[Tech. Adv. Mem. 8123007.]

¶ 8.04 EMPLOYEE STOCK OPTION PLAN PROCEEDS DEDUCTION

Retroactive application of amendment to estate tax deduction upheld. Decedent died on September 29, 1985. The filing deadline was extended and the return for her estate was not due until December 29, 1986. The estate was eligible for an estate tax deduction for sales of employer securities to employee stock ownership plans (ESOPs) that was enacted by Congress as part of the Tax Reform Act of 1986 (TRA '86). TRA '86 became law on October 22, 1986, and the ESOP proceeds deduction was codified at Section 2057. Section 2057 allowed a deduction from the gross estate equal to 50 percent of the proceeds of securities sold to a qualified ESOP. This deduction was repealed in 1989. The executor of the estate seeking to utilize the new deduction on December 5, 1986, purchased stock for $11,206,000 and resold the stock two days later for $10,575,000 to a qualifying ESOP. The executor filed the estate tax return on December 29, 1986, and claimed a deduction of $5,287,000 from the gross estate pursuant to Section 2057. On December 22, 1987, a bill was enacted that denied the deduction pursuant to Section 2057 unless decedent had "directly owned" the securities before death, and it applied the decedent ownership requirement retroactively as if TRA '86 as originally enacted had contained that requirement. The estate was audited, and it was determined that there was a total deficiency of $3,385,333, of which $2,501,161 was attributable to the disallowance of the ESOP proceeds deduction.

Held: For the IRS. The Supreme Court held that the validity of retroactive tax legislation is governed by the following due process standard: whether "the retroactive application of a statute is supported by a legitimate legislative purpose furthered by rational means." The Court explored the legislative history of Section 2057 and found that when Congress initially enacted Section 2057, it estimated a revenue loss from the deduction of around $300 million over a five-year period. Because of the absence of a decedent ownership requirement, however, that figure quickly ballooned to as much as $7 billion. The 1987 amendment was clearly meant as a curative measure. Congress' purpose in enacting the amendment was neither illegitimate nor arbitrary. In addition, the amendment was enacted promptly and established only a modest period of retroactivity. Therefore, its retroactive application met the requirements of due process.

[Carlton, 114 S. Ct. 2018, 73 AFTR2d 94-2198, 94-1 USTC ¶ 60,169 (1994).]

CHAPTER **9**

Administration Expenses

¶ 9.01 QUALIFIED EXPENSES, GENERALLY

Sixth Circuit rules administration expenses must be necessary to be deductible. Decedent died in 1989. The estate spent $750,000 on upkeep and maintenance of a 150-acre country estate near Cleveland and sought to deduct this amount as an administration expense. The estate argued that the costs were deductible because the estate reasonably anticipated an estate tax audit and delayed distribution of the real property in order to retain sufficient assets to pay a potential tax deficiency. The Tax Court analyzed the deductibility question solely under state law, in accordance with Park, 475 F2d 673, 31 AFTR2d 73-1442, and ruled in favor of the IRS. The Sixth Circuit initially affirmed the Tax Court but subsequently decided to rehear the case before the entire Sixth Circuit. The Sixth Circuit ruled that *Park* was incorrectly decided and overruled the decision. Before decedent's death, her husband established three trusts: (1) a charitable trust; (2) a marital trust; and (3) a residuary trust. The marital trust, over which decedent had a general power of appointment, held the 150-acre estate, known as Ripplestone, and other substantial assets. Her will partially exercised the power by appointing some assets to the charitable trust, some to her estate to pay estate taxes, and the remainder to her husband's residuary trust. Prior to Ripplestone's sale on April 20, 1994, the IRS audited the estate over the value of Ripplestone. The estate challenged the deficiency in the Tax Court, where the parties eventually reached agreement on the value. However, the estate continued to pursue a claim for a deduction of $757,356 for the costs to maintain and sell Ripplestone following decedent's death. Based on its reading of state (Ohio) law, the Tax Court allowed the estate to deduct the costs of maintaining Ripplestone only through March 16, 1990, rather than through the date on that Ripplestone was sold. The Tax Court found that Ripplestone's maintenance was necessary only until March 16, 1990, to allow the Cleveland Museum of Art to select items from decedent's art collection, in accordance with the terms of her will. The Tax Court ruled that after the selection was complete and the executor filed the estate tax return, Ripplestone's retention was no longer necessary under Ohio law. Thus, the martial trust should have transferred Ripplestone to the husband's residuary trust. The estate argued that the costs of maintaining Ripplestone were administration expenses allowed under Ohio law and were therefore deductible. The IRS argued that expenses must be actually and necessarily incurred under Regulation § 20.2053-3(a) to be deductible. The IRS contended that the statutory phrase, "administration expenses," is not self-defining, and that the regulation provides a permissible construction of the statue.

    Held: Reversed for taxpayer. The Sixth Circuit said that Code Section 2053(a) compels a two-part test for deductibility: First, an expense must be one of the four types of expenses specifically enumerated in the statue. Second, it must be "allowable by the laws of the jurisdiction . . . under which the estate is being administered." The Sixth Circuit agreed with the IRS that the phrase "administration expenses" is neither self-defining nor unambiguous and found that the regulation's construction of that phrase to include only those expenses "actually and necessarily" incurred in the administration of decedent's estate to be a permissible one. The court held it was therefore bound by that construction. The court said that the factual record was not clear enough for it to decide whether the estate should be permitted to deduct the expenses of maintaining Ripplestone. The estate said it was necessary to delay distribution pending an audit that it reasonably believed to be inevitable in light of the large size of the gross estate (around $23 million). The Sixth Circuit said that the estate's theory may be meritorious as several state probate courts have approved the reservation of assets against the possibility of a tax audit and a deficiency assessment. It remanded the case to the Tax Court to determine the appropriate facts to resolve the issue.

[Estate of Millikin, 125 F3d 339, 80 AFTR2d 97-6347, 97-2 USTC ¶ 60,287 (6th Cir. 1997).]

Administrative expenses reduced residual bequest. Decedent's will bequeathed the residue of her estate to charity. It also authorized payment of all taxes from the residue, and administrative expenses from postmortem income earned by the estate. Although state law generally required that administrative expenses be paid from principal unless the will directed otherwise, the Florida probate court held that decedent's will authorized payment from postmortem income. The executor therefore paid the administrative expenses from postmortem income and did not reduce the estate's charitable deduction by those expenses. The IRS disallowed the charitable deduction to the extent of the administrative expenses and attributable estate taxes. The estate argued that the expenses should not reduce the residual charitable gift because state law permitted the payment from postmortem income. In addition, since the estate had actually paid the expenses from income and not from principal, the charity would receive the full charitable bequest deducted by the estate. The IRS contended that the residue of the estate, and thus the charitable gift, should be reduced by the administrative expenses and attributable taxes. According to the IRS, that state law permitted the administrative expenses to be paid from postmortem income should not dictate their source for federal estate tax purposes.

Held: For the IRS. Section 2031 defines "gross estate" in terms of the date-of-death value of decedent's property. Under Section 2051, the taxable estate is determined by reducing the gross estate by deductions, including administration expenses under Section 2053(a)(2). Reading all three provisions together, the court concluded that the value of decedent's estate on the date of death was, for estate tax purposes, the sole source from which administrative expenses could be deducted. The court observed that while state law determines property rights, federal law determines how those rights are taxed. Payment of administrative expenses from income under state law did not necessarily mean that the administrative expenses could be included in the residual gift for estate tax purposes, even if the charity received the full bequest for which the deduction was claimed. The proper avenue of inquiry was the bequest to the charity under the will according to federal law.

[Burke, 994 F2d 1576, 72 AFTR2d 93-6705, 93-2 USTC ¶ 60,146 (Fed. Cir. 1993), cert. denied, 510 US 990 (1993).]

Retroactive amendment of ESOP deduction upheld. Decedent's estate claimed a deduction for the sale of stock to an employee stock option plan (ESOP). The IRS disallowed the deduction based upon the retroactive amendment to Section 2057 (now repealed) that required decedent to have owned the stock on the date of death. The district court rejected the estate's argument that the retroactive application was a denial of due process.

    Held: Affirmed for the IRS. The IRS gave fair warning in Notice 87-13, 1987-1 CB 432, of the retroactive application of the amendment. In addition, the change did not amount to a wholly new tax.

[Ferman, 993 F2d 485, 72 AFTR2d 93-6713, 93-1 USTC ¶ 60,140 (5th Cir. 1993).]

Selling costs are held deductible where will permits sale of realty. Decedent established a testamentary trust to which he devised his estate after several specific bequests. The residue included two rental properties that the trustee did not want included in the testamentary trust. Thus, the executrix sold the properties on the open market, and on the estate tax return deducted the selling expenses as administration expenses. This was a permissible deduction under New York law. The executrix argued that selling the property was necessary to distribute the residuary estate to the testamentary trust, and also contended that Section 2053(a) provides that if the expenses are allowable under local law as administration expenses, they are deductible. The IRS argued that under Regulation § 20.2053-3, the expenses were not deductible, because they were not incurred to pay decedent's debts; expenses of administration; or taxes, or to preserve the estate or to effect the distribution. The IRS also contended that the expenses were incurred for the benefit of the testamentary trustee, not that of the estate.

    Held: For the estate. The court agreed with the estate that expenses of selling property are deductible as an administration cost for estate tax purposes where decedent's will specifically permitted such a sale. The court followed the reasoning in Sternberger, 207 F2d 600 (2d Cir. 1953), rev'd on other grounds, 348 US 187 (1955), and found that the real property was not specifically devised or intended to be distributed in kind. The controlling facts were that the executrix actually sold the real estate, and the proceeds became part of the residue. Because the trustee did not want the rental property in the trust, it was necessary for the executrix to sell the property in order for the residuary estate to be distributed to the trustee.

[Estate of Vatter, 556 F2d 563, 39 AFTR2d 77-1582, 77-1USTC ¶ 13,169 (2d Cir. 1976).]

No charitable deduction but ranching expenses were necessary for administration. Decedent resided on a historic parcel of land in Florida that consisted of approximately 1,160 acres and included decedent's 120-year-old residence; a family cemetery; a one-room schoolhouse; an Indian burial mound, and other structures and sites. In addition, decedent owned and operated a cattle ranch on approximately 7,700 acres about twenty miles from her home. Six years before her death, she established a revocable trust, that during her life acquired a portion of the residential property and the entire cattle ranch and related lands. Under her will, the remaining portion of her residential land was transferred to the trust at her death. The trustees sold a portion of the ranch lands, followed shortly thereafter by sales of the cattle business and the remaining ranch lands. The trustees continued to operate the ranch until its sale and claimed the related expenses as deductible estate administration expenses. The IRS denied the deductions. The trust agreement requested that decedent's home, "insofar as possible, be set aside by the Trustees as a historical site," with the "designation of this site and management . . . in the discretion of the Trustees." A portion of the residential realty was donated to the local water district, which had agreed to transfer the residence and the other historical sites to a Florida agency that would preserve the sites and keep them open to the public. When petitioning the Tax Court to protest the denial of the administration expenses, the estate also claimed that the trustees' transfer of property to the water district without consideration constituted a charitable transfer that was eligible for an estate tax deduction.

Held: For the IRS, in part. The charitable deduction was denied. It was the trustees, exercising the wide discretion afforded to them, who made the charitable transfer, rather than decedent. The trustees had the power to set aside decedent's home as a historic site without making a contribution to a qualifying organization, and thus the value of the transfer to a charitable entity was not presently ascertainable at the date of decedent's death. Therefore, the possibility that the property would not be transferred to a qualifying organization was not so remote as to be negligible. The ranching expenses were allowed, however. The trust's continuation of the ranching business was necessary for the preservation of the estate and was a necessary step in liquidating the estate's assets. The ranch land likely would have reverted to muck and swamp if the cattle were no longer grazing there. The value of the ranch lands remaining after the first sale, when the cattle finally were sold, depreciated in value, as compared with the price obtained on the first sale.

[Estate of Lockett, 75 TCM 1731, RIA TC Memo. ¶ 98,050 (1998).]

Return preparation fee paid to family member is reduced. Decedent's daughters were the executors of his estate, and his son-in-law prepared the estate tax return. The IRS disallowed the estate's deduction of $57,650 for executor's commissions that were never paid to the executors. At trial, the estate claimed that the fee was for the son-in-law's preparation of the estate tax return. The son-in-law asserted that he spent over 1,000 hours in connection with preparing the return during a six-month period.

    Held: For the IRS, in part. The estate primarily consisted of a residence and some marketable securities. The amount claimed was excessive in light of the estate's relative simplicity, and a deduction was allowed for only $2,000.

[Estate of Stimson, RIA TC Memo. ¶ 92,242, 63 TCM (CCH) 2855 (1992).]

Payment from decedent's son to surviving spouse is not deductible. Despite the fact that he was the sole beneficiary under decedent's will, decedent's son agreed to pay decedent's surviving spouse cash and property worth $171,324 in return for any interest that the spouse may have possessed in the estate. Decedent's estate claimed a marital deduction for the settlement payment. The IRS disallowed the deduction.

    Held: For the IRS. The payment did not qualify for the marital deduction, because the surviving spouse had no enforceable right. The payment also did not qualify as a claim against the estate, because decedent had no obligation to make the payment. In addition, the claim was not an administrative expense, because the son made the payment to decedent's surviving spouse for personal reasons.

[Estate of Suzuki, TC Memo. (P-H) ¶ 91,624, TCM (CCH) 1550 (1991).]

IRS rules on deductibility of sales expenses and late-payment interest on additional estate tax. The IRS ruled that if a qualified heir disposes of a portion of qualified property to a person who is not a member of the family of the qualified heir, after a decedent's estate has made a special-use valuation election under Section 2032A, and the qualified heir incurs sales expenses and late-payment interest on the additional estate tax imposed by Section 2032A(c), neither the sales expenses nor the interest on the additional tax is deductible under Section 2053(a)(2) in computing the decedent's taxable estate.

[Rev. Rul. 90-8, 1990-1 CB 173.]

IRS determines valuation date for deductible foreign expenses and claims. An executor paid expenses with respect to property that was located in a foreign country and was includable in decedent's gross estate. Decedent also incurred debts in that country. The deduction for administration expenses was based on the exchange rate in effect on the date of actual payment. Generally, the law provides that claims are valued by the exchange rate on the date of death or on the alternate valuation date. Where post-death events are considered in valuing claims, however, the exchange rate on the date of payment applies.

[Rev. Rul. 80-260, 1980-2 CB 277.]

Interest paid on delayed distribution of bequest was not deductible administration expense. Decedent died in February 1990. His revocable trust provided for a pecuniary bequest in trust for his daughter, son-in-law, and their issue. The trust was funded in September 1993. A Pennsylvania state statute required the payment of interest on a pecuniary bequest from a trust. The estate paid the statutory interest on the pecuniary bequest and then claimed that the interest was deductible as an administration expense.

The IRS disagreed and concluded that interest paid pursuant to state law on the delayed distribution of a pecuniary bequest is not a deductible administration expense under Section 2053. The IRS stated that, given the purpose of the interest payments (i.e., ensuring allocation of trust income equitably among the beneficiaries), the payments could not properly be viewed as a deductible expense of administering the estate.

[Tech. Adv. Mem. 9604002.]

Costs of selling residence were deductible administration expenses. Decedent's entire probate estate passed to his adult child, *A*, as did the nonprobate property held jointly by decedent and *A*. The probate property consisted of a condominium apartment, stocks, and mutual funds. The jointly held property consisted of bank and brokerage accounts. After decedent's death, *A*, who was also the executor, sold the condominium and deducted the sale expenses as administration expenses under Section 2053(a). It was contended that the costs of selling the condominium were not deductible as administration expenses because the sale was for *A*'s benefit and was not necessary to settle the estate, since there was enough cash in the joint bank accounts to pay the administration expenses.

The IRS ruled that the costs of selling the condominium were deductible administration expenses. Since there were no cash assets in the probate estate, a sale of some probate assets was necessary to pay the expenses of administration.

[Tech. Adv. Mem. 9342002.]

Expenses of running decedent's business are not administration expenses. Decedent died, leaving a motel and restaurant business worth approximately $2 million, or over half his estate. From the time of decedent's death until the business was sold two years later, the business incurred $1.9 million of operating expenses, that the personal representative sought to deduct as administration expenses under Section 2053(a)(2). The IRS stated that the expenses were incurred in the ongoing conduct of business and were not deductible as administration expenses. The expenses went beyond maintaining the value of the business or settling the estate. The underlying issue here may have been the overlap between income tax and estate tax rates.

[Tech. Adv. Mem. 9132003.]

¶ 9.02 ATTORNEY FEES AND EXECUTOR COMMISSIONS

Estate tax deductions for unpaid portions of attorney fees and executor's compensation are allowed, despite collateral agreement with the IRS. Decedent's estate, valued at $5,316,255, claimed deductions of $100,000 each for executor's compensation and attorney fees on the estate's federal estate tax return. At the time the return was later audited, $55,300 of executor's compensation and $55,000 of attorney fees had been paid. The estate furnished the IRS with a declaration made under penalties of perjury that the total amount of the fees had been or would be paid. The IRS nevertheless denied allowance of any amounts of the fees in excess of those that had already been paid. Under local law, compensation to the executor and to the attorney for the estate of $100,000 was prima facie reasonable, and compensation in that amount was allowable to each. The IRS stated that if the estate had agreed with the IRS on other issues in dispute, the unpaid fees probably would have been allowed; that is, allowance or disallowance of the fees depended on agreement with respect to other issues. The estate argued that the IRS should have allowed all of the fees before they were paid entirely.

Held: For the estate. The court found that there was no indication in the record that the IRS had any reason to believe the remaining agreed amounts would not be paid and that there was no reason to believe the amounts were unreasonable. The court stated that the Code, regulation, and *Internal Revenue Manual* do not contemplate collateral disagreements. The requirements for allowing the deduction of unpaid fees are that they be agreed upon, that they be reasonable, and that the IRS be reasonably satisfied that the amounts will be paid. Contrary to the IRS's position, the existence of unrelated disagreements cannot figure into whether unpaid fees may be deducted. Accordingly, the estate tax deduction for the unpaid portions of attorney fees and executor's compensation were allowed.

[Boatmen's First Nat'l Bank of Kansas City, 705 F. Supp. 1407, 89-1 USTC ¶ 13,795, 63 AFTR2d 89-1510 (WD Mo. 1988).]

Tax Court asserts right to review probate expenses allowed by state court. The IRS disallowed certain administrative deductions on an estate tax return, contending that the law firm bill was not sufficiently specific; there was no itemized breakdown of the services rendered by each attorney. However, affidavits submitted to the state court and the Tax Court described in detail the various services performed by the firm for the estate.

Held: For the estate, in part. The Tax Court stated that attorney fees, which were claimed as administration expenses on the estate tax return and were approved by a state surrogate's court, cannot be challenged by the IRS, unless the IRS can show that there has been fraud, overreaching, or excessiveness by the attorney or surrogate. The court cited Regulation § 20.2053-1(b)(2), which provide that the decision of a state court allowing an administration expense will generally be accepted if it appears that the state court actually passed upon the merits of the claim. The Tax Court concluded that though the bill was not itemized, the affidavits provided the necessary information. Consequently, the expenses for the attorney fees were held to be deductible. Similarly, executor's commissions that were awarded by the state court following the state statutory rate were deductible. The Tax Court stated that an executor's commissions that are fixed by a state court and actually paid are deductible. However, the court found that fees for investment counseling, bank custodial services, and real estate maintenance were not adequately documented to establish that they were necessarily incurred for preserving the estate, as required by Regulation § 20.2053-3(d)(1). Thus, though Section 2053(a) provides that administration expenses allowed by a state court may be deducted in calculating the taxable estate, the Tax Court held that it was nevertheless entitled to review that court's decision to verify that the allowed expenses were properly incurred.

[Estate of DeWitt, TC Memo. (P-H) ¶ 87,502, 54 TCM (CCH) 759 (1987).]

¶ 9.03 BROKERAGE FEES

Underwriting commission is held to be deductible fee, not mere profit on stock sale. In order to satisfy debts, taxes, and expenses, and to make distributions, decedent's estate was forced to sell a large block of stock comprising 11 percent of all outstanding shares. Because of the "blockage" factor, the only practical method of selling the stock was a registered secondary offering. A firm commitment agreement was entered into with an underwriting company, under which the estate was to receive $39 per share and was to cover incidental costs. The underwriters could terminate the agreement in the event of certain contingencies, among them a "material adverse change" in the net asset value of the corporation. Although the agreement did not stipulate a public selling price, the stock registration statement indicated that it would be $42 per share and stated that the $3 excess was the underwriters' commission. The estate maintained that the $3 per share was an expense necessary to effect the sale and was therefore deductible under Section 2053(a)(2). The IRS argued that the agreement with the underwriters constituted a sale for $39 per share, that all of the risk passed from the estate to the underwriters under the agreement, and that the $3 per share was simply the underwriters' profit upon resale and was unrelated to the administration of the estate.

Held: For the estate. Reversing the Tax Court's decision, the Seventh Circuit held that underwriters' commissions paid by an estate in conjunction with a sale of stock are deductible administration expenses under Section 2053(a)(2). The court thereby joined the Ninth Circuit, which in Estate of Joslyn, 566 F2d 677 (9th Cir. 1977), reversed the Tax Court in a similar case. The Tax Court found that the underwriters not only could rescind the agreement if the value of the stock dropped but also that under the Securities and Exchange Commission's regulations underwriters are prohibited from purchasing stock for their own accounts. The Tax Court stated that it would be unlikely for them to enter a transaction in direct violation of federal law. The IRS argued that under Regulation § 20.2031-2, the "blockage" factor already benefitted the estate by causing the shares to be valued lower for estate tax purposes. To allow the $3 per share differential caused by that factor to be deducted at this point would have created a "double deduction" effect. This IRS argument was similarly rejected on appeal.

[Jenner, 577 F2d 1100, 42 AFTR2d 78-6422, 78-2 USTC ¶ 13,251 (7th Cir. 1978).]

Estate deduction for underwriter's spread is approved. In order to raise cash to meet certain extraordinary administrative expenses, taxpayer, an estate, entered into a firm commitment underwriting agreement with a brokerage house for the sale in a secondary offering of 250,000 shares of stock held by taxpayer. Under the agreement, the underwriter would sell the shares to the public for $19.25 a share. However, the underwriter was obligated to pay the taxpayer only $18.01 a share. The underwriter thus earned $288,750 from the sale of the 250,000 shares. This sum was taken by the underwriter directly from the proceeds of the offering. Taxpayer claimed the $288,750 underwriter's spread as a deductible administrative expense under Section 2053. The local probate court had in fact allowed the deduction. The IRS and the Tax Court, however, disallowed the deduction on the ground that taxpayer had merely sold the stock to the underwriter for $18.01 a share. The $288,750 spread was simply the underwriter's profit. In fact, nowhere in the agreement between taxpayer and the underwriter was taxpayer obligated to pay the underwriter a set fee or commission. Taxpayer was merely entitled to receive $18.01

a share even if the underwriter was not able to sell any or all of the shares to the public.

Held: Reversed for the estate. The underwriter's discount in such a secondary stock offering was in substance a brokerage fee and was therefore a deductible administrative expense for estate tax purposes. The court found that the underwriter's spread was actually an expense incurred by taxpayer. The court analogized the transaction to situations where a brokerage fee is charged for the sale of property. Such brokerage fees are deductible administrative expenses. In addition, the court argued that the deductibility of an underwriter's spread on the sale of securities to meet debts and obligations of an estate can be inferred from the holding in Huntington, 36 BTA 698 (1937). In that case, taxpayer sold promissory notes to an underwriter at a discount and later bought them back at a premium in order to raise cash to meet estate obligations. The court held that the entire amount of the premiums and discounts was a deductible administrative expense. It should be noted that the lower court had found the *Huntington* case to be totally inapposite on the ground that the discounts and premiums were readily identifiable as interest expenses incurred by the estate as a result of its borrowing the money involved.

[Estate of Joslyn, 566 F2d 677, 41 AFTR2d 78-1464, 78-1 USTC ¶ 13,227 (9th Cir. 1977).]

Tax Court denies deduction, despite approval under New York law. Executors of decedent's estate determined that it was necessary to raise cash to pay estate taxes. Executors had a choice of either selling a cooperative apartment or making an early withdrawal from a time-deposit bank account. The estate sold the cooperative, incurring selling expenses. The IRS denied the deduction of selling expenses under the rule set forth in Regulation § 20.2053-3(a), despite the fact that such expenses were approved by a probate court that correctly applied New York state law. Regulation § 20.2053-3(d)(2) provides that expenses of selling property of the estate are deductible "if the sale is necessary in order to pay the decedent's debts, expenses of administration, or taxes, to preserve the estate or to effect distribution."

Held: For the IRS. An estate's administration expenses allowable under state law are not necessarily deductible on the federal estate tax return. According to the Tax Court, administration expenses were allowable under New York law but did not meet the requirements of Section 2053(a). Section 2053(a) does not require that state law alone govern deductibility of expenses from the gross estate. The court held that Regulation §§ 20.2053-3(a) and 20.2053-3(d)(2) supply a definition of "administrative expenses," as that term is used in Section 2053(a)(2), that is both reasonable and consistent with the statute.

[Estate of Posen, 75 TC 355 (1981).]

Broker's leasing commission is deductible estate expense. Decedent died in July 1973. Among his assets was a shopping center valued at death in excess of 35 percent of the gross estate. Thus, the executor elected to pay the estate taxes on the installment method under Section 6166. Ownership of the shopping center was left one half to decedent's son and one half in trust for decedent's daughter. The will provided that estate taxes were to be deducted from the bequests. Decedent's son was named executor and trustee. He was empowered to continue operating the shopping plaza, and he decided to do so. In 1975, the largest tenant, a dry goods merchant, went bankrupt and eventually vacated the plaza. A broker was contacted to find a replacement tenant, and, when one was found in 1976, the broker was paid a commission of $110,000. The estate deducted the commission as an administration expense under Section 2053(a)(2). The IRS, on audit, assessed a deficiency, finding that decedent's son exercised the power in his capacity as trustee rather than as executor, and thus the commissions were not estate administration costs.

Held: For the estate. Despite the fact that the payments were made three years after decedent's death, they were nevertheless properly deductible as administration expenses. The court found that the leasing expense was necessary to the proper settlement of the estate and directly related to paying the estate tax. The court noted that the executor's election to pay the estate taxes in installments under Section 6166 was made to enable decedent's heirs to pay the taxes out of the earnings of the business. The new lease made continued payments possible. Without it, the property would have been sold or the mortgage on it would have been foreclosed. The deferral of estate taxes would have ended, and payment delays would have been subject to interest. More fundamentally, without the lease, the property would have been worth far less than its value in the gross estate. Thus, the court noted that the IRS's argument that a foreclosure or sale would not have affected the net value of the estate was "ludicrous."

[Estate of Papson, 73 TC 290 (1980).]

No deduction is allowed for cost of executing hypothetical closing transactions. During his life, decedent sold put and call options. Decedent's executors included the cash and investments of decedent's brokerage account in his gross estate, and they wanted to deduct what would have been the cost of executing closing transactions on the options on the date of decedent's death. These transactions could have eliminated the estate's potential obligations under all the outstanding options.

In technical advice, the IRS stated that the profit or loss on the options was uncertain, and therefore no deduction was allowable for the closing transaction costs. In reaching its conclusion, the IRS stated that contingent liabilities are deductible if they are reasonably certain to be paid, but no deduction is allowed if the contingency makes it uncertain whether decedent's estate will ever be called upon to pay the claim.

[Tech. Adv. Memo. 8204017.]

¶ 9.04 FUNERAL EXPENSES

Funeral expenses deductible under Section 2053 are not subject to Section 642(g) waiver. Decedent died in 1955. His estate, through its executor, decedent's surviving spouse, filed its 1955 income tax return, claiming a deduction for funeral expenses paid during the taxable year. A statement purporting to waive the right to deduct funeral expenses from the gross estate was attached to the return. The IRS assessed a deficiency based on its disallowance of the funeral expense deduction, citing Section 642(g). That section provides that amounts allowable as a deduction from gross estate under Section 2053 shall not be allowed as a deduction in computing taxable income, unless a statement is filed waiving the estate tax deduction.

Held: For the IRS. The purpose of Section 642(g) is to avoid the possibility of a double deduction for items of a character that would properly be deductible for both estate tax and income tax purposes. The court concluded that funeral expenses are not of such a character, because they "have nothing to do with the determination of taxable income." Thus, funeral expenses that are otherwise deductible under Section 2053 are not subject to waiver under Section 642(g).

[Estate of Yetter, 35 TC 737 (1961).]

Funeral expenses do not include establishment of the fund for education of priests. Decedent's estate deducted as a funeral expense monies paid to establish a fund for the education of priests as a memorial to his deceased family members. In addition, $28,000 in attorney fees were claimed as administration expenses. The IRS disallowed the claimed funeral expenses and limited the attorney fees deduction to $9,200.

Held: For the IRS. The establishment of a scholarship fund for the education of priests as a memorial for deceased members of the family cannot be considered a funeral expense under applicable state law or the estate tax regulations. The payment represents a bequest for the benefit of members of decedent's family, unrelated to the funeral. Furthermore, the estate failed to meet its burden of proof that the attorney fees were reasonable. The attorney fees were not supported by a surrogate's court order approving the fees, nor did the attorney keep any records concerning the amount of time he expended working on the estate in his capacity as attorney.

[Calcagno, TC Memo. (P-H) ¶ 89,677, 58 TCM (CCH) 1042 (1989).]

Decedent's bequest for perpetual care of family cemetery does not qualify for deduction by estate as funeral expense, because decedent was not buried in family cemetery. In his will, decedent left fifteen acres of land, including one acre on which a family cemetery was located, to the trustees of five local churches, along with $10,000 for the development, improvement, maintenance, and beautification of a community cemetery. If the churches did not accept this land, the $10,000 would go into a trust to provide a burial place for members of decedent's family, and the money was to be used to maintain and beautify the family cemetery. Upon decedent's death, the churches did not accept the land, and a trust was established with the $10,000 to maintain the family cemetery. Decedent's wife predeceased him and was buried at another local cemetery. Decedent left no instructions as to where he wished to be buried, and his executors buried him in the same cemetery as his wife. On the estate tax return, the $10,000 placed in trust was deducted as a funeral expense. The IRS disallowed this deduction.

Held: For the IRS. The court held that the $10,000 was not an expense to the estate at all. Rather, it was merely a bequest for the benefit of the family cemetery. According to the court, the term "funeral expenses" meant expenses incurred in connection with decedent's funeral and does not include expenses of the funeral of another or the perpetual care of the burial place of others. The court distinguished a case where decedent bequeathed $25,000 for the perpetual care of a mausoleum in which she was to be interred along with her son, his wife, and his lineal descendants. The court stated that in that case, the expenses were clearly occasioned by and directly related to decedent's own burial and only secondarily to funerals of members of her family. The estate argued that under Regulation § 20.2053-2, funeral expenses include a reasonable expenditure for a burial lot for either decedent or his family, including a reasonable expenditure for its future care. The court acknowledged that though this regulation may be interpreted to cover expenses incurred exclusively for members of decedent's family, the sounder interpretation would be that such expenses incurred on behalf of family members must be incurred in conjunction with decedent's own funeral.

[Estate of Tuck, TC Memo. (P-H) ¶ 88,560, 56 TCM (CCH) 828 (1988).]

Funeral expense deduction must be reduced to reflect recovery in wrongful death action. Although proceeds of wrongful death actions are concededly not includable in the gross estate, any recovery attributable to funeral expenses will reduce the allowable deduction under Section 2053(a)(1).

[Rev. Rul. 77-274, 1977-2 CB 326.]

Whether decedent-wife's estate can deduct her last illness and funeral expenses depends upon husband's liability under state law. Using two fact patterns, the IRS set forth rules for the deductibility of funeral and last illness expenses by the estate of a decedent-wife. In jurisdictions where the husband is primarily liable for such expenses, but the wife's estate is secondarily liable, a Section 2053 deduction is available where the wife directs her estate to pay such expenses, or where the husband is insolvent. Expenses must be actually paid and approved by the local court. In states where the estate is primarily liable in all cases, a deduction is permitted for all expenses actually paid and allowed by the local court. Revenue Ruling 65-300, 1965-2 CB 375 is superseded.

[Rev. Rul. 76-369, 1976-2 CB 281.]

¶ 9.05 INTEREST PAID

[1] Taxes, Generally

Interest on back taxes owed by a decedent are held fully deductible to extent of post-death accrual. Decedent died intestate on July 8, 1960, leaving only his children as his heirs-at-law. On November 14, 1962, the IRS proposed deficiency assessments of federal income taxes owed by decedent for taxable years preceding his death. The estate administrator disputed the asserted deficiencies and entered into negotiations with the IRS that concluded with a settlement reached on May 28, 1964. The estate administrator paid a total of $79,310 in back taxes, which the IRS allowed as a Section 2053 deduction, along with penalties. As to interest on the deficiencies, however, the IRS permitted a deduction for only that part of total interest that accrued on the principal amount prior to the date of death. The estate administrator argued that all interest should be deductible.

Held: For taxpayers. The court looked to state law and determined that interest that the administrator permits to accrue for some beneficial purpose is an expense of administration entitling the administrator to a credit under state law. The court held that in the present case, the postmortem accrued interest was incurred in a proper defense of claims filed against the estate, and was therefore fully deductible for federal estate tax purposes.

[Maehling, 20 AFTR2d 5997, 67-2 USTC ¶ 12,486 (SD Ind. 1967).]

Interest on pre-death tax deficiencies is held chargeable to estate principal, not to post-mortem income. Decedent, who was the founder of a cosmetics empire, died in 1975. His will provided for estate taxes to be paid out of the noncharitable residuary, with the net effect of protecting the charitable bequests from diminution and assuring both a maximum charitable deduction and a minimum of federal estate taxes. In administering the estate, the executors paid at least $214,472 in interest for income tax liabilities predating decedent's death. At issue in the Claims Court was the question whether the interest expense should have been charged to the principal of the estate or to estate income. The New York probate court is governed by state law that permits the interest to be paid out of post-mortem income, thereby preserving the maximum charitable contributions. The IRS contended, however, that for federal estate tax purposes, no deference to state laws was required, and that the expense should have been charged to principal.

Held: Summary judgment for the IRS granted. The court found that the accounting practice adopted in New York respecting pre-death interest was "at fatal variance" with the long-standing federal tax principle that a decedent's estate must be valued at the date of death for purposes of deducting later-incurred administration expenses. Accordingly, the interest was chargeable to the principal, thereby reducing the charitable deduction.

[Rifkind, 5 Cl. Ct. 362, 54 AFTR2d 84-6453, 84-2 USTC ¶ 13,577 (1984).]

IRS rules on deductibility of sales expenses and late-payment interest on additional estate tax. The IRS ruled that if, after a decedent's estate has made a special-use valuation election under Section 2032A, the qualified heir disposes of a portion of the qualified property to a person who is not a member of the family of the qualified heir, and the qualified heir incurs sales expenses and late-payment interest on the additional estate tax imposed by Section 2032A(c), neither the sales expenses nor the interest on the additional tax is deductible under Section 2053(a)(2) in computing the decedent's taxable estate.

[Rev. Rul. 90-8, 1990-1 CB 173.]

Foreign death tax interest is deductible from gross estate. The IRS ruled that interest paid by a U.S. resident to a foreign taxing authority incurred as a result of late payment of a foreign death tax is deductible as an administrative expense under Section 2053(a)(2) to the extent that it is deductible under the law of the state in which the estate is administered.

[Rev. Rul. 83-24, 1983-1 CB 229.]

Interest on state death taxes is deductible expense. Interest expense incurred on state death taxes by an estate incident to a deferral, late payment, or deficiency federal estate tax is an administration expense deductible under Section 2053 to the extent allowable under local law.

[Rev. Rul. 81-256, 1981-2 CB 183.]

Estate can claim post-death interest on income tax deficiency on estate tax or income tax return. At the time of decedent's death, his federal income tax returns for prior years had been audited and a tax deficiency had been proposed. Decedent died while the amount of the assessment of the proposed deficiency was in dispute. After contesting the proposed deficiency, the executor of the estate agreed to a settlement that included interest accruing after decedent's death. In addition, the executor paid to the state in which decedent resided at the time of his death an income tax deficiency and post-death interest thereon that resulted from adjustments in the federal income tax liability. The post-death interest on the federal and state income tax deficiencies, incurred while the executor of decedent's estate was contesting imposition of the taxes, is deductible as an administration expense under Section 2053(a)(2) to the extent allowable under local law. However, the estate may waive the right to deduct the interest on its federal estate tax return in order to deduct it on the fiduciary income tax return under Section 642(g).

[Rev. Rul. 69-402, 1969-2 CB 176.]

[2] Deferred Taxes

Deduction is allowed for interest on deferred estate taxes, but only as interest accrues. Decedent died on September 9, 1979, leaving her majority interest in the family business, a small specialty steel company located in Baltimore, Maryland. In order to avoid having to sell the stock to satisfy estate taxes, the personal representative elected to pay in installments under Section 6166 over a fifteen-year period. The estate tax return showed a total tax due of $297,844, of which $53,287 was included with the return. The balance of $244,556 was deferred under Section 6166. In calculating the tax due, the personal representative sought to deduct the projected, but as yet unaccrued, interest that would be owed to the government as a result of the election. The IRS denied the interest deduction and assessed a deficiency.

Held: For the estate. Under Section 2053, a deduction is allowed for certain expenses incurred in connection with the administration of an estate if the expenses are permissible under state law. Under Maryland law, interest incurred on estate taxes is an allowable expense chargeable against the principal of an estate. Thus, the estate had sustained its burden of showing that it was entitled to deduct the interest on the deferred estate tax. However, its interest deduction was limited to such interest as had actually accrued, in accordance with the procedures set forth in Revenue Ruling 80-250, 1980-2 CB 278.

[Snyder, 582 F. Supp. 196, 54 AFTR2d 84-6470, 84-1 USTC ¶ 13,564 (D. Md. 1984).]

Interest on deferred taxes is held to be administration expense under Sections 212 and 57. A taxpayer trust was established by decedent, who died in 1981. The major asset in his adjusted gross estate was stock in a closely held business within the meaning of Section 6166. The estate made an election under Section 6166 to defer payment of its federal estate tax liability attributable to the stock to avoid the necessity of an immediate or forced sale of the stock. As a result of this election, the trust paid $1,950,509 in interest on the deferred federal estate tax liability as required by Section 6166(f)(1). The interest amount was allowed as an administrative expense under local law. The trust treated the interest paid as an administration expense under Section 212 and therefore as a deduction for a cost incurred in connection with the administration of a trust within the meaning of Section 57(b)(2)(B)(i). As a result, the trust determined that it was not liable for alternative minimum tax under Section 55. In its notice of deficiency, the IRS claimed that the interest expense was deductible only as interest under Section 163, and therefore the trust was subject to the alternative minimum tax. The IRS stated that the interest expense was not allowable as a deduction under Section 212, because it was specifically allowable under Section 163. In the IRS's view, Section 212 is not necessary for, and does not expressly cover, expenses that are specifically deductible under other sections of the Code. The reference in Section 57(b)(2)(B)(i) to costs paid in connection with the administration of the estate or trust should be read to mean those administration costs that are not otherwise covered by specific itemized deductions such as Section 163.

　　Held: For the estate. The court stated that Sections 212 and 163 are of equal dignity and are not inconsistent with each other. Therefore, the interest expense in issue was allowable as a deduction under Section 212 because it satisfied the test for deductibility under that section, even though it is also allowable under Section 163. Consequently, the court held that the interest expense qualified as a deduction for a cost paid or incurred in connection with the administration of an estate or trust within the meaning of Section 57(b)(2)(B)(i). Accordingly, the trust was not subject to the alternative minimum tax imposed by Section 55.

[Estate of Ungerman, 89 TC 1131 (1987).]

Tax Court fashions special remedy for estate caught in procedural problem. Following his appointment as personal representative of decedent's estate, the petitioner timely filed an election with the IRS to pay estate taxes in ten equal installments pursuant to Section 6166. On the initial estate tax return, he deducted an estimate of the amount of federal and state interest to be accrued over the full ten-year deferral period. The IRS disagreed with the timing and method used by petitioner, arguing that an administration expense cannot be claimed for interest that has not actually accrued prior to the date on which the return was filed. Taxpayer asserted that such an estimate was proper because the amount of the claimed deduction was ascertainable and reasonably accurate within the meaning of Regulation § 20.2053-1(b)(3). The issue was presented to the Tax Court, which held that the estate could deduct federal and state interest on deferred taxes only as they actually accrued. The court based its ruling on Regulation § 20.2053-1(b)(3), finding that the amount of interest was not ascertainable, because of fluctuations in the applicable interest rates and the possibility that the estate would prepay the taxes or that its liability to pay would be accelerated by operation of law. Immediately following this adverse decision, the petitioner moved for a reconsideration of its opinion. In support, petitioner argued that by operation of Section 6512(a) and in view of certain language used in the court's opinion, the estate would be unable to claim deductions for interest accrued after entry of final judgment.

Held: For the estate. Section 6512(a) provides that if a taxpayer files a timely petition with the Tax Court after receiving a ninety-day notice, no credit or refund shall be allowed, and no suit may be instituted thereafter in any court. As a result, the estate would be without a judicial or administrative remedy in respect of tax matters arising after the entry of final judgment. Although Revenue Ruling 80-250, 1980-2 CB 278, and Revenue Procedure 81-27, 1981-2 CB 548, provide a procedure to enable estates to deduct accrued interest on deferred estate taxes, the estate would most likely be unable to avail itself of such relief by reason of Section 6512(a). The court commented on the harshness of the effect of Section 6512(a) in such cases and granted the petitioner's motion. It considered alternative remedies and determined that in view of the strictures of Section 7459(c), which requires that Tax Court decisions specify a dollar amount, its only option was to keep the case on its open docket until such time as the estate's tax liability is fully satisfied.

[Bailly, 81 TC 949 (1983).]

Interest on estate tax installments is held deductible. Taxpayer estate incurred liability for interest to the IRS for deferred payment of estate taxes. The deferral prevented a forced sale of assets, which would have been necessary to pay taxes. The state court, correctly applying local law, allowed the estate's deduction of such interest as an administrative expense. The IRS contended that where interest was paid on debt created to pay the tax, a deduction is proper. In the situation of interest paid as a result of an extension of time as in the present case, however, Section 6601(e)(1) states that interest is to be assessed, collected, and paid in the same manner as tax. Therefore, according to the IRS, such interest is to be treated as part of the tax for this purpose. Because the tax is not deductible, neither is the interest.

Held: For the estate. Since interest on a loan to pay estate tax is deductible, the result should not be different when, in effect, the loan was from the IRS in the form of an extension of time to pay tax. Thus, the estate's deduction was proper. The court flatly refused to follow a circuit court case supporting the IRS's position, Ballance, 347 F2d 419 (7th Cir. 1965), which was decided under the 1939 Code. There the court denied a deduction for interest paid on installment payments of estate tax on the ground that the 1939 Code (Sections 890 and 891) required that interest on estate taxes be collected as part of the tax.

[Estate of Bahr, 68 TC 74 (1977), acq. 1978-1 CB 1.]

Estate is permitted to switch interest deductions from income tax to estate tax expense. An estate deducted interest incurred pursuant to Section 6166A as a fiduciary income tax expense. No waivers were filed under Section 642(g), and the statute of limitations expired. The estate then decided that it wished to deduct the interest on the estate tax return as an administrative expense. The IRS ruled that the estate may do this. In addition, under the doctrine of equitable recoupment, the amount of the estate tax overpayment is reduced by the deficiencies and the interest on them resulting from deducting the interest on the fiduciary income tax returns for years closed by the statute of limitations. Although Section 6166A has been repealed by the Economic Recovery Tax Act of 1981, the equitable recoupment doctrine applies to new Section 6166.

[Rev. Rul. 81-287, 1981-2 CB 183.]

Acceleration of estate tax interest deduction is barred. The IRS ruled that interest incurred on account of a deferral of estate taxes may be deducted only as it accrues. Accordingly, no deduction is allowed for an estimate of the future interest expense. Since Revenue Ruling 78-125, 1978-1 CB 292, and the IRS's acquiescence in Estate of Bahr, 68 TC 74 (1977), the IRS has allowed deductions for interest incurred as a result of estate tax deferrals under Sections 6161, 6163, 6166, and 6166A. (The expense must be allowable under local law.) Under Regulation §§ 20.2053-1(b)(3) and 20.2053-3(a), an expense may be deducted before it is incurred if it is ascertainable with reasonable certainty. Here, however, the executor may elect to accelerate the payment of deferred estate taxes.

Alternatively, an acceleration may be mandated under Section 6166A(h) if certain conditions allowing the deferral terminate. Accordingly, any estimate of future interest charges is necessarily vague and uncertain. Thus, the deduction is allowed only when the interest accrues. The deduction should be claimed annually at the time when the installment payment is due. Because the deduction will affect the rest of the installments, they should be recomputed accordingly. Refunds will be made only when the entire tax liability has been paid.

[Rev. Rul. 80-250, 1980-2 CB 278.]

Interest on deferred estate tax is deductible. In Revenue Ruling 78-125, the IRS revoked Revenue Ruling 75-239, 1975-1 CB 304, and ruled that projected interest on deferred estate taxes is deductible for estate tax purposes. In Revenue Ruling 75-239, the IRS had relied on Section 6601(e)(1) in arguing that the interest was equivalent to a tax and hence not deductible. The IRS acknowledged in Revenue Ruling 78-125 that payment of interest to the IRS was equivalent to interest payable to a third party where an estate has borrowed funds to pay its tax liability.

[Rev. Rul. 78-125, 1978-1 CB 292.]

[3] Loans and Debts

Borrowing O.K. to pay tax instead of deferring it. Decedent died owning class B nonvoting stock in a closely held corporation with FMV of $4.8 million and voting stock with a value of $770,000. The taxable estate was $12.4 million, including $5.5 million of gift tax that had been paid on gifts made within three years of death. This generated federal and state death taxes of $7.4 million, and the estate had to use its class B stock to provide most of the funds to pay the taxes and expenses (after selling assets that were to be disposed of first). The estate could have deferred the payment of approximately 40 percent of the federal tax by making an election under Section 6166. Instead of making the Section 6166 election and selling some class B stock, however, the estate borrowed $5.5 million from the corporation in March 1990. That loan was replaced with a lower-rate bank loan several months later, after a shareholders' agreement was amended to permit the pledge of stock. In December 1991, the corporation redeemed approximately two thirds of the estate's class B stock for $6.75 million, paying $4.4 million with a note that had a payment schedule identical to the bank loan. In January 1993, the corporation prepaid its note to the estate, and the estate prepaid the bank loan. Decedent's will incorporated by reference the Tennessee state law permitting an estate to borrow and pay interest, but limited the authorization to the extent "applicable." In reliance on the will, the estate's personal representatives did not obtain probate court approval of the loans. The estate deducted $1.2 million of interest it had paid to the corporation and the bank as an administrative expense. The IRS concluded, however, that the borrowings were not authorized and denied the deduction. Section 2053(a)(2) allows a deduction for administration expenses that are allowed by the law of the state in which the estate is being administered. The expenses must be "necessarily incurred" in the collection of assets, payment of debts, or the distribution of property, according to Regulation § 20.2053-3(a). The IRS argued that the borrowing was not permitted, because the general authorization in the will was overridden by decedent's intent that a Section 6166 election be made. Although the will did not mention Section 6166, the IRS said that decedent wanted the election made to conform to shareholders' agreements. Under these agreements, if the personal representatives of the estate had made a Section 6166 election, they would have maintained discretion as to the timing and number of shares to be offered to the corporation.

Held: For the estate. The court pointed out, that absent a Section 6166 election, the corporation was still obligated to purchase shares to provide funds for death taxes (through a Section 303 redemption), so the election was not required by the agreements, and the general authorization in the will applied. Moreover, borrowing all required funds from the corporation, instead of having stock redeemed under the shareholders' agreements, was in the interest of the estate. If a Section 6166 election had been made, $5.3 million still would have been required for nondeferable taxes and other expenses, and even after using other assets, it would have been necessary to sell 61 percent of the class B stock to provide the funds required for taxes and expenses. This would have left the estate in a precarious position with the remaining tax liability almost equal to the value of the remaining class B stock (although the estate also had other assets). The personal representatives had anticipated that the value of the class B shares would increase and provide the requisite funds, and they had acted reasonably in borrowing to postpone a sale. Furthermore, even if they had made a Section 6166 election, they would have still incurred interest expense. The interest fell within a line of cases approving a deduction for interest on money borrowed to pay an estate tax to avoid a sale of assets on unfavorable terms. Thus, discounts and premiums (the equivalent of interest) on $9.5 million of notes issued by an estate to raise money for estate taxes and to avoid forced sales of closely held business interests were deductible as administrative expenses in Estate of Huntington, 36 BTA 698 (1937). Although a California state court had approved the issuance of the notes in *Huntington,* this is not necessary, since Regulation § 20.2053-1(b)(2) provides that a deduction will not be denied because court approval was not obtained, if the expense would be allowable under local law. Here, the state's supreme court had approved a similar loan, so the interest was a proper expense under state law.

[McKee, 72 TCM 324, RIA TC Memo. ¶ 96,362 (1996).]

Future payment of interest is held deductible as administration expense. Decedent died in 1981 owning a majority interest of 5,130 shares in a closely held family corporation. After a trust for decedent's widow had been established and amounts for payment of administration expenses and state inheritance taxes had been set aside, there remained approximately $20,000 in liquid assets to pay federal estate taxes of $204,218. Rather than sell the stock in the closely held corporation, the executors of the estate, including decedent's son, who was also a cotrustee of the trust and president and board member of both the corporation and its wholly owned subsidiary, decided to borrow the $204,218 from the wholly owned subsidiary of the corporation. The loan, for which approval was sought and obtained from the supervising probate court, was evidenced by an unsecured promissory note. According to the terms of the note, interest accrued at a fixed rate of 15 percent per year, the prime rate at the time. Principal and interest were due in a single payment in 1997, fifteen years after the date on which the note was made. Prepayment of principal or interest was prohibited. The fifteen-year maturity date was set to coincide with the spouse's life expectancy. Her longevity was used as the measuring rod for the length of the note, because, upon her death, the assets in her trust would be available to satisfy (at least in part) the note obligation. On its federal estate tax return, the estate deducted, as an administration expense, $459,491—the amount representing the total interest due on the note in 1997. The IRS assessed a deficiency in decedent's federal estate tax based upon its determination that the interest was not deductible as an administration expense because the interest was not actually and necessarily incurred.

Held: For the estate. The Tax Court held that the future single interest payment incurred on the loan made by the estate to pay its federal estate tax was a deductible administration expense under Section 2053(a)(2). The court reasoned that under Regulation § 20.2053-3(a), the interest expense was "actually and necessarily incurred" because the loan was bona fide, repayment of the loan was intended by both the borrower and the lender, and there were insufficient liquid assets in the estate to pay the tax.

[Estate of Graegin, TC Memo. (P-H) ¶ 88,477, 56 TCM (CCH) 387 (1988).]

Estimated future interest payments on borrowed funds cannot be deducted in full. Decedent died in 1982. His estate consisted almost entirely of stock of a closely held corporation. No election to extend the time for payment of the estate tax was made pursuant to Section 6166. There was an insufficient amount of funds available to pay the federal estate tax, and a forced sale would have been required to convert estate assets into sufficient cash. Therefore, the executor borrowed funds on behalf of the estate to pay the tax obligation. The principal amount of the loan was to be repaid over a period of six years, with 10 percent interest payable annually. The loan could be fully repaid at any time at the executor's option, without penalty. If the executor failed to make any payment on time, the remaining payments could have been accelerated at the lender's option. On the federal estate tax return filed for the estate, the executor deducted $25x as the estimated total amount of future interest to be paid during the loan term. The $25x was allowable as an administrative expense under applicable local law.

The IRS determined that because the loan was obtained to avoid a forced sale of assets, the loan was reasonably and necessarily incurred in administering the estate. Therefore, interest incurred on the loan was deductible as all expense of administration under Section 2053(a)(2). The IRS cautioned, however, that for Section 2053(a)(2) deduction purposes, the possibility of prepayment renders any estimate of future interest vague and uncertain within the meaning of Regulation § 20.2053-1(b)(3). In this case, because accelerated payment could have been made at the executor's option or could have been required upon failure to make a timely scheduled payment, the $25x estimated future interest expense was not allowable as a deductible administrative expense. Rather, such future interest expenses become deductible only as they accrue.

[Rev. Rul. 84-75, 1984-1 CB 193.]

Interest payments on decedent's obligation are not deductible administrative expenses. Decedent left an installment note obligation bearing interest at 6 percent. The executor elected to have the estate's assets valued on the alternative valuation date and, in addition, determined that it was necessary to keep the estate open until decedent's obligations matured to avoid selling estate assets at sacrifice prices.

The IRS ruled that the interest on decedent's installment obligation accruing after decedent's death is not a deductible administrative expense. The exigency of avoiding sacrifice sales should not be confused with the necessity of paying interest on an obligation of the decedent. Had decedent lived, the interest obligation would have existed independent of any conditions requiring continuation of the estate.

[Rev. Rul. 77-461, 1977-2 CB 324.]

CHAPTER **10**

Charitable Deduction

¶ 10.01 CHARITABLE ORGANIZATIONS AND PURPOSES

Third Circuit reverses lower court finding that bequests to cemetery associations qualify for Section 2055. Decedent died testate in December 1976. By the terms of the will, the residuary estate was to pass to a cemetery association for the construction of a new utility building, with the balance to be added to the cemetery's endowment fund. The executors claimed a Section 2055 charitable deduction of $370,901, representing the total amount distributed. The IRS, however, disallowed the deduction on the strength of long-standing case law precedent establishing the rule that cemetery associations do not fall within the statutory definition of a "charitable organization." The case was heard in federal district court, where the IRS argued that under the traditional view, cemetery associations cannot qualify under Section 2055, because they lack the required "religious, charitable, scientific, literary, or educational purposes." The estate argued successfully that the Supreme Court's opinion in Bob Jones University, 461 US 574 (1983), required a reevaluation of the prevailing view. The district court noted that the Supreme Court, in considering the tax status of a university as a charitable organization under Section 501, stated that in order for an organization to be entitled to exempt status, it must meet certain common-law standards of charity and must "serve a public purpose." Applying the public purpose standard, the district court ruled that the cemetery association was a charitable organization for purposes of Section 2055, and that therefore the estate was entitled to the claimed deduction.

Held: Reversed for the IRS. At the outset, the Third Circuit stated that "in light of the framework of the Internal Revenue Code," the district court was not free to apply the *Bob Jones University* common-law concept of charity to a case involving a Section 2055 deduction. That case dealt only with Section 501(c)(3), which governs the determination of organizations entitled to exemption from taxation under the income tax provisions. The deductibility of contributions made to such an organization is covered in Section 170. Thus, concluded the court, "charitable" organizations are exempt from taxation under Section 501(c)(3) and contributions to charitable organizations are deductible from taxpayer's income under Section 170(c)(2)(B). Other subsections of these two statutes provide explicitly for nonprofit cemeteries, thereby suggesting that such organizations are not encompassed within the meaning of "charitable organizations." The court examined legislative history relating to the adoption of Section 170 and found that although Congress amended Section 170 in order to "extend" the definition of charitable organization to include cemetery associations for income tax purposes, it failed to adopt a corresponding extension amendment for estate tax purposes. In view of the clear distinction drawn by Congress in its treatment of cemetery associations under the income and estate tax laws, the court was constrained to conclude that *Bob Jones University* was not controlling.

[Mellon Bank, 762 F2d 283, 56 AFTR2d 85-6481, 85-1 USTC ¶ 13,615 (3d Cir. 1985), cert. denied, 475 US 1032 (1986).]

Bequests to cemetery associations are not deductible for lack of charitable or religious purpose. By the terms of her will, decedent bequeathed a large portion of her estate to two nonprofit cemetery associations. She left $25,000 for the perpetual care of the family burial plot to one of the associations, and a 50 percent portion of her residuary estate, approximately $2.5 million, to the other association. The executor of her estate claimed that the two cemetery associations were "charitable" or "religious" entities within the meaning of Section 2055(a)(2), thus entitling the estate to a deduction for the two bequests. The IRS denied the claimed deduction, arguing that the associations did not have a primarily charitable or religious purpose.

Held: For the IRS. The court found that the activities of the cemetery associations were not historically infused with such charitable services as providing free or low-cost burials to constitute "charitable" activities in accordance with Section 2055(a). In addition, the associations were found not to be "religious" entities under Section 2055(a), because they did not operate under the ownership, supervision, or affiliation of any particular church.

[Child, 540 F2d 579, 38 AFTR2d 76-6278, 76-2 USTC ¶ 13,150 (2d Cir. 1976), cert. denied, 429 US 1092 (1977).]

Estate is denied charitable deduction for gift to organization, despite fact that no notice of its revocation of exempt status was published in *Internal Revenue Bulletin.* An estate claimed a charitable deduction for a gift to an organization that distributed funds to private schools. The IRS denied the claimed deduction on the ground that the organization was dropped from the IRS's cumulative list of exempt organizations. The estate contended that it was nevertheless entitled to the deduction because no notice of the revocation of the organization's exempt status was published in the *Internal Revenue Bulletin.*

Held: For the IRS. Although no notice of this revocation was published, the organization was dropped from the IRS's cumulative list of exempt organizations. The Tax Court concluded that this was sufficient notice to the public, despite the fact the executor relied on the organization's affidavit, stating that it was still exempt. The court also rejected the estate's argument that the non-exempt organization held the funds in constructive trust for the other charitable beneficiaries.

[Estate of Clopton, 93 TC 275 (1989).]

Trusts used for missionaries' retirement qualified for charitable deduction. Decedent's will established two subtrusts for the purpose of implementing a church's missionary work. The IRS argued that the estate was not entitled to a charitable deduction because the trust income was used for the retirement of individual missionaries.

Held: For the estate. Decedent's intent was to benefit the general public. The church had sufficient control over the funds to ensure that the charitable purposes would be followed to qualify the bequests for the charitable deduction.

[Estate of Hubert, 66 TCM 1064, RIA TC Memo. ¶ 93,482 (1993).]

Charitable deduction allowed for bequest to church for celebrating masses. A charitable deduction was allowed under Section 2055 for a bequest made to a church for the celebration of masses for decedent's previously deceased relatives. Masses would have been celebrated regardless, and the bequest became part of the church's general funds.

[Rev. Rul. 78-366, 1978-2 CB 241.]

Contributions to integrated state bar pursuant to timely pledge are deductible. Under Revenue Ruling 77-232, 1977-2 CB 71, contributions to an integrated state bar made on or after July 5, 1977, are not deductible charitable contributions for estate or gift tax purposes. If a legally binding pledge to make such a contribution was made before that date, however, the actual contribution made after that date is deductible.

[Rev. Rul. 78-129, 1978-1 CB 67.]

Pet cannot be life beneficiary of charitable remainder annuity trust. Decedent created, by his will, a purported charitable remainder annuity trust that provided payments for the care of decedent's pet animal for its life. In a state where such a trust is permitted under state law, regardless of whether the pet's interest is enforceable, no estate tax charitable deduction arises from it, because an animal is not a "person" to whom an annuity payment may be payable. In a state where such a trust is void at its inception, however, so that the remainder is accelerated into a present interest, a charitable deduction may be taken.

[Rev. Rul. 78-105, 1978-1 CB 295.]

Where testator fails to limit use of gifts, estate can deduct gift to nonprofit hospital, but not to fraternal order. An individual died testate in March 1986. Under her will, her residuary estate was to be distributed to ten named organizations in equal shares, without any stated restriction or limitation on the use of the gift. The estate claimed a deduction under Section 2055 for the gift made to each organization. The examining agent questioned whether the bequests to two of the organizations would be deductible. One organization was a nonprofit hospital, a Section 501(c)(3) organization, that charged reasonable fees and reported net taxable unrelated business income of less than $1,000 for 1985. The other organization was a fraternal order operating under the lodge system and was tax-exempt under Section 501(c)(4). The fraternal organization agreed to use the bequest exclusively for charitable purposes. Furthermore, the local probate court issued a decree interpreting decedent's will to state that decedent intended that the entire residuary estate be devoted exclusively to religious, charitable, or other exempt purposes.

The IRS stated that even though the testator failed to require that her gift be used exclusively for charitable purposes, the estate was entitled to deduct the gift to the nonprofit hospital, but not to deduct the gift to the fraternal order. The IRS explained that the fact that the hospital charges reasonable fees for services or has insubstantial unrelated business taxable income would not prevent the organization from being described in Section 2055(a)(2). Furthermore, Section 2055 does not require that the donor of a gift to a Section 2055(a)(2) organization earmark the gift for charitable purposes in order for the estate to qualify for a charitable deduction. The IRS noted, however, that the fraternal organization is described in Section 2055(a)(3), which, among other things, requires that under the terms of the instrument of transfer, the gift must be used exclusively for charitable or religious purposes. The fraternal organization's agreement to use the bequest exclusively for charitable purposes did not convert a nonspecific gift from decedent into a specific gift for charitable use as required by Section 2055(a)(3). Citing Levey v. Smith, 103 F2d 643 (7th Cir. 1939), cert. denied, 308 US 578 (1939), the IRS concluded that the probate court order was not dispositive of the issue of the testator's donative intent, because of the absence of parol evidence showing that the testator had communicated this donative intent to the legatee.

[Tech. Adv. Mem. 8901007.]

¶ 10.02 COMPLETED TRANSFERS

Marital trust with general power of appointment may lose distribution deduction. Decedent's estate plan included a testamentary marital trust in which his wife was given a general power of appointment. She exercised the power by assigning her interest in trust corpus to a private charitable foundation. The estate made periodic distributions to the marital trust, which promptly passed the payments along to the foundation. The estate deducted the amounts of these distributions to the extent of its distributable net income. The IRS refused to recognize the marital trust for federal tax purposes, arguing that, as provided in Regulation § 1.663(a)-2, Section 661(a) does not permit a deduction to an estate or trust for distributions not otherwise qualifying under Section 642(c). The estate contended, however, that Regulation § 1.663(a)-2 (which denies a charitable deduction unless Section 642(c) applies) lacks statutory support and was invalid. Further, the estate claimed that Section 661(a)(2) permits a deduction for any other amounts properly paid or required to be distributed to the exclusions of Section 633(a). Section 663(a) precludes a distribution deduction for charitable distributions that qualify under Section 642(c). Because nonqualifying charitable distributions are not excluded from Section 661, the distributions should be deductible under that Section.

Held: For the IRS. The court found that the marital trust was not a recognizable tax entity. Because of the wife's "powers" over the trust corpus and income, the grantor trust provisions of Section 678 would require the wife to be treated as owner of the trust assets. The court used this section not merely to reallocate income to the wife but also to declare the trust invalid for tax purposes. Thus, the distributions were treated as passing directly from the estate to the foundation, and thus were not deductible. The court held that distributions for charitable purposes are deductible only if they qualify under Section 642(c). Thus, the rule set forth in Regulation § 1.663(a)-2 is valid.

[Estate of O'Connor, 69 TC 165 (1978).]

No charitable deduction but ranching expenses were necessary for administration. Decedent resided on a historic parcel of land in Florida that consisted of approximately 1,160 acres and included decedent's 120-year-old residence; a family cemetery; a one-room schoolhouse; an Indian burial mound, and other structures and sites. In addition, decedent owned and operated a cattle ranch on approximately 7,700 acres about twenty miles from her home. Six years before her death, she established a revocable trust, which during her life acquired a portion of the residential property and the entire cattle ranch and related lands. Under her will, the remaining portion of her residential land was transferred to the trust at her death. The trustees sold a portion of the ranch lands, followed shortly thereafter by sales of the cattle business and the remaining ranch lands. The trustees continued to operate the ranch until its sale and claimed the related expenses as deductible estate administration expenses. The IRS denied the deductions. The trust agreement requested that decedent's home, "insofar as possible, be set aside by the Trustees as a historical site," with the "designation of this site and management . . . in the discretion of the Trustees." A portion of the residential realty was donated to the local water district, which had agreed to transfer the residence and the other historical sites to a Florida agency that would preserve the sites and keep them open to the public. When petitioning the Tax Court to protest the denial of the administration expenses, the estate also claimed that the trustees' transfer of property to the water district without consideration constituted a charitable transfer that was eligible for an estate tax deduction.

Held: For the IRS, in part. The charitable deduction was denied. It was the trustees, exercising the wide discretion afforded to them, who made the charitable transfer, rather than decedent. The trustees had the power to set aside decedent's home as a historic site without making a contribution to a qualifying organization, and thus the value of the transfer to a charitable entity was not presently ascertainable at the date of decedent's death. Therefore, the possibility that the property would not be transferred to a qualifying organization was not so remote as to be negligible. The ranching expenses were allowed, however. The trust's continuation of the ranching business was necessary for the preservation of the estate and was a necessary step in liquidating the estate's assets. The ranch lands likely would have reverted to muck and swamp if the cattle were no longer grazing there. The value of the ranch lands remaining after the first sale, when the cattle finally were sold, depreciated in value, as compared with the price obtained on the first sale.

[Estate of Lockett, 75 TCM 1731, RIA TC Memo. ¶ 98,050 (1998).]

Estate may not deduct payment of non-enforceable charitable pledges. Shortly before his death, decedent invited friends, family, and representatives of twenty charitable organizations to a party to celebrate his ninetieth birthday. At the party, decedent announced that he would establish a $10,000 charitable remainder annuity trust for each charity represented at the party, with family members and others as the income beneficiaries. Before he died, decedent wrote letters to a number of the charities to reaffirm his intent to make the gifts. He died before he could establish the trusts, however. The personal representative eventually paid $10,000 to seventeen of the twenty charities, or a total of $170,000. An additional $30,000 was divided among the three other charities and six individuals, who presumably would have been the income beneficiaries of the trusts that were to have been established for those three charities. The entire $200,000 was deducted on the estate tax return as a claim against the estate. The estate argued that Section 2053(a)(3) permitted the deduction for the payments to the charities. That section provides for a deduction for such claims against the estate as are allowable by the laws of the jurisdiction under which the estate is being administered—in this case Florida. An allowable claim is one that is enforceable under state law.

Held: For the IRS. The Tax Court determined that under Florida law, a promise to contribute to a charitable organization is enforceable under the doctrine of promissory estoppel if the promisor makes a promise that he reasonably expects to induce action or forbearance of a substantial character by the promisee. In this case, the court found there was no indication that decedent expected to induce the donee organizations to take or forbear from taking any action of a substantial character in response to his promises. Although representatives of the twenty donee-charities attended decedent's ninetieth birthday party, decedent did not have an expectation of benefit. The Tax Court cited Estate of Sochalski, 14 TCM 72, ¶ 55,019 P-H Memo. TC (1955). There, a decedent promised in writing to make a gift to a church organization but died before making the gift. His wife, as executrix, made the gift and deducted it. The court held that the estate was not entitled to a deduction, because decedent's promise was not an enforceable obligation in the state in which the estate was administered. With respect to the payments to the six individuals in the instant case, the same analysis presumably would apply. Rather than discussing whether the individuals could have enforced decedent's promises, however, the court held that the payments were not deductible, because they were not contracted bona fide for adequate and full consideration in money or money's worth. Adequate and full consideration in money or money's worth is consideration that (1) augmented decedent's estate; (2) bestowed a right or privilege not previously held by decedent; or (3) discharged an existing claim of decedent. Because the estate acknowledged that decedent did not receive adequate consideration under this test, the estate could not deduct the amount paid to the individuals.

[Estate of Levin, 69 TCM 1951, RIA TC Memo. ¶ 95,081 (1995).]

Retention of right to dividends precludes charitable deduction. Under decedent's will, the executor was to hold the stock of certain corporations until completion of administration, to pay dividends distributed with respect to the stock during that period to an individual. Therefore, the executor was to transfer the stock to charity. The estate claimed an estate tax charitable deduction.

The IRS stated that a vested right to receive dividends, even for a specific period, is an interest in property. Thus, an interest in the stock passed under the will to both a charitable and noncharitable beneficiary. Because this split interest is not in one of the three forms enumerated in Section 2055(e)(2), the charitable deduction was disallowed.

[Rev. Rul. 83-45, 1983-1 CB 233.]

Amount of charitable contribution subject to spouse's allowance is determined. The portion of decedent's estate contributed to charity was subject to a spouse's allowance—a fixed monthly support payment to the surviving spouse, payable during the estate administration period and terminable on death or remarriage during that period. The IRS ruled that the property in which the spouse had an interest because of the allowance was a nondeductible split interest under Section 2055(e)(2). However, the portion certain to be distributed to charity was deductible.

[Rev. Rul. 83-20, 1983-1 CB 231.]

Charitable deduction is allowed where transfer is not made via trust. Decedent bequeathed his residuary estate to a living trust created by him several years prior to death. The living trust was includable in his gross estate. The trust provided that at decedent's death, 10 percent of the corpus, as augmented by decedent's residuary estate, was to be paid in fee simple to a qualified charity. State law provided that the charity was entitled to receive 10 percent interests in each and every asset comprised in the trust corpus as well as 10 percent of all income prior to distribution. Because the trust was required to make an immediate distribution of any assets to which the charitable beneficiary was entitled and, therefore, did not have the power to hold such assets, the trust was merely a distribution mechanism; therefore, the charitable interests were not transferred "in trust" within the meaning of Section 2055(e)(2) and Regulation § 20.2055-2(e)(2)(i). Therefore, a charitable deduction was allowed under Section 2055(c).

[Rev. Rul. 75-414, 1975-2 CB 371.]

Tennessee estate may take charitable deduction on gift of remainder to charity. Decedent bequeathed a life interest in eighty-six acres in Tennessee to an individual. On the individual's death, the property was to be sold and the proceeds given to a charitable beneficiary. Tennessee law permits the charity to elect to take the property against the will. The IRS stated that the estate was entitled to a charitable deduction because of the charity's right to take against the will under local law.

[Priv. Ltr. Rul. 8141037.]

¶ 10.03 TESTAMENTARY INTENT

Charitable deductions are allowed where trustee's discretion is limited by local law. Decedent created a revocable trust that gave the trustee "absolute discretion" to pay certain testamentary charitable bequests from the corpus. Decedent's probate estate was insolvent at her death. The IRS argued that the bequests paid by the trustee were subject to a condition precedent under Regulation ¶ 20.2055-2(b) and disallowed the charitable deductions.

Held: For the estate. In light of decedent's clear intent, the trustee had a fiduciary duty under local law to pay the bequests, notwithstanding the discretionary language contained in the trust instrument itself.

[State St. Bank & Trust Co., 634 F2d 5, 47 AFTR2d 81-1558, 80-2 USTC ¶ 13,376 (5th Cir. 1980).]

Trustees' discretion does not defeat charitable purpose of trust. Decedent's will contained a charitable bequest in trust to be used, at the trustees' discretion, exclusively to foster and to promote patriotism. Three years after decedent's death, the trustees executed a document further limiting the trust purpose to charitable purposes. The IRS denied the charitable deduction for the trust assets.

Held: For taxpayer. The trustees' discretion did not prevent the trust's charitable purposes. In addition, the subsequent document further limited the trustees' discretion.

[Buder, 92-2 USTC ¶ 60,105, 70 AFTR2d 92-6189 (ED Mo. 1992), aff'd, 7 F3d 1382, 93-2 USTC ¶ 60,149, 72 AFTR2d 93-6758 (8th Cir. 1993).]

Nonapportionment clause is not given effect in order to preserve charitable contribution. Decedent's will provided that pre-residuary estate taxes were to be paid from the residuary. Another clause provided that no taxes should be apportioned to any recipient of a taxable portion of the estate. The residuary, divided in six equal parts, included five individual beneficiaries and a charitable trust.

Held: The court entered judgment in which the residuary was reduced by pre-residuary taxes, then divided into six equal parts, with the tax burden falling on the five individual beneficiaries. The nonapportionment clause was self-contradictory and ambiguous, and if etrece, would have exhausted the charitable contribution with tax liability. The testator could not have intended this result.

[Endicott Trust Co., 37 AFTR2d 76-1516, 75-2 USTC ¶ 13,111 (NDNY 1975).]

Charitable deduction is allowed. Decedent left property in trust with instructions that the trustees should accumulate the income until enough capital was accumulated to build a hospital. The IRS denied a charitable deduction.

Held: For the estate. Decedent's intent that the trust property vest in the village where the hospital would be located overrides the normal state law rule that an undevised remainder interest in trust passes through intestacy.

[Estate of Orphanos, 67 TC 780 (1977), acq. 1977-2 CB 2.]

IRS illustrates estate tax burden where half of residue goes to charity under clear direction against apportionment. Decedent's will directed that all taxes were to be paid out of the residue of his estate, with no part to be apportioned to any beneficiary. The remainder was to be divided equally between charity and decedent's son. In the instant case, because there was a clear unambiguous direction against apportionment, all taxes would be subtracted, and the remaining residue would be divided equally between the beneficiaries.

[Rev. Rul. 76-359, 1976-2 CB 293.]

The IRS does not allow extrinsic evidence to "clarify" that bequest is for charitable purposes when intent is clear from will. An individual died, leaving a will that provided for a cash bequest to a fraternal society. The will stated that the bequest was made "without reservation as to use, but it is my wish that it be maintained at compound interest for eventual use in acquiring its own building." Decedent's representative stated that the testator's intent was to make a charitable bequest and asserted that parol evidence should be admitted to prove the testator's intent.

The IRS stated that under Section 2055, the bequest to the fraternal society did not qualify for the estate tax charitable deduction. The IRS took the position that the will did not restrict the use of the bequest exclusively to purposes described in Section 2055(a)(3), noting that the bequest was "without reservation as to use," even though decedent's will expressed the desire that it be used by the fraternal society to acquire its own building. The IRS concluded that decedent's bequest was clear from the "four corners" of the will, adding that extrinsic evidence is admissible only to determine the testator's intent when intent is ambiguous.

[Priv. Ltr. Rul. 8704004.]

¶ 10.04 REFORMATION AND AMENDMENTS

Charitable remainder interest was "presently ascertainable" and therefore deductible. Decedent provided in her will for a life interest for her long-time employee, including a monthly payment plus payment of medical expenses; income taxes; and improvements to a house. The remainder was to be distributed to charity. After decedent's death, the estate obtained a reformation of the will in state court, changing the noncharitable beneficiary's interest solely to a flat amount annually. The reformation was sought to qualify for the estate tax charitable deduction under Section 2055. The district court held that the remainder interest was reformable and that the interest was "presently ascertainable" at decedent's death and so qualified for the charitable deduction.

Held: Affirmed for taxpayer. The ability of the trustee to pay for improvements to the house occupied by the noncharitable beneficiary or to pay his income taxes did not preclude the remainder interest from being "presently ascertainable." The improvements to the house were limited to those that would maintain its condition as of decedent's death. The power to invade principal to pay the life beneficiary's income taxes did not give him a significant volitional power over the charitable remainderman.

[Wells Fargo Bank, 1 F3d 830, 72 AFTR2d 93-6728, 93-2 USTC ¶ 60,144 (9th Cir. 1993).]

Nonreformable split-interest trust is denied charitable deduction. Decedent's will established a trust to benefit his sisters, to maintain a family gravesite, and to make charitable donations. The estate sought a refund of estate taxes for its contribution to the charitable trust, claiming that the will created three trusts. The IRS argued that the will created a split-interest bequest and denied the refund. The district court allowed the refund.

Held: Reversed for the IRS. The will unambiguously created a single trust to serve three purposes, only one of which involved a charitable bequest. All three were to be funded from the same property. The trust, however, did not qualify as a charitable remainder annuity trust, unitrust, or pooled income fund. Qualified reformation of the trust was impossible, because the noncharitable beneficiary's interest could not be measured.

[Estate of Johnson, 941 F2d 1318, 91-2 USTC ¶ 60,084, 68 AFTR2d 91-6049 (5th Cir. 1991).]

Charitable transfer made as result of will contest settlement is held not to constitute tainted split interest. Decedent, an Oklahoma rancher and horseman with substantial oil and gas interests, died in 1976, leaving an estate valued in excess of $1 million. In 1974, decedent had executed a revocable inter vivos trust providing for specific bequests to relatives, together with instructions to the trustee that he should, in his "sole and uncontrolled discretion," apply any part of the trust income to the care of decedent's sister. The trust also directed the trustee to hold and manage the trust property and income for the benefit of charities, including the establishment of grants and scholarships to further "high standards in horse breeding." Following decedent's death, the heirs launched a will contest in state court, contesting the validity of the trust as a testamentary instrument and seeking a full distribution of trust assets in accordance with the state rules of intestacy. Immediately prior to the entry of final judgment, the heirs and trustees entered into a comprehensive settlement of the issues and agreed to the creation of a private charitable foundation to hold specific properties and to carry out decedent's charitable intent. The estate then filed its final estate tax return, claiming a charitable deduction equal to the value of the property to be held by the newly created foundation. On audit, the IRS disallowed the claimed deduction on the ground that it constituted a nonqualified split-interest testamentary trust. Under Section 2055(e)(2), a deduction is disallowed whenever a split interest does not meet the definition of a charitable remainder annuity trust, a charitable remainder unitrust, or a pooled income fund. The estate conceded that the charitable interest in issue did not fall within the statutory requirements, but argued that there was no split interest transfer and, consequently, no basis for disallowance. As viewed by the estate, the charitable interest passed directly to the foundation, without an intervening or simultaneous noncharitable interest in the same property.

Held: For the estate. The court rejected the IRS's argument that the charitable interest was traceable to a nonqualifying split interest, and in the process questioned the IRS position in a number of revenue rulings that draw a distinction between the right of a spouse to elect against a will and the right of the heirs to undertake a will contest. The court noted that in both instances, there is a postmortem abrogation of the dispositive provisions of the will, but that neither circumstance amounts to a postmortem will amendment that would result in the creation of a tainted split interest. Accordingly, the court determined that the amount taken outright by an otherwise qualified charitable organization or used pursuant to the settlement of a bona fide will contest qualifies for the deduction in Section 2055(a)(2).

[Flanagan, 810 F2d 930, 59 AFTR2d 87-1212, 87-1 USTC ¶ 13,718 (10th Cir. 1987).]

Unpaid estate tax is held not subject to interest charges, despite subsequent reformation. Decedent died in 1977, leaving a will that passed the residue of his estate to a testamentary trust. Under the terms of the trust, two named individuals were to share all trust income for life, with the remainder passing to two charities. The estate filed an estate tax return in which it claimed the Section 2055(a)(2) charitable deduction for the value of the interest passing to the two charities. At the same time, the executor requested technical advice from the IRS on whether a planned reformation of the trust under state law would qualify the estate for the charitable deduction. The IRS issued a technical advice memorandum in which it stated that the proposed reformation would qualify for the deduction. Upon audit, the IRS made no assessment of estate tax liability based on the technical advice memorandum. However, the IRS eventually assessed interest on the grounds that estate taxes were due at the time of filing the estate tax return and that no deduction was allowable at that time, because the reformation had not yet been effected. The trustees paid the interest and sought a refund in federal district court. The lower court granted summary judgment for the IRS, holding that interest on unpaid taxes is based on the amount of tax due on the date on which the estate tax return is required to be filed. The court found that because the estate tax liability arises on the date of the decedent's death, a subsequent reformation has no effect on the existence of the initial obligation. The court noted a clear indication in Section 2055 that an executor is required to file a return on or before the due date in all cases, including those situations where the reformation has not yet been accomplished.

Held: Reversed for the estate. The Fourth Circuit rejected the district court's reasoning and held that the amendment converting bequests of charitable remainders into gifts related back to the date of decedent's death. The court concluded that no interest was owed to the IRS, primarily because the reformation was expressly made retroactive.

[Oxford Orphanage, Inc., 775 F2d 570, 56 AFTR2d 85-6588, 85-2 USTC ¶ 13,643 (4th Cir. 1985).]

Estate is entitled to charitable deduction for scholarship foundation. Decedent's will left a residence to his wife and established a trust of the remainder of his estate to establish a scholarship fund for students at the University of Arkansas. The portion of the will establishing the scholarship foundation, to be administered by a bank, directed that from the net income of the trust, the trustee was to pay decedent's wife $100 per month. The wife elected to take against the will. An order of an Arkansas probate court, based on an agreement between the bank as executor of the estate and the wife, decreed that the wife would receive nothing from the will, but the estate was ordered to pay the wife a lump sum of $50,000 plus $600 per month during her lifetime. The wife received the monthly payments until her death on August 31, 1975.

On July 30, 1976, the probate court closed the estate of the husband, except for a determination of the tax liability question involved in the instant case, and authorized the foundation to commence operation of the trust. It found that the foundation was the sole residuary beneficiary of the husband's will and transferred the accounting responsibility for the trust to a state chancery court. The bank, as executor of the husband's estate, filed a federal estate tax return showing that no federal estate taxes were due and claiming a charitable contribution to the scholarship foundation in the amount of $439,556. The IRS took the position that the bank had not complied with Section 2055(e)(2). Section 2055(e)(2) provides that an estate tax charitable deduction is not allowed for transfers of property to a trust that has both charitable and noncharitable interests unless, in the case of a remainder trust, the trust is in one of three qualifying forms: a charitable remainder annuity trust, a charitable remainder unitrust, or a pooled income fund.

The IRS sent a deficiency notice to the bank. The bank paid $122,657 pursuant to the deficiency notice, and then applied to the Arkansas chancery court for an order amending the trust to comply with Section 2055(e)(2). The chancery court entered an order amending the trust to comply with Section 2055(e)(2). In the instant refund suit, the federal district court found that the foundation qualified as a charitable use pursuant to Section 2055(a). The district court concluded that the wife was never a beneficiary of the husband's will, that she was entitled to nothing by virtue of the trust created in his will, and that Section 2055(e)(2) was not applicable. The bank thus was awarded the $122,657 that it had previously paid under the deficiency notice.

Held: Affirmed for the bank. The district court correctly ruled that Section 2055(e) was not applicable. Section 2055(e)(2) applies when the noncharitable and charitable interests pass "from the decedent" and are "in the same property." Although the wife's noncharitable interest "passed from the decedent," even though she did not take under decedent's will, Section 2055(e)(2) was not applicable, because the noncharitable and charitable interests were not in the same property. The $50,000 lump sum plus the $600 per month for life in which the wife had an interest were capable of being measured and severed from the solely charitable property in the residuary estate. This was the only property in which a noncharitable interest existed. The remainder of the property was not subject to diversion for a noncharitable purpose and was certain to be received by the scholarship foundation.

This case involved none of the abuses that Section 2055(e) was enacted to prevent. The charitable deduction sought by the estate did not exceed the actual benefit to the charity, and the value of the charity's interest was ascertainable. The estate was thus entitled to the charitable deduction.

[First Nat'l Bank of Fayetteville, 727 F2d 741, 53 AFTR2d 84-1594, 84-1 USTC ¶ 13,558 (8th Cir. 1984).]

Direct transfer to charity, if made pursuant to will amendment, is held sufficient to cure nondeductible split-interest bequest. By the terms of decedent's will the residue of his estate was to be placed in trust for the lifetime benefit of certain individual beneficiaries, with the remainder to be paid over to designated charities. After concluding that the testamentary trust created a split-interest transfer that did not qualify for a deduction under Section 2055(e), the estate filed a petition in state court seeking judicial reformation to conform with the statutory requirements. By the terms of a court-approved settlement, the remainder trust was eliminated and the estate instead paid $45,000 outright to the intended charities.

The IRS, however, determined that the direct transfer did not conform to the requirements of Section 2055(e)(3), which provide generally for the recognition of certain will amendments made to conform to the split-interest rules in Section 2055(a). In the view of the IRS, Section 2055(e)(3) sets forth the rule that a nonconforming split-interest can be saved only if it is amended to one of the three trust forms outlined in Section 2055(d)(2)(A). Thus, because the settlement called for an outright transfer instead of a charitable remainder annuity, a charitable remainder unitrust, or a pooled income fund, the IRS argued that the amendment failed to qualify for a deduction.

Held: For the estate. The district court found that the provisions of Section 2055(e)(3) are not the exclusive means of saving a nondeductible split interest, and that the attempt by the IRS in Temporary Regulation § 24.1(h)(1) to so provide is no substitute for actual congressional action on the issue. The court followed the reasoning in Flanagan, 810 F2d 930 (10th Cir. 1987), and noted that the charitable transfer involved no intervening or simultaneous noncharitable interest in the same property. Because none of the abuses that Section 2055(e) was intended to eliminate were present, such a direct transfer by judicial amendment was fully deductible.

[Estate of Strock, 655 F. Supp. 1334, 59 AFTR2d 87-1258, 87-1 USTC ¶ 13,717 (WD Pa. 1987).]

Elimination of beneficiaries is not qualified reformation of split-interest trust. After decedent's death, the trustees of a revocable trust with a charitable remainder attempted to reform the trust to qualify for a charitable deduction. Although the reformation eliminated the noncharitable beneficiaries, it did not change the split-interest trust into an annuity trust, unitrust, or a pooled income fund as required by Section 2055(e)(2). The IRS denied the deduction.

Held: For the IRS. Congress provided very specific statutory means for reforming nonqualify charitable trusts. The trustee's actions split the trust assets, removed beneficiaries, and created an entirely new legal entity. Although the modified trust appears to meet the requirements of Section 2055(a), the IRS is entitled to the estate taxes based on the trust's dispositive provisions that existed at decedent's death.

[Estate of LaMeres, 98 TC 294 (1992).]

Missed deadline for qualified reformation of trust results in denial of charitable deduction. Decedent's will created a split-interest charitable trust, with the income payable to her son for life and the remainder going to six specified charities. The trust failed to comply with the form requirements for deduction under Section 2055(e)(2)(A), not qualifying as a charitable annuity trust, charitable remainder unitrust, or pooled income fund. A year and a half after the estate tax return was filed, the estate petitioned the state court to reform the trust. The IRS disallowed charitable deductions for the remainder interests, asserting that the reformation was not commenced within ninety days after the last date for filing the estate tax return.

Held: For the IRS. Generally, charitable bequests are deductible from the value of the gross estate in computing decedent's taxable estate. However, a split-interest bequest is deductible only if formulated in terms of one of the forms set out in Section 2055(e). The estate failed to timely institute judicial proceedings to change the trust's remainder interest into deductible interests within the prescribed deadline. Consequently, there was no qualified reformation, and charitable deductions for those interests were disallowed.

[Estate of Hall, 93 TC 745 (1990), aff'd without published op., 941 F2d 1209 (6th Cir. 1991).]

IRS concludes that there is nonqualifying remainder where contingency cannot be cured. Decedent, *D,* died testate in 1984. Under the provisions of the will, *D* bequeathed a farm to a child, *A,* for life with remainder to *C,* an organization charitable under Sections 170(c), 2055(a), and 2522(a). The will further provided that if *B*, another child, survives *A*, the remainder in the farm was to vest in *B* instead of in *C*. *A* and *B* were both forty-five years old as of *D*'s death.

The IRS ruled that no deduction was allowable under Section 2055 for such a bequest of a contingent interest in a farm. Section 2055(e)(3) provides that under certain conditions, a bequest that fails to meet the requirements of Section 2055(e)(2) may be amended or conformed through qualified probate or judicial reformation proceedings to meet the requirements of Section 2055(e)(2). One of the conditions is that a deduction for the bequest would have been allowable under Section 2055(a) at the time of the decedent's death but for Section 2055(e)(2). The IRS noted that in a previous ruling, Revenue Ruling 77-374, 1977-2 CB 329, it had considered a charitable remainder trust that was created after the enactment of Section 2055(e) and concluded that even though the trust was in a form that met the requirements of Section 2055(e)(2), no deduction would be allowable, because the bequest to the charity was too contingent. The ruling also concluded that the contingency could not be removed under the amendment and conformation provision of Section 2055(e)(3). This was because the restrictions on contingent bequests that are described in Regulation § 20.2055-2(b) relate to Section 2055(a), rather than to Section 2055(e). These restrictions have been an inherent part of Section 2055(a) since prior to the 1969 Tax Reform Act, and were not affected by that Act.

In the present case, because the ages of *A* and *B* were equal, the actuarial probability that *B* will survive *A* and divest the charity of its remainder interest in the farm is 50 percent. This exceeds the 5 percent limit referred to in Revenue Ruling 77-374. Thus, the possibility that the charitable remainder transfer in this case will not take effect in possession and enjoyment was not so remote as to be negligible. The fact that the bequest was in the form of a remainder interest in a farm, which meets the requirements of Section 2055(e)(2), does not permit allowance of the deduction. The amendment and conformation provisions of Section 2055(e)(3) could not be employed to remove the contingency and thereby avoid disallowance of the charitable deduction.

[Rev. Rul. 85-23, 1985-1 CB 327.]

Judicial reformation of a testamentary charitable remainder trust does not affect applicability of Section 2055(e)(3). Under Revenue Ruling 76-545, 1976-2 CB 289, when a noncharitable income beneficiary of a defective testamentary charitable remainder trust dies before the due date of the testator's estate tax return, the governing instrument is deemed amended under Section 2055(e)(3) to meet the requirements of Section 2055(e)(2) applicable to interests created in a will executed before 1979. Judicial reformation of the governing instrument initiated after the income beneficiary's death, to provide for a 5 percent annuity, does not alter the result. Therefore, under Temporary Regulation § 24.1(h)(2)(i) (implicitly extended to apply to periods beyond its original scope), the amount of charitable deduction is to be determined as if a 6 percent annuity was payable from the date of death of testator for the expected (not actual) life of the decreased income beneficiary as of such date.

[Rev. Rul. 82-97, 1982-1 CB 138.]

Section 2055(e)(3) does not apply to gift tax charitable deduction. Section 2055(e)(3)allows the amendment of trusts that do not qualify as charitable remainder annuity trusts, charitable remainder unitrusts, or pooled income funds. The IRS ruled that Section 2055(e)(3) applies only where a federal estate tax deduction is not otherwise allowable and that it has no application to irrevocable trusts for purposes of the gift tax charitable deduction.

[Rev. Rul. 77-132, 1977-1 CB 297.]

Charitable deduction is allowed. Decedent created a testamentary trust with income payable to his widow for life, with the remainder going to charity. The trust did not qualify as a pooled income fund under Section 642 or as a charitable remainder unitrust under Section 644. The widow died before the due date of the estate tax return. A deduction was allowed under Section 2055(a) as if the governing instrument had been amended to meet the requirements of Section 2055(e)(2)(A).

[Rev. Rul. 76-545, 1976-2 CB 289, clarified by Rev. Rul. 82-97, 1982-1 CB 138.]

Pre-1973 charitable remainder trust amended pursuant to Section 2055(e)(3) qualified as charitable remainder unitrust. Decedent executed a charitable remainder trust before 1973. Following decedent's death, the trustee amended the trust pursuant to Section 2055(e)(3). The IRS ruled that the amended trust qualified under Section 664(d)(2) as a charitable remainder unitrust even if it did not contain certain mandatory provisions that had been suspended in certain cases by Regulation § 1.664-1(g)(2). Thus, a deduction for the remainder interest would not be disallowed under Section 2055(e)(2)(A).

[Rev. Rul. 76-370, 1976-2 CB 286.]

Failure to reform trust in time precludes charitable deduction. *A* died, leaving a will that devised a life estate in real property to *B*. On *B*'s death, the real property was to pass to Trust *X*. *A*'s will also provided for pecuniary bequests to two individuals. The residue of the estate also was to pass to Trust *X*. Trust *X* authorized the trustee to distribute money at the trustee's discretion to organizations dedicated to the care of animals. The trustee was also authorized to pay any real estate taxes or other charges on the real property devised to B for life and to pay $20,000 to another individual as the trustee deemed appropriate. If the individual died before receiving the $20,000, it would remain part of Trust X. Finally, the trustee had to pay $3,000 per year to the individuals named in the will. If one of them died, the survivor would receive the $3,000 per year for five years. The remainder of Trust X was to be paid to an organization that cared for animals. Prior to filing the estate tax return, the estate received permission from the probate court to make partial distributions to the individual beneficiaries and to Trust X. The estate made the distribution to Trust X and claimed an estate tax charitable deduction pursuant to Section 2055 for the residue of the estate. Thirteen months after the estate tax return was filed, the estate received permission to modify the terms of Trust X and the will to conform with Section 2055(e)(3)(B). Under the modification, Trust X was divided into a charitable remainder annuity trust with sufficient principal to pay the $3,000 annuity and a separate charitable trust with a wholly charitable purpose funded with the balance of the X funds. Section 2055(a) allows a deduction from the gross estate for amounts paid to charity and other specified uses. Under Section 2055(e)(2), however, where property passes for a charitable *and* noncharitable use, no deduction is allowed unless either (1) in the case of the remainder interest, such interest is in a trust that is a charitable remainder annuity trust or charitable remainder unitrust or a pooled income fund or (2) in the case of any other interest, the interest is in the form of a guaranteed annuity of a fixed percentage distributed yearly of the fair market value (FMV) of the property. An instrument can be reformed to comply with Section 2055(e)(2) as long as all payments to persons other than the charitable organization are expressed in either specific dollar amounts or a fixed percentage of the FMV of the property. If not, then the instrument can be reformed only if a judicial proceeding is commenced to change the interest into a qualified interest not later than the ninetieth day after the last date (including extensions) for filing the estate tax return. Here the trustee of Trust X was authorized to make distributions to noncharitable individuals that were not expressed in terms of specific dollar amounts or a fixed percentage of the value of the property. For example, the trustee was authorized to pay any real estate taxes attributable to the real property devised to B for life. Also, the payment of the $20,000 bequest was discretionary and could not be properly characterized as a specific dollar amount. Thus, the estate had to commence reformation proceedings within ninety days after the filing of the estate tax return. It did not do this, however, until thirteen months after the estate tax return was filed. The estate relied on Craft, 74 TC 1439 (1980), to argue that the division and the distribution of the estate assets prior to filing the estate tax return was a reformation of the estate sufficient to comply with Section 2055(e)(2). The distribution to Trust X prior to the filing of the estate tax return was to a split-interest trust providing for both charitable and noncharitable purposes, including a $20,000 bequest to an individual and two $3,000 annuities for individuals. Until thirteen months later, Trust *X* was not a wholly charitable trust and this earlier distribution was not eligible for the estate tax charitable deduction. In addition, the earlier distribution was not made pursuant to the provisions of Trust *X*, in contrast to the trust in *Craft*, which authorized a segregation of assets. Therefore, no charitable deduction was allowable.

[Tech. Adv. Mem. 8950001.]

Reformation of trust instrument results in charitable deduction for partial remainder interest. An individual left a will that provided for the reformation of a trust. The will provided for the residue of the estate to pass to the trust. The trustee was directed to pay all of the income to decedent's son for life. Upon his death, one third of the remainder was to pass to a charity, and two thirds would pass to a noncharitable organization. The IRS stated that the interest passing to the charity would not qualify as an interest in a charitable remainder trust as defined by Section 664. However, the IRS concluded that a deduction would be allowed if the trust were reformed in accordance with Section 2055(e)(3). The IRS noted that the reformation may require the establishment of two separate trusts.

[Priv. Ltr. Rul. 8849050.]

¶ 10.05 COMPUTATIONS

Administrative expenses reduced residual bequest. Decedent's will bequeathed the residue of her estate to charity. It also authorized payment of all taxes from the residue, and administrative expenses from postmortem income earned by the estate. Although state law generally required that administrative expenses be paid from principal unless the will directed otherwise, the Florida probate court held that decedent's will authorized payment from postmortem income. The executor therefore paid the administrative expenses from postmortem income and did not reduce the estate's charitable deduction by those expenses. The IRS disallowed the charitable deduction to the extent of the administrative expenses and attributable estate taxes. The estate argued that the expenses should not reduce the residual charitable gift because state law permitted the payment from postmortem income. In addition, since the estate had actually paid the expenses from income and not principal, the charity would receive the full charitable bequest deducted by the estate. The IRS contended that the residue of the estate, and thus the charitable gift, should be reduced by the administrative expenses and attributable taxes. According to the IRS, that state law permitted the administrative expenses to be paid from postmortem income should not dictate their source for federal estate tax purposes.

Held: For the IRS. The court agreed with the IRS. Section 2031 defines "gross estate" in terms of the date-of-death value of decedent's property. Under Section 2051, the taxable estate is determined by reducing the gross estate by deductions, including administration expenses under Section 2053(a)(2). Reading all three provisions together, the court concluded that the value of decedent's estate on the date of death was, for estate tax purposes, the sole source from which administrative expenses could be deducted. The court observed that while state law determines property rights, federal law determines how those rights are taxed. Payment of administrative expenses from income under state law did not mean that they could be included in the residual gift for estate tax purposes, even if the charity received the full bequest for which the deduction was claimed. That was irrelevant—the proper inquiry was the bequest to the charity under the will according to federal law.

[Burke, 994 F2d 1576, 72 AFTR2d 93-6705, 93-2 USTC ¶ 60,146 (Fed. Cir. 1993), cert. denied, 510 US 990 (1993).]

Increased charitable deduction allowed after state court determined expenses. Decedent's will placed the bulk of her estate in two residuary charitable lead trusts providing for fixed annuity payments to charity for twenty years. Her children were the remainder beneficiaries of one trust, her grandchildren of the other. After numerous lawsuits by the beneficiaries and creditors were resolved, the state probate court allocated only 27.5 percent of the expenses to the residue. The IRS argued that the will required that all administrative expenses were to be paid out of the residue. The Tax Court agreed with the IRS.

Held: Reversed for the estate. The state court decree settled a bona fide will contest and was binding on the IRS. Therefore, the estate tax charitable deduction had to be computed on what the charities received under the settlement.

[Estate of Warren, 981 F2d 776, 71 AFTR2d 93-2160, 93-1 USTC ¶ 60,127 (5th Cir. 1993).]

Section 2055(c) is interpreted. From part of his estate, decedent created a trust with income for life, coupled with a power of appointment, to his wife. If she failed to exercise the power, then a life estate would pass to his stepchildren and the remainder would pass to his stepgrandchildren. All state inheritance taxes on this part of the estate were to be paid out of another part of the estate bequeathed to charity. State law provided for a 9 percent inheritance tax on transfers to stepchildren, but a 15 percent tax on transfers to stepgrandchildren. In calculating the charitable deduction under Section 2055(c), the estate decreased the deduction by inheritance taxes computed at the rate of 9 percent only, claiming that the different rate treatments accorded by state law were unconstitutional. The IRS argued that the possibility that the higher rate would be imposed was not so remote as to be negligible and, under Regulation § 20.2055-2(b)(1), computed the decrease in the charitable deduction at the 15 percent rate. The district court declared the state law unconstitutional and held for the estate.

Held: Reversed and remanded for the IRS. Both stepchildren and step-grandchildren have contingent interests in the trust. Thus, even if decedent's wife fails to exercise the power, part of the transfer should be taxed at each of the rates, and the district court should determine the amount of charitable deduction accordingly.

[Estate of Kunkel, 689 F2d 408, 50 AFTR2d 82-6204, 82-2 USTC ¶ 13,491 (3d Cir. 1982).]

Unambiguous will dictates that all administration expenses be deducted from residuary estate in computing charitable deduction. Decedent's will provided for the establishment of two charitable annuity trusts out of the residue of her estate, with the trust corpus passing to her children and grandchildren at the end of the annuity period. The will specifically provided that all administration expenses be satisfied from her residuary estate prior to its passage to the charitable remainder trusts. The Texas probate court instructed the administrators of the estate to allocate a portion of the administration expenses to the income of the estate. The IRS determined a deficiency in the estate tax liability, arguing that for the purposes of calculating the charitable annuity deduction, the residuary estate had to be reduced by the full amount of the administration expenses as indicated by the will. The estate contended that the probate court's allocation was proper and should be observed for federal estate tax purposes.

Held: For the IRS. Decedent's will unambiguously directed that all administration expenses be paid from the residuary estate prior to its passing to the charitable trusts. The express language of the will, as well as the statutory and decisional law of Texas, require that all administrative expenses be deducted from the residuary corpus in calculating the amount of the charitable deduction for federal estate tax purposes.

[Warren, 93 TC 694 (1989).]

Residue of estate qualifying for charitable deduction must be reduced by executor's commissions. Decedent died in 1981, leaving a will providing for the residue of her estate to go to an organization exempt under Section 501(c)(3). An estate tax return for decedent's estate was timely filed. On the return, a deduction in excess of $1.2 million was claimed for bequests to charity. The residue amount was calculated by reducing the gross estate by the specific bequests, debts, funeral expenses, and administrative expenses, except for executor's commissions. The executor's commissions were instead deducted on the estate's income tax return. The IRS issued a notice of deficiency, in which it determined that the charitable deduction claimed by the estate for the bequest of the residue should be reduced by the amount of the executor's commissions deducted by the estate on its income tax returns.

Held: For the IRS. The court stated that the issue must be decided by determining, under applicable state law, in this case South Carolina, the amount of the residuary estate bequeathed to the charity for which a charitable deduction is sought. It found that under South Carolina Code § 21-35-190, in the absence of a provision in the will to the contrary, the administration expenses of an estate are to be charged to, and to reduce the amount of, the estate's residue. Furthermore, under Section 2055, an estate is allowed a deduction for the amount of all bequests to charity to the extent that the transferred property is required to be included in the gross estate. Thus, the estate is entitled to deduct only the amount actually passing to the charitable beneficiary. Since, under state law, the residuary estate was reduced by the amount of executor's commissions, the amount actually passing to the charitable beneficiary was also so reduced. The proper amount of the charitable deduction was, therefore, properly reduced by the administrative expenses paid from the residue.

[Horne, 91 TC 100 (1988).]

Ambiguous language in will triggers California apportionment statute: charitable deduction thus is not reduced by share of estate tax. Decedent's will, as originally written, made several specific bequests and left the residue to a family trust. The will provided that all estate and inheritance taxes were to be paid out of the residue of the estate, without apportionment. During the eleven years between the will's execution and decedent's death, seven codicils were executed, substantially altering decedent's estate plan. At death, the bulk of decedent's estate was disposed of through two testamentary trusts. Two thirds of the estate went to a family trust, and one third went to a charitable trust. On decedent's estate tax return, a charitable deduction was claimed for one third of the gross residual estate. The IRS reduced this deduction by a share of the estate tax, on the ground that the entire residual estate bore the burden of such tax.

Held: For the estate. Under Section 2055(c), if estate tax is chargeable to or payable out of a charitable bequest, the charitable deduction is reduced by the amount of taxes so chargeable. Thus, the court looked to the applicable California state apportionment statute, and it held that the charitable deduction was not to be reduced to reflect a share of the estate tax liability. Under the apportionment statute, which is typical of most state apportionment statutes, property that is excluded or deductible from the gross estate in computing taxable estate is generally not charged with any portion of the federal estate tax liability. California courts have consistently interpreted this statute as requiring apportionment only to property that creates the tax. Exceptions to the rule are allowed only where the testator's intent to the contrary is clear and unambiguous. The court held that though decedent's original intent, that is, to charge the estate tax to the residue, was clear, the codicils made it unclear whether his intent withstood the changes in his estate plan. The court noted that in the sixth codicil, the phrase "notwithstanding anything contained herein to the contrary" established that the codicil's language is to control any inconsistent language in the original will. This codicil provides that if one third of decedent's estate does not qualify for the charitable deduction, then the entire charitable bequest is revoked. In referring to "estate," it is not clear whether decedent meant his gross residuary estate or his net residuary estate. The court held that resolution of the ambiguity was not crucial to the case. Rather, the mere presence of such ambiguity as to the apportionment of estate taxes makes the general apportionment rules of the state applicable.

[Estate of Brunetti, TC Memo. (P-H) ¶ 88,517, 56 TCM (CCH) 580 (1988).]

Future accrued interest does not reduce estate tax deduction. In this revenue ruling, the IRS has revised its previous position that an estimate of post-death interest payable out of the residuary estate on deferred Federal estate taxes must reduce the deduction for a residuary charitable bequest taken on the estate tax return. The IRS changed its position in response to holdings in several recent tax cases—Estate of Richardson, 89 TC 1193 (1987); Estate of Street, 974 F2d 723 (6th Cir. 1992); and Estate of Whittle, 93-1 USTC ¶ 60,141 (7th Cir. 1993). In *Richardson*, the Tax Court held that estimated interest payable on federal and state estate taxes and on deficiencies with regard to such taxes should not reduce the marital deduction claimed for the residuary estate, but should instead be charged against income earned by the estate. In *Street*, the Sixth Circuit, following *Richardson*, reached the same conclusion on the ground that the interest owed is an obligation that arises after decedent's death.

In *Whittle*, a surviving spouse's estate claimed an estate tax credit for the tax previously paid by her husband's estate on his share of joint tenancy property. The husband's estate had deferred payment of the estate tax it owed so the payments made were actually accrued interest. The IRS claimed that the husband's estate should have been reduced by the interest payments as administration expenses, which would, in turn, reduce the credit for prior taxes paid and increase the surviving spouse's taxes. The Tax Court and the Seventh Circuit disagreed with the IRS, finding that the accrued tax payments were not administration expenses nor otherwise an obligation of the husband's estate because they resulted from an election by the surviving joint tenant. Therefore, they did not reduce the Section 2013 credit taken for tax paid on prior transfers.

In response to these cases, the IRS has issued this ruling, which revokes Revenue Ruling 82-6, 1982-1 CB 137, modifies Revenue Ruling 66-233, 1966-2 CB 428, and Revenue Ruling 73-98, 1973-1 CB 407, and clarifies Revenue Ruling 80-159, 1980-1 CB 206.

Revenue Ruling 82-6 held that, for purposes of the estate tax charitable deduction, the value of a charitable residuary bequest must be reduced by an estimate of the maximum amount of interest that is expected to be paid on deferred estate taxes when the taxes and interest thereon are to be paid out of the residue of the estate. This ruling is now revoked. In Revenue Ruling 66-233, the value of a residuary bequest transferred by prior decedent is reduced by any administrative expenses payable out of such bequest. This ruling is modified to reduce the residue by administrative expenses other than interest accrued on obligations payable from the residuary estate.

Revenue Ruling 73-98 states that the value of a charitable residuary bequest is reduced by administrative expenses payable from the income of the residuary estate. This ruling is modified to apply to administrative expenses other than interest accruing on obligations payable from the residuary principal or income.

Lastly, Revenue Ruling 80-159 concludes that the value of a residuary marital bequest is not reduced by interest paid on deferred estate taxes if state law requires that both the deferred tax and the accrued interest be paid from portions of the estate other than the residuary marital bequest. This ruling is clarified to state that the residuary marital bequest cannot be reduced by the accrued interest on deferred taxes even if state law requires that the deferred tax and interest be paid from the marital bequest portion of the estate.

[Rev. Rul. 93-48, 1993-2 CB 270.]

IRS gives sample of apportionment of taxes where residuary is to bear taxes and remainder is split between charity and decedent's son. Decedent had specified that all taxes would be paid from the residue of his estate, with the remainder being divided equally between charity and decedent's son. In accord with New York case law, because there is no clear direction in the will against statutory apportionment of taxes among residuary beneficiaries, the New York apportionment statute is applied. Thus, the pre-residuary tax liability is subtracted from the overall residue, and the balance of the taxes is imposed on the noncharitable residuary beneficiary. A sample computation is furnished.

[Rev. Rul. 76-358, 1976-2 CB 291.]

¶ 10.06 EFFECT OF PROBATE

Charitable transfer resulting from deed contest of estate property is not deductible. In 1967, decedent's mother made outright conveyances to him of eight tracts of real property in fee, plus three other parcels in which she retained a life estate. In 1973, decedent died and by his will left two of the tracts to his brother for life. The remaining property passed into a residuary trust created for the benefit of the mother for her lifetime. Upon her death, the property was to pass to two local churches in fee. Soon after decedent's death, the brother initiated a suite against the executor of his estate to set aside the mother's original conveyances of the property on the ground of undue influence. Before the case came to trial, however, an agreement was reached whereby decedent's brother was to receive a certain amount of real property in fee, whereas the mother's life interest in the trust was dissolved. The effect of the agreement was to vest title of the remaining property in the two churches. The executor of decedent's estate claimed a charitable deduction under Section 2055 for the value of the property passing to the two churches. The IRS disallowed the deduction, arguing that the property was obtained by the churches through purchase, not by inheritance.

Held: For the IRS. The court found that because the original testamentary plan was not followed, and because the beneficiaries agreed to redistribute the property, the churches did not obtain the property through inheritance or with respect to the testamentary scheme. As a result, a deduction under Section 2055 was denied because no testamentary transfer was actually made.

[Estate of Burgess, 622 F2d 700, 45 AFTR2d 80-1797, 80-1 USTC ¶ 13,354 (4th Cir. 1980).]

Charitable deduction for split-interest bequest is limited to actuarial value. Decedent's will provided for a split-interest bequest to his children and grandchildren in trust, with a remainder interest going to a charitable organization. The trust provided for a pooled income fund; thus, the estate was allowed to deduct the actuarial value of the remainder interest, which was $14,746. As a result of a will contest, the charity received $250,000 outright, which the estate claimed as a deduction. The IRS argued that the estate was allowed only the actuarial value.

Held: For the IRS. The deduction was limited to the actuarial value because the charity had an enforceable right under state law only to that amount. The money received in excess of the actuarial amount was given by the heirs, not by decedent.

[Terre Haute First Nat'l Bank, 91-1 USTC ¶ 60,070, 67 AFTR2d 91-1217 (SD Ind. 1991).]

Tax Court upholds charitable estate tax deduction, despite existence of voidable forced heir's rights in donated property. Decedent died in 1980, survived by her children and grandchildren. Under the terms of her will, approximately $12.5 million was left to a charitable foundation for which the estate claimed a charitable estate tax deduction under Section 2055. The IRS disallowed the claimed charitable deduction on the ground that it was voidable by the exercise of a forced heir's interest under state law. A legitime, or forced heir's, interest is that portion of a parent's estate of which he cannot disinherit his children without legal cause. All of decedent's children and grandchildren had previously waived their rights to claim their forced heir's interest in the charitable bequest. Section 2055 allows a federal estate tax deduction for charitable devises and bequests to qualified donee organizations. Under Regulation § 20.2055-2(b)(1), however, where a charitable devise or bequest is contingent upon the happening of a precedent event or condition, or upon the happening of a subsequent event or condition, a charitable deduction is not allowed unless the possibility of the occurrence of the event or condition is so remote as to be negligible.

The IRS argued that the possibility that decedent's forced heirs would exercise their legitime interests was not so remote as to be negligible. The IRS also argued that in order for the charitable devise to be deductible, the forced heirs would have had to file disclaimers of their legitime interests as provided under Section 2518. The estate, however, relied on a line of cases that have allowed charitable estate tax deductions where the charitable bequest was explicit in the will, where under state law the bequest to charity was merely voidable, and where the charitable donee actually received the full amount of the bequest with respect to which the charitable deduction was claimed.

Held: For the estate. The Tax Court noted that under local law, a testamentary disposition that impinges on a legitime interest is not void but merely voidable. The court found that relevant case law and Example 6 of Regulation § 20.2055-2(e)(1)(i) supported the estate's position. Under Example 6, a testator devised real property to charity. The charitable devise could have been defeated by the exercise of the surviving spouse's statutory dower rights. The example concludes that the surviving spouse's unexercised dower rights are to be ignored, and that the charitable deduction is to be allowed. The court stated that the cases and regulations look beyond the voidable character of the gifts or disclaimers and treat the gifts or disclaimers as effective and final, at least in those situations where the gifts or disclaimers in question are never voided. In other words, the mere voidability of a gift or disclaimer in these situations is not regarded as creating a contingency that fails the "so remote as to be negligible" test of the regulations under Section 2055.

With respect to the IRS's argument that each of the forced heirs should have filed disclaimers that qualified under Section 2518, the court stated that paragraph 4 of Section 2518(b) makes it clear that the disclaimer provisions apply only where the interest in the property being disclaimed will be transferred to the decedent's spouse or a person other than the person making the disclaimer as a result of the disclaimer. The court stated that under the will, the devise and bequest in question passed to the foundation immediately upon the death of decedent. The transfer of ownership to the foundation occurred as a testamentary gift from the decedent, not as a result of disclaimers executed by the forced heirs. Therefore, Section 2518 disclaimers were not required. Accordingly, the estate's deduction was upheld by the court.

[Longue Vue Found., 90 TC 150 (1988), acq. 1989-1 CB 1.]

Estate's payment to charity to satisfy its claim to a split-interest remainder trust was deductible as charitable contribution, even though trust was not qualified remainder trust. Decedent's will left the residue of his estate to a trust, with income from the trust being payable to his child for life and the remainder being payable to a charity. The bequest did not comply with the requirements for a qualified trust. Therefore, no deduction would have been allowed. Decedent's child, in good faith, contested the validity of the will and accepted an immediate payment from the estate in settlement of the claim. The charity then received the balance of the estate. A deduction from the gross estate is allowed for all bequests, legacies, devises, or transfers to specified beneficiaries, including certain charitable institutions. Under Section 2055(e)(2), however, when a remainder interest in property passes or has passed from decedent for a charitable purpose, and an interest in the same property passes or has passed from decedent for a noncharitable use, no deduction is allowed unless the charitable remainder interest is a charitable remainder annuity trust, a charitable remainder unitrust, or a pooled income fund. The IRS concluded that a deduction was allowable because the settlement did not create split interests. That is, the interests passing to the charitable and uncharitable beneficiaries were not interests in the same property. Thus, in situations involving settlements of bona fide will contests, the IRS will no longer challenge the deductibility of payments to charities solely because they were made in lieu of split interests that would not otherwise be allowable deductions. The IRS will continue to scrutinize will contests, however, to make sure that related settlements are not attempts to secure a deduction by instituting and then settling a collusive contest. As a result of this decision, the IRS will no longer follow Revenue Ruling 77-491, 1979-2 CB 332, and Revenue Ruling 78-152, 1978-1 CB 296, to the extent that these rulings would have denied the deduction.

[Rev. Rul. 89-31, 1989-1 CB 277.]

IRS rules that state mortmain statute does not block estate charitable deduction. D, a resident of State X, died in 1982. Under D's will, executed in 1980, D's farm was bequeathed to A, D's spouse, for life. The remainder interest in the farm was bequeathed to charitable organization Y, an organization described in Section 2055. State X has a mortmain statute that provides that a charitable organization may not retain a bequest of real estate for more than ten years. Under this statute, if *D*'s farm is held by *Y* for ten years after the death of *A*, the farm will revert to other beneficiaries of *D*'s estate. Thus, *Y* must sell the farm within ten years or be divested of all right, title, and interest therein. State *X* statute has no comparable provisions concerning inter vivos transfers.

The IRS noted that although in this case the mortmain statute required the charity to either sell the property within ten years of receiving it or be divested of all right, title, and interest in the property, such circumstance does not lend itself to abuse. The charity was receiving the farm in its original form and could sell the property for itself in the way most advantageous and most likely to realize the full value of the property. Accordingly, a Section 2055 charitable deduction was allowed in this situation.

[Rev. Rul. 84-97, 1984-2 CB 196.]

Payment to charity resulting from acceleration of trust interest is not deductible, because acceleration was not due to bona fide will contest. An individual had created an inter vivos charitable income trust agreement. The agreement established a charitable lead annuity trust to take effect at death. The annuity payments under the trust would be paid to two qualified charities for twelve years. Upon termination of the trust, the corpus was to be distributed equally to the individual's three grandchildren. On August 18, 1987, the beneficiaries under the trust entered into a settlement agreement to accelerate the interests of the trust. On August 19, 1987, the court approved the settlement agreement and directed the personal representative to pay the charities $800,000. The settlement agreement was initiated because the decedent's grandchildren threatened to contest the will. Prior to her death, decedent directed her counsel to prepare a codicil to her will removing the charities and the charitable lead trust as beneficiaries for the estate and substituting her grandchildren. It was never approved. Decedent had indicated to at least one heir that the estate plan had been modified in the grandchildren's favor. Upon learning that the codicil had not been executed, the heirs went into settlement. They also sued the attorney who failed to have decedent sign the codicil prior to death.

The IRS stated that the estate does not qualify for a charitable deduction under Section 2055(a) for the value of the payment made to the charitable organizations in satisfaction of the settlement agreement. If, in settlement of a bona fide will contest, a decedent's estate makes an immediate payment to a qualifying charity in satisfaction of the charity's claim to a split interest trust, the estate is entitled to a charitable deduction under Section 2055(a), citing Revenue Ruling 89-31, 1989-1 CR 277. The IRS distinguished the present situation because the arguments presented by decedent's grandchildren did not constitute a bona fide will contest. Analyzing the arguments, the IRS concluded that the grandchildren could not effectively challenge the charities' interest under the will and trust.

[Priv. Ltr. Rul. 8945004.]

Executor's discretion to select assets that satisfy pecuniary bequest to charity permit estate to claim charitable deduction. Under decedent's will, the excess of his estate over a specified sum was to pass to a charitable trust that decedent created in a separate instrument. The will also provided that all taxes were to be paid only from the residuary estate. The executor of decedent's estate, using the values that were determined for federal estate tax purposes, was to select the assets that would pass to the trust.

The IRS stated in technical advice that under the State of Washington's requirements for fiduciaries, the executor's discretion to select assets for the pecuniary bequest to charity is a power that permits decedent's estate to qualify for a charitable deduction under Revenue Procedure 64-19, 1964-1 (Part 1) CB 578. Revenue Procedure 64-19 concerned a fiduciary who is to select assets to satisfy a pecuniary bequest by using federal estate tax values. The revenue procedure stated that if, under state law, such a fiduciary "must distribute assets, including cash, fairly representative of appreciation or depreciation in the value of all property thus available for distribution, in satisfaction of such pecuniary bequest ..., the marital deduction is determinable and may be allowed in the full amount of the pecuniary bequest." The IRS stated that the revenue procedure also applies to the charitable deduction.

[Tech. Adv. Mem. 8339005.]

¶ 10.07 PERSONAL RESIDENCE REMAINDERS

Charitable deduction is disallowed for remainder in salt-mining royalty. An estate deducted under Section 2055(a) a bequest to a church of a remainder interest in royalties from salt mined on decedent's ranch. Although decedent had also bequeathed a life interest to his spouse, the estate argued that the remainder qualified under Section 170(f)(3)(B)(i) or Section 170(f)(3)(B)(ii).

Held: For the IRS. The salt royalty did not constitute a "personal residence or farm," and the remainder was not an undivided portion of decedent's entire interest.

[Estate of Brock, 630 F2d 368, 47 AFTR2d 81-1563, 80-2 USTC ¶ 13,379 (5th Cir. 1980).]

Tax Court determines that personal residence remainder in sale proceeds may qualify under Section 2055(e)(2). Decedent by her will left her personal residence to her husband for life. On his death, it was to be sold and the proceeds were to be distributed among four qualified charities. The IRS disallowed a deduction for the present value of the property because it did not pass directly to the charities as, according to the IRS, was required by the Code. It contended that all the charities got was a nondeductible remainder interest in the proceeds. At issue was the effect of Section 2055(e)(2), which provides an exception to the general rule that a deductible transfer of a remainder interest to a charity must be in the form of a charitable remainder annuity trust, unitrust, or a pooled income fund. Under that section, an interest described in Section 170(f)(3)(B) is not subject to the general rule. Such interests include a remainder interest in a personal residence or farm.

Held: For the estate. The court found that the requirement in Section 2055 for qualified interests to charities was enacted to prevent situations where a deduction would be taken for a charitable contribution that was in excess of what the charity would receive. The court held that such a potential for abuse was not present in this situation. The one possibility for abuse—that the executor would not sell the property at its fair market value—was guarded against by remedies under state law that were available to the remaindermen. As a practical matter, a charity receiving a residence, or an interest in one, would sell it as soon as practicable. Indeed, noted the court, the institution could sell the interest prior to the life tenant's death. The provision in the will merely facilitated matters.

[Estate of Blackford, 77 TC 1246 (1981).]

Charitable deduction is allowed for value of charitable remainder interest in proceeds from sale of decedent's personal residence if, under the local law, charity has option to take residence instead of sale proceeds. Decedent executed a will on July 7, 1978, and died on August 5, 1980. Under the will, decedent devised a personal residence to a beneficiary for life. At the beneficiary's death, the residence was to be sold and the proceeds distributed to an organization that was a charity within the meaning of Section 2055(a). Section 2055(a) provides that in determining the taxable estate of a decedent, a deduction from the value of the gross estate is allowed for the amount of all bequests, legacies, devises, or transfers to be used exclusively for religious, charitable, scientific, literary, or educational purposes. Under the local law's doctrine of equitable reconversion, between the time of the equitable conversion of the realty to personalty by the decedent's devise of the proceeds from the sale of the residence and the time of actual sale, the property could be reconverted to its original character as realty if the entity entitled to the property should elect to take the property in its reconverted form as realty. Advice was requested from the IRS regarding whether a charitable deduction is allowable under Section 2055(a) for the value of a remainder interest in a personal residence where, under the terms of decedent's will, the residence is to be sold and the proceeds distributed to charity, but local law permits the charity to elect distribution of the residence itself.

The IRS stated that a charitable deduction is allowable under Section 2055(a) for the value of a charitable remainder interest in the sale proceeds to be distributed from the sale of a decedent's personal residence if, under local law, the charity has the option to take the residence instead of the sale proceeds. The interests described in Section 170(f)(3)(B) include a remainder interest, not in trust, in a personal residence. Thus, if a decedent devises to charity a remainder interest in a personal residence and bequeaths to a noncharitable beneficiary a life estate in such property, the value of the remainder interest is deductible under Section 2055.

[Rev. Rul. 83-158, 1983-2 CB 159.]

Personal residence left in trust with remainder to charity does not qualify for estate tax charitable deduction. Decedent left a personal residence in trust for the lifetime use of his child, with the remainder going to charity. Because the house was left in trust, it does not qualify under the exception for remainder interests in personal residences under Regulation § 20.2055-2(c)(2)(ii). Nor does it qualify as remainder interest left in trust, because the trust is not a charitable remainder annuity trust, unitrust, or pooled income fund.

[Rev. Rul. 76-357, 1976-2 CB 285.]

Bequest of ranch to trust for term of years, with remainder going to charitable foundation, qualifies for deduction. Decedent bequeathed the residue of his estate in trust to a bank trust. A portion of the estate consisted of a ranch, which, under the terms of the will, was to be operated as a model ranch by a Section 501(c)(3) foundation. Upon termination of the trust after twenty-one years, the ranch was to pass from the trust to the foundation. The IRS stated that the bequest qualified for a charitable deduction because the ranch passed to a trust for twenty-one years subject to a restriction that only a qualified Section 501(c)(3) organization may operate the ranch, or supervise its operation consistently with the organization's exempt purpose. Because the trust instrument did not provide for any potential use of the trust corpus or income for noncharitable purposes, the transferred interest was not a split interest for purposes of Section 2055(e). The IRS said that the payments to the bank for trustee's services would not be considered payments for noncharitable purposes.

[Priv. Ltr. Rul. 8414005.]

Estate may not claim charitable deduction for outright bequest of partial remainder interest in residence and farm. Under decedent's will, the remainder fee interest in a residence and a farm was to pass outright to three charities and two individuals. Decedent's executor claimed a federal estate tax charitable deduction for the value of the charitable remainder interests in the home and farmland.

The IRS stated in technical advice that the estate may not claim a charitable deduction under Section 2055(e)(2) for the bequest to charity. Relying on Estate of Blackford v. Comm'r, 77 TC 1246 (1981), Estate of Boeshore v. Comm'r, 78 TC 523 (1982), and Revenue Ruling 76-544, 1976-2 CB 288, the IRS stated that a charity must receive an entire remainder interest in an outright bequest of a residence or farm for purposes of a charitable deduction. Further, the IRS said, Section 2055(e)(3) does not permit the reformation of this transfer, because the charitable interest is not held by a charitable remainder trust.

[Tech. Adv. Mem. 8341009.]

¶ 10.08 NONQUALIFYING REMAINDERS

No charitable deduction because amount of bequest not determinable. On May 9, 1981, decedent executed a will containing a number of specific bequests, including a bequest of $5,000 to his long-time housekeeper. The residue of his estate was divided equally between Princeton University and Johns Hopkins University. On August 21, 1982, decedent executed a codicil to his will, which deleted the gift to his housekeeper and added the following new clause that empowered his personal representatives,

> in their sole and absolute discretion, to compensate persons who have contributed to my well-being or who have otherwise been helpful to me during my lifetime by allocating to each of them such items of tangible personal property, or by transferring securities, or by giving them cash, or any combination of tangible personal property, securities or cash, as my Personal Representatives determine is a fair bequest for services rendered.

Each such bequest was limited to one percent of his gross probate estate. Decedent died on November 14, 1984, and his will and codicil were filed for probate. In accordance with the codicil, his personal representatives made bequests to his housekeeper, and his friend and guardian. The housekeeper received $10,000 and decedent's friend and guardian received $15,000. These were the only bequests made pursuant to the discretion provided in the codicil. On July 23, 1985, the personal representatives filed a federal estate tax return listing a gross estate of $2,584,500, and claiming a charitable deduction of $2,105,100 for the residue bequeathed to Princeton and Johns Hopkins. The IRS disallowed the deduction for the charitable bequest to the two universities. The IRS stated that on the date of death, the value of any beneficial interest in property transferred to charity was not presently ascertainable, and even if such interest had been ascertainable, the legatee, devisee, donee, or trustee was empowered to divert the entire property to a use that would have rendered it nondeductible had it been directly so bequeathed, devised, or given by decedent. Therefore, the IRS determined that the charitable deduction was not allowable.

Held: For the IRS. The appellate court first cited the regulations, which provide that to be deductible as a charitable gift, the value of a testamentary remainder interest must be "presently ascertainable, and hence, severable from the noncharitable interest." According to the court, ascertainability at the date of death of the amount going to the charity is the test. To be presently ascertainable, the power of the trustee to divert corpus from the charities must be restricted by a fixed standard. The Fourth Circuit then cited Merchant's Bank of Boston, Executor, 320 US 256 (S. Ct. 1943), which held that where the extent to which principal might be used was not restricted by a fixed standard, the remainder bequest to charity was not ascertainable. The circuit court found that there was no fixed standard that could be applied to the discretion given to decedent's personal representatives. They had sole and absolute discretion to compensate persons who had contributed to his well-being or who had been otherwise helpful to him during his lifetime. There was no limit to the number of persons who could be compensated, and there were no standards for determining such elements as "contribution," "my well-being," and "have been otherwise helpful to me during my lifetime." The court noted that decedent had lived sixty years and there might be many persons who had been helpful to him in various degrees throughout his lifetime; no standard for measuring these terms existed. The Fourth Circuit concluded that this lack of a definite standard made the amount of the charitable bequest under the Marine will uncertain and unascertainable. When this factor was combined with the unlimited number of individuals who could receive such bequests, the charitable deduction was denied. According to the court, the fact that only two persons received bequests was of no consequence because this could not be determined at the time of death so as to affect ascertainability.

[Estate of Marine, 990 F2d 136, 71 AFTR2d 93-2182, 93-1 USTC ¶ 60,131 (4th Cir. 1993).]

Attempt to obtain charitable deduction by terminating split-interest trust fails. Decedent's will created a split-interest trust. The estate claimed a charitable deduction for the charity's remainder interest, that the IRS denied as a nondeductible split-interest bequest. One year later the estate paid the charity the present value of the interest, terminated the trust, and sought to deduct the payment as a charitable contribution. The Tax Court found that taxpayer had terminated the trust to obtain the deduction, and denied the deduction.

Held: Affirmed for the IRS. Taxpayer could have obtained the deduction only by timely modifying the trust into a charitable remainder annuity trust, unitrust, or pooled income fund under the relief provisions of Section 2055(e)(3).

[Burdick, 979 F2d 1369, 92-2 USTC ¶ 60,122, 70 AFTR2d 92-6287 (9th Cir. 1992).]

Eleventh Circuit upholds Tax Court ruling on split-interest charitable deductions. Decedents, who were husband and wife, died in 1978 and 1976, respectively. The wife's will created a marital deduction trust for the benefit of the husband, which trust was subject to a power of appointment. Within six months of the wife's death, the husband signed an affidavit specifying his interest to exercise the power in favor of certain charitable organizations. At the same time, the husband executed his will and exercised his power for the benefit of the charities. Both estates claimed charitable deductions equal to the value of the charitable trust remainder. The IRS denied both deductions. In the case of the wife's estate, the IRS determined that the remainder did not satisfy the requirements of Section 2055(e)(2), that governs split-interest gifts to charity. The husband's deduction was denied because it was conditioned on the allowance of the charitable deduction to the wife's estate.

Held: For the IRS. The court rejected the estates' argument that Section 2055(e)(2)(A) limits actual—but not deemed—split-interest transfers to charity. The plain language of Section 2055(e)(2)(A) operates as a limitation of the Section 2055(b)(2) deemed transfer rules; therefore, the charitable deductions were properly disallowed.

[Estate of Flanigan, 743 F2d 1526, 54 AFTR2d 84-6518, 84-2 USTC ¶ 13,592 (11th Cir. 1984).]

¶ 10.09 ANNUITY TRUSTS

[1] Charitable Lead Trusts

Prepayment clause disallows charitable lead deductions. Donor transferred funds to an irrevocable trust and directed that a portion of the funds be paid to a charity to ten years, after which time the trust was to terminate and the remaining funds were to be paid to the donor's child. The trustee had the discretion to use trust income or principal to commute and prepay the future annuity payments to the charity. The prepayment amount was based on the discount rate and the method used to calculate the present value of annuity payments under the regulations, in effect at the time of the prepayment. Section 2522(c)(2)(B) provides that when a donor transfers an interest in property to or for a charitable purpose and an interest in the same property passes to or for a noncharitable use, no deduction is allowed for the transfer unless the interest is in the form of a guaranteed annuity.

Under Regulation § 25.2522(c)-3(c)(2), a guaranteed annuity must satisfy two requirements: (1) The annuity must represent the right to receive periodic payments over a specific period of time and (2) the exact amount payable under the annuity must be determined as of the date of the gift. The interest in this case failed to meet both requirements. It did not represent the right to receive periodic payments over a specified period of time, because the number of payments depended upon whether, and to what extent, the trustee decided to prepay the charitable annuity. Similarly, the exact amount payable could not be determined as of the date of the gift, because the amount of each payment depended on whether the trustee decided to prepay.

[Rev. Rul. 88-27, 1988-1 CB 331.]

Payments from charitable lead trust qualify as deductible guaranteed annuity. On November 21, 1988, a trustor created a revocable inter vivos trust that was to pay him all of the income therefrom during his lifetime. Upon the trustor's death, the trust established a charitable lead trust to be funded by the stock of a publicly traded company. The charitable trust provided for guaranteed annual annuities that would be paid to charitable beneficiaries to be designated by the remaindermen. The guaranteed annuities would be paid for fifteen years. At the termination of the trust, the principal would be distributed in equal shares to the trustor's children.

The IRS stated that the proposed annuity payments meet the requirements of a guaranteed annuity under Regulation § 20.2055-2(e)(2)(vi)(a). Consequently, a charitable deduction would be allowable to the estate for the value of the guaranteed interest passing to the charity.

[Priv. Ltr. Rul. 8946022.]

Charitable lead interests qualify as guaranteed annuity. An individual died in 1986 and was survived by two individuals who were forty-eight and fifty years old, respectively. A trust was established during the individual's lifetime and became irrevocable upon his death. The residue of the trust was to be distributed under the following plan. As long as the two surviving individuals were living, three Section 501(c)(3) charities would receive $1,000 per year. The two individuals would receive all of the income of the trust in excess of $3,000 per year. If the younger of the two were to die first, the annual payments to the charities would cease, and one-half of the trust corpus would be distributed to the charities. Upon the other individual's death, the remaining assets were to be distributed to the charities. If the older individual were to die first, the same distribution would occur. The individuals sought to reform the trust, effective on the date of the grantor's death, by dividing it into three separate trusts. One of the trusts was to be a charitable lead trust, which would pay $1,000 per year to each of the charities, and, upon the death of the younger individual, one half of the assets were to be distributed to the second trust, and the other half, if the older individual did not survive, would be distributed to the charities in three equal shares. The second and third trusts each would receive one half of the residue of the original trust after the first trust was funded. The second and third trusts provided for the payment of a unitrust amount equal to 9.57 percent of the income value of the trust assets or limited to the income from the trust for that year. The second trust provided for payment of the unitrust amount to the older individual for life. After the death of the eldest, the income was to be paid to the younger individual. Upon the surviving individual's death, the assets of the trust were to be distributed to the charities in equal shares. The third trust provided for the payment of the unitrust amount to the younger individual, and, upon his death, the assets were to be distributed in three equal amounts to the charities. The IRS stated that the charitable lead interests provided for in the first trust qualified as a guaranteed annuity under Section 2522(c)(2)(B). The IRS then stated that the two remaining trusts qualified as charitable remainder unitrusts under Section 664(d)(2) for any year in which they would continue to meet the definition of, and function exclusively as, charitable remainder unitrusts. The IRS concluded that the proposed reformation would be a qualified reformation under Section 2055(e)(3)(B), and therefore that the estate of the grantor would be entitled to a charitable deduction under Section 2055(a) for the present value of the qualified charitable interests after the reformation.

[Priv. Ltr. Rul. 8834050.]

[2] Charitable Remainder Trusts

IRS rules that charitable remainder trust cannot be subject of qualified subchapter S trust election. The IRS took the position in this revenue ruling that a trust that qualifies as a charitable remainder trust under Section 664 cannot be the subject of a qualified subchapter S trust (QSST) election under Section 1361(d)(2). If stock of an S corporation is transferred to a charitable remainder trust (other than a trust described in Section 1361(c)(2)(A)(iii)), the corporation's subchapter S election is terminated because the charitable remainder trust is not an eligible shareholder. The corporation may be eligible for relief from inadvertent termination of its subchapter S election under Section 1362(f).

[Rev. Rul. 92-48, 1992-1 CB 301.]

Annuity interest passing to charity preceded by life interests to private individuals does not qualify as guaranteed annuity interest. Decedent's will created a qualifying charitable remainder annuity trust paying a 6 percent annuity to his surviving spouse for life, then in equal shares to three individuals for their lives. Upon the death of any of the individuals, their share of the annuity was to go to a designated charitable organization, and upon the death of the last, the trust was to terminate with the remaining corpus to go to the charitable organization.

The IRS ruled that the annuity amount passing to charity upon the deaths of the individual recipients is not a guaranteed annuity interest within Section 2055(e)(2)(B), because the obligation to pay does not begin at decedent's death and was preceded by an obligation to pay the annuity for a private interest. Therefore, no deduction for the annuity value is allowable under Section 2055(a). However, the value of the charitable remainder interest is deductible.

[Rev. Rul. 76-225, 1976-1 CB 281.]

¶ 10.10 UNITRUSTS

[1] Charitable Lead Trusts

Estate qualifies for Section 661 deduction where Section 642(c) deduction is unavailable. An individual's will provided for certain preresiduary bequests and left an amount equal to one half of the adjusted gross estate in a marital deduction trust. The residuary estate passed to a charitable lead trust. The clause creating the charitable trust instructed the trustees to pay annually an amount equal to 6 percent of the fair market value of the trust assets to charitable organizations selected by the trustees. The will allowed payment of this unitrust amount to be deferred until the end of the taxable year in which the trust was completely funded. On the twenty-fifth anniversary of decedent's death, the trust payments were to cease and the principal was to become payable or be held in trust for decedent's grandchildren or "more remote descendants." The executors elected a tax year ending March 31, and during the tax year ending March 31, 1983, they made pro rata distributions to the two trusts, distributing 53 percent to the marital trust and 47 percent to the charitable trust. No other distributions were made during the tax year ending March 31,

1983, and funding of the charitable trust was not completed in 1983. The estate reported no taxable income for its 1983 tax year, as a result of a Section 661(a) deduction taken for the distributions. An examining agent proposed to disallow the deduction and any alternative deduction claimed under Section 642(c).

The IRS stated that the estate was entitled to a Section 661 deduction to the extent of distributable net income. The IRS stated that allowing the deduction was not inconsistent with Regulation § 1.663(a)-2 or the decisions in Mott, 462 F2d 512, 199 Ct. Cl. 127 (Cl. Ct. 1972), cert. denied, 409 US 1108 (1973), and O'Connor, 69 TC 165 (1977). Those authorities, the IRS noted, stated that amounts paid, permanently set aside, or to be used for charitable purposes were deductible only as provided by Section 642(c). But the IRS continued, "There is no inconsistency because a determination that there is more than a remote possibility that amounts distributed to the charitable lead trust may never be paid to a charitable beneficiary means that an amount distributed to such trust is not paid or permanently set aside for charitable purposes."

[Priv. Ltr. Rul. 8603002.]

[2] Charitable Remainder Trusts

Reformation was not available for CRT under 1978 will. Decedent's husband executed his will on November 9, 1978, and died on December 31, 1978. Decedent's husband's will established a purported charitable remainder trust (CRT). Decedent died on January 4, 1987, leaving her residuary estate to her late husband's CRT. The CRT was to pay income to decedent for her life, and upon her death, to decedent's husband's daughter. Upon the death of decedent and the daughter, the trust was to be divided into a number of shares equal to the number of then living children of the daughter and any then deceased child of the daughter who had left then surviving issue. Each such share was to receive a payment of $75,000 of principal at such time. The remainder was to be distributed to eleven charitable organizations. The IRS argued that decedent's pour-over was not eligible for a claimed charitable contribution deduction, because the CRT was ineligible for the charitable deduction. In addition, the IRS argued that the amount of the charitable bequest (i.e., the remainder interest) could not be ascertained. The estate acknowledged that the CRT did not comply with the requirements of the Code relating to the charitable deduction, but asserted that the trust should be afforded reformation relief under current Section 2055(e)(3)(C). The estate contended that the trust was not subject to the requirement that reformation be sought by December 31, 1981. The estate also claimed that the CRT contained an ascertainable reformable interest.

Held: For the IRS. Section 2055(e)(2)(A) disallows an estate tax charitable deduction for a bequest to a CRT unless the trust meets certain requirements. Section 2055(e)(3) grants an estate the opportunity to bring a bequest's provisions into compliance with Section 2055(e)(2) through reformation. The current savings provision, in effect since 1984, permits an estate tax charitable deduction if the governing instrument contains a reformable interest prior to reformation and reformation of the governing instrument occurs. (See Section 2055(e)(3)(C).) The court held, however, that Section 2055(e)(3) as in effect before 1984 applied and that, therefore, the CRT was not eligible for reformation. The court refused to apply the current savings provision. In reaching this result, the court reviewed the history of the rules permitting reformation of split-interest trusts. The savings provision of Section 2055(e)(3) was originally enacted in 1974 and subsequently amended in 1976, 1978, and 1980. The savings rule in effect prior to 1984 applied to wills executed or trusts created before December 31, 1978, and allowed a charitable deduction provided that the non-complying instrument was amended or conformed on or before December 31, 1981. In 1984, a permanent rule permitting the reformation of charitable trusts was enacted. This amendment did not apply, however, to reformations to which Section 2055(e)(3) as in effect on July 17, 1984, applied. In the instant case, decedent's husband's will was governed by the law as in effect on July 17, 1984 (i.e., the pre-1984 savings provision), because he executed his will on November 9, 1978, and died on December 31, 1978. The estate argued that under the IRS's position, any individual who died today and executed a will before 1979 could not seek reformation under the 1984 rule. The court pointed out the flaw in that argument, stating that such an individual's estate is established after July 18, 1984, and thus is subject to the 1984 rule. In other words, Section 2055(e)(3) as in effect on July 17, 1984, would not apply to such an estate, because the estate did not exist at that time. The estate also contended that the 1984 rule applied to the CRT because the trust was created *on* December 31, 1978, decedent's husband's date of death, and not *before* December 31, 1978. The court held, however, that the pre-1984 rule applies not only to trusts created before December 31, 1978, but also to wills executed before that date.

[Estate of Reddert, 925 F. Supp. 261, 77 AFTR2d 96-1947, 96-1 USTC ¶ 60,230 (DNJ 1996).]

Deduction for unitrust preceded by private unitrust is approved. Decedent devised his residuary estate to a charitable unitrust. A distribution of 6 percent of the value of the trust assets was to be paid annually to decedent's spouse, child, and grandchildren. Upon the death of the spouse, the distribution was to be paid to the child, the grandchildren, and the charity in the amounts of 58 percent to the individuals and 42 percent to charity. The remainder was to pass to charity on the death of the individual beneficiaries. The IRS allowed an estate tax deduction for the present value of the charitable remainder, but sought to disallow the deduction for the present value of the charitable unitrust interest on the ground that Regulation § 20.2055-2(e)(2)(vi)(e) denied a deduction when a private unitrust preceded the charitable unitrust. Taxpayer contended that the regulation was invalid because the devised unitrust interest satisfied the statutory requirements.

Held: For the estate. The court declared the regulation invalid for its failure to harmonize with the origin and purpose of the statute. Prior to the enactment of Section 2055(e), split interests of income or principal could be devised to charity and a deduction was allowed for the value computed under tables with an assumed interest rate. The assets, however, could be invested in such a way as to discriminate against the charitable beneficiary. As a result, the charitable deduction based on the tables was often greater than the amount the charity actually received. This manipulative investing was the abuse that Section 2055 was designed to abolish. All charitable nonremainder interests must be in the form of a guaranteed annuity or a unitrust, which is an annual payout of a fixed percentage of the value of the trust assets and is not tied merely to the income of the trust. The incentive to manipulate investments has been eliminated. The court concluded that the abuse that Section 2055 was enacted to prevent was not present here. All the income interests were unitrust income, and no power to invade, alter, amend, or revoke existed. According to the court, Congress did not deem the sequential payments, standing alone, a sufficient threat to the charitable benefit to deny a deduction. Moreover, the result in *Boeshore* is parallel to the rules applied to charitable remainder trusts, which permit a preceding private unitrust interest. The invalid regulation, said the court, is interpretive, rather than legislative, and thus is entitled to less weight.

[Estate of Boeshore, 78 TC 523 (1982).]

Method for computing deferred payments clarified for charitable remainder unitrusts. For governing instruments of charitable remainder unitrusts, the sample provisions in Revenue Procedure 90-30, 1990-1 CB 534, and Revenue Procedure 90-31, 1990-1 CB 539, correctly apply the method for computing deferred payments. As an alternative, the IRS has provided a sample provision that modifies the erroneous language in Revenue Ruling 88-81, 1988-2 CB 127, and Revenue Ruling 82-165, 1982-1 CB 117. This ruling is effective for testamentary charitable remainder unitrusts created by decedents dying after July 20, 1992, other than any testamentary charitable remainder unitrust created under a governing instrument executed before July 20, 1992, which is not amended after July 20, 1992.

[Rev. Rul. 92-57, 1992-2 CB 123.]

IRS rules that charitable remainder trust cannot be subject of QSST. The IRS ruled that a trust that qualifies as a charitable remainder trust under Section 664 cannot be the subject of a qualified subchapter S trust (QSST) election under Section 1361(d)(2). If stock of an S corporation is transferred to a charitable remainder trust (other than a trust described in Section 1361(c)(2)(A)(iii)), the corporation's S election is terminated, because the charitable remainder trust is not an eligible shareholder. The corporation may be eligible for relief from inadvertent termination of its S election under Section 1362(f).

[Rev. Rul. 92-48, 1992-1 CB 301.]

Payment of death taxes out of trust corpus disqualifies charitable trust. The IRS ruled that where a grantor made a transfer to a charitable remainder unitrust, and where a part of such trust may be includable in grantor's gross estate and state law provides that federal and state death taxes are payable from the trust corpus, such payment of death taxes violates Section 664(d)(2)(B). That section disallows payment of any amount, except the unitrust amount, to any person other than a charitable organization. Therefore, the unitrust does not qualify for a charitable deduction under Sections 170 and 2522. If, instead, however, a secondary life beneficiary of the unitrust is liable for the death taxes, the trust does qualify for such a charitable deduction.

[Rev. Rul. 82-128, 1982-2 CB 71.]

Estate tax deduction is allowed only for portion of unitrust remainder to qualifying organization. Decedent's testamentary trust meets the requirements of a charitable remainder unitrust described in Section 664. Upon termination of the trust, 75 percent of the remainder interest would be transferred to three organizations, all of which qualify as charitable under both Sections 2055(a) and 170(c). The remaining 25 percent of the trust assets would, upon termination, be distributed to an organization that meets Section 170(c) requirements, but that was not described in Section 2055(a).

The IRS ruled that an estate tax charitable deduction is allowable only to the extent of the portion of the remainder passing to the three organizations qualifying under both sections.

[Rev. Rul. 77-385, 1977-2 CB 331.]

Estate tax charitable deduction is disallowed for charitable bequest in trust. Decedent's residuary estate was bequeathed to a trust: 50 percent of both income and corpus was to benefit charity and 50 percent was to benefit decedent's spouse. The IRS ruled that no contribution deduction would be allowed under Section 2055(e). Where an interest in property goes partly to charity and partly to a person for a noncharitable purpose, no charitable deduction is allowed (unless it is a charitable remainder trust). In this case, if decedent had set up two separate trusts, the deduction would have been allowed.

[Rev. Rul. 77-97, 1977-1 CB 285.]

Death is not equivalent to disclaimer. Decedent died, leaving a testamentary charitable remainder unitrust. Before the due date of the estate tax return, the lifetime beneficiary died. At that time, no distributions had been made under the will of decedent. The beneficiary's death is not a disclaimer under Section 2055(a), so only the present value of the remainder interest is allowable as a charitable deduction.

[Rev. Rul. 76-546, 1976-2 CB 290.]

Deduction for charitable remainder interest not disallowed where trustee has power to add and/or substitute additional remaindermen. Taxpayer created a charitable remainder unitrust, with the remainder going to an organization described in Sections 170(c), 2055(a), and 2522(a). The trustee was given the power, during the grantor's life, to add or substitute additional organizations described in Section 170(b)(1)(A). Because any organization specified therein is covered by Section 2522(a), there is no possibility that the remainder would go to other than approved organizations. Thus, the deduction for the remainder is not disallowed.

[Rev. Rul. 76-371, 1976-2 CB 305.]

Division of unitrust assets into two separately maintained parts results in disqualification as charitable remainder trust. A provision in an otherwise qualifying charitable remainder unitrust directs that following the death of the survivor of the grantor or his spouse, the trust assets must be divided into two equal parts to be operated separately for the respective benefit of *A* and *B*, the grantor's children. The IRS said that this provision disqualified the trust because the divided assets could earn income at different rates, resulting in a total distribution of less than the amount required by Section 664(d)(3).

[Rev. Rul. 76-310, 1976-2 CB 197.]

Ruling determines qualifications of unitrust for income, estate, and gift tax charitable deductions. A taxpayer transferred property to the *X* foundation as trustee of a Section 664(d)(2) charitable remainder unitrust. The *X* foundation is an organization described in Sections 170(c), 2055(a)(2), 2106(a)(2), 2522(a), and 2522(b), and is also the remainder beneficiary of the trust. The taxpayer was the life beneficiary of a unitrust amount. The governing instrument of the trust contained a provision that if, upon the termination of the trust, the *X* foundation were not an organization described in

Section 170(c), then final distribution would be made to one or more organizations that qualified under Section 170(c). The possibility that upon the termination of the trust, the X foundation would not be a Section 170(c) organization was so remote as to be negligible.

The IRS ruled that the transfer of property to the X foundation as trustee entitled taxpayer to an income tax charitable deduction under Section 170(a) for the value of the remainder interest, because the trust was a charitable remainder unitrust within the meaning of Section 664(d)(2). In addition, the transfer qualified for the charitable gift tax deduction under Section 2522(a) to the extent of the value of the remainder interest, despite the fact that the trust instrument provided for alternative remaindermen. This was because, at the time of transfer, the named charitable remainderman, the X foundation, was a qualified charity within the meaning of both Sections 170(c) and 2522(a), and the possibility that the X foundation would not be both a Section 170(c) and Section 2522(a) organization upon the termination of the trust was so remote as to be negligible. Whether taxpayer's estate would be entitled to an estate tax charitable deduction under Section 2055 would depend on the qualification of the charitable remainderman under Section 2055 on the date of taxpayer's death.

[Rev. Rul. 76-307, 1976-2 CB 56.]

Trust ceased to qualify as CRT when option was transferred to trust. Taxpayer, who had established a charitable remainder unitrust, entered into an agreement with the trustee under which the trust would have the right to acquire a fee interest in certain encumbered real estate by paying a specific sum of money to taxpayer. It was contemplated that the trust would not exercise this purported option, but instead would assign the option to a third party purchaser in exchange for an amount equal to the difference between the FMV of the real estate at the time of the assignment and the exercise price of the option. The trust was to use the sale proceeds to invest in income-producing securities, which would be held by the trust to pay the unitrust amount.

The IRS ruled that upon the transfer of the purported option to the trust, the trust ceases to qualify as a charitable remainder trust (CRT), even if it was otherwise qualified. Because no income tax or gift tax charitable deduction is allowable in this instance, the trust cannot be a CRT in every respect and cannot function exclusively as a CRT from its inception.

[Priv. Ltr. Rul. 9501004.]

Estate reforms will to obtain deduction for charitable remainder unitrust. An individual died testate, his will directing that the residue of his estate pass in trust for the benefit of his brother, his sister-in-law, and three organizations. The trust's terms direct annual distribution of income to the brother and sister-in-law. Upon their death, $5,000 of the corpus should be distributed to an organization to which contributions are not deductible. The remainder of the corpus is to be split evenly between two organizations described in Sections 2055(a)(2) and 2055(a)(3), respectively, to which contributions are deductible. At the grantor's death, the trust did not qualify as a charitable remainder trust under Section 2055(e)(2). After the noncharitable organization designated to receive $5,000 filed an irrevocable disclaimer, the estate obtained a court order reforming the grantor's will by substituting a reformed residuary trust that qualifies as a charitable remainder unitrust. Under the reformed trust, the two income beneficiaries would receive a unitrust amount equal to the lesser of trust income or 7.6 percent of the net fair market value of the trust assets determined annually. Upon the income beneficiaries' deaths, the remainder would be distributed to the two charitable donees.

As a result of the reformation, however, the difference between (1) the actuarial value, as of the date of the grantor's death, or the charitable remainder interest in the reformed trust and (2) the actuarial value, as of the date of the grantor's death, of the charitable remainder interest in the trust prior to reformation, exceeded 5 percent of the actuarial value, as of the date of the grantor's death, of the charitable remainder interest in the trust prior to reformation. Accordingly, the estate proposed to further reform the will to narrow this difference in actuarial values to no more than 5 percent. Under the reformed will, the disclaiming organization's share will be deposited in a separate trust that does not qualify for a charitable deduction. Meanwhile, the unitrust amount payable is the lesser of trust income or 8.8 percent of the net fair market value of the assets determined annually.

The IRS stated that the estate had accomplished a qualified reformation under Section 2055(e)(3)(B), and that the trust's governing instrument would qualify as a charitable remainder unitrust under Section 664. The IRS also stated that a charitable contribution deduction would be allowed under Section 2055(a), based on the present value of the remainder interest created by the reformed trust.

[Priv. Ltr. Rul. 8952026.]

Testamentary trust is CRT and supporting organization. Decedent's will created a testamentary trust that received the residue of decedent's estate. The trust income was to be distributed to decedent's wife, and the remainder was to be distributed for the benefit of a tax-exempt organization described in Section 509(a)(1). The trust agreement provided that after the death of decedent's wife, all of the trust's income was to be distributed to the tax-exempt organization. The trust's required annual distributions to the tax-exempt entity would represent almost 80 percent of the entity's unrestricted contributions and over 25 percent of its total unrestricted nonoperating revenues. Both decedent and his wife served as directors of the tax-exempt entity.

The IRS stated that decedent's testamentary trust was a tax-exempt charitable remainder trust under Section 642(c)(2)(A). The IRS also stated that the trust was a supporting organization described in Section 509(a)(3).

[Priv. Ltr. Rul. 8718048.]

¶ 10.11 VALUATION

Charitable deduction is denied where amount is not presently ascertainable. Decedent's will established a charitable trust. His daughter was a 50 percent income beneficiary for a term of years. The trustee was empowered to invade the remaining income, that otherwise went to a convent of which the daughter was a member, for her support. She assigned her interest to the convent. The district court held that the bequest to the convent was not eligible for a charitable deduction.

Held: Affirmed for the IRS. No charitable deduction is available, because the amount of the bequest was not presently ascertainable.

[Estate of Cotter, 633 F2d 214, 46 AFTR2d 80-6218, 80-2 USTC ¶ 13,372 (6th Cir. 1980).]

Actuarial tables set value of charitable trust remainder, although life tenant was ill. Decedent's will established a charitable remainder trust. The IRS valued the charitable deduction for the trust by the actuarial tables in the regulations. The estate argued for a higher value to reflect the fact that the life tenant was ill when decedent died, and died seventeen months later himself.

Held: For the IRS. The life tenant's death was not so imminent to justify abandoning the actuarial tables. The court added, apparently as dicta, that the trust, in which one of the remaindermen was noncharitable, did not qualify for a charitable deduction.

[Eager, 43 AFTR2d 79-1287, 79-1 USTC ¶ 13,289 (CD Cal. 1978).]

Present value of deferred interest in unitrust is includable in life beneficiary—decedent's estate computed. Decedent was the life beneficiary of a charitable remainder unitrust. The trust provided that the obligation to make payments to the life beneficiary commences upon the trustor's death, but that actual payment could be deferred until the end of the taxable year in which the trust becomes fully funded. Decedent's beneficiary died two years after the trustor's death, but before the trust was fully funded. The IRS ruled that the present value of the deferred interest includable in decedent's estate be computed with reference to the terms of the trust. In the instant case, the trust provided for computation of such interest in accordance with Regulation §1.664-1(a)(5)(ii), and the IRS explained this computation.

[Rev. Rul. 77-471, 1977-2 CB 322.]

Unitrust valuation is explained. The IRS set forth in a published ruling an acceptable method for the valuation of unitrust assets where payments have been made to a beneficiary prior to the annual valuation date. The net value of the trust assets was computed on the first day of the trust's tax year, and an estimated unitrust amount was computed from that value. On the annual valuation date, the actual unitrust amount payable is computed on the net value of the trust assets, without adding the amount of prior payments back into the trust. If there was an amount due from a beneficiary as a result of an overpayment, that amount was to be treated as a trust asset. An amount that was due to a beneficiary as a result of an underpayment was treated as if paid prior to computing the net value of the trust assets.

[Rev. Rul. 76-467, 1976-2 CB 198.]

CHAPTER 11

Marital Deduction

¶ 11.01 DEDUCTIBLE INTERESTS, GENERALLY

Marital deduction denied for property transferred to trust. Decedent's property was transferred to a testamentary trust for the benefit of the surviving spouse. The will required that the net income from the trust be paid to the spouse at the trustee's discretion. The IRS's denial of a marital deduction for the trust property was sustained by the district court.

    Held: Affirmed for the IRS. The trust, by its plain language, entitled the beneficiary to neither all nor a specific portion of the income from the entire interest for life, but rather allowed the survivor only as much income as the trustees in their discretion distributed. The trust also made no provision for the frequency of the distributions.

[Wisely, 893 F2d 660, 90-1 USTC ¶ 60,017, 65 AFTR2d 90-1183 (4th Cir. 1990).]

Disclaimer of tax benefit adds to marital deduction. Decedent's will directed the executor to pay from the probate estate the estate tax on life insurance proceeds passing to decedent's son. Decedent's son, however, who was the policy's beneficiary, disclaimed the benefit. In addition, decedent's son gave the estate a check for the estimated tax due. The estate claimed that this amount was restored to the bequest to decedent's spouse and qualified for the marital deduction. The IRS contended that the direction to the executor was not an interest in property that could be disclaimed. Therefore, the amount did not qualify for the marital deduction.

    Held: For the estate. If an insurance policy is included in a decedent's estate because decedent retained an incident of ownership, Section 2206 permits the estate to require that the beneficiary of the policy reimburse the estate for the allocable federal estate tax in the absence of a will direction to the contrary. Section 2518 provides that if a person makes a qualified disclaimer of an interest in property, it is as if that interest were never transferred to the disclaimant. The Seventh Circuit noted that under Wisconsin state case law, a direction that state inheritance taxes, which would otherwise be paid by the legatees, be paid out of the residue of the estate constitutes a transfer of an interest in the estate. Thus, such a direction is a bequest of an interest in property. The IRS conceded that if the will had bequeathed an amount to the son to reimburse him for paying the estate tax, there would have been no question that Section 2518 applied to disclaimer of this bequest. The court concluded that no distinction existed between a direction and a bequest, because state law provided that the son's disclaimer was one of a property interest. The court noted that a common form of a bequest is the forgiveness of a debt owed the testator. If the intended recipient disclaims it and insists on repaying the debt, such a disclaimer should be effective under Section 2518. Thus, the court rejected the IRS's position that a direction in the will is not a bequest. In the instant case, because it transferred an interest in property, it was a bequest.

[Estate of Boyd, 819 F2d 170, 59 AFTR2d 87-1272, 87-1 USTC ¶ 13,720 (7th Cir. 1987).]

Divorce invalidated after death negates marital deduction. Decedent was a New York state resident from the time of his first marriage until the time of his death. A New York court declared his Mexican divorce decree invalid after he admitted the invalidity to reduce the waiting time on his second marriage in Connecticut. The IRS denied the estate's claim to a marital deduction, contending that there was no "widow" or "widower" for purposes of the marital deduction.

Held: For the IRS. Previously, in the context of income tax issues, the Second Circuit decided it would ignore decrees invalidating a divorce in another jurisdiction, even a foreign one. Borax, 349 F2d 666 (2d Cir. 1965); Wondsel, 350 F2d 339 (2d Cir. 1965). The Second Circuit abandoned this position on the issue of the surviving spouse in the instant case. It recognized that the New York decree invalidating the Mexican divorce had federal estate tax consequences. Decedent was always a New York state resident, as were his first and second wives. His will was probated in New York. For purposes of Section 2056, New York law determined his marital status. (The first wife elected against the will and, quite consistently, the IRS admitted that her share qualified for the marital deduction.)

[Estate of Goldwater, 539 F2d 878, 38 AFTR2d 76-6263, 76-2 USTC ¶ 13,146 (2d Cir. 1976), cert. denied, 429 US 1023 (1976).]

Validity of decedent's foreign divorce may affect estate plan. Decedent, his widow, and their former spouses were all residents of Wisconsin. Decedent, after initially obtaining a divorce in Mexico, was then divorced from his first wife in Wisconsin. The widow obtained a Mexican divorce in which her first husband appeared. Decedent and the widow were then married in Wisconsin. The validity of that marriage was never questioned until the proceedings determining the Wisconsin tax on his estate. A bequest to a widow bore a lower rate of tax than a bequest to a stranger. The Wisconsin court decided that the widow's Mexican divorce had no effect in Wisconsin, and that in fact she therefore was not a widow under state law. The IRS maintained that no marital deduction was proper, because there was no surviving spouse.

Held: For the IRS. The Seventh Circuit noted that the original purpose of the marital deduction was to equalize the estate tax burden between couples in community property and common-law states. Therefore, state law plays a dominant role in deciding whether an estate qualified for the deduction. Because all decedent's ties were with Wisconsin and his will was probated in Wisconsin courts, the Seventh Circuit saw no choice but to apply Wisconsin law on his marital status.

[Estate of Steffke, 538 F2d 730, 38 AFTR2d 76-6248, 76-2 USTC ¶ 13,145 (7th Cir. 1976), cert. denied, 429 US 1022 (1976).]

Marital deduction is not lost because of challenge to foreign divorces. The surviving spouse was married in Pennsylvania, moved to Connecticut, and then moved to New York when he separated from his first wife. Subsequently, he obtained a Nevada divorce decree, and in that action served his wife in Vermont while she was still a Connecticut resident. The first wife moved to require the Nevada decree set aside in New York. Decedent, who had been in California, appeared in that action and lost. He returned to California, married his second wife there, and lived with her in California until her death. Her will was probated in California. The IRS claimed that for federal estate tax purposes, because of the New York decree, the widower was not a surviving spouse of the California marriage, although there had been no challenges to the validity of the marriage there. Accordingly, the IRS refused to permit a claimed marital deduction.

Held: For the estate. The court determined that only California had an interest in the validity of the marriage, and because it had voiced no doubts, the widower was a surviving spouse. The Second Circuit considered the New York action between the widower and his first wife completely extraneous. It soundly rejected the IRS's belief that the opinion of the last court of competent jurisdiction to pass on the validity of a marriage controlled the validity of a subsequent marriage.

[Estate of Spaulding, 537 F2d 666, 38 AFTR2d 76-6245, 76-2 USTC ¶ 13,144 (2d Cir. 1976).]

Marital deduction fails—Tax Court confirms there is no sanity clause. Decedent's will left the residue of her estate to a revocable trust she had established with her husband. The trust agreement provided for an *A-B* arrangement when the first spouse died, with *Trust B* being the credit-shelter trust and *Trust A* receiving the bulk of the assets. The couple expressed their specific intention that *Trust A* qualify for the marital deduction, and be funded only with appropriate assets. The estate claimed a $920,000 marital deduction and reported no estate tax liability. However, the surviving spouse had to remain competent in order to continue to receive distributions of income or principal from *Trust A*; once the survivor was determined to be incompetent (defined in the instrument as being unable to handle his own affairs), "said spouse shall take no benefits hereunder and this Trust shall be treated and distributed as if said spouse had died." On the death—whether real or deemed—of decedent's husband, the remaining assets were to be distributed pursuant to his directions as expressed in a testamentary power of appointment. In the absence of an effective disposition in that manner, the remainder was to be divided into six shares for the couple's children. The IRS stated that the trust was a Section 2056(b) terminable interest, ineligible for the marital deduction. The estate made two arguments. First, it contended that the testamentary general power allowed decedent's husband to dispose of the marital property at any time before his death or incompetency. Alternatively, it argued that the trust was conditioned on qualification for the marital deduction. Without the qualification, the trust failed and decedent's estate tax must be computed as if it (and the fatal language) did not exist.

Held: For the IRS. The court did a chapter-and-verse explanation of the Section 2056 requirements. The estate tried to distinguish a similar case—*Estate of Tingley*, 22 TC 402 (1954)—that dealt with legal incapacity. It noted that in the instant case, the power of appointment was activated by the survivor's incompetency; the power in *Tingley* could be lost for reasons besides incapacity. The court, however, stated that the critical fact in both cases was the possibility that the survivor would lose power over the corpus on the happening of the contingency of incompetency: a terminable interest. In rejecting the alternative argument, the Tax Court also declared that the estate "has set forth no good reason why we should disregard the validity of the Trust." The mere fact that the settlors intended the trust to qualify for the marital deduction did not save it. They had other purposes, including qualification for medical assistance after the survivor's incompetency by distributing the trust's assets to family members.

[Estate of Walsh, 110 TC 393 (1998).]

Surviving spouse's interest in trusts qualified for marital deduction. Before her death, decedent and her husband established two trusts. She and her husband were the settlors; initial trustees; and lifetime beneficiaries of both trusts. Their children were the secondary beneficiaries. Decedent's estate tax return claimed a marital deduction for the trust interests passing to her husband at her death. The estate took the position that these interests qualified as a life estate with a general power of appointment under Section 2056(b)(5). The IRS disagreed.

Held: For taxpayer. The trust provisions granted the surviving spouse the power to demand that the trustee invade or consume any or all of the property for his own benefit without any duty to account to the remaindermen. Such powers constituted a general power of appointment, which, coupled with the husband's right to income for life, satisfied the requirements of Section 2056(b)(5).

[Flake, 68 TCM 1232, RIA TC Memo. ¶ 94,573 (1994).]

Community property interest in revocable trust qualifies for marital deduction. Decedent and his wife transferred their community property to a revocable trust. On the death of either spouse, the property was to be held in trust for the benefit of the survivor, who would be the sole trustee and would have the power to appoint the trust property. The estate claimed the marital deduction for decedent's interest in the trust. The IRS argued that the trust interest did not qualify, because the surviving spouse had only (1) the power to revoke the trust with respect to her half of the community property that funded the trust and (2) a terminable interest in the other half of the corpus.

Held: For taxpayer. The survivor had the unrestricted power to appoint all of the trust property to herself. Although the trust instrument did not provide for the trust income to be paid annually, state law required payments to be made at reasonable periods.

[Estate of Wilson, RIA TC Memo. ¶ 92,479, 64 TCM (CCH) 576 (1992).]

Bequest to satisfy debt qualifies for marital deduction. Decedent left a bequest to satisfy a debt of his surviving spouse, for which he was not liable. The bequest qualified for the marital deduction because it was indistinguishable from a situation in which decedent bequeathed the money to his wife who subsequently used it to pay the debt.

[Rev. Rul. 79-383, 1979-2 CB 337.]

Marital deduction lost when children allowed mother to keep property without probating will. Decedent's will bequeathed personal property to the surviving spouse and established a family trust and a marital trust. The family trust was a credit shelter trust (to be funded with an amount equal to decedent's remaining unified credit and state death tax credit). The balance went to the marital trust. All the income of the marital trust (and discretionary distributions of principal) was payable to the surviving spouse. She had a special power, exercisable in her will, to appoint the property between her two children with decedent. If she did not exercise her power of appointment, the principal of the marital trust was to be added to the family trust. The family trust provided for discretionary distributions of income and principal to the surviving spouse and, at her death, the remaining principal was to be distributed to the two children. The share of a deceased child would pass to that child's issue. The surviving spouse and the children asked a local court for permission to enforce an agreement they had made not to probate the will. The court granted permission, and the surviving spouse received all decedent's property outright under the Virginia state's intestacy law. If decedent's will had been probated, a qualified terminable interest property (QTIP) election could have been made for the marital trust, and it would have qualified for the marital deduction. By not probating the will, however, the marital deduction was lost. Although the surviving spouse received decedent's entire estate, it did not "pass" from decedent, according to the IRS.

Section 2056(a) allows the marital deduction for property included in an estate passing from a decedent to the surviving spouse. If, as a result of a will controversy, a property interest is surrendered to the surviving spouse, it is regarded as passing from a decedent only if it was a bona fide recognition of enforceable rights of the surviving spouse in decedent's estate, according to Regulation § 20.2056(c)-2(d)(2). This requirement is presumed to be satisfied when a probate court enters judgment in an adversarial proceeding after a genuine and active contest, but it is not necessarily satisfied by an agreement not to probate a will. Active contest or not, the surviving spouse must still have an underlying enforceable claim under state law, according to Ahmanson Foundation, 674 F2d 761, 48 AFTR2d 81-6317, 81-2 USTC ¶ 13,438 (9th Cir. 1981). In the instant case, the IRS concluded that the surviving spouse never had an enforceable claim to the amount she received. Neither she nor the children possessed any right other than their rights under the will. Although the surviving spouse could have elected to take a statutory share against the will, this right was never exercised or even mentioned. There were no arm's-length negotiations reflecting underlying rights. Thus, the surviving spouse received the property from her agreement with the children and not from decedent. In Estate of Carpenter, 75 AFTR2d 95-2084, 95-1 USTC ¶ 60,194 (4th Cir. 1995), property transferred to a widow after genuine arm's-length bargaining did not qualify for the marital deduction, because her interest under the will would not have qualified. Here, the IRS disallowed the entire marital deduction as not reflecting enforceable rights, although the surviving spouse by taking against the will or accepting the will would have received a smaller interest qualifying for the deduction. The marital deduction would, nevertheless, have been salvaged if the agreement between the surviving spouse and the children had been a qualified disclaimer of the children's interest under Section 2518(b). An individual making a qualified disclaimer is treated as never having received the property, and it passes directly to the person entitled to receive it as a result of the disclaimer, under Regulation § 25.2518-1(b). Consequently, the children would have no part in the transaction, and the surviving spouse's interest would have passed to her from decedent.

The agreement not to probate the will failed to satisfy the formal requirements for a qualified disclaimer, but Section 2518(c)(3) provides that a transfer of property is treated as a qualified disclaimer, even though all of the formal requirements are not met, if three requirements are satisfied: (1) the transfer is made within the normally required nine-month period for a qualified disclaimer; (2) the person making the disclaimer did not accept any interest in the property; and (3) the property passes to the individual who would have received the property under a qualified disclaimer. Unfortunately, the third requirement was not satisfied, because the property would not have passed to the surviving spouse if the children had made qualified disclaimers. Instead, the property in the family trust would have passed to their issue. Thus, the surviving spouse received her interest at their direction, that is incompatible with a qualified disclaimer.

[Tech. Adv. Mem. 9610004.]

IRS revises its position: loan guarantees will not automatically reduce marital deduction. On December 21, 1990, the IRS issued Private Letter Ruling 9113009, which concerned taxpayer, who had personally guaranteed loans made to corporations in which he owned an equity interest and loans made to his children that allowed them to acquire interests in other corporations. Taxpayer was interested in establishing a revocable inter vivos trust. Under the terms of the trust, if his wife survived him, at his death, the assets in the revocable trust would be transferred to two new trusts—an estate trust and a marital trust. The amount passing to the estate trust would equal two times the net value cost of making payments on guarantees given by taxpayer that were outstanding on the date of his death. The "net value cost" was defined as the present value of all payments the estate trust could reasonably be expected to bear on the outstanding guarantees. The estate trust was given exclusive responsibility for making any payments owed by taxpayer as a result of the guarantees. The balance of the revocable trust would pass to the marital trust, which would be structured as a QTIP trust. Taxpayer sought a ruling that the assets in the estate trust, less (1) any amounts needed to pay federal or state death taxes and (2) the net value cost of any outstanding loan guarantees, would qualify for the marital deduction. He also requested a ruling that the assets in the marital trust, except to the extent that they were used to pay federal or state death taxes, would qualify for the marital deduction. The IRS determined in Private Letter Ruling 9113009 that the assets in the estate trust would qualify for the marital deduction only to the extent that they exceeded the face value (rather than the present value) of any outstanding loan guarantees. The IRS based its decision on the fact that the estate trust could be called on at any time to pay the guarantees in full. With regard to the marital trust, the IRS ruled that it would not qualify for the marital deduction at all if the estate trust were not funded sufficiently to cover the full amount of the outstanding loan guarantees. The IRS reasoned that any claims not covered by the estate trust could be enforced against the marital trust. Thus, a portion of the property could be appointed to someone other than the surviving spouse, in violation of the QTIP rules. The IRS subsequently indicated, through public statements and a letter to an accountant, that it was rethinking its position on the effect of the existence of loan guarantees on the marital deduction. In March 1992, the IRS announced that it planned to revise Private Letter Ruling 9113009. That revision issued in this ruling, and Private Letter Ruling 9113009 was withdrawn.

In the instant ruling, the IRS stated that an asset passing to the surviving spouse that is encumbered should be valued in the same manner as if it were a gift to the spouse. If such asset were eligible for the marital deduction, the deduction would not be reduced by the entire unpaid balance of the loan subject to the guarantee unless it appeared likely that (1) the borrower would default after the estate trust was funded; (2) the assets in the estate trust would be used to pay the entire outstanding balance on the loans; and (3) the trust's subrogation rights against the original borrower appeared to be worthless. According to the IRS, holding an asset subject to a loan guarantee is similar to holding a note payable. In the case of a note, there is a risk of loss if the borrower defaults. Nevertheless, it is well settled, stated the IRS, that "an asset in the form of a promissory note that passes from a decedent to or for the benefit of a surviving spouse is ordinarily eligible for the marital deduction, whether the note passes outright to the spouse or to an estate trust described in Regulation § 20.2056(e)-2(b) or to a marital trust described in Section 2056(b)(5) or Section 2056(b)(7)." If assets passing from a decedent to, or for the benefit of, the spouse are subject to a loan guarantee, the spouse or trustee is subject to a risk of loss if the borrower defaults and is unable to repay the loan. If that occurred and the spouse or trust were called on to pay the loan, the spouse or trust would be subrogated to the lender and would become a creditor of the borrower for the amount paid. The spouse or trustee would then be in the same position as if the asset inherited was a promissory note. The IRS found that "[i]n either case, neither the borrower nor the lender possesses an 'interest in' or a 'power to appoint' property as those terms are used in Section 2056(b)." Therefore, the QTIP requirements are not violated. The IRS concluded that the mere presence of a loan guarantee as an encumbrance on assets passing from taxpayer at death would not ordinarily cause the complete disallowance of the marital deduction that would otherwise be allowable for the estate trust or the marital trust. According to the IRS, this would be true regardless of whether taxpayer had any financial interest in the borrower.

[Priv. Ltr. Rul. 9409018.]

¶ 11.02 COMPUTATIONS

[1] Amount Deductible

Expenses paid from income do not reduce marital deduction. Decedent died with an estate worth more than $30 million. Litigation ensued as to bequests and collateral matters. Many individuals were involved. Consequently, the estate's administration expenses reached $2 million. A settlement agreement divided the $26 million remaining principal of the residuary estate between a trust for charities and trusts for the surviving spouse. Decedent's will authorized the payment of administration expenses from either principal or income, as permitted by Georgia state law. The estate paid $500,000 of these expenses from principal and $1.5 million from income. The IRS acknowledged that the transfers to the trusts qualified for the marital or charitable deduction. The expenses that were paid from principal clearly reduced these deductions by the amount of the expenses charged to the principal of the respective trusts. (This did not increase the taxable estate, because a deduction for administration expenses replaced the marital or charitable deduction that was lost, but there was no income tax deduction for the administration expenses charged to principal.) The IRS stated that the $1.5 million of administration expenses paid from estate income likewise reduced the estate tax marital and charitable deductions dollar for dollar, just as if they had been paid from principal. (In the IRS's view, the price of an income tax deduction was the loss of an equal estate tax deduction and an increase in the taxable estate.)

Held: Affirmed for the estate. The Supreme Court affirmed the decision of the Eleventh Circuit that allowed the deductions. (The Sixth Circuit had accepted the IRS's position in Estate of Street, 974 F2d 723, 70 AFTR2d 92-6220 (6th Cir. 1992), and the Supreme Court granted certiorari in *Hubert* to resolve the conflict.) The Court issued four opinions, none of which commanded a majority. Seven justices agreed that the marital deduction was allowable in full because the expenses paid from income allocable to the marital share were not "material," but they differed in their analyses and in how to determine materiality. (Although the opinions concentrated on the marital deduction, the conclusion applied equally to the charitable deduction.) Four justices decided that the amount of the marital deduction depended on the net value (as of decedent's death) of the interest passing to the surviving spouse, determined as if there was a gift to the spouse, as provided in Regulation § 20.2056(b)-4(a). The value would not be reduced unless the administration expenses charged to income were "material." Applying gift tax valuation principles and a case (Ithaca Trust Company, 279 US 151, 7 AFTR 8856 (1929)) that used actuarial tables as of the date of a decedent's death while ignoring a decisive event several months later, these justices decided that projected values had to be used to evaluate the effect of administration expenses. Thus, to determine materiality, the date of death value of projected administration expenses chargeable to income had to be compared with the date of death value of the expected future income. The threshold of materiality might be crossed when the anticipated income used to determine the fair market value (FMV) of the surviving spouse's interest is relatively small, so that the anticipated income used to pay administration expenses might be material in comparison. Also, in determining materiality, the nature of the surviving spouse's interest should be taken into account, so that complete ownership of property—or a QTIP—would support a larger amount of administration expenses than a bequest of income before being considered material. In the instant case, the Tax Court decided, without elaborating, that the trustee's discretion to pay administration expenses from income was not material. Although substantial litigation costs might have been anticipated in light of the size and complexity of the estate, these were not necessarily material, because of the large income the trust corpus might have been expected to generate. Thus, there were no grounds to reverse the Eleventh Circuit's reliance on the Tax Court's opinion. The IRS asserted that the reduction of the marital deduction was mandated by an example in Regulation § 20.2056(b)-4(a), which requires that "material limitations" on a surviving spouse's right to income from property be taken into account in determining the value of his or her interest. A situation to which this rule may be applied, according to the regulation, is a bequest in trust for the benefit of a surviving spouse when the income from the property between a decedent's death and the funding of the trust is to be used to pay administration expenses. The IRS stated that the example was on point, but the Tax Court stated that the IRS was delving too deeply because the regulation treats this as a situation in which the use of income to pay administration expenses *may* be material, not that it *is* necessarily material. The IRS also argued that allowing an income tax deduction while not reducing the marital deduction was the equivalent of a double deduction. This argument overlooked the fact that the marital deduction is for property and not per se for income. Thus, the use of income to pay administration expenses, consistent with state law and short of the materiality threshold, does not require a reduction of the marital deduction. Three concurring justices thought that the valuation theory (determining materiality by comparing the date of death value of expected future administration expenses chargeable to income to the date of death value of the expected future income) was only one of a number of possible solutions in the absence of guidance in the statute and the regulations. Thus, it was just as reasonable to compare *actual* administration expenses with an estimate of the income that would be generated by the marital bequest during the spouse's life, as the Tax Court had done (or to compare the discounted present value of the projected income stream from the marital bequest when actual administration expenses are allocated to income with the projected value when the expenses are allocated to principal, as urged in a brief submitted by an organization of trust and estate counsel). Instead of advocating one of these methods, the concurring opinion relied on Revenue Ruling 93-48, 1993-2 CB 270. There, the IRS acknowledged that the marital deduction is not ordinarily reduced when an executor uses income from the surviving spouse's bequest to pay interest on deferred federal taxes. Thus, not every burden on the income of the marital share requires that the marital deduction be reduced. Therefore, the concurring justices concluded that there is a quantitative materiality test under which the marital deduction is affected only when the administrative expenses charged to income reach a "certain quantum of substantiality." The concurring justices noted that, as matter of first impression, the $1.5 million of administration expenses charged to income seemed material, even in light of the size of the estate. Nevertheless, they voted to affirm because of the procedural history of the case.

[Estate of Hubert, 117 S. Ct. 1124, 79 AFTR2d 97-1394, 97-1 USTC ¶ 60,261 (1997).]

Administration expenses reduce marital deduction. For several years after decedent's death, the estate filed fiduciary income tax returns on which administration expenses were claimed as deductions. On audit of the estate tax return, the IRS reduced the marital deduction by administration expenses and by interest accruing on federal estate tax and state inheritance tax deficiencies. The Tax Court ruled against the IRS. Relying on Estate of Richardson, 89 TC 1193 (1987), it determined that because the administration expenses and interest were chargeable to income (and not to principal), they would not reduce the marital deduction.

Held: Reversed in part for the IRS. On appeal, the Sixth Circuit reversed the Tax Court's holding with respect to the administration expenses. Regulation § 20.2056(b)-4(a) requires the marital deduction to be reduced to reflect the income used by the estate to pay administration expenses. Income earned by the estate from the date of death until distribution builds up the marital share, whereas expenses paid from income during this period have the effect of decreasing the amount of estate property distributable to the spouse. Therefore, payment of administration expenses from the estate's income must reduce the marital deduction to correspond to the assets in the estate at the death of decedent.

Richardson, on which the Tax Court relied, was distinguished on the ground that *Richardson* dealt only with post-death liability for interest on estate taxes, not with both administration expenses and interest. The Sixth Circuit concluded that Estate of Roney, 33 TC 801 (1960), aff'd, 294 F2d 774 (5th Cir. 1961), should be followed. There the marital deduction was reduced for administration expenses paid from income. Although *Roney,* unlike the instant case, involved a state statute requiring administration expenses to be paid from principal, the Sixth Circuit in the instant case ruled that Regulation § 20.2056(b)-4(a) controls the tax treatment of administration expenses paid from income, regardless of state law or decedent's will. With respect to the interest expenses, the Sixth Circuit affirmed the Tax Court's holding and also agreed with *Richardson* that the marital deduction is not decreased by such expenses. Unlike administration expenses, which accrue at death, interest on taxes accrues after death. Thus, estate income used to pay such interest would not affect the size of the estate at the date of death. Moreover, the marital deduction, which is fixed at death, is not diminished by the payment from income of interest expenses that accrue after death.

[Estate of Street, 974 F2d 723, 92-2 USTC ¶ 60,112, 70 AFTR2d 92-6220 (6th Cir. 1992).]

Marital deduction was reduced by estate taxes charged to marital share.
Taxpayer died in 1981 prior to the changes to Section 2056, which removed
the 50 percent cap on the estate tax marital deduction. Her assets, including insurance proceeds, came to approximately $14,400, of which only $3,254 was
actually part of the probate estate. She was the life tenant of an inter vivos
trust in which her husband held the remainder interest. This trust, which was
included in her taxable estate, was worth $781,764 on the date of her death.
Another $850,000 was included in her taxable estate under the gift-in-contem-
plation-of-death rules as they existed at the time of her death. Her gross estate
for tax purposes was therefore $1,648,250. Decedent's husband was to receive
the remainder interest in the trust, plus, under the terms of her will, up to 50
percent of her adjusted gross estate. Decedent left the typical type of will that
was in existence at the time of her death. The will contained a 50 percent
formula marital bequest to her husband and charged the nonmarital share of
the estate with the payment of estate taxes. Because of charitable deductions
that were available for the gifts in contemplation of death, estate taxes totaled
$72,852. Because the probate estate possessed only $3,254, the remainder of
the taxes necessarily had to be paid out of the inter vivos trust, which passed
to her husband and which otherwise would have qualified for the marital deduction. Because the amount passing to decedent's husband was reduced by
this tax payment, the IRS similarly reduced the marital deduction by the
amount of the tax paid out of the trust and increased the taxes payable by the
estate by $22,972.

Held: For the IRS. The Seventh Circuit reasoned that the marital deduction must be reduced by the estate taxes paid by the trust, which ultimately reduced the remainder interest passing to the surviving spouse. Accordingly, the
court upheld the increased tax assessment of $22,972 caused by this reduction
in the marital deduction. This holding was based on the principle that Section
2056(b)(4) allows a marital deduction only for the amount that a surviving
spouse actually receives. Because the amount received by the surviving spouse
was reduced in this case by the estate taxes paid, the court reasoned that the
marital deduction must be correspondingly reduced. The tax allocation clause
in the will was held to be irrelevant because the actual tax payment came from
another source. As the court noted, "had decedent been less generous during
her life, and the estate larger on her death, the taxes would have been
smaller."

[Martin, 923 F2d 504, 91-1 USTC ¶ 60,055, 67 AFTR2d 91-1174 (7th Cir.
1991).]

**Ninth Circuit holds that state inheritance taxes are not deductible from
gross estate in calculating unlimited marital deduction.** Decedent bequeathed his entire estate of approximately $20 million to his surviving wife.
The estate paid $2,299,121 in state inheritance taxes. Federal estate taxes were

assessed on the taxable estate, which consisted of the sum of the estate's debts, expenses, and the state taxes. The estate paid the federal taxes and subsequently filed suit seeking a full refund of all federal estate taxes paid, arguing that the Code's unlimited marital deduction offset any amount of federal estate taxes due, because decedent had bequeathed his entire estate to a surviving spouse. The IRS refused to refund the taxes paid, taking the view that the portion of the gross estate used to pay state and federal estate taxes did not pass to the surviving spouse and consequently did not qualify for the marital deduction. The federal district court held for the IRS, and the estate appealed.

Held: Affirmed for the IRS. The court of appeals stated that despite the extensive legislative history indicating the congressional intent to eliminate all taxes on interspousal transfers, the unlimited marital deduction is nevertheless subject to Section 2056(b)(4)(A), that states, "There shall be taken into account the effect which ... any estate, succession, legacy, or inheritance tax, has on the net value of the property passing to the surviving spouse." The court also rejected the estate's argument that though Section 2056(b)(4)(A), on its face, excludes any state and federal taxes from the deduction, the subsection was impliedly repealed by the enactment of the unlimited marital deduction under the Economic Recovery Tax Act of 1981. Accordingly, the estate was not entitled to a refund.

[Chiles, 843 F2d 367, 61 AFTR2d 88-1365, 88-1 USTC ¶ 13,763 (9th Cir. 1988).]

Seventh Circuit rejects exclusion of marital property encumbrances in calculating credit under Section 2013. Decedent died on December 2, 1978, sixteen months after her husband's death. The husband left property valued at $435,000, $336,500 of which qualified for the marital deduction. In calculating decedent's estate tax, the executors claimed a credit of $19,366 pursuant to Section 2013, which sets forth a formula for determining an estate's credit for tax on prior transfers. The executors adjusted the value of the property received from the husband's estate by reference only to those taxes and obligations chargeable to the nonmarital portion of her inheritance. The IRS allowed only $8,310 of the credit, on the ground that all encumbrances relating to the property, both marital and nonmarital, were to be deducted from the value of the property.

Held: For the estate. By the plain language and legislative history of Section 2013(d)(2), the value of transferred property must be reduced by the entire amount of all encumbrances and obligations, without regard to whether the property qualifies for the marital deduction. The court rejected the estate's argument that the credit was designed to account for taxes paid only on property that is taxable to the transferor as being contrary to the statutory scheme of Section 2013.

[Reed, 743 F2d 481, 54 AFTR2d 84-6503, 84-2 USTC ¶ 13,586 (7th Cir. 1984), cert. denied, 471 US 1135 (1985).]

Marital deduction was not allowed for post-death appreciation of marital share. Decedent died on January 23, 1988. He was a New Jersey resident and was survived by a second wife who was significantly younger than he. Decedent's son qualified as executor. Decedent's will bequeathed his stock in three close corporations to the children of his first marriage in varying percentages. The residue of his estate was left to his surviving spouse. After payment of the funeral expenses, medical expenses, debts, and specific bequests, the entire probate estate would have been consumed, leaving no residue. Accordingly, despite her status as the surviving spouse, decedent's wife would have received property consisting only of decedent's half interest in their cooperative apartment worth $108,000 and insurance proceeds of $38,889. Since her elective share of decedent's augmented estate under New Jersey law exceeded the property to which she was entitled under the will, plus the nonprobate property she received, she invoked her legal right of election under state law against the estate. The estate answered the widow's complaint and asked that the court fix the value of the surviving spouse's elective share as she had requested. This matter was settled by written agreement, dated December 28, 1988, pursuant to which decedent's surviving spouse was entitled to receive specific properties. Both she and the estate were represented by counsel in the lawsuit and the settlement, and there was no dispute that the settlement was negotiated at arm's length. The parties stipulated that the settlement of her lawsuit was "inclusive of any and all rights of the surviving spouse to share in any post-death appreciation of assets included as part of the augmented estate." On the estate tax return, the estate claimed a marital deduction of $629,107, which included advances by the estate; a car; a cash payment of $400,000; an interest in a card shop (that was given no value); a cooperative apartment worth $108,000; and proceeds of life insurance equal to $38,889. The IRS decreased the marital deduction by $143,546. The marital deduction allowed in the deficiency notice represented decedent's surviving spouse's one-third share of the "augmented estate" under New Jersey law, which was computed to equal all of decedent's assets at the date of death, using the date of death values shown on the estate tax return, as adjusted in the notice of deficiency, and reduced by debts and expenses.

 Held: For the IRS. The Tax Court indicated that the sole issue was the proper amount of the marital deduction for amounts paid to the surviving spouse in settlement of her elective share under New Jersey law. The court then turned to Section 2056(a), which allows the marital deduction, and Section 2031(a), which provides that the value of the gross estate is determined by the value of decedent's property "at the time of his death." The statutory scheme of Section 2056, the foundation for deductibility of testamentary spousal transfers, is that the value of the transferred property qualifying for the marital deduction must be included in decedent's gross estate and that such value must be determined as of the date of death. The court stated that the marital deduction must be based on the value of the property involved as of the date of death, and that the parties had stipulated that the settlement of decedent's surviving spouse's lawsuit included any rights she might have to share in the post-death appreciation of assets that formed part of the augmented estate. Accordingly, the settlement was not calculated simply by reference to decedent's estate as it existed at death. The court found that the marital deduction claimed on the return necessarily exceeded her elective share of the sum of date of death values of properties included in the estate. Therefore, the court determined that the IRS properly disallowed the portion of the marital deduction attributable to post-death increases in the value of the estate assets. Moreover, the taxpayer-estate failed to show that the assets given to decedent's surviving spouse did not include a negotiated portion of the enhancement of the estate after decedent's death. The estate relied on Estate of Hubert, 101 TC 314 (1993), aff'd, 76 AFTR2d 95-6448, 95-2 USTC ¶ 60,209 (11th Cir. 1995). The court stated, however, that that case did not discuss the statutory and regulatory provisions at issue here, which limit the marital deduction to the taxable value included in the gross estate, measured at the date of death. Regardless of the holding in *Hubert* as to the availability of the marital deduction in a settlement context, part of the settlement in the instant case included increases in the value of estate assets that occurred after death and that were consequently not included in the gross estate. The court held that that portion of the settlement was clearly not eligible for the marital deduction. The estate also cited a New Jersey case, In re Estate of Cole, 200 NJ Super. 396, 491 A2d 770 (1984), which indicated that a surviving spouse's elective share is to be valued as of the date of distribution rather than at the date of death. In response, the court noted a long-standing settlement that while state law governs the rights created in property, federal law determines how those rights may be taxed. Hence, even assuming that *Estate of Cole* correctly interprets New Jersey law, it is irrelevant under the Code because post-death appreciation in the estate's assets may not be included in the measure of the marital deduction. Therefore, the IRS's denial of part of the marital deduction was upheld.

[Estate of Agnello, 103 TC 605 (1994).]

Tax Court reaffirms its position that marital deduction is not reduced by administration expenses. Decedent died on March 12, 1987, an Oklahoma resident. She left a will under which the residue of her estate was allocated to two trusts—a residuary (nonmarital) trust and a marital trust. The maximum amount eligible for the unified credit was to be placed in the nonmarital residuary trust, with the balance going to the marital trust. Decedent's husband was to receive all the income from both trusts. The trustee had discretion to pay him as much of the principal of the marital trust as the trustee deemed necessary for the surviving spouse's care, comfort, support, maintenance, and medical attention. Upon the husband's death, the assets in the marital trust would pour over into the residuary trust and be held for the benefit of decedent's issue. Decedent's will gave her executors discretion to elect to deduct administration expenses on either the estate tax return or the income tax return. The executors elected to take the deductions on the fiduciary income tax return. The IRS issued a notice of deficiency, contending that the marital deduction should have been reduced by the administrative deductions taken on the income tax return. The right to take an estate tax deduction for property passing to the surviving spouse is found in Section 2056. Section 2056(b)(4) provides that in valuing the interest passing to the surviving spouse, one must take into consideration any taxes or other encumbrances that may reduce the surviving spouse's interest. This is addressed further in Regulation § 20.2056(b)-4(a), which states, in part:

> In determining the value of the interest in property passing to the spouse account must be taken of the effect of any material limitations upon her right to income from the property. An example of a case in which this rule may be applied is a bequest of property in trust for the benefit of decedent's spouse but the income from the property from the date of decedent's death until distribution of the property to the trustee is to be used to pay expenses incurred in the administration of the estate.

Oklahoma law mandates that if the will specifies the assets from which expenses are to be paid, the will controls. Otherwise, Oklahoma law requires that administrative expenses be charged against income. Furthermore, under the state statute, any will of a decedent dying after 1981 that contains a maximum marital deduction formula is construed to be referring to the unlimited marital deduction enacted by ERTA. The estate claimed that the provisions of decedent's will and Oklahoma law required that the administration expenses be charged against income, and therefore, provisions of the estate tax statutes and regulations discussing a reduction in the marital deduction did not apply. The estate cited for support the Tax Court's earlier decision in Estate of Street, RIA TC Memo. ¶ 88,553, even though it had been reversed by the Sixth Circuit, 974 F2d 723 (6th Cir. 1992). (The appellate court, however, did agree with the Tax Court that the marital deduction should not be reduced for interest on taxes that accrues after death.) Alternatively, the estate argued that the Sixth Circuit's decision in *Street* was factually distinguishable because it involved a single marital trust of the entire residue, rather than two trusts, one of which qualifies for the marital deduction and one which does not. Unlike the situation in *Street*, in the instant case there was a nonmarital share that was more than adequate to cover the estate's expenses. The IRS argued that the Sixth Circuit's opinion in *Street* was correct. The circuit court relied on Regulation § 20.2056(b)-(4)(a) in finding that the estate tax statute and regulations require that the marital deduction be reduced for administrative expenses. According to the Sixth Circuit, income received by the estate during administration increased the value of the marital share, and therefore, expenses paid should reduce the marital deduction.

Held: For the estate. Citing Estate of Hubert, 101 TC 314 (1993), the court reaffirmed its interpretation of Regulation § 20.2056(b)-4(a) and its rejection of the Sixth Circuit's analysis. The court went on, however, to sustain taxpayer's alternative argument that *Street* was distinguishable as involving a single (marital) trust of the entire residue. Here, the income of the separate nonmarital trust meant that the marital trust was not burdened by the administration expenses to any degree whatsoever. It was clear that, under the will and state law, the administration expenses were not to be charged against the principal or income of the marital share.

[Estate of Allen, 101 TC 351 (1993).]

Marital deduction is reduced by estate taxes. In 1976, decedent transferred his sole proprietorship to a revocable trust and granted the trustees discretionary power to pay out of principal any or all estate, inheritance, or any other taxes due by reason of his death. The trust included no provision expressly relating to the federal estate tax marital deduction. Decedent died in 1982, survived by his wife. His will also provided for the payment of all estate, inheritance, and succession taxes out of the residuary. The IRS reduced the amount of the marital deduction claimed by the estate based on the amount of state inheritance tax on the property passing to the surviving spouse and also for unpaid state and federal income taxes owed by decedent at the time of his death. The estate argued that decedent intended that all taxes were to be paid from the trust.

Held: For the IRS, in part. The Tax Court held that the marital deduction was reduced by the state inheritance tax because the trustees had discretionary power to pay that tax. However, the state inheritance tax was not reduced by the outstanding federal and state income taxes, because no law required the surviving spouse to pay decedent's unpaid income taxes.

[Estate of Reid, 90 TC 304 (1988).]

Control premium is added to block of stock passing to surviving spouse for purposes of marital deduction. When decedent died in July 1982, he owned 100 percent of the stock of a corporation. The stock was valued in his federal estate tax return at $2,834,033. Under decedent's will, his surviving wife received 51 percent of the stock of which the estate claimed a $1,996,038 marital deduction under Section 2056. The estate arrived at the stock valuation for marital deduction purposes by adding a "control premium" of 38.1 percent to the stock's value as reported in the gross estate. The IRS determined a deficiency in the estate tax. The IRS contended that the estate was not entitled to increase the value of the controlling interest in the corporation for purposes of the marital deduction above a strict 51 percent share of the value of all stock as reported in the gross estate.

   Held: For the estate. The Tax Court held that changes can be wrought in the value of an asset in a decedent's gross estate by provisions in his will that change some of the asset's characteristics. In this case, decedent, by breaking his controlling interest and giving it to his surviving spouse, created a new and different asset that carried the control premium for valuation purposes. The court stated that assets can be valued differently for purposes of Sections 2031 and 2046.

[Estate of Chenoweth, 88 TC 1577 (1987).]

IRS rules on applicable marital deduction for second limitation on credit for prior transfers. Decedent died in July 1986, survived by a spouse. The value of decedent's gross estate was $3.3 million, and allowable deductions for debts and expenses were $200,000. Decedent bequeathed the residue of the estate, $2.4 million, to the spouse. A marital deduction was allowable for this amount. The estate claimed a credit for tax on prior transfers under Section 2013 based on a transfer of $500,000 that decedent received from the estate of his parent who died in 1984. The IRS ruled that in determining the "second limitation" on the credit for tax on prior transfers, the marital deduction allowable is $2.4 million. In computing the estate tax on the reduced gross estate under Section 2013(c)(1)(B) for estates of transferees dying after 1981, the applicable marital deduction is the value of the property passing to the surviving spouse without any proportionate reduction and without limitation as to amount.

[Rev. Rul. 90-2, 1990-1 CB 169.]

Expenses paid from income still reduce marital deduction. In the ruling discussed below, administration expenses paid from the income of an estate reduced the marital deduction just as if they were paid from principal. Decedent's entire residuary estate went to a trust under which stock in a family corporation passed to decedent's children, and the remaining property was divided between two shares of a marital trust. One share was funded with an amount equal to decedent's remaining $1 million generation-skipping transfer (GST) tax exemption, and the other with the balance of the trust property. The income of both marital shares was payable to the surviving spouse quarterly. Upon her death, the principal of the generation-skipping share will be distributed to decedent's grandchildren, and the remaining principal of the marital share will be distributed to decedent's children. Decedent's will authorized the estate's administration expenses to be paid either from principal or from income earned by the estate before the funding of the marital trust. The personal representative paid them from income, and the estate claimed an income tax deduction. The estate also claimed a full marital deduction for the date of death FMV of the property passing to the marital trust. The IRS reduced the marital deduction by the administration expenses, however, just as if they had been paid from the principal of the marital trust.

An estate's administration expenses are deductible on either its estate tax return or its income tax return (if an estate tax deduction is waived under Section 642(g)). To be deductible from income, however, the will or state law must authorize the payment from income. If administration expenses are paid from principal, the marital deduction is reduced by these expenses (which otherwise would have gone into the marital trust), but this is offset by an estate tax deduction for the expenses. Even if administration expenses are paid from income and claimed as an income tax deduction, the marital deduction is nevertheless reduced, according to Estate of Street, 974 F2d 723, 70 AFTR2d 92-6220, 92-2 USTC ¶ 60,112 (6th Cir. 1992). There, the Sixth Circuit reasoned that administration expenses accrue as of a decedent's death (except for interest on estate taxes). Therefore, the expenses reduce the residue of the estate regardless of whether they are chargeable to income or to principal. Otherwise, if an estate's assets could be augmented by subsequent income, its deductions might exceed the value of the estate available for distribution to the surviving spouse. Also, the surviving spouse receives the same reduced amount whether $1 of administration expenses is paid from income or principal. The court based its reasoning on Regulation § 20.2056(b)-4(a), that states that a material limitation on the surviving spouse's right to income reduces the marital deduction. An example of this is property held in trust for a surviving spouse when income on the property from the date of a decedent's death until the distribution of the property to the trust is used to pay administration expenses. Since this appeared to be on point, the regulation was dispositive.

The IRS adopted the circuit court's reasoning to reduce the marital deduction by the administration expenses. The Tax Court, however, rejected the circuit court's reasoning, in Estate of Hubert, 101 TC 314 (1993), aff'd, 63 F3d 1083, 76 AFTR2d 95-6448, 95-2 USTC ¶ 60,209 (11th Cir. 1995). The regulation relied on by the Sixth Circuit was only a valuation provision, in the Tax Court's view, and the use of income to pay administration expenses was not necessarily a material limitation that reduced the deduction, since this income was insubstantial viewed against a lifetime of income to be received by the surviving spouse. Also, the estate was not improperly boosting the deduction by using income to fund the expenses, because the income was not included in the gross estate. Therefore, no further adjustment was required.

[Tech. Adv. Mem. 9617003.]

Taxes payable from marital share reduce deduction. According to the ruling discussed below, a qualified disclaimer made by a surviving spouse to allow immediate funding of a generation-skipping trust generated estate tax payable from a marital trust, which further reduced the marital deduction. Decedent's will directed the distribution of all probate assets to a revocable trust established by decedent and spouse during decedent's life. Under the trust, decedent's assets were to be allocated to a family trust and to a marital trust. The marital trust was to be funded to minimize taxes in decedent's estate and was divided into two separate trusts. The first trust was a QTIP trust. It used decedent's remaining $1 million GST tax exemption by a reverse QTIP election under Section 2652(a)(3), that permits decedent to be the transferor for GST tax purposes even though the trust is includable in the surviving spouse's estate because of the QTIP election. After the surviving spouse's death, the trust was to be distributed to generation-skipping trusts for the benefit of decedent's grandchildren and more remote descendants. The second marital trust provided for the payment to the surviving spouse of all income and certain principal. After the surviving spouse's death, the remaining principal was to be payable to trusts for decedent's daughters. Decedent's personal representatives would elect to qualify this trust as a QTIP trust. The family trust was funded with decedent's assets that do not pass to the marital trust. The surviving spouse wanted to disclaim the entire interest in the first marital trust. Under the terms of the trust, a disclaimed interest would pass to the generation-skipping trusts as if the surviving spouse had predeceased decedent. Any taxes generated by the disclaimer would be paid from the second marital trust. The estate asked the IRS whether this provision would be given effect so that the taxes would reduce the marital share of the surviving spouse.

The IRS explained that if the disclaimer is qualified under Section 2518, the surviving spouse is treated as never having received the disclaimed property. Consequently, the first marital trust will no longer qualify for the marital deduction, and estate tax will be due. Under Revenue Ruling 79-14, 1979-1 CB 309, if an executor has discretion to pay estate taxes from a marital trust, the marital deduction is reduced by the taxes that could have been paid from the trust, whether or not the taxes are in fact paid from the trust. In the instant case, the direction to pay taxes from the second marital trust would be given effect, and the marital deduction would be reduced by federal and state estate and inheritance taxes paid from that trust or that could have been paid from that trust. Furthermore, the additional taxes caused by this reduction of the marital deduction would generate additional taxes, that would in turn reduce the marital deduction.

[Priv. Ltr. Rul. 9541035.]

[2] Allocation of Taxes

Taxes properly allocated to taxable portion of estate in accordance with state law. Decedent's will provided bequests to several trusts for the benefit of her children. Decedent left the residue of her estate to her husband, who also was the beneficiary of an irrevocable intervivos trust previously created by decedent. While the will mentioned the residue as the source of funds to pay the estate tax, other provisions of the will referred to "other sources" and granted the executors the authority to minimize taxes. The executors paid the estate tax from the taxable portion of the estate rather than from the residue, which qualified for the marital deduction. The IRS issued a notice of deficiency contending that, based on the will, the tax should have been paid from the residue, thus reducing the martial deduction. The Ohio state probate court concluded that the executors acted properly in apportioning the estate taxes in accordance with the state apportionment statute. The Tax Court, however, agreed with the IRS.

Held: Reversed for the estate. In adjudicating property rights, federal courts are bound by the rulings of a state's highest court. Here, the will contained no specific and clear intent that the estate taxes be paid in a manner contrary to the apportionment statute, and the Ohio Supreme Court previously held that such intent was necessary to avoid application of the statute.

[Estate of Swallen, 98 F3d 919, 78 AFTR2d 96-6905, 96-2 USTC ¶ 60,248 (6th Cir. 1996).]

Estate tax burden cannot be shifted to entirety property. The estate of decedent, who died in 1978, included both probate and nonprobate property. The probate property consisted primarily of real estate in Kentucky. The nonprobate property included decedent's residence in Virginia and a checking account held with his wife in tenancy-by-the-entirety. Under decedent's will, his wife received a life estate in the Kentucky real property, and his daughter took the remainder interest. Thus, the Kentucky property was not eligible for the marital deduction available under Section 2056(b)(1). Decedent also directed that "all death duties" on the Kentucky real estate were to be paid out of other assets of his estate. The residue of the estate was left to decedent's wife, who was also named as the executor. At the time the will was written, there were sufficient assets in the residue of the probate estate to pay the state and federal estate taxes and the administration expenses; however, this was no longer true by the time decedent died. Payment of taxes and administration expenses had completely depleted the residue, making it ineligible for the marital deduction. In 1982, the IRS issued a notice of deficiency. The IRS determined that because of the tax provisions in the will, the estate taxes attributable to the Kentucky property should have been taken out of the Virginia property held in tenancy-by-the-entirety. This reduced the marital deduction on the Virginia property and increased total estate taxes. The Tax Court ruled in the IRS's favor, finding that decedent had the right, under Virginia Code Annotated § 64.1-165, to specify the assets from which estate taxes were to be paid. This right overrode the general apportionment statute found in Virginia Code Annotated § 64.1-162, by which estate taxes were allocated against the assets that generated the tax (except to the extent that a beneficiary of an interest can benefit from any exemptions, deductions, and exclusions under Virginia law). Because the tenancy-by-the-entirety property was included in the taxable estate, the Tax Court concluded that the estate taxes could be shifted to that property, reducing the marital deduction. On appeal, the Fourth Circuit affirmed the Tax Court's decision. It found a distinction between property includable in the gross estate but not taxable because of an exemption, and property not includable in the estate. The Fourth Circuit agreed with the Tax Court that decedent had authority to allocate estate taxes against nonprobate assets, even if that would reduce the marital deduction. The marital deduction is determined under federal law, not under state law, stated the court, and it is reduced by any encumbrances against that property. The court was also not persuaded by the argument that a person owning property in tenancy-by-the-entirety cannot invade the property without his spouse's consent. It found that this rule did not apply in the case of an estate, because ownership of the property was solely in the spouse (though the IRS still had authority to tax the property). The estate requested an en banc rehearing of the Fourth Circuit's ruling.

Held: Reversed for the estate. Sitting en banc, the Fourth Circuit reversed its earlier ruling in a 6-5 opinion. It saw a different relationship between the federal and state statutes. The court focused on the fact that even though nonprobate assets are part of the taxable estate and the federal estate tax is actually imposed on the executor, an executor has control only over probate assets. Prior to the enactment of the Virginia apportionment statute in 1946, estate taxes could be paid only out of probate assets. Virginia Code Annotated § 64.1-162 gave an executor the right to collect estate taxes from nonprobate assets, in "the proportion that the value of the [nonprobate] asset bears to the [gross estate less exemptions, deductions, and exclusions]." The statute also preserved an existing right that testators had to create their own scheme for apportioning taxes among their *probate* assets. The court determined, however, that if the testator creates such a scheme, then the apportionment statute is not applicable: "The provisions of the will . . . shall be given effect to the same extent as if this article had not been enacted." In that case, the executor could not collect estate taxes from the nonprobate property. Applying this rule to the present case, the court concluded that when decedent included an apportionment clause in his will, he limited the source of those tax payments to probate assets. The court summarized its opinion by finding that decedent lacked the power to impose taxes created by probate assets on tenancy-by-the-entirety property and that therefore all of the entirety property passed to his spouse and qualified for the marital deduction.

[Estate of Reno, 945 F2d 733, 91-2 USTC ¶ 60,083, 68 AFTR2d 91-6035 (4th Cir. 1991).]

Provision in will that death taxes be paid from residue does not diminish surviving spouse's interest in the residue. Decedent died in 1983. His will contained specific legacies to his surviving spouse and others, and it directed that 50 percent of the residue was to be paid to his surviving spouse. Death taxes were also to be paid from the residue of the estate. In determining its marital deduction for purposes of the federal estate tax, the estate reduced the value of the surviving spouse's interest in the residue of the estate by her pro rata share of the federal estate tax due on her specific legacies, but did not reduce the value of her interest in the residue by any of the federal estate tax due on the residue itself. The IRS determined a deficiency in the estate tax on the ground that the value of the surviving spouse's interest in the residue should have been reduced by a pro rata share of the federal estate tax due on the residue itself, thus reducing the marital deduction accordingly. The estate contended that the amount passing to the spouse, and thus eligible for the marital deduction, was not responsible for any death taxes allocable to the residual interests.

Held: For the estate. The Tax Court noted that state law provided that in the absence of a contrary provision in the will, death taxes were to be apportioned to the respective interests of the beneficiaries. However, any exemption or deduction allowed by reason of the relationship of a beneficiary to decedent was to inure to that beneficiary. The Tax Court reasoned that this deflected estate taxes from the marital deduction portion of a residuary interest. Nevertheless, the marital deduction portion of the residue was responsible for nearly half the taxes on the specific legacies, and, under Section 2056(b)(4)(A), this amount did not qualify for the marital deduction.

[Estate of Phillips, 90 TC 797 (1988).]

Interest paid on death taxes is held not to reduce marital deduction. Decedent died in 1982, survived by his wife. His will basically divided his residual estate into a unified credit shelter trust and the balance to his surviving spouse. The will provided that decedent's wife was to receive that portion of the residue of his estate required to obtain the maximum allowable marital deduction. It also contained a provision that any amounts paid out of the residuary estate for inheritance, succession, or estate taxes were to be charged against that portion of the residuary estate that was devised to the trust. The IRS later assessed a deficiency and contended that the interest due on the deficiency resulted in a reduction in the allowable marital deduction. The IRS's theory was that the interest was chargeable against principal of the estate, not against its income; therefore, the assets available to fund the marital share were reduced. The IRS also argued that decedent's will provided for payment out of the residuary estate of all fees and expenses that were incident to the administration of the estate, and asserted that interest on federal estate taxes is incident to the administration of an estate.

Held: For the estate. Although agreeing that interest on estate taxes is incident to the administration of an estate, the court felt that that was not determinative of whether the interest should have been charged against the principal or the income of the estate in this case. The court stated that decedent had specifically provided that the death taxes were to be charged against the nonmarital share of the residuary estate, and had emphasized many times in his will that his goal was to obtain the maximum marital deduction. Also, it was more natural and equitable that interest on deferred estate and inheritance taxes be chargeable to the income from the estate and that it was clearly the intention of decedent through the language in his will that the marital share not be burdened with interest on estate taxes. The court found no cases on point to affirm or refute its holding, but it cited several cases dealing with the chargeability of administration expenses and death taxes themselves, as related to the marital deduction, to support its holding.

[Estate of Richardson, 89 TC 1193 (1987).]

Tax apportionment clause decreased marital deduction. Decedent bequeathed half of her residuary estate to her surviving spouse. The other half went to a trust. Her will expressly indicated that all estate tax paid be borne by the residuary estate, "as an expense of administration without apportionment and without contribution or reimbursement from anyone . . . , including beneficiaries." Decedent's estate disagreed with the IRS over the apportionment of estate taxes between the husband's and trust's portions of the residuary. The estate argued that the husband's portion was free from all estate tax; the trust was supposed to pay federal estate tax. The IRS, on the other hand, imposed an equal tax burden on husband and trust, splitting the tax burden fifty-fifty between them. Section 2056(a) allows a federal estate tax marital deduction from a decedent's gross estate for the value of property interests passing from decedent to the surviving spouse. Section 2056 does not specify how taxes are to be apportioned among the interests comprising the estate, however. In general, state law governs how the estate tax burden is allocated among the estate's assets. Under the Texas state law applicable in this case, in the absence of specific directions regarding apportionment in decedent's will, the estate tax burden is apportioned according to the taxable value of each recipient's respective interests in the estate. The statute thus takes the marital deduction into account; because the marital portion adds no value to the taxable estate, no estate tax would be apportioned to the surviving spouse's bequest. When the will does specify apportionment among recipients, Texas law allows decedent's wishes regarding the estate tax burden to be fulfilled. Thus, decedent is allowed to "opt out" of the statutory framework of federal estate tax apportionment, in favor of his or her own plans. In this case, the estate claimed decedent's will did not "opt out" of the statutory framework, claiming that any of the residuary estate going to the husband still qualified for a marital deduction. The IRS, nevertheless, countered that decedent had "opted out," that the husband's share of the residuary estate no longer fully qualified for the marital deduction since decedent's will specified her own plan.

Held: For the IRS. According to *Fine*, 90 TC 1068 (1988), the "without apportionment" language in decedent's will regarding the residuary estate meant two things: (1) The maximized marital deduction safeguarded by state statute did not apply, and (2) specific bequests under the will did not bear the burden of any of the taxes due. Thus, by putting an express provision in her will regarding apportionment of the residuary, decedent negated the state law that would have shielded her husband from estate taxes through the marital deduction. Therefore, there could be no apportionment of the tax burden within the residuary. The estate then argued that the applicable statute was not law when the will was drafted. By this token, the estate should not have been limited by the statute. That, the Tax Court said, did not negate the plain meaning of the will that the estate tax not be apportioned within the residuary estate, however. The estate was limited by the language of the statute. After all, decedent could have altered the will before she died after the statute became law. There was a six-year window of opportunity between the law's enactment and her death. This highlights the importance of reviewing wills periodically to determine whether they should be revised because of law changes. The estate also argued that the phrase "without apportionment" meant that only the trust had to pay estate taxes; the husband's portion was supposed to pay nothing because no tax was due on a bequest to him. The court, however, said that this interpretation was contrary to the plainly recognized meaning of the phrase "without apportionment." Also, the Tax Court was unwilling to assume that decedent would have wanted an interpretation in favor of the husband over the trust. Testimony indicated that she wanted to provide for her children (through the trust), as well as her surviving spouse.

[Miller, 76 TCM 892, RIA TC Memo. ¶ 98,416 (1998).]

Value of property passing to surviving spouse is not reduced by interest on unpaid tax. Decedent's will provided for a specified legacy free of estate tax to his parents with the remainder passing equally to his spouse and child. The estate elected to pay the tax in installments and accrued the interest thereon. State law required that tax and interest be paid from the beneficial interests that generated the tax, except where specifically exonerated by the will. The value of the property passing to the spouse was not reduced by the interest for purposes of the marital deduction. The bequest to the spouse did not give rise to any taxes.

[Rev. Rul. 80-159, 1980-1 CB 206.]

¶ 11.03 WILL CONSTRUCTION

[1] Testamentary Intent

Bequest does not qualify for marital deduction. In his will the testator, a Tennessee resident who died in 1976, stated the following: "I hereby give and bequeath all of my personal property to my wife, Mozell Evans. I do hereby direct and instruct my said wife to use a portion of said personal property in the event the same becomes necessary for the use and benefit of my daughter, Marie Manley." The will further stated that the testator intended "to give to my wife, Mozell Evans, all of my personal property to use as she so desires and in the event any of said personal property remains after the death of my wife, Mozell Evans, I give and bequeath the same to my two grandchildren, Marvin Keith Evans and Jeffrey Manley, to share and share alike." On audit, the IRS raised the issue of whether the testator's will created an estate in his widow qualifying for the marital deduction permitted by the federal estate tax law. The district court held that the bequest did not so qualify.

Held: Affirmed for the IRS. The controlling statute was Section 2056 as it existed prior to amendment by the Economic Recovery Tax Act of 1981. Whether a bequest of personal property qualified for a marital deduction was a federal question to be determined under federal law. However, the issue of exactly what kind of interest the widow received was to be determined under Tennessee law. The cardinal rule in construing a will under Tennessee law is that the intent of the testator must prevail over all other rules of construction, except those founded upon public policy and the necessity of sustaining established principles of law. The testator's widow did not receive under the will an unlimited power to appoint the entire estate in the personal property to herself or to her estate. Thus, the bequest did not qualify for the marital deduction.

[Evans, 719 F2d 201, 52 AFTR2d 83-6459, 83-2 USTC ¶ 13,542 (6th Cir. 1983).]

State court modification of trust instrument is ineffective to save marital deduction. Decedent established an inter vivos trust for his family's benefit that directed the trustees to pay decedent's spouse "so much of the net income . . . as . . . (she) may from time to time require to maintain . . . (her) usual and customary standard of living." The trustees were also authorized to pay the principal of the trust to accomplish this end. Upon the spouse's death, the trust corpus was to be distributed to decedent's children in equal shares. In addition to the trust, decedent executed a pour-over will providing for the distribution of property to the trustees for administration as part of the trust. After the trust was established, decedent directed his accountant to review the instrument. Decedent indicated that he was not concerned with creating the maximum marital deduction, but rather wanted some indication that the trust would provide financial security for his wife and that it would not create a tax problem. No further efforts were made to modify the trust. After decedent's death in 1983, his estate was advised that the trust as drafted would not qualify for the estate tax marital deduction, because the trust instrument did not provide for distribution of all trust income to the surviving spouse. The trustees petitioned the state court for modification of the trust to qualify it for the marital deduction. The IRS was not made a party to that proceeding. A decree modifying the trust was entered by the state court, and this court also specifically authorized the executor of decedent's estate to make the QTIP election. The IRS denied the marital deduction for the trust on the ground that all income was not payable to the surviving spouse as required by Section 2056(b)(7)(B)(ii).

Held: For the IRS. The estate's contention that the trust was ambiguous and that decedent intended the surviving spouse to receive all of the income from the trust was rejected. The language was not ambiguous, and thus there was no reason to examine the circumstances surrounding the trust execution. Even if the court did look at the surrounding circumstances, it would find that decedent's interest was in providing security to the spouse rather than in maximizing the marital deduction. In addition, the state court modification represented a substantial change in the trust instrument after the IRS secured rights under the original trust. The IRS's right to estate taxes accrues based on the trust instrument as it existed at the time of death. Accordingly, the Tax Court would not give effect to a local court order that modified the trust instrument after the IRS acquired rights under its provisions. This case was distinguished from prior cases where retroactive change was allowed because a mistake had been made.

[Estate of Nicholson, 94 TC 666 (1990).]

General direction in will to maximize marital deduction is held to be ineffective. Decedent died in 1983, survived by his wife. His will directed that certain specific property was to pass to his widow; that all federal and state death taxes were to be paid out of the residuary estate, without apportionment; that his widow was to receive one half of the residuary estate, with the remainder divided equally among his brother and two nephews; and that any power, duty, or discretionary authority granted to the executor was to be void to the extent that its exercise caused his estate to lose all or any part of the tax benefit afforded by the marital deduction under federal and state laws. On decedent's federal estate tax return, the estate reported the surviving spouse's portion of the residuary estate as eligible for the marital deduction without reduction for taxes and administrative expenses. In its notice of deficiency, the IRS determined, pursuant to the terms of decedent's will, that the allowable marital deduction must be reduced by the portion of the estate's administrative expenses and estate and inheritance tax burden allocable to the surviving spouse's share of the residuary estate, thereby increasing the taxable estate. The estate argued that the surviving spouse's one-half interest in the residuary estate was not required to bear a proportionate share of the taxes, because the will mandated that the executor take no action that would have the effect of reducing the allowable marital deduction. Only by interpreting the will in this way, the estate contended, could decedent's intent to maximize the allowable marital deduction be effectuated.

Held: For the IRS. The court noted that the will provided that taxes were to be paid out of the residuary estate without apportionment. The "without apportionment" language, according to the court, meant that the maximized marital deduction safeguarded by the state probate code did not apply, and that the specific bequests to decedent's widow were not to bear any portion of the taxes due. Decedent could not, without more than a general limitation on the exercise of executors' discretion, be found to have intended the widow's share of the residuary to be free of taxes while the remaining distributees of the residuary bore the full amount of taxes. Accordingly, the IRS's deficiency was upheld.

[Estate of Fine, 90 TC 1068 (1988).]

Marital deduction is reduced by debt of estate, despite agreement of beneficiaries and local court decree. Before he died, decedent had made a loan to one of his sons. The amount of the unpaid loan plus accrued interest totaled $210,615.97. At the time of his death, decedent owed this same amount to a bank. In his last will, decedent devised various parcels of real property to his two sons and left the residue of his estate to his surviving spouse. He directed in the will that all his debts be paid from his residuary estate. He further directed that if he was survived by his wife, the son to whom he had provided the loan was required to pay the balance of the loan to the estate within 120 days of decedent's death. After his death, decedent's surviving spouse and two sons, who together constituted all of the beneficiaries under decedent's last will, agreed to allow the son to pay his $210,615.97 debt to the estate by paying the estate's identical debt to the bank. The IRS determined that the $210,615.97 owed by decedent's son was required to be included in the gross estate and that the marital deduction was required to be reduced by the amount that decedent owed the bank. After the estate received the IRS's notice of deficiency, it filed an ex parte petition with the probate division of the local district court and was granted an order construing the will that decedent intended to pass real property to his son encumbered by decedent's debt to the bank, and that decedent did not intend his debt to the bank to become an obligation of his estate. The IRS was not a party to this proceeding. The estate argued that the debt was not required to be paid out of decedent's estate, and therefore did not reduce the estate's marital deduction. In support of its position, the estate pointed to the construction of decedent's will given by the probate division of the state district court.

Held: For the IRS. The Tax Court noted that it was not bound by the construction given decedent's will by the state district court, because under local law, the state district court lacked jurisdiction to reform decedent's will. The Tax Court concluded that if decedent had intended to allow his son to satisfy his debt to him by taking the property subject to the mortgage, he would have said so in his will, and that under local law, the terms of decedent's will required the debt to be paid from the residuary estate. Accordingly, the Tax Court held that the debt reduced the estate's marital deduction as the IRS had determined.

[Estate of Preisser, 90 TC 767 (1988).]

Estate is entitled to marital deduction for half of jointly held property. Decedent and his wife died simultaneously in an automobile accident. Decedent's will provided that in a simultaneous death situation, "it shall be presumed that my wife predeceased me." The IRS denied the marital deduction for one half of jointly owned property on the ground that the wife did not survive the husband under the will provision.

Held: For the estate. Under New York law, decedent is presumed to be survived by his spouse unless the dispositive document provides otherwise. Here the jointly held property passed outside of the will, so the will's provision did not override the presumption.

[Estate of Racca, 76 TC 416 (1981), acq. 1982-2 CB 2.]

Marital deduction is governed by state abatement statute where estate is insufficient to satisfy all legacies. Decedent's estate consisted of property sufficient to pay all debts and taxes, but not enough to pay all of decedent's legacies in full. On its tax return, the estate claimed a marital deduction, under Section 2056, of $250,886. The IRS determined a deficiency in estate tax, based largely on its findings that the marital deduction was $122,799. The IRS argued that the estate lacked sufficient property to satisfy the full legacy left to the surviving spouse.

Held: For the IRS. The calculation of the marital deduction is limited under Section 2056 to the value of property passing to the surviving spouse. Because the property from which debts and taxes are payable, and the order of such payments, are governed by state law, it is necessary to look to state abatement statutes in order to ascertain those legacies that must yield in a situation where the legacies exceed the value of the estate. In the instant case, the court found that state classification of general and specific legacies under the abatement statute resulted in a radically reduced marital deduction when each separate legacy was considered. In its determination, the court looked to decedent's testamentary intent and applied state law accordingly.

[Estate of Short, 68 TC 184 (1977), acq. 1977-2 CB 2.]

Extrinsic evidence is used to establish that amendment to trust creates marital deduction, but deduction is disallowed. An individual established a will in 1978 that made specific bequests to the spouse, with the balance of the estate passing to a revocable trust. The trust provided that upon the death of the individual or the spouse, the trust would be divided into a marital share, consisting of the surviving spouse's interest in their community property, and a family share, consisting of decedent's interest in the community property. The marital share could be revoked by the surviving spouse, but the family share became irrevocable upon the individual's death. The beneficiaries of the family share were to be the surviving spouse and the couple's daughter. The corporate trustee had discretionary authority to distribute the income and principal as it deemed proper. Upon the death of the surviving spouse, the property was to pass one-half in trust for decedent's daughter and one-half in trust for decedent's grandchildren.

In 1983, the individual amended the dispositive provisions of the trust to provide that when the terms of the trust provided for a share of the estate to be subject to the maximum estate tax marital deduction, that expressed intent should be considered as referring to the unlimited estate tax marital deduction. Because the individual's 1978 estate plan had never contemplated the use of the marital deduction, however, the 1978 trust contained no references to "one-half of a settlor's federal adjusted gross estate" or to the "maximum marital deduction." Thus, the 1983 trust amendment did not refer to any language, dispositive or otherwise, found within the trust.

In 1984, the individual died, and the estate's personal representative distributed the tangible personal property and real estate to the surviving spouse following the will's specific bequests. The representative distributed $325,000 to the family share of the trust, and, because the marital share of the trust had been revoked by the surviving spouse and replaced by a new revocable grantor trust, the estate's remaining assets were distributed to the new trust. As a result of this distribution plan, which was approved by a state probate court in 1985, the surviving spouse received 75 percent of decedent's estate outright. The estate claimed a marital deduction for the assets distributed to the surviving spouse, including those assets distributed to the marital share portion of the trust.

The IRS stated that under Section 2056, extrinsic evidence was admissible to establish the effect of the 1983 amendment to the trust. The IRS noted, however, that no evidence was presented to show that decedent intended to alter the dispositive scheme of the trust to qualify for the unlimited marital deduction. In particular, the IRS noted, there was no evidence to establish decedent's intent to revoke the interests of the child and the grandchildren in all but 25 percent of the estate. "Given the fact that the marital deduction had never figured heretofore in decedent's dispositive scheme, it is unlikely, as a matter of fact, that decedent ever contemplated the distribution of the estate approved by the state court," the IRS concluded. The IRS further concluded that the 1983 amendment would not affect the dispositive provisions of the trust for federal estate tax purposes. The IRS stated that the highest state court in the jurisdiction would have required clear and convincing evidence of a mistake to reform the trust, and no such evidence was available. The distribution approved by the lower state court was not binding for federal estate tax purposes.

[Priv. Ltr. Rul. 8706014.]

[2] Formula Clauses

Because decedent's intent was to minimize estate taxes, not to maximize marital deduction, ERTA transitional rule, ERTA § 403(e)(3), is inapplicable to limit the estate's marital deduction. The Tax Court held that the estate was entitled to the unlimited marital deduction allowed by Economic Recovery Tax Act of 1981 (ERTA) because the estate had established that decedent's will did not contain a maximum marital deduction clause formula within the meaning of the transitional rule of ERTA § 403(e)(3). The Tax Court based its decision on the following facts. Decedent executed his will and marital trust on March 2, 1981 (prior to ERTA's effective date), and died on April 22, 1982. His will funded the marital trust under a formula requiring the trust to be funded with the lesser of (1) an amount equal to the maximum marital deduction allowable under the federal estate tax and (2) the amount that, after taking into account all credits, exemptions, and deductions, other than the marital deduction, would result in the elimination of all federal estate tax on decedent's estate. At the time the will and this trust were executed, the law provided for a marital deduction equal to the greater of $250,000 and 50 percent of the gross estate. In 1981, Congress enacted ERTA, which repealed this provision and allowed an unlimited marital deduction. Neither decedent's will nor the trust was amended after the enactment of ERTA. The IRS assessed the estate on the ground that it was not entitled, under the ERTA § 403(e)(3) transitional rule, to ERTA's unlimited marital deduction.

    Held: Affirmed for the estate. The transitional rule was intended to preserve decedent's intent where a marital deduction formula clause was used. Without such a transitional rule, a formula clause under the ERTA change to the marital deduction might cause more property than decedent intended to pass to his spouse. Here the provision used by decedent was intended to minimize his estate taxes, not to limit the property bequeathed to his spouse to the maximum marital deduction allowable. Accordingly, the transitional rule was inapplicable.

[Bruning, 888 F2d 657, 89-2 USTC ¶ 13,821, 64 AFTR2d 89-5950 (10th Cir. 1989).]

Marital deduction is limited to one half of adjusted gross estate where formula clause is used in decedent's pre-1981 will. Decedent executed his will in 1964, making no subsequent amendments or codicils prior to his death in 1983. The will provided for a fractional marital bequest in an amount equal to the maximum marital deduction allowable in determining the federal estate tax. Under current law, the marital deduction is unlimited, but prior to the Economic Recovery Tax Act of 1981 (ERTA), the maximum amount of the marital deduction was the greater of $250,000 or one half of the adjusted gross estate. Under ERTA transitional rules, Section 2056 as it existed prior to ERTA applies to pre-ERTA wills. Thus, estates passing by wills executed and not amended before September 12, 1981, cannot take advantage of the unlimited marital deduction. Each state may, however, enact provisions making the amended Section 2056 applicable to wills executed before ERTA. Kentucky, the state of decedent's domicile, has not enacted any such statute. The purpose of this transitional rule is to prevent an unintended testamentary disposition in wills executed before the enactment of ERTA that contain maximum marital deduction formula clauses. The estate claimed an unlimited marital deduction on the ground that the language of the will showed an intent on decedent's part that changes in federal law concerning the marital deduction were to apply to his estate. The IRS asserted that no such intention was evident and that the transitional rule thus should apply.

Held: For the IRS. The court stated that the purpose of the transitional rule is to preserve, rather than defeat, the testator's intent. There was no specific language in the will that showed that decedent intended the marital bequest to change if federal tax law changed. The will states that he intended to bequeath a share "equal to the maximum marital deduction allowable," and this is precisely the type of provision addressed by the transitional rule in ERTA. The court cited several cases in which clauses almost identical to the aforementioned were held to be formula clauses to which the transitional rule applied. The transitional rule was, therefore, properly applied by the IRS to limit the marital deduction available to decedent's estate.

[Liberty Nat'l Bank & Trust Co., 867 F2d 302, 89-1 USTC ¶ 13,797, 63 AFTR2d 89-1550 (6th Cir. 1989).]

Unlimited marital deduction is allowed in pre-ERTA will. Decedent died in 1982. His will, executed in 1980, contained a standard marital deduction provision that provided that his surviving spouse would receive minimum amount necessary to secure the lesser of (1) the maximum marital deduction allowable for federal estate tax purposes or (2) the minimum marital deduction that, after taking into account the unified credit available to his estate for federal estate tax purposes, would result in no federal estate tax. On audit, the IRS reduced the marital deduction claimed by the estate on its federal estate tax return on the ground that the interest passing to the surviving spouse was determined by a formula marital deduction will provision that was not modified or amended after the enactment of Section 403(e) of the Economic Recovery Tax Act of 1981 (ERTA). Because decedent did not modify his will to allow the unlimited marital deduction, the IRS claimed that the allowable marital deduction was reduced to one-half of the adjusted gross estate. The estate contended, on the other hand, that it was entitled to an unlimited marital deduction under Section 2056 because decedent's will did not contain a maximum marital deduction formula.

Held: For the estate. The court stated that in 1981, Congress enacted ERTA, which permitted interspousal transfers to be made free of tax and thus amended Section 2056 to provide for an unlimited marital deduction. This new deduction was applicable to estates of those decedents dying after December 31, 1981. Congress enacted ERTA's transitional rule to cover those situations where decedents with pre-1981 formula clauses died in 1982 or later years, as did decedent in the instant case. The transitional rule provided that the new provision for an unlimited marital deduction would apply to wills executed prior to September 14, 1981, that contained maximum marital deduction formula clauses, only if (1) the formula was amended before decedent's death to refer specifically to the unlimited marital deduction or (2) a state statute applicable to the estate was enacted construing the old maximum marital deduction formula clauses as referring to the new unlimited marital deduction. Because there was no such state statute in decedent's state, the court resolved the case on the maximum marital deduction formula clause issue. The court stated that the formula marital deduction provision in decedent's will was not, in the words of ERTA § 403(e)(3)(B), "a formula expressly providing that the spouse is to receive the maximum amount of property qualifying for the marital deduction allowable by Federal law"; rather, it was a formula expressly providing that the spouse was to receive the minimum amount necessary to ensure that decedent's estate pays the least amount of federal estate tax. Consequently, it was clear that decedent never intended by this provision to pass to his spouse the greater of $250,000 or 50 percent of the value of his adjusted gross estate (unless, of course, one of these amounts turned out to be the minimum amount necessary to ensure that decedent's estate paid the least amount of federal estate tax). The court concluded, therefore, that the formula marital deduction provision in decedent's will was not a "formula" within the meaning of ERTA § 403(e)(3)(B) and that ERTA § 403(e)(3) did not preclude the estate from qualifying for an unlimited marital deduction under Section 2056.

[Estate of Neisen, 865 F2d 162, 89-1 USTC ¶ 13,790, 63 AFTR2d 89-1509 (8th Cir. 1988).]

Extrinsic evidence is not allowed to negate effect of formula clause on marital deduction. Decedent executed her will in 1977 and did not alter, amend, or revoke it prior to her death in 1982. Her will devised to her surviving husband that portion of her separate property and, to the extent necessary, her community property that would equal the maximum marital deduction provided by the Code. Decedent's estate was valued at $319,000 and consisted entirely of community property. Her surviving spouse disclaimed all he was entitled to under the will, except $70,300 in cash and notes. Decedent's estate claimed a marital deduction in that amount. The IRS disallowed the deduction on the ground that decedent's will contained a maximum marital deduction formula within the meaning of Section 403(e)(3) of the Economic Recovery Tax Act of 1981 (ERTA), and therefore the unlimited marital deduction under Section 2056 of the Code (as that section applies to the estates of decedents dying after December 31, 1981) was not applicable to decedent's estate. Decedent's estate contended that her will did not contain a maximum marital deduction formula within the meaning of ERTA § 403(e)(3), and therefore the estate should have been allowed the unlimited marital deduction available under the law effective in 1982, the date of decedent's death. The estate argued that under local law, decedent's will was ambiguous because her testamentary intent could not be definitely determined from the four corners of the instrument. On this basis, the estate concluded that the court should have disregarded the document's express language and, instead, pieced together, from extrinsic evidence, an overriding intent on the part of decedent to minimize federal estate taxes.

Held: For the IRS. The court stated that it was not free to wander outside the confines of a testamentary instrument to determine, under state law, the intent of a decedent where the language contained in that instrument caused it to fall squarely within a set of criteria established by Congress. The court said that any ambiguity in decedent's will was caused by changes in the available marital deduction, not, as the estate seemed to suggest, from the language of the will itself. The court noted that Congress, in enacting the unlimited marital deduction, recognized that this change in federal estate tax law could create ambiguities in existing wills (such as decedent's) that expressly referenced and depended on the then-existing marital deduction. It provided a method for resolving such ambiguities in ERTA § 403(e)(3). Once the criteria set out in this transitional rule had been met, the court stated that it could not vary or change the result prescribed by Congress based on an after-the-fact state law argument as to what decedent may or may not have intended. Because the court concluded that the marital deduction provision in decedent's will was a marital deduction formula to which ERTA § 403(e)(3) applied, the marital deduction available to decedent's estate was determined under Section 2056(c) of the Code as in effect prior to the repeal by ERTA. Accordingly, the IRS's allowance of the marital deduction was sustained.

[Estate of Christmas, 91 TC 769 (1988).]

Full marital deduction is allowed for recomputation of gross estate under Section 691(c). Taxpayer's husband died in 1975. His employment contract provided that his annual bonus payments would continue to be paid to his spouse after his death. The husband left most of his other property to a trust. After payment of taxes, debts, and the expenses of administering the husband's estate, the trust property was divided into a marital part and a nonmarital part. The marital part consisted of property equal in value to the maximum marital deduction allowable to his estate, less the value of nontrust property includable in the gross estate that passed to taxpayer and qualified for the marital deduction. The bonus payments were such nontrust property. Thus, the value of the right to the payments was subtracted from the maximum marital deduction in determining the marital part. The marital part passed to taxpayer and was eligible for the marital deduction. The nonmarital part consisted of the remainder of the trust property. Taxpayer did not report all of the bonus payments in 1976 and 1977. The IRS and taxpayer subsequently agreed that the payments were includable in taxpayer's gross income as income in respect of a decedent (IRD). They disagreed, however, about the amount of the deduction allowable to taxpayer pursuant to Section 691(c)(1)(A) (deduction for estate tax), as a consequence of including the bonus payments in her gross income. The controversy centered on how to calculate the estate tax attributable to the bonus payments. Section 691(c)(2)(C) provides that the amount of estate tax attributable to the IRD is the difference between the actual estate tax and the estate tax computed without including the IRD in decedent's gross estate. The parties disputed the effect of the exclusion of the bonus payments on the marital deduction. The IRS contended that the exclusion of the bonus payments resulted in a reduction of the marital deduction. Taxpayer argued that the full maximum marital deduction should be allowed, because the will provided for a full marital deduction bequest and there were sufficient nonIRD assets in the estate to fund the formula marital deduction.

Held: For the estate. The court found that the purpose behind Section 691 is to provide a deduction to those required to include IRD in their gross income to offset, at least in part, the estate tax attributable to the inclusion of that IRD in the gross estate of a decedent. Although no guidance existed in the statute or the legislative history on the specific point at issue in the present case, the court concluded that taxpayer's method was consistent with the purpose of the statute. The formula bequest required that taxpayer receive property equal in value to the maximum marital deduction out of the assets of the estate available for distribution. In the recomputation, there was no IRD available in the recomputed gross estate to satisfy the marital bequest. The bequest, therefore, by its own terms, had to be funded to its full extent by nonIRD property. Thus, the full maximum marital deduction, subject only to the Section 2056 50 percent limitation, was allowable in the recomputation of taxpayer's husband's estate.

[Estate of Kincaid, 85 TC 25 (1985).]

Marital deduction is limited by ERTA maximum formula clause transition rule. An individual executed his will on October 24, 1980, and died on November 28, 1984. The will created two funds. The first fund consisted of a fractional share of decedent's residuary estate that would equal the maximum allowable federal estate tax marital deduction less the value of all interests passing to the benefit of his wife. This included life insurance. These interests were limited to the extent that they were included in determining decedent's gross estate and were allowable as a marital deduction for federal estate tax purposes. Only those assets that would qualify for the marital deduction would be allocated to the first fund. The second fund would consist of the balance of decedent's residuary estate after deducting fractional shares allocated to the first fund. The will also stated that any taxes not otherwise included in the gross estate would not be apportioned, but should be paid out of the residuary estate. The spouse also was granted a lifetime power to require distribution of the trust corpus to herself and a testamentary general power of appointment for the first fund. A separate trustee would control the second fund.

The IRS stated that the federal estate tax marital deduction is limited to the greater of $250,000 and one half of decedent's adjusted gross estate. The IRS noted that the marital clause in decedent's will was a maximum marital deduction formula clause within the meaning of the transitional rule of ERTA § 403(e)(3). The IRS further noted that the will did not contain specific language indicating that decedent intended that subsequent changes in the federal estate tax marital deduction law should apply to his estate.

The IRS rejected the estate's position that decedent's intent was to take advantage of the full amount of the marital deduction. The IRS took the position that the will contained a maximum marital deduction formula clause, because it directed the trustee to fund the marital trust only with assets that qualify for the marital deduction. The IRS stated that this referred to the quality of the property used to fund the trust, not to the quantity thereof.

[Tech. Adv. Mem. 8914001.]

IRS finds that clause in 1977 will referring to "present law" requires that dollar limitation in old law be applied. An individual who died in 1984, survived by his spouse and three children, provided in his 1977 will that he would devise and bequeath as much out of his separate property to his wife as was eligible for the marital deduction under present law. The residue of the estate was to be bequeathed to his children in equal shares. The will directed that all inheritance, succession, estate, and similar taxes that might become payable with respect to the property be apportioned among the legatees, devisees, and recipients of the property. The children executed a disclaimer with respect to certain property otherwise passing to them under the residuary clause of the will. Under local law, the property passed to the spouse under the intestacy statutes of the state. Because more than 35 percent of the estate consisted of a closely held business, the executor elected, under Section 6166, to make installment payments of the portion of the estate tax liability that was attributable to the closely held business.

The IRS indicated that the marital deduction was limited to the greater of $250,000, or 50 percent of the adjusted gross estate. Noting that the will provision was executed before the enactment of Section 403(e) of the Economic Recovery Tax Act of 1981, the IRS reasoned that the will provision would be subject to the quantitative limits of Section 2056(c). The IRS determined that the provision was not a maximum marital deduction, because the will provided for the deduction under present law and required that the bequest be selected from separate property. The IRS also determined that the value of the intestate property received by the surviving spouse was subject to reduction by the estimate of the maximum amount of interest payable on the deferred estate tax under Section 6166 to determine the marital deduction under Section 2056. The IRS noted that under common law, absent direction, the intestate property is first used to pay the estate's administration expenses, and it reasoned that the disclaimed property that passed to the spouse constituted intestate property. Finally, the IRS concluded that the estate could not deduct, as an expense of administration under Section 2053(a)(2), an estimate of the maximum amount of interest payable on the deferred estate tax under Section 6166. The IRS reasoned that the interest would be deductible under Section 2053(a) only when it accrued.

[Priv. Ltr. Rul. 8714010.]

IRS takes position that provision of trust restatement is formula maximum marital deduction clause under ERTA § 403(e)(3). An individual who died in 1984 provided in a will drafted in 1980 that upon his death the remainder of his estate was to pour over to an inter vivos life insurance trust. The trust, which was originally drafted in 1970, provided for a maximum marital deduction. In 1981, the trust was restated to provide that if the individual's wife survived him, the trustee should set aside out of trust principal the minimum pecuniary amount sufficient to achieve the maximum federal estate tax deduction. The restatement of the trust was prepared and reviewed by members of the individual's law firm who were estate tax specialists and who were aware of the marital deduction transition rule in Section 2002(d)(1)(B) of the Tax Reform Act of 1976, Pub. L. No. 94-455. The individual was not an estate tax specialist. The trust was subsequently amended, but the amendments were dispositive in nature and did not make any changes to the formula marital bequest.

The IRS stated that the amount referred to in the restated trust's marital deduction clause should not exceed the greater of $250,000 or 50 percent of the adjusted gross estate. The IRS determined that the original trust language might have avoided the transitional rule of ERTA § 403(e)(3), concluding that the individual knew how to express a maximum marital deduction clause in terms that would have anticipated the federal law changes. That section of the law applies, the IRS noted, where an individual died after 1981 and the formula clause was not amended to refer to the unlimited marital deduction.

[Priv. Ltr. Rul. 8708003.]

IRS takes position that Section 2056(b)(7) election is effective for trust property. A husband and wife executed a revocable trust naming a trustee who, after satisfying specific devises, was to divide the property at the husband's death into three new trusts. One trust was to receive the wife's undivided one-half interest in community property and the wife's separate property. The second trust would receive an amount of property representing what the husband owned in excess of the unified credit equivalent including the specific devises. Any property disclaimed by the wife and any remaining property would go to the third trust. The husband's will authorized his personal representative to make the Section 2056(b)(7) election with respect to property held in the second new trust. The trust agreement stated that the personal representative was to make the election for all or a fraction of the trust property to obtain the largest possible marital deduction for the individual reduced by the amount that would increase the taxable estate to the largest possible amount that would result in no federal estate tax liability. The language of the will was unclear whether the permissible reduction in the marital deduction was also relevant with respect to the funding of the second new trust.

The IRS determined that the trust agreement provided for a reduction formula that related only to the fraction of the trust for which a Section 2056(b)(7) election was to be made, and that the trustee had no discretion over the funding of the trust. Accordingly, the IRS determined that the trust was properly funded by the trustee and that the estate's personal representative made an effective election under Section 2056(b)(7) with respect to the includable portion of the trust property.

[Priv. Ltr. Rul. 8609003.]

Disclaimed property passing to surviving spouse is unaffected by formula clause. Decedent's will provided that his wife receive property "having a value equal to the maximum marital deduction as finally determined in my federal estate tax proceedings, less the aggregate amount of marital deductions, if any, allowed for such tax purposes by reason of property ... passing ... to my said wife otherwise than pursuant to the provisions of this item." Nine months after decedent's death, his son and daughter, their children, and decedent's siblings and their children disclaimed interest in the estate. The son also disclaimed interests in shares of stock that were to pass to him under the will. All of the disclaimed property passed to the surviving spouse.

The IRS concluded that the clause quoted above is a formula clause. However, the IRS determined that the disclaimers were valid under Section 2518, so the property that passed to the surviving spouse was unaffected by the formula clause. Accordingly, the unlimited marital deduction of Section 2056(a) applied to that property.

[Priv. Ltr. Rul. 8510023.]

[3] Savings Clauses

Tax Court holds Minnesota spouse allowance to be nonterminable interest qualifying for marital deduction. Decedent, a resident of Minnesota, died intestate on September 15, 1980. He was survived by his wife and their three children. The widow petitioned the probate court for a "spouse allowance" under Minnesota law. The probate court thereafter issued an order directing the estate to pay her $27,000 (payable in $1,500 monthly installments) as a spouse allowance. Decedent's estate contended that under Minnesota law, the spouse allowance was a nonterminable interest within the meaning of Section 2056, and therefore was subject to the marital deduction in its entirety. On audit, the IRS determined a deficiency in decedent's estate tax on the ground that under Minnesota law, the spouse allowance was a terminable interest and thus did not qualify for the deduction.

Held: For the estate. The court, in rejecting the IRS's contention that there was no vested right under Minnesota law to a spouse allowance, concluded that the grant language of the Minnesota spouse allowance statute was mandatory, not permissive. The court also rejected the IRS's argument that the spouse allowance was not indefeasibly vested. The court stated that the right to the spouse allowance vested on the date of decedent's death and was not defeated by the surviving spouse's subsequent death or remarriage as claimed by the IRS. Accordingly, the court upheld the estate's deduction of the spouse allowance.

[Radel, 88 TC 1143 (1987), acq. 1987-2 CB 1.]

Savings clause does not negate marital deduction. Decedent left his widow $100,000 in his will in satisfaction of the terms of an antenuptial agreement. Under state law, her dower interest would have come to $500,000. She brought an action to set aside the antenuptial agreement and to claim her dower rights. Before a court decision was handed down, she reached an agreement with the estate. Under the agreement's terms, she was to get $400,000 immediately, but $300,000 would have to be returned if the entire amount did not qualify for the marital deduction.

The IRS ruled that in approving the marital deduction claimed by the estate, a transfer that otherwise qualified for the marital deduction would not become a terminable interest, because it was conditioned on IRS approval.

[Rev. Rul. 76-199, 1976-1 CB 288.]

Savings clause renders inconsistent clause ineffectual and saves marital deduction. An individual willed his residuary estate to two funds. One fund consisted of a fraction of the residuary estate, the numerator of which was the maximum marital deduction allowable, less all other property passing to his wife, and the denominator of which was the value of his residuary estate. The trustee of the first fund was empowered to appoint the principal of the fund to the wife, their son, or their son's children. Only the wife would receive the income from the first fund, and only she could unilaterally withdraw from the principal. The will stated that if any provision in the will prevented a federal estate marital deduction with respect to the first fund, the provision would not apply.

The IRS stated that the first fund qualifies for the marital deduction. The IRS noted that the provision that would allow the trustee to invade principal for the health or maintenance of the son would normally disqualify the fund from the marital deduction. The IRS concluded, however, that New York law would not give effect to that provision, because of the savings clause that renders any provision contrary to a marital deduction ineffectual.

[Priv. Ltr. Rul. 8437093.]

¶ 11.04 SPOUSAL CLAIMS AND ELECTIONS

Assets received by surviving spouse under settlement agreement were not eligible for marital deduction. Decedent died on October 2, 1987, survived by his wife and daughter from a previous marriage. After leaving certain property to each of them outright, he created a testamentary trust in which his wife had a life estate and his daughter had a remainder interest. It was clear from the language of the trust that he wanted his wife to live comfortably after his death, as evidenced by the fact that the wife could draw on trust assets for her needs without limitation. Two banks that were approached to be corporate trustees found a conflict between this right of the spouse and the testator's intention to leave his daughter a portion of the trust in the form of a remainder interest. After some negotiation, a family settlement was reached, under which the trust assets were divided equally between the two beneficiaries. The estate claimed a marital deduction of $464,795 for the trust assets received by the spouse. The IRS disallowed $422,464 of the deduction on the ground that the property passing to the spouse was terminable interest property under Section 2056. The estate contended that the spouse received a general power of appointment over the trust assets. Under Section 2056(b)(5), a life estate accompanied by such a power can qualify for the marital deduction if certain requirements, including the following, are met: (1) the spouse must have the power to appoint the entire interest to herself or her estate, and (2) the power must be exercisable by the spouse alone and in all events (whether exercisable by will or during her life).

The estate asserted that the only issue in question was whether the spouse had the power to appoint the entire interest to either herself or the estate. The taxpayer-estate then argued that the spouse had the power to appoint property to herself and that this was sufficient. In order for the assets to qualify for the marital deduction, under Section 2056(b)(5) and Regulation § 20.2056(b)-5(a)(3), the spouse did not need to have a power to appoint to her estate if she could appoint to herself. The issue, though, was whether the spouse in this case had the right to exercise the power of appointment under any and all circumstances.

Held: For the IRS. According to the Fourth Circuit, the regulations and case law make clear that a surviving spouse's power of appointment does not qualify for the marital deduction under Section 2056 if the exercise of the power requires the "joinder or consent of any other person." The court concluded that the Supreme Court of North Carolina would have ruled in the instant case that the will did not give the surviving spouse the power to appoint assets to herself to the deprivation of the remainder beneficiary. Thus, she did not have sufficient rights in the trust assets to qualify them for the marital deduction. The estate argued that it was still entitled to claim a marital deduction because "the distribution of . . . assets to decedent's wife pursuant to the Family Settlement Agreement . . . passed to her in recognition of her enforceable rights in an arms-length settlement of a legitimate will controversy." Under Section 2056(a), only property that passes from decedent to the surviving spouse qualifies for the marital deduction. Regulation § 20.2056(c)-2(d)(2) explains further that if property is assigned to a surviving spouse as a result of a will controversy, it is treated as having passed from decedent if the assignment "was a bona fide recognition of enforceable rights of the surviving spouse in decedent's estate." The test, said the court, is "whether the interest reaches the spouse pursuant to state law, correctly interpreted—not whether it reached the spouse as a result of good faith, adversary confrontation." The court indicated that the proper focus is on the spouse's rights under the terms of the testamentary trust, not on any subsequent rights she may have received from the settlement agreement. Because the court had previously determined that the trust did not give the spouse a life estate with a general power of appointment that qualified for the marital deduction under Section 2056(b), she could not have received such an interest under the terms of the settlement agreement, not even an arm's-length agreement.

[Estate of Carpenter, 52 F3d 1266, 75 AFTR2d 95-2084, 95-1 USTC ¶ 60,194 (4th Cir. 1995).]

Marital deduction is denied where spouse surrenders rights to nonprobate property. As part of a settlement with decedent's daughters, the surviving spouse surrendered her survivorship right to joint tenancy property and her statutory election right to decedent's property. The IRS disallowed the marital deduction, contending that under the will contest provisions of Regulation § 20.2056(e)-2(d), the property never passed to the surviving spouse. The district court agreed.

    Held: Affirmed (in part) for the IRS. Although the will contest regulation does not apply to property passing outside the will, its rationale does. To the extent that a surviving spouse surrenders property rights, such property does not pass to the spouse.

[Schroeder, 924 F2d 1547, 91-1 USTC ¶ 60,059, 67 AFTR2d 91-1180 (10th Cir. 1991).]

Eighth Circuit holds that Tax Court is required to make independent determination of enforcement of surviving spouse's dower claims against estate under state law at time settlement was reached and is required to consider constitutionality of state dower statute at time of settlement. The IRS appealed a Tax Court decision holding that an estate was entitled to an estate tax marital deduction of $90,000, based upon a settlement payment made to decedent's surviving spouse. On appeal, the IRS argued that the Tax Court had erred in allowing the marital deduction without first making an independent determination whether decedent's surviving spouse had an enforceable claim against the estate under the Arkansas dower election statute at the time the settlement agreement was reached. The IRS also argued that the Tax Court had erred in allowing as the marital deduction the full $90,000 paid to decedent's surviving spouse, because an enforceable one-third dower interest in decedent's estate would have amounted to less than $56,000.

    Held: Reversed and remanded for the IRS. The Tax Court was required to make an independent determination of the enforcement of the surviving spouse's dower claims against the estate under state law at the time the settlement was reached. Specifically, the Tax Court was required to consider the constitutionality of the Arkansas dower statute at the time of settlement. The Tax Court failed to do so. The Eighth Circuit remanded the case for a determination of the constitutionality of the Arkansas dower statute at the time the settlement was reached.

[Estate of Brandon, 828 F2d 493, AFTR2d 87-6139, 87-2 USTC ¶ 13,733 (8th Cir. 1987).]

Marital deduction was not allowed for post-death appreciation of marital share. Decedent died on January 23, 1988. He was a resident of New Jersey and was survived by a second wife who was significantly younger than he. Decedent's son qualified as executor. Decedent's will bequeathed his stock in three close corporations to the children of his first marriage in varying percentages. The residue of his estate was left to his surviving spouse. After payment of the funeral expenses, medical expenses, debts, and specific bequests, the entire probate estate would have been consumed, leaving no residue. Accordingly, despite her status as the surviving spouse, decedent's wife would have received property consisting only of decedent's half interest in their cooperative apartment worth $108,000 and insurance proceeds of $38,889. Since her elective share of decedent's augmented estate under New Jersey law exceeded the property to which she was entitled under the will, plus the nonprobate property she received, she invoked her legal right of election under state law against the estate. The estate answered the widow's complaint and asked that the court fix the value of the surviving spouse's elective share as she had requested. This matter was settled by written agreement, dated December 23, 1988, pursuant to which decedent's surviving spouse was entitled to receive specific properties. Both she and the estate were represented by counsel in the lawsuit and the settlement, and there was no dispute that the settlement was negotiated at arm's length. The parties stipulated that the settlement of her lawsuit was "inclusive of any and all rights of the surviving spouse to share in any post-death appreciation of assets included as part of the augmented estate." On the estate tax return, the estate claimed a marital deduction of $629,107, which included advances by the estate, a car, a cash payment of $400,000, an interest in a card shop (which was given no value), a cooperative apartment worth $108,000, and proceeds of life insurance equal to $38,889. The IRS decreased the marital deduction by $143,546. The marital deduction allowed in the deficiency notice represented decedent's surviving spouse's one-third share of the "augmented estate" under New Jersey law, which was computed to equal all of decedent's assets at the date of death, using the date of death values shown on the estate tax return, as adjusted in the notice of deficiency, and reduced by debts and expenses.

Held: For the IRS. The Tax Court indicated that the sole issue before it was the proper amount of the marital deduction for amounts paid to the surviving spouse in settlement of her elective share under New Jersey law. The court then turned to Section 2056(a), which allows the marital deduction, and Section 2031(a), which provides that the value of the gross estate is determined by the value of decedent's property "at the time of his death." The statutory scheme of Section 2056, the foundation for deductibility of testamentary spousal transfers, is that the value of the transferred property qualifying for the marital deduction must be included in decedent's gross estate and that such value must be determined as of the date of death. The court stated that the marital deduction must be based on the value of property involved as of the date of death, and that the parties had stipulated that the settlement of decedent's surviving spouse's lawsuit included any rights she might have to share in the post-death appreciation of assets that formed part of the augmented estate. Accordingly, the settlement was not calculated simply by reference to decedent's estate as it existed at death. The court found that the marital deduction claimed on the return necessarily exceeded her elective share of the sum of date of death values of properties included in the estate. Therefore, the court determined that the IRS properly disallowed the portion of the marital deduction attributable to post-death increases in the value of the estate assets. Moreover, the taxpayer-estate failed to show that the assets given to decedent's surviving spouse did not include a negotiated portion of the enhancement of the estate after decedent's death. The estate relied on Estate of Hubert, 101 TC 314 (1993). The court stated, however, that that case did not discuss the statutory and regulatory provisions at issue here, which limit the marital deduction to the taxable value included in the gross estate, measured at the date of death. Regardless of the holding in *Hubert* as to the availability of the marital deduction in a settlement context, part of the settlement in the instant case included increases in the value of estate assets that occurred after death and that were consequently not included in the gross estate. The court held that that portion of the settlement was clearly not eligible for the marital deduction. The estate also cited a New Jersey case, In re Estate of Cole, 200 NJ Super. 396, 491 A2d 770 (1984), which indicated that a surviving spouse's elective share is to be valued as of the date of distribution rather than at the date of death. In response, the court noted that it has long been settled that while state law governs the rights created in property, federal law determines how those rights may be taxed. Hence, even assuming that *Estate of Cole* correctly interprets New Jersey law, it is irrelevant under the Code because post-death appreciation in the estate's assets may not be included in the measure of the marital deduction. Therefore, the IRS's denial of part of the marital deduction was upheld.

[Estate of Agnello, 103 TC 605 (1994).]

Elective share had to be reduced by pro rata share of decedent's debt. The surviving spouse opted to take her elective share under Tennessee state law and selected unencumbered assets of the estate to fund that amount. The issue was whether the estate was entitled to a marital deduction for the elective share amount awarded or whether the elective share had to be reduced by a pro rata share of the estate's secured debt.

Held: For the IRS. The elective share must be reduced by a pro rata share of decedent's secured debt in determining the marital deduction. State law subjected all estate assets, including those chosen to fund the elective share, to liability for a pro rata share of decedent's secured debt.

[Estate of Williams, 103 TC 451 (1994).]

Marital deduction is limited to bequest amount where state dower law is unconstitutional. Decedent's will provided a $25,000 cash bequest to his surviving spouse, who instead filed an election to take against decedent's will, pursuant to Arkansas's dower statute, thereby renouncing all benefits under decedent's will. Under the Arkansas statute in effect at the time of the settlement, a female surviving spouse electing to take against the will was entitled to a dower interest amounting to one third of a decedent husband's property held during their marriage. Decedent's estate was valued at $167,172 at the date of his death. However, his surviving spouse had brought suits to invalidate transfers of property made by decedent and his first wife prior to their deaths. After protracted negotiations, the estate and the surviving spouse entered into a settlement agreement under which the surviving spouse accepted the sum of $90,000 cash in return for a full and complete release of any and all claims she held against decedent's and others' estates. In the estate tax return, the entire $90,000 was deducted as a marital deduction. In the notice of deficiency issued to the estate, the IRS allowed only $25,000 as a marital deduction, on the ground that the surviving wife did not have a legally enforceable claim against the estate in excess of that amount, because the Arkansas dower statute was unconstitutional at the time the settlement was reached. The estate contended that the settlement was a bona fide recognition of the surviving spouse's rights under the law, and that the settlement amount was properly deductible by the estate as a marital deduction pursuant Section 2056.

Held: For the IRS. The Tax Court held that under Orr v. Orr, 440 US 268 (1979), the Arkansas dower statute was held to be unconstitutional under the equal protection clause at the time the settlement was reached. Thus, a dower interest did not pass to the spouse. The court stated that a good faith settlement or judgment of a lower state court must be based on an enforceable right, properly interpreted under state law, in order to qualify as passing pursuant to the estate tax marital deduction. The court stated that the will, not the settlement agreement itself, determined the source and nature of the surviving spouse's legal rights. Hence, the court was not concerned with whether the settlement agreement was based on an enforceable right. Even if the surviving spouse had been successful in her claims to invalidate the property transfers of decedent and his first wife, those properties would have been placed back into the estate. In that event, the surviving spouse would have had an enforceable right, for purposes of the estate tax marital deduction, to only those properties through decedent's will. Thus, she did not have an enforceable right for estate tax purposes against the estate for more than $25,000 as provided in the will. The marital deduction was thus limited to $25,000.

[Estate of Brandon, 91 TC 829 (1988).]

Homestead does not qualify for marital deduction upon surviving spouse's disclaimer of life estate therein. Decedent, a resident of Minnesota, died intestate on September 15, 1980. He was survived by his wife and their three adult children. At the time of his death, he owned farmland that was included in his gross estate at a value of $210,000, of which $158,400 was attributable to the homestead of decedent and his surviving spouse. In March 1981, the surviving spouse disclaimed her life estate in the homestead, which had passed to her under state law, and the estate thereafter claimed a marital deduction of $52,800, the value of a one-third fee interest in the homestead. The estate claimed that the surviving spouse's disclaimer had caused the Minnesota laws of descent and distribution to provide her with a one-third fee interest in the homestead property. The essence of the estate's theory was based upon the legal fiction that treats a disclaiming spouse as predeceasing a decedent with respect to the property. The estate theorized that if the spouse had predeceased decedent, then the homestead provisions would have become inoperative. Thus, she would have received a fee interest in the homestead property that would have qualified for the marital deduction. The IRS disallowed the claimed marital deduction.

Held: For the IRS. Minnesota statutes provide for a homestead interest to pass from a decedent to a spouse. If there are children, the spouse receives a life estate, with the remainder going to the children. The court, in following the IRS's arguments, stated that the spouse's disclaimer of her life estate in the homestead merely caused an acceleration of the children's interest from a remainder to a fee simple absolute. Thus, the spouse's interest in the disclaimed homestead property did not qualify for the marital deduction, because it passed directly to the children from decedent. Accordingly, the marital deduction was properly denied.

[Radel, 88 TC 1143 (1987), acq. 1987-2 CB 1.]

Amounts paid for release of dower rights qualify for marital deduction. Decedent's surviving spouse elected to receive her dower interest in decedent's real property, but the executor could not conveniently satisfy her request. Rather than petition the state court for commutation of her dower interest, she settled with the estate. The IRS ruled that this settlement qualified for the marital deduction because it was a bona fide compromise resulting from her enforceable right of commutation, and the amount of the settlement was not greater than that which she would have received had the court decided the issue.

[Rev. Rul. 83-107, 83-2 CB 159.]

¶ 11.05 TERMINABLE INTERESTS

[1] Deductibility, Generally

Probate court decision does not govern QTIP election. Decedent's will created a testamentary trust for the benefit of his surviving spouse that gave the trustee (his son) absolute discretion to pay the spouse income or principal for her health, education, and support. As originally created, the trust was not qualified terminable interest property (QTIP) (e.g., it did not meet Section 2056's requirement that the surviving spouse be entitled to all income, payable at least annually), and therefore was not eligible for the estate tax marital deduction. Recognizing the trust's non-QTIP status, the spouse asked the California state probate court to modify it to bring it in accord with Section 2056. This request was not challenged by decedent's son or the representative of decedent's minor grandchildren (potential beneficiaries). The spouse told the court that decedent intended the trust to qualify for the QTIP election. The will, however, was not ambiguous, and no documentary or other evidence supporting this contention was submitted. Nevertheless, the probate court granted the request and entered an order clarifying that the trust income was payable to the spouse at least annually. After the probate court's reformation order became final, the estate filed the final federal estate tax return claiming a marital QTIP deduction covering the trust. The IRS, which was not notified of and did not appear at the probate hearing, disallowed the deduction. Based on its construction of California law, the Tax Court decided for the IRS. Although agreeing with the IRS and the Tax Court that the probate court's reformation decision was erroneous under state law, the estate still maintained its entitlement to treat the trust as QTIP. The estate based its position on the fact that the probate court order was final when the QTIP election was made.

Held: For the IRS. The Ninth Circuit decided that the probate court decision was not binding for purposes of determining the estate's federal tax liability based on the Supreme Court's decision in Estate of Bosch, 387 US 456, 19 AFTR2d 1891 (S. Ct. 1967). *Bosch* stands for the proposition that a state trial court's decision in a nonadversarial proceeding on a property interest's character under state law is not controlling for federal estate tax purposes, and that a federal court is entitled to make its own determination of the state law's applicability if the state's highest court has not ruled on the issue. The nonadversarial probate court proceeding in this case was, as in *Bosch,* "brought for the purposes of directly affecting federal estate tax liability" and was "determinative of federal estate tax consequences." Thus, under *Bosch,* the Tax Court was not bound by the probate court's reformation decision. Further, the estate's attempts to circumvent *Bosch* were nonavailing. The estate argued that, since the probate court order was final and unappealable as of the alleged "measuring date" for federal tax purposes (e.g., the QTIP election date), *Bosch* did not apply and the probate court order was binding for federal tax purposes. Regardless of the proper measuring date, however, this argument was irrelevant because under *Bosch*, even a final state court decision may be ignored for federal tax purposes. In addition, the appeals court rejected the estate's reliance on Revenue Ruling 73-142, 1973-1 CB 405, in which the IRS stated that a final, unappealable state court order determining the estate tax consequences of a trust was binding even though the decision was contrary to state law. In that ruling, the state court proceedings, which resulted in the removal of the trust from decedent's estate, were brought by decedent himself for an interpretation of the trust instrument, and bound decedent before his death. In contrast, the probate court proceedings here were brought by the estate to modify decedent's will after his death for the express purpose of avoiding federal estate taxes.

[Estate of Rapp, 140 F3d 1211, 81 AFTR2d 98-1151, 98-1 USTC ¶ 60,304 (9th Cir. 1998).]

Joint bank account is held not to qualify under marital trust rules, because of terminable interest exception. Decedent, a resident of Kansas, died testate on July 24, 1977. During the period from April 1971 to September 1976, he used his own funds to purchase 334 certificates of deposit (CDs) from two local banks. At the time of his death, the CDs were worth a total of $460,000. As a part of his estate plan, decedent caused each certificate to be issued jointly in his own name and in the name of one of his several beneficiaries, including his wife. The CDs were kept by decedent in his safe deposit box. All accrued interest was paid to decedent. For estate tax purposes, the estate reported the jointly owned CDs in gross estate. The $7,851 interest that accrued on the CDs from the date of the last payment to the date of death, however, was not included in the gross estate. The IRS contended that the interest was a part of gross estate, and a notice of deficiency was issued to collect estate tax thereon.

Decedent also had a joint tenancy bank account in the amount of $32,621 in his name and in the names of his wife and son. The full amount of this account was included in the marital deduction on the estate tax return. The account was opened on April 20, 1965, in all three names. On August 2, 1977, after decedent's death, the wife and son signed a new signature card as joint tenants. On April 19, 1978, the son filed a written disclaimer of any interest in the account, and a new signature card was signed by only the decedent's wife. The son then filed a gift tax return showing a gift conveyance of one half of this joint tenancy account to his mother. There was also reported on the estate tax return two shares of stock valued at $185, held jointly by decedent and his wife. This amount was included in the marital deduction.

Upon audit of the federal estate tax return, the IRS determined that (1) decedent's estate should be increased by $7,851, the amount of accrued interest to the date of death on the 334 CDs; (2) the marital deduction should be decreased by $16,310, one half of the joint tenancy bank account, and by $92, one half of the shares of stock; and (3) the marital deduction should be reduced by $1,383, the wife's share of the state inheritance tax, and by $9,408, the wife's share of the funeral and administration expenses. On February 2, 1981, the estate was assessed additional taxes and interest in the amount of $14,063. The estate paid the tax and filed a claim for refund, which was denied.

Held: For the IRS, in part. With respect to the accrued interest issue, the Tenth Circuit noted that estate taxation under the joint tenancy rules of Section 2040 is not prevented or affected by state property laws or contract terms that vest ownership in the survivor immediately upon death. It thus rejected the estate's contention that the accrued interest should not be included in decedent's gross estate, because it passed to the joint tenant immediately upon decedent's death. With regard to the joint tenancy bank account, the legal status of the account at the time of decedent's death governed the tax consequences. The fact that the son had since disclaimed his interest in the account did not change the fact that at the time of his father's death, he had the power to withdraw all of the funds in the account, thus making the wife's interest in the account a nondeductible terminable interest. Therefore, one half of the amount of the joint tenancy bank account at the date of death, $16,310, did not qualify for the marital deduction.

The IRS conceded that the marital deduction should not be reduced by one half of the value of the two shares of stock. As for the family settlement agreement, it was invalid because it was not supported by consideration. Because there was no valid agreement, it was not necessary to decide what effect such an agreement would have on the marital deduction. The plaintiffs' contention that the IRS could not reduce the marital deduction by the amount of the wife's share of the state inheritance tax because the state of Kansas did not assess any tax against the wife was rejected. The state of Kansas imposed an inheritance tax chargeable against the interests of each beneficiary in proportion to the amount of the shares of the estate received by each. The wife's proportionate share of the inheritance tax was chargeable to her under this provision. The marital deduction thus had to be reduced by the amounts of $1,383 and $9,408, the surviving spouse's pro rata share of the state inheritance tax and the funeral and administration expenses.

[Jeschke, 814 F2d 568, 59 AFTR2d 87-1235, 87-1 USTC ¶ 13,713 (10th Cir. 1987).]

Bequest does not qualify for marital deduction. A dairy farmer whose wife worked with him on the farm executed a will in 1963, bequeathing to his wife "the use, income and profits, of and from, all my personal property, including the dairy livestock and the farm machinery and equipment, for and during her lifetime, with the right to use so much of the principal thereof for her needs and the needs of my children as she in her discretion may deem necessary." The will further stated that "on her death I give all of such property then remaining to my children equally." At the time of the execution of the will, as well as at the time of his death in 1977, decedent and his wife had three children. The issue in the case was whether the bequest to the surviving spouse qualified for the estate tax marital deduction. The Tax Court held that the bequest did not qualify for the marital deduction.

Held: Affirmed for the IRS. Under New York law, a power to consume as was involved in this case is limited by a standard of good faith, thus not constituting a "power in the surviving spouse to appoint ... in all events" under Section 2056(b)(5) and applicable regulations. The essential concern under New York law is whether a spouse has absolute discretion to invade his life estate at will, without regard to any good faith obligations toward the remaindermen. The precise form in which that absolute discretion is granted is not determinative. What is required is certification or some equally specific provision fulfilling the good faith requirement. In this case, there was nothing to take the place of or fulfill the good faith requirement. Thus, the bequest did not qualify for the marital deduction.

[Estate of Foster, 725 F2d 201, 53 AFTR2d 84-1582, 84-1 USTC ¶ 13,555 (2d Cir. 1984).]

Stock qualifies for marital deduction, despite subsequent recapitalization.
Decedent's will gave common nonvoting stock (in a family corporation that was to be converted by the executor to nonvoting preferred stock) to a marital trust. The district court disallowed the marital deduction for this stock because the preferred stock would be "acquired ... by the executor" under Section 2056(b)(1)(C) and was thus a terminable interest.

Held: Reversed for the estate. The property passing to the widow was the common stock subject to exchange, not the preferred stock, so the bequest was deductible. A trial is necessary to determine the value of the stock as affected by the recapitalization.

[Provident Nat'l Bank, 581 F2d 1081, 42 AFTR2d 78-6458, 78-2 USTC ¶ 13,255 (3d Cir. 1978).]

Fourth Circuit rules on formal bequest acceptance; marital deduction is not lost. Decedent, in his will, provided that the surviving spouse was to have the option of taking enough properties from his residuary estate to obtain the maximum allowable marital deduction. The election was to be made in writing. A failure to make the statement was considered a rejection of the property, in which case the property would go into a residuary trust. Income from the trust was to be distributed to the wife and children at the discretion of the trustee. The two sons had a remainder interest in this trust. The wife elected to accept the property which was claimed as part of the marital deduction. The IRS argued that if the surviving spouse could elect to accept or reject a bequest, the fact that she could reject the bequest, which could put the property into the possession or enjoyment of another person, rendered it a terminable interest.

Held: For the estate. The Ninth Circuit rejected the IRS's argument and accepted the reasoning of the Tax Court. The mere requirement of a formal written acceptance did not distinguish this case from those holding that a right of election against a will is not a disqualification to claim the property as part of the marital deduction, as long as the interest that passes to the surviving spouse is not terminable.

[Estate of Mackie, 545 F2d 883, 39 AFTR2d 77-1578, 76-2 USTC ¶ 13,166 (4th Cir. 1976).]

No deduction for bequest to spouse and charities. Decedent left the residue of his estate ($1,475,968) to his wife as trustee of a trust for her benefit. The will provided that the trustee pay his wife the entire net income of the trust. It also provided that upon his wife's death or remarriage, the trustee must distribute the balance of the trust to four charities designated in the will. The trust did not provide his wife with any power of appointment. The trust was not a qualified unitrust, annuity trust, or pooled income fund. A tax liability of $358,846 was reported and paid with a timely filed estate tax return. No marital deduction was claimed on the return, nor was a charitable deduction claimed for any residual value of the trust. In an amended return filed twenty days after the filing of the original return, the estate claimed a marital deduction of $1,475,968, the full amount of the bequest to the trust, and sought a refund of the entire tax of $358,846. The estate did not claim any charitable deduction in either the original or amended return, and it did not elect to claim a marital deduction for QTIP, pursuant to Section 2056(b)(7), in either return.

Held: For the IRS. The court held that the bequest did not qualify for the marital deduction, because the interest passing to the surviving spouse was terminable. Section 2056(b)(1) provides that if (1) the surviving spouse's interest is terminable, (2) the interest passes to any other "person," and (3) that person gets the opportunity to enjoy the interest, no marital deduction is allowed. In this case, decedent's wife's income interest was terminable because it ended upon her remarriage. Upon the occurrence of that contingency, the interest was to pass to charities, and the charities would have the opportunity to enjoy the interest passed to them. The trustee argued that the charities were not "persons" within the meaning of the statute. The court rejected this argument as yielding an absurd result: An estate could transfer interests to a spouse with the remainder to any entity other than a human being (or perhaps a corporation) and always be entitled to a marital deduction. This is clearly contrary to congressional intent. An exception to the terminable interest rule is provided for QTIP. Qualifying for the QTIP exception requires, among other things, that (1) the property pass from decedent, (2) the surviving spouse be entitled to income for life, and (3) the executor elect, on the tax return, to treat the property as QTIP. A contingent interest is fatal to a QTIP election. Because the estate in the instant case did not make the QTIP election on either tax return, and because decedent's wife's life estate was contingent on her not remarrying, the interest passed to her was not QTIP.

The trust also failed to qualify under the exception to the terminable interest rule for charitable remainder trusts. This type of charitable trust includes only a charitable remainder annuity trust or a charitable remainder unitrust under Section 664. Because the charitable remainder at issue was not determinable upon decedent's death, the trust did not qualify as either an annuity trust or a unitrust. The trustee contended that, because the bequest passed entirely to the spouse and the charities, it would be contrary to the spirit of the law to deny the estate a marital deduction. The trustee sought support for this argument in a footnote in the legislative history of the statute, which provides that "[t]he general rules applicable to qualifying income interests may provide similar treatment where a decedent provides an income interest in the spouse for her life and a remainder interest to charity." The court found that this footnote did not support the trust's position. Decedent's wife did not have a qualifying income interest, because her income was contingent on not getting remarried. The use of the conditional "may" in the legislative history shows that what follows is only hypothetical, and the trust did not match the facts of the hypothetical. The footnote contemplates only a life estate transfer upon the death of the surviving spouse. It does not discuss contingencies such as remarriage. Hence, the court refused to expand the express language of the Code. Legislative history can assist in deciphering unclear statutes, but the statute in question provides "uncommonly clear and cohesive language, particularly for tax provisions."

[Roels, 928 F. Supp. 812, 79 AFTR2d 97-1099, 96-2 USTC ¶ 60,234 (ED Wis. 1996).]

Marital deduction allowed for real, but not personal, property. Decedent's will left his wife his residuary estate, provided she "survived distribution." The IRS disallowed the marital deduction attributable to the residuary estate on the ground that the surviving spouse received a terminable interest.

Held: For taxpayer (in part). Because the personal property left to the spouse was contingent upon her surviving until it was actually distributed to her and there was no requirement under the will or Washington state law that such property be distributed within six months after decedent's death, the spouse's interest in the personal property was a terminable interest and so was not eligible for the marital deduction. On the other hand, the real property left to the spouse qualified for the marital deduction because under state law, title to the realty vested immediately upon decedent's death and therefore the real property was deemed to have been distributed to the spouse immediately at death.

[Estate of Bond, 104 TC 652 (1995).]

Estate may deduct spousal allowance provided under state law. Two months after decedent's death, the surviving spouse petitioned the state court and received her statutory allowance. The surviving spouse also disclaimed her life estate in the homestead, which immediately passed to decedent's three children. The estate deducted the spousal allowance and the surviving spouse's one-third interest in the homestead. The IRS disallowed two thirds of the statutory allowance and the entire homestead deduction. The estate argued that the spousal allowance was not a terminable interest under Section 2056 and qualified for the marital deduction. Furthermore, the waiver of the homestead resulted in a one-third fee interest under state law and was deductible.

Held: For the estate (in part). The spousal allowance was deductible because state law was not discretionary and did not contain any contingencies. Thus, the allowance was a nonterminable interest. However, the waiver of the homestead passed the property directly to the children, and no marital deduction was allowed for that interest.

[Estate of Radel, 88 TC 1143 (1987), acq. 1987-2 CB 1.]

Survivorship requirement in decedent's will results in failure of marital deduction under terminable interest rule. Prior to their marriage in 1911, decedent and her husband entered into a prenuptial contract by which they agreed that all property owned by each party prior to the marriage, together with property coming to each party during the marriage, was to remain separate property. They also waived California community property rights and all rights as an heir or a surviving spouse. By the terms of her 1974 will, however, decedent devised to her husband a certain condominium, together with its contents, that had been her separate property. The devise further provided, however, that if the husband failed to survive the probate of the estate, the condominium and its contents were to pass instead to her son. In a later codicil, decedent created a $75,000 testamentary trust to provide income for the remainder of the husband's life. The husband did, indeed, survive probate, and the condominium was distributed to him in 1978. Thereafter the estate claimed a marital deduction of $117,175, representing the value of the condominium and its contents. The IRS disallowed the item in full, arguing that the requirement of survival constituted a terminable interest under Section 2056. In the Tax Court, the estate's position was that the disputed term "fails to survive distribution of my estate" should have been interpreted as being synonymous with the phrase "fails to survive my death" in order to effectuate decedent's intent. The estate argued that decedent's language was ambiguous and that extrinsic evidence was admissible to prove decedent's testamentary intent.

Held: For the IRS. By the terms of Section 2056(b)(3), an interest passing to the surviving spouse under a survivorship contingency shall not be considered as a terminable interest if (1) the surviving spouse's death will cause a termination of the interest within a period not exceeding six months of the date of decedent's death and (2) such termination does not in fact occur. The court, looking to California law, concluded that the phrase "fails to survive distribution of my estate" had a well-established technical meaning under state law and that it plainly created a survivorship requirement measured only by the period of probate administration, not by a period not exceeding six months. Accordingly, the court concluded that the husband's interest was terminable for purposes of Section 2056, and, accordingly, the estate's claimed deduction was disallowed.

[Estate of Harmon, 84 TC 329 (1985).]

Tax Court holds widow's allowance to be terminable interest not qualifying for marital deduction. Decedent married his second wife on October 3, 1972, and remained married to her until his death on November 18, 1977. Decedent left his entire estate to the children of his first marriage. The widow petitioned the probate court to fix a widow's allowance under the Texas Probate Code. The probate court awarded her a widow's allowance of $13,750. Decedent's estate contended that the widow's allowance was subject to the marital deduction in its entirety. In a notice of deficiency, the IRS determined that under Texas law, the widow's allowance is a terminable interest and thus does not qualify for the deduction.

Held: For the IRS. The Tax Court held that the widow's allowance was a terminable interest and did not qualify for the marital deduction under Section 2056. Interests passing to the surviving spouse that are nevertheless "terminable" under Section 2056(b) do not qualify for the marital deduction. In order to escape the terminable interest limitation, the interest passing to the surviving spouse must be indefeasible and unconditional as of the moment of decedent's death. Under Texas law, the entitlement of a widow to a widow's allowance is contingent upon her not having separate property adequate for her maintenance. Thus, it is not indefeasible and unconditional as of the moment of decedent's death, because it would never come into being if the widow had separate property that was adequate for her maintenance.

[Estate of Snider, 84 TC 75 (1985).]

Charitable remainder annuity trust arrangement is held disqualified for marital deduction. Decedent, a resident of Florida, died testate on February 14, 1977. Over a period of four years prior to the date of death, she transferred a sizable block of corporate common stock to three charitable remainder annuity trusts pursuant to agreements that provided for periodic annuity payments to decedent for life and then to her husband if he survived her. Upon the death of the survivor, the remainder of the trust was to pass outright to charities named in decedent's will. The will also included a bequest to a marital trust for the benefit of her husband in an amount equal to the maximum allowable under Section 2056. She further directed that taxes and administrative expenses were to be paid out of the residue of the estate, which in turn was bequeathed to one of the inter vivos trusts. The IRS determined that the value of the annuities payable to the surviving spouse under the terms of the trusts did not qualify for the Section 2056 marital deduction. In its presentation to the Tax Court, the IRS contended that decedent's will passed a "terminable interest," which is defined in Regulation § 20.2056(b)-1(b) as an interest in property that terminates or fails on the lapse of time or on the occurrence or the failure to occur of some contingency. The IRS argued that the trust annuities payable to the surviving spouse did not constitute "property," but only interests in property, and that because the trust corpus was to pass to the charities on the death of the surviving spouse, the purported marital deduction was improper under Section 2056(b)(1). The estate maintained that the property in this case was the right to receive annuity payments, and that a marital deduction calculated on the value of the annuity payments, not trust corpus, should be allowed.

Held: For the IRS. The Tax Court found that the annuities constituted nondeductible terminable interests and that the assets in the trust corpus must be treated as the underlying property in cases such as this. The court based its holding on several authorities, most notably Meyer, 364 US 410 (1960), which rejected a substantially similar taxpayer argument respecting life insurance. The critical point in the Tax Court's view was that the "rights to receive annuity payments look to the underlying trust assets for their realization." As such, the rights to annuity payments cannot be viewed as the property under Section 2056; therefore, the annuities do not qualify for the marital deduction.

[Estate of Leach, 82 TC 952 (1984), aff'd without published op., 782 F2d 179 (11th Cir. 1986).]

Pecuniary bequest does not create terminable interest. A residuary bequest to the spouse qualified for the marital deduction, even though the subsequent valuation of a pecuniary bequest to another beneficiary seriously depleted the assets actually passing to the spouse. Here use of a pecuniary bequest guaranteed that full advantage would be taken of the credit shelter amount for the maximum savings in both estates. The assets in decedent's gross estate had a FMV of $900,000 at the date of death. The will contained a pecuniary bequest of $600,000 to decedent's child and gave the residue to the spouse. As a result of the October 1987 stock market crash (which occurred more than six months after decedent's death, but before the estate tax return was due), the value of the assets in decedent's gross estate declined by roughly $200,000. Local law required that the assets used to satisfy the pecuniary bequest be valued at the date of payment. After such payment and expenses, the residue passing to the spouse was $55,000, compared with the $250,000 value of the residue at the date of death. If assets used to fund a pecuniary bequest are valued at a time other than distribution, the payment may differ from the bequest. In Revenue Procedure 64-19, 1964-1 CB 682, the IRS explained that a marital deduction may fail under the terminable interest rule if a pecuniary bequest *to the spouse* is to be satisfied with assets valued at the date of death and if the executor has no duty to use assets that fairly represent the appreciation and depreciation of all available assets. A marital deduction is generally allowed, however, where a pecuniary bequest to the spouse is satisfied with assets valued at the distribution date. However, the pecuniary bequest was not to the spouse.

The IRS ruled that if a pecuniary bequest is required to be paid with assets valued at time of payment, the possibility that a decrease in the estate value may result in a smaller residuary bequest to the spouse does not create a terminable interest. The IRS's ruling does not indicate the size of the marital deduction available on the estate tax return. Presumably, it would be valued as of the same date used for valuing the gross estate. (In the facts of this ruling, the alternate valuation date of Section 2032A is not a factor, because the drop in values occurred more than six months after decedent's death.) Thus, in this ruling, the $900,000 gross estate would be offset by the $250,000 marital deduction, even though both had subsequently declined.

[Rev. Rul. 90-3, 1990-1 CB 174.]

IRS rules that marital bequest contingent on trust funding is nondeductible terminable interest. Decedent died testate, leaving a bequest to a power of appointment trust described in Section 2056(b)(5). This type of trust, more popular before the enactment of the qualified terminable interest property (QTIP) rules of Section 2056(b)(7), grants to the surviving spouse a general power of appointment over the property passing to the marital trust. If the spouse did not survive until the later of sixty days after the date of decedent's death or the date on which the trust was funded, the property otherwise funding the trust would pass to decedent's children. Decedent's spouse survived decedent by more than sixty days, and pursuant to the terms of the will, that was probated immediately after decedent's death, the residue of decedent's estate was placed in trust for the benefit of his spouse. Under the applicable probate code, a will may be admitted to probate, and an application for letters testamentary can be made, up to four years after decedent's death. Creditors of decedent may present their claims to the executor for six months after the letters testamentary are granted. Property devised and bequeathed by a will vests immediately in favor of the beneficiaries of the property. An income beneficiary's right to income is determined by the date specified in the trust instrument or, if one is specified, the date on which the asset becomes subject to the trust.

This probate code also provides that an asset subject to a testamentary trust becomes subject to the trust on the death of a testator even though there is an intervening period of administration.

In this ruling, the IRS recited the terminable interest provisions of the Code, noting that under Section 2056(b)(3), an interest will not be considered terminable if it should fail on the death of a spouse that occurs within six months after decedent's death and if termination or failure of the interest does not in fact occur. In sum, a marital bequest may be conditioned upon the spouse surviving for a period of up to 180 days after decedent's death. According to Regulation § 20.2056(b)-3(d), a residuary estate devised and bequeathed to a surviving spouse is a nondeductible terminable interest if the spouse is required to be living on the date of the distribution of decedent's estate, even though the spouse survived until the date of distribution. Under applicable state law, the will could be admitted to probate for four years after decedent's death and for another six months would be required for creditors to present their claims. Because funding the trust could occur more than six months after the date of death (at which the surviving spouse could be deceased), the IRS concluded that at the time of decedent's death, funding of the marital trust was contingent upon the spouse's surviving for more than six months after the death of decedent. The IRS concluded that the surviving spouse's interest in the marital trust could fail or terminate upon her death and that her interest in the trust was terminable under Section 2056(b)(1). This result occurred even though the applicable state law treated the spouse's interest as having vested at the time of decedent's death, entitling the spouse to income from the date of decedent's death. Similarly, the result was not affected by the fact that the spouse survived the funding of the trust. The critical fact was that the surviving spouse's interest could be defeated at a point more than six months after the date of decedent's death.

[Rev. Rul. 88-90, 1988-2 CB 335.]

[2] Life Estates With Powers of Appointment

Disclaimed power need not pass to anyone. Decedent's will directed the trustee of a residuary trust to use the income and principal for the support and maintenance of his wife. However, the trustee also had the power to use the principal for the college education of decedent's children. Because Section 2056(b)(7)(B)(ii)(II) provides that a trust qualifies for the marital deduction only if no person can appoint any part of the trust property to anyone besides the surviving spouse, the trust did not qualify for the marital deduction. To circumvent this, the trustee disclaimed his invasion power and furnished each child and the wife with a copy of the executed disclaimer. Section 2518 provides that in order for a disclaimer to qualify

1. It must be in writing.
2. It must be timely.
3. The disclaimant must not have accepted the interest or power or any of its benefits.
4. The interest must pass, without any direction from the disclaimant, to either the surviving spouse or someone other than the person disclaiming.

If a qualified disclaimer is made, the interest is treated as though it never passed to the disclaimant but instead passed directly to the person subsequently entitled to it. The IRS contended that the fourth requirement was not met, because the power the trustee disclaimed did not pass to anyone.

Held: For the estate. The court noted that Regulation § 25.2518-(2)(e)(1) provides that if a power of appointment is disclaimed, the disclaimer qualifies as long as there is no direction by the disclaimant as to the transfer of the interest subject to the power or with respect to the transfer of the power to another person. The court concluded that there was no specific requirement that the disclaimed interest pass to anyone. The IRS then argued that, despite the disclaimer, the children continued to have an interest in the trust because the corpus could be used for their college education. However, the court noted that the children had been notified of the disclaimer and had not objected and were therefore unable to claim any interest in the trust. As a result, the court determined that the disclaimer was valid in qualifying the residuary trust for the marital deduction.

[Cleaveland, 62 AFTR2d 88-5992, 88-1 USTC ¶ 13,766 (CD Ill. 1988).]

Different powers of appointment are necessary for marital deduction and gross estate inclusion. Decedent's husband created a trust with income going to decedent upon his death and the remainder going to her estate. When the husband died, the IRS disallowed a marital deduction because decedent did not possess a power of appointment for Section 2056(b)(5) purposes. Upon decedent's death, the remainder was included in her gross estate because she had a power of appointment over it under Section 2041(a)(2). The estate argued that the IRS is equitably estopped from taking those inconsistent positions.

Held: For the IRS. Determination of the existence of a power of appointment for purposes of one section does not control the question of whether a power of appointment exists for purposes of another section. Thus, inconsistent positions were not taken.

[Smith, 557 F. Supp. 723, 51 AFTR2d 83-1328, 83-1 USTC ¶ 13,511 (D. Conn. 1982).]

Marital deduction is not disqualified, despite fact that widow's power over corpus extends solely to fixed-dollar share. Decedent died on May 12, 1977. After making specific testamentary bequests, his will provided that the residuary of the estate was to be placed in trust for the benefit of his wife as well as certain other heirs and charitable beneficiaries. The trustee was directed to determine the wife's share pursuant to a formula clause set forth in the will. The wife's share was expressed as a fixed-dollar amount that was to be approximately equal to the maximum federal estate tax marital deduction allowable in determining decedent's taxable estate. At the time of decedent's death, the unlimited marital deduction, introduced by the Economic Recovery Tax Act of 1981, was not in effect. The will further provided that if the wife survived decedent for a period of six months, she was to receive a testamentary power of appointment over that part of the trust corpus that was equal to her lifetime share. In addition, the will contained a savings clause that stated that decedent intended "to cause the portion of this trust equal in amount to the wife's share to qualify for the marital deduction allowed by the federal estate tax laws, therefore, if the entire amount subject to the power of appointment . . . shall not qualify for the marital deduction, then the power shall be exercisable over all of the trust principal constituting my wife's share as it exists upon the death of my wife."

On its return, the estate claimed a marital deduction equal to one-half of the adjusted gross estate. The claimed deduction consisted of the wife's specific bequests plus her portion of the residuary estate. On audit, the IRS refused to allow the deduction to the extent that it included the value of the wife's share of the residuary. The estate argued that the wife's legacy was not a terminable interest under Section 2056(b)(5), which provides that if the surviving spouse is entitled for life to all of the income from a specific portion of trust property, coupled with a power of appointment over such portion, the interest will qualify for the marital deduction. The IRS contended, however, that the wife did not receive a power of appointment over a specific portion. In support, the IRS relied on Regulation § 20.2056(b)-5(c), which requires that the surviving spouse's power of appointment must constitute the right to appoint a fractional or percentile share of the property. Moreover, the regulation provides that if the surviving spouse's power of appointment is over only a specific sum out of a larger amount, then the interest is not a deductible interest. The estate admitted that the power of appointment extended only to a fixed dollar amount, but argued that insofar as the regulation required that the power of appointment be expressed as a fractional or percentage interest, or its equivalent, it was invalid.

Held: For the estate. The wife's share of the trust qualified in full for the marital deduction. The court ruled that Section 2056(b)(5) does not require that a specific portion of a residuary trust be expressed as a fractional or percentile share in order to fall within the exception to the terminable interest rule. In the court's view, Congress used the term "specific portion" in its general and unambiguous sense, and therefore did not intend to require a fixed dollar amount.

[Estate of Alexander, 82 TC 34 (1984), aff'd without published op., 760 F2d 264 (4th Cir. 1985).]

Tax Court interprets testamentary provision. The IRS disallowed a marital deduction for a transfer to a trust for the benefit of decedent's husband. The IRS argued that the trust was a terminable interest that did not give the husband an unlimited power of appointment and which provided that whatever power he had would cease upon disability.

    Held: For the estate. Correct interpretation and application of state law indicate that the power of appointment is unlimited and does not cease upon disability. Thus, the estate is entitled to a marital deduction under Section 2056(b)(5).

[Estate of Smith, 79 TC 974 (1982), acq. 1984-2 CB 2.]

Personal property passed to surviving spouse does not qualify for marital deduction, because spouse received life estate in such property and did not possess power of appointment. Decedent and his wife executed a joint and mutual will stating that each spouse would give to the surviving spouse all of the personal property, and that upon the death of the surviving spouse, all of the property would go to the couple's four children. Upon decedent's death, the estate filed a return claiming a marital deduction for the property that passed to the surviving spouse under the will. The IRS disallowed the deduction, claiming that the surviving spouse received only a terminable interest in the property and that therefore it did not qualify for the marital deduction.

    Held: For the IRS. The court found that under applicable Illinois state law, a joint and mutual will becomes irrevocable upon the death of the first spouse, and the property must be disposed of according to the plan set forth in the will. Thus, the surviving spouse received only a life estate in the property, which, pursuant to Section 2056(a), is a nonqualifying terminable interest and does not qualify for the marital deduction. If, however, a life estate is coupled with a power of appointment, it does qualify for the marital deduction. To qualify a life estate under this exception, five conditions must be met:

1. The surviving spouse must be entitled to all of the income from the entire interest or from a specific portion of the entire interest or to a specific portion of all of the income from the entire estate.
2. The income must be payable at least annually.
3. The spouse must have the power to appoint the entire interest of the specific portion to either herself or her estate.
4. The power must be exercisable by the spouse alone and must be exercisable in all events.

5. The entire interest must not be subject to a power in any other person other than the surviving spouse.

Because under Illinois law the interests of the remaindermen become vested at the time of the first spouse's death, the power of appointment, if any, was not exercisable by the surviving spouse alone or in all events. Thus, the life estate was not coupled with a power of appointment meeting the five conditions, and it did not qualify for the marital deduction.

[Estate of Grimes, TC Memo. (P-H) ¶ 88,576, 56 TCM (CCH) 890 (1988), affd sub nom. Bartlett, 937 F2d 316, 68 AFTR2d 91-6015, 91-2 USTC ¶ 60,078 (7th Cir. 1991).]

Trust is not eligible for marital deduction if support payments to another may cut off spouse's income interest. Decedent's will established a trust with a life estate and a power of appointment of the remainder to the wife. However, the spouse's life estate is subject to a direction for the trustee to pay to one of decedent's parents, out of income, amounts necessary to support the parent in his customary standard of living. No marital deduction is allowable for the wife's interest, because she has an unqualified right to none of the trust income. If an emergency arose, decedent's parent might need all of the trust income for support.

[Rev. Rul. 79-86, 1979-1 CB 311.]

Interest in trust does not qualify for marital deduction, because surviving spouse may not receive all of trust's net income. A couple executed a revocable inter vivos trust and transferred some realty interests to it. Prior to the transfer, various parcels of the real estate were owned by the wife, her husband, and by the couple as joint tenants with right of survivorship. The wife died, and all of the real estate was included in her estate. The trust provided that the surviving settlor would be the sole trustee and would be entitled to all of the trust's annual net income. Upon the death or legal incapacity of the surviving settlor, four persons were designated as cotrustees.

The IRS stated that the surviving spouse's interest in the trust did not qualify for the marital deduction under Section 2056(b)(5). The IRS reasoned that the surviving spouse was not entitled to all of the trust's income on an annual basis, because "assurance of annual distributions of all trust income is dependent upon the surviving spouse acting as trustee." The IRS stated that the trust provided for annual distributions or otherwise as the trustee considered desirable. Because the surviving spouse could become incapacitated, his authority to act as trustee was contingent, and there would be no assurance that the surviving spouse would receive all of the trust's net income. The IRS distinguished Revenue Ruling 55-518, 1955-2 CB 384.

[Priv. Ltr. Rul. 8546008.]

[3] QTIP: Qualified Terminable Interest Property

Provision allowing bargain sale of trust property killed QTIP marital deduction. Decedent died on November 25, 1988, survived by his wife and his son, who were named as co-executors by decedent's will. For many years, decedent served as the chief executive officer of a company. On the date of his death, he owned 52 percent of the company's capital stock. These shares had a book value of $1,390,178 and a FMV of $1,520,067. Decedent's will provided that if she survived him, the company stock would go to a trust for his wife. The net income of the trust was to be payable to her at least annually, and at her death the trust was to terminate, and the stock was to be distributed outright to decedent's son. The son was named as trustee of the QTIP trust, but his authority to manage the trust was made subject to several conditions. As long as he continued in the day-to-day management of the company, the voting rights of the stock were to be vested in him. But if, for any reason, he became unwilling or unable to continue active management of the company, the voting rights were to be vested in decedent's wife or, if she was no longer living, in the fiduciary of the trust. As soon as practicable after the son gave up day-to-day management, the fiduciary was to offer to sell the trust's stock to him at book value. If the sale was not effectuated, then the fiduciary was to select other potential buyers and offer reasonable terms for the stock's sale. After decedent wrote his will, the company elected S status, effective on January 1, 1987. Eleven months after decedent's death, the directors of the company approved a redemption of his shares from the trust. On the same date, the son, as trustee, entered into an agreement with the company to redeem the shares. The company agreed to pay the trust $1,520,067 for the shares, with $100,000 paid at the closing and the balance paid in quarterly installments over a twenty-year period, with 8.5 percent interest. Decedent's federal estate tax return, filed on November 29, 1989, showed a QTIP marital deduction of $1,520,067, representing the value of the stock willed to the trust. In examining the return, the IRS ruled that the trust did not qualify for QTIP treatment. The IRS said that the trust did not give decedent's wife a qualifying income interest for life because, in the event that the son ceased day-to-day management of the company, the will obligated him, as trustee, to offer to sell the stock to himself at book value—a price substantially below the FMV of the stock at the time. Such a transaction would effectively diminish the value of the trust's corpus, which runs counter to the QTIP requirement that "no person has a power to appoint any part of the property to any person other than the surviving spouse." The IRS said that the bargain sale would reduce the trust's principal and remove property from the wife's estate. If a QTIP election were allowed, this, in turn, would permit property that had already avoided taxation in decedent's estate to escape taxation in his wife's estate as well. The IRS said eligibility for QTIP treatment must be determined at the moment of death.

The estate argued that, at the time of the election, the trust owned none of the shares because they had already been redeemed at FMV, and decedent's son thus had no right to purchase them at a bargain price. The estate reasoned that, with no possibility of a bargain sale, the corpus of the trust was not subject to diminution, and no obstacle to QTIP eligibility remained.

Held: For the IRS. The Court of Federal Claims and the Federal Circuit disallowed the deduction because the trust established by decedent's will was clearly ineligible for QTIP treatment; the will explicitly subjected the trust's value to diminution through the potential sale of its assets at a bargain price to someone other than the surviving spouse. Accordingly, the company's post-mortem redemption of the shares devised to the trust by decedent's will did not bring the trust into compliance with the statutory requirements for QTIP eligibility.

[Estate of Rinaldi, 82 AFTR2d 98-7127 (Fed. Cir. 1998).]

QTIP not snubbed when spouse fails to get stub income. Decedent died in 1986, and his will divided the estate into two shares, one of which funded a trust that paid income to his wife in quarterly installments during her lifetime. The trust terminated upon his wife's death. Trust principal and all undistributed income were payable to decedent's niece. Quincy State Bank was the personal representative for decedent's estate. It elected to treat about half of the trust assets as QTIP. After the IRS examined the estate tax return, it allowed the QTIP deduction and issued a closing letter. Under Section 2056(b)(7), QTIP is property that passes from a decedent in which the surviving spouse has a qualifying income interest for life and for which a QTIP election has been made. To be a qualifying income interest, the surviving spouse must be entitled to all income from the property, payable at least annually, during her lifetime. QTIP qualifies for the unlimited marital deduction in Section 2056(a) and is taxed in the surviving spouse's estate under Section 2044.

Decedent's wife died in 1989. Quincy State Bank also served as personal representative for her estate. The bank omitted the value of the trust assets on the estate tax return for this estate. When the IRS audited the return, it included the trust property on which the QTIP election had been taken and assessed a deficiency. The bank, however, argued that the property was not includable in decedent's wife's estate, because she had not been entitled to *all* income—income accumulating after the last payment date and prior to her death (the "stub" income) went to the niece—so the QTIP election was invalid. The IRS, on the other hand, contended that Section 2056(b)(7) is satisfied if the surviving spouse controlled all of the income that had been distributed. By the time decedent's wife's estate was disputing this point with the IRS, the limitations period had expired with respect to decedent's estate tax return. Thus, the bank's conflicting positions on decedent's and his wife's returns sought to keep the property out of both spouses' taxable estates. The Tax

Court held that the requirements of Section 2056(b)(7) were not met, because decedent's wife did not have control over the stub income. Six of the sixteen judges, however, dissented.

Held: For taxpayer. The Eleventh Circuit began its analysis by characterizing the marital deduction as serving the dual purposes of (1) equalizing the tax treatment between those in common law and community property states, and (2) treating a couple as one economic entity. The goal of the deduction, said the court, was to permit property to pass untaxed from the first spouse to die to the survivor; property that passed untaxed was then expected to be taxed in the survivor's estate. Qualified terminable interest property—i.e., property interests that could end before the surviving spouse's death and thus escape taxation in the survivor's estate—generally could not qualify for a marital deduction prior to the enactment of the QTIP rules. In response to the rise in divorce and remarriage rates, the court said that Congress enacted the QTIP provisions in 1981 so the first-to-die spouse could better provide for the upkeep of the surviving spouse of a second marriage while having more control over the distribution of excess assets to children from a first marriage. Legislative history, however, did not address the stub income issue. Therefore, the court analyzed how it could further the goals of the marital deduction framework. The second goal, i.e., treating the married couple as one financial entity, entails letting property pass between spouses free of transfer tax, but taxing it when the surviving spouse dies. The IRS's position, said the court, comports with this by requiring the wife's estate to abide by the prior QTIP election. The Eleventh Circuit rejected the Tax Court's reading of Regulation § 20.2056(b)-5(f) as requiring the surviving spouse to have the power to dispose of stub income. That regulation says that "it is sufficient if [stub income] is subject to the spouse's power to appoint." Rather, the Eleventh Circuit said that the person with power to appoint trust principal should be treated as having power to appoint stub income. Then the stub income would be taxed along with the principal in the surviving spouse's estate. This appellate court pointed out that the flush language of Section 2056(b)(7) permits the property to be appointed to someone other than the surviving spouse upon or after that spouse's death without disqualifying the trust from a marital deduction. Furthermore, the 1981 addition of the QTIP rules was intended to liberalize availability of the marital deduction.

Finally, the Eleventh Circuit pointed out the following policy reasons for its position: (1) to provide certainty in estate planning because trust instruments set up in accordance with the IRS's advice would not be questioned, (2) to meet standard trust practices, since the Tax Court's interpretation of the statute would require the unusual practice of distributing income daily in order to have no accumulated income when the surviving spouse dies, and (3) to increase tax collections and further the congressional intent of taxing all previously deducted property.

[Estate of Shelfer, 86 F3d 1045, 78 AFTR2d 96-5177, 96-2 USTC ¶ 60,238 (11th Cir. 1996).]

Assets included in estate because of prior QTIP election. Decedent and his wife were married residents of Texas, which is a community property state. In 1980, they purchased a renewable term insurance policy on decedent's life. In 1983, decedent's wife died testate; her will left decedent certain property interests that he, as executor of her estate, elected to deduct from her estate by making a QTIP election. In 1986, decedent died, leaving his estate as the sole beneficiary of approximately $650,000 in life insurance proceeds. His personal representative excluded from the gross estate one half of the term life insurance benefit paid to the estate and those property interests that had passed from decedent's wife to decedent on her death in 1983. Decedent had made a QTIP election in his wife's estate in 1983 and deducted the property at issue from her estate by claiming the marital deduction. Now, however, his estate advanced the argument that this election was defective. The estate took the position that the income interest decedent received could not constitute a "qualifying income interest for life," as required by Section 2056(b)(7)(B). Upon decedent's wife's death, decedent received two types of interests in property. She bequeathed him specifically defined interests in their home and other real property, and her will also created a residuary trust whose income was to be paid to decedent during his lifetime. Her will assigned him a life estate in the family home, but permitted him to sell it provided that the proceeds from such sale were invested in another home for him, with any balance to be added to her estate's residuary trust. Decedent's estate argued that since no provision of her will nor Texas law precluded the accumulation of trust income (as opposed to its current distribution), the possibility existed that some of this income might be distributed to someone other than decedent. His estate contended that the QTIP election was defective. Decedent's wife's will provided that all the income from the trust was to be paid to decedent for as long as he lived "monthly or at the end of such other periods as may be necessary or desirable in the discretion of the Trustee." The IRS issued a notice of deficiency, and the Tax Court held that both the life insurance proceeds and the other aforementioned interests were properly includable in decedent's estate.

Held: Affirmed for the IRS (in part). The Fifth Circuit held that although the provisions of the will plainly granted the trustee some latitude in determining when income distributions should be made, reading this clause to allow the trustee to exercise absolute discretion in choosing when to pay decedent income was unwarranted. Decedent's wife's will specifically stated that payments of income should be made periodically, and the inclusion of the word "monthly" evidenced an intent to distribute the income at more frequent intervals than "reasonableness" requires. There was no authorization in the will for the trustee to accumulate income during decedent's life, and decedent was also given a "five and five" power. The court reasoned that since decedent was entitled to require distributions of principal annually under the five and five power, it was unlikely that decedent's wife did not intend him to take distributions of income as often. Consequently, the court ruled that decedent had received a qualifying income interest for life.

With respect to the life insurance proceeds, the court concluded that half the insurance proceeds were excludable from decedent's estate because they represented decedent's wife's community property. Regulation § 20.2042-1(b)(2) excludes life insurance proceeds payable to the estate to the extent they belong to decedent's spouse under state community property law. Here, it was clear that under Texas law, if life insurance is purchased during a marriage and paid for with community funds, the policy rights or incidents of ownership and the right to receive the proceeds in the future constitute community property. The IRS argued that the marital community was dissolved at decedent's wife's death, and any community property interest in the policy terminated upon expiration of the last one-year term of the policy paid with community funds. Alternatively, the IRS asserted that her community interest was capped at half the cash surrender value or the interpolated terminal reserve value of the policy at her death, which would have been zero. The court examined community property law and concluded that the community interest was not terminated by a zero cash surrender value at the time of decedent's wife's death. In other words, a number of valuable property rights continued for decedent's wife's estate, including the right to renew the policy annually at stated premiums with no evidence of insurability. In addition, the premium rates were fixed under the terms of the policy, and the dividends increased as the policy was renewed for extended terms. Therefore, by continuing coverage after decedent's wife's death, decedent apparently reaped some benefit from the prior four years of insurance. Based on this factor, the court held that half the proceeds should be attributable to decedent's wife's estate and, hence, excludable from decedent's estate.

[Estate of Cavenaugh, 51 F3d 597, 75 AFTR2d 95-2049, 95-1 USTC ¶ 60,195 (5th Cir. 1995).]

Estate may adopt wait-and-see approach and determine amount of QTIP on date of election. On September 24, 1984, decedent executed a trust agreement that provided for the establishment of a QTIP trust and a children's trust or credit shelter trust. The QTIP trust was to be funded with the amount elected under Section 2056(b)(7) by the executor after decedent's death. This trust contained typical QTIP provisions specifying that all income would be distributed to the surviving spouse at least quarterly and that no one could grant income or principal to anyone other than the surviving spouse during her lifetime. Decedent's spouse was named as trustee. Simultaneously, decedent executed a will naming his spouse as executrix of his estate. The will gave her almost complete discretion to determine the amount of the QTIP election. It also contained a provision indicating that decedent anticipated that his executor would elect to minimize the estate tax payable by his estate. Decedent died in March 1987; the surviving spouse qualified as executrix. On December 3, 1987, she appointed approximately $1.2 million of the estate to the QTIP trust and used the unified credit and administrative costs to reduce the taxable estate to zero. She then filed an estate tax return, claiming that the entire value of the QTIP trust was exempt from taxation under Section 2056(b)(7) by making the requisite QTIP election. The IRS disallowed the marital deduction. The IRS argued that the QTIP election should be disallowed because the executrix's power to determine the amount of the election constituted an impermissible power to appoint property away from the surviving spouse under Section 2056(b)(7)(B)(ii)(II). In response, the spouse pointed out that under the terms of the trust agreement, no property in the QTIP trust could be appointed away from her until after her death. Once the property was distributed to the trust, it clearly met all the requirements of Section 2056(b)(7)(B) and should qualify for the QTIP deduction.

Held: For taxpayer. The Sixth Circuit stated that it agreed with prior cases in the Fifth and Eighth Circuits (Estate of Clayton, 976 F2d 1486 (5th Cir. 1992), and Estate of Robertson, 15 F3d 779 (8th Cir. 1994), respectively) that the estate here was eligible for the marital deduction. The court indicated that estimating in advance of death how much property to commit to QTIP to minimize estate taxes is a problem for the estate planner. This is what led decedent in the instant case not to designate specific QTIP property in his will but rather to grant his wife as executrix the authority to decide what amount of property would be subject to the QTIP election when the time came to make it. According to the court, it is often impossible to designate prudently what should be committed as QTIP far in advance of death. By statute, the election can be made only after death. Therefore, no property anywhere can meet the definition of "qualified terminable interest property" until after decedent's death. The court reasoned that it would be contrary to the policy and meaning of the statute, as well as counter-intuitive and against common sense, to apply the definition before the election is satisfied. The Sixth Circuit held that the date of the election is the proper date for deciding whether property meets the requirements set forth in Section 2056(b)(7). The court noted that its decision was consistent with the purpose of Congress to liberalize the requirements surrounding the marital deduction. The 1981 amendments to Section 2056 made a number of changes, each of which expanded the scope of the marital deduction. In this spirit, the court determined that an interpretation favoring the allowance of the deduction in this case was in keeping with congressional intent. Such an interpretation recognizes that wills are often drafted long before death and that family situations and the value of assets may change dramatically. There is no reason to interpret Section 2056(b)(7) to require that a will identify QTIP far in advance of death and thereby deny taxpayers the full advantage of the marital deduction for such property. The election provision is plain enough and seems purposely worded to avoid this estate planning problem. The court indicated that its decision was reinforced by *Clayton* and *Robertson*, which reached the same conclusion. The Fifth Circuit in *Clayton*, after detailing the legislative history of Section 2056(b)(7), took the IRS to task for overzealous revenue collection. The Sixth Circuit in the instant case stated, however, that the *Clayton* court unnecessarily created a legal fiction that the QTIP election is somehow considered retroactive to the date of death. The Sixth Circuit found this treatment of the election unnecessary for the reasons previously stated. According to the court here, the election provision is plain on its face and need not be read retroactively.

[Estate of Spencer, 43 F3d 226, 75 AFTR2d 95-563, 95-1 USTC ¶ 60,188 (6th Cir. 1995).]

Fifth Circuit reverses Tax Court on executor's QTIP discretion. Decedent's will used a fairly standard *AB* trust approach. The portion of the residue of his estate that would be sheltered by the unified credit passed to Trust *A* for the benefit of his surviving spouse. That bypass trust did not meet the requirements for the marital deduction. Trust *B*, however, was designed to hold qualifying terminable interest property and to meet the requirements for the marital deduction imposed by Section 2056(b)(7). The will emphasized decedent's intent that the assets in the trust qualify for the deduction if the executor made a timely election. If the executor failed to elect QTIP treatment for any of the assets passing to Trust *B*, however, those assets would become a part of Trust *A*. The QTIP election was made for an undivided 56 percent interest in residuary assets (worth almost $1.1 million). The remaining 44 percent interest poured over to Trust *A*. Under Section 2056(b)(7)(B)(ii)(II), the QTIP election is not available if, during the surviving spouse's life, any person has the power to appoint any part of the property to any person other than that spouse. The IRS argued successfully in the Tax Court that the default provision of the will defeated the marital deduction. The Tax Court held that the QTIP election gave the executor control over trust assets that was tantamount to a power to appoint property away from the spouse. Thus, the issue facing the appellate court was whether the default to Trust *A* tainted the entire bequest and caused the assets in Trust *B* to be ineligible for the marital deduction. Although the statute permitted a partial QTIP election, the IRS contended that any QTIP trust that poured nonelected property over to another trust was fatally flawed.

Held: Reversed for the estate. The Fifth Circuit agreed with the estate that the property to be tested for compliance with the QTIP rules was the 56 percent for which the election was made, not, as the IRS and Tax Court had determined, the entire residue of the testator's estate (the maximum with which Trust *B* could have been funded if a total QTIP election were made). Accordingly, the surviving spouse had the requisite life income interest in the property. It was clear to the appellate court that the estate's entitlement to a QTIP deduction was not meant to be abrogated simply because making a *partial* election for a separate interest in the property resulted in a portion of the estate's residue passing to the bypass trust. The IRS's call for a narrow reading of the QTIP rules was rejected. In enacting the unlimited marital deduction, Congress clearly favored deferring estate tax until the death of the surviving spouse. It is the terminable interest provisions, which are an exception to this broad rule, that should be narrowly construed, the court said. QTIP—as an exception to that exception—should be as liberally construed as the marital deduction itself. The IRS's position would deny the marital deduction for *all* otherwise eligible property if occurrences after the testator's death, such as a QTIP election, prevented even a *part* of the otherwise eligible property from passing to the spouse. The Fifth Circuit found nothing that even remotely supported this "strained result," which would require it to ignore the "overarching truism that many acts must be done and many facts must be determined *after* the death of the testator in order to determine the taxable estate."

[Estate of Clayton, 976 F2d 1486, 92-2 USTC ¶ 60,121, 70 AFTR2d 92-6262 (5th Cir. 1992).]

Ninth Circuit upholds QTIP, despite trust provision permitting accumulation of income. Decedent, who died in 1986, had established an inter vivos trust that, upon his death, split into three smaller trusts. One of these subtrusts was denominated a marital deduction trust. The principal asset of the trust was the family farm. The initial trustees of this trust were the decedent's wife and her son. The trust agreement provided that the entire net income of the trust was to be distributed in quarter-annual or other convenient installments (but at least annually). The trust, however, did contain an accumulation proviso that read as follows: "If the income so payable to the Surviving Settlor shall, at any time or times, exceed the amount which the Trustee deems to be necessary for his or her own needs, best interests and welfare, the Trustee may accumulate the same as the Trustee deems advisable." The estate claimed a marital deduction for the trust property under Section 2056(b)(7), but the IRS denied the deduction because of the aforementioned accumulation provision. The Tax Court upheld the denial of the marital deduction, and the estate appealed to the Ninth Circuit. It was stipulated that if the marital deduction were not available, the estate would owe over $8 million in taxes, and the surviving spouse would have to sell the family farm.

Held: Reversed for the estate. The critical issue in this case was whether the surviving spouse had a "qualifying income interest for life" as required by Section 2056(b)(7). Most particularly, the issue was whether the surviving spouse was entitled to all of the income from the property because of the accumulation provision. According to Proposed Regulation § 20.2056(b)-7(c)(1), one requirement of the term "qualifying income interest for life" is that the surviving spouse is entitled for life to all of the income from the property, payable at least annually. The court examined the accumulation provision and decided that the testator's intent was such that the trustee could not, in effect, accumulate any income. The Ninth Circuit first noted that the trust was denominated a marital deduction trust and cited language of the trust instrument to the effect that

> The intention and direction of the Settlor is that all the property allocated to the marital deduction trust (1) may qualify for the marital deduction as qualified terminable interest property, (2) may be elected pursuant to Internal Revenue Code Section 2056 by the Deceased Settlor's personal representative to qualify as terminable interest property, and (3) may not be taxed as part of the Deceased Settlor's estate but shall only be taxed as part of the Surviving Settlor's estate at the Surviving Settlor's death.

Although the Tax Court had determined that this language was merely a gratuitous statement of intent, the Ninth Circuit felt that this language clearly demonstrated that the settlor wished the marital trust to qualify as QTIP if the trustee so elected. The court then noted that the accumulation provision stated that the trustee may accumulate income in excess of the amount necessary for the surviving spouse's "needs, best interest and welfare." The trust agreement did not define the term "best interest." As the estate's argument indicated, it would not be in the surviving spouse's best interest for the trustee to be forced to sell the family farm so that the estate could pay in excess of $8 million in taxes out of the marital deduction property. Consequently, the estate argued that the trustee of the marital deduction trust actually possessed no discretion to accumulate income. To effectuate the settlor's intent, the trustee would have to pay all of the income of the trust to the surviving spouse for her life. In other words, the estate contended that paying the surviving spouse such amounts of the income necessary for her best interest meant paying her all of the income, because to do otherwise would force her to sell the family farm. The Ninth Circuit concluded that although the trust could have been more clearly drafted, the court's choice was between two plausible readings of the trust agreement—only one of which effectuated the settlor's clearly manifested intent that the trust qualify for the marital deduction. If the accumulation proviso were to be read as granting the trustee unlimited discretion, the QTIP deduction would be lost. The court reasoned that the trustee did not have such discretion, and, accordingly, the trust qualified for the marital deduction.

[Estate of Ellingson, 964 F2d 959, 92-1 USTC ¶ 60,101, 69 AFTR2d 92-1475 (9th Cir. 1992).]

Lifetime use of marital residence qualifies as QTIP. Decedent granted her husband an interest in a residence pursuant to a codicil to her will, which provided, "I give, devise and bequeath to my residuary devisees and legatees ... my residence located at 1352 Willoughby Road, Birmingham, Jefferson

County, Alabama, ... subject, however, to the right of my husband, to occupy said property for as long as he desires. During the time my said husband occupies said property he shall pay the ad valorem taxes on said property and shall keep the same fully insured against fire and other perils, and in a reasonable state of repair." After decedent's death, her husband lived in the house until his subsequent death. Decedent's estate claimed a marital deduction equal to the value of her residence, but the IRS disallowed the deduction. The estate filed a complaint in federal court, requesting a refund of estate taxes with respect to that deduction for the value of the residence. The district court granted summary judgment to the IRS, and the estate appealed to the Eleventh Circuit.

Held: For the estate. The Eleventh Circuit stated that the issue was whether the transfer of the lifetime interest to decedent's husband qualified under Section 2056 as QTIP property. It was conceded that the transfer met two of the three QTIP requirements: (1) the property passed from decedent and (2) the executor made a proper and timely QTIP election. Consequently, the only question on appeal was whether decedent's husband's interest in the residence was a qualifying income interest for life. According to Section 2056(b)(7)(B), the surviving spouse has a qualifying income interest if he or she is entitled to all the income from the property, payable annually or more frequently, and if no one has the power to appoint any part of the property to anyone other than the surviving spouse. The IRS argued that decedent's will gave her husband only the right to physically live in the residence, and did not give him the right to all of the income (such as rents) as required. The Eleventh Circuit turned to Alabama law to determine whether that will gave him only a right to physically live in the house or whether he also had the right to any rents. In making this examination, the Eleventh Circuit found no Alabama cases that considered whether a will provision granting another the right to occupy a residence for as long as desired gave that beneficiary a right to the rents in the property for life. The court did find cases in some other jurisdictions construing similar provisions to establish a life estate. There were contrary determinations in some other jurisdictions. In light of this confusion in authority, the Eleventh Circuit determined to construe the will in its entirety according to the testator's intent. Decedent's intention was found to be providing her husband with a means to live out his life comfortably. She did not require that he physically live in the residence. The court concluded that if she intended that he forfeit his interest if he ceased physical occupation of the house, common sense dictated that such a requirement would have been included in the will. According to the court, decedent did not intend that if her husband needed to vacate the residence for a reason such as an illness, he would not be entitled to the rents from that residence. The court held that the testator's intention was to provide him with a life estate in the house to be used as a residence as he desired, and as a consequence he was entitled to the rents from the residence. The IRS also focused upon the language in the codicil that decedent's husband was to live in the residence as long as he desired.

The IRS reasoned that this interest could terminate prior to husband's death, and, hence, the will conveyed something less than a life estate. The court stated that although he might be able to relinquish his interest in this residence, it was an action completely dependent on his personal will and did not differ from any life estate that could be renounced or given away before death. The court concluded that decedent intended that her husband should have the degree of beneficial interest equivalent to a life estate and found a qualifying income interest for life existed.

[Estate of Peacock, 914 F2d 230, 90-2 USTC ¶ 60,051, 66 AFTR2d 90-6015 (11th Cir. 1990).]

Spouse need not get stub income for trust to be QTIP. Taxpayers placed all their property in a family trust. On the first spouse's death, the trust was divided, with each spouse's share transferred to separate trusts. The trust containing decedent's property was subject to the surviving spouse's right to receive distributions of all of the income at least quarterly. A QTIP election was made, and the resulting marital deduction eliminated any estate tax liability. Three weeks after the estate tax return was filed, the surviving spouse died. To avoid inclusion of this trust in the second decedent's estate, an amended return was filed for the first decedent, claiming that the QTIP election was invalid. Accordingly, the amended return reflected an estate tax of $380,000, whereas the second decedent's return showed a tax of $162,000. The IRS contended that the original QTIP election was valid, resulting in a total estate tax of more than $835,000, entirely attributable to the second decedent's estate. The basis for the estate's claim that the QTIP election was invalid was that the trust provided for the stub income to go to beneficiaries other than the surviving spouse or her estate. To qualify as QTIP, Section 2056(b)(7)(B) provides that the surviving spouse must be entitled to all of the income from the property for life, payable at least annually. According to the estate, because the income that accrued after the last distribution prior to the spouse's death was not payable to the spouse or her estate, the statutory requirement was not met.

Held: For the IRS. As long as the income was payable at least annually, it was sufficient that the spouse be entitled to all regular distributions of income for life. It was neither realistic nor required that the trust immediately pay out income each day on which it accumulates. Under the court's reading, the legislative history confirmed this meaning of the statute. The court also gave effect to Proposed Regulation § 20.2056(b)-7(c)(1). Finally, the court held that even though it was not payable to her, the undistributed income was includable in the second decedent's estate under Section 2044. The undistributed income was part of the QTIP in which decedent had a qualifying income interest.

[Estate of Howard, 910 F2d 633, 90-2 USTC ¶ 60,033, 66 AFTR2d 90-5994 (9th Cir. 1990).]

QTIP election must be clearly and unequivocally indicated. Decedent died testate, leaving the residue of his estate to a trust, with the provision that the net income therefrom be paid to his wife and, upon her death, that the remaining trust property be paid to three qualified educational institutions. Upon her death, the will was admitted to probate, and a federal estate tax return filed. On the return, the estate answered "no" to the question concerning the QTIP election under Section 2056(b)(7), and failed to identify any property that qualified for the election on Schedule M. The IRS disallowed a portion of the claimed marital deduction, asserting that the estate had not established that an election was made to treat any portion of the property passing to decedent's wife as a QTIP. The estate filed for a redetermination of the deficiency and argued that despite its negative answer to Question 12 on the return, its return as a whole demonstrated an intention to make a QTIP election.

Held: For the IRS. Section 2056(b)(7) requires a manifestation of an affirmative intent to elect qualified terminable interest treatment. If an election is made, the property is included in the estate of the surviving spouse. The decision whether to make the election requires an analysis of both spouses' potential tax liabilities, and may or may not be advised, depending upon the circumstances. The section does not allow a taxpayer to adopt a wait-and-see approach. Without the requirement of a clear and definite election, taxpayer could argue later that he had never intended to make an election.

[Higgins, 897 F2d 856, 90-1 USTC ¶ 60,011, 65 AFTR2d 90-1231 (6th Cir. 1990).]

Duty of consistency mandates trust's inclusion. Decedent's predeceasing husband's will created a trust benefitting decedent and their two adult children. The trust corpus consisted of terminable interest property in which decedent had an income interest for life. The husband's will authorized the trust to be treated as a QTIP, and named decedent and their son as co-executors. When decedent died on April 21, 1991, the trust had not been funded. The two children were decedent's only beneficiaries, and were the co-executors of her estate. The husband's estate tax return reported a $1,877,372 gross estate and claimed a $1 million marital deduction for the trust. The husband's estate tax return did not list the trust as terminable interest property, or make a QTIP election for it. Because the husband's estate did not treat the trust as QTIP, decedent's estate contended that the trust was not includable in her estate under Section 2044, which provides that a surviving spouse's estate includes terminable interest property if a QTIP election had been made. The IRS countered that, despite the lack of the QTIP election, the value of the trust was includable in decedent's gross estate under the duty of consistency (the limitations period on assessments against the husband's estate had expired).

Held: For the IRS. Under Section 2056, a predeceasing spouse's estate may claim a marital deduction for the value of certain property passing to the surviving spouse. The deduction is available with respect to terminable interest property, however, only if the predeceasing spouse's estate treats the property as QTIP. Thus, if the QTIP election is made, the property may be covered by the marital deduction, but that property is then subject to tax in the surviving spouse's estate. Because the trust was covered by the husband's estate tax marital deduction, the IRS argued that allowing decedent's estate to also avoid tax on it would violate the duty-of-consistency rule against allowing a taxpayer to benefit from an earlier year's error that cannot be corrected due to the expiration of the limitations period. The duty of consistency applies if: 1) taxpayer previously made a factual representation or reported an item for one tax year; 2) the IRS acquiesced in or relied on that representation; and 3) taxpayer subsequently, after the limitations period for the earlier year expired, attempts to change that representation.

Although the duty refers to inconsistent representations a single taxpayer makes, it may also apply to bind one taxpayer to another taxpayer's representations if the two taxpayers share a sufficient identity of interests. Thus, the duty was potentially applicable to the two estates here if they shared the requisite identity of interests. Finding that the estates were a single economic unit, that decedent had acted as co-executor of the husband's estate with her son (who also was co-executor of her estate), and that the estates shared the same adult beneficiaries, the court stated that the estates' interests were sufficiently aligned to subject them to the duty. The court then determined that, because the three requisite elements existed, the duty was in fact applicable in this case. First, the husband's estate had represented that the trust was eligible for the marital deduction and that it was not terminable interest property (which would be ineligible for the marital deduction absent a QTIP election). Second, the IRS, by accepting the husband's estate's return without auditing it before the limitations period expired, had acquiesced in or relied on this representation. Third, decedent's estate, in labeling the trust as terminable interest property, took a position inconsistent with that of the husband's estate after the limitations period on assessments against his estate had expired. Thus, the duty applied; so, decedent's estate could not avoid the tax on the trust that the husband's estate had already deferred—even though the trust was terminable interest property for which no QTIP election had been made.

[Estate of Letts, 109 TC 290 (1997).]

Tax Court concedes executor discretion O.K. for QTIP trust. Decedent died on July 1, 1987, with assets in excess of $7 million. His will provided for a bequest of a controlling interest in a family corporation to a son and bequests to his surviving spouse. The residue of his estate was divided between a marital trust and a family trust. The net income of the marital trust was payable to the surviving spouse at least quarterly and the trustees had an invasion power to maintain her standard of living. Upon her death the remaining principal was to be added to the family trust. The family trust provided for income and principal to be distributed among the surviving spouse, decedent's children, and the issue of any deceased children, in the sole discretion of the trustees. The estates' personal representatives had discretion to make a QTIP election for all or any part of the estate in excess of the specific bequests, expenses, taxes, unified credit, and any deductions. If they made the QTIP election for the maximum amount, all of it was to be distributed to the marital trust, and the family trust would not be funded until the surviving spouse died. Any amount for which they did not make the QTIP election was to go to the family trust. The personal representatives made a QTIP election for the maximum amount and the family trust was not funded. Section 2056(a) allows a marital deduction for property passing from a decedent to decedent's surviving spouse. Generally, the marital deduction is denied for a "terminable interest," i.e., a property interest that will terminate after a period of time, or on the occurrence of an event. A life estate is a terminable interest and, without more, would be ineligible for the marital deduction. Section 2056(b)(7), however, allows the marital deduction for life estates that are "qualified terminable interest property," which is defined as property satisfying three conditions: (1) It passes from decedent; (2) the surviving spouse has a qualifying income interest for life; and (3) an election has been made. For a qualifying income interest, the surviving spouse must be entitled to all the income from the property, payable at least annually, and no person can have the power to appoint the property to anyone other than the surviving spouse. The IRS disallowed the marital deduction for decedent's trust because any property for which a QTIP election was not made went to the family trust in which the surviving spouse did not have a qualifying income interest. Therefore, argued the IRS, the surviving spouse's receipt of a qualifying income interest was contingent on the personal representatives' election, and they had the power to appoint the property to someone other than the surviving spouse. In three earlier cases, the Tax Court had accepted the IRS's argument and been reversed by the Fifth, Sixth, and Eighth Circuits. The circuit courts thought that the third requirement, that the election "has been made," suggested a special testing date. In Estate of Clayton, 976 F2d 1486, 70 AFTR2d 92-6262, 92-2 USTC ¶ 60,121 (5th Cir. 1992), the Fifth Circuit concluded that when a QTIP election is made it is retroactive to decedent's death, so the personal representative never has discretion. The Sixth Circuit held that the date for determining whether the property qualifies for the QTIP election is the date the election is made, in Estate of Spencer, 43 F3d 226, 75 AFTR2d 95-563, 95-1 USTC ¶ 60,188 (6th Cir. 1995).

Held: For taxpayer. The Tax Court decided to follow the three circuit courts without specifying the precise reasoning that led to its acceptance of this result. The court cautioned, however, that its decision did not pass on the validity of Regulation § 20.2056(b)-7(d)(3), which states that an income interest that is contingent on an executor's QTIP election is not a qualifying income interest regardless of whether the election is made. The regulation is effective for estates of decedents dying after March 1, 1994, so it will have to be dealt with in a future Tax Court decision.

[Estate of Clack, 106 TC 131 (1996).]

Trustees' disclaimer cannot create marital deduction. Decedent's will poured the residue of the estate into an existing inter vivos trust. At decedent's death, this trust was divided into two separate trusts: the Family Trust and the Memorial Trust. Under the terms of the Memorial Trust, the trustees were to pay the net income of the trust to the surviving spouse during her lifetime. The trustees were also authorized, however, to pay medical, funeral, and burial expenses for three relatives of decedent from either income or principal. In addition, the trustees were authorized to pay educational benefits for certain individuals from trust income or principal. The trustees had the right to terminate the trust if they determined that it was so small that it was difficult to manage and did not accomplish the purposes for which it was established under decedent's will. After decedent's death, in an effort to obtain a marital deduction for a portion of the Memorial Trust, the trustees disclaimed some of their powers under the trust agreement. Members of decedent's family also disclaimed specified trust benefits (e.g., certain medical benefits). A state probate court confirmed the disclaimers. A qualifying income interest for life, as required by Section 2056(b)(7), exists if (1) a surviving spouse is entitled to all of the income from the property payable at least annually and (2) no person has a power to appoint any of the property to anyone other than the surviving spouse. The IRS disallowed the marital deduction on the ground that the surviving spouse did not have a qualifying income interest for life, because

1. The trustees could pay the medical and educational benefits from the income of the trust.
2. The amount of the medical benefits and the number of educational beneficiaries were unlimited, and thus the trustees conceivably could appoint the entire trust to someone other than the spouse.
3. The trustees had the power to terminate the trust.
4. The trustees had the power to allocate income to principal and thereby defeat the spouse's income interest.

Although the estate conceded that the trust had failed to meet the requirements of QTIP, the estate contended that the disclaimers cured the defects in the trust agreement to permit a marital deduction.

Held: For the IRS. The Tax Court agreed with the IRS that the trustees did not have the authority to change the unambiguous terms of the trust agreement. The court rejected the trustees' attempts, through renunciation of certain powers, to substitute their view of decedent's intent and to rewrite the trust agreement to allow a marital deduction that neither the will nor the trust agreement provided for. According to the court, the trustees sought to disclaim powers and duties that would amount to a renunciation of their trusteeships. Such a renunciation could not be effective, particularly if it was for the sole purpose of changing the tax results. The state probate court order confirming the disclaimers was not binding on the Tax Court. Thus, although disclaimers are frequently used to remedy a defective QTIP trust, the court refused to permit this where the result would be to rewrite the trust.

[Estate of Bennett, 100 TC 42 (1993).]

Exchange of homestead right for residual share of decedent's estate does not qualify as QTIP. Because decedent's will predated his marriage, it did not mention his surviving spouse. State law, however, provided that decedent's wife was entitled to a homestead right. In settlement of this right, she took a share of decedent's residual estate. The surviving spouse argued that the homestead right would have qualified for a marital deduction as a QTIP interest and that the portion of the residual share of the estate received in exchange for that right also qualified. She claimed that (1) the homestead right passed from decedent; (2) her interest was a QTIP interest; and (3) the remote possibility of her abandonment of her homestead right was not enough to deny an estate tax deduction. She asserted that it was unlikely that she would abandon her right to occupy the home, because it was worth more than $1 million and the remainder belonged to children from decedent's previous marriages. The IRS, on the other hand, contended that the homestead right under state law was not a qualified terminable interest, and that the exchange of a nonqualifying interest for a qualifying interest did not cure the defect. The state law allowed the surviving spouse to occupy the marital home as long as he or she lived. The right could be lost, however, if the surviving spouse abandoned the homestead. Also, the right to live on the property could not be sold or conveyed.

    Held: For the IRS. The Tax Court looked to state law to determine the deductibility of the surviving spouse's residual share. It rejected the surviving spouse's claim that it was unlikely that she would abandon the homestead, because it was based on speculation, not on any evidence of her actual intent. It is the possibility, not the probability, that an interest will terminate or fail that determines whether the surviving spouse's interest is a qualifying income interest for life. Although the homestead right is similar to a life estate, it is different and distinguishable in that the homestead right is personal to the surviving spouse and the right to live on the property cannot be sold or conveyed. Thus, the surviving spouse has a significantly restricted, or *terminable*, power over the homestead property. As a result, decedent's estate was not entitled to a marital deduction for the surviving spouse's share of the residual estate received in exchange for her homestead right. The residual share of decedent's estate that the surviving spouse received in exchange for her homestead right was similar to a payment for her statutory interest and was not a QTIP interest.

[Kyle, 94 TC 829 (1990).]

Although surviving spouse elected to take her statutory share against will, property transferred to inter vivos trust under decedent's will was QTIP. Decedent established an inter vivos trust solely to receive the residue of his probate estate. The trust agreement granted decedent's spouse an interest in the trust that would qualify for the marital deduction. After decedent's death, his surviving spouse elected to take her statutory share in lieu of her rights under decedent's will. After payment of the will's specific bequests and the spouse's statutory share, the executors distributed the residue to the inter vivos trust. On the estate tax return, the executors claimed a marital deduction based on the value of the property distributed to this trust. The IRS disallowed the marital deduction, on the ground that the property transferred to the trust was not a QTIP under Section 2056(b)(7).

Held: For the estate. Because the trust was an inter vivos trust, not a testamentary trust, the spouse's election did not affect the QTIP status of the property distributed to the trust. First, the spouse's election did not, under local law, cause her to relinquish any rights that she had in the inter vivos trust. Second, the spouse's election against the will did not prevent her from being deemed to receive property that "passed from decedent" as required under Section 2056 and its applicable regulations.

[Estate of Harper, 93 TC 368 (1989).]

Tax Court finds no qualified terminable interest property trust where trustee had power to invade corpus for benefit of decedent's son and brother during surviving spouse's life. Under the testamentary trust established by decedent, the trustee was given the power to invade the trust's corpus for "any emergency needs which affect the support, maintenance and health needs of any beneficiary" of the trust. This power was subject solely to the trustee's own discretion. The beneficiaries of the trust included decedent's son and decedent's brother, who were expressly granted (under other provisions of the trust) rights to the trust corpus after the death of decedent's surviving spouse. On the estate tax return, a marital deduction was claimed that included the value of the surviving spouse's income interest. The IRS disallowed the marital deduction to the extent that it was attributable to the value of the surviving spouse's life income interest, on the ground that the interest in the trust granted to such spouse was a terminable interest that did not qualify for the marital deduction.

Held: For the IRS. The trustee's power to invade corpus, during the surviving spouse's life, for the benefit of decedent's son and brother prevented the spouse's trust interest from qualifying as an income or annuity interest as described in Sections 2056(b)(7)(B) and 2056(b)(7)(C). Despite the estate's argument that the discretionary invasion power was intended to be effective after the surviving spouse's death, under state law, the trust provision (clear on its face) is given its plain meaning; that is, the invasion power was intended to be effective during the surviving spouse's life. The fact that decedent's son was severely disabled lends credence to this conclusion.

[Estate of Bowling, 93 TC 286 (1989).]

QTIP election is allowed, despite conditions imposed by will. Decedent's will left a life estate in certain property to her husband on the condition that he pay the real estate taxes and mortgage on the property. If he failed to make the payments, the life estate would terminate and the property would pass to their daughter. The IRS argued that because failure to pay the taxes or the mortgage would terminate the life estate, the interest did not qualify for the marital deduction as a QTIP under Section 2056(b)(7)(B)(ii)(I).

Held: For the estate. The court noted that the conditions for preserving the property that were contained in the will were also contained in the deed of trust by which the property had been transferred to decedent and the surviving spouse. Additionally, state law obligates a life tenant to preserve the property in much the same manner as the will required. The court acknowledged that there was a possibility that a situation might occur where the obligations imposed on the surviving spouse by the will would not exactly coincide with those under the deed of trust or state law, but it felt that the possibility was so remote that it could be ignored. Therefore, the property qualified for the marital deduction, because decedent's estate was entitled to make a QTIP election as to the property.

[Novotny, 93 TC 12 (1989).]

IRS rules that acquisition by spouse of remainder interest in QTIP trust gives rise to a gift. Under the facts of the ruling, a decedent who died in 1993 created a trust under his will for the benefit of his spouse and child. The surviving spouse was entitled to all the income from the trust, payable at least annually, for her lifetime. Upon her death, the balance of the trust was to be distributed to her adult child. The executor of decedent's estate elected QTIP treatment for the trust, and deducted the value of the trust on the estate tax return. Subsequently, the surviving spouse purchased her child's remainder interest in the QTIP trust. She gave her child a promissory note for the present value of the remainder interest. All the assets in the trust were then distributed to the surviving spouse. She used a portion of the assets to pay off the promissory note. A question arose as to whether the transaction caused a taxable gift to be made by the surviving spouse to her child. The surviving spouse argued that it did not because she had received full and adequate consideration (the remainder interest in the QTIP trust) in exchange for the promissory note she issued to her child. The IRS disagreed, finding that she had made a "disposition" of her income interest which generated a taxable gift under Section 2519.

The estate tax marital deduction is a special tax benefit that allows property to pass to a surviving spouse without payment of estate tax on the first spouse's death. The tax deferral continues until the surviving spouse dies or disposes of the property during her lifetime. When either of these events happens, a transfer tax—either estate or gift tax—is paid. The estate tax marital deduction is allowed under Section 2056(b)(7) for assets passing to a trust that meets the requirements for QTIP (the property must pass from decedent to a QTIP trust, and the surviving spouse must be entitled to all the trust income for life). The tax is deferred under Sections 2519 and 2044 for as long as the surviving spouse retains the life-time income interest in the trust. Section 2519(a) establishes the existence of a taxable gift if an interest in the QTIP trust is disposed of during life. The statute provides that "any disposition of all or part of a qualifying income interest for life in any property to which this section applies shall be treated as a transfer of all interests in such property other than the qualifying income interest." The statute further states that it specifically applies to any property for which a deduction was allowed with respect to the transfer of such property to the donor under Section 2056(b)(7). Section 2044 includes in the surviving spouse's estate property for which a marital deduction was claimed. This section provides that "the value of the gross estate shall include the value of any property to which this section applies in which decedent had a qualifying income interest for life." Section 2044 also expressly applies to any property for which a marital deduction was allowed under Section 2056(b)(7). Under Section 2519, a surviving spouse who disposes of all or part of her qualifying income interest in a QTIP trust is treated as having made a gift of the remainder interest in the underlying property (i.e., all interests other than the qualifying income interest). The term "disposition" is interpreted broadly, as explained in the legislative history of the 1981 enactment of Section 2519. In this Ruling, the IRS cited HR Rep. No. 201, which states: "The bill provides that property subject to a [QTIP election] will be subject to transfer taxes at the earlier of (1) the date on which the spouse disposes (either by gift, sale, or otherwise) of all or part of the qualifying income interest, or (2) upon the spouse's death." Section 2511(a) makes clear that the gift tax rules apply whether the transfer is in trust or otherwise, whether the gift is direct or indirect, and whether the property is real or personal, tangible or intangible. If the qualifying income interest is disposed of for less than adequate and full consideration in money or money's worth, under Section 2512(b) the gift equals "the amount by which the value of the property exceeded the value of the consideration." The ruling then discussed commutations. A commutation occurs when property is divided proportionately between the life income beneficiary and the remainderman, based on the respective values of their interests. In the context of QTIP trust, a commutation results in a taxable disposition of the surviving spouse's qualifying income interest, which generates a gift under Section 2519 of the remainder interest. A sale by the surviving spouse of her income interest is essentially the same as a commutation. The IRS decided that examples of sales and commutations in the regulations and in Estate of Novotny, 93 TC 12 (1989), were similar to the present transaction. In each situation, the surviving spouse's income interest was terminated, and the surviving spouse received outright assets with a value equal to that of her income interest. Similarly, after the transaction the remainderman owned assets equivalent to the value of his remainder interest in the trust. Therefore, the IRS ruled that the sale of the remainder interest to the spouse was a disposition of the spouse's income interest. The ruling concluded that under Section 2519, the spouse made a taxable gift equal to the value of the remainder interest in the QTIP trust.

[Rev. Rul. 98-8, 1998-7 IRB 24.]

IRA distributions to trust qualify for marital deduction. Decedent died in 1988, survived by his spouse. He designated the trustee of a testamentary trust established under his will as the beneficiary of all amounts payable from the individual retirement account (IRA). Under the distribution option he irrevocably selected, the account balance as of his death had to be distributed to the trust in equal annual installments over the spouse's life expectancy. The income earned on the undistributed portion of the account balance received during a calendar year had to be distributed to the trust annually by the close of the calendar year. On the spouse's death, any undistributed balance of the IRA had to be distributed to the trust. Under the terms of the trust, all trust income was payable annually to the spouse, and no one had power to appoint trust principal to any person other than the spouse. Accordingly, the trust met the requirements of a qualified terminable interest property trust. In addition, under the terms of the trust and state law, the installments of the IRA balance paid to the trust became trust corpus. All trust expenses normally allocated to corpus, including income tax payable on the IRA distributions, had to be charged to corpus. Both the income earned on the undistributed portion of the IRA balance payable to the trust and the income earned by the trust on the distributed portion of the IRA were payable currently to the spouse as income beneficiary of the trust. Although the marital trust qualified for the marital deduction under Section 2056(b)(7), the issue was whether the IRA itself also qualified. In order for the IRA to qualify, the surviving spouse must be entitled to all of the income from the property payable at least annually.

The IRS ruled that because the IRA had to distribute all income for the calendar year to the trust by the close of the year, and because the trust had to distribute all income currently to its beneficiary, the trust operated as a mere conduit for payment to the spouse of the annual income earned in the IRA. Thus, the income earned on the undistributed portion of the IRA was considered "payable annually" for purposes of Section 2056(b)(7), even though it was payable in the first instance to the trust, not to the spouse. The spouse therefore had a qualifying income interest for life in the IRA. Accordingly, on the spouse's death, any undistributed balance held in the IRA, as well as any portion of the IRA balance previously distributed to the trust, would be includable in the spouse's gross estate.

[Rev. Rul. 89-89, 1989-2 CB 231.]

Qualified disclaimer invalidates QTIP election. The estate made a valid QTIP election with respect to a certain interest left to the spouse. The spouse subsequently made a Section 2518 qualified disclaimer of the interest. The IRS ruled that the disclaimer is valid, and the spouse is treated as never having received the interest. Therefore, there is no qualified terminable interest under Section 2056(b)(7)(B). Thus, the QTIP election notwithstanding, marital deduction is not allowable.

[Rev. Rul. 83-26, 1983-1 CB 234.]

Marital deduction lost if rights end with incompetency. An interest in a trust failed to qualify for the marital deduction because the surviving spouse's rights depended on his remaining competent in this ruling. Decedent and her surviving spouse had transferred most of their assets to a revocable trust. During their joint lives, both were trustees, and the survivor would continue as the sole trustee until the need to appoint a successor arose. Decedent's probate estate poured over to the trust. The trustee was authorized, but not required, to pay all the trust's income to the survivor and apply principal for his support or for luxuries. Individually, the surviving spouse had sweeping powers. He could withdraw all (or part) of the principal, revoke the trust, and appoint any remaining principal by will. If the surviving spouse was declared incompetent, however, his interest in the trust and his powers terminated as if he were dead. The trust principal would then be distributed as he had appointed by will or, if the will was silent, to his children. Generally, under the terminable interest rule, a surviving spouse's interest that will terminate or fail with the passage of time or when an event or condition occurs does not qualify for the marital deduction. Section 2056(b)(5) provides an exception to this rule for a life estate in property with a power of appointment in the surviving spouse. This interest qualifies for the marital deduction if the five requirements of Regulation § 20.2056(b)-(5)(a) are satisfied:

1. The surviving spouse is entitled for life to all of the income from the interest.
2. The income is payable to the surviving spouse at least annually.
3. The surviving spouse has the power to appoint the entire interest to the surviving spouse or the surviving spouse's estate.

4. The power of appointment (whether exercisable by will or during life) is exercisable by the surviving spouse alone and in all events.
5. No one other than the surviving spouse has the power to appoint any part of the property to anyone else.

The IRS said that the trust failed to satisfy the first condition because the trustee was not required to distribute income to the surviving spouse. If income were accumulated, it would not necessarily be distributed to the surviving spouse if he were subsequently declared incompetent. The first condition is satisfied, nevertheless, if a surviving spouse has the right, exercisable at any time and in all events, to terminate the trust by having the corpus distributed to himself, according to Regulation § 20.2056(b)-5(f)(6). The income requirement also is satisfied if the surviving spouse can require annual distributions to himself, under Regulation § 2056(b)-5(f)(8). Despite the surviving spouse's powers to obtain all the trust principal, the IRS said that neither regulation applied, because the trust could terminate without his having exercised the powers if he first became incompetent. Therefore, they were not exercisable in all events. The Tax Court had concluded that a surviving spouse's power to invade corpus was not sufficient to save the marital deduction under the predecessor of Section 2056(b)(5) when the right to receive income and to withdraw corpus terminated if the spouse became legally incompetent, as in Estate of Tingley, 22 TC 402 (1954), aff'd sub nom. Starrett, 223 F2d 163, 47 AFTR 1225 (1st Cir. 1955). In the ruling, the estate contended that the surviving spouse's testamentary power to appoint the entire corpus of the trust (which was not present in the case) preserved the deduction. This power governed the disposition of the trust if the surviving spouse became incompetent (just as if he had died) and, therefore, argued the estate, decedent's power of appointment was exercisable in all events. The IRS pointed out, however, that the surviving spouse could become incompetent before his will exercised the power. Therefore, it was not exercisable in all events.

[Tech. Adv. Mem. 9644001.]

Trust with IRA can get QDT and QTIP tax breaks. A U.S. taxpayer who is married to a noncitizen received a positive response from the IRS to an estate planning arrangement in this ruling. Taxpayer had set up a marital trust that named his wife and another individual as trustee. If the wife is not a U.S. citizen at the time of his death, one of the trustees must be a citizen or domestic corporation and have the right to withhold tax on distributions. The trustees must distribute net income from the trust, at least quarterly, to the wife. They also may make discretionary distributions from principal for her "support in reasonable comfort, maintenance, and health" and pay expenses of her last illness and funeral. Any accrued and undistributed income at her death is payable to her estate. The trustees also are to distribute to the estate the amount of the estate tax on the trust property. Then, the remaining corpus goes to the couple's children. Taxpayer has two IRAs that designate the marital trust as the primary beneficiary. If taxpayer has begun taking required distributions from the IRAs before his death, the annual distributions to the trust are to be the greatest of the following: (1) all IRA income; (2) the current method of distributions being made at his death; (3) the required minimum distributions under Section 408(a)(6); and (4) the required minimum distributions under Section 401(a)(9). If taxpayer dies before required minimum distributions have begun, annual distributions must be at least the greatest of the following: (1) all trust income; (2) an amount based on the joint life expectancy of the wife and oldest contingent beneficiary; (3) the required minimum distribution under Section 408(a)(6); and (4) the required minimum distribution under Section 401(a)(9).

The IRA distributions made to the trust will be allocated to principal, except to the extent of the income earned by the IRAs (which will be allocated to income). If these distributions are less than the income, the trustees must require that additional distributions be made. If the wife is not a U.S. citizen at taxpayer's death, the trustees must elect to qualify the trust as a qualified domestic trust (QDT) for marital deduction purposes. The IRS ruled that the trust satisfies the QDT requirements in Section 2056A(a) because the U.S. trustee and withholding requirements, among other rules, are met. In addition, the marital trust and IRAs satisfy the QTIP requirements in Section 2056(b)(7) because all income will be paid to the spouse at least annually (in this instance, at least quarterly), and no one can appoint property to anyone other than the wife during her lifetime. With respect to the IRAs, the income will be distributed via the trust but will go to the wife frequently enough and in at least the minimum required amounts.

[Priv. Ltr. Rul. 9544038.]

Wife's interest in residence fails to qualify as QTIP. Decedent left an interest in his personal residence to his wife, directing in his will that she could use and occupy it for her life unless she moved out or remarried. The remainder interest in the residence was left to his sons. In an attempt to qualify the wife's interest for QTIP treatment, the sons and grandchildren executed disclaimers of any interest in the residence that they had that might arise during the wife's lifetime.

The IRS stated that although beneficiaries may disclaim one interest in property while retaining another interest in the same property, they may not disclaim a part of a single interest. To qualify for a partial disclaimer, the interest disclaimed must be separately created by the transferor or it must be a separate portion of an interest. The IRS concluded that there could not be a partial disclaimer of the remainder interest of the beneficiaries that might come into existence on the wife's moving or remarrying. Without such a disclaimer, the wife could not have a "qualifying interest for life" in the residence, as required for QTIP treatment. Thus, her interest in the residence could not be a QTIP interest.

[Priv. Ltr. Rul. 9140004.]

Trust funded with closely held stock fails to qualify for QTIP. Decedent's trust for the surviving spouse was funded with closely held stock that had not paid dividends regularly and that could be purchased by the son at book value during the surviving spouse's life. The IRS took the position in technical advice that the trust failed to qualify for QTIP. The son's right to purchase the stock at book value (that was less than FMV) gave him a power to withdraw property from the trust. Thus, the son had a power to appoint a portion of the property to a person other than the surviving spouse, in violation of Section 2056(b)(7). The IRS determined that the son's power to withdraw property could not be construed as giving the spouse the right to income from a specific portion of the trust. The spouse did not receive a qualifying income interest for life, because she lacked an adequate right to income. The spouse had no legally enforceable right to establish an adequate income flow, because the son's voting right gave him the power to accumulate profits and withhold dividends.

[Tech. Adv. Mem. 9139001.]

Lifetime use and right to 50 percent of sale proceeds from marital residence qualifies as QTIP. Testator died on January 25, 1988, and bequeathed to his spouse the right to occupy their principal residence. The will provided that if the spouse vacated the premises prior to her death, the premises would be sold at a price and at terms established by the executor. In such an event, 50 percent of the proceeds would be paid to the testator's son, and the remaining 50 percent would be added to the corpus of a marital trust that concededly qualified as a QTIP.

The IRS took the position in technical advice that the right to occupy the residence until the sale, coupled with the right to income from 50 percent of the sale proceeds until the death of the spouse, constituted a right to the lifetime enjoyment of one half of the property interest represented by the residence. Therefore, the surviving spouse was held to have a qualifying income interest for life in at least 50 percent of the residence for purposes of Section 2056(b)(7).

[Tech. Adv. Mem. 9040001.]

General power to appoint does not preclude QTIP deduction. Decedent's wife received a QTIP under a will that gave her the power to appoint up to $5,000 or 5 percent of the QTIP property annually to whomever she liked. A deduction for a trust for a surviving spouse is available to the estate if the surviving spouse is entitled to all of the income from the trust property annually during her life, and no person has a power during the spouse's life to appoint any part of the property to any person other than the spouse. The wife's general power to appoint the property did not violate Section 2056(b)(7), because the appointment of property to her included the power to exercise such dominion and control over the property that she could give it to whomever she wished. Furthermore, the IRS noted that the legislative history provided that a spousal power of appointment would not preclude the deduction where the exercise of the power was subject to the transfer tax. Because a general power is subject to the transfer tax, it is consistent with the provisions of Section 2056. Thus, the QTIP deduction was allowed.

[Tech. Adv. Mem. 8943005.]

Contingent upon executor electing to treat trust as QTIP, income interest does not qualify for marital deduction. An individual died testate in 1985, leaving his wife and two children. A trust had been created in 1977 and was amended in 1984. Under the terms of decedent's will, the executor of the estate was directed to make several advisable elections. The elections included, but were not limited to, an election to treat all or part of any property passing to the surviving spouse as constituting a qualifying income interest for life for marital deduction purposes. The trust directed the trustee to set aside, out of the trust's estate, an amount to be held as a marital deduction trust. Specifically, the amount to be set aside was to be the smallest amount that, if allowed as a federal estate tax marital deduction, would result in the smallest possible federal estate tax being owed. In relation to funding the marital trust, the executor could elect to have all or part of the marital trust treated as QTIP for federal estate tax purposes. In addition, any portion of the marital trust that was not QTIP would be used to fund a second trust. If the executor should fail to elect that the marital trust qualify for the marital deduction, the property, which would have comprised the marital trust, would pass instead to the second trust. The provisions in the second trust called for distributions of income to the surviving spouse and decedent's descendants and their spouses.

The IRS stated that the surviving spouse's income interest in the marital trust would not qualify for marital deduction treatment under Section 2056(b)(7). The IRS reasoned that the surviving spouse's income interest in the trust would be contingent upon the fiduciary's election to treat the property as QTIP. Because the spouse's interest would be contingent upon a fiduciary's election, the IRS concluded that it would not be passing from decedent to the surviving spouse.

[Tech. Adv. Mem. 8916002.]

Spouse's income interest in marital deduction trust does not qualify for Section 2056(b)(7) election if interest is contingent on QTIP election. An individual died testate. His will provided that his residuary estate was to be divided into two separate trusts, a family trust and a marital deduction trust. The family trust was to be funded with an amount of property that would produce a tentative tax equal in value to the federal estate tax unified credit. During the surviving spouse's life, the family trust was to be held, applied, and distributed by the fiduciary for the benefit of the spouse and decedent's children and descendants. At the spouse's death, the family trust would terminate. The remainder would be distributed to decedent's children and descendants. The marital deduction trust consisted of the balance of the residuary estate not included in the family trust. The will provided that if decedent's wife survived him by sixty days, the trustee would distribute the balance of the trust estate not passing into the family trust into the marital deduction trust. If such action had the effect of passing property into the marital deduction trust that did not qualify for the federal estate tax marital deduction, however, then the nonqualifying property would be distributed into the family trust.

The IRS stated in technical advice that the surviving spouse's interest in the marital deduction trust would not qualify for the Section 2056(b)(7) election, because her income interest in the trust would be contingent on the trustee's election to treat the property as QTIP. Section 2056(b)(7) provides that QTIP is treated as passing to the surviving spouse and that no part of such property shall be treated as passing to any person other than the surviving spouse. The IRS noted that though the marital deduction trust may have met the income and power of appointment requirements of Section 2056(b)(7), the family trust did not. Under the will, the fiduciary was granted discretionary authority to elect to treat the property passing into the marital deduction trust as QTIP. If the fiduciary failed to elect that the marital deduction trust qualified for the marital deduction, then the property that would have comprised the marital deduction trust would pass instead to the family trust. As part of the family trust, the property would not be eligible for a marital deduction under Section 2056(b)(7). The IRS therefore concluded that the spouse's interest in the marital deduction trust should not be regarded as passing from decedent to the surviving spouse for purposes of Section 2056. The IRS concluded that the surviving spouse should not receive a qualifying income interest for life in any part of the assets of the marital deduction trust, and that no portion of the marital deduction trust qualified for the Section 2056(b)(7) election.

[Tech. Adv. Mem. 8901003.]

Conditional election of QTIP is valid. An individual died in May 1986. The residue of his estate passed into a trust created by the will. The wife was given a power, as trustee, to appoint one half of the trust assets to herself during her lifetime, but she did not possess a power of appointment as described in Section 2056(b)(5). The wife also was given an 80 percent share in the "income" from the trust. The trust defined "income" as taxable income as reported on the tax return, however, rather than the items of income that might be reflected on the tax return but do not enter into the computation of taxable income. Included in the property that funded the trust were tax-exempt municipal bonds, representing approximately 5 percent of the gross estate. The estate claimed a marital deduction for one half of the trust, stating that if this portion did not qualify for a marital deduction under Section 2056(b)(5), the executor would elect to treat one half of the trust as a QTIP qualifying for the marital deduction under Section 2056(b)(7).

The IRS took the position in technical advice that the surviving spouse would have a deductible QTIP interest equal to 50 percent of the value of all of the estate assets that would fund the trust. A QTIP election that is conditioned on property not otherwise qualifying for a marital deduction is not the equivalent of a revocable election, the IRS explained. Further, the IRS stated that the expression of the surviving spouse's income interest by reference to taxable income would not require a disallowance of a deduction under Section 2056 for any part of the surviving spouse's interest in the trust. The amount of the deductible interest would be determined by reference to the surviving spouse's maximum assured income interest, the IRS concluded, because that interest, in 50 percent of the trust property, would be less than the surviving spouse's nominal 80 percent income interest. The municipal bonds could be sold by the surviving spouse as the initial trustee, the IRS noted, so that this tax-exempt income would not accumulate in the trust, because of the trust document's failure to provide for the distribution of tax-exempt income. The wife would be assured only of a maximum income interest of 50 percent, the IRS concluded, because if all of the trust assets were sold, she would receive 50 percent of the proceeds, and her nominal 80 percent interest in the trust income would disappear with the trust's termination. Finally, the IRS concluded that it is not necessary to identify specific trust assets that represent the surviving spouse's principal interest.

[Tech. Adv. Mem. 8841001.]

Property placed in trust qualifies for QTIP election. An individual's will provided for a bequest of certain personal property to his wife and for a devise of the remainder of his property to a remainder trust created under the will. The remainder trust agreement directed the trustee to "pay the net income from the trust to (the individual's) wife until her death," if she survived the individual by thirty days. The executor provided sufficient information on the estate tax return to allow the estate tax examiner to determine that the executor had made an election under Section 2056(b)(7) for treatment of the trust property as QTIP. The will did not state how often the trustee was to make payments of income from the trust property to decedent's wife. Accordingly, the successor trustee filed a petition in a district court of the appropriate state seeking an order construing the provisions of the will governing the payments of income. The district court found that the provisions of the will were silent regarding the frequency with which payments of income were to be made. The court then found that in a case where a trust agreement does not specify the income beneficiary's rights, the income must be distributed at least annually.

The IRS took the position that the trust provisions in decedent's will satisfied the requirements of Section 2056(b)(7), including the requirement of annual payments of income. Accordingly, the IRS allowed a marital deduction for the QTIP. The IRS stated that the only provision of state law applicable to interpret the terms of the trust was a statute declaring that, absent contrary trust provisions, the trustee shall perform all duties imposed by common law. The IRS determined that the general rule under common law requires payment of income at least annually. The IRS determined that the state's supreme court, if presented with the issue, would affirm the district court's decision. Such a determination, the IRS stated, is mandated by Estate of Bosch, 387 US 456 (1967), which held that a federal agency should decide how the state supreme court would rule in assessing the effect of a trial court's decision.

[Priv. Ltr. Rul. 8715004.]

Interest passing to spouse is QTIP, even though it does not require annual payout of income. An individual died in 1984, survived by a spouse and two adult children. His will bequeathed his personal property to his spouse, and his real property was to be divided in equal shares between his two children, subject to the condition that the net rents and revenues from the real property be paid to the spouse during her lifetime. The will also expressed the desire that the children control decedent's one half of the community real property, subject to the surviving spouse's management of the entire community real property. The will made no provision for the payment of debts, administration expenses, or estate taxes. During the nine-month period after decedent's death, the spouse executed a disclaimer with respect to certain parcels of real property that, under local law, caused the properties to pass directly to the children. The estate made a Section 6166 election to make installment payments for a portion of the federal estate tax liability that was attributable to a closely held business. The estate tax return also indicated that the property acquired by the spouse was acquired as QTIP. The spouse's interest in the real estate was presented to the District Office in the form of a trust, but the trust instrument did not specify whether income from the property was to be paid at least annually, and there was no state statute that required distributions of trust income at least annually. Under the trust, the children, who were its trustees, had the discretion to determine the frequency of the income payments.

The IRS stated that the interest passing to the spouse satisfied the requirement under Section 2056(b)(7)(B)(i) that income from the property be payable annually or at more frequent intervals. The IRS reasoned that under trust law in "virtually all jurisdictions, if a trust instrument or will directs the payment of income to beneficiaries, but the time for payment is not fixed by the instrument, the income may not be accumulated. Rather, the income must be paid out at reasonable intervals, that is, on a quarterly or semi-annual basis, or as the income is received." The IRS cited Egavian v. Egavian, 232 A2d 789 (RI 1967) to support its holding. The IRS also stated that the value of the personal property passing to the spouse was to be reduced by the estimated maximum amount of interest that would be payable on the deferred federal estate tax. To the extent that personal property was not available, the IRS further indicated, the interest would be payable from the spouse's interest in the residuary real property. The IRS reasoned that the applicable Texas law provides that in the absence of a provision that provides otherwise, all administration expenses, debts, and estate taxes are to be paid from the corpus of the residue, with the personal property in the residue being used first. The IRS cited Republic Nat'l Bank of Dallas, 334 F2d 348 (5th Cir. 1964), to support its holding. In considering the amount of administration expenses deductible under Section 2053(a), the IRS concluded that no deduction was allowable with respect to the estimated amount of total interest to be paid on the deferred estate tax, with the interest being deductible only when accrued. The IRS noted that though interest expense for deferred federal estate taxes is deductible under Section 2053(a), it can be deducted only when accrued. The IRS cited Revenue Ruling 80-250, 1980-2 CB 278, for the proposition that no deduction was allowed for estimated future interest expenses.

[Priv. Ltr. Rul. 8705002.]

IRS revokes prior technical advice indicating that residual trust corpus is QTIP. An individual died in 1982. His will provided for the payment of debts, expenses, and death taxes; made specific bequests of tangible personal property and residential real estate to his spouse; and provided that all of the residue of the estate would pass to the trustee of a revocable trust. The bulk of the estate consisted of the proceeds of insurance policies on decedent's life, payable directly to the trustee of the revocable trust. The probate estate was insufficient to pay debts and expenses, and therefore nothing passed under the residuary clause of the will. The revocable trust provided that during the individual's lifetime, the trustee was to pay to him or for his benefit so much of the annual net income and principal as he requested. Alternatively, in the absence of a request or in the event of the individual's incapacity, the trustee was to pay him so much of the income and principal as the trustee, in its discretion, deemed desirable for the support, maintenance, health, and education of the individual and his wife and of their issue living under his or her care or supervision. The revocable trust further provided for the creation of three separate trusts upon the decedent's death: a unified credit trust, a marital trust, and a residual trust. The unified credit trust was not in issue, and the marital trust satisfied the requirements of Section 2056(b)(2). The executor elected under Section 2056(b)(7) to claim a marital deduction for the entire amount of property passing to the residual trust. The individual's will provided that during his wife's lifetime, the trustee should pay at least quarterly to her, or apply for her benefit, all of the net income and "so much of the principal of the trust as the trustee in its sole discretion deems advisable for her comfortable support, maintenance, health, and/or education and that of any of the settlor's issue under her care and supervision." The surviving spouse was given a testamentary power to appoint the residual trust corpus among decedent's issue. In the event that the wife did not exercise any of the powers of appointment, the property subject to such power was to be held in separate trusts. There was to be one trust for each living child of decedent and one trust for each deceased child leaving issue.

In a prior ruling, Private Letter Ruling 8526009, the IRS had taken the position that the corpus of the residual trust was QTIP under Section 2056(b)(7). In the instant ruling, the IRS revoked its prior ruling and indicated that the property passing under the terms of the residual trust failed to qualify as QTIP. Citing Regulation § 20.2056(b)-5(j), the IRS reasoned that the trustee's power to distribute residual trust property to the spouse for the maintenance and support of decedent's "issue," which could include adult children for whom the surviving spouse would have no legal obligation of support, violated the requirement under Section 2056(b)(7) that no person have the power to appoint any part of the property to any person other than the surviving spouse during her lifetime. This was so, the IRS concluded, even though all payments for the benefit of the issue would be initially payable to the spouse, because she would be bound by a fiduciary standard "in her custody and disbursement of such invasions."

[Priv. Ltr. Rul. 8701004.]

Disclaimers do not create qualifying income interest for life. Decedent's will provided for a marital deduction equal to the "maximum marital deduction allowable in determining the federal estate tax payable." The spouse irrevocably disclaimed her interest, except her right to income for life, and the children irrevocably disclaimed their interests and powers to act as trustee to invade corpus for the support, education, last illness, and funeral expenses of decedent's other descendants. None of the children disclaimed their beneficial right to have the trust corpus invaded for their own support, education, last illness, and funeral expenses. The day after the disclaimers were filed, the estate tax return was filed with a QTIP election under Section 2056(b)(7)(B)(v), which, if valid, would reduce the federal estate tax to zero.

The IRS stated that the disclaimer did not effectively extinguish the rights of the surviving spouse and the children to allow other descendants to enforce the provisions of the trust for the spouse's and children's benefit. Accordingly, the marital deduction was disallowed under Section 2056(b)(7) because the surviving spouse was not assured of income from a qualified portion of the corpus for her entire lifetime.

[Priv. Ltr. Rul. 8605004.]

QTIP election is held valid, despite errors in filling out estate tax return forms. An individual died testate with a will providing specific bequests and a residual bequest to fund a trust. The surviving spouse had an income interest in the trust for life under Section 2056(b)(7)(B)(ii). If the estate made the proper election, the trust would be QTIP. On the estate tax return, the estate's personal representative answered "yes" to the question, "Do you elect to claim a marital deduction for an otherwise nondeductible interest under Section 2056(b)(7)?" On Schedule M of the return, however, the personal representative failed to indicate a QTIP election. An entry was made for certain "Qualified Terminal [sic] Interest Property," and two of the estate's assets were listed. The IRS stated that under the facts and circumstances of the case, a QTIP election was properly made. The National Office noted that the estate "manifested a clear intent to make a QTIP election" by answering "yes" to the above-noted question on the estate tax return.

[Priv. Ltr. Rul. 8602005.]

QTIP final regulations offer refund opportunity. Final regulations clarify that an executor's discretion in making a QTIP election does not prevent property from qualifying for the marital deduction. The regulations let taxpayers make a retroactive election that can produce tax refunds. In general, the estate tax marital deduction is not available for life interests in property. Section 2056(b)(7), however, provides an exception for QTIP. Such property must:

1. Pass from decedent.
2. Give the surviving spouse a qualifying income interest for life (i.e., entitlement to all income from the property, payable at least annually, and no one has the power to appoint any part of the property to someone other than the surviving spouse).
3. Be the subject of an irrevocable QTIP election made by the executor on the estate tax return.

Suppose a decedent's will establishes a trust that will pay the surviving spouse a qualifying income interest for life from the portion of the trust that the executor elects to treat as QTIP. Their child is the beneficiary of the portion of the trust for which the election is not made. Under regulations issued in 1994, the surviving spouse's income interest specifically could not be a qualifying income interest for life (and hence not eligible for the marital deduction). Now, Regulation § 20.2056(b)-(7)(d)(3) has been amended so that the contingency of an executor's election, or fact that a portion of the property for which the election was not made passes to someone else, does not prevent a qualifying income interest for life from being eligible for the marital deduction. This liberalization conforms with various court decisions (e.g., *Estate of Clack*, 106 TC 131 (1996).

The new regulations apply to estates for which estate tax returns were due after February 18, 1997. It also applies to estates with earlier return due dates—for which the limitations period in Section 6511(a) did not expire— that did not make the QTIP election because the surviving spouse's income interest was contingent on the executor's election and whatever the election did not cover would go to someone other than the surviving spouse. Refund claims should be made on Form 843 with a revised recapitulation and Schedule M of Form 706. The new regulations should be referred to on the Form 843. Also, that form should bear this signed statement: "The undersigned certifies that the property with respect to which the QTIP election is being made will be included in the gross estate of the surviving spouse as provided in section 2044 of the Internal Revenue Code, in determining the federal estate tax liability on the spouse's death."

[TD 8779, 1998-36 IRB 11.]

PART III

TAXATION OF ESTATES AND BENEFICIARIES

CHAPTER **12**

Estate Tax

¶ 12.01 IMPOSITION OF TAX

[1] Generally

State law determines when missing person is considered dead. *X* was missing for seven years. His property was placed in receivership, but he retained title. Under state law, *X* could not be declared dead until fourteen years after his disappearance. *X*'s estate tax return was due within nine months following the fourteen-year period, unless death was established earlier by a state court decision transferring title.

[Rev. Rul. 80-347, 1980-2 CB 342.]

[2] Foreign Estates, Interests, and Decedents

French resident's estate is not entitled to unified credit. Decedent was a citizen and resident of France. His estate included property in California. The estate claimed that it was entitled, under the U.S.-France Tax Treaty, to compute the estate tax by using the unified credit for U.S. citizens and residents. The Tax Court held that decedent was allowed only the nonresident unified credit for $3,600.

Held: For the IRS. The treaty could not be reasonably construed as overruling the Code, either expressly or implicitly, to permit decedent to use the unified credit allowed to U.S. citizens and residents.

[Estate of Arnaud, 895 F2d 624, 65 AFTR2d 90-1196, 90-1 USTC ¶ 60,006 (9th Cir. 1990).]

Decedent is held to be U.S. citizen. Decedent's estate claimed a refund for gift taxes based on the theory that decedent was not a U.S. citizen. The district court held for the IRS. Although decedent married a Mexican citizen and executed a certificate of Mexican nationality, she did not execute an oath renouncing her U.S. citizenship and evidenced no intent to renounce her citizenship. Moreover, her estate was estopped from claiming that she renounced her U.S. citizenship, because, through her actions and representations subsequent to her marriage, she represented herself as a U.S. citizen.

Held: Affirmed for the IRS. The district court properly granted summary judgment in favor of the IRS. The estate was estopped to deny a long line of representations of decedent's U.S. citizenship.

[Matheson, 532 F2d 809, 37 AFTR2d 76-1555, 76-1 USTC ¶¶ 9,304, 13,129 (2d Cir. 1976), cert. denied, 429 US 823 (1976).]

Claims Court, citing Tax Court decision, construes U.S.-Swiss treaty liberally in finding full availability of unified credit. Decedent was an Irish national who was a domiciliary of Switzerland at the time of his death in 1980. Although he was neither a resident nor a citizen of the United States, the bulk of his estate was located in the United States and subject to U.S. federal estate tax. The estate filed its estate tax return, paying $131,284 in tax and claiming a unified credit of $3,600. The estate later reconsidered its claimed credit and sued for a refund on the basis of a total credit of $38,210. In support of this position, the estate noted that Section 2102(c)(1) provides a maximum credit of $3,600 for nonresident foreigners, but allows a maximum credit of $42,500 for residents and citizens. However, the estate argued in the Claims Court that the U.S.-Swiss estate tax treaty, in Article III, provides for a Swiss national to receive a pro rata portion of any specific exemption otherwise available to a U.S. citizen.

Held: For the estate. Citing a 1983 Tax Court case dealing with similar issues under a U.S.-Italian treaty, the Claims Court held that the term "specific exemption" was intended to apply to estate tax credits, including the unified credit as applied to foreign estates. The IRS argued that the term was to be applied only to exemptions that were formerly a part of federal estate tax. Credits were therefore not covered. The Claims Court, like the Tax Court before it, rejected this contention in view of the rule propounded by the Supreme Court for liberal construction of tax treaties.

[Mudry, 11 Cl. Ct. 207, 59 AFTR2d 87-1202, 86-2 USTC ¶ 13,706 (1986).]

U.S.-Canadian estate tax convention does not preclude United States from imposing federal estate tax on transfer of life insurance proceeds and death benefits from retirement annuity contracts and retirement plan owned by U.S. citizen domiciled in Canada at death. Decedent died a citizen of the United States but a domiciliary of Canada. At the time of death, decedent owned interests in Canadian life insurance and annuity contracts for which he designated a Canadian citizen as beneficiary. His estate did not include the value of the proceeds from the various contracts in the gross estate, on the ground that pursuant to the Convention for the Avoidance of Double Taxation of Estates between Canada and the United States, the proceeds from decedent's life insurance policy and annuity contracts need not be included in his gross estate for federal estate tax purposes. The estate reasoned that because Canada imposes no estate tax, and because the situs of the death benefits, as determined by Article II of the Convention, was in Canada, there was no U.S. estate tax on the transfer. The estate argued, alternatively, that it was inequitable to require inclusion of the proceeds, because the amounts were never in decedent's possession. The IRS contended that the proceeds were includable in the gross estate.

    Held: For the IRS. The Tax Court stated that the U.S.-Canadian estate tax convention does not prevent the United States from imposing federal estate tax liability on the transfer of property interests at death by U.S. citizens domiciled in Canada. The federal estate tax on the transfer of the benefits of decedent's interests in the retirement plan and annuity contracts was imposed by reason of decedent's citizenship, not because of the situs of the beneficiary's benefits, policies, or payors. Section 2001 imposes a tax on "the taxable estate of every decedent who is a citizen or resident of the United States." Because decedent was a U.S. citizen, the situs of the property in which he held an interest was irrelevant. The court noted that the estate made no argument that Section 2033, 2039, or Section 2042 did not apply to the transfer of interests that the IRS sought to tax. There appeared to be no argument to construct. The court also concluded that there were no equitable principles applicable to this case.

[Estate of Taylor, TC Memo. (P-H) ¶ 89,112, 56 TCM (CCH) 1498 (1989).]

Nonresident aliens are allowed portion of unified credit. In Revenue Ruling 81-303, 1981-2 CB 255, the IRS ruled that the term "specific exemption" referred to in the U.S.-Switzerland Estate and Inheritance Tax Convention did not include the Section 2010 unified credit. Thus, a Swiss resident was entitled to only the smaller exemption allowed under Section 2102(c)(1). The IRS has since ruled that as a result of the 1988 amendments to Section 2102(c) (effective for decedents dying after November 10, 1988), a credit is allowed in an amount that bears the same ratio to $192,800 as the value of the gross estate situated in the United States at the time of death bears to the value of the entire gross estate. This ruling applies to any treaty with language similar to the

U.S.-Swiss convention, for example, those treaties with Australia, Finland, Greece, Italy, Japan, and Norway.

[Rev. Rul. 90-101, 1990-2 CB 315.]

Alien's estate is taxable under Section 2001. Decedent entered the United States as a nonimmigrant alien under a G-4 visa, which did not limit the duration of his stay. At the time of death, he was domiciled in the United States, having formed the intent to remain indefinitely. Thus, he was a U.S. resident, and his estate was taxable under Section 2001.

[Rev. Rul. 80-363, 1980-2 CB 249.]

[3] Computations

Decedent's prior tax years are netted for estate liability. Decedent showed income tax overpayments for some prior tax years and liabilities for others. Decedent's short-year return showed a net operating loss that could be carried back to prior years. Although there were overpayments in three of those years, the overpayments were more than offset by tax liabilities for the remaining four years. Thus, the testator showed a net tax liability at his death of approximately $745,000. The estate treated gross overpayments as an asset of the estate and gross outstanding liabilities as a debt of the estate. The IRS netted all overpayments and tax liabilities to produce a single debt. The estate's treatment resulted in a larger amount passing to the spouse, and hence an increased marital deduction. The Tax Court determined that the estate was required to offset gross income tax overpayments against gross income tax liabilities within any single year, but was not obliged to offset net income tax liabilities against net income tax overpayments for different years.

Held: For the IRS. The Third Circuit stated that the estate could have no reasonable expectation that a refund would be awarded. Mere expectancies do not rise to the level of property interests, which are generally includable as assets in an estate. Furthermore, the Internal Revenue Manual Section 30(55)9 indicates that offsets are to be applied as a matter of course. Where the IRS has refrained from exercising its discretion to offset an overpayment against a tax liability, this restraint was done solely to prevent recoveries of refunds and therefore to benefit the Treasury.

[Estate of Bender, 827 F2d 884, 60 AFTR2d 87-6123, 87-2 USTC ¶ 13,730 (3d Cir. 1987).]

Executor recoups overpayment of estate tax against income tax deficiency. The IRS assessed an income tax deficiency against decedent for years 1947 through 1950. The executor paid the deficiency and filed a claim for a refund of estate taxes based upon the deduction of decedent's income tax liability. The claim for refund of estate taxes was filed after the expiration of the period of limitations and was therefore disallowed. A second claim was filed for refund of income taxes on the theory of equitable recoupment, asking that the barred estate tax overpayment be offset against the income tax. This second claim was timely, but it was also disallowed. In a suit based upon the second claim, the district court held that the executor was entitled to recover.

Held: Affirmed for the estate. The theory of equitable recoupment was applicable because both claims arose out of the same subject matter and transaction. The estate tax deduction for which a refund would have been available was germane to the same subject matter as the income tax deficiency, and the executor was entitled to offset the overpayment of estate tax against the income tax. Although there was fraud involved in the income tax deficiencies, this did not prevent the application of the equitable recoupment doctrine. This situation was not a result of fraud on taxpayer's part.

[Bowcut, 287 F2d 654, 7 AFTR2d 506-B, 61-1 USTC ¶ 11,992 (9th Cir. 1961).]

Credit used for estate tax cannot apply to gift tax as well. Decedent sold a farm to her grandson on the installment method and treated the value of the land as equal to the price her grandson paid for it. Thus, decedent believed there was no gift component. She died the next year. She did not file a gift tax return, and no gifts were reported on the estate tax return. Thus, at her death, the entire amount of the unified credit was applied to the estate tax liability. The IRS subsequently determined that the value of the land sold to decedent's grandson exceeded the sales price, and the difference resulted in a taxable gift. The determination was made after the statute of limitations ran with respect to adjustments to the estate tax. Section 2505(a) provides for the unified credit against the gift tax, whereas Section 2010(a) provides for the unified credit against the estate tax. Although the unified credit rules are set forth in separate sections for gift and estate taxes, the credit is, in effect, a single unified credit. Any part of the unified credit used against gift taxes generally reduces the credit available to be used against the estate tax. In Revenue Ruling 79-160, 1979-1 CB 313, the IRS ruled that the gift tax is reduced by the amount of unified credit allowable at the time of the transfer. Revenue Ruling 79-398, 1979-2 CB 338, states that the unified credit is mandatory and must be used when computing the gift tax.

The IRS concluded that where the full amount of the credit was used to offset the estate tax liability and the statute of limitations ran with regard to an estate tax assessment, the credit was unavailable to offset the gift tax. Although generally a three-year statute of limitations applies to assessments (where a tax return has been filed), there is no statute of limitations if such return (including a gift tax return) has not been filed. Moreover, the receipt by the estate of an estate tax closing letter does not estop the IRS from assessing a liability against the estate for gift taxes if the limitations period has not expired. Also, the IRS's acceptance of the estate tax return as filed did not prevent the IRS from assessing a gift tax liability against the estate. Finally, Regulation § 25.2502-2 provides that if a donor dies before paying the gift tax, the tax becomes a debt of the estate, payable by the executor. Liability of the executor exists for the unpaid gift tax to the extent of payments made of any part of other debts before the IRS claim, if the executor was aware of the debt. Otherwise, under Section 6324(b), the transferee liability of the donees is limited to the value of the gift received.

[Priv. Ltr. Rul. 8743001.]

Results of couple's gift-splitting on estate tax are charted. A husband established taxable gifts in 1977 and 1979, and, under Section 2513, he and his wife treated the 1977 gifts and part of the 1979 gifts as being made half by each. The husband died in 1982. His surviving spouse paid the gift taxes on the 1977 and 1979 gifts by using checks drawn on the couple's joint checking account. All funds in the account were attributable to the husband, and half the balance of the account was reported on Schedule E (jointly held property).

The IRS stated that the amount includable on line 4 (adjusted taxable gifts) of the husband's federal estate tax return was the value of the gifts after considering gift-splitting treatment under Section 2513. Therefore, half the value of the gifts that were subject to Section 2513(a) treatment, plus the total value of the gifts that were not subject to gift-splitting treatment, should be included on line 4. The IRS concluded that under Section 2035(c), the amount includable on Schedule G(A) (gift tax gross-up) was the amount of gift tax that decedent paid on the 1977 and 1979 gifts. The amount of gift tax paid by the wife was not includable in the husband's estate. This result was dictated by the finding that under Missouri law, the couple held the joint checking account as joint tenants.

[Priv. Ltr. Rul. 8515001.]

¶ 12.02 CREDITS AGAINST TAX

[1] Prior Transfers

Prior transfer credit not reduced by interest on deferred estate tax payments. Decedent and her predeceased husband held their assets as joint tenants. When her husband died, decedent elected to defer the estate tax and interest began to accrue. The IRS argued that the interest reduced the Section 2013 credit for tax on prior transfers because the interest should have been deducted from the first estate. The Tax Court disagreed.

Held: Affirmed for the estate. The interest payments were not administration expenses that reduced the first estate, because no probate estate had been created on the husband's death. Most of the property was held in joint tenancy, and the obligation to pay the tax, as well as the benefit of the deferral, was decedent's.

[Estate of Whittle, 994 F2d 379, 71 AFTR2d 93-2203, 93-1 USTC ¶ 60,141 (7th Cir. 1993).]

Usufruct interest passing in simultaneous death has no value for credit on prior transfers. Decedent and his wife died simultaneously in a car accident. State law presumed that the wife predeceased decedent. For purposes of the tax credit on prior transfers, taxpayer valued the usufruct interest by using the actuarial tables. The IRS argued that the interest had no value. The district court agreed with taxpayer.

Held: Reversed for the IRS. The interest passing between the couple had no value, and no credit was allowed. The regulations permit use of a common-sense approach, rather than the actuarial tables, to value the usufruct.

[Estate of Carter, 921 F2d 63, 91-1 USTC ¶ 60,054, 67 AFTR2d 91-1176 (5th Cir. 1991), cert. denied, 502 US 817 (1991).]

Prior transfer credit is allowed for life interest. Before his death, decedent's husband established both a marital and a nonmarital deduction trust for her. The trust instrument provided that the trustee's powers were to be liberally construed in allowing distributions of interest or principal. Consequently, she could continue to maintain herself in the manner to which she had been accustomed. Her estate claimed that the value of her life estate in the nonmarital deduction trust, although not includable in her estate, was entitled to the credit on prior transfers. The IRS argued that the value of decedent's interest could not be determined, because the trustee had the power to invest trust funds in nonproductive assets, to invade principal for the benefit of the children, to accumulate income, and to distribute income to the children rather than to decedent. The IRS contended that if an interest is subject to contingencies that make it incapable of valuation in accordance with recognized valuation principles, there can be no credit.

Held: For the estate. Relevant state law indicated that although the trustee was granted broad investment powers under the instrument, the trustee was nevertheless required to exercise such powers in a fiduciary capacity. The instrument required that the trustee exercise his powers primarily for decedent's benefit and only secondarily for the children's benefit. Consequently, investing in nonproductive assets for the benefit of the children (as ultimate takers) would be a violation of the trustee's fiduciary responsibility under state law. Although the trustee was authorized to pay income or principal to beneficiaries other than decedent, the instrument required first and foremost that she be maintained in her accustomed manner. This allowed a reasonable estimate of her needs. The court indicated that the situation was similar to that in Estate of Lloyd, 650 F2d 1197 (Ct. Cl. 1981), where the Court of Claims held that a life estate was reasonably capable of valuation, even though the trustee was empowered to invade principal for the benefit of persons other than the surviving widow.

[Estate of Weinstein, 820 F2d 201, 59 AFTR2d 87-1279, 87-1 USTC ¶ 13,722 (6th Cir. 1987).]

Second Circuit affirms Tax Court's adoption of IRS method of calculation respecting multiple prior transfers. During 1975, decedent's mother, father, and husband died. In each instance, decedent inherited property from the respective estates. Following decedent's own death in 1978, her estate claimed a tax credit on prior transfers under Section 2013. The IRS determined that the estate failed to compute the previously paid tax separately in respect of each transferor. Under Section 2013, the credit is limited to the amount of federal estate tax that is attributable to the transferred property in the decedent's estate. That is, the credit the difference between the decedent's estate tax as computed by including the value of the transferred property in the gross estate and as computed by excluding the value of the transferred property from the gross estate. The credit is then reduced by an applicable percentage, which depends on the number of years that have lapsed between the deaths of the transferor and the decedent. The IRS, citing Regulation § 20.2013-6, contended that in the case of multiple transferors, the limitation must be apportioned among the transferors to that credit and must be computed separately for each transferor. The estate, however, argued that the credit should be the lesser of the aggregate amounts of tax paid by the transferor estates or the aggregate amount of tax attributable to the property in decedent's estate.

Held: Affirmed for the IRS. The Second Circuit stated that when property included in an estate is derived from a prior transfer from another estate, Sections 2013(a) and 2013(b) allow the recipient estate a credit for estate tax paid on the property by the donor estate. Section 2013(c), however, limits the credit to the amount by which the transferred property increases the estate tax liability of the recipient estate. Where there is only one transferor, the Section 2013(b) credit (called the "first limitation" in Regulation § 20.2013) and the Section 2013(c) limitation of credit (called the "second limitation" in Regulation § 20.2013) is easily computed. The lesser of these two figures is the actual credit available to the decedent's estate. The Second Circuit agreed with the Tax Court that the computational method advocated by the IRS was consistent with the applicable legislative history. That position, apart from being consistent with the language and purpose behind Section 2013, is also consistent with the mathematical example contained in the Senate Report. Since the example was placed in the *Congressional Record* to show how Section 2013 is to be applied, the IRS could reasonably rely on it as a model for fashioning its own regulations.

[Estate of Meyer, 778 F2d 125, 86-1 USTC ¶ 13,650, 57 AFTR2d 86-1486 (2d Cir. 1985).]

Ninth Circuit denies Section 2013 credit where estate asset is incapable of valuation. Decedent's mother died in 1969, leaving a will that created a trust naming decedent and his two children as trustees. All income was to be distributed to decedent and to his wife for their lives, as well as whatever portion of the principal was reasonably necessary for their support, maintenance, and welfare, if, in the opinion of the trustees, their other resources were insufficient for that purpose. Principal and accumulated income remaining at the death of the life tenants were to be distributed to their then-living descendants. The trustees were given broad investment powers, including the choice of unsecured, unproductive, underproductive, overproductive, or wasting assets. When decedent died within the ten-year period of Section 2013, his estate claimed that it was entitled to a credit for the estate tax paid by his mother's estate with respect to the life interest. The credit applies to any beneficial interest received by a transferee. A life estate qualifies as a credit even though it is not included in the decedent's estate. The credit is based on the value at which the transferred property was included in the transferor's estate for federal tax purposes. The IRS sought to deny the credit, arguing that the administrative powers vested in the trustees were so broad that decedent's life interest was not capable of being valued as of his mother's death.

Held: For the IRS. In what it admitted was an unfair result, the Ninth Circuit found that a terminable life estate was incapable of valuation and therefore is not entitled to a credit under Section 2013. The court noted that this was apparently the first case in which a Section 2013 credit had been denied on these grounds, although similar situations have arisen in connection with an estate tax charitable remainder trust under Section 2055, and a gift tax exclusion for a donor's retained interest under Section 2503. In general, where a trustee's powers are so circumscribed either by the instrument or by state law that the value of the interest in question is "accurately calculable," the tax benefit has been allowed. Although the trust instrument in the present case concededly lacked the requisite standard, taxpayer argued that state law filled the gap. The court rejected this argument. Examining the general plan of the trust instrument as required by state court decisions, the court found that the transferor (decedent's mother) intended to vest the trustees with broad discretion so that they could manage the trust fund flexibly in order to produce a great deal of, or very little, income. In light of the burden on taxpayer to establish entitle-ment to the credit, the court concluded that an investment in non-income-pro-ducing assets would not have constituted an abuse under state law.

[Holbrook, 575 F2d 1288, 42 AFTR2d 78-6419, 78-2 USTC ¶ 13,249 (9th Cir. 1978).]

For purposes of credit for prior transfers, value of property is determined on basis of net gift to transferee. Decedent relinquished her community prop-erty interest in return for a life estate in her husband's community property. The value of the property relinquished at her husband's death exceeded the value of the interest she acquired. The Tax Court allowed a credit for estate taxes paid by the husband's estate on the life interest. The court reached this result because the transferred property was not excluded from decedent's estate.

Held: Reversed for the IRS. Decedent purchased the life estate, and the Section 2013 credit is not available for purchases.

[Estate of Sparling, 552 F2d 1340, 40 AFTR2d 77-6207, 77-1 USTC ¶ 13,194 (9th Cir. 1977).]

Decedent's life estate in trust received from her spouse less than ten years before her death qualified for estate tax credit for prior transfers. Dece-dent's husband predeceased her by less than ten years, leaving an estate com-prising an inter vivos trust. Upon the husband's death, the trust was split between a marital deduction trust and a residual trust, in which decedent had a life estate. Decedent withdrew her marital share and placed it in her own inter vivos trust. Under the terms of the residual trust, the trustee was to pay to or apply for the benefit of the grantor's wife the net income from the residual trust, and any net income not disbursed was to be added to principal. The at-torney who drafted the trust document explained to decedent's husband that the terms of the residual trust were not intended to give the trustee discretion over whether to pay income to the wife. The clause directing that income not disbursed was to be added to principal was intended only to manage income not distributed in the event of the wife's death. Decedent died in 1982, and her estate claimed an estate tax credit under Section 2013 for her life interest in the residual trust. Under Section 2013, an estate may take a credit for any es-tate tax paid by the estate of a prior decedent relating to property transferred by the prior decedent to the present decedent. The IRS disallowed the credit on the ground that the value of the residual trust was not definitely ascertaina-ble. The IRS construed the clause concerning application of undistributed net income to principal as giving the trustee discretion over whether to pay income to the beneficiary.

Held: For the estate. The court stated that the IRS's disallowance of the credit rests on the settled principle that a credit is permissible only where the property interest involved is susceptible to valuation in accordance with recognized valuation principles. For life estates, Regulation § 20.2013-4 provides that the value of the interest is determined as of the date of the transferor's death on the basis of recognized valuation principles. Revenue Ruling 67-53, 1967-1 CB 265, states that if a trustee possesses the power, in absolute and uncontrolled discretion, to pay out net income to the beneficiary of a trust or to apply such income to principal, the beneficiary's interest cannot be valued according to recognized valuation principles. Therefore, under such circumstances, a Section 2013 credit is not allowed. The court concluded that the crux of the dispute was the interpretation of the aforementioned clause in the trust document and that such interpretation must be made pursuant to local law. The court found that under settled trust construction principles, a trustee's power to accumulate income should not be implied, absent "strong and clear language" to that effect. According to the court, no such language existed in the present case; instead, the clause used the mandatory "shall," indicating that the grantor's intention was for the income to go to the beneficiary. The second part of the clause can easily be construed to apply only to distribution after the death of the beneficiary. Evidence from the trust's drafter of the intent of the grantor convinced the court that its construction of the trust was correct. Furthermore, the IRS failed to provide any evidence that the grantor intended the contrary. The court thus allowed the credit and upheld taxpayer's claim for refund of estate tax overpaid.

[Boryan, 690 F. Supp. 459, 62 AFTR2d 88-5965, 88-2 USTC ¶ 13,775 (ED Va. 1988), aff'd, 884 F2d 767, 64 AFTR2d 89-5916, 89-2 USTC ¶ 13,814 (4th Cir. 1989).]

Interest on deferred tax does not reduce tax credit on prior transfers. Decedent's husband died on February 23, 1981, leaving decedent as the sole heir. Decedent's husband's will was not offered for probate, because virtually his entire estate, consisting of farmland, common stock, treasury notes, and bank deposits, passed to decedent by joint tenancy. Decedent, in possession of her husband's property, filed a federal estate tax return and elected to pay a portion of the estate tax in installments, pursuant to the provisions of Section 6166. The total amount of interest liability assessed and paid with respect to the Section 6166 election was $113,948. (Decedent's husband died prior to the enactment of the unlimited marital deduction, which would have eliminated all estate taxes in the event that his situation occurred today.) Decedent died on March 22, 1985, while a domiciliary of the state of Illinois. Her personal representative filed a federal estate tax return, including as an asset property received from decedent's husband's estate valued at $2,931,505. A tax credit on prior transfers under Section 2013 was claimed with respect to this property. The IRS filed a notice of deficiency against decedent's estate, determining that additional estate taxes of $19,584 were due. This deficiency arose out of the

IRS's contention that the estate tax credit for prior transfers must be reduced because of the interest paid as a result of the Section 6166 deferral of estate taxes by her husband's estate. The IRS contended that the value of the property received from decedent's husband must be reduced by the amount of interest paid under Section 6166. The IRS reasoned that under the Illinois Principal and Income Act, interest on federal estate taxes is charged against principal, not against income. Additionally, such interest under Illinois law is a deductible administration expense. Furthermore, in computing the tax credit on prior transfers of property, the gross value of the prior transfer must be reduced by the amount of claims against the transferor's estate, including estate taxes and administration expenses, regardless of whether they are claimed as deductions on the estate tax return. Consequently, in computing the credit to which decedent's estate was entitled, the IRS reasoned that the amount of interest paid by virtue of the election to defer payment of estate taxes due from the prior transferor must be deducted from the gross value of the property. Decedent, in contrast, contended that because all property passed to her by joint tenancy, there was no estate under Illinois law against which to make a claim.

Held: For the estate. The court stated that the critical factor in this case is the interpretation of the phrase "the value of the property transferred," used in Section 2013. In interpreting that phrase, the court first noted that decedent obtained her interest in the property of her deceased husband as a surviving joint tenant, not as a devisee, legatee, or heir. Thus, she obtained the property free and clear of any obligations of her deceased husband, except any that might specifically be imposed in her capacity as a joint tenant. There was no probate estate. The liability of decedent with respect to the estate tax of her deceased husband was founded on Section 6324(a)(2), which imposes a direct liability for such tax on a surviving tenant, independent of the operation of state law. This liability imposed no obligation for interest on the estate tax. This second liability was created after the death of decedent's husband in a manner similar to a mortgage that decedent might have placed on her surviving joint tenancy interest. The court concluded that the interest payments were incurred not to preserve the estate of decedent's husband, but rather to protect the surviving joint tenancy of decedent. Although the court noted that decedent did incur a liability for the interest on the deferred estate taxes, it stated that its analysis was not for the purpose of determining the ultimate liability for such interest, but in the context of determining whether such interest should reduce the credit for the estate tax on prior transfers. It further stated that in considering whether there should be such a reduction, it was irrelevant that the interest was not deducted by decedent's husband's estate for either estate or income tax purposes. Based on this reasoning, the court held that the credit on prior transfers to which the taxpayer's estate was entitled should not be reduced by the interest paid, because of the Section 6166 deferral of estate taxes by the transferor's estate.

[Estate of Whittle, 97 TC 362 (1991), aff'd, 994 F2d 379, 93-1 USTC 60,141, 71 AFTR2d 93-2202 (7th Cir. 1993).]

Credit for prior tax on transfers is disallowed. Decedent was one of the three income beneficiaries of a trust under the will of her predeceased husband. The trustee, at his absolute discretion, was authorized to invade the trust corpus and to distribute the trust income and the trust corpus to beneficiaries other than decedent. The IRS disallowed decedent's estate's claim for a credit for tax paid on prior transfers.

Held: For the IRS. Decedent had no absolute right to any fixed amount of the trust income. The value of decedent's income interest in the trust could not be ascertained on the date of the husband's death. Therefore, her estate was not entitled to a tax credit on prior transfers.

[Estate of Pollock, 77 TC 1296 (1981).]

Decedent's gross estate is not reduced by amounts subject to marital deduction. During a two-year period, decedent was predeceased first by his daughter and then by his wife. The daughter died intestate, with half of the property being distributed to decedent and half to the wife. Petitioner claimed that the value of the daughter's property received from the wife's estate should be reduced by the marital deductions used to determine the wife's estate tax liability.

Held: For the IRS. Section 2013 was intended as a method of valuing the credit for estate taxes previously paid, not for valuing property in the gross estate.

[Estate of La Sala, 71 TC 752 (1979).]

Decedent's interest was an annuity for purposes of calculating tax credit on prior transfers. Decedent husband, age 91, died five months after his wife. He was the beneficiary of a residuary trust under his predeceased wife's will. That trust provided for an annuity of $300,000 per year during the decedent husband's life plus a five and five power of withdrawal. The issue was the amount of tax credit on prior transfers that could be claimed by decedent's estate. The amount of the credit depends on the value of the property interest transferred to decedent. Here, the IRS disallowed a portion of the credit based on a lower valuation for decedent's interest in the trust. The IRS argued that the interest was not an annuity. Rather, the interest was for a term certain because of the high probability that the corpus would be depleted within four years.

Held: For the estate. The estate properly characterized and valued decedent's interest in his wife's residuary trust for purposes of calculating the tax credit on prior transfers. His predeceased wife intended to give him an income stream for life. The high probability that the corpus would be depleted within four years did not make the interest a term certain.

[Estate of Shapiro, 66 TCM 1067, RIA TC Memo. ¶ 93,483 (1993).]

IRS rules on applicable marital deduction for second limitation on credit for prior transfers. Decedent died in July 1986, survived by a spouse. The value of decedent's gross estate was $3.3 million, and allowable deductions for debts and expenses were $200,000. Decedent bequeathed the residue of the estate, $2.4 million, to the spouse. A marital deduction was allowable for this amount. The estate claimed a tax credit on prior transfers under Section 2013, based on a transfer of $500,000 that decedent received from the estate of his parent, who died in 1984. The IRS ruled that in determining the "second limitation" on tax credit on prior transfers, the marital deduction allowable was $2.4 million. In computing the estate tax on the reduced gross estate under Section 2013(c)(1)(B), for estates of transferees dying after 1981, the applicable marital deduction is the value of the property passing to the surviving spouse, without any proportionate reduction and without limitation as to amount.

[Rev. Rul. 90-2, 1990-1 CB 169.]

Granting of incidents of ownership in life insurance policy is not transfer of property to which Section 2013 applies. *W* died owning a life insurance policy on *H*'s life, the value of which was includable in her estate. The insurance was left to a residuary trust for the benefit of their children. *H*, as trustee, possessed incidents of ownership that led to the inclusion of the policy proceeds in his gross estate. The IRS ruled that the Section 2013 credit on prior transfers is not available to *H*'s estate. Although *H* possessed incidents of ownership, he did not have a direct beneficial interest in the property.

[Rev. Rul. 77-156, 1977-1 CB 269.]

[2] State Death Taxes

State gift tax payment is held not to constitute deductible claim against estate. Decedent gave property to her children in 1973 and, as a result, incurred an obligation of $32,193 in Oklahoma state gift taxes. She died less than one year later, without having paid the taxes. Because her gift was made less than one year before her death, the gift property was included in her gross estate for purposes of calculating both state death taxes and federal estate taxes. After her death, but before her estate filed either the state death tax return or the federal estate tax return, her executors paid the $32,193. Although this payment was ostensibly a payment of a gift tax, the Oklahoma Tax Commission, in assessing state death taxes, treated it as an advance payment of state death taxes. The Commission based its calculation of state death taxes due exclusively on the state death tax statute, and then allowed a credit against those state death taxes of $32,193. The estate paid, in addition to the $32,193, a sum of $120,239 in state death taxes. The total state death taxes calculated by the Oklahoma Tax Commission and paid by the estate were in the sum of $152,332. In calculating the federal estate taxes due, the IRS allowed the estate a tax credit for state death taxes paid in the amount of $152,332, reduced to the statutory maximum amount allowable. The estate filed a refund claim, contending that it was also entitled to a deduction for the $32,193 ostensibly paid as a gift tax. The issue before the district court was whether the estate was entitled to a federal estate tax credit and a federal estate tax deduction for the $32,193 that it had paid to Oklahoma.

Held: For the IRS. The court stated that a gift tax payment was analogous to a contingent payment. If death occurs within one year of the gift, the gift tax payment loses its gift tax character and becomes instead a credit against the then due and owing state death taxes. If, as in the present case, the gift taxes are not paid before death and if death occurs within one year, the nature of the tax reported on the gift tax return is a defeasible obligation that is extinguished at death. Thus, when death occurs within one year after making a gift, payment of the contingent gift tax is converted into a credit against death taxes due to the state. If the gift tax remains unpaid on the date of death, the obligation to pay the tax as a gift tax is defeated, and the only obligation due to the state on that date is payment of death taxes on both the gifted property and the remainder. The fortuitous payment of the amount of the $32,193 was nothing more than an installment on the yet-to-be-calculated state death taxes. Oklahoma treated the payment in a similar manner when it gave the estate a credit in the exact amount of the purported gift taxes paid after the death of decedent. Accordingly, the court concluded that the $32,193 shown on decedent's gift tax return ceased to be an obligation of the estate instantly upon her death.

[First Nat'l Bank & Trust Co. of Tulsa, 789 F2d 1393, 57 AFTR2d 86-1559, 86-1 USTC ¶ 13,663 (10th Cir. 1986).]

Credit for state death taxes is available only if actually paid. On a timely filed tax return, decedent's estate claimed a credit for state death taxes. The IRS allowed only a portion of the credit and claimed that the estate did not substantiate a greater payment.

Held: For the IRS. The credit was allowed for state death taxes actually paid. Under Section 2011, an estate may claim a credit against its federal estate tax for any state death taxes paid. The estate argued that it was entitled to claim a credit for the entire amount of state death taxes being paid on an installment basis. The court held that there was no authority for such a contention and that Section 2011(a) requires actual payment of the state death tax before a credit may be claimed. Actual payment involves the outlay of cash or its equivalent, which does not include the accrual of state death tax liability. Thus, the estate was entitled to a credit only on the amount of the state death tax actually paid.

[Estate of Spillar, TC Memo. (P-H) ¶ 85,529, 50 TCM (CCH) 1285 (1985).]

IRS rules on state death tax credit in cases where estate elects installment payments under Section 6166. Decedent died in 1984, leaving a gross estate composed of a corporation's stock and miscellaneous personal property. The value of his interest in the corporation exceeded 35 percent of adjusted gross estate. Decedent's stock interest qualified as an interest in a closely held business as defined in Section 6166(b)(1). The estate could therefore elect to pay in ten annual installments the portion of the federal estate tax attributable to the interest in the closely held business. A similar provision under the law of the probating state permitted the estate to elect to pay in ten annual installments the portion of the state death tax attributable to an interest in the closely held business. Deferred and installment payments, plus interest, were required under state law in the same manner provided for in Section 6166 as in effect on the date of death.

The personal representative of the estate made a timely election under Section 6166 to pay part of the federal estate tax in ten equal annual installments and made a similar election under state law to pay part of the state death tax in ten annual installments. The representative timely paid in a single day the nondeferred portion of the federal estate tax, the first installment of the deferred estate tax, the nondeferred portion of the state death tax, and the first installment of the deferred state death tax. When the federal estate tax return was filed, the estate claimed a credit under Section 2011 for the total amount of the state death tax liability, including the state death tax paid and the state death tax that the estate expected to pay in installments over the next nine years. The IRS was asked to rule on the extent to which a credit for state death taxes existed, given these facts.

In the IRS analysis, the fact that the estate had elected to pay in ten annual installments made Section 2011(c)(2) applicable; thus, the estate qualified for the Section 2011 credit for state death taxes paid for the period ending before the date of the expiration of the ten-year period elected for paying the federal estate tax. At such time as the estate tax return was filed, however, only the state death taxes actually paid would qualify for the Section 2011 credit on the estate tax return. If necessary, after all state death taxes had been paid, a claim for refund could be made for an overpayment of tax, but only after the federal estate tax liability had been paid in full.

[Rev. Rul. 86-38, 1986-1 CB 296.]

IRS reverses its position on state gift tax treatment. The IRS announced that state gift taxes on a transfer of property that is later included in the decedent's state inheritance tax base are not an asset of the estate if paid before death, are deductible as a claim against the estate if not paid before death, and are not deemed "inheritance taxes" under Section 2011 in either case. The IRS has revoked Revenue Ruling 75-63, 1975-1 CB 294, and Revenue Ruling 71-355, 1971-2 CB 334, in which it had ruled to the contrary on each issue. The IRS's actions complement its acquiescences in Estate of Gamble, 69 TC 942 (1978), and Estate of Lang, 613 F2d 770 (9th Cir. 1980), aff'g in part and rev'g in part 64 TC 404 (1975).

[Rev. Rul. 81-302, 81-2 CB 170.]

Death tax credit is denied until state taxes are paid. Decedent's estate owed $20 million in state taxes, 80 percent of which would ordinarily have been due within six months of decedent's death. The executor obtained a three-and-a-half-year extension for payment of all but $5 million. The estate claimed the maximum deduction allowed under Section 2011(b), $15 million. Under Section 2011(a), a credit for state death tax may be taken against federal estate tax only if the state death taxes are paid by the time of the later of the following dates: (1) the due date for filing the federal estate tax return or (2) the first date prescribed under state law for the payment of death taxes, without regard to any extension of time. Regulations § 20.2011-1(c)(2) provides that evidence of the payment of state death taxes must be submitted with the federal return or soon thereafter. Because state death taxes are often paid at about the time the federal return is filed, a grace period is provided to obtain credit evidence.

The IRS concluded that when state death taxes are paid late, the allowable credit does not relate back retroactively to the due date of the federal return. Instead, the estate can claim a refund on the overpaid estate tax. Since the estate took the credit for taxes that had not in fact been timely paid, there was an underpayment, the interest on which was due from the date on which the federal return was due to the date on which the state tax was paid. Thus, the estate owed interest on $10 million for two years.

[Tech. Adv. Mem. 8947005.]

[3] Foreign Death Taxes

French estate tax paid on decedent's real property in France gives rise to credit against U.S. estate tax. Decedent, a U.S. citizen, died while a resident of France. Under French law, an estate tax was paid on her property, both real and personal, located in France. The executor of her U.S. estate did not report for U.S. estate tax purposes the personal and real property located and subject to estate tax in France. The IRS included such French property in decedent's gross estate and assessed the estate for additional estate tax. The executor argued that the assessment was a treaty violation, because it imposed a double estate tax on the decedent's French assets.

Held: For the estate. Decedent's French property was subject to U.S. estate tax, but a U.S. tax credit for the French estate tax imposed on such property prevents double taxation. The mere fact that the U.S.-France Tax Treaty was executed when U.S. law exempted real property located outside the United States from estate tax does not mandate that the then-existing U.S. law be applied to all future situations covered by the treaty. Here, allowing a tax credit prevents the double taxation that is impermissible under the treaty.

[Norstar Bank of Upstate NY, 644 F. Supp. 1112, 58 AFTR2d 86-6395, 86-2 USTC ¶ 13,697 (NDNY 1986).]

No estate credit for Canadian provincial estate tax. Taxpayer, the estate of a U.S. citizen residing in Canada, paid an estate tax to the Province of Ontario on two bank accounts located there. Taxpayer then claimed a credit against U.S. estate taxes under the U.S.-Canada Estate Tax Treaty.

Held: For the IRS. No credit is available, because the taxes referred to in the treaty are those imposed by the national government, not its political subdivisions. Additionally, the Section 2014 credit is unavailable, because the bank accounts were not connected with any Canadian trade or business and are therefore deemed to be situated outside Canada under Sections 2101 and 2105.

[Borne, 577 F. Supp. 115, 52 AFTR2d 83-6444, 83-2 USTC ¶ 13,536 (ND Ind. 1983).]

Tax Court holds that tax paid to Canada is not estate tax for which credit is allowed. Decedent was a U.S. citizen and a resident of Iowa. At the time of his death, he owned land in Canada. The Canadian authorities assessed a tax on the property based on the property's appreciation in value between January 1, 1972, and the date of decedent's death. On decedent's estate tax return, a foreign death tax credit was taken for the tax paid to Canada. The IRS disallowed the credit, but allowed the estate to deduct the Canadian tax.

Held: For the IRS. Section 2014 allows a credit against an estate tax for the amount of any estate, inheritance, legacy, or succession tax actually paid to a foreign country. The court held that in order for a foreign tax to qualify under Section 2014, it must be substantially equivalent to an estate tax as the term is understood in the United States. In Knowlton v. Moore, 178 US 41 (1900), the Supreme Court defined the term "estate tax" as an excise tax upon the privilege of transferring property of a decedent upon his death. The section of the Canadian Income Tax Act under which the tax in question was imposed provides that upon the death of a decedent owning capital property in Canada, the decedent is deemed to have disposed of the property immediately before his death. The court held that this tax was imposed on neither the transfer of property nor the power to transfer property at death. The focus was on the recognition of gain, not on the taxing of the transfer of property from the decedent to a beneficiary. The tax therefore was not the substantial equivalent of an estate tax as understood in the United States.

[Estate of Ballard, 85 TC 300 (1985).]

Tax Court permits full credit for estate taxes paid on foreign bank deposits. On May 3, 1978, decedent, a United States citizen, died intestate in Madrid, Spain. He left $182,262 in two Spanish banks, together with a furnished condominium valued at $18,088. The estate paid $27,516 in inheritance taxes to the Spanish government, and claimed that amount as a foreign tax credit. The IRS disallowed that portion of the credit representing taxes paid on the bank accounts, contending that they were not situated abroad within the meaning of Section 2014, because decedent was deemed to be a nonresident of Spain. The estate took the position that the bank deposits were located within Spain in every practical and economic sense, and that under pertinent statutory provisions, they should have been treated as located within Spain for federal estate tax purposes.

Held: For the estate. The determination of situs under Section 2014 is to be made with reference to the general rules of Code Subchapter B of Chapter 11, which governs the estate taxation of decedents who were neither U.S. citizens nor U.S. residents. Section 2104(c) states the rule that the location of debt obligations is governed by the location of the obligor, not the obligee. Thus, the obligations of a Spanish bank are treated as property located within Spain. Where Section 2104(c) speaks of debt obligations held by a nonresident, however, not a citizen of a foreign country, the context requires that such words be read out of the statute as pertaining only to situations directly arising under Section 2104. The Tax Court concluded that the governing principles, not the strict rules of Section 2104, should be applied in Section 2014 situations, and that the results must accord with the purpose and intent of Section 2014. Accordingly, the full amount of estate taxes paid to the Spanish government were eligible for the credit.

[Estate of Schwartz, 83 TC 943 (1984), acq. 1986-1 CB 1.]

[4] Unified Credit

Noncitizen who died abroad was a U.S. resident for estate tax purposes. Decedent was a Pakistani citizen who lived most of his life in India and Pakistan. Decedent's father had immigrated to the United States and, along with other immigrated family members, established a farming and real estate business in California. Decedent and his mother did not move to the United States with the father. When decedent's father died in 1958 and left most of the business to decedent, decedent stayed in Pakistan and one of his sons moved to California to help run the business. The son remained in California and eventually obtained U.S. citizenship in 1982. Decedent made his first trip to the United States on a temporary visitor visa in 1971, when he was sixty-one years old. He stayed until his visa expired in 1974. Decedent wanted to get a permanent resident visa at this time, but was told he had to wait until after his son obtained U.S. citizenship. Decedent's visa-related application materials indicated he intended to leave his wife and other children in Pakistan and to stay permanently in the United States. Decedent was ultimately granted a visa and green card in 1985, registering him as a resident alien and authorizing him to live permanently and work in the United States. Decedent came to the United States in January 1985 and stayed until December 1986, in a bedroom his son built for him in the son's home. Decedent obtained a Social Security number and worked for the family business, but did not join any social organizations or obtain a library card. Also, decedent spoke only his native language and understood no English. Decedent decided to return to Pakistan in December 1986 to formalize a business agreement with certain relatives. He applied for a U.S. reentry permit, which was sent to his U.S. address. His son, who signed decedent's returns under a power of attorney, did not read the permit's warning that a resident alien who claims nonresident alien status for income tax purposes "may be regarded as having abandoned his [U.S.] residence." Decedent never read the permit, never used it, because of failing health, and died on February 25, 1991, without ever returning to the United States. Decedent's accountants, who did not personally know him, used Forms 1040NR for his pre-1985 and post-1985 income tax returns. A Form 1040 was used for his 1985 tax year. The 1986-1991 returns were amended, however, in 1992 (by the family attorney), and the estate tax return was filed on the basis of decedent's U.S. residency. The estate tax return indicated that decedent was "domiciled" in the United States when he died, and claimed the full $192,800 unified credit under pre-Taxpayer Relief Act of 1997 Section 2010. The IRS disagreed with the estate's position, arguing that decedent was no longer a U.S. resident when he died.

   Held: For the estate. Because the estate of a noncitizen, nonresident decedent is generally entitled under Section 2102 to only a limited, $13,000 credit against the taxable estate, the estate's eligibility for the full (versus the limited) credit hinged on decedent's resident status at his death. For estate tax purposes, a decedent's residence depends on his or her "domicile" at death, which in turn, depends on whether decedent lived in the United States and intended to remain indefinitely. Here, the court believed decedent intended to live in the United States permanently when he moved to California in 1985. Notably, decedent started seeking permanent U.S. residency back in 1975, ultimately obtained a permanent resident visa, green card, and Social Security number, and was part of a family with a long immigration history. Moreover, decedent had $760,000 in business and property interests in the United States and over $70,000 in his U.S. bank account when he died. In contrast, his only Pakistan asset was a fifteen-acre family farm. The court found these facts clearly indicative of an intent to reside in the United States indefinitely, while decedent's failure to obtain a library card or driver's license, or to bring his wife and family with him, were irrelevant. The court also concluded that decedent had not abandoned his U.S. domicile when he returned to Pakistan. Long, continued absence does not necessarily prove that an intent to return—even a doubtful intent—has changed. Thus, decedent's intent to return (evidenced by his reentry permit and substantial U.S. property holdings) did not necessarily change just because he did not, in fact, return. Further, this intent was not negated by his income tax nonresident alien return filings. Because the income tax rules base resident status on either legal residency or substantial presence in the United States, the court did not view decedent's income tax status to be determinative of his estate tax resident status (which was premised solely on his domicile). The court further supported its finding with the facts that decedent never saw the returns and that his son signed them without fully reading them himself. Thus, based on the record as a whole, the court found that decedent had intended to live in the United States indefinitely, and had not changed that intent at the time he died in Pakistan. Consequently, decedent was a U.S. resident whose estate was not subject to the limited $13,000 credit under the estate tax rules.

[Khan, 75 TCM 1597, RIA TC Memo. ¶ 98,022 (1998).]

Nonresident aliens are allowed portion of unified credit. In Revenue Ruling 81-303, 1981-2 CB 255, the IRS ruled that the term "specific exemption" referred to in the U.S.-Switzerland Estate and Inheritance Tax Convention did not include the Section 2010 unified credit. Thus, a Swiss resident was entitled to only the smaller exemption allowed under Section 2102(c)(1). The IRS later ruled that as a result of the 1988 amendments to Section 2102(c) (effective for decedents dying after November 10, 1988), a credit is allowed in an amount that bears the same ratio to $192,800 as the value of the gross estate situated in the United States at the time of death bears to the value of the entire gross estate. This ruling applies to any treaty with language similar to that of the U.S.-Swiss Convention, for example, the treaties with Australia, Finland, Greece, Italy, Japan, and Norway.

[Rev. Rul. 90-101, 1990-2 CB 315.]

Disclaimer of fractional portion of IRA allows widow to maximize the unified credit available to her husband's estate. When A died, he held an individual retirement account (IRA) of which his wife, B, was the beneficiary. Under Section 408(d)(3)(C)(ii), B could roll over the account when she inherited it. However, she decided to disclaim part of the account. The portion disclaimed was to go into a trust established by her husband for the benefit of *B* and their children. Because the trust was included in *A*'s taxable estate, exempted only to the extent of the unified credit, *B* wanted to disclaim only that portion of the IRA that would not have brought the trust above the credit limit. Although she was herself a beneficiary of the family trust, disclaimers of interests by spouses were not precluded, even if the spouse received another interest in the property disclaimed. *B* was therefore able to use a fractional disclaimer to assure that the maximum amount is included free of estate tax in the family trust.

[Priv. Ltr. Rul. 8922036.]

¶ 12.03 EXEMPT INTERESTS AND PROPERTY

Supreme Court finds housing bonds are not exempt from estate tax. Decedent died in 1982 owning project notes, housing agency bonds issued under the authority of the Housing Act of 1937. His estate included them on the estate tax return as taxable assets. In August 1984, the estate filed an amended estate tax return claiming that the Project Notes were exempt from estate taxation. The claim for a refund was denied, but in a later refund action, the district court concluded that the project notes were tax-exempt when the returns were filed, relying on the reasoning of Haffner, 585 F. Supp. 354, 84-1 USTC ¶ 13,571 (ND Ill. 1984), aff'd, 757 F2d 920, 85-1 USTC ¶ 13,611 (7th Cir. 1985). The district court also held that Section 641 of the Deficit Reduction Act unconstitutionally denied the estate due process and equal protection under the law as guaranteed by the Fifth Amendment. In *Haffner*, it was held that project notes were exempt from estate taxation. Section 641 of the Deficit Reduction Act of 1984 mandates that project notes are not exempt from estate taxation after the effective date of the Act (June 19, 1984) and forbids any refund for estate taxes paid on project notes prior to that date if a refund claim had not been previously filed. A direct appeal to the Supreme Court was then taken by the IRS.

Held: Reversed for the IRS. The Supreme Court began by reciting the principle that exemptions from taxation are not to be implied and must be unambiguously proved. It then indicated that well before the Housing Act was passed, an exemption of property from all taxation had an understood meaning—that property was exempt from direct taxation, but that certain privileges of ownership, such as the right to transfer the property, could be taxed. On the rare occasions when Congress had exempted property from estate taxation, it generally explicitly referred to that tax rather than to "all taxation." Accordingly, because this exemption did not specifically refer to estate taxation, the Court felt that such an exemption was not intended by Congress. The Court then reviewed the estate's reasons for exception in addition to its reliance on the specific language of the statute. These arguments included the fact that Section 20 of the Housing Act of 1937, which also contained an exemption from taxation for bonds of a U.S. Housing Authority, contained a specific exemption from that exclusion for estate and inheritance taxes. Thus, it was argued that if Congress did not intend the term "all taxation" to include estate tax, it would have specifically said so. Also cited was a statement made in the floor debate over the 1937 Act by one senator who indicated that the exemption in Section 5(e) included estate taxation as well as a similar statement of an individual who was the first Chief Economist of the U.S. Housing Authority. The Court summarily rejected these arguments and indicated that they did not overcome the requirement that an exemption from estate taxation be expressly stated. Accordingly, the project notes were included in the estate and the subsequent claim for refund was denied.

[Wells Fargo Bank, 485 US 351, 108 S. Ct. 1179, 61 AFTR2d 88-1345, 88-1 USTC ¶ 13,759 (1988).]

Deficiency notice for failure to include public housing bonds in estate is valid. Decedent's estate listed tax-exempt public housing bonds on the estate tax return, but excluded their value from the gross estate, based upon Haffner, 757 F2d 920 (7th Cir. 1985). The IRS included the bonds in the estate. The Tax Court agreed and rejected the argument that Section 642 of the Deficit Reduction Act of 1984 prevented the IRS from issuing a notice of deficiency until the courts decided the includability of such bonds.

    Held: Affirmed for the IRS. Section 642 was merely a reporting provision and did not preclude the issuance of a notice.

[Estate of Pollenz, 925 F2d 1066, 91-1 USTC ¶ 60,062, 67 AFTR2d 91-1186 (7th Cir. 1991), cert. denied, 502 US 910 (1991).]

¶ 12.04 ESTATE TAX DEFERRAL

[1] Elections

IRS is not estopped from reversing its position as to election to defer payment of estate tax. Decedent died in 1979, leaving an estate, 90 percent of which consisted of capital stock in a close corporation. An estate tax return was filed, and the executor made an election under Section 6166 to pay the tax due in installments. After initially accepting the election, the IRS reversed its position, assessed the remaining amount due, and assessed additional estate taxes plus interest. The estate paid the amount assessed and then filed a claim for refund.

Held: For the IRS. Section 6166 permits a taxpayer to defer payment of estate tax if a lump-sum payment would require the taxpayer to sell assets used in an ongoing business, thereby disrupting or destroying the business. The court found that the purpose behind this section was to give relief to family members who had inherited nonliquid assets of a small business. The court held that because decedent's estate was mainly composed of liquid assets, it did not qualify for the deferral election. The estate could easily satisfy its tax liability by selling stock or real estate without disrupting its trade or business. The court also held that the IRS was not estopped from rejecting the election by its initial acceptance. Such an estoppel would be available only if the taxpayer had relied on the IRS's original position to such a degree that it would be unconscionable to allow a reversal of position. The court stated that such a case would arise if a taxpayer had sold off its liquid assets in reliance on the IRS's acceptance of the election and then had no liquid assets with which to satisfy the claim. In the present case, the estate failed to show any circumstances that would make the allowance of the IRS's reversal of position unconscionable.

[Estate of Green, 56 AFTR2d 85-6549, 85-2 USTC ¶ 13,634 (ND Tex. 1985).]

IRS is barred from revoking estate's election. Farmland and crops constituted approximately 90 percent of the value of decedent's estate. The executor filed an election to pay the estate tax attributable to the farming interests in installments pursuant to Section 6166. Because a portion of the farmland was rented at death on a cash-rent basis, that portion constituted investment property, rather than a business, and was ineligible for Section 6166 installment treatment. Nevertheless, the IRS acquiesced in the election for over three years by submitting to the executor annual statements for interest payments due. During that time, the executor, in reliance on the validity of the election, disposed of certain estate assets and distributed farm income. Revocation of the election would have caused the deferred estate tax to become immediately due and payable. The executor sued for summary judgment affirming his right to pay the tax in installments under Section 6166. The IRS argued that the suit was barred by the Anti-Injunction Act.

Held: For the estate. The IRS is prohibited from revoking an estate's Section 6166 election after acquiescing in the election for more than three years. Because the estate had relied on the election and distributed some of its assets, the IRS was estopped from subsequently disavowing the election. The court concluded that the Anti-Injunction Act did not bar the executor's action, because of (1) the likelihood that the estate would be substantially damaged by revocation of the election and (2) the absence of any legal remedy as to the estate. Because the assessment was not disputed, the Tax Court was unavailable. Moreover, the fact that the ultimate tax liability was not disputed precluded any refund action. The court reasoned that under Shapiro, 424 US 614 (1976), the implication exists that due process would be denied upon a showing of potential irreparable injury and in the absence of any remedy for an expeditious determination of the rights of the aggrieved party. The Anti-Injunction Act would apply, however, in the presence of an adequate remedy as to the aggrieved party.

[Parrish, 558 F. Supp. 921, 51 AFTR2d 83-1335, 83-1 USTC ¶ 13,507 (CD Ill. 1982).]

Tax Court denies review of Section 6166 election on jurisdictional grounds, despite related deficiency assessment. Following decedent's death, her executor elected under Section 6166 to extend the time for payment of estate taxes. The IRS, in its subsequent notice of deficiency, determined an estate tax deficiency of $1.27 million, based in part upon an increase in the valuation of stock in decedent's closely held business. The IRS also disallowed a Section 2053 administration expense for interest on the estate tax arising as a result of the Section 6166 election. In its petition to the Tax Court, the estate alleged as error the IRS's disallowance of the interest expense, and also, in a separate allegation of error, the underlying denial of the Section 6166 election. The IRS argued that as set forth under the decision in Estate of Sherrod, 82 TC 523 (1984), the Tax Court was without jurisdiction to decide the propriety of an IRS denial of a Section 6166 election, because the denial is not attributable to a deficiency. The estate contended that where, as here, the IRS determines a deficiency in part based on its denial of the election, the Tax Court acquires jurisdiction to review the legal sufficiency of the denial.

Held: For the IRS in part. In a two-part decision, the Tax Court concluded that though it had no jurisdiction to review the disallowance of the Section 6166 election, it nevertheless had jurisdiction to consider whether the interest expense was deductible under Section 2053. Looking to *Estate of Sherrod*, the court again ruled that it was completely without jurisdiction over matters concerning the denial of an estate tax deferral election, even where a deficiency results from the related disallowance of an interest expense deduction claimed under Section 2053. Accordingly, the court consented to review the narrow issue raised in respect to the deduction, but indicated that it would not examine the estate's underlying qualification under Section 6166.

[Estate of Meyer, 84 TC 560 (1985).]

IRS rules on state death tax credit in cases where estate elects installment payments under Section 6166. Decedent died in 1984, leaving a gross estate composed of a corporation's stock and miscellaneous personal property. The value of his interest in the corporation exceeded 35 percent of the adjusted gross estate. Decedent's stock interest qualified as an interest in a closely held business as defined in Section 6166(b)(1). The estate could therefore elect to pay in ten annual installments the portion of the federal estate tax attributable to the interest in the closely held business. A similar provision under the law of the probating state permitted the estate to elect to pay in ten annual installments the portion of the state death tax attributable to an interest in the closely held business. Deferred and installment payments, plus interest, were required under state law in the same manner provided for in Section 6166 as in effect on the date of death. The personal representative of the estate made a timely election under Section 6166 to pay part of the federal estate tax in ten equal annual installments and made a similar election under state law to pay part of the state death tax in ten annual installments. The representative timely paid in a single day the nondeferred portion of the federal estate tax, the first installment of the deferred estate tax, the nondeferred portion of the state death tax, and the first installment of the deferred state death tax. When the federal estate tax return was filed, the estate claimed a credit under Section 2011 for the total amount of the state death tax liability, including the state death tax paid and the state death tax that the estate expected to pay in installments over the next nine years. The IRS was asked to rule on the extent to which a credit for state death taxes existed, given these facts.

In the IRS analysis, the fact that the estate had elected to pay in ten annual installments made Section 2011(c)(2) applicable, and thus the estate qualified for the Section 2011 credit for state death taxes paid for the period ending before the date of the expiration of the ten-year period elected for paying the federal estate tax. At such time as the estate tax return was filed, however, only the state death taxes actually paid would qualify for the Section 2011 credit on the estate tax return. If necessary, after all state death taxes had been paid, a claim for refund could be made for an overpayment of tax, but only after the federal estate tax liability had been paid in full.

[Rev. Rul. 86-38, 1986-1 CB 296.]

Application of Section 2013 to Section 6166 payments is explained. An estate elected to pay the estate tax in ten installments under Section 6166. The assets were bequeathed to decedent, who died two years later, when two installments had been made. Decedent's estate claimed a Section 2013 credit for estate tax paid on the assets. The IRS ruled that the amount of credit under the Section 2013(b) formula should be computed with reference only to the amount of estate tax installments actually paid by the first estate. Decedent's estate must file a protective claim for the refund of the entire amount potentially due within the period provided in Section 6511. Subsequent refund claims must be filed upon payment of each installment by the first estate by using Form 843.

[Rev. Rul. 83-15, 1983-1 CB 224.]

Estate may defer tax on deficiency, despite failure to make election. An individual died, and the estate timely filed its estate tax return on February 13, 1981, paying the $115,787 tax in full. The IRS examined the estate tax return and determined that assets in the estate included a closely held business, which represented approximately a 74 percent interest of the adjusted gross estate. The estate agreed to a $67,449 deficiency and filed a notice of election under Section 6166 within sixty days after issuance of the deficiency notice and demand for payment. The estate cited Regulations § 20.6166-1(i), Example (1)(i), arguing that because 74 percent of the estate was a closely held business as of the estate return filing date, the estate "could have had a maximum deferral of $135,560, or 74 percent of the corrected tax liability." Therefore, the estate contended that it had prepaid $68,111, or about one half of the tax that it could have paid in installments. The estate further argued that because of the prepayment of one-half of its deferrable tax, no portion of the tax that the estate elected to pay in installments would be due until approximately the sixth installment.

The IRS took the position that the agreed-upon deficiency was payable in installment payments under Section 6166(h). The IRS noted that the estate did not make a Section 6166(a) deferral election with the timely filed return. Therefore, the estate could not have deferred 74 percent of the tax reported and paid with the return as it argued. Consequently, 26 percent of the $67,449 deficiency was due by February 17, 1981, and the balance, or 74 percent, was payable in ten equal installments beginning February 17, 1986, a five-year deferral.

[Tech. Adv. Mem. 8846001.]

Estate qualifies for installment payments; IRS charts effect of deficiency. A woman leased farm property to her children. Under the leases, she received one third of the crops and paid one fifth of the fertilizer costs for the farm. The tenants used their own equipment on the farm. The woman instructed the tenants not to grow sunflowers on the land in 1977, decided when to sell her share of the crops, and decided with the tenants how much fertilizer to apply. When the woman died, the estate elected to value the farm under Section 2032A, but filed a tardy estate tax return, thus disqualifying the estate for special-use valuation. No negligence penalty was asserted for the late filing, but a deficiency was assessed on audit because of the ineffective special-use valuation. The estate then elected to pay the deficiency in installments under Section 6166(h).

The IRS stated that the woman's farming activities were sufficient to qualify the estate for paying the state taxes in installments under Section 6166. The IRS also stated that the estate could pay its deficiency in installments, unless the deficiency, or any part of it, was due to negligence. Finally, the IRS concluded that the negligence of the attorney in filing the estate tax return late would not prevent the estate from using Section 6166(h) unless that negligence also extended to the deficiency.

[Priv. Ltr. Rul. 8432007.]

[2] Interest Payments

Interest on deferred tax does not reduce credit for tax on prior transfers.
Decedent's husband died on February 23, 1981, leaving decedent as her husband's sole heir. Decedent's husband's will was not offered for probate, because virtually his entire estate, consisting of farmland, common stock, treasury notes, and bank deposits, passed to decedent by joint tenancy. Decedent, as the person in possession of the property of her husband, filed a federal estate tax return and elected to pay a portion of the estate tax in installments, pursuant to the provisions of Section 6166. The total amount of interest liability assessed and paid with respect to the Section 6166 election was $113,948. (Decedent's husband died prior to the enactment of the unlimited marital deduction, which would have eliminated all estate taxes in the event that this situation occurred today.) Decedent died on March 22, 1985, while a domiciliary of the state of Illinois. Her personal representative filed a federal estate tax return, including as an asset property received from decedent's husband's estate valued at $2,931,505. A credit for tax on prior transfers under Section 2013 was claimed with respect to this property. The IRS filed a notice of deficiency against decedent's estate, determining that additional estate taxes of $19,584 were due. This deficiency arose out of the IRS's contention that the estate tax credit for prior transfers must be reduced because of the interest paid as a result of the Section 6166 deferral of estate taxes by her husband's estate.

The IRS essentially contended that the value of the property received from decedent's husband must be reduced by the amount of interest paid under Section 6166. The IRS reasoned that under the Illinois Principal and Income Act, interest on federal estate taxes is charged against principal, not against income. Additionally, such interest under Illinois law is a deductible administration expense. Furthermore, in computing the credit for the tax on prior transfers of property, the gross value of the prior transfer must be reduced by the amount of claims against the transferor's estate, including estate taxes and administration expenses, regardless of whether they are claimed as deductions on the estate tax return. Consequently, reasoned the IRS, in computing the credit to which decedent's estate is entitled, the amount of interest paid by virtue of the election to defer payment of estate taxes due from the prior transferor must be deducted from the gross value of the property. Decedent, in contrast, contended that because all property passed to her by joint tenancy, there was no estate under Illinois law against which to make a claim.

Held: For the estate. The court stated that the critical factor in this case is the interpretation of the phrase "the value of the property transferred" as used in Section 2013. In interpreting that phrase, the court first noted that decedent obtained her interest in the property of her deceased husband as a surviving joint tenant, not as a devisee, legatee, or heir. Thus, she obtained the property free and clear of any obligations of her deceased husband, except any that might specifically be imposed in her capacity as a joint tenant. There was no probate estate. The liability of decedent with respect to the estate tax of her deceased husband was founded on Section 6324(a)(2), which imposes a direct liability for such tax on a surviving tenant independently of the operation of state law. This liability imposed no obligation for interest on the estate tax. This second liability was created after the death of decedent's husband in a manner similar to a mortgage that decedent might have placed on her surviving joint tenancy interest.

The court concluded that the interest payments were incurred not to preserve the estate of decedent's husband but rather to protect the surviving joint tenancy of decedent. Although the court noted that decedent did incur a liability for the interest on the deferred estate taxes, it stated that its analysis was not for the purpose of determining the ultimate liability for such interest, but in the context of determining whether such interest should reduce the credit for the estate tax on prior transfers. It further stated that in considering whether there should be such a reduction, it was irrelevant that the interest was not deducted by decedent's husband's estate for either estate or income tax purposes. Based on this reasoning, the court held that the credit on prior transfers to which taxpayer's estate was entitled should not be reduced by the interest paid, because of the Section 6166 deferral of estate taxes by the transferor's estate.

[Estate of Whittle, 97 TC 362 (1991), aff'd, 994 F2d 379, 93-1 USTC 60,141, 71 AFTR2d 93-2202 (7th Cir.).]

Estate tax liability paid on installment method is subject to increase in interest rate. Taxpayer's estate elected in 1974 to pay its outstanding estate tax liability on the installment method pursuant to Section 6166. In 1975, Congress changed the interest rate from 4 percent to a higher variable rate. Taxpayer argued that the rate change as applied violated the constitutional due process requirement.

Held: For the IRS. Taxpayer had no vested right in the 4 percent interest rate; the election was no more than a privilege, which is not entitled to constitutional protection.

[Estate of Papson, 81 TC 105 (1983).]

Tax Court joins IRS in rejecting estimated interest deduction on Section 6166 payments. Following decedent's death in 1978, his estate reported a $9.02 million adjusted gross estate, $5.89 million of which represented the value of decedent's interest in a closely held business enterprise. The executor elected to have the payment of estate taxes deferred pursuant to Section 6166. At the time of decedent's death, Section 6166 provided that a portion of the estate tax liability could be deferred if the value of the closely held business interests exceeded 65 percent of adjusted gross estate. Interest was payable under the statute in the same way provided for in Section 6166 following the 1981 ERTA amendments. On the final estate tax return, the executor, a commercial bank, claimed an interest expense deduction in accordance with Section 2053(a)(2) for the total amount of interest that it estimated would be incurred as a result of the election. The IRS, however, disallowed the deduction, arguing that the estimated amount was not in compliance with the requirements of Section 2053.

The IRS cited Regulation § 20.2053-1(b)(3), which states that an estimated amount can be deducted only where the amount (1) can be ascertained with reasonable certainty and (2) will be paid. In the IRS's view, an estimate of interest due under Section 6166 can never satisfy the test, because there is always the possibility of fluctuation in the applicable interest rate, as well as the chance that there will be a voluntary or involuntary acceleration of the estate tax liability. The estate claimed that it satisfied the certainty test by using a method based on the average yield to maturity of Treasury obligations maturing over the deferral period to estimate the total interest to be incurred. Also, given the illiquid nature of the closely held assets, the estate argued, there was virtually no possibility of acceleration.

Held: For the IRS. The Tax Court refused to accept the estate's argument that its method of valuation had a demonstrated certainty, despite the fact that Congress had considered adopting such a method during 1982. Because the proposed legislation was not adopted, the force of the estate's argument was lost, and the court held that there was no showing that reasonable certainty would be achieved by the use of such a method. As to the certainty of the payment test, the regulation requires that the interest "will be paid." The fact that the estate could voluntarily or involuntarily accelerate payment rendered the tax liability uncertain as a matter of law. Accordingly, the estate was confined to an interest deduction equal to the amount actually accrued.

[Estate of Hoover, TC Memo. (P-H) ¶ 85,183, 49 TCM (CCH) 1239 (1985).]

When time to pay estate tax payment has been extended and deficiency is assessed after estate has timely made at least one payment, 4 percent interest rate is applied to determine amount of interest that should have been paid in each annual payment. When the value of an interest in a closely held business is included in determining decedent's gross estate, the executor may elect to pay all or part of the estate tax in up to ten equal install-ments, provided that the interest in the business exceeds 35 percent of the ad-justed gross estate. This election provides liquidity relief to an estate in which decedent's interest in a closely held business is a significant part of the gross estate. If such an election is made, the estate makes only annual interest pay-ments during the initial five-year period on the tax attributable to the business. Under Section 6601(j), during the deferral period, interest accrues at the rate of 4 percent, rather than at the prevailing rate under Section 6601(a). When a de-ficiency attributable to decedent's interest in the business is assessed during the five-year deferral period, it is generally prorated to the scheduled tax in-stallments, and interest is imposed at the rate of 4 percent. If the deficiency is assessed after one or more of the annual interest payments have been made, the interest payments that were made before the deficiency was assessed will be less than the payments that would have been made had the correct liability been shown on the return. If the 4 percent rate of interest were applied to the interest that should have been paid in past annual interest payments from the date on which the interest was due until the date of notice and demand for such interest, the estate would be in a better position than if the tax liability had been reported correctly on the return. Under Section 6166(f)(1), an estate is obligated to pay the interest on the full amount of its unpaid tax annually, and the 4 percent rate of interest extends only to the date on which the interest should have been paid.

According to the IRS, Congress did not intend that an estate with a defi-ciency be entitled to the 4 percent rate of interest for any period beyond the date on which the annual interest payment on the full amount of unpaid tax was due. Thus, the IRS concluded that interest on any underpayment of inter-est accrues at the prevailing rate from the date on which the interest should have been paid had the return shown the correct tax liability.

[Rev. Rul. 89-32, 1989-1 CB 307.]

[3] Amount Deferred

Overpayment of estate tax liability is applied to unpaid installments. Two estates elected under Section 6166 to defer a portion of the estate tax due. Al-though the IRS initially issued notices of deficiency, alleging that the stock of the closely held corporation owned by decedents (husband and wife) had been undervalued, it was eventually agreed that it had in fact been overvalued. The overpayments included portions of the installment payments that would not have been due had the correct value for the stock been given on the estate re-turns. As to these amounts, the estates sought refunds, with interest. The IRS contended that the matter was resolved by Section 6403, which provides that when a taxpayer pays makes an installment payment for more than the correct amount, the overpayment is to be credited to unpaid installments. Only if the amount already paid by taxpayer exceeds the ultimate amount due would a refund be due the taxpayer. The estates countered that this provision should not apply to Section 6166, in that Section 6166(g) should be the exclusive list of situations under which the benefits of the section would be curtailed. To apply Section 6403 would, in effect, accelerate the payments due. This, the estates argued, would be contrary to the congressional intent behind Section 6166, which is to allow deferral of estate taxes on family farms and closely held businesses. The IRS's approach, according to the estates, substantially reduced the benefits of deferral.

Held: For the IRS. The court disagreed with the estates' argument, holding that the IRS appropriately credited the overpayments toward the future, corrected installments. Although the estates correctly stated the policy of the statute, the court concluded that Section 6166(g) is not the exclusive delineation of situations in which the benefits of the section are curtailed. Although no specific mention of Section 6403 is made in Regulations § 20.6166-1(i), the example demonstrates the correct treatment of overpayments of installments, indicating that overpayments should be credited toward subsequent installments.

[Estate of Bell, 92 TC 714 (1989), aff'd, 928 F2d 901, 67 AFTR2d 91-1198, 91-1 USTC ¶ 60,065 (9th Cir. 1991).]

Mortgages on property in closely held business are relevant to determination of decedent's interest for estate tax deferral. After decedent's death, her surviving spouse continued the couple's real estate development proprietorship. Decedent's interest in the proprietorship included property that was subject to mortgages with interest rates below those prevailing on her death. The estate elected to defer the federal estate tax attributable to decedent's interest in the closely held business.

The IRS took the position in technical advice that if real property used in a closely held business is mortgaged, the mortgages are relevant to determining the value of a decedent's interest in the business for purposes of deferring federal estate tax.

[Tech. Adv. Mem. 8343002.]

Value of closely held business should not be reduced by income tax attributable to predeath earnings. An estate elected under Section 6166 to pay a portion of the estate tax in installments. The estate claimed as a deduction on the estate tax return the income tax payable on income earned from estate assets prior to decedent's death, less estimated tax payments. The estate's income tax liability was attributable to all earnings, including the earnings from a closely held business.

The IRS took the position in technical advice that "in calculating the value of 'the closely held business amount' for purposes of section 6166(a)(2)(A) of the Code, the value of the closely held business should not be reduced by the federal income tax liability attributable to earnings from the closely held business prior to the decedent's date of death." The IRS reasoned that personal liabilities of a decedent are not considered in determining the net value of a closely held business.

[Tech. Adv. Mem. 8234001.]

[4] Active Business Requirement

Holding company is not active trade or business qualifying for Section 6166A deferral. Decedent's estate included voting stock in a bank holding company that owned 98 percent of a bank. The executor sought deferral of the estate taxes attributable to the estate's interest in the holding company through the application of Section 6166A, which allows installment payments of tax over ten years for certain closely held businesses. The IRS argued that the stock did not qualify for the installment method, because it did not satisfy the active trade or business requirements of Regulation § 20.6166A-(c)(1), which provides that in order for the stock of a corporation to qualify as an interest in a closely held business, it is necessary that the corporation be engaged in carrying on a trade or business at the time of the decedent's death.

Held: For the IRS. The court found from the evidence presented at trial that the holding company was not in and of itself carrying on an active trade or business. At the time of decedent's death, the holding company had no office or telephone, its office consisted of a file in the desk drawer of an officer of the bank, its bank account consisted of $1,000, which was used to pay the income tax preparation fees for the holding company, and the holding company did not have any income. The court stated that although the holding company held the stock of an active business, the holding company did not actively supervise or control the subsidiary corporation. The decision making and the running of the bank was conducted by its officers and directors, who did not directly act for or report to the parent holding company. The court rejected the estate's argument that if a holding company has no reason to exist, except as an entity to hold the ownership of a qualifying trade or business, then the holding company should be treated as the qualifying trade or business for purposes of Section 6166A. The court noted that Congress amended Section 6166A, adding Section 6166(b)(8), which permits certain holding company stock to be treated as a stock in a business company. However, the court said that the amendment did not apply retroactively to the estate's case. Accordingly, the estate was not entitled to deferral treatment.

[Estate of Moore, 87-2 USTC ¶ 13,741 (ED Tex. 1987).]

Farm property is not closely held business for purposes of Section 6166 installment payments. At the time of decedent's death in 1979, she owned two farms. She did not personally operate the farms, but had an arrangement with an unrelated individual to operate them. The arrangement was a cross between a fixed cash rental lease and a typical share-cropping arrangement. Decedent was to receive a percentage of the crop production, with a minimum payment of $600 annually. She would also share a portion of the expenses. Every spring the individual would discuss with decedent what fertilizer and weed control would be used, what crops would be planted, and what expenses would be incurred during the year. Although decedent was kept well informed, she did not participate in any of the decisions, and it was clear that the individual had the ultimate responsibility for making the decisions. Decedent was unable to participate in the day-to-day farming operation because of her impaired vision. For the three years prior to her death, decedent listed her occupation as retired on her income tax returns, which included Form 4835, designed for nonparticipating owners of agricultural property. After decedent's death, her executors claimed that the estate was entitled to make estate tax payments in installments pursuant to Section 6166. They alleged that the two farms were interests in closely held businesses and constituted more than 65 percent of the adjusted gross estate (the test for decedents prior to the enactment of the Economic Recovery Tax Act of 1981 (ERTA)).

Held: For the IRS. The district court recognized that the issue was whether the farms were being managed and operated in a manner that would qualify them as a trade or business under Section 6166. It noted that the IRS had previously ruled that farm property is eligible to qualify for Section 6166 treatment. Its qualification, however, must then be judged in accordance with the guidelines that have been established by the IRS. These guidelines indicate that Section 6166 was intended to give relief for businesses that were actively managed and operated by the decedent, not for businesses that provided only a passive income for the decedent.

The court characterized decedent's activities as passive, not the type of active participation envisioned by Section 6166. Although she did bear a portion of the expenses, and although the individual kept her well informed of the activities, she really made no management decisions and did not actually participate in the operation of the farms. The fact that there was a share-cropping arrangement did not per se disqualify the farms, but there had to be active participation by decedent in the management decisions about the use and cultivation of the farms and a periodic observation of the operations. The court felt that decedent had acknowledged her lack of active participation in the management and operation of the farms by showing her occupation as retired and filing Form 4835. Although decedent may well have received income that was dependent upon crop production from the farms, that alone was not enough without a showing of active participation. The court held that decedent did not "cultivate, operate or manage" the farms as required by Revenue Ruling 75-366, 1975-2 CB 472, and therefore that her estate was not entitled to the installment payment option provided by Section 6166.

[Schindler, 87-2 USTC ¶ 13,735 (ND Ohio 1987).]

Estate tax deferral for real estate. The IRS held in this ruling that the estate of a decedent who owned a real estate business could qualify for the closely held business estate tax deferral relief in Section 6166, despite the characterization by Revenue Ruling 75-365, 1975-2 CB 471, of an owner-manager's rental commercial property as not being an interest in a closely held business for purposes of Section 6166.

The ruling distinguished between properties for which decedent, as landlord, was responsible for performing daily janitorial services from other commercial rental properties decedent had owned. Only with respect to the former did the IRS determine that decedent's level of activity satisfied the trade or business requirement of Section 6166.

[Priv. Ltr. Rul. 9832009.]

Deferral election limited to active business assets. Decedent owned 18 percent of the voting stock of a corporation engaged in developing and constructing rental real property. Decedent also owned 39 percent of the stock of a corporation that managed real estate (all developed by the first corporation) for itself and four partnerships in which decedent held major interests. Each corporation had fewer than ten shareholders. The corporations shared approximately twenty-five employees, including seven of decedent's children or their spouses. All the employees were paid by the development corporation, and it was reimbursed by the management corporation for its share of the payroll and overhead in serving as common paymaster. The management corporation's assets included six apartment complexes, a shopping center, three mobile home courts and individual mobile home rental units, storage and warehouse facilities, land either held for development or leased, and an interest in a partnership owning and operating apartment complexes. The management services included screening prospective tenants; maintaining common areas; installing and repairing household fixtures; maintaining water, heating, and sewer systems; painting; disposing of garbage and satisfying recycling requirements; making ordinary plumbing and electrical repairs; mediating tenant disputes; providing 24-hour emergency service; maintaining records; and, preparing reports for government agencies.

Under Section 6166, an estate can elect to pay the estate tax attributable to an interest in a "closely held business" in (up to) ten installments beginning with the fifth year after the tax was originally due. To be eligible, the value of the closely held business must exceed 35 percent of the adjusted gross estate.

Section 6166(b)(1)(C) provides that stock of a corporation carrying on a trade or business is an interest in a closely held business if 20 percent or more in value of the voting stock is included in the gross estate or if the corporation had fifteen or fewer shareholders. Under Section 6166(c), interests in two or more businesses may be treated as interests in a single closely held business for purposes of the 35 percent test if 20 percent or more of the total value of each business is included in determining the value of a decedent's estate. Decedent did not actually own 20 percent of the stock of the development and construction corporation, but his stock could be aggregated with the management corporation's stock because Section 6166(b)(2) attributes stock of family members to a decedent for purposes of the 35 percent test.

The more serious problem for the estate was whether all the management corporation's real estate interests were part of a qualifying trade or business. Even if a corporation is carrying on a trade or business, under Section 6166(b)(9), nonbusiness assets are subtracted in determining the value of the interest that qualifies for the election. Furthermore, a trade or business must be an active business that would be disrupted by the sale of assets to pay tax, if it is to qualify under Section 6166, according to Revenue Ruling 75-365, 1975-2 CB 471. Therefore, the management of income-producing properties that do not form part of an active enterprise is not a business for purposes of Section 6166 (even if expenses are deducted as business expenses under Section 162). Thus, when an individual repurchased eight homes that he had sold as part of a home-building operation, his renting, repairing, and maintaining them was only an investment activity in Revenue Ruling 75-367, 1975-2 CB 472.

In the instant ruling, the development corporation was engaged in a trade or business qualifying under Section 6166. Likewise, the management corporation's rendering of services to other entities qualified as a trade or business. In addition, the properties owned by the management corporation for which it provided substantial services were part of an active trade or business. This included all the buildings where the full range of management services were provided to tenants. Where the services provided were not substantial, however, the properties were mere investment assets. Consequently, the IRS held that only property used in the active business, regardless of ownership, was covered by a Section 6166 election to defer the payment of estate tax. Thus, real property held solely for investment did not qualify, even though it was owned by a corporation conducting an active real estate business.

[Priv. Ltr. Rul. 9634006.]

Life insurance policy used as collateral for proprietor's business loans cannot be considered business asset for purposes of estate tax deferral. An individual died in 1986. Prior to his death, he operated a variety of businesses as a sole proprietor. The individual had purchased a life insurance policy, which was used at various times as collateral to secure bank loans to purchase properties used in his business. Upon his death, a bank, in its capacity as creditor, received the $500,000 insurance proceeds. The estate argued that because the policy was used as collateral for business loans, the policy should be considered in determining the value of decedent's interest in a closely held business for purposes of the estate tax deferral under Section 6166. The estate included the $500,000 life insurance proceeds in determining the value of decedent's interest in the business. The cash value of the policy immediately before death was zero.

The IRS took the position that the $500,000 proceeds from the insurance policy could not be treated as an asset actively used in decedent's trade or business. The IRS concluded that though Section 6166A was repealed by the Economic Recovery Tax Act of 1981, the regulations under Section 6166A are still considered in determining whether decedent owned an interest in a closely held business. The IRS looked to Section 6166(b)(9), which provides that the value of any interest in a closely held business shall not include the value of the portion of such interest that is attributable to passive assets held by the business. The IRS stated that in the case of a sole proprietorship, each asset is examined at the time immediately preceding decedent's death to determine whether the asset was actively used in the business and that passive assets are not taken into account. The IRS concluded that the life insurance policy was merely a passive asset, and the fact that it was used as collateral to secure loans did not change that characterization.

[Tech. Adv. Mem. 8848002.]

Decedent's business interest is eligible for estate tax installment payments. An individual established, and was the sole beneficiary of, a revocable trust that had as one of its assets several residential rental properties. The individual personally managed, maintained, and operated these properties as a trade and business. The individual had to withdraw from the active management of the business because of a disabling illness in mid-1985, but continued to advise his son about the operation of the business until mid-1986, after which time he relinquished all business duties to his son. The individual died. The properties constituted more than 35 percent of decedent's adjusted gross estate.

The IRS stated that decedent's business interest qualified under Section 6166(b)(1)(A) as an active trade or business interest in a closely held business. The IRS also indicated that any federal estate liability tax attributable to the business interest may be paid in up to ten installments, with a five-year grace period for the first payment and with an annual 4 percent interest rate. The IRS distinguished Revenue Ruling 75-365, 1975-2 CB 472.

[Priv. Ltr. Rul. 8741076.]

General partnership interest qualifies as interest in closely held business under Section 6166. An individual owned a one-sixth general partnership interest in some ranchland when she died. The individual also owned a limited partnership interest. Before her death, the individual and her husband had operated the ranchland with the husband's brothers and their spouses through a general partnership. Later the owners had executed a limited partnership agreement to operate the ranching business. Ownership remained in the hands of the brothers, who leased the ranchland to the limited partnership on a net-lease basis. The limited partnership paid lease rentals based on the average price received for bulls sold at the "annual October bull sale." When the husband died, the lease agreement remained in effect, and the individuals stayed actively involved in managing the property.

The IRS stated that the general partnership interest owned by the individual qualified as an interest in a closely held business under Section 6166. Citing Revenue Rulings 75-366 and 75-367, 1975-2 CB 472, the IRS concluded that the ranchland was not held as a passive income-producing investment. The IRS noted that the general partnership interest was an interest in an ongoing business enterprise.

[Priv. Ltr. Rul. 8601005.]

Vendor liens do not qualify as interests in closely held business. A self-employed sole proprietor subdivided and sold plots of land from time to time. When she died, 95 percent of her estate consisted of promissory notes secured by vendor liens representing the unpaid balances from the sale of land. The IRS stated that the vendor liens did not qualify as an interest in a closely held business for purposes of Section 6166. The IRS characterized the notes as "mere ownership of investment assets." The private ruling relied on Revenue Ruling 75-365, 1975-2 CB 461; Revenue Ruling 75-366, 1975-2 CB 472; and Revenue Ruling 75-367, 1975-2 CB 472.

[Priv. Ltr. Rul. 8514037.]

Net-leased property does not qualify for estate tax deferral. When decedent died, decedent owned stock in a closely held business that qualified under Section 6166. Decedent also owned real property consisting of a lot and building used exclusively by one of decedent's closely held corporations. Decedent leased the property to the corporation on a net-lease basis. The IRS stated that the real estate leased on a net-lease basis to decedent's corporation did not qualify as an interest in a closely held business for purposes of Section 6166. The IRS stated that net leased property did not satisfy the active business test.

[Priv. Ltr. Rul. 7451014.]

[5] Aggregation of Businesses

Fractional oil interests are part of decedent's sole proprietorship. A petroleum engineer operated his oil business as a sole proprietorship. He held and developed oil properties. When he participated with others in working interests, he elected not to be treated as a partnership. He also owned interests of less than 20 percent in several working interests, and he held royalty interests in others. He participated in decisions regarding the working interests, even those for which he was not the operator, and he also worked on the royalty interests. The engineer died in 1979.

In technical advice, the IRS took the position that both the royalty interests and the working interests of less than 20 percent were part of the engineer's interest in a closely held trade or business for purposes of Section 6166; that is, they were part of the engineer's sole proprietorship. To require each interest to qualify separately as a trade or business, the IRS said, "places undue emphasis on the mode of tenancy and fractional nature of these interests and ignores the existence of the [engineer's] oil and gas proprietorship."

[Tech. Adv. Mem. 8419002.]

[6] Acceleration

[a] Generally

Estate is entitled to refund where it made full payment after erroneous acceleration notice. Following decedent's death in 1978, his estate elected deferral and installment payment of estate taxes pursuant to Section 6166. That section allows a qualifying estate to defer payment of the tax due on that portion of the estate represented by a closely held business (including a farm) for up to five years, after which time the tax must be paid in up to ten equal installments. During the five-year deferral period, only interest payments are due. When the estate failed to make its first payment of interest on time, the IRS sent the estate a notice stating that because it had failed to make the required interest payment, the estate's deferred payment status was being terminated; it also sent the estate a bill for the total amount of tax, plus interest and penalty, declaring that the entire amount was due because of the missed payment.

After borrowing more than $500,000 from a bank at market rates, the estate paid the entire amount demanded by the IRS. The estate then filed claims for refunds of both the penalty assessed and the principal amount of the tax that had qualified for deferral. The estate also requested reinstatement of the installment payment schedule. The IRS denied the estate's claim for refund, even though it admitted that under Revenue Ruling 82-120, the acceleration notice was improperly issued. At the time of the IRS's demand to the estate for full payment, Section 6166(g)(3) permitted acceleration after an "installment" payment had been missed. Under Revenue Ruling 82-120, however, interpreting Section 6166, an "installment" means a principal payment as opposed to an interest payment during the five-year deferral period. The IRS nevertheless contended that because the entire accelerated amount paid by the estate did not exceed the total estate tax due, Sections 6402 and 6403 did not allow a refund. These sections permit a refund of taxes prematurely paid to the extent that there is an overpayment. The estate asserted that if Sections 6402 and 6403 were to be interpreted in the manner suggested by the IRS, it would totally negate the benefits of deferred payments confirmed under Section 6166. The estate suggested that the proper application of Sections 6402 and 6403 is to credit overpayments against taxes then due—not to liabilities, that by law become due in the future.

Held: For the estate. The court stated that because the IRS admitted that it had wrongfully revoked the installment plan and demanded full and immediate payment, the amount paid cannot be construed as an overpayment. Instead, it was a forced payment of a tax that was prematurely, and therefore erroneously, assessed and collected. The court said that to allow Sections 6402 and 6403 to operate as the IRS claimed would negate the benefits of Section 6166, to which both parties agreed the estate was entitled. Because the IRS wrongfully revoked the estate's deferral status when it accelerated all future payments, the court concluded that Sections 6402 and 6403 were not applicable to deny the estate's refund claim, and the court reinstated the estate's deferral payment status.

[Novak, 88-1 USTC ¶ 13,765, 71A AFTR2d 93-4998 (D. Neb. 1988).]

Late payment does not necessarily void election. Decedent's estate elected under Section 6166 to pay federal estate taxes in regular deferred installments. The estate failed to make a payment due on December 8, 1978, but sent the amount owed to the IRS on April 23, 1979. Notice and demand for payment was issued on May 14, 1979. The IRS sought to void the election and accelerate all amounts due under the authority of Regulations § 20.6166-3(c), which states that an election to defer estate tax payments under Section 6166 is always lost if a payment is not made on time. The taxpayer argued that a default in payment of an installment can be cured by a late payment if the payment is made before notice is given by the district director.

Held: For the estate. In refusing to follow Regulations § 20.6166-3(c), the court took the position that where payment is made prior to the issuance of notice and demand by the IRS, the election can still be in force. In so holding, the court was strongly influenced by the decision in Lake Shore Nat'l Bank,

419 F2d 958 (7th Cir. 1959), which implied this result but did not squarely reach the issue. In *Lake Shore Nat'l Bank*, involving Section 6166, an estate also failed to make a payment on time. It paid the installment after notice and demand was issued, and the court was asked to decide which interest rate was applicable, the special 4 percent rate or the then-general rate of 6 percent. The 6 percent rate was held to apply to the past-due installment from its due date, because no further extension was in effect with respect to that payment; but the court seemed to hold that the 4 percent rate continued to apply to the balance of the tax until the notice was given, at which time the 6 percent rate became applicable until the balance of the tax was paid. The court accepted this reasoning in holding that the taxpayer's installment election was still valid. It emphasized that Congress intended to give some degree of flexibility in handling late installments, because those estates that were late were most often those in need of the relief of Section 6166. The court concluded that the IRS had failed to exercise the discretionary authority conferred upon it by statute.

[Delguzzi, 46 AFTR2d 80-6192, 80-2 USTC ¶ 13,364 (WD Wash. 1980).]

IRS rules on effect of state death tax credit in acceleration case. *A* died in 1982, leaving an interest in *X* corporation, a closely held business, exceeding 35 percent of the adjusted gross estate. *A*'s personal representative elected to pay the portion of the estate tax attributable to the closely held business in ten equal installments under Section 6166. *A*'s personal representative timely paid the nondeferred portion of the estate tax and the first installment of the deferred tax on January 10, 1983. In order to pay a state death tax liability, some shares of *A*'s stock of *X* were redeemed on January 11, 1983, in a redemption of stock under Section 303. The proceeds (an amount less than the maximum amount of credit permitted under Section 2011(b)) were paid to the state for death taxes on January 9, 1984. The proceeds, when added to prior distributions, amounted to a disposition of more than 50 percent in value of the estate's interest in *X*. The IRS was asked to rule on whether a state death tax credit is equivalent to a payment of tax imposed by Section 2001 for purposes of avoiding the acceleration of federal estate tax installment payments under Section 6166(g)(1)(B).

The IRS noted that Revenue Ruling 83-15, 1983-1 CB 224, holds that when the federal estate tax is being paid in installments under Section 6166, only the amount of the installment actually paid is to be used in computing the credit for the tax on prior transfers under Section 2013 for the estate of the transferee-decedent. In Revenue Ruling 84-11, 1984-1 CB 201, an adjustment was made by the IRS in 1982 to increase the value of a 1977 gift. Although no gift tax could be assessed for the gift, because the period of limitations had expired, the ruling holds that the adjustment does increase the total sum of the gifts because the use of the unified credit under Section 2505 does not result in a payment or assessment of the gift tax that would preclude such adjustment under Section 2504(c). Section 6166(g)(1)(B) requires a payment of the tax imposed by Section 2001. Only those credits that are based on an actual federal tax payment may be regarded as tax paid for purposes of Section 6166(g)(1)(B). An example of such a credit is a credit of the amount of an overpayment of an installment under Section 6403. Other credits do not represent actual payments of tax but do satisfy the tax liability. This is true of the unified credit against the gift tax. Other examples are the investment credit, foreign tax credit, and the energy credit. The state death tax credit falls into this category; it offsets the estate tax liability but is not based on an actual payment of that tax. Accordingly, the IRS ruled that the application of a state death tax credit is not equivalent to an amount of tax paid for purposes of avoiding acceleration of federal estate tax installment payments under Section 6166(g)(1)(B).

[Rev. Rul. 85-43, 1985-1 CB 356.]

Stock redemption does not accelerate deferrals when made to fund bequest and to pay taxes and expenses. When a man and his wife both died in 1980, he owned 1,921 of the 1,987 sole class of stock shares outstanding in a closely held corporation. His wife and son owned the remaining shares, fifty-three and thirteen shares, respectively. Both estates filed elections under Section 6166 for the extension of time for payment of estate tax attributable to their respective stock interests in the corporation. The husband's estate qualified for the extension under Section 6166, and the wife's estate qualified pending a determination whether her estate had the required interest in a closely held business. Both estates wished to raise cash to pay their respective federal and state death taxes and administration expenses. To this end, each estate proposed to redeem some of its stock in the corporation to raise money. The husband's estate was to transfer shares in the corporation to the wife's estate to fund the bequest to the wife under the husband's will.

The IRS took the position that the distribution of stock from the husband's estate to his wife's estate would not be an accelerating event for purposes of his estate's Section 6166 deferral. It also stated that the amount that either estate receives for redemption of stock would be treated as a distribution in full payment in exchange for the stock to the extent that it is used for the payment of estate tax and accrued interest. Further, the amount that either estate receives in redemption of its stock would not be treated as withdrawals or distributions for purposes of accelerating estate tax deferrals.

[Priv. Ltr. Rul. 8839013.]

IRS takes position on transfer of closely held business interests between heirs' accelerated estate tax payments. Decedent bequeathed to her two sons a farm consisting of three tracts of land. The executor elected to extend payment of the estate tax under Section 6166, because the farm was operated as a closely held business and represented 96 percent of the gross estate. The children of one of the sons sold one tract of land to the other son and proposed to do the same with one of the remaining two tracts of land.

The IRS stated that the proposed sale would be a disposition under Section 6166 and would accelerate estate tax payments under Section 6166(g)(1)(A). The IRS reasoned that because the source of cash would be from outside the estate, the purpose behind Section 6166 would be thwarted, because the closely held business would not be reshuffled within the estate.

[Priv. Ltr. Rul. 8730006.]

Estate's sale of farm assets to pay off mortgages is not disposition of interest in business. An individual owned a farming business at the time of his death. Mortgages on the farm property had become delinquent, and the estate wanted to sell off part of the property to satisfy the mortgages. The IRS stated that the sale of a portion of the farm property to pay off the mortgages would not be a disposition of an interest in the business or a withdrawal of funds from the business if the proceeds were applied to the mortgages. The IRS added that any proceeds received in excess of the mortgages would be considered a disposition under Section 6166(g)(1)(A).

[Priv. Ltr. Rul. 8441029.]

Division of farm estate into parcels does not accelerate tax payments; operation on cash rental basis does. An individual who owned two tracts of farmland operated them on a share-rent basis. Tenants worked the land and shared a percentage of the crops and expenses with the farm owner. He shared in the major decisions. The owner died in 1981. His two heirs continued to operate the farmland on the same basis as decedent. The estate elected to pay the tax on the land in installments. The two heirs divided the farm, and each took one parcel.

The IRS stated that the division of the farm by the heirs is not a triggering event under Section 6166(g)(1)(A) and should not cause an acceleration of the estate tax. The IRS also stated, however, that a discontinuance of the farm use of the land would constitute a triggering event. The IRS concluded that the straight cash rental operation of the land would be inconsistent with the qualified use of the land.

[Priv. Ltr. Rul. 8339023.]

Distribution of estate assets does not accelerate deferred estate tax. An interest in a closely held business was part of decedent's estate. The coexecutors of the estate elected under Section 6166 to pay the estate tax attributable to the business interest in ten installments. The coexecutors proposed to distribute the estate assets to the heirs and then to close the estate. The estate heirs included decedent's grandsons, who proposed to transfer the interests received from the estate to grantor trusts for their own benefit. When the grandsons reached age 35, the trusts were to terminate, and the grandsons were to receive the trusts assets. The grandsons had powers of appointment over their trusts. The IRS stated that the distribution of the estate assets and the transfer to the grantor trusts would not accelerate the deferred estate tax under Section 6166.

[Priv. Ltr. Rul. 8326023.]

[b] Corporate transactions

Trust's stock in corporation qualified as interest in closely held business. From September 1981 until August 1986, the date of individual's death, 100 percent of a corporation's stock was owned by the family trust, which was a grantor trust. The stock was the trust's only asset. The individual's estate included 100 percent of the stock as well as securities and bank accounts. The value of the real estate assets of the corporation exceeded 35 percent of the individual's adjusted gross estate. The executors wanted to pay the tax allocable to the value of the shares in the corporation in installments. The corporation was engaged in the purchase, renovation, management, and rental of older commercial properties. At the time of individual's death, the corporation owned three parcels of land; the corporation had been paid for by a fourth parcel seized through eminent domain. The corporation later purchased a fifth parcel of land and instituted a suit claiming that the land taken by eminent domain was worth more than the corporation had paid. In December 1986, the corporation was liquidated under Section 331, and all of its assets were distributed to the family trust. Real estate assets were held in the name of a trust that was to act as the nominee for the family trust. The family trust would continue to run the business previously engaged in by the corporation until December 2006.

The IRS, citing Revenue Ruling 75-365, 1975-2 CB 471, Revenue Ruling 75-366, 1975-2 CB 472, and Revenue Ruling 75-367, 1975-2 CB 472, took the position that the stock in the corporation qualified as an interest in a closely held business under Section 6166(b)(1). The IRS further stated that the cash on hand in the corporation at the time of individual's death attributable to payment from eminent domain was not a passive asset under Section 6166(b)(9). The remaining amount from the eminent domain payment also would not be a passive asset if reinvested in commercial realty within three years, or at a later date approved by the IRS. If the amount were not timely reinvested, it would be considered a "disposition" under Section 6166(g) as of the first day of the replacement period. Finally, the IRS concluded that the liquidation of the corporation under Section 331 and the distribution of all assets to the family trust were not a disposition or withdrawal of an interest in a

closely held business under Section 6166(g). Therefore, there was no acceleration of the estate tax payable in installments.

[Priv. Ltr. Rul. 8829013.]

**Division of family corporation into two corporations does not result in ac-
celeration of estate tax payments.** Decedent's estate included 18,627 shares
of a total of 50,000 shares of the common stock of a family-operated farm and
ranching corporation. The other shareholders were decedent's wife and five
children. Of the 50,000 shares of common stock, 1,525 shares of the corporation were redeemed to pay estate taxes, with the balance of decedent's shares
being distributed to the wife and children. The estate elected to specially value
decedent's stock interest under Section 2032A and to pay in installments a
portion of the tax attributable to decedent's interest under Section 6166. None
of the shares distributed to decedent's wife and children were sold, distributed,
or transferred by them. The family proposed to divide the corporation into two
corporations, primarily to eliminate family disputes that adversely affected the
business. The transaction represented a vertical division of the corporation,
separating the ranching and farming businesses. The corporation was to create
a new corporation (Newco), which would transfer a stock interest, representing
42.67 percent of the operating assets and liabilities of the corporation, to
Newco in exchange for all of the common stock of Newco. The corporation
then would distribute all of the common stock of Newco to certain individuals
and trusts in a non-pro rata distribution in exchange for their shares of the corporation's common stock.

The IRS stated that the proposed division of the corporation into two corporations would not be a disposition by the estate of an interest in a closely
held business under Section 6166(g)(1)(A), because it would qualify for an exception under Section 6166(g)(1)(C). Therefore, the disposition would not accelerate estate tax payments. The IRS concluded that the transaction was
merely a change in form.

[Priv. Ltr. Rul. 8740031.]

**Change of form that does not materially alter interests or business does
not result in acceleration under Section 6166.** An individual died in 1981,
owning 94 percent of one corporation and 100 percent of a second corporation.
Decedent provided for the creation of four testamentary trusts. His estate
elected to pay estate tax in installments under Section 6166. The estate
planned to liquidate the corporations and distribute their assets to the shareholders, who were immediately to contribute the assets to a limited partnership
in which the estate would be a limited partner. The partnership would not receive any assets other than those that were distributed by the two corporations
upon their liquidation, and the fair market value of the estate's interest in the
corporations would not change, because of the formation of the limited part-

nership. Upon termination of the estate, its assets would be distributed to the testamentary trusts.

The IRS stated that the proposed transaction would not constitute a disposition under Section 6166(g), because the business had not been materially altered and the interest of the estate in the business had not changed. The transfer of the estate's interest to the testamentary trusts was sanctioned by Section 6166(g)(1)(D) and would not result in acceleration of the deferred tax. The IRS also stated that the distribution of current earnings from the partnership would not constitute a withdrawal of funds from the closely held business under Section 6166(g).

[Priv. Ltr. Rul. 8534073.]

Distribution of interest in closely held corporation is not disqualifying disposition. In 1981, an individual died, survived by two daughters, a son, and a wife. His gross estate consisted largely of closely held business interests, including the stock of a corporation. An election was made to pay estate tax in installments under Section 6166. Decedent's will provided that half of his shares in the corporation would pass to his wife and that the other half would be put in trust for his children until the youngest reached the age 21. At the date of death, the youngest child was over age 21. The estate redeemed some of its stock to pay nondeferred federal and state estate taxes. The estate then made a distribution to the surviving spouse of almost all of her interest in the stock. The estate planned to distribute equal shares of almost all of the remaining stock to decedent's two daughters and son. Two additional shares were to be distributed jointly to the daughters, the son, and the surviving spouse to account for fractional share interests. The estate was then to terminate. After the termination, the corporation was to redeem the interest of the daughters, including their fractional interests in the two shares. The redemption would be for cash and promissory notes. The surviving spouse and the son were to redeem a portion of their stock before the due date for an installment payment of the estate's tax obligation.

The IRS stated that a distribution of the stock to decedent's children would not constitute a disposition under Section 6166(g)(1)(A)(i) that would result in an acceleration of the deferred portion of the estate tax by reason of Section 6166(g)(1)(D). The IRS also stated that the two daughters would completely terminate their interests in the corporation under Section 302(b)(3) after the redemption. The IRS further stated that changes in the value of the closely held stock after it has been valued for federal estate tax purposes would not result in prospective or retrospective changes in the percentage decrease in the interest of the closely held business for purposes of determining the dispositions. Finally, it concluded that the redemption of shares held by decedent's spouse and his son would not be treated as distributions as long as the amounts came within amounts provided for in Section 303(a).

[Priv. Ltr. Rul. 8534071.]

**Corporation's obligation to pay decedent's estate may result in termina-
tion of Section 6166 extension.** An individual owned 2,600 shares of the
7,500 outstanding shares of a closely held corporation. The corporation and its
shareholders agreed that the corporation would buy, and the shareholders' estates would sell, the shares held by each estate, so that the purchase would be
treated as a Section 303 redemption. The agreement also gave the corporation
the option, in the event that an estate elected to pay estate tax in installments,
to pay the redemption price for the redeemed stock in installments, with interest, over the same period that the estate tax was paid. When the individual
died, his estate elected to pay estate tax in installments. The estate borrowed
$700x from the corporation to pay the state inheritance tax of $600x. When
the estate filed its federal estate tax return, $100x was paid as the nondeferred
portion of the tax. Later the corporation redeemed 1,856 shares of the estate's
stock for $5,000x, payable over the estate tax deferral period. The estate did
not receive any cash at the time of the redemption, but the previously borrowed $700x was credited against the $5,000x redemption price.

The IRS stated that the corporation's commitment to pay the estate
$5,000x constituted the receipt of money or other property by the estate under
Section 6166. Whether the aggregate value of the $700x and the obligation re-
ceived by the estate at the date of the distribution exceeded the Section 2001
tax that was paid by the estate within one year after the distribution was a factual question, the IRS said. If it did exceed that amount of tax, the IRS concluded, then the extension for payment of tax under Section 6166 would cease
to apply. The IRS said that Sections 6166(g)(1)(B) and 303 do not require a
creditor's obligation to be a "cash equivalent" or "readily tradable" to be considered "property." The value of the obligation at the date of the distribution,
however, is relevant, the IRS said, citing Revenue Ruling 65-289, 1965-2 CB
86.

[Priv. Ltr. Rul. 8506004.]

**Distribution of stock and liquidation of corporation are not dispositions of
closely held business interests.** Decedent's estate included all of the stock of
a corporation that operates a hotel, several office buildings, and a real estate
development business. The corporation had two subsidiaries. A partnership
was to be organized by the estate and the surviving spouse. Interests in real estate and the stock of the corporation were to be transferred to the partnership
by each party in exchange for partnership interests. The corporation and its
subsidiaries planned to liquidate and distribute their assets to the partnership.
After the liquidation, the partnership planned to sell two properties and use the
proceeds to reduce the mortgage on those properties and to reduce other debts
of the partnership. The IRS stated that none of the events outlined above

would be a disposition of an interest in a closely held business under Section 6166(g)(1)(A).

[Priv. Ltr. Rul. 8452043.]

[c] Partnership transactions

Transfer of use of property between partnerships does not constitute disposition by estate of interest in closely held business. The IRS stated that the transfer of property by a partnership to another partnership, with the transferor retaining an interest as a general partner, is not a disposition of an interest in a closely held business under Section 6166(g)(1)(A)(i). The IRS also indicated that sale of other property, with the proceeds used to discharge debts of the partnership, likewise does not constitute a disposition under Section 6166(g)(1)(A)(i). The IRS stated, however, that the withdrawal of funds, within the meaning of Section 6166(g)(1)(A)(ii), occurs to the extent that such proceeds are used to pay the federal estate tax liability (plus the accrued interest) of the estate.

[Priv. Ltr. Rul. 8841006.]

Part sale of business and part transfer to partnership and stock redemptions do not accelerate estate tax. Decedent's estate consists of a sole proprietorship and a 51 percent stock interest in a family corporation. The estate sold a 60 percent interest in the sole proprietorship and was operating the business with the purchasers. The estate proposed to transfer its remaining interest in the business to a limited partnership. The estate planned to have the corporation redeem stock between 1985 and 1993 to pay the federal estate taxes.

The IRS stated that the interests in the proprietorship and the corporation qualified as interests in a closely held business under Section 6166. The IRS also indicated that if the proposed stock redemption qualified under Section 303, the redemption and the sale of the interest in the proprietorship would not accelerate the deferred federal estate taxes as long as there were no other dispositions. In addition, the IRS concluded that the transfer of the remaining interest to the partnership would not accelerate the deferred taxes.

[Priv. Ltr. Rul. 8226156.]

[d] Exchanges

Estate's exchange of undivided interests in woodlands does not accelerate estate tax installment payments. Decedent's estate consisted primarily of undivided interests in woodlands and stock in a company. The estate elected to pay its federal estate tax liability on the installment basis under Section 6166. The estate managed the woodlands and the company, the principal asset of which also was woodlands. The proposed exchange of woodlands potentially would result in the transfer of more than 50 percent of the company. The proposed exchange would also result in the consolidation of land ownership involving the estate and the "family group," which consisted of decedent's relatives. The undivided interests in the land had to be partitioned to effect the proposed exchange.

The IRS indicated that the proposed exchange of undivided interests would not accelerate the estate tax installment payments under Section 6166(g)(1)(A). The IRS explained that the proposed exchange would not materially alter the estate's interest in the timber business and therefore would not constitute a "disposition." The IRS cited Revenue Ruling 66-62, 1966-1 CB 272.

[Priv. Ltr. Rul. 8722075.]

Surviving spouse who runs closely held business is permitted to exchange parcel of land for more suitable property. Decedent left a closely held business to his wife, who operated it as the sole proprietor. Because of the growth of the business, the existing space was no longer sufficient, and decedent's wife wished to exchange one of the parcels of land in the proprietorship for larger property. The transaction would result in an exchange of specific assets held by the proprietorship, not in an exchange of an "interest in" the closely held business.

The IRS took the position that there would be no acceleration of the estate-tax installments under Section 6166(g)(1)(A), and that the exchange would not be considered a disposition of interest or withdrawal of funds from the business.

[Priv. Ltr. Rul. 8512025.]

Beneficiaries' exchange of undivided interests in farms for fee interests does not accelerate estate tax installments due. Two beneficiaries of decedent's estate received an undivided one-half interest in two farms. The estate made an election to pay the estate tax in installments under Section 6166. The beneficiaries proposed to divide the two farms between them, with each receiving a fee simple title to a portion of the farm acreage. No boot or other consideration would be involved in the proposed exchange.

The IRS indicated that as long as the land continued to be used for farming, the proposed exchange would not constitute a "disposition, sale, exchange, or withdrawal" under Section 6166(g)(1)(A), and would not result in an acceleration of the balance of the estate tax payable in installments.

[Priv. Ltr. Rul. 8509025.]

Like-kind exchange is not disposition of closely held business. Two devisees of an estate planned to enter into a like-kind exchange of farm property to provide for the ownership of contiguous parcels by each devisee. Both parcels were of similar fair market value. The IRS stated that the exchange would not be a disposition under Section 6166(g)(1)(A)(i).

[Priv. Ltr. Rul. 8452134.]

¶ 12.05 PAYMENT OF TAX

[1] Flower Bonds

Purchase of flower bonds pursuant to power not voided by decedent's comatose condition. During May 1972, decedent had suffered a mild stroke at age 81 while vacationing in Vermont. His son immediately came to his side, and the question of estate planning was raised and discussed between them. It was decided that the purchase of government flower bonds to be redeemed at par for the payment of estate taxes would be an advantageous investment. Accordingly, decedent executed a power of attorney specifically authorizing his personal lawyer to purchase flower bonds on his behalf. On June 6, 1972, decedent suffered a massive stroke and lay comatose until he died on June 27. In the meantime, his lawyer, acting pursuant to the power of attorney, had completed the purchase of flower bonds in the face amount of $775,000 a week prior to the date of death. The estate subsequently tendered them for redemption at par to be credited towards the estate tax liability. On audit, however, the IRS determined that the flower bonds could not be used at par, because of the decedent's comatose condition at the time of purchase. The IRS argued that under local (New York) law, the incapacity of decedent caused the power to lapse by operation of law, and that therefore the purported purchase on behalf of decedent was a nullity.

Held: For the estate. The court found that under local law, the exercise of a power on behalf of a comatose principal is at most a voidable—but not a void—act. Accordingly, the purchase of flower bonds under decedent's power was legally sufficient to vest title in decedent prior to death. The court ruled that the existence of an inchoate right to disaffirm the purchase was not determinative of whether the bonds were properly included in gross estate.

[Manny, 645 F2d 163, 47 AFTR2d 81-1630, 81-1 USTC ¶ 13,400 (2d Cir. 1981).]

Court of Claims has sole jurisdiction to hear suits to compel redemption of flower bonds. Following decedent's death in 1972, the estate tendered its entire holdings of U.S. flower bonds to the Treasury for redemption. After some delay, the Treasury redeemed half of the $200,000 face amount, but returned a reissued bond for the balance of $100,000 to the estate, claiming that the deceased owned only half of the bonds because the bonds were community property. The estate thereupon filed suit in federal district court to compel redemption. The court decided on the merits that a full redemption was proper and issued a writ of mandamus to enforce judgment. The IRS appealed, arguing that the district court lacked jurisdiction.

Held: Reversed and remanded for the IRS. The district court was without jurisdiction to entertain the estate's suit. By statute, the Court of Claims (as then constituted) has exclusive jurisdiction over contract actions against the United States where the amount in controversy exceeds $10,000. At the same time, federal district courts have original jurisdiction of actions that arise under the laws of the United States. In the case of flower bonds, which are contracts, jurisdiction lies only in the Court of Claims as provided in the Tucker Act.

[Lee v. Blumenthal, 588 F2d 1281, 43 AFTR2d 79-1264, 79-1 USTC ¶ 13,274 (9th Cir. 1979).]

Incompetency does not void purchase of flower bonds. Decedent set up a trust, granting the trustee liberal managerial and investment powers, specifying only that written notice of proposed transactions be given to him. The trustee purchased the flower bonds while decedent was comatose, two days prior to the date of death. No notice of the transaction was given. The IRS argued that the trustee had breached its fiduciary duty by purchasing the bonds without notice and that therefore it had never held indefeasible title to the bonds. The taxpayer-estate argued that absolute ownership is not required. Taxpayer maintained that the only requirements that had to be met were (1) that the bonds be in trust at the time of death and (2) that the trust terminate in favor of the decedent, both of which occurred.

Held: For the estate. The court did not base its decision on whether indefeasible ownership in trust is a requirement under these circumstances. It held rather that under general principles of trust law, the trustee had acted properly and that, consequently, no challenge to the validity of the transaction should be sustained. The court determined that, given the unanticipated circumstances and, particularly, the extremely broad powers that decedent had granted to the trustee, the trustee was properly carrying out the purposes of the trust by purchasing the flower bonds (i.e., minimizing the erosion of the trust corpus through taxation).

[Estate of Glenny, 42 AFTR2d 78-6474, 78-2 USTC ¶ 13,259 (WDNY 1978).]

Claims Court upholds higher interest where flower bond redemption is delayed. The executor of decedent's estate submitted $50,000 par value flower bonds, carrying a 3.5 percent coupon, in partial payment of the estate tax. The Bureau of Public Debt demurred, requesting proof of the decedent's mental capacity at the time the bonds were purchased. This action was taken in accordance with the IRS position that if bonds are bought while the decedent is incapacitated and unaware of the purchase, the bonds are not redeemable at face value. However, the courts have generally rejected this approach if there was a valid power of appointment (which remained valid under local law) outstanding at the time of decedent's incapacitation. The bonds were finally redeemed nearly three years after they were first offered for redemption. The estate contended that damages resulting from the IRS's refusal to redeem the flower bonds should have been assessed from the date on which the bonds were tendered for redemption. The IRS argued that damages should have been assessed from the date on which the IRS made the determination to redeem the bonds.

Held: For the estate. The court held that the failure to redeem when first offered meant that the IRS was in breach of contract. The remedy in such situations is to put the injured party in as good a position as he would have been in had the breach of contract never occurred. Because the estate had to make a cash payment of the tax while waiting for the bond redemption dispute to be resolved, the court held that it could recover the interest it paid. Further, the estate was entitled to the statutory rate paid on refunds retroactively from the point when the cash payment was made until the date on which the IRS issued the estate a refund.

[Cavanagh, 12 Cl. Ct. 715, 60 AFTR2d 87-6113, 87-2 USTC ¶ 13,727 (1987), motion for reconsideration denied, 14 Cl. Ct. 60, 61 AFTR2d 88-1322, 88-1 USTC ¶ 13,745 (1987).]

Damages arising from IRS's refusal to accept flower bonds. The IRS at first accepted the estate's tender of flower bonds as payment for its estate tax liability but then later refused to accept them. It returned them to the estate after having held them for more than a year, and assessed interest penalties for late payment. The estate paid the penalty and transferred the bonds, with an adjusted basis equal to their fair market value (FMV), to the estate's distributees, who eventually sold them and recognized capital gains. The estate and distributees claimed various damages, including attorney fees.

Held: For the estate (in part). The refusal to accept the flower bonds constituted a breach of contract. The estate is entitled to damages equal to the difference between the contract price (the bonds' face value) and the market price (their FMV) at the time of breach, that is, when they were tendered, not when they were returned. The estate is entitled to a refund of the penalty, but the IRS may offset against such refund amounts of coupon interest on the bonds paid to the estate for the period during which the bonds were held by the government. It is also entitled to offset the amount of increase in the estate tax that would have been incurred had the bonds been properly valued at their face value instead of at FMV. The distributees are not entitled to any damages for the capital gains that they recognized, instead of the capital loss they should have recognized, because such damages were not proximately caused by the breach. The estate is not entitled to attorney fees, because the government's conduct was not reprehensible.

[Estate of Berg, 687 F2d 377, 231 Ct. Cl. 466, 50 AFTR2d 82-6193, 82-2 USTC ¶ 13,486 (1982).]

Tax Court decides valuation issue. The IRS, on audit, raised a question about the valuation in decedent's estate of flower bonds used to pay an estate tax deficiency and the interest accrued thereon. The taxpayer granted that the bonds should be included in the estate at face value to the extent that they were used to cover the estate tax deficiency. The taxpayer argued, however, that with respect to the bonds' use to pay the interest, they should be included in the estate only at their FMV. The taxpayer based its claim on the requirement that assets must be valued at the time of death, at which time the interest element had not even existed and could not possibly have been known. Consequently, it argued, the valuation of the bonds in excess of their fair market value would be impermissibly based on events subsequent to death.

Held: For the IRS. The court concluded that the taxpayer's reasoning, if sound, would also apply to the deficiency, with respect to which the valuation of the bonds at face value were not challenged by the taxpayer. The court analogized this situation to estate administration expenses (such as attorney fees arising from the litigation of an estate tax question), which validly reduce a deficiency subsequent to death and correspondingly reduce the use of flower bonds. The court also held that the impossibility of computing accurately the interest figure (because it is dependent upon the date of payment of the deficiency) does not alter the result. Again, the court cited administration expenses and charitable and marital deductions, which often cannot be precisely computed at the date of death, yet are approximated for estate tax purposes. The court simply held fast to the principles of Revenue Ruling 69-489, 1969-2 CB 172, and held that flower bonds that may be used for estate taxes, deficiencies, and interest must be valued in the estate at face value. The court did, of course, allow the estate a deduction for interest paid.

[Buchholtz, 70 TC 814 (1978).]

Flower bonds used to pay deficiency determined by Tax Court are valued at face value. Decedent purchased certain flower bonds prior to his death. At decedent's death, certain of these bonds were used to pay federal estate taxes and were valued at face value for purposes of computing the gross estate. The remaining bonds, which were not so used, were valued at fair market value. The IRS contended that even the bonds not redeemed at face value should be valued at face, because they could be applied in satisfaction of a subsequent estate tax deficiency.

Held: For the estate in part. Additional bonds used to pay a deficiency determined by the Tax Court are to be valued at face value, and any remainder should be valued at fair market value.

[Estate of Hill, 64 TC 867 (1975), aff'd without pub. op., 568 F2d 1365 (5th Cir. 1980).]

IRS may reinstate flower bonds previously redeemed in settlement of overpaid estate taxes. Decedent died on May 15, 1980. On February 15, 1981, the executor of the estate filed a federal estate tax return, reporting $800x in tax. In order to pay the tax, the estate redeemed flower bonds bearing interest at 3.5 percent, due February 15, 1990, with a par (face) value of $800x and a fair market value of $600x. On February 15, 1982, the estate filed a claim for refund for $200x. Advice was requested as to the following issues:

1. Whether in the case of an overpayment of estate tax the government may reinstate flower bonds previously tendered at par in payment of the tax

2. If so, the proper rate and amount of interest due on such overpayment.

The IRS ruled that flower bonds previously redeemed in settlement of an overpayment of federal estate tax may be reinstated under these facts, and that interest will be paid at the applicable rate established under Section 6621 in lieu of the contractual rate. Such interest will be calculated on the fair market value of the bonds at the time they are redeemed, from the date of the overpayment to the date reinstatement is made.

[Rev. Rul. 84-38, 1984-1 CB 250.]

Flower bonds are valued at par, despite tax deferral. In this revenue ruling, the IRS illustrated the problems that can arise for an estate holding flower bonds that elects under Section 6166 to pay a portion of the estate tax in installments. The IRS took the position that the flower bonds that could have been used to pay the deferred portion of the tax (but that were instead sold) had to be included in the gross estate at their par value rather than at the lower market value. The estate elected to pay the portion of the tax attributable to a closely held business in installments beginning five years after the due date of the return. The executor paid the nondeferred portion of the estate tax with flower bonds and sold the rest. Because those bonds could have been used to pay the deferred portion, they had to be valued at par.

The IRS position is consistent with the holding in Estate of Simmie, 69 TC 890 (1978), aff'd, 632 F2d 93 (9th Cir. 1980). There an estate that sold bonds in excess of the amount needed to pay the tax was later forced to include them at par when the IRS determined a deficiency; that the bonds had been sold after the estate tax return was filed was irrelevant to the issue of their value. The planning required is clear: Determine the amount of the estate tax that cannot be deferred, and limit flower bond holdings to that amount (either when purchasing or by disposing of the excess before the decedent's death). Otherwise, the excess bonds will be valued at par and will increase the gross estate. If it is too late to decrease the flower bonds held by the estate, the executor must decide whether to dispose of them in order to obtain a better yield, or to keep them to pay the tax.

[Rev. Rul. 81-228, 1981-2 CB 171.]

[2] Transferee Liability

Transferee's liability for unpaid estate tax was independent obligation arising on due date of estate tax return. Taxpayer was a one-third beneficiary of his father's $150,000 life insurance policy. The IRS and the estate agreed to an approximate $62,000 estate tax deficiency, which the estate failed to pay. The IRS assessed taxpayer, as a transferee of the estate, for the $50,000 insurance proceeds plus interest. The Tax Court agreed with the IRS, finding that taxpayer was personally liable for interest on the underlying $50,000 assessment. Taxpayer argued that his status as a transferee was to be determined under state law. He also sought to have the estate tax redetermined. Finally, he contended that his total liability, including interest, was limited to the $50,000 he received.

Held: Affirmed for the IRS. The Eleventh Circuit quickly disposed of the first two arguments. Section 6324(a)(2) is an independent source of federal liability, so there was no reason to look to state law. Further, under the doctrine of res judicata, taxpayer, who was in privity with the estate, was bound by the earlier Tax Court decision upholding the estate tax deficiency. Finally, the appellate court held that (1) under Section 6601, taxpayer was subject to interest on his liability as transferee and (2) Section 6324(a)(2) limited only the underlying obligation and not the interest thereon. The court noted that under Section 6601(e)(1), any reference in the Code to "tax" also generally refers to "interest imposed by this section on such tax." Thus, the transferee liability for estate tax under Section 6324(a)(2) includes any interest accrued on the underlying tax. In that situation, the limitation applies to the interest as well. Nevertheless, the liability imposed on a transferee under Section 6324(a)(2) is not itself a tax liability, which could be collected—with appropriate interest and penalties—under other Code provisions. Rather, it is an independent liability, the collection of which is provided for under Section 6901(a). That Section states that a transferee's liability for estate taxes (among other items) is "subject to the same provisions and limitations as in the case of the taxes with respect to which the liabilities were incurred." Thus, interest may be imposed on that liability under Section 6601 as if it were a tax liability. Furthermore, the court said, common sense indicates that it is unlikely Congress would alter the traditional rule that one who holds government funds must pay interest for the period the person enjoys the benefits of possession. The court noted that under Section 6601(a), interest is imposed on an unpaid tax liability from "the last date prescribed for payment" of the tax. Since no such date is given for a transferee's liability for unpaid estate tax, under Section 6601(b)(5) the date is deemed to be when the liability arises. That is, interest starts to accrue when the estate fails to pay the tax and the transferee is in possession of the transferred property. In the instant case, taxpayer received the insurance proceeds before the estate return was due. Thus, interest on taxpayer's independent liability as transferee ran from the due date of the estate return.

[Baptiste, 29 F3d 1533, 74 AFTR2d 94-7477, 94-2 USTC ¶ 60,178 (11th Cir. 1994).]

IRS is upheld on imposition of transferee liability and inclusion of joint interests in gross estate. Decedent died on November 4, 1964. The estate failed to prepare its final estate tax return within the time allowed by statute, and, upon receiving the late return, the IRS imposed a late filing penalty in addition to other assessments for wrongful exclusion of certain assets from the gross estate. In the meantime, decedent's two daughters and daughter-in-law had received distributions of estate property; therefore, the IRS sought to collect the deficiencies from them as transferees pursuant to Section 6901(a). The heirs challenged the IRS's assessments on the following grounds:

1. There was reasonable cause for the late filing.
2. The additions to gross estate concerned a joint bank account and other property that were not includable in gross estate.
3. Transferee liability was not proper as applied to them.

Held: Affirmed for the IRS. The court found as a preliminary matter that transferee liability under Section 6901(a) requires a showing of a sufficient legal or equitable basis under state law that justifies such derivative liability. The court found ample support under Illinois law for the recovery of taxes against transferees, which recovery was limited only to the date-of-death value of the property actually received by the individual transferee. Accordingly, Section 6901(a) was properly applied to the heirs. The court also upheld the Tax Court's findings relative to the includability of the disputed property in gross estate and rejected the heirs' argument that the IRS had failed in its "proof" by not showing signature cards in respect of each separate account. The stipulations of counsel prior to trial established a sufficient ground upon which the Tax Court could reasonably have concluded that the joint interests wee includable. In addition, the court summarily rejected the claim that reasonable cause justified the late filing, because the record contained no credible evidence in support thereof.

[Berliant, 729 F2d 496, AFTR2d 84-1619, 84-1 USTC ¶ 13,563 (7th Cir. 1984), cert. denied, 469 US 852 (1984).]

Insolvency of estate limits personal liability of executors for unpaid estate tax. Decedent died, leaving a solvent estate, which was composed primarily of stock in two closely held corporations. The executor commenced distributions to decedent's wife. Meanwhile, the value of the stock declined, throwing the estate into insolvency. The IRS proceeded under 31 USC § 192 and sought to collect the entire unpaid estate tax from the executor in his personal capacity.

Held: Reversed and remanded for the executor. An executor is not personally liable where bequests have been distributed from a solvent estate that later becomes insolvent. The court found that the executor's liability extended only to distributions made after the estate was insolvent. Thus, the insolvency of an estate will not be applied retroactively to taint prior distributions. The court cited Lutz, 295 F2d 736 (5th Cir. 1961), where a corporation's president was held not liable for making distributions to creditors instead of to the government prior to the corporation becoming insolvent. In *Lutz*, the court said that to allow retroactive liability would go beyond the intent of Congress and "would subject corporate officers to the harsh rule that whenever they paid any debt at a time when the corporation owed money to the government, no matter how solvent the corporation, they would be personally liable should the corporation eventually be unable to repay the government debt." This same logic applied equally to the estate in the present case, concluded the court. In addition, the court reviewed the Tax Court's factual determination of insolvency and held that it was not supported by the evidence. The court also increased the valuation of certain assets and reduced the amounts of certain liabilities, thereby determining that insolvency occurred as of a later date than had been determined by the Tax Court.

[Schwartz, 560 F2d 311, 40 AFTR2d 77-6225, 77-2 USTC ¶ 13,201 (8th Cir. 1977).]

Failure to assess transferee bars estate tax liability. Taxpayer was decedent's surviving spouse and although she was originally appointed personal representative, she was removed and replaced by two of decedent's sons from a previous marriage. The estate filed its return and the IRS assessed additional taxes. Subsequently, the IRS and the estate reached a settlement regarding the taxes due, but the estate failed to pay what it owed, despite apparently having the funds to do so. Taxpayer had received more than $400,000 from the estate, which demanded that she pay a pro rata share of the assessed taxes, interest, and penalties. The probate court found that the penalties and interest were due to the negligence of the personal representatives and ordered her to pay only the portion of the *tax* attributable to the assets she had received. The IRS collected part of the balance from the estate, but the remainder was unpaid. The IRS then informed taxpayer that she owed taxes on her late husband's estate but would not tell her how much because she was not a personal representative. The IRS had never assessed the surviving spouse for the taxes and the time for doing so had now passed. Thus, she contended that she could not be held liable as a transferee. Under Section 6324(a)(2), transferees of estate property generally may be held personally liable for any unpaid estate taxes to the extent of the date-of-death value of the property. The court noted that under Section 6901, the liabilities of transferees must be assessed. Section 6901(h) includes as a transferee any person liable under Section 6324(a)(2).

The IRS argued that an assessment was not necessary under Section 6324(a)(2), relying on Russell, 461 F2d 605 (10th Cir. 1972) (Russell II), rev'g and remanding 327 F. Supp. 632 (D. Kan. 1971) (Russell I).

Held: For taxpayer. The court rejected this argument, however, and adopted the reasoning and analysis of *Russell I*, which held that the IRS could not ignore the procedural requirements of Section 6901 before proceeding under Section 6324(a)(2). The court doubted the precedential value of *Russell II*, even in the Tenth Circuit. There, after the district court found for the IRS on remand, the Tenth Circuit affirmed but limited its holding to the specific facts of the case (532 F2d 175 (10th Cir. 1976) (Russell III)). In the *Russell* cases, the transferee was the surviving spouse and the executrix of the estate. She was aware of the jointly held property in the estate and also knew it was the only asset available to pay the tax following the estate's insolvency. Here, taxpayer was not the personal representative of the estate, and she was prevented from learning of the estate's financial condition and its tax liability. Moreover, the estate had sufficient funds to pay the tax, interest, and penalties owed, and the failure to pay was directly attributable to the personal representative's negligence, which was beyond taxpayer's control.

The court noted that this case makes clear why an assessment should be required before transferee liability will be enforced. The IRS, in effect, maintained that an assessment against the estate is sufficient notice to any transferees of taxes due. Here, this obviously was not true. Finally, if the IRS were not required to first make an assessment under Section 6901 before pursuing transferee liability under Section 6324(a)(2), it could wait as long as thirteen years following the filing of the estate tax return before notifying a transferee of any possible estate tax liability. This would deny taxpayer the fundamental due process afforded by the assessment provisions.

[Schneider, 71A AFTR2d 93-4973, 92-2 USTC ¶ 60,119 (DND 1992).]

Transferee liability is imposed on beneficiaries. Decedent's executor paid the applicable state inheritance tax and claimed a deduction on the federal estate tax return. However, the check used to pay the state tax was dishonored. The IRS requested proof that the tax had been paid, but the executor never responded. The estate's assets were transferred to the beneficiaries. After assessing a deficiency and unsuccessfully attempting to collect the estate tax, the IRS issued a notice of transferee liability to the beneficiaries. The taxpayers argued that the procedural requirements for transferee liability had not been followed.

   Held: For the IRS. The transferees' argument that the estate was not insolvent before, the transfer was rejected or as a result of the transfer being rejected. In addition, the IRS was not required to seek payment from the estate before proceeding against the transferees, because such effort would have been futile. Finally, under Illinois state law, the transferees had substantive liability.

[Gumm, 93 TC 475 (1989), aff'd without published op., 933 F2d 1014 (9th Cir. 1991).]

Transferee cannot be held liable for transferor's estate tax if assessment expires and extinguishes transferor's liability before assets are transferred. The period of limitations on assessment of an additional estate tax against an estate expired. At that time, there was neither an outstanding consent to extend the period nor an IRS notification of any proposed additional liability for estate tax. Four months later the estate distributed assets to taxpayer. Within one year from the expiration of the limitations period, the IRS executed a Reopening Memorandum and issued a notice of liability to the transferee-taxpayer.

   Held: For taxpayer. The Tax Court held that Section 6901 does not create a separate liability for the transferee. Instead, it merely provides for a secondary method of enforcing the liability of the transferor. Thus, as long as the transferor's liability is extinguished before the assets are transferred under the will, the transferee cannot be liable for any additional tax. The court emphasized that this rationale does not apply where the assets are transferred before the period of limitations against the transferee expires. Thus, in such a case, under Section 6901(c), the IRS would have an additional year after the original limitations period expired to assess the taxes.

[Illinois Masonic Home, 93 TC 145 (1989).]

Tax Court holds transferee liable for decedent's estate tax deficiency. Taxpayer was the executrix of decedent's estate, from which she also received certain property. After taxpayer filed an estate tax return for decedent's estate, the IRS assessed a deficiency, an addition to tax, and interest against taxpayer. A notice of transferee liability against taxpayer was subsequently issued by the IRS. Taxpayer argued against the determination of transferee liability, but he made no argument against the deficiency and addition to tax determination. Taxpayer contended that the IRS's notice of transferee liability was not timely.

Held: For the IRS. The court ruled that there was no merit in taxpayer's argument that, since she had made a request for prompt assessment of tax under Section 6501(d), a notice of transferee liability would be timely only if issued within thirty months. The notice had, in fact, been issued two days short of four years later. The court found that Section 6501(d) was not applicable to estate tax returns and that there was no evidence that taxpayer had filed a request for prompt assessment of tax. The proper period of limitations is the three years provided under Section 6501(a), plus an additional year with respect to transferors as provided by Section 6901(a). The notice was therefore timely. The court also rejected taxpayer's argument that liability extends to a transferee only if all remedies against the estate have been exhausted. Section 6324 provides that for estate tax purposes, a transferee's liability for estate tax is a primary obligation resting directly on the transferee. Thus, taxpayer was liable for decedent's estate tax to the extent that the property received by her was includable in decedent's taxable estate.

[Eggleston, TC Memo. (P-H) ¶ 85,327, 50 TCM (CCH) 333 (1985).]

Executor is liable for payment of taxes. Decedent had not paid income taxes for several years prior to death. The amount of taxes, interest, and penalties exceeded the value of the assets of the estate. The executor paid the mortgage, state income taxes, and debts to general creditors. The executor was deemed chargeable with knowledge of the taxes due, and he was personally liable for them.

[Rev. Rul. 79-310, 1979-2 CB 404.]

[3] Stock Redemptions

IRS rules on effect of Section 6166 in stock redemption cases. The IRS ruled that the exclusion in Section 6166(g)(1)(B) applies to a Section 303 redemption if (1) the cumulative amount of Section 303 redemptions as of the date of the redemption is less than or equal to the total amount of estate tax payments as of the due date of the following estate tax payment (or, if earlier, the date that is one year after the distribution pursuant to the redemption), or (2) the amount of the redemption is less than or equal to the amount of the estate tax payments made within the permitted period.

[Rev. Rul. 86-54, 1986-1 CB 356.]

Redemption of stock held in closely held corporation does not result in acceleration of federal estate tax installments. When decedent died in 1983, decedent owned stock in a closely held corporation. Decedent's estate elected to defer payment of the federal estate tax attributable to decedent's interest in the corporation. The estate also elected to defer the payment of its state inheritance and estate tax. The estate proposed to enter into a series of independent redemptions on or within one year prior to the date when each installment of deferred federal estate tax and interest came due and each installment of deferred state inheritance and estate tax and interest came due.

The IRS took the position that the Section 303 stock redemptions with respect to the installments of deferred federal estate tax and interest would qualify as redemptions under Section 6166(g)(1)(B) and thus would not be withdrawals or distributions under Section 6166(g)(1)(A). Based on Revenue Ruling 86-54, 86-1 CB 7, the IRS stated that Section 6166(g)(1)(B) may be applied, based interchangeably on the cumulative method and the redemption-by-redemption method. The cumulative method requires that the total cumulative amount of the current redemption and all prior redemptions not exceed the total cumulative amount of all federal estate taxes paid on or before the close of the permitted period. The redemption-by-redemption approach provides that the amount of each Section 303 redemption must not exceed the amount of federal estate taxes paid during the permitted period. The IRS also stated that based on Revenue Ruling 85-43, 1985-1 CB 356, the stock redemptions with respect to the deferred state inheritance and estate tax did not qualify under Section 6166(g)(1)(B). Thus, the IRS concluded that such redemptions would be treated as withdrawals or distributions under Section 6166(g)(1)(A).

[Priv. Ltr. Rul. 8701023.]

Corporation redeems stock to enable estate to pay death taxes and related expenses. A corporation's majority shareholder died in 1983. The shareholder owned 5,750 shares of the firm's stock when the shareholder died. The shareholder's three daughters each owned 750 shares. All of the shares held by the estate of the shareholder were to be distributed to a testamentary trust. The shares placed in the trust were to be divided into an "electing for marital deduction portion" and a "nonelecting for marital deduction portion." The corporation was then to redeem 2,615 shares of stock from the first portion and 142 shares from the second portion. Consideration for the redemption was to consist of cash and property. The IRS took the position that the redemption would qualify under Section 303(a), provided that the requirements of Section 303(b) were satisfied.

[Priv. Ltr. Rul. 8546057.]

Stock redemptions by parent company and its subsidiaries qualify as redemptions to pay death taxes. All of a company's common stock represented more than half the value of decedent's estate after allowable deductions. This stock was to pass to decedent's beneficiaries, subject to the pro rata payment of federal estate tax. Decedent's widow elected a one-third interest in all of the estate's assets under state law. Her elective share would not be reduced by federal state taxes. To enable the estate and the beneficiaries to pay death taxes, and to preserve the relative voting power of each beneficiary, the company issued a new class of nonvoting common stock to the estate. The estate then sold small amounts of the nonvoting stock to the company's subsidiaries. The company redeemed almost one third of the stock issued to the estate, and the estate distributed all of the remaining common and nonvoting common to decedent's widow and beneficiaries.

The IRS stated that the company's distribution of nonvoting common stock should not result in taxable income to the estate under Section 305(a). The nonvoting common stock is not Section 306 stock. The proposed redemption of the nonvoting common stock from the estate and the sales to the company's subsidiaries qualified for sale or exchange treatment under Sections 303(a), 303(c), and 304(a)(2).

[Priv. Ltr. Rul. 8336044.]

Redemption to pay death taxes qualifies; estate tax is not accelerated by redemptions to pay estate tax installments. A deceased shareholder's estate held stock of two closely held companies that constituted more than half of the estate's assets after allowable deductions. To enable the estate to pay death taxes and administrative expenses, one of the companies redeemed one third of each of its two classes of common stock, which the estate distributed to the deceased shareholder's daughter. There were to be subsequent redemptions between 1984 and 1993 to pay estate taxes, which the estate elected to pay in installments.

The IRS took the position that the redemption of stock from the daughter would qualify under Section 303(a), as would the subsequent redemptions. The corporation's redemption of the daughter's stock did not result in a dividend distribution to the estate under Section 301, by application of Sections 305(b) and 305(c). The subsequent redemptions to pay estate tax installments would qualify under Section 6166(g)(1)(B). None of the distributions in redemption of stock accelerated the time to pay the estate tax installments under Section 6166(g)(1)(A).

[Priv. Ltr. Rul. 8318036, modified in Priv. Ltr. Rul. 8329035.]

[4] Apportionment of Estate Tax

Apportionment of estate taxes reduces marital and charitable deductions.
The tax clause in decedent's will did not refer to the residuary estate. The IRS
contended that the will required the subtraction of all death taxes before formulating the residue. Taypayer argued that the state apportionment statute applied, which exempted property qualifying for a charitable or marital deduction
unless decedent directed otherwise.

   Held: For the IRS. The testator intended that the taxes be paid "off the
top" of the residuary. The state apportionment statute was inapplicable.

[Estate of Ransburg, 765 F. Supp. 1388, 68 AFTR2d 91-6026, 91-1 USTC ¶
60,052 (SD Ind. 1990).]

Tax Court rules on apportionment of taxes and expenses under state law.
Decedent's will directed the payment of all debts, expenses, and taxes as soon
after his death as was convenient. Decedent bequeathed a life estate to his
spouse, with a remainder going to his children, a sum of money going to a religious organization, and the residue going to his spouse. The IRS argued that
the will directed the apportionment of estate taxes out of the residue, thus reducing the marital deduction.

   Held: For the estate. The will did not expressly direct the apportionment
of estate taxes. State law applied to apportion the taxes against the life estate.

[Estate of Shannon, TC Memo. (P-H) ¶ 90,614, 60 TCM (CCH) 1361 (1990).]

**Ambiguous language in will triggers California apportionment statute;
charitable deduction thus is not reduced by share of estate tax.** Decedent's
will, as originally written, made several specific bequests and left the residue
to a family trust. The will provided that all estate and inheritance taxes were to
be paid out of the residue of the estate, without apportionment. During the
eleven years between the will's execution and decedent's death, seven codicils
were executed, substantially altering decedent's estate plan. At death, the bulk
of decedent's estate was disposed of through two testamentary trusts. Two
thirds of the estate went to a family trust, and one third went to a charitable
trust. On decedent's estate tax return, a charitable deduction was claimed for
one third of the gross residual estate. The IRS reduced this deduction by a
share of the estate tax, on the ground that the entire residual estate bore the
burden of such tax.

   Held: For the estate. Under Section 2055(c), if estate tax is chargeable to
or payable out of a charitable bequest, the amount deductible is reduced by the
amount of taxes so chargeable. Thus, the court looked to the applicable state
(California) apportionment statute and held that the charitable deduction was
not to be reduced to reflect a share of the estate tax liability. Under the appor-

tionment statute, which is typical of most state apportionment statutes, property that is excluded or deductible from the gross estate in computing the taxable estate is generally not charged with any portion of the federal estate tax liability. California courts have consistently interpreted this statute as requiring apportionment only to property that creates the tax. Exceptions to the rule are allowed only where the testator's intent to the contrary is clear and unambiguous. The court held that though decedent's original intent, that is, to charge the estate tax to the residue, was clear, the codicils made it unclear whether his intent withstood the changes in his estate plan. The court noted that in the sixth codicil, the phrase "notwithstanding anything contained herein to the contrary" established that the codicil's language is to control any inconsistent language in the original will. This codicil provides that if one third of decedent's estate does not qualify for the charitable deduction, then the entire charitable bequest is revoked. In referring to "estate," it is not clear whether decedent meant his gross residuary estate or his net residuary estate. The court held that resolution of the ambiguity was not crucial to the case. Rather, the mere presence of such ambiguity as to the apportionment of estate taxes makes the general apportionment rules of the state applicable.

[Estate of Brunetti, TC Memo. (P-H) ¶ 88,517, 56 TCM (CCH) 580 (1988).]

IRS determines who pays estate taxes when will does not. Decedent's probate estate was valued at over $1 million, but his nonprobate estate was valued at over $4 million. The will directed that once debts other than taxes were paid, the probate property was to be put into a revocable trust. This trust provided for half of the trust assets to pass to the surviving spouse, and the other half to pass to the decedent's child and grandchildren. The will also provided that the estate was liable for any estate taxes without charging them against the interest of any beneficiary (including the trust). The trust provided that the trustee had the authority to pay any estate taxes. State law as to the distribution of property at death governs the impact of the federal taxes on the beneficiaries, unless the governing instrument provides for the burden of tax to be apportioned otherwise. Under state case law, if taxes attributable to nonprobate property are to be paid from the probate estate, the executor has no right of contribution against the nonprobate beneficiaries. State courts had also held that when the will indicates that taxes were to be paid by the beneficiaries in their proportionate shares, no tax was to be paid by the spouse's share, because that share had no portion of the taxable assets of the estate. The will provided only for the estate tax to be paid from the (probate) estate, and also that the tax should not be charged against any of the beneficiaries.

Thus, balancing the requirements of state law, the IRS indicated that the estate tax should be paid first out of the probate funds. Because these funds were insufficient to pay the estate tax, however, no funds would pass by will to the revocable trust for either the spousal or nonspousal shares. The trust was therefore responsible for payment of part of the federal estate taxes, but the IRS concluded that this contribution would come only from the nonspousal share.

[Tech. Adv. Mem. 9010005.]

[5] Fiduciary Liability

Executor who failed to timely file return and paid only portion of estate tax shown to be due was liable as fiduciary for unpaid estate tax, interest, and penalties. The executor of decedent's estate, after obtaining two extensions, filed the estate tax return late. Additionally, only 10 percent of the estate tax liability shown to be due on the return was paid at that time. Along with the return, the executor submitted a letter stating that there were insufficient funds to pay the entire estate tax liability, because the estate consisted mostly of unimproved real property. The letter also requested approval to pay the remaining estate tax in installments. Six months after filing the estate tax return the executor filed an amended return, based on lower values for the estate's property, and claimed a refund of estate tax already paid. Subsequently, the executor filed, and was granted, a final accounting that reserved only $15,000 for payment of taxes. At this time, the outstanding balance of estate tax due as shown on the original estate tax return was far in excess of $15,000. The IRS assessed the executor for the unpaid estate tax, penalties, and interest.

Held: For the IRS. Under the facts, the executor is liable for the taxes, penalties, and interest as a fiduciary.

[Bank of the W., 93 TC 462 (1989).]

¶ 12.06 COMPLIANCE AND PROCEDURE

[1] Penalties and Interest

U.S. Supreme Court holds circuit court has no jurisdiction to forgive interest and statutory late payment penalties in reviewing Tax Court case. Decedent's estate made a late election for special-use valuation of decedent's undivided interest in a farm. The IRS disallowed the election as being untimely under Section 2032A and assessed deficiency and late payment penalties. The estate argued that the time for making the election under Section 2032A had been extended retroactively by the Economic Recovery Tax Act of

1981 (ERTA). The Tax Court, however, rejected the estate's contentions and sustained the deficiency. The IRS assessed interest and penalties. The Sixth Circuit affirmed the Tax Court, but forgave the estate the interest and penalties. It noted that the interest and penalties exceeded the assessed tax and concluded that the interest and penalties should be forgiven "in order to achieve a fair and just result."

Held: Reversed for the IRS. The Supreme Court stated that the Sixth Circuit had clearly exceeded its jurisdictional bounds; its only jurisdiction was to review the decision of the Tax Court, and its duty was to affirm or reverse the decision. It was not empowered to proceed further to decide other questions relating to interest and penalties—questions that were not presented, and could not possibly have been presented, to the Tax Court—or to grant relief that the Tax Court itself had no jurisdiction to provide. The Supreme Court noted that the estate was not without an opportunity to litigate the validity of the interest and the late-payment penalty. The proper procedure was for it to pay the interest and penalty and then to sue for a refund in an appropriate federal district court or in the Claims Court.

[McCoy, 484 US 3, 108 S. Ct. 217, 60 AFTR2d 87-6150, 87-2 USTC ¶ 13,736 (1987).]

Supreme Court holds that late filing penalty cannot be excused for good-faith reliance on estate attorney. Following his mother's death in September 1978, the respondent was named executor and retained a lawyer to serve as attorney for the estate. The lawyer informed the executor that the estate was required to file a federal estate tax return, but he did not mention the deadline for filing, which was June 14, 1979. Although the executor was a businessman, he had no experience in the field of federal taxation, other than having been executor of his father's estate twenty years before. The record showed that the executor relied on the attorney for instruction and guidance and that he fully cooperated in providing all relevant information concerning the estate. On several occasions during the spring and summer of 1979, the executor inquired about the progress of the probate proceedings and the preparation of the estate tax return, only to be assured each time that he would be notified when the return was due and that it would be filed "in plenty of time."

When the executor called the lawyer on September 6, 1979, he learned for the first time that the return was by then overdue. Apparently, the lawyer had overlooked the matter because of a clerical oversight in omitting the filing date from the lawyer's "master calendar." Eventually, the return was filed on September 13, 1979, three months late. Acting pursuant to Section 6651(a)(1), the IRS assessed a failure-to-file penalty of $17,124, together with interest of $1,326. The estate resisted the penalty assessment, arguing that the circumstances fell within the exception of Section 6651(a)(1), which states that no penalty shall be assessed if it is shown that the failure to file was "due to reasonable cause and not due to willful neglect." To this, the IRS has added, in Regulations § 301.6651-1(c)(1), an additional requirement that the taxpayer must show that he "exercised ordinary business care and prudence and was nevertheless unable to file the return within the prescribed time." The district court and the Seventh Circuit held for the estate, finding that the executor's reliance on counsel was reasonable cause for purposes of Section 6651(a)(1).

Held: Reversed for the IRS. The Supreme Court noted that Congress established two standards for proving the exception: that the failure did not result from willful neglect and that the failure was due to reasonable cause. The term "willful neglect," according to the Court, means a conscious, intentional failure or reckless indifference, whereas reasonable cause requires the taxpayer to demonstrate that he exercised ordinary business care and prudence, but nevertheless was unable to file the return within the prescribed time. In addition, the Court noted that Congress placed the duty to file squarely on the executor, not on some agent or employee of the executor. Although engaging an attorney to assist in probate proceedings is plainly an exercise of ordinary care and prudence, it is not reasonable for him to assume that the attorney will discharge the executor's plain statutory duty.

The Court drew a distinction between delinquent filings and reliance on advice of counsel, holding that reliance on professional advice could constitute reasonable grounds, because taxpayers customarily rely on an accountant or an attorney in tax matters that are beyond the ken of an ordinary "layperson." By contrast, the Court found that a simple failure to comply with a filing deadline was an entirely different matter in that no special training or effort is required to ascertain the scope of an executor's duties. Accordingly, the Court reversed the Seventh Circuit and permitted the IRS to reimpose the penalty, stating that the failure to make timely filing by reason of reliance on an agent does not constitute reasonable cause under Section 6651(a)(1).

[Boyle, 469 US 241, 105 S. Ct. 687, 55 AFTR2d 85-1535, 85-1 USTC ¶ 13,602 (1985).]

Unpaid estate tax is held not subject to interest charges, despite subsequent reformation. Decedent died in 1977, leaving a will that passed the residue of his estate to a testamentary trust. Under the terms of the trust, two named individuals were to share all trust income for life, with the remainder going to two charities. The estate filed an estate tax return in which it claimed the Section 2055(a)(2) charitable deduction for the value of the interest passing to the two charities. At the same time, the executor requested technical advice from the IRS on the question whether a planned reformation of the trust under state law would qualify the estate for the charitable deduction. The IRS stated that the proposed reformation would qualify for the deduction. Upon audit, the IRS made no assessment of estate tax liability based on the technical advice memorandum. The IRS eventually assessed interest, however, on the grounds that estate taxes were due at the time of filing the estate tax return and that no deduction was allowable at that time, because the reformation had not yet been effected. The trustees paid the interest and sought a refund in federal district court. The lower court granted summary judgment for the IRS, holding that interest on unpaid taxes is based on the amount of tax due on the date on which the estate tax return is required to be filed. The court found that because estate tax liability arises on the date of a decedent's death, a subsequent reformation has no effect on the existence of the initial obligation. The court noted a clear indication in Section 2055 that an executor is required to file a return on or before the due date in all cases, including those situations where the reformation has not yet been accomplished.

Held: Reversed for the trustees. The Fourth Circuit rejected the district court's reasoning and held that the amendment converting bequests of charitable remainders into gifts related back to the date of decedent's death. The court concluded that no interest was owed to the IRS, primarily because the reformation was expressly made retroactive.

[Oxford Orphanage, Inc., 775 F2d 570, 56 AFTR2d 85-6588, 85-2 USTC ¶ 13,643 (4th Cir. 1985).]

Reliance on mistaken advice of counsel does not constitute reasonable cause for failing to file timely estate tax return. Decedent died in 1977, and the executrix retained the services of an attorney to handle the affairs of the estate. Although the attorney correctly advised the executrix that it would be necessary to file an estate tax return, he erroneously believed that the return was due one year after decedent's death. The return was in fact due on July 10, 1978, nine months after decedent's death. On the advice of the attorney, the executrix hired an accountant to prepare the estate tax return, and over the next few months, she made inquiries of the accountant concerning his progress in preparing the return. The executrix discharged the accountant for neglecting the return, and on June 15, 1978, she employed another accountant. As a result of his erroneous belief concerning the filing deadline, counsel for the estate did not provide the second accountant with any information about the estate, including the date of decedent's death, until August 2, 1978. Upon being informed of the date of death, the second accountant immediately realized that the return was past due. He therefore sought an extension of time for filing the return and submitted a check signed by the executrix as payment of estimated taxes owed by the estate. The accountant eventually filed the estate tax return on October 10, 1978, whereupon the IRS assessed a penalty under Section 6651(a)(1) for failure to file a timely return, and an additional penalty under Section 6651(a)(2) for late payment. The executrix brought an action in federal district court seeking recovery of these amounts plus administrative expenses incurred in connection with her refund claim. The executrix argued that she had exercised ordinary business care and prudence in relying on the advice of the attorney for the estate and the second accountant regarding due dates and penalties. The district court granted summary judgment in favor of the IRS.

Held: Affirmed for the IRS. Under Sections 6651(a)(1) and 6651(a)(2), a taxpayer is liable for delinquency penalties unless the failure to file a timely estate tax return and pay the amount owed was due to reasonable cause. The executor or executrix has a personal and nondelegable duty to file a timely return, and reliance on the mistaken advice of counsel is not sufficient to constitute reasonable cause for failing to fulfill that duty.

[Estate of Kerber, 717 F2d 454, 52 AFTR2d 83-6446, 83-2 USTC ¶ 13,541 (8th Cir. 1983), cert. denied, 469 US 1188 (1985).]

Seventh Circuit rules on value claim at date of decedent's death. Five years after the date of death, decedent's estate received $1 million from its claim against certain life insurance companies. Decedent had taken out over $1.4 million of life insurance and shortly thereafter was killed when the car he was driving was struck by a train. Eyewitness accounts and decedent's previous behavior raised a suspicion of suicide. The insurance companies refused to pay the claims on the ground of suicide exclusions, material misrepresentations made by the insured, and technical insufficiencies. The estate tax return was filed a year and a half late and listed the value of the insurance claims as zero. The executor sued the insurers, and two years later the estate was awarded $1 million. The IRS assessed estate taxes and the 25 percent late filing penalty of Section 6651(a) on the full $1 million. The executor sued for a refund, arguing that the amount subject to the penalty should be the value of the claims as of decedent's date of death, not the actual amount recovered. The IRS based its argument on Regulation § 20.2042-1(a)(3), which states that the amount of life insurance to be included in an estate is "the full amount receivable under the policy." The IRS claimed that this regulation distinguishes life insurance from other assets that are valued at their date-of-death FMVs under Section 2031.

Held: For the estate. The 25 percent penalty for filing the estate return late should be assessed only upon the value of the claim as of the date of death, not upon the actual amount recovered or the face value of the policies. The Seventh Circuit stated that under the IRS's strict interpretation of Section 2042, the entire $1.4 million face value of the policies would have to be included, a result that it termed "harsh and seemingly irrational." Even assuming that the estate could later claim a refund on the amount not recovered from the insurance companies, it would still have to advance the inflated estate tax with funds it might not have. The court cited the legislative history of Section 2042 and reasoned that the section's purpose was to determine the includability, but not the valuation, of life insurance policies.

[American Nat'l Bank & Trust Co., 594 F2d 141, 43 AFTR2d 79-1297, 79-1 USTC 13,284 (7th Cir. 1979).]

Penalty for late filing of estate tax return is upheld on ground that failure to file lacked reasonable cause. Decedent died on June 13, 1983, leaving a will that named her son as executor of the estate. The executor was informed by his attorney that a federal estate tax return would be required if the value of the estate exceeded $275,000, and that such return was due March 13, 1984. The bulk of the estate consisted of three parcels of land. To determine the value of the estate, the executor consulted with his brother, a developer, and examined the County Tax Assessors 1980 tax statements for the estate properties. He did not, however, obtain professional appraisals or investigate comparable sales in the area. The executor valued the property at $145,000, which brought the total value of the estate to $270,878. The probate referee appraised the total assets of the estate at $395,483, with a value of $288,333 assigned to the real property. The executor then filed a federal estate tax return on May 16, 1984, with payment of the tax due. The IRS assessed a late filing penalty in the amount of $6,807. The executor appealed the imposition of this penalty.

Held: For the IRS. The court stated that the late filing penalty can be avoided only upon the showing that the failure to timely file the return was due to reasonable cause and not due to willful neglect. After reviewing the facts, the court concluded that though there was no evidence of willful neglect on the executor's part, he failed to provide evidence that he exercised ordinary business care and prudence. The court based this conclusion on several factors, including that the executor's estimate of the real property's value was made on incomplete and outdated information and that he had neglected to obtain a professional appraisal. This conduct constituted a failure to exercise ordinary business care and prudence. Furthermore, the executor was aware of the filing requirements, but chose to rely on real property valuations that had little current reality. Thus, the penalty for late filing of the return was properly assessed.

[Charman, 88-2 USTC ¶ 13,780, 62 AFTR2d 88-6019 (SD Cal. 1988).]

Under Supreme Court's "bright line" holding in *Boyle*, executor may not avoid late filing penalty by showing reliance on accountant who prepared return. Decedent died on March 9, 1978, and a professional executor employed by a bank was appointed by the state court. An initial six-month extension for filing the federal estate tax return was approved. A second request, dated June 8, 1979, however, asking for an extension from June 6, 1979, to October 9, 1979, was rejected. The estate filed the return on November 20, 1979. The IRS assessed a delinquency penalty. The taxpayer paid the assessed penalty and sought a refund of the penalty amount, on the ground that he had "reasonable cause" for late filing. The bases of his claim were that he relied on assurances made by the accountant who prepared the estate's return that the extension to October 9, 1979, had been obtained, and also that he believed there was no tax due, because of the charitable remainder.

Held: For the IRS. Under the Supreme Court's decision in Boyle, 469 US 241 (1985), an executor cannot delegate the responsibility of filing a timely federal estate tax return. Accordingly, the executor's reliance in this case cannot be reasonable cause. Second, the erroneous belief that no tax is due does not relieve an executor from the responsibility of filing a return. Thus, it does not constitute reasonable cause.

[Estate of Cox, 637 F. Supp. 1112, 86-2 USTC ¶ 13,681, 58 AFTR2d 86-6354 (SD Fla. 1986).]

Advanced years and poor health of administrator and attorney combine to establish reasonable cause for late filing. After decedent died on August 6, 1981, her brother, age 78, was appointed to serve as administrator of the estate. Prior to the date of death, the brother, who was in chronic poor health, had served as decedent's conservator. As such, he retained an attorney to handle legal matters concerning the conservatorship. The same lawyer was thereafter retained as the estate attorney, largely because of his familiarity with decedent's personal and business affairs. The attorney, who had practiced for fifty-five years, understood that he would be responsible for the preparation and filing of all tax returns for the estate. He was aware that the federal estate tax return was due on May 6, 1982, nine months after decedent's death, pursuant to Section 6075. He did not, however, inform the brother of the due date for filing the return. During the early part of 1982, the attorney began experiencing severe chest pains. Around April 24, 1982, he was hospitalized for tests because of his chest pains. On April 26, 1982, shortly after being discharged, he suffered urinary problems and was again hospitalized. During this stay in the hospital, he underwent prostate surgery and was treated for his heart condition. He was released from the hospital on May 3, 1982, three days before the federal estate tax return was due. After his release, the attorney eventually returned to his office and resumed work on a limited basis, gradually increasing his workload over a period of several weeks. The attorney filed the federal estate tax return on August 5, 1982. Pursuant to Sections 6651(a)(1) and 6651(a)(2), the IRS subsequently assessed penalties against the estate for late filing of the estate tax return and for late payment of estate tax due. The estate paid $8,430.40 in satisfaction of the penalty and associated interest, and brought an action in federal district court for a refund, arguing that there was reasonable cause to excuse the late filing.

Held: For the estate. In the view of the district court, the executor's age, poor health, and lack of experience in estate administration excused him from taking steps to determine his responsibilities in face of the emergency situation created by the attorney's hospitalization. Because the executor was unable to exercise ordinary care, he was relieved of duties normally expected of estate administrators.

[Brown, 630 F. Supp. 57, 57 AFTR2d 86-148, 86-1 USTC ¶ 13,656 (MD Tenn. 1985).]

Underreporting a decedent's bank account can be a valuation understatement. After decedent's death, a number of recently written, but undelivered, checks were found in his car. Three $10,000 checks, drawn on one bank account, had notations that they were gifts. Another check for $61,000, drawn on a second bank account, stated that it was for a past loan and reimbursement of expenses. On the estate tax return, the estate underreported the values of the bank accounts by the outstanding checks.

Held: For the IRS (in part). Underreporting the value of a bank account can be a valuation understatement within the meaning of prior Section 6660. In the context of the estate tax, bank accounts are "property" to which Section 6660 applied.

[Estate of Owen, 104 TC 498 (1995).]

Penalty for late filing of estate tax return is upheld; offhand response cannot be relied on. The executor of an estate shared offices with an attorney who handled state inheritance matters. When asked by the executor when the estate tax was due, the attorney replied that to the best of his knowledge, the return and payment were due eighteen months after decedent's death, but that the executor should verify that information with his accountant. Although the executor did engage an accountant to prepare the return, he did not check the due date with him, and apparently the accountant did not volunteer that information. As a result, the return was filed eight months late, and a late filing penalty was assessed.

Held: For the IRS. In Boyle, 469 US 241, 85-1 USTC ¶ 13,602, 55 AFTR2d 85-1535 (S. Ct. 1985), the executor, a man with extensive business background, hired an attorney who negligently missed the filing date. The Supreme Court, in *Boyle*, held that the failure to timely file a tax return is not excused by the taxpayer's reliance on an agent and such reliance is not, therefore, "reasonable cause" to avoid the late filing penalty. The Court reasoned that it required no special training or effort to ascertain a deadline and make sure that the deadline is met. The Court did say that taxpayer is not required to get a second professional opinion. The executor in the instant case used this language to contend that he was entitled to rely on the attorney's advice. The Tax Court, however, held that there was no advice rendered by the attorney. The attorney had not been retained to advise about federal estate tax matters and had not received any compensation for any such advice. The executor himself was an attorney and shared an office with the other attorney. Therefore, the executor knew the nature of that attorney's practice, and it would not have been reasonable for the executor to rely on the attorney's offhand comment.

[Newton, TC Memo. (P-H) ¶ 90,208, 59 TCM (CCH) 469 (1990).]

Tax Court, applying *Boyle* standard, finds reasonable cause excuses non-filing. For a substantial period of time prior to her death in 1972, decedent engaged in a pattern of making gifts to members of her family for which gift tax returns were regularly filed. In several cases, the gifts were made to separate trusts established for the benefit of decedent's children. During late 1970, she made equal gifts of stocks and bonds to various family members, including her three sons, their wives, and their children. She reported the total value of these gifts as $100,465 on the gift tax return filed with the IRS in April 1971. In late 1971, she made further gifts of stock, which were reported as having a value of $126,516. During this same period, however, she also made cash advances to one of her sons, for which no gift tax returns were filed. In 1970, there was a cash advance of $50,000, and a further $296,500 advance was made during the early part of 1971. Decedent also drew checks in payment of outstanding loans made to the son by local banks, and she assigned a block of stock to him in 1971. This latter transaction was the subject of an "Agreement to Loan Corporate Stock" that attempted to characterize the stock assignment as a loan. In sum, the advances to the son totaled $756,666 during 1970 and 1971. When the family attorney and accountant became aware of these advances, he advised decedent that no gift tax return was necessary if the advances were indeed loans. The IRS, however, determined that the entire amount of $756,666 constituted taxable gifts.

Held: For the IRS. The estate conceded liability for gift tax on the entire assessed amount prior to trial, but it chose to contest the assertion by the IRS of penalties under Section 6651(a)(1). The estate argued that the penalty was not proper, because decedent relied on professional advice in not filing a gift tax return. The Tax Court, applying the test in Boyle, 469 US 241 (1985), held that reasonable cause had been established by evidence that decedent consulted with counsel on the necessity of compliance, and that she relied on his erroneous advice. The court noted that the law does not require that a taxpayer challenge the advice of professionals or seek second opinions merely to assure compliance. Because the evidence showed that reasonable effort was made to comply, the penalty was not appropriate.

[Estate of Buring, TC Memo. (P-H) ¶ 85,610, 51 TCM (CCH) 113 (1985).]

[2] Closing Agreements

Closing agreement is held fully enforceable by IRS and bar to readjustment of basis in corporate notes. At the time of his death in 1975 from drug abuse, decedent was the controlling shareholder of a closely held corporation in the videotape business. In 1974, the corporation arranged for a business loan from a commercial bank that required decedent to guarantee the loan personally. As part of the guarantee, decedent acquired two life insurance policies and assigned them to the bank. The bank was designated as the beneficiary, under an arrangement that provided for the estate to receive an interest in the corporation's promissory notes to the extent that the proceeds of the policy satisfied the notes. Because of the circumstances of decedent's death, the insurance company asserted a complete defense to payment of the policy amount. The bank and the estate then entered into an agreement under which the bank would relieve the corporation of liability on the loan, and they would work jointly to collect the insurance proceeds. The insurance company soon agreed to settle and paid the bank $4.2 million, after which the bank assigned the estate an interest in the corporation's promissory notes to the extent of the $4.2 million. On its estate tax return, the estate attributed no value to the life insurance policies on decedent's life. It maintained that the estate possessed only a subordinated interest in such policies. The IRS disputed this treatment, and, after extensive discussion and negotiation, the estate and the IRS entered into a statutory closing agreement under Section 7121 to settle the value for purposes of inclusion in the gross estate. The closing agreement also stipulated an agreed-upon unadjusted basis in the subordinated notes for income tax purposes. Thereafter, in 1980 and 1981, the notes were repaid in full, and the estate paid income tax on the capital gains as computed in accordance with the basis figure set forth in the closing agreement. Later the estate, having reconsidered its position, filed amended returns for 1980 and 1981, claiming entitlement to refunds on the ground that its basis in the notes should have been increased by the $4.2 million paid to the bank by the insurance company.

Held: For the IRS. A closing agreement, once entered into and approved in accordance with Section 7121, is final and conclusive as between the parties in all matters affected thereby. In the absence of a showing of fraud, misrepresentation, or malfeasance, the agreement may not be disavowed by any party or annulled by a court. The estate made no showing of fraud, misrepresentation, or malfeasance, and the essential facts urged in support of the basis adjustment were known by the parties as of the date of the closing agreement. Accordingly, the court refused to abrogate the agreement and denied the refund claim.

[Estate of Johnson, 88 TC 225 (1987), aff'd without published op., 838 F2d 1202 (2d Cir. 1987).]

IRS could reopen examination of estate's return after issuing closing letter. An estate tax return was audited, and, after the audit, the IRS issued an estate tax closing letter. The letter stated that it did not constitute a formal closing agreement under Section 7121. A year and a half later, the IRS reopened the examination of the estate's return and issued a deficiency notice.

The estate contended that the deficiency notice was invalid because the IRS lacked the authority and jurisdiction to reopen the closed examination.

Held: For the IRS. The IRS had the authority to reopen the examination because the closing letter was not a closing agreement.

[Estate of Bommer, 69 TCM 2541, RIA TC Memo. ¶ 95,197 (1995).]

Tax Court finds sufficient grounds to reopen estate tax return, despite issuance of IRS closing letter. Following decedent's September 2, 1972, death, his estate filed a delinquent estate tax return bearing the date July 13, 1980. The estate corrected errors in data in the filing of a second return, dated August 3, 1980. The second return was selected for audit by the IRS, and the examining agent focused on the value of certain property owned by decedent at the time of his death. Six months later the estate's first return was also selected for audit in the course of the IRS's routine selection procedure. In response, the estate's attorney contacted the examining agent to whom the first return had been assigned and expressed his need for a closing letter with respect to the first return. Unaware of the ongoing audit of the second return, the agent surveyed the first return and stamped it "closed." The District Director, in reliance on the agent's action, issued an estate tax closing letter. A few weeks later the agent who had been conducting the audit of the second return spoke with the estate's attorney and learned of the closing letter for the first time. The IRS then advised the estate that the case was being administratively reopened in order to pursue the proposed changes advanced by the auditor of the second return. After an attempt at settlement failed, the IRS issued its notice of deficiency, and the matter was presented to the Tax Court. The estate's sole contention was that the case was erroneously reopened and that therefore the notice of deficiency was invalid. It argued that either the IRS did not follow the guidelines for reopening a case as set forth in Revenue Procedure 81-35, 1981-2 CB 588, or that the IRS had failed to provide written notification as required by Section 7605(b). The estate further argued that the failure to give proper notice of the reopening caused it to rely detrimentally on the closing letter.

Held: For the IRS. The cited revenue procedure states that the IRS will not reopen any case closed after examination by a District Office, Service Center, or Office of International Operations to make an adjustment unfavorable to the taxpayer, unless other circumstances exist that indicate the failure to reopen would be a serious administrative omission. In upholding the IRS, the court noted the following:

1. Two returns were submitted by the estate.
2. The attorney for the estate affirmatively sought an expedited review.
3. There was nothing to indicate that the attorney notified the IRS that the two returns had been filed.

4. The attorney said nothing about the second return when contacted by the agent auditing the first return.

5. The attorney did not check for verification with the auditor examining the first return when he received the closing letter.

These facts, in the court's view, indicated an administrative error on the part of the IRS that could have been avoided if the estate and its attorney had acted in good faith. From this, the court concluded that a "failure to reopen would be a serious administrative omission" within the meaning of Revenue Procedure 81-35, and that the reopening of the case and the resulting deficiency had been properly asserted.

[Estate of Keeler, TC Memo. (P-H) ¶ 84,632, 49 TCM (CCH) 243 (1984).]

[3] Litigation Costs and Fees

Measure of net worth for attorney fees included distributed assets. After prevailing in an action challenging a tax assessment, an estate sought attorney fees. The IRS conceded that an estate could do so but contended the estate did not satisfy the maximum net worth requirement. The estate was valued at over $2 million on decedent's date of death, but distributions reduced the value below that threshold prior to the estate's filing the complaint. The lower court sided with the estate.

Held: Reversed for the IRS. The net worth requirement for an estate is not determined when the complaint is filed, but must take into account any assets previously distributed.

[Estate of Woll, 44 F3d 464, 75 AFTR2d 95-354, 95-1 USTC ¶ 60,187 (7th Cir. 1994).]

District court awards litigation costs to estate. The estate claimed the maximum marital deduction under prior law, but the IRS contended that the marital deduction should not be applied before the payment of federal estate taxes. The IRS's contention was rejected, and the estate sought litigation costs.

Held: For the estate. The IRS's position was unreasonable, and litigation costs were awarded. Under Indiana state law, the estate was entitled to the marital deduction before reduction for the taxes, even though the estate would have insufficient probate assets to pay the taxes afterward.

[Martin, 90-2 USTC ¶ 60,044, 71A AFTR2d 93-5044 (ND Ind. 1990).]

Successful estate is denied litigation costs. An estate was the prevailing party with respect to issues involving a split-gift election and the decedent's percentage ownership in a family business. The estate sought litigation costs, and the IRS argued that its position was substantially justified.

Held: For the IRS. The IRS's position had a reasonable basis in both law and fact.

[Estate of Lenheim, RIA TC Memo. ¶ 91,021, 61 TCM (CCH) 1700 (1991).]

Estate is denied litigation costs in case involving valuation of stock. After reconsidering its bench opinion, the Tax Court determined decedent's stock to be worth $12.45 per share, without relying on any one expert's opinion. The IRS had asserted a value of $46 per share, and the estate valued the stock at $10 per share. The estate then sought litigation costs.

Held: For the IRS. The IRS's position was substantially justified, despite its gross overvaluation of the stock. The IRS had placed reasonable reliance on an expert opinion, so that the "position of the U.S." was reasonable.

[Estate of Feldmar, TC Memo. (P-H) ¶ 89,096, 56 TCM (CCH) 1414 (1989).]

[4] Jurisdiction

Pursuant to the Anti-Injunction Act, federal courts do not have jurisdiction to review IRS decision denying installment payment of estate taxes. Decedent died, leaving an estate, 98 percent of which consisted of ranchland. The estate filed a timely tax return, electing to pay the taxes due in installments pursuant to Section 6166. The IRS proposed an increase to the estate tax liability and denied the installment election. During the audit and the ensuing appeal, the IRS continued to bill the estate pursuant to the Section 6166 election. The IRS issued a ninety-day letter containing its determination of the tax deficiency but was silent as to the installment issue. The estate filed a petition with the Tax Court, seeking to estop the IRS from denying the Section 6166 election. The IRS filed a motion to strike all references to Section 6166, contending that the Tax Court lacked jurisdiction to determine the method of payment of taxes. The Tax court granted the IRS's motion, and the estate was informed that the installment method of paying taxes was denied. The estate brought this action appealing the denial.

Held: For the IRS. The U.S. District Court held that it lacked proper jurisdiction to review the IRS decision to deny the installment method election under Section 6166. The court relied principally on the Anti-Injunction Act, Section 7421 of the Code, which states that "no suit for the purpose of restraining the assessment or collection of any tax shall be maintained in any court." The court noted that the prohibition against taxpayers questioning the assessment or collection of taxes under the Anti-Injunction Act has been strictly enforced and consistently upheld. The Act is designed to protect the

IRS's need to assess and collect taxes as expeditiously as possible with a minimum of interference from the courts. The Act does not apply to actions brought by parties for whom an alternative remedy has not been provided. In the instant case, however, a suit for refund was an adequate remedy available to the taxpayer, and thus the Act is an absolute bar to suit seeking injunction against collection of a tax.

[McEachen, 89-1 USTC ¶ 13,794, 63 AFTR2d 89-1568 (D. Neb. 1988).]

Declaratory Judgment Act does not bar estate's action to void tax levy. The IRS made a tax assessment against the taxpayer-estate. The IRS then seized some real property belonging to the estate without first giving the estate notice as required by Section 6631. The estate thereafter sought a declaratory judgment under the Declaratory Judgment Act, 28 USC § 2201(a), challenging only the procedural validity of the tax levy, not the merits of the asserted tax liability. The IRS contended that the court lacked subject matter jurisdiction to declare the levy void, because the Declaratory Judgment Act does not allow cases "with respect to federal taxes."

Held: For the estate. The court stated that in order to determine whether the Declaratory Judgment Act barred the estate's action, it had to determine whether the action was allowed under 28 USC § 7421(a), the Anti-Injunction Act, because a suit that is allowed under 28 USC § 7421(a) is not barred by the Declaratory Judgment Act. That section provides in part that, except as provided in 28 USC § 6213(a), no suit for the purpose of restraining the assessment or collection of any tax shall be maintained in any court by any person, regardless of whether such person is the person against whom such tax was assessed. The court stated that the language of Section 7421(a) does not apply to a taxpayer's suit to enjoin a levy imposed before notice of deficiency, during the ninety-day period after that notice, or while a petition is pending in the Tax Court. The court noted that though the estate's claim in this case arose under 28 USC § 6331, the Supreme Court in Shapiro, 424 US 614 (1976), has included the notice and demand procedures of Section 6331 in suits permitted under the exception provided in 28 USC § 6213(a). The court concluded that the estate's action arose directly under Section 6331 and therefore fit within the statutory exception under Section 6213(a) to the Anti-Injunction Act. Accordingly, because the action was allowed under the Anti-Injunction Act, it was not barred by the Declaratory Judgment Act.

[Powelson, 88-1 USTC ¶ 13,747, 71A AFTR2d 93-4994 (D. Or. 1987).]

[5] Refunds and Returns

Estate is allowed to recover interest paid on deficiency where retroactive revision in estate tax provisions results in refund of deficiency. Decedent left half of his estate in trust for the benefit of his companion during her lifetime, with the remainder to be paid to the Shriner's Hospital on her death. Upon the companion's death six months later, the remainder was paid to the hospital, and decedent's estate filed its final tax return, claiming a charitable deduction for the entire trust amount. The IRS disallowed the charitable deduction and assessed a deficiency because the testamentary split-interest trust as established in the will did not meet the requirements of Section 2055(e)(2). The estate paid the deficiency with interest and did not challenge the assessment within the statute of limitations. Under the Deficit Reduction Act of 1984 (DEFRA), Section 2055(e)(3)(F) was revised to provide that if an income beneficiary of a split-interest charitable remainder trust dies before the estate tax is due, the will establishing the trust is deemed reformed as of the date of death to create a gift passing directly to the charity. The provision was made retroactive to include the period affecting the estate in the present case, and the estate was entitled to obtain a refund for the excess estate tax paid, even though the statute of limitations had run. After the IRS failed to act upon the request for refund, the estate filed suit in Claims Court. In that action, the IRS conceded that the refund for estate tax paid was due, but contended that the interest assessed upon late payment of the tax should not be refunded. The IRS based its contention on a provision in DEFRA that prohibits the IRS from paying interest on refunded taxes when the refund is available only because of the retroactive waiver of the period of limitations. The Claims Court upheld the IRS on the interest issue, and the estate filed an appeal.

Held: For the estate. The appellate court held that the provision on which the IRS relied to deny the claim for refund of interest paid was not applicable in the present case. It concluded that the provision refers solely to interest paid by the IRS to the taxpayer, not to any interest paid to the IRS. According to the court, the congressional intent behind the reformation provision requires treatment as if the amended trust were actually in the will. The provision, in effect, eliminates the basis on which the tax was imposed, and thus no tax was ever due. The court further held that if no tax was due, there could be no ground for assessing a deficiency or for charging interest on a late payment. The estate was therefore entitled to a refund for interest paid on the deficiency.

[Shriners Hosp., 862 F2d 1561, 88-2 USTC ¶ 13,789, 63 AFTR2d 89-1507 (Fed. Cir. 1988).]

Protest letter to IRS is not claim for refund. The IRS assessed a deficiency attributable to a decrease in the marital deduction claimed by an estate. After the estate protested, the IRS reconsidered, but increased the deficiency. The estate responded with a thirty-seven-page letter to the IRS that outlined why the full marital deduction should have been permitted. The last page of the letter asked for a refund. As the result of negotiations between the estate and the IRS, the estate agreed to an additional assessment and signed a Form 890-AD (Offer of Waiver of Restrictions on Assessment and Collection of Deficiency in Tax and of an Acceptance of Overassessment). Although execution of the form generally precludes a later refund claim, the estate attached a proviso to the form, stating that it reserved the right to file a refund claim on the marital deduction issue. The estate then paid the additional assessment and sued for a refund. In the district court, the estate argued that it had claimed a refund when it filed the Form 890-AD. The district court rejected this argument, concluding that no refund claim had been filed, and dismissed the suit.

The Seventh Circuit reviewed Section 7422(a), which requires that a claim for refund be filed before suit can be instituted. Regulations § 301.6404-2(b) states that the claim must set forth in detail both the ground on which the refund is sought and the facts sufficient to apprise the IRS of the basis for the claim. The estate argued that either its letter and other information given to the IRS served as an informal claim for a refund, or the Form 890-AD sufficed. With regard to the latter argument, the estate cited Revenue Ruling 68-65, 1968-1 CB 555, which provides that a taxpayer has made a valid claim for a refund if the taxpayer has agreed to an overassessment on Form 890-AD.

Held: For the IRS. The court rejected the Form 890-AD argument, because the estate had not agreed to an overassessment; rather, it had agreed to a deficiency. Thus, the ruling did not apply. Moreover, the proviso added by the taxpayer to the form reserved only a right to file a future refund claim. The proviso language was inconsistent with an interpretation that either the form or the taxpayer's prior letter constituted a claim for a refund. As for the estate's letter, the court adopted the test set forth in American Radiator & Standard Sanitary Corp., 318 F2d 915, 63-2 USTC ¶ 9525 (Ct. Cl. 1963). Under this test, an informal refund claim must meet the following tests: (1) The action must be in writing and (2) the claim must be sufficient to apprise the IRS that a refund is sought and to focus attention on the merits of the dispute, so that the IRS can make an examination if it so wishes. Thus, for example, in *American Radiator*, notations on the taxpayer's income tax return, combined with knowledge of the revenue agent auditing the taxpayer, added up to an acceptable informal refund claim.

In this case, however, the court found that although the alleged refund claim had been in writing, the second prong of the test was not satisfied. A proper claim would inform the IRS that a refund was being sought and would contain all facts necessary to determine that a reduction in tax liability was involved. Although the letter stated that a refund was claimed, most of it simply argued why the full marital deduction should be allowed. The court concluded that the marital deduction issue was raised in the context of the deficiency assessment, not a potential refund. The court contrasted this with a situation in which the substantive question underlying the refund claim is being litigated at the time the claim is made. In such a situation, the court stated, the IRS is aware of the litigation and is put on notice that the taxpayer expects to receive a refund if the litigation is decided in the taxpayer's favor. Because the IRS was not on notice as to the claim in the present case, however, the suit had not been instituted in accordance with Section 7422(a), and accordingly had properly been dismissed.

[Martin, 833 F2d 655, 60 AFTR2d 87-6037, 87-2 USTC ¶ 13,742 (7th Cir. 1987).]

Litigation costs against murdering heir are held nonrefundable for want of timely refund claim. Decedent was murdered in 1977 by her son. In her will, she left her considerable estate to him as the sole heir. Following his entry of a no-contest plea to reckless homicide, decedent's relatives commenced an action in state court challenging the son's inheritance on the ground that common law bars a murdering heir from collecting his testamentary bequests. While this litigation was in progress, the estate's personal representative in 1978 filed the estate tax return and paid taxes exceeding $400,000. In 1979, the litigation was settled by an agreement under which the son took a small portion of the estate. The victorious relatives then filed a refund claim based on deductions for their reimbursed attorney fees. The refund claim was filed in 1983, but the IRS refused to honor it on the ground that Section 6511(a) requires a refund claim to be submitted not later than three years after the filing date of the estate tax return or two years after the payment. The IRS determined that more than five years had passed since the payment and filing of the estate's taxes. The district court dismissed the refund suit, and an appeal followed.

Held: Affirmed for the IRS. The five-year lapse since the payment and filing of the estate's return rendered the refund claim untimely, and dismissal by the trial court was proper. The court rejected the estate's argument that though a contingent administrative expense can be preserved for reduction by means of filing a timely protective refund claim, the personal administrator in this case would have been in breach of his fiduciary duties had it done so. The court declined to make a finding that such a breach would have existed under applicable state law and held instead that the estate had simply failed to protect itself at the proper time.

[Swietlik, 779 F2d 1306, 57 AFTR2d 86-1497, 86-1 USTC ¶ 13,652 (7th Cir. 1985).]

Standing to sue for refund of estate taxes is not limited to actual payor. Decedent died intestate. Although he never appointed executors, his three surviving brothers continued to run the corporations that were the major assets of decedent's estate. The corporations paid the estate tax. In the refund suit, the

IRS contended that neither the corporations nor the brothers had standing to sue.

 Held: For the taxpayers. The brothers had standing as executors because of the Section 2203 definition of "executor" as any person in possession of the property of the decedent. The Sixth Circuit further held that attorney fees of the refund litigation were an allowable administration expense and therefore were deductible.

[DeNiro, 561 F2d 653, 40 AFTR2d 77-6246, 77-2 USTC ¶ 13,205 (6th Cir. 1977).]

Verbal communication with IRS attorney regarding refund does not constitute informal claim. Decedent's residuary estate was to pass under the will to two charitable organizations. The description of one of the charities was vague, however, and the executor filed suit seeking judicial guidance. While the suit was pending, the estate tax return was filed, claiming deductions for both charitable bequests. An IRS attorney contacted the executor and advised him that because half the residuary estate could pass to decedent's heirs at law, who were not tax-exempt, the estate should pay the potential tax to avoid interest charges. The attorney further stated that the IRS would refund the tax if the disputed bequest ultimately went to a charity. The estate paid the additional tax, and, after the limitations period had run, the court identified the second charity and awarded it the balance of the residuary estate. The estate filed a claim for refund, and the IRS denied it as being time-barred.

 Held: For the IRS. The estate's earlier communications with the IRS were neither a formal nor informal refund claim. In addition, the IRS is not bound by the statements of the IRS attorney.

[Miller, 67 AFTR2d 91-1203, 91-1 USTC ¶ 60,061 (WD Va. 1991), aff'd, 949 F2d 708, 68 AFTR2d 91-6073, 91-2 USTC ¶ 60,092 (4th Cir. 1991).]

Refund claim cannot double as protective claim. The estate had borrowed money to pay the estate tax. Within three years of the date on which the estate tax return was filed, it made a successful refund claim arising from the first two years' interest paid on the loan. After the statute of limitations expired, the estate filed another refund claim based on additional interest paid. The IRS denied the claimed deduction.

 Held: For the IRS. Although interest paid on a loan to pay estate taxes is a deductible administration expense, a deduction cannot be taken for estimated future interest expenses. Problems arise because the interest generally will be paid after the estate tax return is filed, and the estate must wait until the interest payments are definite to claim a refund. An estate that will be incurring interest in the future can file a protective claim within the limitations period. Such a claim can be supplemented with a formal claim once the interest is paid. The later claim relates back to the date of the protective claim and is thus timely. Protective claims are not recognized in the Code or regulations but are authorized by case law. Under Mills, 890 F2d 1133 (11th Cir. 1989), the protective claim need not comply with all formal claim requirements, as long as its defects are remedied by amendment (even after the statutory period has expired). The informal claim should, however, adequately apprise the IRS that a refund is sought for certain years. An informal claim does not exist merely because the IRS might be able to deduce from information in its possession that taxpayer might desire a refund. Furthermore, a claim involving the same ground for a different period is not adequate. Thus, because the earlier refund claim did not put the IRS on notice that a refund claim also would be sought for a subsequent year, it was not an adequate protective claim.

[Pickett, 90-2 USTC ¶ 60,030, 71A AFTR2d 93-5037 (ND Fla. 1990).]

Payment of taxes in full is jurisdictional prerequisite for maintaining tax refund action in federal district court. In 1988, taxpayer filed suit in federal district court seeking recovery of federal estate taxes and interest erroneously and illegally assessed and collected. At the time the complaint was filed, taxpayer had an outstanding tax liability. The IRS argued that it is a well-settled rule that federal district courts lack subject matter jurisdiction over suits to recover estate taxes erroneously or illegally assessed and collected prior to payment in full. Taxpayer argued that payment in full after suit had begun conferred jurisdiction upon the court.

Held: For the IRS. Citing Church of Scientology of Colorado, 499 F. Supp. 1085, 81-1 USTC ¶ 9236 (D. Colo. 1980), the court stated that the prepayment requirement is a condition precedent to filing an action in district court for the recovery of such taxes. The jurisdictional prerequisite must be satisfied prior to or at the time suit is filed. The court noted that the parties may not cure such a jurisdictional prerequisite after the fact; jurisdiction must exist at the time suit is filed.

[Whiteman, 89-1 USTC ¶ 13,804, 63 AFTR2d 89-1571 (D. Idaho 1989).]

Foreign death tax assessment following payment of U.S. estate tax does not give rise to interest claim on refund. Decedent, a citizen of the United States, died on May 25, 1977, while domiciled in the Republic of Ireland. Her estate consisted of assets located in Ireland and in the United States. On her estate tax return filed in 1978, the estate claimed a foreign tax credit, based on the assumption that the estate would be assessed Irish death duties in the amount of $293,938. As a result of the claimed credit, the estate reported no U.S. estate tax liability. Thereafter the IRS disallowed the credit on the ground that no Irish death duties had actually been assessed. The estate paid the resulting deficiency, but the Republic of Ireland later assessed death duties totaling $174,992. The estate then filed a claim for refund of the entire amount of federal estate taxes and interest paid. The IRS failed to respond administratively, and the estate brought suit in federal district court. The basis for the estate's contention was that the payment made to the IRS constituted an overpayment under Section 6401(a)(4).

Held: Claim for interest denied. The district court found that the general rule as to payments of interest on overpayments was not controlling, because Section 6611 is subject to the exceptions set forth in Section 6612(c). Among these exceptions is the rule in Section 2014(e), which provides that no interest can be paid with reference to funds based on foreign death taxes. The same rule is reiterated in the language of the estate tax treaty between the United States and Ireland in Article 6(2). Accordingly, the district court awarded a refund of the amount of tax paid without interest or attorney fees.

[Estate of Daley, 55 AFTR2d 85-1582, 85-1 USTC ¶ 13,609 (CD Ill. 1984).]

Refund suit is dismissed as premature. On May 31, 1983, the IRS received a claim for refund of estate taxes paid by an estate. On August 5, 1983, the executrix of the estate filed the instant suit seeking a refund. The IRS moved to dismiss the suit on the ground that the court had no jurisdiction, because the plaintiff had failed to comply with the requirements of the governing statutes and regulations controlling suits seeking refund of estate tax payments.

Held: IRS's motion to dismiss granted. The relevant statutory provisions were Sections 7422(a) and 6532(a)(1), which provide that no suit for a tax refund can be brought until six months after a claim for refund is filed with the IRS. The purpose of these statutes is to provide the IRS with sufficient time to review the rule on a claim. The record reflected that six months had not elapsed between the receipt of the claim by the IRS and the filing of the instant lawsuit.

[Magouirk, 53 AFTR2d 84-1624, 84-1 USTC ¶ 13,554 (WD La. 1983).]

Mere fact that estate has elected to pay estate tax due in installments or qualified for Section 6166 deferral does not permit it to file refund claim before paying all tax due. The estate reported a federal estate tax liability of $81,338. The estate prepaid $39,000 of this liability and elected to pay the $42,388 balance in installments. The IRS assessed the reported tax liability on April 30, 1984, crediting the estate with the $39,000 payment. Prior to March 1987, the estate had not received any communications from the IRS indicating that it did not qualify to pay the estate tax in installments or to defer the tax under Section 6166. In fact, the IRS, in 1984, 1985, and 1986, sent the estate notices of interest due, which the estate paid. On March 13, 1987, the IRS assessed the estate for additional taxes in the amount of $127,324 and determined that the estate did not qualify to pay the $42,388 balance reported on the return in installments or pursuant to a Section 6166 deferral as argued by the estate. The estate paid the $127,324 assessment but not the $42,388 unpaid balance of the tax reported on the estate tax return. On July 27, 1987, the estate filed a claim for refund of the $127,324 payment. The IRS sought to dismiss the estate's suit on the ground that the court lacked jurisdiction to hear the claim because the estate still owed $42,388, the balance of tax due.

Held: For the IRS. In general, full payment of an IRS assessment is a jurisdictional prerequisite to the bringing of a refund action. Further, neither Section 6166, permitting a deferral in the payment of estate tax, nor qualification for installment payment of tax is an exception to the full payment rule.

[Rocovich, 18 Cl. Ct. 418, 89-2 USTC ¶ 13,819, 64 AFTR2d 89-5942 (1989), aff'd, 933 F2d 991, 67 AFTR2d 91-1210, 91-1 USTC ¶ 60,072 (Fed. Cir. 1991).]

IRS is presumed to have received timely mailed return unless it can show otherwise. Even though decedent's estate tax return was not sent by certified or registered mail, a postal official testified that she had accepted and postmarked the envelope prior to the due date of the return. The IRS, however, argued that under Section 7502, a timely mailed return is timely filed only if the return is actually, not presumptively, delivered to it. The IRS also argued that under Section 7502(c), proof of delivery can be made only when a return is sent by registered or certified mail.

Held: For the estate. According to the court, neither Section 7502 nor its legislative history indicates that Congress intended to exclude the common-law presumption of delivery created by proof of a properly mailed document. Thus, because the IRS was unable to present positive evidence to the contrary, the court held that the timely mailed return was delivered. The court found it only coincidental that the corresponding state tax returns had not been received by the state tax authority.

[Estate of Wood, 92 TC 793 (1989), aff'd, 909 F2d 1155, 90-2 USTC ¶ 60,031, 66 AFTR2d 90-5987 (8th Cir. 1990).]

Tax Court holds that no refund is due where estate overpays installment. Two estates elected under Section 6166 to defer a portion of the estate tax due. Although the IRS initially issued notices of deficiency, alleging that the stock of the closely held corporation owned by decedents (husband and wife) had been undervalued, it was eventually agreed that it had in fact been overvalued. The overpayments included portions of the installment payments that would not have been due had the correct value of the stock been given on the estate returns. As to these amounts, the estates sought refunds, with interest. The IRS contended that the matter was resolved by Section 6403. That section provides that when a taxpayer pays as an installment in more than the correct amount, the overpayment is to be credited to unpaid installments. Only if the amount already paid by taxpayer exceeds the ultimate amount due would a refund be due the taxpayer. The estates countered that this provision should not apply to Section 6166, in that Section 6166(g) should be the exclusive list of situations under which the benefits of the section would be curtailed. To apply Section 6403 would, in effect, accelerate the payments due. This, the estates argued, would be contrary to the congressional intent behind Section 6166, which is to allow deferral as to estate taxes on family farms and closely held businesses. The IRS's approach, according to the estates, substantially reduced the benefits of deferral.

Held: For the IRS. The court disagreed with the estates' argument, holding that the IRS had appropriately credited the overpayments toward the future, corrected installments. Although the estates had correctly stated the policy of the statute, the court concluded that Section 6166(g)is not the exclusive delineation of situations in which the benefits of the Section are curtailed. Although no specific mention of Section 6403 is made in Regulations § 20.6166-1(i), the example demonstrates the correct treatment of overpayments of installments, indicating that overpayments should be credited toward subsequent installments.

[Estate of Bell, 92 TC 714 (1989), aff'd, 928 F2d 901, 67 AFTR2d 91-1198, 91-1 USTC ¶ 60,065 (9th Cir. 1991).]

Nonfiduciary bank need not file Form 1041. As a result of prolonged litigation over a contested will, an estate administrator was not appointed. The taxpayer bank held money for the estate and paid interest on it, without performing any administrative duties. The IRS ruled that the bank was not a fiduciary and was not required to file Form 1041.

[Rev. Rul. 82-177, 1982-2 CB 365.]

Two-year refund period applies to estate tax installments. An estate's failure to file a supplemental return claiming interest and other administration expense deductions each time it made an installment payment, or file a protective refund claim, precluded its claim for a refund covering the payments it made over the entire ten-year installment period, in this ruling. Taxpayer elected to pay the portion of its estate taxes attributable to a closely held business interest in installments. Taxpayer timely made annual payments of just interest for the first four years, followed by combined installment payments of tax and accrued interest over the next ten years. The IRS received taxpayer's final installment payment on December 23, 1993. On December 12, 1995—within two years of its final payment—taxpayer filed a claim for a refund of the interest it paid during the entire installment period and for other administration expenses from 1986 through 1996. The IRS acknowledged that taxpayer had overpaid its estate tax and interest. Nevertheless, the IRS stated that it was prevented from granting taxpayer's claim by Section 6511(b)(2)(B), which limits refunds to payments made in the two years preceding the refund claim (if the claim is not filed within three years of the return filing date, which clearly was the situation here). The IRS relied on Revenue Procedure 81-27, 1981-2 CB

548. As noted in that procedure, a refund claim for estate taxes paid in installments cannot be made until the installment payments made to date exceed the final estate tax liability. This scheme poses potential limitations period problems because more than two years may elapse between the payment of interest with earlier installments and the eventual overpayment of the tax.

Under the procedure, however, an estate can file a supplemental return claiming interest and other administration expense deductions each time an installment payment is made. As long as this is done in accord with Revenue Procedure 81-27, the IRS will recompute the estate tax liability using the increased deduction and apply any overpayment to the next installment. Then, if the total estate tax liability is less than the total installments paid, a refund claim "can be filed . . . within the applicable period of limitations" (in Section 6511(b)(2)(b)). Alternatively, a taxpayer can preserve its claim by filing a protective refund claim within the statutory period. In this instance, taxpayer neither followed Revenue Procedure 81-27 (e.g., taxpayer paid each installment in full and filed no supplemental returns claiming interest or other administration expense deductions), nor filed a protective refund claim. Instead, taxpayer waited until after paying the final installment to claim a refund for interest and other expenses it had paid over the whole ten-year installment period. Taxpayer argued that the Section 6511(b) two-year limitations period did not bar its claim because its entire deferred estate tax was not paid until the last installment was made (thus reasoning that the limitations period did not start to run on any of the deferred tax until it made its final payment on December 23, 1993). Taxpayer relied on Revenue Procedure 81-27 and a statement in *Bailly*, 81 TC 246 (1983), that "no . . . limitations [period] problem can arise with earlier payments since no overpayment can occur until the final installment is paid." The IRS found, however, that taxpayer's reliance was misplaced. The IRS pointed out that Revenue Procedure 81-27's provision for filing a refund claim is premised on a taxpayer's following the procedure. Similarly, the *Bailly* court statement that the limitations period would not be a problem with respect to earlier installments was made in the context of a taxpayer following Revenue Procedure 81-27. Since taxpayer here did not follow that procedure, however, or file a protective refund claim, the two-year limitations period did apply to its claim for a refund of the estate taxes and interest it paid in installments—even though it had clearly overpaid.

[Tech. Adv. Mem. 9828002.]

[6] Assessment and Collection

Signatures of each coexecutor are not necessary to enforcement of Form 890 waiver. The taxpayer and his brother were the sole beneficiaries and coexecutors of their mother's estate. In 1979, an estate tax return was filed with the IRS, bearing the signatures of the taxpayer's coexecutor and the attorney who represented the estate. Included in the gross estate was a parcel of property valued at $165,000 that was bequeathed to the taxpayer's coexecutor. Within four months, however, the property was sold for $212,000. Following an audit, the IRS determined a deficiency based on the apparent undervaluation, and a Form 890 (waiver of restrictions on assessments) was executed by the taxpayer's coexecutor and the attorney. Thereafter the IRS demanded payment of the deficiency from the taxpayer, on the ground that he was liable under Section 6901(a)as a transferee of estate assets. The taxpayer contended that because he did not sign the Form 890 waiver, the waiver was invalid as it applied to him. In support, the taxpayer noted that the Form 890 signed by the coexecutor constituted a confession of judgment against the estate at a time when it was insolvent and that it was an act outside the ordinary course of estate administration. Because the coexecutor was himself bankrupt at the time, the taxpayer argued that the waiver should be treated as a personal confession of judgment, which, under local law, could not bind the estate without the signatures of both executors.

Held: For the IRS. Under established principles, the assent of a coexecutor is not required to bind the estate to the actions of one of the executors. The execution of a Form 890 is an act within the ordinary course of estate administration, and, where an executor does not object at the time to the acts of his coexecutor, he may not later complain of the result. As to the taxpayer's status as a trustee, the court applied Section 6901, which provides a means by which the IRS can pursue its claim against a transferee. The actual liability of the transferee is determined under the applicable state law. Ohio state law provides that any conveyance made by a person who is, or who will thereby become, insolvent is fraudulent as to creditors, without regard to actual intent if there was no fair consideration. If a fraudulent conveyance has been made, the creditor may then generally attach or levy on the property conveyed. In the present case, the beneficiaries of the estate received a distribution of estate assets. This distribution rendered the estate insolvent and was without consideration from the beneficiaries. Thus, the distribution was a fraudulent conveyance by definition of the state law.

[Ewart, 814 F2d 321, 59 AFTR2d 87-1248, 87-1 USTC ¶ 13,715 (6th Cir. 1987).]

IRS is estopped from reopening return after sending Form L-154 to taxpayer. After the estate filed its estate tax return, it received from the IRS Form L-154, which states that the return was accepted and will not be reopened unless certain conditions occur. The estate later filed a refund claim and the IRS issued a notice of deficiency based on a higher valuation of certain assets. The estate argued that the issuance of Form L-154 had estopped the IRS from opening the case.

Held: For the taxpayer. The IRS had intended the estate to rely on the form and was therefore bound by it. The estate relied on it to its own detriment, because it might not have filed the refund claim had the form stated that a refund claim would reopen the case. Had the refund claim been based on the valuation of those assets, however, the IRS would not have been estopped from arguing that they were undervalued on the return.

[Law, 51 AFTR2d 83-1343, 83-1 USTC ¶ 13,514 (ND Cal. 1982).]

Letter addressed to beneficiary that demanded payment of estate taxes is held not to constitute statutory notice of deficiency. The taxpayer was the sole surviving relative of decedent, who died in 1980, leaving a gross estate of $3 million. The estate consisted primarily of cash and marketable securities. Although the taxpayer, a beneficiary of the estate, hired counsel to administer the estate and an accounting firm to prepare a Form 706 (estate tax return), the return was not timely filed, nor was the tax of $1.08 million timely paid. The taxes as shown on the return were not paid until more than three years after the date of death. The IRS assessed a late filing penalty, together with a late payment penalty and sought to collect the balance owed from the taxpayer as transferee. By way of a letter dated January 24, 1986, an IRS official sent a demand notice to the taxpayer, saying that he was required to make payment of $1.10 million, "which is the extent of the value, at the time of decedent's death, of property received by you as spouse, beneficiary, transferee, trustee, surviving tenant, or person in possession of property by reason of the exercise, nonexercise, or release of a power of appointment." The agents who participated in sending the letter were not authorized to issue statutory notices of deficiency or notices of transferee liability. The taxpayer thereafter filed a Tax Court petition seeking a redetermination of the asserted $1.10 million deficiency. The IRS moved to dismiss the petition for lack of jurisdiction, on the ground that no statutory notice of deficiency had been issued pursuant to Section 6212.

Held: IRS motion to dismiss granted. The Tax Court, in a case of first impression, noted that although no particular form of notice is required, the notice must, at a minimum, convey to the addressee that a deficiency has been determined. The letter sent to the taxpayer, according to the court, simply did not set forth such a deficiency and only advised of a demand for payment based on transferee liability. This, coupled with the fact that the IRS official had no delegated authority to issue a notice of deficiency, led the court to dismiss the taxpayer's petition for lack of jurisdiction.

[Kellogg, 88 TC 167 (1987).]

Notice of deficiency is valid, but petition to Tax Court is untimely. At the time of her death in 1978, decedent was a domiciliary of Nevada and the owner of real property in both Nevada and California. In accordance with the terms of decedent's will, the Nevada court appointed her brother as coexecutor. The brother retained counsel for the estate in Nevada, and also retained counsel in California to represent the estate in ancillary proceedings respecting probate of the California real property. The Nevada court entered its order of November 24, 1981, directing the executors to make a distribution of the estate's assets, except for $25,000 to be used for the payment of a potential estate tax deficiency. The court further stipulated that it was retaining jurisdiction until the estate was finally closed. On August 29, 1979, the estate filed its federal estate tax return, together with a check drawn on a California bank and signed by the brother in partial payment of the estate's total liability. The return listed the names and addresses of the three Nevada coexecutors. In the following December, one of the brother's coexecutors wrote another check drawn against the same California bank for additional federal estate taxes, and signed the accompanying return as the personal representative. In March 1982, the IRS issued a notice of deficiency against the estate and mailed one copy to the Nevada attorney who had signed the December 1979 return and mailed the other copy to the brother, using his California address. The Nevada attorney had since removed himself to Utah, and consequently the only notice of deficiency actually received was that addressed to the brother. By the end of the ninety-day statutory period, the estate had not filed a Tax Court petition, and the IRS moved to dismiss. In a subsequent hearing, the estate asserted that the IRS notice was invalid, because it was not sent to the last known address of the estate or to the proper estate representative as indicated on the first return.

Held: For the IRS. The court found that the IRS was not on notice that the estate had designated anyone in particular to receive correspondence from the IRS, and therefore it was justified in sending copies to the brother, an executor, as well as to the last attorney of record. The fact that one of the executors did in fact receive the notice of deficiency without delay was itself reasonable compliance with the IRS's duty to provide adequate notice of an assessed deficiency.

[Estate of McElroy, 82 TC 509 (1984).]

[7] Statute of Limitations

Supreme Court holds that taxpayer's incompetence does not extend the refund claim limitations period. A senile 93-year-old taxpayer mailed a $7,000 check to the IRS along with an application for an automatic extension of the time to file his 1993 return. He died 4½ years later without ever filing the return. Decedent's daughter discovered the payment in administering his estate and filed a refund claim. Section 6511(a) requires that a refund claim be filed within either three years from the date of the return or two years from the time the tax was paid. If the claim is not timely filed, no refund is allowed, under Section 6511(b)(1). (The estate's claim was filed with the return so the three-year limit was satisfied.) Even if the claim is filed within the three-year period, Section 6511(b)(2)(A) limits the refund to the tax paid in the prior three years plus the period of any filing extension. (This barred the estate's claim, because the tax had been paid more than three years earlier.) Also, if the claim is not filed within the three-year period, the refund cannot exceed the portion of the tax paid within the prior two years, under Section 6511(b)(2)(B). The Ninth Circuit held that the limitations period remained open while decedent was incompetent, under the doctrine of equitable tolling, because it was unconscionable for the government to keep the money. This doctrine had been applied against the U.S. in Irwin v. Dept. of Veterans Affairs, 489 US 89 (1990), an employment case, and Congress had never said it could not apply in a tax case.

   Held: Reversed for the IRS. The Supreme Court reversed. The highly detailed technical language that is repeated in several different ways in Sections 6511(a) and 6511(b), accompanied by a listing of particular exceptions in Section 6511(d), leaves no room for unmentioned exceptions. Also, equitable tolling, by introducing case-by-case exceptions, could create an administrative nightmare by forcing the IRS to address large numbers of otherwise late refund claims.

[Brockamp, 117 S. Ct. 849, 79 AFTR2d 97-986, 97-1 USTC ¶ 50,216 (1997).]

Return based on estimates starts limitations period. Decedent died on April 16, 1983. The estate obtained the maximum extension, until July 16, 1984, to file the estate tax return. On March 16, 1984, the estate's attorneys sent the IRS $30,000, which an accompanying letter described as an estimated payment based on known values and guesses as to the value of property that would accrue to the estate. Form 706 was filed on the extended due date. It provided a value for every part of the gross estate noted on the form but did not include any supporting schedules indicating how those values were arrived at. A check for $15,500, the remaining liability, was enclosed with the return. Several days before the due date, the attorneys wrote the IRS that it was necessary to estimate the value of nine items because of difficulties in valuation, and the return might have to be revised because there were still too many unknown quantities for the return to be considered accurate. The estate was audited, and the IRS asked for the missing schedules. On January 8, 1990, the estate filed an amended return that included the schedules and showed a refund due of $18,600, plus interest. The IRS said the original return was a valid return and the limitations period for a refund had expired. A district court granted a refund because it viewed the original return as merely a tentative estimate of liability, not a bona fide return able to start the limitations period, so the claim was timely.

Held: Reversed for the IRS. The Ninth Circuit reversed because the lower court had misapplied a Supreme Court decision. The Supreme Court had held that a tentative or estimated income tax return was insufficient to start the limitations period, in Florsheim Brothers Drygoods Co., 280 US 453, 8 AFTR 10281, 2 USTC ¶ 485 (S. Ct. 1930). *Florsheim* was distinguishable, however, because it involved income tax. By contrast, tentative estate tax returns are not permitted. The estate tax regulations contemplate the valuation difficulties that confront some taxpayers and provide leeway. Thus, although Form 706 must be filed before the expiration of any extension period, it is to be as "complete as possible," according to Regulation § 20.6081-1(c). Consequently, if precise determinations cannot be made, the estimated values for various categories of assets are to be used to calculate the tax, and the return is a valid return. *Florsheim* also was distinguishable since the tax form there was designated a tentative return (because the law that applied was enacted less than three weeks before returns were due) so the characterization of the return as tentative did not depend on the taxpayer's intent. In the Ninth Circuit's view, a taxpayer cannot suspend the limitations period by claiming that the return might have to be amended or by withholding requisite schedules. The lower court also had concluded that the estate's remittances were deposits, not payments, so the limitations period did not apply. Since the return was valid, however, this conclusion was clearly incorrect. A remittance of the amount shown on a return as due, even if there is no precise calculation, is a payment unless it is expressly designated a deposit, according to Blatt, 34 F3d 252, 74 AFTR2d 94-6311, 94-2 USTC ¶ 50,453 (4th Cir. 1994). Here, there was no designation of any remittance as a deposit. In fact, the estate had described its remittances as payments. The Ninth Circuit has allowed the refund of erroneously paid income tax after the expiration of the limitations under the doctrine of equitable tolling, in Brockamp, 67 F3d 260, 76 AFTR2d 95-6735, 95-2 USTC ¶ 60,213 (9th Cir. 1995). Here, however, there were none of the exceptional circumstances that might justify the application of this doctrine. So the court denied the estate's refund claim.

[Zeier Estate, 80 F3d 1360, 77 AFTR2d 96-1653, 96-1 USTC ¶ 60,228 (9th Cir. 1996).]

Gifts are subject to estate tax even if gift tax statute of limitations has expired. Decedent began a gift-giving program in 1979. She filed gift tax returns for each year from 1979 through 1985, the year she died. In 1984, decedent made gifts of $20,000 in Atlanta, Georgia Project Notes (project notes), which, at that time, were supposedly exempt from gift tax under the Housing Act of 1937. A statement to this effect was included on decedent's 1984 gift tax return. The $20,000 in project notes was not listed as a taxable gift on the return. Decedent did not have to pay any gift tax in 1984 owing to use of the annual gift tax exemption and a portion of her unified credit. If the project notes had been included on the return, there still would have been no tax liability because the tax incurred would have been offset by the unified credit. At the time that decedent's 1984 gift tax return was filed, there was also case authority that said that project notes were not subject to estate tax. This decision was overruled in 1988 by the Supreme Court in Wells Fargo Bank, 485 US 351 (S. Ct. 1988). The statute of limitations period for assessing additional tax on the 1984 gifts expired April 15, 1988. Although the Supreme Court's decision in *Wells Fargo Bank* was issued prior to April 15, 1988, the IRS apparently made no effort to isssue a deficiency notice or assess gift tax on the project notes prior to the expiration of the statute of limitations. The IRS stated that its inaction was due to the fact that no gift tax would have been owed, because it would have been offset by the unified credit. Upon a review of decedent's estate tax return, the IRS determined that the $20,000 in project notes should have been added to adjusted taxable gifts on the estate tax return, so it issued a deficiency notice to the estate. The estate opposed the assessment, and the issue went before the Tax Court. The Tax Court ruled in favor of the IRS.

Held: Affirmed for the IRS. The estate claimed that the IRS was barred from assessing estate tax on the project notes because they were not listed as taxable gifts on the 1984 gift tax return, and that the IRS was barred by the statute of limitations from issuing a deficiency notice assessing gift tax on those notes. The court agreed that the statute of limitations barred further assessment of gift tax, but reasoned that this did not prevent the IRS from including those nontaxed gifts on the estate tax return as adjusted taxable gifts if the statute of limitations for estate tax had not expired. The estate tax statute, Section 2001, states that "adjusted taxable gifts" means "the total amount of taxable gifts (within the meaning of section 2503) made by the decedent after December 31, 1976, other than gifts which are includable in the gross estate of the decedent." "Taxable gifts" is defined in Section 2503 as "the total amount of gifts made during the calender year, less the deductions provided in subchapter C (section 2522 and following)." As the Tax Court noted, "Nowhere in section 2522 and following or elsewhere in the Internal Revenue Code is there any provision for the deduction of gifts on the basis that the statute of limitations has run."

The Fourth Circuit found that not including the project notes on the estate tax return would allow the estate to claim a larger unified credit deduction than it was entitled to, effectively rewarding a taxpayer for not reporting a taxable transaction. The court noted that if the project notes had been transferred prior to 1981, they would have automatically been included on the estate tax return under Section 2035, either as transfers in contemplation of death or transfers made within three years of death. (The statute was amended in 1976 to limit its application to gifts made within three years of death. In 1981, this section was effectively repealed except for certain circumstances.) According to the circuit court, the unification of the gift and estate taxes was not done to allow taxpayers to avoid paying estate tax. One cannot avoid estate tax, if the statute of limitations on estate tax has not run, by not paying gift tax when due and then relying on the expiration of the gift tax statute of limitations. The estate made an alternate claim that the IRS was prohibited by Section 2504(c) from revaluing gifts made by decedent. That section states that if the period for assessing tax on gifts made in a preceding calender year has expired, and if tax was assessed or paid for such year, then the value of the gift for purposes of any future computation is the value used in computing tax in that preceding year. The court concluded that Section 2504 is irrelevant to the issue being addressed because it relates solely to valuation of property for gift tax purposes. The court would not extend the section's application to estate tax issues. The court also refused to address the IRS's other arguments as to why Section 2504(c) was inapplicable.

[Estate of Prince, 986 F2d 91, 71 AFTR2d 93-2167, 93-1 USTC ¶ 60,128 (4th Cir. 1993), cert. denied, 510 US 816 (1993).]

Statute of limitations on collection of estate tax is suspended while decedent's assets are under control of local probate court. Decedent's estate was submitted for probate in 1963, and the local probate court retained control over substantially all of the estate's assets. The IRS determined a deficiency on the estate's taxes and sought to file suit to collect the unpaid taxes more than six years after the date of the assessment. In an earlier decision of the same case, Silverman, 621 F2d 961, 80-2 USTC ¶ 13,360 (9th Cir. 1980), the appellate court had held that the statute of limitations was not suspended if there were substantial assets, not under the probate court's control, against which the IRS could have levied during the period of limitations. Thus, the court remanded the case for determination whether substantial assets became available for levy more than six years prior to commencement of the action to collect. On remand, the district court found that no substantial assets were available for levy by the IRS and that the statute of limitations was thus suspended during the period that the assets were under the control of the probate court. The estate brought this appeal, arguing that a distribution of one half of the community property was made to the surviving spouse more than six years before the commencement of the action to collect the taxes, and that this constituted substantial assets that were available for levy.

Held: For the IRS. The appellate court held that though one half of the community property was distributed to decedent's spouse, such property is excluded from the gross estate of decedent and thereby from the taxable estate. Because the surviving spouse's share of the community property was not part of the taxable estate, it was not liable for any portion of the estate tax. It could not, therefore, be levied against to satisfy the estate tax assessment. Thus, the court affirmed the district court's holding that substantially all of the state's assets were under the control of the probate court.

[Silverman, 859 F2d 1352, 88-2 USTC ¶ 13,785, 62 AFTR2d 88-6014 (9th Cir. 1988), cert. denied, 493 US 1036 (1990).]

Court rejects equitable recoupment argument where proceeds of predeath sale are taxable as capital gains to decedent and subject to inclusion in gross estate. Prior to his death, decedent was the owner of 20 percent of the outstanding shares of stock in a cooperative apartment building in New York City. In 1949 and 1950, the stock was sold to the tenant-owners of the building, and the proceeds were distributed to decedent and his associates. Decedent died on December 26, 1950, following the completion of the sales, but before he had paid any tax on the resulting gain. His executrix included in the gross estate the value of his 20 percent cooperative interest. On December 12, 1960, the IRS assessed a $28,011 deficiency against decedent's 1949 income, on the ground that the sale of his 20 percent interest in 1949 resulted in capital gains of $112,046. The deficiency was paid, and on September 26, 1961, the estate filed a claim for refund, which was partially settled when the IRS allowed a $14,084 reduction in estate taxes to offset the additional taxes due on decedent's lifetime income. The estate then brought the instant suit for refund, alleging three causes of action.

The first involved the executrix's claim that a refund of estate taxes was due because of the erroneous inclusion in gross estate of the fair market value of the decedent's 20 percent interest in the cooperative building. The second prayed for recovery of income taxes paid by the estate on the capital gains realized from the sale. The third cause of action asserted that under the doctrine of equitable recoupment, the estate should be permitted to recover estate taxes, notwithstanding the statute of limitations, on the ground that the IRS had collected a double tax—both estate tax and income tax—on the same sale transaction. In essence, therefore, the estate argued that once the IRS taxed the sale proceeds as income, it could not later tax the same property as part of the estate corpus.

On May 12, 1972, the district court, in the first reported decision in the case, denied the parties' cross-motions for summary judgment on the equitable recoupment claim. The court held that because a factual dispute existed concerning the IRS's method of computing the estate tax value of the 20 percent interest, summary judgment did not lie for either party. After a two-day trial, the case was decided in the second reported decision, with the court entering judgment on June 30, 1972, in favor of the IRS. The court found that the income that decedent had derived from the sale of the corporation's stock was predeath income, because the sale took place prior to the actual date of death and decedent had the unrestricted use of his share of the proceeds. Accordingly, the court determined that there were two taxable events: the sale of stock giving rise to capital gains for income tax purposes and the existence of such proceeds or a claim thereto as an asset of decedent's estate.

Held: On appeal, judgments below affirmed. The Second Circuit determined that the court below properly held that the doctrine of equitable recoupment, announced in the seminal case of Bull, 295 US 247 (1935), was inapposite as a means by which the estate could bypass the statute of limitations. (Neither court applied the mitigation of limitation provisions in Sections 1311 et seq., because they apply only to income taxes, not to estate taxes.) The theory of equitable recoupment is that one taxable event should not be taxed twice, once on a correct theory and again on an incorrect theory. In the present case, however, no such double tax effect existed, because the gain was properly taxed both as income and as corpus. There was no showing by the estate of inconsistent treatment of the item on the part of the IRS, and, in all respects, the 20 percent interest was treated correctly by the government.

[Minskoff, 490 F2d 1283, 33 AFTR2d 74-1442, 74-1 USTC ¶ 12,969 (2d Cir. 1974).]

Tax on undeclared dividends included in stock valuation is held subject to equitable recoupment. Decedent's wholly owned corporation held title to a block of 8 percent cumulative preferred stock in a newspaper. The stock, which had a par value of $128,000, carried with it some twenty years of dividend arrearages valued at approximately $210,000. For estate tax purposes, the executors valued the stock by adding the total of the dividend arrearages to the stock's par value. The distributees received the dividend arrearages over the next four years, and each year they declared the dividends on their income tax returns, but reported them as nontaxable dividends. After the expiration of the three-year statute of limitations for refund claims, the distributees received deficiency notices based on their exclusion of the dividends from their taxable income. The distributees paid the deficiencies and sued for a refund in federal district court, where summary judgment was granted for the IRS.

Held: Reversed for taxpayers. The court ruled that the dividend arrearages did not constitute income in respect of a decedent, because there was no "right to income" in decedent at the time of his death as required by Regulations §1.691(a)-(1)(b). The court pointed out that even assuming that the arrearage was a right to receive income, such right was in the decedent's wholly owned corporation, not in decedent personally. Equitable recoupment was held to apply because the IRS was in effect doubly taxing the same fund. The court concluded that it would be inequitable to permit the IRS to levy an income tax without granting a credit for the previously paid estate tax, regardless of the statute of limitations.

[Boyle, 355 F2d 233, 17 AFTR2d 21, 66-1 USTC ¶¶ 9145, 9225 (3d Cir. 1966).]

Statute of limitations does not bar refund. Taxpayer-administrator sued for a refund of estate taxes. The IRS conceded that it had overassessed the value of the estate but claimed that taxpayer had failed to file suit within the statute of limitations. Although the estate failed to sue within the limitations period, estate representatives had had ongoing communications with the IRS officer handling the case that led them to believe that the estate's claim was being reconsidered and that a refund would be granted consistent with the resolution of a related dispute.

Held: For taxpayer. The IRS is estopped from denying relief, on the ground that the statute of limitations had expired. Taxpayer's reliance on the understanding that it thought it had with the IRS was reasonable.

[Howard Bank, 759 F. Supp. 1073, 91-1 USTC ¶ 60,053, 66 AFTR2d 90-5985 (D. Vt. 1990), aff'd, 948 F2d 1275 (2d Cir. 1991).]

Claim for refund is barred by statute of limitations, even though facts giving rise to claim occurred four years after filing of return. Decedent died in 1977, leaving her estate to her son. A federal estate tax return was filed in 1978, and the tax shown thereon was paid. Shortly after the probate proceedings began, decedent's two brothers and brother-in-law contested the will. A settlement was reached in 1982, and the probate court declared the attorney fees incurred during the litigation to be deductible from the estate as administrative expenses. The estate filed a claim for refund in 1983. The IRS refused to take action on the claim and contended that the claim was barred by the statute of limitations. The estate argued that the limitations period did not begin to run until the event giving rise to the claim had occurred, that is, the 1982 probate court order declaring the attorney fees deductible from the gross estate.

Held: For the IRS. Under Section 6511(a), a claim for a refund must be filed within three years of the date on which the return was filed or within two years of payment of the tax, whichever is longer. The court held that because this was the only authority as to the events triggering the period of limitations, the estate's argument was therefore without merit.

[Swietlik, 56 AFTR2d 85-6520, 85-2 USTC ¶ 13,622 (ED Wis. 1985), aff'd, 779 F2d 1306, 57 AFTR2d 86-1497, 86-1 USTC ¶ 13,652 (7th Cir. 1985).]

IRS questionnaire started running of limitations period. When decedent died in 1980, her estate elected under Section 2032A to value property based on its qualified use as a farm. Taxpayer, decedent's daughter, inherited an interest in the property and immediately leased it to her brother, who was also an heir, under a cash rental arrangement. In 1987, the IRS sent a questionnaire to the estate that was designed to monitor qualifying uses of specially valued property. The estate returned the questionnaire on January 11, 1988, and disclosed the cash rental. Based on "additional information," the IRS prepared substitute Forms 706-A (U.S. Additional Estate Tax Return) to impose recapture tax against the heirs on the ground that there had been a cessation of qualified use. The returns (unsigned by taxpayer or other qualified heirs) were completed by the end of November 1989. It was not until June 6, 1991, however, that the IRS issued deficiency notices to the heirs. Section 2032A permits an estate to value property that a decedent or a family member used in farming or in a trade or business based on its agricultural or business use and not its highest and best use. This benefit is limited to a $750,000 reduction in the estate's value and applies only if:

1. Basically, at least 50 percent of the gross estate consists of qualified real or personal property, and the real property is at least 25 percent of the gross estate.
2. A decedent or a family member materially participated in a "qualified use" of the real property, that is, farming or a trade or business, on the date of death and for five out of the eight preceding years.
3. The real property is left to a "qualified heir," which includes a decedent's spouse and ancestors, and lineal descendants (and their spouses) of a decedent and a decedent's spouse and parents.

If specially valued property is disposed of or no longer used for a qualified use within ten years (fifteen years for decedents dying before 1982) after a decedent's death, Section 2032A(c) imposes a recapture tax. Under Section 2032A(f), the period for assessing recapture tax on specially valued property expires three years from the date that the IRS is notified of the disposition or disqualifying use as prescribed by regulations (which have not been issued). Taxpayer contended that the statute of limitations had expired because the IRS failed to issue deficiency notices within three years of being notified of the cessation of qualified use, as required under Section 2032A(f). In the absence of regulations, taxpayer claimed that the questionnaire constituted the required notice. The IRS argued that the limitations period had not expired, because (1) the questionnaire was not notice under 2032A(f); (2) the IRS did not determine the recapture tax based solely on the questionnaire; (3) the notices were timely because they were issued within three years of the IRS's notification to taxpayer that there was a cessation of qualified use; and (4) notification under Section 2032A(f) can be accomplished only by filing Form 706-A and paying the recapture tax.

Held: For taxpayer. The Tax Court cited Sections 1033(a) (nonrecognition of gain on involuntary conversion) and 1034 (deferral of gain on sale of a residence), which include notice requirements similar to Section 2032(f). The regulations under those sections require only that notification contain all details of the transaction and be filed with the district office where the return was filed. The questionnaire submitted by taxpayer satisfied these requirements. The court found it irrelevant that the IRS acquired additional information before issuing the deficiency notices, since almost all examinations to some degree corroborate information that the IRS has. The IRS's contention that the limitations period ran from the date that the IRS notified taxpayer of its position was also rejected. Section 2032A(f) requires notification *from* a taxpayer. Further, the absence of a return filing requirement to start the limitations period under Sections 1033 and 1034 rebutted the IRS's contention that only Form 706-A constituted required notice. Since the estate responded to the questionnaire on January 11, 1988, the limitations period expired on January 11, 1991, and the notices issued on June 6, 1991, were invalid. Taxpayer first argued that renting the land to a qualified heir was not a disqualifying use. The Tax Court rejected this argument based on Williamson, 70 AFTR2d 92-6244, 92-2 USTC ¶ 60,115 (9th Cir. 1992), aff'g 93 TC 242 (1989), in which the Ninth Circuit concluded that Section 2032A(c)(1)(B) requires qualified heirs to put the property to the qualified use. The court noted that Section 2032A(b)(5)(A) permits only *spouses*, not other heirs, to rent to family members for cash without causing a cessation of qualified use.

[Stovall, 101 TC 140 (1993).]

Transferee cannot be held liable for the transferor's estate tax if assessment expires and extinguishes transferor's liability before assets are transferred. The period of limitations on assessment of an additional estate tax against the estate had expired. At that time, there was neither an outstanding consent to extend the period nor an IRS notification of any proposed additional liability for estate tax. Four months later the estate distributed assets to taxpayer. Within one year from the expiration of the limitations period, the IRS executed a Reopening Memorandum and issued a Notice of Liability to the transferee-taxpayer.

Held: For taxpayer. The Tax Court held that Section 6901 does not create a separate liability for the transferee. Instead, it merely provides for a secondary method of enforcing the liability of the transferor. Thus, as long as the transferor's liability is extinguished before the assets are transferred under the will, the transferee cannot be liable for any additional tax. The court emphasized that this rationale does not apply where the assets are transferred before the period of limitations against the transferee expires. Thus, in such a case, under Section 6901(c), the IRS would have an additional year after the original limitations period expired to assess the taxes.

[Illinois Masonic Home, 93 TC 145 (1989).]

Notice of deficiency is timely where no request for prompt assessment is made. Decedent died in March 1984, and his personal representative gave notice to creditors as provided under local law, directing all persons having claims against the estate to present their claims within four months of the notice. The IRS filed no claims for income tax liability during the four-month period specified by the notice, and the estate made no written request for a prompt assessment of taxes pursuant to Section 6501(d). In December 1984, the assets were distributed in accordance with the order of the court, the estate was closed, and the personal representative discharged. It was later discovered that decedent had failed to report on his 1982 federal income tax return $75,847 in interest income. A notice of deficiency for decedent's 1982 income tax was therefore issued to his estate in October 1985. The estate contended that the notice of deficiency sent was not timely, because it was mailed after the final distribution of the estate was made and after the personal representative was discharged. The IRS argued that because no request under Section 6051(d) was made and the notice was mailed within three years of the date of decedent filing his 1982 income tax return (on April 15, 1983), the notice was timely and valid.

Held: For the IRS. The court stated that if an executor or personal representative of an estate can shorten the three-year period of limitations for assessment of a deficiency against the estate merely by distributing the assets of the estate and being discharged, there is no need for the provisions of Section 6501(d) shortening the period of limitations upon proper request of the executor or personal representative. The predecessor of Section 6501(d) was enacted to allow an executor to have the period shortened to enable a more expeditious distribution of the estate. The court noted that because Section 6501(d) provides a manner of shortening the period of limitations on assessment of a deficiency against an estate, the three-year period remained in effect because a proper request under the section was not made. Thus, the court concluded that the notice of deficiency was valid and timely.

[Estate of Walker, 90 TC 253 (1988).]

Surviving spouse does not receive decedent's shorter limitations period. Decedent and her husband had electronically filed their 1993 joint return on February 21, 1994. Decedent's husband died on February 12, 1995, leaving decedent as the sole heir and executrix of his estate. On March 24, 1995, decedent (as executrix) submitted a "Request for Prompt Assessment Under Internal Revenue Code Section 6501(d)" (Form 4810) with respect to her husband's 1992 through 1995 tax years. The IRS received the request on March 29, 1995, and on June 15, 1995, notified decedent that her husband's 1992 and 1993 tax returns had been accepted as filed. The husband's estate was closed in August 1995; decedent died on February 20, 1996. On February 21, 1996, the IRS mailed a notice proposing changes to the couple's 1993 joint return. The IRS then issued decedent and her husband a deficiency notice for their 1993 year on July 2, 1996. Decedent's executor responded by filing a Tax Court petition, claiming that the IRS was barred from making an assessment for the 1993 tax year by the limitations period and under the doctrine of equitable estoppel.

Held: For the IRS. Section 6501(a) provides the general rule that the IRS must assess any tax within three years after the date taxpayer files a return. Section 6501(d) provides an exception to this rule for assessments against deceased taxpayers. Under Section 6501(d), if an executor requests a prompt assessment against a decedent, the IRS generally has only eighteen months from the request date to make an assessment. The IRS argued that, because Section 6103(d)(3) provides that a husband and wife filing a joint return are jointly and severally liable for any resulting tax assessment, the IRS could proceed against decedent and her husband jointly or individually for the full assessment. The IRS's position was supported by Garfinkel, 67 TC 1028 (1977), which held that the normal three-year limitations period continued to apply against a surviving spouse, even though the eighteen-month period precluded the IRS from proceeding against the pre-deceased spouse. The court reasoned that, because the surviving spouse was severally liable for the joint deficiency, the IRS was entitled to the full three-year period to make an assessment against that spouse. Here the court agreed that the shortened eighteen-month limitations period applied only to the husband, not decedent. Moreover, the notice was timely under both the eighteen-month and the three-year periods. The court flatly rejected the executor's argument that *Garfinkel* did not apply because it was based on an "antiquated version of the tax code" (1954 Code) and "paternalistic thought." In fact, the 1954 version was no different than the current version of the applicable section. Further, the executor failed to prove that the IRS made a misrepresentation on which taxpayer relied to support an estoppel theory. The executor argued that the IRS's no-change letter misrepresented that the IRS accepted the 1993 return as filed, and that the letter was relied on by the attorney closing the husband's estate. The court found, however, that the IRS's no-change letter had no effect on the estate because taxpayer would have been liable as the estate's sole beneficiary. Thus, the IRS was not estopped or time-barred from making as assessment against decedent for the joint deficiency—for which she was severally liable.

[Estate of Severt, 75 TCM 1651, RIA TC Memo. ¶ 98,034 (1998).]

Executor liable though period extended by co-executor. Taxpayer was the attorney for an estate and served as co-executor along with the sole beneficiary. During 1978, estate assets the beneficiary had taken home to have appraised were burglarized. On June 4, 1979, the estate tax return was filed claiming a $38,000 theft loss. The IRS disallowed the loss on the theory that the assets had been distributed to the beneficiary prior to the theft. On July 24, 1981, the co-executors agreed to a $12,700 deficiency, which was assessed on December 7, 1981. Distributions were made to the beneficiary before the assessment and even after the assessment when she became needy. In 1987, taxpayer refused an IRS request to extend the six-year limitations period for collecting the deficiency, but in October the co-executor signed a tax collection waiver (Form 900) extending the period to December 31, 1993. Shortly before this period expired, the IRS sent taxpayer a notice of personal liability. Although the estate had paid almost the entire deficiency, it owed $31,000 in interest. The estate tax is a personal liability of the executor, under Section 2002, and if the payment of an estate's debts or distributions to beneficiaries leaves insufficient assets to pay the tax, the executor must make the IRS whole. Under Section 6901(c)(3), the tax can be assessed against the executor for up to one year after the liability arises, or the IRS can use the normal limitations period for assessing the underlying tax liability.

Taxpayer argued that the limitations period had expired because he and his co-executor had agreed to the original deficiency by executing Form 890 (Waiver of Restrictions on Assessment and Collection of Deficiency) on July 24, 1981, and under Section 6502, the IRS has only six years to collect the tax. When the co-executor agreed to extend the collection period on October 16, 1987, this was more than six years after the date of the Form 890. Unfortunately for taxpayer, the six-year collection period ran from the date of the assessment (i.e., the date the IRS recorded the tax liability), not the date of the waiver. Since the assessment was in December 1981, the co-executor's extension was timely. Because the taxpayer had refused to extend the collection period, he argued that he was not bound by the co-executor's unilateral extension, particularly since state (Virginia) law does not permit a personal representative to waive the protection of a limitations period.

Held: For the IRS (in part). The court pointed out that one co-executor could bind an estate to a federal tax liability regardless of state law requirements, according to Ewart, 85 TC 544 (1985), aff'd, 814 F2d 321, 59 AFTR2d 87-1248, 87-1 USTC ¶ 13,715 (6th Cir. 1987). Some of the payments to the beneficiary had been made when she was in difficult personal circumstances (she ended up comatose in a nursing home and the IRS made no effort to collect the tax from her), and taxpayer was trying to resolve the estate's tax situation. Nevertheless, this could not affect taxpayer's liability.

The court had to decide, in a case of first impression, whether taxpayer was also liable for interest accruing after the notice of personal liability was mailed to him. The Tax Court had held a transferee liable for interest accruing after transferee liability arose on unpaid estate tax, and that liability was not even limited to the value of the property received, in Baptiste, 100 TC 252 (1993), aff'd, 29 F3d 1533, 74 AFTR2d 94-7477, 94-2 USTC ¶ 60,178 (11th Cir. 1994), aff'd in part and rev'd in part 29, F3d 433, 74 AFTR2d 94-7455, 94-2 USTC ¶ 60,173 (8th Cir. 1994). Here, the court concluded that the *Baptiste* rationale should not be extended to taxpayer's situation so as to hold him liable for subsequent accruing interest, because unlike a transferee, he had received no benefit from the property that had been distributed.

[Singleton, 71 TCM 3127, RIA TC Memo. ¶ 96,249 (1996).]

Doctrine of equitable recoupment governs estate's adjustment for over-payment on estate tax return. An estate elected to pay in ten installments the federal estate tax on the qualifying part of a closely held business. Later the election was terminated, and payment of the outstanding tax was extended under Section 6161. On audit, the federal estate tax liability was corrected. The estate then claimed an estate tax deduction for its interest payments under Section 6161. The estate claimed income tax deductions for the interest payments but realized no tax benefit for them. The estate did not file a Section 642(g) waiver with the income tax returns. The limitations period for the income tax returns had expired.

In technical advice, the IRS determined the interest on unpaid federal estate tax that is deductible under Section 2053(a)(2) and the resulting net federal estate tax. The IRS stated that the doctrine of equitable recoupment applies to reduce the estate's overpayment on the federal estate tax return by the amount of deficiencies on the income tax return for which assessment is barred under the statute of limitations. The IRS explained how to do the computation.

[Tech. Adv. Mem. 8409005.]

[8] Estate Tax Liens

Eighth Circuit holds that estate tax lien is durational, not limitational. Section 6324(a)(1) imposes a special tax lien upon the gross estate of a decedent to ensure the payment of federal estate tax. The lien, which goes into effect automatically, applies to all the assets in the estate, except those allowed by a court to be used for the payment of debts, administration expenses, and other charges against the estate. The lien lasts for ten years from the date of death, unless the tax liability incurred is paid sooner. When decedent died on June 30, 1984, the special tax lien at issue was automatically imposed on his estate. On September 27, 1993, the government commenced a suit to foreclose the lien. The government's motion for summary judgment was denied by the district court on May 9, 1994. The court granted the appellees' motion for summary judgment and ordered the government not to levy execution pursuant to the divested lien. The court ruled that the properties in question were divested of the lien and that the appellees (a revocable trust and a corporation) held the property free and clear of any estate tax lien claimed by the government. The government did not file its notice of appeal until July 6, 1994, more than ten years after decedent's death. The appellees argued that the government's appeal was moot because the lien expired on June 30, 1994. The question before the court of appeals was whether the ten-year period of the lien was durational or limitational. If it was durational, the government had to enforce the lien within ten years. If the period was limitational, it would be sufficient for the government to have filed a complaint within ten years. If the government was successful in its complaint, it could then enforce the lien, even though the date of enforcement would be more that ten years after the date of death.

Held: For taxpayer. The Eighth Circuit held that the plain language of the statute states that the lien lasts for ten years, not that the government has ten years to file a complaint. Citing Cleavenger, 517 F2d 230 (7th Cir. 1975), the circuit court stated that the ordinary meaning is presumed to be the intended one unless such interpretation would defeat the purpose of the statute. The court also noted that durational liens are not uncommon; for example, a durational period is used in the case of a judgment lien. According to the court, there are some benefits that result from a durational scheme. The ten-year period is a bright line for a title examiner or purchaser of property. If more than ten years have passed since the date of death, these parties can presume that there will be no title problems due to the tax lien. On the other hand, whenever a transaction occurs within the ten-year period, a red flag will be automatically raised to check for a lien. The government contended that a durational period is detrimental because it rewards delay and encourages defendants to act slowly in reaching a resolution of the case. The Eighth Circuit believed that there are sufficient other safeguards to prevent this. All parties in district court have an obligation to expedite litigation, and they can face penalties if they do otherwise. Furthermore, a durational period creates incentives for the government to move the case along. The government also argued that a durational period encourages frivolous appeals. The court disagreed because a taxpayer filing a frivolous appeal may be subjecting himself to sanctions as well as the cost of the appeal. Additional reasons why a taxpayer would not unnecessarily delay resolution are the fact that interest accrues on the unpaid tax liability, and, until the liability is resolved, taxpayer cannot do anything with the property. The court chastised the government for arguing about delays when its own delays are what caused the instant case to be more protracted than it would have been under a durational period. The government waited nine years before filing its complaint, and the dispute over the lien was still going on more than ten years after the lien arose. If the lien period were found to be limitational, that would allow the government to wait until the last day of the tenth year before filing its claim and to litigate the claim for many years after the ten-year period had expired. The Eighth Circuit did not think that is what Congress intended with respect to this statute. The court concluded that "the statute places a reasonable burden on the government to prosecute its claim diligently before it expires." The government had conceded that it is unusual for a foreclosure under a Section 6324 lien not to be completed within ten years. Therefore, the court believed that ruling that the lien period is durational was not an unreasonable result. The court then held that the government's appeal was moot.

[Davis, 52 F3d 781, 75 AFTR2d 95-1817, 95-1 USTC ¶ 60,193 (8th Cir. 1995).]

Ten-year period of special estate tax lien is held to be limitational, not durational. Decedent died on July 27, 1977, leaving property to the taxpayer. The IRS thereafter assessed deficiencies against the estate for unpaid federal estate tax and interest. On May 22, 1987, the IRS instituted suit against the taxpayer to recover outstanding estate taxes allegedly owed by taxpayer as transferee of property belonging to decedent's estate. The IRS sought to foreclose the special estate tax lien imposed upon the property of decedent's estate pursuant to Section 6324(a)(1) and to obtain a judgment of personal liability against the taxpayer pursuant to Section 6324(a)(2). Section 6324(a)(1) provides, in part, that unless estate tax is paid in full, or becomes unenforceable by reason of a lapse of time, a lien results upon the gross estate of a decedent for ten years from the date of death. The taxpayer contended that the special estate tax lien created by Section 6324(a)(1) had lapsed and that its duration was not extended by the IRS filing suit within the ten-year period.

Held: For the IRS. The court stated that the durational rule urged by the taxpayer not only would discourage cooperation between the parties during litigation leading to amicable settlement of claims but also would encourage taxpayers to use any means at their disposal to hinder progress of their case. The court stated that this is not what Congress intended in enacting the ten-year provision in Section 6324(a)(1). Thus, the court found that the ten-year period set out in the statute is merely limitational. Accordingly, the Tax Court concluded that because the IRS instituted the action on May 22, 1987, within ten years of the death of decedent, its action was filed in a timely manner.

[Harrell, 61 AFTR2d 88-1328, 88-1 USTC ¶ 13,746 (MD Fla. 1987).]

Estate tax lien takes priority over alleged purchaser under Section 6324. Decedent died in 1975. By the terms of his will, decedent left his undivided, 50 percent interests in two large tracts of real estate in eastern Pennsylvania to his niece. The other joint owner (decedent's sister-in-law) challenged the will in probate court. The parties finally reached a settlement in 1978, in which the property was to be divided between them and a portion was to be sold. During the years following decedent's death, the value of the property fell sharply as the result of changed market conditions and the opening of a landfill dump on an adjacent parcel of land. Consequently, the parties were unable to dispose of the property for a price even approaching its date-of-death value of $304,000. During this time, both state and federal estate taxes remained unpaid, and during 1980 and 1981, both taxing authorities filed liens against the property. In defense of her interest, the sister-in-law opposed the IRS's foreclosure action by contending that she was the purchaser of the portion of the decedent's property that was conveyed to her in settlement of the will contest.

Held: Summary judgment for the IRS granted. The court found that federal estate tax liens attach to estate property at the time of the decedent's death pursuant to Section 6324. Even assuming that the sister-in-law was justified in asserting the status of a purchaser, the fact remained that the IRS's special estate tax lien arose prior to the settlement agreement, and therefore the IRS lien took priority over the sister-in-law's interest.

[Estate of Young, 592 F. Supp. 1478, 55 AFTR2d 85-1519, 84-2 USTC ¶ 13,594 (ED Pa. 1984).]

CHAPTER 13

Income Tax

¶ 13.01 INCOME IN RESPECT OF A DECEDENT

[1] Generally

Post-death deal could not transform estate into alimony trust. When a couple divorced in 1973, the ex-husband agreed to pay the ex-wife alimony. In October 1987, her estate filed a claim against his estate for $480,000 in unpaid alimony. To settle the claim, his estate established her estate as its sole beneficiary. In 1989, the ex-husband's estate had distributable net income (DNI) of $8,700 and a capital loss of $1,300, and it paid the ex-wife's estate $362,000. Her estate distributed the payment to its beneficiaries, and taxpayers (the couple's sons). Taxpayers, applying the DNI rules, reported only their share of the DNI (as passing from the ex-husband's estate to the ex-wife's estate and thereafter to them), reduced by the capital loss (that flowed through when the estates terminated). The IRS stated that the payment to the ex-wife's estate was income in respect of a decedent (IRD) and, therefore, it was not limited by the DNI (and the capital loss) of the ex-husband's estate as it would have been in the case of a distribution to a beneficiary. This increased the DNI of the ex-wife's estate, which passed to taxpayers. Section 71(a) includes alimony in income. Lump-sum payments of alimony arrearages remain alimony, according to Olster, 751 F2d 1168, 55 AFTR2d 85-919 (11th Cir. 1985), and other cases. Alimony that is collected by an estate is taxable to the estate (or its beneficiaries) as IRD under Section 691. Section 691 applies to income that a decedent had a right to receive but that was not reportable under his or her method of accounting prior to death. The IRD retains the character it would have had in the hands of a decedent when it is received by that decedent's estate or a beneficiary. Also, there is no step-up in basis, although Section 691(c) allows a deduction for any estate tax attributable to the IRD. Taxpayers contended that the ex-husband's estate became an alimony trust when it settled the claim. Under Section 682, an ex-wife is the beneficiary of an alimony trust established by her ex-husband, and this, according to taxpayers, brought the normal trust-beneficiary rules into play and limited the income of the ex-wife's estate to the DNI of the ex-husband's estate.

Held: For the IRS. The Tenth Circuit acknowledged that taxpayers' reading of Section 682 was reasonable (on the assumption that the pre-1984 version, which clearly made the payment alimony, did not apply to the post-1984 settlement). Nevertheless, the court sided with the IRS (without deciding whether taxpayer's interpretation of Section 682 was correct), since the ex-husband's estate could not be an alimony trust. Although the title of Section 682 mentions estates, its substantive provisions are limited to trusts. This is a logical conclusion, since Section 682 cannot operate as intended after the grantor dies. Thus, in excluding trust income from the income of an ex-husband who establishes an alimony trust and includes it in the ex-wife's income, Section

682 refers to income that otherwise would have been includable in the ex-husband's income under the grantor trust rules of Sections 671 through 678. These sections, however, do not apply after the grantor dies; therefore, they cannot apply to an estate. In addition, Section 682 is not intended to permit a post-death agreement to convert a decedent's alimony obligation into an alimony trust. Instead, the alimony remains fully taxable as IRD. Although the ex-wife's estate was required to include the payment in income, there was no corresponding tax benefit from a deduction. The ex-husband had not paid alimony, and his estate had insufficient income to use the deduction. Nevertheless, the ex-spouses were separate taxpayers. In addition, no matching benefit requirement existed.

[Kitch, 103 F3d 104, 79 AFTR2d 97-301, 97-1 USTC ¶ 50,124 (10th Cir. 1996).]

SCIN income at death taxed to decedent-obligee's estate. Decedent deferred more than $500,000 in gain from the sale of stock in his company to each of his four children, by taking in exchange self-cancelling installment notes (SCINs) payable over twenty years. Under the terms of the sale, each SCIN would be cancelled as if fully paid on the death of decedent prior to the final payment of principal and interest. The interest rate was above market to compensate decedent (age 53 at the sale) for assuming the risk that he would die before receiving full payment. He lived to receive only two installments on the notes. The IRS contended that the cancellation of the SCINs triggered the remaining deferred gain, which should be recognized by the estate, or, alternatively, by decedent on his final return. The IRS cited Sections 691 (IRD) and 453B (gain or loss on disposition of installment obligations). Section 453B(f) provides that when an installment obligation between certain related parties is cancelled, the obligee recognizes income to the extent of the difference between the obligee's basis in the note and its face value. Similarly, under Section 691, the cancellation of an installment note is a transfer, resulting in IRD equal to the face value of the note less its basis to decedent. Taxpayers argued that the cancellation did not generate income. They claimed that the "automatic cancellation" of the SCINs was not covered by the cancellation provisions in Sections 453B(f) and 691(a)(5). Those statutes were meant to prevent abuses that occur when a note is cancelled by an act subsequent to the contract, and were not meant to apply to a cancellation resulting from a term of the obligation itself. According to taxpayers, with a SCIN, the price the obligor pays depends on when the obligee dies. Thus, the obligor's basis in the acquired property is the amount paid on the note; since there is no step-up to the FMV at the date of death, no abuse occurs.

   Held: For the IRS. According to the court, even though these sections were meant as anti-abuse provisions, they nevertheless apply to SCINs. The court also noted that GCM 39503 (May 7, 1986), which concerns SCINs, concluded that the obligor's basis in the acquired property is the note's face value. The rationale of the GCM is that because the obligee is taxed on the property's appreciation under Section 453B, the obligor should benefit from a step-up in basis. Thus, the injustice presumed by taxpayers only occurs if the obligor and obligee are not treated consistently. Finally, the Eighth Circuit held that, under Section 691(a)(2), the estate is taxed on its transfer of the right to receive IRD. Under Section 691(a)(5)(A)(iii), cancellation of an installment obligation (i.e., the right to receive IRD) on the death of decedent is a transfer by decedent's estate. The Tax Court found the cancellation to be a "disposition" taxable to decedent under Section 453B, rather than a "transmission of installment obligations at death," which, according to Section 453B(c), is covered by Section 691. The Eighth Circuit rejected this reasoning as "nebulous," however. Instead, it applied the "unambiguous" language of Section 691(a)(5)(A)(iii), which states that cancellation on the obligee's death is a transfer by the estate, taxable under Section 691(a)(2).

[Frane, 998 F2d 567, 72 AFTR2d 93-5268, 93-2 USTC ¶ 50,386 (8th Cir. 1993).]

Crop-shares are IRD. During her lifetime, decedent owned two plots of land, which she leased for farming purposes. One lease entitled her to a share of "all crops grown" annually, and the other entitled her to a share of "the net proceeds of all crops grown." Payments for crops produced from both plots in the year of her death were received subsequently by her estate, and were included as part of the gross estate in its federal estate tax return. The IRS argued that each form of rent constituted income in respect of a decedent (IRD).

    Held: For the IRS. The rents, both in cash and in crops, were properly taxed to the estate as IRD. The court noted that the predecessor of current Section 691 does not define precisely the term "income in respect of a decedent." Among the factors that it considered were that the rents arose directly from economic activities that occurred prior to decedent's death and were not attributable in any way to acts performed by the estate or to unrealized passive appreciation of property owned at the time of death. In addition, the rents were fully accruable to decedent on the date of her death, and would have been income to decedent had she lived to receive them. Based on these facts and others, the court deemed the rents to be IRD. The court found the cash rents to be indistinguishable from any other kind of cash rent that might have arisen. Regarding the crop rents, the court ruled that they were taxable only when finally sold for the account of the estate.

[Davison Estate, 292 F2d 937, 155 Ct. Cl. 937, 8 AFTR2d 5,178, 61-2 USTC ¶ 9584 (Ct. Cl.), cert. denied, 368 US 939 (1961).]

Heir's claim of right relief does not extend to decedent's tax overpayment. Decedent and her aunts engaged in oil and gas leases with a large oil company in the 1970s from which they derived royalties. Decedent reported her royalty income and paid taxes on it from 1975–1980. Subsequently, after a court found that the company had been overcharging for the oil, the company sued the leaseholders to recoup the overpaid royalties. The company sued decedent individually in 1988, and as executrix of the estates of her aunts—who had pre-deceased her and left her their interests in the leased property. Decedent died in 1990, and the estate settled the company's claims in 1992 for $681,840. The settlement covered the company's claims for the excess royalties paid to both decedent and her aunts. Based on earlier litigation, taxpayer and the IRS agreed that Section 1341(a)(5) entitled taxpayer to an income tax overpayment with respect to the years (1975–1980) decedent reported and paid tax on the repaid royalties. The issue in the instant case focused on the appropriate method to compute the overpayment. Section 1341 provides relief for taxpayers who are forced to repay amounts they previously included in income under a claim of right (i.e., items a taxpayer appeared to have an unrestricted right to, but was required to later restore). Instead of taking a deduction, a taxpayer may reduce the repayment year's tax under Section 1341(a)(5), based on the tax that would have been paid in the earlier years if the amount received under the claim of right had not been included in income. Under Section 1341(b), to the extent the reduction exceeds taxpayer's repayment year tax liability, the excess is a creditable or refundable overpayment. In the instant case, the estate filed a 1992 income tax return reporting $8,338 in tax, which the estate computed without deductions for the settlement payment. Taxpayer argued that, because the settlement was a claim against the estate, decedent's 1975–1980 royalty income should be recomputed using the entire $681,840. The IRS countered that the estate could use only the portion representing the excess royalties decedent reported and paid tax on, not the amounts attributable to her aunts.

Held: For the IRS. The court found that the statute clearly restricts its relief to a taxpayer's previously reported income items that taxpayer is later found not to have an unrestricted right to, and is required to repay. In the instant case, decedent did not receive or pay tax on any of the royalties paid to her aunts in 1975–1980. Based on the statute's plain language, therefore, the estate, standing in the shoes of decedent, could not use the repayment of the aunts' royalties to its benefit. Consequently, only that portion of the settlement representing the royalties decedent personally received and reported was taken into account in computing her Section 1341 relief. Contrary to the IRS's attempt to further restrict taxpayer's relief, however, taxpayer's overpayment was not limited under Section 1341(b). The court pointed out that the statute contained no qualification on the final overpayment computation, but simply allowed the portion of the prior years' decreased tax liability that was not used in recomputing taxpayer's 1992 tax to also be considered an overpayment. Thus, Section 1341 did limit the amount of relief, but did not limit the final overpayment.

[Estate of Smith, 110 TC 12 (1998).]

IRD is not includable in distributee's income. Taxpayer's husband's will provided that his residuary estate be established in trust for her benefit. Rentals owed to the husband, which were accrued but unpaid at the date of death, were included as an asset of his estate. The husband reported his income on the cash basis.

Held: For the estate. The rentals, when collected, although includable in the trust's gross income as IRD, were not includable in taxpayer's gross income, because their distribution to taxpayer was not a taxable distribution. The court followed its earlier decision in Huesman, 16 TC 656, aff'd, 198 F2d 133, 42 AFTR 320, 52-2 USTC ¶ 9395 (9th Cir. 1952). The Code makes no provision for taxing IRD to anyone but the recipient (here, the trust itself). The court also ruled that $5,000 withheld from distribution by the trustees as a "reserve for repairs" and $2,000 withheld as a "reserve for trustees' commissions" as determined by a state court were properly withheld as being unavailable to taxpayer, and consequently these amounts were not distributable income to be included in her income.

[Estate of Carruth, 28 TC 871 (1957), acq., 1957-2 CB 4.]

Section 691 overrides distribution rules, according to Tax Court. At the time of his death, decedent held a promissory note securing payment for the sale of cattle. The note was payable in eight equal installments, with annual interest of 7 percent on the unpaid balance. Pursuant to the terms of the will, his estate succeeded to the right to receive payments on the note. At the time of distribution to the beneficiaries, there was a balance due on the note of $198,908. The estate distributed to decedent's beneficiaries the right to receive the installment payments on the promissory note, which represented to the beneficiaries the right to receive IRD pursuant to Section 691. The estate claimed that it was entitled to a distribution deduction pursuant to Sections 661 and 662, but the IRS disallowed the deduction.

Held: For the IRS. Although Sections 661 and 662 generally govern distributions, a deduction is provided to an estate for distributions to beneficiaries under Section 661, and Section 662 requires beneficiaries to include such distributions in gross income. Section 691, however, provides special rules for income to which a decedent had a right or entitlement at or prior to death, but that was not included in gross income. Such income is designated "income in respect of a decedent." Generally, Section 691 requires such income to be reported by the person receiving the income when it is actually received, regardless of whether the recipient is an estate or an individual. When the right to receive such income is distributed by an estate, the distribution rules of Sections 661 and 662 conflict with the provisions of Section 691, because Section 691 property receives no step-up in basis under these circumstances, unlike most property acquired from a decedent. If allowed a deduction for the distribution of Section 691 property, the estate would escape income tax on the amount of the distribution. Given the well-suited principle that a specific statute controls a general one, the Tax Court held that Section 691 overrules Sections 661 and 662 under these circumstances, and it disallowed the distribution deduction.

[Estate of Dean, TC Memo. (P-H) ¶ 83,276, 46 TCM (CCH) 184 (1983).]

[2] Wages, Fees, and Commissions

Postmortem executive bonus is held to be IRD under Section 691. Decedent was an executive in a large corporation at the time of his death in 1969. For several years prior to 1969, he participated in the company's bonus plan under which executive officers were awarded annual bonuses. The amount of the bonus was determined each January for the previous year. On March 2, 1970, three months after the date of death, the company awarded decedent a postmortem bonus consisting of 1,786 shares of stock and $285,763 in cash. In accordance with company policy, the bonus was paid in annual installments beginning in 1973. Some ten years prior to his death, decedent established a revocable trust, with a residuary pour-over provision in his will. In accordance with this scheme, the right to receive future installment payments was transferred from the estate to the trust, and, as each installment became due, the company made payments directly to the trustee as decedent's designated beneficiary. The trust reported the bonus payments in income for the years 1970 through 1973 and valued them as of the time of distribution. When the payments were made during 1973, 1974, and 1975, the estate reported only the difference between the amount earlier included in income and the actual amount of the distribution. The estate claimed a corresponding deduction under Section 661(a)(2) equal to the FMV of each bonus distribution received by the trustee. On audit, the IRS claimed that each bonus constituted IRD within the meaning of Section 691 and that each bonus installment received was includable in the trust's gross income for the year of actual payment. The Tax Court held that although decedent had no legal right to receive the payments on the date of death, he nevertheless possessed a "right" to the bonus under Section 691, because it was substantially certain that he would receive the bonus. Consequently, the Tax Court ruled that the bonus payments constituted IRD as argued by the IRS.

Held: Affirmed for the IRS. In general, Section 691(a)(1) provides that all IRD not includable in decedent's last return or in a prior return must be included in the taxable income of the estate, of a person entitled to receive the amount directly from decedent, or of a person entitled to receive the amount as an estate beneficiary. In Regulation § 1.691(a)-1(b), "income in respect of a decedent" (IRD) is defined as including amounts to which a decedent was entitled as gross income but that were not properly includable in computing his taxable income for the year ending on the date of death. The court noted that IRD includes three categories of income: (1) all accrued items of a cash-basis decedent; (2) income accrued solely by reason of decedent's death in the case of an accrual-method decedent; and (3) income to which decedent had a contingent claim at the time of death. The key test, in the court's view, for determining whether decedent had a "right" or was "entitled" to the postmortem bonus should be based on the likelihood that at the time of death, he would have received the bonus, regardless of whether he had a legal right to do so. Thus, where decedent provided services for which he had a reasonable and substantial expectation of being rewarded, any bonus awarded subsequent to his death for such prior services constitutes IRD. The court noted that the company had consistently awarded bonuses to executives and that it had made a tentative decision to make the award prior to the date of death. Accordingly, the court affirmed the ruling of the Tax Court, finding that the bonus payments were Section 691 IRD.

[Rollert Residuary Trust, 752 F2d 1128, 55 AFTR2d 85-685, 85-1 USTC ¶ 13,603 (6th Cir. 1985).]

Decedent's right to income does not have to be legally enforceable to constitute IRD under Section 691. Decedent was the proprietor of an insurance agency that sold insurance primarily for one insurance company. Under the terms of the compensation contract into which decedent had entered with this company, decedent was entitled to receive commissions on all initial insurance policy premiums and on all renewal premiums. Although there was no provision in this contract for making postdeath payments, the company had a long-standing policy of making postdeath payments to the beneficiaries named by deceased agents. This policy was embodied in a corporate resolution that authorized the company to pay a 5 percent commission on renewal premiums in effect at an agent's death to a named beneficiary over a period of three years. When decedent died, the insurance company assumed control of his agency and purchased all of the fixtures and furniture of the agency for a lump sum. In addition, the executors of decedent's estate agreed to release the insurance company from all claims and to transfer all rights to decedent's insurance business. In return, the insurance company agreed to pay benefits to the estate under its policy, which provided for 5 percent commissions on renewal premiums for three years. The IRS determined that the commissions paid by the company under its benefits policy constituted IRD under Section 691. The estate contended that the commissions were the proceeds from the sale of decedent's agency business. The district court found that the commissions were not IRD under Section 691, because decedent had no legally enforceable right to receive them under the terms of his compensation contract with the company. Accordingly, the district court held that the commissions were to be treated as the proceeds from the sale of decedent's agency.

Held: Reversed for the IRS. The district court erred in its determination that a right to income must be a legally enforceable right in order for the income to constitute IRD. If this were the case, parties could simply circumvent the provisions of Section 691 by failing to provide for compensation for a decedent's services in a binding contract. Thus, for purposes of Section 691, a right to income exists not only when there is a legally enforceable right but also when there is a substantial certainty that benefits directly related to decedent's past economic activity will be paid to his heirs or to his estate upon his death. Here decedent had a sufficiently certain right to receive the 5 percent commissions on the renewal premiums under the company's long-standing policy of paying such benefits. This policy, which was embodied in the resolutions adopted by the company, together with the company's practice of paying such benefits, even absent a contractual obligation to do so, compels the conclusion that decedent had a right to the renewal commissions. Accordingly, the commissions constituted IRD under Section 691.

[Halliday, 655 F2d 68, 48 AFTR2d 81-5819, 81-2 USTC ¶ 9652 (5th Cir. 1981).]

Redemption price for stock included taxable fee. Decedent owned 71.43 percent of an incorporated law firm that specialized in personal injury and products liability law. In 1973, the shareholders executed a shareholder agreement that obligated the firm to purchase a deceased shareholder's stock for the sum of the following amounts: (1) the shareholder's purchase price for the stock; (2) a share of the earned but unpaid corporate profits or dividends; (3) any earned but unpaid salary of the deceased shareholder; (4) unreimbursed expenses incurred or loans made by the shareholder; (5) 25 percent of the firm's net receipts after the shareholder's death for cases decedent brought to the firm; (6) 10 percent of the net receipts on other cases pending when the shareholder died; (7) 25 percent of the net receipts during the three years after the shareholder's death from business clients that the deceased brought to the firm; and (8) 50 percent of the proceeds of life insurance bought by the firm on decedent's life, to apply to the amounts listed in the above seven items.

In 1988, the shareholders amended the agreement. The amendment affected only decedent's shares. In order to ensure that decedent's widow would be provided with sufficient funds to maintain her lifestyle and to ease the firm's survival without him, the amended agreement provided that the firm would purchase $5 million in insurance on decedent's life. The death benefit was to be the value of his stock and any claims on his behalf for cases or work in process. Decedent died a few months after the agreement was amended. The firm collected on the insurance policies and paid the proceeds to the estate. The firm filed a Form 1099-MISC reporting payment of about $4 million to decedent's estate for nonemployee compensation. The estate then filed a Form 1041, Fiduciary Income Tax Return, that did not include the insurance proceeds in its taxable income; it attached a statement with the return that characterized the insurance proceeds as consideration for decedent's stock in the law firm. The IRS, however, determined that $4 million of the payment was for compensation, and only about $1 million was for the purchase price of the stock. Therefore, the IRS assessed a deficiency of over $1 million. The estate contended that the 1988 agreement fixed the redemption price of the stock at $5 million.

Held: For the IRS. The court pointed out that the agreement stated that the insurance payment was for both decedent's stock and claims for cases or work in process. The estate also argued that the insurance proceeds were a non-operating asset of the firm and should be included in valuing the firm's stock. The court disagreed, however, and stated that the insurance proceeds did not affect the value of decedent's stock, because they were paid entirely to decedent's estate. The court distinguished these facts from cases in which a corporation kept part of the insurance proceeds as working capital; in that event, the proceeds would affect the value of the stock. In valuing the stock, the IRS expert multiplied decedent's percentage ownership in the firm by the sum of the firm's retained earnings and undistributed earnings (net of taxes). He then added decedent's purchase price for his shares and applied a control premium. This computed to an amount greater than the stock purchase price would have been under the 1973 agreement. Finally, to the extent the payments were not for decedent's stock, they were IRD under Section 691 and, as such, taxable when received. Furthermore, Section 1014(c) provides that such payments are not eligible for the step-up in basis that inherited property generally receives under Section 1014.

[Estate of Cartwright, 71 TCM 3200, RIA TC Memo. ¶ 96,286 (1996).]

Bonus awarded after death is not included in gross estate. A corporation had a bonus incentive plan under which an employee was eligible for a bonus based on salary. The bonus was awarded and paid in installments, provided that the individual was still employed. If the employee were to die, the amounts would be paid to his legal representative at the same times and in the same amounts as if the employee were alive. At the date of death, a deceased employee was awarded bonuses, parts of which were still unpaid. In addition, six months after decedent's death, the employer awarded decedent an additional bonus based on services rendered during the year of his death.

The IRS ruled that the predeath award should be taxed to the estate as IRD, because, although conditional, it became a fixed right at death. The postdeath award would receive exactly the same income tax treatment, because it was based upon compensation for services. Only the predeath award was includable in the gross estate, however, because rights under the postdeath award did not arise until after death.

[Rev. Rul. 65-217, 1965-2 CB 214.]

[3] Retirement and Death Benefits

Tax effects of lump-sum distribution of IRA to nonspouse beneficiary. The IRA of decedent, *A*, was distributed in a lump sum to his child, *B*, the designated beneficiary. *A* made nondeductible contributions to the IRA, and the IRA held assets that had appreciated.

The IRS ruled that the amount of the distribution equal to the balance in the IRA at *A*'s death, less nondeductible contributions, was IRD and was includable in *B*'s income in the year he received the distribution. The rest of the distribution, which represented appreciation and income accruing between the date of death and the date of distribution, was not IRD but was taxable income to *B* pursuant to Sections 408(d) and 72. For the year in which IRD was included in *B*'s income, *B* was allowed a deduction for the estate tax attributable to that IRD.

[Rev. Rul. 92-47, 1992-1 CB 198.]

IRS rules that survivor benefits are IRD. A contract between an employer-corporation and an employee provided that if, upon retirement, the employee rendered services as requested by the employer, the employee would then be paid a specified sum for life each year thereafter. In addition, the contract provided that upon the employee's death, before or after his retirement, his widow would receive one half the amount payable to her husband as long as she lived, except for termination in the event of remarriage. Under the terms of the contract, the employee was not required to contribute any amounts, and the employer was obligated to make only the payments as agreed. The husband's rights under the contract were not nonforfeitable. The husband died on January 1, 1972, while actively employed. Upon his death, the widow became the primary annuitant. She received her first payment on January 5, 1972. The IRS was asked to rule on whether survivor benefit payments received by the widow pursuant to the terms of the employment contract were includable in her gross income as income IRD under Section 691(a).

The IRS ruled that the payments to the widow arose from a specific provision in the employment contract. The widow acquired her right to the payments by reason of her husband's death and did nothing to earn these payments. Decedent rendered the services that gave rise to the payments for his services. Therefore, the payments received by the widow were IRD.

[Rev. Rul. 73-327, 1973-2 CB 214.]

Surviving spouse has IRD upon receipt of income element in vested community interest. In the year following his wife's death, taxpayer received a lump-sum cash distribution payable to him as a retiree from an exempt employee's trust to which he had made contributions. Because the entire amount received was vested in the husband at the time of the wife's death, it was community property in which the wife had a one-half interest.

The IRS ruled that the part of the property that represented the surviving spouse's one-half share of community property should be considered to have been acquired from decedent under Section 1014(b)(6). The one-half share of community property that was includable in the estate of decedent should be considered to have been acquired from decedent under Section 1014(b)(1). Under Section 1014(a), the basis of property in the hands of the person acquiring the property from decedent is its FMV at the date of death or applicable valuation date. The income element embodied in a vested community interest in an employee's trust passes to the surviving spouse as a right to IRD and, as such, acquires no basis under Section 1014(a).

[Rev. Rul. 68-506, 1968-2 CB 332.]

[4] Interest Income

Unearned discount included in face amount of mortgage notes is not IRD where notes are valued at date-of-death FMV. Before his death in 1958, decedent was in the business of lending money on notes secured by real estate mortgages. In a typical transaction, he would loan, as the mortgagee, $8,000 in return for a note in the amount of $10,000 plus interest, payable over four years. As he received payments on account, he allocated 80 percent to principal and 20 percent to discount, reporting the latter as income in the year paid. At the time of his death, the mortgage was entering its third year, so that decedent was paid $4,000 of the face amount, $800 (20 percent) of which was allocated to discount income and $3,200 (80 percent) of which was allocated to principal. At that time, the total discount income accrued was $1,000, leaving $200 of discount earned but unpaid. On its federal estate tax return, the estate valued the note at the balance due of $6,000, less 7 percent to reflect the high rate of interest. Thereafter the note was paid in full to the estate, which reported $1,200 attributable to discount and taxable as Section 691 IRD. In due course, however, the estate sought a refund, claiming that only the $200 of discount earned but unpaid at the date of decedent's death constituted IRD. In the estate's view, the notes were properly included in gross estate at their FMV, but the estate argued that taxable IRD constituted only the difference between the amounts received and FMV. The district court found for the IRS in a ruling that concluded that all payments attributable to discount, earned or unearned, constituted IRD.

Held: Reversed for the estate. IRD includes payments attributable to decedent's lifetime activities, even though decedent may not have the right to demand payment before the date of death. However, IRD does not include payments "in the nature of return" after death or property passing to the estate, such as rents, royalties, or interest on a coupon bond. The unearned discount in the present case was within the latter class, ruled the court, whereas the earned discount of $200 clearly fell within the former. The court further concluded that the basis of the property in the hands of decedent's transferee was its FMV on the date of death, not the increment subsequently realized on its disposition or satisfaction.

[Levin, 373 F2d 434, 19 AFTR2d 573, 67-1 USTC ¶ 9196, reh'g denied, 373 F2d 439, 19 AFTR2d 831, 67-1 USTC ¶ 9272 (1st Cir. 1967).]

Estate is not permitted to revoke election under Section 454(a). When decedent died in 1984, she owned Series E savings bonds. Her estate elected under Section 454(a) to include in her 1984 gross income the increase in redemption value of the savings bonds for that year. Decedent may have reported the interest income on the bonds annually, upon disposition, or at maturity, rather than by election under Section 454(a). Her estate nevertheless made the election (that resulted in a heavier tax burden on the estate) to benefit strangers to the estate who were erroneously believed to be joint owners of the bonds and who previously agreed to reimburse the estate for the added taxes. Upon discovering that the strangers to the estate were not in fact joint owners of the bonds, the estate requested permission to revoke the election and requested a refund of the added taxes. The IRS denied the request. In this refund action, the estate argued that it was entitled to revoke the election, because it was made in good faith reliance upon a material mistake of fact.

Held: For the IRS. The court stated that an election under Section 454(a) may not be retroactively revoked, even when made in a good faith reliance on a material mistake of fact. The court added that the estate could not avail itself of the rule even if the contrary were true, because no amendment was sought to correct a factual mistake and because the bona fides of the estate in electing a method of reporting bond income that resulted in a heavier tax burden on the estate was questionable in any event. Accordingly, the IRS's denial of the change of election request and refund was proper.

[West, 701 F. Supp. 695, 89-2 USTC ¶ 9409, 63 AFTR2d 89-1374 (WD Ark. 1988).]

Surviving co-owner of Series E bonds is taxable under Section 691 on all bond interest accruing prior to co-owner's death. Taxpayer's mother purchased several Series E U.S. Savings Bonds and placed them in her and tax-payer's names as co-owners. During her lifetime, taxpayer's mother did not report interest accrued on the bonds, nor, because of her minimal income, did she file any tax returns. Upon his mother's death, taxpayer acquired complete ownership of the bonds. The estate did not file an income tax return reflecting any interest income accruing prior to taxpayer's mother's death. Taxpayer re-deemed the bonds, receiving amounts that included all of the accrued interest. Taxpayer did not report this interest on his return. The IRS determined that the accrued interest was taxable to taxpayer as IRD under Section 691.

Held: For the IRS. Under Section 454, interest accruing on Series E bonds is not taxable before redemption, unless the holder elects otherwise. Be-cause taxpayer's mother never made this election, she was not taxable on the accrued interest. Accordingly, under Section 691(a)(1), taxpayer must report as income the interest that accrued on the bonds prior to his mother's death.

[Apkin, 86 TC 692 (1986).]

[5] Proceeds of Sale

Proceeds from sale are not IRD where decedent's estate performs substan-tive acts under sales contract. Decedent was in the cattle raising and selling business. Approximately four months prior to his death decedent entered into a livestock sales contract, which provided that decedent was to raise 3,300 calves and sell them to the purchaser. The terms of the contract further pro-vided that decedent was to designate the dates of delivery upon five days' no-tice, except that one group of calves was to be delivered no later than November 1, and the other group was to be delivered no later than December 15. In addition, the calves were to be from three to eleven months old and were to be in merchantable condition. The purchaser advanced the sales price to decedent, and the risk of loss was on decedent until delivery. Decedent died on November 9, without having delivered any calves or having designated any delivery dates. Following his death, decedent's estate assumed responsibility for the calves, and in December, the estate delivered 2,929 calves to the pur-chaser. On its fiduciary return, decedent's estate reported as gain from the sale of the calves the difference between the FMV of the calves on the date of de-cedent's death and the sales proceeds. The IRS determined that the gain from the sale of the calves constituted IRD. Accordingly, the IRS recomputed the gain by subtracting decedent's adjusted basis in the calves from the sale pro-ceeds. The Tax Court applied the following four-factor test to determine whether the sale proceeds constituted IRD:

1. Whether decedent entered into a legally significant arrangement re-garding the subject matter of the sale.

2. Whether decedent performed the substantive acts required as preconditions to the sale.
3. Whether material economic contingencies existed at the time of decedent's death that might have disrupted the sale.
4. Whether decedent would ultimately have received the sale proceeds if he had lived.

The Tax Court found that the livestock sales contract was a legally significant arrangement, that there were no material economic contingencies existing at the time of decedent's death, and that if decedent had lived, he would have received the sale proceeds. However, based upon its finding that decedent had not performed the substantive acts required under the contract, since on the date of his death not all of the calves were in deliverable condition, the Tax Court held that the sale proceeds were not IRD. On appeal, the IRS argued that the Tax Court had improperly applied the test that it had adopted and that under a proper application of that test, the portion of the sale proceeds that was allocable to calves in deliverable condition on the date of decedent's death constituted IRD.

Held: Affirmed to the estate. Under Section 691, in determining whether income is IRD, the focus is upon decedent's right or entitlement to the income as of the date of decedent's death. Under a contract of sale, decedent ordinarily does not have a right to the sale proceeds unless he has performed the substantive acts required by the contract prior to his death. In the instant case, delivering the calves and feeding and caring for them prior to delivery were substantive acts required by the contract. In fact, until the calves were actually delivered, decedent bore the risk of loss. The estate performed the substantive acts required by the contract when it fed and cared for the calves and delivered them to the purchaser. In essence, the estate's performance was performance of the contract. In arguing that a portion of the sale proceeds was IRD, the IRS incorrectly emphasized that some of the calves were in deliverable condition on the date of decedent's death. It is the status of the contract itself, not the status of the subject matter of the contract (calves), to which one must look in determining whether substantive acts have been performed under the contract and whether decedent would have been entitled to the proceeds (or portion thereof) on the date of death. Here it was not until after decedent's death that the right to the sale proceeds arose. Accordingly, the sale proceeds were not IRD, and the estate was therefore entitled to a stepped-up basis in computing the gain from the sale.

[Estate of Peterson, 667 F2d 675, 49 AFTR2d 82-424, 82-1 USTC ¶ 9110 (8th Cir. 1981).]

Sixth Circuit finds IRD where, at time of death, decedent was entitled to specific performance of purchase agreement on tender of deed. At the time of her death in 1967, decedent was the owner of a 256-acre farm in Kentucky.

During 1966, she executed a contract with a real estate agent by which she conveyed the right to purchase the farm for $4,000 per acre. The intended buyer was the Ford Motor Company, which was planning the construction of a large truck assembly plant in the area. In addition to creating the option, the contract empowered decedent to accept partial payment of the purchase price in the form of other farm or investment property that Ford's agent agreed to help her find. There was also a liquidated damages provision that was intended to protect the agent in the event that Ford's plans changed after exercising the option. The contract extended over a period of six months, and within that time, Ford's agent exercised its option, and Ford set about immediately to prepare the site for construction. In the meantime, the agent located and acquired suitable replacement property, but decedent died before she could take possession. Consequently, the property, plus a cash payment, were transferred to the estate.

On its fiduciary income tax return, the estate excluded all gain realized from the sale of decedent's farm. The IRS, however, insisted that the replacement property and cash represented IRD under Section 691, and, accordingly, it assessed a deficiency. At issue in the district court was the interpretation of Regulation § 1.691(a)-1(b), that defines IRD as "those amounts to which a decedent was entitled as gross income but which were not property includable in computing his taxable income for the taxable year ending with the date of his death." The IRS argued that decedent became entitled to the purchase price on the date when the option was exercised. The district court held for the estate, finding that though all contract conditions precedent had occurred as of the date of death, there was still the possibility of a default and settlement under the liquidated damages provisions of the contract. The parties foresaw the possibility that Ford would choose not to make the final purchase after its agent had exercised the option; therefore, the liquidated damages provision was inserted to protect the agent from liability. Because of this conceivable eventuality, the court determined that decedent was not necessarily entitled to the proceeds of sale on the date of death.

Held: Vacated and remanded for the IRS. The Sixth Circuit found that as of the time of her death, decedent was entitled under state law to specific performance of the contract merely by tendering her deed; therefore, this right to demand payment caused the replacement property and cash to be regarded as IRD. In reaching this conclusion, the appellate court panel considered the enforceability of the contract as an aspect of entitlement to payment of purposes of applying the rule set forth in Regulation § 1.691(a)-1(b). The court's adoption of this view resulted from its rejection of the IRS's "economic activities" test, which would greatly expand the scope of Section 691.

[Claiborne, 648 F2d 448, 47 AFTR2d 81-1369, 81-1 USTC ¶ 9365 (6th Cir. 1981), reh'g denied (1981).]

Sale of realty completed after death did not constitute IRD. Decedent entered into a contract for the sale of real property owned by him, but the sale was not completed until after his death. The contract —entered into on April 8, 1985—contained a number of provisions, among which was a requirement that the seller comply with all notices of violations of law or municipal ordinance, including housing, building, fire, health, and labor conditions. Prior to the completion of the sale, it was discovered that there were a number of housing department violations with respect to this property. A re-inspection of the property was undertaken. At the time of decedent's death on June 2, 1985, however, one violation remained uncorrected. As a result, decedent's attorney entered into negotiations with the purchaser's attorney, resulting in the purchaser agreeing to take title to the property subject to the one remaining housing violation in return for a $2,250 reduction in the purchase price. The closing of the sale occurred on July 30, 1985, approximately two months after decedent's death. The IRS concluded that the gain on the sale of the property was IRD because the contract had been entered into prior to decedent's death. Section 691(a) provides that IRD that is not properly includable in any taxable year of decedent must be included in the recipient's gross income if the recipient acquires from decedent the right to receive that amount. Although the Code does not define the term "income in respect of a decedent," Section 691(a)(1) clearly states that a right to receive the amount must have been acquired from decedent in order for the amount to be IRD. Taxpayer argued that decedent's contract with the buyer was subject to a number of conditions that were not satisfied at the time of decedent's death, and such unfulfilled conditions prevented treatment of the income as IRD under Section 691.

Held: For the estate. The Tax Court noted that decedent must acquire a *right* to receive the income in order for IRD to be created. In contrast, if the estate acquires a mere expectancy from decedent, any amount received pursuant to that expectancy does not constitute IRD. In order for an amount to be IRD, decedent must have entered into a legally significant arrangement (such as a contract), and decedent must have performed the substantive nonministerial acts required of him as preconditions for the sale. The IRS had previously ruled that gain on a sale of a residence is IRD where decedent signed a sales contract, accepted a down payment, and then died before closing the sale. IRD was created because decedent left only ministerial obligations to be performed by his executor. In the instant case, the contract of sale required the removal of all the municipal violations that had not been complied with at the time of decedent's death. Accordingly, to close the sale, decedent's attorney was required to undertake negotiations resulting in a reduction of the purchase price. The court noted that although this was not a large reduction in price, the nature of the acts that were required to be undertaken was more significant than the dollar amount. Therefore, the court ruled for taxpayer.

[Estate of Napolitano, 63 TCM 3092, RIA TC Memo. ¶ 92,316 (1992).]

[6] Royalty Payments

IRS rules on Section 691 taxation of royalty payments. Decedent, an inventor, entered into nonexclusive licensing agreements with various corporations in 1957 covering the manufacture and sale of articles under a patent that he owned. In consideration thereof, the corporations agreed to pay taxpayer specified royalties upon the sale of the articles. Decedent died in 1958. Under the terms of his will, the patent and licensing agreements were devised to a trust. Under the terms of the trust indenture, the trustee, who was also the executor of decedent's estate, was empowered to do all acts necessary for the proper control and management of the trust property, including the power to collect the royalty payments due or accrued under the licensing agreements at or after decedent's death and to pay such income in regular installments to decedent's widow. Advice was sought as to the applicability of Section 691 to the post-mortem royalty payments.

The IRS concluded that the royalty payments due and accrued at the date of the inventor's death, which were paid to decedent's executor, constituted IRD under Section 691(a) and thus were includable in the gross income of decedent's estate, because such items of income were considered to have been earned during the inventor's lifetime. Under Section 691(c), the estate was entitled to deduct that portion of the estate tax imposed upon the estate that was attributable to the inclusion in such estate of the right to receive such amount. However, those royalty payments paid after the inventor's death, and attributable to sales concluded by the licenses subsequent to the date of his death, could not be considered IRD, but were items of ordinary income includable in the gross income of the recipient under Section 61(a), because decedent had not sold the patent and therefore had not earned the payments during his lifetime. The licensees were granted only certain nonexclusive rights in the inventor's patent. There was neither a transfer of all of the substantial rights to the patent nor a transfer of an undivided interest therein.

In summary, the IRS concluded that if a contract entered into between an inventor and a manufacturer constitutes merely a "license" to use the inventor's patent in return for the payment of royalties, not a "sale," royalty payments due and accrued under the contract at the date of death of the inventor constitute IRD under Section 691(a). Where the contract constitutes a "license," royalty payments accrued after the date of death of the inventor are ordinary income includable in the gross income of the recipient under Section 61.

[Rev. Rul. 60-227, 1960-1 CB 262.]

Royalties paid to author's heirs constitute IRD. In 1937, taxpayer's father (the "author") entered into an agreement with certain publishers whereby he transferred to the publishers the sole right to publish his manuscript, including all revisions and future editions. The agreement provided that the copyright be taken out in the name of the publishers. The author agreed to revise the book or to cooperate with the publishers with the revision of the book. The publishers agreed to pay the author a royalty of 10 percent of the retail selling price. The author died in 1952. In the same year, his widow was appointed executrix of his estate. Because the estate of the author was the sole owner of all rights, title, or interest arising out of this contract, and because the publishers desired to publish future editions of the books, the widow, as executrix of the estate of the author, and a trade association entered into an agreement with the publishers on July 1, 1953. The parties agreed to prepare and to supply to the publishers later editions in accordance with the terms and conditions of the original contract executed in 1937. The association agreed to provide the services of an editor whose name would appear on the title page of the book, together with the name of the author. The publishers agreed to pay the executrix and the association royalties based on the selling price of the book, with such payments to be made in designated percentages and by separate checks. The widow died in January 1955, and, pursuant to the terms of her will, her daughter began receiving the royalty payments under the contract executed on July 1, 1953.

Section 691(a) provides that the amount of all items of gross IRD that are not properly includable in respect of the taxable period in which falls the date of decedent's death or a prior period (including the amount of all items of gross income in respect of a prior decedent, if the right to receive such amount was acquired by reason of the death of the prior decedent or by bequest, devise, or inheritance from a prior decedent) shall be included in the gross income, for the taxable year when received, of (1) the estate of decedent, if the right to receive the amount is acquired by decedent's estate from decedent; (2) the person who, by reason of the death of decedent, acquires the right to receive the amount, if the right to receive the amount is not acquired by decedent's estate from decedent; or (3) the person who acquires from decedent the right to receive the amount by bequest, devise, or inheritance, if the amount is received after a distribution by decedent's estate of such right.

In view of the foregoing, the IRS ruled that royalty payments received by taxpayer under the contract executed by her deceased mother, as executrix of the estate of her father, constituted taxable income to her under the provisions of Section 691(a). Under Section 691(c), however, taxpayer was entitled to deduct that portion of the federal estate tax imposed upon her mother's estate that was attributable to the inclusion in the estate of the right to receive such amount.

[Rev. Rul. 57-544, 1957-2 CB 361, distinguished and clarified, Rev. Rul. 60-227, 1960-1 CB 262.]

[7] Partnership and Corporate Interests

Partnership receivables are IRD and therefore are not subject to basis step-up. Prior to his death in 1960, decedent was a 50 percent partner in an architectural and engineering firm that ceased business in 1957. At decedent's death, the partnership interest became the property of his estate and was thereafter placed in decedent's testamentary trust. The partnership owned certain accounts receivable with a face value of $518,000 and a FMV of $454,991. The accounts receivable were for services previously rendered by the partnership and had a basis of zero prior to the date of decedent's death. Thereafter the partnership elected under Section 754 to adjust the basis of its partnership interest as provided in Sections 743(b) and 755. This resulted in an increase of basis in the partnership's accounts receivable from zero to an amount approximately one half of their face value. The trust used as its basis the date-of-death FMV of the accounts receivable. The IRS later determined that collections made on the accounts receivable constituted IRD under Section 691. Consequently, in the IRS's view, the date-of-death value of the partnership interest did not include the FMV of decedent's share of the receivables, and, moreover, the partnership's Section 754 election had no effect on basis. The IRS relied on Section 1014(c), that denies a date-of-death basis step-up in the case of property that constitutes a right to receive an item of IRD under Section 691. The trust argued that the partnership provisions of the Code adopted the "entity theory" of partnerships and that the plain meaning of such provisions requires the conclusion that the inherited partnership interest is separate and distinct from the underlying assets of the partnership. Therefore Sections 691 and 1014(c) have no application.

Held: Affirmed for the IRS. The accounts receivable are separate from the rest of the partnership assets because they are IRD; therefore, the IRS properly applied the rule set forth in Section 1014(c). The fact that the receivables arose directly from decedent's lifetime services clearly placed them within the class of assets subject to Section 691. Therefore, the rule of Section 1014(c), which requires separate treatment for property giving rise to IRD, prevents the use of any method that increases basis and thereby avoids taxes on what is essentially unrealized ordinary income.

[Quick Trust, 444 F2d 90, 27 AFTR2d 71-1581, 71-1 USTC ¶ 9489 (8th Cir. 1971).]

Fifth Circuit adopts "entitlement test" for application of Section 691 to postdeath payments. Prior to his death, decedent and other members of his family entered into negotiations for the sale of their controlling stock in a closely held chain of hotels. Following initial discussions with the buyers, decedent and the other stockholders executed a written contract with the buyers on August 4, 1960, in which they agreed in principle to sell either the stock or the assets of all of the corporations in the chain. In connection with the written agreement, the parties placed cash and the corporate stock in escrow, pending a favorable ruling on a tax matter and other stipulated contingencies. On January 30, 1961, decedent died, and his will was probated one week later. In the following month, on February 23, 1961, the purchase was closed, and a total of $3.53 million was paid to the estate for decedent's stock. The estate income tax return filed for the period reflected a basis in the stock of $3.53 million, which was its FMV on the date of decedent's death. Accordingly, no gain was reported by the estate or by any of the beneficiaries. The IRS determined, however, that the proceeds from the final sale constituted IRD under Section 691 and that long-term capital gain of $3.45 million had been realized on the sale. The resulting deficiencies were paid in full by the respective parties, and suits for refund followed the IRS's administrative refusal to honor their refund claims. Taxpayers contended that no sale occurred prior to decedent's death and that therefore the proceeds were not taxable. The IRS argued successfully in federal district court that the transaction was completed by decedent prior to his death and that all that remained to complete the transaction was the closing and payment. In reaching its conclusion that the sale proceeds were IRD, the district court stated that the applicable test was whether the post-death payments were in fact due to the services performed by, or the economic activities of, decedent during his lifetime.

Held: Affirmed for the IRS as modified. The Fifth Circuit, in its per curiam opinion, concluded that the district court's test was too "open-minded and somewhat inadequate" as precedent when considered in relation to the statutory provisions of Section 691. The court allowed that it was "pertinent" to inquire whether the income received after death was attributable to activities and economic efforts of decedent in his lifetime, but found that the proper analysis would focus on whether such activities and efforts gave rise to a right to receive the income prior to death. Without such a right to income, there would be no Section 691 taxable income, regardless of how great decedent's activities and efforts were prior to death. The court added that its "entitlement" test looks to the totality of decedent's rights on the date of death to determine whether postdeath income was derived therefrom.

[Trust Co. of Ga., 392 F2d 694, 21 AFTR2d 311, 68-1 USTC ¶ 9133 (5th Cir. 1967), cert. denied, 393 US 830 (1968).]

Under terms of will, estate is required to report partnership earnings as IRD. *A*, a member of the *M* partnership, died on September 15, 1964. Both *A* and the *M* partnership reported income on the cash receipts and disbursements method of accounting and used a calendar-year accounting period. *A*'s distributive share of the taxable income of *M* partnership for the period January 1, 1964, through September 15, 1964 (the date of his death), was $50x, of which $20x was distributed to *A* prior to his death. Under the terms of his will, *A* bequeathed to each of five beneficiaries an equal portion of the right that he possessed at the date of his death to receive undistributed amounts of his share of the profits earned and realized by the partnership from the beginning of 1964 to the date of his death. He also bequeathed to those beneficiaries in equal shares any guaranteed amounts to which he had a right under the terms of the partnership agreement. Pursuant to the terms of the will, on December 1, 1964, the executor of the estate assigned to each beneficiary a one-fifth interest in these two rights. The bequest to the five beneficiaries specifically excluded A's right to undistributed amounts of his share of profits earned and realized by the partnership before the 1964 calendar year. The estate reported income on the cash receipts and disbursements methods of accounting and used a fiscal-year accounting period ending February 28. Although Section 691 and the regulations thereunder provide special rules for the reporting of IRD, those rules do not govern the time for reporting a deceased partner's distributive share of partnership income for the partnership's taxable year in which decedent died. Instead, Section 706 is applicable. Under Regulation § 1.706-1(c)(3)(ii), a deceased partner's distributive share of partnership income for the partnership's taxable year in which decedent died is includable in the gross income of the estate or other successor in interest in its taxable year within which or with which the taxable year of the partnership ends. This inclusion is applicable even though there may not have been a distribution by the partnership of the amounts involved.

A's estate became successor in interest upon his death, and, as such, it became the owner of the partnership interest held by decedent. Because the estate did not assign to the five beneficiaries the right to receive undistributed amounts of his share of profits earned and realized by the partnership before 1964, the estate remained the successor in interest to the entire partnership interest of decedent as of the end of the partnership taxable year ending December 31, 1964. Accordingly, decedent's estate should be required to include in its gross income in its first taxable year $50x, the amount of the distributive share of partnership taxable income for the partnership taxable year ending December 31, 1964.

[Rev. Rul. 68-215, 1968-1 CB 312.]

[8] Deduction for Taxes

Tenth Circuit resolves conflict over interplay of Section 691(c) and Section 1202 deductions. Prior to his death, decedent contracted to sell a 640-acre parcel of land for a contract price of $1.1 million. The transaction was established on an installment basis whereby decedent agreed to convey one acre for each $2,000 paid by the purchaser. On the date of decedent's death, the balance due was $1.06 million, and the estate treated the unpaid balance as IRD under Section 691. Taxpayer, who was decedent's heir and surviving spouse, received several payments from the purchaser in the years following the date of death. She reported these amounts as long-term capital gains and claimed the capital gains deduction as provided under Section 1202. In addition, she deducted her share of estate taxes pursuant to Section 691(c). On audit, the IRS recomputed taxpayer's Section 1202 deduction by deducting the allocable Section 691(c) estate tax from the net capital gain before applying the Section 1202 percentage deduction.

Held: For taxpayer. Although 691(c) states that the deduction for estate taxes "shall be allowed," it provides no guidance for determining the proper method of calculation relative to Section 1202 or any other deductions provided by the Code. The court looked to the expressed purpose of Section 691(c) and determined that Congress sought to alleviate the double taxation effect of Section 691(a) without limitation or exception. Thus, in applying Sections 691(c) and 1202, taxpayer is entitled to the maximum possible advantage, and therefore may take the Section 691(c) deduction after applying the Section 1202 capital gains deduction.

[Quick, 503 F2d 100, 34 AFTR2d 74-5861, 74-2 USTC ¶ 9700 (10th Cir. 1974).]

Full marital deduction is allowed for recomputation of gross estate under Section 691(c). Taxpayer's husband died in 1975. His employment contract provided that his annual bonus payments would continue to be paid to his spouse after his death. The husband left most of his other property to a trust. After payment of taxes, debts, and the expenses of administering the husband's estate, the trust property was divided into a "marital part" and a "nonmarital part." The "marital part" consisted of property equal in value to the maximum marital deduction allowable to his estate, less the value of nontrust property (the bonus payments) includable in his gross estate that passed to taxpayer and qualified for the marital deduction. Thus, the value of the right to the payments was subtracted from the maximum marital deduction in determining the "marital part." The "marital part" passed to taxpayer and was eligible for the marital deduction. The "nonmarital part" consisted of the remainder of the trust property. Taxpayer did not report all of the bonus payments in 1976 and 1977. The IRS and taxpayer subsequently agreed that the payments were includable in taxpayer's gross income as IRD. They disagreed, however, over the amount of the deduction allowable to taxpayer pursuant to Section 691(c)(1)(A) (deduction for estate tax), as a consequence of including the bonus payments in her gross income. The controversy centered on the computation of the estate tax attributable to the bonus payments. Section 691(c)(2)(C) provides that the amount of estate tax attributable to the IRD is the difference between the actual estate tax and the estate tax as computed without including the IRD in decedent's gross estate. The parties disputed the effect of the exclusion of the bonus payments on the marital deduction. The IRS contended that the exclusion of the bonus payments resulted in a reduction of the marital deduction. The estate argued that the full maximum marital deduction should be allowed, because the will provided for a full marital deduction bequest. In addition, there were sufficient non-IRD assets in the estate to fund the formula marital deduction.

Held: For the estate. The court found that the purpose behind Section 691 is to provide a deduction to those required to include IRD in their gross income to offset, at least in part, the estate tax attributable to the inclusion of that IRD in the gross estate of a decedent. Although no guidance existed in the statute or the legislative history on the specific point at issue in the present case, the court concluded that taxpayer's method was consistent with the purpose of the statute. The formula bequest required that taxpayer receive property equal in value to the maximum marital deduction out of the assets of the estate available for distribution. In the recomputation, there was no IRD available in the recomputed gross estate to satisfy the marital bequest. The bequest, therefore, by its own terms, must be funded to its full extent by non-IRD property. Thus, the full maximum marital deduction, subject only to the Section 2056 50 percent limitation, was allowable in the recomputation of taxpayer's husband's estate.

[Estate of Kincaid, 85 TC 25 (1985).]

¶ 13.02 TAXABLE INCOME AND DEDUCTIONS OF ESTATES

[1] Income

[a] Generally

Fiduciary bond requirement is held not to bar constructive receipt of tax refund. Decedent, an incompetent Osage Indian, died in 1932. The estate executor, the federal Osage Indian Agency, filed an estate tax return and remitted full payment of all taxes shown on the return. Decedent's heir and sole beneficiary died in 1967. Three years later, in 1970, the federal government changed its position on the taxability of Osage Indians and remitted $150,241 to the Agency as executor of decedent's estate. Following its receipt of the refund, the executor notified the estate of decedent's beneficiary of the availability of the refund. As a part of its notice, the executor advised the beneficiary's estate of the need to post a bond prior to releasing the refund. After much delay, the beneficiary's estate finally obtained the requisite bond, and in 1974, the

Agency paid the refund to the beneficiary's estate. The IRS determined that the beneficiary's estate was in constructive receipt of the refund during 1970, and, accordingly, the IRS assessed an income tax deficiency based on the interest that accrued on the $150,241 refund from 1970 to 1974.

Held: For the IRS. The court found that there had, indeed, been constructive receipt of the refund in 1970, and therefore the asserted deficiencies were upheld. The court found no authority to support the estate's claim that the need to post a fiduciary bond in a probate proceeding amounts to a substantial limitation or restriction sufficient to postpone income recognition under the doctrine of constructive receipt.

[Estate of Shelton, 612 F2d 1276, 45 AFTR2d 80-566, 80-1 USTC ¶ 9151 (10th Cir. 1980), cert. denied, 449 US 873 (1980).]

Estate cannot recharacterize postmortem income as part of gross estate in order to reduce federal estate tax liability. On her death in 1948, decedent, a resident of the District of Columbia, left an estate valued at $16.83 million. The will provided for several specific bequests and directed the executors to place the residue of the estate in trust for certain named charities. Once the specific bequests, debts, administration expenses, and taxes were satisfied, however, the estate was completely exhausted. The total amount of the residuary estate before taxes was $8.26 million. The estate taxes amounted to $9.19 million. However, the estate realized income of $1.16 million during the period of administration. The executors were therefore able to pay the entire amount of taxes and to use the balance of $238,979 to fund the charitable trust. Not content with this result, the executors claimed in the instant refund suit that the $1.16 million of income should have been included in the gross estate. By adopting this position, the executors sought to lower the estate's overall tax liability and increase the amount available for charitable purposes, to the extent that a larger charitable deduction from the gross estate would have reduced the taxable estate. The IRS challenged the refund claim by pointing out that postmortem income is simply not part of the gross estate, but rather is taxable as estate income. The estate's argument in support of its novel position was that under District of Columbia law, an estate's income becomes part of the principal and is therefore available to pay debts, taxes, and administration expenses. Consequently, the estate contended that it should be treated as if the taxes were paid out of income rather than from amounts that entered the gross estate on the death of death.

Held: For the IRS. The Court of Claims refused to recharacterize as part of the gross estate amounts that were undeniably income, and it rejected the estate's attempts to ignore the clear dictates of statutory law. Under elementary principles of applicable estate and income tax law, postmortem income in excess of estate debts, administration expenses, and taxes is reportable as income and channels into the residuary to be disposed of in accordance with the testator's will. Regardless of local probate law governing the administration of estates, an estate's postmortem income is never part of the gross estate for federal tax purposes. The court pointed out that the estate taxes were almost entirely paid during 1949 and 1950, whereas the estate's books first recorded the transfer of postmortem income to principal account in 1952. Moreover, the court was unmoved by the executors' equitable arguments because the estate was fully entitled to deduct all charitable contributions from income under the law as codified in Section 170.

[Waldrop, 137 F. Supp. 753, 49 AFTR 27, 56-1 USTC ¶ 11,588 (Ct. Cl. 1956).]

Estate realizes income from discharge of indebtedness where creditors fail to file timely claim. On his death, decedent and his wife owned all of the stock in two corporations to which decedent was indebted in the amounts of $30,000 and $3,000. The corporations did not timely file claims for these debts. The estate claimed a $33,000 estate tax deduction. The IRS determined that the estate realized $33,000 in income from the discharge of indebtedness.

Held: For the IRS. The Wisconsin statute provides that all claims against an estate are forever barred unless filed within the time period established by the probate court, and thus the corporate debts were extinguished on February 21. Furthermore, the fact that the estate was not enriched economically is not of consequence, because the cancellation relieved the estate from liability for the debts.

[Miller, 76 TC 191 (1981).]

Restitution of income is taxable to estate. A New Jersey decedent's will left his entire estate to his parents. The will was admitted to probate, and letters testamentary were issued to the father, who distributed the estate pursuant to the terms of the will. About nine years later it was discovered that decedent was below the minimum age to make a valid will. Under the laws of intestate distribution, the estate passed to decedent's two infant children. The mother, who resided in New York, was divorced from decedent about four months before his death. After some time the property and earnings thereon since the date of death were paid over to the estate. However, nothing was immediately distributed to the infant beneficiaries, because a proceeding was to be brought in New Jersey to remove the estate assets from New Jersey to New York. The income amounted to $11,940. The IRS maintained that this income was taxable to the infant beneficiaries and/or to the estate, which had filed no income tax returns. The beneficiaries and estate argued that this was not income but mere "restitution," and as such was not taxable.

Held: For the IRS. The income was fully taxable to the estate. According to the Tax Court, there was no question that this constituted "gross income" under the definitions set forth in the Code, and that the only remaining question was to determine the party liable for the tax. The income cannot be taxed to the beneficiaries until distribution, which took place long after the payment of the income to the estate. There was no state law requiring that the income be currently distributed to the beneficiaries. Because the income was not in fact paid to them, this was not income distributed currently pursuant to Section 652. Therefore, it was properly taxable to the estate.

[Bowen 34 TC 222 (1960), aff'd per curiam, 295 F2d 816, 8 AFTR2d 5763, 61-2 USTC ¶ 9757 (2d Cir. 1961).]

Tax Court finds no tax liability on estate's part for decedent's unproved theft of money. Decedent, who died in 1984, named taxpayer, her daughter, as a beneficiary of her estate. The will was never probated, and no estate was opened, because there were no assets in decedent's estate. After investigation, the IRS determined that decedent and taxpayer did not report $548,000 that was stolen from decedent's husband in 1964. The IRS accused taxpayer and decedent of theft and asserted a deficiency against her estate and taxpayer, who was the executrix.

Held: For the estate. The Tax Court reviewed the evidence presented and concluded that there was no conclusive proof that decedent or taxpayer had stolen the money as alleged. The allegation of theft was first reported to the police nine months after the theft occurred, and at the time decedent and her husband were embroiled in domestic difficulties.

[Estate of Hollingsworth, TC Memo. (P-H) ¶ 87,095, 53 TCM (CCH) 163 (1987).]

IRS rules on TIN compliance relative to reporting estate's interest income. Decedent died on October 1, 1983. On the date of death, he had two savings accounts, both of which carried his taxpayer identification number (TIN). One account was in his name only. It earned interest of $500 from January 1, 1983, to decedent's death, and an additional $60 from the date of death to November 1, 1983, when decedent's spouse, the executrix of his estate, closed the account. The other account was in decedent's name and in his spouse's name as joint owners with rights of survivorship. At decedent's death, his spouse became sole owner. This account earned $3,000 in interest from January 1, 1983, to decedent's death, and an additional $1,200 from the date of death until December 31, 1983. As executrix, the spouse notified the bank in which the accounts were held of decedent's death on November 1, 1983, and provided it with the estate's identifying number, as well as the spouse's own Social Security number, by filing Form W-9 (Payer's Request for Taxpayer Identification Number).

The IRS was asked to rule on the question of whose TIN should be used by a financial institution for reporting interest payments credited to single-owner and joint accounts after the death of the account owner under facts such as those presented. After reviewing the relevant statutory and regulatory authority, the IRS concluded that decedent's Social Security number must be used for both accounts to report interest earned prior to his death. After the date of decedent's death, the estate's employer identification number must be used to report the $60 paid to the estate in 1983. In addition, the Social Security number of the spouse must be used to report $1,200 payable to the spouse after decedent's death.

[Rev. Rul. 84-73, 1984-1 CB 240.]

Previously unrecognized gain inherent in notes held by decedent need not be recognized as of date of death. On three separate occasions prior to her death, decedent sold oil and gas interests on real property to one or more of her sons or to a third party. In each case, the purchaser issued a promissory note for the property. Decedent used the installment method of reporting gain from the sales. On those occasions involving a third-party purchaser, the third party reconveyed the property to one or more of the individual's sons immediately after purchasing the property. The sons assumed the third party's liability on its notes to decedent and often conveyed other property to the third party. During decedent's lifetime, interest payments on the notes were regularly made by the obligors. After her death, however, the obligors made no interest payments, and her estate made no demand for interest payments. Decedent's will bequeathed the notes to her sons. Each son might receive notes on which he was the obligor, as well as notes on which the obligor was one or more of the other sons. The notes did not provide for automatic cancellation upon decedent's death. The estate took no action under applicable state law to cancel the notes. A state statute prevented the estate from delivering the estate's assets (including the notes) to the beneficiaries until administration was closed, a move that could not be accomplished until after the estate had taken possession of the notes.

The IRS took the position that the estate would not be required to recognize the previously unrecognized gain inherent in the notes as of the date of the individual's death. The IRS also stated that the failure of the executors to enforce the notes and to collect the amounts due and payable would not be treated as a cancellation of the notes, as long as the notes would not be canceled under state law. The IRS concluded that all or a portion of the previously unrecognized gain inherent in the notes would have to be recognized by the estate in the first year in which

1. The notes are distributed, in whole or in part, to the obligors;
2. The notes are canceled under state statute;
3. The notes become unenforceable;
4. The administration of the estate terminates under Regulation § 1.641(b)-3;

5. Any other event occurs that would be considered a cancellation or a transfer of the notes under temporary or final regulations promulgated under Section 691 or Section 453B.

Finally, the IRS added that if none of these five listed events occurred, and principal payments were made, then the estate would have to report gain on such payments using the installment method.

[Priv. Ltr. Rul. 8806048.]

Exchange of stock for debentures of equal value is not self-dealing. A testamentary trust was established as the depository of stock owned by an estate. The coexecutors of the estate were the cotrustees of the trust. One of the companies whose stock the estate owned proposed to purchase its own stock and that of another company owned by the estate and, in return, gave the estate the company's interest earning debenture in an amount equal to the FMV of the stock as determined by an independent appraiser.

The IRS stated that the redemption, receipt, and holding of the debenture by the estate or the trust would not constitute an act of self-dealing under Section 4941, except to the extent that the value of the stock exceeded the value of the debenture. The IRS also indicated that the payment of cash to the estate and the receipt by the estate of cash in exchange for stock would not constitute self-dealing, except to the extent that the value of the stock exceeded the cash received. The IRS relied upon Regulation §53.4941(d)-1(b)(3).

[Priv. Ltr. Rul. 8528079.]

[b] Capital gains

Liquidation proceeds arising from condemnation settlement are held to be IRD and not subject to basis adjustment. At the time of his death on November 15, 1973, decedent was a major stockholder in two corporations in business in New York. One of the companies operated a local bus line and the other owned and managed a bus garage and maintenance facility. On March 30, 1973, local officials initiated a condemnation action for the acquisition of all of the assets of the two corporations. On June 1, 1973, the court granted the municipality's petition and caused the corporations' assets to be transferred on the following day. The corporations claimed, however, that the original value placed on the assets by the municipality was far short of FMV. As a part of its order of condemnation, the court placed the issue of valuation on its special calendar and directed that the municipality pay its proposed purchase price to the corporations in installments pending further proceedings. The two companies received a portion of these payments in July 1973, whereupon they promptly dissolved and liquidated under Section 337. A final settlement was reached on the issue of FMV in 1976, with the municipality agreeing to make a further payment. Meanwhile, decedent died in November 1973, and his estate included the total amount of the initial liquidation distribution in the gross estate. After decedent's death, the balance of the initial court-order payments were made to the corporation and distributed in 1974; but the estate did not report any of this gain on its 1974 income tax returns. After receiving the final settlement in 1976, the estate reported a long-term capital gain with respect to the operating corporation and a long-term capital loss with respect to the real estate corporation on its fiduciary income tax return for that year. In its notice of deficiency, the IRS determined that the estate realized capital gains income in 1974. In addition, the IRS concluded that there was additional capital gains income reportable in 1976.

In making this determination, the IRS asserted that the liquidating distributions constituted IRD under Section 691, and that therefore Section 1014 did not provide a step-up in the estate's basis for the stock. Section 1014(a) provides generally that the basis of property in the hands of a taxpayer acquiring the property from decedent is its FMV at the date of death. Section 1014(c), one of the exceptions to the general rule of Section 1014(a), states, however, that there shall be no such step-up in respect of property constituting a right to receive an item of IRD under Section 691.

Held: For the IRS. The issue squarely presented to the Tax Court was whether the gains from liquidation of the corporations received by decedent's estate in 1974 and 1976 were IRD. The controlling definition of IRD, as set forth in Regulation §1.691(a)-1(b), is that it refers to "those amounts to which a decedent was entitled as gross income but which were not properly includable in computing his taxable income for the taxable year ending with the date of his death." Applying this language and the principles enunciated in several cited cases, the Tax Court held that the right to receive payments was IRD under Section 691. The court found that the liquidation of the two companies progressed to the point where as of November 15, 1973, decedent was entitled to, and had a right to receive, the liquidation proceeds that were thereafter payable. Decedent was required to do nothing further in order to receive his full share of corporate proceeds, inasmuch as the corporations—and not the various shareholders—were responsible for pursuing the litigation.

[Estate of Bickmeyer, 84 TC 170 (1985).]

[c] Effect of state law

Waiver of community property rights has no effect for income tax purposes. Taxpayer was executor of a California decedent's will that created a trust for the benefit of decedent's wife. The trust was, however, conditioned on the wife's waiving her right to take one half of the community property. The wife waived such right and exercised her powers under the will. On the estate income tax return, only half of the income from the administered property was reported, and the other half was reported on the wife's income tax return. The IRS claimed that all of the income should have been reported on the estate's income tax return, and a deficiency was assessed against the estate for half of the income. The district court held that all of the income was taxable to the estate, on the ground that the wife's waiver of her community property rights was binding under California law and would be followed for tax purposes.

Held: Reversed for the estate. The income was taxable half to the estate and half to the wife. The court first pointed out that in a case where the estate is composed entirely of community property in which the husband and wife had equal interests at the time of death, the widow would own half of the income, and the estate could not be taxed on more than the other half. In such a case, the widow's half would never become part of the estate. The court ruled that the effect of the widow's waiver was not substantially different from such a case. On the issue of whether the waiver was binding under state law, the court held that the will and the waiver were each dependent on the other, but did not, in and of themselves, resolve into a binding contract between the spouses, so that neither one could change the relationship without the consent of the other. Even assuming that the wife was estopped upon the husband's death from revoking her waiver, thereby placing what had been her half of the community property into the estate, she still retained the power and right to receive half of the trust corpus, thereby reinstating herself in the same legal relationship to the community property in which she stood prior to her husband's death. Alternatively, setting aside the assumption of a valid contract, the court held that the substance of the transaction was that the wife was a trustee of half of the community property. Because the will explicitly gave the wife the right to withdraw and to control half of the trust corpus, half of the trust income would be taxable to the wife under the "grantor trust" rules.

[Gibson Estate, 245 F2d 524, 51 AFTR 581, 57-1 USTC ¶ 9653 (9th Cir. 1957).]

[2] Deductions

[a] Generally

Executor is denied right to change election to deduct expenses on estate income tax return. The executors filed timely income tax returns for 1953 and 1954. A statement was attached to each return waiving the right to claim administration expenses of the estate as deductions on the federal estate tax return and electing to treat such expenses as deductions in determining the net income of the estate. Later, the executors determined that none of the deductions for 1953, and only part of the deductions for 1954, were of income tax benefit to the estate. At a time when both income tax returns and the estate tax return were open for examination and under consideration by the IRS, the executors filed a statement with the District Director changing their elections and claiming the right to take all of the 1953, and part of the 1954, administrative expenses as an estate tax deduction. The IRS determined, however, that the waivers filed with the fiduciary income tax returns operated as an irrevocable relinquishment of the right to claim the administrative expenses as estate tax deductions.

Held: For the IRS. The right to change the election was denied. The regulations permit a taxpayer to defer an election, but when that election is made, the regulations say it is final. A mistake as to tax consequences does not entitle taxpayer to a second choice.

[Darby, 323 F2d 792, 12 AFTR2d 6308, 63-2 USTC ¶ 12,186 (10th Cir. 1963).]

Funeral expenses deductible under Section 2053 are not subject to Section 642(g) waiver. Decedent died in 1955. His estate, through its executor, decedent's surviving spouse, filed its 1955 income tax return, claiming a deduction for funeral expenses paid during the taxable year. A statement that purported to waive the right to deduct funeral expenses from the gross estate was attached to the return. The IRS assessed a deficiency based on its disallowance of the funeral expense deduction, citing Section 642(g). That section provides that amounts allowable as a deduction from the gross estate under Section 2053 shall not be allowed as a deduction in computing taxable income, unless a statement is filed waiving the estate tax deduction.

Held: For the IRS. The purpose of Section 642(g) is to avoid the possibility of a double deduction for items of a character that would properly be deductible for both estate tax and income tax purposes. The court concluded that funeral expenses do not fall into this category, because they "have nothing to do with the determination of taxable income." Thus, funeral expenses that are otherwise deductible under Section 2053 are not subject to waiver under Section 642(g).

[Estate of Yetter, 35 TC 737 (1961).]

Section 754 adjustment is permissible, even though partner-estate claims Section 2053 deduction for partnership liabilities. An individual held a partnership interest. On his death, his estate made the election under Section 754 to adjust the basis of partnership property as provided in Section 743. The partnership's principal asset was an apartment building, and the upward basis adjustment created a loss under Section 1231 when this property was transferred to settle a creditor's claim. The partnership's acquisition of the building was financed with a recourse note on which decedent and the other partners were jointly and severally liable. Decedent's estate, in computing its estate tax liability, claimed a deduction under Section 2053 for the partnership liabilities. The examining agent disallowed the deduction. He contended that Section 642(g) applied because the partnership liabilities are an element of decedent's basis in the partnership, thus contributing towards the Section 1231 loss. (Section 642(g) provides that amounts deductible under Section 2053 may not be deducted for income tax purposes.)

In technical advice, the IRS took the position that the liabilities created a double tax benefit, but that Section 642(g) did not apply. The IRS reasoned that the basis increase was not a double deduction. The IRS further reasoned, however, that Regulation § 1.755-1(a)(1)(ii) precludes a basis adjustment that causes an asset's basis to exceed its FMV. Thus, the partnership did not correctly compute the basis adjustment. (The IRS did not state the effect of this holding on the Section 1231 loss.) The IRS further indicated that the partnership's settlement with creditors resulted in discharge of indebtedness income. The insolvency exception to recognizing discharge of indebtedness income is applied at the partner level, not at the partnership level. Because decedent's estate was insolvent both before and after its settlement with creditors, it fell within the exception. A portion of the settlement represented a disposition of property under Section 1001, however, and the estate must include its distributive share of the gain from the disposition in its gross income.

[Tech. Adv. Mem. 8348001.]

[b] Distributable property

Bankrupt estate may not deduct distributions to creditors in computing its taxable income. Prior to the effective date of the Bankruptcy Tax Act of 1980, taxpayer was appointed as trustee of a bankrupt estate. While the estate was in the process of liquidation, it earned over $320,000 from interests, dividends, rents, and the sale of property. The trustee claimed that no tax was due on this income, on the ground that a bankrupt estate in the process of liquidation is not a taxable entity. The IRS filed a proof of claim against the estate for taxes plus interest due on the income earned by the estate. The bankruptcy court held that the trustee must pay income tax on the income of the bankrupt estate, but that no interest was due on these taxes. The bankruptcy court further held that in computing the taxable income of the bankrupt estate, the trustee could deduct any distributions made, or that could have been made, to the creditors of the estate. The district court affirmed the decision of the bankruptcy court, and the IRS appealed.

Held: Reversed in part for the IRS. Income of an individual's bankrupt estate is taxed as income of an estate under Section 641. Thus, the trustee was required to file a fiduciary return and to pay tax on the income of the bankrupt estate. The trustee was also liable for interest on delinquent taxes. However, the trustee was not entitled to deduct distributions to creditors in computing its taxable income. The trustee argued that because the provisions of Section 661 entitle a decedent's estate or trust to deduct distributions to beneficiaries in computing its taxable income, a bankrupt estate should be able to deduct the distributions to its creditors. This argument was rejected because it is clear from the provisions of Section 662 and the purpose of the bankruptcy laws that Congress did not intend to allow individual bankrupt estates to deduct distributions to creditors from gross income. First, if a bankrupt estate were allowed a deduction under Section 661 for distributions to creditors, the creditors would be required to include such distributions in income under Section 662. This result clearly was not intended, because it would require creditors to treat whatever portion of the principal debt that they received as if it were income. Second, if an individual's bankrupt estate were allowed to deduct the distributions that it made or could have made to creditors, this could place creditors in a better position after bankruptcy than they were in before bankruptcy. Before bankruptcy, the debtor must pay income taxes and then pay creditors. If, during bankruptcy, deductions are allowed for distributions to creditors, then creditors could be paid out of the bankrupt estate's gross income, unreduced by taxes. Congress did not intend this incongruous result.

[Williams, 667 F2d 1108, 49 AFTR2d 82-1430, 82-1 USTC ¶ 9112 (4th Cir. 1981).]

Widow's allowance paid out of estate principal is fully deductible under Section 661(a)(2). Following the death of her husband, taxpayer was awarded a statutory widow's allowance pursuant to an order of the state probate court. The court decreed that the sum of $1,000 was to be paid to taxpayer each month, but it did not specify whether the payments were to be made from corpus or from income. During 1963 and 1964, the estate claimed a deduction of the widow's allowance for income tax purposes and reported that all payments were made from corpus. At the same time, taxpayer did not include such payments in her own gross income, contending that they were not taxable under Section 662. The IRS, however, concluded that the widow's allowance was not deductible by the estate, because it was paid out of corpus, not out of income. The estate argued that the payments were clearly "any other amounts properly paid or credited or required to be distributed" by the estate pursuant to Section 661(a)(2).

Held: For the estate. Congress specifically envisioned that amounts paid from estate corpus could be deducted under Section 661(a)(2), because the operative statutory limitation refers only to whether the amount is "required" to be distributed, not to whether it originates from corpus rather than income. The court noted that certain IRS regulations acknowledge the deductibility of amounts paid from sources "other than income," and therefore the IRS's position in the present case was at odds with its own published interpretation of the governing law. Consequently, the court upheld the estate's deduction in full.

[Estate of McCoy, 50 TC 562 (1968), acq. 1973-1 CB 2.]

Section 663 "specific sum of money" includes bequest of specific amount to be satisfied out of unspecified assets. Decedent's will provided that a specific trust be funded with cash or property, at the discretion of the executor, having a date-of-distribution value of $2,000. The executor satisfied this bequest with securities owned by decedent having a distribution value of $2,000 and an adjusted basis of $2,500.

The IRS ruled that a bequest of unspecified cash or property with a total stated value is deductible by an estate under Section 663 because the monetary value of bequest is ascertainable under the terms of the will as of the date of decedent's death. When an estate satisfies such a bequest with property, however, the election under Section 643(d)(3) is not available, because the act of satisfying such a bequest is a taxable event to the estate.

[Rev. Rul. 86-105, 1986-2 CB 82.]

Equalization directive triggers taxable gain for estate. Decedent's will provided that the residue of his estate be divided between his two adult children after first taking into consideration the date-of-death value of 100,000 shares of stock he transferred to one of the children prior to his death. The will also provided that any assets distributed in kind be valued at the date of distribution. The residuary estate consisted solely of 60,000 shares of the same stock that were worth 50 percent more at the time of distribution than at the date of death. Thus, the estate was able to pay only 90 percent of the equalization amount to the legatee who did not receive the inter vivos gift and nothing to the other legatee.

The IRS advised that the estate must realize the 50 percent increase in the value of the stock as taxable gain. Under Regulation § 1.661(a)-2(f)(1), whenever an estate distributes property other than money to any beneficiary in satisfaction of a specific dollar amount, the estate realizes gain or loss as measured by the difference between the amount of the bequest satisfied and the basis to the estate of the distributed property. Although Section 663(a) provides an exception to Section 661(a) for amounts properly paid or credited as a gift or bequest of a specific sum of money under the governing instrument, the instant distribution does not qualify, because neither the amount of money nor the identity of the specific property was ascertainable as of the date of decedent's death.

[Rev. Rul. 82-4, 1982-1 CB 99.]

Will provision for abatement of specific bequests did not render amounts of bequests unascertainable. Decedent's will listed gifts of specified sums and property for several beneficiaries. The will provided that if the aggregate value of the gifts exceeded 50 percent of the estate's assets after the payment of death taxes and administration expenses, then all but one of the gifts was to be proportionately reduced until the aggregate value equaled 50 percent of the estate. The residue of the estate was to pass to three other beneficiaries.

The IRS stated that the gifts of specified sums and property are bequests of specific sums of money and of specific property under Section 663(a)(1). The IRS also stated that despite the abatement provision, the kind and amount of each specific bequest could still be ascertained on decedent's death.

[Priv. Ltr. Rul. 8346062.]

[c] Expenses and losses

Partner's share of partnership loss is completely allocated to partner's estate where partner dies during year. A limited partnership was organized in 1968 to develop and to operate a shopping center in Phoenixville, Pennsylvania. Decedent, one of several general partners, owned 59.52 percent of the partnership at the time of his death on August 22, 1975. In 1975, the year of decedent's death, the partnership suffered a loss of $313,684.79. Decedent's 59.52 percent share amounted to $186,705.19. Because decedent's estate succeeded to his interest in the partnership midway through the year, the issue arose of how that loss should be allocated between decedent's short taxable year and the estate's. The plaintiff's solution (the estate and its coexecutors) was to divide the loss pro rata between them, based on the portion of the year (234 days) that decedent was alive. The tax return filed by decedent's' widow claimed $119,696 of the loss, and the estate's return claimed the remaining $67,009.19. The IRS disallowed the portion of the partnership loss claimed on decedent's final return by his widow. The IRS contended that the entire $186,705.19 loss must be allocated to the estate. The plaintiffs contested the IRS's determination in the Tax Court. The Tax Court ruled in favor of the IRS, and the plaintiffs appealed.

Held: Affirmed for the IRS. If a partnership's taxable year is not deemed closed prior to the end of its usual taxable year, all of the income or loss attributable to a deceased partner's share for that year must be allocated to his estate. If the partnership year were deemed to close on a partner's death, then the pro rata allocation urged by the plaintiffs would be proper. Section 706(c)(2)(A)(ii) states that "the taxable year of a partnership with respect to a partner who dies shall not close prior to the end of the partnership's taxable year." The court could not overlook the plain statutory language of Section 706(c)(2)(A)(ii), despite policy arguments advanced by the plaintiffs, such as the contention that Section 706(c)(2)(A) runs counter to the broad tax policy of allowing partnerships great freedom in allocating profits and losses among partners. The plain language of Section 706(c)(2)(A)(ii) prevented the plaintiffs from making the pro rata allocation.

[Estate of Applebaum, 724 F2d 375, 53 AFTR2d 84-508, 84-1 USTC ¶ 9117 (3d Cir. 1983).]

Commissions paid with respect to sale of testamentary trust property cannot be deducted by estate. By the terms of his will, decedent directed that his collection of historical documents was to be held in trust and disposed of by sale, with the proceeds being distributed to named beneficiaries. The collection consisted of books, maps, manuscripts, and other properties initially valued at $2 million. Within two years after the date of death, the gradual sale of the properties commenced, and within another three years, the sale was completed. The gross proceeds realized from the sale totaled $3.1 million, and the sales commissions over the three-year period totaled $490,292. The executors treated the commissions as estate expenses and deducted that amount from the gross estate under Section 2053. The IRS, however, preferred to allocate the commissions as an expense of the testamentary trust rather than of the estate. The Tax Court agreed with the IRS and denied the deduction, finding that the distribution in this case was the transfer of property to the trust and that the estate should be held to the testamentary form that decedent established. The Tax Court refused to disregard the trust as merely superfluous and found that the expenses could be deducted only by the trustees, not by the estate executor.

Held: Reversed for the estate. The Third Circuit determined that the sole purpose of the trust was to effect the distribution of decedent's estate. Because the duty of sale and distribution imposed upon the trustees was a duty normally performed by the executor, the estate should be entitled to the deduction. The court noted that under state law, where a trustee performs services of this nature, amounts paid in connection with these services are allowable as estate administrative expenses, regardless of the strict distinction between estate and trust entities. Thus, the court allowed the estate to deduct the selling expenses and rejected the view adopted by the IRS and the Tax Court as being "too narrow and technical for us to accept."

[Estate of Streeter, 32 AFTR2d 73-6212, 73-2 USTC ¶ 12,934 (3d Cir. 1973).]

Tax Court permits estate to depreciate postmortem right to receive income where it is based on surviving partner's use of invested capital. Prior to his death in 1947, decedent was a member of a partnership that operated a motion picture theater on premises leased from a third party. The governing partnership agreement provided that in the event of the death of either partner, the survivor would continue the business for a stated term, and that the personal representative of the deceased partner would be entitled to receive a portion of partnership income until the partnership terminated by operation of the agreement. Following decedent's death, the surviving partner operated the theater in accordance with the partnership agreement for the balance of the term, which expired in 1950, and paid the estate half of all net profits. The IRS required that the estate include in gross income the value of decedent's income rights, and the estate paid an appropriate estate tax on the agreed amount. The IRS also concluded that for income tax purposes, the estate was not entitled to a deduction for depreciation of the partnership interest. The estate argued that its right to receive income for a period of years was an exhaustible intangible asset that could be amortized under current Section 167.

Held: For the estate. Because the estate's right to receive income was limited to a stated period, this right constituted an exhaustible asset that could be amortized and deducted by the estate over its useful life. The court rejected the IRS's argument that the interest in controversy was not "the type of asset" subject to depreciation, and chided the IRS for failing to support its case with a fully articulated position. The court stressed the fact that the partnership payments were made in return for the use of capital assets, and it concluded that the right to receive payments from the surviving partner was a property interest subject to depreciation.

[Howell, 24 TC 342 (1955), nonacq. 1963-1 CB 5.]

Interest required to be paid by state law on delayed legacy distributions is deductible under Section 163. The IRS was presented with a question regarding the manner in which interest is deductible by an estate and includable in the gross income of its legatees. Specifically, in what manner is interest deductible where the time of payment of a legacy of a specific sum of money or of specific property under a will is deferred by the executors for administration purposes, and where the executors are required by state law to pay interest on such legacies. Under state law, this interest is allowed as a deduction in computing the estate's income. In addition, a question arose of whether the federal income tax treatment would be affected if the executors paid the interest out of principal rather than out of income.

The IRS noted that Regulation § 1.663(a)-1 provides that a gift or bequest of a specific sum of money or of property that is required by the specific terms of the will or trust instrument and that is properly paid or credited to a beneficiary is not allowed as a deduction to an estate or trust under Section 661. In addition, it is not included in the gross income of a beneficiary under Section 662, unless, under the terms of the will or trust instrument, the gift or bequest is to be paid or credited to the recipient in more than three installments. Thus, the treatment for federal income tax purposes of a bequest of a specific sum of money or of specific property is governed by the provisions of Section 661, Section 622, and Section 623. Interest that is required by state law to be paid with regard to a legacy of a specific sum of money or of specific property is not considered to be a part of such legacy. Rather, such interest is considered to be an amount payable with regard to an indebtedness incurred by the estate.

Accordingly, the IRS ruled that interest required by state law to be paid with regard to a legacy of a specific sum of money or of specific property is deductible by the estate under the provisions of Section 163(a) and is includable in the gross income of the beneficiary entitled to such legacy under the provisions of Section 61(a)(4). Sections 661 and 662 do not apply, because the relationship between the parties is that of dcbtor and creditor rather than that of estate and income beneficiary. Furthermore, the fact that interest is paid from principal rather than from income does not affect its deductibility by the estate under Section 163(a), nor does it affect its includability in the gross income of the beneficiary under Section 61(a)(4).

[Rev. Rul. 73-322, 1973-2 CB 44.]

Expenses allocable to tax-exempt income are estate tax deduction. Decedent's estate received approximately $200,000 in income during the period of administration, of which $25,000 was tax exempt. Consequently, only $70,000 of $80,000 in administration expenses was deductible for income tax purposes, with the remaining $10,000 apportioned to the exempt income. Nonetheless, the $10,000 was deductible for estate tax purposes. The IRS ruled that the allocation was not a prohibited double deduction.

[Rev. Rul. 59-32, 1959-1 CB 245, clarified, Rev. Rul. 63-27, 1963-1 CB 57.]

[d] Charitable transfers

Estate cannot deduct gross income distributed to satisfy charitable bequest where will does not require payment of bequest out of estate gross income. Decedent's will directed that 10 percent of his gross estate was to be paid to a specific charity. However, there was no requirement that it be paid solely from estate assets or estate income. The estate satisfied the bequest in part with estate assets and in part with income earned by the estate. The estate claimed an estate tax deduction for the entire amount of the charitable bequest under Section 2055(a)(2), as well as an income tax deduction under Section 661(a)(2) for "income distributed" for that portion of the bequest satisfied with cash reflected in the estate's "distributable net income." The IRS challenged the estate's income tax deduction, arguing that such a deduction could be claimed only under Section 642(c). In this case, the IRS stated the Section 642(c) deduction was unavailable because the bequest need not have been paid out of estate income.

Held: Reversed for the IRS. As indicated in Regulation § 1.663(a)-2, an estate's charitable distributions are deductible, if at all, under Section 642(c). The blanket deduction under Section 661(a)(2) for income "properly paid ... for such taxable year" cannot be read literally. Taxpayer's contention that Section 661(a)(2) is a clear directive and that the regulation is invalid ignored the fact that in enacting Section 661(a)(2), Congress did not intend to permit income and estate tax deductions for the same charitable gift.

[United States Trust Co., 803 F2d 1363, 58 AFTR2d 86-6152, 86-2 USTC ¶ 9777 (5th Cir. 1986).]

Second Circuit holds that estate's income tax charitable deduction must be determined without regard to its effect on amounts available for distribution. Under decedent's will, her residuary estate was to be apportioned among certain charitable organizations. The estate filed its income tax return without claiming a deduction under Section 642(c) for amounts payable to such organizations. As a result, payment of the estate's income tax liability consumed the entire residuary estate, leaving no amount available for distribution to these organizations. Pursuant to Revenue Ruling 73-266, 1973-2 CB 408, the organizations, as residuary legatees, filed a suit for refund of income tax, claiming a Section 642(c) deduction for amounts payable to them. They argued that the estate's Section 642(c) deduction should be determined by the amount payable to them, without regard to the estate's income tax liability and its effect on the amount of the residuary estate. The IRS argued that an estate's Section 642(c) deduction is based on the amount actually paid to charitable organizations.

Held: Affirmed for taxpayers. An estate computes its Section 642(c) deduction without regard to the effect that the estate's potential income tax liability may have on the amount distributable to charities. The estate had $2.4 million of taxable income without regard to any Section 642(c) deduction. Since $1 million was used for nondeductible administration expenses, the residuary estate totaled $1.4 million. If, as the charitable organizations contended, the estate determined a $1.4 million deduction for the amount of the residuary estate, the estate's taxable income would be $1 million ($2.4 million taxable income less a $1.4 million deduction), and its tax liability (using a 70 percent rate) would be $700,000. Thus, $700,000 ($1.4 million residuary estate less $700,000 tax) would be payable to the charitable legatees. The IRS contended that because the Section 642(c) deduction cannot include money used to pay taxes, the initial deduction of $1.4 million would be reduced by the first-determined tax of $700,000. The recomputed deduction of only $700,000 ($1.4 million reduced by $700,000 tax) would result in a higher redetermined tax liability of $1.19 million (70 percent of ($2.4 million less $700,000)). This redetermined tax would require a recomputed deduction of a lesser amount, which would then result in a higher redetermined tax, and so on. Consequently, under the IRS's method, the tax liability would consume the entire residuary estate, leaving no amounts distributable to the charitable residuary legatees. The court determined that this method was inconsistent with Congress's general policy of encouraging charitable gifts.

[Hartwick College, 801 F2d 608, 58 AFTR2d 86-5846, 86-2 USTC ¶ 9690 (2d Cir. 1986).]

Estate cannot deduct income set aside for charity while will contest is pending. Decedent's will directed that the residuary estate was to pass to charity. During probate, decedent's sister led a will contest action, which was settled by giving the challengers 50 percent of the residuary. While the contest was pending, the residuary estate was producing income, and the estate attempted to take a charitable deduction for the entire amount, honoring the will's direction that the entire residuary estate pass to charity. The IRS disallowed the deduction, claiming that the residuary was not been "permanently set aside" for charity as required by Section 642(c)(2), because of the will contest. The estate filed a refund suit, but the district court found for the IRS. The estate appealed to the Ninth Circuit.

Held: Affirmed for the IRS. The income cannot be said to have been "permanently set aside" for charity when a pending will contest ultimately results in a partial distribution to a noncharitable beneficiary. The amount actually distributed and received by the charity, not the amount of the bequest as set forth in the will, controls the amount of the deduction. Thus, only 50 percent of the income produced by the residuary qualified for a charitable deduction.

[Estate of Wright, 677 F2d 53, 50 AFTR2d 82-5024, 82-1 USTC ¶ 9389 (9th Cir. 1982), cert. denied, 459 US 909 (1982).]

Estate cannot deduct charitable gifts of corpus in computing estate gross income. Decedent died in 1962, leaving a gross estate in excess of $36 million. Under the terms of his will, two thirds of the estate after payment of debts, expenses, and specific bequests was left to decedent's tax-exempt charitable foundation. The residue of the estate, together with income earned during the period of administration, was left in trust for a named beneficiary. During taxable years 1963 through 1965, the executors made payments out of estate corpus to the foundation and claimed a corresponding estate tax charitable deduction. They also asserted the right to claim a deduction from estate taxable income under Section 661(a)(2), which allows a deduction for any amount properly paid, credited, or required to be distributed for the taxable year. The IRS conceded that a literal reading of Section 661(a)(2) would permit the deduction, but it argued that the section must be read in the context of the entire statutory scheme of Subchapter J. When so viewed, the IRS contended, it becomes clear that the distribution to the charitable organization in this case can be deducted only if the distribution qualifies under Section 642. According to Section 642(c), an estate or trust may only take a charitable deduction for an amount paid if the amount was paid from gross income, not from corpus.

Held: For the IRS. The Court of Claims concluded that amounts paid, permanently set aside, or to be used for charitable purposes are deductible only as provided in Section 642(c), regardless of the fact that Section 661 would otherwise seem to apply without limitation. In its reading of Section 661, and of Section 662, which provides for the inclusion of distributable income by the beneficiary, the court found an implicit congressional intention that only amounts paid from income are subject to the deduction in Section 661. There-fore, the estate was not entitled to deduct its charitable contributions to the ex-tent paid from corpus.

[Mott, 462 F2d 512, 199 Ct. Cl. 127, 30 AFTR2d 72-5193, 72-2 USTC ¶ 9557 (1972), cert. denied, 409 US 1108 (1973).]

¶ 13.03 INCOME TAXATION OF ESTATE BENEFICIARIES

[1] Income

[a] Generally

Beneficiary is not estopped to prove her probate property has value higher than that reported by estate. Taxpayer was a beneficiary of the estate of her grandmother, who died in 1969. Prior to the grandmother's death, there was an acrimonious intrafamily dispute concerning attempts by various fac-tions to gain control of the family's manufacturing business. In order to equal-ize taxpayer's overall interest with other members of the family, the grandmother left taxpayer an extra block of stock to cure the disparity. The ex-ecutors of the estate resisted taxpayer's claim to the additional shares, how-ever, and after prolonged discussions, an agreement was reached whereby taxpayer received a $200,000 corporate debenture in lieu of the stock. On her tax return for the year of settlement, taxpayer reported interest income from the debenture. The IRS insisted, however, that she also realized taxable gain as the result of exchanging her right to receive stock valued at $47,630 for the $200,000 debenture. In the IRS's view, the difference of $152,370 was ordi-nary income. The district court made extensive findings of fact and entered summary judgment for the IRS. The lower court determined that the debenture was issued in full settlement of taxpayer's claims and that she should be es-topped from asserting that the shares of stock had a value any higher than the $47,630 previously accepted by the IRS.

Held: Reversed and remanded for taxpayer. An acquiescence by the beneficiary to the executor's valuation of property for estate tax purposes did not estop her from later claiming that she inherited stock with a basis higher than that reported by the executors. The court found that taxpayer was not involved in the administration of the estate and that the IRS did not rely on any representations made by her concerning the value of the disputed shares. Therefore, taxpayer should be free to present evidence to the court to support her contention that the stock's value on the date of death was higher than the $47,630 previously accepted by the IRS.

[Shook, 713 F2d 662, 52 AFTR2d 83-5868, 83-2 USTC ¶ 9564 (11th Cir. 1983).]

Use of estate income credited to beneficiaries' accounts to pay taxes creates liability for repayment. Decedent, who died in 1948, devised his estate in trust for the benefit of members of his family. The trust property included decedent's interest in three operating businesses, plus certain real property. By the terms of the will, the executors were directed to pay all administration costs and taxes before making any distributions to beneficiaries, and they were empowered to sell or to mortgage any of the trust's real property for such costs and taxes. At the same time, the will provided that the executors were to have the discretionary power to pay from estate income any part thereof to the beneficiaries during the period of administration and before the business property was transferred to the trust. The executors deemed it preferable not to exercise their power to sell or to encumber the real property, and instead used net income from the trusted business for the payment of death taxes. On the trust's books, the executors recorded all income received and credited each beneficiary's separate account. As cash payments were made, they were charged to the separate accounts and recorded as loans to the trust. Meanwhile, the executors organized a holding company to take possession of the assets of decedent's businesses. In transferring the property from the trust, the executors caused the newly formed corporation to repay the beneficiaries' loans. The IRS refused to accept the estate's characterization of these transactions and assessed deficiencies on the basis that the loan "repayments" were taxable income to the beneficiaries. The IRS contended that the net income, although posted to the account of the beneficiaries, remained part of the estate because decedent had not empowered the executors to make any distributions until after the payment of costs and taxes. Thus, in the IRS's view, the beneficiaries never possessed control of trust income and therefore could not make loans. Accordingly, the IRS concluded, the loan "repayments" by the corporation were taxable dividends.

Held: For the beneficiaries. Income from the unincorporated businesses was properly credited to the beneficiaries' accounts pursuant to the executor's power to make discretionary payments of estate income. The restriction on distributions was intended by decedent to ensure that taxes were promptly paid. This purpose was not incompatible with the desire to provide estate income distributions in cases where the executors saw fit to provide advances. The subsequent use of such money for tax payment was properly characterized as loans, and consequently the later repayments thereof by the trust could not be construed as dividends.

[Harris, 370 F2d 887, 19 AFTR2d 411, 67-1 USTC ¶ 9152 (4th Cir. 1966).]

Interest on bequest is taxable. Under the will of a California decedent, taxpayer was bequeathed $100,000. Decedent died in 1949, and in 1954 the Superior Court of Los Angeles County entered a decree whereby taxpayer was to receive $113,666. This amount constituted satisfaction of the $100,000 bequest, plus $13,666 compensation for delay in payment under the California Probate Code, which provided, in substance, that general pecuniary legacies, if not paid within one year of decedent's death, would bear annual interest thereafter at 4 percent. The IRS sought to tax the $13,666 as interest, but the federal district court held that the entire $113,666 was a bequest to taxpayer paid in one lump sum and that no portion of the payment was taxable as interest income. That court held that even if taxable as interest income, the $13,666 would not be income to taxpayer until 1955 under the conduit theory of taxation.

Held: Reversed for the IRS. The California statutory interest was includable in taxpayer's gross income. The court pointed out that the Supreme Court has held that the term "interest" as used in a revenue act bears the ordinary and well-known meaning of compensation for the use or forbearance of money. Furthermore, Section 61 specifically includes interest in its definition of "gross income," and by regulation provides that the term "interest" includes interest on legacies. As to the lower court's conduit theory, the court pointed out that taxpayer was a recipient of a money legacy and was not an income beneficiary of the estate. Under Section 662, the conduit theory applies only to estate income distributions. Thus, the payment to taxpayer in 1954 was gross income to him in that year.

[Folckemer, 307 F2d 171, 10 AFTR2d 5456, 62-2 USTC ¶ 9691 (5th Cir. 1962).]

Life tenant is found liable for capital gains. Taxpayer was bequeathed a life interest in her husband's property, with a power to consume principal as necessary for her support, comfort, and health. Taxpayer reported net capital gains from the sale of securities that were part of the principal of the life estate. The income was reported on fiduciary returns filed by taxpayer as a legal life tenant under the name of the "Harrison B. Riley Trust." After taxpayer's death, the executor of her estate sought a refund of taxes that she had paid on the capital gains. The IRS rejected the refund claim, on the ground that decedent was taxable as a fiduciary.

Held: For the IRS. The will provision permitting the life tenant to consume principal imposed a fiduciary duty on taxpayer in making withdrawals from principal. Thus, she was liable as a trustee for capital gains taxes on sales of principal assets. The narrow powers of taxpayer in the instant case justify treating her as a fiduciary.

[Security First Nat'l Bank, 181 F. Supp. 911, 5 AFTR2d 1069, 60-1 USTC ¶ 9327 (SD Cal. 1960).]

Court rejects novel "balancing" argument and finds beneficiary is fully subject to tax under Section 662(a)(2)(B). Taxpayer was the beneficiary of a testamentary marital trust created by her husband, who died in 1954. The trust consisted of one half of the estate's residuary assets. The husband also created four other trusts for the benefit of his children, consisting of the other half of the residuary estate. Taxes and expenses were to be paid solely from the second half of the residuary, not from the marital trust half. During 1955, and prior to the ultimate distribution of the residuary estate, the executors made total distributions of $36 million to taxpayer and other beneficiaries. Of this amount, taxpayer received 76 percent. Distributable net income for the taxable year was approximately $1 million. On audit, the IRS contended that taxpayer was taxable on her ratable 76 percent share of the entire distribution pursuant to Section 662(a)(2)(B), which provides that where the amounts distributed to all beneficiaries exceed the distributable net income of the estate, each beneficiary shall include in gross income an amount bearing the same ratio to distributable net income as the total amount distributed to such beneficiary bears to the total of the amount distributed to all beneficiaries. Taxpayer argued that despite the plain language of Section 662(a)(2)(B), she was required to include only 50 percent—not 76 percent—of the distributable net income in gross income. She attempted to demonstrate that part of her distribution was from corpus, and that whenever the executors paid taxes, they made an equivalent distribution to her from corpus. She asserted that the only reason she received more than 50 percent was that the executor, consistent with local practice, made distributions of principal to her in order to "balance" death tax payments and other principal distributions to the children's trusts. Thus, she disclaimed any tax avoidance motive in the transactions, and argued that Section 662(a)(2)(B) was not applicable.

Held: For the IRS. Under Section 662(a)(2)(B), the lack of a tax avoidance motive is irrelevant. Therefore, the IRS was upheld in its insistence that the full amount of distributable net income attributable to taxpayer was includable in her gross income. Neither the will nor local law required the executors to make such "balancing" distributions, and therefore Section 662(a)(2)(B) must be applied without reference to the executors' purpose or intent.

[Harkness, 469 F2d 310, 199 Ct. Cl. 721, 30 AFTR2d 72-5754, 72-2 USTC ¶ 9740 (1972), cert. denied, 414 US 820 (1973).]

Pecuniary legatees are not taxable on "interest" in excess of estate income. Decedent's will provided for specified dollar legacies, or shares of such legacies, to various beneficiaries. The estate was administered over the course of four years, during which time it reported considerable taxable net income. No distribution was made until the fourth year. State law provided that pecuniary legatees were entitled to interest at a fixed rate on their legacies until paid without regard to the amount of income actually earned by the estate.

Held: For taxpayers. To the extent that payments exceeded the actual income of legacy funds during the year in which the legacies were paid, such payments were not includable in the beneficiaries' taxable income for that year. The payments were either a distribution from accumulated income, in which case only the income for the year in question would be taxable, or a portion of the corpus, in which case they were totally nontaxable to the beneficiaries.

[Davidson, 149 F. Supp. 208, 50 AFTR 1948, 57-1 USTC ¶ 9462 (Ct. Cl. 1957).]

Expatriation during year does not create two separate tax years for purposes of timing receipts from testamentary trust. Taxpayer changed her status through expatriation from a U.S. citizen to a nonresident alien on December 23, 1975. On November 20, 1975, taxpayer received a distribution from a testamentary trust, comprising both distributable net income and an accumulation distribution. Although the distribution was received before her expatriation, taxpayer reported it as taxable income during the period after she became a nonresident alien, which subjected the distribution to a lower tax rate. The IRS contended that the distribution was actually received before taxpayer's change in status and thus was subject to the graduated tax rates of U.S. citizens.

Taxpayer maintained that under Sections 668(a) and 662(c), as they were then in force, the accumulation distribution should be includable in income during the period after expatriation. This argument was based on the provision in Regulation § 1.668-1A(a) which states that an accumulation distribution is includable when paid, unless the taxable year of the beneficiary differs from the taxable year of the trust. In such a case, the amount is includable, pursuant to Section 662(c), in the tax year of the beneficiary that coincides with or encompasses the end of the tax year of the trust. Taxpayer argued that under Regulation § 1.871-13(a)(1), by virtue of her change in status on December 23, 1975, she had two tax years, and that the end of the trust's tax year coincided with the end of the tax year in which she was a nonresident alien.

Held: For the IRS. The entire amount of the distribution from the testamentary trust was includable in income during the period before taxpayer's change in status and subject to the tax rates applicable to U.S. citizens. The court concluded that taxpayer's change in status did not function to create two separate tax years under Section 441(b)(3) and Section 443(a). Section 441 defines a "short tax year" as a period of less than twelve months for which a return is made. Such a short period, however, must arise out of one of three specific circumstances authorized under Section 443. These circumstances are:

1. When taxpayer changes his annual accounting period;
2. When taxpayer is not in existence for an entire taxable year;
3. When the Secretary terminates taxpayer's taxable year for jeopardy.

In the present case, taxpayer met none of the circumstances and in fact filed only one return for 1975, a Form 1040-NR, attaching a schedule of income allocations between the two periods. Hence, the court reasoned, taxpayer had but one tax year bifurcated into two periods.

[Furstenberg, 83 TC 755 (1984).]

Decedent's annuity distribution is taxable to surviving spouse. Taxpayer received a distribution from his deceased spouse's annuity policy. He claimed that the payments were received in his capacity as executor of the estate and thus were not includable in his income.

Held: For the IRS. Taxpayer was named as the beneficiary under the annuity contract, and the payments were taxable to him.

[Knight, TC Memo. (P-H) ¶ 90,252, 59 TCM (CCH) 661 (1990).]

Residence devised to taxpayers for rendering care to decedent until her death is held to be gross income. In 1959, taxpayers, husband and wife, entered into an enforceable agreement with an elderly woman whereby the elderly woman agreed to leave her residence to taxpayers in her will, provided that they would live with her and perform certain services for her for the remainder of her life. Taxpayers fully performed their obligations under the agreement and were devised the residence in 1980. Taxpayers did not report the value of the residence as income on their joint income tax return for 1980. The IRS determined a deficiency in their 1980 income tax, on the ground that the residence constituted compensation for services taxable as income under Section 61(a)(1). Taxpayers contended that they received the residence as a bequest specifically excludable from gross income under Section 102(a).

Held: For the IRS. Citing Wolder, 58 TC 974, 979 (1972), aff'd in part and rev'd and remanded in part, 74-1 USTC ¶ 9266, 493 F2d 608 (2d Cir. 1974), the court stated that whether the value of the residence constituted a bequest or compensation for services depended on the intention of the parties to the agreement and their performance in accordance with those intentions. The court found that there was an agreement to render services in payment for a specific will provision and that there was performance in accordance with the stated intentions. The court noted that the will provisions regarding the residence stated, "I am required to devise and bequeath to [*taxpayers*] for services rendered, my home." Accordingly, the residence constituted taxable income under Section 61(a)(1).

[Miller, TC Memo. (P-H) ¶ 87,271, 53 TCM (CCH) 962 (1987).]

Under state law, surviving spouse is not liable for self-employment tax while operating family business as "independent executrix." Prior to his death in 1973, decedent, a resident of a community property state, operated a producing oil and gas lease as an independent operator. He was subject to, and paid, self-employment tax on the full amount of income derived from the operation of the lease. Taxpayer, his surviving spouse, was engaged in the occupation of housewife prior to her husband's death. She did not pay self-employment tax. By his will, decedent appointed his surviving spouse the independent executrix of his estate. She duly qualified as independent executrix and received letters testamentary on January 3, 1974, from the local court. The will provided, and the court so ordered, that after taxpayer was sworn in as executrix, no further action would be taken by the court in the administration of the estate other than to receive in due course an inventory, appraisement, and list of claims of the estate. The inventory, appraisement, and list of claims were approved by the court on August 28, 1974. Taxpayer, pursuant to the terms of the will, inherited her deceased husband's entire estate. The IRS, asserting that taxpayer was operating the lease in her individual capacity, claimed that she was required to pay self-employment taxes on the oil and gas earnings.

Held: For taxpayer. The Tax Court held that in no sense was taxpayer carrying on a trade or business in her individual capacity and that during the taxable period at issue, she was serving as executrix of the estate. Under state law, the status of an independent executrix is solely administrative, even though this was a community property jurisdiction.

[Huval, TC Memo. (P-H) ¶ 85,568, 50 TCM (CCH) 1452 (1985).]

When can the surviving spouse roll over decedent's IRA? A surviving spouse who receives proceeds from her husband's IRA through a third party (such as at the discretion of a trustee), rather than directly from her husband, cannot roll over the proceeds into an IRA for her benefit in a tax-free transaction. This was the conclusion of the ruling cited below. Such a rollover will be allowed only if there is a way to circumvent the third party's control.

Decedent, who was survived by a spouse, had an IRA that named his estate as its beneficiary. He rolled over into the IRA assets from a qualified retirement plan. Under his will, he provided that if the real and personal property passing to his spouse did not equal the maximum amount eligible for the marital deduction, additional assets equal in value to the remaining amount of the available deduction were to be transferred to a marital trust for the benefit of his spouse. She would be entitled to all of the income from the trust and to distributions of principal at the trustee's discretion for maintenance, support, illness, misfortune, or emergencies. Upon the spouse's death, any remaining assets in the trust were to be distributed pursuant to a power of appointment exercised by the wife in her will. A bank was the personal representative of decedent's estate. The bank used a portion of the IRA proceeds for administrative expenses and intended to transfer the remaining IRA funds to the surviving spouse through the marital trust. The surviving spouse then planned to roll the funds over into an IRA for her benefit. Two rulings were requested from the IRS: (1) that decedent's IRA did not represent an inherited IRA within the meaning of Section 408(d)(3)(C) with respect to his spouse and (2) that, pursuant to Section 408(d)(3), the spouse was not required to include in income distributions from decedent's IRA that were rolled over into an IRA for the spouse.

The IRS reviewed the grantor trust rules of Sections 671 through 678 and determined that the surviving spouse would not be treated as the owner of the marital trust under Section 678 because, although she had a testamentary power of appointment over the trust assets, exercisable in her will, and she could appoint assets to her creditors or her estate, she had no power to vest the corpus of the trust in herself during her life. The IRS then examined the IRA rules in Section 408. Generally, under Section 408(d)(1), IRA distributions from funds generating a tax deduction when contributed to the IRA are includable in the recipient's gross income. There is an exception under Section 408(d)(3) for distributions that are rolled over to another IRA as provided in Sections 408(d)(3)(A) and 408(d)(3)(B). The entire amount received must be rolled over within sixty days of receiving the distribution. This rule does not apply if, within the one-year period ending on the day of the receipt of the funds, the recipient received any other distributions from an IRA that were rolled over. The IRS also discussed an "inherited IRA," which, under Section 408(d)(3)(C)(ii), is one that is acquired by the individual for whom it is maintained by reason of the death of another individual, and the surviving individual was not the spouse of decedent. Such a recipient cannot avoid including distributions from an inherited IRA in her taxable income by rolling the amounts over into another IRA, according to Section 408(d)(3)(C)(i). The IRS applied these rules to the facts of this ruling. According to the IRS, the surviving spouse did not qualify as a distributee of her husband's IRA for purposes of Section 408, because she was not the personal representative of the estate, she was not treated as the owner of the marital trust under Section 678, and distributions to her were made only pursuant to the trustee's unlimited discretion to invade principal for her benefit—not due to any right she had to receive funds directly. Therefore, she would not be taxed under Section 408(d) for any amounts distributed to her from her husband's IRA, but she would also be ineligible to roll any assets over into an IRA for her own benefit under Section 408(d)(3).

[Priv. Ltr. Rul. 9445029.]

[b] Effect of state law

Provisions of state law are held determinative on whether estate's distribution is treated as paid from income. Taxpayer was the widow and sole residuary legatee under the will of her husband, who died in 1955. During 1957, the local probate court ordered the estate to make a partial distribution of shares of corporate stock to taxpayer. The value of the shares distributed was $162,025, an amount exceeding the estate's distributable net income of $29,076 for the taxable year. The IRS, citing Section 661 and Section 662, determined that taxpayer received an amount includable in her gross income equal to the distributable net income on the year, and that the estate was entitled to a corresponding deduction. Taxpayer disputed the IRS's conclusions and argued that state law barred a distribution from estate income where, as here, the estate had not yet paid its outstanding debts, taxes, and administration expenses. She therefore contended that she could not be deemed to have received estate income by virtue of the stock distribution. The IRS argued simply that the distribution satisfied Sections 661 and 662 because the stock was an amount "properly paid" within the meaning of these two sections.

Held: For taxpayer. Because the distributed amounts were, under state law, subject to recall because they were made prior to the payment of outstanding estate liabilities, the distribution was not taxable under Section 662. Where there is no testamentary provision to the contrary, general state law controls for tax purposes on the question of whether a distribution of property is made from income or from estate assets. Thus, because governing state law required that income from the estate be used first to pay taxes and other expenses, and because the income was in fact so used, taxpayer was not in receipt of any amount subject to Section 662.

[Bohan, 456 F2d 851, 29 AFTR2d 72-739, 72-1 USTC ¶ 9286 (8th Cir. 1972).]

[c] Prenuptial agreements

Antenuptial agreement did not waive surviving spouse's right to retirement plan benefit. Decedent was the chief executive officer of a wholly owned corporation and the sole participant of its employees profit sharing plan (the Plan). The Plan was a qualified profit sharing plan subject to the rules and provisions of the Employee Retirement Income Security Act of 1974 (ERISA) and the Code.

Decedent was married three times. His last marriage occurred nine months prior to his death. Before the marriage, decedent's wife executed an antenuptial agreement (the Agreement), forgoing any right to decedent's property upon his death. The Agreement read, in part, as follows:

> Each party hereby waives and releases to the other party and to the other party's heirs, executors, administrators and assigns any and all rights and causes of action which may arise by reason of the marriage between the parties ... with respect to any property, real or personal, tangible or intangible ... now owned or hereafter acquired by the other party, as fully as though the parties had never married.

Decedent's sole heir was his son from his first marriage. Decedent's son brought an action against decedent's wife in Supreme Court, New York County, requesting a declaration that he was the sole beneficiary of the Plan benefits. Decedent's wife removed the action to federal district court and filed a counterclaim seeking a declaration that she was the rightful recipient of the benefits and that the antenuptial agreement did not effectively waive her rights. Both parties moved for summary judgment. The district court granted decedent's wife's motion. Decedent's son appealed the ruling.

Held: Affirmed for decedent's wife. Summary judgment is appropriate if, based on the evidence presented, there is no genuine issue of material fact and the moving party is entitled to prevail as a matter of law. The parties in this case agreed that there was no dispute over material facts and that the sole issue was whether the antenuptial agreement was an effective waiver of decedent's wife's benefits under decedent's retirement plan. Decedent's son argued that New York law should be relied on for guidance because ERISA did not address the effectiveness of an antenuptial agreement as a spousal waiver. The court ruled against any application of New York law because ERISA supersedes any and all state laws that may apply to an employee benefit plan. Furthermore, the court pointed out that ERISA sets out plainly the requirements for an effective spousal waiver of benefits. These requirements are as follows:

> (2) Each plan shall provide that an election [of a waiver] ... shall not take effect unless—(A)(i) the spouse of the participant consents in writing to such election, (ii) such election designates a beneficiary (or form of benefits) which may not be changed without spousal consent (or the consent of the spouse expressly permits designations by the participant without any requirement of further consent by the spouse), and (iii) the spouse's consent acknowledges the effect of such election and is witnessed by a plan representative or a notary public.

The Agreement signed by decedent's wife did not satisfy these requirements and did not designate a beneficiary or acknowledge the effect of the
waiver. Moreover, decedent's wife was not decedent's spouse at the time that
she signed the agreement. Decedent's son also argued that the district court's
interpretation of the statute and the Agreement conflicted with Congress's intent in enacting the statute. According to decedent's son, the purpose of the
statute was to protect nonworking spouses who contributed services to their
families but had no financial security from such contributions. He took the position that there was no indication that Congress intended to disinherit decedent's children from a previous marriage. Thus, the statute must be interpreted
broadly under decedent's son's line of reasoning. The court disagreed. Though
it was likely that Congress had not anticipated a situation where two older,
wealthy individuals were married for only a number of months, and it was
clear that Congress did intend to protect long-term partners, by the same token,
the statute did not indicate an intent to disenfranchise newlyweds. Furthermore, decedent's son's interpretation of the statute would require that the individual circumstances of each waiver request be examined, which is difficult to
do when one of the main parties is deceased. One purpose of the ERISA provisions was to set established procedures that would eliminate the need for extensive case-by-case examination and that would be a safeguard against fraud.

[Hurwitz v. Sher, 982 F2d 778, 93-1 USTC ¶ 50,282 (2d Cir. 1992), cert. denied, 508 US 912 (1993).]

**Payments by testamentary trust in accordance with prenuptial agreement
are taxable to surviving spouse to extent paid out of trust income.** Taxpayer and her late husband entered into a prenuptial agreement. On December
27, 1928, taxpayer agreed to accept on her husband's death $5,000 annually
for her life in lieu of any and all claims of dower that she might possess
against his estate. In 1942, the husband instituted divorce proceedings in local
court. Shortly thereafter he executed his last will and testament, which made
no provision for taxpayer beyond that set forth in the prenuptial agreement.
Eight months later, with the divorce action still pending, the husband died. According to the terms of his will, a trust was established to provide for the annual $5,000 payments and to furnish support for their minor son. Taxpayer
renounced the will and repudiated the prenuptial agreement in an effort to
claim her elective share pursuant to state statute. A suit was filed, and eventually a negotiated settlement was reached under which taxpayer would receive
the $5,000 annuity as originally planned. The court approved the settlement,
and payments commenced in 1944.

During the taxable years in question, 1950 through 1953, the trustees reported on their fiduciary returns that the $5,000 was paid from current trust in-
come. Consistent with the trust's treatment of the annual payments, the IRS
demanded that taxpayer include such payments in her gross income. She there-

upon commenced an action in state court challenging the trustee's right to pay the annuity from income when the trust was formed primarily to provide support for the son. The state court heard the action and declined to rule directly on the merits of taxpayer's claim. The court instead characterized the trust's liability to her as a charge against the entire trust estate "payable from principal if necessary." It further found that the income of the trust was intended for the support of the son, and that therefore taxpayer was not a beneficiary of the trust estate or the income thereof. In the subsequent Tax Court proceeding concerning assessed deficiencies for 1950 through 1953, taxpayer contended that the state court's opinion should be read as directing the trust to pay the annual $5,000 out of corpus, in which case she would have no tax liability for the years in question. The IRS based its position on provisions of the 1939 Code (the predecessors to Section 662 and related sections), which required that a trust beneficiary include in gross income those amounts paid from the trust's distributable income. From this, the IRS concluded that because the payments were made at regular intervals from either income or trust principal, they were taxable to the extent that they were not in excess of distributable income. The Tax Court held for the IRS, rejecting taxpayer's argument that the $5,000 represented her share of the marital estate as agreed to in the prenuptial contract. In the Tax Court's view, the decision rendered by the local court did not preclude the trustees from making the payments from income, and therefore, to the extent so characterized by the trust, taxpayer was required to report the payments as taxable income.

Held: Vacated and remanded for taxpayer. The Fourth Circuit was in full agreement with the basic legal findings of the lower court, but reversed for a determination of the division of trust income between taxpayer and her son. Under the settlement agreement as adopted by the state court, taxpayer's annual payments could be made from income or principal, and therefore it was not clear from the record whether the payments actually made were derived from income. Accordingly, the court remanded the case to the Tax Court for a determination of the source of such payments.

[Offutt, 276 F2d 471, 5 AFTR2d 1111, 60-1 USTC ¶ 9354 (4th Cir. 1960).]

[d] Prolonged estate administration

Estates terminated for unreasonably long administration periods have income attributed to beneficiary. Taxpayer's mother died in 1968, leaving all of her property in trust for her son, with decedent's husband serving as trustee. Decedent's husband died in 1969, naming taxpayer as independent executor of his estate. By July 1971, the wills of the two decedents were admitted to probate, federal and state estate taxes were paid, and all other formal steps of independent administration were completed. However, taxpayer failed to close

the estates. The IRS determined that the administration period was unduly prolonged, terminated the estates for federal income tax purposes, pursuant to
Regulation § 1.641(b)-3(a), as of the end of 1976, and attributed the income
reported by the estates from 1976 to 1981 to taxpayer as beneficiary under the
wills. Immediately thereafter taxpayer received permission from a state probate
court to continue the administration of the estates, and, citing Frederich, 145
F2d 796 (5th Cir. 1944), argued that the period of administration approved by
the state probate court should be used to determine when income should be attributed to an estate or beneficiary.

    Held: For the IRS. Regulation § 1.641(b)-3(a), which authorizes the ter-
mination of an estate for federal income tax purposes where the period of administration has been unduly prolonged, is valid. *Frederich* was overruled by
Estate of Bosch, 387 US 456 (1967), which recognizes the IRS's right to impose a reasonableness standard.

[Brown, 890 F2d 1329, 65 AFTR2d 90-448, 90-1 USTC ¶ 50,026 (5th Cir.
1989).]

Eighth Circuit upholds IRS on undue period of administration argument.
Decedent and his brother, taxpayer, were business partners providing services
for various railroads. In 1944, decedent died, and taxpayer was named in the
will as his sole heir and executor. Accordingly, on the date of death, taxpayer
held 45 percent of the stock personally and the balance of 55 percent in his capacity as executor. The estate tax liability of decedent's estate was finally determined in June 1954, nearly ten years after the date of death. From that time
until 1957, the estate continued in existence, with the estate reporting all income attributable to decedent's partnership share. The IRS assessed deficiencies against taxpayer for 1956 and 1957, based on its conclusion that the
estate's administration period was unduly prolonged and that taxpayer should
be taxed on the estate's income for that period. Taxpayer argued that the
twelve-year period of administration was necessitated by the need to respond
to certain estate and income tax controversies and to defend against lawsuits
and Labor Department actions.

    Held: For the IRS. The evidence showed that the only matter pending in
relation to the administration of the estate that could reasonably be considered
a cause for not closing that administration prior to 1955 was certain litigation
that ended in September 1955. Nothing in the record supported taxpayer's
claims that the estate had substantial matters outstanding in 1956 and 1957,
and therefore judgment was entered for the IRS respecting deficiencies assessed for 1956 and 1957.

[Miller, 333 F2d 400, 14 AFTR2d 5066, 64-2 USTC ¶ 9579 (8th Cir. 1964).]

**Estate administration is not unduly prolonged where executors have "seri-
ous" litigation pending, plus unresolved claims to personal property.** At

the time of her death in 1957, decedent possessed cash assets in excess of $1 million plus numerous interests in oil and gas properties and farmland. Her debts totaled less than $30,000. As a result of her dealings in relation to a working interest in an oil project, decedent in 1953 entered into an agreement with a major oil company whereby she relinquished her ownership rights for a royalty interest. The agreement provided, inter alia, that decedent would retain an option to repurchase certain oil-related equipment in order to recover its salvage value. She was also involved as a defendant in a lawsuit, pending since 1952, in which the plaintiff sought to recover possession of certain property and compensation for oil allegedly extracted therefrom by the defendants. By 1960, three years after the date of death, the executors satisfied all of decedent's specific bequests and all claims against her estate, except for the two outstanding matters involving the repurchase option and the lawsuit. The executors continued their negotiations in both matters and eventually settled the repurchase controversy in 1964. In that same year, they made an offer to settle the lawsuit for a lump-sum cash payment. The IRS began an audit of the estate in 1963, six years after the date of death, and concluded that the estate remained open for an unreasonable length of time. Consequently, the IRS assessed deficiencies based on its determination that the beneficiaries should have been taxed on all estate income arising after 1960. The executors argued that the pending litigation and property claims were sufficient justification for keeping the estate open, and they disputed the IRS's attribution of estate income to the beneficiaries.

Held: For the estate. Under governing law, the rule is established that the period of administration or settlement of an estate is the period that is actually required by the executor to fulfill the ordinary duties of administration, such as the collection of assets, the payment of debts, and the settlement of claims. The period of administration cannot, however, be unduly prolonged, and, if such period is unreasonably prolonged, the IRS may consider the estate closed for federal income tax purposes after the expiration of a reasonable period for administration. The question of whether the estate administration was unreasonably prolonged is one of fact, to be determined under all of the relevant circumstances affecting the executor in the diligent discharge of his duties. In the instant case, the evidence showed that the claims against the estate were nominal in comparison to its total value, but the fact remained that the unresolved litigation was of a "serious" nature, affecting properties that were a significant part of the estate. In view of the need to pursue the repurchase claim and to defend against the pending lawsuit, the court concluded that the estate was not held open for an unreasonable period and that the beneficiaries were therefore not liable for tax on post-1960 estate income.

[Wylie, 281 F. Supp. 180, 21 AFTR2d 972, 68-1 USTC ¶ 9286 (ND Tex. 1968).]

Court of Claims refuses to find eighteen-year period of administration unreasonable. Prior to his death in 1938, decedent served as the president of a family owned and operated bottling business. His estate consisted largely of his stock holdings in the company, but at the same time, it had an aggregate indebtedness of $108,142. Because the stock generated substantial annual income, the executrix chose to pay the indebtedness solely from income in order to avoid a sale of the stock. The local probate court assented to the arrangement and ordered that the estate should remain open until the debt was fully extinguished. As a result, the estate's administration period extended from 1938 through the end of 1956, a period of eighteen years. The IRS, however, determined that the estate's administration period was unduly prolonged, and it assessed deficiencies based on its attribution of estate income to the beneficiary.

Held: For the estate. Because there was a bona fide purpose in keeping the estate open, the period of administration was not unreasonably prolonged. The court paid great deference to the judgment of the state probate court and refused to "disregard" or "lightly" weigh its findings. The record showed that when the stock was finally disposed of in 1956, the estate realized a substantial profit and promptly retired its debt. From this, the court concluded that the decision to avoid an untimely sale was based on sound business factors and was necessary to keep the estate open. In addition, there was no indication that tax considerations played any part whatsoever in the estate's liquidation plan. Consequently, the deficiencies were dismissed, and the estate itself was permitted to report all gross income for the disputed period.

[Carson, 317 F2d 370, 161 Ct. Cl. 548, 11 AFTR2d 1471, 63-1 USTC ¶ 9469 (1963).]

Jointly held survivorship property cannot be unduly retained by estate. Decedent died in 1953, leaving a will that named her husband as executor and bequeathed to him her entire estate, consisting of various real estate and partnership interests in a cattle business. The estate tax return was filed in September 1954. For income tax purposes, however, the estate stayed open until July 1957. The IRS took the position that the estate's administration period was unduly prolonged and, accordingly, assessed deficiencies against the husband, as taxpayer, for taxable years 1953 through 1956. The IRS's principal contentions involved:

1. Certain real property, owned jointly by decedent and taxpayer, the IRS viewed as vesting in taxpayer on the date of death;
2. Certain community property that, according to the IRS, also vested in taxpayer by operation of California community property law; and
3. Certain income-producing partnership interests that the IRS concluded were unnecessarily administered by the estate.

Taxpayer disputed each of these assertions, arguing that he and decedent did not own "true" joint tenancy property and that the duration of administration was justified by the need to litigate a tax matter and to defend against a negligence suit filed against the estate.

Held: For the IRS, in part. On the issue of the real estate owned jointly by the parties prior to decedent's death, the Tax Court found that title thereto passed to taxpayer on decedent's death and that taxpayer was fully taxable on all income arising from that property. Under California law, a presumption of joint tenancy arises where record title is taken by a husband and wife jointly. In the absence of evidence to rebut that presumption, the Tax Court concluded that a valid joint tenancy existed. Accordingly, the IRS's deficiency was sustained as to income arising after taxpayer's acquisition of full title by virtue of his survivorship rights. On the other issues, however, the Tax Court found that the estate's administration period was not unreasonably prolonged. The court flatly rejected the IRS's argument that taxpayer's expectancy of receiving the property under the will, when coupled with his management duties as estate executor, necessarily resulted in such complete domination over estate assets as to require that he be taxed as the full beneficial owner. The court concluded that under state law, taxpayer was subject to substantial restraints in dealing with estate property, and that his interest was secondary at all times to the estate's superior claim and to his fiduciary duties with respect to the disputed property. The court found that the estate was justified in delaying distribution of property in view of the pending lawsuit and the existence of a tax controversy then being litigated. Consequently, judgment was entered to reflect the disallowance of the assessments based on estate income from the property retained to satisfy such claims.

[Petersen, 35 TC 962 (1961).]

[e] Support allowances

Ninth Circuit finds widow's allowance payable from estate income is fully taxable to her. Following the death of taxpayer's husband, the local probate court ordered that she was entitled to receive a widow's allowance and that it be paid expressly from the estate's income. The IRS contended that the estate's income distributions to taxpayer were therefore taxable to her. Taxpayer argued successfully in federal district court that Sections 643(c), 661(a), and 661(b) do not purport to tax that part of a widow's allowance that is paid to her by court order out of estate income. The basis of her argument was that she was a widow, not an "heir, legatee or devisee," within the meaning of the statutes.

Held: Reversed for the IRS. The court examined the statutory scheme for taxing estates under Subchapter J and concluded that a widow who derives her right to receive an allowance from estate income is a beneficiary as fully as if she were an "heir, legatee or devisee." Consequently, the receipt of estate income by one who is not a creditor, and who derives the right to income by virtue of the decedent's death, subjects them to tax under Subchapter J.

[James, 333 F2d 748, 14 AFTR2d 5017, 64-2 USTC ¶ 9576 (9th Cir. 1964), cert. denied, 379 US 932 (1964).]

Minor children of decedent are held to be fully taxable on estate support payments under Section 662(a)(1). Following decedent's death in 1967, taxpayers, his minor children, received monthly support allowances paid by the estate pursuant to a probate court order. The estate deducted these payments on its fiduciary income tax returns for 1967 and 1968, but not on its federal estate tax return. Taxpayers treated the amounts in a similar fashion and did not include them as gross income. The IRS determined, however, that taxpayers were fully taxable on all amounts received. The IRS based its position on Section 662(a)(1), which provides that a beneficiary shall include in gross income the amount of income for the taxable year required to be distributed currently to such beneficiary, regardless of whether the amount is to be paid from income or corpus, to the extent that such amount is paid out of estate income. Thus, the items to be reported in gross income are limited to the extent that all current estate distributions exceed distributable net income (DNI). Taxpayers conceded that the estate had DNI in excess of the amounts paid for support, but they argued that the distributions were paid to them not as estate beneficiaries, but rather as minor children entitled to their father's support without tax liability.

   Held: For the IRS. Because the payments were made solely by reason of the father's death, taxpayers were to be treated as estate beneficiaries fully subject to taxation under Section 662(a)(1). The court noted that Section 643(c) defines the term "beneficiary" as including, expressly without limitation, heirs, legatees, and devisees. Given this broad legislative intent, the court was constrained to include taxpayers within Section 643(c), despite the fact that they received the payments as a statutory right in preference to most other estate charges.

[Cameron, 68 TC 744 (1977).]

[f] Will contests

Lump-sum compromise settlement of claim against residuary beneficiary is excludable under Section 102(a). Taxpayer was the son of Jean Paul Getty (JPG) and Adolphine Getty (AHG). Prior to their marriage, AHG and JPG had entered into a prenuptial agreement, which was amended on several occasions after their marriage. The couple obtained a Mexican divorce in 1932, and

AHG subsequently tried to attack the validity of the divorce. In a letter to AHG, JPG threatened that if AHG pursued this course of action, he would leave nothing to taxpayer. Originally, taxpayer was to be treated equally with JPG's other children under his will, but prior to writing the letter to AHG, JPG executed a codicil reducing taxpayer's bequest to $5,000. In 1934, a trust was established by JPG and his mother, into which JPG contributed $1 million in stock of Getty Oil and his mother contributed $2.5 million in promissory notes made by the corporation. Jean Paul Getty was named trustee of the trust. The purpose of this trust was to transfer control of Getty Oil to JPG while providing his mother with assurance regarding the financial security of JPG and his issue. Jean Paul Getty was to receive the income from the trust during his lifetime and then to his children in certain proportions, but JPG could waive his right to the income, in which case it would be distributed to the children in certain proportions. The terms of the trust were such that taxpayer's income interest was limited to $3,000 in all events, and his half-brothers received $9,000 each and were to share equally in any income remaining after the initial distributions. The trust was to terminate upon the death of the last surviving son of JPG and was then to be distributed among all of JPG's grandchildren per stirpes. The rationale behind the inequality of the income distributions was that taxpayer was expected to acquire a sizable inheritance from his maternal grandfather. In 1935, after AHG returned to California upon JPG's request, JPG amended his will to provide for an equal distribution to taxpayer, but the terms of the trust were not amended. Taxpayer's maternal grandfather lost his wealth when the Nazis came to power, and taxpayer inherited nothing from him. In 1940, it was discovered that there was no language in the trust document rendering it irrevocable, and JPG's mother informed him that if the trust was revocable, she wished to revoke it to render it more equitable in its income distributions. Jean Paul Getty then brought an action against his mother and sons to declare the trust irrevocable. In this action, taxpayer, then only eleven years old, was represented by his mother, AHG. Adolphine Getty signed and delivered certain pleadings that JPG had asked her to sign after he gave her his assurance that the inequality of the trust would be rectified. Jean Paul Getty's mother executed a new will that provided for a testamentary trust for taxpayer in the amount of $200,000 and for his half-brothers in the amount of $50,000 each. This was to remedy the inequality of the 1934 trust. Over a course of years, JPG continued to clarify to taxpayer and AHG that he intended to nonetheless remedy the inequality of the 1934 trust. In the 1960s and 1970s, however, JPG stated that the inequality was remedied by his mother's testamentary trusts, which were by then established. Upon JPG's death, taxpayer received 2,000 shares of Getty Oil, then valued at $330,000, some personal effects, and a life interest in a home in Italy, from which he received $1.5 million when it was sold. Jean Paul Getty's other sons received only nominal bequests under the will. Taxpayer received no more than $3,000 in income from the 1934 trust. After JPG's death, taxpayer brought an action against the trustees and beneficiaries of the 1934 trust and JPG's estate and its residuary beneficiary, the J. Paul Getty Museum (the Museum). Taxpayer claimed that JPG's promise to equalize the treatment of taxpayer with the treatment of his half-brothers under the 1934 trust was never accomplished. In 1980, the Museum, upon advice of counsel, entered into a settlement with taxpayer for $10 million in exchange for taxpayer dropping the claim against the Museum. Taxpayer did not report receipt of this settlement in his income tax return for 1980, on the ground that the amount was received in lieu of an outright bequest under JPG's will. The IRS claimed that the amount was not a bequest, devise, or inheritance, because taxpayer did not directly challenge JPG's will. The Tax Court sustained the IRS's determination that the $10 million was includable in taxpayer's 1980 income tax return as ordinary income. On appeal, taxpayer attempted to demonstrate that the $10 million he received from the trustees of the museum fit into the exclusion provided by Section 102(a).

Held: Reversed for taxpayer. The Tax Court's factual conclusions indicated that taxpayer satisfied his burden of persuasion. Even though taxpayer did not show that, had JPG remedied the inequality, he necessarily would have done so with a bequest of property, taxpayer did show and the Tax Court found that JPG probably would have done so with a bequest of property. This was all that the burden of persuasion by a preponderance of the evidence required in this case. The $10 million settlement payment was excludable from taxpayer's 1980 gross income.

[Getty, 913 F2d 1486, 66 AFTR2d 90-5517, 90-2 USTC ¶ 50,502 (9th Cir. 1990).]

Will contest settlement paid in installments out of estate income is taxable income to recipient. Decedent died testate in 1950 and was survived by his wife, taxpayer. By the terms of his will, decedent provided for the establishment of a trust containing all of his property plus his stock in a realty company, with directions to pay the larger of one fourth of the divided income or $500 per month to taxpayer. In further dispositions of the bulk of his estate, decedent made generous provisions for a number of other relatives and their lineal descendants. Taxpayer challenged the validity of her husband's will during probate, alleging noncompliance with statutory formalities of execution. The probate court held that the will was valid and properly executed. The court entered its order accordingly. Thereafter, taxpayer appealed and sought a jury trial de novo on the essential issues. The motion was granted, and, in 1951, after two days of trial testimony, taxpayer and the estate entered into a stipulated settlement, which the trial court entered of record as its final judgment in the case. The compromise agreement provided in part that taxpayer was to receive a fixed monthly amount in exchange for her relinquishment of all claims and rights in decedent's estate. During taxable years 1956 and 1957, taxpayer received the payments as agreed. The estate fiduciary tax return showed the amounts as being paid out of estate income. Taxpayer, however, did not report the amounts in her gross income. The IRS assessed deficiencies based on its conclusion that the payments constituted taxable income from "an interest in an estate or trust" pursuant to Section 61(a)(15). Taxpayer argued that the payments were excludable from gross income under Section 102, which permits a taxpayer to receive property from an inheritance tax-free. She also argued that the payments were derived from the settlement agreement, not from estate or trust income. Thus, in taxpayer's view, the payments were paid to her by the beneficiaries of the trust as consideration for the relinquishment of her marital rights under the will, and that they therefore represented installment payments made in lieu of her inheritance.

Held: For the IRS. Under Section 102(b), the exclusion of inherited property from gross income is expressly inapplicable to amounts received by an heir that are paid from estate or trust income. In the present case, both the will and the settlement agreement provided for taxpayer to receive amounts solely from income. There was no indication that she was paid a lump sum in installments pursuant to a liability owed by the other beneficiaries. The court reviewed several earlier decisions involving essentially the same issue and concluded that taxpayer's payments were received through inheritance and were in fact made from trust income at monthly intervals.

[Williams, 36 TC 195 (1961).]

Settlement in estate dispute is held not to be taxable income. Taxpayer's natural father married taxpayer's stepmother in June 1956. In 1968, the father and stepmother acquired legal title as joint tenants to real property located in Santa Barbara County, California. Approximately ten years later taxpayer's father executed a grant deed concerning his interest in the property to taxpayer. The deed was signed by taxpayer's father, notarized, and recorded approximately two years thereafter in the local county recorder's office. Taxpayer's father died on June 5, 1980. Twelve days later taxpayer's stepmother filed a civil complaint in Santa Barbara Superior Court to set aside the 1978 deed to taxpayer. Five months later, taxpayer filed a cross-complaint in the same court, naming his stepmother as a cross-defendant. This cross-complaint alleged that taxpayer acquired an undivided half-interest in the property in the 1978 deed. He also requested a judicial determination as to his interest in the property and requested a partition of it. Taxpayer and his stepmother continued court proceedings. After approximately three years of litigation and twenty-five court filings over this property, a settlement was reached. Taxpayer's stepmother agreed to pay taxpayer $390,000, and both parties agreed to execute a stipulation for entry of judgment stating that the 1978 deed was null and void. Taxpayer agreed to execute and deliver a quitclaim deed in which he would disclaim any interest in the property. The settlement agreement specifically stated that the covenants therein and the $390,000 payment to taxpayer were "in lieu and instead of any inherited interest in the property." The settlement agreement also stated that taxpayer's stepmother would pay and hold the petitioner harmless for all federal estate and gift taxes and California inheritance and gift taxes. Taxpayer received the $390,000 in the taxable year 1983, but did not report the settlement amount as income on his tax return. Taxpayer contended that the settlement payment was excludable from gross income pursuant to Section 102, because it was in lieu of a gift or any inherited interest in the property. The IRS contended the amount received either was capital gain from the sale of the property or was paid as part of a nuisance settlement.

Held: For taxpayer. The court first noted that taxpayer did not receive the $390,000 payment by gift, devise, bequest, or inheritance, but rather by settlement of a lawsuit. Regardless of whether a dispute is resolved through litigation or settlement, the nature of the underlying action determines the proper tax consequences. The taxability of a settlement is controlled by the nature of the litigation. The nature of the litigation is in turn controlled by the origin and character of the claim that gave rise to the litigation. The court stated that in characterizing a settlement payment for tax purposes, the test to be applied is stated most simply as follows: "In lieu of what were the damages awarded?" The court then examined the settlement agreement, which specifically stated that the payment was in lieu of any inherited interest in the property described in the grant deed. The origin and character of the dispute involved the validity of a gratuitous transfer of an interest in real property to taxpayer by his father, pursuant to the 1978 deed. Taxpayer's stepmother requested the court to declare that deed null and void, whereas taxpayer requested a partition of his alleged interest in that property. Accordingly, the court concluded that the underlying claim arose from the dispute as to the validity of a gratuitous transfer of the property to taxpayer. The payment of the settlement proceeds represented a payment for any interest that may have been acquired from the gratuitous transfer by his father pursuant to the 1978 deed. The settlement payment was therefore held to be properly excludable from taxpayer's 1983 gross income under Section 102(a).

[Vincent, RIA TC Memo. ¶ 92,021, 63 TCM (CCH) 1776 (1992).]

IRS rules on treatment of income during will contest. *A* died in 1972, leaving personal property and real property that was disposed of by decedent's last will. The personal property was decedent's estate for purposes of Section 641(a)(3). All interests in the real property, including the right to collect income therefrom, passed to *B*, the devisee under the will. The will was contested, and the income from the personal property collected by the executor was not paid or credited to any legatee or other beneficiary during the period from *A*'s death to February 1974, when the will was upheld. During the will contest, the rents from the real property devised to *B* were collected on *B*'s behalf by *C*. The applicable state statute and the court with jurisdiction over the will contest imposed no restrictions on the disposition of the income derived from the properties during the will contest.

The IRS cited Regulation § 1.641(a)-2, which provides that the gross income of an estate consists of all items received during the taxable year, including, among other items, income received by estates of deceased persons during the period of administration or settlement of the estate. Accordingly, the IRS ruled that the executor must include in the estate's gross income the income received relating to the personal property subsequent to the date of *A*'s death. The IRS further indicated that if a taxpayer receives earnings under a claim of right and without restriction as to its disposition, taxpayer has received income, even though there is a claim that taxpayer is not entitled to retain the earnings, and even though taxpayer may be required subsequently to return an equivalent amount. Therefore, the income derived from the real property was includable in *B*'s gross income, notwithstanding the will contest.

[Rev. Rul. 75-339, 1975-2 CB 244.]

[2] Deductions

Bequest of proceeds, not property, prevented loss deduction. Decedent's will provided that if his estate contained a particular parcel of rental real estate, the parcel was to be sold and up to $400,000 of proceeds divided equally between his brother and sister. The remainder of the estate was to go to another individual. After the brother and sister expressed an intention to contest the will, they entered into a stipulation with the other party concerning the division of property. Among other things, the stipulation removed the ceiling on the proceeds amount the brother and sister could receive and provided that they would pay selling costs from the proceeds. The property was eventually sold for $355,000—less than its $435,000 date-of-death value. On the theory that he was a half-owner of the property, the brother deducted half of the difference between the property's date-of-death value (i.e., his purported basis in the property) and the sale proceeds from the property as a Section 165 loss on his tax return. The IRS, however, contended that he could not claim a loss because he never owned the property.

Held: For the IRS. Under both the will and the stipulation, the court determined that the heir possessed only an expectancy to proceeds from the property's sale; he never inherited (or had title to) the underlying property itself. Rather, the estate owned the property. Therefore, the heir possessed no basis in the property and could not deduct a loss on its sale.

[Hummel, 81 AFTR2d 98-2246 (SD Ind. 1998).]

Charitable deductions of estate are not excess deductions on termination.
Taxpayer was the sole income beneficiary of a residuary trust established by
an estate. In the year in which the estate terminated, the residuary trust
claimed the estate's excess deductions under Section 642(h)(2). Although the
excess deductions had no effect on the taxable income of the trust, they did
substantially reduce taxpayer's taxable income as the trust's sole income beneficiary. In computing its excess deductions on its final return, the estate included its Section 642(c) charitable contribution deductions in its total
deductions. Had the estate not included these charitable contribution deductions, it would not have had excess deductions. The IRS determined that the
estate had no excess deductions that could be claimed by taxpayer under Section 642(h)(2), because the charitable contribution deductions were improperly
included in the estate's computation of excess deductions. Taxpayer contended
that the amount by which the estate's total deductions (including its Section
642(c) charitable contribution deductions) exceeded its gross income was an
excess deduction under Section 642(h)(2). Taxpayer further contended that to
the extent that the amount of the excess deduction did not exceed the estate's
noncharitable contribution deduction, it was deductible by her under Section
642(h)(2) as a beneficiary of the estate.

    Held: For the IRS. Section 642(h)(2) expressly provides that if, on the ter-
mination of an estate, the estate has excess deductions other than Section
642(b) or Section 642(c) deductions, the beneficiaries may claim those excess
deductions. Therefore, when an estate computes its excess deductions for purposes of Section 642(h)(2), it must disregard its charitable contribution and
personal exemption deductions. The charitable contribution deductions are allowed only in the computation of the estate's taxable income and are not allowed to be claimed for the benefit of noncharitable beneficiaries. Thus,
because the estate's noncharitable and nonpersonal exemption deductions did
not exceed its gross income, there was no excess deduction for taxpayer to
claim under Section 642(h)(2).

[O'Bryan, 75 TC 304 (1980).]

[3] Basis of Distributed Property

Only portion of property included in estate gets basis step-up. Decedent
had a life estate in a trust created by her husband at his death. She also had
two powers over the trust:

1. She could withdraw the greater of either 5 percent of the trust corpus
   or $5,000 per calendar year for her life.
2. She had a limited power of appointment over 5 percent of the trust,
   which she could exercise in favor of her late husband's lineal de-

scendants and their spouses alone. She could not exercise the power of appointment in favor of herself, her creditors, her estate, or the creditors of her estate.

At the time of decedent's death, the FMV of the trust's corpus was $755,759; $600,000 of this was attributable to the family home, which was worth only $259,000 at the husband's death. It was sold for $600,000 after decedent's death. Because of the limited power of appointment, 5 percent of the trust's value was included in decedent's estate. Taxpayer in the instant case, however, was not the late husband or decedent, but their daughter. Taxpayer had a 30 percent remainder interest in the trust and received 30 percent of the trust's proceeds following her mother's death. She asserted that the trust's basis in the home was its FMV on her mother's date of death. The IRS, however, computed the basis as 95 percent of the FMV at the husband's death, plus 5 percent of the FMV at decedent's death.

    Held: For the IRS. According to Section 1014(a), property acquired from a decedent generally receives a basis equal to its FMV at the date of decedent's death. Section 2041(a)(2) states, however, that only the portion of the property over which decedent had a power of appointment was includable in her estate. Thus, decedent's estate correctly included only 5 percent of the trust. On the other hand, this means that only 5 percent of the trust qualified for a stepped-up basis. Therefore, the IRS's calculation of basis was accurate.

[Prokopov, 82 AFTR2d 98-6792, 98-2 USTC ¶ 60,329 (2d Cir. 1998).]

Basis of property is stepped up to date-of-death value, despite lack of legal title. Decedent died on March 28, 1975, leaving an estate valued at $7,213,604. Under his will, the residuary estate was to be divided between a marital trust and a residuary trust. Decedent's wife was the income beneficiary of both trusts and had a general power of appointment over the corpus of the marital trust. Decedent's wife died in November 1981. In her will, she exercised her power of appointment over the corpus of the marital trust by appointing it to an inter vivos trust for the benefit of her three grandchildren. At the time of her death, the trusts established under decedent's will were not yet funded. The assets in decedent's estate substantially increased in value to $28,184,342. In June 1982, decedent's estate sold all the stock it held in Danbury Fair, Inc. The net proceeds from the sale totaled $25,399,454. In computing the capital gain, the estate used as its basis the value of the stock at the time of decedent's death, $1,779,993. It reported a capital gain of $23,691,521 and paid capital gains tax of $4,719,784. Shortly thereafter the estate distributed $2,563,596 to the marital trust.

    In August 1982, decedent's wife's estate filed its federal estate tax return, which included the $2,563,596 in the marital trust, treating it as a pecuniary or fixed bequest. The IRS determined that the bequest to the marital trust should have been treated as a fractional share bequest (a proportionate share of the residue) rather than as a pecuniary bequest and that the appreciation in value of that proportionate share should have been included in decedent's wife's estate. This increased the value of the trust by approximately $6,300,000, to $8,863,596, and increased the estate tax by $3.4 million. Approximately one year later decedent's estate filed a claim for refund of $1,485,882 for an alleged overpayment of fiduciary income tax. The estate argued that because decedent's wife's estate included the appreciated value of the property in the marital trust on its estate tax return, decedent's estate could use the stepped-up basis to determine the amount of capital gain on the sale of the property. The IRS denied the refund claim, and the estate sued. The district court ruled in favor of the IRS, finding that decedent's estate could not use the step-up in basis to calculate its capital gain. The estate appealed the ruling.

Held: For taxpayer. Section 1014, which regulates the computation of basis in property received from a decedent, generally provides that the basis of property in the hands of a person "*acquiring* the property from a decedent or to whom the property *passed* from a decedent" (emphasis added) is the property's FMV at decedent's death. The IRS contended that decedent's estate always possessed the property in the marital trust. Therefore, it never "acquired" anything from decedent's wife's estate, so decedent's estate could not use the value of the stock at her death as its basis in the stock that was sold. The Second Circuit disagreed and found that the IRS had not applied the definition of "property" consistently. It was an undisputed fact that the power of appointment that decedent's wife held over the assets in the marital trust caused those assets to be included in her estate, even though the marital trust had not yet been funded. Decedent's wife was the beneficial owner of such assets for estate tax purposes until she died. At her death, her appointee, the inter vivos trust, acquired her interest in the property. Although the executor of decedent's estate was responsible for managing, liquidating, and distributing the assets in his estate and retained legal title to those assets, his estate did not "possess any real ownership interest in the property." It simply held or managed the property on behalf of the beneficiaries of the marital trust. Similarly, although the estate was liable for paying the capital gains tax arising from the sale of property that had not yet been distributed to the marital trust, the tax payment came from the proceeds of the sale. Consequently, the tax burden actually fell on the beneficiaries of the trust. The circuit court concluded that whether decedent's estate could use the stepped-up basis depended on whether decedent's wife's appointee, the inter vivos trust, could have used the stepped-up basis to calculate capital gains on sales of marital trust property after decedent's wife's death. The court determined that decedent's wife's appointee could use the stepped-up basis. Although the inter vivos trust did not actually hold the stock when it was sold, it acquired a beneficial interest in the stock through decedent's wife. The court reviewed the provisions of Section 1014 that describe the basis of property acquired from a decedent. According to the court, Congress did not intend to interpret the words of acquisition in Section 1014—

"acquiring" and "passed from"—literally. The opinion cited one of a number of examples found in Section 1014(b) of how property can be acquired from a decedent. Under Section 1014(b)(4), "property passing without full and adequate consideration under a power of appointment exercised by decedent by will" is property acquired from decedent. Also cited was Regulation § 1.1014-4(a)(1), which states that the basis of property acquired from a decedent is uniform in the hands of any persons possessing or enjoying the property under a will or other instrument, regardless of whether the property is possessed or enjoyed by an executor or administrator, an heir, a legatee or devisee, or a trustee or beneficiary of a trust.

The fact that decedent's estate delayed distributing the assets to the marital trust did not affect the basis. The court pointed out that to say otherwise would allow executors to manipulate tax consequences by their decisions regarding when to distribute estate assets. Decedent's wife's appointee, the inter vivos trust, was deemed to have acquired the stock upon decedent's wife's death, and such appointee could use the stepped-up basis. Decedent's estate, which was holding and managing the property for the appointee, could also use the stepped-up basis when determining the amount of capital gain upon the sale of the property.

[Connecticut Nat'l Bank, 937 F2d 90, 91-2 USTC ¶ 60,079, 68 AFTR2d 91-5170 (2d Cir. 1991).]

Basis step-up was denied for installment notes. Taxpayer and her deceased husband jointly held several mortgage notes they received in their 1986 sale of three condominiums. The couple elected to report the sale gains under the installment method (which allowed them to pay tax on the gain as the sale proceeds were received over several years, rather than as a lump sum in the sale year). After her husband died in 1987, taxpayer continued to report the gain in accordance with their earlier installment election. Once the notes were paid in full in 1993, taxpayer filed amended returns claiming refunds on the gain she had reported in the years following her husband's death. Taxpayer based her claim on the premise that she was entitled to a step-up in basis in the notes after her husband died. Using the alleged basis step-up, taxpayer concluded that she had overcalculated and overreported the gain for those post-death years. The court disagreed. Section 1014(a) provides a step-up in basis in certain property that passes or is acquired from decedent. The basis of such property in the recipient's hands becomes the property's FMV at the date of death or at an alternative valuation date if an election was made under certain circumstances. Under Section 1014(c), however, this basis step-up is not available for IRD. Under Section 691, IRD includes income items reportable by a decedent under the installment method.

Held: For the IRS. The court first addressed Section 1014's applicability to decedent's interest in the jointly held notes. The court rejected taxpayer's attempt to avoid the Section 1014(c) limitation with her contention that the 1986 sale was a sale of investment properties and that the mortgage notes were investment assets, not income instruments. Regardless of this "investment" characterization, the gain on the sale was income that was reportable in installments; as such, it constituted an item of IRD. Thus, taxpayer had no right to a basis step-up on the transfer of her deceased husband's interest in the notes. The court then turned to Section 1014's applicability to taxpayer's own one-half interest in the notes. Under Section 1014(b), property that is considered to have been acquired or passed from a decedent includes a surviving spouse's one-half share of community property if one half of that community interest was includable in decedent's estate. Standing alone, this provision seemed to provide taxpayer a basis step-up for her one-half interest in the notes. Nevertheless, the court found that the installment notes did not fit within the statute's basis step-up framework; taxpayer could not simply rely on this subsection and override Section 1014(c)'s express declaration that the step-up does not apply to IRD. The court noted that, although taxpayer's separate community interest was not technically IRD, her interest would qualify for the basis step-up only by virtue of its fictional characterization as property passing from decedent (i.e., taxpayer's interest, although not actually passing through decedent's estate, would be treated as a constructive transfer from decedent under Section 1014(b)). The court reasoned that taxpayer could not take advantage of this fictional transfer treatment without paying heed to the limitations the statute also places on such transfers. Thus, reading the statutory provisions in context, the court concluded that the jointly held mortgage notes were property representing IRD, and the notes retained that character in taxpayer's hands. As such, the notes did not qualify for a basis step-up under Section 1014.

[Holt, 39 Fed. Cl. 525, 97-2 USTC ¶ 50,929, 80 AFTR2d 97-7677 (1997).]

Surviving joint tenant gets step-up for 100 percent of pre-1977 interest. On the death of her husband in 1991, taxpayer became the sole owner of a co-op apartment that they had purchased in 1972 as joint tenants with right of survivorship. The full $700,000 date-of-death value of the apartment, which cost $44,000, was included in the husband's estate tax return. Taxpayer sold the apartment in 1993 for $720,000 and, after increasing the $700,000 basis for commissions and other selling expenses, reported no gain on the sale for federal income tax purposes. Taxpayer argued that because the joint tenancy was created prior to 1977, and because she provided no part of the consideration for the purchase, the contribution rule of Section 2040(a) applied and, consequently, under Section 1014, she was entitled to a stepped-up basis in 100 percent of the property. According to the IRS, because taxpayer's husband died after 1981, as a matter of law the 50 percent inclusion rule of Section 2040(b)(1) applied and thus taxpayer was entitled, under Section 1014, to step up the basis of only half the property. Accordingly, the IRS found the basis to be approximately $428,000 (i.e., half of the original cost basis ($22,000) plus half of the date-of-death value ($350,000) plus selling expenses ($56,000)). After allowing the then-applicable Section 121 one-time exclusion of $125,000 of gain from the sale of a principal residence, the IRS determined a $167,000 gain on the sale. Section 1014 generally provides that the basis of property acquired from a decedent is the FMV of the property on the date of decedent's death or on the alternate valuation date. Under Section 1014(b)(9), however, a surviving joint tenant is deemed to have acquired property from decedent only to the extent the property was required to be included in decedent's estate. The portion of the property not included in decedent's estate retains the survivor's adjusted basis. Before 1977, Section 2040 provided that the gross estate included the value of all property held by decedent and another person in a joint tenancy or tenancy by the entirety, except for the part of the entire value that was attributable to consideration furnished by the other person. Thus, the rule established a "contribution test" to determine the portion of jointly owned property included in a decedent's estate. The statute created a rebuttable presumption that the value of the entire property was includable in the deceased joint tenant's estate, and the burden of showing original ownership or contribution to the purchase price by the surviving joint tenant fell on the estate. Section 2040(b), added by the Taxpayer Relief Act of 1976, created a special rule whereby, for certain "qualified joint interests" of a husband and wife created after 1976, only one-half of the value of the property so owned was includable in decedent's gross estate, without regard to which spouse furnished the consideration to acquire the jointly held property. Section 2040(c) through Section 2040(e) were added by the Taxpayer Relief Act of 1978, to provide a mechanism whereby an election could be made to treat joint interests created prior to 1977 as "qualified joint interests." Finally, in 1981 ERTA repealed Section 2040(c) through Section 2040(e) and redefined "qualified joint interest" to eliminate the requirement that the creation of the joint interest be treated as a gift. The 1981 amendments applied to the estates of decedents dying after 1981. The operational provision of Section 2040(b)(1) providing for 50 percent inclusion was not changed, however.

Held: For taxpayer. The issue, according to the Tax Court, was whether Section 2040(b)(1) applies to joint interests created before 1977, where the deceased joint tenant died after 1981. The court found that it did, and it rejected the IRS's position that the 1981 amendment to the definition of "qualified joint interests" in Section 2040(b)(2) somehow modified the effective date provision of Section 2040(b)(1). Gallenstein, 975 F2d 286, 70 AFTR2d 92-5683 (6th Cir. 1992), dealt with the same issue. The Tax Court in the instant case followed the Sixth Circuit's reasoning in holding that Congress, merely by changing the definition of "qualified joint interests" in Section 2040(b)(2), did not expressly repeal the effective date of Section 2040(b)(1). An express repeal can be found only where a subsequent statute expressly states that it repeals a portion of the former statute. The court also could not find that the effective date was impliedly repealed. Absent evidence of an affirmative intention to repeal, an implied repeal can be found only where two acts are in irreconcilable conflict or where a subsequent act covers the whole subject of an earlier act. The two acts here peacefully co-exist, as Section 2040(b)(1) applies to a "qualified joint interest" created after 1976, while Section 2040(b)(2) merely redefines "qualified joint interest" for estates of decedents dying after 1981. In addition, because the two statutes in the instant case are not mutually exclusive, the court could not conclude that the later statute filled the entire area of law, thereby rendering the prior statute ineffective. Moreover, the express repeal of Section 2040(c) throughSection 2040(e) was persuasive evidence that Congress did not also intend to repeal Section 2040(b)(1)'s effective date. Finally, the court rejected the IRS's concern regarding the potential for abuse where a surviving spouse furnished the entire consideration for the jointly held property. The IRS speculated that the estate of the deceased joint tenant could purposely fail to carry its burden of proving that the survivor furnished any of the consideration, resulting in 100 percent of the property being included in decedent's gross estate under Section 2040(a). In addition, according to the IRS, a corresponding step-up in the survivor's basis for 100 percent of the property with no concurrent increase in estate tax (because of the unlimited marital deduction). The IRS argued that Congress did not intend this result. According to the court, however, the IRS simply misunderstood the operation of the burden of proof in this situation. For estate tax purposes, Section 2040(a) raises a rebuttable presumption that decedent furnished the entire consideration for the jointly held property. For income tax purposes, however, Section 1014(b)(9) allows a step-up in basis only for property "required to be included" in decedent's gross estate. Thus, in the income tax setting—the context in which the instant case arose—taxpayer has the burden of proving that decedent furnished the consideration for the jointly held property in order to receive a step-up in basis.

[Hahn, 110 TC 140 (1998).]

Tax Court resolves basis question arising from conditional testamentary devise of property. Taxpayer's father died testate in 1940, and by his last will devised to taxpayer a tract of partially developed land in Pennsylvania. The father stipulated, however, that taxpayer's legacy was to be conditioned on his payment of a lifetime annuity to his mother, plus the sum of $2,000 to his brother, to be paid in monthly installments. In 1958, the state condemned part of the land for highway construction, and in 1959, taxpayer received payment in compensation. On his 1959 income tax return, taxpayer elected under Section 1033 not to recognize gain, indicating his intention to replace the condemned property. By the end of the statutory replacement period, however, his expenditures for substitute property were lower than the basis of the condemned property, and therefore he was required to include the difference as income. For purposes of calculating the taxable amount, taxpayer contended that his basis was equal to the FMV of the property at the time of his father's death, plus the amounts paid to his brother and mother as required under the testamentary conditions. By the IRS's reckoning, however, the actuarial value of the annuity and the discounted value of payments to the brother were in excess of the FMV of the land on the date of death. The IRS further maintained that taxpayer's payments to his family members were gifts to the extent that they were in excess of FMV. Therefore, the IRS concluded that taxpayer was a purchaser of the property from his father's estate and that he had a Section 1012 cost basis equal to FMV.

Held: The Tax Court carefully examined the extensive factual record and concluded that there was a substantial equivalence between the FMV of what taxpayer received and the anticipated payments that he undertook to make. Consequently, it rejected the argument that he made taxable gifts. The court found that taxpayer had made a purchase of the property; therefore, his basis should be determined under Section 1012, not under Section 1014 as it pertains to inherited property. Accordingly, the court held that taxpayer's basis was equal to the discounted value of the obligations without regard to the stipulated FMV, thereby rejecting the arguments of both the IRS and taxpayer.

[Vaira, 52 TC 986 (1969), acq. 1971-2 CB 3.]

Basis is determined from date of death, despite intervening life estate. Taxpayer received real property through a devise, subject to an intervening life estate and limited power of appointment. Taxpayer took sole possession when the life estate ended and the power lapsed. He later sold the land to his three children, who assumed the mortgage, but held a right to cancel the sale. They transferred the land to voluntary trusts for two years, after which time the land was reconveyed to taxpayer. In computing long-term capital gain, taxpayer used as his basis the FMV of the land when the life estate ended. The IRS used the date on which the land passed under the will, decedent's date of death. Taxpayer responded by arguing that in any case, no sale had occurred.

Held: For the IRS. The possibility that the sale could be canceled did not make the exchange conditional, and the right to cancel was not unrestricted. The correct valuation date for the land was the date of death for the original transfer by will.

[Juden, TC Memo. (P-H) ¶ 87,302, 53 TCM (CCH) 1154 (1987), aff'd, 865 F2d 960, 63 AFTR2d 89-595, 89-1 USTC ¶ 9142 (8th Cir. 1989).]

IRS rules on basis effect of distribution of excluded foreign-situs real estate. *D*, who was a citizen and a resident of *Z*, a foreign country, died in 1982. *D* owned real property located in *Z*. *B*, a U.S. citizen, inherited the real property in accordance with the laws of *Z*. At the time of *D*'s death, the real property had a basis of $100x and a FMV of $1,000x. Because the real property was located outside the United States, and because D was a nonresident alien, the value of the property was not includable in D's gross estate under Section 2103 for purposes of the federal estate tax. B sold the real property in 1983 for $1,050x, claiming a basis of $1,000x and a gain of $50x.

The IRS ruled that B inherited the real property from D, and that such property was within the description of property acquired from a decedent under Section 1014(b)(1). Therefore, B would be entitled to a stepped-up basis under Section 1014(a). Under Section 1014(b)(9)(c), Section 1014(b)(9) does not apply to property described in Section 1014(b)(1); hence, the requirement of Section 1014(b)(9) that property be included in the value of a decedent's gross estate does not apply.

[Rev. Rul. 84-139, 1984-2 CB 168.]

Surviving spouse's share of community property reacquired from revocable trust is considered acquired from decedent-spouse for basis purposes. In 1958, a husband and wife who lived in California transferred their community property to a revocable trust. Under the trust instrument, either spouse could, while both were alive, alter, amend, or revoke the trust. Income was to be applied for the benefit of the grantors. Therefore, under Section 676(a), they were treated as the owners of the trust property, and, under Section 671, the income, deductions, and credits of the trust were included in computing the grantors' taxable income. In 1965, one of the spouses died, and the trust was divided into two separate trusts—one being the community interest of the husband and the other being the community interest of the wife. Income from decedent's share, which was in an irrevocable trust, was to be paid to the survivor and another individual. The survivor also received the income from his or her separate trust. For purposes of Section 1014(b)(6), the husband and wife continued to own the property transferred to the revocable trusts as community property.

The IRS ruled that in computing the gross estate under Sections 2033, 2036(a)(1), and 2038(a)(1) for the first decedent, one half of the community interest in the property held in the revocable trust was includable. The surviving spouse's interest in one half of the property in the revocable trust was considered to have been acquired from decedent under Section 1014(b)(6), and the basis of this one-half interest was determined under Section 1014(a).

[Rev. Rul. 66-283, 1966-2 CB 297.]

Right to reacquire property barred basis step-up. A surviving spouse was denied a step-up in basis for property includable in his wife's estate in the ruling cited below, because he retained the right to reacquire the property from a revocable trust. Approximately one month before her death, decedent and her spouse established a revocable living trust that was funded with jointly held property. Either spouse could have revoked the trust during their lives, which would have resulted in each spouse receiving a one-half interest in the property free of the trust. Upon the death of the first spouse, decedent's one-half interest in the property would pass to the survivor. In addition, either spouse could direct the trustee in writing to use the trust assets to pay the taxes and debts of the first spouse to die. Neither spouse exercised the revocation right, and the surviving spouse did not direct the trustee to pay decedent's expenses.

The executor included the one-half trust interest of both spouses in the estate. The surviving spouse's interest was included under Section 2041, which provides that an estate includes any property over which decedent had, at death, a general power of appointment. A general power of appointment includes a power to appoint to (1) decedent, (2) decedent's estate, (3) decedent's creditors, or (4) creditors of decedent's estate. Under Section 1014(a), the basis of property passing from decedent to a beneficiary is the FMV at the date of death, or an alternate valuation date. Property passing from decedent includes property acquired through the exercise or nonexercise of a power of appointment. Section 1014(e) provides that this step-up in basis does not apply under the following conditions:

1. Decedent acquired the appreciated property by gift during the one-year period ending on the date of death.
2. The property is acquired from decedent by, or passes from decedent to the donor or the donor's spouse.

The estate requested a ruling as to whether the surviving spouse's one-half interest in the trust was eligible for a basis step-up under Section 1014(a), or ineligible under Section 1014(e).

The one-year rule of Section 1014(e) was intended to prevent taxpayers from making gifts of appreciated property to a family member in anticipation of a basis step-up upon the family member's death. According to the legislative history, Congress viewed such transactions as lacking substance because the donor never ceded complete control of the property. The IRS ruled that the inheritance was ineligible for a step-up in basis because the surviving spouse's power to reacquire the property represented control over his one-half interest in the trust which was retained until decedent's death. Under these circumstances, a step-up in basis was "unintended and inappropriate" under Section 1014(e).

[Tech. Adv. Mem. 9308002.]

¶ 13.04 COMPLIANCE AND PROCEDURE

Change in accounting method does not justify adjustments under Section 481. A business owner used the cash basis method of accounting. After his death, the estate used the same method of accounting, but the IRS insisted that it change to the accrual basis method in order to reflect income clearly. The IRS recomputed the estate's income on this basis, including as income certain accounts receivable that were assets of the estate collected by it during the tax year in question and representing sales made by decedent prior to his death. The estate contended that the IRS effectively changed the method of accounting in decedent's last return, making the estate's income subject to adjustments under the provisions of Section 481(b)(4)(A).

Held: Affirmed for the IRS. The Sixth Circuit affirmed the Tax Court's holding that the adjustments were not proper. No change in accounting was in fact made on decedent's return, and, because the estate was a separate taxable entity from decedent and the tax period in question was its first year to file a return, there was no "preceding taxable year" under which the estate's income was computed using a different method. Although Section 691(a)(3) allows the character of receipts to be the same to the estate as it would have been to decedent, that section does not activate Section 481.

[Biewer, 341 F2d 394, 15 AFTR2d 398, 65-1 USTC ¶ 9245 (6th Cir. 1965).]

Administrator fails in effort to enjoin wrongful IRS tax levy. Taxpayer's husband died in 1980. In 1984, the IRS sent a notice of deficiency to taxpayer, as administratrix of the husband's estate, relating to his income tax liability for 1978 and 1979. Taxpayer and decedent filed joint returns for 1972 through 1977, but not for 1978 or 1979. Taxpayer filed a separate return for 1979, but never filed a 1978 return. In 1985, the IRS sent a notice of levy to taxpayer's employer seeking to enforce collection of the taxes owed by the deceased husband. The IRS eventually released the levy after inquiry by the employer. Thereafter taxpayer brought an action in federal district court to enjoin the IRS from further enforcing the levy against her.

Held: For the IRS; injunctive relief denied. The court determined that the issue was moot because the IRS released the levy. In addition, no threat of another wrongful levy existed. Taxpayer's contention that reoccurrence was possible was rebutted by an IRS employee's testimony that all computerized records were adjusted to eliminate the possibility of the issuance of another wrongful collection notice.

[Haywood, 642 F. Supp. 188, 58 AFTR2d 86-5983, 86-2 USTC ¶ 9812 (D. Kan. 1986).]

Constructive fraud created transferee liability. Taxpayers were the heirs of their mother's estate. Distributions to them from the estate left insufficient funds to pay the estate's income taxes. The IRS imposed transferee liability based on Florida state law against fraudulent conveyances.

Held: For the IRS. The effect of the conveyance was to hinder or to delay income tax collection. Thus, the transfers were constructively fraudulent under the relevant state law and transferee liability was properly imposed.

[LeBeau, 63 TCM 3177, RIA TC Memo. ¶ 92,359 (1992).]

Request for extension of time to file Form 1041 establishes tax year. An executor filed a request for an extension of time to file a fiduciary income tax return, indicating a calendar tax year. He also paid 25 percent of the estimated tax due for the period from decedent's death in August to December 31. An extension was duly granted by the IRS. When the return was finally filed, however, the executor based the return on a fiscal year rather than on a calendar year. The IRS disallowed the use of a fiscal year, holding that the filing of a request for extension indicating December 31 as the final day of the taxable year established the accounting period for the estate. Any change to another accounting period requires the IRS's prior approval.

[Rev. Rul. 69-563, 1969-2 CB 104.]

CHAPTER 14

Determining Taxable Gift Transfers

¶ 14.01 TAXABLE TRANSFERS

[1] Generally

Trustee's transfer of trust property was not a gift. Taxpayer transferred shares of stock in his closely held company to his three children. He created irrevocable trusts for two of his children and gave a third child his shares outright. The third child later bought the remaining shares owned by taxpayer. Subsequent to the creation of the trusts for his children, some of the stock in the trusts was transferred to trusts for two grandchildren. Taxpayer and his attorney were co-trustees of the trusts. The trust agreement specified that all decisions were to be made unanimously and that taxpayer had no right to act as sole trustee. Moreover, the grantor and trustees were prohibited from purchasing, exchanging, or otherwise dealing with or disposing of trust assets for less than adequate or full consideration in money or money's worth. The trustees made such a disposition in 1986 when they, as directors of the closely held company, authorized a recapitalization of the company. Pursuant to the recapitalization, the common stock held by the trusts was exchanged for preferred stock with a value substantially less than that of the common stock. The trustees did not seek court approval for the transfer. In addition, the transfer was performed without informing the trust beneficiaries, two of whom were minors. The IRS contended that the transaction was actually a gift by taxpayer to the third child, who presumably held the common stock, that increased in value as a result of the recapitalization. The Tax Court ruled that a gift did occur, resulting in the imposition of a gift tax deficiency of $978,960, and negligence penalties of $575,953.

Held: Reversed for taxpayer. The Second Circuit said that New York law applied when determining ownership of the transferred securities because the trusts were created in New York and the recapitalization occurred there. New York courts have emphasized strongly the duties and obligations of trustees. Although taxpayer and his attorney orchestrated the recapitalization in their positions as directors of the closely held company, they were still trustees of the trusts. Their positions as corporate officers could not supersede or supplant their duties and obligations as fiduciaries. Therefore, the Second Circuit concluded that the Tax Court erred as a matter of law in holding that taxpayer did not make the transfer in his capacity as trustee. Furthermore, if taxpayer acted alone, as the Tax Court held, his actions violated the provision in the trust agreement requiring the trustees to act jointly. The appellate court then cited Section 288 of the Restatement (Second) of Trusts and Comment: (a) thereunder, which state that if a trustee transfers trust assets in a manner which breaches the trustee's fiduciary duty, and the transferee is aware of the breach, the transferee does not take the property free of the trust, even if he paid value for the property. The transferee holds the property in a constructive trust for the beneficiary of the original trust, and such beneficiary can compel the transferee to return the property to the trust. A transfer is not a gift, and not subject to gift tax, until any power to revoke or recall the gift has terminated. This is true regardless of whether the right to reclaim the property was expressly reserved by the donor, or arose by indirection or operation of law. Because an individual who receives trust property as a result of a breach of trust holds the property in a constructive trust, and has an obligation to return it to the trust, the transfer is not a gift. This conclusion is supported by Regulation § 25.2511-1(g)(1), which states in part:

> A transfer by a trustee of trust property in which he has no beneficial interest does not constitute a gift by the trustee (but such a transfer may constitute a gift by the creator of the trust, if until the transfer he had the power to change the beneficiaries by amending or revoking the trust).

It was clear from the trust agreement that taxpayer did not retain any beneficial interest in the trust property. Because he was not the owner of the property, the transfer was not a gift to the transferee. Furthermore, although taxpayer was acting in his position as a corporate director when he initiated the recapitalization, he was still a trustee with all the related duties and obligations. Since the property was not transferred for adequate value, his actions as a trustee violated his fiduciary duty.

[Saltzman, 131 F3d 87, 80 AFTR2d 97-8365, 97-2 USTC ¶ 60,295 (2d Cir. 1997).]

Payment by jointly and severally liable donor of entire state gift tax constitutes further gift to codonor. In 1976, taxpayer made gifts resulting in both Wisconsin and federal gift tax liability. Under Wisconsin law, the donor and donee were jointly and severally liable for payment of the state gift tax. Taxpayer paid the full amount of Wisconsin gift tax arising from these gifts. The IRS asserted that payment of the Wisconsin tax resulted in an additional gift to his donee for federal gift tax purposes, equal to one half of the state tax paid. Specifically, under Wisconsin law, the donor and donee are each responsible for half of the tax liability. Taxpayer, by paying the full amount of the Wisconsin tax, satisfied the donee's share of such liability. Taxpayer argued that under federal tax law, a joint and several liability for taxes requires each obligor to be responsible for the full liability. Therefore, as noted in Regulation § 25.2511-1(d) with regard to the joint and several tax liabilities of spouses, full payment of a joint tax liability is not a gift to the nonpaying obligor.

Held: For the IRS. The full payment of joint tax liability results in a gift.

[Doerr, 58 AFTR2d 86-6327, 86-1 USTC ¶ 13,670 (ED Wis. 1986), aff'd, 819 F2d 162, 59 AFTR2d 87-1275, 87-1 USTC ¶ 13,721 (7th Cir. 1987).]

Failure to convert preferred stock is taxable gift. Taxpayer owned common stock and Class A nonvoting, noncumulative, 7 percent preferred stock of a corporation in which the only other shareholders were members of her family. The Class A stock was convertible into Class B preferred, which was entitled to a 7 percent cumulative dividend. In addition, the holders of Class B preferred could require the corporation to redeem it for a stated amount plus accumulated dividends. Taxpayer created an irrevocable trust for her grandchildren and transferred her common stock to the trust. The IRS then claimed that by failing to convert her Class A stock to Class B stock, taxpayer made a continuing gift to the other common stockholders to the extent of the forgone accumulated dividends on the Class B preferred ($181,370 per year). Taxpayer contended that there was no gift, because the corporation did not liquidate or sell the stock that it held. In taxpayer's view, until the value of that stock was realized and distributed to the common shareholders, no value was transferred to them.

Held: For the IRS. The court concluded that taxpayer relinquished her right to accumulate unpaid dividends of $181,370 per year. To the extent that the stock owned by the corporation increased in value enough each year to have paid the entire cumulative dividend, taxpayer made a gift to the common shareholders. There was enough increased value in the stock to support the accumulated dividend if taxpayer converted her Class A preferred. In addition, the absence of a requirement to pay cumulative dividends to the preferred on redemption would positively affect the value of the common stock.

[Snyder, 93 TC 529 (1989).]

Forgone dividends on preferred stock of family corporation did not result in gifts to owners of common stock. In 1982, taxpayer merged his three wholly owned corporations into a new corporation of which he received all common stock. He then gave his children 10 percent of these shares and exchanged the remaining common stock for noncumulative preferred as part of the reorganization. One issue before the court was whether the failure, from 1983 through 1986, of corporation's board of directors to declare or to pay dividends on the preferred stock gave rise to taxable gifts to taxpayer's children, the holders of the common stock.

Held: For taxpayer. Based on the evidence presented, the board of directors had valid business reasons for not voting to pay dividends, and the failure to pay dividends did not constitute a gift to the common shareholders. Taxpayer demonstrated that the company needed to expand its inventory and open new stores in new locations to remain competitive and that it had a longstanding practice of not assuming debt.

[Daniels, 68 TCM 1310, RIA TC Memo. ¶ 94,591 (1994).]

Surviving spouse's purchase of QTIP remainder is a gift. A surviving spouse's purchase of a remainder interest in a qualified terminable interest property (QTIP) trust gave rise to a taxable gift. This prevented the surviving spouse from shifting the value of the remainder interest out of her estate at no transfer tax cost. Taxpayer's husband's will established a trust that gave taxpayer a qualifying income interest for life. Taxpayer was not given a general power of appointment over the trust property, and the remainder was to be distributed outright to taxpayer's adult child on taxpayer's death. The husband's estate elected to treat the trust property as a QTIP and claimed a marital deduction for it. Subsequently, taxpayer acquired her child's remainder interest with a promissory note for the interest's face value. The trustee then distributed all of the trust assets to her; she subsequently used some of those assets to satisfy the note. The net effect was a termination of the trust, with taxpayer gaining assets equal to the value of her life interest and the child gaining assets equal to the remainder interest's value. Taxpayer contended that she received full and adequate consideration for the promissory note, therefore no taxable gift resulted from the transaction. The IRS disagreed. Under Section 2056, an estate may claim an estate tax marital deduction for a QTIP in which a surviving spouse is given a qualifying income interest for life. This defers the tax on the property until the spouse dies or makes a lifetime gift of the income interest. Pertinent to the transaction in the instant case was Section 2519, that treats a spouse's "disposition" of any part of a qualifying income interest in a QTIP as a gift of the remainder. The IRS found that "disposition" includes relinquishments or terminations of a surviving spouse's right to receive income. Therefore, the IRS concluded that, because the transaction was a sale or commutation terminating taxpayer's income interest in the QTIP, the transaction effected a disposition of that interest for Section 2519 purposes. A commutation is a proportionate division of trust property between the life and remainder beneficiaries. Commutations in the QTIP context are essentially sales of the spouse's income interest for a payment equal to the interest's value. Further, sales and commutations are expressly characterized as dispositions in Regulation § 25.2519-1. Because the transaction essentially mirrored the regulatory examples, terminated the trust and left taxpayer and child with assets equalling their respective income and remainder interests' values, it was considered a commutation of taxpayer's income interest. Thus, taxpayer's purchase of the QTIP remainder was treated as a disposition of her income interest, resulting in a deemed gift under Section 2519. To further support this conclusion, the IRS pointed out that the receipt of an asset that does not effectively increase the recipient's gross estate is generally not considered adequate consideration for transfer tax purposes. The IRS concluded that, because the full QTIP trust was already subject to estate or gift tax, taxpayer's receipt of the remainder interest did not increase the value of her taxable estate. Thus, the transfer resulted in a gift, taxable under Sections 2511 and 2512.

[Rev. Rul. 98-8, 1998-7 IRB 24.]

Enforced promise to make gift is taxable. A parent promised his sixteen-year-old child in writing in 1972 that if the child graduated from college, he would give him $10,000. The child graduated in 1977, and the parent refused to pay. In 1978, the child sued successfully for the payment and received the full amount in that year.

The IRS ruled that the gift was made in 1977, when the child graduated from college, thus causing the promise to become binding. The IRS ruled that for gift tax purposes, a gift occurs when a promise to make the gift becomes binding, even if the donee must sue to enforce the gift and it is paid in a later year.

[Rev. Rul. 79-384, 1979-2 CB 344.]

IRS rules on tax effects of gift of stock option. In the ruling discussed below, taxpayer is an employee of X corporation and holds a number of options to purchase X's stock. The ruling states that these options would be taxable under Section 83. For most nonqualified options, Section 83 typically creates a taxable transaction when the option is exercised, leaving the employee taxable on the difference between the option price and the fair market value (FMV) of the stock on the date of exercise. The employer receives a corresponding deduction at that time. Because such options generally are not susceptible to valuation when they are granted, the critical time for taxation is the time of exercise. Most such options are not transferable by corporate employees. The instant ruling indicates, however, that the corporate employer intends to amend its plan to permit limited transferability of options granted or to be granted. The class of permitted transferees will be limited to immediate family members, partnerships in which the only partners are members of the employee's immediate family, and trusts established solely for such immediate family members. Once the plan is amended, taxpayer intends to transfer the options to certain of his immediate family members. Each option will remain subject to the provisions of the plan and therefore will be exercisable as provided by the plan. After the transfer, the family member will have the sole responsibility for determining whether and when to exercise the options. The IRS indicated that, in this case, the options do not have a readily ascertainable FMV at the date of the grant. Also, because the transfer of the options to the family member will not be pursuant to an arm's-length transaction, they will not be considered disposed of under Regulation § 1.83-7(a).

Based on these facts, the IRS issued a number of rulings. First, the transfer of the stock options to the family members will be a completed gift for gift tax purposes. The amount of the gift will be the FMV of the options transferred on the date of the gift. The IRS noted that the FMV of the options for gift tax purposes will be determined under Regulation § 25.2512-1. Factors such as the possibility that the terms of the options may permit the options to be exercised without payment, and the possibility that the committee designated by the employer's board of directors may allow the exercise of the options without payment, should be considered in valuing the options for gift tax purposes. In addition to this conclusion, the IRS ruled that the transfer of the stock options to the family members will not cause the recognition of taxable income or gain to taxpayer. If, however, the family member subsequently exercises the options, taxpayer (or taxpayer's estate if taxpayer is not living) will be deemed to receive taxable compensation under Section 83, and the corporate employer will receive a corresponding deduction under Section 162. If the family member exercises the stock options, this individual's basis in the stock acquired will be its FMV on the date of exercise, which consists of the consideration paid by the family member and the income taxed to taxpayer or to taxpayer's estate under Section 83. The IRS also ruled that the transfer of the stock options to the family members will not be subject to Section 2701 or 2703 of ¶ 14 and that, once the gift is complete, neither the stock options nor the stock obtained upon exercise of the options will be includable in taxpayer's estate.

[Priv. Ltr. Rul. 9616035.]

Grantor's payment of income tax liability of trust may be an additional gift to remaindermen. *A* and *B* each transferred shares of *X*, an S corporation, to irrevocable grantor trusts that they created. Each trust was structured as a grantor-retained annuity trust (GRAT). Among other provisions, each trust agreement required the trustee to reimburse the grantor for the income tax liability paid by the grantor with respect to trust income not distributed to the grantor.

The IRS stated that if there were no reimbursement provision, an additional gift to a remainderman would occur when the grantor paid tax on any income that would otherwise be payable from trust corpus. Because there was a reimbursement provision in this situation, however, the IRS ruled that if the income of either trust exceeds the annuity amount, the income tax paid by the grantor on trust income not paid to the grantor will not constitute an additional gift to the remaindermen of the trust.

[Priv. Ltr. Rul. 9444033.]

Forgone dividends were a continuing gift. Taxpayer capitalized a corporation in return for all of the corporation's common and preferred shares. The preferred shares had a liquidation value roughly equal to the initial capitalization, but a noncumulative dividend of less than one percent. When the shares were issued, the prevailing rate of dividends on preferred stock was over 11.5 percent. Shortly after forming the corporation, taxpayer transferred all of the common stock to his children and, in the following year, transferred a portion of the preferred shares to his wife. Even after these transfers, however, taxpayer retained a majority vote in the corporation. Section 2511 provides that the gift tax applies whether a transfer is direct or indirect. Not all apparent transfers are gifts; for example, an incomplete transfer where the donor can recover the transferred property is not a gift.

Taxpayer sought to rely on Anderson, 56 TCM 553 (1988), where the Tax Court included previously transferred common shares in the value of decedent's retained preferred shares because he had the right to liquidate the corporation, thereby recovering the value of the common shares. Since taxpayer had a liquidation right, any funds left with the company by reason of the low dividend rate were not completed gifts. The IRS pointed out that taxpayer was entitled only to the return of his original investment upon liquidation. He could not, as in *Anderson*, recover the full value of the corporation, since its value had increased over the years. The IRS looked instead to Snyder, 93 TC 529 (1989), which concluded that where a preferred shareholder did not exercise the right to convert her noncumulative shares to shares having a cumulative dividend, there was a gift of the lapsed dividends. Taxpayer had the voting power to increase dividends on the preferred shares and should have done so. The only reason taxpayer was satisfied with the low yield was his desire to benefit his children. The forgone dividends were continuing gifts to the extent of the difference between the dividends paid and the market rate when the preferred stock was issued.

[Tech. Adv. Mem. 9301001.]

[2] Full and Adequate Consideration

Summary judgment is improper when genuine issue of fact exists whether decedent's payment to bank to release collateral securing loan to her husband was for full and adequate consideration or was gift to husband. In January 1976, decedent's husband obtained a $50,000 loan from a bank. Decedent delivered $100,000 in bonds, purchased with her own funds, to serve as security for the loan. In 1977, her husband increased the demand loan by $90,000 to pay income taxes owed for past years. Between June 1977 and January 1978, the husband repaid approximately $50,000 of the loan, reducing the balance to $90,000. In February 1978, decedent used her own funds to reduce the outstanding balance to $23,000. Her husband died in February 1979, and decedent repaid the balance of the loan out of assets of her husband's estate, thereby obtaining the release of her bonds. She died in 1980, and the bonds, in addition to other assets, were included in her estate. The IRS took the position that the $67,000 payment to the bank, made within three years of her death, was a gift to her husband that was includable in the gross estate. Decedent's estate argued that (1) the payment was made to obtain release of the bonds held as collateral for the loan and (2) it was, in effect, payment of the joint tax obligation, and thus was not includable in the gross estate. Both sides moved for summary judgment, and the district court held for the IRS.

Held: Vacated and remanded for the estate. Summary judgment was inappropriate on the issue of whether decedent made the $67,000 payment for full and adequate consideration. No discussion or evidence was submitted on whether, by payment of the $67,000, a suretyship arrangement arose between decedent and her husband. The existence of a taxable gift by decedent to the husband would turn on whether the husband's estate had sufficient assets to repay the entire loan or the $67,000 to decedent. To the extent that he had insufficient funds to repay, decedent's payment to the bank to preserve her collateral would be for full and adequate consideration. The court also noted that the IRS's argument that the pledge itself was a gift would not cause the payment to be included in decedent's estate, such pledge having occurred more than three years prior to her death.

[Abrams, 797 F2d 100, 58 AFTR2d 86-6350, 86-2 USTC ¶ 13,683 (2d Cir. 1986).]

Property settlement found to be made for adequate and full consideration results in basis step-up. While their divorce action was pending, a husband and wife entered into a comprehensive court-approved property settlement. Among the contested assets were 6,600 shares of zero-basis corporate stock that the husband had acquired in exchange for certain patent rights. It was agreed that the husband and wife would take 2,400 and 2,000 shares, respectively, as their separate property, and that the remaining 2,200 shares would be placed in an educational trust for the benefit of their minor children. The agreement was incorporated into the court's final decree, and, together with other stipulations and undertakings, was accepted in exchange for relieving the husband of the obligation to provide further support and maintenance for the wife and children. Shortly after the transfer the trustee sold 1,000 shares of the stock at FMV. The trust reported no gain on the sale, contending that it had received a stepped-up FMV basis upon the husband's conveyance of the stock pursuant to the settlement agreement. In support, the trust relied on Section 2516, which provides that transfers made pursuant to certain property settlements do not constitute taxable gifts but are deemed to have been made for adequate and full consideration where entered into for the purpose of furnishing support or for the relinquishment of marital rights. In the trust's view, the stock transfer qualified under Section 2516 as an exchange rather than as a gift; therefore, the basis of the stock in the hands of the trustee was equal to FMV. The IRS maintained that the transfer was a gift and that the trustee had a carryover basis of zero.

Held: For the trust. The court rejected the IRS's contention that there was taxable gain under Section 644 and held that the initial stock transfer fell squarely within the rule of Section 2516. In substance, the property settlement agreement was part of the overall resolution of the husband's and wife's respective interests. The court concluded that the husband should be deemed as having received full and adequate consideration in the form of the wife's release of her marital rights. Thus, the step-up in basis occurred at the time of the husband's transfer to the trustee. Therefore, no gain resulted under Section 644 on the trust's later sale of the property at the same FMV.

[St. Joseph Bank & Trust Co., 716 F2d 1180, 52 AFTR2d 83-5946, 83-2 USTC ¶ 13,537 (7th Cir. 1983).]

Contribution to corporation triggers gift tax. Taxpayer contributed real estate to a newly created corporation in exchange for 34 percent of the stock. The balance was held by her sons, who made no contribution. The IRS argued in the district court that this constituted a gift to her shareholder-sons. However, the jury found that the transfer to the corporation was made "in the ordinary course of business," and the court held that under Regulation § 25.2511-8, it was considered to have been made for adequate and full consideration and was no gift.

 Held: Reversed for the IRS. No reasonable person would have entered into this transaction with the knowledge that 66 percent of the stock was held by strangers. There was no evidentiary basis for the jury to conclude that this was a transfer in the ordinary course of business, and the undisputed facts permitted no resolution other than a judgment for the IRS.

[Kincaid, 680 F2d 1220, 50 AFTR2d 82-6175, 82-2 USTC ¶ 13,484 (5th Cir. 1983).]

Court determines that taxpayer's wife received stock in exchange for her equitable interest in land, not as gift. Taxpayer and his wife were married in 1939. At that time, their individual and combined assets were minimal. In 1940, taxpayer, after consulting with his wife, purchased ranchland on the installment basis. Both taxpayer and his wife worked during the period in which the installments were paid, and their salaries were deposited in a single joint account, the funds from which were used to pay the installments. Taxpayer, however, took title to the land in his name only. In 1943, taxpayer prepared, but never recorded, a deed reflecting the transfer of an undivided half-interest in the land to his wife. In 1978, taxpayer, his wife, and their sons formed a corporation. Taxpayer and his wife then transferred their ranch and some cattle to the corporation; each received 43.7 percent of its stock. During the period from 1979 to 1981, taxpayer and his wife made equal gifts of stock, and their sons executed a "gift adjustment agreement" under which the number of shares they received would be adjusted to reflect any change in valuation. In effect, the agreement sought to freeze the amount of the gifts by adjusting the number of shares given to support the amount of the gift originally reported. The IRS asserted gift tax deficiencies against taxpayer and his wife, on the ground that the wife's receipt of her interest was a gift from taxpayer; that the sons received stock with a value higher than that assumed by taxpayer and his wife; and that the "gift adjustment agreement" was ineffective to freeze the value of such gifts.

Held: For taxpayer. Since the taxpayer's wife was an equitable owner of an undivided one-half interest in the ranch (state law would have imposed a resulting trust in her favor), her receipt of a 43.7 percent stock interest was not a gift. In addition, the court found that the gift adjustment agreement was void as contrary to public policy, and thus the amount of the stock gifts was not frozen.

[Ward, 87 TC 78 (1986).]

Stock sale and redemption was not taxable gift. Decedent owned 52 shares (100 percent) of stock in a soft drink bottling corporation. In 1982, she sold two of the shares to her son and the corporation redeemed the remaining fifty shares in exchange for notes and an account receivable. The IRS determined that the sale and redemption was a taxable gift from decedent equal to the FMV of the corporation ($800,000) less (1) the FMV of the notes given by the son ($305,000) and (2) the account receivable assigned to decedent in connection with the redemption (approximately $55,000). Thus, the IRS contended that decedent dispersed approximately $440,000. The estate argued that the sale and redemption was an arm's-length transaction in which decedent received at least as much as she gave, so that there was no gift element to the transaction. According to the estate, the combined value of the notes given by the son and the corporation almost exactly offset the value of the corporation.

Held: For the estate. As a starting point, the court disputed the $800,000 used as the value of the corporation. This was a preredemption value that omitted the very transaction that resulted in the alleged gift. The court found that $500,000 (the value computed approximately nine months before the sale and redemption) was the best estimate. Thus, decedent's son received a company worth $500,000 that was burdened with approximately $645,000 of debt (the face amount of the notes that the corporation gave to redeem decedent's shares) and relieved of an account receivable worth $55,000. In addition, the corporation had other mortgages and restrictions, which resulted in a total devaluation of approximately $700,000. The corporation also had the continuing obligation to pay the redemption notes, which affected its cash flow. As a result, decedent's son became the 100 percent shareholder of a company that had substantial negative stockholder's equity and essentially was insolvent. Since he gave notes with a face amount of approximately $26,000, decedent received substantially more than she transferred. Therefore, no gift was made.

[Estate of Bruce, 65 TCM 2848, RIA TC Memo. ¶ 93,244 (1993).]

Taxpayer's below FMV sales to sons are held to be taxable gifts. On December 13, 1976, taxpayer's husband died, leaving a will that bequeathed half of his estate to her outright, with a life estate in trust funded by the balance of his property naming their children as remaindermen. In April 1977, taxpayer sold 160 shares of nonpublicly traded stock to her two sons for $16,200, which was the price her husband paid. In December 1977, she and the estate jointly sold two parcels of land to the sons for $200,000, which was the value established by a December 1976 appraisal. Taxpayer sold no property to her daughter. In November 1978, her sons executed notes in payment of the stock but never paid principal or interest thereunder. Taxpayer reported neither of the sales as gifts. On audit, the IRS determined that the sales were gifts to the extent of the difference between the FMV of the stock and the land and their purchase prices. The probate decree for the husband's estate was filed on June 11, 1981. At that time, taxpayer's attorney had reason to believe that the December 1976 appraisal substantially undervalued the husband's estate. Accordingly, taxpayer believed that she was entitled to a larger outright bequest. This shortage resulted in the trust's receiving a larger corpus. The IRS determined that taxpayer made a gift to her children (the remaindermen) as a consequence of this shortage.

Held: For the IRS. Both the sale of stock and the sale of land occurred at less than FMV. Consequently, a gift equal to the difference between value and price existed, unless it could be shown that the sales were made in the ordinary course of business. A sale occurs in the ordinary course of business if the sale is bona fide, at arm's length, and free of any donative intent. Further, where a transfer occurs between family members, the presumption is that it is a gift. With respect to the stock sale, the court held that no attempt was made to ascertain the stock's FMV (taxpayer used her husband's cost basis), and no attempt was made to enforce payments by the sons. The court observed that the notes were not executed until a year after sale and that no payments were ever made on the notes. As to the sales of land, taxpayer used an appraisal that was later determined to have been erroneous and that was prepared one year prior to the sale. In addition, she made no attempt to ascertain the land's true market value at the time of sale. On this basis, the court concluded that the sales were not bona fide, at arm's length, and free of donative intent. The imputed transfer to the residuary trust of the outright bequest shortage was not a completed gift to the remaindermen, because taxpayer could have obtained an amendment of the probate decree's distribution provisions at any time during the taxable year.

[Bergeron, TC Memo. (P-H) ¶ 86,587, 52 TCM (CCH) 1177 (1986).]

Sale of option for nominal consideration, if enforceable, is subject to gift tax. Taxpayer sold to his son, for nominal consideration, an option to purchase realty. The option was enforceable under state law, regardless of the adequacy of consideration. The son exercised the option. The IRS ruled that the sale of the option was a completed gift of the difference between the amount paid and the option's FMV.

[Rev. Rul. 80-186, 1980-2 CB 280.]

Voluntary payment by one heir to another is gift. Decedent made separate, unconditional gifts to two heirs. Upon his death, the will directed that the residuary estate be divided equally between the two heirs. In addition, the will directed that the lifetime gifts be valued as of the date of death and be included in the residuary estate. To equalize the portions, one heir gave a portion of his advancement to the other. State law did not require the donee to return an advancement to an estate when the amount was greater than the amount due under the will. The IRS said that this voluntary payment was a gift. Taxpayer was under no compulsion to effect the transfer and received no consideration for doing so.

[Rev. Rul. 77-372, 1977-2 CB 344.]

IRS determines estate and gift tax consequences of will allocation agreement. A husband and wife executed a "transmutation agreement," changing community property into separate property and a will "allocation agreement." Under the allocation agreement, the wife's interest in her husband's individual retirement account (IRA) became his separate property, and his interest in their other assets became his wife's separate property. They also executed identical wills, each of which provided that assets of decedent's estate with a value equal to the allowable unified credit would pass to a family trust that would pay its income to the surviving spouse. The allocation agreement was effective only if the husband predeceased the wife. According to that agreement, if the husband died first, the wife would transfer all of her interest in her separate assets to her husband's estate and would receive a lifetime annuity from the IRA in exchange. When a decedent gives property to his spouse, the value of the gift is deductible under Section 2523(a). In the instant case, when, pursuant to the agreement, the wife transferred her interest in her husband's IRA for separate ownership of other assets, her interest exceeded the value of the property she received in exchange. As a result, the wife made a gift to her husband that qualified for the marital deduction. Because the execution of the allocation agreement did not result in a present transfer of property, there was no transfer subject to gift tax. The transfer to the husband's estate was subject to the gift tax at that time. Because the transfer was to an estate, however, no marital deduction was available. Therefore, though the signing of the allocation agreement produced no taxable gift, its future implementation would do so. Regarding whether the assets transferred to the husband's estate would be included in the wife's estate in any case, taxpayer argued that because she intended to exchange the assets for a life estate, the assets should no longer be included in her estate. Under Section 2036(a), assets transferred to which a life estate is retained are not included in the decedent's gross estate if the transfer was for "adequate and full" consideration. Thus, to avoid the inclusion under Section 2036, the value of the annuity the wife receives from the IRA must be equal to or greater than the value of the non-IRA assets. Because this can be determined only when the contingency of the husband dying before the wife occurs, the IRS declined to give an opinion on the effect of Section 2036 on the estate plan.

[Priv. Ltr. Rul. 8929046.]

[3] Loans and Compensation Distinguished

Supreme Court holds that intrafamily, interest-free demand loans result in taxable gifts equal to value of use of money lent. Decedent was the owner of a closely held corporation, along with his wife, his son, and his son's family. Between 1971 and 1976, decedent and his wife loaned substantial sums to their son and the corporation. Over this five-year period, the outstanding balances for the loans from decedent to his son varied from $144,715 to $342,915. The outstanding balances for decedent's loans to the corporation ranged from $207,875 to $669,733. During the same period, decedent's wife loaned $226,130 to her son and $68,651 to the corporation. With two exceptions, all of the loans were evidenced by demand notes bearing no interest. Decedent died in 1976, leaving a gross estate for federal estate tax purposes of $3,464,011.

The IRS audited decedent's estate and determined that the loans to the son and the corporation resulted in taxable gifts to the extent of the value of the use of the loaned funds. The IRS then issued statutory notices of gift tax deficiency both to decedent's estate and to his wife. Decedent's wife and the estate sought redetermination of the deficiencies in the Tax Court. The Tax Court concluded that intrafamily, interest-free demand loans do not result in taxable gifts and held that the loans were not subject to the federal gift tax. The court of appeals reversed, holding that gratuitous interest-free demand loans give rise to gift tax liability.

Held: Affirmed for the IRS. The interest-free demand loans shown by the record in this case resulted in taxable gifts of the reasonable value of the use of the money lent. Transfers of property by gift, by whatever means elected, are subject to the federal gift tax. The gift tax was designed to encompass all transfers of property and property rights having significant value. The use of valuable property—in this case, money—is itself a legally protectible property interest. Thus, the interest-free loan of funds is a "transfer of property by gift" within the contemplation of the federal gift tax statutes. Congress has provided generous exclusions and credits designed to reduce the gift tax liability of the great majority of taxpayers. Congress has the power to provide a similar exclusion for the gifts that result from interest-free demand loans, but any change in the gift tax consequences of such loans is a legislative responsibility, not a judicial one. Until such a change occurs, the court is bound to effectuate Congress' intent to protect the estate and income tax systems with a broad and comprehensive tax upon all "transfers of property by gift."

[Dickman, 465 US 330, 104 S. Ct. 1086, 53 AFTR2d 84-1608, 84-1 USTC ¶ 13,560 (1984), reh'g denied, 466 US 945 (1984).]

Transfers from religious leader to relatives are gifts, not compensation. Less than seven months prior to his death, decedent, the leader of a religious group, transferred real property to certain members of his immediate family, who were responsible for maintaining a high level of security around him at all times. The property was procured by decedent in connection with perceived security risks. Decedent was renowned for his generosity, and at no time did decedent's relatives provide protection with an expectation of payment for their services. The estate did not pay gift tax on the transfers and argued that the property was transferred in consideration for services rendered and as part of a continuing security effort. The IRS determined that the transfers were gifts made in contemplation of death, and, as such, should be included in decedent's gross estate.

   Held: For the IRS. Section 2501(a) imposes an excise tax on gifts made during a calendar quarter. A "gift" is defined as any transfer of property not compensated by full and adequate consideration. The subjective intent of the transferor is not controlling. Rather, the gift tax is imposed based upon an objective analysis of the facts and circumstances surrounding the transfer. The transfers were made for zero consideration in money or money's worth. They were in keeping with decedent's legendary generosity. In addition, the transferees of the properties rendered their services without any expectation of repayment. Their reward was in the form of increased spiritual tranquility in knowing that they rendered services to enhance and protect the life of their father and leader of the religious order. Finally, decedent's gifts were made within three years prior to decedent's death, and consequently were presumed to have been made in contemplation of death under Section 2035(a). The estate failed to rebut this statutory presumption, and therefore the value of the gifts must be included in decedent's gross estate.

[Estate of Elijah Muhammad, TC Memo. (P-H) ¶ 90,211, 59 TCM (CCH) 478 (1990), aff'd, 965 F2d 520, 70 AFTR2d 92-6194, 92-2 USTC ¶ 60,103 (7th Cir. 1992).]

Severance payments are not gifts, but compensation. Taxpayer was a key employee of a privately held corporation that was sold to a larger publicly held corporation. The stockholders of the privately held corporation, in a continuation of an employment contract with taxpayer, agreed to pay him a certain sum of money to remain with the buyer-corporation to ensure that it became as profitable as possible, because its degree of profitability determined the amount of money that the stockholders were to receive under the purchase price formula contained in the contract of sale. Subsequently, taxpayer was discharged, and he entered into a severance agreement with the former shareholders that provided for payments for which he was not entitled under the continuing employment agreement. The severance agreement required that taxpayer:

1. Not accept employment in competition with the buyer corporation for a period of twenty months
2. Refrain for two years from disclosing confidential information he had received
3. Not impugn or denigrate the reputation of the corporation or its former stockholders

Failure to comply with any of these prohibitions would have resulted in taxpayer forfeiting the remaining payments due under the severance agreement. On his 1982 federal income tax return, taxpayer did not include in income that portion of the severance payments to which he was not entitled under the employment contract, contending that they were voluntary and hence constituted nontaxable gifts. The IRS claimed that the payments were includable in income as compensation.

Held: For the IRS. The court found that the severance payments were made to taxpayer in order to compensate him for his past contributions and for his compliance with the restrictive covenants. The court therefore concluded that the totality of the facts amply demonstrated that the payments were not motivated by a detached and disinterested generosity, and that the former stockholders did not intend such payments to be gifts. Accordingly, the court held that the entire amount of the severance payments constituted compensation, and that they should have been included in taxpayer's income in the years received.

[Schwartz, TC Memo. (P-H) ¶ 89,097, 56 TCM (CCH) 1417 (1989).]

Statute of limitations may turn loan into a gift. The IRS has taken the position that when a creditor fails to enforce a debt obligation (within the family context) and the statute of limitations runs, the creditor may be charged with having made a gift. This position makes necessary close monitoring of interest-free demand loans to ensure that the goal of avoiding gift taxes is not subverted. A taxpayer loaned $500,000 to his child in return for a promissory note payable on demand, bearing interest at the market rate. The parties intended that the note be enforceable. Under state law, however, upon the passing of three years, the statute of limitations on loan recoveries ran without taxpayer having recovered the loan. The child had financial resources when the statute ran. The IRS ruled that a taxable gift occurred upon the running of the statute. Under Regulation § 25.2512-8, a transfer made in the ordinary course of business (i.e., that is bona fide, at arm's length, and free from donative intent) is not a gift.

[Rev. Rul. 81-264, 1981-2 CB 185.]

[4] Donative Intent

Fifth Circuit finds valid donation inter vivos under Louisiana law. Taxpayer was a resident of New Orleans, Louisiana, where he lived with his invalid mother. During the years in question, the mother's income was small, and her medical expenses were high. In 1975, taxpayer spent on his mother's behalf over $9,000 for doctor's fees and other medical expenses. This figure more than doubled during the following year, and rose to over $22,000 in 1977. Because taxpayer had insufficient funds of his own in 1975 to provide for his mother, his mother executed a general power of attorney in favor of her son on May 15, 1975, naming him her agent and attorney-in-fact. In October 1975, acting under this power of attorney, taxpayer withdrew all of the funds on deposit in a number of accounts registered in the name of the mother, or jointly in the names of the mother and taxpayer, and redeposited these funds in accounts registered solely in his name. The total withdrawn was $42,537. On his federal income tax returns for 1975, 1976, and 1977, taxpayer asserted a dependency exemption for his mother, argued that he was an unmarried head of a household, and contended that he was entitled to deductions for the medical expenses that he had paid on behalf of his mother. To convince the IRS that the funds spent on her behalf belonged to her son and not to her, the mother executed an affidavit in 1979 stating that it had been her intent in 1975 to make a gift of all of the proceeds of the accounts withdrawn by taxpayer. She also simultaneously filed a gift tax return, and later an amended return. The IRS asserted a deficiency, however, and determined that for the three years at issue, taxpayer was entitled to neither an exemption for his mother nor to head of household status, because his mother's annual gross income exceeded $750. The IRS also disallowed the claimed deductions for the mother's medical expenses, on the ground that the money spent for her care was in fact her own. Taxpayer filed a petition in the Tax Court seeking a redetermination. The Tax Court, concluding that there had not been a donation inter vivos under Louisiana law, ruled that taxpayer was not entitled to medical expense deductions under Section 213.

Held: Reversed for taxpayer. A valid donation inter vivos under Louisiana law occurred in this case. When the mother executed the general power of attorney and appointed taxpayer her agent and attorney-in-fact, she made a payment cum animo donandi (with the intention of giving) and intentionally procured a gratuitous enrichment for him. The donation was complete when taxpayer subsequently exercised the power of attorney and withdrew the funds on deposit, converted them into cash, and redeposited them in his name. The mother's affidavit, executed in 1979, stated that it had been her intention in 1975 to make a gift of the funds. The uncontradicted evidence showed, therefore, not only that taxpayer's mother had the requisite donative intent when she created the power of attorney, but also that the power of attorney was in existence when she executed the affidavit. The intent therefore also existed when taxpayer exercised the power. Because the substantive requirements of divestment and donative intent were met, the donation was valid. Taxpayer was entitled to medical expense deductions under Section 213.

[Ruch, 718 F2d 719, 52 AFTR2d 83-5337, 83-2 USTC ¶ 9257 (5th Cir. 1983).]

Evidence of intent is admissible, but is not mandatory to prove gift. A jury determined that taxpayer had fraudulently underpaid gift taxes. Taxpayer sought to set aside the verdict based upon prejudicial error in the jury instructions on the consideration of donative intent. Taxpayer claimed that Regulation § 25.2511-1(g)(1) bars evidence of intent.

Held: For the IRS. The regulation does not preclude the consideration of donative intent but merely allows for the application of the gift tax to a gratuitous transfer without specific proof of such intent. Except for two transfers where ownership rights never passed, ample evidence was presented for a jury to reach the same verdict as that arrived at here.

[Heyen, 731 F. Supp. 1488, 90-1 USTC ¶ 60,014, 65 AFTR2d 90-1245 (D. Kan. 1990), aff'd, 945 F2d 359, 68 AFTR2d 91-6044, 91-2 USTC ¶ 60,085 (10th Cir. 1991).]

Prepayment discount is held not to be gift. In 1982, taxpayer was indebted to a lending institution for $32,960.68, the remaining principal amount due on a loan. The indebtedness was evidenced by a promissory note secured by a mortgage on taxpayer's residence; it bore an interest rate of 8.5 percent per year on the unpaid balance and had a ten-year term remaining. The lending institution offered to cancel the note and the mortgage in return for a discounted amount of $24,720.50, representing the FMV of the note as of the date paid. Taxpayer agreed, paid the amount, and received a canceled note and satisfaction of the mortgage. Taxpayer thus received a discount of $8,240.17 for prepayment of the note, which amount represented the difference between the face value of the note (remaining principal amount) and the amount paid by him. Taxpayer did not report the discount as income, and the IRS then determined a tax deficiency for the amount of the discount. Taxpayer contended that the discount was a gift and therefore was not taxable to him.

Held: For the IRS. The court stated that because the lending institution had not acted out of a detached and disinterested generosity, the discount could not be considered a gift. Further, Section 108, which provides exceptions to the recognition rule where there is business property, was inapplicable because a personal residence was involved in this case. Taxpayer also failed in his argument that the discount reduced the basis of his property and should not have been recognized until he disposed of the property. According to the court, this could have provided an escape hatch only if the value of the property had fallen below the unpaid principal amount of the mortgage, which did not happen here. Consequently, taxpayer had to recognize as income the discount received for prepayment.

[Sutphin, 14 Cl. Ct. 545, 61 AFTR2d 88-990, 88-1 USTC ¶ 9269 (1988).]

Intrafamily transfers that lack donative intent are not gifts. Taxpayer made purported gifts to his children in the form of two checks. The first check was returned to taxpayer when the second check was transferred. Taxpayer then borrowed the money from the children, executed demand notes, and made timely interest payments that he deducted. The IRS disallowed the deductions, arguing that no gift had been made.

Held: For the IRS. The transfers to taxpayer's children were not completed gifts, because there was no donative intent, and thus there was no valid loan.

[Muserlian, TC Memo. (P-H) ¶ 89,493, 58 TCM (CCH) 100 (1989), aff'd, 932 F2d 109, 67 AFTR2d 91-912, 91-1 USTC ¶ 50,204 (2d Cir. 1991).]

Tax Court finds that taxpayers lack donative intent and gift of religious center is sham. Taxpayers formed a general partnership for the purpose of helping a religious center that was deeply in debt. The partnership purchased the center for $250,000 by using a mortgage note of $228,000, and then leased it back to the religious organization that ran the center. The FMV of the property was $480,000. The center failed to pay its rent and defaulted on the lease. Consequently, the partnership decided to either sell the center or donate it to someone with the financial capability of assuming the mortgage. The partnership authorized a title company executive to act on its behalf in locating a donee, instructing him to make the gift only on condition that the mortgage was assumed or satisfied. The executive contacted a small storefront church that was in dire need of money. He informed the pastor that if he accepted the center, he could sell it at a profit, but never informed him of any obligation regarding the outstanding mortgage. Acting as escrow agent, the executive obtained and recorded quitclaim deeds from members of the partnership, purportedly conveying the center to the small church. The executive then offered the pastor $10,000 if he would sign corporate documents showing that the board of trustees of the church had accepted and received the center as a gift. The executive also had the pastor sign a purchase agreement by which the church purportedly would sell the center for $510,000 to a partnership organized by the title company executive. The executive then executed a warranty deed by which the church conveyed title to his partnership. After being pressured by taxpayers' partnership that originally bought the center, he acquired a loan and satisfied the mortgage note taken out by the first partnership. Taxpayers claimed a charitable deduction for the purported gift of the center from the first partnership to the church. The IRS disallowed the deductions.

Held: For the IRS. In reviewing the facts, the court concluded that the purported gift was nothing more than a scam by the title executive to acquire the center for his own personal benefit. The court stated that it was clear that the church had never benefited from the gift. In fact, the church's congregation and board knew nothing of the gift and received no money from the purported sale of the center to the title executive's partnership. The court also held that taxpayer lacked the requisite donative intent. It found that taxpayer, after buying and leasing the center, simply desired to satisfy the mortgage. The court held that taxpayer had failed to carry the burden of proving that the transaction was in substance a gift or that it had possessed the requisite donative intent. Thus, the IRS disallowance of the deduction was proper.

[Suna, TC Memo. (P-H) ¶ 88,541, 56 TCM (CCH) 720 (1988), aff'd, 893 F2d 133, 65 AFTR2d 90-607, 90-1 USTC ¶ 50,021 (6th Cir. 1990).]

[5] Disclaimers

Disclaimer of interest created before enactment of gift tax results in taxable gift. In 1917, taxpayer's grandfather established an irrevocable inter vivos family trust. His wife and children were the primary life income beneficiaries. Upon the death of the survivor of them, the trust was to terminate. The corpus would be divided equally among his living and deceased grandchildren, with the issue of a deceased grandchild taking his or her share. The trust terminated on June 27, 1979. Taxpayer, a grandchild, was entitled to one thirteenth of the corpus. On August 23, 1979, she disclaimed five sixteenths of her interest in the trust, which then passed in equal shares to her five children. Although she had learned of her contingent interest in the trust in 1931 when she reached age 21, and she had been receiving income from the trust since her father died in 1966, her disclaimer was valid under state law. Taxpayer reported the disclaimed interest on her gift tax return but did not treat it as a taxable gift. On audit, the IRS contended that the disclaimed interest was a taxable gift and issued a deficiency notice for $7,468,671. The IRS argued that the disclaimer was untimely and was not excepted from gift tax under Regulation § 25.2511-1(c) because it was not made "within a reasonable time" after taxpayer had "knowledge" (at age 21) of the transfer by her grandfather that created her interest in the trust. The IRS relied on Jewett, 455 US 305 (1982), in which the Supreme Court held that the "transfer" referred to in Regulation § 25.2511-1(c) occurred at the creation of the interest being disclaimed (in this case when the trust was created), and not when that interest was finally ascertained or became possessory (noncontingent). The estate argued that the gift tax rules did not apply, because the transfer creating the trust occurred prior to the enactment of the gift tax. For this reason, the transfer was not a "taxable transfer" as referred to in the revised version of Regulation § 25.2511-1(c); therefore, the "reasonable time" limitation would not apply. The estate distinguished Jewett by pointing out that the trust there was created in 1939, after the enactment of the gift tax.

Held: For the IRS. The Supreme Court granted certiorari "to determine whether a disclaimer made after enactment of the gift tax statute, of an interest created before enactment, is necessarily free of any consequent federal gift taxation." The Court held that it was not. Sections 2501 and 2511 tax the transfer of property by gift whether it is in trust or not, direct or indirect, and whether the property is real or personal, tangible or intangible. The Court has repeatedly stressed that the intent of the gift tax statutes was to embrace all kinds of gratuitous transfers of value. In *Jewett,* the Court held that the gift tax rules apply to an indirect transfer, resulting from a disclaimer, of a contingent future interest in a trust. These rules are subject, of course, to the exception for a disclaimer made "within a reasonable time after knowledge of the transfer" (the creation of the trust), as described in Regulation § 25.2511-1(c). According to the Court, it was clear that if Regulation § 25.2511-1(c) applied to taxpayer's disclaimer (and she did not disclaim within a reasonable time), then her disclaimer resulted in taxable gifts. She had the knowledge and capacity to make a disclaimer as early as her twenty-first birthday, when she first learned of her interest in the trust. The determination of the amount of "reasonable time" within which she could disclaim "must be based upon the gift tax's purpose to curb avoidance of the estate tax," reasoned the Court. As the Court noted in *Jewett,* the practical effect of a disclaimer is to reduce one's taxable estate and confer a gratuitous benefit on the natural objects of one's bounty. The purpose of the gift tax, then, was to prevent an avoidance of death tax by taxing inter vivos transfers. The Court stated that the opportunity to disclaim and thereby avoid gift and estate tax "should not be so long as to provide a virtually unlimited opportunity to consider estate planning consequences." The period of forty-seven years taken by taxpayer could not be considered reasonable. By that time she was certainly in a position to make a fairly accurate determination as to whether she would need the trust assets or whether it would be better to remove them from her estate. The Court then addressed the estate's two arguments. The first was that, by its own terms, the regulation did not apply to the facts of the case, and therefore, the taxability of the transfer depended upon the effectiveness of the disclaimer under state law. The estate's second argument was that Regulation § 25.2511-1(c), by its language, applies only to transfers from a decedent, either by will or by the law of descent and distribution. The regulation makes no reference to a disclaimer of an inter vivos transfer. Therefore, a strict reading of the regulation suggests that it would not apply to taxpayer's interest. The Court said that even if one or both of the estate's arguments are sound, the estate cannot avoid taxability by relying on the state law rule that disclaimed property passes directly from decedent to the next beneficiary in line. This runs counter to the Court's position in *Jewett* and the general rule that, though state law creates interests and rights, federal law determines to what extent those interests will be taxed. Under state law, a disclaimer is generally treated as relating back to the original transfer of the disclaimed interest, creating a transfer directly from the original donor to the new beneficiary. According to the Court, this is done to prevent the disclaimant's creditors from reaching the disclaimed property. Since the reasons for defeating creditors provide no valid reasons for also defeating gift tax, this legal fiction is not followed in federal tax law. A disclaimed interest is treated as passing from the disclaimant to the new beneficiary, and the transfer is subject to taxation unless the exception in Regulation § 25.2511-1(c) applies. The Court recognized that when the gift tax statute was enacted, Congress stipulated that it would not apply to a transfer made on or before the date of enactment (June 6, 1932). The estate claimed that the transfer referred to is the original transfer to the trust in 1917, so the gift tax statute does not apply. The Court disagreed, finding that though the statute does not apply to transfers that occur prior to enactment of the Act, it does apply to interests created before the Act that are transferred after enactment.

[Irvine, 114 S. Ct. 1473, 73 AFTR2d 94-1721, 94-1 USTC ¶ 60,163 (1994).]

Taxpayer does not file disclaimer within reasonable time after obtaining knowledge of transfer creating his interest; disclaimed interest is subject to gift tax. In 1917, taxpayer's grandfather established an inter vivos trust in which taxpayer received a contingent remainder interest upon his birth in 1922. In 1979, the trust terminated upon the death of the last life tenant, and, within two months thereafter, taxpayer partially disclaimed his interest in the trust. As a result of the disclaimer, taxpayer's children received his interest in the trust. The IRS argued that the disclaimer was a transfer subject to gift tax. Taxpayer contended that the disclaimer was made in accordance with state law and involved a refusal to accept a property interest created in 1917, a year that was prior to the enactment of the 1932 gift tax statute. Accordingly, taxpayer argued that there should have been no federal gift tax consequences. The IRS, on the other hand, contended that even though taxpayer may have complied with state law, he had not complied with Regulation § 25.2511-1(c), which provides that a beneficiary must make a disclaimer within a reasonable time after knowledge of the existence of a transfer to him. The IRS argued that taxpayer knew of the existence of the contingent remainder as early as 1941 but did not disclaim his interest until 1979. Thus, the IRS maintained that the disclaimer was not made within a reasonable time. The district court granted summary judgment in favor of taxpayer.

Held: Reversed and remanded for the IRS. Applying Jewett, 455 US 305 (1982), the Eleventh Circuit held that taxpayer did not file his disclaimer within a reasonable time after obtaining knowledge of the transfer creating his interest, causing the disclaimed interest to be subject to the gift tax.

[Ordway, 908 F2d 890, 66 AFTR2d 90-5998, 90-2 USTC ¶ 60,035 (11th Cir. 1990).]

Transferee liability for tax deficiency and interest on gift is limited by disclaimer. Decedent died in 1937, and his will established a trust that provided that the income generated from the trust was to be paid to decedent's wife, with the remainder left in equal shares to decedent's daughters. In 1970, after decedent's wife had died, the daughters renounced all rights that they had in the remainder of the trust. At that time, the FMV of the remainder of the trust exceeded $10 million. Approximately ten years later the IRS sent notices of gift tax deficiency both to the executor of one of the daughters' estates and to that daughter's two children for transferee liability with regard to the deficiency. The Tax Court upheld the IRS's finding that the estate owed a gift tax of almost $5 million plus interest from the date of renunciation in 1971 to the date of payment. Because the two children each received a portion of their mother's share from decedent's trust, they were held liable as transferees for the deficiency and interest owed by their mother's estate. On appeal, the children argued that the imposition of transferee liability on them was improper, because the IRS had not established, in accordance with state law, that their mother was insolvent at the time of renunciation. In addition, the two children asserted that even if transferee liability had existed, the amount of the deficiency was improper, because it exceeded the value of the gift that they had received.

Held: For the estate, in part. The Third Circuit held that though transferee liability did exist on the children, the amount due the IRS could not exceed the value of the gift that they received. The question of whether the children's mother had been insolvent at the time of renunciation had no bearing on whether transferee liability existed, because donee liability is determined by federal law, not state law, and under federal law, transferee liability is not dependent on the insolvency of the donor. In addition, Section 6324(b) as written at the time of the gift provided that the amount of transferee liability for gift tax was only to be the extent of the value of such gift. In addition, the court stated that this "value of the gift" limitation was applied to the amount of interest for which a donee could be liable; therefore, both the interest and the tax deficiency could not exceed the value of the gift that the children received at the time of renunciation.

[Poinier, 858 F2d 917, 62 AFTR2d 88-6000, 88-2 USTC ¶ 13,783 (3d Cir. 1988), cert. denied, 490 US 1019 (1989).]

Donor is liable for federal gift tax for paying state gift tax for which donees are liable. In 1976, taxpayer made substantial gifts to six donees and paid the entire federal and state gift tax on the six gifts. Because taxpayer paid the entire state tax on the gifts, the IRS assessed additional federal gift taxes against him. He paid the assessed amount and sued for a refund.

Held: For the IRS. Unlike the federal gift tax statute, which places responsibility for paying the tax on the donor, the state gift tax statute imposes the tax upon both the donor and the donee and imposes joint and several liability upon the donor and the donee if the tax is not timely paid. If one person pays the tax, the statute implicitly provides that he may bring a claim for contribution against his coobligor. There is no right to contribution, however, unless a person reserves the right to contribution in writing on his return. Taxpayer did not reserve his right to contribution on his state gift tax return. The court stated that by paying the entire state gift tax while foreclosing any right to recover through a claim for contribution, he extinguished the liabilities of the donees at the expense of his taxable estate. His actions had the same practical effect as if he had simply given the donees cash to pay their proportionate share of the state tax obligation. His net worth was decreased by an amount equal to the donees' proportionate share of the tax while the donees' net worth was increased by the same amount. The court noted that although taxpayer achieved this result without physically transferring money to the donees, it was irrelevant. Accordingly, the refund was denied.

[Doerr, 819 F2d 162, 59 AFTR2d 87-1275, 87-1 USTC ¶ 13,721 (7th Cir. 1987).]

Creation of "partitionable" joint tenancy does not transfer right of survivorship until death of one joint tenant. In 1953, taxpayer and her husband acquired a farm, which they held as joint tenants with a right of survivorship. Taxpayer's joint tenancy interest was a taxable gift from her husband. In 1978, taxpayer's husband died, and in the following year, taxpayer disclaimed the interest in the farm acquired under the right of survivorship. The husband's half of the farm went to their daughter. Under applicable state law, a joint tenant had an unfettered right to partition jointly owned property and thereby terminate any rights of survivorship. Citing Jewett v. Comm'r, 455 US 305 (1982), the IRS determined that taxpayer's disclaimer was untimely, because the gift of the survivorship interest was made in 1953. Accordingly, the IRS assessed taxpayer for making a taxable gift to her daughter of one half of the farm.

Held: Reversed for the IRS. Gifts of future interests, even though they may be contingent upon the donee surviving another person, are nonetheless transfers of wealth or current value and thus are taxable gifts when transferred. The value of such gifts, as in *Jewett,* may be actuarially determined. Where the contingent future interest may be defeated by the voluntary act of the donor, however, no gift is made until the donee's rights are vested or until they ripen into a present interest. Because taxpayer or her husband could have defeated the right of survivorship merely by exercising the discretionary right to partition the farm, no gift of the right of survivorship or the property to which it applied was made until taxpayer's husband died in 1978. Accordingly, taxpayer's 1979 disclaimer was timely.

[Kennedy, 804 F2d 1332, 59 AFTR2d 87-1191, 86-2 USTC ¶ 13,699 (7th Cir. 1986).]

Disclaimer of joint interest after death of joint tenant is held valid. Taxpayer purchased realty in her own name and thereafter placed it in joint tenancy with her spouse, who subsequently predeceased her. Upon her spouse's death, taxpayer disclaimed her survivorship interest in the realty under Section 2518. The IRS contended that taxpayer's disclaimer with respect to the realty originally owned by her was not a qualified disclaimer within the meaning of Section 2518. The underlying principle of Section 2518 is to treat a transfer creating an interest as if it had never occurred where the transferee makes a qualified disclaimer. The IRS's contention was based on the reasoning that the creator of her own survivorship interest cannot thereafter disclaim that interest. Taxpayer's position rested upon the holding that the transfer occurred at the time of death of the joint tenant, when the survivorship interest could have passed to her. This theory assumes that each joint tenant owns an undivided interest, but that a survivorship interest does not pass until the time of a joint tenant's death or some other event, such as partition.

Held: For taxpayer. The Tax Court stated that the rationale in McDonald, 853 F2d 1494 (8th Cir. 1988), reversing the Tax Court's previous holding in this case (89 TC 243 (1987)), compelled it to agree with taxpayer. The Tax Court stated that under the Eighth Circuit's rationale, taxpayer and decedent were joint tenants at the time of the transfer (decedent's death). Under that rationale, the disclaimer concerned the survivorship interest being transferred (as a matter of law) to taxpayer. Accordingly, taxpayer was entitled to disclaim the survivorship interest.

[McDonald, TC Memo. (P-H) ¶ 89,140, 56 TCM (CCH) 1598 (1989).]

Estate tax is avoided on life estate of disclaimed property. Decedent's husband predeceased her and left her all of his property. Since he had intended to change his will to include their son, the surviving spouse decided not to offer the will for probate, so that the property would pass under the laws of intestacy. Later the son became concerned that his mother's income was not sufficient, and he conveyed a life estate in his share of the property to her. To make sure that she would not receive property under the will, decedent executed a disclaimer in it. The IRS asserted that the agreement to disregard the will constituted a gift from decedent to her son. Further, because she received a life estate, the property was includable in her gross estate.

Held: For the estate. The Tax Court disagreed with the IRS on both of its assertions. As to the agreement to disregard the will, the court concluded that it was a voluntary arrangement, thus indicating a gift. The execution of the disclaimer superseded the agreement, however, and the agreement became a nullity. Contrary to the assertion of the IRS, the disclaimer was not given in return for the life estate. They were two separate transactions. Thus, there was no gift tax. In deciding that the voluntary agreement by itself would have generated a gift, the Tax Court was bound by the decision in Estate of Vease, 314 F2d 79, 63-1 USTC ¶ 12,131, 11 AFTR2d 1800 (9th Cir. 1963). Otherwise, the court indicated, it would have come to a contrary conclusion. The IRS also lost on the life estate issue, because decedent did not transfer property and retain the estate as required by Section 2036.

[Estate of Anderson, TC Memo. (P-H) ¶ 88,423, 56 TCM (CCH) 78 (1988).]

IRS outlines gift tax consequences of partial disclaimer for remainder interests. Taxpayer had a contingent remainder interest in four trusts. Taxpayer planned to make a partial disclaimer of the interests, and those interests were to pass to taxpayer's descendants who were living at the time of the contingent event.

The IRS stated that a disclaimer made within nine months of the discovery of the interests would be deemed to have been made within a reasonable time under Regulation § 25.2511-1(c). The IRS expressed no opinion on when taxpayer had knowledge of the existence of the interests or the effectiveness of the disclaimer under local law.

[Priv. Ltr. Rul. 8601017.]

[6] Insurance

Effects of paying life insurance premiums with community funds. Decedent, a resident of Louisiana, purchased an insurance policy on his life. He designated his spouse as the owner of the policy, so she held all the incidents of ownership over the policy. The premiums for the policy were paid by the insured and his spouse out of community funds. When the insured died, the life insurance proceeds were paid to their child, who was designated as the beneficiary by the spouse. The issues of this ruling were (1) whether any of the proceeds were includable in the insured decedent's estate under Section 2042 and (2) whether, if the surviving spouse/owner designates a third party to receive the policy proceeds, the death of the insured and the payment of the proceeds cause the spouse to make a gift of the proceeds to the beneficiary under Section 2511.

Section 2042(2) includes in a decedent's estate the proceeds of an insurance policy on his life payable to a named beneficiary if the decedent possessed any incidents of ownership in the policy at his death. Under Regulation § 20.2042-1(c)(2), the term "incidents of ownership" includes not only legal ownership but also the power to change the beneficiary; to surrender, cancel, or assign the policy; to revoke an assignment; to pledge the policy for a loan; or to obtain from the insurer a loan against the surrender value of the policy. The determination of whether a decedent held such incidents of ownership depends on state law. Generally, if an insurance policy is acquired by a spouse living in a community property state and the policy premiums are paid from community property funds, the proceeds of the policy are community property. The rule is different in Louisiana, however, where the presumption that property held by either spouse during a marriage is community property does not apply to a life insurance policy transferred from one spouse to another. In Catalano, 429 F2d 1058 (5th Cir. 1969), the Fifth Circuit ruled that an insurance policy unconditionally owned by the insured's wife was, as a matter of law, part of the wife's separate estate. In holding that insurance policies are contractual in nature, and not governed by the Civil Code, the court of appeals followed a long-standing position taken by the Louisiana Supreme Court. Later cases determined that the use of community funds to pay the premiums on such a policy would not alter the separate property status of the policy or cause incidents of ownership to be attributed to the insured. Applying these holdings to the facts of the ruling, the IRS concluded that the insurance policy was the sole property of the surviving spouse and that no incidents of ownership were attributable to the insured decedent. Consequently, under Louisiana law, none of the proceeds was includable in decedent's gross estate under Section 2042. The IRS noted, however, that if the insurance contract had specifically stated that the policy was to be held as community property, half the proceeds would have been included in decedent's estate.

The second issue in this ruling concerns the taxation of gifts. Section 2511 makes clear that taxable gifts include transfers in trust or otherwise, direct as well as indirect transfers, and property that is real, personal, tangible, or intangible. Under Regulation § 25.2511-1(a), the assignment of the benefits of a life insurance policy may be a taxable transfer. Regulation §25.2511-1(h)(9) explains that if community funds are used to purchase insurance on the life of a spouse, and a third person is named as the beneficiary, then the payment of the proceeds constitutes a completed gift by the surviving spouse as to one

half of the proceeds. The other half is considered to have passed to the beneficiary from the decedent. This rule does not apply in Louisiana, though, because in that state, the use of community funds to pay the premiums does not
make the policy a community asset if the policy is owned by one spouse.
Since all the proceeds are considered to be the separate property of the surviving spouse, upon the death of the insured the payment of the proceeds is
treated as a completed gift by the surviving spouse to the beneficiary. The
value of the gift is the total proceeds—not just half. Thus, the IRS found that
because the surviving spouse held all the incidents of ownership, including the
right to designate and change the beneficiary, she made a gift to the beneficiary of all the proceeds upon her husband's death. This ruling revokes Revenue
Ruling 48, 1953-1 CB 392, and Revenue Ruling 232, 1953-2 CB 268, which
applied the general rule regarding the estate and gift tax treatment of life insurance proceeds in community property states to Louisiana and Texas. These
earlier rulings can still be relied on, however, for estate tax purposes by the estate of a Louisiana decedent who acquired a policy on his life prior to November 14, 1994, and died before May 15, 1995. For gift tax purposes, the prior
rulings can be relied on by the spouse of a Louisiana decedent who died
before May 15, 1995, if the spouse acquired a policy on the decedent's life
prior to November 14, 1994.

[Rev. Rul. 94-69, 1994-2 CB 241.]

Transfers of group-term policies may be gifts. The IRS ruled that a transfer
of an employee's interest in a group-term policy as a trust is a gift if the employee's consent is needed to cancel the policy. This modifies Revenue Ruling
76-490, 1976-2 CB 300, without citing that revenue ruling. There the IRS
stated that an assignment of such a policy was not a taxable gift, because the
policy did not have an ascertainable value by virtue of the employer's power
to cancel it by not making future premium payments. The policy in the instant
revenue ruling was a typical group-term arrangement, with the employer's payment keyed to the increase in the policy's cash surrender value. Although the
corporation was the owner, taxpayer-employee's consent was needed to cancel,
surrender, or assign the policy. Taxpayer transferred all rights to the policy to
a trust for the benefit of taxpayer's child.

   The IRS said that the terminal reserve value of the policy at the time of
the transfer, less the employer's payments, was a taxable gift. Any future premium payments made by taxpayer would also be gifts. Typically in such arrangements, however, the employer pays all the premiums after the first few
years. Thus, there would not be any payments required from the employee.

[Rev. Rul. 81-198, 1981-2 CB 188.]

**Premium payments under assigned insurance policy are not excludable
under Section 2503(b).** An employee assigned the benefits of a life insurance

policy (payments made for employee by employer) to an irrevocable trust, with the proceeds being held in trust at employee's death and the income therefrom payable to the trust's beneficiaries. The IRS ruled that the present payment of premiums is a gift by the employee of a future interest and does not qualify for the annual exclusion under Section 2503(b).

[Rev. Rul. 79-47, 1979-1 CB 312.]

Premiums qualify for annual exclusion in insurance trust. An employer purchased a master group insurance policy insuring the lives of his employees. The policy covered the employees until they reached age 65, but if an employee left the company prior thereto, his coverage would then terminate. An employee created an irrevocable trust and assigned to it all of his rights under the policy. Under the terms of the trust, the beneficiary of his estate was to receive the entire proceeds of the policy immediately on the employee's death.

The IRS determined that the initial transfer of the policy into the trust was not a taxable gift, because the interest that the employee transferred had no ascertainable value. This was the case because neither the employee nor the trust had the right to compel the employer to make any of the premium payments. But when the employer actually made a premium payment, a taxable gift did occur. Each premium payment made by the employer was compensation to the employee. But the employee's prior assignment of his rights under the group-term policy caused these payments to inure to the benefit of the trust beneficiary. The employee is deemed to have made a gift of these premium payments, despite the employer's actual transfer of the funds directly to the insurance company. Thus, the transaction is viewed as two transfers: first from the employer to the employee, and then from the employee to the beneficiary. The premium payment is considered a payment of a present interest that qualifies for the annual exclusion.

[Rev. Rul. 76-490, 1976-2 CB 300.]

Insurance trust beneficiaries' premium payments are not gifts to insured. A life insurance policy on an individual's life funds a life insurance trust of which the grantors and the beneficiaries are the same persons. The beneficiaries pay the premiums in proportion to their shares in the proceeds. The IRS ruled that the beneficiaries' payment of the premiums does not constitute a taxable gift, because the beneficiaries are making the payments for their own benefits. Citing Revenue Procedure 82-37, 1982-1 CB 491, the IRS refused to decide whether the proceeds of the policy would be included in the insured's gross estate for federal estate tax purposes.

[Priv. Ltr. Rul. 8316092.]

¶ 14.02 COMPLETED GIFTS

[1] Generally

Family gifts could relate back to prior year, Fourth Circuit agrees. Donor-decedent had given his son power of attorney to make gifts to family members, which the son used to write checks for $10,000 each on December 14, 1985. Similar gifts to some of the same individuals were made during 1986. The first set of checks was deposited on December 31, 1985, and cleared decedent's account on January 2, 1986, the same year as the second checks cleared. Decedent died in 1987, and the IRS sought to include the second gifts in the estate as taxable gifts (i.e., 1986 gifts in excess of the annual exclusion). Regulation § 25.2511-2 provides that a gift is complete when the donor no longer has power to change it. Under Maryland state law, donors retain control over their checks (e.g., the power to stop payment) until the checks are accepted by the drawee bank. The Tax Court agreed with the IRS that the gifts were not completed until they were honored by decedent's bank in 1986, but it applied the relation-back doctrine to find for the estate. Under that doctrine, once the checks were honored, the gifts were completed for gift tax purposes on the date they were deposited.

Held: For taxpayer. The Fourth Circuit agreed, although a dissenting opinion sided with the IRS on the grounds that the regulations were clear and use of the relation-back doctrine was therefore invalid.

In affirming the Tax Court's ruling, the appellate court reviewed the evolution of the relation-back doctrine:

1. *Charitable gifts.* The Tax Court first applied the doctrine in Estate of Spiegel, 12 TC 524 (1949), an income tax case involving charitable contributions, which permitted charitable deductions in the year checks were delivered. The doctrine was extended to the estate tax in Estate of Belcher, 83 TC 227 (1984), where charitable donations were mailed prior to the donor's death but not paid until after. The charitable donation context is fundamentally different from family gifts in that donations included in the estate would be deductible on the estate tax return.

2. *Post-death presentment.* In both McCarthy, 806 F2d 129 (7th Cir. 1986), and Estate of Gagliardi, 89 TC 1207 (1987), checks given to relatives were not cashed until after the donor's death. The courts rejected use of the relation-back doctrine in these cases out of concern that it could foster abuse if donors issued checks with the understanding they would not be cashed until after the donor's death. The Fourth Circuit agreed with these decisions but pointed out that con-

cern about fostering estate tax avoidance was not present in *Metzger,* because the checks were cashed a year before decedent's death.

3. *Delayed presentment.* In Estate of Dillingham, 88 TC 1569 (1987), aff'd, 903 F2d 760 (10th Cir. 1990), noncharitable gift checks given on December 24, 1980, cleared the donor's bank on January 28, 1981, while the donor was still alive. The relation-back doctrine was not applied, however, because the delay in cashing the checks (i.e., over thirty days) cast doubt on whether they were unconditionally delivered in December.

[Metzger, 38 F3d 118, 74 AFTR2d 94-7486, 94-2 USTC ¶ 60,179 (4th Cir. 1994).]

Uncashed checks to individuals are not completed gifts. On or near December 24, 1980, decedent gave six checks for $3,000 each to six individuals. The checks were presented to the bank for payment on or about January 28, 1981. Around that time decedent gave the beneficiaries second checks for $3,000 each, which were also presented for payment on or about January 28. Decedent, a resident of Oklahoma, died on June 7, 1981. The IRS issued a deficiency notice to decedent's estate on April 8, 1985, claiming that it owed additional federal estate taxes of $369,644. A second notice was issued on April 19, 1985, asserting a deficiency of $70,814 in federal gift tax for the quarter ending December 31, 1980. On June 28, 1985, the estate filed a petition in Tax Court stating that the three-year statute of limitations in Section 6501(a) barred the IRS's claim in the estate tax case. The IRS responded that the six-year statute of limitations found in Section 6501(e)(2) applied because the amounts omitted from the estate tax return exceeded 25 percent of the gross estate. The estate then argued that the gifts were completed in 1980 because payment on the checks related back to the date on which the checks were delivered. The IRS disagreed, stating that the relation-back doctrine does not apply to noncharitable gifts. The IRS also contended that decedent did not relinquish dominion and control over the checks in 1980. The Tax Court held for the IRS, agreeing with both of its arguments. The estate appealed, asserting that the IRS has the burden of proof in showing that the six-year statute of limitations applies, and that it had failed to satisfy this burden of proof. Both parties agreed that for gift tax purposes, if the checks were completed gifts in 1980, they qualified for the annual exclusion found in Section 2503(b). Conversely, if the checks did not constitute gifts until 1981, then it was agreed that they did not qualify for the exclusion in 1980. With respect to the estate tax deficiency, both sides agreed that if the checks were gifts in 1980, then the sum of the original checks and the additional checks ($36,000) was not omitted from decedent's gross estate, the six-year statute of limitations did not apply, and recovery of any estate tax deficiency was barred by the three-year statute of limitations. Conversely, if the gifts were made in 1981, $36,000 was omitted from decedent's gross estate, and the six-year statute of limitations applied; therefore, assessment of any deficiency was not barred by the three-year statute of limitations.

Held: For the IRS (in part). The IRS has the burden of showing that the six-year statute of limitations was applicable. To do so, the IRS had to prove that the omitted amounts should have been included in the gross estate and that such amounts exceeded 25 percent of the gross estate. The IRS met its burden as a matter of law through the facts as stipulated. According to Regulation § 25.2511-2(b), a gift is complete when "the donor has so parted with dominion and control [over the property] as to leave in him no power to change its disposition." A gift is incomplete if "a donor reserves the power to revest the beneficial title to the property in himself." The IRS therefore had to establish that decedent did not part with "dominion and control" over the funds in her checking account when she distributed the six checks in December 1980. To determine whether the facts showed that the decedent had retained dominion and control, the court had to look to state law. The Supreme Court had ruled years before that "state law creates legal interests but the Federal statute determines when and how they shall be taxed." Under Oklahoma law, unless a check is given in exchange for consideration, the drawer's liability to the payee is canceled if the drawer stops payment on the check. Because the checks were cashed on or near the same day, it is conceivable that decedent did not have sufficient funds in her checking account when the checks were delivered and that she asked the beneficiaries to wait until January to cash the checks. If this was the situation, the court's ruling correctly prevented decedent and her estate from receiving an unearned and unwarranted gift tax benefit.

[Estate of Dillingham, 903 F2d 760, 90-1 USTC ¶ 60,021, 65 AFTR2d 90-1237 (10th Cir. 1990).]

Checks drawn and delivered before, but not cashed until after, decedent's death are includable in gross estate. During May 1980, decedent had her son draw nine checks of $3,000 each for certain relatives. Although all of the checks were mailed before decedent's death on May 24, 1980, none of them were cashed until after that date. The estate did not include the $27,000 represented by these checks in decedent's gross estate, on the ground that the gifts came under the Section 2503(b) $3,000 gift exclusion. The IRS assessed a deficiency on the ground that under state law, the gifts were not complete at death, and thus Section 2035, which reflects the $3,000 exclusion for determining inclusion in the gross estate, was inapplicable.

Held: For the IRS. In the absence of consideration from the payee to the drawer of a check, state law provides that a timely filing of a stop-payment order operates to extinguish any liability of the drawer to the payee. Thus, under applicable state law, decedent failed to relinquish total dominion and control over the checks at the time of her death. State law also provides that partially complete gifts are revoked at death. Accordingly, the checks were not completed gifts for federal estate and gift tax purposes, and Sections 2035 and 2503(b) were inapplicable. The relation-back doctrine for checks is applicable only to transfers that, if included in gross estate, would entitle the estate to an offsetting deduction (e.g., charitable gifts and decedent's legal obligations).

[McCarthy, 806 F2d 129, 59 AFTR2d 87-1193, 86-2 USTC ¶ 13,700 (7th Cir. 1986).]

Creation of "partitionable" joint tenancy does not transfer right of survivorship until death of one joint tenant. In 1953, taxpayer and her husband acquired a farm, which they held as joint tenants with right of survivorship. Taxpayer's joint tenancy interest was a taxable gift from her husband. In 1978, taxpayer's husband died, and, in the following year, taxpayer disclaimed the interest in the farm acquired under the right of survivorship. The husband's half of the farm went to their daughter. Under applicable state law, a joint tenant has an unfettered right to partition jointly owned property and thereby terminate any rights of survivorship. Citing Jewett v. Comm'r, 455 US 305 (1982), the IRS determined that taxpayer's disclaimer was untimely because the gift of the survivorship interest was made in 1953. Accordingly, the IRS assessed taxpayer for a taxable gift to her daughter of one half of the farm.

Held: For taxpayer. Gifts of future interests, even though they may be contingent upon the donee surviving another person, are nonetheless transfers of wealth or current value, and thus are taxable gifts when transferred. The value of such gifts, as in *Jewett,* may be actuarially determined. Where the contingent future interest may be defeated by the voluntary act of the donor, however, no gift is made until the donee's rights are vested or until they ripen into a present interest. Because taxpayer or her husband could have defeated the right of survivorship merely by exercising the discretionary right to partition the farm, no gift of the right of survivorship or the property to which it applied was made until taxpayer's husband died in 1978. Accordingly, taxpayer's 1979 disclaimer was timely.

[Kennedy, 804 F2d 1332, 59 AFTR2d 87-1191, 86-2 USTC ¶ 13,699 (7th Cir. 1986).]

Joint and mutual will giving spouse life estate and remainder to their children did not give rise to gift to children on death of first spouse. In 1951, a husband and wife executed a joint and mutual will. The will disposed of the joint property by providing the surviving spouse with a life estate and giving their children the remainder. The only restrictions with regard to the property were that it was to be managed carefully and that it was to be distributed in accordance with the remainder provision of the will. The wife died in 1964, and her estate included only her half interest in the joint property. The will was not, however, admitted to probate. The husband died in 1977, and the

1951 will was admitted to probate. The IRS asserted that the husband was liable for gift tax in 1964 when his wife died, reasoning that the 1951 will then imposed upon the husband a contractual obligation to make gifts to their children. The husband's estate filed a petition contesting the IRS's assessment of a gift tax deficiency. The Tax Court held that the 1951 will, without being probated, was not a joint and mutual will, and that it did not create a contractual obligation on the part of the husband when his wife died in 1964. Accordingly, no gift was made to the children in that year.

   Held: Affirmed for taxpayer. The 1951 will was a joint and mutual will, even though it was not admitted to probate. Thus, in 1964, it imposed a contractual obligation on the husband vis-à-vis the remainder interest in the joint property. However, the terms of that contract did not so restrict the husband's ability to control the property such that a gift to the children was completed in 1964. Specifically, the husband was not liable for waste; the property was subject to his debts, funeral expenses, and estate taxes; and he could encumber it freely.

[Estate of Lidbury, 800 F2d 649, 86-2 USTC ¶ 13,688, 58 AFTR2d 86-6365 (7th Cir. 1986).]

Property passing to surviving spouse by joint and mutual will is deemed completed gift to heirs of surviving spouse because disposition of property is limited by ascertainable standard. In 1973, taxpayer and her husband executed a joint and mutual will. The will provided that the surviving spouse would receive the deceased spouse's property in fee simple and specified, in great detail, the disposition of the property at the death of the survivor. In 1978, taxpayer's husband died. While taxpayer was hospitalized, her attorney filed a gift tax return and paid taxes on all of her property, under the assumption that the joint and mutual will functioned to make a valid gift from taxpayer to her beneficiaries. Subsequently, taxpayer challenged this payment as erroneous and sought a refund. The district court granted taxpayer's motion for summary judgment on the refund claim.

   Held: Reversed for the IRS. The court stated that it must look to the state court decision giving judicial construction of the will. The state court had construed the will as being joint and mutual. Pursuant to Illinois state law, such arrangements are interpreted as giving the survivor the equivalent of a life estate in the couple's assets. Such wills are deemed irrevocable, and the surviving spouse is thus prohibited from alienating or disposing of the property, except as necessary to provide for the spouse's health, support, comfort, or maintenance. The district court held that the will created a gift from the surviving spouse to the beneficiaries. Because the surviving spouse was able to invade the corpus for comfort, however, the court ruled that disposition of the property was not limited by an ascertainable standard and thus was an incomplete gift not subject to gift tax. The Seventh Circuit did not agree with this reasoning. In looking at the state court's decision construing the will, the Seventh Circuit found that the state court had placed significant constraints on taxpayer's liberty to dispose of the property. The state court had held that although entitled to the income from the property, taxpayer was entitled to invade the corpus only for her "health, support, comfort and maintenance." The state court permitted the sale of some of the assets, but only in order to acquire "investment of equal or more value." Further, the state court prohibited taxpayer from disposing certain parcels of real estate until all of the other assets had been consumed first, and required that the proceeds of the real estate be used for her health, support, comfort, and maintenance. The Seventh Circuit felt that these restrictions were sufficiently stringent to form an ascertainable standard limiting her interest. The gift was therefore completed and was subject to federal gift tax.

[Pyle, 766 F2d 1141, 56 AFTR2d 85-6521, 85-2 USTC ¶ 13,626 (7th Cir. 1985).]

Unenforceable private annuity payable out of trust funds does not reduce value of trust for gross estate purposes. In anticipation of receiving an inheritance, decedent established a trust during 1965 and transferred to it his remainder interest in a trust created by his grandfather in 1931. The grandfather's trust originally contained stock in two corporations engaged in the resort hotel business. Prior to 1965, the grandfather's trust was a plaintiff in a shareholders' derivative suit that had been filed against the two corporations. The case was settled before trial, and, in exchange for its stock, the trust received cash plus a $1.34 million mortgage note payable over a term of twenty years. The mortgage note remained in the grandfather's trust until decedent's remainder interest ripened into ownership, at which time the trustees of decedent's trust received title to his interest in the note. Under the terms of the original settlement, it was agreed that a portion of each annual installment from the note would be paid to decedent's mother as a lifetime annuity. In accordance with this agreement, the trustees of decedent's trust paid $25,000 to the mother each year. Decedent died in 1972 and was survived by his mother. The executors of his estate included the mortgage note in gross income but discounted its FMV to reflect the continuing liability to pay the mother's annuity. On audit of the estate's tax liability, the IRS determined that the full value of the note was includable, without the claimed reduction. In defense, the estate argued that the agreement creating the mother's annuity constituted a completed gift and that the reduction in FMV of the note was proper for gross estate purposes.

Held: For the IRS. Under state law, the agreement was not a completed transfer of an interest in property but was merely a promise to make a gift in the future. The court pointed out that though a donor may effect a completed, present gift of a future interest, the agreement in the present case did not constitute an irrevocable assignment as required under Regulation § 25.2511-2(b), because the mother had no enforceable right to receive the annual payments. The court also noted that though the 1965 trust transfer was itself a completed gift, the fact that the annuity was to terminate on the earlier of the decedent's or the mother's death rendered the entire note includable in gross estate.

[Grossinger, 723 F2d 1057, 53 AFTR2d 84-1574, 84-1 USTC ¶ 13,550 (2d Cir. 1983).]

Gift tax exclusion for checks expires with donor. The donor and her husband executed a power of attorney appointing their son attorney-in-fact in May 1985. No reference to making gifts was contained in this power of attorney. Shortly before the donor's death on September 28, 1992, the son drew six checks against her bank account payable to himself, his wife, his brother, his nieces, and two other people. None of these checks were cashed until after the donor's death. The IRS contended that the checks were incomplete gifts during the donor's lifetime. As such, the funds represented by the checks should be includable in her gross estate. A gift is not complete until the donor has parted with dominion and control so as to leave him or her with no power to change its disposition (see *Estate of Metzger*, 100 TC 204 (1993), generally aff'd, 38 F3d 118, 74 AFTR2d 94-7486 (4th Cir. 1994).

Held: For the IRS. Local law determines whether the donor parted with dominion and control. The District of Columbia law that applied in this case, DC Code Announcement § 28:3-409(1), provided that a check or other draft does not, of itself, operate as an assignment of any funds in the hands of the drawee available for its payment, and the drawee is not liable on the instrument until he or she accepts it. Because the donor can revoke the gift by stopping payment on the check or withdrawing the funds prior to the drawee's acceptance of the check, the gift remains incomplete until the donee presents the check for payment and the check is accepted by the drawee. The court was not persuaded by the estate's argument that, as the donor was unable to stop payment on the checks because of her failing health, the checks were not revocable and were complete on delivery. The mere possession of a power to revoke, not the ability to exercise it, is controlling (see *Estate of Alperstein*, 71 TC 351 (1978), aff'd, 613 F2d 1213, 45 AFTR2d 80-1708 (2d Cir. 1979)). The court thus found that, because the donor possessed the power to revoke the checks and the bank did not accept or pay the checks until after her death, they were not completed gifts under local law. The court also rejected the estate's argument that the gifts were deemed complete under the relation-back doctrine. Under that doctrine, the drawee's payment of the checks relates back to the date the checks were issued (i.e., prior to the donor's death). Although the relation-back doctrine has been applied under particular circumstances in other cases, the Tax Court has specifically declined to apply it where non-charitable gifts were made by check and the donor died while the checks were still outstanding (see *Estate of Gagliardi,* 89 TC 1207 (1987)). The relation-back doctrine was applied to checks given as charitable contributions because the estate would receive an offsetting deduction under Section 2055 if the funds were included in the estate (see *Estate of Belcher,* 83 TC 227 (1984)). The doctrine was also applied with respect to noncharitable donees when the issue was in which year gifts were made; the checks were deposited in the recipients' banks during December, but did not clear the donor's bank until January—and the donor remained alive at this time (see *Estate of Metzger*). Since the donor in the instant case retained dominion and control over the checking account until her death, the checks were not completed gifts during the donor's life, and were, therefore, includable in her estate.

[Estate of Newman, 111 TC 81 (1998).]

Spouse's annuity is included in shareholder's estate. Decedent was a director of a corporation in which he owned 83 percent of the voting stock. Approximately one month prior to decedent's death, the board of directors adopted a plan providing for the payment of an annuity to the surviving spouses of corporate officers who met certain eligibility requirements and died while still employed by the company. The plan could be amended or terminated by the board. At the time of adoption of the plan, decedent was the only eligible officer. Upon decedent's death, the corporation began paying the annuity to his widow. The IRS contended that the benefit was includable in the estate of decedent as a revocable transfer under Section 2038, which provides that a revocable transfer is includable in a decedent's estate where the decedent (1) held a property interest in the annuity; (2) transferred the property interest; and (3) retained a power to amend or terminate the transfer.

Held: For the IRS. With respect to the first element of Section 2038, the court concluded that decedent, in remaining in the employment of the company, had effectively accepted the company's offer to make the annuity payments. This meant that the annuity was procured as a result of decedent rendering services to the company and was deferred compensation. The estate contended that the plan was revocable and did not amount to a property interest, but merely an "expectancy" of a future benefit. The court noted, however, that (1) the plan's terms seemed to indicate that no amendment could be made having an adverse impact on the benefit without the written consent of the eligible officer and his spouse and (2) the fact that decedent owned 80 percent of the corporation's stock made it highly unlikely the plan would be terminated without his approval. The third element for inclusion in an estate pursuant to Section 2038 is that decedent must have retained the power to "alter, amend, revoke, or terminate" the transfer. The court noted that though decedent did not have such a right in his individual capacity, as the majority shareholder, he was able to do so in conjunction with other members of the board of directors. The court believed that the ability of the other board members to go against decedent's wishes was largely illusory. In rejecting the IRS attempt to impose a gift tax, the court concluded that because of this retained power, there had been no completed gift during decedent's lifetime.

[Estate of Levin, 90 TC 723 (1988), aff'd by unpublished op., 891 F2d 281 (3d Cir. 1989).]

Survivor's benefit paid under nonelective company plan is held not to be taxable gift. From 1950 until his death in 1979, decedent was an employee of a company that maintained an unfunded, uninsured survivor's income benefit plan covering decedent and other employees. The noncontributory plan automatically covered all employees and was not subject to any power in the employee to alter, amend, revoke, or terminate benefits, or to designate named beneficiaries. By its terms, the plan was payable only to a surviving spouse or to the children or parents of a covered employee. Following the death of decedent, plan benefits were paid to his surviving spouse in monthly installments. The value of the plan was not included in gross estate. Following audit, the IRS determined that a taxable gift of the present value of plan benefits was made by decedent on the date of death. In the IRS's view, the gift was completed on the date of death, because it had not previously been susceptible of valuation.

Held: For the estate. After noting that it was "unclear precisely what the [IRS] argues in this case," the Tax Court found that decedent had made a taxable gift of an interest in the plan to his wife, largely because he never had an identifiable ownership or property interest in the benefits. The benefits were paid out of the several assets of the employer; an employee's rights in the plan never vested in any way; and the payment of benefits was at all times subject to the employer's separate and exclusive right to revoke or amend the plan at any time. In the absence of any enforceable right or interest, decedent had no "property" to transfer. Thus, a gift could never have been made.

[Estate of DiMarco, 87 TC 653 (1986), acq. 1990-2 CB 1.]

Fractional interest gifts upheld. In 1984, decedent decided she would make a series of annual gifts to each of her three children to pare down her taxable estate. She intended to give in each year 1984, 1985, and 1986, a one-ninth fractional interest in a residence in which she had been devised a life estate by her mother. The residence's FMV on the devise date was $90,000 and the life estate's value was $54,470. Mistakenly believing she had been devised a fee simple interest rather than a life estate, decedent executed a deed in 1984 purporting to transfer one-ninth fee simple interests to each child. Furthermore, due entirely to a scrivener's error not noticed by any of the parties, the deed described the transferred interest as her *entire* interest, rather than the intended fractional interests. Still unaware of the scrivener's error, and pursuant to her stated intent, decedent deeded additional fractional interests to her children again in 1985 and 1986. Later, in 1987, when the life estate mistake was discovered, the children quitclaimed their interest to decedent's trust—to allow a sale of the property in fee simple. Shortly thereafter, decedent transferred $90,000 to the children, and sold the property in 1988 for $90,000. The IRS determined that decedent made an unreported, taxable gift of her entire interest in the property in 1984, or in the alternative, that the whole 1984 transfer was illusory and that she made a $90,000 gift to the children in a later year. The estate countered that she transferred only three one-ninth interests in 1984, which transfers were not taxable gifts under Section 2503(b)'s annual exclusion from the federal gift tax for the first $10,000 of gifts a donor makes to each donee in a tax year.

Held: For decedent. The Tax Court agreed that decedent gave only the fractional interests she intended to in 1984 (and in 1985 and 1986). Under Regulation § 25.2511-1(g)(1), the gift tax applies only to transfers of beneficial interests in property, not transfers of bare legal title; and under Regulation § 25.2511-2(c), a gift is not complete if the donor reserves the right to revest beneficial title in herself. What real property interest is transferred in a particular case depends on the law of the state where that property is located (in this case, Georgia). Here, the fact that the deed recited a greater interest in the residence than decedent had did not void the transfer in its entirety; the deed simply transferred (fractions of) the life estate interest that she did have. Furthermore, the scrivener's error would not have been effective to transfer decedent's entire interest under Georgia law. So, the 1984 deed transferred only bare legal title to her entire interest, leaving decedent with an unqualified right to defeat the transfer of all but three-ninths of her interest immediately thereafter. Thus, decedent had a right to reform the deed and revest title to herself with respect to the other six-ninths interest. Consequently, decedent did not make a completed gift in 1984 with respect to that six-ninths interest for federal gift tax purposes, despite the deed's language. Also, her 1985 and 1986 gifts of the remaining fractional interests were complete in those years; and the IRS's alternative argument that decedent's 1987 $90,000 transfer to the children was gratuitous was not supported by the facts, which clearly showed that the $90,000 was consideration for the children's interest in the property. Finally, twelve $10,000 checks that decedent made out to the three children and other family members in 1985 through 1988 were completed gifts of present interests under Section 2503(b). For 1985 and 1986, however, the gifts to the children were not excludable from the gift tax to the extent that the total cash and property she transferred to each of them exceeded $10,000.

[Estate of Holland, 73 TCM 3236, RIA TC Memo. ¶ 97,302 (1997).]

No gifts from late checks until following year. On December 31, 1983, taxpayer mailed to his sons and hand delivered to his daughters checks intended as gifts for 1983. Each check was endorsed for deposit in savings accounts maintained by the children under the employee savings plan at the family's closely held corporation. The checks were not presented to taxpayer's bank for payment until January 11, 1984. Under Regulation § 25.2511-2(b), a gift is completed if the donor has given up all power to affect the disposition of the gift for the benefit of himself or someone else. The IRS's position was that a check must clear the donor's bank by the end of the year because until then, the donor can stop payment on it. The IRS therefore argued that the gifts were ineffective for 1983 due to taxpayer's failure to cede control over the gifts during that year and that an additional gift tax liability should be imposed for 1984. Taxpayer argued that the relation-back doctrine applied to make the gifts effective for 1983. In Metzger, 100 TC 204 (1993), the Tax Court applied the doctrine to validate gift checks deposited on December 31 that did not clear the donor's bank until January 2 of the following year. Under this view, the checks clearing in 1984 related back to and validated taxpayer's delivery of the gifts in 1983.

Held: For the IRS. The Tax Court noted that application of the relation-back doctrine in Metzger was based on (1) proof that the donor intended to make a gift and (2) deposit of the check within the year for which favorable tax treatment was sought and within a reasonable time of issuance. In this case, however, the checks were endorsed to an in-house account at a family-owned corporation, which cast doubt on taxpayer's intent to make a gift, as did taxpayer's failure to show that funds were available in his account to pay the checks by the end of the year. Thus, the relation-back doctrine did not apply and the transfers were gifts for 1984.

[W.H. Braum Family Partnership, 66 TCM 780, RIA TC Memo. ¶ 93,434 (1993).]

Use prior to gift does not accelerate donation. Taxpayer donated a house to her town for use as a library by entering into a lease agreement in 1983. The town was to pay annual rent, and taxpayer agreed to pay an equal amount as an annual charitable contribution in support of the library. In fact, the town never paid rent, and taxpayer never made the contributions. The lease was for one year and thereafter from year to year, subject to the right of either party to cancel. Taxpayer reserved the right to inspect the property and to make any repairs or improvements that she deemed necessary. No alterations or additions could be made by the town without prior consultation with taxpayer. The town maintained an insurance policy on the property in taxpayer's name. An option was given to the town to purchase the property for $1 during the running of the lease. The option could be terminated by taxpayer at any time and also provided that after the exercise of the option by the town, taxpayer could defer the closing and delivery of the deed for up to three years, during which time the lease would remain in effect. Toward the end of 1983, after transforming the house into a library, the town informed taxpayer that it would exercise its option. The deed transferring the property to the town was dated December 31, 1985, was delivered on December 31, 1986, and was recorded on January 30, 1987. During that entire time, the property was used as a library. The IRS denied a charitable deduction until the year in which the deed was physically delivered.

Held: For the IRS. A deduction is allowed under Section 170(a) for a charitable contribution paid during the taxable year. The timing of a charitable contribution is analyzed exactly like the timing of a gift. The six essential elements of a bona fide inter vivos gift are

1. A donor competent to make a gift
2. A donee capable of accepting a gift
3. A clear and unmistakable intention of the donor to absolutely and irrevocably divest title, domain, and control of the donated property
4. The irrevocable transfer of present legal title and dominion and control of the entire gift to the donee so that the donor can no longer exercise any act of dominion or control over it
5. Delivery of the gift by the donor to the donee of the gift
6. Acceptance of the gift by the donee.

All six factors must be met for qualification as an inter vivos gift or a charitable contribution. Here, because taxpayer did not irrevocably transfer present legal title and dominion and control of the entire gift to the town, so that taxpayer could not exercise any further act of dominion and control in 1983 or 1984, she was not entitled to a charitable contribution deduction at that time. Regulation § 1.170-1(b) provides that a contribution is made at the time of delivery, but there is no guidance as to when delivery is made. Therefore, the court looked to state law, which provides that a deed must be delivered for conveyance of title to occur. A state court defined "delivery" as that point when the parties manifest their intention to make the instrument an operative and effective integration of their agreement regarding the property. Taxpayer did not intend the deed to be operative in 1983 or 1984. During the period between the exercise of the option and physical delivery of the deed, the town continued to seek permission from taxpayer before making any changes or improvements to the property. Taxpayer objected to certain changes and exercised her dominion and control by seeing that these changes were not made. She was still named as insured on the property, and the town recognized that it did not yet hold legal title. Thus, although the property was being used as a library in 1983 and 1984, taxpayer did not deliver the property at the time for purposes of the charitable contribution deduction. The proper time for the deduction was 1986, the year in which the deed was physically delivered.

[Dyer, TC Memo. (P-H) ¶ 90,051, 58 TCM (CCH) 1321 (1990).]

Intrafamily transfer of building is not sale. Taxpayer, an attorney, transferred a building he owned to his son and daughter. The transfer was made primarily because the father feared that he might lose the property in a malpractice suit. Taxpayer claimed that the transfer was an installment sale under an oral sales agreement. The IRS argued that the transfer was a gift completed in 1978 by deed.

Held: For the IRS. A gift had been made in 1978, when taxpayer left the signed deed with his law partner to give to his son, and the partner delivered it to the son.

[Belli, TC Memo. (P-H) ¶ 89,403, 57 TCM (CCH) 1172 (1989).]

Gifts granted by decedent's son pursuant to power of attorney are not includable in gross estate. About two and one-half months before her death, decedent executed a power of attorney appointing her son as her attorney-in-fact. Among other things, the power of attorney allowed the son to grant and convey any property, both real and personal, owned presently or in the future by decedent. When she executed the power of attorney, decedent had a history of giving gifts to her children qualifying for the gift tax exclusion. Between the date on which the power of attorney was executed and decedent's death, the attorney-in-fact transferred $10,000 each to himself and five other family members of decedent. Upon decedent's death, the estate did not include the $60,000 given out by her attorney-in-fact. The IRS determined that this amount was properly included in gross estate, because the attorney in fact was unauthorized to make such gifts. The IRS contended that the language of the power of attorney allowed the attorney-in-fact to engage only in business transactions on decedent's behalf.

Held: For the estate. The court applied local New Jersey law to determine whether the power of attorney authorized the attorney-in-fact to make gifts on behalf of decedent. The court found that the power of attorney included "a broad grant of power to do and perform all and every act and thing whatsoever requisite and necessary." It also includes the specific power to grant and convey property owned presently or in the future by decedent. The court ruled that the IRS had failed to provide any evidence in support of the notion that the power to grant and convey is inappropriate gift language in New Jersey. The court acknowledged that the language might be somewhat ambiguous, but it was confident that on close scrutiny of the personal circumstances or the power's creation and the personal concerns of decedent for her family members, a New Jersey court would sustain the attorney-in-fact's authority to make such gifts. The $60,000 in gifts was therefore properly excludable from the gross estate of decedent.

[Bronston, TC Memo. (P-H) ¶ 88,510, 56 TCM (CCH) 550 (1988).]

Tax Court determines that under local law, decedent made completed gift of bonds. Decedent's husband owned several bonds with an aggregate principal value of $150,000. On March 11, 1982, decedent's husband went to his safe-deposit box with his daughter and removed the bonds from the box. He then handed the bonds to his daughter informing her that he wished to make a gift of the bonds to a family partnership in which his five children were the partners. Attached to the bonds were transfer forms. These forms were not filled in, but the bonds were taken by the husband and daughter to their attorney's office and left there. Decedent's husband died shortly thereafter, and, after his death, the transfer forms were executed on behalf of his estate by his personal representatives. In his will, the husband left a life interest to decedent in a trust comprising one half of his estate, with the remainder going to whomever decedent appointed in her will. Upon decedent's death, the IRS issued a notice of deficiency, increasing her taxable estate by over $80,000, $75,000 of which was to take into account her ownership of the bonds that she inherited from her husband. Decedent's estate argued that she had never inherited the bonds, because her husband had made an effective inter vivos transfer of the bonds to the family partnership.

Held: For the estate. The court looked to the applicable provisions of North Dakota law in determining whether there was an effective inter vivos transfer of the bonds. Under the state law, which was an enactment of the Uniform Commercial Code, the bonds held by decedent's husband were securities in registered form. Upon delivery of securities, the "purchaser" acquires the rights that the transferor had or had authority to convey. "Purchaser" is defined to include one who received securities as a gift. If a registered security is delivered without proper endorsement by the transferor, the transferee becomes a bona fide purchaser only as of the time the endorsement is supplied. As against the transferor, however, the transfer is complete upon delivery, and the purchaser has a specifically enforceable right to have any necessary endorsement supplied. Thus, as between parties to the transfer, all that is required to effect the transfer is delivery with an intent to change ownership, and the lack of an endorsement does not affect the validity of the transfer as between these parties. The court held that because decedent's husband made a physical transfer of the bonds with the requisite donative intent, a valid gift was made. Furthermore, under state law, the donee had a specifically enforceable right to compel endorsement; thus, the daughter, as agent for the family partnership, received delivery of the gift, along with a means of obtaining control over them (i.e., the right to compel endorsement). Because decedent's husband had no remaining interest in the bonds once the gift was effected, they were not part of his estate, they did not pass to decedent, and they were not includable in her gross estate.

[Estate of Novetzke, TC Memo. (P-H) ¶ 88,268, 55 TCM (CCH) 1116 (1988).]

Preconditions on stock option exercise affect gift date. In this ruling, the IRS determined that an employee's transfer of a nonstatutory stock option to a child for no consideration was not a completed gift until certain preconditions to the option's exercise were satisfied—raising the possibility of an increased gift tax on such transfers (i.e., when the stock's value increases between the time of transfer and when the preconditions are ultimately satisfied). Under taxpayer's employer's stock option plan, employees were awarded nonstatutory stock options that were not traded on an established market. The plan provided that an option granted to taxpayer was exercisable only after taxpayer performed certain additional services. The plan also provided that employees could transfer their options to immediate family members (or to a trust for their benefit). The transferee was then entitled to determine whether and when to exercise the option, subject to the employee's satisfaction of the additional services requirement and the exercise period dates, and obligated to pay the exercise price. Shares acquired on the exercise of an option were freely transferrable.

Taxpayer here transferred her option for no consideration to one of her children before she had satisfied the option exercise's additional services requirement. Although the transfer clearly resulted in a gift, the question was when that gift was complete. Relying on Revenue Ruling 80-186, 1980-2 CB 280, the IRS determined that the gift here was not complete when taxpayer made the transfer. In Revenue Ruling 80-186, the IRS determined that a parent's transfer to a child for nominal consideration of an option to purchase real property for less than fair value within a set period was a completed gift on the transfer date, provided the option was binding and enforceable on that date. Here, the option was not binding and enforceable until the service preconditions on exercise were satisfied. Since taxpayer had not yet satisfied the preconditions when she transferred the option to her child, she did not have enforceable property rights that were transferrable for federal gift tax purposes at that time. Thus, the gift of the nonstatutory stock option was not complete until the service preconditions were satisfied. Also, if the transferee were a skip person for generation-skipping transfer tax (GSTT) purposes, the GSTT would apply at the same time as the gift tax.

[Rev. Rul. 98-21, 1998-18 IRB 7.]

Gratuitous transfer of legally binding promissory note is completed gift. On August 1, 1977, D gratuitously transferred to A a promissory note in which D promised to pay A a sum of money on December 31, 1982. The note was legally enforceable under state law. On May 30, 1982, D died. The note had not been satisfied at D's death. The IRS was asked for advice regarding the gift and estate tax consequences if a donor-decedent gratuitously transfers a legally binding promissory note that has not been satisfied at decedent's death.

The IRS ruled that the gratuitous transfer of a legally binding promissory note is a completed gift under Section 2511. If the note has not been satisfied at the promisor's death, no deduction is allowed under Section 2053(a)(3) for the promisee's claim with respect to the note. The completed gift is not treated as an adjusted taxable gift in computing the tentative estate tax under Section 2001(b)(1). In the case of a legally enforceable promise for less than an adequate and full consideration in money or money's worth, the promisor makes a completed gift under Section 2511 on the date when the promise is binding and determinable in value, rather than when the promised payment is actually made. In such a case, the amount of the gift is the FMV of the contractual promise on the date it is binding. In this case, *D* made a completed gift under Section 2511 on August 1, 1977, the date on which *D*'s promise was legally binding and determinable in value. No deduction was allowable under Section 2053 for *A*'s claim as promisee on *D*'s note, because the note was not contracted for an adequate and full consideration in money or money's worth. Because the note had not been paid, the assets that were to be used to satisfy *D*'s promissory note were a part of *D*'s gross estate. Therefore, *D*'s 1977 gift to *A* was deemed to be includable in *D*'s gross estate for purposes of Section 2001. Thus, *D*'s 1977 gift was not an adjusted taxable gift as defined in Section 2001(b). Consequently, the value of *D*'s 1977 gift was not added under Section 2001(b)(1)(B) to *D*'s adjusted taxable gifts in computing the tentative estate tax under Section 2001(b)(1). The holding of this ruling applied only to the extent that the promissory note remained unsatisfied at *D*'s death.

[Rev. Rul. 84-25, 1984-1 CB 191.]

Transfer of stock options to employee's child was a completed gift. An employee owned vested stock options received from his employer, a publicly held corporation. The options are exercisable from the date they vest until they expire. The options expire ten years from the grant date, or sooner in the case of termination of the employee's employment. Currently, the options are not transferable other than by will or the laws of descent and distribution. The company will amend the stock option plans so that options will also be transferable to members of the employee's immediate family, among others. Under another proposed amendment, the employee will no longer be able to consent to the company's termination, modification, or amendment of the plan that adversely affects the rights of the grantee of the options. The employee intended to transfer a portion of each of three fully vested stock options to his child. The IRS determined that this transfer to the child will be a completed gift on the date of the transfer. Moreover, the transferred portion of the options will not be included in the employee's estate.

[Priv. Ltr. Rul. 9514017.]

Forgone dividends were a continuing gift. Taxpayer capitalized the corporation in return for all the corporation's common and preferred shares. The preferred shares had a liquidation value roughly equal to the initial capitalization, but a noncumulative dividend of less than one percent. When the shares were issued, the prevailing rate of dividends on preferred stock was over 11.5 percent. Shortly after forming the corporation, taxpayer transferred all of the common stock to his children and, in the following year, transferred a portion of the preferred shares to his wife. Even after these transfers, however, taxpayer retained a majority vote in the corporation. Section 2511 provides that the gift tax applies whether a transfer is direct or indirect. Not all apparent transfers are gifts; for example, an incomplete transfer where the donor can recover the transferred property is not a gift.

Taxpayer sought to rely on Anderson, 56 TCM 553 (1988), where the Tax Court included previously transferred common shares in the value of decedent's retained preferred shares because he had the right to liquidate the corporation, thereby recovering the value of the common shares. Since taxpayer had a liquidation right, any funds left with the company by reason of the low dividend rate were not completed gifts. The IRS pointed out that taxpayer was entitled only to the return of his original investment upon liquidation. He could not, as in *Anderson*, recover the full value of the corporation, since its value had increased over the years. The IRS looked instead to Snyder, 93 TC 529 (1989), which concluded that where a preferred shareholder did not exercise the right to convert her noncumulative shares to shares having a cumulative dividend, there was a gift of the lapsed dividends. Taxpayer had the voting power to increase dividends on the preferred shares and should have done so. The only reason taxpayer was satisfied with the low yield was his desire to benefit his children. The forgone dividends were continuing gifts to the extent of the difference between the dividends paid and the market rate when the preferred stock was issued.

[Tech. Adv. Mem. 9301001.]

Gifts made under durable power of attorney are ruled revocable. The taxpayer executed a broad, durable power of attorney on December 30, 1983, appointing another individual as his attorney-in-fact. Although this power of attorney was durable and provided for a comprehensive list of acts that the attorney could perform, it did not contain any express power authorizing the holder to make gifts of taxpayer's property. The taxpayer had a history of making gifts to his children, which practice the attorney-in-fact continued once taxpayer went into a nursing home. During the period from 1986 to 1989, gifts were made to taxpayer's children and twenty grandchildren, and the attorney-in-fact signed all the checks. The attorney-in-fact also signed the federal gift tax returns reporting these transfers. After the death of taxpayer's spouse, the attorney-in-fact, who was appointed conservator of the spouse's estate, obtained a court order ratifying the previous gifts made by this individual as attorney-in-fact for taxpayer, with "said ratification being effective as of the date of each gift."

In reviewing this issue, the IRS essentially relied on its long-stated principle that powers of attorney are to be given technical, rather than popular, meanings and are to be strictly construed. The IRS cited Estate of Casey, 91-2 USTC ¶ 60,091, 58 AFTR2d 91-6060 (4th Cir. 1991), in which the Fourth Circuit, applying Virginia law, stated that the failure to specifically authorize an attorney-in-fact to make gifts for the principal rendered such gifts revocable, incomplete, and includable in the gross estate of the donor. The IRS also cited Nebraska law for the proposition that powers of attorney are to be strictly construed. The IRS concluded that because the power of attorney did not confer on the attorney-in-fact the express grant of authority to make gifts, the gifts made by the attorney-in-fact were revocable and incomplete for gift tax purposes. The IRS further determined that the state court order retroactively approving the gifts could not validate the tax consequences for federal gift tax purposes. It cited Sinopoulo v. Jones, 154 F2d 648, 46-1 USTC ¶ 9220, 34 AFTR 1124 (10th Cir. 1946), to the effect that a state court order making a reformation of a trust retroactive to the date of its execution did not affect the rights of the government under the tax laws. The court in *Sinopoulo* held that as between the parties to an instrument, a reformation relates back to the date of the instrument; but as to third parties, the reformation is effective from the date thereof. The IRS concluded that the gifts were incomplete for federal gift tax purposes until the court order in November 1989. Such transfers became a gift of a present interest as of the date of the court order, and the annual exclusion of $10,000 per donee was allowable under Section 2503 against the total gifts confirmed on that date.

[Tech. Adv. Mem. 9231003.]

IRS takes position that proposed assignment of remainder interest is gift. Under a trust that became irrevocable at the settlor's death in 1953, one of the settlor's grandchildren received a life estate in farm property. At that grandchild's death, the farm was to pass either to her children or, if she had no children, to her then-surviving siblings. The life beneficiary had an adopted child who was not a descendant under the terms of the trust, because she was not the biological child of the life beneficiary. The beneficiary stated that she would not have any other children. Because the two remaindermen believed that the adopted child should be entitled to possession of the farm as if she were the life beneficiary's natural descendant, an agreement was entered into whereby the farm was to be distributed to the adopted child if she survived the life beneficiary or to the adopted child's estate if she did not survive the life beneficiary. The trust instrument also contained a spendthrift provision under which payments to each trust beneficiary were to be made to no one else, and under which no interest of any beneficiary could be assignable in anticipation of payment for such beneficiary's debts, obligations, or liabilities.

The IRS stated that the remainder interests created by the trust were vested remainders subject to divestment, which were alienable under the relevant Illinois state law, and that the spendthrift provision was no barrier to the proposed assignments. Accordingly, the assignments were complete for purposes of Section 2511 and were subject to gift tax. The IRS determined that the spendthrift clause was included only to govern income beneficiaries, not to limit parties who might wish to assign remainder interests that would otherwise succeed to their possession and enjoyment free of trust.

[Priv. Ltr. Rul. 8624014.]

[2] Transfers in Trust

Eighth Circuit reverses Tax Court's decision on when completed gift occurs. In 1975, decedent, a Nebraska resident, incorporated his business (Farms), which owned and operated various ranches and farms. Decedent received 5,000 shares of stock in Farms. During the next few years, he made gifts of stock to various family members so that as of January 1, 1981, stock ownership in Farms was as follows: decedent, 2,757 shares; decedent's son, 1,945 shares; decedent's daughter-in-law, 55 shares; decedent's three grandchildren, 81 shares each. On January 2, 1981, decedent created a trust (Trust), to which he transferred his 2,757 shares in Farms. Decedent's son and daughter-in-law were named as trustees. Decedent, as grantor, retained authority to remove any trustee and to appoint a successor. The trustees had authority to distribute principal or income to any of the beneficiaries or to the trustees, but not to the grantor. A beneficiary had no right to a distribution of principal until the trust terminated. The trust was to continue for twenty-five years unless extended or terminated earlier by the trustees. The trustees had broad powers to manage, sell, or otherwise deal with trust assets. Beneficial interest in the trust was divided into 100 Class A certificate units, each representing a one percent–pro rata interest in income and corpus. Neither the trust nor the trustees had any power or control over the beneficial interest certificates. Decedent received the 100 units in exchange for his Farms stock. There was no restriction on his ability to transfer the certificates.

On January 2, 1981, decedent transferred fifty units to his three grandchildren jointly with their father, so that each child and his father jointly held sixteen and two-thirds units of beneficial interest in the trust. Decedent filed a gift tax return for the period ending March 31, 1981, showing taxable gifts of $184,560 and gift tax due from the transfer of the fifty units. On January 2, 1982, decedent transferred twenty-three units to his grandchildren (six units each) and his son and daughter-in-law (five units held in tenancy in common). On the 1982 gift tax return, decedent reported taxable gifts of $39,682, with no gift tax due. On January 16, 1984, decedent's son was appointed as the guardian and conservator of decedent. In February 1985, the son petitioned the county court for a declaration allowing the trustees to make gifts of his father's remaining units in the trust to the son and his family members for estate-planning purposes. The court approved the petition. According to the declaration approved by the court, the grantor relinquished his right to remove trustees and appoint successors, and he relinquished any rights to income.

On February 18, 1985, the trustees purported to cancel all previous transfers of units of beneficial interest by decedent. The trustees repeated this effort on November 1, 1985, when they then assigned the 100 units in the following manner: twenty-five units held in tenancy in common by decedent's son and daughter-in-law, and twenty-five units held by each of decedent's grandchildren. On the gift tax return filed for 1985, the trustees reported a gift valued at $86,530 and no tax due. The IRS issued a notice of deficiency, claiming that a completed gift was not made by decedent or the trustees until February 18, 1985, that the gift was of 2,757 shares of Farms stock, and that the taxable value of the gift was $1,132,438. The IRS then added a 30 percent addition to tax under prior law, because of the valuation understatement. The Tax Court held in favor of the IRS.

Held: Reversed and remanded for the estate. The Eighth Circuit found no merit in the estate's argument that the transfer of the stock to the trust in 1981 was a completed gift. The court, however, agreed with the estate that the 1981 and 1982 transfers of beneficial certificates completed part of the gift. The court concluded that the gift was complete with respect to fifty certificates on January 2, 1981. The same logic applied to decedent's transfer of twenty-three certificates on January 2, 1982. The court also concluded that the final completion of the gift of the remaining twenty-seven certificates occurred on November 1, 1985. The court reversed the Tax Court's conclusion that a completed gift occurred on February 18, 1985, and remanded the case for further proceedings.

[Estate of Vak, 973 F2d 1409, 92-2 USTC ¶ 60,110, 70 AFTR2d 92-6239 (8th Cir. 1992).]

Taxpayer makes taxable gift when he relinquishes right to receive corpus of trust in favor of his children. The will of a testator who died in 1953 provided for a trust that was to pay half of all income to taxpayer for its twenty-year term. At the end of the term, that portion of the corpus that was the source of the income was to be turned over to taxpayer, if living, or to his children, if taxpayer were deceased. Taxpayer regularly received income over the entire twenty years. On April 9, 1973, one day after the trust terminated, taxpayer disclaimed his interest in the corpus, and as a result, the assets, valued at $2.5 million, passed to his children. Taxpayer and his wife filed a gift tax return for the second quarter of 1973, in which return they advised the IRS of the disclaimer, but did not treat it as a taxable gift. The IRS disagreed and assessed gift taxes and interest. Taxpayer died in October 1973, and in 1977, his estate paid his share of the deficiency and interest, and his wife paid the remainder. After denial of their administrative claims, they brought suits for refund of their 1973 gift taxes.

Held: For the IRS, on this issue. Although under the standards of Section 2518, a disclaimer of the right to receive property in favor of another, such as in the instant case, is explicitly subject to gift tax, that section of the Code was not enacted until 1976. The legislative history indicates that no inference may be drawn from the enactment as to the prior law in effect in 1973, the year in question. It was thus necessary to look at the more general provisions of the Code and regulations prior to the later amendments. The Code levies the gift tax on every "transfer of property by gift . . . by any individual" (Section 2501(a)(1)), whether the gift is direct or indirect, and whether the property is real or personal, tangible or intangible (Section 2511(a)). Regulation § 25.2511-1(c) provides that in the absence of facts to the contrary, if a person fails to refuse to accept a transfer to him of ownership of a decedent's property within a reasonable time after learning of the existence of the transfer, he will be presumed to have accepted the property. Taxpayer received the income from the trust property for twenty years before repudiating his interest in it and did not disclaim his interest until one day after the trust terminated and he was absolutely entitled to the corpus. Thus, taxpayer made a taxable gift in 1973, when, after having received the income of the trust during its twenty-year term, he relinquished his right to receive the corpus in favor of his children.

[Estate of Bunn, 3 Cl. Ct. 547, 52 AFTR2d 83-6462, 83-2 USTC ¶ 13,543 (1983).]

Transfers among family members are gifts. In 1953, decedent started a small sawmill business in Branscomb, California, which was operated as a partnership under the name of Branscomb Enterprises. Decedent and his two sons were partners, with one son also serving as trustee for decedent's daughter, a limited partner. On January 1, 1955, the partners formed another partnership, Hardwood Investment Company (HIC). Each held a one-third general partnership interest in HIC. The partnership interest in decedent's name was the community property of decedent and his wife. On July 16, 1955, decedent executed his will, directing that his entire separate estate and all of the community property, including his wife's share, pass to a testamentary trust. In a separate document, the wife consented in writing to the provisions of the will affecting the disposition of their community property. It was provided in the will that if the wife revoked her consent and elected to take her statutory share in lieu of the testamentary provisions, the will was to be given effect as if she had predeceased him, except for certain specific bequests.

Decedent died on March 8, 1958, survived by his wife and children. In 1971, the wife withdrew her consent to the disposition of her share of community property made by her husband's will and, pursuant to state court order, received a one-half interest in the community property held in trust. Because decedent was a one-third partner in HIC at the time of his death, the wife received a one-sixth interest pursuant to the 1971 court order, with the remaining one-sixth interest in HIC being divided into equal shares for the children. On January 1, 1973, the wife transferred her interest in HIC to her two sons in equal shares in exchange for a promissory note in the amount of $573,365, to be paid in four equal installments without interest. Subsequently, she exchanged the promissory note for a lifetime annuity.

On January 1, 1973, an additional one-eighth interest in HIC was transferred to the daughter; the daughter did not transfer any money to HIC in 1973, however, nor was there any written agreement that she would pay any amount for such interest. For tax purposes, taxpayers contended that the wife's transfer of the partnership interest to her sons in exchange for the promissory note was a transfer in the ordinary course of business, and hence was not subject to the gift tax even if the value of the wife's interest exceeded the value of the note. Taxpayers further contended that the January 1, 1973, transaction in which the daughter had gained a one-eighteenth interest in HIC was also a transfer in the ordinary course of business, or, in the alternative, that a $300,000 payment made to HIC by the daughter in 1978 should be recognized as consideration for the one-eighteenth interest that she received on January 1, 1973. The IRS denied these contentions.

Held: For the IRS. Transactions within a family group are subject to special scrutiny, and the presumption arises that a transfer among family members is a gift. A transfer by a mother to her sons of her interest in a family partnership, structured totally by the family accountant, with no arm's-length bargaining, cannot be characterized as a transaction in the ordinary course of business. Thus, the wife was found to have made a gift to the sons equal to the excess value of the one-sixth interest in HIC over the face amount of the note. Similarly, the wife and sons made taxable gifts to the daughter in 1973 that were equal to the excess of the FMV of the partnership interests over the value of any consideration received therefor. The court concluded that taxpayers had not met their burden of proving that the $300,000 was consideration paid in exchange for the one-eighteenth partnership interest acquired by the daughter.

[Harwood, 82 TC 239 (1984), aff'd without published op., 786 F2d 1174 (9th Cir. 1986).]

Entirely voluntary distribution power of trustee vis-à-vis grantor earmarks completed taxable gift. The IRS ruled that a transfer of property to an irrevocable inter vivos trust wherein the trustee is given discretionary power entirely voluntary under the instrument and applicable state law, to distribute income and principal to the grantor constitutes a completed taxable gift of the entire value of the property transferred. Although the trustee has an unrestricted power to distribute trust assets to the grantor, the grantor cannot require that such distribution be made, nor can he use the trust assets by going into debt and relegating his creditors to the trust. (Revenue Ruling 62-13, 1962-1 CB 181, is clarified.)

[Rev. Rul. 77-378, 1977-2 CB 347.]

Entire value of property transferred in trust is subject to gift tax where donor's interest cannot be valued. Taxpayer-donor created a trust with net income to A and B for their joint lives and to the survivor for life, and thereafter with discretion to accumulate or distribute income to C or D, or both. The trust was to terminate on the last to occur of ten years plus one day, A's death, or B's death. The trustee had absolute discretion to change the form of assets, to sell the assets, and to allocate all of the proceeds to income and none to principal. The IRS ruled that the donor's retained interest was incapable of valuation. Therefore, the entire value of the property transferred in trust was subject to gift tax.

[Rev. Rul. 76-275, 1976-2 CB 299.]

Transfer of property to discretionary trust whose assets are subject to claims of creditors is not completed gift. Grantor created an irrevocable inter vivos trust the income from which could be paid, in the absolute discretion of the trustee, to the grantor or accumulated and added to the principal. Under the law of the state in which it was created, the trust was a discretionary trust, and the entire property of the trust could be subjected to the claims of the grantor's creditors. Accordingly, the grantor retained dominion and control over the trust property, because he could enjoy all of the trust income by relegating the creditors to the trust for settlement of their claims. The grantor's transfer of property to the trust did not constitute a completed gift for federal gift tax purposes.

[Rev. Rul. 76-103, 1976-1 CB 293.]

Contingent interests do not reduce a GRAT gift. The right to receive the balance of an annuity payable from a grantor-retained annuity trust (GRAT), if the grantor died before receiving all the payments, was not a qualified interest that reduced the value of the gift to the remainderman, according to this ruling. A grantor set up a trust with a five-year term, funding it with cash. He retained an annuity in a fixed amount, payable annually for five years. After the trust term, the principal was distributable to the grantor's issue. If the grantor died before receiving the entire annuity, the remaining payments were to be made to his spouse, provided that she was then alive and the grantor had not revoked her interest. If the spouse did not survive of if the grantor revoked her interest, the balance of the annuity was payable to the grantor's estate. Section 2702 provides special rules for valuing transfers to a trust set up for the benefit of certain family members if the grantor retains an interest in the trust. Under Section 2702(a)(2), the grantor's retained interest is valued at zero unless it is a qualified interest. (A qualified interest is valued using tables under Section 7520.) A qualified interest must entitle the grantor to a fixed amount payable annually ("qualified annuity interest") or a fixed percentage of the FMV of the property determined and payable annually ("qualified unitrust interest"), or it must be a "qualified remainder interest," according to Section 2702(b). (The reservation of "income" does not satisfy either requirement.) A qualified remainder interest must be payable to the remainder beneficiary or his or her estate in all events, and the other interests in the trust must be qualified annuity or unitrust interests.

The IRS decided that the gift to the grantor's issue was not reduced by the value of an annuity payable *in all events* for five years, since the interests of the spouse and the estate did not qualify. Rather, the only qualified interest was the grantor's right to receive an annuity payable annually for five years or until his prior death, which had a lower value than an annuity for a term certain. The estate's interest was not a qualified annuity based on Regulation § 25.2702-3(e), Examples 1 and 5. In Example 5, a donor transferred property to a trust and retained the right to receive qualified unitrust payments (equal to 5 percent of the value of the trust property valued annually) for a ten-year term. If the donor died within the ten years, the payments were to be made to his estate for the remaining portion of the ten-year term. In Example 1, if the donor died before receiving all the payments (of an annuity), the corpus reverted to the donor's estate. Both examples concluded that the only qualified interest was the donor's right to receive the unitrust or annuity amount during the term of the trust or until the donor's prior death. The interests that depended on the donor's death (e.g., the remaining unitrust payments in Example 5) did not qualify, because they were contingent. The IRS decided that these examples were on point, except for differences as to the amount or precise nature of the interests that reverted, which were not material differences. Here, the spouse's contingent right to receive an annuity if the donor died prior to the end of the trust term raised an additional issue, because it was revocable by the grantor. If a transfer in trust is an incomplete gift, it is not subject to Section 2702, according to Section 2702(a)(3)(A)(i) and Regulation § 25.2702-1(c). For this exception to apply, however, the entire gift must be incomplete. Thus, in Regulation § 25.2702-2(d), Example 6, a spouse had a nonqualifying income interest that was revocable and followed still another nonqualifying income interest. The incomplete-gift exception did not apply to the spouse's interest, however, because all the other interests in the trust were not incomplete.

Therefore, the entire transfer in trust was a gift to the remainder beneficiary. Here, only the spouse's interest was revocable, so the incomplete-gift exception likewise did not apply. In addition, since her interest was contingent, it could not be subtracted from the value of the gift.

[Tech. Adv. Mem. 9707001.]

Gift of life insurance does not endanger exclusion. Taxpayer transferred several life insurance policies on his life that were subject to policy loans to an irrevocable trust and named his wife as trustee. Later he purchased the policies for their net cash surrender value from the trustee, who terminated the trust. Taxpayer gratuitously contributed the policies to a newly established irrevocable trust. Under Section 101(a)(2), however, if a life insurance contract is transferred for valuable consideration, the transferee's exclusion of the proceeds received is limited to the value of the consideration paid for the policy, plus the net premiums and other amounts paid for the policy. This limitation does not apply when either (1) the transfer is to the insured, his partner, his partnership, or a corporation in which he is a shareholder or officer or (2) the transferee's basis for the policy is determined in whole or in part by reference to the transferor's basis. In addition, when the transfer is gratuitous, the limitation does not apply, and all of the death benefits are excluded. The transfer of the policies from the older trust to taxpayer was for valuable consideration, because taxpayer paid for the policies. The limitation on the exclusion of death benefits did not apply, because the transfer was to the insured. Thus, the transaction satisfies the first exception, and the amount realized on the trustee's sale is the amount paid by taxpayer plus the outstanding policy loans. Revenue Ruling 69-187, 1969-1 CB 45, deals with a husband's transfer to his wife of a life insurance policy on the husband's life that was subject to an indebtedness. Her interest in the policy was acquired in part for consideration and in part by the gift. Therefore, the wife's basis in the policy was determinable in part by reference to the basis of the policy in the husband's hands. That revenue ruling holds that upon the husband's death, the proceeds are paid to the wife solely by reason of the insured's death and are excludable from her gross income.

Citing that revenue ruling, the IRS concluded that taxpayer's transfer of the policies to the new trust was part sale and part gift. Thus, the new trust's bases in the policies are determined by reference to taxpayer's basis. According to Regulation § 1.101-1(b)(3), if the final transfer in a series is for valuable consideration, the transferee can exclude the amount that the transferor could have excluded if no transfer had occurred, but only if the transferee's basis is determined by reference to the transferor's. Thus, the new trust can exclude the amount of proceeds that taxpayer could have excluded if the new trust's basis in the policies is determined, at least in part, by reference to taxpayer's basis. The new trust meets this condition because the transfer of the policies to it is a gift to the extent to which taxpayer's adjusted basis in the policies exceeds the policy loans.

[Priv. Ltr. Rul. 8951056.]

Trust properties transferred in 1985 and held by grantor's agent until recorded in 1986 are completed taxable gifts in 1986. An individual created an irrevocable trust for the benefit of his descendants that was initially funded in late December 1985 with $30,000. The trust provided that any net income earned during the grantor's life would be paid to the grantor's descendants for their health and welfare at the trustee's discretion. Regarding subsequent additions to the trust, the trust provided that each descendant and spouse would have a noncumulative right, within thirty days after notice that the property had been added, to withdraw a pro rata share of the addition. The trust further provided that if, upon termination of the power of withdrawal, the person holding such power were deemed to have made a taxable gift for federal gift tax purposes, then the power of withdrawal would not lapse. Instead, the power of withdrawal would continue to exist, relating to the amount that would have been a taxable gift, and would terminate only when the termination would not result in a taxable gift. The trust also provided that the donor of any subsequent property would have the right, in writing, to exclude any individual with a power of withdrawal from exercising that power as to any property subsequently added by the donor. On December 27, 1985, the grantor executed a deed of transfer of parcel *A* to the trust, followed by the execution of a deed of transfer of parcel *B* on December 30, 1985. Both deeds were recorded on January 6, 1986. Prior to their recording, the grantor's attorney, acting as the grantor's agent, held the deeds. At no time prior to January 6, 1985, did the trustee have control over the deeds. The grantor executed a deed of transfer for parcel *C*, which was recorded on March 19, 1986, and was given to the trustee at that time. The grantor and his spouse elected to split the gifts and filed the appropriate Form 709, reporting the initial funding of the trust and parcels *A* and *B* in 1985. The grantor and his wife reported the gift of parcel *C* in 1986. In addition, the grantor and his spouse each claimed seven annual exclusions on their 1985 returns. As a result of changes in the generation-skipping transfer tax laws caused by the 1986 Act, the grantor and the spouse amended their 1985 generation-skipping transfer tax returns in August 1986, with each claiming a refund of $1,700 based on the use of $5,000 of the $2 million grandchild exclusion.

The IRS took the position that the transfers of parcels *A* and *B* were not completed gifts subject to federal gift tax until 1986. The IRS noted that leaving the deeds with the grantor's attorney-agent was not a completed gift for Section 2511 purposes, because the grantor retained the power to revoke the deeds until they were in the hands of the trustee or the trustee's agent. Citing Crummey, 397 F2d 82 (9th Cir. 1968), and Revenue Ruling 80-261, 1980-2

CB 279, the IRS further indicated that the transfer of property to the trust over which the beneficiaries have the right of withdrawal was a present interest that qualified for the annual gift tax exclusion under Section 2503(b), provided that there was no impediment to the appointment of a guardian under local law for any minors involved. The IRS also indicated that each time a beneficiary permitted a power of withdrawal to lapse, the beneficiary would be deemed to have made a pro rata gift of their portion to the trust, to the extent that the portion exceeds the greater of $5,000 or 5 percent of the contribution. The IRS also cited Proctor, 142 F2d 824 (4th Cir. 1944), cert. denied, 323 US 756 (1944), and Revenue Ruling 86-41, 1986-1 CB 300, to find that the condition that the right of withdrawal will not lapse is a condition subsequent. Accordingly, the IRS concluded that the condition was not valid. The IRS stated that although the contributions to the trust would not result in a direct skip to the trust for the benefit of the grantor's grandchildren, they would constitute a transfer to the grandchildren for purposes of Section 1433(b)(3) of the 1986 Act. Therefore, the IRS concluded that the contributions would not qualify for the $2 million grandchild exclusion. The donor's power to keep beneficiaries from exercising their right of withdrawal of specific contributions did not constitute a retention of control under Section 674. The IRS therefore concluded that the donor was not subject to taxation under Section 671. Once the property was transferred to, and became part of, the trust, the IRS reasoned, the donor's power could no longer affect the beneficial enjoyment of the property.

[Tech. Adv. Mem. 8901004.]

Transfer of S corporation stock to trusts is completed gift, notwithstanding grantor's reversionary interest. An individual proposed to transfer stock of an S corporation into two irrevocable trusts. Both trusts were to terminate on the earlier of the death of the grantor or eight years. The grantor was to receive all of the income from the trusts on an annual basis. If the grantor were still living upon the expiration of the eight-year period, the principal of the trusts would then pass to another trust for the benefit of the grantor's children. Under the terms of both trusts, if the individual were to die before the eight-year term expired, he would have a testamentary general power of appointment over the trust principals. Under the terms of one of the trusts, if the grantor were living at the expiration of the eight-year term and had no living descendants, the trust principal was to revert to him. Under the terms of the other trust, if the grantor survived the eight-year period, then his spouse was to have a special power of appointment in favor of any descendant of the grantor's father. Failure to exercise the power would result in the principal being distributed to a third trust. The shareholders of the S corporation agreed to pay the shareholders a minimum annual dividend equal to the sum of state and federal taxes payable by any shareholder.

The IRS stated that the grantor would not retain control over the property transferred to the trusts, because the general power of appointment he would retain can be exercised only upon his death. Therefore, the retained power of appointment would not prevent the transfer of the stock to the trusts from being considered a complete gift for gift tax purposes. The IRS then stated that the possibility that the grantor may die before the expiration of the eight-year term would affect the value of the interests transferred. The IRS concluded that the grantor's reversionary interest could not be actuarially valued, because at the time of the proposed transfer, the grantor had two living children who themselves might have had children. The IRS stated that when a retained interest cannot be actuarially valued, it may be excluded from the value of the completed gift. Therefore, the value of the reversionary interest would not reduce the value of the gift or the property transferred. Lastly, the IRS provided the formula to determine the value of the grantor's retained interest.

[Priv. Ltr. Rul. 8830052.]

Transfer to trust results in taxable gift, but retained income interest and contingent remainder are excluded. An individual transferred cash and publicly traded securities to an irrevocable trust, with her two children named co-trustees. The individual retained the right to receive all of the net income produced from the trust until 1997. If the individual (trustor) was still living at that time, then all of the remaining principal was to be distributed outright to the children or to their estates in equal amounts. The children had not designated the trustor as a beneficiary of their respective estates. If the trustor should die before 1997, the trust would terminate, and the principal would be distributed as the trustor directed by a general power of appointment. If the power lapsed, then the trust principal would be divided directly between the two children or their respective estates. The trust also had a provision that allowed distribution of corpus to pay income taxes.

The IRS stated that the income interest, which would terminate in 1997 or earlier if the trustor were to die, clearly was not a taxable gift, because the trustor retained an interest. The IRS then stated that at the time of the transfer, the amount of the corpus was a completed gift because the trustor had retained no interest in it. Thus, the gift tax applied at the time of the transfer to the entire value of the property less the trustor's retained income and contingent reversionary interest. Lastly, the IRS provided the actuarial factor to be used to compute the value of the property and gift tax on the transfer.

[Priv. Ltr. Rul. 8815005.]

Gift tax is assessed at time trust is set up when donor lacks power to recapture property. A donor set up a trust providing that the trustee should hold the principal for three years after the instrument date or his death, whichever should occur first. During the term of the trust, the trustees would pay net income to the donor. If the trust were to terminate after three years, the trustees then would hold the principal for the donor's wife and living heirs. The trust further provided that if the donor had died before the expiration of the three-year term, he would have had a general power to appoint the trust property in his will.

The IRS stated that the donor made a completed gift under Section 2511 to his wife and living descendants, and that the gift tax was due when the transfer occurred. The IRS reasoned that the donor's power to recapture the transferred property was not subject to a condition within his control, because his testamentary power to appoint the trust assets was contingent upon the donor dying before a specified date. The IRS distinguished Revenue Ruling 54-537, 1954-2 CB 316. The IRS also concluded that under Section 2512, the value of the trust assets when the trust was funded was the amount of the gift, and that the regulations under that section set out a formula to compute the value of the gift and the remainder interest.

[Priv. Ltr. Rul. 8727031.]

Transfers to trust are completed gifts, despite donor's testamentary power to appoint trust assets. In 1981, an individual created two trusts. The first trust provided that the trustee would pay the trust income to the individual until the earlier of March 1, 1988, or the individual's date of death, and then distribute the trust principal to her living descendants. The first trust also provided that if the settlor died before March 1, 1988, she would retain a general power to appoint the trust property by will. The second trust was identical to the first trust, except that the date of March 1, 1991, was used in place of March 1, 1988.

The IRS stated that the individual made a complete gift of the assets given to the trusts when the trusts were created. The IRS distinguished Revenue Ruling 54-437, 1954-2 CB 316, and concluded that the settlor's power of appointment was not subject to a condition that was within her control and that the gifts were subject to tax in 1981.

[Priv. Ltr. Rul. 8546001.]

¶ 14.03 POWERS OF APPOINTMENT

Property passing to surviving spouse under joint and mutual will is deemed completed gift to heirs of surviving spouse, because disposition of property is limited by ascertainable standard. In 1973, taxpayer and her husband executed a joint and mutual will. The will provided that the surviving spouse would receive the deceased spouse's property in fee simple and specified in great detail the disposition of the property at the death of the survivor. In 1978, taxpayer's husband died. While taxpayer was hospitalized, her attorney filed a gift tax return and paid taxes on all of her property, under the assumption that the joint and mutual will functioned to make a valid gift from taxpayer to her beneficiaries. Subsequently, taxpayer challenged this payment as erroneous and sought a refund. The district court granted taxpayer's motion for summary judgment on the refund claim.

Held: Reversed for the IRS. The court stated that it must look to the state court decision giving judicial construction of the will. The state court had construed the will as being joint and mutual. Pursuant to Illinois state law, such arrangements are interpreted as giving the survivor the equivalent of a life estate in the couple's assets. Such wills are deemed irrevocable, and the surviving spouse is thus prohibited from alienating or disposing of the property, except as necessary to provide for the spouse's health, support, comfort, or maintenance. The district court held that the will created a gift from the surviving spouse to the beneficiaries. Because the surviving spouse was able to invade the corpus for comfort, however, the court ruled that disposition of the property was not limited by an ascertainable standard and was thus an incomplete gift not subject to gift tax. The Seventh Circuit did not agree with this reasoning. In looking at the state court's decision construing the will, the Seventh Circuit found that the state court had placed significant constraints on taxpayer's liberty to dispose of the property.

The state court had held that although entitled to the income from the property, taxpayer was entitled to invade the corpus only for her "health, support, comfort and maintenance." The state court permitted the sale of some of the assets, but only in order to acquire "investments of equal or more value." Further, the state court prohibited taxpayer from disposing of certain parcels of real estate until all of the other assets had been consumed, and required that the proceeds of the real estate be used for her health, support, comfort, and maintenance. The Seventh Circuit felt that these restrictions were sufficiently stringent to form an ascertainable standard limiting her interest. The gift was therefore completed and was subject to federal gift tax.

[Pyle, 766 F2d 1141, 56 AFTR2d 85-6521, 85-2 USTC ¶ 13,626 (7th Cir. 1985), cert. denied, 475 US 1015 (1986).]

Release of settlor's power to amend trust constitutes taxable gift. Taxpayer elected, as a condition of taking under her husband's will, to place her share of community property in trust, retaining a power of appointment that permitted her to make gifts to her children and to charity. Four years later she released the retained power. The Tax Court held that this release constituted a taxable gift of the remainder interest in the trust.

Held: Affirmed for the IRS. The transfer to the trust was not a complete gift to the remaindermen at that time, because of the retained power of appointment. The retention of such power by her as settlor was, in effect, the retention of a power to alter or amend the trust, the release of which constituted a taxable gift. Taxpayer should not credit consideration received at time of transfer in trust against the amount of the gift. Section 2512(b) determines the value of the gift at the time it became complete, and only consideration received then is taken into account.

[Robinson, 675 F2d 774, 50 AFTR2d 82-6116, 82-1 USTC ¶ 13,470 (5th Cir. 1982), cert. denied, 459 US 970 (1982).]

Life income beneficiary's inter vivos transfer of income rights is held to constitute taxable gift. Decedent's father died in 1973, leaving property in trust for decedent, with income payable to her for life. The remainder was subject to a special power of appointment in decedent to be exercised inter vivos or by her will. During 1974, decedent exercised her special power of appointment and transferred the entire trust corpus in favor of a separate trust created by her son. She also filed a gift tax return in respect of the final quarter of 1974, but no mention was made of the exercise of the power. Following decedent's death in 1977, the estate filed its estate tax return without including in gross estate an amount attributable to decedent's life income interest in the trust or her exercise of the special power of appointment. The IRS subsequently assessed a deficiency on the ground that decedent's inter vivos exercise of the special power effected a taxable gift of her life income interest. Acknowledging that Section 2514 applies by its terms only to general powers of appointment, the IRS argued that the life income interest transferred by decedent was separate from the corpus, and, because only the corpus was the subject of the special power, the transfer of the income interest should be treated and taxed separately. The estate cited two cases, Walston, 8 TC 72 (1947), aff'd, 168 F2d 211 (4th Cir. 1948), and Self, 142 F. Supp. 939, 49 AFTR2d 1913, 56-2 USTC ¶ 11,613 (Ct. Cl. 1956), in support of its contention that decedent's interest in the income of the trust should be treated as extinguished, not transferred, upon exercise of the special power.

Held: For the IRS. The IRS argued persuasively that neither court in *Walston* ruled contrary to its present position, because each court ruled that under the facts, taxpayer only held a special power over the income interest and was directed by the will to transfer the income interest to a named party. The Tax Court examined *Self* and determined that the Court of Claims ignored the fact that in *Walston,* taxpayer did not have an unrestricted right to enjoy income for life, or the power to make an inter vivos transfer of such income. The Tax Court concluded that, given these factual distinctions, the two cases were not controlling. Accordingly, the court held that an inter vivos transfer by a life tenant with an absolute power over income constitutes a taxable gift, regardless of Section 2514.

[Estate of Regester, 83 TC 1 (1984).]

Multiple *Crummey* powers possessed by sole beneficiary are to be aggregated for purposes of annual gift tax exclusion. In situation 1, an irrevocable trust was created, with one beneficiary receiving the trust income for life and another receiving the remainder interest. The life-income beneficiary was given the right to withdraw up to $5,000 from each contribution to the trust. The trustee was to give notice to this beneficiary upon receipt of a contribution, and the beneficiary maintained the right to withdraw for a sixty-day period following receipt of notice. The beneficiary was given notice twice, but failed to exercise his rights on both occasions. In situation 2, the grantor established two separately administered irrevocable trusts on the same terms and conditions as those of the trust in situation 1. During the year, the grantor made one contribution to each of the trusts, but the life-income beneficiary did not exercise his right to withdraw. The issues raised were whether a taxable gift resulted from the successive lapses of two noncumulative powers to withdraw trust corpus within one calendar year, and, if so, what the amount of such a gift would be.

The IRS ruled that in both situations, the life-income beneficiary was deemed to have made a gift as a result of the lapse of his right to withdraw. The amount taxable was the aggregate amount subject to the power to withdraw that exceeds the $5,000 exemption provided in Section 2514(e), less the value of the beneficiary's retained interest in that amount. Section 2514(c) defines a "general power of appointment" as a power exercisable in favor of the possessor of the power, the possessor's estate, the possessor's creditors, or the creditors of the possessor's estate. Under Section 2514(b), the exercise or release of a general power of appointment created after October 21, 1942, is treated as a transfer of property by the individual possessing such power for federal gift tax purposes. Under Section 2514(e), the lapse of a general power of appointment created after October 21, 1942, like the release of such a power, results in a transfer for federal gift tax purposes. With respect to any calendar year, however, this rule applies only to the extent that the value of the property subject to the elapsed powers exceeds the greater of $5,000 or 5 percent of the aggregate value of the assets ("the five-and-five exemption") on which the exercise of the lapsed powers could have been performed. The language of Section of 2514(e) states that the exemption applies "with respect to the lapse of powers during any calendar year." Thus, under these circumstances, only one five-and-five exemption under Section 2514(e) is available for all lapses of powers of appointment in a single trust in a calendar year, and the beneficiary is entitled to only one $5,000 exemption per calendar year.

[Rev. Rul. 85-88, 1985-2 CB 201.]

IRS rules on release of general power of appointment. *G* was sole trustee of a trust established by his parent. The trust instrument provided that during *G*'s lifetime, income was to be accumulated or paid to *G* at the trustee's discretion. *G* named his two children and a corporation as cotrustees. He then relinquished all interest in the trust, accelerating the remainder interests and terminating the trust. *G*'s power as sole trustee to distribute all income to himself was a general power of appointment, released when three more trustees were appointed. The value of the released power was subject to gift tax under Section 2514(b). When all additional rights were later released, *G* made a gift under Section 2511.

[Rev. Rul. 79-421, 1979-2 CB 347.]

Exercise of power of appointment with income interests is taxable gift. Taxpayer had an income interest, coupled with a special power of appointment in trust property. At age 65, she exercised the power in favor of one of her children. Exercising the power resulted in a taxable gift because taxpayer also had an income interest in the property subject to the power.

[Rev. Rul. 79-327, 1979-2 CB 42.]

Release of power of appointment is not subject to gift tax, because it was created before statutorily established date of October 1942. A father established an irrevocable indenture of trust divided into four shares, one for each of his children. The two sons were granted the right to purchase from the trustees any part of the stock that constituted the corpus of the trust. The first of the sons died in 1978, without ever having exercised this right, which was thus extinguished as to him. The second surviving son released his right to purchase the stock from the trust. Section 2514(b) provides that the exercise or release of a general power of appointment created after October 1942 shall be deemed a transfer of property by the individual possessing the power.

The IRS determined that the second son's right to purchase was a general power of appointment as described in Section 2514. The IRS stated, however, that the release of the power was not subject to gift tax, because the power was created before October 1942. Hence, the unconditional and complete release of the right to purchase was not deemed a transfer for federal gift tax purposes under Section 2051, 2511, or 2514.

[Priv. Ltr. Rul. 8839059.]

¶ 14.04 JOINT INTERESTS

Where property held in joint tenancy is subject of joint and mutual will giving surviving spouse life interest in decedent's joint interest, surviving spouse is held to have made gift of remainder interest in such property

upon decedent's death. Taxpayer and his wife made a joint and mutual will in which each promised that the survivor would dispose of his or her interests in jointly held property according to the terms of the will. The will stipulated that in regard to real property held in joint tenancy, the portion of such property belonging to the first deceased would go to the children and grandchildren in fee simple, subject to a life estate of the surviving spouse. Taxpayer's wife died first, and, under applicable state law, the will thus became irrevocable. The wife's interest in the jointly held real estate passed to the children and grandchildren, subject to a life estate of taxpayer, and was taxable to her estate. The IRS claimed that by virtue of the will becoming irrevocable upon the wife's death, taxpayer made a completed gift of the remainder interest in his portion of the property. Taxpayer argued that there was no completed gift, because, under the will, he had retained the right to consume the entire value of the property.

Held: For the IRS. The court held that the appropriate tax treatment under such wills depends on the language in the will. The court stated that a gift occurs only when the donor has parted with dominion and control to leave him with no power to change its disposition. A gift does not, however, require donative intent, but rather only that beneficial ownership be conveyed for less than full consideration. Upon his wife's death, taxpayer became legally obligated to convey both his and his wife's interests in the property to the children and grandchildren according to the plan of the will. The court said that the effect of this was as if taxpayer had given all of his real property to his heirs, retaining a life interest. According to the court, such a scenario would have resulted in gift tax. Taxpayer argued that this scenario did not accurately portray the situation, because he retained the power to consume the entire value of the land. State law treats joint wills of this kind as reserving the right to consume corpus of the bequest only under certain circumstances, such as when the survivor incurs steep medical bills. Taxpayer contended that because he had this right to consume the corpus, there was no certainty that the remaindermen would take anything until taxpayer's death. The court rejected this argument, pointing out that under Illinois law, the surviving spouse does not have unlimited power to dispose of the property, unless the will clearly states otherwise. Rather, he has a duty to preserve the estate as well as to distribute what remains according to the will's directions. Because of this peculiarity in Illinois law, the court held that a completed gift was made when taxpayer's wife died.

[Grimes, 851 F2d 1005, 88-2 USTC ¶ 13,774, 63 AFTR2d 89-1526 (7th Cir. 1988).]

Withdrawals from joint account are not gifts. Decedent and her nephew had a joint bank account, with all funds in the account supplied by decedent. The lower court found that decedent was incompetent at the time the account was established, and decedent was declared incompetent during the period in which the nephew made withdrawals from the account. The nephew asserted that the withdrawals constituted gifts to him.

Held: For the IRS. Decedent lacked capacity to make a gift at the time of the withdrawals. The lower court's determination that decedent lacked capacity to make a gift even before she was declared incompetent is not clearly erroneous.

[Estate of Bettin, 543 F2d 1269, 38 AFTR2d 76-6313, 76-2 USTC ¶ 13,159 (9th Cir. 1976).]

Part of survivor annuity under qualified plan is taxable gift if employee can withdraw employer contributions before retirement. Taxpayer participated in a qualified profit-sharing plan that entitled him to withdraw up to one half of the employer contributions from the plan after fifteen years of service. When he retired, he received a joint and survivor annuity for himself and his wife. The gift tax exclusion in Section 2517 for annuity payments under qualified plans does not apply when taxpayer constructively received part of his account before retirement. Because he constructively received half of his account after fifteen years of service, one half of the value of the annuity rights of the wife was a taxable gift.

[Rev. Rul. 78-399, 1978-2 CB 250.]

Transfers to ease probate can generate gift tax. A ninety-year-old woman individually owned two pieces of real estate. She transferred title to a joint tenancy with right of survivorship to her sole heir, her daughter. The IRS ruled that the mother had made a gift of one half of the property at the time the title was transferred. This was based on Regulation § 25.2511-1(h), which states that if a taxpayer owns property individually and transfers the title to a joint ownership with rights of survivorship where the rights may be defeated by either party severing an interest, a gift has been made of one half of the property. In such a joint tenancy, an interest may be severed by the transfer of one or both interests to other parties.

The IRS declined to indicate whether the property would be includable in the mother's estate, because that involved application of the estate tax to a living person. In such situations, the IRS is very restrictive in its rulings. Since, apparently, the mother furnished all of the consideration for the property, the full value would be includable in her estate. That being the case, the basis of the property after the mother's death would be the FMV of the property at death, or the alternate valuation date, whichever would be applicable.

[Priv. Ltr. Rul. 8805019.]

Provision for annuity to spouse of civil servant under Civil Service Retirement Spouse Equity Act generates taxable gift. In two similar rulings, the

IRS stated that the transfer of a survivor annuity to a federal employee's spouse, upon the employee's retirement, under the Civil Service Retirement Spouse Equity Act of 1984, constitutes a taxable gift. Under that Act, a married civil servant automatically receives a reduced annuity at retirement and thereby provides a survivor annuity to his wife, unless the couple files a joint waiver. In the two private rulings, the waiver was not filed. The IRS stated that the survivor annuity was transferred to the spouse in connection with services rendered to the employer. The IRS noted that the taxable transfer occurred when the employee retired and that the transfer did not qualify for the annual gift tax exclusion.

[Priv. Ltr. Ruls. 8715010, 8715035.]

IRS takes position that survivor annuity is gift. A married civil servant who retired on or after May 7, 1985, was receiving a reduced retirement annuity in order to provide a survivor annuity for his spouse. The IRS stated that the right to receive the survivor annuity that was irrevocably provided to the civil servant upon his retirement was transferred to his wife and thus constituted a gift. The IRS also indicated that the gift of the annuity was completed upon the retirement of the civil servant. The IRS further indicated that the amount of the gift was the present value of the survivor annuity attributable to the civil servant's contributions into the plan.

[Priv. Ltr. Rul. 8708008.]

¶ 14.05 ANNUITIES

Amount of transferred stock exceeding value of private annuity received constitutes taxable gift. A husband, his wife, and their son entered into an agreement to transfer the husband's and wife's stock in a jointly owned company to the son. They wanted to make the transfer at less than FMV but did not want to make a gift of their entire interest in the corporation. Therefore, they agreed to make the transfer to their son for a monthly annuity of $600 until their death. The three asked the IRS for a ruling as to the value, determined actuarially, of the private annuity.

The IRS concluded that under Sections 2512(a) and 2512(b), the amount by which the value of the 650 shares of company stock transferred exceeded the value of the consideration received in the form of a private annuity was a taxable gift. The IRS calculated the present value of an annuity of $600 per month, first payment due in five years and three months thence, paid until the death of the survivor of two people both age 67 ($12 \times \$600 \times 3.9303 \times 1.0450$ (factor for monthly payments of $29,571.58)). The computation was based on Regulation § 25.2512-5(a). The IRS would not speculate on the value of the stock.

[Priv. Ltr. Rul. 8903076.]

CHAPTER **15**

Valuation of Property

¶ 15.01 FACTORS AND METHODS

Actuarial tables used for cancer victims. Decedent had extensive holdings in television and radio broadcasting when he was diagnosed with esophageal cancer in May 1985. Despite treatment, by September his condition was considered "systemic," with a 2–3 percent overall survival rate. Six courses of chemotherapy were administered from October 1985 through March 1986, a period which saw a temporary remission as well as a suicide attempt. Nevertheless, the oncologist reported in February that decedent was "certainly a candidate for long term control which fulfills medical and lay criteria for curability . . . [There was a] risk that the disease might recur, but . . . the possibility that [the] disease has been permanently eradicated is definite and significant and . . . should form the basis for . . . planning for the future." On decedent's sixty-fifth birthday, March 5—a date on which his chances of surviving for more than one year were approximately 10 percent, according to undisputed expert testimony—decedent entered into a private annuity transaction with his son and a family trust. He transferred remainder interests to them in return for $250,000 and an annuity priced so that its aggregate present value would equal the present value of the remainder interests, using the life expectancy tables in the regulations. By May 1986, the cancer recurred and decedent died in September. The IRS claimed that decedent's life expectancy was sufficiently predictable—and in fact was less than one year—to make use of the tables unnecessary and erroneous. Thus, the IRS contended the remainder interests were undervalued and the annuity overvalued. The Tax Court agreed and imposed $12.5 million in additional gift and estate taxes. It held that the use of the tables was improper because decedent's life expectancy—of approximately one year—was reasonably predictable at the time of the transfer. In the first appeal, the Fifth Circuit reversed (77 F3d 477, 96-1 USTC ¶ 60,220, 77 AFTR2d 96-666 (5th Cir. 1995)) on the substantive valuation questions, and remanded as to the use of the actuarial tables. The appellate court indicated it was unable to discern whether the Tax Court followed Revenue Ruling 80-80, 1980-1 CB 194, or found reason to depart from it: "The Tax Court's opinion is both ambiguous and ambivalent regarding the revenue ruling, as it holds that [decedent] had a life expectancy of one year, a finding that would suggest to us under the express language of the revenue ruling that death was not clearly imminent."

Held: For decedent. The Fifth Circuit noted that the actuarial tables in the regulations "have not always been vigorously enforced by the courts." "Tolerated" as an administrative necessity, the tables "have been discarded where an actual value can be calculated in a suitably reliable way." The Fifth Circuit observed that the cases in which the courts decided to "allow departure from the harshness of the tables were without exception favorable to taxpayers in ultimate result. . . . Here, of course, the [IRS] seeks departure at taxpayer's expense. This distinction is not wholly irrelevant. . . . " In Revenue Ruling 80-80 the IRS attempted to clarify its position as to use of the tables, which it described as properly applicable to the vast majority of individual life interests even though the health of a particular individual may be better or worse than that of an average person. If the actual facts of an individual's condition are exceptional, however, the IRS would find departure from the tables to be appropriate. The ruling concludes that the tables should be applied if valuation of a life interest is required for estate or gift tax purposes unless, at the time of the transfer, the individual is known to have been afflicted with an incurable physical condition that is in such an advanced stage that death is clearly imminent. The court emphasized the ruling's explanation that "death is not clearly imminent if the individual may survive for a year or more and if such a possibility is not so remote as to be negligible." The IRS argued that the court was not bound to follow Revenue Ruling 80-80, and alternatively that the ruling did not mandate use of the tables as argued by the estate because there was sufficient evidence of decedent's actual life expectancy. The appellate court held that the ruling's clear standard was met by the estate: "Whatever 'negligible' might mean in a closer case, we are certain that it does not refer to a one-in-ten chance." It characterized the IRS's argument under the ruling as "meritless" and rejected the Tax Court's alternative holding that it would have reached the same result in this case if it had applied Revenue Ruling 80-80. The ultimate issue, therefore, became the correctness of the Tax Court's choice not to apply Revenue Ruling 80-80. The appellate court recognized that the Tax Court "has long been fighting a losing battle with the various courts of appeals over the proper deference to which revenue rulings are due." Virtually every circuit recognizes some form of deference, but "the Tax Court stands firm in its own position that revenue rulings are nothing more than the legal contentions of a frequent litigant, undeserving of any more or less consideration than the conclusory statements in a party's brief." The Fifth Circuit noted that the Tax Court's position was not without some merit. Furthermore, the Fifth Circuit acknowledged that revenue rulings are "odd creatures" clearly less binding on the courts than the statute or regulations, "but probably (and in this circuit certainly) more so than the mere legal conclusions of the parties." This case, however, did not require a direct resolution of the deference issue. The usual position of the adversaries with respect to a revenue ruling was reversed: Here, the IRS that argued (somewhat vaguely, as the court commented in a footnote) that the ruling did not apply. A well-established rule in the Fifth Circuit provides that IRS will be held to its published rulings where the law is unclear, and may not depart from them in individual cases. According to the appeals court, decedent went to great lengths to structure the transaction so as to comply with the law, and relied on Revenue Ruling 80-80. Where the IRS has specifically approved a valuation methodology, like the actuarial tables, in a published ruling, it "will not be heard to fault a taxpayer for taking advantage of the tax minimization opportunities inherent therein."

[Estate of McLendon, 135 F3d 1017, 81 AFTR2d 98-963 (5th Cir. 1998).]

IRS can revalue gifts for estate tax purposes. Decedent died in 1986. In 1977, 1978, 1981, 1982, 1985, and 1986, decedent made various gifts of land and minerals to members of her family. Gift tax returns were timely filed for the gifts made in 1977, 1978, 1981, and 1982. None of the returns were examined or audited, though the IRS did correct a mathematical error on the 1981 return. In 1977, the gift amount was less than the annual exclusion, therefore, no gift tax was due. In 1978, 1981, and 1982, the gift tax owed was offset by the unified credit. When decedent's estate filed the estate tax return, it valued the prior taxable gifts at $196,000. The IRS adjusted the value of the gifts to $1,068,600, an increase of $872,600. The estate paid the additional tax generated and filed for a refund, which led to this case in district court. The estate argued that the statute of limitations applicable to the gift tax computation barred the IRS from revaluing the taxable gifts for estate tax purposes. The IRS claimed that the statute of limitations applied only to gift tax calculations.

Held: For the IRS. Estate tax is computed under Section 2001(b) by adding the value of adjusted taxable gifts made by decedent to the value of decedent's taxable estate, and subtracting the gift tax that would have been payable under Chapter 12 (the gift tax provisions in the Code). According to Section 2001(b), the term "adjusted taxable gifts" refers to the total amount of taxable gifts within the meaning of Section 2503. Section 2504(c) provides a limitations period of three years during which a gift can be revalued for gift tax purposes. The court examined the language of all of the statutes and determined that Section 2504(c) did not apply to the estate tax calculation. In analyzing Section 2504, it noted that the language of the statute defined its application "for the purpose of computing the tax under this chapter [Chapter 12]," which means that it does not necessarily apply to another chapter. The court then discussed the estate tax statutes, pointing out that in Section 2001(c), Congress could have defined "adjusted taxable gifts" by referring to "Chapter 12," which would have included all of the gift tax statutes. Instead, Congress referred solely to Section 2503, which makes no reference to Section 2504 or to the gift tax statute of limitations. The court also noted that the credit given in the estate tax computation is for gift taxes that *would have been* payable under Chapter 12. If there were a prohibition on revaluing gifts for estate tax purposes, Congress could simply have given a credit for taxes that *had been* paid. The phrase "taxes that would have been payable" suggests that gifts can be revalued for estate tax purposes, but the estate receives credit for taxes it would have paid, therefore, the IRS cannot indirectly recoup the lost gift tax by increasing estate tax. The court stated that it was aware of the decision in Boatmen's, 705 F. Supp. 1407, 89-1 USTC ¶ 13,795, 63 AFTR2d 89-1510 (WD Mo. 1988), but felt compelled to follow the ruling in Smith, 94 TC 872 (1990).

[Stalcup, 792 F. Supp. 714, 91-2 USTC ¶ 60,086, 68 AFTR2d 91-6057 (WD Okla. 1991).]

Claims Court resolves valuation question regarding untransferred remainder interests. In 1970, taxpayer created a trust containing his remainder interest in a certain trust that had been formed by his mother in 1927. The IRS assessed a gift tax on the ground that taxpayer's execution of the trust document constituted a taxable gift under Section 2501(a)(1). The Claims Court, after trial, determined that taxpayer's execution of the trust agreement in 1970 expressed his assent to the terms of the agreement and his intention to be bound thereby. In its 1984 opinion, reported at 4 Cl. Ct. 705, 53 AFTR2d 84-1624, 84-1 USTC ¶ 13,565, the Claims Court specifically left the issue of valuation open for further proceedings, because there were portions of the trust property that were not transferred in the gift conveyance. In subsequent proceedings, the IRS and taxpayer disputed the proper method of computing the value of the remainder interest. The IRS established the value by ascertaining the value of taxpayer's remainder and subtracting therefrom his gift tax liability and the present value of the interest he retained when he established the 1970 trust. Taxpayer, however, maintained that because the interests transferred in 1970 were not capable of valuation based upon the facts known at the time, the valuation should be based on subsequent events that would result in the tax being imposed on the property actually transferred, rather than on property and interests that were never transferred.

Held: For the IRS. The IRS properly determined the gift tax value of the 1970 conveyance, and the Claims Court adopted its figures as part of the final entry of judgment. The court noted that the IRS applied the method of valuation set forth in Regulation § 25.2511-1(e), which states that if the donor's retained interest is not susceptible to measurement on the basis of generally accepted valuation principles, the gift tax is applicable to the entire value of the property subject to the gift.

[Carpenter, 7 Cl. Ct. 732, 55 AFTR2d 85-1585, 85-1 USTC ¶ 13,612 (1985), aff'd without published op., 790 F2d 91 (Fed. Cir. 1986).]

Gift value of interest-free loans for federal gift tax purposes can exceed state usury law limits. From 1981 through 1984, taxpayer made interest-free demand loans to her two children. On her gift tax returns for those years, taxpayer valued the gift element of the loans at the amount of interest that could legally be charged under state law. On audit, the IRS assessed a deficiency in taxpayer's gift tax liability for those years on the ground that for purposes of valuation of the gift element of the loans, Revenue Procedure 85-46, 1985-2 CB 507, mandates interest rates based upon the lesser of (1) the statutory rate for refunds and deficiencies and (2) the annual average rate for thirteen-week Treasury bills (both of which were higher than the state usury law limit that taxpayer used).

Held: For the IRS. The Tax Court stated that Section 2501(a)(1) imposes the gift tax "on the transfer of property by gift." The value of a gift is defined as the price at which such property would change hands between a willing buyer and a willing seller, neither being under any compulsion to buy or to sell, and both having reasonable knowledge of the facts. According to the court, in the case of an interest-free demand loan, the right to use the money is considered "property" that comes within the scope of the gift tax statute. The gift tax is imposed on the reasonable value of the use of the money lent. Therefore, the court concluded that the proper valuation of the gift element of an interest-free demand loan does not depend on how much interest the lender can legally extract from a particular borrower but is based on the reasonable value of the use of the borrowed funds. Concluding that Revenue Procedure 85-46 is a fair and reasonable method for determining the reasonable value of gifts resulting from interest-free demand loans, the court upheld the IRS's deficiency against taxpayer.

[Estate of Arbury, 93 TC 136 (1989).]

Tax Court upholds IRS's interest rates in valuing gift loans. Taxpayer made interest-free demand loans of approximately $70 million to three irrevocable trusts for various family members. Taxpayer valued the gift loans, which were repaid by 1984, by using the rates specified in Regulation §§ 25.2512-5(e) and 25.2512-9(e). In a notice of deficiency, the IRS determined that the value of each taxable gift should have been determined using the interest rates in Revenue Procedure 85-46, 1985-2 CB 507. Pursuant to the procedure, the interest rate for valuation was the lesser of (1) the statutory interest rate for refunds and deficiencies in Section 6621 or (2) the annual average rate for three-month Treasury bills.

Held: For the IRS. The court stated that the IRS's use of the lesser of the statutory interest rate for refunds and deficiencies or the annual average rate for three-month Treasury bills, pursuant to Revenue Procedure 85-46, was proper for valuing gifts that arose from interest-free demand loans. In so holding, the court explicitly affirmed the IRS's unilateral action when it issued Revenue Procedure 85-46.

[Cohen, 92 TC 1039 (1989), aff'd, 910 F2d 422, 66 AFTR2d 90-6004, 90-2 USTC ¶ 60,034 (7th Cir. 1990).]

IRS explains how to request Statement of Value to substantiate value of art. The IRS issued a revenue procedure informing taxpayers how to request from the IRS a Statement of Value that can be used to substantiate the value of art for income, estate, or gift tax purposes. A taxpayer who complies with the procedure may rely on the Statement of Value in completing the tax return that reports the transfer of art. The procedure generally applies to an item of art that has been appraised at $50,000 or more and has been transferred (1) as a charitable contribution, (2) by death, or (3) by lifetime gift.

A taxpayer must submit to the IRS a request for a Statement of Value for an item of art before filing the estate or gift tax return that first reports the transfer of the item. The procedure sets forth the information (including an appraisal) that must be included in the request. A copy of the Statement of Value, regardless of whether taxpayer agrees with it, must be attached to, and filed with, taxpayer's return. The procedure applies to requests for Statements of Value submitted after January 15, 1996.

[Rev. Proc. 96-15, 1996-1 CB 627.]

IRS rules on gift tax valuation of assigned group term insurance policy. *X* formed an agreement with an insurance company providing for a master group term insurance policy on the lives of *X* employees. The employees did not hold a contractual right to require *X* to maintain the group term contract. The premiums on the group term policy were payable annually by *X* in advance on March 1. The employees were not required to contribute toward the payment of the premium. There were no permanent insurance benefits as defined in Regulation § 1.79-0 provided under the group term policy. *D*, an employee of *X*, assigned all right, title, and interest in the group term life insurance policy on *D*'s life to an irrevocable trust for the benefit of *D*'s children. *D* was fifty-four years old on March 1, 1984, when *X* paid an annual premium on the group term policy. The amount of insurance coverage under the group term policy on *D*'s life at that time was $80,000. The IRS was asked to ascertain the value of the policy for purposes of Section 2512.

The IRS noted that the actual cost of life insurance coverage purchased by an employer for an employee can be determined by analyzing the insurance contract. Where more than one employee is covered by the same contract, the total premium cost should be actuarially apportioned among the covered employees. In some instances, particularly where large numbers of employees are concerned, the actual cost allocations may involve complex computations and may be difficult for an individual employee to obtain.

On the basis of Revenue Ruling 76-490, 1976-2 CB 300, the IRS concluded that because *D* previously made an irrevocable assignment of all right, title, and interest in the group term policy, *D* made a gift on March 1, 1984, when *X* paid the annual premium on the group policy. Thus, the IRS stated that if *X*'s plan of group term life insurance meets the nondiscrimination requirements of Section 79(d), or if *D* is not a key employee within the meaning of Section 79(d)(6), an acceptable method of determining the value of the gift under Section 2512 is based upon Table I in Regulation § 1.79-3(d)(2).

[Rev. Rul. 84-147, 1984-2 CB 201.]

Taxable gift reduced by gift tax recipients paid. The IRS ruled that, in reporting the transfer of her income interest in qualified terminable interest property (QTIP) property, the donor/surviving spouse properly reduced the remainder's amount by the gift tax paid by the donees. Decedent was a U.S. citizen who died in 1986. Under his will, his surviving spouse was granted a qualifying income interest for life in a trust for which a QTIP election was made. When the spouse disclaimed her interest in 1994, the corpus passed to the remainder beneficiaries, who agreed to pay all the resulting transfer taxes. The spouse reported the transfer of the qualifying income interest as a taxable gift under Section 2511, and the transfer of the remainder interest (the corpus minus the qualifying income interest's value) as a taxable gift under Section 2519. Taxpayer treated the remainder transfer as a net gift—reducing the actuarial value of the remainder by the attributable gift tax. Under Section 2511, the gift tax is imposed on a direct or indirect transfer, whether the transferred property is real or personal, tangible or intangible, and whether the transfer is in trust or otherwise. Section 2512(b) provides that when property is transferred for less than full consideration, the amount of the property's value that exceeds the consideration's value is a gift. Under Section 2519, any disposition of a qualifying income interest for life in QTIP property is treated as a transfer of all the property interest other than the qualifying income interest. Further, the value of a Section 2519 transfer is the fair market value (FMV) of the entire property less the qualifying income interest's value. The gift tax rules provide that the gift tax is the donor's personal liability. Section 2207A(b), however, shifts the burden, but not the liability, for paying the gift tax on a Section 2519 transfer to the donee. In such a situation, the donee provides the donor consideration for the gift by paying the gift tax (i.e., the donee's payment reimburses the donor for a tax that the donor would otherwise be liable to pay out of his or her own funds). The IRS stated that this statutory scheme implies net gift treatment for a Section 2519 transfer. In Revenue Ruling 75-72, 1975-1 CB 310, the IRS ruled that, in determining a gift's value, the gift tax paid by a donee could be deducted from the transferred property's value if such payment was a condition of the transfer. Thus, the gift's value was the transferred property's FMV less the gift tax the donee paid. As in that ruling, the transfer terms in the instant case required the donees to pay the gift tax. Based on the statutory scheme and in accord with the IRS's prior ruling, therefore, the surviving spouse's Section 2519 transfer was a net gift to the extent that the donees paid the gift tax. Thus, the gift's value was properly reduced by the gift tax the donees paid.

[Tech. Adv. Mem. 9736001.]

IRS values transfer of property for gift tax purposes. The life income beneficiary of a trust had a five-or-five appointment power over the corpus. In addition, the beneficiary had the power to appoint corpus to any person, except the beneficiary, the beneficiary's estate, or the creditors of the beneficiary's estate. On July 1, 1987, the beneficiary directed $657,500 of the assets to a second trust. Immediately before the transfer, the value of the corpus was $1,112,415. The IRS concluded that the beneficiary made a taxable transfer equal to the difference between the value of the income interest plus the general power to invade corpus before the exercise of the nongeneral power and the value of the income interest plus the general power to invade corpus after the exercise of the nongeneral power. The IRS determined that the present worth of the right to receive all of the income each year, plus the greater of $5,000 or 5 percent of the declining principal payable until the death of a person seventy-two years old, was $771,456. The IRS determined the value after the transfer to be $315,482. Accordingly, the IRS valued the amount of the gift as $455,873.

[Priv. Ltr. Rul. 8825080.]

¶ 15.02 STOCK, SECURITIES, AND REAL ESTATE

Stock gift reduced for built-in capital gains. Taxpayer held all stock in a C corporation that owned and leased space in a commercial building. From 1991 to 1993, she made gifts of the corporation's stock to her son and two grandchildren. When she valued the stock for gift tax purposes, taxpayer lessened its value by the amount the capital gains tax would have been had the corporation liquidated, or sold or distributed the property, at the times of the gifts. The IRS sent her a deficiency notice, claiming she was not allowed to lessen the stocks' value by the amount the capital gains tax would have been. The tax, the IRS stated, was too speculative. Taxpayer contended she lowered the stock's value because any prospective buyer would have insisted on paying market value minus capital gains tax. The IRS argued that a hypothetical buyer would have been able to avoid the capital gains tax altogether by purchasing and continuing to lease the real estate as a corporation. Further, the amount of the capital gains tax or the property's value in the future was impossible to predict.

    Held: For taxpayer. The FMV of property given as a gift is based on a hypothetical transaction between buyer and seller—the buyer seeking to maximize profit. Common business practice, thus, dictates that a hypothetical buyer would take capital gains taxes into consideration. Therefore, taxpayer was allowed to lower the value of her stock by capital gains tax for gift tax purposes. This holding comports with that of *Estate of Davis*, 110 TC 530 (1998), in which the Tax Court held that the built-in capital gains tax on a corporation's stock should be taken into consideration when determining the FMV of the stock. Traditionally, reductions in the value of closely held stock by potential capital gains tax liabilities at the corporate level were not allowed unless evidence existed that a liquidation or a sale of assets was likely. The court in the instant case attributed this to the former ability of corporations to avoid recognition of gain by distributing appreciated property to shareholders prior to liquidation. Ever since the Tax Reform Act of 1986 (TRA '86) repealed the *General Utilities* doctrine, however, the capital gains tax cannot be avoided when a corporation liquidates. Thus, the payment of capital gains tax is no longer speculative, and the court rejected the IRS's references to pre-TRA '86 court decisions. The payment of capital gains tax in the instant case was, therefore, assured on the sale of the property or liquidation of the corporation.

Thus, taxpayer was allowed to use the lesser value for gift tax purposes. This holding was reached based on the facts that capital gains tax was certain, and a buyer would be reasonably expected to take the tax into consideration.

[Eisenberg, 155 F3d 50, 82 AFTR2d 98-5757, 98-2 USTC ¶ 60,322 (2d Cir. 1998).]

Valuation tables did not reflect value of retained income interest. In 1985, taxpayer and his wife each transferred twenty shares of stock to five grantor retained income trusts (GRITs). Under the terms of the trusts, taxpayers retained income interests in the stock for the life of the trusts (two to four years). Upon the trusts' termination, the stock would pass to their children. At the time of the transfer, the stock was worth $9,639 per share. Taxpayers' basis in the stock was $115 per share. The dividend distribution in the previous three years had been $13 per share, which was a yield of 0.2 percent. The trustee was authorized to hold the stock and not worry about diversifying, so as to avoid capital gains taxes. Though the stock historically had a low dividend rate, for purposes of the gift tax return taxpayers valued their short-term retained income interests at 25 percent to 30 percent of the total value of the stock by using the gift tax actuarial table, Table B, found in Regulation § 20.2512-5(f). This table assumed a 10 percent return for income interests. (Currently, interests are valued under Section 7520.) The IRS disagreed with this valuation and assessed deficiencies for 1985 and 1986 based on the full value of the stock, which was $9,639 per share. The IRS had argued that the entire value of the stock should be treated as a gift because, as stated in Regulation § 25.2511-1(e), "the donor's retained interest is not susceptible of measurement on the basis of generally accepted valuation principles." Taxpayers contended that Regulation § 25.2512-5 required that a retained income interest be valued using Table B. The IRS asserted that a valuation under Table B produced a "patently unreasonable result." Therefore, argued the IRS, valuation should be determined under Regulation § 25.2511-1(e). Taxpayers challenged the IRS's position, and the Tax Court ruled in their favor.

　　Held: For the IRS (in part). The Eighth Court agreed with the Tax Court that the interests retained by taxpayers were "susceptible of measurement" within the meaning of Regulation § 25.2511-1(e). The stock had a stated per share FMV, and it had paid a small, but consistent, dividend in prior years. Therefore, a valuation expert should have been able to place a value on the retained income interests using generally accepted valuation principles. The problem was not that the interests could not be valued, but that their valuation under Table A was a "wildly unrealistic measurement." The circuit court also agreed with the Tax Court that Regulation § 25.2511-1(e) applies only if the property interests are subject to contingencies that are indeterminable and that make it more likely than not that the interests will have no value. The stock did produce some income, so the retained interests were not worthless. They should not be valued at zero as suggested by the IRS, ruled the Eighth Circuit. The appellate court decided that the retained interests should also not be valued under actuarial Table B. The court referred to the dominant regulation, Regulation § 25.2512-1, which states that value "is the price at which such property would change hands between a willing buyer and a willing seller." After stating this governing principle, Regulation § 25.2512-1 refers taxpayer to Regulation § 25.2512-5 "for further information concerning the valuation of other particular kinds of property." According to the court, this language did not suggest that the latter regulation should override the dominant principle. The Eighth Circuit based its decision in part on the fact that historically courts have not universally applied the actuarial tables if the tables would produce a skewed result. The appellate court cited the Tax Court opinion in Weller, 38 TC 790 (1962), which stated that the use of the tables "must be sustained unless it is shown that the result is so unrealistic and unreasonable that either some modification in the prescribed method should be made, or complete departure from the method should be taken, and a more reasonable and realistic means of determining value is available." Since the circuit court did not approve of the value proposed by either of the parties, it remanded the case to the Tax Court for a more realistic determination of the value of the retained interests and the gift interests.

[O'Reilly, 973 F2d 1403, 70 AFTR2d 92-6211, 92-2 USTC ¶ 60,111 (8th Cir. 1992).]

Safe harbor interest rates do not apply to below-market sale for gift tax purposes. Taxpayers transferred land to their sons under a contract that provided for annual installment payments and 6 percent interest. The IRS used an 11 percent interest rate to determine the present value of the contract and assessed gift tax based on the difference between the present value and fair market value. Taxpayers argued that the Section 483 safe harbor interest rates applied. The Tax Court agreed with the IRS position.

Held: Affirmed for the IRS. The safe-harbor interest rates do not limit the rate allowed in valuing an installment sales contract for gift tax purposes.

[Krabbenhoft, 939 F2d 529, 91-2 USTC ¶ 60,080, 68 AFTR2d 91-6021 (8th Cir. 1991).]

Donor's transfer of real estate to her children under real estate installment sale contract bearing interest at 6 percent is not partial gift, even though market interest rates are much higher. Donor entered into a contract with her three children for the conditional sale of her farm. Under the terms of the contract, each child received a one-third share of the farm, which at that time had a FMV of $582,000. In return, the children agreed to pay 6 percent interest on an agreed-upon sale price of $386,000. Donor filed a gift tax return and reported a gift of $184,000, which equaled the difference between the FMV of the farm and the contract sales price. Because the taxes owed on the $184,000 gift did not exceed the unified credit, donor reported that no taxes were due. The IRS determined that the discounted value of the consideration that donor was to receive under the contract was only $134,298.20, because the market rate of interest at the time of the gift was 18 percent, not the 6 percent provided for in the contract with her children. Based on the revised value of the gift, the IRS assessed the donor taxes, that no longer were exceeded by the unified credit. Donor appealed this assessment, arguing that Section 483 provided a safe harbor and permitted her to charge a 6 percent rate of interest on the land sale, without either income or gift tax consequences. The IRS responded that the 6 percent safe harbor interest rate contained in Section 483 applied only to income taxes and did not have anything to do with the valuation of the gift made to the donor's children. The Tax Court affirmed the IRS's imposition of gift taxes, and donor then appealed the decision to the Seventh Circuit.

Held: For donor. The court stated that although the valuation of property for gift tax purposes was not directly related to the imputation of taxes on installment contracts, a taxpayer who complied with Section 483 and charged a safe harbor rate of interest should not be penalized, even though the safe harbor rate was considerably lower than the market rate of interest. The safe harbor rate of interest provided for in Section 483 was held by the court to apply, by the clear terms of the statute's language, to all provisions of the Code. A review of the legislative history of Section 483 was found to be unnecessary because a statute's legislative history is used to interpret a statute only if its wording is ambiguous or completely at variance with the statute's purpose. By charging her children 6 percent interest in the land sale contract, the donor was found to have followed the Code; therefore, she had properly insulated herself from any adverse income tax consequences.

[Ballard, 854 F2d 185, 88-2 USTC ¶ 13,779, 62 AFTR2d 88-5988 (7th Cir. 1988).]

IRS cannot revalue gift of stock for estate tax purposes more than three years after the gift was made and gift taxes were paid. Decedent's wife gave her children stock. Tax returns showing the stock's value were timely filed, and the gift tax was paid. Decedent had consented to have the gifts considered as made by him, so that half their value was reported on his estate tax return, filed more than three years later. The IRS tried to increase the value of the gifts, claiming that they were originally undervalued. The IRS conceded that Section 2504(c) prevented it from revaluing the stock for gift tax purposes after the gift tax had been paid and the statute of limitations had run. It argued that it could nevertheless revalue the gifts to determine the amount of taxable gifts for estate tax purposes.

Held: For the estate. The court concluded that the unified system of estate and gift taxation compels the application of Section 2504(c), that deals with gift taxes, to estate tax calculations. Under the unified system, decedent's estate is taxed at the rate that it would have paid if the gifts had remained in the estate. Once the rate is established, the gift's value is removed from the estate. The taxable estate value, excluding the gift value, is then taxed at the rate that was calculated including the gift. Adding the previously taxed gifts and then removing the tax paid boosts the tax rate applied to the remaining estate. Thus, the estate argued, if the IRS increases the gift's value, it would tax the estate on the amount by which the gift allegedly was undervalued. The federal district court agreed. Taxpayers would face undue burdens if there were an indefinite limitations period. They would be forced to retain records relating to a gift made many years before death and would have difficulty planning if the value and tax effect of gifts could not be fixed until after death.

[Boatmen's First Nat'l Bank, 705 F. Supp. 1407, 89-1 USTC ¶ 13,795, 63 AFTR2d 89-1510 (WD Mo. 1989).]

Taxpayers fail to prove that value of stock reported on gift tax return is excessive. Taxpayers were stockholders in a family-owned business known as the Blue Bird Body Company, that manufactured school buses and mobile homes. During 1976, taxpayers each made gifts of a portion of their respective shareholder interests to members of their family in sixteen separate transactions affecting 97,000 shares, or 17 percent of the total outstanding stock. Each donor filed a gift tax return that reported the shares as having a value of $39 each, based on the year-end book value for 1976. Subsequently, taxpayers filed suit for a refund of gift taxes, claiming that the shares had an FMV of only $16. In support of their revaluation, taxpayers presented extensive evidence that tended to show that the bus market was seriously depressed during the relevant taxable year, and that the company's earnings, projected sales, and profits were at sufficiently low levels to justify the $16 per share figure.

Held: For the IRS. The court examined the evidence and determined that taxpayers had not carried their burden of proving with sufficient certainty that the original value was excessive. In placing a value on corporate stock that is not traded on the open market, it is necessary to produce evidence of the company's net worth, its prospective earning power, its dividend-paying capacity, and prospective earning power, as well as the value of goodwill. In addition, there must be an analysis of the economic outlook in the industry, the company's position in the industry, and the relative strength of its management in relation to competitors. Because taxpayers failed to present a thorough analysis by using each of the relevant factors, the court concluded that they had not carried their burden and therefore were not entitled to the claimed refund.

[Luce, 4 Cl. Ct. 212, 53 AFTR2d 84-1565, 84-1 USTC ¶ 13,549 (1983).]

Built-in gains tax results in valuation discount. This case involved gifts of stock in a closely held company whose main asset was common stock. In valuing the stock for gift tax purposes, taxpayer applied a discount factor for the built-in gains tax that would be due if the corporation were liquidated or the shares were sold. The facts in this case did not indicate that any of the parties involved in the gifts intended to liquidate the corporation or sell the shares. The IRS argued that no discount should be applied because the shareholders could avoid the built-in gains tax by electing S corporation status and then holding the assets for ten years, as provided in Section 1374(d)(7).

Held: For taxpayer. The court held that a discount was appropriate. Valuation is based on the price that a hypothetical willing buyer would pay a willing seller. Such a buyer would pay less for stock in a company whose assets were subject to the potential built-in capital gains tax than it would if there were no such tax. In addition, the restrictions on S corporation shareholder eligibility, said the court, would impermissibly limit the pool of hypothetical willing buyers if the S election route were taken. Further, the assumption that the stock would not be sold within ten years would have reduced the marketability of the closely held company shares. As for the size of the discount, the court held that the full $25.66 million of built-in capital gains tax should not be taken as the discount. Rather, the court selected $9 million as an amount that fell within the range of discounts determined by expert witnesses.

[Estate of Davis, 110 TC 530 (1998).]

Discount factor does not apply to value of interest in trust with wasting assets. Taxpayer deeded his mineral interests to a trust for a term of years for the benefit of his children and grandchildren. The net income less a 15 percent depletion reserve was distributed to the beneficiaries. Taxpayer argued that for gift tax purposes, the value of the interests should also be reduced by a discount factor determined under Table B of Regulation § 25.2512-5(f).

Held: For the IRS. Use of the discount factor was unrealistic because the subject matter of the trusts was property containing gas reserves and a lease of the gas, that is, wasting assets that would have been exhausted by the time the term of years expired.

[Froh, 100 TC 1 (1993), aff'd, 46 F3d 1141, 95-1 USTC ¶ 60,189, 75 AFTR2d 95-808 (9th Cir. 1995).]

Tax Court examines valuation of close corporation stock that is not publicly traded. Four shareholders owned all of the stock of a nonpublicly traded corporation. They reorganized the capital structure of the corporation as part of their estate planning. Following the reorganization, each of the four shareholders held equal amounts of voting common stock, nonvoting common stock, and nonvoting preferred stock. Each transferred his voting common stock to a separate trust, and three of the four transferred their nonvoting common to separate trusts. On their gift tax returns and on the estate tax return of one of the shareholders, the voting common was valued at $6.30 per share and the non-voting common was valued at $0.63 per share. The IRS rejected these values. At trial, experts for both taxpayer and the IRS based their stock valuations in part on those of similarly situated (nature of business or earnings-financial structure) companies that were publicly traded (i.e., a market-comparable approach). In addition, taxpayer's expert made a discount cash flow analysis of the stock values, whereas the IRS's expert made an analysis of the book values of assets held by the corporation and its subsidiaries.

Held: Both of the experts improperly resorted to the market-comparable approach, because the publicly traded corporations that were used for reference were not in the same line of business as the corporation. Instead, the discounted cash flow approach was in this instance a more reliable measure of value. Although discounts for both minority interest and lack of marketability were granted at 25 percent and 20 percent, respectively, the court noted that the higher discounts claimed by the taxpayer improperly took into account the fact that the gift transfers resulted in 75 percent of the corporation's stock being held in trust. The nature and circumstances of other donees in contemporaneous transfers do not affect the value of a gift as transferred at the donor's side of the gift.

[Northern Trust Co., 87 TC 349 (1986).]

Inflation in value at monthly rate of 30 to 40 percent is taken into account by Tax Court in gift valuation case. In 1967, decedent, who was then eighty years old, owned property located near an airport in Kansas City, Missouri. The area had recently attracted interest on the part of real estate developers who were anticipating rapid commercial development. Decedent spurned the advances of an interested developer and decided instead to leave the property by will to her relatives and to the long-term tenant farmers who inhabited the place. After obtaining advice from her lawyer, she formed a corporation, transferred the property to it, and caused it to issue stock to her intended beneficiaries. She took back a promissory note from the corporation in the principal amount of $480,000. During the following year, the shareholders sold their stock for an aggregate selling price of $2.5 million. Following decedent's death, the IRS asserted gift tax liability, arguing that the property was transferred for less than adequate and full consideration.

Held: For the IRS. The Tax Court found that the FMV of the property was $726,122 on the date of transfer and that a taxable gift was made to the extent that this figure exceeded the face amount of the note. Based on expert testimony and a fully developed record, the court determined that prices rose at a rate of 20 to 30 percent each month between the date of transfer and the sale of stock.

[Ketteman Trust, 86 TC 91 (1986).]

Value of gift subject to mortgage is determined. Taxpayer owned property mortgaged to her father, who died before the mortgage note became due. He bequeathed the note to her and appointed her executrix. Taxpayer then made a gift of the mortgaged property and subsequently transferred the note to herself as legatee. The IRS argued that in computing the property's value for gift tax purposes, its FMV should not be decreased by the amount of mortgage liability, because taxpayer held the mortgage note prior to making the gift, and the liability was therefore extinguished.

Held: For the taxpayer. Taxpayer held the note, prior to the gift, as executrix, not as legatee. The fact that she may have been able to distribute the note to herself before making the gift and thereby cancel the mortgage was irrelevant.

[Laughinghouse, 80 TC 425 (1983).]

Value of unregistered stock is determined. A donor made a gift of the unregistered stock in two investment companies, each funded with the unregistered stock of a publicly owned corporation, cash and real property. The IRS challenged the valuation of the gift.

Held: For taxpayer (in part). Because taxpayer was a "control" person under Securities and Exchange Commission regulations, he could not sell the shares before they were registered, but he could have had the shares registered. Thus, the value of the stock was that of the publicly traded shares on the date in issue, less a discount.

[Estate of Piper, 72 TC 1062 (1979).]

Transaction's form controlled valuation of gifts to children. This case stemmed from a dispute with respect to the value of interests in real property that taxpayer, a builder, developer, and manager of rental real estate in New York City, attempted to give to his children. On December 30, 1976, for the purpose of making gifts, he conveyed interests in twenty-two buildings, consisting of twenty apartment buildings and two office buildings located in the boroughs of Queens and Brooklyn, to his children individually or to trusts created for their benefit. Prior to the conveyances, twenty of the buildings were held by taxpayer individually and operated as sole proprietorships, and two were held by partnerships in which the taxpayer held a 96 percent interest and his children, or trusts for their benefit, held the remaining 4 percent. Also on December 30, 1976, taxpayer formed twenty partnerships with his children or their trustees. Each of the partnerships was to own and operate one of the twenty buildings that were formerly held by taxpayer individually as sole proprietorships. Each of the buildings was conveyed to taxpayer and the donees as tenants in common, doing business as the particular partnership formed to hold the respective building conveyed. The deeds were recorded on December 30, 1976. A business certificate for partners for each partnership was filed with the county clerk of Queens County on that date as well. Taxpayer conveyed to each donee a 7.5 percent interest in each of the buildings subject to the outstanding mortgages. All the buildings were encumbered with mortgages, and the residential real property was subject to New York City rent control laws. A substantial dispute arose between the IRS and taxpayer regarding the value of the interests transferred. Taxpayer contended that the interests transferred were interests in partnerships, while the IRS argued that taxpayer had transferred interests in real property. Each side produced valuation experts who gave widely different views of the value of the properties transferred. Of particular note and concern is the fact that taxpayer's valuation experts, operating under the assumption that interests in partnerships were transferred, discounted the value of the partnership interests for both minority interest and lack of marketability. The IRS's experts valued the interests as interests in real property, claiming a far lesser discount.

Held: For the IRS. The Tax Court first determined that the interests transferred were interests in real property rather than partnership interests. In reaching this conclusion, the court relied heavily on the form of the transaction, noting that the real property was deeded to taxpayer and his children as tenants in common—thus, creating the gift. The court also reasoned quite correctly that taxpayer could not have created a one-person partnership by himself in which he subsequently transferred interests to his children. Consequently, the conclusion was reached that taxpayer conveyed interests in the buildings to his children which were subsequently conveyed to the partnerships and operated under the partnership agreement. The significance of this holding is that it allowed the court largely to refute the testimony of taxpayer's valuation expert who calculated discounts based upon the conclusion that interests in partnerships were transferred. The court stated that inasmuch as it had held that the gifts consisted of interests in real property, and not partnership interests, taxpayer's expert's report contained fundamental flaws and did not aid in ascertaining the appropriate minority discount. Taxpayer's expert did not rely on the amount of discount applicable to fractional interests in real property of the type transferred in the instant case in arriving at his figure. The court determined that the expert had not demonstrated that the partnership interests were comparable to interests in real property, and it rejected his testimony and accepted the testimony of the government expert who arrived at a substantially lower discount.

The government in the instant case also presented the argument—which was rejected by the Tax Court—that it was inappropriate to allow a minority discount in valuing gifts of an entity controlled by family members. The court rejected this argument based on the holdings of Estate of Bright, 658 F2d 999 (5th Cir. 1981), and Estate of Lee, 69 TC 860 (1978).

[LeFrak, 66 TCM 1297, RIA TC Memo. ¶ 93,526 (1993).]

Guidance on valuing compensatory stock options for transfer tax purposes. This revenue procedure offers taxpayers welcome guidance on valuing certain compensatory stock options to purchase publicly traded stock. It sets out an option pricing method that takes into account factors similar to those established by the FASB in SFAS No. 123 (Accounting for Stock-Based Compensation). If the procedure's requirements are followed, the IRS will treat the value of covered options as properly determined for gift, estate, and generation-skipping transfer tax purposes. The procedure is applicable only to the valuation of nonpublicly traded compensatory stock options (i.e., options granted in connection with the performance of services, including options subject to Section 421) on stock that is publicly traded on an established securities market on the valuation date. Taxpayers may make such a valuation using a generally recognized option pricing model (such as the Black-Scholes model or an accepted version of the binomial model) that takes into account certain specified factors on the valuation date, provided the factors are reasonable, the model is properly applied, the option grantor is subject to SFAS No. 123 for the fiscal year encompassing the valuation date, the underlying stock is common stock, and no discount can be applied to the valuation produced by the pricing model. The specified factors that must be taken into account are:

1. The option's exercise price and expected life.
2. The underlying stock's current trading price, expected volatility, and expected dividends.
3. The risk-free interest rate over the remaining option term.

The procedure generally requires taxpayers to use *either* the maximum remaining term of the option on the valuation date, or the procedure's specific "Computed Expected Life" calculation (in Section 4.03), to determine the option's expected life. If, however, any one of the following conditions is present on the valuation date, the maximum remaining term must be used:

1. The option transferor is not the person to whom the company granted the option.
2. Excepting transfers at death, the transferor is not an employee or director of the company on the valuation date.
3. Excepting instances involving the transferor's death or disability, the option does not terminate within six months of the transferor's termination of employment (or service as a director).
4. The option by its terms is transferable to, or for the benefit of, persons who are not the natural objects of the transferor's bounty or charitable organization.
5. Excepting instances involving the transferor's death, the option's exercise price is not "fixed" on the valuation date.
6. Excepting instances involving the transferor's death, the option's terms and conditions are such that, if they applied to all options granted in the fiscal year encompassing the valuation date, the

weighted-average expected life for the year would have been more than 120 percent of the weighted-average expected life actually reported for the year.

7. The company is not required by SFAS No. 123 to disclose an expected life of the options granted in the fiscal year encompassing the valuation date.

The procedure also stipulates that the expected volatility and expected dividends factors must be determined using the expected volatility and expected dividends as disclosed in accord with SFAS No. 123 in the publicly traded company's financial statements for the applicable fiscal year. Further, the risk-free interest rate must be determined using the valuation date yield to maturity of zero-coupon U.S. Treasury Bonds with a remaining term nearest to the option's expected life. Finally, taxpayers must indicate their reliance on this procedure by writing "FILED PURSUANT TO REV. PROC. 98-34" on the applicable return.

[Rev. Proc. 98-34, 1998-18 IRB 15.]

Family control not aggregated for transfers of stock. When a donor transfers shares in a corporation to each of the donor's children, a factor of corporate control in the family will not be considered in valuing the transferred interests, according to this ruling. This reverses a longstanding position of the IRS and makes it less costly to make gifts of stock in closely held corporations. Taxpayer owned all of the single outstanding class of stock of a corporation. He transferred all of his shares by making simultaneous gifts of 20 percent of the shares to each of his five children. When a gift is made in property, its value at the date of the gift is the amount of the gift. The value of stocks or bonds is the FMV per share or bond on the date of the gift. Under Regulation § 25.2512-2(f), the degree of control of the business represented by the block of stock to be valued is among the factors to be considered in valuing stock when there are no sales prices or bona fide bid or asked prices.

Revenue Ruling 81-253, 1981-1 CB 187, holds that, ordinarily, no minority shareholder discount is allowed with respect to transfers of shares of stock between family members if, based upon a composite of the family members' interests at the time of the transfer, control of the corporation exists in the family unit. For this purpose, control may be either majority voting control or de facto control through majority relationships. Revenue Ruling 81-253 also states that the IRS will not follow Estate of Bright, 658 F2d 999, 48 AFTR2d 81-6292, 81-2 USTC ¶ 13,436 (5th Cir. 1981). There, decedent's undivided community property interest in shares of stock, together with the corresponding undivided community property interest of decedent's surviving spouse, constituted a control block of 55 percent of the shares of a corporation. The court held that, because the community-held shares were subject to a right of partition, decedent's own interest was equivalent to 27 percent of the outstanding shares. Therefore, it should be valued as a minority interest, even though the shares were to be held by decedent's surviving spouse as trustee of a testamentary trust.

The IRS has now concluded that, in the case of a corporation with a single class of stock, notwithstanding the family relationship of the donor, the donee, and other shareholders, the shares of other family members will not be aggregated with the transferred shares to determine whether the transferred shares should be valued as part of a controlling interest. Thus, it will follow the holding in *Estate of Bright.* Under this ruling, the minority interests transferred to the children should be valued for gift tax purposes without regard to the family relationship of the parties.

Example. Carl owns 40 percent of the single class of stock of a corporation, his wife owns an additional 30 percent, and his two brothers each own 15 percent. Carl gives a 5 percent interest in the corporation to his son. Under Revenue Ruling 81-253, the 5 percent interest would have been considered part of the majority interest and valued accordingly. Now, the instant ruling permits a minority discount to be applied to the valuation of the transferred shares.

[Rev. Rul. 93-12, 1993-1 CB 202.]

IRS rules on gift tax consequences of stock recapitalization. During his lifetime, decedent owned 100 percent of the voting shares of a corporation. He died in 1980, leaving a will that provided for the creation of two testamentary trusts. Trust *A* provided his spouse with a lifetime income interest and a general testamentary power of appointment over the corpus. Trust *A* was funded with shares of common stock worth $120x. Trust *B* provided the spouse with a life income interest and their child with the remainder interest. Trust *B* was funded with shares of common stock worth $80x. In 1982, the stock of the corporation was recapitalized. This resulted in two new classes of stock, voting common and nonvoting preferred. Preferred stock worth $50x was allocated to Trust *A*, and common stock worth $150x was allocated to Trust *B*. The trustees of Trust *A* acquiesced in the recapitalization, and the wife executed a release, valid under local law, in which she agreed not to challenge the trustee's action with respect to the recapitalization. She died in 1985, when the fair market value of the preferred stock held by Trust *A* was $55x and the fair market value of the common stock held by Trust *B* was $225x.

The IRS ruled that for purposes of the gift tax, the release by the surviving spouse had to be treated as a transfer of property to the child as the owner of the remainder interest in Trust *B*, for which the surviving spouse did not receive adequate and full consideration. The value of the gift as a result of the recapitalization of the corporation was equal to the present value of the remainder interest in $70x worth of stock that was shifted from Trust *A* to Trust *B*.

[Rev. Rul. 86-39, 1986-1 CB 301.]

Blockage discount blocked by separate valuations. The IRS concluded, in this ruling, that a transfer of stock to a trustee who was instructed to divide it into nine parts, benefiting three individuals, had to be valued as nine separate gifts. As a result, the transfer would not qualify for the same blockage discount as it would have if all the transferred stock was valued in its aggregate. The donor established three trusts with identical terms, except for the age at which the beneficiaries obtained a power of appointment. The trustee was to divide the initial corpus of each trust into three equal shares, one for each of the donor's three grandchildren. The grandchildren obtained powers of appointment over their share in the first trust at age 25, the second trust at age 30, and third trust at age 35. The donor gave the trustee shares of stock to fund the trusts. The donor filed nine separate gift tax returns and reported the FMV of the transferred stock as the mean stock exchange price on the day of transfer, reduced by a blockage discount. This discount reflected the depression in price that would be caused by selling all the shares transferred to the trustee at once. The IRS, however, said that each of the nine gifts must be valued separately; on their own, the individual gifts would qualify for a smaller, if any, blockage discount. The IRS explained that, unlike the estate tax, which is imposed on the aggregate of all of decedent's assets, the gift tax applies to property passing from the donor to each donee. Furthermore, Regulation § 25.2512-2(e) provides for a blockage discount when the size of a block of stock to be valued for "each separate gift" is so large as to depress the market price. Thus, even simultaneous gifts of similar property (as in this ruling) are evaluated separately when arriving at a valuation for gift tax purposes.

The IRS cited two cases that followed this position:

- In Rushton, 498 F2d 88, 34 AFTR2d 74-6287 (5th Cir. 1974), the donor made sixteen separate gifts of stock over four days and aggregated the gifts made on each day to determine the blockage discount. The court rejected the aggregation as violating the regulation, which it said was a legitimate exercise of the IRS's discretion. Rather, the court held that the blockage concept must be applied to each individual gift.
- In Calder, 85 TC 713 (1985), the donor created four trusts, benefiting a total of six individuals, and funded them with 1,226 paintings that the donor had inherited. While the estate had figured the blockage discount based on the aggregate number of paintings, the court held that the donor had to compute separate discounts based on the size of each of the six gifts.

The IRS concluded in the ruling that although there were only three beneficiaries, the segregation of the stock into three trusts of which they were each beneficiaries meant that there were nine gifts. Had the donor used one trust with provisions providing different powers of appointment at different ages, there would have been only three gifts. In any event, given how the trusts were structured, the blockage discount concept must be applied to the number of shares involved in each of the nine gifts.

[Tech. Adv. Mem. 9719001.]

Gift sheltered by unified credit can be revalued years later. When the unified credit completely shelters a gift from tax, this ruling explains that the usual limitations period for adjusting the gift's value does not apply. On the other hand, a limitations period on refunds can make the ability to revalue the gift irrelevant. The ruling involved a donor who made gifts of fractional interests in different parcels of real estate in 1982, 1989, and 1991. These gifts were valued without taking minority interest discounts. The values exceeded the annual gift tax exclusion, so they were taxable gifts for which gift tax returns were filed. The 1982 and 1989 gifts, however, were fully sheltered by the donor's unified credit—with no gift tax due; the 1991 gift was partially sheltered, and gift tax was paid. The donor died in 1994, and on April 13, 1995, the personal representative of the donor's estate filed a refund claim for the 1991 gifts. The refund sought was based on reducing the value of the 1991 gifts by a minority discount factor. The refund claim did not refer to the 1982 or 1989 gifts. When the representative met with someone from the IRS on October 31, 1995 to discuss the refund claim, the representative stated that discounts should also be taken to adjust the value of the earlier gifts in order to compute the gift tax on the 1991 gifts. Because of the cumulative nature of the gift and estate taxes, revaluing earlier gifts can affect the transfer tax due on later gifts or bequests. Simply stated, Section 2502(a) sets the gift tax on one transfer at the excess of the tentative tax on the sum of all taxable gifts made in that and prior years, over the tax that would be due on the sum of taxable gifts made in prior years. Thus, the lower the value of gifts made in prior years, the lower the transfer tax bracket in which the current gift will be taxed.

Under Section 2504(c), if tax was paid on a gift and the limitations period for assessing tax on that gift has expired, the value used in computing the tax is to be used in determining the tax on subsequent gifts. The theory behind this rule is that the IRS and taxpayer have accepted the value for gift tax purposes, so certainty should be given to that value. Thus, if gift tax had been paid on the 1982 and 1989 gifts, the estate's representative could not revalue those gifts. The ruling, however, points out that when the unified credit fully shelters a gift from tax, no gift tax is paid, so Section 2504(c) does not apply. That situation was discussed in Revenue Ruling 84-11, 1984-1 CB 201, with the IRS concluding that when no tax is due because of the unified credit, an undervaluation of the gift may have little or no current tax consequences. Thus, that valuation should not get the stamp of finality. Although this reasoning permits the value of the 1982 and 1989 gifts to be adjusted when the donor's taxable gifts for prior years are determined, the ruling's discussion of another issue undercuts the apparent benefit. Permitting the revaluation of earlier gifts is not the same as authorizing refunds. Under Section 6511(a), refund claims must be filed within three years from the time the return was filed or two years from when the tax was paid. The estate's representative argued that, by raising he minority discount issue for 1991 gifts, it necessarily raised the issue for earlier gifts because the valuation of earlier gifts affects the gift tax due on the 1991 gift. The IRS, however, concluded that the valuation of property is a factual issue, and the fact that a minority interest is appropriate with respect to one piece of property does not mean that the same—or even any—minority discount is automatically appropriate for interests in another piece of property. Thus, the refund claim concerning the 1991 gifts did not notify the IRS that refunds were being claimed for the 1982 and 1989 gifts. The estate's amendment of its claim to request refunds for these earlier years was a new claim. As such, it was made after the limitations period expired. Therefore, refunds attributable to gifts made in those years were not available.

[Tech. Adv. Mem. 9718004.]

Cousins are not family for estate freeze rules. The special valuation rules of Section 2701 did not apply to taxpayer's contribution to a partnership, because the partnership was not controlled by taxpayer and family members, in this ruling. Interests held by taxpayer's cousins and the spouse of a sibling did not count in determining control. Taxpayer made a capital contribution to a limited partnership that was engaged in an active business. The contribution was designated priority capital, required to be repaid in two years, and allocated net operating profits keyed to the short term federal rate. Immediately before the contribution, taxpayer and taxpayer's children had direct and indirect interests aggregating 20 percent in the partnership's capital and profits. (They owned stock in the corporate general partner, and the children held their interests through a separate partnership.) Taxpayer's sibling and the sibling's children had an aggregate interest of 17 percent, and the sibling's wife had a 13 percent interest. Fifty percent of the partnership interests was held by the taxpayer's cousin and the cousin's spouse and children (directly and indirectly through ownership of 50 percent of the stock of the general partner and a partnership of the children). Section 2701 provides special rules for valuing interests in family-controlled corporations and partnerships for gift tax purposes. Under these rules (effective in October 1990), the classic entity freezes (e.g., with parents receiving noncumulative preferred stock and the children receiving common stock) no longer work. This is accomplished, in part, by assigning a zero value to rights to receive priority distributions that either are not required to be made at a fixed rate or are not cumulative. Thus, if Section 2701 applied in the ruling, taxpayer's right to profits for the preferred capital contribution would be valued at zero because it was not cumulative (although there was a fixed rate by reference to a specified market interest rate). If qualifying cumulative preferred distributions (assumed in an initial valuation) are not made, they eventually may be treated as gifts (in an amount increased by compounding). In addition, rights to liquidate an entity and recover a preferred capital contribution or convert a preferred interest into a junior equity interest (e.g., common stock) are assigned a zero value. Furthermore, the value of all junior equity interests is at least 10 percent of the value of the entity so that, regardless of the parents' yield from qualifying distributions on their preferred interests, there is a minimum gift when their children receive the junior equity interests. These rules apply to transfers of an interest in (or a contribution to) a partnership or corporation only if the transferor and "applicable family members" have "control" of the entity immediately before the transfer. Under Section 2701(b)(2), these persons have control if they hold 50 percent of the stock (by value or vote) of a corporation. For a partnership, control is holding 50 percent of the capital or profits interests or, in the case of a limited partnership, any interest as a general partner. Applicable family members (counted in determining control) are a transferor's spouse, ancestors, ancestors of the spouse, and spouses of any ancestor, under Section 2701(e)(2). In addition, descendants of the transferor's parents or the transferor's spouse are considered applicable family members in determining control, under Section 2701(b)(2)(C). Thus, interests held by grandparents, children, grandchildren, brothers, sisters, nieces, and nephews of the transferor are taken into account. Furthermore, an individual is treated as holding interests owned indirectly through another entity, under Section 2701(e)(3). Therefore, in the ruling, taxpayer and the relatives were allocated their proportionate shares of the partnership interests owned by the various entities.

The IRS explained that taxpayer was not subject to Section 2701, because the requisite control was not present. The only interests that counted towards control were those held directly and indirectly by taxpayer, taxpayer's children, the sibling, and the sibling's children, which totalled only 37 percent of the interests. Thus, the interests held by the sibling's spouse, the cousin, the cousin's spouse, and the cousin's children were not taken into account. Furthermore, although the transferor and applicable family members held a one third interest in the corporate general partner, the IRS did not treat them as holding the general partnership interest it owned, which would have established control independently. The IRS determined "control" under Section 2701 as it read prior to the recent legislation. The 1996 Act changed the wording and the placement of part of the definition of "control" (reflected in the references above), but made no change in substance.

[Priv. Ltr. Rul. 9639054.]

Sale and simultaneous redemption of stock constituted a single transaction. The donor owned 60 percent of the voting stock of a close corporation; child *A* owned 20 percent of the voting stock, and two other children each owned 10 percent. When the donor was terminally ill, she sold half her shares (i.e., 30 percent of the stock of the corporation) to child *A*. Simultaneously, the donor redeemed her remaining shares. In setting the purchase price for the sale and redemption, the donor treated the 30 percent blocks of stock as two separate minority blocks rather than as a single 60 percent majority block. After the sale and redemption, the donor owned no interest in the corporation, and child *A* held a 71.4 percent controlling interest.

The IRS ruled that for gift tax purposes, the sale and simultaneous redemption constituted a single integrated transfer of a controlling interest in the corporation to child *A*. The value of the transfer includes a control premium. According to the IRS, Revenue Ruling 93-12, 1993-1 CB 202, did not apply in this case because here, child *A* was the sole transferee of the controlling interest.

[Tech. Adv. Mem. 9504004.]

Valuing simultaneous gifts of stock to eleven family members. On May 1, 1990, the donor, who owned 100 percent of the stock of *X* corporation, transferred all his stock via equal gifts to each of his eleven children, who then owned the corporation. Citing Revenue Ruling 93-12, 1993-1 CB 202, the IRS ruled that the value of the gift to each donee is calculated by considering each gift separately and not by aggregating all the donor's holdings in the corporation immediately before the gift. The application of any discounts for lack of marketability is determined in connection with each separate gift. Whether the donor owns 100 percent of the corporation or a lesser controlling interest prior to the gift and whether the donees are family members or third parties are not determining factors in valuing a block of stock transferred or in deciding whether a separate gift is subject to a minority interest discount. The percentage of control represented by each gift of stock (including the potential swing vote value), as well as other financial data and factors affecting the value of the transferred stock, must be included in the valuation for gift tax purposes.

[Tech. Adv. Mem. 9449001.]

No minority discount is available on transfer to donor's issue of shares in family corporation. An individual transferred publicly traded stock to a new corporation in exchange for all of the outstanding common and preferred shares of the new corporation. Both classes of stock were entitled to one vote per share. The corporation subsequently reinvested the publicly traded stock. The individual gave all of her common shares in the corporation to her children and grandchildren. On her gift tax return, she subtracted estimated future income taxes on unrealized capital gains from the value of the net assets that the common stock represented. She claimed a further discount in the value of the stock on the ground that it was a minority interest, lacked marketability, and was a nondiversified portfolio.

The IRS stated in technical advice that the "unity of ownership" theory under Revenue Ruling 81-253, 1981-2 CB 187, prohibits a minority discount for the shares that the donor gave to her relatives. The revenue ruling concludes that, absent family discord, no minority discount is allowed for transfers of a corporation's shares among family members if the family controls the corporation at the time of the transfer. The IRS further stated that the revenue ruling prohibited a discount on the other grounds that the donor posited. The IRS also stated that the revenue ruling would not preclude the donor from claiming discounts on grounds that fell outside the scope of the revenue ruling.

[Tech. Adv. Mem. 8338009.]

PART V

GIFT TAXATION

CHAPTER **16**

Applying the Gift Tax

¶ 16.01 COMPUTATIONS AND CREDITS

Supreme Court holds that reduction of unified credit for specific exemption gifts is constitutional, notwithstanding inclusion of such gifts in gross estate under Section 2035. On September 28, 1976 (within the transitional period of the change by the Tax Reform Act of 1976 of the specific exemption to the unified credit system), decedent made gifts of $45,000 to five persons.

No gift tax was paid, because he claimed the $3,000 annual exclusion for each gift and used his entire $30,000 specific exemption. Decedent died two years after he made these gifts, and the gifts were included in his gross estate under Section 2035. The estate claimed its entire unified credit on the estate tax return. Pursuant to Section 2010(c), the IRS reduced the credit because of the specific exemption claimed on the 1976 gifts. Taxpayer argued that the retroactive application of Section 2010(c) was a denial of due process. The district court held for taxpayer.

Held: Reversed for the IRS. First, Section 2010(c) reduces the unified credit for amounts allowed as a specific exemption. The specific exemption is considered allowed, even though it results in no tax benefit as, for example, where the gifts are included in the gross estate under Section 2035. In determining whether the provision effects a denial of due process, the critical question is not whether Section 2010(c) has a retroactive effect, but whether that effect is so "oppressive as to transgress" the constitutional notion of due process. In the instant case, the estate paid no more tax under the 1976 Act system than it would have paid under prior law. Further, the adverse consequence asserted to have been the result of Section 2010(c) was caused principally by the inclusion of the 1976 gifts in the gross estate under Section 2035, which was not enacted in the 1976 Act.

[Hemme, 476 US 558, 106 S. Ct. 2071, 58 AFTR2d 86-6320, 86-1 USTC ¶ 13,671 (1986).]

Reduction of unified credit by IRS is held not to constitute an assessment or collection of tax. Taxpayer gave stock to several donees in 1982 and 1983. On the gift tax returns for those years, taxpayer stated the value of the stock to be $40 per share. Because the gifts were distributed among several donees, the exclusion available for each transfer resulted in a showing of no taxable gifts on taxpayer's returns. The IRS thereafter advised taxpayer that its own valuation of the stock was $110 per share, which resulted in a finding of taxable gifts in 1982 and 1983. As a result, the IRS applied portions of taxpayer's unified credit to satisfy the gift tax amounts. Taxpayer filed an action in federal district court seeking full reinstatement of the unified credit. The IRS contended that the court lacked jurisdiction under Section 1346(a)(1), because taxpayer did not seek recovery of a tax assessed or collected. The IRS also maintained that its notification that a portion of taxpayer's unified credit had been applied to satisfy a gift tax that would otherwise be owed did not constitute an assessment of a tax. In addition, there had been no collection of tax. Section 1346(a)(1) provides that district courts have jurisdiction in any civil action against the United States for the recovery of any internal revenue tax alleged to have been erroneously or illegally assessed or collected, or any penalty claimed to have been collected without authority or any sum alleged to have been excessive or in any manner wrongfully collected under the internal revenue laws. Taxpayer contended that even if the reduction of his unified credit was not a tax assessed or collected, it was at least "any sum" as that term is employed in Section 1346(a)(1).

Held: For the IRS. The court adopted the IRS's position, stating that application of a portion of an individual's unified credit does not constitute an assessment or collection of tax for purposes of federal district court jurisdiction pursuant to Section 1346(a)(1). The court also rejected taxpayer's interpretation of the term "any sum" as being too expansive. Accordingly, the action was dismissed for lack of jurisdiction.

[Reilly, 61 AFTR2d 88-1332, 88-1 USTC ¶ 13,752 (SD Ind. 1987).]

Transitional rules of Section 2010(c) are explained. Decedent made a Section 2513 election to be treated as the donor of half the gift made by his wife after September 8, 1976, and before 1977, and used the Section 2521 specific exemption. Section 2010(c) provides for a decrease in the Section 2010 unified credit by 20 percent of the Section 2521 exemption used for gifts made between these dates. Decedent's estate did not reduce the credit under Section 2010(c).

Held: For the IRS. The statutory language and legislative history of Section 2010(c) indicate that the section applies to gifts made by a deemed donor under Section 2513, and the credit should therefore be decreased.

[Estate of Gawne, 80 TC 478 (1983).]

Value of gift is reduced by gift tax paid by donee. The value of a gift is reduced by the amount of gift tax the donee actually pays when the donee has agreed to pay the gift tax. The value of the gift is not reduced, to the extent that the donor's unified credit is used.

[Rev. Rul. 81-223, 1981-2 CB 189.]

Spouse's failure to consent to decedent's gift bars estate from splitting gift tax liability. An individual lent his grandson $350,000 in May 1984. The two executed a non-interest-bearing note that required no payment until May 1989. The principal was payable to the individual. Although the individual was married when the note was executed, the spouse was not a party to the note. On November 18, 1984, the spouse died. On December 31, 1984, the individual made gifts of $10,000 each to several family members. On March 26, 1985, the individual died. On April 16, 1985, the individual's estate filed a gift tax return reporting the December 31, 1984, gifts. On August 16, 1985, the spouse's estate filed its estate tax return, reporting no gifts made during 1984. Finally, on December 23, 1985, the individual's estate filed its estate tax return, which did not list the $350,000 loan as an adjusted taxable gift. Later, the individual's estate conceded that the individual made a taxable gift of

$132,677 on the date on which the promissory note was executed. The individual's estate contended that the gift should be split between the individual's estate and the spouse's estate. The IRS contested this treatment, arguing that the spouse had not signified consent to the gift as required by Section 2513(a)(2).

The IRS took the position that the taxable gift made with the non-interest-bearing $350,000 loan could not be split between the individual's and the spouse's estates. Citing Regulation §25.2513-2(b)(1), the IRS concluded that when the federal gift tax return was filed by the individual's estate on April 16, 1985, it signaled the termination of the estate's opportunity to demonstrate that the spouse consented to a split gift. The IRS rejected the individual's estate's argument that, under the rationale of Frieder, 28 TC 1256 (1957), the estate's April 16, 1985, gift tax return reported only gifts made when the individual was unmarried (widowed) and therefore did not constitute a "spouse return" for purposes of Section 2513(b)(2). The IRS distinguished *Frieder* on its facts and emphasized that in the instant case, the gifts made during the marriage and out of marriage were made by the same person and were reportable on the same return.

[Tech. Adv. Mem. 8843005.]

Credit used for estate tax cannot apply to gift tax. Decedent sold a farm to her grandson on the installment method and treated the value of the land as equal to the price her grandson paid for it. Thus, she believed that there was no gift component. She died the next year. She had not filed a gift tax return, and no gifts were reported on the estate tax return. Thus, at her death, the entire amount of the unified credit was applied to the estate tax liability. The IRS subsequently determined that the value of the land sold to decedent's grandson exceeded the sale price, and the difference was a taxable gift. The determination was made after the statute of limitations had run with respect to adjustments to the estate tax. Section 2505(a) provides for the use of the unified credit against the gift tax, whereas Section 2010(a) provides for the use of the unified credit against the estate tax. Although the unified credit rules are set forth in separate sections for gift and estate taxes, the credit is, in effect, a single unified credit for estate and gift tax purposes. Any part of the unified credit used against gift taxes generally reduces the credit available for estate tax purposes. In Revenue Ruling 79-160, 1979-1 CB 313, the IRS ruled that the gift tax is reduced by the amount of unified credit allowable at the time of the transfer. Revenue Ruling 79-398, 1979-2 CB 338, takes the position that the unified credit is mandatory and must be used when computing the gift tax.

The IRS concluded that where the full amount of the credit was used to offset the estate tax liability and the statute of limitations had run with regard to an estate tax assessment, the credit was unavailable to offset the gift tax. Although generally a three-year statute of limitations applies to assessments (where a tax return has been filed), there is no statute of limitations if such return (including a gift tax return) has not been filed. Moreover, the receipt by the estate of an estate tax closing letter does not estop the IRS from assessing a liability against the estate for gift taxes if the limitations period has not expired. Thus, the IRS's acceptance of the estate tax return as filed did not prevent the IRS from assessing a gift tax liability against the estate. Finally, Regulation § 25.2502-2 provides that if a donor dies before paying the gift tax, the tax becomes a debt of the estate, payable by the executor. Liability of the executor exists for the unpaid gift tax to the extent of payments made of any part of other debts before the IRS claim, if the executor was aware of the debt. Otherwise, under Section 6324(b), the transferee liability of the donees is limited to the value of the gift received.

[Priv. Ltr. Rul. 8743001.]

Use of unified credit is mandatory. Taxpayer made his first gift in 1977 and filed a gift tax return for the quarter ending June 30, 1977. He computed the tax under Section 2502 and did not use the unified credit under Section 2505. The IRS has concluded that the use of the unified gift tax credit is mandatory. The memorandum relies on the "shall be allowed" language in Section 2505(a) and on the statute's provision that the credit be reduced by amounts "allowable" in prior years.

[Tech. Adv. Mem. 7953011.]

¶ 16.02 EXEMPT TRANSFERS

Transfer of proceeds of allotment property is held not subject to gift taxation. Taxpayer was an American Indian who received certain allotment rights over federal timberland property pursuant to the General Allotment Act of 1887. By the terms of the Act, an American Indian otherwise qualifying for special status is exempt from taxation on the proceeds from the sale of timber products. Taxpayer transferred part of the proceeds from timber sales to a nonqualifying individual and claimed that the transfer was exempt from federal gift tax. The IRS argued successfully in federal district court that the action was a taxable gift.

Held: Reversed for taxpayer. The court analyzed the case of Squire v. Copoeman, 351 US 1 (1956), and concluded that the Supreme Court's broad ruling in respect of the nontaxability of allotment property proceeds extends to the gift tax as well as to the income tax.

[Kirschling, 746 F2d 512, 54 AFTR2d 84-6540, 84-2 USTC ¶ 13,596 (9th Cir. 1984).]

Nonresident alien's gift of stock in U.S. company to U.S. resident is not taxable. A nonresident alien individual was the sole shareholder of a U.S. corporation. The individual planned to give his shares in the corporation to his daughter, who was a U.S. resident. The IRS stated that the transfer would be a gift of intangible property exempt from gift tax under Regulation § 25.2501-1(a)(3)(i). The IRS stated that only gifts of real estate or tangible personalty that are in the United States when transferred subject a nonresident alien to gift tax.

[Priv. Ltr. Rul. 8342106.]

¶ 16.03 CHARITABLE DEDUCTION

[1] Generally

Charitable contribution deduction denied for lack of appraisal. In 1990 and 1991, taxpayers contributed shares of a corporation to charities that they valued at $33,000 and $88,000, respectively, based on arm's-length sales of stock in the company. The company was actively traded but not publicly traded during those years. Taxpayers did not obtain any appraisals of the donated stock. While conceding that taxpayers accurately valued the shares, the IRS denied the deductions because the appraisal requirements in Regulation § 1.170A-13(c) were not met. This regulation requires that qualified appraisals be obtained and appraisal summaries attached to the tax returns on which deductions are claimed for donations of more than $10,000 of nonpublicly traded stock.

Held: For the IRS. The Fourth Circuit, affirming the Tax Court's decision, agreed that the deductions could not be claimed because the substantiation requirements in the regulation were not met. Further, the court rejected taxpayers' assertion that they be allowed to deduct $10,000 in each of the years—an amount for which an appraisal would not be required—because they had already claimed higher values and had not satisfied the regulatory substantiation requirements. The court also stated that taxpayers did not qualify for the "substantial compliance" exception recognized in Bond, 100 TC 32 (1993). In Bond, taxpayers had obtained a professional appraisal that lacked all the information needed for a "qualified appraisal," but did attach a complete appraisal summary to the income tax return.

[Hewitt, 166 F3d 332, 98-2 USTC ¶ 50,880, 82 AFTR2d 98-7164 (4th Cir. 1998).]

Self-dealing bars charitable deduction. X transferred funds to a charitable trust, of which his child Y was trustee. Y was permitted to borrow from the trust, subject to repayment by the time the trust terminated. Under Section 2522(c)(1), X's transfer would not qualify for a charitable deduction. The trust constituted a private foundation that permitted self-dealing within the meaning of Section 508(e).

[Rev. Rul. 80-271, 1980-2 CB 282.]

Percentage of guaranteed annuity qualifies for gift tax charitable deduction. Section 2522(c) provides that no deduction is allowed for the transfer in trust of a charitable lead interest, unless the charitable interest is in the form of a guaranteed annuity or a fixed percentage of the trust corpus. The regulations require that in order to qualify as a guaranteed annuity, the amount to be paid annually must be determinable as of the date of gift. The IRS ruled that a fixed percentage of a guaranteed annuity payable at least annually to a charitable organization is a determinable amount and is therefore deductible under Section 2522.

[Rev. Rul. 77-327, 1977-2 CB 353.]

Gift of less than taxpayer's entire interest in policy does not qualify for gift tax charitable deduction. The IRS issued a ruling that sets forth the gift tax consequences of Revenue Ruling 76-143, 1976-1 CB 63. Revenue Ruling 76-143 involved two situations where gifts of the cash surrender value of insurance policies were made to a charitable institution, but taxpayer retained certain rights, including the right to name or change the beneficiary and to assign the balance of the policy. The IRS indicated that the gift tax charitable deduction would be disallowed under Section 2522(c) for both of these situations, because they were gifts of less than taxpayer's entire interest and were not undivided interests in the policies.

[Rev. Rul. 76-200, 1976-1 CB 308.]

Retained easement not a prohibited partial interest. The IRS ruled that a taxpayer's retained easement on charitably donated property was not a prohibited partial interest under Sections 170(f) and 2522(c), so it did not defeat taxpayer's charitable contribution and gift tax deductions, in this ruling. Taxpayer owned property in fee simple, on which was situated a main house, a new house, and a guest cottage. The only access from all three structures to a public road was via one paved driveway. Taxpayer subdivided the property into two lots and donated the lot containing the main house to an exempt, nonprofit educational and scientific research organization. The deed, however, reserved in taxpayer a nonexclusive easement for pedestrian and vehicular ingress and egress over the donated lot's driveway. The deed provided that taxpayer could not park on or block the driveway; that the donee was responsible for all driveway maintenance costs; and that the donee could terminate the easement with proper notification and payment. The donee planned to use the property for educational purposes—i.e., as a conference center, meeting place, and re-treat—and stated that the easement would not interfere with such use. Tax-payer sought a ruling that the retained easement would not defeat the charitable contribution and gift tax deductions for the donated lot. Under Sec-tions 170(a) and 170(c), a taxpayer can deduct certain contributions he or she makes to a qualified exempt organization, such as a nonprofit educational and scientific organization. Here, there was no question that the donee was a quali-fied charitable organization eligible to receive tax deductible contributions. Nonetheless, taxpayer's deduction for the contributed lot could be denied under Section 170(f)(3) as a contribution of a prohibited partial interest in property, *unless* the contribution was considered an "undivided portion" of tax-payer's entire property interest. Regulation § 1.170A-7(b)(1)(i) defines this un-divided portion as consisting of a "fraction or percentage of each and every substantial interest or right" that a taxpayer owns in the property. Based on the statute and the regulation, the test for determining the applicability of the undi-vided portion exception to an otherwise prohibited partial interest contribution is the substantiality of the rights or interests that the donor retains.

Here, the IRS found that taxpayer's retained easement rights were so in-substantial that they would not affect the donee's use of the contributed lot; so, in effect, the donation was considered to have been a transfer of taxpayer's en-tire interest in that lot. The IRS reasoned that, as taxpayer could not park on or block the driveway, and would not interfere with the donee's use of the lot, taxpayer's rights to the driveway were insubstantial in nature. Thus, the excep-tion applied and the retained easement was not a prohibited partial interest under Section 170(f)(3) that would destroy taxpayer's charitable contribution deduction for the contributed lot. The IRS also concluded that taxpayer's re-tained easement rights would not destroy the Section 2522(a) gift tax deduc-tion for qualified charitable gifts. Regulation § 25.2522(c)-3(c) denies a charitable gift tax deduction for the transfer of partial interests in property, *un-less* such interest is a qualified "deductible interest." Akin to the Section 170 rules, the regulation defines a deductible interest as an undivided portion of a donor's entire property interest; and the test again is whether the donor's re-tained rights are so insubstantial that the donor is considered to have trans-ferred his or her entire interest. Based on its conclusion under Section 170 that taxpayer's retained easement rights were not substantial in nature, and that the donation was consequently a transfer of taxpayer's entire property interest, the IRS concluded that the retained easement was similarly not a prohibited partial interest for gift tax purposes. The IRS did rule, however, that the deductions both had to be reduced because in determining the charitable contribution in-come and gift tax deductions, the contribution must be reduced by any consid-eration received in return for the contribution. Here, the IRS determined that the driveway maintenance costs the donee agreed to pay were consideration for taxpayer's contribution. Thus, the deductible contribution had to be reduced by the present value of those costs.

[Priv. Ltr. Rul. 9729024.]

IRS revokes private ruling regarding charitable gift of life insurance. The IRS revoked Private Letter Ruling 9110016, that addressed the issue of whether charitable deductions would be allowed to a donor who applied for a life insurance policy and immediately transferred the policy to charity. Private Letter Ruling 9110016 had concluded that no charitable deduction would be allowed for income, gift, or estate tax purposes, because the donor's executor or heirs would have an enforceable right under New York state law to recover the policy proceeds from the charity. This conclusion was based in part on existing New York statutes and related case law. Subsequent to the issuance of Private Letter Ruling 9110016, the state retroactively amended the New York Insurance Code to provide that an insured person may immediately transfer a newly purchased life insurance policy to charity. Thus, the IRS revoked the prior ruling.

[Priv. Ltr. Rul. 9147040.]

[2] Annuity Trusts

Gift tax charitable deduction is denied where excess income is paid to noncharitable remaindermen. Where the income of a charitable lead trust in excess of that needed to fund the guaranteed annuity is paid over to noncharitable remaindermen, a gift tax charitable deduction will be denied. In a ruling, however, the IRS indicated that if the excess over the guaranteed annuity were added to the trust corpus, a deduction would be allowed even if neither the trust instrument nor state law required the trust to operate within the restrictions of Sections 4943 and 4944, which impose a penalty tax on excess business holdings and jeopardizing investments, respectively. The guaranteed annuity interest payable to the charity cannot exceed 60 percent of the trust corpus. Section 4947(b)(3)(A) provides that Section 4943 and 4944 do not apply if the income interest of the trust is devoted solely to charitable purposes.

[Rev. Rul. 88-82, 1988-2 CB 336.]

IRS charts gift tax consequences of grantor's transfer of life interest in charitable remainder annuity trust. In 1980, grantor created a charitable remainder annuity trust as described in Section 664(d)(1). He retained the annuity interest in the trust for life. The remainder beneficiary was a charitable organization as described in Sections 170(c) and 2522(a). In 1984, grantor transferred the annuity interest in the trust to the charity.

On these facts, the IRS stated that under Regulation § 1.170A-7(a)(2)(i), grantor's transfer of his entire life annuity interest qualified for an income tax charitable deduction. It also qualified for a gift tax charitable deduction. Following the 1984 transfer, grantor retained no interest in the trust and had not made, at that time nor at any prior time, a transfer from the trust for private purposes. Although the transfer of the remainder interest to the charity divided his prior interest, the transfer was for charitable purposes, not private purposes. Consequently, in order to qualify for a gift tax charitable deduction, the 1984 transfer did not need to be in the form described in Section 2522 and Regulation § 25.2522(c)-3(c)(2). Accordingly, grantor's transfer of the life annuity interest to the named charity qualifies for a gift tax deduction under Section 2522.

[Rev. Rul. 86-60, 1986-1 CB 302.]

IRS approves of charitable remainder trust in detailed revenue ruling. In 1984, *A* created a trust funded with $250,000 in cash. The trust instrument provided that the trustee was to distribute at the end of each taxable year an annuity of $20,000 to certain charities described in Sections 170(c), 2055(a), and 2522(a). The trust was to terminate on the earlier of a period of thirty years after the funding of the trust, or twenty-one years after the death of the last survivor of *A*'s children living on the date when the trust was created, in favor of *A*'s surviving issue. When *A* created the trust, *A* had three adult children, ages 55, 60, and 63. In assessing whether annuity interests that will continue for a term of years or for a period of lives in being plus a term of years qualify as guaranteed annuity interests under Section 2522(c)(2)(B), the IRS noted at the outset that a charitable remainder trust must be in the form of a guaranteed annuity or a fixed percentage distributed yearly of the FMV of the property (to be determined yearly). A guaranteed annuity is an arrangement under which a determinable amount is paid periodically, but not less often than annually, for a specified term or for the life or lives of an individual or individuals, each of whom must be living at the date of the gift and can be ascertained at such date. For example, the annuity may be paid for the life of *A* plus a term of years. An amount is determinable if the exact amount that must be paid under the conditions specified in the instrument of transfer can be ascertained as of the date of the gift. In this case, the annuity interests were payable for the lesser of a term of years or for a period of lives in being plus a term of years. As of the date on which the trust is created, each of the possible payment periods was an allowable payment period described in Regulation § 25.2522(c)-3(c)(2)(v), and the lesser value of the two can be computed as provided in Regulation § 25.2522(c)-3(d)(2)(iv). When the annuity interests terminate, such interests will have continued for a term of years or for a period of lives in being plus a term of years. Accordingly, the annuity interests in this case meet the definition of, and qualify as, guaranteed annuity interests as described in Regulation § 25.2522(c)-3(c)(2)(v).

[Rev. Rul. 85-49, 1985-1 CB 330.]

Purchaser of annuity from charitable organization is allowed charitable deduction. Taxpayer paid a charitable organization $100x for an annuity that was worth $5x. The annuity was payable from the organization's general funds. The taxpayer could deduct under Section 2522 the amount by which 100x exceeded the present value of the annuity. Section 2522(c) did not preclude the deduction, because taxpayer retained no interest in the funds that he transferred.

[Rev. Rul. 80-281, 1980-2 CB 282.]

Tax consequences of trust providing guaranteed annuity interest and remainder interests are outlined. An individual plans to create an irrevocable trust. The trust agreement would provide that for a fifteen-year period, the trustee will distribute $162,500 annually to organizations described in Section 170(c) and 2522(a). At the end of that period, trust corpus and income would be held for the use and benefit of the grantor's grandchildren. On termination of the trust, trust assets would be distributed to the grandchildren or their issue.

The IRS took the position that the proposed trust would be classified as a trust under Regulation § 301.7701-4(a). The IRS stated that the grantor would not be treated as the owner of any portion of the trust under Sections 673, 674, 676, and 677. The IRS further stated that whether the grantor would be treated as owner of the trust under Section 675 would depend on how the trust was operated. The IRS concluded that taxpayer would not be treated as the owner of the trust under Section 667, except to the extent that current trust income would be applied to support a trust beneficiary whom the grantor is legally obligated to support. The IRS also concluded that the grantor would be allowed to deduct, under Section 642(c)(1), amounts of gross income paid to organizations described in Section 170(c), except to the extent of the trust's unrelated business income under Section 681(a), during the period of the deduction. The IRS determined that the trust's charitable annuity is a guaranteed annuity interest in trust under Section 2522(c). The IRS further determined that the grantor would be entitled to a gift tax charitable deduction in an amount equal to the present value of the interest passing to the charities described in Section 2522(a). The IRS stated that the gift of the remainder interest in trust is a generation-skipping gift. The IRS also stated that termination of the annuity interest at the end of the fifteen-year term is a taxable termination under Section 2612 subject to the generation-skipping transfer tax under Section 2601.

[Priv. Ltr. Rul. 8729051.]

Grantor does not own charitable lead trust. An individual planned to transfer preferred stock in a closely held company to a trust. The trust instrument provided for the payment of an annuity equal to 10 percent of the initial net FMV of the trust corpus to a charitable organization. The annuity was to be paid out of principal if the income was insufficient. The term of the trust was for the life of the grantor. On termination, the assets were to be distributed for private purposes. If the charitable beneficiary ceased to be an organization described under Section 170(c), 2055(a), and 2522(a), the payment was to be made to an alternative organization, named in the trust instrument.

The IRS stated that because the grantor had no power to amend or modify the trust, the initial transfer of property to the trust would constitute a taxable transfer under Section 2511 and would be subject to tax under Section 2501. The IRS stated that a gift tax charitable deduction under Section 2522 may be taken for the present value of the annuity as computed under Regulation § 25.2512-5. The IRS further stated that the trust would qualify as a trust under Regulation § 301.7701-4(a). The IRS concluded that the grantor would not be treated as the owner of the trust under Sections 673, 674, and 676. Moreover, the IRS concluded that none of the factors that would cause the grantor to be treated as owner under Section 675 were present.

[Priv. Ltr. Rul. 8706019.]

Charitable annuity trust qualifies as guaranteed annuity. A U.S. citizen planned to establish a charitable annuity lead trust to pay a guaranteed annuity amount to one or more charitable organizations. The term of the trust was to be fifteen years from the date of execution. The trust instrument contained prohibitions against self-dealing, excess business holdings, and incurring taxable expenditures.

The IRS stated that the charitable annuity described in the trust instrument qualified as a guaranteed annuity under Section 2522(c)(2)(B). Accordingly, the donor would be entitled to a charitable deduction under Section 2522.

[Priv. Ltr. Rul. 8550042.]

IRS allows deduction for charitable annuity trust. The IRS took the position that an individual may claim a gift tax deduction for the present value of payments made to charitable organizations from a charitable annuity trust. The payments would be made for sixteen years, and the remaining income (after the required distributions to the charitable organizations) and principal of the trust would pass to the children of the individual.

[Priv. Ltr. Rul. 8421060.]

Grantor of proposed guaranteed annuity charitable trust is not owner; gift tax deduction is allowed. The IRS stated that the grantor of a proposed ten-year guaranteed annuity charitable trust would not be the owner of the trust. The annuity would be a "guaranteed annuity" under Regulation § 25.2522(c)-3(c)(2)(v). A gift tax charitable deduction under Section 2522, equal to the present value of the guaranteed annuity, would be allowed when property is transferred to the trust. The IRS provided the actuarial factor needed to compute the present value of the guaranteed annuity.

[Priv. Ltr. Rul. 8344021.]

[3] Unitrusts

Donor need not specify recipients of charitable lead unitrust interests to obtain gift tax deduction. The donor created a ten-year-and-one-month trust that required annual payments to a charitable lead unitrust interest. In order to obtain a gift tax charitable deduction, it was not necessary for the donor to specify the charitable recipients of the payments. The trustee may be empowered to choose the recipients from charities that meet the requirements of Section 2522(a).

[Rev. Rul. 78-101, 1978-1 CB 301.]

No deduction is allowed for charitable interest. A taxpayer created an irrevocable trust providing for the annual payment of trust income to charity, with the remainder passing to the taxpayer's children. The trust instrument provided that the annual payment to charity be of an amount equal to the lesser of the trust income for the taxable year or a fixed percentage of the net FMV of the trust corpus. Taxpayer sought to qualify the charitable income interest as a deductible unitrust interest under Section 2522.

The IRS ruled that because the charitable interest consists only of the right to receive the lesser of a sum certain (the trust income) or a fixed percentage of the net FMV of the trust corpus, it is not a unitrust interest within the meaning of Regulation § 25.2522(c)-3(c)(2)(vi). Under that regulation, a charitable interest must consist of an irrevocable right to receive payment of a fixed percentage of the net fair market value of the trust corpus in order to qualify as a unitrust interest. Because the charitable income interest is not a unitrust interest, no deduction for the value of that interest is allowed under Section 2522(a) or Section 2522(c).

[Rev. Rul. 77-300, 1977-2 CB 352.]

Transfer to charitable unitrust receives limited deduction. Grantor proposed to create a charitable lead unitrust for a term of ten years. The beneficiary would be a private foundation. If the foundation would not be qualified under Sections 170(b)(1)(A) and 170(c) at the time of the contribution, then the trustees would select an organization that would qualify. At the termination of the trust, the foundation would be the trustor. The unitrust amount would be an amount equal to 5 percent of the net FMV of the trust property to be determined annually. Payments would first be made from trust income and then, to the extent that income would be insufficient, from the principal. Additional contributions to the trust would be permitted. Further, in the case of an additional testamentary contribution to the trust, the trustee's obligation to pay the amount apportionable to the additional testamentary gift would begin on the date of the contributor's death, but payment could be deferred to the end of the trust's taxable year. The trustees would be prohibited from any acts of self-dealing under Section 4941.

The IRS stated that, assuming that the trust meets the requirements of Section 671 for grantor trusts, the trust would qualify as a charitable lead unitrust under Section 170(f)(2)(B). The IRS then stated that because the grantor would have no power to amend, modify, or revoke the trust, the initial transfer of property to the trust would be a taxable transfer under Section 2501, except to the extent of any deduction allowable. The IRS determined that the trust would meet the definition of a unitrust interest under Regulation § 25.2522(c)-3(c)(2)(vii), because it would have an irrevocable right under the terms of the instrument to a fixed percentage of the net FMV, determined annually, of the property that funds the unitrust. The IRS also stated that because a gift to a charitable lead unitrust is deemed to be a gift "for the use" of the charity, not a gift "to" charity, the income tax deductions would be limited to 30 percent of adjusted gross income under Regulation § 1.170A-8(a)(2). The unused deductions for gifts for the "use of" a charity cannot be carried forward and used to offset income in the future years. Therefore, the transfers to the trust would not be deductible by the transferor for federal income tax purposes as a contribution to a private foundation as provided by Section 170(c). The IRS concluded that no gain or loss would be recognized by the grantor upon the transfer of property to the trust.

[Priv. Ltr. Rul. 8824039.]

Funding of trust is completed gift with respect to spouse, not with respect to charities. A grantor planned to transfer appreciated securities to a trust. The grantor was to retain a life interest for himself and grant a contingent life interest to his wife. The remainder was to be donated to charity. The grantor retained the right to name new charitable beneficiaries and to change the interests of beneficiaries between themselves.

The IRS stated that the trust qualified as a charitable remainder unitrust under Section 664. The IRS further stated that the funding of the trust constituted a completed gift of contingent income to the grantor's spouse. The IRS concluded that on the funding of the trust, a gift tax marital deduction would be allowable under Section 2523(a) for the present value of the grantor's spouse's contingent-income interest. The IRS also concluded that the funding of the trust would not constitute a completed gift of the remainder interest under Sections 2501 and 2511. The IRS refused to take a position on the application of the estate tax to the trust.

[Priv. Ltr. Rul. 8702040.]

Unitrust qualifies for charitable deduction. A grantor proposed to create a charitable unitrust. Under the trust, the trustees would pay an amount equal to 5 percent of the FMV of the trust assets to charitable organizations. The unitrust amount was to be prorated on a daily basis for a short taxable year. The trust allowed for additional contributions from the grantor. The IRS stated that the proposed trust qualifies as a unitrust under Regulation § 25.2522(c)-3(c)(2)(vi). The IRS also stated that the present value of the unitrust interest may be deducted under Section 2522, and it supplied the actuarial factor for valuing the unitrust interest.

[Priv. Ltr. Rul. 8052068.]

¶ 16.04 MARITAL DEDUCTION

Underfunding of testamentary trust after estate accounting is approved constitutes taxable gift. Decedent died on July 1, 1977. His will provided for a bequest of $200x to be used to establish a testamentary trust for the benefit of his surviving spouse. The will provided that trust income was payable to the spouse for her life and that a general power of appointment over the trust assets may be exercised by her at any time. The terms of the trust met the general requirements for a marital deduction. The residue of the estate was bequeathed to the couple's child. Decedent's executor filed a timely estate tax return for the estate on March 20, 1978, claiming a marital deduction of $200x for the bequest to establish the trust. At that time, the executor believed that the trust for the benefit of the spouse would eventually be fully funded. The trust was established by the executor and initially funded with $100x on April 1, 1979. Final funding of the trust was delayed, however, until the administration of decedent's estate could be completed. On July 15, 1983, the executor distributed an additional $60x worth of tangible and intangible assets to the trust. Income was paid to the spouse with respect to the $160x worth of corpus for the period between decedent's death and the time the amounts were placed in trust. The remaining $40x worth of the bequest was never distributed to the trust. In order for the remaining $40x portion of the bequest to be satisfied, the executor would have had to sell some of decedent's farmland that would otherwise become a part of the residue for the benefit of the child. The executor's final account showing that only $160x worth of assets had been distributed to the trust was approved by an order of the local probate court on July 22, 1983. The spouse did not object or attempt to appeal the order of the court, which became final on August 22, 1983.

The IRS was asked to rule on the estate and gift tax consequences of these facts. It concluded that the estate tax marital deduction allowable to the estate for the bequest in trust was $200x, and that the distribution of $40x to the child was a taxable gift by the spouse. The IRS noted that the spouse could have recovered the $40x amount by routinely asserting in the local probate court the right as beneficiary under the will to have the bequest adequately satisfied. Even though the estate would have had to sell or sever some of the farmland, the spouse still could have made a claim for full satisfaction of the bequest.

[Rev. Rul. 84-105, 1984-2 CB 197.]

Gift subject to buy-sell can get marital deduction. Gifts of terminable interests do not qualify for the marital deduction. That does not, however, prevent a spouse from ensuring the opportunity to regain property given as a gift should the recipient choose to dispose of it. In the instant ruling, the IRS held that a gift of stock subject to a buy-sell agreement qualified for the marital deduction. Section 2523(a) allows donors to deduct gifts made to their spouses in computing taxable gifts. Section 2523(b) provides an exception for terminable interests. No deduction is allowed if the transferred interest will fail due to the lapse of time or the occurrence (or nonoccurrence) of an event or contingency.

In the ruling, a wife gave her husband an outright gift of stock in a closely held corporation subject to a buy-sell agreement. The agreement provides that, if the husband wishes to sell his shares, the corporation and then the wife have a right of first refusal to purchase them at the price offered by a third party. Similarly, if the couple divorce or the husband predeceases the wife, the corporation and then the wife have the option to purchase the shares at their FMV. That value would be determined by an independent appraisal. Thus, in all situations, the buy-sell agreement provides that the husband or his estate will be paid FMV for the stock. Therefore, the IRS held that the husband's interest will not terminate and the buy-sell restriction does not affect the gift's eligibility for the marital deduction.

[Priv. Ltr. Rul. 9606008.]

¶ 16.05 PAYMENT OF TAX

[1] Net Gifts

Supreme Court holds that net gifts trigger income to donor. In 1972, taxpayer transferred 17,025 shares of stock in a closely held company outright to his son and 17,024 shares of stock in the same company to each of two irrevocable trusts created for the benefit of each of his two daughters. When the gifts were made, the son executed separate agreements, on behalf of himself and as trustee to each of the two trusts, pursuant to which each donee agreed to pay its share of taxpayer's federal and state gift taxes as a condition to receiving the gifts. The stock was valued at $7.80 per share, and therefore the total value of the 51,073 shares transferred was $398,369. The net gift reported on the federal gift tax return was $316,869, which generated a gift tax liability of $62,992. To satisfy the federal gift tax liability, the son, acting in his individual capacity and as trustee of the two trusts, borrowed $62,992 from the company that issued the stock. Each loan was represented by a separate check payable to the order of the respective borrower. By August 15, 1972, the son paid the gift tax, individually and as trustee of the two trusts, by endorsing the loan checks to the order of the IRS. In December 1972, each trust sold approximately 2,700 shares of stock to the company at $7.80 per share to pay the principal and interest on the loans from the company. The son paid the principal and interest on his personal loan with his own funds. State gift taxes were paid in 1973, and additional federal gift taxes were paid by the donees in 1975 after an audit led to an increase in the value of the transferred shares. Taxpayer did not report any income in 1972 due to the stock transfers. As a result of an audit, the IRS assessed a deficiency, asserting that taxpayer had realized a long-term capital gain to the extent that the $62,992 in federal gift taxes paid in 1972 by the donees exceeded taxpayer's basis of $51,073 ($1 per share) in the transferred shares. The IRS did not contend, however, that the additional gift tax liabilities discharged by the donees in 1973 and 1975 were part of taxpayer's amount realized in 1972.

Held: For the IRS. In a decision ending the issue of whether a gift of appreciated property, subject to the condition that the donee pay the donor's gift tax liability (i.e, a net gift), results in taxable gain to the donor, the Court ruled that a donor realizes taxable income to the extent that the gift taxes paid by the donee exceed the donor's adjusted basis in the transferred property. The court held that the donee's payment of the donor's gift tax liability was income to the donor under the rule laid down in Old Colony Trust Co., 279 US 716 (1929). Without acknowledging the threshold question whether a net gift constitutes a taxable transaction, the Court indicated that the donee's assumption of the donor's gift tax liability pursuant to the transfer constitutes the requisite economic benefit for realization of income.

[Diedrich, 457 US 191, 102 S. Ct. 2414, 50 AFTR2d 82-5054, 82-1 USTC ¶ 9419 (1982).]

Eighth Circuit rules on case involving net gifts. Decedent died on June 27, 1980. Less than three years before his death, decedent and his wife gave stock valued at $2,399,044 to three irrevocable trusts established for the benefit of their grandchildren. The donation was designed as a net gift; that is, the trust instrument required, as a condition of the gift, that the trustees satisfy all gift tax liability arising from the donation of stock. Accordingly, the donee trusts paid a gift tax of $612,700, and decedent and his wife reported the gift at a value of $1,786,340. After decedent's death, the gift of stock was included in decedent's gross estate on the estate tax return pursuant to Section 2035(a). The stock's value on the date of decedent's death had declined to $2,196,180, and the executors followed the then-established practice of subtracting the amount of the gift tax paid by the donee trusts from the value of the gift included in the estate, for an includable total of $1,583,480. Decedent's executors filed the estate tax return on March 25, 1981. Three weeks earlier the Eighth Circuit had decided Diedrich, 643 F2d 499 (8th Cir. 1981), which had held for the first time that a donee's payment of the gift tax on a net gift creates taxable income for the donor. After the Supreme Court affirmed the Eighth Circuit's decision in Diedrich, 457 US 191 (1982), the executors of decedent's estate agreed to recognize the gift tax paid by the donees, less the adjusted basis in the stock, as income to the estate. The executors paid the additional income tax resulting from the donees' 1978 payment of the gift tax and deducted this payment as a claim against the estate under Section 2053(a)(3). The estate's additional tax liability created by *Diedrich* was forgiven by Congress in the Tax Reform Act of 1984. As a result, the estate received a full refund of all income tax that it had paid on the donees' 1978 satisfaction of the gift tax liability for the gift of stock. The IRS took the position that the estate should include, in addition to the value of the net gift itself, the amount of the gift tax paid by the donees. In a petition to the Tax Court, the estate sought a redetermination of this decision, claiming that it rested on a misinterpretation of Section 2035(c). In his amended answer, the IRS sought to disallow the estate's deduction under Section 2053(a)(3) for the income tax liability that had been imposed under *Diedrich*, but that had subsequently been forgiven by the Tax Reform Act of 1984. The Tax Court held that the estate was entitled to deduct, as a claim against the estate under Section 2053(a)(3), the income tax that was subsequently refunded. The IRS appealed on this issue. The Tax Court further held that the donees' 1978 tax payment on the net gift was includable in the gross estate under Section 2035(c). The estate cross-appealed this determination.

   Held: For the IRS. A decedent's executors may not deduct as a claim against the estate under Section 2053(a)(3) an income tax liability that is subsequently forgiven by Congress. In addition, decedent's gross estate must, under Section 2035(c), include the amount of any gift tax paid by the donees of any net gift made within three years of decedent's death. Accordingly, the Tax Court's judgment was affirmed in part and reversed in part.

[Estate of Sachs, 856 F2d 1158, 62 AFTR2d 88-6000, 88-2 USTC ¶ 13,781 (8th Cir. 1988).]

[2] Transferee Liability

Transferee liability for tax deficiency and interest on gift is not permitted to exceed value of gift received. Decedent died in 1937, and his will established a trust that provided that the income generated from the trust was to be paid to his wife, with the remainder being left in equal shares to his daughters. In 1970, after decedent's wife had died, the daughters renounced all rights they had in the remainder of the trust. At that time, the FMV of the remainder of the trust exceeded $10 million. Approximately ten years later the IRS sent notices of gift tax deficiency both to the executor of one of the daughters' estates and to her two children for transferee liability with regard to the deficiency. The Tax Court upheld the IRS's finding that the estate owed a gift tax of almost $5 million plus interest from the date of renunciation in 1971 to the date of payment. Because the two children each received a portion of their mother's share from decedent's trust, they were held liable as transferees for the deficiency and interest owed by their mother's estate. On appeal, the children argued that the imposition of transferee liability on them was improper, because the IRS had not established, in accordance with state law, that their mother was insolvent at the time of renunciation. In addition, the two children asserted that even if transferee liability existed, the amount of the deficiency was improper, because it exceeded the value of the gift they had received.

Held: For the estate, in part. The Third Circuit held that though transferee liability did exist on the children, the amount due the IRS could not exceed the value of the gift that they received. The question whether the children's mother had been insolvent at the time of renunciation had no bearing on whether transferee liability existed, because donee liability is determined by federal law, not by state law, and under federal law, transferee liability was not dependent on the insolvency of the donor. In addition, Section 6324(b), as written at the time of the gift, provided that the amount of transferee liability for gift tax was only to be to the extent of the value of such gift. In addition, the court stated that this "value of the gift" limitation also applied to the amount of interest for which a donee could be liable, and therefore both the interest and the tax deficiency could not exceed the value of the gift that the children received at the time of renunciation.

[Poinier, 858 F2d 917, 88-2 USTC ¶ 13,783, 62 AFTR2d 88-6006 (3d Cir. 1988), cert. denied, 490 US 1019 (1989).]

Lien is perfected when refiled within allowable statutory period. The plaintiff was the sublessee of a gas station that had been an asset in the estates of both decedents, who were husband and wife. Their son served as executor of the estates, and, in this capacity, he originally leased the gas station to the sublessor of the plaintiff. Subsequent to the lease and the assignment, the IRS made assessments against both estates for unpaid gift taxes. In partial settlement, the executor assigned rental income from the property to the IRS. The executor then sold the property to the plaintiff's lessor. Following this the IRS instituted procedures to collect upon its conflicting claim and sought to recover against the property. The plaintiff contended that the IRS action was improper because title to the gas station had been conveyed out of the estate and was no longer the separate property of a transferee liable on the original deficiency.

Held: For the IRS. The IRS was entitled to rents payable by the plaintiff to the plaintiff's lessor. The court upheld the validity of the IRS's lien against the property because all notices and demands had been sent to the property holder within the time provided for by law. The IRS's lien was perfected in accordance with statute, and therefore the claim of lien was proper. The fact that the IRS had refiled its original lien within the statutory period did not adversely affect its validity.

[Chevron, Inc., 705 F2d 1487, 52 AFTR2d 83-6403 83-1 USTC ¶ 13,523 (9th Cir. 1983).]

Indirect transfer of property by gift, where heavily encumbered by mortgages, cannot create transferee liability. In 1972, taxpayer's parents formed a corporation, and, in 1977, they transferred the stock to taxpayers. In the following year, 1978, the parents transferred real property to taxpayers individually, along with a further 3,599 acres that were transferred to the corporation. The acreage alone was valued in excess of $1 million. Later in 1978 the IRS issued a notice of deficiency to the parents, asserting liability for their 1973 income taxes. The matter was taken to the Tax Court, which entered judgment for the IRS. The amount of the judgment ($475,544 plus additions to tax) was never collected. Subsequently, in 1981, the corporation filed a voluntary petition in bankruptcy, following which the IRS made a jeopardy assessment of the parents for unpaid gift taxes arising from the 1978 transfers of property. On March 7, 1983, the bankruptcy court entered an order allowing the IRS's secured claim based on the assertion against the bankrupt of transferee liability for the parent's income and gift tax. The IRS also asserted a deficiency against taxpayers, again as transferee-donees of the parents.

Held: For the IRS, in part. With respect to taxpayers' liability for unpaid gift tax resulting from the 1978 transfers, taxpayers argued successfully that their liability as transferees should have been limited to the net FMV of the property, computed as FMV less encumbrances as of the date of transfer. The court found that taxpayers were transferees of only the property given to them personally, not of the property transferred to the corporation. The IRS had argued that taxpayers were indirect donees. Under Section 6324(b), a transferee's liability is limited to the extent of the value of the gift. Applying this standard, the court found that the IRS had failed to prove that the transfer of heavily encumbered property to the corporation resulted in any net value to taxpayers. Accordingly, taxpayers were held not to be liable as transferees for unpaid tax relating to the property held by the corporation.

[Tilton, 88 TC 590 (1987), acq. 1987-2 CB 1.].

Annual Exclusion

¶ 17.01 EXCLUDABLE AMOUNTS

Transfers to trust fail to qualify for gift tax exclusion. Taxpayer created trusts with a testamentary power of appointment. If the power was not exercised, the corpus would pass to the donee's "heirs at law." The IRS claimed that the transfers did not qualify for the gift tax annual exclusion.

Held: For the IRS. In order to qualify, the corpus must pass to the donee's estate if the donee dies before age 21. "Heirs at law" is insufficient.

[Ross, 652 F2d 1365, 48 AFTR2d 81-6275, 81-2 USTC ¶ 13,424 (9th Cir. 1981).]

Gift tax return cannot be amended to claim exemption after time for filing original return expires. In December 1976, taxpayers made several gifts. They subsequently filed a federal gift tax return on February 10, 1977. They did not, however, claim the $30,000 specific exemption when they filed the return. Such lifetime exemption for $30,000 was permitted by Section 2521, subsequently repealed by the Tax Reform Act of 1976 for gifts made after the end of that year, and was an elective provision at the donor's discretion. On February 9, 1980, taxpayers filed an amended gift tax return claiming the benefits of the exemption and a refund for the gift taxes paid. The IRS disallowed the claim for a refund, arguing that the time to file the original return had expired; thus, the election not to claim the exemption was irrevocable.

Held: For the IRS. The court held that the election not to use the gift tax exemption became irrevocable on February 15, 1977, the last day allowed by law to file gift tax returns for gifts made during the last quarter of 1976. The Tax Court pointed out in its opinion that under general principles of tax law, an election made on a return cannot be changed once the period for filing such return has expired. The IRS has the discretion to allow an amendment to a return only under the following three specific circumstances:

1. The amended return must have been filed prior to the date prescribed for filing a return.
2. Taxpayer's treatment of the contested item in the amended return was not inconsistent with his original return.
3. Taxpayer's treatment of the item in the original return was improper, and taxpayer elected one of several allowable alternatives in the amended return.

The court found that the amended return was filed by taxpayers after the period for filing the original return had expired, thus rendering the first circumstance inapplicable. The position taken on the amended return was opposite to that taken on the original return, thus rendering the second circumstance inapplicable. The treatment of the exemption by taxpayers was not improper; thus, they did not qualify under the conditions of the third circumstance. Finally, the court held that the present case was distinguishable from Richardson v. Comm'r, 126 F2d 562 (2d Cir. 1942), which allowed a retroactive election of the specific exemption. In *Richardson*, taxpayer did not elect the exemption, because he believed that there was no liability for gift taxes. In the present case, however, taxpayers were fully aware of their liability for gift taxes and made an intentional election not to use the exemption. Therefore, they must abide by their decision.

[Pearce, 55 AFTR2d 85-1541, 84-2 USTC ¶ 13,598 (D. Kan. 1984).]

Tax Court rules on transfers from revocable trusts and the annual exclusion. In September 1971, decedent, Lee D. Jalkut, created the Lee D. Jalkut

Revocable Trust (the Revocable Trust). Jalkut funded the trust by transferring to it his entire estate, including his personal residence, bank and brokerage accounts, and publicly traded stocks. Jalkut appointed himself as trustee and retained the power to amend or to revoke. In 1973, Jalkut amended the trust to authorize the trustees to pay the grantor any amounts of income or principal that the grantor requested. If the grantor became unable to manage his affairs, the trustees could use income and principal to care for the grantor or his descendants. The trustees were also authorized to continue to make any payments or gifts that the grantor had been making prior to becoming disabled. In 1984, Jalkut was diagnosed with inoperable cancer. Later that year he amended the trust again to include instructions for the distribution of the trust property after his death. After making specific bequests, the balance of the property was to be held in trust for the benefit of Jalkut's children. This amendment to the Revocable Trust also named the replacement trustees. In November 1984, Jalkut established an irrevocable trust for the benefit of his grandchildren (the Family Trust). The trust was funded by transferring to it $40,356 of mutual fund shares that had been held in the Revocable Trust. Jalkut established a second irrevocable trust in December 1984 for the benefit of Anna S. and Jane Jalkut (the Jalkut Trust). This trust was funded by transferring $20,000 from the Revocable Trust. On January 25, 1985, the replacement trustees were notified by Jalkut's physician that Jalkut was no longer capable of managing the Revocable Trust. Rosehelen Klein-Fields and Nathan M. Grossman assumed the position of cotrustees. On that day, they made the following transfers from the Revocable Trust:

1. $40,000 to the Family Trust
2. $20,000 to the Jalkut Trust
3. $10,000 to Michael Jalkut
4. $10,000 to Theresa Jalkut

Lee Jalkut died on February 6, 1985. Nathan Grossman was appointed as executor of Jalkut's estate. In November of that year, Grossman filed the federal estate tax return, on which the total gross estate was valued at $1,152,139. No transfers of assets were included in the gross estate under Section 2035 or Section 2038. The IRS determined that there was a $55,184 deficiency in the estate tax due. The IRS claimed that the $140,356 in transfers from the Revocable Trust in 1984 and 1985 should have been included in the estate under Sections 2035 and 2038. Grossman, as executor of the estate, contended that the value of the Revocable Trust was includable in decedent's gross estate only under Section 2033 (which excludes annual exclusion gifts). Sections 2035 and 2038 did not apply, because decedent did not divest himself of beneficial ownership of the assets when he transferred them to the Revocable Trust. The transfers made in 1984 and 1985 all qualified for the gift tax annual exclusion and were excludable from the gross estate under Section 2035(d)(1). Alternatively, Grossman argued that the IRS should look past the technical form of the transfers to their substance to treat all the transfers as if Jalkut had withdrawn the assets from the Revocable Trust and then made the transfers. Lastly, Grossman contended that it would be unjust to include transfers made within three years of death in the estate if deathbed transfers that qualify for the annual exclusion are not includable for decedents who die after 1981.

Held: For the IRS. The Tax Court began its response by stating that Section 2038, not Section 2033, determines whether property transferred to a trust was includable in an estate, and that generally the value of a revocable trust at decedent's death was includable. The court next considered whether the transfers *from* the Revocable Trust were includable in the gross estate under Section 2035(d)(2) or Section 2038(a)(1). Grossman claimed that annual exclusion gifts were not includable in the estate, because of Section 2035(d)(1). The court disagreed because of the provisions in Section 2035(d)(2). Grossman then claimed that Section 2038(a)(1) did not apply to annual exclusion gifts. He cited a number of letter rulings to support his claim. The court noted that such rulings have no precedential force, but said that "the number of rulings reveals that the issue is one of significant importance to estate planners." The court disagreed with Grossman's claim that annual exclusion gifts were beyond the reach of Section 2038. It decided that the determination whether the transfers would be included under Section 2038 depended on the particular terms of the trust agreement. While Jalkut was acting as trustee, he was the sole permissible beneficiary of the trust income and principal. The only way trust assets could have been transferred to a third party was for Jalkut to withdraw the income or principal for his own use and then give it to the transferee; thus, Jalkut, not the Revocable Trust, was the transferor. Therefore, the transfers in 1984 were not a relinquishment under Section 2038 of Jalkut's power to influence the enjoyment of trust property transferred; they were excludable gifts under Section 2035(d)(1). A different situation arose after Jalkut became disabled and could no longer act as trustee. At that point, the replacement trustees had authority to transfer trust principal and income to persons and entities other than Jalkut. Transfers made by the replacement trustees could not be treated as withdrawals by Jalkut for his own use. They were, however, relinquishments by Jalkut, through the trustees, of his power to alter, amend, revoke, or terminate the trust with respect to the assets transferred, as described in Section 2038(a). Consequently, these transfers were includable in Jalkut's estate under Section 2035(d)(2).

[Estate of Jalkut, 96 TC 675 (1991).]

Gifts made by attorney-in-fact excluded from estate. Decedent died on September 13, 1992, at age 97, a resident of Keyes, Oklahoma. On August 16, decedent was hospitalized with a broken hip resulting from a fall. On September 1, she returned home, where she was cared for by home health care nurses and by her family until her death. Decedent had been ill for ten years so her death was not unexpected. In 1987, decedent purchased twenty-one separate annuities, naming various nieces and nephews, a sister-in-law, and a former brother-in-law, as annuitants. Decedent was the owner of each annuity, and the annuitant was named as contingent owner, to whom ownership would pass when decedent died. Decedent did not file any gift tax returns during the ten years prior to her death. During that time she made small cash gifts within the annual exclusion amount, and transferred some bonds and certificates of deposit. Two months before her death, decedent executed a durable power of attorney, naming three relatives (including the former brother-in-law) as attorneys-in-fact. The power of attorney did not contain explicit gift-giving authority. Decedent was considered mentally competent to handle her affairs at all times. She was concerned about retaining control of her assets at the time she executed the power of attorney. Decedent was present when the power of attorney was discussed with the drafting lawyer. She signed the document, although she needed some assistance in determining where to sign, due to failing eyesight. Before falling and injuring herself, decedent cashed two annuities after the annuitants had died. Decedent told her insurance agent that she intended to pay the taxes owed on the proceeds and then give the face amount, $10,000, to the heirs of the deceased annuitants. At that same time, decedent mentioned to several people, including her accountant and her insurance agent, that she was considering giving the remaining nineteen annuities to the various annuitants. Prior to meeting with her lawyer to discuss the power of attorney, decedent told one of the attorneys-in-fact that she did wish to make such gifts. On or about August 27, 1992, the attorneys-in-fact transferred the nineteen remaining annuities to the annuitants. Before processing the transfers, the insurance agent consulted with decedent's attorney to confirm that the attorneys-in-fact had authority to make the gifts. He was told that they did have such power. At the same time, the attorneys-in-fact created a revocable living trust for decedent. Decedent did not personally sign the trust agreement; it was executed by the attorneys-in-fact. After her death, decedent's property was distributed pursuant to the trust rather than under her will. A federal gift tax return for 1992 was filed by decedent's estate on May 1, 1993. It listed gifts to nineteen relatives which were made on August 27 or 28, or September 12. The gifts, which totaled $293,249, included the nineteen annuities, three Series E bonds, and $4,000 in cash. Nineteen $10,000 exclusions were claimed, resulting in a net taxable gift of $103,249. The federal estate tax return was filed on June 9, 1993. After the above gifts were made, the total gross estate exceeded $973,000. The IRS audited the return and assessed a deficiency of $61,381. It challenged the authority of the attorneys-in-fact to make gifts since that authority was not specifically granted in the durable power of attorney. The IRS argued that the gifts were incomplete, invalid, or revocable, and that therefore the value of all the gifts must be included in the gross estate.

    Held: For the estate. The Tax Court held that the gifts were completed gifts and excludable from decedent's estate even though there was not a specific gift-making authorization in the power of attorney. The Tax Court found that in Oklahoma, such gifts are complete if there was an intent by decedent to make the gifts, and there was delivery to, and acceptance by, the donee. The Tax Court in the instant case recognized that some states do not allow attorneys-in-fact to make gifts unless there is specific gift-giving authority in the power of attorney. Oklahoma does not have such a rule. The court then tried to determine how Oklahoma courts would rule on this issue. It believed that the Oklahoma Supreme Court would look for "clear, explicit, and convincing" evidence of intent. It noted that in Rolater, 542 P2d 219, 233 (Okla. Ct. App. 1975), the Court of Appeals of Oklahoma could not find any "hard evidence or cogent circumstances" to indicate that decedent intended for her attorney-in-fact to make gifts. The Tax Court felt that such evidence and such circumstances were present in the instant case, and that therefore, the gifts in question were valid.

[Estate of Neff, 73 TCM 2606, RIA TC Memo. ¶ 97,186 (1997).]

Gifts of real property qualify for annual gift tax exclusion. In 1980, *A* owned ten acres of income-producing real estate and transferred three of those acres to *B*. At that time, the land was correctly appraised at $1,000 per acre. In 1981, *A* transferred two of *A*'s remaining seven acres to *B*. The land was correctly valued at $1,500 per acre. In 1982, *A* transferred to *B* the remaining five acres, which were appraised at $2,000 per acre. Because the value of each transfer was equal to the annual exclusion available in the respective years of transfer, *A* did not file federal gift tax returns for the transfers, and consequently paid no gift taxes. Advice was requested from the IRS as to the gift tax consequences where, under the circumstances of this ruling, the donor transfers specified portions of real property equal in value to the annual gift tax exclusion allowable under Section 2503 in effect for the years of the transfers.

The IRS determined that where a donor transfers, on an annual basis, a specified portion of real property, the donor has made a completed gift each year of the portion transferred, and each gift qualifies for the annual exclusion under Section 2503. Because *A* made a completed gift of only a portion of the property in every year, only that portion transferred to *B* each year was subject to the gift tax. Each of the gifts qualified for the annual exclusion under Section 2503 because, under the terms of the transfers, *B* received the present unrestricted right to the immediate use, possession, and enjoyment of an ascertainable interest in the real property. Because separate annual gifts were involved, and the value of each gift was equal to the annual gift tax exclusion in effect for the year of transfer, *A* could use the exclusion for each annual gift.

[Rev. Rul. 83-180, 1983-2 CB 169.]

Estates included transfers from living trusts. In the ruling cited below, decedent established a trust in 1983 under which the trustee was to distribute income or principal to decedent or otherwise as she directed. If her doctor certified in writing that she was incapable of handling her financial affairs, the trustee could pay trust income or principal to her for her benefit or for that of her dependents. In 1988 and 1989, decedent asked the trustee to make eleven gifts of $10,000 each and five gifts of $5,000 each from the trust to specified individuals. She died in 1989, and her estate included the date-of-death value of the trust, but not the value of the transfers, in the gross estate. Section 2035(a) provides that a gross estate includes the value of all property interests transferred by a decedent within three years before death. Although under Section 2035(d)(1) this rule generally does not apply to decedents dying after 1981, Section 2035(d)(2) provides that it does apply to a transfer of an interest in property that is included in a decedent's estate under Section 2036 (transfers with retained life estate), Section 2037 (transfers taking effect at death), Section 2038 (revocable transfers), or Section 2042 (life insurance proceeds), or that would have been so included if a decedent had retained the interest. In addition, Section 2038(a) provides that the gross estate includes the value of property to the extent of any interest that a decedent transferred without receiving adequate and full consideration in money or money's worth. This provision applies if, at death, the enjoyment of the interest is subject to any change through exercise of a power by a decedent (alone or with any other person) to alter, amend, revoke, or terminate, or when such power is relinquished during the three years ending on the date of death. According to Revenue Ruling 75-553, 1975-2 CB 477, if decedent creates a revocable trust with the remainder payable to a decedent's estate, the corpus that is payable to the estate is decedent's property under Section 2033 (property in which decedent had an interest). In Estate of Jalkut, 96 TC 675 (1991), acq., decedent created a revocable trust that provided for the payment of all net income and principal as he requested during his life. If he became unable to manage his affairs, the trustee could pay income and principal to decedent or his descendants. During the three years before decedent's death, he became incompetent, and transfers were made to persons other than decedent while he was competent and incompetent. At his death, the trust was distributed to third parties.

The Tax Court held that decedent in the instant case was the sole permissible beneficiary while he was competent. Thus, the transfers to persons other than decedent during this period were withdrawals preceding gifts by decedent. Since transfers to or for the benefit of his descendants when he was incompetent were authorized by the trust, the court found no reason to recharacterize the transfers as withdrawals by decedent followed by transfers to third parties. Rather, they were relinquishments under Section 2038(a) of decedent's power to alter, amend, revoke, or terminate the trust with respect to the transferred property. Because the transfers would have been includable in the gross estate under Section 2038 if retained by decedent, they were held to be includable under Section 2035(d)(2). The IRS held that the corpus remaining at dece-dent's death was includable in her gross estate under Section 2038, citing Rev-enue Ruling 75-553 and *Jalkut.* Since decedent's doctor never certified that she was incompetent, the trustee could distribute income or principal directly to any donees designated by decedent orally or in writing. Thus, the transfers were a relinquishment under Section 2038(a) of her power to amend or to re-voke the trust. In addition, since the transfers would have been includable in the estate under Section 2038 if retained by decedent, they were also includ-able under Section 2035(d)(2).

[Tech. Adv. Mem. 9318004.]

¶ 17.02 PRESENT INTERESTS

Exclusion not available where trust is funded by non-dividend-paying cor-porate stock. Taxpayers, husband and wife, established trusts for their chil-dren and grandchildren with stock in their closely held corporation. Each trust was to last for twenty years, or until the corporation redeemed the shares or the beneficiary died. The adult beneficiaries were to receive the income from their trusts quarterly. The trustees were to accumulate the income for the mi-nor beneficiaries until they reached their majorities, although the trustees also had the discretion to apply income for the minors' support and maintenance. The IRS examined the transfers and determined that neither the trust corpus nor the income interest qualified for the annual exclusion. The IRS concluded that the trust corpus was clearly a future interest and that the income interest, though theoretically qualified, was ineligible.

   Held: For the IRS. The court examined the underlying facts and circum-stances and concluded that the income interests were incapable of valuation. The corporation did not pay dividends for eleven years, and its historical growth rate made it unlikely that it would pay dividends in the foreseeable fu-ture. There was also a restriction on the beneficiaries' right to the income. If one of the beneficiaries died, forcing the corporation to redeem his stock, the corporation could not pay dividends for the next three years. Finally, the trust-ees had little real opportunity to revalue the stock into assets that would pro-duce income. Before the trustees could sell, they were required to procure the consent of the other shareholders. The corporation could redeem the shares at any time, but only if it possessed the necessary surplus. Also, the corporation was obligated to buy in the shares, but, again, only if it possessed sufficient surplus. On this basis, the court denied the claimed annual exclusion.

[Berzon, 534 F2d 528, 37 AFTR2d 76-1601, 76-1 USTC ¶ 13,140 (2d Cir. 1976).]

Substantial restriction on gift disqualifies minor's trust. Decedent established trust accounts for twelve of her grandnieces and grandnephews. Paragraph 1 of each trust provided that until termination of the trust, the income and principal were to be expended for the benefit of the beneficiary in such amounts as the trustee deemed advisable (1) for the preparatory school, college, university, graduate school, or technical school education of the beneficiary, or (2) in the event of an accident, illness, or disability affecting the beneficiary or, in the event of the death or disability of either or both of the beneficiary's parents, for the care, support, health, and education of the beneficiary. "As to educational expenditures hereunder, the trustee shall consult with the beneficiary's father [father's name], or in the event of his death, with his mother [mother's name]." Each trust account was established with an initial contribution of $10,000. Additional contributions of $10,000 each were made to eleven of the accounts prior to decedent's death on April 20, 1987. Upon audit, the IRS determined that the twenty-three transfers of $10,000 each were not excludable taxable gifts. As a result, additional taxes and interest were assessed in the amount of $153,826. The estate paid the assessed amount and subsequently sued for a refund.

Under Section 2503(c), a gift tax exclusion is provided for transfers in trust for the benefit of a minor. Section 2503(c) is interpreted by Regulation § 25.2503-4(b)(1), which provides that a transfer will not fail to satisfy the conditions of Section 2503(c) by reason of the mere fact that there is left to the discretion of a trustee the determination of the amounts, if any, of income or property to be expended for the benefit of minors and the purposes for which the expenditure is to be made, *provided there are no substantial restrictions* under the terms of the trust instrument on the exercise of such discretion. The IRS contended that paragraphs 1(a) and 1(b) of the trust instruments imposed a substantial restriction under the regulations and that the IRS was therefore entitled to summary judgment.

Held: For the IRS. The trusts in question imposed substantial restrictions on the exercise of the trustee's discretion. In addition, the trust instruments did not qualify under Section 2503(c). The court noted that provisions in trust instruments providing that trust funds may be expended as may be necessary or if the minor's needs are not otherwise adequately provided for have been held not to constitute substantial restrictions. These holdings were reached on consideration that the restrictions imposed on a guardian under state law were at least as great. Similarly, a trust provision that stated that no income or principal was to be paid for support or maintenance that the settlors were legally obligated to provide a beneficiary did not constitute a substantial restriction, because the provision really ensured that the increase in the beneficiaries' present interest would be used to supplement, not duplicate, rights already held by the minors under state law. The court noted that in all of the cases finding no substantial restriction, the purposes for which the funds could be expended were broad, and the controversy surrounded a restriction on expenditures for those broad purposes. In contrast, when the purposes for which trust funds could be expended have been narrower, a substantial restriction has been found. The court in the instant case noted that the purposes for which any beneficiary's trust funds could be expended were limited to providing for the education of the beneficiary, or, in the event of an accident, illness, or disability affecting the beneficiary, or in the event of the death or the disability of either or both of the beneficiary's parents, for the care, support, health, and education of the beneficiary. According to the court, it was apparent from reading the trust instruments that the intent of the settlor of the trusts was to provide for the education of the beneficiaries. This wish of the settlor would not constitute a substantial restriction, as long as the trustee possessed as much discretion to expend trust funds for the beneficiaries' benefit as a guardian would under Illinois law. Under Illinois law, a guardian has a duty to manage a ward's estate frugally and to expend income and principal of the estate as necessary for the comfort and suitable support and education of the ward, his children, and relatives who depend on, or who are entitled to, support from him and as the court otherwise determines to be in the best interest of the ward. The district court held that the trustee here possessed less power to expend the trust assets for the benefit of the minor beneficiary than would a guardian under Illinois law. Consequently, these trusts were held to provide a substantial restriction on the discretion of the trustee and could not qualify under Section 2503(c).

[Illinois Nat'l Bank of Springfield, 756 F. Supp. 1117, 91-1 USTC ¶ 60,063, 67 AFTR2d 91-1194 (CD Ill. 1991).]

Proposal to pay annual gift out of lottery annuity is gift of present interest. An individual bought a winning lottery ticket with community funds in a community property state. The state will pay the individual $250,000 each year for the next twenty years. The individual and his spouse proposed to pay three individuals approximately $3,000 each per year. The couple requested rulings on the estate and gift tax consequences of the transaction.

The IRS stated that the gifts to the three individuals were present interest gifts and, because they were under the $10,000 exclusion limit of Section 2503(b), there would be no gift tax consequences.

[Priv. Ltr. Rul. 8940010.]

Transfers of shares of trust are present interests qualifying for annual gift tax exclusion. An individual executed a trust on December 29, 1987, naming himself as trustee. He then deeded his entire interest in some waterfront property to the trustee in trust. He deeded a one-half interest in the trust to his wife. He then executed a deed of gift whereby he transferred to each of eight donees a fractional interest in his interest in the trust, with a value of $10,000 each. All of the donees were adults, and all but one were his children. The trust provided that the trustee would pay the net income from the trust at least annually to the beneficiaries in proportion to their interests. Upon the trust's termination, the trustee was to distribute the principal of the trust in proportion to the beneficiary's interests. The beneficiaries would be allowed to enjoy the free use of the trust property, provided that they did not waste it. The trust was to terminate upon the affirmative vote by beneficiaries who had more than a 50 percent interest in the trust.

The IRS stated that the transfer by the trustee to the eight donees of the fractional shares constitute gifts of present interests in property, which qualify for the annual gift tax exclusion under Section 2503(b). The IRS noted that Regulation § 25.2503-3(b) provides that an unrestricted right to the immediate use of property or to the income from property is a present interest in property. Because each of the eight donees was given an unrestricted right to the immediate use, possession, or enjoyment of the trust property, the IRS noted, each had a present interest in the property. Therefore, the interest should qualify for the exclusion to the extent of the value of each of the donee's present interests in the trust of up to $10,000.

[Priv. Ltr. Rul. 8906026.]

Children's trust qualifies for gift tax exclusion. An individual established a trust for her two children under which the trustee must pay the trust income to the children or to their custodian quarterly. The trust may terminate when the children reach age 21, at the trustee's discretion. The trustee must distribute a child's share of the trust as the child directs by will, if the child dies before reaching age 21. The IRS stated that the income interest of the gift to the trust qualifies for the gift tax annual exclusion under Section 2503(b). The IRS also provided factors for valuing the beneficiaries' interests.

[Priv. Ltr. Rul. 8330070.]

Income interest in trust for minor qualifies for annual gift tax exclusion. A grantor established a trust for a minor beneficiary to pay, at least quarterly, the entire net income of the trust to the beneficiary or to a custodian for him under the Uniform Gifts to Minors Act. The principal was to be distributed to the beneficiary or his estate upon his death or when he reaches age 21, whichever occurs first. The IRS stated that the income interest of the donor's gift to the trust qualifies for the gift tax annual exclusion under Section 2503(b).

[Priv. Ltr. Rul. 8327060.]

¶ 17.03 FUTURE INTERESTS

Gift to corporation is future interest to shareholders. Decedent's family formed a corporation in 1981, with decedent as president and chairman of the board. She did not own any corporate stock. Two weeks after the incorporation, decedent sold 267 acres of land to the corporation, to be paid for in monthly installments over the next twenty years. Starting in 1982, decedent forgave the corporation $30,000 of its debt for the land. In each of the three following years she forgave the corporation $50,000, $25,000, and $42,000, respectively, for a total debt forgiveness of $147,000. Five years later, in 1990, the corporation sold all its land, converted its assets to cash, and dissolved. The IRS audited the estate and assessed it a deficiency because the forgiveness of debt involved did not qualify for the $10,000 per donee annual exclusion. Section 2503(b) excludes the first $10,000 of a gift from the gift tax as long as the gift is not a future interest. Regulation §§ 25.2503-3(a) and 25.2503-3(b) differentiate between present and future interests:

1. Present interests are unrestricted rights to immediate use, possession, or enjoyment of property or income from property.
2. Future interests commence in use, enjoyment, or possession at some future time (e.g., remainder interests).

The Code and the regulations both do not apply these definitions to gifts made to corporations. Revenue Ruling 71-443, 1971-2 CB 337, states, however, that although a gift to a corporation is a gift to its shareholders, the corporation takes title to the gift. Shareholders can use, possess, or enjoy the gift only when the corporation liquidates or declares a dividend—which requires votes by the corporation's directors, at the very least. This lag in time necessary for such voting makes the gift a future interest. The estate argued that no binding authority required the gifts be future interests. Further, the estate cited numerous tax treatises and text books that supported finding gifts to corporations to be gifts of present interests to the shareholders. The estate contended that the debt forgiveness, thus, was an indirect gift to the shareholders, which they could have cashed in immediately by selling their stock at higher prices.

Held: For the IRS. According to *Disston*, 325 US 225, 33 AFTR 857 (1945), taxpayer bears the burden of showing that the gift is not of a future interest. The court found that decedent's estate did not meet the burden. The court reasoned that to allow taxpayers to claim that an interest was a present interest merely because they could sell it at an increased price after it was given as a gift would effectively dissolve the distinctions between present and future interests. The court refused to dissolve such distinctions. The present fair market value (FMV) of a gift, thus, did not make the gift a present interest if it could not be used at the time it was given. Based on this reasoning, the estate was not allowed to claim decedent's gift was a present interest when given. Therefore, it was a future interest and did not qualify for the $10,000 per donee exclusion from gift tax. The estate pointed out that the exclusion would have applied if the gift had been structured in a different way. For example, decedent could have exchanged the land for corporate stock, and then the stock given to the other shareholders. The stock would have been a present interest, thus qualifying for the $10,000 exclusion. Because the gift was not structured in this way, however, the favorable gift tax treatment did not apply.

[Stinson, 82 AFTR2d 98-6944 (ND Ind. 1998).]

Gifts of future interests made within three years of death do not qualify for $3,000 exclusion and are thus included in decedent's gross estate. In August 1980, decedent discovered that she had contracted a fatal illness. In the following month, she listed her residence for sale with a broker. The residence was later sold in 1983 for $62,000. Immediately after listing her home, decedent executed her will and an instrument purporting to transfer as a gift to each of sixteen named individuals a $3,000 present interest in her residence. This instrument was notarized but not recorded or delivered to any of the donees. None of the donees took possession of the residence, and each received $3,000 from decedent's estate by executing a release of his rights in the residence. On the estate tax return, the residence was listed at a value of $75,000, and a deduction of $48,000 was claimed for liens (i.e., the interests given to decedent's donees). The IRS challenged the treatment of the "gifts" as liens and included the entire value of the residence in the gross estate.

Held: For the IRS. As in effect at the time of death, Section 2035 included in gross estate all gifts made within three years of death. Section 2035(b) excluded from this rule any gift to a donee if decedent was not required to file a gift tax return for such year on gifts to that donee under Section 6019(a). Section 2503(b), which defines "taxable gifts," provided for a $3,000 exclusion from taxable gifts only for gifts of present interests. A gift of a present interest in property conveys the present right to use, possess, and enjoy the property (not the mere vesting of legal title). Accordingly, under this standard, the interests that decedent conveyed in her residence were gifts of future interests, in this case rights to share in the sale proceeds of the residence to the extent of $3,000 per donee. Such gifts do not qualify for the $3,000 exclusion, and thus are included in their entirety in decedent's gross estate under Section 2035. The court also held that the value of decedent's residence for estate tax purposes was not affected by the existence of the sixteen fractional interests in the residence held by the donees. Under Section 2035, the interest included in the estate is the interest held by decedent before the transfer-triggering application of Section 2035.

[Babbitt, 87 TC 1270 (1986).]

Tax Court holds that taxpayer is not entitled to annual gift tax exclusion, because no present interest is transferred and blockage discount in valuation is to be applied to each gift separately. Taxpayer set up four separate trusts. Two of the trusts had one beneficiary each, whereas the other two trusts had two beneficiaries each. To each trust, taxpayer transferred property that she had received from her husband's estate. On taxpayer's gift tax return, the gifts were valued at the same amount claimed on her husband's estate tax return. Taxpayer also claimed the annual gift exclusion for six separate gifts. The IRS determined that although the property had not increased in value since the death of taxpayer's husband, the "blockage" discount used to value the property for the estate tax was not appropriate for gift tax purposes. The IRS contended that the blockage discount should be based on six separate transfers, with each transfer's impact on the market being considered independently. The IRS also argued that taxpayer was not entitled to the annual exclusion for the transfers.

Held: For the IRS. The court first examined the question of the blockage discount. A blockage discount is allowed on the postulate that a large block of a certain asset is more difficult to sell than a small block. The IRS has contended that blockage discounts are not appropriate in the gift tax area, because gifts, unlike property passing to an estate as a result of death, are contemplated events that can be manipulated to lessen adverse consequences. The court found, however, that the gift tax regulations contradicted the IRS's position. Regulation § 25.2512-2(e) permits the use of blockage discounts in the valuation of property for gift tax purposes. Taxpayer argued that a discount should be applied to the property on an aggregate basis in order to take into account the time necessary for an orderly liquidation. The IRS, on the other hand, contended that the blockage discount must be applied to each gift separately. On this issue, the court ruled for the IRS.

The court examined a number of prior cases dealing with similar issues, and found that blockage discounts were generally applied to each separate gift rather than to consolidated gifts. The court then looked to the question of the gift tax exclusion. After first noting that taxpayer's position that six separate gifts were made was well supported by the law, the Tax Court then ruled that taxpayer was not entitled to the annual gift tax exclusion, because the gifts did not create present interests in the property. For gift tax purposes, a present interest in property is defined as an unrestricted right to immediate use, possession, or enjoyment of the property. In Fondren, 324 US 18 (1945), the Supreme Court refined this definition by stating that the annual exclusions are available only if the donee receives "the right to substantial economic benefit." When the gift is made in trust, taxpayer may claim the annual exclusion only if three requirements have been met:

1. The trust will receive income.
2. Some of the income will flow to the beneficiary.
3. The income going to the beneficiary can be ascertained.

The court applied these criteria to the present case and found that taxpayer was not entitled to the annual exclusion. At the date of transfer, the beneficiaries had the right to periodic distributions of income; however, the corpora of the trusts in question merely consisted of the gifts. There was no showing that the trust assets would generate income for distribution to the beneficiaries. Taxpayer did not, for example, show that the gifts would generate rental income or, for that matter, any other type of income. Thus, none of the requirements in the Supreme Court definition were met.

[Calder, 85 TC 713 (1985).]

Annual distribution of accumulated income is gift of future interest. Donor established a trust providing for an annual distribution of income earned during the year to beneficiaries living at the time of distribution. Donor claimed the annual exemption on the gift, and the IRS disallowed it, arguing that this was a gift of future interest.

Held: For the IRS. Because the trust did not create a continuing present right to the income as it was generated, it was an accumulation trust, which delays the right of enjoyment of the gift until the date of distribution. Donor therefore had made a gift of a future interest that is ineligible for the annual exclusion.

[Estate of Kolker, 80 TC 1082 (1983).]

Gifts to trust are gifts of future interests for purposes of annual exclusion where trustee-beneficiaries are not required to distribute income and distributions of income require their unanimous consent. In 1979, taxpayer established a trust, naming his three daughters as trustees. The primary beneficiaries were the three daughters, with their husbands and children named as second beneficiaries. Each daughter and her family were given a one-third interest in the trust. Income and distribution of corpus were within the sole discretion of trustees, but unanimous approval was required for any such distributions. The trust agreement did not require that any distribution be made to any beneficiary prior to termination of the trust. Further, the trustees could withhold distributions from a particular beneficiary. Taxpayer claimed use of the Section 2503 annual exclusion for the gift of property to the trust. The IRS disallowed taxpayer's use of the exclusion and argued that because the beneficiaries of the trust held only future interests in both income and principal, there was no transfer of a present interest as required for claiming the exclusion.

Held: For the IRS. Under Section 2502, the exclusion is allowed only for gifts of present interests. Although taxpayer intended that the beneficiaries should receive a present interest in trust income, the fact that all distributions were within the discretion of the trustees and required their unanimous consent made it less than certain that distributions of income would be made. The fact that the trust regularly distributed income was immaterial; it is not the fact of distribution but the right to distribution that is determinative. To show a present income interest in the beneficiaries, taxpayer must prove that:

1. The trust will receive income.
2. Some portion of the income will flow steadily to the beneficiary.
3. The portion of the income flowing out to the beneficiary can be ascertained.

Factors (2) and (3) were not shown in this case.

[Ritland, TC Memo. (P-H) ¶ 86,298, 51 TCM (CCH) 1458 (1986).]

Non-income-producing stock is not eligible for annual exclusion. Taxpayer received certain stock in a statutory merger, subject to a two-year restriction against selling, pledging, or otherwise disposing of the shares, except by gift, where the donee also agrees to the restrictions. No dividends on the stock were payable or anticipated. Taxpayer made a gift of the stock to his children. The IRS ruled that this is a gift of a future interest, which is not eligible for the annual exclusion either for the stock value or for an income interest in the stock.

[Rev. Rul. 76-360, 1976-2 CB 298.]

Extension of income interest in trust is gift of future interest for which Section 2503(b) annual exclusion is unavailable. Taxpayer created an irrevocable trust with income going to the beneficiary for five years, valued the interest actuarially and claimed the annual exclusion thereof. A year later he extended the term of the income interest for ten years and sought to treat it in the same manner. The IRS ruled that the later transfer constitutes the gift of a future interest, for which the annual exclusion is unavailable.

[Rev. Rul. 76-179, 1976-1 CB 290.]

Too many restrictions turned partnership interest gift into future interest. A widow's gifts of limited partnership interests to various family members and trusts did not qualify for the annual gift tax exclusion, even though title vested in the donees, because the gifts were of future (not present) interests in property, according to this ruling. Taxpayer was a childless widow who, in 1993 and 1994, made gifts of varying percentages of her limited partnership interest to thirty-five family members and seven trusts (which she had established for the benefit of her seven minor grandnieces and grandnephews). Taxpayer had formed the partnership on December 22, 1992, and on December 31, 1992, had contributed a 95 percent interest in a leased industrial building worth $2.5 million to the partnership in exchange for a 90.6 percent limited partnership interest. That same day, she had also transferred the remaining 5 percent interest in the building to her solely owned S corporation, which immediately transferred that interest to the partnership in exchange for a 5 percent general partnership interest. The other 4.4 percent of the partnership was transferred to certain family members in exchange for another building that taxpayer had previously given to them. The partnership agreement gave the general partner sole discretion over income distributions and the right to retain funds "for any reason whatsoever." Also, no limited partnership interest other than the donor's was assignable, and limited partners could withdraw or be substituted only under certain circumstances. After giving away her remaining partnership interest to the thirty-five family members and trusts in 1993 and 1994, the family members held a 95 percent limited partnership interest and the S corporation owned the 5 percent general partnership interest. Taxpayer claimed that the 1993 and 1994 gifts were excludable from the gift tax under Section 2503(b) as gifts of up to $10,000 of present interests in property. The IRS, however, found that the gifts did not qualify for the exclusion. Section 2503(b) and Regulation § 25.2503-3 provide that the annual gift tax exclusion applies only to gifts of present, not future, interests in property. A future interest is generally an interest—whether vested or contingent—whose use, possession, or enjoyment is restricted to begin at some time in the future.

Because of the agreement's restrictions on the limited partners' right to income and other prohibitions on their interests, the IRS determined that taxpayer's 1993 and 1994 transfers were gifts of future, not present, interests. Central to its decision was the general partner's right to retain funds for any reason whatsoever. The IRS found that this gave the general partner authority to retain funds for nonbusiness reasons and showed that the limited partners were not assured a present right to the income. In addition, the IRS noted that the agreement prohibited any limited partner other than the donor from assigning a limited partnership interest. Further, the IRS stated that the agreement's proviso that the limited partners could join to liquidate the partnership in certain circumstances did not change the character of their interests from future to present. Thus, although vested, the interests transferred lacked the immediate economic benefit of a present interest and were gifts of future interests only. As such, the gifts did not qualify for the Section 2503(b) annual gift tax exclusion.

[Tech. Adv. Mem. 9751003.]

¶ 17.04 *CRUMMEY* POWERS

Withdrawal right of contingent beneficiaries is present interest. Before her death, decedent contributed property worth $70,000 in each of two years to an irrevocable trust with seven beneficiaries—her two children (who were the primary beneficiaries) and her five minor grandchildren (who had contingent remainder interests). Each beneficiary had the right to withdraw an amount up to the gift tax annual exclusion within fifteen days of contributions by decedent. The IRS disallowed gift tax exclusions for the grandchildren on the ground that their *Crummey* withdrawal powers were not gifts of present interests.

    Held: For taxpayer. The correct test of a *Crummey* power is the beneficiaries' legal right to demand payment from the trustee, rather than the likelihood of actually receiving present enjoyment of the property. In this case, each grandchild had the right to withdraw corpus, and the trustees would be unable to legally resist such demands. The good health of decedent's children did not mean that it was impossible for them to predecease her (in which case the grandchildren's interests would vest). There was no agreement or understanding among the parties that the grandchildren would not exercise their withdrawal rights. Moreover, decedent intended to benefit her grandchildren.

[Estate of Cristofani, 97 TC 74 (1991), acq. in result in part, 1992-1 CB 1.]

Tax Court approves use of *Crummey* powers for contingent beneficiaries. Decedent set up an irrevocable trust to which she transferred a commercial building. The primary trust beneficiaries were decedent's adult son and daughter. The trust also had sixteen contingent remainder beneficiaries, who were the daughter's children and grandchildren and the son's wife and children. Under the terms of the trust, for a thirty-day period following a transfer of property to the trust, both the primary and the contingent beneficiaries were given the right to demand immediate distribution to them of trust property up to the $10,000 gift tax annual exclusion amount (*Crummey* powers). The beneficiaries all received notices of their rights, but none of them exercised his or her right to demand a distribution from the trust. Annual exclusions were claimed for the interests of the sixteen contingent beneficiaries. The IRS denied these annual exclusions.

    Held: For taxpayer. Citing Estate of Cristofani, 97 TC 74 (1991), the court held that the contingent beneficiaries' interests qualified for sixteen annual exclusions. The fact that none of the beneficiaries exercised their rights to demand distribution did not imply that the beneficiaries had agreed with decedent-grantor not to do so, and the court refused to infer any understanding.

[Estate of Kohlsaat, 73 TCM 2732, RIA TC Memo. ¶ 97,212 (1997).]

Multiple *Crummey* powers possessed by sole beneficiary are to be aggregated for purpose of annual gift tax exclusion. In situation (1), an irrevocable trust was created, with one beneficiary receiving the trust income for life and another receiving the remainder interest. The life-income beneficiary was given the right to withdraw up to $5,000 from each contribution to the trust. The trustee was to give notice to this beneficiary upon receipt of a contribution, and the beneficiary maintained the right to withdraw for a sixty-day period following receipt of notice. The beneficiary was given notice twice, but failed to exercise his rights on both occasions. In situation (2), the grantor established two separately administered irrevocable trusts on the same terms and conditions as those of the trust in situation (1). During the year, the grantor made one contribution to each of the trusts, but the life-income beneficiary did not exercise his right to withdraw. The issues raised were whether a taxable gift resulted from the successive lapses of two noncumulative powers to withdraw trust corpus within one calendar year, and, if so, what the amount of such a gift would be.

The IRS ruled that in both situations, the life-income beneficiary was deemed to have made a gift as a result of the lapse of his right to withdraw. The amount taxable was the aggregate amount subject to the power to withdraw that exceeds the $5,000 exemption provided in Section 2514(e), less the value of the beneficiary's retained interest in that amount. Section 2514(c) defines a "general power of appointment" as a power exercisable in favor of the possessor of the power, the possessor's estate, the possessor's creditors, or the creditors of the possessor's estate. Under Section 2514(b), the exercise or release of a general power of appointment created after October 21, 1942, is treated as a transfer of property by the individual possessing such power for federal gift tax purposes.

Under Section 2514(e), the lapse of a general power of appointment created after October 21, 1942, like the release of such a power, results in a transfer for federal gift tax purposes. With respect to any calendar year, however, this rule applies only to the extent that the value of the property subject to the lapsed powers exceeds the greater of $5,000 or 5 percent of the aggregate value of the assets ("the five and five exemption") on which the exercise of the lapsed powers could have been performed. The language of Section 2514(e) states that the exemption applies "with respect to the lapse of powers during any calendar year." Thus, under these circumstances, only one five-and-five exemption under Section 2514(e) is available for all lapses of powers of appointment in a single trust in a calendar year, and the beneficiary is entitled to only one $5,000 exemption per calendar year.

[Rev. Rul. 85-88, 1985-2 CB 201.]

Year-end demand right does not qualify transfer for annual exclusion. Shortly before the end of the taxable year, donor created and funded an irrevocable trust for the benefit of the donee, with the remainder going to another. The trust instrument gave the donee the power to demand distribution of $3,000 per year. However, neither the donor nor the trustee informed the donee of the demand right before it had lapsed. The transfer was not a present interest eligible for the annual exclusion under Section 2503, because the donee lacked knowledge of the existence of the power and thus had no opportunity to exercise it before it lapsed.

[Rev. Rul. 81-7, 1981-1 CB 474.]

Waiver of *Crummey* notice precludes use of annual exclusion. In this ruling, the IRS took the position that a waiver by a holder of a power of withdrawal of the right to receive notification regarding his or her right of withdrawal as to future gifts prevents the holder from having the immediate use, possession, and enjoyment of the property (i.e., a present interest in the property). Therefore, according to the IRS, the transfer does not qualify for the gift tax annual exclusion under Section 2503(b). The ruling concludes that a donee must have current notice of any gift in order for that gift to be a transfer of a present interest that qualifies for the gift tax annual exclusion.

[Tech. Adv. Mem. 9532001.]

IRS tightens availability of annual gift tax exclusion for *Crummey* powers. A donor created three trusts—A, B, and C. Trust A provided that its income was to be distributed at least annually to the donor's children (a son and a daughter). Under Trust B, the income was to be distributed to the husband's sister, and, upon his sister's death, if either of the donors were still alive, the income would be distributed in equal shares to the donor's children. Trust C provided that the income was to be distributed annually to the donor's children. All of the trusts were to terminate upon the death of the surviving spouse. At that time, the principal would be distributed in equal shares to the children or their descendants if they did not survive. If no descendant survived when the trust terminated, the principal would be distributed one fourth to one donor's sister, one fourth in equal shares to two brothers, and the remainder to charitable organizations selected by the trustee. Each trust provided fourteen *Crummey* powers—one for each of the grantor's children, grandchildren, son-in-law, daughter-in-law, sister, and the wife's brothers. All of these powers contained typical *Crummey* language providing for notice to the *Crummey* power holders and giving the trustee the authority to satisfy the right of withdrawal, either with cash or in kind. The donors filed gift tax returns and listed a gift to each of the fourteen individuals with the *Crummey* power as qualifying for the annual gift tax exclusion.

In reviewing this situation, the IRS declared that the critical issue was whether the beneficiaries ever expected that any of them other than the children would enjoy any bona fide rights in the trust. The IRS looked to the case of Deal, 29 TC 730 (1958), involving a sale of property by a mother to her children, in which the children gave a series of demand notes for the purchase price. The notes were canceled by the mother one-by-one in an amount equal to the annual gift tax exclusion. The Tax Court concluded that the donor was not entitled to the annual exclusion, because there was never an intention to enforce the notes. The entire value of the transaction was held to be a taxable gift in the year of the purported sale. The IRS applied the *Deal* rationale to the trusts. The IRS concluded that the children would not exercise their *Crummey* rights, because both of them had future rights in the trust under the life insurance policy. None of the other twelve beneficiaries had ever exercised their withdrawal rights, despite numerous opportunities to do so. Because the IRS could find no reason for their failure to exercise these rights, it found that the beneficiaries had reached a prior understanding with the donors that the withdrawal rights would never be exercised. The IRS analyzed whether each of the trust beneficiaries had a sufficient interest in the trust property for the annual exclusion to apply. If they did not, the donors should not be able to make transfers of property to the trust and parlay those transfers into the annual exclusion. According to the IRS, the donors intended that the property transferred to the trust would remain there for the ultimate benefit of their children.

If the donors had intended the other twelve family members to receive a pro rata portion of the donated property, they could have transferred the property to them outright or given them rights to income or principal of the trust. Because that was not done, the IRS concluded that it was never intended that the *Crummey* rights conferred on the other twelve beneficiaries would be exercised. The purpose in adding these other family members as beneficiaries was simply to avoid the federal gift tax through a proliferation of annual gift tax exclusions. According to the IRS, the children were the sole donees for purposes of the Section 2503(b) annual exclusion with respect to transfers made to the trust.

[Tech. Adv. Mem. 9045002.]

Gift with thirty-day withdrawal right is covered by exclusion. Taxpayer created an irrevocable trust, under the terms of which the trustee was required to inform the beneficiary promptly in writing of any contribution to the trust and of her right to withdraw the contribution. The beneficiary had thirty days after receipt of the notice to exercise her right and withdraw the lesser of (1) $10,000 (or $20,000 if, at the time of the contribution, the donor was married), or (2) the total contribution made to the trust. The withdrawal right was not cumulative, so that it would lapse if it was not exercised. With the exception of the withdrawal right, the beneficiary was not entitled to anything until she reached age 60. The withdrawal provision of this trust was designed to avoid Section 2503(b), which provides that the exclusion for the first $10,000 of gifts ($20,000 if the donor's spouse consents to split them) does not apply to gifts of future interests. In Crummey, 397 F2d 82, 68-2 USTC ¶ 12,541, 22 AFTR2d 6023 (9th Cir. 1968), it was held that a beneficiary has a present interest if he is given the power to demand immediate possession and enjoyment of corpus or income. To determine whether the gift is a present or future interest, however, it is necessary to consider not only the terms of the trust but also the circumstances in which the gift was made. If the delivery of property to a trust is accompanied by limitations upon the donee's present enjoyment of the property in the form of conditions, contingencies, or the will of another, either under the terms of the trust or under other circumstances, the interest is a future interest even if the enjoyment is deterred for only a short time. The issue is when enjoyment begins, not when title vests. Although gifts to such trusts are made in contemplation that a beneficiary will not exercise the right of withdrawal, the right must be exercisable, even if the beneficiary is a minor. Here the trustee was required to give prompt notice to the beneficiary of the contributions to the trust. The thirty-day period following the notice was deemed adequate to allow the beneficiary to exercise her right of withdrawal.

Thus, the IRS concluded that an annual exclusion under Section 2503 was available. What constitutes an adequate time to withdraw a contribution has been the subject of several rulings. The thirty-day period was among the shortest periods, if not the shortest, approved by the IRS.

[Priv. Ltr. Rul. 8813019.]

Trust contribution qualifies for annual gift tax exclusion. An individual created an irrevocable trust for the benefit of her husband, son, mother, and aunt. Under the trust agreement, the trustees, in their discretion, could distribute the net income of the trust to a named beneficiary. The grantor's husband was appointed guardian for the benefit of their minor son. Upon the death of the survivor of the husband, son, mother, and aunt, the undistributed income and principal was to be distributed to or for the benefit of the grantor's issue. The trust was to be funded with cash, liquid assets, or income-producing assets. The grantor's son or his guardian had the right to withdraw the value of any gift to the trust within sixty days following receipt of notice of the gift from the trustees or within thirty days of such receipt, if the transfer occurred within sixty days of December 31. The trustees were required to notify the grantor's son or his guardian of any property transferred to the trust, within seven days of the transfer. The withdrawal powers did not apply to property transferred to the trust after November 23 of any year.

Citing Crummey, 397 F2d 82 (9th Cir. 1968), the IRS stated that with the exception of a property transfer to the trust between November 23 and the end of the year, the proposed transfer to the trust would qualify for the annual gift tax exclusion under Section 2503(b).

[Priv. Ltr. Rul. 8712014.]

CHAPTER **18**

Compliance and Procedure

¶ 18.01 FILING OF RETURNS

Taxpayer must prove gift tax return was filed. Decedent conveyed a farm to his daughter in 1977. In 1983, decedent died, and a timely estate tax return was filed that indicated the farm transfer and the fact that no gift tax was paid. The IRS determined that no gift tax return was filed and assessed a deficiency. In 1986, the IRS sent a no-change letter with reference to a gift tax return filed in 1977. The estate argued that the statute of limitations had expired, but the IRS countered that the statute of limitations had not run, because a gift tax return was never filed.

Held: For the IRS. The estate failed to sustain its burden of proving that a gift tax return was filed. Decedent's meticulously kept diaries were not proof that a return was filed. In addition, no canceled check, proof of mailing, or copy of the return was produced. The fact that a no-change letter was (mistakenly) mailed to the estate did not prove that a gift tax return was filed.

[Small, TC Memo. (P-H) ¶ 89,048, 56 TCM (CCH) 1189 (1989).]

¶ 18.02 EXAMINATION OF RETURNS

Successive examinations of gift documents are held not to violate Section 7605. During an estate tax audit, an IRS examiner discovered that in previous years, decedent made a series of gifts to a family member without reporting or paying gift tax. In discussions with the estate's attorney, the IRS examiner proposed a compromise by which the estate would file past returns and report agreed amounts of taxable gift transfers. In subsequent examination proceedings against the donee, the examining agent requested access to the same records previously used to determine the gifts for purposes of assessing gift tax against the estate. The donee, in Tax Court, complained that the second request and examination was improper under Section 7605, which forbids an IRS agent, unless upon authority of a delegated official, from examining the same matters for the same year more than one time.

Held: For the IRS. The facts showed that the documents in question, though perhaps in the custody of the donee, were actually those of the estate. Therefore, multiple examinations were not conducted as to the donee. In addition, the IRS had copies of the books and records in its possession; therefore, it was not clearly shown that the IRS acted upon its second examination in assessing the deficiency complained of by the donee.

[Estate of Slutsky, TC Memo. (P-H) ¶ 83,578, 46 TCM (CCH) 1423 (1983).]

¶ 18.03 REFUND CLAIMS

Informal claim for gift tax refund is allowed. Taxpayer transferred property that, if owned by taxpayer prior to the transfers, would be includable in her gross estate. Taxpayer's ownership of the property, however, was contested at the time, and restoration was sought in state court. During the pendency of the proceedings, the estate filed returns claiming a credit against the estate tax liability for gift taxes paid on several of the contested transfers. The executor also sent to the IRS a letter seeking to avoid any penalty or interest against the estate relating to the gift tax returns and requesting an extension of time to pay gift taxes until a judicial determination was made concerning the validity of the transfers. The executor's affidavit attached to the letter set forth in detail the facts surrounding the gifts and the state court action for restoration of the transferred property. The IRS denied this request, and the executor paid the tax. Subsequent to the filings and tax payments, the state court ruled that decedent did not own the property. Therefore, no estate or gift taxes should have been paid on the transferred property. The district court found that the estate's letter to the IRS and the attached affidavit clearly set forth the facts and the legal basis on which a claim would be made in the event that the transferred property was restored to another claimant. This was sufficient to alert the IRS of the circumstances upon which a claim for refund would be based, whereas the documents adequately stated a legal basis for the claim.

Held: Affirmed for the estate. According to the Sixth Circuit, the IRS was on notice that if the estate lost in state court, there would be no gift tax or estate tax liability. It was sufficient for the estate to advise the IRS of the contingency and the estate's probable position if that contingency occurred. Thus, the claim for refund was not barred, despite the fact that no formal claim was filed within three years of filing the gift tax return or within two years from the payment of the tax.

[Estate of Hale, 876 F2d 1258; 89-2 USTC ¶ 13,810, 63 AFTR2d 89-1576 (6th Cir. 1989).]

IRS, following *Dickman*, offers procedural guidance for indirect gift tax refund claims. Following the Supreme Court's resolution of gift tax treatment of interest-free demand loans in Dickman, 465 US 330 (1984), the IRS issued detailed rules on the appropriate method to be used in obtaining gift tax refunds. If a gift tax return is filed prior to the date of decision, taxpayers are entitled to claim gift tax overpayments attributable to the interest-free loan, but only if the year is one for which a refund claim would otherwise be considered timely filed within the limitation period for refunds allowed under Section 6511. A refund may also be claimed for any demand loan gift that was reported in a previously filed gift tax return if the gift was valued on the basis of a valuation in excess of the valuation determined pursuant to standards established by the IRS in this procedure. However, this allowance is valid only if the year is one for which a refund claim would otherwise be considered timely filed within the limitation period for refunds allowed under Section 6511.

[Rev. Proc. 85-46, 1985-2 CB 507.]

¶ 18.04 EQUITABLE RECOUPMENT

Supreme Court rejects equitable recoupment claim. In 1976, taxpayer paid a gift tax on payments received from her deceased employer's estate, but paid no gift taxes for monies received in 1977. After an audit of her 1976 and 1977 income tax returns, the IRS asserted deficiencies, arguing that the money received was for services rendered and should have been reported as income. Taxpayer petitioned the Tax Court for a redetermination of the deficiencies without raising an equitable recoupment claim for the gift tax paid in 1976. The case was settled in 1983, with the parties agreeing to a stipulated decision that taxpayer owed less tax than the amount asserted in the income tax deficiencies. In 1984, taxpayer filed a district court action for a refund of the gift tax paid in 1976, even though the applicable statute of limitations had run. Taxpayer argued that the suit was timely under the doctrine of equitable recoupment set forth in Bull, 295 US 247 (1935), and that the gift tax liability was eliminated by the earlier Tax Court settlement. The court dismissed the suit for lack of jurisdiction, and the court of appeals reversed.

Held: For the IRS. The district court lacked jurisdiction over the refund claim. In *Bull*, equitable recoupment of estate tax was sought as part of a timely action for refund of income tax, an action over which there was no question of the court's jurisdiction. A party litigating a tax claim in a timely proceeding may seek recoupment of a time-barred, but related and inconsistent, tax growing out of the same transaction. In the instant case, however, taxpayer sought to invoke equitable recoupment in an independent action as the sole basis for jurisdiction, thus distinguishing it from *Bull*. The case did not come within any of the exceptions to the statutory limitations period; therefore, the IRS was immune from suit under settled principles of sovereign immunity.

[Dalm, 494 US 596, 110 S. Ct. 1361, 90-1 USTC ¶ 60,012, 65 AFTR2d 90-1210 (1990).]

¶ 18.05 EQUITABLE ESTOPPEL

Equitable estoppel is denied with respect to increased gift tax liability. During his life, decedent and his wife gave eighteen separate residential properties to their children. The properties were reported as having an aggregate value of $765,590 on the federal gift tax returns of decedent and his wife, and a gift tax of $3,707.70 was reported and paid with each of their returns. The IRS, in a notice dated August 20, 1984, stated that the amount of $138,685.59, including additional gift tax, penalties, and interest, was due. A second notice claimed an amount due of $140,803.69. Taxpayer's counsel wrote to the IRS requesting an explanation of the amount claimed. In January 1985, taxpayer's counsel received a letter handwritten on notepaper from the IRS Problem Resolution Office, which stated that a "tax decrease" had been applied, and that the correct tax was $3,707.00. An adjusted amount of $4,306.25 was paid. Several months after the payment was made, the IRS made additional requests for information (inspection reports), with which taxpayers complied. The IRS issued a notice of deficiency on April 14, 1987. Taxpayers argued equitable estoppel against the IRS with respect to the increased gift tax liability.

   Held: For the IRS. Equitable estoppel can be invoked against the IRS only in cases where taxpayer would otherwise sustain a profound and unconscionable injury in reliance on the IRS's action as to require, in accordance with justice and fair play, that the IRS should be estopped from inflicting that injury. There was no false statement or misleading silence by the IRS. The additional request for information after payment was made should have been sufficient to alert taxpayers that the IRS would be reviewing the inspection reports, with a view toward evaluating their gift tax liability. In addition, there was no reasonable reliance. The note of January 1985 was handwritten on a small piece of paper signed by an individual who never indicated her position or title at the Problem Resolution Office and containing nothing to indicate actual or apparent authority to enter into any sort of "binding resolution." Furthermore, taxpayers suffered no detrimental reliance.

[Bennett, TC Memo. (P-H) ¶ 89,681, 58 TCM (CCH) 1056 (1989), aff'd, 935 F2d 1285 (4th Cir. 1991).]

¶ 18.06 JURY INSTRUCTIONS

Evidence of intent is admissible, but is not mandatory to prove gift. A jury determined that taxpayer fraudulently underpaid gift taxes. Taxpayer sought to set aside the verdict based upon prejudicial error in the jury instructions on the consideration of donative intent. Taxpayer claimed the Regulation § 25.2511-1(g)(1) barred evidence of intent.

   Held: For the IRS. The regulation does not preclude the consideration of donative intent, but merely allows for the application of the gift tax to a gratuitous transfer, without specific proof of such intent. Except for two transfers where ownership rights never passed, ample evidence was presented for a jury to reach the same verdict as in the instant case.

[Heyen, 731 F. Supp. 1488, 90-1 USTC ¶ 60,014, 65 AFTR2d 90-1245 (D. Kan. 1990), aff'd, 945 F2d 359, 68 AFTR2d 91-6044, 91-2 USTC ¶ 60,085 (10th Cir. 1991).]

¶ 18.07   LITIGATION COSTS AND FEES

Legal fees charged to taxpayers, one of whom was attorney rendering services reflected in such fees, are held not fully payable by IRS under Section 7430. Following the filing of a petition in Tax Court contesting the assessment of federal gift taxes, the IRS and taxpayers entered into a stipulated decision that relieved taxpayers from the payment of all asserted tax deficiencies. Taxpayers thereupon moved the court to award attorney fees pursuant to Section 7430 and Tax Court Rule 231. The court held that taxpayers were entitled to litigation costs, but the IRS later objected to the amount of the award on the grounds that one of the taxpayers was a member of the law firm representing taxpayers and that his time devoted to the case was improperly billed as part of the litigation expenses.

Held: For taxpayers, in part. The Tax Court concluded that all of the taxpayers, except for the attorney, met their burden of proof and that an award of attorney fees, subject to statutory limitations, was appropriate. The court disallowed the payment of fees to the attorney on the ground that the attorney was in effect a pro se litigant who, under the rule of Frisch, 87 TC 838 (1986), was not entitled to recover the value of his own services.

[Minahan, 88 TC 516 (1987).]

¶ 18.08   RES JUDICATA AND COLLATERAL ESTOPPEL

Separate income and gift tax determinations may be made for same transaction. Taxpayer transferred real estate to a corporation in which his wife was a shareholder. The IRS determined an income tax deficiency against the wife, and the parties entered into a settlement agreement. Taxpayers argued that the IRS was precluded from subsequently determining gift tax liability for the same transaction and period under Section 6212, res judicata, or collateral estoppel.

Held: For the IRS. Nothing in the statute prohibits the determination of more than one type of tax in connection with the same transaction. In addition, res judicata did not apply, because each tax is a separate and distinct liability, and the parties were not collaterally estopped. Collateral estoppment did not occur because the court entered the parties' agreed decision without considering the merits.

[Towe, RIA TC Memo. ¶ 92,689, 64 TCM (CCH) 1424 (1992).]

PART VI

GENERATION-SKIPPING TRANSFER TAX

CHAPTER **19**

Applying the Transfer Tax

¶ 19.01 TAXABLE TRANSFERS

General power subjects 1974 trust to GST. Decedent's husband died in 1974. His will established a marital trust for decedent with all the income paid to her for life. She also had the right to withdraw up to one half of the principal during her life and a general power of appointment exercisable in her will, as was then required for the marital deduction. If she did not exercise the power, the trust principal was to be distributed to a trust for the husband's grandchildren from a previous marriage. Decedent died in 1987, and the trust was included in her estate under Section 2041. Her will directed the payment of the estate tax generated by the trust, but otherwise specifically declined to exercise the power. The IRS stated that the trust became liable for the generation-skipping transfer (GST) tax when decedent's power lapsed and the remaining property was transferred to the grandchildren's trust. The GST tax is imposed on a trust at the maximum estate tax rate then in effect, multiplied by an "inclusion ratio," each time an interest in a trust passes to or is distributed to a grandchild (or other "skip" person). The inclusion ratio gives effect to the grantor's $1 million GST exemption and may exempt all or a portion of a transfer from the tax. The GST tax does not apply to generation-skipping transfers from a trust that was irrevocable on September 25, 1985. The grandfathering is lost, however, for corpus subsequently "added" to the trust. Furthermore, if a general power of appointment over a trust lapses (or is released or exercised), the portion of the trust that was subject to the power is treated as then "added" to the trust, under Temporary Regulation § 26.2601-1(b)(1)(v)(A). Thus, the property in a trust subject to a general power of appointment held by a surviving spouse that lapses on his or her death is treated as if it were distributed to him or her and then recontributed to the trust, in Temporary Regulation § 26.2601-1(b)(1)(v)(D), Example 1. (By contrast, a special power of appointment, under which the power holder cannot appoint to himself or herself, his or her estate, or the creditors of his or her estate, does not subject the trust to the GST tax.) The marital trust claimed that the regulation was invalid because the statute exempts all transfers from the trust unless established out of corpus "added" to the trust after September 25, 1985. The trust argued that there could not have been an addition when the assets in the trust, after the lapse of the power, were the same as before.

　　Held: For the IRS. The Second Circuit rejected this argument because defining "added" in simple arithmetic terms ignored the principle that a general power of appointment is tantamount to ownership of property for tax purposes. Therefore, decedent, by permitting her power to lapse, was properly treated as if she were the actual grantor of the trust. Although the trust was irrevocable even before there was any GST tax, there was no unfairness in subjecting it to the tax. The effective date provision was intended to rescue taxpayers who were locked into inflexible arrangements in reliance on the pre-existing law. By contrast, decedent's general power of appointment, while enabling the husband to obtain the marital deduction, also provided the flexibility to handle any changes in the law.

[E. Norman Peterson Marital Trust, 78 F3d 795, 77 AFTR2d 96-1184, 96-1 USTC ¶ 60,225 (2d Cir. 1996).]

Parent's death does not move child into next generation after QTIP transfer. Decedent's will created two trusts. The first trust paid decedent's wife $1 million for life, with the remainder going to decedent's grandchild. The second trust was similar, with the remainder interest paid to decedent's child and a contingent remainder paid to the grandchild. Both trusts elected qualified terminable interest property (QTIP) treatment to qualify for the marital deduction. In addition, the $1 million trust made a reverse QTIP election for generation-skipping transfer (GST) tax purposes. Decedent's child predeceased the surviving spouse, and both trusts were distributed to the grandchild. With respect to the $1 million trust, the IRS ruled that the transfer to the grandchild was not a direct skip. Thus, the grandchild did not move into the next generation level. For the other trust, however, the grandchild did move up a generation because no reverse election was made.

[Rev. Rul. 92-26, 1992-1 CB 314.]

Recapitalization is taxable gift for GST tax purposes. An irrevocable generation-skipping trust was created and funded with common stock. Pursuant to a recapitalization plan, the trust stock was exchanged in an E reorganization for new common stock. Immediately before the exchange, the stock was worth $900; after the recapitalization, it was worth $1,000. The exchange of stock by the trust was a taxable gift for purposes of the GST tax, because the recapitalization reduced the value of the grantor's stock and increased the value of the trust's stock.

[Rev. Rul. 89-3, 1989-1 CB 278.]

No income or GST tax on trust partition. When decedent died in 1958, his income interest in a trust—which was created in 1957 by his mother's will—became payable equally to his spouse and their three children. By its terms, the trust would continue until it terminated on the later of the spouse's death or the youngest child's attaining age 35. The trust also provided that if a child died before the trust terminated, that child's share was payable to his or her surviving spouse, and then to his or her issue, per stirpes. No beneficiary was entitled to the trust corpus until the trust terminated, at which time the trustee would distribute one share to each surviving beneficiary and one share, per stirpes, to any deceased beneficiary's issue. The trustee was authorized to make final distributions in kind and equalize the distributed shares with cash or other securities or property. The applicable state law allowed non-pro rata distributions. After the children all reached age 35 and while decedent's spouse was still alive, the trust was divided into three separate trusts for the benefit of each child. The trust's assets, 90 percent of which consisted of a publicly traded company's stock, were divided on a pro rata, or equivalent non-pro rata, basis; 75 percent of each trust's income passed to the respective beneficiaries, and the balance passed to decedent's spouse. The partition terms provided that if one of the children died before termination (on decedent's spouse's death), his or her 75 percent would be paid to his or her surviving spouse—or issue, per stirpes—or if no spouse or issue, to the other trust beneficiaries (decedent's other children and spouse). At termination, the trusts were to be distributed to the beneficiaries, or their issue, per stirpes.

The first question was whether the partition triggered the realization of taxable income or gain or loss. Gains from dealings in property are generally includable in gross income. Regulation § 1.1001-1(a) provides that the gain or loss realized on a property's exchange or its conversion to cash is treated as income or as loss sustained. A partition of joint property, however, is not a taxable disposition where the co-owners sever their interest without gaining new or additional interests. Thus, such a partition does not trigger gain or loss. In the instant case, the IRS ruled that the trust's division into three separate trusts was a partition that did not trigger the realization of income or gain or loss. The IRS distinguished Revenue Ruling 69-486, 1969-2 CB 159, in which it found a trustee's in-kind, non-pro rata distribution of trust property equivalent to a pro rata distribution followed by a taxable exchange. Central to that ruling was the fact that the trustee was not authorized by the trust or local law to make a non-pro rata distribution. In contrast, the trustee in the instant case was authorized to make non-pro rata distributions on the basis of fair market value (FMV), and was not required to make pro rata distributions with respect to each trust asset. The IRS then turned to the GST issue, considering whether the partition caused the original trust to lose its GST tax exemption and triggered GST tax with respect to the three separate trusts. The Section 2601 GST tax is imposed on certain transfers to skip persons—which include individuals two or more generations below the transferor. Taxable GSTs generally include a taxable transfer of a property interest to a skip person, a trust distribution to a skip person, or a termination of a trust interest that leaves only skip persons with an interest in the trust property. Although the trust in the instant case was a generation-skipping trust, it was exempt from the GST tax under Regulation § 26.2601-1(b), that provides an exemption for trusts that were irrevocable on September 25, 1985. The exemption applies, however, only to the extent no additions were made to the irrevocable trust after that date. Further, the exemption is lost if any change in the quality, value, or timing of an interest in the trust is made. Because the trust was irrevocable on September 25, 1985, and no additions were made after that date, it was clearly entitled to the GST tax exemption before the partition. Moreover, by its terms, the partition did not impermissibly modify any beneficial trust interest. Thus, provided there are no future additions, the GST tax exemption would continue to apply to the trust and to any GSTs from the three trusts.

[Priv. Ltr. Rul. 9737017.]

Grandchild not skip person for GST after parent dies. Taxpayer's gifts to her grandchildren were not subject to the GST tax because they moved up one generation after the daughter died, according to the ruling discussed below. Taxpayer's husband died when their daughter was a year old. Ten years later, the daughter was adopted by the deceased husband's sister. The daughter died in 1991, survived by a son and a daughter. Taxpayer remained close to the daughter and the grandchildren and, in 1995, she gave the granddaughter $125,000 in order to buy a house. In taxpayer's will, she bequeathed her tangible personal property to the granddaughter and established her and the grandson as the beneficiaries of a trust consisting of two-thirds of the residuary estate. (There were no other beneficiaries of an older generation.) The GST tax is imposed at the maximum estate tax rate then in effect on transfers to a "skip person." The tax applies when there is a direct transfer to a skip person ("direct skip") or when an interest in a trust passes to or is distributed to a skip person. There is an annual exclusion of $10,000 and a $1 million exemption, which for a trust is given effect through an inclusion ratio. A skip person is an individual who is two or more generations below the generation to which the transferor is assigned. If the individual is a "lineal descendant" (i.e., a lineal descendant of the transferor's grandparent), the generation assignment is made by comparing the number of generations between the transferor's grandparent and the transferor to the number of generations between the grandparent and the individual, according to Section 2651(a)(1). (A similar rule applies to lineal descendants of a spouse's grandparent.) Thus, the grandchild of the transferor's brother and the transferor's grandchild are both skip persons, and a transfer to either of them would be a direct skip.

Under Section 2612(c)(2), there is an exception for a transfer to the children of a predeceased child in determining whether a transfer is a direct skip. Following the death of a transferor's child, that child's children move into the next generation and are no longer skip persons (and the children of grandchildren also move into the next generation). This rule also applies to the child of the transferor's spouse or former spouse. Under Section 2613(a)(2), a trust is a skip person if all interests in the trust are held by skip persons. (A trust is also a skip person if there is no person who has an interest in the trust (e.g., the trust is for afterborn grandchildren) and distributions can be made only to skip persons.) A transfer to such a trust may trigger GST tax. At the same time, the predeceased child exception applies to a transfer to the trust when it is established and to distributions from the trust that are attributable to that transfer under Section 2612(c)(2). Thus, there was no taxable skip when the grandparent established a trust for the child of a deceased child, with income payable to the grandchild for five years and the principal then to be distributed to the grandchild, according to Regulation § 26.2612-1(f), Example 6. (Where the income was first payable to the grandparent's spouse for two years, however, the trust could not be a skip person and the predeceased child exception did not apply, in Example 7.) The IRS was required to decide whether the predeceased child exception applied to taxpayer's 1995 transfer to the granddaughter and to the transfers in her will. If taxpayer's daughter had not been adopted, the answer would have been clear. As a result of the daughter's death in 1991, the granddaughter and the grandson would have moved into the next generation for purposes of determining whether transfers to them were direct skips. Thus, the GST tax would not have applied to the 1995 gift to the granddaughter and to the bequest of tangible personal property to her in taxpayer's will. In addition, the predeceased child exception would have applied to the residuary trust, and transfers to the trust for the grandchildren and distributions to them from the trust would not have been subject to the GST tax. The daughter's adoption complicated matters. Under state law, an adopted child is not a lineal descendant of his or her natural parents for purposes of intestate succession. Standing alone, this terminated the relationship between taxpayer and the daughter and rendered the predeceased child exception inapplicable. Fortunately, under a special provision of state law, adoption by a close relative of the daughter (her father's sister) had no effect on the daughter's relationship with her predeceased father's family. Thus, she remained the daughter of taxpayer's predeceased spouse, and the predeceased child rule applied to her just as if she had not been adopted.

[Priv. Ltr. Rul. 9709015.]

Generation-skipping exemption applied to withdrawal power. A trust grantor's remaining GST tax exemption can be allocated to a gift that was subject to a beneficiary's lapsed $5,000 withdrawal right, according to the ruling discussed below. For income tax purposes, however, the beneficiary is the owner of the portion of the trust to which the withdrawal right applied during the year it was in effect. In 1994, decedent created a life insurance trust. During her life, income and principal were distributable for the maintenance and support of her two nieces and their five children and grandchildren. In addition, each beneficiary had a power, exercisable for thirty-three days following a contribution to the trust, to withdraw one-seventh of the contribution, not to exceed $10,000. (The donor's gift, however, never exceeded $5,000 per donee.) At decedent's death, the remaining principal was to be divided into equal shares for each niece, with each having a power to appoint her share to her descendants by will. The trust was to continue for at least ninety years after decedent's death. Decedent transferred $17,000 to the trust, which the trustee used to purchase a life insurance policy on decedent's life. Decedent died within thirty-three days of the transfer, and the beneficiaries thereafter declined in writing to exercise their withdrawal rights. The beneficiaries' withdrawal rights complied with Crummey, 397 F2d 82, 22 AFTR2d 6023, 68-2 USTC ¶ 12,541 (9th Cir. 1968), therefore establishing seven gift tax exclusions available to decedent for what would otherwise have been nonqualifying gifts of future interests. The estate, however, wanted assurance that decedent's GST tax exemption could be applied to her gift despite the withdrawal rights. Because the nieces did not have general powers of appointment, their trust shares were not includable in their estates. Therefore, if an exemption from GST tax is not available, each time an interest in the trust passes to, or is distributed to, a child or other descendant of a niece (a "skip person") there would be a taxable termination or a taxable distribution subject to GST tax at the then maximum estate tax rate. An annual GST tax exclusion of $10,000 exists, similar to the gift tax exclusion, but it applies only if the skip person is the sole beneficiary of the trust. In addition, however, every individual has a $1 million GST tax exemption. If the exemption is applied against all transfers to a trust, the trust will never be subject to GST tax. Because decedent's trust would continue for at least ninety years, it is almost certain that terminations and distributions would occur, so it was important for the estate to identify the transferor for GST tax purposes and to use the transferor's exemption promptly to cover the gift. If the exemption is applied on a timely filed gift tax return, the value of the transfer against which the exemption is applied is the value of the trust at the date of the gift. Otherwise, the applicable value is the value when the exemption is applied. Since the insurance policy became payable shortly after decedent's transfer, the difference was considerable.

The IRS ruled that decedent was the transferor for GST tax purposes, and her exemption could be applied on a timely filed gift tax return. Generally, under Section 2652, the transferor for GST tax purposes is the last person in whose hands the property was subject to gift or estate tax. Under Section 2514(b), the lapse of a general power of appointment during the life of the power holder ordinarily is a gift. Section 2514(e), however, excepts the lapse of powers, during any year, that do not exceed the greater of $5,000 or 5 percent of the total value of assets out of which the lapsed powers could be satisfied. Since the beneficiaries' *Crummey* powers were within the Section 2514(e) limits and, consequently, the lapse of the powers were not transfers for gift tax purposes, the IRS stated that they were likewise not transfers for GST tax purposes. Therefore, under Section 2642(b), decedent's exemption could be applied to the transfer, valued at only $17,000, on a timely filed gift tax return. For income tax purposes, however, the beneficiaries were the owners of the trust in 1994. Section 678 provides that persons other than the grantor be treated as the owners of any portion of a trust as to which they have the power to vest income or principal in themselves. Since each beneficiary could have withdrawn one seventh of the principal of the trust in 1994, each was the owner of that portion of the trust under Section 678. Consequently, under Section 671, the corresponding percentage of the items of income, deduction, and credit of the trust was reportable by each beneficiary.

[Priv. Ltr. Rul. 9541029.]

Beneficiaries' disclaimers permitted amounts to pass free of GST. Decedent bequeathed the residue of her estate to her grandchildren. The grandchildren and a guardian ad litem for the great-grandchildren disclaimed a portion of the residue based on a formula, so that the maximum that could pass free of GST would pass to the grandchildren. The disclaimed amount passed to decedent's daughter.

The IRS ruled that the disclaimers were qualified disclaimers involving a specific pecuniary amount. The IRS further concluded that the executrix could allocate decedent's $1 million GST exemption to the property bequeathed to the grandchildren that remained after they made the disclaimers. Proper allocation of the exemption would result in no GST on the bequests to the grandchildren.

[Priv. Ltr. Rul. 9203028.]

GST tax is inapplicable where grandchildren's mother dies before transfer and grandchildren have unrestricted right to assets. An individual died in 1988 and left a will executed in 1985. He was suffering from a mental disability on October 22, 1986, that precluded him from changing the disposition of his property. He did not regain his competence prior to his death. The will provided that trusts were to be established for each of his grandchildren living at his death, to be funded with property included in his gross estate. It further provided that if, at the time that his or her trust was to be set apart, a grandchild attained the age at which he or she was entitled to withdraw principal, that grandchild would have an unrestricted right to withdraw the trust corpus and income as of decedent's death. Two of decedent's grandchildren, who were the children of decedent's deceased daughter, exercised their right of withdrawal and attained the age to exercise that right under the terms of the will. The will also provided that a marital trust be established for the benefit of decedent's surviving spouse. It further provided that when the spouse died, the remaining principal was to be divided equally between decedent's two children and the then-living issue of these children. Because one daughter did not survive decedent's spouse, upon the death of the spouse, the share of the marital trust to be held in trust for that daughter was added to the share to be held in trust for the benefit of that daughter's two children.

The IRS stated that the GST tax would not apply to any transfer to or distribution from the grandchildren's trusts, any transfer from the marital trust to the issue trusts upon the death of decedent's surviving spouse or any subsequent distributions from the issue trusts, or any transfer to the issue trusts (or outright to the issue of decedent's daughters) upon the termination of a daughter trust. The IRS also stated that the predeceased child exception provided by Section 2612(c)(2) would apply to any transfer from the marital trust to the issue trusts for the benefit of the grandchildren or to any distribution to them from any issue trust established for their benefit. The IRS further stated that the GST tax would not apply to any transfer to or distribution from either of the grandchildren's trusts established for the benefit of the grandchildren or to any distribution by the executors directly to the grandchildren in accordance with the exercise of the right of withdrawal under the will. The ruling cited below assumes that the aggregate transfers to the grandchildren would not exceed $2 million.

[Priv. Ltr. Rul. 9002029.]

Single QTIP split, followed by reverse QTIP election, is acceptable and trusts are treated as separate trusts for purposes of GST tax. A trust instrument provided that upon the settlor's death, the trust would be divided into a marital trust that would qualify for the estate tax marital deduction as QTIP under Section 2056 and a residuary trust (the family trust). The trust further provided that if the trust created would be partially exempt from the GST tax by reason of an allocation of the GST tax exemption to it, the trustee could, before the allocation, divide the trust into two separate trusts of equal or unequal value to permit allocation of the GST tax exemption solely to one trust that would be entirely exempt from GST tax. The trustee would not make discretionary distributions from the income or principal of the exempt trust to beneficiaries who are nonskip persons, as long as any readily marketable assets remain in trusts other than the exempt trust. The trust further provided that upon division or distribution of an exempt trust and a nonexempt or partially exempt trust, the trustee may allocate property from the exempt trust first to a share from which a generation-skipping transfer is more likely to occur. The trustee wished to divide the QTIP trust into two QTIP trusts, one to be funded with property having an estate tax value equal to the amount of decedent's GST tax exemption that remained after a portion of the exemption was allocated to the family trust. The two QTIP trusts had identical terms. The division of the QTIP trust would be made on a fractional basis. The numerator of the fraction was equal to the amount of decedent's GST tax exemption that remained available after the allocation of a portion thereof to the residuary trust. The denominator was the estate tax value of the QTIP trust prior to division. Each asset in the trust was split between the two QTIP trusts on the basis of this fraction. Similarly, any distribution would be allocated between the two trusts on the basis of this fraction.

The IRS stated that the division of a single QTIP trust into two QTIP trusts for the purpose of making a reverse QTIP election with respect to one of such trusts is permissible under Section 2654(b) when the property transferred to the reverse QTIP trust is fairly representative of the net appreciation or depreciation in the value of all property for such use. The IRS also ruled that the two QTIP trusts existing after the division should be treated as separate trusts for all GST tax provisions in Chapter 13 of the Code.

[Priv. Ltr. Rul. 9002014.]

Disclaimed property qualifies for grandchild exclusion for purposes of GST tax. An individual died on March 2, 1988, survived by a son, three sons of a deceased daughter, a daughter, and the daughter's two daughters. Before her decease, the individual transferred all of her assets to two revocable trusts. The first trust held the balance of her assets and provided specific bequests, including giving a limited partnership interest to the daughter; if the daughter should die, it would pass to the family trust. The balance would be divided into two equal shares: one share would pass to a second family trust for the three grandsons, and the other would pass to the first family trust for her granddaughters. The second trust held her cash and marketable securities and was to be used to pay estate taxes, administrative expenses, and certain bequests. The balance of the second trust was to be distributed one half to the three grandsons and one half to the daughter. The daughter wished to disclaim her interest in the limited partnership to the extent possible to avoid the GST tax. She also wished to disclaim her power over the trusteeship of the first trust. The first family trust would be divided into two shares for each of her daughters. The shares would be divided into an exempt share and a nonexempt share. The exempt share would consist of an amount equal to the then-remaining unused portion of the trustor's GST tax exemption under Section 2631(a). The nonexempt share would be further divided into a grandchild exclusion share for the grandchild exclusion under Section 1433(b)(3) of the Technical and Miscellaneous Revenue Act of 1988 (TAMRA). The daughter's interest in the partnership would pass to the first family trust and be allocated among the various shares of that trust. The amount of property passing to each of the granddaughters was $500,000, that would qualify for the Section 2631 exemption.

The IRS stated that the disclaimed interest by the daughter in the partnership would be a qualified disclaimer under Section 2518. The disclaimer would relate to the greatest percentage of interest in the partnership that could be disclaimed without resulting in a GST tax under Section 2631. The passage of the disclaimed portion of the partnership to the first family trust, plus property from the decedent's first trust, would be a transfer subject to estate tax. The distribution of such property to the first family trust would be a transfer of property to a trust in which all of the interest would be held by skip persons under Section 2613(a)(2)(A). Therefore, the transfer would constitute a direct skip under Section 2612(c). In addition, the transfers to the exempt share trusts for the benefit of the granddaughters would not be subject to the GST tax. Finally, the IRS concluded that the property that passed to the grandchild exclusion trusts for the granddaughters' benefit would not be treated as a direct skip under Section 1433(b)(3) of TAMRA, provided that the $2 million per grandchild exclusion was not exceeded.

[Priv. Ltr. Rul. 8907028.]

Gift and GST taxes handicap sprinkling trust. During the grantor's life, the income of a trust was payable at the trustee's discretion to the grantor's descendants for their health, education, and support. At the grantor's death, half the trust was to be held for the benefit of the grantor's daughter and her descendants and half for the grantor's son and his descendants. At the death of the grantor's daughter, the half preserved for her was to be distributed to her descendants. The same provision applied to the grantor's son. When any property was added to the trust, each descendant had a noncumulative right to withdraw a pro rata share of the addition within thirty days of receiving notice of the addition. If, upon the termination of any power of withdrawal, the person holding the power was deemed to have made a taxable gift for federal gift tax purposes, the power would not lapse until the termination and would not result in a taxable gift.

The IRS determined that when property was added to the trust and the powers of withdrawal lapsed, gifts were made by the holders of the *Crummey*-power. Regulation § 25.2514-1(b)(1) provides that where a beneficiary may appropriate or consume the principal of a trust, he has a power of appointment. When he may do so on behalf of himself, it is a general power. Under Section 2514(e), the lapse of a general power is a transfer of the property subject to the power to the extent that the property exceeds the greater of $5,000 or 5 percent of the aggregate value of the covered property. Because no one beneficiary retains an exclusive lifetime benefit from the trust or a power to control the disposition of the trust at death, each lapse of a power is a completed gift. The IRS concluded that any attempt to value one income beneficiary's interest in property reverting to the trust on lapse of a power of withdrawal would be no more than a guess. Consequently, there was no reduction of the gift for any reversionary interest for purposes of calculating the value of the completed gifts. Also, the IRS deemed invalid the provision in the trust by which the withdrawal rights were declared not to lapse if a gift was found to be made because of the termination. Such a provision was a condition subsequent and was void as contrary to public policy, because its operation would either defeat the gift or otherwise render the examination of returns ineffective. The grandchildren of the grantor were "skip persons" within the meaning of Section 2613(a). Gifts to skip persons are "direct skips" and are subject to the GST tax unless the transfer is to a grandchild of the transferor prior to 1990 and the aggregate transfers from the transferor to a grandchild do not exceed $2 million. However, a transfer in trust is not treated as a transfer to a grandchild. Consequently, contributions to the trust are subject to the GST tax. The value of the transfer that constituted a direct skip is each grandchild's pro rata portion of each contribution.

[Priv. Ltr. Rul. 8901004.]

Direct funding for generation-skipping beneficiaries is excluded from GST tax provisions. An individual executed a will in 1976 and added a codicil to it in 1979. At age 89 in 1985, the individual was adjudged incompetent, and his condition was certified as irreversible. One of the trusts in his will provided distributions to later generations—or generation-skipping beneficiaries. This trust would be funded with either direct funds from the individual's residuary estate or with pour-back funding from his wife's estate. The individual's wife was also adjudged incompetent in 1986, and her condition was certified as irreversible.

The IRS stated that direct funding for the generation-skipping beneficiaries would be excluded from the GST tax provisions under Section 1433(b)(2)(C)(i) of the Tax Reform Act of 1986. The IRS noted that this private ruling is based on the assumption that the individual would not regain competence and dispose of the property before his death. The IRS offered no opinion on the pour-back funding issue.

[Priv. Ltr. Rul. 8734012.]

¶ 19.02 TRANSITION RULES

Distributions to trust are excepted from GST tax. An individual's will, executed on August 3, 1984, provided for the disposition of her property and revoked her prior will and codicils. The individual died on April 4, 1986. The third article of the will created a trust for the benefit of an heir. Under its terms, the heir received an income interest for life, and the remainder interest was bequeathed to several nieces and nephews or their issue, by representation, if the nieces or nephews did not survive the heir. The residue of decedent's estate, under the fourth article of the will, would be paid to the trustees of a second trust. The second trust would be divided into two family trusts. One of these trusts would be further divided into shares to be separately held and administered for the benefit of the nephews and nieces. At issue was whether the distributions from these trusts would be subject to the tax on generation-skipping transfers under Section 2611.

The IRS stated that under Section 1433(b)(2)(A) of the Tax Reform Act of 1986 and Temporary Regulation § 26.2601-1(b)(2), the distributions to the trusts would be excepted from the GST tax provisions of the Code. The IRS noted that the Tax Reform Act of 1986 and the temporary regulations provide that the GST tax does not apply to any generation-skipping transfer occurring on or before October 22, 1986. In addition, it does not apply to any generation-skipping transfer under a will executed before the date of enactment if decedent dies before January 1, 1987.

[Priv. Ltr. Rul. 8905057.]

GST tax is inapplicable to proposed qualified disclaimers. Decedent died testate, survived by his wife, two sons, and six grandchildren. Decedent suffered from a disease affecting his mental functions and, by October 22, 1986, lacked the mental capacity to execute a new will. Under his will, the individual bequeathed a life estate in certain items to his wife, with the remainder passing first to his sons, then per stirpes. The will further provided that certain items of tangible personal property would pass to the sons as tenants in common, with the property passing to the grandchildren if the sons died before decedent. Decedent also bequeathed specific items of tangible personal property to both sons, individually. If both sons died before decedent, the items were to be included in the individual's residuary estate, passing to residuary trusts established under the will to benefit decedent's grandchildren. Decedent also bequeathed the balance of his tangible personal property to his sons in equal shares. If both sons died before decedent, the balance of the tangible property was to pass into the residuary trusts for the benefit of the grandchildren. The sons proposed to make qualified disclaimers of their personal interests in one or more of the tangible personal property items bequeathed to them under the will. The disclaimers would be made within nine months of the date of decedent's death. The disclaimed property would pass under the will either directly to, or in trusts for the benefit of, the individual's grandchildren.

The IRS stated that the GST tax would not be applicable to the proposed qualified disclaimers. The IRS determined that under the provisions of Section 2518, the qualified disclaimers resulted in (1) the disclaimed interests being considered to have passed under the trusts to the individual's grandchildren or (2) the disclaimed interests passed in the form of a direct skip. The IRS noted that the transfers would be considered as having occurred after October 22, 1986, because of the individual's mental disability. Therefore, amendments made to the GST tax by the 1986 Tax Reform Act would be inapplicable to the proposed transfers under Section 1433(b)(2)(C) of the Act. In addition, the transfers would not be subject to the GST tax provisions, because of the retroactive repeal of the provisions by Section 1433(c)(1) of the Act. The IRS did not offer an opinion on whether the proposed disclaimers were qualified.

[Priv. Ltr. Rul. 8815034.]

Transfers from trusts to grandchildren are GSTs, but are eligible for transitional rule obviating transfer tax. An individual died testate in October 1986. The individual's will provided that one half of the residue of the estate was to be distributed to a trust benefiting the decedent's daughter and five of the decedent's grandchildren. One half of the trust corpus, or one fourth of the residue, was to be distributed outright to the decedent's daughter. The remaining trust corpus was to be divided into five equal shares to be held for five separate subtrusts, benefiting each of the five grandchildren. The subtrust beneficiaries were entitled to principal and income from the trust as the trustee deemed necessary for the beneficiaries' upkeep, health, and education until age 25. At age 25, the beneficiaries were entitled to distribution of the principal and any accumulated income. Three of the five grandchildren were at least twenty-five years old, and their shares were distributed upon funding of the trust.

The IRS stated that the transfers in trust for the benefit of the grandchildren were generation-skipping transfers under Section 2611. The transfers to the three grandchildren, age 25 or over, were direct skips. In addition, the transfers to the underage grandchildren were direct skips to trusts, with the interests being held for them by skip persons. The IRS further determined that because the individual died before January 1, 1987, and because the will was executed before October 22, 1986, the transitional rule of Section 1433(b)(2)(B) of the 1986 Tax Reform Act was applicable. Therefore, the transfers to and from the trust were not subject to the Section 2601 tax.

[Priv. Ltr. Rul. 8740017.]

PART VII

TRUSTS AND TRUST ENTITIES

CHAPTER **20**

Taxable Trusts

¶ 20.01 RECOGNITION AND VALIDITY

[1] Legal Sufficiency

Taxpayer is denied deduction for management fee paid to controlled trust. Taxpayer, a dentist, was grantor, sole beneficiary, and cotrustee, with his wife, of a trust. After executing the trust indentures, taxpayer contracted with the trust, by which the trust agreed to manage taxpayer's dental practice in return for a management fee of 60 percent of his gross income. On his 1980 tax return, taxpayer reported $159,091 in gross income from the dental practice; he then deducted a management fee of $95,000 allegedly paid to the trust. On audit, the IRS disallowed the management fee and assessed a deficiency. The Tax Court held for the IRS on the management fee deduction, finding that the fee was never paid to the trust and that the trust device was an invalid anticipatory assignment of income. Taxpayer appealed, arguing that the trust was not an anticipatory assignment of income, because it was not a family trust.

Held: Affirmed for the IRS. The Seventh Circuit noted that in the typical family trust case, a taxpayer's income and property are transferred into a trust controlled by taxpayer; the trust then pays taxpayer's personal expenditures and sometimes returns part of his wages to taxpayer as a management fee. The court stated that although taxpayer did not transfer all his income to the trust and did not require the trust to pay him a fee or salary, the income-splitting effect was similar to that of the typical family trust; that is, the trust declared part of taxpayer's income, and he declared the rest. The court stated that where a taxpayer attempts to shift income to an entity under his unfettered control, the IRS can disregard the form of the transaction. The court also found that the $95,000 management fee was never actually paid. Accordingly, the claimed deduction was denied, and the deficiency was upheld.

[Pfluger, 840 F2d 1379, 61 AFTR2d 88-857, 88-1 USTC ¶ 9221 (7th Cir. 1988), cert. denied, 487 US 1237 (1988).]

Trust's transfer of lease with reversion in grantor is held as impermissible assignment of income. Taxpayer owned certain improved real property in Illinois for use in his construction contracting business. In 1959, he leased the property to his closely held corporation for a term of eleven years at $475 per month. During the following year, 1960, he placed the lease in an accumulation trust for the benefit of his two children. The trust was to last for ten years and one day, after which the lease would revert to taxpayer. The trustee, a commercial bank, expressly disclaimed any and all responsibility for the active management of the property. During the years 1962 through 1964, the trustee collected the rents and reported them as income. The IRS conducted an audit for those taxable years and determined that the rental income should have been taxed in full to taxpayer, not to the trust. At trial, the IRS asserted that the trust transfer was void under the doctrine of assignment of income. Taxpayer contended that the lease transfer was not an assignment of the mere right to receive income, but that it constituted the bona fide transfer of all rights and title to income-producing property for a term of years.

Held: For the IRS. The facts showed that taxpayer merely assigned a stream of income and not the underlying asset itself, because he specifically reserved the right to a revestment of title in the property at the conclusion of the lease term. The court cited the opinion by Justice Holmes in Lucas v. Earl,

281 US 111 (1930), in which the Court viewed a lease in a similar case to be evidence of the manner in which income was to be distributed, and was not itself a recognizable property interest. Because taxpayer did not part with title, the court concluded that there had been an impermissible assignment of income.

[Iber, 409 F2d 1273, 23 AFTR2d 69-1001, 69-1 USTC ¶ 9293 (7th Cir. 1969).]

Transfer of residence to trust is held to be sham. Taxpayers, husband and wife, subscribed to a home-study course and purchased materials with step-by-step instructions designed to enable them to create and to maintain a family trust. They established themselves as the grantors, two of the three trustees, and the sole beneficiaries of the trust, the corpus of which consisted solely of their residence. After the purported transfer of their residence to the trust, taxpayers continued to pay the property tax, the mortgage, and the home insurance; to deduct the property tax and mortgage payments on their personal income tax return; and to use and to enjoy the home in precisely the same manner as before the purported transfer. The IRS thereafter levied upon the residence to satisfy taxpayers' unpaid federal income tax liabilities. The trust then brought a wrongful levy suit against the IRS, arguing that it, not taxpayers, was the legal owner of the real property at issue, and that all federal tax liens and levies upon the residence should therefore have been removed. The IRS contended that the trust was formed by taxpayers as a device to thwart the collection of their unpaid income tax liabilities in question.

Held: For the IRS. The court stated that where trustees have the power to use and dispose of a trust's property as if they owned it, the trust is a sham without legal significance and should be disregarded. The court concluded that the transfer of title to the residence to the trust while taxpayers retained their use and enjoyment of it was a sham transaction. As such, the transaction lacked economic substance, and would not be recognized for tax purposes. Because the trust was void, the court upheld the validity of the IRS's levy.

[Gastineau Equity Trust, 687 F. Supp. 1422, 61 AFTR2d 88-920, 88-1 USTC ¶ 9314 (CD Cal. 1987).]

Family trust lacking economic purpose is disregarded for tax purposes. Taxpayers, husband and wife, were the trustors and trustees of a trust. Their four adult sons were designated as the trust beneficiaries. The trust assets consisted of two parcels of realty, two automobiles, two life insurance policies, and household furnishings and personal items such as clothes and jewelry, all possessions of the husband and wife. No deeds or other documents were ever executed evidencing the transfer of the realty to the trust. The sole source of income for the trust was the personal earnings of the husband, but no income tax returns had been filed on behalf of the trust reflecting that income. Checks for the husband's services, which were paid to the trust, were cashed by the husband and wife, and these funds were then used to pay their personal living expenses. The IRS levied against the property in the trust in order to satisfy unpaid federal taxes owed by the husband. The IRS took the position that the trust was a family trust and a sham. In support of this position, the IRS cited the grantor's failure to deed the real property to the trust, the apparent absence of any distributions of trust income to the beneficiaries, and the use by the trustees of trust funds to pay their living expenses. Taxpayers contended that the IRS wrongfully levied against the property belonging to the trust to satisfy their alleged tax liabilities.

Held: For the IRS. The court stated that it concurred with the IRS that the trust lacked economic reality and should therefore be disregarded for tax purposes. The court stated that the family trust is a time-worn tool of tax avoidance, the legitimacy of which has been repeatedly and overwhelmingly rejected. The court concluded that the IRS properly seized the trust property held in the name of the trust in order to satisfy taxpayers' tax liabilities.

[Schmidt Liberty Trust, 61 AFTR2d 88-318, 88-1 USTC ¶ 9144 (WD Okla. 1987).]

Tax Court strikes down family trust-and-leaseback arrangement under form-over-substance doctrine. Taxpayer and his wife were the owners of a two-story building that they held as tenants-by-the-entirety. The lower floor was used by taxpayer as his medical offices, and the upper floor served as the personal residence of taxpayer and his wife. During 1960, taxpayer transferred the property to a ten-year trust, with the wife serving as trustee and their children named as beneficiaries. In a simultaneous transaction, the wife, acting in her trustee capacity, entered into an agreement by which the trust leased the ground floor to taxpayer for a term equal to the life of the trust in exchange for a monthly rent of $75 while the trustee also rented the upper story to taxpayer for a two-year term at a monthly rent of $350. On his personal federal income tax return for the years 1960 through 1962, taxpayer claimed a business expense deduction for the rental payments. In addition, he reported depreciation on 50 percent of the adjusted basis of the property for the period prior to the trust transfer. The trust, in turn, included the rental payments as income and took full depreciation deductions. The IRS, however, treated the trust transfer as a nullity and assessed deficiencies on the basis of the disallowed deductions. The case was brought to the Tax Court, where the issue, as presented by both parties, was whether the trust was valid under state law.

Held: For the IRS. The Tax Court initially found that state law was irrelevant and that the determinative issue was whether the transaction possessed sufficient economic reality to warrant recognition for federal tax purposes. In applying a "form-over-substance" analysis, the court identified several major factors that led it to conclude that the transaction lacked economic reality:

1. Taxpayer completely dominated the trustee.
2. Taxpayer retained the power to decide whether the property could be sold by the trustee.
3. Taxpayer retained a reversionary interest.
4. The conveyance and leases were never recorded.
5. The property was subject to outstanding mortgage indebtedness that the trust paid out of its rental income, thereby leaving no amounts for distribution to the beneficiaries.
6. Taxpayer and his wife claimed a homestead exemption on the property under state law.

The Tax Court stressed that no one factor should be viewed as determinative of the ultimate issue, and expressly based its holding on a "totality" of all relevant factors. It concluded by finding that the trust should be ignored and that taxpayer's liability for federal income tax should be computed without regard to the 1960 conveyance.

[Furman, 45 TC 360 (1966), aff'd per curiam, 381 F2d 22, 20 AFTR2d 5244, 67-2 USTC ¶ 9589 (5th Cir. 1967).]

IRS rules that state law is determinative as to validity, for tax purposes, of testamentary trust to provide care for decedent's surviving pet. *A*, a resident of State *X*, died testate in 1976. Under the terms of *A*'s will, *A*'s entire property passed to designated individuals, including a residuary legatee, with the exception of a fund established to care for *A*'s pet. The income of the fund, to the extent required, was to be used for the animal's maintenance. Upon the death of the animal, the corpus of the fund was to be distributed to *A*'s heirs, if living, or their descendants. Because the life of an animal is not a proper measuring life in being under the rule against perpetuities in State *X*, the bequest in trust to provide for the care of the animal was void from its inception. Accordingly, because the bequest in trust for the care of the pet was void from its inception, a valid trust was never created for purposes of Section 641. Further, the property passed to the residuary legatee pursuant to the law of State *X*, because no contrary intention appeared in the will, and the income earned on such property is includable in the income of the residuary legatee in the year in which the income is received.

[Rev. Rul. 76-486, 1976-2 CB 192.]

[2] Intent to Create a Trust

Trust created in exchange for dower rights results in taxation of beneficiary on distributions. Following their marriage, taxpayer's parents entered into an agreement in 1914 wherein the mother surrendered her future dower rights in the property of the father in exchange for the father's promise to create a trust for the benefit of taxpayer and her mother. An inter vivos trust was created according to the terms of the 1914 agreement, and income-producing property was transferred to the trustees. Once taxpayer's rights under the trust fully ripened, she received a payment of trust income annually. During 1935, however, a controversy arose between the trustees and income beneficiaries concerning the possible exhaustion of trust principal and the proper construction to be given to the 1914 agreement. The matter was heard and finally adjudicated in state court. As a part of its decree, the state court construed the agreement as creating a fully constituted trust entity for all purposes under state law. From the time taxpayer first received distributions from the trust, she duly reported the amounts in gross income and was taxed thereon. For taxable years 1953 through 1958, however, she ceased reporting the income and was eventually assessed deficiencies by the IRS. In support of her actions, taxpayer alleged that the 1914 agreement did not in fact create a trust, and that the agreement provided only for the creation of a collateral mortgage security arrangement as payment for the mother's release of dower rights. Taxpayer therefore concluded that the payments were inherited nontaxable incidents of property rather than trust income.

    Held: For the IRS. The 1914 agreement created a valid trust, and all payments received by taxpayer were taxable income under Section 662. Looking to the intent of the parties as expressed in the agreement, as well as to the state court's earlier findings, the court concluded that the agreement was unambiguous and therefore could not be construed as a "security arrangement" or other form of "mortgage." The court noted this case was distinguishable from other cases dealing with postmortem will compromises wherein the parties agree to certain payments in lieu of dower rights and, for tax purposes, such payments are considered inherited property. In the instant case, the release of inchoate dower rights for the promise of future payments was not equivalent to a compromise of a present claim to inheritance.

[Hanover Bank, 40 TC 532 (1963), acq. 1964-2 CB 5.]

House transferred to mother by son to avoid attachment by wife is not considered to be held in trust. Decedent died on March 23, 1982. At that time, she still held the deed to a house, that she bequeathed to her son by will. She gained ownership of the house through a series of transactions inspired by her son's fear that his ex-wife would attach the house (their marital residence) if ownership remained in his name. Decedent allowed her son to live in the house after the transfer. Decedent never resided in the house or rented it to anyone. Pursuant to decedent's will, the house was bequeathed to her son and, in the event that he did not survive her, to her daughter. The value of the house was not included in decedent's gross estate. The IRS claimed that under Section 2033, the value of the house should be included in decedent's gross estate.

Held: For the IRS. Decedent owned the house in fee simple absolute at the time of her death. The facts did not support the contention by the estate that the house was held in constructive trust by decedent for her son. Additionally, the estate did not establish that an understanding existed between decedent and her son to establish an express trust. Further, because the son did not purchase the property at the time he transferred it to decedent, no resulting trust arose.

[Estate of Saunders, TC Memo. (P-H) ¶ 89,537, 58 TCM (CCH) 282 (1989).]

Precatory conditions on use of income do not give rise to trust. In her last will and testament, decedent provided for the creation of a trust that was to pay $25,000 annually to taxpayer, who had been decedent's husband. The testamentary trust also expressed in precatory language decedent's wish that taxpayer apply the annual amount to the maintenance of a home for himself and/ or their daughters. By express language, decedent disclaimed any intention of pressing an enforceable obligation upon taxpayer to use the funds in the manner indicated. In addition, the trust was to terminate on taxpayer's death, or earlier if he so elected, with corpus to revert to a separate testamentary trust for the benefit of the daughters. Taxpayer, in reporting trust distributions for federal tax purposes, claimed that the amounts received were nontaxable, because they were subject to a condition that they be used for the purposes specified in the will. The IRS rejected taxpayer's assertion that he was a fiduciary and determined that the amounts were fully taxable, regardless of whether part of the distributions were actually expended for the benefit of the daughters.

Held: For the IRS. The income received from the trust was not subject to a fiduciary duty; therefore, taxpayer must include the entire amount in gross income. The court held that taxpayer's legal argument was without the necessary factual foundation, because the will, by express provision, rebutted the existence of any obligation to expend the income for a certain purpose.

[Osborne, TC Memo. (P-H) ¶ 57,199, 16 TCM (CCH) 905 (1957).]

¶ 20.02 TAXABLE AS ASSOCIATION OR CORPORATION

Ten-year trust is taxable as corporation. The beneficiary of a testamentary trust created a new trust to hold title to the inherited property on the expiration of the original trust. The trust agreement gave the trustees broad management powers and allowed them, with approval of a majority of beneficiaries, to select successor trustees to distribute earnings to beneficiaries at their discretion.

The Tax Court found that the trust was created for the purpose of conducting a business enterprise and was, during each of the years in question, an association taxable as a corporation.

Held: Affirmed for the IRS. For purposes of reclassifying a trust as an association, the courts look to five factors:

1. Continuity of the entity throughout the trust period.
2. Centralized management.
3. Continuity of the trust uninterrupted by death among the beneficial owners.
4. Transferral method of beneficial interests.
5. Personal liability limitation of participants in respect of property involved in the undertaking.

The court ruled that the trust possessed four of the five attributes. Because the instrument granted power to a surviving trustee to appoint a successor from among the beneficiaries, the trust was a continuing entity. Among the broad powers of centralized management were "full and complete management and control of all of said property" by the trustees. The continuity of the trust was not to be interrupted by the death of any beneficial owners. In addition, the trust agreement provided for a transferral method of beneficial interests, with the provision that such transfer be made upon notice to the other beneficiaries. Finally, as demonstrated by the large profits made through the trust's business activities, the primary purpose of the trust was business activity rather than orderly liquidation.

[Cooper, 262 F2d 530, 3 AFTR2d 354, 59-1 USTC ¶ 9154 (10th Cir. 1958), cert. denied, 359 US 944 (1959).]

Testamentary trust is not corporation, because of lack of associates engaging in business for profit. Decedent in his will established a testamentary trust to which most of his property, including his business, was transferred. Under the trust, his wife, children, and grandchildren were to share income interests. Three of his children were named trustees and were charged with maintaining the trust's assets, including decedent's business, that they were to "operate so long as it was profitable to do so." After decedent's death in 1964, the trustees operated the company and managed, invested, and reinvested the trust's assets. They made distributions of income and principal in accordance with decedent's detailed instructions. These instructions generally required that one third of the trust's income be paid to decedent's wife and that the balance be distributed to his three children (or their surviving issue). The trustees were also granted (1) the power to distribute additional income to decedent's wife for her needs and (2) broad powers to pay additional income or to invade corpus in the event of a beneficiary's serious illness. The trust was to terminate when decedent's youngest living grandchild turned age 21, and it was to distribute its assets equally to the grandchildren. The trustees met informally: No votes were taken, and no minutes were kept at these meetings. There were no governing bylaws, and no certificates of beneficial interest in the trust were ever issued. Although the will was silent on whether such interests were transferable, it is clear from the will that decedent intended that only his blood relatives share in the trust's income and assets. The IRS determined that the trust was a corporation and taxed a trust distribution to taxpayer as a dividend.

Held: For taxpayer. The two distinguishing characteristics between a trust and a corporation are (1) associates and (2) an objective to conduct business and divide the gains therefrom. Unless a trust has both of these factors, it is not taxed as a corporation. Here the trust did not have associates and thus was not a corporation. There was no planned or common effort among the beneficiaries to combine for conducting business. As beneficiaries, they possessed no control over or any right to participate in trust affairs. In addition, they could not vote or appoint the trustees. The beneficiaries neither created nor contributed to the trust; their interests in the trust were not transferable; and only a few of them participated in trust affairs. Accordingly, they could not be treated as associates. The trust therefore was not an association.

[Bedell, 86 TC 1207 (1986), acq. 1987-1 CB 1.]

IRS provides detailed analysis illustrating trust taxable as corporation. *D*, an individual taxpayer, created an arrangement that he named "The *D* Family Estate (A Trust)" and referred to as a "pure trust," an "equity trust," or "constitutional trust" (hereinafter referred to as the Family Estate). Taxpayer transferred to the Family Estate substantially all of his real and personal property, including his sole proprietorship retail clothing establishment, in exchange for certificates representing all of the "units of beneficial interest" in the Family Estate issued under the terms of the governing instrument. *D*, his wife, and his son were named "trustees" of the Family Estate. After transferring the property to the Family Estate, *D* retained one half of the units of beneficial interest and assigned the remaining units equally to his wife and son. Such units of beneficial interest, evidenced by certificates, are described in the governing instrument as "transferable." Considering the governing instrument as a whole, it appears that a certificate holder may, without the consent of other certificate holders or "trustees," transfer his entire interest in the Family Estate by sale, exchange, or otherwise. The governing instrument states that the Family Estate shall continue for a period of twenty years unless the "trustees" unanimously determine to terminate it at an earlier date. It is further provided that the death, insolvency, or bankruptcy of any certificate holder, or the transfer of his units of beneficial interest in the Family Estate by gift, devise, or descent, shall not operate as a dissolution of the Family Estate, or in any manner affect the Family Estate or its operations or mode of business. The governing instrument provides that affirmative action, except for early termination of the arrangement, may be tolerated only upon a majority vote of the "trustees." The "trustees," in whom the property of the Family Estate is vested, are authorized to enter into and conduct any imaginable business or enterprise under the name of "*D* Family Estate (A Trust)." The "trustees" are to be guided by the governing instrument and their own resolutions as recorded in the minutes. Thus, under the authority inherent in the governing instrument, the "trustees" have the power to make distributions to holders of units of beneficial interest. The governing instrument of the Family Estate specifically provides that the "trustees" "shall continue in business, conserve the property, commercialize the resources, extend any established line of business in industry or investment," and engage in any business activity whatsoever.

The IRS concluded that based on all relevant authorities, the *D* Family Estate possessed a preponderance of corporate characteristics over noncorporate characteristics, and that under Section 7701, it is an association taxable as a corporation, rather than as a trust, for federal income tax purposes.

[Rev. Rul. 75-258, 1975-2 CB 503.]

Each grantor bank in common trust is to be treated as owner of its portion of trust. The IRS's advice was requested as to whether, in the case of a trust established under New York State law by several savings banks as their medium for certain security transactions, the grantor banks should take as their own the deductions attributable to the trust. The banks entered into a trust agreement with a trust company in order to fulfill the requirements of a New York law enabling banks to make certain investments. Under the provisions of the trust instrument, the trustee acquired as part of the trust corpus certain mortgages and issued certificates of participating interest to each grantor bank.

The IRS ruled that since the trust could not vary the investment portfolio of the trust, the trust would not be considered an association taxable as a corporation. Noting that the interests in the income of the trust, including capital gains, were reserved to the grantors in proportion to their respective contributions, the IRS also ruled that under the provisions of Section 677(a), each grantor bank would be treated as the owner of an aliquot portion of the trust. In addition, each grantor bank would be so treated under the provisions of Section 674(a), because the beneficial enjoyment of the corpus and the income therefrom was subject to a power of disposition in each bank as to its proportionate interest. Each bank's power of disposition exists by reason of a power to assign that was expressly reserved in the governing instrument and also by New York State law ruling that grantors cannot create a spendthrift trust with respect to reserved interests, but necessarily retain a power to convey them or to cause them to be reached by persons to whom they are under legal obligation. Because each bank was an owner of a portion of the trust, all income, deductions, and credits attributable thereto would be treated as those of that bank under Section 671.

[Rev. Rul. 61-175, 1961-2 CB 128.]

Trust authorized to lease interests in oil and gas operations is not taxable as association. The corpus of the trust under consideration in the instant ruling consisted solely of "nonworking interests," such as oil and gas royalties, oil payments, and similar participations in hydrocarbons. The powers granted to the trustees did not extend beyond those necessary to the incidental preservation of the trust property, the collection of the income therefrom, the payment of expenses, and the disbursement of the net proceeds of the trust to the beneficial owners. The trustees may sell or deal with assets of the trust only upon authorization in writing by all of the beneficial owners. Furthermore, the trustees had no discretion in the matter of investment, reinvestment, accumulation, or distribution of the trust net income. Trusts of this type are held to be strict investment trusts. It was proposed to include in the trust corpus certain mineral fee interests, that would be acquired subject to an existing oil and gas lease, and other similar interests that would be leased by the trustees if and when the opportunity presented itself. The so-called mineral fee interests represent fee simple title to the minerals in place. The owner of such an interest is privileged either to exploit the minerals himself or to lease the same to a company operating for that purpose. The owner of a mineral fee interest that has been leased for oil and gas purposes is not charged with any of the cost or burdens of developing or operating the property. Where mineral fee interests are included in the trust corpus, and, under the trust agreement, the trustees do not have authority to exploit the mineral by developing and operating the property, but may only, with approval in writing of a particular contract by all the owners of beneficial interest, lease to an operating company for such purpose, and the income from such interest constitutes a royalty, the inclusion of the mineral fee interests in the trust corpus does not, in itself, result in the trust being treated as an association taxable as a corporation. Accordingly, the IRS ruled that the inclusion of mineral fee interests in the corpus of the trust does not result in the trust being treated as an association taxable as a corporation.

[Rev. Rul. 57-112, 1957-1 CB 494.]

Revocable trust, marital accumulation trust, and marital income trust are trusts, not associations taxable as corporations. A sole grantor created a fully revocable and amendable trust. The grantor was engaged in the oil and gas business. Under the terms of the revocable trust, a marital accumulation trust and a marital income trust were required to be created upon the death of the original grantor. The trustee was authorized to carry on the grantor's oil and gas activities and planned to continue a management contract with a subchapter S corporation, which had managed the oil and gas properties during the grantor's lifetime. The terms of the revocable trust called for the grantor's daughter to become the sole trustee upon the death of the grantor. The daughter also was to be the sole trustee for each marital trust. The sole beneficiary of each of the trusts was the grantor's wife. Under the terms of the revocable trust, the residue of the trust estate was to be distributed between the marital trusts.

The IRS stated that the revocable trust, the marital accumulation trust, and the marital income trust were trusts, not associations taxable as corporations. The IRS applied the factors found in Curt Teich Trust No. One, 25 TC 884 (1956), acq. 1956-2 CB 8; Elm St. Realty Trust, 76 TC 803 (1981), acq. 1981-2 CB 1; and Estate of Harry Bedell, Sr., Trust, 86 TC 1220 (1986), acq. in result, 1987-2 CB 1, in determining that the beneficiaries of a trust were not considered to be associates in a joint enterprise for profit.

[Priv. Ltr. Rul. 8842043.]

¶ 20.03 TRUST CLASSIFICATION

[1] Generally

Trust created to provide perpetual care is complex trust. The grantor created a trust for the purpose of providing perpetual care for cemetery lots owned by the grantor and located in the trustee's cemetery. During the tax year in question, the trust had total income of $544 and total expenses of $487. The $57 surplus was retained by the cemetery to meet extraordinary expenses, such as structural repairs to a mausoleum.

Held: For the IRS. The trust did not qualify as a "simple" trust under Section 642(b), and therefore was entitled to an exemption of $100 rather than the $300 claimed on its tax return. Section 642(b) provides that a simple trust must be required by its governing instrument to distribute all of its income currently. Because the trust agreement specifically authorized the trustee "to apply the surplus of income, if any, to the improvement and embellishment of said lots," as the trustee did in fact do, the trust agreement did not require that all of the trust's income be applied to the lots as it accrued. Furthermore, the court held that the result was not changed by Regulation § 1.651(a)-2(a), which provides that retention of income for a reasonable reserve to keep trust corpus intact, such as a depreciation reserve, does not prevent a trust from being a simple trust. In this case, the accumulations were maintained to fulfill the trust's purpose rather than to keep the trust corpus intact.

[Clark Trust, 49 TC 456 (1968).]

Partnerships comprising charitable remainder trusts are classified as partnerships. An entity operated an educational organization and, in order to facilitate contributions to support its educational and charitable activities, acted as the trustee of several charitable remainder trusts. The entity invested the trust assets separately in accordance with the separate investment objectives. In order to accomplish more efficient investment management, the entity proposed to cause the trusts to form three general partnerships investing in stocks, bonds, and cash equivalents, respectively. To accomplish the formation of the three partnerships, the trusts were to contribute their assets to a partnership with appropriate investment objectives. In exchange for the contribution of trust assets to the three partnerships, each trust would receive units of interest in the appropriate partnership. Therefore, the entity would be able to commingle and jointly invest the trust assets. The terms of the partnership agreements were identical, except for the investment objectives, and the units were not transferable by any partner. The entity, as trustee, however, could cause the trust's assets to be withdrawn from the partnership. The agreements and the entities were to be subject to the Uniform Partnership Act. The IRS stated that each of the three partnerships should be classified as partnerships for federal income tax purposes. Therefore, formation of the partnerships would not establish entities subject to federal income tax separate from the trusts that were to be the partners.

[Priv. Ltr. Rul. 8847003.]

Trust that merely holds title is not trust. An entity's general partner was a limited partnership whose general partners were corporations. Thus, the IRS conditioned the instant ruling, stating that the corporations must have substantial assets that can be reached by the second-tier partnership's creditors. Two of the general partners of the first-tier partnership transferred mortgaged land to two trusts. The trustee did not have the usual responsibility to protect and conserve the trust property. The trustee's only duty was to make the mortgage payments out of recent proceeds. The trust settlors, who were also the beneficiaries, planned to sell part of their interests in the trust to the second-tier partnership.

The IRS ruled that an entity formed under a state's version of the Uniform Limited Partnership Act will be treated as a partnership for tax purposes. The IRS stated that the trust would not be treated as a partnership or as a taxable trust. The IRS added that the trustee must file a notice of fiduciary relationship under Section 6903.

[Priv. Ltr. Rul. 8346089.]

[2] Bankruptcy Proceedings

Bankruptcy trust is taxable as trust. A fund was established under a plan for the reorganization of a bankrupt firm. The creditors' committee elected a disbursing agent who had the right to make appropriate distributions, invest moneys in the fund, increase the fund by protecting the firm's and the creditors' rights, and retain investigators. The plan was also governed under an agreement between the agent and the debtors. The IRS stated that the disbursing agent was a trustee and that the fund was a taxable trust under Section 641. The IRS relied on Revenue Ruling 69-300, 1969-1 CB 167, to reach its conclusion.

[Priv. Ltr. Rul. 8524052.]

Funds created as result of bankruptcy do not constitute trusts. A corporation filed a petition in bankruptcy. The court appointed a trustee to operate the business and manage the property of the corporation. The company was reorganized and continued under a new name, and several funds were set up to settle accounts with the company's creditors. The income on these funds was retained by the funds, either individually or as a group. The trustee may invest the funds only as permitted under the court's order.

The IRS stated that the trustee qualifies as a fiduciary under Section 7701(a)(6) and that the funds do not constitute trusts, because the trustee's duties toward them are generally ministerial. The IRS also stated that the company's income would not include interest on the funds.

[Priv. Ltr. Rul. 8340026.]

Funds held under bankruptcy plan are not trust. A subsidiary and its parent filed for bankruptcy. They proposed a plan for disbursing their assets, and a disbursing agent was named by the bankruptcy court. The assets were placed in an interest-bearing fund. Before the fund could be distributed, it earned $750,000.

The IRS stated that under Section 337 of the Bankruptcy Act (which defines the role of a "disbursing agent") and Revenue Ruling 71-119, 1971 CB 163, the interest-bearing fund is not "property held in trust" within the meaning of Section 641(a). Consequently, no fiduciary income tax return need be filed by the disbursing agent under Section 6012.

[Priv. Ltr. Rul. 8012024.]

[3] Corporate Liquidations

Corporation acting as fiduciary is not taxable on distributions to beneficiaries. Three stockholders of a corporation on the verge of liquidation formed a new corporation and conveyed bare legal title in certain real property to the new corporation as trustee. The trust agreement provided for the distribution of net income from the trust property to the three shareholders as trust beneficiaries after the trustee had performed its enumerated duties of rent collection and property preservation. The three stockholders simultaneously formed a partnership to carry on the business of the old corporation, and the partnership leased the trust property to a third party. The corporation did not conduct any business other than management of the property. Taxpayer, as trustee of an express trust, claimed the right to deduct the net income distributed to the beneficiaries from its receipts. The IRS argued that the corporation was taxable on the income, on the ground there was no valid trust.

Held: For taxpayer. The mere collection and transmittal of the rents, with such incidental activities as negotiating with tenants and keeping the property in repair, do not require taxpayer to be engaged in business any more than would have been the case if an unrelated fiduciary had done the same. Further, there was no showing that a valid trust existed under local law. Accordingly, taxpayer, as trustee, was not taxable on the income currently distributed to the beneficiaries.

[Caswal Corp., TC Memo. (P-H) ¶ 60,143, 19 TCM (CCH) 757 (1960).]

IRS rules on liquidating trust involving nonsalable notes. Pursuant to a plan of complete liquidation, corporation X entered into an agreement to sell all of its operating assets to Y, an unrelated corporation. Assets that were not susceptible of distribution in kind of shareholders or marketable at a fair price within the twelve-month period from the date of the adoption of the plan of liquidation, and any assets needed to provide for actual or contingent liabilities, were transferred to a trust established under state law for the benefit of the shareholders of X corporation. The trust agreement provided that the trust was organized for the purpose of administering, liquidating, and distributing the trust corpus, and that the trust was not empowered or authorized to carry on any profit-making business. All assets of the trust were to be distributed, and the trust was to terminate as soon as practicable following liquidation of substantially all of the known assets of the trust and the satisfaction of all known probable transferee liabilities of the beneficiaries. Among the assets transferred to the trust were two notes and related mortgages from corporation Y due ten years from the date of the sale of X's assets to Y. At the time the notes were transferred to the trust, they were not salable at or near their face value, for the following reasons:

1. The interest rates on the notes were substantially below the market rate for obligations of this type.
2. The obligor had no personal liability on the notes.
3. The notes were of a high-risk nature, because the properties securing them were special-purpose buildings not suitable for general occupancy.

However, the trustees planned to sell the notes as soon as market conditions permitted them to dispose of the notes at or near their face value. The large number of shareholders made it impractical to distribute the notes and the mortgages directly to the shareholders.

The IRS analyzed Regulation § 301.7701-4(d) and concluded that the transfer of the notes to the trust, with the possibility that they may remain in the trust until maturity, should be considered neither an unreasonable prolongation of the trust nor a business activity indicating that the declared purpose of liquidation has been lost or abandoned. The use of business skill and judgment awaiting a favorable opportunity for sale of the notes, and, in the absence of such opportunity, the collection of the installments of principal and interest due on the notes, would not convert the liquidation into a business enterprise. The facts disclosed that the primary purpose of the trust was the liquidation of the assets transferred to it, and is activities were reasonably necessary to, and consistent with, the accomplishment of such purpose. Accordingly, if the trust operated in accordance with the terms of the trust agreement, it should be not an association taxable as a corporation, but a liquidating trust within the meaning of Regulation § 301.7701-4(d).

[Rev. Rul. 75-379, 1975-2 CB 505.]

Holders of beneficial units in liquidating trust are trust's owners. A liquidating corporation intended to sell all of its assets except its mineral properties. The corporation would place the mineral properties in a trust for the benefit of its shareholders. The shareholders would receive beneficial units in the trust equal to their shares in the corporation on the funding date. The trustee must sell the properties and collect income on them pending their sale. The sale proceeds would be distributed to the trust's beneficiaries. The IRS stated that the holders of the beneficial units in the trust would be taxed under the grantor trust rules as the owners of the trust's corpus and income.

[Priv. Ltr. Rul. 8351101.]

[4] Investment Trusts

Organization formed to hold title to property is trust. *A*, *B*, and *C*, owners of a commercial building and the land on which it was situated, established a trust that provided that a bank, as trustee, was to oversee the daily operations of the property, distribute trust income, and conserve the property. As beneficiaries, *A*, *B*, and *C* had the right to approve all agreements entered into by the trustee and, in addition, were personally liable for the trust's debts.

The IRS ruled that the arrangement was a trust for federal income tax purposes and concluded that *A*, *B*, and *C* were the owners of the trust and were taxable on its income. Generally, an arrangement is treated as a trust under the Code if it can be shown that the purpose of the arrangement is to vest in trustees the responsibility for the protection and conservation of property for beneficiaries who cannot share in the discharge of this responsibility. It is distinguished from the arrangement in Revenue Ruling 78-371, 1978-2 CB 344, that was taxable as a corporation because the trustees were empowered to sell, raze, lease, or mortgage the trusted property.

[Rev. Rul. 79-77, 1979-1 CB 448.]

IRS details tax status of investment trust. The trust, whose corpus consisted of a portfolio of municipal obligations, was formed to provide its investors with continuing tax-free income over a reasonable period of time. It was to terminate upon the maturity, redemption, sale, or other disposition of the last obligation held thereunder, but in no event was the trust to extend beyond December 31, 2023. The trust could be terminated under certain circumstances if the value of the trust decreased to less than $2 million, and was required to be terminated if the value of the trust decreased to less than $1 million. In order to protect its investors from early termination of the trust as a result of bond issuers exercising the privilege of redeeming outstanding high-interest-rate bonds from the proceeds of newly issued lower-interest-rate bonds, the trust agreement permitted limited reinvestment of certain funds under specified limited conditions during the first twenty years of the trust's existence. Reinvestment was permitted only of funds derived from the redemption by the issuing municipality of municipal obligations prior to maturity, and was limited to municipal obligations maturing no later than the last maturity date of the municipal obligations originally deposited in the trust. The original corpus consisted solely of bonds rated at least "medium grade" by specified bond-rating organizations, and reinvestment was further limited to new offerings of municipal obligations that were similarly rated. Funds derived from early redemption were distributed to certificate holders, unless, within twenty days of receiving such funds, the trustee made a commitment to reinvest them.

Based upon these facts, and in view of Regulation §§ 301.7701-2(a)(2) and 301.7701-4(c), the IRS determined that the existence of a power to sell trust assets does not give rise to a power to vary the investment. Rather, it is the ability to substitute new investments, and the power to reinvest, that would require an investment trust to be classified as an association. In addition, a power to vary the investment of the certificate holders exists where there is a managerial power under the trust instrument that enables a trust to take advantage of variations in the market to improve the investment of the investors. Therefore, in the instant case, the power in the trust agreement permitting reinvestment of the proceeds of redemptions over which the trust has no control, was a managerial power that enabled the trust to take advantage of variations in the market to improve the investment of the investors. It therefore was a power to vary the investment of the certificate holders within the meaning of Regulation § 301.7701-4(c). Accordingly, the IRS concluded that the trust in the instant case should be classified as an association taxable as a corporation for federal income tax purposes.

[Rev. Rul. 78-149, 1978-1 CB 448.]

Four common trust funds qualify as common trust fund. A bank maintained two common trust funds. Each fund was limited to specific investments, and its permissible investments differed from those of the other fund. The bank proposed to establish two more funds. Each of the new funds also was to be limited to specific investments, which would differ from those of the other funds. Participants in the original funds would receive proportional units of participation in the new funds, and they would receive cash for fractional units. All of the funds would be maintained for the collective investment of money contributed by the bank in its capacity as fiduciary of any estate or trust.

In two similar rulings, the IRS stated that the funds would qualify as common trust funds under Section 584(a). The cashing-out of the fractional units of participation, the IRS stated, would constitute a withdrawal under Section 584(e). Except for these cash-outs, the IRS determined that no gain or loss would be realized on the transactions. The IRS concluded that any new fund created by the bank under the same terms as the other funds within a year would qualify as a common trust fund.

[Priv. Ltr. Ruls. 8902006, 8902007.]

Corporation's transfer of oil and gas income interests to trusts results in shareholder-owned grantor trusts. A publicly held oil and gas corporation created two trusts. The company transferred to the trusts income interests carved out of oil and gas properties. In exchange for the income interests, the trusts issued ownership units equal to the number of outstanding shares in the corporation. The corporation then assigned the trust units to a trustee for the benefit of its shareholders. Each shareholder was issued one beneficial unit in each trust for each share of stock owned.

The IRS stated in technical advice that the trusts are to be classified as fixed investment trusts. The IRS determined that because there is no power to vary the investments in the trusts, they would be treated as trusts for tax purposes. The IRS further determined that the trust unit owners, not the corporation, should be regarded as the settlors of the trusts and that the trusts should be treated as grantor trusts.

[Tech. Adv. Mem. 8412003.]

[5] Litigation Settlements

Payments of contested liability to trust are not deductible by cash-basis payor where claimant was neither party to, nor aware of, trust. Partnership A, in which taxpayer was a partner, entered into a joint venture arrangement with X. Under this agreement, A agreed to contribute funds, upon X's invoice, to drill the acreage X contributed to the venture. Believing that X had breached this agreement, A did not contribute funds invoiced by X. Consequently, X sued A for breach of contract. While litigation was pending, A formed a trust with an independent bank as trustee to which A paid amounts equal to the claims made by X. X was not a party to this trust, nor was he aware of its existence. A deducted amounts paid to the trust as if they were paid to X. The litigation was settled with a payment by A to X. A did not have to resort to the funds held by the trust. The trust's funds and interest income thereon were returned to A. On audit, the IRS challenged the claimed deduction.

Held: For the IRS. The payments to the trust were not deductible by A or its partners under Section 461(f) of the Code and Regulation § 1.461-2(c)(1)(ii). This regulation allows a deduction of payments to certain trusts by analogy to escrow arrangements. The regulation was held to be valid insofar as it required that the claimant be a party to the trust agreement.

[Rosenthal, 11 Cl. Ct. 165, 58 AFTR2d 86-6125, 86-2 USTC ¶ 9776 (1986).]

Income from trust owned by United States is tax-free. Pursuant to a court-approved settlement, the United States established a trust to pay for the medical expenses of an individual who was injured at a federally operated medical facility. Under the terms of the settlement and trust agreement, the trust's net income and its corpus would be distributed in payment of the individual's medical expenses to the extent necessary. In addition, any net income in excess of incurred medical expenses would be accumulated and added to corpus. Upon the death of the individual, the remaining corpus and accumulated net income would revert to the United States.

The IRS ruled that because any remaining corpus and accumulated net income would revert to the United States, the United States was considered to be the owner of the entire trust under Section 667(a)(2), and because the United States is not subject to federal income tax, the trust's income would not be taxable. This is so regardless of whether the trust income is distributed to the individual beneficiary or is accumulated. In addition, any distributions made to the individual would be excludable from the individual's gross income under Section 104(a)(2), because they would be in settlement of the individual's tort claim.

[Rev. Rul. 77-230, 1977-2 CB 214.]

Settlement fund deposited with U.S. District Court is not trust. Pursuant to a settlement agreement, a corporation deposited a sum of money with a federal district court for the purpose of paying claims made against it. These claims arose under an action brought in that court by shareholders of the corporation, who alleged misstatements and omissions in registration statements filed by the defendant corporation pursuant to the Securities Act of 1933. The court issued a final judgment and appointed a special master to administer the fund and take all ministerial steps necessary to effect the settlement.

Neither the court nor the master had title to the settlement fund, that was to be distributed to the claimants on a pro rata basis after payment of administration expenses. During the holding period, the sum would earn income. The court and master wished to know whether the settlement fund was "property held in trust" within the meaning of Section 641(a), and whether one or the other must file Form 1041, the fiduciary income tax return. The IRS ruled that the settlement fund is not a trust under Section 641(a), nor are the court and special master "fiduciaries" within the meaning of Section 7701(a)(6). Therefore, no fiduciary income tax return need be filed.

[Rev. Rul. 71-119, 1971-1 CB 163.]

Settlement fund is not trust. A bank sold commercial paper issued by its parent corporation to several purchasers. The corporation defaulted, and the purchasers brought a class action suit against both parties. The bank sold its assets and created a bank fund under the control of a conservator. The corporation filed for bankruptcy. In settlement of the suits filed against the bank, the conservator organized a fund to make distributions to the purchasers. A dispute arose between the bankruptcy trustee of the corporation and the committee managing the fund over the terms of the settlement. In 1985, however, the trustee and the conservator made final payments to the fund. The fund held the balance of the undistributed principal and interest and was awaiting a final court order authorizing a distribution to the purchasers. After the distribution, the purchasers were to receive slightly less than 100 percent of the principal amount of the commercial paper held by them before the default.

Citing Revenue Ruling 71-119, 1971-1 CB 163, the IRS stated that the fund was not a trust within the meaning of Section 641(a). The IRS also declared that the members of the fund committee were not fiduciaries within the meaning of Section 7701(a)(6). Accordingly, the IRS stated, the fund was not subject to Section 6012 and was not required to file an income tax return.

[Priv. Ltr. Rul. 8611013.]

Interest on settlement fund is not income. Several wrongful death or personal injury actions arising out of a fire were settled. The settlement agreement provided for a fund to be established to receive the settlement money and additional money that would be contributed as other suits were settled. The administrator of the trust could disburse funds only by leave of the court, and the funds could be invested only in short-term U.S. government securities.

The IRS stated that the fund was not a trust held for the purpose of protecting or conserving its contents, and that the administrator did not have the ordinary duties of a trustee. The IRS concluded that the administrator did not have to report interest from the fund as income under Section 641(a).

[Priv. Ltr. Rul. 8417023.]

[6] Trusts As S Corporation Shareholders

IRS rules on retroactive effect of state court order reforming trust to be QSST. The IRS ruled that a state court order, which retroactively reforms a trust to meet the requirements of a qualified subchapter S trust (QSST), does not have retroactive effect for purposes of determining the trust's eligibility to be a shareholder of an S corporation. The IRS will not follow Flitcroft, 328 F2d 449 (9th Cir. 1964).

Rev. Rul. 93-79, 1993-2 CB 269.

IRS rules on separate share of trust as QSST. The IRS ruled that a substantially separate and independent share of a trust, within the meaning of Section 663(c), is not a qualified subchapter S trust (QSST) if there is a remote possibility that the corpus of the trust will be distributed during the lifetime of the current income beneficiary to someone other than that beneficiary. The IRS also held that if a shareholder inadvertently causes a termination of an S corporation by transferring stock to a trust that does not meet the definition of "QSST," relief may be requested under Section 1362(f) and the regulations thereunder.

[Rev. Rul. 93-31, 1993-1 CB 186.]

QSST rules override trust law for sales of S corporation stock. The IRS ruled that if a QSST sells stock in an S corporation, the beneficiary must recognize gain or loss, even if local trust law allocates the gain or loss to corpus rather than to income. The ruling states that the trust sold "all or part" of its stock in the S corporation. The IRS thus emphasized that the result would be the same, regardless of whether the trust continued to own an interest in the S corporation or disposed of its entire interest in the stock sale. The QSST is a Subpart E trust only with respect to the S stock, not as to the other assets. Thus, the consideration received for sale of the stock would not be "owned" by the beneficiary. The narrow issue is whether the Subpart E status terminated just before or just after the sale. The ruling concluded that the gain on the sale was Subpart E income.

[Rev. Rul. 92-84, 1992-2 CB 216.]

Trust language that permits distribution of corpus to persons other than beneficiary results in denial of QSST status. A trust held shares of an S corporation. C and D were the successive income beneficiaries. The trust instrument provided that corpus could be distributed only on the termination of the trust, but if the trust no longer held S stock, the trust could terminate and distribute assets to C and D or to their issue. Section 1361(d)(3)(A)(iv) indicates that a trust is not a QSST unless it provides that on the termination of the trust during the life of the current income beneficiary, the trust must distribute all of its assets to that beneficiary. That requirement was not met in this case, because the trust could terminate during C's lifetime, and the assets could be distributed to C, D, or their issue. Thus, the trust's terms did not ensure that C would be the only distributee of trust assets during C's lifetime. Accordingly, the trust was not a QSST, and the subchapter S election was invalid.

[Rev. Rul. 89-55, 1989-1 CB 268.]

Treatment of split-dollar arrangement between S corporation and trust. A and B, husband and wife, wanted to establish a split-dollar life insurance arrangement between their wholly owned S corporation and a trust created by the husband for their children and grandchildren. The policy acquired by the trust was a survivorship life policy on A and B. As part of the transaction, the husband would transfer enough S stock to the wife so that each would hold in a revocable trust a 50 percent interest in the corporation. On the death of the first to die, that spouse's 50 percent interest would pass to a trust for the surviving spouse. The survivor would make a qualified subchapter S trust (QSST) election under Section 1361(d)(2) so that the trust would be a permitted S shareholder.

The IRS concluded that the surviving spouse's execution of a QSST election would not cause the attribution of incidents of ownership in the insurance policy to the spouse so as to cause inclusion of the proceeds in the spouse's estate under Section 2042. (Regulation § 20.2042-1(c)(6) was cited.) The IRS, however, expressed no opinion as to the tax consequences of the transaction under Section 7872, relating to below-market loans.

Priv. Ltr. Rul. 9348009.

Trusts with *Crummey* powers are eligible S shareholders. A grantor set up trusts to benefit each of his eight children. The trusts provided that the trustee must notify the beneficiary whenever the grantor made a distribution of assets to the trust, and, within a certain period after that notice, the beneficiary could withdraw the assets (the *Crummey* power). A gift of assets to a beneficiary accompanied with these powers is a present interest and thus is eligible for the gift tax exclusion. None of the beneficiaries exercised their withdrawal powers, and the donated assets remained in the trusts. Income was to be distributed quarterly, or as needed, to the beneficiaries until their deaths, at which time the principal and any accrued income was to be distributed in accordance with the beneficiaries' wills. The assets in the trusts were shares of a corporation wishing to elect subchapter S status. One of the permissible shareholders of an S corporation is a grantor trust. Under Section 1362(c)(2)(A)(i), such a trust qualifies if all of it is treated under the grantor trust rules as owned by an individual who is a citizen or resident of the United States. The grantor trust rules provide that a grantor who is treated as the owner of any portion of the trust must include all of the tax items of the trust in his or her individual return. Section 675 provides that the grantor is treated as the owner of any portion of a trust if, under the terms of the trust or its operation, administrative control is exercised primarily for the benefit of the grantor rather than the beneficiary. Under Section 677, the grantor is treated as the owner if the trust income may be:

1. Distributed to the grantor or the grantor's spouse
2. Held or accumulated for future distribution to the grantor or the grantor's spouse
3. Applied to the payment of premiums on policies of insurance on the life of the grantor or his spouse

Amounts paid or distributed for the support or maintenance of a beneficiary whom the grantor is obligated to support are considered under Section 677(b) to be paid and taxed to the grantor. Under Section 678, a person other than the grantor is the owner of the trust if the person (1) has a power exercisable solely by himself to vest principal or income in himself or (2) has previously partially released this power and retains enough control so that he would be the owner if he were the grantor. In this case, each beneficiary had the power to vest in himself the principal of each of their trusts. When they failed to exercise this power, the funds were held in trust for them only, with the income to be distributed to them. Thus, the beneficiaries were the trust owners, not the grantor. As individual owners of trusts, the trusts were eligible shareholders of an S corporation, and the corporation could elect subchapter S status.

[Priv. Ltr. Rul. 9009010.]

[7] Qualified Personal Residence Trusts

Fair market rent allows grantor to remain when trust ends. Qualified personal residence trusts (QPRTs) included parcels of real estate and outbuildings adjoining a personal residence in this ruling. At the termination of the trusts, the grantor can continue to reside on the property, while excluding it from her estate, by leasing it at FMV. The grantor resided on an estate in an affluent area where other properties were of comparable size. She set up two QPRTs, each with an undivided 50 percent interest in the property. The property transferred included the house in which she lived with the underlying real estate, four outbuildings, including a caretaker's residence and a pool building, and two adjacent parcels of real estate. The trusts were identical except that one had a three-year term and the other a five-year term. At the expiration of each trust, its interest in the property would pass outright to taxpayer's issue if she is then alive. Otherwise, the interest will pass as provided in her will, or to a trust she establishes, or to her estate. During the term of each trust, taxpayer has the right to enter into a lease of the property held by the trust, effective on the termination of the trust, at a fair market rental. Apart from this, the interests may not be transferred directly or indirectly to the grantor, the grantor's spouse, or an entity controlled by the grantor's spouse. Section 2702 sets up special rules for valuing transfers to trusts for the benefit of close family members when the grantor retains an interest in the trust. Generally, the grantor's retained interest in such a trust is valued at zero unless it is a qualified interest or certain tangible property. (A qualified interest must be a qualified annuity interest, a qualified unitrust interest, or a qualified remainder interest.) Thus, the transfer of securities to a trust in which the grantor reserves the right to income for a term of years is valued as if the grantor's retained interest had a zero value. Under Section 2702(a)(3)(A)(ii), these rules do not apply to a personal residence trust, so the grantor's gift is reduced by the value of the retained interest, as determined using prescribed annuity tables. To qualify, the trust's property must consist of a residence to be used as a personal residence by persons holding term interests in the trust. (Thus, two spouses with interests in the same residence may transfer their interests to the same trust, but only the spouses may have term interests in the trust.) In addition, a personal residence trust may hold the proceeds for damage to, or destruction or involuntary conversion of, the residence, if these must be reinvested in a new residence within two years; and a *qualified* personal residence trust may hold cash required for expenses, or to purchase a residence or make improvements, and insurance policies on the residence. The residence of a term holder must be his or her principal residence or one other residence (applying the definitions in Sections 1034 and 280A(d)(1) but without attributing occupancy under Section 280A(d)(2)), according to Regulation § 25.2702-5(c)(2)(i). The interest transferred may be an undivided interest in a residence that otherwise qualifies. A personal residence may include appurtenant structures used by the term holder for residential purposes and adjacent land not in excess of that which is reasonably appropriate for residential purposes, taking into account the residence's size and location, under Regulation § 25.2702-5(c)(2)(ii). (Household furnishings and other personal property, however, may not be included.)

Here, the IRS decided that the interests transferred qualified as a personal residence. All the land and structures were used for residential purposes and the combined size of the three parcels was comparable to that of other residential properties in the area. The IRS also addressed the consequences of the grantor's leasing one or both of the undivided interests after the termination of a trust. Section 2036(a) includes in the gross estate the value of property transferred by a decedent (other than by a bona fide sale for full consideration) if decedent retains the possession or enjoyment of the property. Thus, the donor's continued occupancy of a transferred residence rent free until his death resulted in the inclusion of the property in his estate, in *Revenue Ruling* 70-155, 1970-1 CB 189. There was no inclusion, however, when a decedent and his spouse transferred a farm to their children and leased it at a FMV rent, in *Estate of Barlow*, 55 TC 666 (1971). Even though decedent ceased paying rent after two years because of medical problems and the children did not evict him, the obligation to pay the rent at the time of the transfer and the absence of an agreement (express or implied) that it would not be enforced, negated the retention of the possession or enjoyment of the property. Applying *Barlow*, the IRS concluded that, if the grantor survived the term of a trust, the interest held by the trust would not be included in her estate, even if she had exercised her right to lease the interest at a fair market rental and was living on the property at her death.

[Priv. Ltr. Rul. 9714025.]

Final regulations on QPRTs. The IRS has issued final regulations permitting the reformation of a personal residence trust (PRT) or qualified personal residence trust (QPRT) to comply with the applicable requirements for such trusts. The final regulations also provide that the governing instrument of a PRT or QPRT must prohibit the sale of the residence held in the trust to the grantor, the grantor's spouse, or an entity controlled by the grantor or the grantor's spouse. If the grantor dies before the end of the retained trust term, the final regulations do permit the distribution (for no consideration) of the residence to any person (including the grantor's estate) pursuant to (1) the terms of the trust, or (2) the exercise of a power retained by the grantor under the terms of the trust. The final regulations also permit an outright distribution (for no consideration) of the residence to the grantor's spouse after the end of the retained term pursuant to the express terms of the trust.

[TD 8743, 1998-7 IRB 26.]

CHAPTER 21

Taxation of Grantors and Grantor Trusts

¶ 21.01 GRANTOR TRUST DEFINED

[1] Generally

Life tenant is taxable on undistributed income of "trust" that she controls. In 1946, taxpayer received by testamentary disposition a life estate in her deceased husband's property. Decedent's will provided that taxpayer would possess the right to consume corpus "as may be required by her for her personal support and maintenance, the reasonableness thereof to be determined by her." The remainder was to be paid over to the parties' children. During 1955 and 1956, taxpayer received and reported income distributions that in both years were considerably less than the net distributable income of the estate. The IRS, on examining taxpayer's returns, assessed deficiencies, on the theory that all of the distributable income was taxable to her.

Held: Affirmed for the IRS. Under Section 678(a) of the grantor trust rules, a person other than the grantor may be treated as the owner of any portion of a trust with respect to which such person has a power exercisable solely by himself to vest the corpus or the income therefrom in himself. In the instant case, the will did not create a trust, and no trust was created, in fact, at any time. Even had a trust been created, Section 678(a) would nevertheless cause the entire amount of trust earnings to be taxed to taxpayer. The fact that taxpayer took less than the available distributable income, or the fact that the will permitted her to make "reasonable" withdrawals of income, were held to be immaterial in determining taxpayer's liability for tax. Thus, the full amount was properly includable in gross income.

[Koffman, 300 F2d 176, 9 AFTR2d 995, 62-1 USTC ¶ 9326 (6th Cir. 1962).]

Beneficiaries are taxable on income, despite attempts to show lack of intent to make trust transfers. During 1954, taxpayers established a trust under Illinois state law for the benefit of their three minor children. The trust corpus consisted of various oil and gas royalty interests. By the terms of the trust instrument, taxpayers named themselves trustees, with the power to pay income and principal to the beneficiaries "as may be necessary" for their education, comfort, and support. Taxpayers possessed the further power to accumulate all undistributed income and principal until each beneficiary reached age 25, at which time the trust would end and all trust property would be paid to the beneficiaries. The instrument also provided that the beneficiaries, or their guardians, could terminate the trust at any time and compel a full distribution of principal and accumulated income. In its income tax return for 1955, the trust reported "net trust income" of $34,202, and in 1956 it reported "net income" of $30,346. In each return, the amount was treated as a "deduction for distributions to beneficiaries," resulting in no reported taxable income. The minor beneficiaries reported the amounts on their personal returns for the same years. The facts showed, however, that the beneficiaries did not actually receive these amounts, and that they were instead accumulated by the trust. Accordingly, the IRS issued notices of deficiency disallowing the distribution deductions and taxing the trust on its income. Taxpayers, as trustees, asserted that the trust was not taxable on the income, advancing two arguments. First, they contended that as donors, they lacked the intention of creating a trust in the original conveyances, and that therefore the transfers should be viewed as vesting absolute title in the children, with taxpayers serving as agents to manage the property on behalf of the beneficiaries. Their second position was that the trust term giving the beneficiaries a right of termination vested full title in such beneficiaries and that the trust transfers were, in effect, outright gifts. In support of this position, taxpayers cited certain gift tax decisions that construed a termination power as tantamount to the transfer of a present interest. In holding that the trust was fully taxable on all income received in the taxable year, the Tax Court rejected the argument that no trust had, in fact, been created, and concluded that the grantors had clearly intended to create a trust. By the very fact of conveying property in trust, subject to a detailed trust instrument whereby title to the property was to vest expressly in the trustees, the Tax Court found that they manifested sufficient intent to create a trust for their children. The court also rejected the theory that an absolute conveyance of title was accomplished as a result of granting the beneficiaries a power of termination. It concluded that gift tax law had no bearing on questions of trust taxation and that the trust itself was taxable on its income, regardless of any unexercised power granted to the beneficiaries.

Held: Reversed for taxpayers. Applying the grantor trust rules in Section 678, the Seventh Circuit determined that the beneficiaries should have been treated as the owners of trust income, because each became vested with the present and fully exercisable right to use all or a part of the trust property simply by making a demand for payment. The court noted that the trust provision for placing the power in the hands of a guardian was not dispositive of the issues, because under state law, such appointment was a "routine" matter in which the federal government had no interest. The necessity of such "routine steps" would have no bearing upon the fundamental question of the legal right of the beneficiaries to terminate the trust. Thus, the court found that each of the beneficiaries became vested with a present right to use all of the property on demand, and, consequently, that they should be treated as the owners thereof under Section 678.

[Brehm Trust, 285 F2d 102, 7 AFTR2d 347, 61-1 USTC ¶ 9151 (7th Cir. 1960).]

Trust funded with demand loan is grantor trust. Taxpayer created a trust for his children's benefit and funded it with $100 and a demand loan with a balance of at least $100,000. Taxpayer had a security interest in the Eurodollar accounts purchased by the trust with the loan proceeds. The IRS argued that the interest income was taxpayer's.

Held: For the IRS. The trust is a grantor trust because taxpayer's ability to demand repayment of the loan enables him to maintain control over the beneficial enjoyment of the trust.

[Kushner, TC Memo. ¶ 91,026, 61 TCM (CCH) 1716 (1991), aff'd without published op., 955 F2d 41 (4th Cir. 1992).]

Trust and grantor are same for replacement property purposes. Taxpayer's property was involuntarily converted into money, and taxpayer's grantor trust purchased replacement property. Under Section 1033(a)(2)(A), the owner of property that is involuntarily converted into money may purchase qualifying replacement property and elect to defer the gain from the conversion. In that event, the gain is recognized only to the extent that the amount realized exceeds the cost of the replacement property. Qualified replacement property is property that is similar or related, in service or in use, to the converted property. If a trust is a grantor trust under Section 671, the grantor is still treated as the owner of the trust assets for income tax purposes. As a result, the grantor includes as income all items of trust income.

In the instant ruling, because taxpayer was treated as the owner of the trust, replacement of the condemned property with the trust was equivalent to taxpayer purchasing the replacement property directly. In reaching its conclusion, the IRS cited Revenue Ruling 70-376, 1970-2 CB 164. The court ruled that property held in a grantor trust was sold by the trust under threat of condemnation. The ruling further provided that the grantor, as the owner of the trust, was the proper taxpayer to elect to defer gain under Section 1033. Revenue Ruling 88-103 amplifies Revenue Ruling 70-376 to indicate that a trust may acquire replacement property.

[Rev. Rul. 88-103, 1988-2 CB 304.]

[2] Adverse Parties

Trustees who cannot meaningfully alter beneficial interests are not adverse parties under grantor trust statutes. During 1975, taxpayers, husband and wife, created a family trust to which they transferred their entire stock in the family manufacturing business, as well as their personal residence and other assets. Their sons also transferred corporate stock to the trust and, like taxpayers, received a number of "units," or negotiable certificates, entitling them to share in trust income. The trust was to continue in existence for twenty years, although the cotrustees, one of taxpayers' sons and certain employees of the manufacturing company, were permitted, at their discretion, to distribute property and income at any time or to close the trust and distribute corpus. In either event, the grantors were entitled to receive distributions in proportion to their certificate holdings. The IRS, on audit, refused to recognize the trust as the sole taxable entity, and, accordingly, deficiencies were assessed against taxpayers pursuant to the grantor trust rules set forth in Sections 671 and 672. Taxpayers argued that they were not taxable under Section 676 (power to revoke) or Section 677 (income for benefit of grantor), because the discretionary powers were exercisable only with the approval of an adverse party.

Held: For the IRS. An adverse party, to whom the grantor must give effective control of the trust if he is to escape taxation on trust income, is defined in Section 672(a) as any person possessing a substantial beneficial interest in the trust that would be adversely affected by the exercise or nonexercise of the power that he possesses regarding the trust. In addition, the statute provides that a person possessing a general power of appointment over trust property shall be deemed to have a beneficial interest. Of the various trustees named, only two were asserted to have any interest in the trust. One of them, taxpayers' son, held a 3.84 percent certificate interest that entitled him only to a share of the assets on termination, but not to any present benefit. The court concluded that though his interest was potentially adverse at termination, it was so minor as to be insubstantial under Section 672(a). The court further determined that the other trustee, who was an employee of the company empowered to exercise discretionary powers of distribution for educational, scientific, or religious purposes, was not an adverse party possessing a general power of appointment. At most, the second trustee possessed a special power of appointment under state law, because the power was exercisable only for named purposes and could not be exercised in the trustee's own favor.

[Paxton, 520 F2d 923, 36 AFTR2d 75-5432, 75-2 USTC ¶ 9607 (9th Cir. 1975), cert. denied, 423 US 1016 (1975).]

Income of family trust is attributable to husband-grantor. Taxpayer bought the building in which his shoe business was being conducted and conveyed the building to a trust. He and his wife served as cotrustees of the trust. Taxpayer, his wife, and their children were the beneficiaries. An unlimited power to amend the trust gave taxpayer the ability to eliminate the interests of beneficiaries other than his wife. The trust instrument established 10 percent of the trust income for the wife and gave the trustees the power to distribute the balance among the other beneficiaries as they saw fit. The Tax Court ruled that taxpayer was taxable on the trust income because of his unfettered control over trust assets.

Held: Affirmed in part for the IRS and reversed in part for taxpayer. The unlimited power of the trustee to amend the trust instrument enabled him to "spray" income among himself and other beneficiaries. The sole holder of such a power would unquestionably be taxable on trust income. In this instance, however, taxpayer was co-holder of the power with his wife, who possessed a 10 percent interest in the income and corpus of the trust. Taxpayer would not be taxable on trust income if it was determined that the wife's interest was a "substantial adverse interest," on the theory that she would be so motivated to protect her interest that she would resist any attempt by him to alter the trust. In this case, the wife can still preserve her interest while joining in a redistribution of the shares of the other beneficiaries. The wife's interest is therefore not so adverse as to relieve taxpayer of the obligation to pay taxes on the 90 percent of trust income that he could control with her cooperation, without eroding her interest. The wife, rather than the husband, is taxable on the remaining 10 percent of trust income, because it is reasonably certain that she would act to prevent taxpayer from adversely affecting her own 10 percent interest.

[Laganas, 281 F2d 731, 6 AFTR2d 5388, 60-2 USTC ¶ 9657 (1st Cir. 1960).]

[3] *Clifford* Trusts

Grantor who did not enforce note is taxed on trust income. A note was given by the partnership in which taxpayer had an interest for funds he lent to the partnership. Later taxpayer bought the interests of the other two partners. He transferred the note into a *Clifford* trust for the benefit of his children, but, as the owner of the business, did not make the payments required by the note. Further, in his capacity as trustee, he did not accelerate the principal, which, under the terms of the trust, he had the right to do. Under Section 675(3), a grantor is the owner of a trust when he has borrowed directly or indirectly the trust corpus or income and has not completely repaid the loan before the beginning of the taxable year, unless the loan is made by a trustee other than the grantor. Direct or indirect borrowing includes any transaction in which a trust extends credit to a grantor. The grantor argued the position that he never borrowed from the trust. Rather, the partnership borrowed money, and then the note was assigned to the trust; only after he purchased the interests of the other partners did he acquire the partnership assets subject to the note and become the obligor on the note. Grantor argued that these events should not be collapsed to establish him as a borrower from the trust. By failing to enforce the note, however, the grantor extended credit to himself on terms different from those contained in the note. This new extension of credit was the economic equivalent of renegotiating a loan with a lender and substituting a new note for a preexisting one, which is new borrowing for purposes of Section 675(3). Thus, because the grantor was the trustee of the trust and borrowed the entire trust corpus, he was the owner of the entire trust. As a result, he was required, pursuant to Section 671, to include in computing his tax liability all items of income, deduction, and credit attributable to the trust.

[Priv. Ltr. Rul. 8802004.]

¶ 21.02 REVERSIONARY INTERESTS

Taxpayer's trust income is taxable under grantor trust rules where taxpayer retains current interest in trust corpus. Taxpayer was the owner of two private annuity contracts, which she received from her wholly owned corporation as a result of the sale of property. In 1976, taxpayer created a trust that was to terminate after a period of ten years plus forty-two days, to which both annuity contracts were assigned. Under the trust agreement, the ordinary income portion of annuity payments (taxable under Section 72(a)) was to be paid to charitable beneficiaries. The remainder of the annuity payments, including the portion excluded under Section 72(b) and the Section 1231 and ordinary gains portions, was to be paid to taxpayer. On the basis of Sections 671 and 673 of the grantor trust rules, taxpayer was assessed for income earned by the trust and paid to the charitable beneficiaries. Taxpayer argued that the assessment was inconsistent with the position stated in Revenue Ruling 67-70, 1967-1 CB 106. She also argued that she was taxable on only a portion of such income under Regulation § 1.671-3(a)(3).

Held: For the IRS. Under Section 673(a), taxpayer was considered the owner of the trust's corpus through her current receipt of the return of capital and the gains portions of the annuity payments. Specifically, under Section 673(a), taxpayer was treated as the owner of a reversionary interest in the trust. Under Section 671, taxpayer was taxable on the income attributable to that reversionary interest. Taxpayer's reliance on Revenue Ruling 67-70 was misplaced, because Section 673(b) was repealed before the trust was formed. Because taxpayer held the entire reversionary interest, Regulation § 1.671-3(a)(3) did not allow a reduction of the portion of the trust income taxable to taxpayer.

[Garvey, TC Memo. (P-H) ¶ 86,200, 51 TCM (CCH) 1026 (1986).]

Grantor may be taxed on income from property added to corpus. The grantor of a trust possessed a reversionary interest in the corpus that would revert to his estate at his death. In the revenue ruling cited below, the court stated that the income therefrom would not be taxable to him under Section 673(a) if his life expectancy, according to appropriate U.S. life and actuarial tables, was more than ten years at the date of the transfer. However, the grantor would be held taxable on the income from that portion of the trust attributable to securities or other property added to the principal of the trust after the date of its creation and within ten years prior to its termination date, as measured by the life expectancy of the grantor on the date that such additions were made.

[Rev. Rul. 56-601, 1956-2 CB 458, as modified by Rev. Rul. 73-251, 1973-1 CB 324.]

Grantor's reversion prevents gain on sales with trust. By retaining a reversion worth more than 5 percent of the initial value of a grantor-retained annuity trust (GRAT), a grantor ensured that she would not recognize gain on distributions of appreciated property from the trust in satisfaction of her annuity or on a sale with the trust. Taxpayer transferred stock to separate trusts for her three children. (Her husband established identical trusts with the same results.) Each trust provided taxpayer with an annuity equal to 13.34 percent of the initial FMV of the trust, payable quarterly for eleven years or until her death, if earlier. The annuity was payable from income and then from principal. After eleven years, each trust continued for the benefit of the child. If taxpayer died before the expiration of the eleven-year term, however, the trust property reverted to her estate. Taxpayer retained a power, in a nonfiduciary capacity, to reacquire trust assets by substituting property of equivalent value.

The trusts incorporated the provisions for a qualified annuity under Regulation § 25.2702-3(b): (1) A fixed percentage of the initial value of the trust as determined for gift tax purposes was payable to the annuity holder at least annually (or the annuity could have been a stated dollar amount, and in either case the annuity could have increased within limits); (2) the annuity was payable for a specified number of years or the life of the annuity holder, or whichever was shorter; (3) additions to the trust were prohibited; (4) commutation of the annuity was prohibited; (5) the annuity was prorated during short years; and (6) no distributions could be made to anyone other than the annuity holder during the annuity term.

Because each annuity was a qualified annuity interest under Section 2702, its value was subtracted from the FMV of the stock transferred to the trust in determining the gift; otherwise, the entire transfer in trust would have been a gift. Taxpayer was fifty-four (on her nearest birthday) at the time of the transfer, and, using the applicable federal rate (7.6 percent for September 1995), each annuity had a value equal to 94.86 percent of the initial corpus of the trust. In addition, each reversion to taxpayer's estate (if she did not survive the eleven-year term) had a value equal to 5.003 percent of the initial FMV. The reversions did not reduce the value of the gifts, but they did provide several advantages. Since each reversion exceeded 5 percent of the initial trust corpus, under Section 673 and Regulation § 1.671-3(b)(3), the trusts were entirely owned by the grantor (taxpayer) with regard to both capital gains and ordinary income. In this circumstance, the grantor is the actual owner of the trust's assets for income tax purposes and cannot recognize gain on a transaction with the trust, according to Revenue Ruling 85-13, 1985-1 CB 184.

Therefore, the IRS ruled that taxpayer would not recognize gain on the payment of an annuity with property or on a sale between herself and a trust. Thus, although the annuity was set at a high rate, taxpayer was assured that if there was insufficient income to provide for the annuity, and it was paid by distributing appreciated stock in satisfaction of the shortfall, there would not be a taxable sale. Furthermore, taxpayer could repurchase the shares at FMV from the trusts, so there would be a step-up in basis in her estate for the shares, without recognizing gain. In addition, if taxpayer died before her interest terminated, there would be an inclusion in her estate. If there were no reversion to taxpayer's estate, the trusts would continue for the benefit of the children, and estate tax would then be payable. The reversion enables taxpayer to take advantage of the marital deduction by providing the husband (if he survives) with a qualifying interest.

[Priv. Ltr. Rul. 9551018.]

¶ 21.03 POWERS OF REVOCATION OR CONTROL

Trust is determined to be grantor trust, but basis step-up is allowed. Taxpayer transferred all of his stock in a real estate holding company to an irrevocable trust created for the benefit of his children. Taxpayer's wife was the trust's sole trustee. Several years after he created the trust, taxpayer purchased the stock from the trustee to enable him to effect a liquidation of the real estate company. The only consideration given by taxpayer for the stock was his own unsecured promissory note. Upon receiving taxpayer's note, the trustee delivered the stock to taxpayer, without retaining any pledge or other security interest in it. Taxpayer then liquidated the company, and, in computing his loss from the liquidation, claimed the face amount of the promissory note as his basis in the company's stock. The IRS determined that taxpayer was not entitled to claim a stepped-up basis for the stock, because taxpayer is treated as the owner of the trust under Section 675(3).

Held: For taxpayer. The Second Circuit agreed with the district court, holding that there was, at least indirectly, a borrowing transaction under Section 675(3). It reversed, however, the lower court's holding that taxpayer was not entitled to a full cost basis in the shares purchased from the trust. The court found that under Section 671, when the grantor is recognized as the owner of the trust, the trust's income is attributed to him. The court held that there is no authority to recharacterize the transaction and disallow a step-up in basis.

[Rothstein, 735 F2d 704, 54 AFTR2d 84-5072, 84-1 USTC ¶ 9505 (2d Cir. 1984), nonacq. Rev. Rul. 85-13, 1985-1 CB 184.]

Identity of taxpayer is determined. Taxpayer *A* and his two sons, taxpayers *B* and *C*, were partners in a partnership engaged in the construction and leasing of nursing homes. In 1963, *A*, *B*, and *C* created a thirteen-year trust, the corpus of which consisted of the partnership's nursing homes. The beneficiaries of the trusts were *B*'s and *C*'s children, and *B* and *C* were named trustees. Under the terms of the trust, all current income was to be distributed at least annually. However, *B* and *C* distributed only amounts sufficient to allow the beneficiaries to pay their income taxes. The remainder of the income was loaned to the partnership and its successor corporation or invested in participation loans with a bank of which *A*, *B*, and *C* owned the majority of the stock. At the end of the thirteen-year trust term, all amounts owed were paid with interest, and the trust corpus and income were distributed to the beneficiaries. The IRS determined that the grantors of the trust were taxable on the trust income under the grantor trust rules.

Held: For taxpayers. Only a portion of the trust income was taxable to the grantors. A loan to a corporation is not a loan to a grantor-shareholder within Section 675. However, a loan to a partnership is equivalent to a loan to the individual partners. Accordingly, because all of the borrowed amounts were derived from ordinary trust income, the grantors were taxable on that portion of the current year's trust income that the total unpaid loans at the beginning of the taxable year bore to the total trust income for prior years and for the taxable year in issue.

[Bennett, 79 TC 470 (1982).]

Interest from revocable trust is taxable to grantors. Taxpayers opened three bank accounts and purchased two certificates of deposit for the benefit of their three children. Taxpayers were designated the joint trustees of each bank account, two of which were revocable by express provision. On each of the certificates of deposit, taxpayers were designated joint tenants, with rights of survivorship, as trustees for their children. The IRS determined that the accounts and certificates of deposit were revocable trusts and that under Sections 671 and 676, taxpayer-grantors were taxable on the interest income of the trusts.

Held: For the IRS. Two of the accounts were revocable trusts because they were expressly designated as such. The third account and the certificates of deposit were deemed to be revocable trusts under applicable California state law, because they contained no provision specifically declaring them to be irrevocable. Because all of the trusts were revocable, taxpayers did not make completed gifts to their children, and, under Sections 671 and 676, taxpayer-grantors were fully taxable on the interest income realized by the trusts.

[Heintz, TC Memo. (P-H) ¶ 80,524, 41 TCM (CCH) 429 (1980).]

IRS, in ruling on grantor trusts, declares that it will not follow *Rothstein* case. In the instant revenue ruling, the IRS ruled that a grantor who acquires the corpus of a trust in exchange for the grantor's unsecured promissory note is considered to have indirectly borrowed the trust corpus. As a result, the grantor is treated as the owner of the trust, and the grantor's acquisition of the trust corpus is not viewed as a sale for federal income tax purposes. The IRS declared that the court's decision in Rothstein, 735 F2d 704 (2d Cir. 1984), insofar as it holds that a trust owned by a grantor must be regarded as a separate taxpayer capable of engaging in sales transactions with the grantor, is not in accord with the views of the IRS. Accordingly, the IRS will not follow *Rothstein.*

[Rev. Rul. 85-13, 1985-1 CB 184.]

Grantor's power to revoke results in taxable income. An individual who owned all of the outstanding stock of a corporation transferred it to a newly created trust and received in exchange a separate certificate of beneficial interest in the trust for each specific share of stock transferred. The trust instrument provided that all of the income of the trust and any distribution of corpus was to be paid to the beneficiaries, based on their respective beneficial interests. The trust could not receive any further transfers of assets, and there was no power under the trust agreement to vary the investment of the trust. Under the provisions of the instrument, the beneficiaries could freely assign or bequeath their certificates of beneficial interest, and their successors in interest were to become beneficiaries of the trust to the extent of the interest they acquire. Beneficiaries were to have the right to vote their share of the stock held in trust through a proxy agreement. The trust instrument further provided that the trust was to terminate on the earlier of the twentieth anniversary of the death of the grantor or when the stock was no longer held in trust. The beneficiaries owning a majority interest in the trust could at any time direct the trustee to sell all, but not less than all, of the stock held in the trust, and such a disposition would terminate the trust.

Based on these facts, the IRS ruled that as long as the grantor had a majority interest whereby he would be able to cause the trustee to sell the trust assets and distribute the proceeds, thus terminating the trust, he would have a power to revoke the trust within the meaning of Section 676. Accordingly, the grantor should be treated as the owner of the trust under Section 676 with regard to the majority interest held by him for such period as he was the majority owner. This is so even though he may be treated as owner of a portion of the trust under other provisions of Part I, Subchapter J, Chapter I, Subtitle A of the Code. In computing his taxable income and credits, he had to include those items of income, deductions, and credits against the tax of the trust as required under Section 671. Furthermore, should the grantor assign certificates of beneficial interest, so that he no longer owned a majority interest in the trust, he would nevertheless be treated as owner of that portion of the trust the income of which was, or might be, distributed to him or his spouse as provided by Section 677(a).

[Rev. Rul. 71-548, 1971-2 CB 250.]

Grantor trust gets nonrecognition treatment on sale to ESOP. A grantor retained a right of revocation for property that he contributed to a trust. Because that was the only property in the trust, the entire trust was effectively a grantor trust. The trust plans to sell qualified stock to the employee stock ownership plan (ESOP) and purchase replacement property as provided in Section 1042(c)(4).

The IRS determined that the situation was analogous to that in Revenue Ruling 66-159, 1966-1 CB 162, in which a grantor trust was permitted to take advantage of the rollover provisions of Section 121 with respect to a principal residence. Similarly, in Revenue Ruling 70-376, 1970-2 CB 164, a grantor was able to elect nonrecognition under Section 1033 when his trust sold condemned property. The IRS concluded that the sale of stock by the trust would be treated as a sale by the grantor, and a purchase of replacement property by the trust would similarly be treated as a purchase by the grantor. Moreover, the grantor would be considered to hold the stock during the time the stock was held by the trust. The grantor would be considered "taxpayer" for purposes of Section 1042, and was the party required to make the appropriate election on his income tax return, according to the ruling.

[Priv. Ltr. Rul. 9041027.]

Trust created to make charitable gifts is grantor trust. The employees of a firm established a trust to make collective gifts to charitable, educational, and civic organizations. Each grantor could contribute cash and property to the trust from time to time. The grantors could revoke their trust shares annually, but only with respect to their individual proportionate interest in the trust. On revocation, that grantor's share would be distributed to the grantor. The trustees had discretion to distribute whatever amounts of income and principal they deemed appropriate to worthy organizations. If any principal or income remained undistributed at the end of the year, the trustees could distribute that principal and income to the grantors. If the grantors had not exercised their right of revocation, the trustees could withhold the distribution and retain those sums in trust. These amounts would be treated as if they had been distributed to the grantors and transferred back to the trust.

The IRS stated that the trust should be classified as a trust under Regulation § 301.7701-4(a). The IRS also stated that the employees of the firm would be treated as the owners of the entire trust under Section 677(a)(2). The IRS concluded that each employee must include the proportionate share of the income, deductions, and credits of the trust in income.

[Priv. Ltr. Rul. 8910018.]

Transfer to trust is not subject to gift tax, because grantor retains power to change income beneficiary. Grantor planned to create an irrevocable trust with a term greater than ten years. All of the net income of the trust was to be distributed at least quarterly. The income was to be distributed to charitable organizations chosen by the grantor after the income had been earned. Grantor specifically reserved the right to change the beneficiaries of the trust at any time before distribution.

The IRS stated that the initial transfer of property to the trust would not constitute a taxable transfer under Section 2511, because grantor was to retain the right to designate the recipients of trust income.

[Priv. Ltr. Rul. 8605036.]

¶ 21.04 INCOME FOR BENEFIT OF GRANTOR

[1] Income Interest

Trust income paid to discharge settlor's gift tax liability is fully taxable to settlor under grantor trust rules. Taxpayer in 1954 executed a single trust instrument whereby she created separate trusts for each of her four children. A local savings bank was named as trustee. Upon executing the trust instrument, taxpayer transferred to the trustees 70,000 shares of stock in the family pen-manufacturing corporation. Taxpayer imposed upon the trustee the affirmative obligation to pay her gift tax liability arising from the transfer. The trustee was bound to secure a loan in an amount sufficient to pay the taxes, using the stock as collateral. Following the stock transfer, the trustee paid the resultant gift tax liability partially with trust income and partially with the proceeds of a loan. On audit, the IRS determined that taxpayer was fully taxable on the amount of trust income used to pay the gift tax. In the IRS's view, the grantor trust rules under Section 644 were applicable, and because the trust paid an obligation of taxpayer, the result was income taxable to her.

Held: For the IRS. Gift tax is a primary and personal liability of the donor, and where a trust uses income (as opposed to corpus or the proceeds of a loan) to discharge the settlor's liability, the amount so expended by the trust is taxable to the settlor. The mechanism cited by the court for imputing income to taxpayer was Section 677, which provides that a grantor will be taxed on distribution from a trust in the absence of a requirement that an adverse party approve the distributions. Thus, to the extent that trust income was applied to discharge taxpayer's indebtedness, taxpayer was taxable under the grantor trust rules.

[Sheaffer, 313 F2d 738, 11 AFTR2d 839, 63-1 USTC ¶ 9272 (8th Cir. 1963), cert. denied, 375 US 818 (1963).]

State court reformation of grantor-trustee power to terminate is held insufficient to avoid grantor trust rules. In 1950, taxpayers executed a single declaration of trust entitled "B&G Realty Trust" and transferred thereto certain properties relating to their business. The trust named as beneficiaries taxpayers and their respective wives and children. The trust instrument appointed taxpayers as trustees and granted them, among other things, the power to:

1. Accumulate income;
2. Exercise discretion in determining when, to whom, and in what amounts distributions to beneficiaries were to be made;
3. Change the terms of the trust, including the beneficiaries;
4. Sell, encumber, or convey trust property; and
5. Terminate the trust at any time prior to the end of its ten-year life with the consent of all adult beneficiaries.

Upon examining the trust instrument and taxpayers' returns, the IRS prepared notices of deficiency asserting that the trust income should be attributed to taxpayers under the grantor trust rules embodied in Subchapter J of the Code. Shortly thereafter one of the trust beneficiaries brought an action in state court to prevent taxpayers from transferring the trust property to themselves and from thereby effecting a termination. The local probate court conducted a hearing on the matter and entered its decree upholding all of the trustees' powers, but limiting their right to alter or amend the trust instrument in such a way as to thwart the beneficiaries' right to prevent a termination. When the matter of the tax deficiencies came before the Tax Court, taxpayers argued that the probate court's decree of reformation had so limited their powers under the trust instrument as to take it out of the grantor trust rules.

Held: Affirmed for the IRS. The appeals court found that the sweeping powers of the trustees, which gave them virtually absolute control over trust property, were not substantially altered by the probate court, and that taxpayers retained sufficient powers to place them squarely within the grantor trust provisions. As the court interpreted the decree, taxpayers were merely foreclosed from terminating the trust outright, but they retained the power to deal with trust assets and the distribution of income, thus keeping for themselves the sole right to enjoy the principal and income at will. Consequently, the court concluded that the income of the trust was properly taxed to the grantors under Section 677.

[Gurich, 295 F2d 845, 8 AFTR2d 5663, 61-2 USTC ¶ 9721 (1st Cir. 1961).]

Rental payments to family trust are held taxable to grantors. Taxpayer-husband was a dentist who practiced through a professional corporation. In 1981, taxpayer-husband and taxpayer-wife executed a trust agreement to last ten years and one month, with taxpayer-wife acting as sole trustee for the benefit of their two sons. Later that year, taxpayer-husband and taxpayer-wife, as co-owners, transferred the real property used in the dental practice to the trustee. Taxpayer-wife as trustee and taxpayer-husband as president of his professional corporation then executed a lease agreement whereby the corporation leased the real property from the trust. On audit of taxpayers' joint federal income tax returns from 1981 through 1983, the IRS determined that under Section 674(a), taxpayers were taxable on the trust income because taxpayer-wife retained the power to sprinkle all or part of the trust income between the beneficiaries. The power to sprinkle income unevenly allows the grantor to control the beneficial enjoyment of trust income, so that under Section 674(a), the grantor is treated as owning that portion of the trust income over which the sprinkling power is retained.

Held: For the IRS. The Tax Court noted that in the critical dispositive language of the trust agreement, there was conspicuously absent the word "equal" as a modifier of the "monthly or other convenient installments" of income distribution requirements. Thus, the language in the trust agreement did not limit the trustee's discretion in dividing distributions between the two beneficiaries. Although not expressly granting the trustee full discretionary powers, the only restriction imposed on her by the trust provision was that all net trust income had to be paid to or applied for the benefit of both beneficiaries at least annually. Accordingly, taxpayers were taxable on the rental payments made to the trust.

[Carson, 92 TC 1134 (1989).]

Tax Court upholds regulation created to prevent use of grantor trust rules for avoiding partnership income following exhaustion of pass-through losses. Taxpayer, a resident of Illinois, created four separate irrevocable trusts for the benefit of named individuals and appointed a nonadverse party to serve as the trustee for each trust. A provision in the trust agreement, that was executed in December 1975, gave the trustee a power to add one or more charitable organizations as beneficiaries to any of the trusts. As a result of this provision, taxpayer, as grantor, was treated as the owner of the four trusts under Section 674(a). On or about December 19, 1975, taxpayer funded each of the trusts with $5,075 in cash, which the trusts immediately transferred to an Illinois investment partnership in exchange for a one-ninth ownership interest. Two days later the investment partnership contributed the money, along with other funds, to a partnership involved in the production of motion pictures. The motion picture partnership thereafter entered into a contract with a major film production company, and, to meet projected expenses, it undertook a nonrecourse loan of $3.27 million. By reason of the grantor trust rules, taxpayer reported a combined loss of $71,462 in 1975 and 1976, followed by $1,544 of income in 1977. On January 1, 1978, the trustee irrevocably renounced his power to add beneficiaries to the trusts. As a result, the trusts ceased to be grantor trusts under Section 674(a), and taxpayer accordingly reported no trust income on his 1978 return. The IRS sent taxpayer a notice of deficiency in respect of 1978, relying upon Regulation § 1.1001-2(c), Example (5). Under Example (5), where the grantor of a trust enjoys the benefits of trust losses arising out of a partnership interest owned by the trust because of the operation of the grantor trust rules, and later, after the partnership begins generating income, the trust ceases to be a grantor trust as the result of the trustee's renunciation of a power, there is considered to be a taxable disposition of the trust's partnership interests by the grantor to the trusts. The IRS determined that by operation of this rule, taxpayer had realized $49,919 in taxable income. At trial, taxpayer attacked the validity of the regulation and argued that he had realized, at most, capital gains on income on the imputed transaction.

Held: For the IRS. The Tax Court noted that the regulation was adopted to frustrate the use of two separate taxing schemes—those of Subchapter K and Subchapter J—to avoid the imposition of tax in a way that Congress clearly had not intended or anticipated. As viewed by the court, Example (5) was a proper use of the IRS regulatory power in that it gave effect to the purpose of Congress, expressed in Section 1001, that the owner of property must be taxed on gains generated by the transfer of property owned by him. Any other result would, according to the Tax Court, place "formalistic" application of taxing measures at odds with the expressed intent of Congress.

[Madorin, 84 TC 667 (1985).]

Tax Court determines amount of grantor's liability based on trust loans of income. Taxpayers, husband and wife, operated an appliance store in Peoria, Illinois. In 1968 and 1969, they acquired undeveloped real property in Peoria and constructed a retail sales facility for use in their appliance business. The property was leased to their wholly owned operating corporation for a period of ten years. In 1972, during the term of the lease, taxpayers transferred the property to a ten-year, irrevocable *Clifford* trust for the benefit of their children, with a reversion to the husband as grantor. The wife was appointed trustee with broad management powers, including the right to "loan trust property to any person with provision for reasonable interest and security." During the period from 1973 through 1974, the wife, in her capacity as trustee, made several cash loans to the husband, each secured by a promissory demand note bearing a market rate of interest. On its federal income tax returns for 1974 and 1975, the trust reported the receipt of rental income with offsetting distribution deductions resulting in zero taxable income. On audit, the IRS discovered that all of the trust income had been loaned to the husband, and that although distribution deductions were taken, the beneficiary children received no money or property from the trust. In its statutory notice of deficiency, the IRS asserted that the husband was taxable on the entire amount of the trust's income. The question presented to the Tax Court was what amount, if any, was taxable to the husband. At issue was Section 675(3) of the grantor trust rules, which provides that a grantor is treated as the owner of "any portion of a trust" if any corpus or income was borrowed by the grantor. The general rule is subject, however, to a statutory exception where the loan provides for adequate interest and security.

Held: For the IRS. The Tax Court summarily rejected taxpayers' argument that the term "any portion" meant the amount borrowed relative to the entire trust. Instead, it construed the term as applying not to what the grantor has actually borrowed, but rather what the borrowing means in terms of dominion and control over the trust. The court specifically rejected any contention that Section 675(3) taxes the grantor on only the part of the trust actually borrowed. Such an interpretation, noted the court, would treat the grantor as only owning the portion he borrowed rather than "the portion of [the] trust" in respect of which the grantor borrowed as specified in the Code. Furthermore, the court stated that such an interpretation would mean, for example, that if the trust had the power to make unsecured loans, the grantor would be taxed on the entire income under Section 675(2). However, if such loans were actually made, then only part of the income would be taxed to the grantor. Thus, under the court's interpretation, the borrowing of any part of trust corpus will result in the entire income being taxed to the grantor unless an exception under Section 675 applies.

[Benson, 76 TC 1040 (1981).]

Trust income used to discharge loan obtained to pay gift tax is not income to grantor. In 1955, decedent created certain irrevocable trusts in favor of her children. The trust corpus consisted of 41,600 shares of stock in a family corporation. At the time of transfer, the stock was valued at approximately $1 million. The trust agreement imposed upon the trustees the obligation to pay any gift tax liability of decedent arising out of the creation of the trusts. The trustees were further empowered to obtain the funds necessary to satisfy the tax by selling corpus or by borrowing the funds and using the stock as security. The trustees chose the latter alternative, and secured a loan from a local lending institution. Decedent herself had no contact with the bank in connection with the loan. During 1956, the trustees paid the gift tax and commenced making periodic payments on the loan by using trust income. For taxable years 1957 and 1958, the IRS assessed deficiencies against decedent, contending that she was taxable on the trust income pursuant to the grantor trust rules under Section 677(a).

Held: For the estate. The income of the trusts used to repay the loan was not income to decedent in 1957 and 1958. The Tax Court acknowledged that in previous holdings, for example, Sheaffer, 37 TC 99 (1962), aff'd, 313 F2d 738, 11 AFTR2d 839, 63-1 USTC ¶ 9272 (8th Cir. 1963), it had found that trust income used to pay a settlor's gift tax liability was taxable to the settlor; but in the present case, the fact that the loan was an arm's-length transaction with a third party distinguished it from earlier cases. Because the settlor was not a party to the loan, her interest in the trust property terminated immediately upon payment of the gift tax. Decedent received no benefit from the fact that the trustees borrowed money to pay the tax rather than selling trust corpus outright to raise cash.

[Estate of Morgan, 37 TC 981 (1962), aff'd, 316 F2d 238, 11 AFTR2d 1231, 63-1 USTC ¶ 9401 (6th Cir. 1963), cert. denied, 375 US 825 (1963).]

Taxpayer-beneficiary is taxable on Illinois land trust income assigned to taxpayer's creditor. Taxpayer transferred real estate to an Illinois land trust. Under the Illinois law of land trusts, a beneficiary holds his interest in the form of personal property, controls the trustee's actions with respect to the real property held by the trust, and reports all income and deductions from the property. The trust sold the property, receiving installment notes from the buyer. When taxpayer could not continue payment of a loan that he had guaranteed, he caused his trustee to assign its interest in the trust to the creditor bank. The purpose of the assignment was to repay the loan with income realized on the installment notes. Taxpayer retained an interest in the trust, as indicated by his renewal of the trust for another twenty-year term and by his continuing right to retain income from the trust by making full payments of the loan balance. Taxpayer did not report the postassignment trust income (capital gain and interest on the notes) or the related deductions. The IRS assessed taxpayer for taxes related to this income. Taxpayer argued that the income was not taxable to him after the assignment.

Held: For the IRS. Taxpayer retained an interest in the trust, because of his ability to redeem such interest by making full payment to his creditors. Accordingly, he did not make a complete and permanent transfer of his trust interest. As such, taxpayer merely assigned a stream of income for the purpose of repaying his loan, and thereby retained enjoyment of such income. He was therefore taxable on such income.

[Pommier, TC Memo. (P-H) ¶ 86,506, 52 TCM (CCH) 766 (1986).]

Grantor-trustee who borrows entire trust corpus is owner of trust, although he repays whole loan with interest in same year as loan. On May 11, 1985, an individual created an irrevocable trust for the benefit of his children. He named himself sole trustee, with the power to borrow trust corpus or income at market rates with adequate security. In 1985, he borrowed and re-paid the entire trust corpus with interest.

The IRS determined that under Section 675(3), the individual who created the trust was the owner of trust property for 1985, even though he did not bor-row the corpus until after the beginning of the trust's taxable year and repaid the loan with interest before the close of such year.

[Rev. Rul. 86-82, 1986-1 CB 253.]

Corporation is deemed to be grantor of trust, and thus may not take de-duction for contribution to trust. A commodity futures exchange established a corporation to clear all trades occurring on the exchange. The corporation was required to guarantee payment when clearing members defaulted on con-tracts traded on the exchange. As a means of meeting his obligation, protecting investors, and promoting public confidence, the corporation created an irrevo-cable trust to provide funds to prevent or mitigate losses of public customers who had claims against defaulting clearing members. In its first taxable year, the trust received a contribution from the corporation. It made no payments to satisfy customers' claims. The corporation, on its income tax return, treated the contribution as a current deduction.

The IRS ruled that the amount of the contribution was not deductible. Section 677(a) provides that a grantor is treated as the owner of any portion of a trust whose income (1) is distributed to the grantor without the approval or consent of any adverse party, or (2) may be distributed to the grantor without the approval or consent of any adverse party at the discretion of the grantor or a nonadverse party or both. Regulation §1.677(a)-1(d) provides, in general, that a grantor is treated as the owner of a portion of a trust whose income (1) is applied in discharge of a legal obligation of the grantor or (2) may be ap-plied in discharge of a legal obligation of the grantor at the discretion of the grantor or a nonadverse party, or both. Section 671 provides that when the grantor is treated as the owner of any portion of a trust, the grantor's taxable income and credits include those items of the trust's income, deductions, and credits attributable to the portion of the trust that the grantor is treated as own-ing. Regulation § 1.671-2(c) provides that an item of income, deduction, or credit included in computing a grantor's taxable income and credits is treated as if the grantor (regardless of whether grantor is an individual) had received or paid it directly. In the present case, because the trust's income and corpus were available to discharge the corporation's legal obligations arising from trades cleared, and because the trustee was not an adverse party, the corpora-tion was deemed to be the owner of the trust and was obliged to include the trust's items of income, deduction, and credit in computing its taxable income. The corporation was not able to take a deduction for the contribution to the trust, but was required to wait until the liabilities to the customers were paid or accrued, depending on the method of accounting that it used.

[Rev. Rul. 85-158, 1985-2 CB 175.]

Grantor is taxable on trust income used to pay his gift tax liability. An individual owned all of the stock of a corporation. He made a gift of such stock in trust for the benefit of his nephew, who was an executive vice-president and treasurer of the corporation. The purpose of the transfer was the orderly transmission of the business to the nephew during the donor's lifetime. The trust initially had no assets other than the stock of the corporation. In connection with the trust, the instrument provided that the gift of all of the stock of the corporation to the trust was made upon the express condition that the trustees assume and agree to pay any federal gift tax that may be incurred as a result of such gift. The trustees further agreed that the trust would promptly pay those taxes with funds to be borrowed by the trust from a bank on security of the donated stock. Section 677 provides, in effect, that the grantor of a trust is taxable on income directed to his benefit or to discharge his legal or contractual obligations. Section 2502(d) provides that the tax imposed by Section 2501 on the transfer of property by gift shall be paid by the donor. In the instant case, the trust was to borrow, with the stock as security, funds sufficient to pay the gift tax. The indebtedness was then to be satisfied from the income of the trust. The liability for the tax was a liability of the donor. Accordingly, the IRS ruled that income of the trust, which was applied by the trustees in satisfying the obligation incurred to pay gift tax of the donor, was taxable to the donor under the provisions of Section 677.

[Rev. Rul. 57-564, 1957-2 CB 328.]

Individual establishes grantor trust for childrens' benefit, but retains qualified income interest. An individual owns 70 percent of an S corporation's outstanding common stock; his children own the balance. The individual proposed to transfer his stock to an irrevocable trust that would pay him income for ten years or until he died. During this income period, the grantor would have the power to require that any underproductive trust property be converted to productive property. If the grantor died within ten years, the corpus and any undistributed income would be distributed to his estate. If the grantor and his son survived the ten-year income period, the trust would pay the income to the son for two years and then distribute the corpus to the son or his estate. If the son did not survive the ten-year income period, then, after year ten, the trust would pay the income to the grantor's daughters for two years and then distribute the corpus to the daughters or their estates.

The IRS stated that the grantor would be deemed to own the entire portion of the trust for ten years under Sections 673 and 677, and that during the ten-year income period, the trust would be a grantor trust and an eligible subchapter S corporation shareholder under Section 1361(c)(2)(A)(i). If and when the trust income was paid to the grantor's son or daughters, the IRS said, the trust would be a qualified subchapter S trust. The IRS also stated that the grantor would be treated as having retained a qualified trust income interest under Section 2036(c)(6). Citing Dickman v. Comm'r, 465 US 330 (1984), the IRS indicated that if, after the initial transfer of stock to the trust, the grantor failed to exercise his right to make unproductive corpus productive, then the lost income on the trust corpus would be recognizable as a taxable gift for each year. The IRS applied Section 7520 to provide the grantor with a present value of his reversion and income interests. Finally, the IRS concluded that for Section 2036(c) purposes, the grantor would not be treated as having retained the enjoyment of nonvoting stock transferred to the trust as a result of the transfer of the nonvoting stock to the trust.

[Priv. Ltr. Rul. 9015024.]

[2] Current Distributions

Complex annuity and stock transactions using foreign situs trust result in taxation under grantor trust rules. In 1955, taxpayer acquired title to a parcel of real property in Los Angeles, on which he constructed a shopping center during 1958 and 1959. Because of a variety of personal and family difficulties, taxpayer's legal counsel advised placing the land and improvements in a trust pursuant to a plan that would pay taxpayer an annual annuity. Accordingly, in 1963, taxpayer created an irrevocable trust under Bahamian law, with a Bahamian bank serving as trustee. Taxpayer's children and numerous relatives were named as beneficiaries, and the trust was initially funded with $1,000. At the same time, taxpayer formed a realty corporation to which he transferred the shopping center in exchange for all of its stock. Shortly thereafter another Bahamian corporation was substituted as trustee, and taxpayer entered into an agreement with it to transfer all of the realty company stock in trust in exchange for an annuity that would pay $75,000 per year to taxpayer and his wife, with full payments to the survivor for life. A month later, on January 2, 1964, the trustee sold the stock to another Bahamian corporation and received the buyer's nonassignable promissory note for $1 million, with principal payable at the end of twenty years. The note provided that the maker would pay annual interest of $75,000, subject to a provision permitting the trustee to "redetermine" principal on the basis of the appraised value of the shopping center in order to increase each year's interest payment. Between 1964 and 1967, taxpayer received $300,000 from the trust. On his 1964 and 1965 federal tax returns, taxpayer reported no income from payments received pursuant to the annuity agreement, on the ground that such amounts were paid under a private annuity arrangement and that no amounts would be taxable until there had been a full return of his basis in the realty stock. The IRS determined that taxpayer was fully taxable on his trust receipts, contending that the substance of the transaction was not a sale, but a transfer of property in trust subject to a reserved right to receive an annual income. The IRS based its position on Section 677(a), which provides that a trust grantor will be taxed as the owner of any portion of a trust whose income, without the approval or consent of an adverse party, is distributed to the grantor. Taxpayer argued that the arrangement was a bona fide sale of the realty company's stock in consideration for a private annuity that did not have an ascertainable FMV. In taxpayer's view, no taxable gain would be realized until he recovered his cost basis in the stock.

Held: For the IRS. Under the grantor trust rules, taxpayer was fully taxable on all $300,000 of trust income. The court found that the transaction was not a sale of property for an annuity, but was rather the creation of a trust with a reserved life estate subject to Section 677(a). Citing Gregory v. Helvering, 293 US 465 (1935), the court applied the rule that substance, not form, controls where a prearranged plan of interrelated steps is carried out for the purpose of achieving a reduction in tax liability. Thus, the court construed the various instruments together and concluded that, in substance, taxpayer created a trust with a reserved life estate, and did not actually sell his stock in exchange for an annuity. In this determination, the court pointed to five factors that, taken together, indicated that no sale had been made:

1. The source of the annuity payments was the trust property itself.
2. The note was nonassignable.
3. The corpus of the trust was to remain intact for ultimate distribution to the beneficiaries.
4. The arrangement did not give taxpayer a down payment, interest on the deferred purchase price, or security for its payment.
5. There was a substantial disparity between the FMV of the stock and the actuarial value of the annuity payments.

[Lazarus, 513 F2d 824, 35 AFTR2d 75-1191, 75-1 USTC ¶ 9387 (9th Cir. 1975).]

First Circuit strikes down attempt to use trust as buyer of property for later sale in exchange for annuity. Taxpayer was an archbishop and the head of the Syrian Church of Antioch in North America. He owned the Dead Sea Scrolls. In 1951, he transferred the Scrolls to a trust, naming himself and another individual as cotrustees with the power to sell, rent, exchange, or hold the Scrolls at the cotrustees' discretion. He also reserved the power to deal in any way he saw fit with trust income, and provided that the trust was subject to his power to amend, revoke, or modify without restriction. In the following year, 1952, he amended the trust by relinquishing his rights to principal and income in exchange for an annuity in the amount of $10,000 per year and, on his death, $2,500 per year to his mother. In addition, the trust was to pay all excess annual income to his church. By express provision, the 1952 amendment also provided that taxpayer could no longer amend or revoke the trust, except to reduce the amount of his or his mother's annual payments. Nearly two years later the Scrolls were sold for $250,000, and the proceeds were invested in securities. During taxable years 1951 through 1953, the trust made no distributions to taxpayer whatsoever. In 1954, the only distribution consisted of two $15,000 payments, ostensibly for his expenses in effecting the sale. In both 1955 and 1956, the trust made $10,000 in distributions to him out of income or principal. Upon examining taxpayer's 1954 personal and fiduciary returns, the IRS determined that capital gains of $123,652 should have been reported and taxed. The case was first heard in the Tax Court, which found that taxpayer was personally taxable on the gain under the grantor trust rules set forth in Section 677(a). That section provides that the grantor of trust property is taxable where the trust's income is or may be either currently distributed to him or accumulated for his personal benefit. On appeal, taxpayer vigorously disputed the Tax Court's decision. He contended that the formation of the trust and the later provision for the payment of an annuity should be characterized as a sale of the Scrolls to the trust in return for the annuity.

Held: Affirmed for the IRS. Taxpayer's transfer of the Scrolls to the trust was in no respect a sale. It was clear that taxpayer sought only to set up a trust to provide himself and his mother with income. Consequently, for tax purposes, the sale of the Scrolls must be taxed to taxpayer under the grantor trust rules in Section 677(a). The court observed that the creation of the trust and the subsequent amendment were two separate events that could not be said to have been part of a single, integrated plan, and, further, that the amendment alone was ineffective to change the settlor-trust relationship into one of creditor and annuitant.

[Samuel, 306 F2d 682, 9 AFTR2d 1840, 62-2 USTC ¶ 9557 (1st Cir. 1962).]

Trustees' assumption of grantors' indebtedness does not trigger grantor trust rules where debt is incurred and trusts are established in contemporaneous transactions. Grantors, husband and wife, were members of a family that was engaged in the wholesale and retail dry goods business in Georgia. The retail part of the business was operated by a closely held corporation, which in turn held a 50 percent interest in a partnership that operated the wholesale part of the business. In 1944, the corporation sold each grantor a $30,000 interest in the wholesale partnership in exchange for their promissory notes, which were payable on demand. In a simultaneous transaction, grantors conveyed their partnership interests to certain newly created trusts for the benefit of their children and grandchildren. As a part of the same overall transaction, the trusts contributed the partnership interests to a new limited partnership. The limited partnership interests were then pledged to the corporation as security for grantors' notes. In addition to providing for these transactions, the governing trust instruments obligated the trustees to assume liability for grantors' entire indebtedness to the corporation. On audit, the IRS determined that grantors were taxable on all trust income that was used to retire the debts. The IRS argued that under the grantor trust rules as codified in Sections 671 et seq., the trust income was being used for the direct benefit of grantors.

Held: For grantors. As a general rule, the grantor trust provisions apply in a case where the trust pays an obligation of the grantor that was incurred prior to and independently of the establishment of the trust, and where the settlor is to receive or participate in trust income after the repayment of the debt. In the instant case, however, the trustees assumed primary liability for payment of the notes at the time of the trusts' formation. The liability of grantors was merely contingent and was enforceable only in the event of default by the trustees. The entire arrangement was undertaken according to a single plan, and therefore grantors received no benefit as a result of the trust's assumption of liability. Moreover, the court held that there was no reservation of future income, nor was there any retained right to benefit from trust corpus once the notes were retired. Under such circumstances, the general rule does not apply; therefore, no part of the trusts' income was properly taxed to grantors.

[Greenwald, 217 F2d 632, 46 AFTR2d 1206, 55-1 USTC ¶ 9114 (5th Cir. 1954), cert. denied, 349 US 905 (1955).]

Tax Court upholds trust-annuity arrangement involving Antilles trustee.
In 1964, taxpayer's lawyer, acting under power of attorney, created a trust and named the Aruba Bonaire Curacao Trust Co., Ltd., trustee. The trust was initially funded with $5. In a contemporaneous transaction, taxpayer entered into an annuity agreement with the trustee under which $371,875 worth of securities was conveyed to the trustee in exchange for an annuity with a present value of $177,500. Between 1965 and 1976, she received periodic annuity payments totaling approximately $24,800 per year. She received several payments after they were due, but she chose not to assert her right to late-payment penalties. In addition, she also received occasional advances and loans from the trust that were never repaid. On audit, the IRS questioned whether the trust was entitled to be recognized for tax purposes, and determined that taxpayer was taxable on all trust income. The IRS argued, inter alia, that the numerous lapses in trust administration, together with occasional failures to observe the necessary formalities, triggered the grantor trust rules.

Held: For taxpayer. The Tax Court followed the decision in LaFargue, 689 F2d 845, 50 AFTR2d 82-5944, 82-2 USTC ¶ 9622 (9th Cir. 1982), aff'd, 800 F2d 936, 58 AFTR2d 86-5859 (9th Cir. 1986), and concluded that the facts in the present case clearly showed that there had been a bona fide trust transfer in exchange for an annuity, and that taxpayer had relinquished sufficient control over her property to avoid imposition of the grantor trust rules. The court examined the circumstances surrounding the informalities and concluded that they did not justify looking through the terms of the annuity agreement to attribute income to taxpayer. Because the fundamental trust transfer was bona fide and the annuity obligations were being met, the court found no basis for applying the grantor trust rules and therefore upheld the entire arrangement.

[Benson, 80 TC 789 (1983).]

Minor can be owner of trust created by court order and is liable for its income. A minor was awarded damages as a result of a personal injury suit filed on his behalf. Pursuant to the court order, an amount of damages was paid into the registry of the court and was transferred to a trust for his benefit. The court order designated a corporation as the trustee. Under the terms of the trust as established by the court, the corporate trustee could accumulate income or distribute both income and corpus as it determined to be reasonably necessary for the beneficiary's health, education, support, or maintenance. The trust was to terminate and all property was to be transferred to the minor beneficiary after he reached age 21. If he were to die before reaching age 21, the trust property would pass to his estate. The trust was not subject to revocation by the minor, but was subject to amendment, modification, or revocation by the court at any time prior to termination. Under state law, if the trust were revoked by the court prior to the beneficiary attaining age 18, the court could enter additional orders concerning the trust corpus and any undistributed income for his benefit. If the trust were revoked by the court after the minor attained age 18, corpus and any undistributed income would be paid over to him.

The IRS ruled that the amount of damages awarded as a result of the personal injury suit should be excluded from the minor's gross income by Section 104(a)(2). As the owner of the damages awarded, however, he was considered the grantor of the trust to which the damages were transferred. Because the income and corpus, by the terms of the trust, were to be distributed currently to the minor or held and accumulated for future distribution to him at the discretion of a nonadverse party, the minor was treated as the owner of the trust pursuant to Section 677(a).

[Rev. Rul. 83-25, 1983-1 CB 116.]

[3] Future Distributions

Trust-leaseback arrangement is held to be grantor trust. Taxpayer, pursuant to a written trust agreement, conveyed certain real estate to a trust for the benefit of his children. Concurrently with the execution of the trust agreement, the property was leased back to taxpayer for use as an office in his medical practice. The trust was irrevocable for a period of ten years and thirty days. Taxpayer did not include in his income the rentals received by the trust, and he deducted the rentals as a business expense. The district court ruled that the taxable trust income for the years in question was not includable in taxpayer's income and that the rent was an ordinary and necessary business expense.

Held: Reversed for the IRS. The taxable income of the trust should have been included in taxpayer's income under Section 677(a)(2), because it was possible for taxpayer to receive accumulated trust income after the expiration of ten years. That section provides that the grantor shall be treated as the owner of any portion of a trust whose income may be held or accumulated for future distribution to the grantor without the approval or consent of any adverse party. The same section contains a clause that excepts certain situations from this general rule, but on these facts, the excepting clause did not apply. Taxpayer was thus subject to the general rule that unless the trustee was found to be an "adverse party" within the meaning of Section 672(a), that defines that term as "any person having a substantial beneficial interest in the trust which would be adversely affected by the exercise or nonexercise of the power which he possesses respecting the trust." Because the trustee in this case had no such beneficial interest, it could not qualify as an adverse party. The court rejected taxpayer's argument that a trustee who is required by law to act solely in the interests of trust beneficiaries is necessarily an "adverse party" within the statute's definition.

[Duffy, 487 F2d 282, 32 AFTR2d 73-6124, 73-2 USTC ¶ 9784 (6th Cir. 1973), cert. denied, 416 US 938 (1974).]

Grantors are owners of trust income that is used to satisfy encumbrances on trust property. A husband and wife transferred to a trust property that was subject to liabilities in excess of the couple's basis in the property. Some of the liabilities were personal liabilities of the husband and wife, and some were nonrecourse liabilities. The couple also planned to refinance the property before the transfer. The trustee was to use trust property to pay the principal and interest on the liabilities; he was to pay the remaining trust income to the couple's adult children—the trust beneficiaries. The trust was to terminate in ten years and three months. The trustee then was to distribute the undistributed net income to the beneficiaries and the trust corpus to the grantors.

The IRS stated that the husband and wife are treated under Section 673 not as the owners of the property transferred to the trust, but as owners of the trust corpus under Section 677(a). Income used to satisfy the principal of debts on the corpus was income to the couple. The IRS concluded that because the grantors were owners of part of the trust income and principal, the transfer of property to the trust was not a disposition, and the couple did not recognize gain from the transfer of unencumbered property.

[Priv. Ltr. Rul. 8217228.]

[4] Support Obligations

Grantor is not taxable where trust funds do not discharge legally enforceable duty under state law. Taxpayer was a physician who practiced out of a building that he owned in Montana. The premises also contained rental space that was used by a pharmacy and by a resident tenant. As a gift, taxpayer deeded the property over to his six minor children and was appointed by the local probate court as their guardian. In this capacity, taxpayer collected rental payments made by the two tenants, as well as those he made to the guardianship pursuant to an unwritten lease. The rental income was applied to the children's insurance, health, and education. In the ensuing tax controversy, the IRS asserted that the conveyance was a sham wholly lacking in a business purpose, and that at a minimum, taxpayer was taxable under Section 677(b) of the grantor trust rules to the extent that the rental income was used to discharge his legal obligations of support.

Held: For taxpayer. The income was properly taxable to the donee children, not to taxpayer. Initially, the court determined that the guardianship was a trust for tax purposes, and that therefore Subchapter J and the grantor trust rules were fully applicable. The court then determined that taxpayer's transfer was not a sham or fraud, because taxpayer sought to (1) provide for his children's welfare; (2) avoid friction with his partners in the medical practice; (3) withdraw his assets from the threat of malpractice suits; and (4) diminish the perceived ethical conflict arising from the ownership of a medical practice in such proximity to a pharmacy. These factors, ruled the court, established "abundant" ground to conclude that tax avoidance was not the compelling motivation. The court went on to find that under Montana law, the payments made by taxpayer in his role as guardian were not enforceable legal obligations, and therefore were beyond the scope of Section 677(b).

[Brooke, 468 F2d 1155, 30 AFTR2d 72-5284, 72-2 USTC ¶ 9594 (9th Cir. 1972).]

Father taxable on income of educational trusts. In April 1959, taxpayer established four trusts to provide income for the payment of tuition and expenses for the education of his four children. Each trust was designed to accumulate income until the beneficiary became age 21, at which time the trust accumulations were to be distributed to the beneficiary. Ten years after the date of their creation, the trusts were to terminate, and the corpus was to revert to taxpayer.

The trustee, a bank, used part of the income to pay school-related expenses during the years 1959 through 1961. The IRS examined the parties' tax returns for the years in question and determined that taxpayer should have reported all trust income on his personal return. The IRS based its determination on the grantor trust rules set forth in Sections 671 et seq. In the IRS's view, the trusts were established to satisfy a legal obligation of the grantor and therefore fell within the rule of Section 677(a).

Held: For the IRS. A long line of judicial precedent applying Section 677(a) has established that trust income that is used to satisfy a legal obligation of the grantor is, in effect, distributable to him, and therefore is taxable in his gross income. The transactions of the trust are regarded as being the same in substance as if the money had been paid to taxpayer and he transmitted it to his creditor. In the instant case, the court found that taxpayer was obligated to each school for the payment of expenses and tuition, and that neither the trusts themselves nor the children individually were responsible for payment. Consequently, the court rejected taxpayer's argument that he was at most secondarily liable, and held him fully taxable on all trust income.

[Morrill, 228 F. Supp. 734, 13 AFTR2d 1334, 64-1 USTC ¶ 9463 (D. Me. 1964).]

Income of grantor trust is taxable to grantor to extent used to discharge support obligation. Taxpayer, a physician, was a shareholder and practiced medicine as an employee of a New Jersey professional service corporation. One of the offices used by the corporation was located in taxpayer's residence. Taxpayer established two irrevocable trusts for the benefit of his six children. Taxpayer, his wife, and a friend of theirs were the trustees. The corpus of each trust was one half of the space in taxpayer's residence that was occupied by the corporation, and the corporation paid rent each year to the trusts. In each of the years in issue, all of the distributed income of the trusts was used for either the college tuition and room and board, or private high school tuition and room and board, for taxpayer's children. The IRS issued a notice of deficiency to taxpayer, claiming that the trusts were grantor trusts, and that the trusts' payment of the children's educational expenses, both at the colleges and at the private high school, constituted a distribution in satisfaction of taxpayer's support obligation to the children within the meaning of Section 677(b). Taxpayer argued that the use of the trust income for educational expenses did not constitute the discharge of a support obligation.

Held: For the IRS. The Tax Court held that the trusts were grantor trusts, and that the education payments were in discharge of taxpayer's support obligation. Under Section 677(b), the income of a trust is taxable to a grantor to the extent that such income is applied or distributed for the support or maintenance of a beneficiary whom the grantor is legally obligated to support or maintain. The New Jersey Supreme Court has held that, depending on financial capability and other circumstances, parents may have an obligation to continue to provide educational expenses for unmarried children over the age of 18. This responsibility may include the duty to assure children of a college or even a postgraduate education. In this case, the petitioner clearly retained the obligation to provide his children with a college education, in light of the background, values, and goals of both the parents and children. The court also held that taxpayer's support obligation extended to providing private high school expenses for a younger child in the same family. Thus, the income of the two trusts, to the extent actually used for tuition and room and board for taxpayer's children, was taxable to him under Section 677(b).

[Braun, TC Memo. (P-H) ¶ 84,285, 48 TCM (CCH) 210 (1984).]

Trust for benefit of grantor's children is not owned by grantor if it is not used to satisfy legal support obligation. An individual planned to create an irrevocable trust for the benefit of his children. Income from the trust was not to be added to principal. During grantor's lifetime, the trustee was empowered to distribute principal or income to grantor's children as necessary for their support and education. On grantor's death, the trust assets were to be distributed to two trusts: one for grantor's spouse and one for the children. The marital trust was to consist of all assets included in grantor's gross estate. Accumulated income would not be put into the marital trust. The trust assets were to include a life insurance policy. The trust agreement prohibited the use of trust income for payment of insurance premiums. Grantor's children had the right to withdraw from the trust a percentage of the value of donated assets. The power existed whenever a donation to the trust was made (including the creation of the trust). Neither the income nor the principal of the trust was to be used to satisfy grantor's legal obligation to support the children.

The IRS stated that each beneficiary of the trust was required to include a pro rata share of income, deduction, and credit of the entire trust. However, the IRS indicated that a beneficiary would not be treated as the owner of any part of the trust if grantor were treated as the owner under Sections 671 and 677. The IRS referred to Regulation § 1.678(b)-1 in reaching its conclusion. The IRS concluded that none of the circumstances that would cause grantor to be treated as the owner of the trust under Sections 673, 674, and 676 existed. The IRS further concluded that grantor would not be treated as the owner of the trust under Section 677 if the trust were not used to support grantor's children. The IRS stated that any property transferred by gift to the trust would constitute a donation to the corpus of the trust. Finally, the IRS stated that grantor's transfers to the trust would qualify for the annual gift tax exclusion under Section 2503(b).

[Priv. Ltr. Rul. 8701007.]

¶ 21.05 BENEFICIARY CONTROL

Grantor trust rules apply even where powers of minor beneficiary are subject to exercise of guardian. *C* is a minor beneficiary of an irrevocable inter vivos trust created by *C*'s parent, *P*, in 1979. Under the terms of the trust agreement, an independent trustee is authorized to accumulate the net income of the trust unless, in the judgment of the trustee, all or part of the current or accumulated net income should be distributed to, or for the benefit of, *C* for *C*'s support, maintenance in reasonable comfort, health, and education until *C* reaches age 25. Also, the trustee may distribute principal to *C* subject to the above standard. The trust also provides that *C* has the noncumulative power in any calendar year to withdraw from principal the lesser of (1) all amounts added to the trust during such year by the grantor or (2) the sum of $3,000. *C* also has the power to withdraw the entire income of the trust until age 25. Unless exhausted by withdrawals or distributions, the trust is to terminate upon the death of *C* or at such time as *C* reaches age 25, and any remaining amount of trust principal and income is to be distributed to *C* or to *C*'s estate. Under applicable state law, *C*, as a minor, is legally incapable of exercising the above powers in the absence of an appointed guardian. Although no legal guardian has been appointed for *C*, there is no impediment under the trust agreement or local law to the appointment of a guardian.

The specific question presented is whether the holder of a power the exercise of which is limited by local law or by a legal or actual disability shall be treated as the owner of any portion of a trust for purposes of Section 678(a). Here, *C*, in the absence of an appointed guardian, is legally incapable of exercising the power; however, *C*'s inability to exercise the power because *C* is a minor does not affect the existence of the power. For purposes of Section 678, it is the existence of a power rather than the capacity to exercise such a power that determines whether a person other than the grantor shall be treated as the owner of any part of a trust. Under Section 678(a), *C*, a minor beneficiary of a trust, is treated as the owner of any portion of the trust with respect to which *C* has a power to vest the corpus or income in *C*, notwithstanding the fact that no guardian has been appointed for *C*.

[Rev. Rul. 81-6, 1981-1 CB 385.]

IRS treats trust grantors of oil and gas net profits interests as owners. Two individuals inherited percentages of a net profits interest in an oil and gas lease. At the time of inheritance, the interests were subject to an assignment executed in favor of a third person who was authorized to reimburse himself out of the proceeds of the net profits interest any sums advanced by him to the original owners of the interest. Acting on the desire of the third party to give the balance owing under the agreement to them, the two individuals transferred their interests in the net profits interest to trusts with bank trustees. The trustees were empowered generally to borrow in the name of the trust and to use part of the proceeds to pay debts of the individuals. The trustees were required to distribute to the individuals monthly amounts for life and to accumulate cash surpluses for future distributions to them. The trustees were also empowered to advance current or surplus cash to the individuals in the event of serious illness, emergency, or decline in the purchasing power of the dollar, or under any other circumstance that the trustee deemed necessary. On the deaths of the individuals, the trusts were to terminate and the assets were to be distributed as their wills directed or under the local laws of intestate succession.

The IRS stated under Section 677 that the two individuals would be treated as owners of the trusts, because the income could be distributed to them or accumulated for future distribution to them without the approval or consent of any adverse party. The IRS stated that the rest of each trust was their percentage interests transferred to the trusts, not the forgiveness of their indebtedness to the third party, which was the inducement to create the trusts.

[Priv. Ltr. Rul. 8532093.]

¶ 21.06 SHAM TRUSTS AND TRUST TRANSFERS

Ninth Circuit strikes down sham trust transfer of family residence. Taxpayers, husband and wife, transferred their interests in the family residence to a so-called family trust created from a kit that had been purchased from the Institute of Individual Religious Studies. The facts showed that despite their careful adherence to the formalities of establishing the trust, there had been no change in taxpayers' use and enjoyment of the property after the transfer, and their personal expenses were paid as expenses of trust administration.

Held: For the IRS. The court, citing Hanson, 696 F2d 1232 (9th Cir. 1983), ruled that the trust arrangement was a sham that could not be recognized for tax purposes. It had no economic effect other than to create tax benefits, and it was intended only to serve as a vehicle for tax evasion. On this basis the court awarded the IRS negligence penalties.

[Neely, 775 F2d 1092, 56 AFTR2d 85-6388, 85-2 USTC ¶ 9791 (9th Cir. 1985).]

Seventh Circuit strikes down dairy farmer's family trust scheme. Taxpayer, a dairy farmer and real estate broker, created a family trust in 1972. He and his wife transferred all of their real and personal property, including a farm and office equipment, together with the wife's future earnings, to the trustees, one of whom was the wife of their bookkeeper. In return, they received shares representing a beneficial interest in the trust for its entire twenty-five-year renewable term. The IRS determined that the trust should be ignored for tax purposes and that under the grantor trust rules set forth in Sections 671 et seq., taxpayer was fully taxable on the farm and real estate income.

Held: For the IRS. The Seventh Circuit began its analysis by noting that "[i]t takes no particular acumen in tax law to know that [these] trusts cannot be treated like ordinary trusts." The court observed that "the real question" was which of several established doctrines the IRS should use in denying the trust's existence as a taxable entity. The court proceeded to invalidate the trust under the anticipatory assignment of income doctrine, as well as the grantor trust rules. In particular, it cited Sections 674(a), 676(a), and 677(a) and, despairing of further analysis, concluded that all income was taxable to taxpayer without regard to the trust.

[Schulz, 686 F2d 490, 50 AFTR2d 82-5562, 82-2 USTC ¶ 9485 (7th Cir. 1982).]

Sixth Circuit upholds Tax Court refusal to recognize family trusts as bona fide limited partners or to provide relief under Section 671. On February 5, 1959, taxpayers, husband and wife, created a limited partnership known as A.K. Co. They contributed two apartment buildings, a large number of shares of publicly traded stock, plus 17,965 shares of Wolverine Shoe & Tanning Corp., a family business of which the husband was president. The governing instruments provided for the allocation of 40 percent of net profits to the general partners and 60 percent to the limited partners. Contemporaneously with the execution of the partnership agreement, taxpayers formed six separate trusts. The husband created three of the trusts, naming their children as beneficiaries, and the wife created the other three trusts for the benefit of their grandchildren. The children's trusts were funded with $100 and 50 shares of Wolverine stock, and the grandchildren's with $100 and 25 shares of Wolverine. In addition, the husband transferred his 60 percent limited partnership interest to the six trusts in exchange for $100 and 80 percent of the net income received by the trusts from the partnership for a period of sixteen years. The children's trusts each held a 15 percent interest in the partnership, and each of the grandchildren's trusts received a 5 percent interest. As a result of these transactions, taxpayers retained a general partnership interest of 40 percent of the profits from the apartment buildings and stock, with the husband receiving 80 percent of the net income from the remaining 60 percent limited partnership interest. By the terms of the instrument conveying the limited partnership interest, it was provided that the husband could reacquire his partnership interest in the event of specified contingencies over which he exercised all practical control. Thus, he retained the right to direct the trustee to make distributions of his periodic payments, and, if no such payments were made during a given year, he could revoke the entire transfer. During taxable years 1965, 1966, and

1967, A.K. Co. distributed a total of $126,000 to the six trusts, less distributions to the husband of $73,663 (net after taxes and expenses). The IRS determined that the trusts were not bona fide partners in the A.K. Co. within the meaning of Section 704(e). The provision permits a party to be recognized as a partner if he owns a capital interest in a partnership in which capital is a material income-producing factor, even if the interest was obtained by gift. The IRS contended that the partnership's entire income was taxable to taxpayers because the trusts were not the "real owners" of their purported 60 percent interest.

Held: Affirmed for the IRS. Although a person may possess a capital interest in a partnership in which capital, not only services, is a material income-producing factor, he will not be recognized as a partner for tax purposes unless the transferor has made a bona fide conveyance of the interest without retaining significant incidents of ownership. The court considered all of the facts presented to the lower court and found that taxpayers possessed both contingent rights to reacquire trust income and principal, as well as the retained right to receive present distributions of trust income. In addition, the major source of income was the Wolverine Co., which was controlled by taxpayers. On the record as a whole, the appellate court concluded that the trusts were not bona fide partners, and that in creating the trusts, taxpayers had no intention of irrevocably parting with dominion and control over trust property. In computing the assessed deficiency, the court rejected taxpayer's argument that the IRS wrongfully disallowed them a credit for the tax paid by the trusts in respect of income subsequently taxed to them. Although Section 671 provides that a grantor is entitled to the same deductions and credits as the trust would be, it does not follow that a tax credit can be claimed by such grantor. The court refused to fashion a relief measure in the instant case, absent congressional or regulatory authority therefor.

[Krause, 497 F2d 1109, 34 AFTR2d 74-5044, 74-1 USTC ¶ 9470 (6th Cir. 1974), cert. denied, 419 US 1108 (1975).]

Invalid trust for benefit of minors results in tax liability to settlor parents. Taxpayers were engaged in extensive disputes with the IRS in regard to their income tax liability. During this period, they set up an inter vivos trust for the benefit of their minor children, apparently to shelter income against tax liens. The instrument designated the beneficiaries, named a trustee, and established a termination date for the trust, but no trust corpus was mentioned, and nothing of any value was transferred to the trustee pursuant to the terms of the instrument.

Held: For the IRS. Taxpayers' actions were not sufficient to create a recognizable trust for tax purposes. The evidence indicated that taxpayers in fact fully controlled the operation and disposition of income, plus the management of the purported trust, and used it as a mere conduit to obtain funds for themselves in the guise of loans. This gave rise to a simple agency relationship, concluded the court, and therefore the property belonged to taxpayers and was fully subject to the tax liens.

[Garcia, 421 F2d 1231, 25 AFTR2d 70-491, 70-1 USTC ¶ 9226 (5th Cir. 1970), cert. denied, 400 US 945 (1970).]

Transferor of property to trust is held to be "owner" of trust and thus is taxable on trust income. Taxpayer was a shareholder in a Wall Street securities firm. The firm received a number of warrants entitling it to purchase the stock of certain corporations. During the year, the firm sought to attract and retain stockholders and employees by periodically assigning a portion of the warrants to them. Taxpayer sold a 64 percent equitable interest in a convertible debenture warrant to a foreign trust. The trust subsequently exercised the warrant and sold the stock. Taxpayer contended that he had sold the warrant to the trust for an annual annuity, and that gain on the sale should be recognized upon receipt of the payments. The IRS argued that the transfer of the warrant was not a bona fide exchange for an annuity, but was rather an outright sale, and that taxpayer recognized the entire gain upon the sale.

Held: For the IRS. The court found that the exchange was not an outright sale, but that taxpayer was nonetheless taxable on the gain, on the ground that taxpayer was the settlor of the foreign trust and was thus subject to tax on income attributable to the trust. The court found that taxpayer had retained effective control over the property purportedly sold to the trust and that the beneficiary of the trust, taxpayer's wife, was given the right to exercise her power of appointment over the trust assets in favor of taxpayer. Because taxpayer made all of his wife's business and financial decisions, he effectively preserved control over the property. Furthermore, it was clear from the evidence that taxpayer also controlled the trustee. The court also found that taxpayer was the settlor of the trust. The named settlor, taxpayer's friend and business associate, was the settlor in name only. The court reached this conclusion based on four factors:

1. The named settlor made only a nominal contribution as compared with a substantial amount transferred by taxpayer.
2. The creation of the trust and taxpayer's transfer occurred in close proximity.
3. The named settlor had a connection to the beneficiary.
4. The named beneficiary of the trust reflected the taxpayer's desires as to the lifetime and testamentary disposition of his property.

Because taxpayer was deemed the settlor of the trust, the grantor trust rules of Sections 671 and 678 were applicable. Under these rules, a taxpayer is taxed on the income attributable to any portion of a trust over which he is deemed to be the "owner." In the present case, taxpayer was considered the owner of the trust because of the effective control he had over the trust. Thus, the gain recognized on the sale of the stock by the corporation was taxable.

[Weigl, 84 TC 1192 (1985).]

Interfamily transfer of trust interest for adequate consideration is found not to be "ritualistic sham." In 1920, taxpayer and her mother established a trust and transferred to it their equal interests in the outstanding stock of a real estate business in Colorado. By the terms of the trust instrument, the mother was granted a life estate in all trust income, and taxpayer was granted a succeeding life estate. On the death of taxpayer, the trust provided that the income should be payable to taxpayer's surviving children for life, and to their issue for a period of twenty-one years. Upon termination of the trust, all assets were to be paid to the surviving issue. The trust further provided that in the event that taxpayer should survive the remaindermen, the trust estate would revert to her. Taxpayer's husband was named as trustee. In 1923, the mother died, leaving taxpayer as the life income beneficiary. Following two U.S. Supreme Court decisions in 1950, taxpayer's legal counsel advised her to dispose of her entire interest in the trust by means of gratuitous transfers in order to avoid having the corpus of the trust included in her gross estate. Because of the considerable value of the stock, taxpayer chose not to make the suggested gratuitous transfers, preferring instead to sell her interest and to generate needed cash. Accordingly, a plan was devised whereby her husband, who still served as trustee, agreed to buy her life interest and her reversion at an arm's-length price to be determined by their son-in-law, who operated the corporation. This plan was adopted and effectuated in 1950 according to a carefully prepared formula to arrive at a fair valuation. The life interest was then formally conveyed to the husband, who thereafter made payments each year through 1954. For federal tax purposes, the husband reported the trust income as a taxable distribution, and taxpayer reported the annual payments of consideration as a nontaxable return of basis. By the end of 1954, she had not yet recovered her full basis. The IRS examined taxpayer's treatment of the transaction and concluded that she was fully taxable on the trust's income, despite the purported transfer. In the IRS's view, the transfer should have been ignored, and the IRS denied any legal effect for tax purposes.

Held: For taxpayer. The Tax Court determined that the transfer was bona fide and that the income interest had been effectively shifted to the husband. The court rejected the IRS's attempts to characterize the transfer as a "ritualistic sham," and found upon close scrutiny that adequate consideration had been paid by the husband, and that the parties were motivated by legitimate estate-planning considerations and a genuine desire to effect the realignment of their respective property interests. The transfer was accomplished by legally sufficient agreements, and, despite the fact that taxpayer received the payments without any liability for tax, the entire arrangement was upheld.

[Evans, 30 TC 798 (1958).]

Assignment of income doctrine and grantor trust rules applied to defeat transfer of insurance sales proceeds to family trust. Taxpayer owned an insurance business, and in 1979 and 1980, he purported to transfer all of his income from insurance sales to a "family trust" that he claimed to have previously created. The IRS determined that the trust should be ignored for tax purposes, and that under the grantor trust rules set forth in Sections 671 et seq. and under the assignment of income doctrine, taxpayer was fully taxable on income derived from his insurance company.

Held: For the IRS. The court stated that the purported conveyance of taxpayer's income to the trust was merely an assignment of income that was an ineffective attempt to shift the incidence of taxation to the trusts. Furthermore, the court held that taxpayer was to be treated as the owner of the entire trust under the grantor trust rules under Sections 671 and 677.

[Schauer, TC Memo. (P-H) ¶ 87,237, 53 TCM (CCH) 793 (1987).]

Tax Court strikes down complex tax-avoidance trust scheme. Taxpayers were members of the same family living in Washington State during taxable years 1976 and 1979. During that period, taxpayers became involved in an organization that was promoting family trust schemes as a means of minimizing or even eliminating income tax liability for its members. Taxpayers themselves formed a so-called ALA trust by which they transferred all of their real and personal property, including businesses, to a trust for which they were named trustees. The trust plan eventually involved four interlocking trusts and a complexity of rules, interests, and organizational documents. The IRS conducted a thorough audit and a criminal investigation that resulted in an indictment and the instant notice of deficiency totaling in excess of $675,000.

Held: For the IRS. The Tax Court upheld the IRS's reconstruction of income by using the bank deposits method and, citing the sham transactions doctrine, held that all trust income was reportable by taxpayers, not by the trusts.

[Ripley, TC Memo. (P-H) ¶ 87,114, 53 TCM (CCH) 262 (1987).]

Family trust is held to violate assignment of income doctrine. In 1975, taxpayers, husband and wife, created a trust to which they conveyed their lifetime services and all of the husband's "earned remuneration accruing therefrom," together with title to other real and personal property. The instrument was called an "express equity pure trust." The trust was used to lease an automobile driven exclusively by taxpayers and for similar purposes. On their 1978 federal income tax return, taxpayers reported income as earned by the trust, and certain nominee payments and consulting fees were reported as deductions from trust gross income. The IRS disallowed the use of the trust for reporting income, and a deficiency was assessed in the amount of $2,949 plus a penalty of $147.

Held: For the IRS. The Tax Court stated that in view of the long series of decisions concerning similar family trust arrangements, all of which have held such assignments of income to be ineffective, there was no doubt that the IRS was correct in ignoring the trust for tax purposes. The court noted that "[i]t is an elementary principle of our tax system that individuals cannot escape taxation by diverting income to some other entity through contractual arrangements." On this basis, the court held that the assignment-of-income doctrine compelled full taxation directly against taxpayers.

[O'Donnell, TC Memo. (P-H) ¶ 86,014, 51 TCM (CCH) 266 (1986).]

Assignment of income doctrine applied to defeat transfer of installment sale agreement to family trust. In 1977, taxpayers sold their 160-acre farm in Illinois to another couple for $325,000. The parties executed an Agreement for Warranty Deed providing for $20,000 down and installment payments over twenty years with a $105,000 balloon payment at the end of the term. Taxpayers elected to report their gain under Section 453. In the year following the sale, however, they established a trust and transferred to it all rights in the installment agreement. They served jointly as trustees under a trust agreement that was by its terms irrevocable for a period of ten years, six months, and two days from its creation. As co-beneficiaries, taxpayers received the principal of each installment payment, and their children received the interest. The IRS assessed deficiencies on the ground that taxpayers were liable for tax on both interest and principal.

Held: For the IRS. The court held that the transfer was an anticipatory assignment of income and that they were fully taxable on all gain and interest under the rule set forth in Lucas v. Earl, 281 US 111 (1930). In form, stated the court, taxpayers did indeed transfer their entire interest in the installment agreement to the trust, taking back a right to receive the principal payments. In substance, however, they conveyed to the trust only the right to receive the interest paid pursuant to the installment agreement, with the trust merely serving as a conduit for the transfer of the principal payments from the purchasers to taxpayers.

[Flacco, TC Memo. (P-H) ¶ 85,393, 50 TCM (CCH) 632 (1985).]

IRS rules on "family estate" trust and assignment of "lifetime services" to trust. In the instant revenue ruling, an individual grantor transferred his personal residence, rental property, and income-producing securities to a "family estate" trust in exchange for all of the "units of beneficial interest" therein, with himself, his spouse, and a third party being named as trustees. The individual was considered the owner of the trust under either Section 674, 676, or Section 677. The IRS ruled that assignment of his "lifetime services" to the trust, that included all remuneration earned by him, regardless of its source, was ineffective to shift his tax burden to the trust.

[Rev. Rul. 75-257, 1975-2 CB 251.]

PART **VIII**

INCOME TAXATION OF TRUSTS

CHAPTER 22

Trust Income

¶ 22.01 TAXABLE INCOME OF TRUSTS

Personal residence held by testamentary trust does not qualify for tax preference exemption on sale of principal residence. Decedent, a California resident who died in 1977, created two trusts in his will. To Trust *A*, he devised his wife's community property interest in their personal residence, subject to her agreement, and to Trust *B*, he devised his own one-half community interest in the residence. The wife was the sole income beneficiary of the two trusts. On November 6, 1978, Trust *A* and Trust *B* both sold their respective one-half interests in the residence for a gross sale price of $465,000. On its fiduciary income tax return for the fiscal year ending July 31, 1979, Trust *B* reported its one-half share of capital gain realized on the sale and claimed an exclusion of 60 percent of such gain as a long-term capital gain deduction. The IRS, on audit, determined that the trust's net capital gain deduction was a tax preference item, and that the trust was therefore subject to the minimum tax under former Section 56. The trust argued that its sale of the personal residence fell within Section 57(a)(9)(D), which states that gain from the sale or exchange of a principal residence (within the meaning of Section 1034) shall not be taken into account as an item of tax preference. In the trust's view, the wife's use of the personal residence should have been imputed to it in order to invoke the exception of Section 57(a)(9)(D).

Held: For the IRS. Although California law treats an income beneficiary as the equitable owner of trust corpus, the Tax Court was not persuaded that such a classification compelled it to find that the property was in any sense the principal residence of taxpayer (in this instance, the trust). Under Section 1034, the property must be "used by taxpayer as his principal residence" in order to qualify for the exception in Section 57(a)(9)(D). Accordingly, the Tax Court ruled that the IRS correctly imposed the minimum tax.

[Lewis Testamentary Trust, 83 TC 246 (1984).]

IRS rules on consequences of "in-substance defeasance" by corporation using trust entity. Corporation X bought $300x of U.S. government securities and contributed them to an irrevocable trust. The trust instrument directed the trustee, a commercial bank, to apply the trust corpus and the interest thereon solely to satisfy the scheduled payments of principal and interest on a $500x outstanding bond issue of X. The trust instrument further provided that neither X nor its creditors were to rescind or to revoke the trust or to otherwise obtain access to the trust assets. Any amount remaining in the trust when the X bonds were retired was to revert to X. Because the government securities yielded 14 percent and the outstanding X bonds yielded only 6 percent, the $300x of government securities, coupled with the earnings thereon, would have generated sufficient funds to service the $500x outstanding debt. Further, the government securities were to provide cash flow (from interest and maturity of those securities) that approximately coincided, as to timing and amount, with the scheduled interest and principal payments on the outstanding X bonds. Moreover, because the assets of the trust were essentially risk-free as to timing and amount of payments of principal and interest, the possibility that X would be required to make future payments on the outstanding bonds was remote. However, X was not legally released from being the primary obligor on the outstanding bonds. The Financial Accounting Standards Board announced, in FASB Statement No. 76, "Extinguishment of Debt" (November 1983), that in trust arrangements such as the one described above, sometimes referred to as "in-substance defeasances," the debtor corporation shall consider the debt to be extinguished for financial accounting purposes. The IRS cited Regulation § 1.61-13(b), which provides that if a corporation, for the sole purpose of securing the payment of its bonds or other indebtedness, places property in trust or sets aside certain amounts in a sinking fund under the control of a trustee who may be authorized to invest or reinvest such sums from time to time, the property or fund thus set aside by the corporation and held by the trustee is an asset of the corporation. Any gain arising therefrom is income of the corporation and shall be included as such in its gross income. For financial accounting purposes, in accordance with FASB Statement No. 76, X was considered by the IRS as having extinguished the debt owed to its bondholders upon the transfer of assets to the trust, because the assets were essentially risk-free, and the likelihood that X would be required to make future payments to the bondholders was remote. However, X was not legally released from the obligation of being the primary obligor on the bonds. Consequently, for federal income tax purposes, X cannot be considered to have discharged the debt owed to its bondholders upon the transfer of assets to the trust.

[Rev. Rul. 85-42, 1985-1 CB 36.]

Trustee must report gain from sale of property on fiduciary income tax return. An individual received, under the will of his father, a life estate in a farm located in Michigan. The remainder in the estate was bequeathed by will to the son's surviving children. The farm barely returned sufficient income to pay the real estate taxes. Michigan law provided that a life tenant in land could (1) file a petition in a chancery court of the county in which the land was situated asking for authority to sell the property; (2) have the court appoint a trustee to take charge of the proceeds received from the sale; and (3) have such proceeds reinvested by the trustee under the order of the court. The life tenant filed such a petition, and the court entered an order authorizing him to sell the property. After the sale, the court appointed a trustee to receive the funds from the sale of the farm. Section 641(a)(1) imposes an income tax on income accumulated in trust for the benefit of unborn or ascertained persons or persons with contingent interests, and income accumulated or held for future distribution under the terms of the will or trust. Advice was requested from the IRS as to whether the gain from the sale of the real estate was to be reported in the year of sale and, if so, whether the life tenant or the court-appointed trustee was required to pay the tax under the circumstances of this case.

The IRS ruled that the trustee should report the gain from the sale of the property on a U.S. fiduciary income tax return, Form 1041, and pay the tax due thereon in the year of sale. Payment of the tax should not be made by the life tenant, nor should it await distribution of the estate to the remaindermen. The income held in the instant case was considered to be income held for future distribution under the terms of the will. The effect of Section 641(a)(1) was to tax the holder of such property as if such holder was a trustee or fiduciary, regardless of whether the local law constituted the holder of the income as a trustee or as a fiduciary.

[Rev. Rul. 59-99, 1959-1 CB 158.]

Trust does not realize income by distributing appreciated corpus. A trust was formed from the residue of an estate as provided in the will of decedent. The will directed that the net income of the trust be paid to the beneficiary until such beneficiary reached a specified age, at which time she would receive one fourth of the corpus or principal of the trust as valued at that time. The balance of the principal was to be retained in the trust, and the net income therefrom was to be distributed to the beneficiary for the next five years, at which time the trust would terminate and the beneficiary would receive the remaining trust principal. The will further provided that the trustees may, where they are required to divide any property into shares or parts or to distribute the same, make such division or distribution in kind or in money, or partly in kind and partly in money, and to that end, to allot specific securities or other property, real or personal, or an undivided interest therein, to any share or part, when the beneficiary of the trust attained the specified age and was entitled to receive a one-fourth distribution of trust principal, then valued at $60x. The trustees proposed to transfer to the beneficiary twenty shares of stock, valued at $15x, which were included in decedent's gross estate for federal estate tax purposes at $7x. Advice was required with respect to the treatment, for federal income tax purposes, of twenty shares of stock to be distributed from the principal of a trust in accordance with the terms of the will. The proposed distribution was not in satisfaction of an obligation of the trust for a definite amount of cash or equivalent value in securities but was rather in the nature of a partial distribution of a share of the trust principal. Accordingly, no sale or exchange was involved.

In view of the facts discussed above, the IRS ruled that neither the trustees nor the beneficiary would realize taxable income by the distribution and receipt of the stock. For federal income tax purposes, the basis of the stock to the beneficiary would be the value of the property as of the date of death of decedent as appraised for federal estate tax purposes, or the value as appraised at the optional valuation date for such purposes.

[Rev. Rul. 55-117, 1955-1 CB 233.]

¶ 22.02 BASIS OF TRUST PROPERTY

Basis of property is stepped up to date of death value, despite lack of legal title. Decedent died on March 28, 1975, leaving an estate valued at $7,213,604. Under his will, the residuary estate was to be divided between a marital trust and a residuary trust. Decedent's wife was the income beneficiary of both trusts and had a general power of appointment over the corpus of the marital trust. Decedent's wife died in November 1981. In her will, she exercised her power of appointment over the corpus of the marital trust by appointing it to an inter vivos trust for the benefit of her three grandchildren. At the time of her death, the trusts established under decedent's will were not yet funded. The assets in decedent's estate had substantially increased in value to $28,184,342. In June 1982, decedent's estate sold all of the stock that it held in Danbury Fair, Inc. The net proceeds from the sale totaled $25,399,454. In computing the capital gain, the estate used as its basis the value of the stock at the time of decedent's death, $1,779,993. It reported a capital gain of $23,619,521 and paid capital gains tax of $4,719,784. Shortly thereafter the estate distributed $2,563,596 to the marital trust. In August 1982, decedent's wife's estate filed its federal estate tax return, that included the $2,563,596 in the marital trust, treating it as a pecuniary or fixed bequest. The IRS determined that the bequest to the marital trust should have been treated as a fractional share bequest (a proportionate share of the residue) rather than as a pecuniary bequest, and that the appreciation in value of that proportionate share should have been included in decedent's wife's estate. This increased the value of the trust by approximately $6,300,000, to $8,863,596, and increased the estate tax by $3.4 million. Approximately one year later decedent's estate filed a claim for refund of $1,485,882 for an alleged overpayment of fiduciary income tax. The estate argued that because decedent's wife's estate included the appreciated value of the property in the marital trust on its estate tax return, decedent's estate could use the stepped-up basis to determine the amount of capital gain on the sale of the property. The IRS denied the refund claim, and the estate sued. The district court ruled in favor of the IRS, finding that decedent's estate could not use the step-up in basis to calculate its capital gain. The estate appealed the ruling.

Held: For the estate. Section 1014, which regulates the computation of basis in property received from decedent, generally provides that the basis of property in the hands of a person "*acquiring* the property from a decedent or to whom the property *passed* from a decedent" (emphasis added) is the property's fair market value (FMV) at the date of death. The IRS contended that decedent's estate always possessed the property that was in the marital trust. Therefore, it never "acquired" anything from decedent's wife's estate. Therefore, decedent's estate could not use the value of the stock at her death as its basis in the stock that was sold. The Second Circuit disagreed and found that the IRS did not apply the definition of "property" consistently. It was an undisputed fact that the power of appointment that decedent's wife held over the assets in the marital trust caused those assets to be included in her estate, even though the marital trust was not yet funded. Decedent's wife was the beneficial owner of such assets for estate tax purposes until she died. At her death, her appointee, the inter vivos trust, acquired her interest in the property. Although the executor of decedent's estate was responsible for managing, liquidating, and distributing the assets in his estate and retained legal title to those assets, his estate did not "possess any real ownership interest in the property." It simply held or managed the property on behalf of the beneficiaries of the marital trust. Similarly, although the estate was liable for paying the capital gains tax arising from the sale of property that had not yet been distributed to the marital trust, the tax payment came out of the proceeds of the sale. Consequently, the tax burden actually fell on the beneficiaries of the trust. The circuit court concluded that whether decedent's estate could use the stepped-up basis depended on whether decedent's wife's appointee, the inter vivos trust, could have used the stepped-up basis to calculate capital gains on sales of marital trust property after decedent's wife's death. The court determined that decedent's wife's appointee could use the stepped-up basis. Although the inter vivos trust did not actually hold the stock when it was sold, it had acquired a beneficial interest in the stock through decedent's wife. The court reviewed the provisions of Section 1014 that describe the basis of property acquired from a decedent. According to the court, Congress did not intend to interpret the words of acquisition in Section 1014—"acquiring"and "passed from"—literally. The opinion cited one of a number of examples found in Section 1014(b) of how property can be acquired from a decedent. Under Section 1014(b)(4), "property passing without full and adequate consideration under a power of appointment exercised by decedent by will" is property acquired from decedent. Also cited was Regulation § 1.1014-4(a)(1), which states that the basis of property acquired from a decedent is uniform in the hands of any persons possessing or enjoying the property under a will or other instrument, regardless of whether the property is possessed or enjoyed by an executor or administrator, an heir, a legatee or devisee, or a trustee or beneficiary of a trust. The fact that decedent's estate delayed in distributing the assets to the marital trust did not affect the basis. The court pointed out that to say otherwise would allow executors to manipulate tax consequences by their decisions regarding when to distribute estate assets. Decedent's wife's appointee, the inter vivos trust, was deemed to have acquired the stock upon decedent's wife's death, and such appointee could use the stepped-up basis. Decedent's estate, which was holding and managing the property for the appointee, could also use the stepped-up basis when determining the amount of capital gain upon the sale of the property.

[Connecticut Nat'l Bank, 937 F2d 90, 91-2 USTC ¶ 60,079, 68 AFTR2d 91-5170 (2d Cir. 1991).]

Property settlement made for adequate and full consideration results in basis step-up. During the pendency of their divorce action, a husband and wife entered into a comprehensive court-approved property settlement. Among the contested assets were 6,600 shares of zero-basis corporate stock that the husband acquired in exchange for certain patent rights. It was agreed that the husband and wife would take 2,400 and 2,000 shares, respectively, as their separate property, and that the remaining 2,200 shares would be placed in an educational trust for the benefit of their minor children. The agreement was incorporated into the court's final decree, and, together with other stipulations and undertakings, was accepted in exchange for relieving the husband of the obligation to provide further support and maintenance for the wife and children. Shortly after the transfer, the trustee sold 1,000 shares of the stock at FMV. The trust reported no gain on the sale, contending that it had received a stepped-up FMV basis upon the husband's conveyance of the stock pursuant to the settlement agreement. In support, the trust relied on Section 2516, which provides that transfers made pursuant to certain property settlements do not constitute taxable gifts but are deemed to have been made for adequate and full consideration where entered into for the purpose of furnishing support or for the relinquishment of marital rights. In the trust's view, the stock transfer qualified under Section 2516 as an exchange rather than as a gift, and therefore the basis of the stock in the hands of the trustee was equal to FMV. The IRS maintained that the transfer was a gift and that the trustee had a carryover basis of zero.

Held: For the trust. The court rejected the IRS's contention that taxable gain resulted under Section 644 and held that the initial stock transfer fell squarely within the rule of Section 2516. In substance, the property settlement agreement was part of the overall resolution of the husband's and wife's respective interests. The court concluded that the husband should be deemed as having received full and adequate consideration in the form of the wife's release of her marital rights. Thus, the step-up in basis occurred at the time of the husband's transfer to the trustee; therefore, no gain resulted under Section 644 on the trust's later sale of the property at the same FMV.

[St. Joseph Bank & Trust Co., 716 F2d 1180, 52 AFTR2d ¶ 83-5946, 83-2 USTC ¶ 13,537 (7th Cir. 1983).]

Court of Claims draws narrow legal distinction in finding trust revocable for basis step-up purposes, thus minimizing its capital gains liability. Decedent was the grantor of an inter vivos trust created in 1931. The trust corpus consisted of 30,000 shares of corporate stock, which were given to him by his father. The trust instrument provided that decedent was to receive the first $80,000 of trust income for life, with the next $12,000 to be paid to his wife for her life, and the balance of any trust income to be paid to their daughter for her life. Decedent also reserved the power to modify, alter, or revoke the trust in whole or in part, with the written consent of his father or his father's executor or other legal representative. An amendment to the trust in 1932 provided that on the death of decedent, two thirds of the corpus should be divided between his wife and their issue. A further amendment in 1934 changed decedent's power of revocation by restricting its exercise so that he could not increase his own or his estate's interest in the income or cause title to any trust property or accumulations to revert to him. In 1945, decedent died, survived by his former wife and two children. Each child received one third of the trust corpus, with the remaining third continuing to be held by the trust for the benefit of the former wife and first-born daughter. The estate was compelled by the IRS to include the value of trust corpus in the gross estate, and, as a result of the increased tax liability, the trustee was forced to dispose of part of the corporate stock. An arrangement was made with the officers of the corporation to purchase the stock in exchange for shares of certain publicly traded stock. In reporting the gain from this transaction, the trustee used as the trust's basis the FMV of the stock on the date of death, rather than the considerably lower original cost basis. The IRS disputed the trustee's use of the higher stepped-up basis and insisted that cost basis was appropriate. The issue at trial centered on whether the statutory basis provisions codified in Section 1014(b)(2) applied to give the trust a stepped-up basis on the date of death. The statute provides that a step-up is proper only where the subject property was transferred by decedent during his lifetime in trust to pay the income for life to, or on the order or direction of, decedent, with the right reserved to decedent at all times before his death to revoke the trust. The IRS contended that the trust was not revocable by virtue of the 1934 amendment.

Held: For the trust. The court held that the 1934 amendment, by which decedent's power to revoke could not be exercised to increase his or his estate's income interest or to revest the trust property in himself, was not sufficient to render the trust irrevocable for purposes of Section 1014(b)(2). It was "perfectly clear" that the amendment did not affect decedent's power to revoke the trust as to the then-existing beneficiaries, and to direct the payment of the trust funds to anyone but himself or his estate. In this determination, the court distinguished between the power to revoke a trust created by a deed of grant and to convert it into an outright gift, versus the power wholly to revoke the original grant and to revest the corpus in the grantor or another. The 1934 amendment barred decedent from exercising the latter right, but the former right remained. The court concluded that this was enough to fall within the basis step-rule of Section 1014(b)(2). At the same time, the court rejected the suggestion that the need to obtain written consent from decedent's father or executor made the trust irrevocable. The father had no adverse interest in the disposition of any part of the trust property; therefore, the law presumed his amenability to the wishes of his son. Accordingly, the trust was entitled to use the higher stepped-up basis in reporting its capital gain on the exchange of stock.

[Bankers Trust Co., 156 F. Supp. 930, 1 AFTR2d 376, 58-1 USTC ¶ 9123 (Ct. Cl. 1957).]

Tax Court determines basis of stock sold by inter vivos trust following grantor's death. Grantor created a trust under an agreement, executed in 1939, between himself and his brother. The two were the owners of substantially all the stock of the United Linen Service Corp. and a related entity. Both parties were actively engaged in the operation of the business. However, their personal enmity began to intrude upon their business dealings. When grantor announced his plans to be married, both the brother and the other directors expressed concern at the prospect of his stock passing to an outside party in the event of his death. Accordingly, corporate counsel prevailed upon grantor to create the subject trust for his own benefit and transfer to it the bulk of his stock interest. The trustee, his brother, was directed to pay to grantor the entire net income derived from the trust property quarterly, plus corpus, when, in his discretion, the trustee deemed it to be advisable. By its terms, the trust was irrevocable, and upon grantor's death, the corpus was to pass to his children. Grantor married in 1939 and remained married until he died intestate in 1946. Shortly after his death, his widow filed suit against the brother in federal district court, alleging that the prenuptial transfer of the stock was fraudulent as to her and her infant daughter. The suit sought damages and an order that she receive one third of all shares held in trust. In 1948, the parties entered into a settlement of the widow's suit, wherein they agreed to have the court enter an order to the effect that decedent's widow was entitled to have one third of the stock transferred to her, but that she would make no such demand if the brother, as trustee, would (1) pay her $80,000 in cash and (2) create an $80,000 trust for the benefit of the infant daughter. The trust thereupon sold a block of 113 shares of the United Linen stock for $368,000, plus 115 shares of the related corporation for $92,000, under installment sales agreements. On its fiduciary returns for the years in which it received payments for the sale of stock, the trust computed its taxable gain by using as its basis the per-share value established by the grantor's estate for estate tax purposes. The IRS disputed the trust's reported gain and determined that the proper basis was the grantor's own cost basis, which resulted in a sizable deficiency.

Held: For the IRS. The trust argued that it was entitled to a stepped-up FMV basis in the stock by virtue of provisions of the 1939 Code that are substantially equivalent to current Section 1014(b)(2). Under those provisions, a trust is entitled to a step-up in basis where property was transferred by decedent during his lifetime in trust to pay the income for life to him or on his own order and direction, with the right at all times to revoke the trust prior to his death. The court rejected the trust's contention, and pointed to express language in the trust agreement that provided that trust corpus was payable to the grantor only in the exercise of the trustee's sound discretion. Because grantor did not reserve a power of revocation, the step-up under current Section 1014(a) was not available. The court further rejected as without merit the trust's argument that the trustee was a nonadverse party and that therefore he was bound to invade corpus upon the direction of the grantor. Consequently, the court upheld the tax deficiencies asserted by the IRS, and ruled that the grantor's cost basis, without adjustment for the amount paid to the widow or for attorney fees or taxes, should control in the calculation of realized gain.

[Trust of Spero, 30 TC 845 (1958).]

Trust cannot adjust basis of assets to reflect payment of transferee estate tax liability. Prior to his death in 1944, decedent created separate trusts for the benefit of his two daughters. The trusts were irrevocable, and each contained a like number of shares in a closely held corporation. The IRS conducted an audit of decedent's estate, and, in 1948, determined that the trust assets were includable in the gross estate. As a result of the assessment of estate tax deficiencies, the trust became liable for a total of $1.9 million in back taxes. The IRS and the trustees agreed to compromise the amount owed. A settlement was reached whereby the trusts paid the IRS $509,428 and $475,243, respectively. They also paid additional state death taxes in the amount of $132,663 and $123,761. The trusts were forced to sell a portion of their stock to pay the taxes, and in reporting their gain, used a cost basis adjusted to reflect the payment of the additional taxes. The IRS rejected the trusts' basis computations and insisted that the taxes could not be added as charges to capital accounts within the meaning of Section 1016(a)(1).

Held: For the IRS. The court found, as a general rule, that transferees of estate property cannot add their derivative tax liability to basis. The overall result would be to allow a recoupment of such taxes on a later sale of the property, thereby defeating the imposition of estate tax. The payments made by the trusts were not expended to preserve or to protect the transferred property, because the liability of a transferee is wholly personal. Accordingly, the proper basis for determining gain was the trust's original carryover basis dating to the original trust transfer.

[Bache Trust, 24 TC 960 (1955), aff'd per curiam sub nom. Michel, 239 F2d 385, 51 AFTR 382, 57-1 USTC ¶ 9286 (2d Cir. 1956).]

¶ 22.03 RECOGNIZING MULTIPLE TRUSTS

Fifth Circuit finds trust instrument provided for creation of separate trust entitles for each beneficiary. In two identical instruments, the grantors, who were brothers, created trusts for the benefit of their respective children. The trustees determined that the trust agreements provided for the establishment of a separate trust for each beneficiary. Upon that theory, they divided the income from the trust funds into separate accounts for each of the ten children involved and computed income taxes on that basis. On audit, the IRS determined that the tax paid by each of the trusts was refundable, and that only two separate trusts were created by the grantors. Upon these determinations, the IRS assessed deficiencies for each of the two trusts in the amount of $1,994. The trustees argued in federal district court that the governing trust instruments should be construed as establishing ten separate trusts, consistent with the intention of the grantors. The IRS contended, however, that the shares of the various beneficiaries under the instruments were so interwoven as to negate any intention to create separate trusts. In support, the IRS emphasized that each instrument provided that upon the death of a beneficiary without issue, his share was to be divided into equal portions and distributed to the remaining children. In the event that a remaining child still retained his share in trust, the portion of the deceased child's share would be added to the fund in trust for the surviving child. The IRS concluded that this and other provisions were not consistent with the argument that the instruments as a whole reflected the grantors' desire to create separate trusts.

Held: Affirmed for taxpayers. The court noted that the grantors' intent was clearly expressed by the terms of the trusts, which required the trustees to divide the corpus into "equal separate and distinct trust funds, creating one such fund for each of the children." In addition, the beneficiaries were entitled to receive distributions only up to their share of the income and corpus, without any right to participate in the balance of the trust corpus. Considering all of the facts and circumstances, the court concluded that the district court's findings of fact were supported by substantial evidence.

[Commercial Bank, 450 F2d 330, 28 AFTR2d 71-5743, 71-2 USTC ¶ 9672 (5th Cir. 1971).]

Retroactive reformation of trust instrument in state court is held ineffective to change federal tax results. Grantor was a one-half owner of an Iowa partnership actively engaged in the business of selling clay products. During 1945, he executed a deed of trust by which he purported to convey part of his interest in the business to a trust for the benefit of his wife and two children. The wife was to receive one third of all annual trust income, and the children were to receive whatever the trustees deemed appropriate for their support, not to exceed one third of all trust income each. In 1946 through 1948, the trustees filed separate annual tax returns for each of the three beneficiaries. The IRS disputed this method of reporting trust income, and treated the annual earnings and distributions of the trust as arising from a single taxable entity. The trustees paid the asserted deficiencies on August 15, 1952, and, on that same day, filed a petition for refund, claiming that the trust deed created three separate trust estates for tax purposes. The grantor filed an action in local equity court a year later for a reformation of the trust instrument. He sought to obtain a ruling that would effectuate his original intention to create three separate trusts. The local court obliged grantor and entered on record a judgment nunc pro tunc (i.e., retroactive). The judgment declared that the trust deed was reformed to reflect the creation of three separate trusts upon the initial signing of the instrument. In subsequent Tax Court proceedings on the 1952 assessment, the court ruled that the IRS correctly treated taxpayer as having created a single trust.

Held: Affirmed for the IRS. The court found that in his initial deed of trust grantor expressly and unambiguously created one trust entity, and that the IRS correctly determined tax liability on that basis. The reformation proceedings in state court were solely for the purpose of lowering the trust's tax burden. Thus the appellate court refused to give effect to the final decree for tax purposes. A taxpayer cannot use an equitable remedy in state court to produce an inequitable result upon the IRS's revenues.

[Estate of Straight, 245 F2d 327, 51 AFTR 552, 57-2 USTC ¶ 9727 (8th Cir. 1957).]

Ninety trusts are not recognized as separate entities. Settlor created ninety identical trusts designating his son as sole beneficiary and his son's father-in-law as trustee. On the same day that he signed the trust instruments, he gave his trustee ninety checks for various amounts totaling $17,740. One check was designated for each trust. The trustee then gave the settlor ninety checks drawn on the trustee's account in the same amounts as those received from the settlor. On the next day, in consideration for the $17,740 and for the benefit of the ninety trusts, settlor conveyed title to the trustee for two houses, his medical clinic and its fixtures, together worth approximately $28,300. The trustee immediately leased the clinic back to settlor for $400 per month. The trustee then resigned, and settlor appointed his wife as trustee, pursuant to a power of appointment contained in the trust instruments. Over the next four years, the new trustee collected all income produced by the trust properties and deposited it in a single bank account. She made several distributions. However, separate checks were issued for each of the "trusts" involved in only one case, a payment of $4,000 to the beneficiary. Thereafter she made distributions in lump-sum checks drawn on the single bank account shared by the ninety trusts. No income tax returns were filed by the trustee to report trust income. The IRS assessed a deficiency, which was paid, and a refund suit was then instituted.

Held: For the IRS. The district court, applying what it called "close scrutiny" of the facts surrounding the case, concluded that this scheme was a mere tax evasion ploy that flouted the purpose of the tax laws. The court characterized the creation of ninety trusts for such a small amount of property as "preposterous." Despite their separate form, these trusts were treated by taxpayer as a single entity. The trustee did not keep ninety separate bank accounts and make ninety separate distributions as required by the terms of the trusts. Instead, she combined the income from all of the trusts into one account and paid lump-sum distributions to the beneficiary. Considering substance rather than form, the court concluded that a single trust existed. Taxpayer's ingenuity failed. Thus, he was required to bear the tax consequences resulting from these acts.

[Boyce, 190 F. Supp. 950, 7 AFTR2d 716, 61-1 USTC ¶ 9257 (WD La. 1961), aff'd per curiam, 296 F2d 731, 8 AFTR2d 6001, 62-1 USTC ¶ 9150 (5th Cir. 1961).]

Tax Court strikes down IRS regulations on consolidation of multiple trusts. On December 14, 1972, the settlor executed a single instrument by which he created two inter vivos trusts. The first of these, referred to as the Simple Trust, was initially funded with 5,000 shares of dividend-paying stock in a public corporation. The second, referred to as the Accumulation Trust, was composed entirely of distributions received from the Simple Trust and from its own accumulated income. The trustees were instructed to make certain mandatory and discretionary distributions of income from the Simple Trust to the principal beneficiary, who was the settlor's daughter. Income not currently distributed to the name beneficiaries was to be distributed to the Accumulation Trust, of which the daughter was also a beneficiary.

Each trust filed a separate income tax return for the years 1974 and 1975. On audit, however, the IRS sought to disregard the separate identities of the two trusts and assessed deficiencies based on a consolidation of all trust income and distributions. In support, the IRS cited Regulation § 1.641(a)-0(c), which requires the consolidation for tax purposes of those multiple trusts that have (1) no substantially independent purposes; (2) the same grantor and substantially the same beneficiary; and (3) the avoidance of either the progressive taxes or the alternative minimum tax for tax preferences as their principal purpose. At trial, the trust argued that the regulation was invalid, contending that the Tax Court's decision in Morris Trusts, 51 TC 20 (1968), aff'd per curiam, 427 F2d 1361, 26 AFTR2d 70-5007, 70-2 USTC ¶ 9490 (9th Cir. 1970), was controlling.

Held: For taxpayer. In *Morris Trusts*, the court held as a matter of law that a finding of tax avoidance was simply not enough to invalidate multiple trusts. The court based its holding on the fact that Congress showed no intention of restricting the income-splitting effect inherent in Subchapter J. In addition, no statutory provision existed making tax avoidance motive a basis for expanding a trust's tax liability. The court noted that following the *Morris Trusts* decision, Congress amended the closely related throwback rule in the Tax Reform Act of 1969, and that it had not expressed a contrary view with respect to multiple trusts. In addition, the court found that whereas Congress chose an objective approach in dealing with multiple trusts under the Section 666 throwback rules, the IRS adopted an incompatible subjective approach in its regulations. The court proceeded to find that the regulation was invalid, because it added restrictions not contemplated by Congress. Accordingly, the court entered judgment for taxpayer pursuant to *Morris Trusts.*

[Stephenson Trust, 81 TC 283 (1983).]

Tax Court finds record sufficient to prove settlor's intent to create multiple trusts. The settlor was heir to a large fortune was placed in trust for him on the death of his father in 1936. He was also a beneficiary of certain other trusts created by his grandparents in 1943 and 1954. During 1960, shortly after the birth of his son, the settlor created a trust containing corporate common stock for the benefit of his son and any afterborn children. The trust instrument described the interest of each child as his "share," or "part," of the trust estate. In 1961, a second child was born. A question arose as to whether the trust instrument effectuated the creation of separate trusts for each beneficiary or a single trust with equal beneficial shares. To clarify the apparent ambiguity, the settlor amended the trust in 1961. Inexplicably, however, the language used in the amendment failed to remove the ambiguity or to state clearly his intentions. Nevertheless, the trustee proceeded on the assumption that each child was the beneficiary of a separate trust. In reporting income during the taxable years in issue, the trustee filed separate trust returns for each of the settlor's children, of whom there were four by 1969. The IRS insisted that one trust existed and assessed deficiencies for 1970 through 1972.

Held: For the trust. The court that the question was whether, as a matter of law, the settlor intended to create a single trust or multiple trusts. The testimony adduced at trial demonstrated that the settlor sought to clarify his intention to create separate trusts by means of the 1961 amendment. The trust instrument was internally consistent in its references to each individual "share" or "part," and the trustee at all times regarded the children as beneficiaries of separate trust estates. Additionally, the form of the beneficiaries' interests was so diverse as to mitigate in favor of finding a single trust entity. The court disregarded the fact that no separate records were kept of each child's interest, and ruled that on the record as a whole, adequate proof existed of the establishment of multiple trusts.

[Moody Trust, 65 TC 932 (1976), acq. 1976-2 CB 1.]

Grantors' tax avoidance motives held irrelevant to recognition of multiple trusts. During 1953, the grantors, husband and wife, each executed ten separate irrevocable declarations of trust by which they purported to create a total of twenty trust entities. The primary beneficiaries were the grantors' son and daughter-in-law. Each instrument was virtually identical, and provided for the accumulation of income for the life of the beneficiaries, with discretion in the trustee to make distributions at any time to maintain the beneficiaries' accustomed standard of living. In addition, the trustee was empowered to combine the corpus of each trust with the corpus of other trusts in pursuance of any management purpose or for convenience. Each trust was funded with an average of $3,000 cash, and each maintained its own bank account, checks, and records. During taxable years 1961 through 1965, the trustee filed twenty separate annual tax returns. The IRS refused to accept the income on separate returns, and assessed deficiencies based on its conclusion that only one trust had been established for tax purposes.

Held: For taxpayer. The Tax Court held as a matter of law that where a grantor abides by state law and makes certain to "dot his i's and cross his t's," there is no basis for declaring the trusts invalid solely because tax avoidance was the underlying motivation. The court stressed the absence of any statutory provision aimed at striking down such an apparent income-splitting scheme and noted that Congress previously considered the question of trust consolidation, but took no action. In view of this legislative background, the court declined to hold that tax avoidance was a ground for consolidation and entered judgment for taxpayer.

[Morris Trusts, 51 TC 20 (1968), aff'd per curiam, 427 F2d 1361, 26 AFTR2d 70-5007, 70-2 USTC ¶ 9490 (9th Cir. 1970).]

Perpetual care fund is taxable as single trust. A cemetery corporation contracted with a local bank in South Carolina whereby the bank agreed to accept certain funds transferred to it irrevocably by the corporation for investment under the direction of the corporation. The fund income was to be paid to the corporation quarterly to be used in honoring its obligation to purchasers of cemetery lots to provide for the perpetual care and maintenance of the cemetery in general, including the specific lots purchased. Each burial lot sold by the corporation carried the oral or written understanding that not less than 10 percent of the purchase price, when paid in full, would be transferred to the trustee (the bank) of the perpetual care fund. The duties of the trustee were limited to the receipt of the trust funds transferred to it by the corporation and the payment of the trust income to the corporation quarterly. When the principal and collected interest of the fund amounted to $1x$, the designated agent of the corporation directed the trustee as to the manner in which such amounts were to be invested. The trustee could make investments, however, when the investments were designated, of less than $1x$. Upon the direction of the corporation, the trustee was required to sell any investment theretofore made upon such terms as directed by the corporation. Under the contract, no owner of any lot sold by the corporation would be considered as possessing any vested benefit or other interest in the perpetual care fund. The corporation was considered the sole beneficiary of such funds. Advice was requested from the IRS as to whether the agreement entered into between the cemetery corporation and the bank should be considered as creating a trust, and, if so, whether it created a single trust or multiple trusts for federal income tax purposes.

The IRS ruled that the agreement was considered a trust instrument within the meaning of Section 641 which provides for the taxation of income of estates and trusts. Therefore, the trust was taxable as a single trust. Under South Carolina law, a requirement existed to create an irrevocable trust for the perpetual care of the grave spaces. Therefore, a trust existed under Section 641 because there was an intention under the trust instrument to create a trust and the legal title to the investments was vested in the trustee, with the corporation as the designated beneficiary. In designating that the income of the trust was to be used for the general care of all the lots sold by the corporation, as well as for the general care of the cemetery, the provisions of the trust instrument indicated that it was the intention of the parties to create a single trust. Accordingly, the trust constituted a single trust for federal income tax purposes.

[Rev. Rul. 59-30, 1959-1 CB 161.]

Division of trust assets into two new trusts to equalize compensation to beneficiaries does not result in income to trusts or to beneficiaries. An entity created a trust. The entity arranged a transfer by the trust of its stock in one foreign corporation to a second foreign corporation in exchange for the stock of the second corporation. The exchange resulted in a potentially huge inequity among beneficiaries who owned only an indirect interest in the second foreign corporation, as compared to those who owned a partnership interest. As a result, the entity decided to divide the trust. The entity assigned 50 percent of the first trust's interest in the partnership to a second newly created trust. The first trust then withdrew shares of common stock in the second foreign corporation and ceased to be a partner in the partnership. The remaining shares of common stock in the second foreign corporation were not distributed to the first trust but would be owned indirectly by the second trust by virtue of its direct ownership of its partnership interest. After the division, half the beneficiaries would hold an interest in one trust, and half would hold an interest in the second trust. The trusts would offer their respective beneficiaries basically the same benefits.

The IRS stated that the proposed division of the trust into two trusts would not be a sale or other disposition or distribution of property and would not result in income, gain, or loss to any trust or beneficiary under Section 367, 661, 662, 663, 741, 751, or 1001.

[Priv. Ltr. Rul. 8949082.]

Partition of trust pursuant to court order does not have adverse tax consequences. A trust provided for the annual distribution of income to the three children of the testator per stirpes. The trustee held no discretion to accumulate the income. The trust also provided for trustee fees and expenses, which could be paid from the corpus or from the income. One of the settlors appointed another individual to serve as trustee upon her death. The trust also had a reinvestment restriction provision. The trustee was forbidden to dispose of certain stock in a corporation that funded the trust. The stock could be sold only to save the trust fund from substantial loss. The value of the corporation's stock declined. Certain beneficiaries of the trust signed an agreement authorizing the sale of a number of shares of the corporation's stock. The capital gain taxes realized from the sale were paid by the trust and allocated to the corpus. Numerous actions and cross-actions were commenced by the beneficiaries as a result of the stock sale by the trustee. These included whether the trustee should be removed, whether the taxes should be paid out of the corpus or income, and whether deviation from the investment restrictions should be permitted. A settlement agreement was entered into whereby the trust was to be partitioned into four parts. Each part was to pay the income to each beneficiary and then to the respective remaindermen.

The IRS stated that with respect to the reinvestment clause issue, there would be no change in the value of any beneficiary's interest as a result of the proposed settlement. The IRS reasoned that it is necessary to determine whether the settlement properly reflected the economic values of the claims of the respective parties in determining whether any gift tax would be imposed because of the settlement agreement. The IRS indicated that the allocation of the capital gain taxes resulting from the sale between the corpus and income likewise did not result in any gift tax liability. The IRS determined that the creation of successor trusteeships and allocation of trustee fees did not deviate from the original article in the trust and did not result in any gift tax. The IRS reasoned that because the trust was partitioned by court order and no corpus would be added to any beneficiary's share as a consequence, the partitioning of the trust did not materially change the value or timing of any of the beneficial interests of the beneficiaries. Thus, the generation-skipping transfer tax (GST) under Section 2601 would not be imposed, because the partitioned trusts would be considered as having been created prior to September 25, 1985. The IRS concluded that the partitioned trusts would be treated as separate trusts for federal tax purposes. The IRS also concluded that none of the beneficiaries would be treated as an owner of the partitioned trusts under Section 678. The IRS stated that to the extent that the amounts that were charged to income and credited to corpus represented items of gross income, those amounts would be includable in the gross income of the trust and, following the division of the trust, in the gross income of each of the trusts. The IRS concluded that none of the trusts or beneficiaries would recognize any gain as a result of the partitioning of the trust pursuant to the settlement order, because there had been no change in their respective beneficial interests. The IRS then determined that the provision in the settlement agreement that called for the appointment of a new trustee would not result in any party realizing income. Further, the IRS determined that the mutual releases signed by all parties would not be viewed as a taxable exchange under Section 1001. The IRS also concluded that the arrangement would not be viewed as a below-market-rate loan under Section 7872. Finally, the IRS concluded that the successor trusts lacked the characteristics of an association taxable as a corporation under Section 7791. Rather, the successor trusts would be classified as trusts under the Code.

[Priv. Ltr. Rul. 8902045.]

CHAPTER **23**

Trust Deductions

¶ 23.01 DISTRIBUTIONS

[1] Generally

No deduction allowed for payments that are not properly paid under terms of trust. Amounts paid by a trust to the settlor's grandchildren during the lifetime of the settlor's husband were deducted by the trust. The IRS determined that these amounts were not properly paid under the terms of the trust agreement and, accordingly, were not deductible under Section 661(a)(2). The trust agreement provided that during the lifetime of the settlor or her husband, trust income was to be distributed to the settlor and, after her death, to her husband. The agreement further provided that after the deaths of both the settlor and her husband, trust income could be distributed to the settlor's grandchildren. The IRS interpreted these provisions to mean that no amounts could properly be distributed to the settlor's grandchildren until after both she and her husband died. The trustees claimed that in accordance with the intent of the settlor and an interpretation of the trust agreement as a whole, the amounts distributed to the grandchildren during the lifetime of the settlor's husband were properly paid for purposes of Section 661(a)(2). The district court agreed with the interpretation of the IRS and disallowed the deduction.

Held: Affirmed for the IRS. Under the express terms of the trust agreement, amounts were distributable to the settlor's grandchildren only after both the settlor and her husband died. Accordingly, the amounts paid by the trustees to the settlor's grandchildren during the lifetime of the settlor's husband were not properly paid and were not deductible under Section 661(a)(2). Furthermore, the state court decision that ratified the actions of the trustees in making these payments was not binding in either the IRS or in the federal courts.

[American Nat'l Bank & Trust Co., 633 F2d 213, 46 AFTR2d 80-6007, 81-2 USTC ¶ 9780 (6th Cir. 1980).]

FMV of stock distributed to income beneficiary must be included in income. Under the terms of the instrument that created a trust, the trustee is required to distribute currently to the beneficiary all of the income of the trust for each year. For the taxable year under consideration, the trustee had sufficient cash on hand to enable him to distribute in cash all of the trust income for that year that he was required to distribute to the beneficiary. In accordance with an agreement with the beneficiary, however, the trustee distributed, in lieu of cash, stock that was a part of the trust corpus and that had a fair market value (FMV) equal to the amount of trust income for that year that was required to be distributed to the beneficiary. The value of the stock so distributed exceeded the basis of the stock in the hands of the trust.

The IRS ruled that the transaction is treated as though the trustee actually distributed to the beneficiary cash in an amount equal to the trust income required to be distributed currently, and as though the beneficiary had purchased the stock from the trustee with cash. The trust is allowed a deduction under Section 651(a), limited by the distributable net income (DNI) of the trust, for the amount of income required to be distributed currently, and the beneficiary must report a like amount in gross income under Section 642(a). The instant transfer, involving stock having a FMV equal to the trust income for the year in question, which income the trustee was required to distribute to the beneficiary, resulted in a capital gain to the trust equal to the difference between the basis of the stock in the hands of the trustee and the amount of the obligation satisfied by the transfer. Further, the basis of the stock in the hands of the beneficiary is his cost, that is, the price he is deemed to have paid for it.

[Rev. Rul. 67-74, 1967-1 CB 194.]

Trust may deduct payments from fund receiving part of its gross income. Under the terms of an irrevocable trust agreement, the trustee was required to set aside a certain portion of the net income of the trust in a separate fund. The trustee was authorized to provide and to maintain out of the fund annuities and/or gifts for the use and benefit of such persons employed by or connected with the grantor's business as the trustee in his uncontrolled discretion may determine and designate as deserving.

The IRS ruled that payments made out of the fund were deductible under Section 661(a)(2) in computing the taxable income of the trust, subject to the limitation that the amount so deductible, when added to amounts otherwise deductible under Sections 661(a)(1) and 661(a)(2), cannot exceed the DNI of the trust. Further, the amounts so deducted by the trust should be included in the gross income of the recipients to the extent provided in Section 662.

[Rev. Rul. 55-286, 1955-1 CB 75.]

Trust cannot claim deduction for gift of trust income where trustees have power to give corpus only. The terms of a will provided for a trust of the residue of the estate, with the income to be paid to the testator's wife and daughter during their lives in the discretion of the trustees. However, the trustees retained the power at any time to terminate the trust and to pay and deliver the whole of the income from, or corpus of, the trust estate within five years to certain designated charitable organizations in such proportion as the trustees in their uncontrolled judgment and discretion determined. The IRS ruled that a donation to charity out of the gross income of the trust prior to a decision of the trustees to terminate the trust would not be pursuant to the terms of the will creating the trust. Accordingly, the trust estate would not be entitled to the charitable deduction authorized under Subchapter J.

[Rev. Rul. 55-92, 1955-1 CB 390.]

Trust qualified for marital deduction despite restriction on the distribution of income in the event of incapacity. A trust for the surviving spouse provided that the trustee must distribute to or for the benefit of the spouse as much income and principal as the spouse directs. If the spouse is incapacitated, however, the trustee may distribute for the spouse's benefit only the amount of income and principal that the trustee determines is necessary or advisable for the spouse's health, support, and maintenance. The trust also gave the spouse the power to amend or to revoke the entire trust at any time during life or at death.

The IRS concluded that the trust qualified for the marital deduction under Section 2056(b)(5). No trust provision terminated the spouse's power to amend or to revoke the trust upon incapacity, nor did any provision prohibit the spouse's power to amend or to revoke from running concurrently with the trustee's discretionary power to restrict the distribution of income in case of incapacity. The spouse had the power, exercisable alone and in all events, to demand payment of the entire trust at any time. Consequently, under Regulation § 20.2056(b)-5(f)(6), the spouse was entitled to all the income of the trust during his life.

[Tech. Adv. Mem. 9511002.]

[2] Distributable Net Income

Trust avoids tax on its share of partnership gains. A trust invested $5 million to become the sole limited partner in a partnership engaged in trading securities. The trust agreement authorized the trustee to distribute net earnings, but not principal, to the income beneficiary. The trust included its $2.9 million share of the partnership's capital gains in the $6.1 million of net earnings distributed to the beneficiary. The capital gains were included in the trust's DNI and deducted by the trust. Section 661 provides a deduction to a trust for distributions to beneficiaries that do not exceed the trust's DNI. (The beneficiaries are taxed on such distributions.) Section 643 defines DNI as the taxable income of the trust with certain modifications. Under Regulation § 1.643(a)-3, capital gains are included in DNI if one of the following conditions is met: (1) they are allocated to income under the terms of the governing instrument or local law; (2) they are actually distributed to beneficiaries during the tax year (even though they are allocated to principal); (3) they are used (pursuant to the terms of the trust or the practice of the trustee) in determining distributions to the beneficiaries; or (4) they are paid to or permanently set aside for a charity. The IRS argued that the trust's capital gains were not part of DNI because they could not be allocated to income. Therefore, they became trust principal, which could not be distributed.

Held: For taxpayer. If the trust owned the securities directly, the IRS would have been correct. The trust, however, owned a partnership interest, not the securities sold. Therefore, the court held that its share of the partnership gain represented net income. The IRS argued that this gave the trustee the power to convert nondistributable capital gains into distributable net earnings, by simply interposing a partnership that owned the securities. The court concluded that the grantor intended the trustee to have this power. After all, if the trustee formed a corporation that sold securities at a profit, the distribution of the profits as a dividend would have been income. Also, at the time the trust was established, case law supported treating partnership gains as income payable to the income beneficiary. Therefore, the grantor could have expected the trustee to treat the gains from a partnership in similar fashion. In addition, the trust permitted investments that could favor either the income beneficiary or the remainder beneficiary. Therefore, an investment permitting the distribution of capital gains to the income beneficiary was consistent with the grantor's wishes. Even if the trust agreement did not supplied an answer, the allocation to income was still proper under Texas state law, under which the allocation must be "reasonable and equitable" to all the beneficiaries. The trustee's allocation to net income met this test because it accorded with the advice of a national accounting firm. Furthermore, although the investment was large in absolute terms, it represented only a small percentage of the trust's principal. Therefore, the allocation of gains to income did not threaten the interests of the remainder beneficiary.

[Crisp, 34 Fed. Cl. 112, 76 AFTR2d 95-6261, 95-2 USTC ¶ 50,493 (1995).]

Tax Court upholds testator's expressed intent that royalty income be added to principal. Taxpayer was the principal life income beneficiary under a testamentary trust created by her father's will. Among the trust's assets were income interests in certain oil and gas properties that were subject to outstanding leases and royalty agreements. The trustees construed certain terms in the will as indicating an intention that royalties and other oil and gas income were to be treated as corpus, and that only the earnings from depositing or reinvesting the royalties and other oil and gas income were to be distributed to taxpayer as income. Consequently, the oil and gas income was not reported as currently DNI. The IRS disputed the trustees' interpretation of the will and determined that all oil and gas income was taxable to taxpayer in the year in which it was received by the trust. In this determination, the IRS proceeded under Section 652, which requires a trust income beneficiary to include in gross income all currently distributable trust income to the extent of "distributable net income."

Held: For taxpayer. The Tax Court examined the trust instrument and concluded that the trustees correctly interpreted the disputed terms. Although state law generally required oil and gas payments to be treated as income to the life beneficiary, the court found that the will effectively provided for a contrary result by express provision.

[Robinett, TC Memo. (P-H) ¶ 62,103, 21 TCM (CCH) 568 (1962).]

Nondividend distribution is not part of trust's DNI. A trust received a nondividend distribution. The fiduciary properly applied it to reduce the adjusted basis of the stock under Section 301(c)(2). The fiduciary also included it in the trust's DNI for the purpose of allocating, under Section 652(b), the deduction for his compensation. The IRS ruled that the distribution was a capital return that was not includable in the trust's DNI. Its use in allocating expenses was erroneous.

[Rev. Rul. 80-165, 1980-1 CB 134.]

Securities distributed by trust to satisfy annuity are includable in gross income of trust, but are excludable from DNI. A testamentary trust was required to pay a flat amount annually to its beneficiary, first out of income and then, if necessary, out of corpus. To meet the $14x difference between the annuity amount ($24x) and its income ($10x), the trust transferred securities to its beneficiary that were worth $14x, but had a basis of $12x in the hands of the trust. Because the will made no provision regarding the treatment of capital gains, local law required that they be allocated to corpus.

The IRS advised that the transaction was to be treated as if the trustee sold the securities to the beneficiary for cash, and immediately afterward distributed the entire proceeds of the sale to her. The trust must include capital gains of $2x in its gross income but is not required to include the capital gains in its DNI. It need report only the $10x ordinary income as DNI. The securities would have a basis of $14x in the beneficiary's hands.

[Rev. Rul. 68-392, 1968-2 CB 284.]

Partial liquidating distribution to trusts qualifies as extraordinary dividend and is excluded from DNI. A closely held corporation had four trusts as shareholders. Because the company liquidated several major assets over the preceding few years, the board decided to make a partial liquidating distribution to all shareholders. The corporation was to pay a dividend of a given number of dollars per share of stock. Most of the company's shares were owned by the trusts. A trustee sought instruction from a court on how to treat the distributions. The court determined that under state law, the extraordinary partial liquidating dividend by the company should be treated as a distribution of principal to be added to the corpus of the trusts. Each trust required that current income be distributed quarterly or annually. The trusts did not permit distributions other than from current income until termination. The trusts did not provide that any amounts were to be paid or set aside for any charitable beneficiary in the year of the liquidating distribution.

The IRS stated that the distribution constituted an extraordinary dividend to the trusts and was excluded from the trusts' DNI under Section 643(a)(4). The IRS determined that the dividend distribution would not constitute income under Section 643(b). The IRS concluded that the retention of the dividend by the trustee would not constitute a gift by the income beneficiaries for gift tax or generation-skipping transfer (GST) tax purposes.

[Priv. Ltr. Rul. 8837081.]

¶ 23.02 EXPENSES

Loss not recognized where grantor sold partnership interest to trust. Taxpayers, husband and wife, established a trust for their grandchildren. On the same day, the husband sold his partnership interest to the trust in exchange for a promissory note. No other property was transferred to the trust. Taxpayers claimed a capital loss on the sale. The IRS disallowed the loss, noting that Section 267(b)(4) precludes loss recognition on a transaction between a grantor and a fiduciary of a trust.

Held: Affirmed for the IRS. Taxpayer was a grantor. He signed the trust document identifying him as such, and intended to create a trust by transferring his property to the trust. There was no evidence to show, as taxpayers claimed, that the trustees purchased the partnership interest and then created the trust. The trustees were unrelated to taxpayers and there was no explanation as to why they would so generously establish a trust for taxpayers' grandchildren. Further, while it is generally true that one cannot become a grantor by transferring property to a trust for consideration, to apply this theory to the facts at issue was nonsensical. The trust itself signed the promissory note, but a trust cannot create itself. A grantor—the creator of the trust—must, by definition, preexist the trust.

[Meek, 133 F3d 928, 81 AFTR2d 98-522, 98-1 USTC ¶ 50,179 (9th Cir. 1998).]

Fees paid by trust for investment advice not subject to 2 percent floor on deductions. A trust was created in 1965 for the benefit of the settlor's family. By 1993, the trust corpus exceeded $4.5 million. The cotrustees had no investment expertise and none of these individuals would agree to serve as cotrustee until an investment adviser was hired to manage and to invest the trust assets. From 1979 to 1991, the cotrustees received investment advice from an investment firm. On its fiduciary income tax return for 1987, the trust deducted the $15,374 in fees paid to the investment adviser. Upon audit, the IRS determined that the investment counselling fees were a miscellaneous itemized deduction under Section 67(a) and allowed the deduction only to the extent that the fees paid exceeded 2 percent of the trust's adjusted gross income (AGI). The Tax Court agreed with the IRS and sustained its determination. Section 67(a) provides that in the case of an individual, miscellaneous deductions for any taxable year are allowed only to the extent that the aggregate of such deductions exceeds 2 percent of AGI. Section 67(e), however, provides that the AGI of an estate or trust is computed in the same manner as in the case of an individual, except that the "deductions for costs which are paid or incurred in connection with the administration of the estate or trust and would not have been incurred if the property were not held in such trust or estate shall be treated as allowable in arriving at adjusted gross income." Consequently, certain expenditures that are unique to trust or estate administration are exempt from the 2 percent floor. The Tax Court, in reviewing this particular case, concluded that the thrust of Section 67(e) is that it applies only to costs that are unique to the administration of a trust. The Tax Court noted that Ohio statutes provide a fiduciary with a detailed list of pre-approved investments, which would obviate the need to incur fees for investment advice.

Held: Reversed for taxpayer. On appeal, the Sixth Circuit stated that Section 67(e) provides an exception to the 2 percent rule that would cover such items as trustee's fees, costs of construction proceedings, and judicial proceedings. Similarly, the investment advisory fees paid by the trust were costs incurred because the property was held in trust, thereby making them eligible for the Section 67(e) exception.

According to the circuit court, a trustee is charged with the responsibility to invest trust assets as a "prudent investor." Although Ohio provides a list of approved investments, the mere selection of an approved investment does not automatically meet the prudent investor standard, and the trustee is not limited to this list of investment options. When a trustee lacks experience in investment matters, professional assistance may be warranted. Here, the trustees lacked investment experience in managing large sums of money and therefore sought the assistance of a professional adviser. Consequently, the Sixth Circuit found that the investment advisory fees were necessary to the continued growth of the trust and were caused by the fiduciary duties of the cotrustees.

[O'Neill Irrevocable Trust, 994 F2d 302, 71 AFTR2d 93-2052, 93-1 USTC ¶ 50,332 (6th Cir. 1993), nonacq. 1994-2 CB 1.]

Legal fees must be capitalized where expended by trust to preserve title. In 1927, the grantor executed an indenture creating a trust for his daughter on her impending marriage. The trust property consisted largely of securities, some of which generated tax-exempt income. By the terms of the indenture, the daughter was to receive the net income for life, with succeeding life estate trusts provided for her issue. In 1953, following the daughter's death, the trust beneficiaries and other interested parties became embroiled in a dispute over the validity and construction of the continuing trusts. After proceedings were instituted in state court, the parties settled their claims, and in 1954, the court entered a stipulated judgment that upheld the validity of the continuing trusts and provided for payments to those whose rights were surrendered. When it filed its fiduciary tax return for 1954, the trustee claimed a deduction of the entire $49,000 in counsel fees incurred in the state court suit. The IRS disallowed the item to the extent of $35,315, on the ground that the fees were partially nondeductible under Section 212 and that they should be capitalized. The IRS also disputed the trust's treatment of legal fees and trustee commissions relative to their allocation between taxable and nontaxable trust income. In the

IRS's view, the trustees erred in excluding from the allocation base certain capital gains and stock dividends properly allocable to principal and therefore not currently distributable. The result was to increase the amount of fees allocable to nontaxable income, thereby lowering the deduction. The issues presented to the court, therefore, were (1) whether the attorney fees expended in determining the trustee's title to trust property were capital expenses or deductible currently and (2) whether the capital gains were properly excluded from the apportioning base for purposes of allocating expenses between taxable and nontaxable income pursuant to Section 265.

Held: For the IRS. On the first issue, the court stated that in ascertaining the character of an expenditure for legal fees, the courts uniformly look first to the primary purpose of the litigation. If the primary purpose was related to title, then the expenditure is capital in nature. In the instant case, the trustee's role in the litigation was to defend its legal title in trust property against claims that the continuing trusts were void and that distributions of all trust property were required. The court concluded, therefore, that the expenditures were capital expenses under Section 263, and were not currently deductible under Section 212. On the second issue, the court looked to the general scheme of trust taxation under Subchapter J and found that though trusts are generally entitled to compute taxable income in the same way as individuals, the modifications set forth in Sections 651 and 643(a), governing the deduction for amounts currently distributable, must be strictly construed. The trustee sought to justify the exclusion of capital gains by noting that Section 643(a) defines "distributable net income" as excluding capital gains that are allocable to corpus. The trustee therefore contended that for purposes of allocating expenses under Section 265 between taxable and nontaxable income, the modifications in Section 643(a) should be applied to prevent the overcollection of tax. In an exhaustive analysis, the court rejected this argument and upheld Treasury regulations under Section 652 that require the inclusion of all capital gains income for purposes of the Section 265 allocation base. The provisions of Subchapter J are not necessarily controlling over the allocation rules in Section 265, and the court was unable to agree that the effect was an overcollection of tax. The court pointed out that the tax benefit of deductions allocable to corpus is generally shifted to beneficiaries under the concept of DNI, and the result in the challenged regulation does not depart from this plain congressional purpose. Accordingly, the court upheld the IRS and ruled that the inclusion of capital gains allocated to corpus for purposes of Section 265 apportionment was not unreasonable.

[Manufacturers Hanover Trust Co., 312 F2d 785, 11 AFTR2d 629, 63-1 USTC ¶ 9250 (Ct. Cl. 1963), cert. denied, 375 US 880 (1963).]

Trust may not deduct expenses made in accordance with its duties as lessor where beneficiary does not receive expenses as "distribution." In 1925, decedent transferred his elaborate mansion to a newly formed corporation in exchange for all of the corporation's stock. He then leased the property from the corporation for the balance of his and his wife's lives, paying a token annual rent of $1. Subsequently, decedent transferred $2 million worth of securities to the corporation to enable it to pay property taxes and to maintain the grounds. On his death in 1935, decedent's stock passed to a testamentary trust for the benefit of his widow. The trustee liquidated the corporation and assumed all of the obligations of the original lease. On its 1966 and 1967 federal income tax returns, the trust attempted to deduct an amount in excess of $300,000 that it expended on general property maintenance. The trustees justified the deductibility of these items under Section 212, which permits a deduction of expenses related to property held for the production of income, or as expenses incurred in the management of trust property. The IRS refused to allow the deductions, and both the Tax Court and the Fifth Circuit upheld the IRS's assertion that Section 212 was inapplicable. The Fifth Circuit, however, remanded the case to the Tax Court with instructions to consider the possible deductibility of the expenses under Section 651 or 661, both of which sections govern trust income tax deductions. On remand, the trust argued that the expenditures were deductible as distributions to the income beneficiary (decedent's surviving spouse).

Held: For the IRS. The Tax Court, on remand, noted initially that the trust's obligation to maintain the property arose as a result of its liquidation of the corporation and its assumption of duties under the outstanding lease. Thus, the court concluded that the trust's maintenance expenses were made in connection with its obligations under the lease, and that the widow received the benefit of such expenditures in her capacity as successor lessee, not as a trust beneficiary. Because Sections 651 and 661 permit a trust to deduct only those items that are properly paid or required to be distributed to the beneficiary, it follows that the beneficiary must receive these distributions in his capacity as beneficiary. Additionally, the court noted that expenses made to preserve trust property are not necessarily for the direct personal benefit of one who is entitled to the lifetime use and enjoyment of such property.

[DuPont Testamentary Trust, 66 TC 761 (1976), aff'd per curiam, 574 F2d 1332, 42 AFTR2d 78-5259, 78-2 USTC ¶ 9515 (5th Cir. 1978).]

Section 212 expenses are disallowed where beneficiary occupies trust property rent-free. In 1932, the settlor created a trust naming himself and his wife as trustees. The trust corpus consisted of 10,000 shares of stock in a family business corporation. By the terms of the governing instrument, income was payable primarily to settlor's son. In 1935, the son purchased land in Virginia, which he later transferred to his wife. By 1948, however, the son was indebted to settlor in the amount of $156,561 arising from a series of loans for property improvements. Settlor arranged to satisfy the indebtedness by having the son convey the Virginia property to the trust in full discharge thereof. To effect the settlement, settlor assigned the debt to the trust, with the understanding that the son would be released from all liability upon his conveyance of the Virginia property to the trustees. In September 1948, the son's wife reconveyed the property to him, and he promptly conveyed it to the trust. The trustees thereupon canceled the indebtedness, and the son was permitted, by agreement, to live on the property rent and tax free. During subsequent years 1952, 1953, and 1954, the trust claimed deductions for insurance, maintenance, repairs, salaries, and taxes expended in connection with the Virginia property. The IRS examined the returns and concluded that the claimed deductions were not allowable under Section 212. The trustees argued that the expenditures were for the management conservation or maintenance of trust property and, as such, were deductible under Section 212(2).

Held: For the IRS. The property was not held by the trust for the income production as required under Section 212, and therefore the expenses were nondeductible. The fact that the premises were occupied rent-free, regardless of the reasons for such occupancy, was determinative of the Section 212 issue. The trustees bore the burden of showing that the property was used in a trade or business within the meaning of Section 162, or that during the taxable years in question, it was held for income production. The failure to sustain the burden, in the court's view, required judgment in favor of the IRS without further inquiry.

[Prince Trust, 35 TC 974 (1961).]

Trust may deduct state income tax paid on retained capital gains in determining its taxable net income and DNI. Advice was requested whether a trust would be allowed a deduction for state income taxes paid as a result of capital gains retained by the trust in accordance with the terms of its governing instrument for the benefit of noncharitable remaindermen. The governing instrument of the trust, an irrevocable inter vivos trust, provided that all of the trust's net income be distributed currently in equal amounts to four beneficiaries. During the taxable year 1972, the trust collected $60x of qualifying dividends of $1x of interest on U.S. government obligations. It also realized capital gains of $200x on the sale of securities and paid $25x of fiduciary income tax, attributable solely to such capital gains, to the Department of Revenue of the state in which the trust was created. As of December 31, 1972, the trustee remitted an amount equal to the dividend income and the interest income, less a trustee's fee of $1x, to the beneficiaries of the trust. The proceeds of the sale of the securities were retained by the trustee as principal and were reinvested, after deducting therefrom the amount of the fiduciary income taxes paid. The retention of the proceeds of the sale was in accordance with applicable local law.

The IRS ruled that the state income tax paid as a result of capital gains retained by the trust was allowable as a deduction in arriving at the taxable income of the trust under Section 641. The IRS further ruled that the state income tax had to be deducted in computing distributable net income, because under Regulation § 1.652(b)-3, state income tax is an expense not directly attributable to a specific class of income and should thus be allocated to the items of income that are included in computing distributable net income (DNI). The resulting reduction in DNI would reduce both the trust's deduction for distributions to beneficiaries and the taxable incomes of the beneficiaries.

[Rev. Rul. 74-299, 1974-1 CB 153.]

¶ 23.03 LOSSES

Losses arising from stock sales between trusts are deemed bona fide. Taxpayer-trust *A* was a testamentary trust created in 1915 under *N*'s will. Taxpayer-trust *B* was formed in 1938 by *N*'s son. Both trusts had the same income beneficiary, but different contingent beneficiaries. In 1975, the trustees of the two trusts met to discuss their portfolios. Both trusts had realized capital gains, and both held stocks that could be sold at a loss to offset the gains. The trustees decided to sell the stocks to realize the losses, but to preserve the consolidated position of the trusts, they decided that each trust would purchase the stock sold by the other and that the transactions would be handled in the securities markets. The sales price used was the most recent bid-and-asked price; the buy and sell orders were placed through a computerized trading service; confirmation slips were issued for all transactions. The trusts used the losses to offset the capital gains, and the IRS disallowed the losses on the ground that they were not bona fide.

Held: For taxpayers. The transactions were final sales with no contingencies, and the prices involved were market prices. The trusts were formed twenty-three years apart by different grantors, and although they had a common trustee, the common trustee was bound by a fiduciary obligation to each trust. Neither trust controlled the other, and the sales effected a change of control, which in turn changed the flow of economic benefits. Furthermore, the trusts had different contingent beneficiaries, so that future changes in the value of the stock would be realized by beneficiaries other than those who would have realized it had the sales not taken place.

[Widener, 80 TC 304 (1983), acq. 1984-1 CB 2.]

Deductions attributable to valid trust may not be claimed by parent-settlor on personal return. Taxpayers, husband and wife, had a child injured at birth. The proceeds from settlement of a malpractice action on his behalf were placed in an inter vivos trust for the child's benefit, with his mother named trustee. Real property was purchased by the mother as trustee with trust assets, and title was recorded in the mother's name as trustee for the child. Taxpayers operated the trust property, which consisted of an apartment complex, and deduced the losses from the operation on their personal income tax return.

Held: For the IRS. The deductions were not proper. Because a valid trust was established, the losses were deductible only by the trust and were not available to taxpayers personally.

[Watkins, TC Memo. (P-H) ¶ 79,270, 38 TCM (CCH) 1062 (1979).]

Business losses are held deductible solely by trust where trust continues by tacit agreement of the beneficiaries. Following decedent's death in 1937, his residuary estate was placed in trust for the benefit of his surviving spouse, taxpayer and his brother. The trust held title to certain savings deposits, securities, and real estate, as well as decedent's plumbing and manufacturing business, and was to terminate in ten years unless the beneficiaries agreed to continue. Taxpayer's mother died in 1948, and by her will, she passed her interest in the trust to the taxpayer. From the date of decedent's death, taxpayer, as trustee, operated the family plumbing business and managed the trust property continuously until 1962. During the years 1959 through 1961, however, the business incurred net losses that were reported on the trust's fiduciary return and were also claimed by taxpayer on his personal return in proportion to his beneficial interest in the trust. The IRS objected to taxpayer's deduction of these amounts on his personal returns and issued appropriate notices of deficiency covering the three-year period. The taxpayer argued to the Tax Court that the deductions were entirely proper because the trust legally terminated in 1947, and that he and his brother held title to the plumbing business as remaindermen.

Held: For the IRS. Because the trust was not actually terminated in 1947, either under the terms of the will or by operation of law, taxpayer's deductions were improper. The evidence presented to the Tax Court showed that the beneficiaries treated the trust as being in existence well beyond the ten-year term. Therefore, the unrebutted inference arose that they agreed to continue the trust in accordance with its express provisions. There was never a distribution of trust property after 1947, and, in each succeeding year, taxpayer prepared and filed fiduciary returns in his capacity as trustee. Consequently, the trust must be treated as a viable entity for tax purposes, with only it, not taxpayer, entitled to deduct the losses.

[Weston, TC Memo. (P-H) ¶ 65,264, 24 TCM (CCH) 1439 (1965).]

Deduction for loss of grantor trust is limited by amount at risk. Shortly after taxpayer created a trust with a cash transfer, the trust purchased an interest in a Section 465(c) oil and gas activity. The trustee paid for the interest with cash and a recourse note. The note provided for full recourse against the trust, and the interest in the oil and gas activity was pledged as security against the note. Although under the grantor trust rules of Sections 671–679, taxpayer is treated as the owner of the entire trust for federal tax purposes, under state law, taxpayer is not personally liable on the trust's note. In the year in which the trust purchased its interest, the oil and gas activity sustained a loss. The amount of loss attributable to the trust's interest exceeded the amount of cash that taxpayer contributed to the trust.

The IRS ruled that because taxpayer is treated as the owner of the entire trust under Sections 671–679, he will also be treated as engaged in the Section 465(c) oil and gas activity for purposes of determining allowable losses. Because under state law, taxpayer is not personally liable on the trust's note, and because only property being used in the activity was pledged as security for the note, under Section 465(b), taxpayer is at risk for only the cash amount he contributed to the trust. Accordingly, taxpayer's deduction for the losses attributable to the trust's interest in the activity is limited under Section 465(a) to the cash amount he actually contributed to the trust.

[Rev. Rul. 78-175, 1978-1 CB 144.]

¶ 23.04 DEPLETION ALLOWANCE

Grantor's intention to retain oil royalties as corpus gives trustee entire depletion allowance. On the death of the testator in 1923, his stockholder interest in a California farming corporation was placed in a testamentary trust. The primary income beneficiary was the testator's widow, who was entitled to receive only the "rents, issues, profits, and income" arising from the stock. Following the testator's death, oil was discovered on the corporation's property, and the corporation later distributed an economic interest in the oil and gas rights to the trust. The major interest so distributed was the right to receive royalties from an oil company that held a lease on the property. Thus, until her death in 1945, the testator's widow received all royalty payments paid to the trust. Following the widow's death, her two surviving daughters became life income beneficiaries under the terms of the testamentary trust, and they, too, received all current royalty payments. The trust also owned the mineral rights of certain other properties in California. During 1948, oil and gas deposits were discovered on this property, and the trustees entered into an agreement with an oil company to develop the site. A provision in the agreement required the trustees to obtain a court determination of their right to enter into the agreement. The trustees thereupon initiated an action for a declaratory judgment in state court. At the outset of these proceedings, a question arose as to whether the royalties should be retained by the trustees, with only the income thereof being distributed to the life beneficiaries. The matter developed into a broad reexamination of the management of the trust and resulted in a court decree that

1. Affirmed the trustee's power to enter into the development agreement;
2. Instructed the trustees to allocate 72.5 percent of the total trust royalty income to the life beneficiaries and the balance to corpus as retained royalties;
3. Required the retained corpus to be invested, with income payable to the life beneficiaries.

In their fiduciary income tax returns for 1952 and 1953, the trustees claimed a ratable portion of the total depletion allowance to the extent of their 27.5 percent interest in the royalties. Consistent with this treatment, the two life beneficiaries deducted the balance of the depletion allowance on their personal returns. On audit, the IRS determined, however, that the income beneficiaries were not entitled to any portion of the claimed depletion. The dispute centered around a provision in the depletion deduction statute, codified in Section 611(b)(3), which states that in the case of property held in trust, the deduction shall be apportioned between income and corpus "in accordance with the pertinent provisions of the instrument creating the trust, or, in the absence of such provisions, on the basis of the trust income allocable to each." The IRS contended that the original testamentary trust granted all depletion allowances to the trustees for deduction by the trust. The life beneficiaries, on the other hand, asserted that there were no "pertinent provisions" in the trust instrument, and that therefore the depletion allowance should be apportioned between income and corpus "on the basis of the trust income allocable to each" as provided in the statute. The IRS acknowledged that no express provision existed in the trust instrument addressing the question directly but contended that the trustees were bound by the will to conserve corpus and therefore had the power to retain royalty income for that purpose. Thus, the IRS rejected the life beneficiaries' position that the state court decree governed the allocation of royalty income and hence the depletion allowances.

Held: For the IRS. There is no language of Section 611(b)(3) to indicate that an apportionment of depletion allowances must be stated in express terms. In the absence thereof, if the intention of the testator can be determined from an examination of the pertinent provisions of the instrument, that intention will be given effect, regardless of whether it is stated in express terms. The state court's decree was based on its finding that the testator indeed manifested an intention to preserve corpus; therefore, the local court required that 27.5 percent of the royalty income was to be retained in trust principal. The Ninth Circuit declared that it was bound by the state court's construction of the testator's intent because the decree was based on a full and fair adversary proceeding. The court then applied the established principle that a trust provision placing a duty upon the trustee to retain part of oil royalties as corpus must be interpreted as a direction that all depletion allowances be deducted by the trustees. Accordingly, the court entered judgment for the IRS upholding the assessed deficiencies.

[Upton, 283 F2d 716, 6 AFTR2d 5576, 60-2 USTC ¶ 9711 (9th Cir. 1960), cert. denied, 366 US 911 (1961).]

Trust leased interests in oil and gas properties to corporation for payments subject to depletion. Under leases, a trust held present and reversionary undivided fractional operating interests in producing oil and gas properties. A corporation held all remaining present interests in these properties. The trust conveyed its interests to the corporation in exchange for monthly payments that equaled the greater of a fixed percentage of the aggregate net proceeds from the properties or a specified minimum amount. These monthly payments were to terminate in 240 months or when all of the oil and gas leases ended. Then the corporation was to make monthly payments to the trust based on the corporation's income and expenditures for the properties.

The IRS stated that the transaction would be a lease for federal income tax purposes and that the trust should retain an economic interest in the properties. On the completion of the transaction, the trust would be the owner of a single economic interest, and its right to receive payments at the end of the 240 months would be a single property under Section 614. All of the payments after the 240-month period would be ordinary income subject to depletion under Sections 611 and 613A, and all of the earlier monthly payments would be ordinary income subject to depletion under Sections 611 and 612.

[Priv. Ltr. Rul. 8337019.]

¶ 23.05 CHARITABLE DEDUCTION

[1] Generally

Trust cannot claim charitable deduction where trust assets are transferred pursuant to terms of settlor's will. In 1959, settlor created an inter vivos revocable trust that he amended on eight separate occasions before his death in 1974. The trust instrument provided for the establishment of separate $50,000 trusts for each of settlor's children living at his death, with each child's trust to be funded by a distribution of trust principal. The children were to receive the income for life, and, upon each child's death, the principal was to be distributed outright to taxpayer, a private foundation. Settlor's trust in its final form also contained a provision that required part of its principal to be paid at settlor's death to "any trust" created by the terms of his will. In fact, however, settlor's will created no such charitable trust but instead provided that the residue of his estate should pass directly to the foundation. The trustees paid all of the trust assets to the foundation and claimed a Section 642 charitable deduction for income tax purposes. The IRS disallowed the deduction on the ground that the trust instrument was not the legal mechanism under which the payments were made. The district court agreed with the IRS that the provision in the settlor's will directing payment of all estate residue to the foundation nullified the term in the trust instrument that called for payments of principal to any testamentary trust.

Held: Affirmed for the IRS. Section 642(c)(1) requires that a deductible payment of a trust must have been made "pursuant to the governing instrument" of the trust itself. This condition was not met, because settlor's will failed to create a charitable trust to receive the payment. Because the trust assets passed to the foundation through the residuary clause of settlor's will, not under the terms of the trust, the foundation was not entitled to receive a Section 642 deduction. The court reached its conclusion after rejecting arguments that the trust was subject to reformation under the state law doctrine of cy pres. The court refused to assume that the doctrine applied or that a state court would exercise its equitable jurisdiction to cause a trust reformation.

[Love Charitable Found., 710 F2d 1316, 52 AFTR2d ¶ 83-5487, 83-2 USTC ¶ 9441 (8th Cir. 1983).]

Trust becomes irrevocable too late to escape 1969 limits on charitable set-asides. Grantor established a revocable trust funded with $3.6 million in 1968. This trust provided him with an income for life. At his death, the assets were to be divided and apportioned into two trusts for family members, with the assets of one trust to be paid over to charity upon the death of the last-named family member. Grantor was rendered incompetent as the result of an illness in December 1969, thereby causing the trust to become irrevocable by operation of law. He died in February 1970. The trustees made charitable set-asides in 1973 and 1974, and claimed charitable deductions for the amounts allegedly "permanently set aside" for charity on the ground that the trust was irrevocable at that time. The IRS disallowed the deductions, but the district court held for taxpayer.

Held: Reversed for the IRS. On October 9, 1969, new rules governing charitable set-asides became effective. These new rules, set forth in Section 642(c), require that instruments pre-dating October 9, 1969, must be irrevocable in order to claim the charitable deduction. The Sixth Circuit held that the controlling date for irrevocability of such trusts was the October 9 date, rather than the date of the set-asides, according to legislative intent behind Section 642(c). Because the trust was still revocable on October 9, 1969, it did not qualify for the charitable deduction.

[Rush, 694 F2d 1072, 51 AFTR2d 83-386, 83-1 USTC ¶ 9103 (6th Cir. 1982), cert. denied, 462 US 1120 (1983).]

Distribution of appreciated property to charity results in gain, which may be offset by charitable deduction. *A*, an individual taxpayer, established an irrevocable trust and funded it with 400*x* shares of *Z* corporation stock. Under the terms of the trust, the trustee was required to pay to qualified charities an annuity equal to 8 percent of the initial net FMV of the transferred stock. The annuity was to be paid annually for a term of ten years and one month after the date of the trust's creation. To the extent that current ordinary income would be insufficient to make payments, the trustee was to make payments from capital gains and, if necessary, from corpus. Upon termination of the trust, the trustee was to distribute the corpus to *A*'s children or to their survivors. In 1983, there was insufficient ordinary income and capital gains to satisfy the annuity to be paid to the qualified charities. Therefore, the trustee paid the deficiency by distributing from corpus some of the shares of stock of *Z* corporation. The stock distributed had a FMV of $48*x* at the time of distribution. The basis of the stock in the hands of the trustee was $38*x*.

The IRS ruled that under the principles of Regulation § 1.661(a)-2(f)(1) and relevant case law, the distribution of appreciated securities caused the trust to realize gain or loss because the distribution satisfied a right to receive a distribution in a specific dollar amount, the trustee's authority to pay the annuity to qualified charities of the trustee's choice notwithstanding. Under Section 642(c), the trust was entitled to a charitable deduction equal to the amount of gain recognized upon the distribution of the appreciated securities. It must first adjust for any deduction provided under Section 1202, however, which allows a 60 percent setoff against income from capital gains.

[Rev. Rul. 83-75, 1983-1 CB 114.]

IRS computes allowable deduction where terminatory charitable trust sells assets for a realized gain. An individual taxpayer died in 1950. Under the terms of taxpayer's will, two trusts were established. One trust, for the benefit of taxpayer's child, was funded with $10*x*, and the other trust, for the benefit of taxpayer's spouse, was funded with the residue of taxpayer's estate. The will further provided that on the death of taxpayer's spouse, the residuary trust for the spouse's benefit was to terminate, and that $20*x* of its corpus was to be paid to the child's trust. The remaining corpus was to be transferred irrevocably to a qualified charitable organization described in Section 170(c). At the time of the spouse's death in 1976, the value of the corpus of the spouse's trust exceeded $20*x*, but the cash in the corpus amounted to only $3*x*. In order to facilitate division and distribution of the assets of the trust, the trustee of the residuary trust sold certain trust assets having a value of $17x. This sale resulted in a gain to the trust of $4x. The $20x in cash was paid to the child's trust, and the remainder of the corpus property was conveyed to the charity in 1976, the same tax year in which the $17x worth of assets were sold.

The IRS reviewed the relevant authorities and determined that in those cases in which the remainder interest in trust assets is payable to charity subject to noncharitable bequests of a specified amount, the charity will also always be at risk with respect to any capital gains income. This risk exists to the extent that the total trust corpus exceeds the specific noncharitable bequests. Accordingly, a deduction under Section 642(c)(1) is allowable in the present case for the lesser of the capital gains realized ($4x) or the amount of the distribution of the remainder of the corpus to the charity. Pursuant to Section 642(c)(4), to the extent that the capital gains in the instant case arose from the sale or exchange of capital assets in 1976 held for more than six months, the amount of the Section 642(c)(1) deduction must be adjusted for any deduction provided in Section 1202. The IRS also ruled that because the amount of $20x paid by the residuary trust was properly paid as a bequest of a specific sum of money in a single payment, it was neither deductible by the residuary trust under the provisions of Section 661 nor includable in the gross income of the trust of which the child was the beneficiary under Section 662.

[Rev. Rul. 78-24, 1978-1 CB 196.]

Charitable bequest paid from trust corpus is not deductible under Section 642(c) as charitable contribution. A decedent's will provided for a bequest to a charitable organization of an amount, in money or property, worth a specified fraction of the adjusted gross estate. The residue of the estate was to be placed in trust. Because the will was silent as to the disposition of income from the estate during the period of administration, state law required that all income earned by the estate during the period of administration be distributed to the residuary legatee. During the taxable year, total cash distributions to the charity and the trust exceeded the estate's DNI.

The IRS ruled that because the amount to be paid to the charity was to be paid from corpus rather than from income, the amounts distributed to the charity would not qualify for the charitable contributions deduction under Section 642(c), nor could the amounts be treated as distribution deductions to beneficiaries under Section 661(a)(2).

[Rev. Rul. 68-667, 1968-2 CB 289.]

Trust may take charitable contribution deduction. An individual executed a will in which the individual left a cash bequest to an inter vivos trust. The trust provided for income to certain named charitable organizations, and, upon the trust's termination in twenty years, the corpus was to be distributed to the same charitable organizations. If, however, any of those organizations were not charitable organizations at the time of the distribution of income or principal, the trustee was not to make a distribution to that organization. Instead, the percentage of distribution for the other organizations that remained qualified would be increased proportionately. The IRS stated that a charitable deduction would be allowed to the estate for the value of the interests passing to the charities.

[Priv. Ltr. Rul. 8839043.]

[2] Charitable Lead Annuity Trusts

Trust's charitable contributions are limited to required annuity payment. Taxpayer, a charitable lead trust, provided that a specified annuity equal to 6.5 percent of the value of the assets be paid to a qualified charitable beneficiary. The trust could make accelerated charitable payments if they were made in commutation of future annuity payments. The trust paid and claimed deductions for amounts exceeding the required annual annuity payment, although it did not commute any future payments. The IRS disallowed the deduction for the excess payments.

Held: For the IRS. Because the trust did not formally compute the present value of the future payments or specifically identify the amount of the future payments satisfied by the current accelerated payments, the excess amounts were not deductible. In addition, they could not be deducted as discretionary distributions, because they were not paid pursuant to the trust instrument.

[Rebecca K. Crown Income Charitable Fund, 98 TC 327 (1992), aff'd, 8 F3d 571, 93-2 USTC ¶ 92-3957, 72 AFTR2d 93-6524 (7th Cir. 1993).]

Distribution of appreciated stock to charity causes trust to recognize gain, offset by charitable deduction. On December 31, 1978, *A*, an individual taxpayer, established an irrevocable trust and funded it with 400x shares of *Z* corporation stock. Under the terms of the trust, the trustee was required to pay to qualified charities an annuity equal to 8 percent of the initial net FMV of the transferred stock. The annuity was to be paid annually for a term of ten years and one month after the date of the trust's creation. To the extent that current ordinary income was insufficient for making payments, the trustee was to make payments out of capital gains and, if necessary, from corpus. Upon termination of the trust, the trustee was to distribute the corpus to *A*'s children or their survivors. In 1983, there was insufficient ordinary income and capital gains to satisfy the annuity to be paid to the qualified charities. Therefore, the trustee paid the deficiency by distributing some of the shares of stock of *Z* corporation out of corpus. The stock distributed had a FMV at the time of distribution of $48x. The basis of the stock in the hands of the trustee was $38x.

The IRS ruled that the distribution of appreciated securities was an "exchange" of the securities, because the distribution satisfied the right to receive a specific dollar amount and therefore resulted in taxable gain to the trust. The trust was entitled to a charitable deduction under Section 642(c), equal to the amount of the gain recognized, less any capital gains deductions claimed by the trust under Section 1202.

[Rev. Rul. 83-75, 1983-1 CB 84.]

Land donated to trust and leased for benefit of charity gives rise to charitable deduction of lease's value. An individual proposed to create a charitable lead annuity trust for the benefit of a charity that qualifies under Section 501(c)(3). The donor planned to transfer real property to the trust, which would exchange a portion of the real property for land of equal value owned by the charity. The trust then would lease the real property acquired in the exchange, along with other real property owned by the trust, to an independent lessee for twenty-five years. The charity would receive an annuity equal to 11 percent of the initial net FMV of the property transferred to the trust, payable for twenty-five years. The trust would terminate after twenty-five years, at which time the corpus was to be placed in two trusts established for the donor's grandchildren.

The IRS stated that the proposed annuity payable under the terms of the trust would meet the requirements of a guaranteed annuity under Section 2522(c)(2)(B) of the Code and Regulation § 25.2522(c)-3(c)(2)(vi). Accordingly, the IRS concluded that a gift tax charitable deduction under Section 2522 equal to the present actuarial value of the guaranteed annuity payable under the trust is allowable in computing the donor's taxable gifts for the calendar year in which the trust would be funded.

[Priv. Ltr. Rul. 8910071.]

[3] Charitable Lead Income Trusts

Trust, but not grantor, may deduct charitable gifts, except to extent of unrelated business income. Y, a bank holding company, created an irrevocable trust that was not to terminate before ten years and one month after the date of its creation. The governing instrument of the trust provided that no additional property would be contributable to the trust after its creation. The net income of the trust was to be distributed to organizations described in Section 170. All income was to be distributed before the close of the year succeeding the year in which the income was received. Capital gains were to be added to corpus.

Y reserved the power to designate income to recipients. Such designation was to be made at any time before or after the income was received. If *Y* failed to designate by the time income was required to be distributed, the trustee would be required to select charitable beneficiaries. Distributions were to be made only from income received by the trust. The trust agreement provided that all powers reserved by *Y* were to be exercised by *Y* in a fiduciary capacity, and that none of the powers was to be construed to permit the trustee to lend any of the principal or income of the trust property, directly or indirectly, to the grantor without adequate interest or security, or to borrow directly or indirectly from the grantor at more than adequate interest or other consideration. Except in the case of permitted distributions, *Y* was prohibited from dealing with or disposing of the principal of the trust property or the income therefrom for less than an adequate consideration. *Y* was precluded from designating any distribution in satisfaction of its own obligation to a charitable organization. Upon the termination of the trust, all of the property comprising the principal of the trust was to be distributed to *Y*. All of the then undistributed income of the trust was to be distributed to or for the use of the charitable organizations described above. The IRS was asked to rule on whether the trust should be allowed a deduction for amounts of gross income paid to charitable beneficiaries under these circumstances.

The IRS ruled that because the terms of the trust required the capital gains to be accumulated for future distribution to *Y*, *Y* should be treated as the owner of the income of the trust with respect to capital gains under Section 677(a). Other items of gross income and deductions and credits attributable to the ordinary income portion of the trust were to be subject to the provisions of Sections 641 et seq. Thus, no deduction would be allowed to *Y* for any amounts of the trust's income paid to charitable organizations. The capital gains allocable to the corpus portion of the trust would be includable in *Y*'s gross income when realized by the trust. The trust itself, however, was to be allowed a deduction in accordance with Section 642(c)(1) for amounts of gross income paid to charitable beneficiaries described in Section 170(c) during its taxable year, or by the close of the following taxable year, except to the extent that it realized unrelated business income within the meaning of Section 681(a).

[Rev. Rul. 79-223, 1979-2 CB 254.]

Grantor bank is not owner of trust. A bank created an irrevocable charitable income trust, naming itself as trustee. Contributions to the trust were held in separate accounts for over ten years. The trust's gross income was distributed annually to charitable organizations, and the corpus reverted to the bank. The bank retained the right to alter beneficiary designations until the distribution date. The distributions were made through a tax-exempt organization of which the bank was a member. The tax-exempt organization held the funds to be distributed for several days in an interest-free account before distributing them to the charitable beneficiaries. The tax-exempt organization did not benefit from the funds. The IRS stated that the bank was not the owner of the trust and that the trust should be allowed a Section 642(c)(1) deduction for the charitable distributions.

[Priv. Ltr. Rul. 8335039.]

[4] Pooled Income Funds

IRS revokes revenue ruling on pooled income funds. In Revenue Ruling 92-108, 1992-51 IRB 5, which involved the requirements of Section 642(c)(5) for qualification as a pooled income fund, the IRS ruled that a fund maintained by a community trust meets the maintenance requirement of Section 642(c)(5)(E) if the donor permits the community trust to choose the charitable organization that will benefit from the remainder interest. The IRS further ruled that a fund maintained by a community trust does not meet the maintenance requirement if the donor may designate the specific charitable organization for whose benefit the community trust will use the remainder interest. In a subsequent revenue ruling, however, the IRS revoked Revenue Ruling 92-108 without discussion.

[Rev. Rul. 93-8, 1993-1 CB 125, revoking Rev. Rul. 92-108, 1992-2 CB 121.]

Ownership of rental real estate does not disqualify pooled income fund. X was a "pooled income fund" as defined in Section 642(c). The governing instrument of the fund provided that the trustees were authorized to invest in real estate. The trustee of X purchased an office building from A, an individual. The selling price of the building was established on the basis of independent appraisals and accounted for the remaining balance on a mortgage that was assumed by X as part of the transaction. X managed and operated the office building. The IRS ruled, without analysis, that X was not disqualified as a pooled income fund under Section 642(c)(5) by its ownership of the office building.

[Rev. Rul. 79-387, 1979-2 CB 247.]

Fund does not qualify in absence of amendment. The IRS ruled that an otherwise qualifying fund whose governing instrument permitted the duration of a beneficiary's income interest to be measured by the life of another did not qualify as a pooled income fund under Section 642(c)(5), and by the value of a remainder under Section 170, 2055, 2106, or Section 2522. This nonqualification stands even though the transfer instrument based the duration of the designated beneficiary's income interest on the beneficiary's life. The fund's governing instrument could be amended to qualify prospectively if the fund did not accept property under a defective transfer instrument.

[Rev. Rul. 79-61, 1979-1 CB 220.]

Pooled income fund qualifies; depreciation and depletion are allocable to income beneficiaries. The IRS stated that a Section 170(b)(1)(A) organization's fund is a pooled income fund under Section 642(c)(5). The IRS also stated that depreciation or depletion deductions are allocable to the fund's income beneficiaries to the extent that those deductions exceed the income set aside by the trustee for the depreciation or depletion reserve. The IRS declared that buildings constructed or renovated and leased back to the organization or another exempt entity must be depreciated by the fund over forty years under the straight-line method. The IRS concluded that the fund would be a split-interest trust and that Section 4947(a)(2) would apply.

[Priv. Ltr. Rul. 8843037.]

Revenue Ruling 82-128 is considered inapplicable to pooled income funds. In a prior ruling, Private Letter Ruling 8208120, the IRS classified a pooled income fund. The trust agreement was amended to conform to the requirements of Revenue Ruling 82-128, 1982-2 CB 71, which states that a trust does not qualify as a charitable remainder trust if federal and state death taxes may be payable from the trust's assets. Subsequently, the trust agreement was again modified by deleting any reference to the revenue ruling. The IRS stated in the instant private ruling that Revenue Ruling 82-128 does not apply to Section 642(c)(5) pooled income funds. The IRS extended the prior ruling to cover the current trust agreement, which is identical to the initial trust agreement.

[Priv. Ltr. Rul. 8352038.]

[5] Charitable Remainder Trusts

Irrevocable trust lacking provision for proration of annuity amount in year of termination does not qualify as charitable remainder trust. Under the provisions of the instrument governing an irrevocable trust, a specified distribution was to be made to the life beneficiary, and, upon the beneficiary's death, the remainder of the trust was to be paid to a Section 170 charitable organization. There was no provision in the trust instrument, however, for determining how the specified distribution was to be prorated in the final taxable year of the trust. There was also no provision that would allow the termination of the specified distribution with the regular payment preceding the date of the life beneficiary's death.

The IRS ruled that because the instrument governing the trust contained no provisions for determining what fraction of the specified annual distribution was to be paid in the year when the noncharitable interest terminated, the trust did not qualify as a charitable remainder trust under Section 664 of the Code and Regulation §§ 1.664-2 and 1.664-3.

[Rev. Rul. 79-428, 1979-2 CB 253.]

Where grantor retains power to substitute himself as trustee and thereby reallocate income among beneficiaries, trust does not qualify as charitable remainder trust. The IRS was asked to determine whether two dissimilar trusts qualified as charitable remainder trusts. In the instant case, the grantor created an irrevocable trust, providing for a specified distribution to himself and another life beneficiary, with the remainder passing to a Section 170(c) charitable organization upon the death of the surviving beneficiary. Under the provisions of the governing trust instrument, the trustee would retain the power to allocate the specified distribution among the beneficiaries, and the grantor would retain the power to remove the trustee for any reason and substitute himself or any other person as trustee. In all other respects, the trust complied with the provisions of Section 664.

The IRS ruled that the trust would not qualify as a charitable remainder trust. A trust is not a charitable remainder trust if any person retains the power to alter the amount to be paid to any beneficiary other than a Section 170(c) charitable organization if that power would cause any person to be treated as the owner of any part of the trust if Sections 673–679 applied to the trust. The grantor's power to substitute himself as trustee established that he would be treated as the owner of this trust, thus disqualifying it.

[Rev. Rul. 77-285, 1977-2 CB 213.]

Sprinkling trust can qualify as charitable remainder trust. A taxpayer created an inter vivos trust and appointed a trust company as the trust's sole, independent trustee. Under the terms of the trust instrument, the trustee retained the power to allocate the specified amount required to be distributed among three individual life beneficiaries. Upon the death of the surviving beneficiary, the remainder of the trust was to pass to a Section 170(c) charitable organization.

The power of the trustee to make a discretionary allocation of the specified amount required to be distributed, the IRS ruled, should not preclude the trust from qualifying as a charitable remainder trust under Section 664. Here, because the power of the independent trustee to make an allocation of the required distribution among the beneficiaries was not a power that would cause any person to be treated as the owner of the trust under the rules of Sections 671–678, the trust qualified as a charitable remainder trust.

[Rev. Rul. 77-73, 1977-1 CB 175.]

IRS denies deduction where contingency involving adoptive children would defeat charitable remainder. The income of a testamentary trust, created in 1960, was required to be paid to A, the testator's wife, for her life. The trustee retained no power to invade the trust principal for A's benefit. Upon A's death, the trust principal was to pass to any of her natural or adopted children then living, or to any descendants of such children. If A were to die leaving no surviving natural or adopted children, or any descendants of such children, the trust principal would be paid to a charitable organization described in Section 170(c)(2). In 1972, the trust realized capital gains from the sale of certain assets. At that time, A was age 60 and had no natural or adopted children. In the state in which A resided, there was no restriction on the age of persons wishing to adopt children. Furthermore, under the local law, capital gains of trusts were required to be allocated to trust principal. The IRS was asked to rule on the issue of whether the trust should be allowed a deduction under Section 642(c).

The IRS noted that where the charitable remainder may be defeated by having issue, a volitional act, the possibility that the charitable transfer will not become effective is not so remote as to be negligible, unless the occurrence of such volitional act is an impossible contingency. The IRS concluded that under the present facts, adoption was a volitional act that could defeat the eventual vesting of the charitable remainder. Because under state law there was no restriction on the maximum age of persons eligible to adopt children, adoption was not an impossible contingency. As a result, the possibility that A would adopt one or more children was not so remote as to be negligible. Therefore, there was a real possibility that the charitable organization would not receive any part of the remainder interest. Accordingly, the trust in the instant case was not allowed a deduction under Section 642(c), because no amount of its gross income would have been permanently set aside for a charitable purpose within the meaning of Section 642(c).

[Rev. Rul. 74-410, 1974-2 CB 187.]

IRS rules on effect of termination provision affecting successive life beneficiaries. The governing instrument of a charitable remainder annuity trust, which otherwise complied with all the requirements of Section 664 and the applicable regulations, provided that the annuity trust amount shall be paid to A for his life in equal quarterly installments on the last day of each calendar quarter, and then to B for her life. The instrument also provided that payment of the annuity trust amount to each life beneficiary shall terminate with the regular payment next preceding the date of death. A died on June 15 of the taxable year. In this situation, payment of the annuity trust amount to *A* termi-nated with the payment on March 31. Further, computation of the annuity trust amount payable to *B* was required to be made from April 1. The IRS was asked to rule on the specific question whether payment of the annuity trust amount to each life beneficiary could terminate with the regular payment pre-ceding the date of death of such beneficiary, or whether such payment must be prorated to the actual date of death.

The IRS cited Regulation §§ 1.664-2(a)(5) and 1.664-3(a)(5), which hold that the provisions for termination of the annuity trust amount payment or the unitrust amount with the regular payment next preceding the termination of the period apply to each life beneficiary in trusts that provide for payments to two or more successive life beneficiaries. Accordingly, in the instant case, the pro-vision of the governing instrument of the charitable remainder annuity trust providing that payment of the annuity trust amount to two or more successive life beneficiaries should terminate with the regular payment preceding the date of death of each life beneficiary complied with the requirements of Section 664 and the applicable regulations thereunder. The IRS also stated that the same result would occur in a situation where the trust is a charitable remainder unitrust.

[Rev. Rul. 74-386, 1974-2 CB 189.]

Twenty-year charitable remainder unitrust providing for alternate income beneficiaries in case of death is held to qualify under Section 664 and reg-ulations. *A* made a gift in 1972 to a university, an organization described in Section 170(c), through a trust. Pursuant to the governing instrument of the trust, the university would serve as trustee of the funds transferred to the trust. The trust instrument provided that each year, quarterly distributions at an an-nual rate of 6 percent of the net FMV of the trust assets, determined annually, be made to *B* for a term of twenty years. If *B* were to die before the expira-tion of the twenty-year term, the payments would be made to *C* for the bal-ance of the twenty-year period remaining. If *C* also died before the expiration of the twenty-year period, the distributions for the balance of the period re-maining would be made to *C*'s heirs at law, excluding the donor and his spouse. At the end of the twenty-year term the balance remaining in the trust was to be distributed to the university. The trust was irrevocable and otherwise complied with the requirements of Section 664 and applicable regulations. The IRS ruled that the trust was a charitable remainder unitrust and the contribu-tion for 1971 to the trust was deductible as a charitable contribution, subject to the Section 170(b) limitation.

[Rev. Rul. 74-39, 1974-1 CB 156.]

Beneficiary's lifetime interest in antiques collection disqualifies annuity trust. The grantor of an irrevocable trust contributed a collection of antiques in addition to income-producing assets to the trust at the time of its creation. The governing instrument of the trust provided that the grantor's spouse, who was the sole income beneficiary of the trust for her life, should have use of the antique collection for her life. At her death, the antique collection and all of the remaining assets in the trust were to be distributed to a charitable organization. In all other respects, the trust instrument complied with the provisions of Section 664 and the regulations applicable thereto concerning creation of annuity amount for a period of years or life, creation of remainder interest in charity, selection of alternative charitable beneficiary if remaindermen do not qualify under Section 170(c) at the time of distribution, computation of an annuity amount in short and final taxable years, prohibition of additional contributions, and prohibitions governing private foundations. Regulation § 1.664-1(a)(3) provides that a trust is not a charitable remainder trust if the provisions of the trust include a provision that restricts the trustee from investing the trust assets in a manner that could result in the annual realization of a reasonable amount of income or gain from the sale or disposition of trust assets.

The IRS ruled that in the instant case, retention of a life estate in the antique collection by the grantor's spouse restricted the trustee from investing all of the trust assets in a manner that could have resulted in the annual realization of a reasonable amount of income or gain from the sale or disposition of trust assets. Accordingly, the trust did not comply with the aforementioned regulations, and therefore did not qualify as a charitable remainder annuity trust under Section 664 and the regulations applicable thereto. Thus, the contribution to the trust was not deductible as a charitable contribution for federal income tax purposes.

[Rev. Rul. 73-610, 1973-2 CB 213.]

Remainder interest in trust containing residence is qualified remainder trust. A husband and wife died within eight months of one another. Together they owned certain real estate as tenants by the entirety. Before their deaths, they transferred their undivided one-half interests in the real estate to two mirror trusts. The husband's trust established the wife as sole beneficiary, with the entire net income to be distributed to the wife during her husband's lifetime. Upon the wife's death, if the husband survived, the trust was to continue for the duration of his life. During this period, the surviving spouse retained the right to live in the marital residence. Some of the net income was then to be distributed to various family members. A majority of the net income was to be distributed to a charitable organization. The mirror trust created by the wife, as grantor, named her husband as lifetime beneficiary and contained similar provisions for the distribution of trust income and corpus upon the husband's death. In addition, the wife was considered the grantor of the trust created for her benefit because both the wife and husband executed reciprocal trusts.

The IRS stated that the unqualified split-interest trust was deemed reformed and treated as if it were a qualified charitable remainder trust under Section 2055(e)(2). In addition, the estate was allowed a charitable deduction for the value of the corpus passing to the charitable organization. The IRS noted that the charitable organization received a remainder interest in trust in the proceeds from the sale of the residence. Because the remainder interest passed under the provisions of a split-interest trust that was deemed reformed on the date of the termination of the trust, a charitable deduction was allowed for this interest.

[Priv. Ltr. Rul. 8912027.]

Wife's contribution of unitrust interest to charity is not deductible, because husband retains right to revoke wife's interest. An individual established a charitable remainder unitrust. Under the terms of the trust, the trustee was to pay 5 percent of the annual interest to the individual for life. Upon the individual's death, the unitrust interest was to be paid to the individual's spouse. The individual retained the right to revoke the spouse's survivorship by will. The individual and the individual's spouse proposed to transfer a portion of their unitrust interest to the beneficiary of the charitable remainder.

The IRS stated that the individual's transfer of the unitrust interest would qualify for a charitable deduction under Regulation § 1.170A-7(a)(2)(i), but the contribution of the spouse's life interest to charity would be ineligible for the charitable deduction, because there would be no assurance that the contingent interest would ever pass to charity. The IRS noted that the gift to the spouse was incomplete and that not only must the spouse survive the individual but the survivorship interest also must be retained. The IRS stated that the question whether the conveyance of the unitrust interest would cause a portion of the trust to merge with the unitrust interest was a question of state law. The IRS determined that if the merger occurs under state law, the trust will continue to qualify as a charitable remainder unitrust if, after the transfer, the trust continued to pay the 5 percent annual interest to the individual. The IRS provided the formula to compute the value of the individual's charitable contribution.

[Priv. Ltr. Rul. 8805024.]

Charitable trust in perpetuity may deduct capital gains under Section 642. An individual died leaving a will that established a testamentary trust. The trust was to pay $25 per year to maintain the individual's cemetery plot. The remainder of the net income of the trust was to be used to benefit the poor. The trust had no termination date under the will. The trustee obtained permission from the court to benefit the poor through donations to public charities. The net income of the trust was far in excess of $25 per year. In addition, it was a virtual certainty that no part of the capital gains earned by the trust would need to be used for maintenance of the cemetery plot. The relevant state law held that a bequest of income in trust without limitation of time and without provision for an estate for years was in effect a bequest of the corpus itself to the income beneficiary. State law also treats capital gains on a perpetual charitable trust as part of the corpus of the trust.

The IRS stated that the capital gains realized by the trust were permanently set aside for a charitable purpose under Section 642(c)(2) and that an irrevocable remainder interest in the corpus was transferred to a charitable organization. The IRS concluded that the trust must be allowed a deduction under Section 642(c)(2) for amounts of capital gain earned each year, except to the extent of unrelated business income under Section 681(a).

[Priv. Ltr. Rul. 8624096.]

CHAPTER 24

Compliance and Procedure in Reporting Income

¶ 24.01 ACCOUNTING METHODS

[1] Generally

Tax Court upholds sale of stock by husband to family trust. Taxpayers, husband and wife, were New Jersey residents during the taxable years in question. Before 1978, taxpayers owned a minority interest in a closely held corporation engaged in the manufacture of aerospace gears. During 1977, a West German manufacturer approached the corporation with an expressed interest in acquiring the corporation as a subsidiary. A purchase preliminary agreement was entered into in principle. The husband was not a good money manager. To avoid him handling the proceeds, taxpayers formed a trust to receive the money and arranged for the trust to purchase the stock under an installment sale before the sale to the West German company. The wife served as trustee, with herself and the couple's children named beneficiaries. The IRS objected to the trust transfer and installment sale characterization of the transaction.

Held: For taxpayers. Applying substance over form, the Tax Court found that a bona fide sale of stock existed by the husband to the trust, and that taxpayers correctly reported the gain under the installment sales rules of Section 453. The trust maintained complete control of the stock and operated independently of the husband in each crucial respect. At no time was the wife or the trust an agent of the husband. The court was satisfied that no sham was intended or accomplished by means of the initial sale to the trust.

[Failla, TC Memo. (P-H) ¶ 86,039, 51 TCM (CCH) 355 (1986).]

IRS rules on transfer of installment obligations to irrevocable reversionary trust. *A*, an individual taxpayer, sold property and accepted a cash down payment and an installment note providing for payment in monthly installments over fifteen years, plus interest at 8 percent on the unpaid balance. The note was prepayable without penalty after the first year. *A* reported the gain on the sale on the installment method of accounting under Section 453. When more than twelve years of installment payments on the obligation were still outstanding, *A* transferred the installment note to an irrevocable trust. Under the terms of the trust, all interest on the note received by the trustee was to be paid currently to *B*, an individual to whom *A* owes no duty of support. The portion of each installment payment representing the deferred profit, as well as the return of capital (principal) was to be paid by the trustee currently to *A*. The trust was terminated ten years and one month after *A* transferred the installment obligation to the trust, at which time the installment note was to be returned to *A*.

After considering the relevant statutory authority, including Section 453B, the IRS ruled that the grantor, *A*, should be treated as owner of that portion of the trust in which the deferred profit portion is included (as well as the return of capital) of the installment obligation. Furthermore, in selling the property for the installment obligation, the grantor created the right to receive payments on the installment obligation. The grantor, by retaining the right to receive the portion of each installment payment representing the deferred profit, as well as the return of capital (principal), could not avoid taxation on the interest income, even though the gift of the interest prior to its payment prevented the income from vesting in taxpayer's possession. Thus, the use of a trust to assign the interest payments to *B* was ineffective for federal income tax purposes. In summary, the IRS determined that (1) the transfer in trust was not a disposition of the installment note by *A*, and *A* should continue to report the deferred profit as installment payments are received by the trust and (2) *A* should continue to include in gross income the interest income as it was received by the trustee.

[Rev. Rul. 81-98, 1981-1 CB 40.]

Accrual-basis beneficiary must include all trust income accrued to date of death in final return. Where all income of a trust was required to be distributed currently to a beneficiary (now deceased) who reported his income under the accrual method of accounting, income earned by the trust to the date of the beneficiary's death was includable in the final return of the deceased beneficiary, within the purview of Section 652(a). Section 652(a) states, in part, that the amount of income for the taxable year required to be distributed currently by a trust shall be included in the gross income of a beneficiary to whom the income is required to be distributed, regardless of whether it is distributed. Section 451(b) states that in the case of the death of a taxpayer whose taxable income is computed under an accrual method of accounting, any amount accrued only by reason of the death of taxpayer shall not be included in computing taxable income for the period in which the date of taxpayer's death falls. That section is not in conflict with Section 652(a), because the amounts included in the gross income of the deceased beneficiary for his last taxable year are so included by reason of the operation of Section 652(a).

[Rev. Rul. 59-346, 1959-2 CB 165.]

Grantor-corporation's accounting period and accounting method control over revocable trust. A calendar-year corporation using the accrual method of accounting was the grantor of a revocable trust that was on a fiscal year basis and used the cash method of accounting. Because the grantor-corporation retained the power to revoke the trust within the meaning of Section 676 in computing its taxable income, it was required, under the provisions of Section 671, to include gross income from all of the trust properties. In addition, the taxable year of, and the method of accounting used by, the trust were disregarded, and the gross income from the trust properties was to be determined by the grantor-corporation as if the trust had not been created. In so ruling, the IRS cited Regulation § 1.671-3(a)(1).

[Rev. Rul. 57-390, 1957-2 CB 326.]

[2] Taxable Year

Life beneficiary's final return must include trust income distributed prior to death, even where trust's fiscal year ends after date of death. At the time of her death on November 29, 1957, decedent owned income interests in two trusts, the Henrici Trust and the Collins Trust. The Henrici Trust kept its books and filed its income tax returns on a February 1 to January 31 fiscal year, and the Collins Trust operated on an April 1 to March 31 fiscal year. Decedent was a cash-basis, calendar-year taxpayer. On April 15, 1958, the estate filed a final income tax return for decedent's taxable year 1957. It reported in gross income decedent's share of the income of the Henrici Trust for its fiscal year ending January 31, 1957, and of the Collins Trust for its fiscal year ending March 31, 1957. Also included was the total amount of Henrici Trust gross income for the 1958 fiscal year, which income was actually distributed to decedent prior to the date of death. There was a similar amount included from the Collins Trust for fiscal year 1958, plus an amount of trust income that was paid to the estate following the date of death. The executor later determined, however, that certain amounts of estate income were improperly included. As part of the subsequent refund claim, the executor claimed that the postmortem distributions of the Collins Trust were not required to be included, nor were the amounts distributed prior to the date of death that related to the 1958 fiscal years of the two trusts. The IRS conceded that the postmortem items were not properly included, but it denied the refund claim with respect to the 1958 fiscal year distributions. At trial in the district court, the IRS argued successfully that sums actually distributed to decedent prior to her death that were earned in a trust year ending after her death were includable in gross income under the rule in Sections 652(c) and 662(c). Known as the "different-taxable-years rule," these provisions state that if the taxable year of the beneficiary is different from that of the trust, the beneficiary must include in gross income an amount based on the income of the trust for any taxable year or years of the trust "ending within or with" the beneficiary's own taxable year. The IRS pointed to Regulation §§ 1.652(c)-(2) and 1.662(c)-(2) in support of its contention that when a life beneficiary of a trust dies, the return for the year of death should include trust income actually received before death, despite the fact that the trust's taxable year ends after the date of death. The executor maintained that the regulations were inconsistent with the plain language of the statutes, and that therefore they were void.

Held: Affirmed for the IRS. The Seventh Circuit found that the problem with which the regulations deal was evidently not contemplated by the statute. Therefore the district court properly rejected the executor's argument that the regulations were in direct conflict with the statutes. As stated by the Supreme Court in South Tex. Lumber Co., 333 US 496 (1948), the focus in such a case is on whether the regulations must be sustained, regardless of the statutory gap. Thus, the Seventh Circuit concluded that the regulations were reasonable because they merely attempted to impose a tax liability on income that the beneficiary, a cash-basis taxpayer, actually received and enjoyed prior to the date of death. The alleged "bunching" of income during a single taxable period was mitigated, according to the court, by the fact that the statute permitted decedent to enjoy the postponement of tax on trust income for several years prior to her death. Therefore, the regulations did not produce an unreasonable effect and were found to be consistent with the overall scheme of Subchapter J.

[Schimberg, 365 F2d 70, 18 AFTR2d 5119, 66-2 USTC ¶ 9527 (7th Cir. 1966).]

Grantor must include trust income in taxable year of constructive receipt, not in accordance with Section 662(c). In 1966, taxpayer, who reported income on a calendar-year basis, executed six written instruments by which he created a separate trust for each of his six children. He appointed his wife and another party as cotrustees and provided that the trusts were to terminate after ten years, with all trust principal reverting to him or to his estate. The trustees were given discretion to distribute the annual net income to the beneficiaries, with a corresponding power to accumulate all undistributed income. Each of the six trusts reported its income by using an April 1 fiscal year. In 1968, the trustees sold stock and debentures that produced substantial net long-term capital gains. The IRS determined, on audit, that taxpayer was subject to the grantor trust rules and that all trust income should be taxable to him pursuant to Section 677(a)(2). Taxpayer acquiesced in the IRS's determination, but insisted that the 1968 capital gains, which were realized during the trust's taxable year ending March 31, 1969, were reportable by him in 1969, not on his 1968 calendar year return as the IRS maintained. Taxpayer brought the case to the Tax Court, arguing that the issue was governed by Section 662(c), which provides that the amount to be included in a beneficiary's gross income shall be based on the distributable net income of the trust, and upon amounts properly paid, credited, or required to be distributed "during the taxable year of the trust."

Held: For the IRS. Taxpayer was not a beneficiary of the trust; therefore, he was not subject to Section 662(c). Although a trust beneficiary under these basic facts would report income on his 1969 personal return, the rule of Section 662(c) is not applicable to one who must report income by virtue of the grantor trust rules. The court determined that the effect of the grantor trust provisions is that the trust is disregarded and that the grantor is considered to be the owner of that portion of the trust in which he has retained an interest. In accordance with this, Regulation § 1.671-2(c) provides that an item of income or deduction included in computing a grantor's taxable income is to be treated as if it were received directly by the grantor, not from the trust. The court reasoned that inclusion of income is not keyed to the trust's distributable income in such a case. Therefore, Section 662(c) does not control. As a result, the court entered judgment for the IRS, requiring inclusion of the item in taxpayer's 1968 return in conformity with Section 451(a).

[Scheft, 59 TC 428 (1972).]

Grantor trust need not use calendar year. The IRS ruled that the taxable year of a grantor trust need not be the calendar year. Section 645 generally requires that a trust be on a calendar year for tax purposes. Although that section does not specifically exclude grantor trusts, Section 671 and Regulation § 1.641(a)-0(b) provide that the general trust provisions of the Code (which include Section 645) do not apply to grantor trusts. The legislative history shows that the purpose of Section 645 was to limit the deferral of income through the use of different tax years for a trust and its beneficiaries. Because a grantor must report all income as if the grantor trust did not exist, this is not a consideration.

[Rev. Rul. 90-55, 1990-2 CB 161.]

Trust is granted extension to file election to treat distribution as being made on last day of tax year. A complex trust filed its return for the year that ended January 31, 1987, on a timely basis. The accountant responsible for preparing the return concluded that the trust owned an interest in a limited partnership. The accountant included the partnership's loss in the trust's computation of taxable income. The trust made a distribution to its beneficiaries on February 5, 1987. Because of the partnership loss, the trust did not treat the distribution as having been made on January 31, 1987. Later the accountant discovered that the trust did not own any interest in the partnership. If the accountant had known this, the trust would have elected to treat the distribution as having been made on January 31, 1987. The accountant prepared a request for an extension to make the election and filed the application. The IRS granted an extension to make the election under Section 663(b). The IRS determined that there was "good cause" for such an extension under Regulation § 1.9100-1(a).

[Priv. Ltr. Rul. 8908005.]

¶ 24.02 RETURNS AND ASSESSMENTS

Expiration of statute of limitations with respect to trust bars assessment against beneficiary with respect to disallowed losses of trust. The IRS disallowed losses claimed by a trust for its investment in two partnerships. The disallowance decreased the loss and increased the income reported by the trust beneficiary. After the period of limitations on assessment had expired with respect to the trust, the IRS mailed timely notices of deficiency disallowing trust losses to the trust beneficiary. The beneficiary argued that the expiration of the periods of limitations on assessment with respect to the trust barred such adjustments.

Held: Reversed for taxpayer. In order for the IRS to adjust tax liability, it must do so at the source of the income; here, the trust. The adjustment cannot be made at the point where the income is distributed; in this case, the beneficiary of the trust. This principle is in keeping with the concept of finality, as embodied in the statute of limitations. The IRS had ample time to audit the trust's returns or obtain an extension, but chose not to do so.

[Fendell, 906 F2d 362, 90-2 USTC ¶ 50,345, 66 AFTR2d 90-5028 (8th Cir. 1990).]

Appointment of administrator to serve as trustee of estate property triggers obligation to file fiduciary returns. In 1903, taxpayer and her late husband executed reciprocal wills that purported to give the survivor a life interest in the property of the other, with the remainder passing to their living heirs. The wills were drafted and executed in Germany in accordance with German law. Although the husband died in New York in 1939, his will was not discovered until 1951 and was not admitted to probate until 1952. The administrator sought guidance from the state court over the construction of certain passages in the will. The state court, by decree entered in 1953, applied applicable German law to the will and determined that it created a life estate in taxpayer, with power to invade principal, and a remainder interest in decedent's two sons. In the meantime, during 1952, capital gains were realized on the corpus, and taxpayer reported these amounts as gross income on her personal return. Following the appointment of an administrator, however, capital gains realized in 1953 and 1954 were reported on fiduciary returns, with the taxes paid from principal. Both parties brought suit for refunds of taxes respectively paid. The district court rejected all of their claims.

Held: Affirmed for the IRS. With respect to the 1952 taxable year, taxpayer at this point held an unfettered power to spend the entire corpus for her own benefit. Therefore, the lower court correctly concluded that taxpayer was not a fiduciary and that the estate property was not then subject to an enforceable trust. Accordingly, taxpayer properly reported the gains as gross income and could not claim entitlement to a refund. The court based its holding on the predecessor statutory provisions to Sections 672 and 678, which treat third parties as the owners of trust property for tax purposes under the grantor trust rules. The court also affirmed a further ruling in the lower court that the 1953 state court decree, appointing a new administrator, effectuated the creation of a new taxable trust entity. Therefore, the 1953 and 1954 fiduciary returns properly reported the capital gains.

[Hirschmann, 309 F2d 104, 10 AFTR2d 5854, 62-2 USTC ¶ 9797 (2d Cir. 1962).]

Family trust is ignored in IRS action for levy. Taxpayers, husband and wife, established a family trust. They transferred their personal residence and its contents, together with their lifetime services and wages, to the trust. The trust was administered initially by taxpayers' eighteen-year-old son and the family physician. Later the doctor resigned, and taxpayers themselves joined their son as cotrustees. Following the creating of the trust, taxpayers used the trust assets as before. Both taxpayers accepted positions working for the trust and executed employment contracts whereby, in exchange for services, they were to receive housing, health care, educational allowances, transportation, and the like from the trust. The fiduciary tax returns filed by the trust showed deductions for salaries, an automobile lease, medical insurance, depreciation on the house, and similar expenses. The IRS challenged the trust on audit and assessed deficiencies against taxpayers individually. Taxpayers, in their capacity as trustees, brought an action for wrongful levy under Section 7426. The IRS moved for summary judgment, contending that its levy against certain trust property in satisfaction of the deficiency was not wrongful.

Held: For the IRS. Under Section 7426(c), in an action for wrongful levy "the assessment of tax upon which the interest or lien of the United States is based shall be conclusively presumed to be valid." Thus, the only issue before the district court was whether the IRS could levy against the trust's property to satisfy the tax assessments against the individuals. The court first concluded that the trust arrangement was "a transparent attempt" to avoid taxes, and ruled that the trust could be ignored for tax purposes. Applying the grantor trust rules under Section 674, the court concluded that taxpayers exercised full powers of disposition over trust property, and therefore the trust was not an independent entity sheltered from a levy for satisfaction of taxpayers' liability.

[Edwards Family Trust, 572 F. Supp. 22, 51 AFTR2d 83-719, 83-1 USTC ¶ 9180 (DNM 1983).]

Trust formed to avoid IRS deficiency collection is held to be transferee. Taxpayer, a family trust entity, was created in June 1977 through the execution of a trust agreement and a transfer by its maker of substantially all of his assets, valued at $100,000. The IRS challenged the transfer, contending that at the time, the transferor, an Ohio resident, was embroiled in Tax Court litigation that subsequently resulted in a judgment of deficiency totaling some $3,379 plus interest and penalties. In the instant proceedings, the IRS attempted to show that because the transfer was without consideration and had the effect of rendering the transferor insolvent, the IRS was entitled to collect from taxpayer trust under the transferee liability rules of Section 6901.

Held: For the IRS. Section 6901 authorizes the assessment of transferee liability, at law or in equity, in the same manner as the liability for income taxes. This provision does not create a new liability, but rather provides a summary remedy for enforcing the existing liability of the transferor. The question before the court was whether, under Ohio state law, the trust was a transferee. Under the controlling Ohio statute, a conveyance made without a fair consideration at a time when the transferor is or will be thereby rendered insolvent is fraudulent as to creditors, without regard to the transferor's actual intent. A conveyance fraudulent as to creditors, therefore, may be invalidated under state law. The court found that taxpayer possessed the requisite intent and that his receipt of an interest in the trust was not consideration.

[Douglas Family Trust, TC Memo. (P-H) ¶ 84,629, 49 TCM (CCH) 234 (1984).]

Revocable trust becomes taxable entity for return purposes at grantor's death. The trustee of a revocable trust filed fiduciary income tax returns (Form 1041) as information returns on behalf of the trust on a calendar-year basis since the trust's inception. The grantor reported the income with respect to the trust and paid the tax thereon. Upon the death of the grantor, when the trust became irrevocable, the trustee desired to file returns for the trust on a fiscal year basis.

The IRS determined that upon the death of the grantor, the trust became a separate entity for federal income tax purposes for the first time, and hence became a new taxpayer. Therefore, the trustee may elect to file the first return for the trust either on the basis of a calendar-year or a fiscal year, without the consent of the IRS, provided that it fulfills the other requirements of a taxpayer filing its first return. For tax purposes, the existence of the trust in this case, prior to the time it became irrevocable, is ignored.

[Rev. Rul. 57-51, 1957-1 CB 300.]

IRS issued final regulations on grantor trust reporting requirements. The IRS released final regulations on the method of reporting for trusts that are treated as owned by grantors or other persons under the grantor trust rules. Subject to certain new limitations, the final regulations retain the optional alternative methods of reporting contained in the proposed regulations. The final regulations clarify that the trustee of a trust that is treated as owned by one or more grantors or other persons may, but is not required to, report using one of the alternative methods.

According to the regulations, a trustee who has reported under one of the alternative methods may report pursuant to the general rule requiring the trustee to file a Form 1041 for any subsequent tax years of the trust, provided prescribed conditions are met. The final regulations make clear that a trustee of a qualified Subchapter S trust (QSST) may not report under an alternative method. The final regulations are generally effective for taxable years beginning after 1995.

[TD 8633, 1996-1 CB 119.]

Taxable Income

¶ 25.01 INTERESTS SUBJECT TO TAX

Dealer intent of trustee cannot be imputed to trust beneficiary for purposes of characterizing gain on the sale of land. Prior to 1953, taxpayer's father acquired an option to purchase approximately 1,160 acres of San Francisco peninsula land that was owned by a corporation. He joined with four other prominent real estate operators, and, in April 1953, they agreed to purchase all of the capital stock of the corporation for $1.15 million. The buyers agreed to liquidate the company and to hold the land for a period of six months in order to qualify for long-term capital gains treatment under then-current law. Their intent was to resell the property at the first opportunity. The purchase was effected during the following month, and the corporation was immediately dissolved. They then held the land as tenants in common. In early 1954, after the six months passed, the property was sold to outside interests at a substantial gain. In addition to his own cash, taxpayer's father contributed $7,000 from a trust in order to finance his portion of the land costs. The trust was created earlier by the father for taxpayer's benefit. Upon dissolution of the corporation, the trust received a conveyance of a one percent undivided interest in the land. In December 1953, two months prior to the land sale, the trust was dissolved, and the trust assets, including the one percent interest in the land, were transferred to taxpayer. On her 1954 return, taxpayer treated her gain on the sale of the land as long-term capital gain. The IRS determined, however, that the gain should have been reported as ordinary income. The IRS contended that the principal aim of the venture was to purchase and to hold the property for later sale to an investment company, and that therefore the land constituted dealer property not within the definition of a "capital asset" under Section 1221.

Held: For taxpayer. The facts showed that taxpayer, a housewife, was quite unaware of the nature of her father's dealings on behalf of the trust, and that she was in no sense engaged in any real estate activity beyond her passive role as trust beneficiary. The court found that the actions of the father, as trustee, were not of a nature sufficient to commit the trust to enter the business of holding property for sale to customers. In such a situation, the trustee's own separate personal motivations in entering the transaction cannot be imputed to the trust or to the beneficiary. Consequently, the income produced by the sale was taxable as capital gain.

[Rosebrook, 318 F2d 316, 11 AFTR2d 1546, 63-2 USTC ¶ 9500 (9th Cir. 1963).]

Widow's renunciation of income from husband's estate shifts tax to succeeding beneficiaries. Taxpayer, a widow entitled to all of the income from a trust under the will of her husband, renounced her right to all except one-thirteenth of the income. The balance passed to her twelve children. Income payment in this way was approved in an accounting by the trustees. The IRS, however, assessed deficiencies against taxpayer, asserting that the entire trust income was taxable to her. The district court held that the state court adjudication was not binding, because it was not an adversary proceeding, inasmuch as the whole family agreed on the redistribution.

Held: Reversed for taxpayer. A decision of a state court, regardless of whether it is adversary in nature, is binding for tax purposes on the question of which party has the right to receive income. This party was therefore liable for the payment of taxes imposed upon an estate beneficiary under the terms of current Section 102(b).

[Gallagher, 223 F2d 218, 47 AFTR 1230, 55-1 USTC ¶ 9485 (3d Cir. 1955).]

Nonresident beneficiary who adopts foreign citizenship must report income realized by trust during taxable year prior to change of status. During 1955, decedent's father created an inter vivos trust under New York State law. Decedent was the sole income beneficiary, and, by the terms of the governing instrument, the trustee was required to distribute all net income "at least annually." The trust's income was solely from non-U.S. sources. For many years prior to his death, decedent was a French resident. On November 24, 1975, he became a French citizen and thereby abandoned his U.S. citizenship.

In respect of his 1975 income taxes, taxpayer filed a nonresident alien income tax return, but reported no taxable income from the trust. The IRS determined that decedent was required to report income representing the total amount of all income actually realized by the trust between January 1, 1975, and November 23, 1975, inclusive. Alternatively, the IRS contended that he was taxable, at the minimum, on the amount of trust distributions actually made to him during the time prior to November 23.

Held: For the IRS. As a general rule, a U.S. citizen who resides abroad for the entire taxable year is taxable on worldwide income. At the same time, a taxpayer who was a nonresident alien throughout the taxable year is taxable only on U.S.-source income or on income effectively connected with the conduct of a trade or business within the United States. In addition, a trust beneficiary is regarded as receiving income from U.S. or foreign sources according to the source of the trust's income, regardless of the situs of the trust or the beneficiary's residency. Where, however, an individual changes his status from nonresident citizen to nonresident alien during the taxable year, the individual's taxable year is to be separated into two periods for purposes of determining the proper amount of income subject to U.S. tax. The court also noted that the taxing scheme of Subchapter J requires that a beneficiary report all income received by a simple trust without regard to the amount actually distributed to the trust. Applying the fundamental principle that a trust beneficiary "realizes taxable income simultaneously with the trust's realization of income," the court held that decedent should be taxed "on the same basis as [he] would have been had he owned the trust assets directly." Consequently, decedent was properly subject to U.S. income tax on the net income actually realized by the trust in that part of the year during which decedent was a U.S. citizen. The court therefore entered judgment upholding the deficiency to the extent of the trust's income realized from January 1 through November 23, 1975.

[Estate of Petschek, 81 TC 260 (1983), aff'd, 738 F2d 67, 54 AFTR2d 84-5424, 84-2 USTC ¶ 9598 (2d Cir. 1984).]

IRS rules on grantor trust beneficiary's Section 121 election. Person *H* died in 1978, leaving a will that provided for the establishment of a marital deduction trust for the benefit of his surviving spouse, *W*. Under the terms of the trust, *W* was entitled to receive all trust income for life and any trust corpus *W* requested from the trustee. The trust agreement also gave *W* the unrestricted power to vest the entire trust corpus or trust income in any person, including *W*. At the time of *H*'s death, *H* and *W* lived in their principal residence since 1970. *H* and *W*'s principal residence was made part of the corpus of the marital trust in 1979, the year in which the trust was established. The residence continued to be *W*'s principal residence until 1983, when it was sold at a price in excess of its adjusted basis. The amount of the gain was less than $125,000. *W* was seventy years old in 1983. In computing her 1983 federal income tax return, *W* treated the gain from the sale of the residence as excludable from gross income under Section 121. At the time of the sale, *W* had not remarried, and neither *H* nor *W* ever elected to use the exclusion provided by Section 121 with respect to any prior sale or exchange. In determining whether a beneficiary who is treated as the owner of a trust that owns the beneficiary's residence is entitled to the one-time exclusion of gain from the sale of a residence, the IRS cited Revenue Ruling 66-159, 1966-1 CB 162. That ruling considered whether the gain realized from the sale by a trust of property used by the grantor as the grantor's principal residence qualified for nonrecognition under Section 1034 (relating to rollover of gain on sale of principal residence). The ruling indicates that because the grantor was treated as the owner of the entire trust under Sections 676 and 671, the sale by the trust was treated as if made by the grantor.

In the present case, under *H*'s will, *W* had the sole power to vest the trust corpus or income therefrom in any person, including *W*. Therefore, under Section 678, *W* was treated by the IRS as the owner of the entire trust for federal income tax purposes, and, under Section 671, was required to include items of income, deductions, and credits attributable to the trust in computing *W*'s taxable income and credits. Because *W* was treated as the owner of the entire trust under Sections 678 and 671, the sale by the trust was treated for federal income tax purposes as if made by *W*. Therefore, if *W* were to make the election under Section 121, she could exclude the gain from the sale of the trust property from gross income, because the requirements of Section 121 had otherwise been met.

[Rev. Rul. 85-45, 1985-1 CB 183.]

IRA left in trust can be rolled over by surviving spouse. Decedent rolled over his retirement plan benefits into an individual retirement account (IRA) and designated a trust as the beneficiary. On his death, the trust was divided into two shares, an exemption trust and a survivor's trust to which the IRA was allocated. The surviving spouse was the sole trustee and beneficiary of the survivor's trust. She wanted to distribute the amount attributable to the IRA to herself under her general power to appoint trust assets by rolling the assets over into another IRA that she established for her benefit within sixty days of the distribution from the survivor's trust. In concluding that such a tax-free rollover was permissible, the IRS noted that the rollover would be tantamount to the surviving spouse's having been named the beneficiary of decedent's IRA.

[Priv. Ltr. Rul. 8920045.]

Grantor trust beneficiary may use alternative method to recover basis in stock of acquired corporation that is trust res. A calendar-year grantor trust, established for the benefit of an individual, owned all of the stock of a corporation involved in retail sales. A second corporation, through its subsidiary, acquired the retail corporation. The acquisition price was a stated amount of money and two contingent notes. The two notes were subject to adjustments based on the acquiring subsidiary's pretax acquisition adjusted income for the period ending with the acquired corporation's taxable year. The acquiring parent corporation also agreed to increase the purchase price by the amount of the trust beneficiary's federal, state, local, or county income taxes attributable to the first corporation's earnings during the acquisition period. After the sale of assets to the acquiring subsidiary, the acquired corporation made a series of liquidating distributions to the trust beneficiary in redemption of all of its stock in the acquiring subsidiary. The individual received all of the contingent obligations payable to the acquiring subsidiary. Citing the growth rate of the acquired corporation and the contingency payment schedule, the trust beneficiary requested that it be allowed to use an alternative method of recovering its basis in the acquired corporation's stock.

The IRS stated that the trust beneficiary's use of normal basis recovery rules set forth in Temporary Regulation § 15A.453-1(c)(3) substantially and inappropriately deferred the recovery of the trust beneficiary's basis. Therefore, the IRS stated that the trust beneficiary was permitted to use an alternative method of basis recovery that allowed him to recover basis at least twice as fast as under the normal basis recovery rules.

[Priv. Ltr. Rul. 8812064.]

¶ 25.02 CURRENTLY DISTRIBUTABLE INCOME

Payments made by corporation to trust-shareholder are not taxable to grantor or to beneficiaries. In 1947, the grantor established an irrevocable inter vivos trust for the benefit of his several children. Trust corpus consisted of all of the stock in a distilling business operated by the grantor. At the time of the trust transfer, however, the Commonwealth of Pennsylvania brought a lawsuit against the grantor for a large sum of money. The creation of the trust and the grantor's transfer of stock rendered him insolvent. He continued to be insolvent during 1950, when the Commonwealth prevailed in the lawsuit and recovered a judgment of nearly $865,000 against the grantor personally. Immediately thereafter the Commonwealth threatened to sue under the state fraudulent conveyance statute to set the trust aside and appropriate the corporate stock in satisfaction of judgment. Under the circumstances, the parties sought to achieve a compromise under which the Commonwealth would receive $756,000 in installment payments over three years in exchange for a full release and the preservation of the trust assets. It was finally agreed, with the consent of the trustees, that the trust assets would be kept intact during the three-year repayment term, and that if such payments fell into default, the trustees would not resist seizure of all the trust assets. The trustees and the grantor also agreed to have the corporation loan the grantor sufficient amounts with which to pay the $756,000 settlement. The details of the agreement were presented to the local orphan's court, which approved the settlement as being in the best interests of the trust and its beneficiaries. During 1951, and in the early part of 1952, the corporation advanced money to the grantor, who delivered it to the Commonwealth pursuant to the agreement. On March 12, 1952, however, the grantor died. His estate continued to make the payments through 1956 from loan proceeds paid by the corporation. On their income tax returns for the years 1952 through 1956, none of the trust beneficiaries reported as income any of the amounts paid by the corporation under its loan agreement with the grantor. The IRS determined, however, that there were deficiencies in the trust income in the amounts of the corporation's advances to the grantor and his estate for each of the years in question. In the IRS's view, the distributions were taxable dividends made out of the corporation's earnings and profits, and therefore the distributions were taxable to the beneficiaries as distributees of the trust, which was the sole shareholder. The beneficiaries argued that the trust was revocable, in that the Commonwealth at any time could have invoked the fraudulent conveyances statute and compelled a transfer of the trust assets. Therefore, under the grantor trust rules, specifically Section 676(a), the grantor and his estate should be taxable on any divided income.

Held: For the beneficiaries. The loans were taxable to the trust as dividends; however, none of the beneficiaries was liable for tax on such amounts. The reality of the situation, as understood by all of the parties and the orphan's court, was that no one ever envisioned that the "loans" would be repaid, and that at all times it was anticipated that the payments would simply result in the depletion of the corporation's assets. The arrangement was acceptable only because the parties found it more beneficial to hold vastly devalued property than to have the stock retracted and the trust dissolved. In light of the "total picture," the court concluded that the grantor and his estate were mere conduits through which the corporation made payments to the Commonwealth in settlement of its claim. The grantor was aging, infirm, and insolvent at the time the payments were made. Since he did not gain economically from satisfaction of the debt, and since he never exercised dominion and control over the loan proceeds, there was no basis for invoking the grantor trust rules, especially where, by its terms, the trust was irrevocable. Having rejected this argument, the court proceeded to find that as contended by the IRS, the payments were dividends made to the trust as sole shareholder. The court determined that the dividends benefited only the trust, however, because with each payment, it was able to preserve its corporate stock against the overriding claims of the Commonwealth. The trust was therefore taxable on the dividends under Sections 316 and 301(c). At the same time, however, the court concluded that none of the dividends represented distributable income taxable to the beneficiaries under Section 652, because the trust's primary liability was to the Commonwealth.

[Binenstock Trust, 321 F2d 598, 12 AFTR2d 5097, 63-2 USTC ¶ 9585 (3d Cir. 1963).]

Trust distributable net income includes "trapping" distribution from estate. Taxpayer, as income beneficiary of a testamentary trust created under her husband's will, was entitled to be paid, at least annually, all of the trust's net income. The estate generated distributable net income and made a principal distribution to the trust, which was income to the trust for tax purposes. Taxpayer reported her share of the trust's income, ignoring the "trapping" distribution from the estate to the trust. The IRS determined that the distribution from the estate, to the extent that it included distributable net income as defined in Section 643(a), was includable in taxpayer's income.

Held: For the IRS. The testamentary trust was required to include in income all trust accounting income, regardless of whether it was distributed. Although the accounting income of the trust is not taxed to a beneficiary to the extent that it exceeds distributable net income, there is no requirement that distributions be traced to principal or income. Instead, the distributable net income concept eliminates the tracing requirement, and presumes that a distribution is made out of a trust's distributable net income, regardless of whether it is actually made from principal or from income.

[Van Buren, 89 TC 1101 (1987).]

Tax Court finds beneficiary fully taxable on trust distributions. On their joint income tax return for 1980, taxpayers reported no income from a certain testamentary trust created in 1971 by the husband's father. Under the terms of the will, the trustee, a bank, was directed to pay $500 per month to the husband for life, with the remainder of current income passing to his sister. For 1980, the trust reported nontaxable distributions of $996 from tax-exempt securities, and taxable distributions of $3,227 from dividends and $566 from trust income. The IRS, noting that taxpayers did not report any trust income, issued a notice of deficiency for $1,406.

Held: For the IRS. Taxpayers argued in their pro se appearance that the husband's trust legacy of $6,000 per year was "fixed" and that the trust should assume the tax burden, as in situations involving divorce decrees. The court rejected this argument and found no merit in the contention that the receipt of a stated amount of income, if fixed by the trust, spares the beneficiary from tax under Subchapter J.

[Mahler, TC Memo. (P-H) ¶ 87,064, 52 TCM (CCH) 1552 (1987).]

Beneficiaries' rights to distributions of capital gain income from trusts are taxable, even though income is not actually distributed. Taxpayers, husband and wife, were the beneficiaries of four trusts. The husband and taxpayers' daughter and son-in-law were the grantors-trustees of two of the trusts. The trust agreements provided that the net income of the trusts was to be distributed to taxpayers as beneficiaries. If any of this income was derived from capital gains, however, then the capital gain income was to be distributed only upon taxpayers' specific request. If taxpayers did not request a distribution of the capital gain income, it was to be added to the corpus of the trusts. Taxpayers created the other two trusts separately. The husband was the grantor-trustee of one trust, and the wife was the grantor-trustee of the other. The trust agreements for both trusts provided that taxpayers as grantors-trustees retained the power to distribute income and principal from the trusts to themselves as beneficiaries, and the power to revoke the trusts at any time. The trusts did not distribute any capital gain income to taxpayers, nor did taxpayers include any of the undistributed capital gains in their gross income. The IRS determined that taxpayers were the owners of the four trusts under Sections 671–679 and that all items of income, deductions, and credits attributable to the trusts were includable in computing taxpayers' taxable income. Taxpayers contended that they should not be taxed on the capital gain income, because it was never actually distributed to them and was intended to be trust corpus.

Held: For the IRS. Under Section 678(a)(1), a person with the power, exercisable solely by himself, to vest the income or corpus of a trust in himself is deemed the owner of the income or corpus. Here, taxpayers clearly retained the power to receive the capital gains income from the first two trusts. Accordingly, they were deemed the owners of this income under Section 678. Under Section 671, the capital gain income was includable in taxpayers' gross income. With respect to the other two trusts, because taxpayers reserved the right to revoke these trusts, they were deemed the trusts' owners under the provisions of Section 676. Consequently, all of the income earned by those trusts was taxable to taxpayers under Section 671. Moreover, the fact that taxpayers did not exercise their power to revoke the trusts was not relevant. It is the retention of the power to revoke, not the actual exercise of that power, that caused taxpayers to be deemed the owners of the trusts and that required the inclusion of the trusts' income in their taxable income.

[Campbell, TC Memo. (P-H) ¶ 79,495, 39 TCM (CCH) 676 (1979).]

Agreement between trustees and beneficiaries regarding interest income from trust property does not affect taxability. The income of a testamentary trust consisting solely of interest from mortgages on the beneficiary's property was required to be distributed periodically. Although the mortgage notes held by the trust required the periodic payment of interest, it was agreed between the beneficiary and the trustees that the beneficiary would pay no interest on the mortgages and that the trustees would distribute no income from the trust.

The IRS ruled that notwithstanding the foregoing agreement, the interest income due on the mortgages held by the trust is includable in the gross income of the trust, and that this same amount, as the distributable income of the trust, is includable in the gross income of the beneficiary. Further, the beneficiary is entitled to a deduction for this interest deemed paid on the mortgages.

[Rev. Rul. 75-68, 1975-1 CB 184.]

Beneficiaries are liable for tax on distributions withheld by trustee pending resolution of legal dispute. Advice was requested whether income of a trust is considered to be distributable currently within the meaning of Sections 651 and 652. The sections state that despite the fact that the terms of the trust require current distribution of income of the trust, it is withheld and not distributed by the trustee pending termination of litigation respecting the proper distribution to be made. In the case of United States v. Higginson, 238 F2d 439 (1st Cir. 1956), the court held that the beneficiaries of an inter vivos trust that by its terms required net income to be paid semiannually to them, were taxable upon net income received by the trustee, but withheld from distribution for approximately four years pending resolution by state courts of an unsuccessful claim that the trust was invalid. The court stated that a decision by the trustees to withhold income, even though in good faith, cannot amend the plain terms of the trust deed.

Pursuant to that ruling, the IRS revoked IT 1733, II-2 CB 169 (1923), and ruled that where the terms of a trust instrument require that trust income is to be distributed currently, suspension of distribution by the trustee pending termination of a legal dispute as to the amounts properly distributable does not shift the liability for the tax from the beneficiary to the trust. As stated in the regulations, the determination whether trust income (as defined in Section 643(b)) is required to be distributed currently depends upon the terms of the trust instrument and the applicable local law. See Regulation § 1.651(a)-2. The fact that the trustee does not comply with such terms, therefore, is not decisive of the question whether trust income is distributable currently. However, extraordinary dividends received by the trust, that the fiduciary, acting in good faith after consideration of the terms of the governing instrument and applicable provisions of local law, determines to be allocable to corpus, would not constitute income required to be distributed currently to an income beneficiary.

[Rev. Rul. 62-147, 1962-2 CB 151.]

Trust to fund supplementary plan does not result in currently taxable income to participants. A company established a trust to pay benefits under its supplementary retirement, disability, and survivor benefits plan. The assets were to remain subject to the claims of the company's general creditors in case of insolvency. The IRS stated that the assets of the trust did not constitute property under Section 83. The IRS also stated that the transfer of assets to the trust and the holding of assets by the trust would not result in the recognition of income to any participant. The IRS concluded that the trust would be classified as a trust for federal income tax purposes and that the company would be the owner of the trust under Section 677 and Regulation § 1.677(a)-1(d).

[Priv. Ltr. Rul. 8834052.]

Expenses and Deductions

¶ 26.01 EXPENSE ITEMS

[1] Generally

Fifth Circuit holds that lack of independent trustee gives rise to disqualifying equity under Section 162(a)(3). Taxpayers were Florida residents who operated a funeral parlor. In 1961, they executed four trust instruments creating separate irrevocable trusts for each of their minor children. The trusts were to terminate after ten years and one day. In a simultaneous transaction, they conveyed title in the funeral home premises to the trustee, who was also the family lawyer. The trustee, in turn, leased the property back to taxpayer for annual rent of $14,040. In 1966, taxpayers executed a subsequent trust agreement whereby they transferred their reversionary interests in the property to a new irrevocable trust for the children. The IRS examined taxpayers' personal joint returns for taxable years preceding the second trust and concluded that they were not entitled to deduct the annual rental payments as claimed. The case was presented to the Tax Court, which entered judgment for taxpayers. The court held that the leasehold interest was not a disqualifying "equity" under Section 162(a)(3), and, primarily on this basis, it rejected the IRS's argument that the trust-leaseback was void for tax purposes.

Held: Reversed for the IRS. The Fifth Circuit focused solely on the issue of the trustee's independence as it bears on the question of determining the existence of an equitable interest under Section 162(a)(3). The critical element, noted the court, was that prior to the execution of the trust, the trustee gave assurances to taxpayers that the funeral home property would be available for rent throughout the term of the trust. Even though the property was leased on a yearly basis, taxpayers nevertheless retained an annual option to renew. The court found that this arrangement gave taxpayers effective control over the property and precluded the trustee from retaining any significant independent powers. The trust was therefore an economic nullity in the court's view, and the retained control, plus the reversionary interest, amounted to an equitable interest in the property sufficient to disqualify taxpayers from claiming Section 162 rental deductions.

[Mathews, 520 F2d 323, 36 AFTR2d 75-5965, 75-2 USTC ¶ 9734 (5th Cir. 1975), cert. denied, 424 US 967 (1976).]

Fifth Circuit strikes down trust-and-leaseback conveyances as lacking business purpose. Taxpayer was a surgeon practicing in Fort Worth, Texas. In 1957, by a single instrument, he created two trusts, with himself as trustee. One trust was for the benefit of taxpayer's son, and the other was for the benefit of his daughter. Each trust was expressly made irrevocable for a period of ten years and two months. In the following month, taxpayer conveyed to the trusts full title to an office building that he used in the conduct of his medical practice, together with all furnishings and equipment. Taxpayer simultaneously entered into a lease agreement with the trusts under which he received the right in his individual capacity to use the building and equipment in exchange for stated annual rentals. On his individual returns for 1958 and 1959, taxpayer deducted the rental payments made to the trusts, claiming them as ordinary and necessary business expenses under Section 162. The IRS refused to recognize the deductibility of the purported rental payments.

Held: For the IRS. The court acknowledged that taxpayer was not subject to the grantor trust rules, under which a grantor who enjoys the power to control beneficial enjoyment and other rights to trust property is regarded as the owner for federal tax purposes. Because the trusts were made irrevocable for a period in excess of ten years, taxpayer was within the exception to the grantor trust rules set forth in Section 673. The court determined, however, that taken as a whole, the creation of the trusts and the consequent leaseback were wholly lacking in a business purpose other than to shift income and to reduce tax liability. The court also concluded that the obligation to pay rent was not ordinary and necessary as required by Section 162. It reasoned that the lease-back was preordained at the time the trusts were created, and that therefore the lease did not create a "necessary" liability to incur the rental expense.

[Van Zandt, 341 F2d 440, 15 AFTR2d 372, 65-1 USTC ¶ 9236 (5th Cir. 1965), cert. denied, 382 US 814 (1965).]

Interest accrued on back taxes prior to trust liquidation may be deducted when paid by transferee beneficiary. Taxpayer was the sole income and principal beneficiary of a trust created in 1935 by his mother and father. On taxpayer's twenty-fifth birthday, in 1944, the trust terminated according to the express terms of the trust agreement. All property was distributed to taxpayer, and the trust itself was dissolved. Taxpayer continued to hold the property for the production of income. At the time of the trust's final liquidation, a dispute was pending between the trust and the IRS regarding the amount of the trust's income tax liability for taxable year 1940. Following the liquidation distributions, a further dispute arose concerning 1941. During 1945, taxpayer and the IRS resolved their differences, and taxpayer made a payment of $23,316 in full satisfaction of the assessed deficiencies. On his 1945 income tax return, taxpayer deducted the entire amount of the accrued interest paid to the IRS with respect to the 1940 and 1941 deficiencies. The IRS disallowed the asserted interest deduction to the extent that it accrued prior to the termination of the trust. The IRS also assessed additional deficiencies in trust income taxes for 1942 and 1943. This dispute was settled by an agreement reached during 1946. Once again, taxpayer deducted the accrued interest, and the IRS disallowed the portion that accrued during the period before the trust was dissolved. The IRS argued that the tax liabilities of the transferor trust were "paid" by taxpayer as transferee in connection with his assumption of a "cost basis" in the assets received in liquidation. Thus, the IRS contended that the accrued interest on the tax deficiencies entered taxpayer's basis and therefore was not deductible when paid.

Held: Affirmed in part for taxpayer, reversed in part for the IRS. The general rule is that interest paid can be deducted only by the party who owed the interest. The court determined that the tax deficiency and accrued interest owed by the trust at the time of termination was an obligation of the trust. This obligation became a charge against trust assets. Thus, taxpayer did not become primarily liable for the payment of back taxes and interest, but rather he was charged with a debt in gross to the IRS, without distinction between principal and interest. Accordingly, the partial disallowance of the claimed deduction was upheld.

[Norton, 250 F2d 902, 1 AFTR2d 622, 58-1 USTC ¶ 9188 (5th Cir. 1958).]

Court rejects rental deductions arising out of trust leaseback of medical offices. In 1956, taxpayers, three physicians practicing as partners, each signed a written instrument by which they conveyed their respective interests in certain partnership property to a trust for a term in excess of ten years. The property consisted of improved real estate that the partners used as their medical offices and that contained other space rented to tenants. In substance, the trust instrument provided for the payment of the net rental income from the property to or for the use of each of taxpayer's several children. On the day following the execution of the trust instruments, the trustee leased the medical offices back to taxpayers for a term of two years at annual rentals of $7,200 payable in advance. For taxable year 1956, the partnership reported a deduction of $1,800 for rental expenses pursuant to Section 162(a)(3). The IRS disallowed taxpayers' distributive share of the claimed expense, arguing that the trust transfers served no business purpose and failed to divest the grantors of such ownership and control of the trust property as to warrant the allowance being claimed. Taxpayers responded that the transactions were actuated by their desire to provide for the education of their children, even though tax savings were an admitted part of the plan. They pointed out that less than half of the trust property was involved in the leaseback, because other tenants occupied the majority of the property. In addition, they claimed that the lease was bona fide because the trustee was independent and they paid full fair rental value to the trusts.

Held: For the IRS. In denying the claimed deductions, the district court pointed to several factors that, taken as a whole, revealed the plan as nothing more than an improper shifting of income among family members. These included the facts, but the court distinguished the following facts in finding for the IRS:

1. The death of a grantor caused the respective trust to become immediately void.
2. The grantors or their estates were the only remaindermen.
3. The grantors reserved the right to settle the accounts of the trustee.
4. The leaseback was designed solely to reallocate income among family members, and for no other purpose.

Consequently, the court found that the trust conveyances were of no force or effect for tax purposes.

[Hall, 208 F. Supp. 584, 10 AFTR2d 5368, 62-2 USTC ¶ 9676 (NDNY 1962).]

Beneficiary of dissolved testamentary trust cannot deduct payments to former co-beneficiaries. By the terms of his will as probated in Texas during 1945, decedent expressed the intention that a trust be created for the benefit of his minor son. The trustee, who was also the executor, was instructed to provide support for the son, then age 14, until he reached age 35. The will also made provision for the payment of specified monthly amounts to decedent's favorite servants. In express terms, the trustee was required to make these payments subject to a general power to reduce or to discontinue them at his sole discretion. Subsequently, the son died before reaching age 35, and the trust thereupon terminated as provided in decedent's will. Taxpayer, decedent's widow, inherited the trust corpus from the son's estate. She continued to make the payments to the servants, and on her 1954 personal return, she treated the payments as deductions from "trust income." The IRS denied the deduction and assessed appropriate deficiencies. At the ensuing trial in federal district court, taxpayer contended that the property passed to her from the son's estate was subject to a trust created by decedent in favor of the servants. She acknowledged that the trust in favor of the son terminated on his death but argued that decedent's will effectively raised a second trust to provide for the servants.

Held: For the IRS. The court examined decedent's will and found that it did indeed require that the trustee make the disputed payments to decedent's servants from trust property. The will was silent, however, on the effect of a trust termination on the monthly payments to the servants. The court resolved the question by finding that the will was so dominated by the trust established for the son that the provision for the servants was "simply an appendage" to the single trust, which created no vested rights in the servants. In view of an expressed intent to provide payments beyond the termination of the son's trust, the court ruled that no trust arose in favor of the servants, and that therefore the property passing to taxpayer was not subject to an obligation to continue payments to the servants. Accordingly, the claimed deduction was found to be improper, and the resulting deficiencies were upheld.

[Green, 6 AFTR2d 5647, 60-2 USTC ¶ 9660 (ND Tex. 1960).]

Rent deduction is allowed on transfer and leaseback of building to short-term trust. During 1954, taxpayer and his wife, as joint owners, completed construction of a building that was thereafter used by taxpayer for his medical practice. In 1956, the couple created an irrevocable short-term trust for the benefit of their children. The trust was to continue for a term of eleven years, with a local bank serving as trustee. The corpus consisted of the land and medical offices, which taxpayer arranged to lease back from the trustee. Three years later, in 1959, taxpayer by deed transferred to his wife full title to his reversionary interest in the property. On his tax returns for 1959, 1960, and 1961, taxpayer claimed business deductions for rent paid on the property to the trustee. The IRS disallowed the rental expense deduction, on the ground that taxpayer retained a prohibited "equity" in the property under Section 162(a)(3) and that the trust-and-leaseback arrangement lacked a bona fide business purpose.

Held: For taxpayer. Under Section 162(a)(3), a trade or business rental deduction is allowed only with respect to property "to which taxpayer has not taken or is not taking title or in which he has no equity." The Tax Court found that one has an "equity" in property when he has a right of redemption, a reversionary interest, a right to specific performance, or, in general, any right that traditionally would have been enforceable by means of an equitable remedy. Because taxpayer relinquished his reversionary interest prior to the taxable periods in issue, he had no equity in the property; therefore, the rental expense limitation in Section 162(a)(3) does not apply. The court further concluded that the transfer and leaseback of business property to a valid irrevocable trust, subject only to the control of an independent trustee, is to be respected for tax purposes without reference to whether a bona fide business reason existed for the transaction. Consequently, as in the instant case, a taxpayer's trust transfer results in a legitimate surrender of all control and interest in title, the arrangement will be respected under the income tax laws.

[Oakes, 44 TC 524 (1965).]

Tax Court upholds deduction for licensing and royalty payments based on transfer of patent to family trust. In 1942, taxpayer began the production of an improved counter chronograph that he designed and patented. His early success in marketing this device led him to consider protecting his patents and providing future income for his family. To this end, taxpayer established three trusts for the benefit of his wife and two minor children. The trusts were irrevocable and were to continue to exist until the children reached their majority. The trustees (his wife, his father, and his accountant) were fully independent and could not be removed or directed by taxpayer under the terms of the governing trust instrument. Taxpayer had no power to alter the status of the beneficiaries, nor did he retain any powers with respect to the accumulation or withholding of income. He had no reversionary interest, no power to change trustees, and the instrument expressly provided that trust income could not be used to discharge any of taxpayer's legal obligations of support owed to the beneficiaries. The corpus consisted of the full and exclusive right, title, and interest in a certain patent application and in all patents arising therefrom. In a contemporaneous transaction, the trustees conveyed to taxpayer a nonexclusive license to manufacture, use, and sell the patented counter chronograph in exchange for a graduated royalty. During the years 1944 through 1946, the taxpayer borrowed some of the royalty income paid to the trusts in order to improve the financial position of his marketing and development company. Also during the same years, taxpayer advanced money to the children to enable them to pay taxes on their taxable trust income. At the close of each year, he offset against such advances the accrued interest on the loans. Furthermore, in 1945, taxpayer purchased a quantity of government bonds and delivered them to the trustees in payment of accrued royalties. The IRS examined these various transactions and determined that taxpayer was personally taxable on all trust income. Specifically, the IRS refused to acknowledge the transfer and license arrangement with respect to the patent application, and disallowed taxpayer's deduction of the royalty payments and the interest paid to the children for the loans. The IRS also sought to tax him on all bond interest received by the trusts in 1945 and 1946. The IRS based its deficiency assessments on the contention that the assignment of the patents to the trusts was invalid, because taxpayer never in substance parted with control of the patents, and that, overall, the plan was a tax avoidance sham.

Held: For taxpayer. The Tax Court examined the terms of the governing trust instrument and concluded that a full, complete, and valid transfer of taxpayer's rights in the patent occurred. The court noted that

1. The assignment and delivery of the patent application was valid under federal patent law;
2. The assignment was irrevocable;
3. The trustees were fully independent;
4. The trust corpus would pass to the beneficiaries on termination of the trust, with no reversionary rights in taxpayer;
5. Taxpayer retained no power to control investments or otherwise affect the beneficiaries' vested rights.

In view of the fact that taxpayer therefore divested himself fully of the trust corpus, the court concluded that the IRS was without statutory authority to allocate trust income to taxpayer or to disallow his deduction of royalties and interest paid to the trustees.

[Potter, 27 TC 200 (1956), acq. 1957-2 CB 6.]

Beneficiary's litigation costs against trustee are deductible. Taxpayer was the beneficiary of a trust. The trustee loaned his wholly owned corporation $250,000 at a below-market interest rate. The beneficiary sought to have a constructive trust imposed upon the profits made by the corporation and the trustee. She thereafter deducted the resulting legal expenses. The IRS alleged that seeking to impose a constructive trust involved the conveyance of title to property, the expenses of which were not deductible under Regulation § 1.212-1(k), because they did not concern the production of income or the management of property held for the production of income.

Held: For taxpayer. The origin of the claim was the loss of taxable income due to breach of fiduciary duty. The beneficiary was attempting to recover, by means of imposing a constructive trust, income lost because of the low rate of interest on the loan. Therefore, her legal expenses were deductible.

[Barr, TC Memo. (P-H) ¶ 89,420, 57 TCM (CCH) 1261 (1989).]

[2] Tax-Exempt Income Allocations

First Circuit requires IRS to use unrealized appreciation in calculating allocation of termination fee to exempt securities. From 1953 to 1969, taxpayer maintained a trust account that included certain tax-exempt municipal bonds, as well as other income-producing securities subject to federal income tax. The trust also realized capital gains and losses from transactions involving its various holdings. When the trust was terminated during 1969, the fair market value (FMV) of the assets included substantial amounts of unrealized capital appreciation. These amounts were reflected in the trustee's termination fee paid under a state statutory formula computed as a percentage of current market value. Taxpayer deducted the full amount of these commissions as expenses for the production of income under Section 212. The IRS disputed the amount claimed and disallowed that portion of the fee that was based on the increased value of the tax-exempt municipal bonds. The IRS proceeded on the theory that Section 265(1) prohibits the deduction of expenses directly or indirectly allocable to the production of tax-exempt income. The Tax Court found for the IRS and sustained its reallocation method based on long-term distributable net income. The Tax Court reasoned that net capital gains income realized over the life of the trust accurately measured the trustee's income-producing activities. Consequently, it concluded that distributable net income, not unrealized appreciation, was the proper basis for allocation of the termination fee.

Held: Affirmed in part for the IRS, and reversed in part for taxpayer. A trust termination fee may be deducted only to the extent that the expense is not directly or indirectly allocable to the production of tax-exempt income. Because capital gains on exempt securities are fully subject to federal tax, and in view of the considerable importance of appreciation in the overall scope of the trustee's duties, the court ruled that such capital appreciation cannot be ignored in calculating an allocation under Section 265. The First Circuit rejected the Tax Court's restrictive view and held that future appreciation was an inferrable objective of taxpayer's trust, particularly because the trustee's compensation was based in large part (over 50 percent) on the appreciated value of corpus at termination. In addition, the court noted that distributable net income was an "annual concept" not readily adapted to a long-term view of a trust's capital value at termination. Such an approach also fails to take fully into account the fact that the trust grantor ultimately faces a tax burden following his reversion of the appreciated property. Thus, though distributable net income forms a proper basis for determining a trustee's annual fee, it is not of controlling relevance in a Section 265 allocation of the trustee's statutory termination fee.

[Fabens, 519 F2d 1310, 36 AFTR2d 75-5248, 75-2 USTC ¶ 9572 (1st Cir. 1975).]

Commissions paid on termination of trust containing tax-exempt bonds are deductible on basis of ratio of taxable to nontaxable income over term of trust. During the years 1910 and 1919, the grantor created two trusts that paid income to his wife and daughters for their lives. The last surviving daughter died in 1958, and during 1959 and 1960, the trust assets were distributed to her issue. Each trust held substantial investments in municipal bonds that paid tax-exempt interest. By the terms of the governing instruments, the trustee was entitled to a periodic commission on trust income, plus an additional fee based on a percentage of the value of corpus at the time of termination. Through the years, the interest income from the municipal bonds was included in the trust income for purposes of determining the trustee's commission, even though such income was excluded from gross income for federal tax purposes consistent with Section 103. At the same time, the trust deducted the commission expense only to the extent that it was paid on taxable income received by the trusts. The entire termination fee, however, was taken as a deduction during 1959 and 1960, when it was paid to the trustee. Because the fees far exceeded taxable income in each year, the beneficiary took the excess deduction against his own income in accordance with the provisions of Section 642. On audit of the fiduciary and individual returns, the IRS refused to permit the beneficiary to deduct any portion of the termination fee based on the tax-free municipal bonds. In support, the IRS cited Section 265, which disallows expenses allocable to tax-exempt income. The IRS prevailed in federal district court, which rejected the beneficiary's argument that the termination fee was unrelated to the production of tax-exempt income.

Held: Reversed and remanded for taxpayer. The court framed the issue as whether the language of Section 265(1) disallowing expenses "allocable" to tax-exempt interest refers only to expenses directly relating to income, or whether it also encompasses expenses indirectly relating to income. The precise question, therefore, was whether such expenses were deductible under Section 212, which permits expenses incurred both for the production of income as well as for the management, conservation, or maintenance of property held for the production of income. The court resolved the issue by referring to Regulation § 1.212-1(a)(1), which provides that an expense may be deducted only where incurred for the production of income that, "if and when realized," will be required to be included in income. In the court's view, the regulation is sufficiently broad to include both interest income as well as taxable gain that would be realized on a later sale of the bonds quite apart from the interest covered by Section 265. Thus, to the extent that municipal bonds produce taxable income, as on a sale, or are held for appreciation, the expenses incurred in their management, conservation, or maintenance are fully deductible under Section 212(2). The court determined that a reasonable basis for determining the extent to which the fee was related to taxable income was to calculate the ratio of taxable income to nontaxable income over the term of the trust.

[Whittemore, 383 F2d 824, 20 AFTR2d 5533, 67-2 USTC ¶ 9670 (8th Cir. 1967).]

Capital gains that enter corpus cannot be used in allocating expenses for Section 652(b) purposes. Taxpayer was the income beneficiary of a trust created under her father's will. By the terms of the trust, the entire net income of the trust, other than capital gains, was payable to her for life. During taxable year 1955, the trust realized $1.4 million of net long-term capital gains, plus tax-exempt bond interest of $308,122, and taxable dividends and interest of $607,497. After auditing taxpayer for 1955, the IRS assessed a deficiency, alleging that the trust erred in computing its distributable income for the year, and that, consequently, taxpayer underreported the amount of distributable income taxable to her under Section 652. The controversy involved the proper allocation of $148,817 in trust expenses. The trustee allocated these expenses pro rata among all tax-exempt and taxable income items, including capital gains. The court thereby concluded an allocation of $23,464 to tax-exempt income, and $125,353 to taxable income. The IRS insisted that the allocation should be made only among the tax-exempt income and taxable income items distributable to the beneficiary (i.e., without regard to the capital gains income). By thus excluding capital gains, the IRS increased the amount of the distribution that must be included in taxpayer's gross income by $32,992.

    Held: For the IRS. Section 652(b) provides that in determining the amount to be included in a beneficiary's gross income under Section 652(a), the deductions reflected in the computation of distributable net income are to be allocated among the various types of gross income required to be distributed. Because the trust stipulated that capital gains were not to be distributed, the capital gains of the trust were not part of the distributable net income and therefore were not an "item of distributable net income" for purposes of allocation under Section 652(b). The court bolstered its analysis by pointing out that Section 643(a)(3) defines "distributable net income" to mean the taxable income of the estate or trust, subject to the rule that capital gains must be excluded to the extent that they are applied to corpus and not distributed to the beneficiary in the taxable year. Thus, capital gains under the instant trust were not part of distributable net income for purposes of Section 652 allocation.

[Tucker, 322 F2d 86, 12 AFTR2d 5368, 63-2 USTC ¶ 9654 (2d Cir. 1963).]

Trust beneficiary may not deduct expenses for producing tax-free income subject to conduit rules of Section 652(b). Taxpayer was the life beneficiary of a testamentary trust created under her father's will. The trust originally owned 110 shares of stock in a local bank, which later merged into another financial institution. As a result, the trust surrendered its 110 shares of the old bank stock in exchange for 880 shares in the new one. Because the merger qualified as a tax-free reorganization, the trust did not recognize gain on the transaction. The trustee treated the receipt of the new shares as an even exchange of trust corpus, and therefore did not allocate any of the shares to income. Taxpayer brought the matter to state probate court and insisted that 509 shares of the new stock constituted income to the trust that should have been currently distributed to her as the life beneficiary. The state court ruled for the trust, finding that the entire 880 shares were properly allocated to trust corpus. As a consequence of her unsuccessful suit, taxpayer incurred legal costs in the amount of $2,865. On her personal return for the taxable year, she claimed the legal fees as a deductible expense. The IRS determined that the item was not deductible and, accordingly, disallowed it in full. At trial, the issue was whether the item was deductible as a nontrade expense for the production of income under Section 212. The IRS argued that taxpayer did not satisfy Regulation § 1.212-1, which permits a deduction only where the expense was incurred in producing income that, if collected, would be taxable to the recipient. The IRS contended that even if taxpayer was successful in compelling a distribution of the shares, she would have received them tax-free by virtue of the nonrecognition rules for exchanges of stock in corporate reorganizations.

Held: Reversed for the IRS. The expense deduction was properly disallowed by the IRS. Under the conduit rules of Section 652(b), property that is tax-free when received by a trust retains its tax-free character in the hands of a beneficiary to whom it is transferred in a current distribution. Since the reorganization nonrecognition rules would have applied to taxpayer in the event of a successful resolution of her suit, the claimed expenses were nondeductible under Regulation § 1.212-1, because taxpayer would have incurred no tax liability.

[Burgwin, 277 F2d 395, 5 AFTR2d 1136, 60-1 USTC ¶ 9368 (3d Cir. 1960).]

IRS rules on allocation of expenses involving tax-exempt income. In 1975, *A* created a simple trust for the benefit of *A*'s child, *B*. The trust instrument provides that the trustee shall distribute, currently, the entire net income of the trust to *B*. The trust instrument does not authorize distributions of corpus during *B*'s lifetime. Capital gains are allocable to corpus under state law. For the taxable year 1976, the trust's income consisted of taxable interest, tax-exempt interest, and capital gains. On the trust's fiduciary income tax return (Form 1041) for 1976, the trustee, in computing distributable net income, allocated its compensation between taxable and tax-exempt income on the basis of a formula that included the trust's capital gains. The IRS was asked to rule on whether a simple trust that does not distribute capital gains, because they are allocable to corpus under the trust instrument or applicable local law, may include, for purposes of computing its distributable net income under Section 643(a), a capital gains in the formula for allocating indirect expenses to tax-exempt income.

The IRS concluded that in the case of an individual taxpayer, there is no division of the taxable income between two or more parties. Therefore, it is proper to allocate expenses under Section 212 to all of the taxable income (including capital gains) of the individual. In the case of a simple trust, however, there may be a division of the taxable income earned by the trust between the trust and its beneficiaries. Therefore, in computing the distributable net income of such trusts, which will determine the amount to be included by the beneficiaries in their gross income, the allocation of indirect expenses must be made only with respect to the income (taxable and tax-exempt) that is to be distributed currently to the beneficiaries by the trust. In the instant case, the trust's capital gains are not included in the computation of distributable net income under the provisions of Section 643. Therefore, the capital gains may not be included in the formula for allocating indirect expenses to tax-exempt income, and the trustee's allocation was improper.

[Rev. Rul. 77-355, 1977-2 CB 82.]

¶ 26.02 DEPRECIATION AND AMORTIZATION

Depreciation must be allocated to income beneficiaries even if trust is not yet established. Taxpayer, an estate in administration, distributed income generated by real property to the income beneficiaries of a trust that will eventually hold such property but that had not yet been established. The IRS contended that taxpayer was not entitled to the entire depreciation deduction with regard to such real property and allocated a pro rata share to the income distributees. The district court found for the IRS.

Held: Affirmed for the IRS. A pro rata share of the depreciation was allocable to the trust beneficiaries. In its review of Section 167(h), the Fifth Circuit found that as a general matter, the statute provides for the depreciation deduction to follow the income from the property. It applied this reasoning to distributions made during the administration of an estate to the income beneficiaries of a testamentary trust that is not yet operative. The court found that it would be anomalous to permit an estate to distribute income that can be identified as coming from a parcel of real property, but to retain the depreciation deduction as an offset against income from unrelated sources.

[Lamkin, 533 F2d 303, 38 AFTR2d 76-5218, 76-2 USTC ¶ 9485 (5th Cir. 1976).]

Life beneficiary of real property trust cannot depreciate building owned by lessee. During 1941, taxpayer's mother leased a parcel of commercial real estate to a national dry goods retailer known as the G.C. Murphy Co. By the terms of the lease, the Murphy Co. was granted the right to demolish existing improvements and to erect a new building on the site. The property and the building were to revert to the mother on the expiration of the leasehold in 1973. The useful life of the building that was eventually constructed exceeded the unexpired term of the lease. When the mother died in 1953, the property and lease passed to her testamentary trust, of which taxpayer was the life beneficiary. In the years 1953 through 1955, taxpayer reported rental income on the property and also sought to take depreciation deductions on the building. The IRS determined that taxpayer's interest in the building was not depreciating in value; therefore, it denied the depreciation deductions. In response, taxpayer argued that she possessed an interest in a wasting asset (as required under Section 167) because the useful life of the building extended beyond the term of the lease. Alternatively, she contended that her deduction represented amortization of the capitalized value of the lease premium. She based this argument on the proposition that the lease was a separate property interest that may be valued apart from all other interests, especially here, where existing lease payments were far in excess of prevailing fair rental value. Thus, taxpayer contended that the difference between the total rentals being paid under the lease and the estimated fair rental value should be amortized over the remaining term.

Held: Affirmed for the IRS. On taxpayer's first argument, the court found that she had no depreciable interest in the building by virtue of her rights under the trust, and that therefore no allowance for depreciation was proper. The court determined that her right of reversion at the end of the leasehold term did not amount to the current possession of an interest in a wasting asset for purposes of depreciation. The court also rejected her second argument, holding that the right to receive rents was merely incident to the trust's ownership of the fee, and that therefore the lease did not constitute a separate capital asset subject to amortization. A favorable lease, producing rents in excess of market value, does not itself constitute a separate asset that can be amortized over its remaining useful life. The court reached this conclusion after noting that even if such a premium were satisfactorily shown to exist under current conditions, there was no assurance that future rental values would necessarily stabilize at that level.

[Schubert, 286 F2d 573, 7 AFTR2d 550, 61-1 USTC ¶ 9217 (4th Cir. 1961), cert. denied, 366 US 960 (1961).]

Remaindermen who buy out life beneficiaries may amortize the purchase price. Decedent, by will, established a testamentary trust that contained stock in a cement company. By the terms of the will, certain named beneficiaries were given an interest in trust income for life, and taxpayers were named as remaindermen to receive the corpus of the trust on the expiration of the life estates. In 1949, approximately seven years after decedent's death, taxpayers began negotiations with the life beneficiaries for the purchase of their life interests. The negotiations were completed in that year, and the income interests were purchased for consideration of $150,465 paid in December. All of the stock was then immediately turned over to taxpayers, and, by operation of state law, the trust terminated. For the years 1952 through 1954, taxpayers claimed as deductions certain amounts representing amortization of their costs in purchasing the income rights of the life beneficiaries on their income tax returns. The IRS disallowed these items, contending that when a remainderman purchases a life or other terminable interest standing ahead of his remainder, the purchased interest merges with the remainder into complete and absolute ownership. Accordingly, in the IRS's view, the capital invested in the purchase could be recouped only at the time of sale or disposition of the trust property, not by means of amortization.

Held: For taxpayers. The court cited Bell, 212 F2d 253 (7th Cir. 1954), for the proposition that amortization under such circumstances is proper, and that the entire purchase price may be recovered over the period of the life expectancy of the former life beneficiaries. The court noted that taxpayers were not buying the stock, but that they were clearly purchasing terminable interests that, notwithstanding their remainder interests, represent wasting, amortizable assets.

[Fry, 31 TC 522 (1958), aff'd without op., 283 F2d 869, 6 AFTR2d 5691, 60-2 USTC ¶ 9738 (6th Cir. 1960).]

¶ 26.03 DEPLETION ALLOWANCE

Allocation of depletion and depreciation deductions is held to benefit income beneficiary, not principal. Decedent, who died in 1953, was for ten years the income beneficiary of a testamentary trust established by her daughter. The trust contained undivided interests in approximately eighty-four oil-producing wells located in Texas. The daughter's will contained certain trust provisions that granted to the trustees the unqualified discretion to allocate trust receipts to income or to corpus, and made no mention of the treatment to be given in allocating such depreciation and depletion deductions as may arise from year to year. On her daughter's death, decedent, as life beneficiary, entered into an agreement with other interested beneficiaries of the will in order to forestall a threatened will contest. By the terms of the settlement, it was provided that a new trust agreement would be entered into by the parties. This subsequent agreement required the trustee to allocate all receipts to principal and income in accordance with Texas state law, which had the effect of causing the entire depreciation and depletion deductions to benefit solely the principal, not the income interests. Nevertheless, decedent claimed entitlement to an allocable share of the deductions on her federal income tax returns. She based her claim on statutory provisions codified in Sections 167(h) and 611(b)(3), which state that allowable deductions shall be apportioned between the income beneficiaries and the trustee in accordance with the pertinent provisions of "the instrument creating the trust," or, in the absence of these provisions, on the basis of trust income allocable to each. Therefore, taxpayer contended that the original testamentary trust controlled the allocation of deductions. Because it contained no special allocation provision, it should follow under the statutes that the apportionment should be made on the basis of trust income, which would thereby benefit her. The IRS convinced the Tax Court, however, that she was not entitled to the claimed deductions, because under the modifying trust agreement, state law controls to compel allocation to principal.

Held: Reversed for taxpayer. The Ninth Circuit rejected the lower court's determination that "the instrument creating the trust" was the subsequent agreement, not the original testamentary trust. In reaching this conclusion, the court noted that the trust modification agreement merely supplemented the original trust and in no way revoked it or otherwise superseded it as the controlling instrument that "created" the trust in the first instance. Accordingly, the Ninth Circuit refused to follow the Tax Court's construction of the later agreement, and applied the statute's unambiguous and plain meaning to the facts presented.

[Estate of Little, 274 F2d 718, 5 AFTR2d 670, 60-1 USTC ¶ 9247 (9th Cir. 1960).]

IRS rules on computation of allocable deductions. The IRS ruled that an estate or trust must compute the deductions for depreciation under Section 167(h) and depletion under Section 611(b), based on properties that it holds in its capacity as a separate taxable person, before apportioning these deductions between the estate or trust and the beneficiaries. The deductions may be allocated to the beneficiaries in amounts greater than their pro rata shares of the estate or trust income.

[Rev. Rul. 74-530, 1974-2 CB 188.]

¶ 26.04 EXCESS DEDUCTIONS

Private foundation may not reduce its excise tax liability through deductions pursuant to Section 642(h). By the terms of his will, decedent created a trust to pay all of its income to his widow for life, and, upon her death, to pay the remainder to decedent's private charitable foundation. The foundation was exempt from income tax under Section 501, but as a private foundation, it was fully liable under Section 509 for excise taxes on its net investment income. Following the death of the life beneficiary in 1970, the trustees sought to claim their statutory distribution fee, which, under state law, was equal to 3 percent of the distributed assets. The foundation prevailed upon the trustees to accept a lesser amount. Eventually it was agreed to settle the controversy for $300,000, or approximately 1.79 percent of the value of the trust's assets. The foundation itself paid the fee directly to the trustees, and thereafter it received a completed distribution of trust assets.

On its 1970 income tax return, the trust claimed the $300,000 item as a deduction against taxable income. The trust's taxable income for 1970 was considerably less than its total deductions, and, consequently, $288,659 of the deductions was not used to offset income. At the same time, the foundation also claimed the $300,000 as a deduction under Section 4940(c)(3)(A) in computing its excise tax liability. The IRS, however, disallowed the foundation's deduction on the ground that it was not paid or incurred for the production or collection of investment income, and also because the distribution fee was an obligation of the trust, not of the foundation. The district court ruled in favor of the IRS under Section 4940, but nevertheless entered judgment for the foundation under Section 642(h), which permits trust beneficiaries to deduct unused trust deductions upon receiving distributions from a terminating trust.

Held: The Fifth Circuit affirmed the district court's findings under Section 4940 but reversed it on the issue of Section 642(h). Section 4940 allows deductions only for ordinary and necessary expenses paid or incurred for the production or collection of investment income, or for the management, conservation, or maintenance of such property. The court held that this language limits the availability of deductible items to only those that have some "nexus with the foundation's investment income activities." The court concluded that the Section 642(h)(2) deduction simply "does not fit" within the statutory framework of Section 4940, and that therefore the foundation was not entitled to deduct any part of its $300,000 payment. The court examined relevant legislative history and found that Congress was fully aware of the limited scope of Section 4940, and that it purposefully narrowed the range of items that could be deducted.

[Whitehead Found., Inc., 606 F2d 534, 44 AFTR2d 79-6056, 79-2 USTC ¶ 9706 (5th Cir. 1979).]

Purchaser of trust interest has no status as "beneficiary" under Section 642(h) for excess deduction allowance. Taxpayer, a practicing lawyer, purchased, for investment purposes, an interest in a testamentary trust. The trust was created in 1925 under the terms of a will probated in Illinois. The remainder beneficiary then sold her entire interest to a group of individuals for total consideration of $31,500. A month later taxpayer acquired his interest by purchase from one of the individual investors. In 1968, the trust terminated, and taxpayer received a distribution of stock having a FMV of $55,788. The trustee reported, however, that for 1968, the trust's deductible expenses exceeded income, and, accordingly, taxpayer claimed his portion of the excess as a deduction on his 1968 personal tax return. The IRS disallowed the deduction, on the ground that taxpayer was not a proper party to claim an excess deduction under Section 642(h). That section provides that upon the termination of a trust or estate, any deductions in excess of the year's gross income shall be allowed as a deduction "to the beneficiaries succeeding to the property" of the estate or trust. The IRS contended that for purposes of Section 642(h), the taxpayer was not a "beneficiary" and therefore was not entitled to the claimed deduction.

Held: For the IRS. The purchaser of an interest in a trust does not "succeed" to the property and therefore cannot be a "beneficiary" for purposes of Section 642(h). The court determined that the use of the phrase "beneficiaries succeeding to the property" indicates that Section 642(h) was intended to refer only to recipients of property by gift, bequest, devise, or inheritance under state succession laws. By entering into the purchase of his interest, taxpayer acquired nothing by bequest, devise, or inheritance; therefore, he was in no sense a "beneficiary."

[Nemser, 66 TC 780 (1976), aff'd without op., 556 F2d 558, 77-1 USTC ¶ 9406 (2d Cir. 1977), cert. denied, 434 US 855 (1977).]

Capital gain deduction of trust under Section 1202 qualifies as Section 642(h) excess deduction. Advice was requested whether the capital gains deduction allowed by Section 1202 in an excess deduction of a trust for the purpose of computing the deduction allowed by Section 642(h) to beneficiaries succeeding to the trust property upon termination of the trust. Section 642(h) provides, in part, that if, on termination, a trust has for its last taxable year deductions other than the deduction allowed under Section 642(b) relating to personal exemption, or the deduction allowed under Section 642(c) relating to charitable contributions, in excess of gross income for such year, the excess is to be allowed as a deduction. This provision is in accordance with regulations prescribed by the Secretary of the Treasury or his delegate, to the beneficiaries succeeding to the property of the trust.

The IRS ruled that the excess deduction is allowed only in computing taxable income. It is not allowed as a deduction in computing adjusted gross income. The excess deduction is to be allocated among the beneficiaries proportionately according to their respective shares in the trust corpus, which must bear the burden of the expenses concerned. Inasmuch as the capital gains deduction is allowable to the instant trust under Section 1202 and qualifies as an excess deduction for the purposes of Section 642(h), taxpayers are entitled to deduct their proportionate share of such excess deduction in computing their taxable income for the year in which the trust terminated.

[Rev. Rul. 59-392, 1959-2 CB 163.]

Beneficiary of trust may not avail himself of dividend exclusion where trust, in its last taxable year, has excess deductions. Advice was requested from the IRS whether a beneficiary of a trust may avail himself of the pre-1964 dividends-received credit and the dividend exclusion provided in Section 34 (repealed) and Section 116, respectively, where the trust, in its last taxable year, has excess deductions within the meaning of Section 642(h)(2). Section 642(h)(2) provides that if an estate or trust has, for its last taxable year, deductions in excess of gross income, the excess is allowed as a deduction to the beneficiaries succeeding to the property of the estate or trust.

The IRS ruled that a beneficiary of a trust may not avail himself of the dividends-received credit or the dividend exclusion where the trust, in its last taxable year, has excess deductions within the meaning of Section 642(h)(2). The pertinent sections of both the Code and the regulations presuppose that the income and deductions of the trust during the last taxable period of the trust are to be computed separately from the income and deductions of the trust beneficiary, and that any excess of income or deductions is thereafter passed on to the beneficiary. Thus, if the estate or trust for its last taxable year has deductions in excess of its gross income, it has no income to pass on to the beneficiary. Hence, there is no dividend income attributable to such taxable year of the trust that would be includable in the beneficiary's return to which the dividend exclusion or dividend credit may be applied.

[Rev. Rul. 59-100, 1959-1 CB 165 (1959).]

Table of IRC Sections

[References are to paragraphs.]

[References are to paragraphs.]

[References are to paragraphs.]

[References are to paragraphs.]

[References are to paragraphs.]

[References are to paragraphs.]

[References are to paragraphs.]

Table of Treasury Regulations

[References are to paragraphs.]

T-9

[References are to paragraphs.]

PROPOSED REGULATIONS

TEMPORARY REGULATIONS

[References are to paragraphs.]

Table of Revenue Rulings, Revenue Procedures, and Other IRS Releases

[References are to paragraphs.]

REVENUE RULINGS

[References are to paragraphs.]

[References are to paragraphs.]

[References are to paragraphs.]

REVENUE PROCEDURES

Rev. Proc.

PRIVATE LETTER RULINGS

Priv. Ltr. Rul.

Priv. Ltr. Rul.

[References are to paragraphs.]

Priv. Ltr. Rul.

8729051	16.03[2]
8730006	12.04[6][a]
8734012	19.01
8740017	19.02
8740031	12.04[6][b]
8741055	3.03
8741076	12.04[4]
8742027	3.03
8743001	12.01[3], 16.01
8802004	21.01[3]
8805019	14.04
8805024	23.05[5]
8806048	2.01[1], 13.02[1][a]
8812064	25.01
8813019	17.04
8815005	14.02[2]
8815034	19.02
8815038	1.04[6]
8824039	16.03[3]
8825080	15.01
8826028	3.03
8827042	3.02[2]
8827072	1.04[4]
8829013	12.04[6][b]
8830052	14.02[2]
8834050	10.09[1]
8834052	25.02
8837081	23.01[2]
8839013	12.04[6][a]
8839043	23.05[1]
8839059	14.03
8841006	12.04[6][c]
8842043	20.02
8843023	2.04[2][b]
8843037	23.05[4]
8847003	20.03[1]
8849050	10.04
8901004	19.01
8902006	20.03[4]
8902007	20.03[4]
8902045	22.03
8903076	14.05
8905057	19.02
8906026	17.02
8906033	2.04[3][c]
8906036	1.04[7]
8907028	19.01
8908005	24.01[2]
8908022	1.04[1]
8910018	21.03
8910071	23.05[2]
8911028	1.04[3]
8912027	23.05[5]
8916032	6.01[1]
8920045	25.01
8922036	1.04[7], 12.02[4]
8928003	7.03
8929046	1.02, 14.01[2]
8933019	2.04[3][d]
8939031	2.04[3][b]
8940010	17.02
8940011	2.04[3][c]

Priv. Ltr. Rul.

8945004	10.06
8946022	10.09[1]
8949082	22.03
8949088	6.01[1]
8951056	14.02[2]
8952026	10.10[2]
9002014	19.01
9002029	19.01
9007034	1.04[1]
9009010	20.03[6]
9014005	1.04[1]
9015024	21.04[1]
9017026	1.04[4]
9041027	21.03
9110016	16.03[1]
9113009	11.01
9128005	4.01[3]
9140004	1.04[6], 11.05[3]
9147040	16.03[1]
9203028	19.01
9203047	6.01[2]
9348009	20.03[6]
9409018	11.01
9413045	7.02
9427030	1.04[2]
9443020	7.01
9444033	14.01[1]
9445029	13.03[1][a]
9501004	10.10[2]
9504004	15.02
9509003	1.04[2]
9511046	7.04
9514017	14.02[1]
9541029	19.01
9541035	11.02[1]
9544038	11.05[3]
9551018	3.01[1], 21.02
9606008	16.04
9616035	14.01[1]
9622036	7.04
9623024	7.04
9636033	7.04
9639053	7.04
9639054	15.02
9706011	1.01
9709015	19.01
9714025	20.03[7]
9729024	16.03[1]
9737017	19.01
9745019	7.04
9832009	12.04[4]
9834006	12.04[4]

TECHNICAL ADVICE
MEMORANDA

Tech. Adv. Mem.

7953011	16.01

GENERAL COUNSEL MEMORANDA

INCOME TAX UNIT REGULATIONS

NOTICES

TREASURY DECISIONS

Table of Cases

[References are to paragraphs.]

[References are to paragraphs.]

[References are to paragraphs.]

[References are to paragraphs.]

[References are to paragraphs.]

[References are to paragraphs.]

[References are to paragraphs.]

[References are to paragraphs.]

Index

[References are to paragraphs (¶).]

I-1

Gift ESTATE AND GIFT TAX DIGEST I-4